# Student, Parent, Teacher
# Internet Resources

**Biology Online** il.biologygmh.com

Access your Student Edition on the Internet so you don't need to bring your textbook home every night. You can link to features and get additional practice with these online study tools.

Check out the following features on your **Online Learning Center:**

**Study Tools**

Concepts In Motion

- Interactive Tables
- Interactive Time Line
- Animated Illustrations
- National Geographic Visualizing Animations

Study to Go
Section Self-Check Quizzes
Chapter Test Practice
Standardized Test Practice
Vocabulary PuzzleMaker
Interactive Tutor
Multilingual Science Glossary
Online Student Edition

**Extensions**

Virtual Labs
Microscopy Links
Periodic Table Links
Career Links
Prescreened Web Links
WebQuest Projects
Science Fair Ideas
Internet BioLabs

**For Teachers**

Teacher Bu
Teaching To

# Safety Symbols

These safety symbols are used in laboratory and field investigations in this book to indicate possible hazards. Learn the meaning of each symbol and refer to this page often. *Remember to wash your hands thoroughly after completing lab procedures.*

| SAFETY SYMBOLS | HAZARD | EXAMPLES | PRECAUTION | REMEDY |
|---|---|---|---|---|
| DISPOSAL | Special disposal procedures need to be followed. | certain chemicals, living organisms | Do not dispose of these materials in the sink or trash can. | Dispose of wastes as directed by your teacher. |
| BIOLOGICAL | Organisms or other biological materials that might be harmful to humans | bacteria, fungi, blood, unpreserved tissues, plant materials | Avoid skin contact with these materials. Wear mask or gloves. | Notify your teacher if you suspect contact with material. Wash hands thoroughly. |
| EXTREME TEMPERATURE | Objects that can burn skin by being too cold or too hot | boiling liquids, hot plates, dry ice, liquid nitrogen | Use proper protection when handling. | Go to your teacher for first aid. |
| SHARP OBJECT | Use of tools or glassware that can easily puncture or slice skin | razor blades, pins, scalpels, pointed tools, dissecting probes, broken glass | Practice common-sense behavior and follow guidelines for use of the tool. | Go to your teacher for first aid. |
| FUME | Possible danger to respiratory tract from fumes | ammonia, acetone, nail polish remover, heated sulfur, moth balls | Make sure there is good ventilation. Never smell fumes directly. Wear a mask. | Leave foul area and notify your teacher immediately. |
| ELECTRICAL | Possible danger from electrical shock or burn | improper grounding, liquid spills, short circuits, exposed wires | Double-check setup with teacher. Check condition of wires and apparatus. Use GFI-protected outlets. | Do not attempt to fix electrical problems. Notify your teacher immediately. |
| IRRITANT | Substances that can irritate the skin or mucous membranes of the respiratory tract | pollen, moth balls, steel wool, fiberglass, potassium permanganate | Wear dust mask and gloves. Practice extra care when handling these materials. | Go to your teacher for first aid. |
| CHEMICAL | Chemicals that can react with and destroy tissue and other materials | bleaches such as hydrogen peroxide; acids such as sulfuric acid, hydrochloric acid; bases such as ammonia, sodium hydroxide | Wear goggles, gloves, and an apron. | Immediately flush the affected area with water and notify your teacher. |
| TOXIC | Substance may be poisonous if touched, inhaled, or swallowed. | mercury, many metal compounds, iodine, poinsettia plant parts | Follow your teacher's instructions. | Always wash hands thoroughly after use. Go to your teacher for first aid. |
| FLAMMABLE | Open flame may ignite flammable chemicals, loose clothing, or hair. | alcohol, kerosene, potassium permanganate, hair, clothing | Avoid open flames and heat when using flammable chemicals. | Notify your teacher immediately. Use fire safety equipment if applicable. |
| OPEN FLAME | Open flame in use, may cause fire. | hair, clothing, paper, synthetic materials | Tie back hair and loose clothing. Follow teacher's instructions on lighting and extinguishing flames. | Always wash hands thoroughly after use. Go to your teacher for first aid. |

**Eye Safety**
Proper eye protection must be worn at all times by anyone performing or observing science activities.

**Clothing Protection**
This symbol appears when substances could stain or burn clothing.

**Animal Safety**
This symbol appears when safety of animals and students must be ensured.

**Radioactivity**
This symbol appears when radioactive materials are used.

**Handwashing**
After the lab, wash hands with soap and water before removing goggles.

# Your Guide to The Illinois Biology Standards

## Table of Contents



Millenium Park, downtown Chicago

# Illinois Standards Correlation

## *Glencoe Biology* correlated to Illinois Standards

**STATE GOAL 11: Understand the processes of scientific inquiry and technological design to investigate questions, conduct experiments and solve problems.**

**Why This Goal Is Important:** The inquiry process prepares learners to engage in science and apply methods of technological design. This understanding will enable students to pose questions, use models to enhance understanding, make predictions, gather and work with data, use appropriate measurement methods, analyze results, draw conclusions based on evidence, communicate their methods and results, and think about the implications of scientific research and technological problem solving.

**A. Know and apply the concepts, principles and processes of scientific inquiry.**

### Early High School

| Standard | | Page |
|---|---|---|
| **11.A.4a** | Formulate hypotheses referencing prior research and knowledge. | Utilized Throughout the Text, for example: 16–21, 173, 519, 590 |
| **11.A.4b** | Conduct controlled experiments or simulations to test hypotheses. | Utilized Throughout the Text, for example: 16–21, 51, 173, 235 |
| **11.A.4c** | Collect, organize and analyze data accurately and precisely. | Utilized Throughout the Text, for example: 16–21, 83, 259, 396 |
| **11.A.4d** | Apply statistical methods to the data to reach and support conclusions. | Utilized Throughout the Text, for example: 217, 420, 590, 646 |
| **11.A.4e** | Formulate alternative hypotheses to explain unexpected results. | 567, 593 |
| **11.A.4f** | Using available technology, report, display and defend to an audience conclusions drawn from investigations. | 653, 983, 1011 |

| B. Know and apply the concepts, principles and processes of technological design. | | |
|---|---|---|
| **Early High School** | | |
| **11.B.4a** | Identify a technological design problem inherent in a commonly used product. | 378 |
| **11.B.4b** | Propose and compare different solution designs to the design problem based upon given constraints including available tools, materials and time. | 51, 235, 783 |
| **11.B.4c** | Develop working visualizations of the proposed solution designs (e.g., blueprints, schematics, flowcharts, cad-cam, animations). | 1011 |
| **11.B.4d** | Determine the criteria upon which the designs will be judged, identify advantages and disadvantages of the designs and select the most promising design. | 1011 |
| **11.B.4e** | Develop and test a prototype or simulation of the solution design using available materials, instruments and technology. | 381 |
| **11.B.4f** | Evaluate the test results based on established criteria, note sources of error and recommend improvements. | Utilized Throughout the Text, for example: 235, 259, 533, 975 |
| **11.B.4g** | Using available technology, report to an audience the relative success of the design based on the test results and criteria. | 1011 |

# Illinois Standards Correlation

**STATE GOAL 12: Understand the fundamental concepts, principles and interconnections of the life, physical and earth/space sciences.**

**Why This Goal Is Important:** This goal is comprised of key concepts and principles in the life, physical and earth/space sciences that have considerable explanatory and predictive power for scientists and non-scientists alike. These ideas have been thoroughly studied and have stood the test of time. Knowing and being able to apply these concepts, principles and processes help students understand what they observe in nature and through scientific experimentation. A working knowledge of these concepts and principles allows students to relate new subject matter to material previously learned and to create deeper and more meaningful levels of understanding.

**A. Know and apply concepts that explain how living things function, adapt and change.**

## Early High School

| Standard | | Page |
|---|---|---|
| **12.A.4a** | Explain how genetic combinations produce visible effects and variations among physical features and cellular functions of organisms. | 270–276, 277–282, 283–285, 296–301, 302–310, 311, 313–315, 326–332, 333–335, 336–338, 340–341, 342–349, 360–362, 363–371, 372–376, 378–379 |
| **12.A.4b** | Describe the structures and organization of cells and tissues that underlie basic life functions including nutrition, respiration, cellular transport, biosynthesis and reproduction. | 182–186, 187–190, 191, 193–200, 201–207, 218–221, 222–224, 225–227, 228–233, 244–247, 248, 250–252, 253–257, |
| **12.A.4c** | Describe processes by which organisms change over time using evidence from comparative anatomy and physiology, embryology, the fossil record, genetics and biochemistry. | 277–282, 283–285, 392–396, 398–400, 401–407, 418–420, 422, 423–430, 431–441, 452–453, 455–460, 461–466, 467–473, 490–496, 498 |

**B. Know and apply concepts that describe how living things interact with each other and with their environment.**

| Early High School | | |
|---|---|---|
| **12.B.4a** | Compare physical, ecological and behavioral factors that influence interactions and interdependence of organisms. | 32–40, 41–44, 45–49, 65–66, 68–73, 74–81, 116–121, 129–131, 133–135 |
| **12.B.4b** | Simulate and analyze factors that influence the size and stability of populations within ecosystems (e.g., birth rate, death rate, predation, migration patterns). | 60–64, 92, 94–99, 100–105, 116–121, 122–128 |

**C. Know and apply concepts that describe properties of matter and energy and the interactions between them.**

| Early High School | | |
|---|---|---|
| **12.C.4a** | Use kinetic theory, wave theory, quantum theory and the laws of thermodynamics to explain energy transformations. | 218–221 |
| **12.C.4b** | Analyze and explain the atomic and nuclear structure of matter. | 148–155 |

**D. Know and apply concepts that describe force and motion and the principles that explain them.**

| Early High School | | |
|---|---|---|
| **12.D.4b** | Describe the effects of electromagnetic and nuclear forces including atomic and molecular bonding, capacitance and nuclear reactions. | 152–155 |

**STATE GOAL 13: Understand the relationships among science, technology and society in historical and contemporary contexts.**

**Why This Goal Is Important:** Understanding the nature and practices of science such as ensuring the validity and replicability of results, building upon the work of others and recognizing risks involved in experimentation gives learners a useful sense of the scientific enterprise. In addition, the relationships among science, technology and society give humans the ability to change and improve their surroundings. Learners who understand this relationship will be able to appreciate the efforts and effects of scientific discovery and applications of technology on their own lives and on the society in which we live.

**A. Know and apply the accepted practices of science.**

**Early High School**

| Standard | | Page |
|---|---|---|
| **13.A.4a** | Estimate and suggest ways to reduce the degree of risk involved in science activities. | 21 |
| **13.A.4b** | Assess the validity of scientific data by analyzing the results, sample set, sample size, similar previous experimentation, possible misrepresentation of data presented and potential sources of error. | Utilized Throughout the Text, for example: 11–15, 533, 623, 681 |
| **13.A.4c** | Describe how scientific knowledge, explanations and technological designs may change with new information over time (e.g., the understanding of DNA, the design of computers). | 4–10, 11–15, 363–371 |

| | | |
|---|---|---|
| **13.A.4d** | Explain how peer review helps to assure the accurate use of data and improves the scientific process. | Utilized Throughout the Text, for example: 11–15, 209, 623, 783 |
| **B. Know and apply concepts that describe the interaction between science, technology and society.** | | |
| **Early High School** | | |
| **13.B.4a** | Compare and contrast scientific inquiry and technological design as pure and applied sciences. | 5–6 |
| **13.B.4b** | Analyze a particular occupation to identify decisions that may be influenced by a knowledge of science. | Utilized Throughout the Text, for example: 372–376, 378–379, 622, 782, 1038 |
| **13.B.4c** | Analyze ways that resource management and technology can be used to accommodate population trends. | 92, 94–99, 100–105, 106, 107 |
| **13.B.4d** | Analyze local examples of resource use, technology use or conservation programs; document findings; and make recommendations for improvements. | 129–131, 133–135, 136, 137 |
| **13.B.4e** | Evaluate claims derived from purported scientific studies used in advertising and marketing strategies. | 14 |

# Standards Practice Countdown

## Week 1

### Monday

1. Which cell part is analogous to the human skeleton? *(Section 7.3)*

**A.** cytoskeleton
**B.** lysosomes
**C.** cilia
**D.** nucleus

### Tuesday

2. Which is a protein that changes the rate of a chemical reaction and is involved in nearly all metabolic processes? *(Section 6.2)*

**A.** amino acid
**B.** nucleic acid
**C.** enzyme
**D.** nucleotide

### Wednesday

3. Viruses can reproduce only under which condition? *(Section 18.2)*

**A.** when they are outside a living organism
**B.** when they carry out respiration
**C.** when they grow or move
**D.** when they are inside a host cell

### Thursday

4. What is the main function of the projections that cover the HIV? *(Section 18.2)*

**A.** They protect the virus and give it its structure.
**B.** They aid in respiration.
**C.** They help the virus invade its host.
**D.** They help the virus move and grow.

### Friday

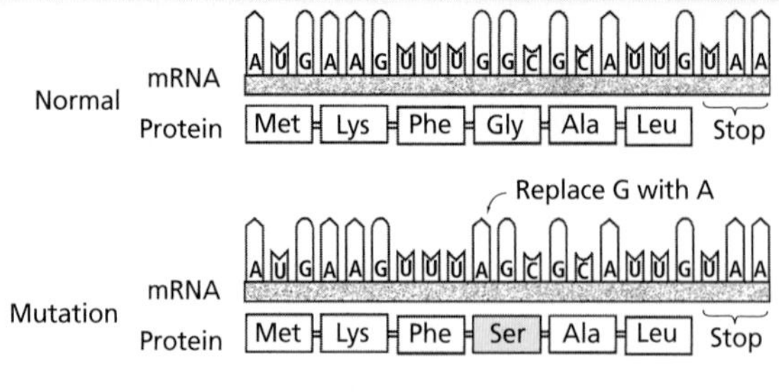

Normal
mRNA A U G A A G U U U G G C G C A U U G U A A
Protein Met Lys Phe Gly Ala Leu Stop

Replace G with A

Mutation
mRNA A U G A A G U U U A G C G C A U U G U A A
Protein Met Lys Phe Ser Ala Leu Stop

5. What kind of mutation is shown in the figure above? *(Section 12.4)*

**A.** deletion
**B.** insertion
**C.** inversion
**D.** translocation

# Week 2

## Monday

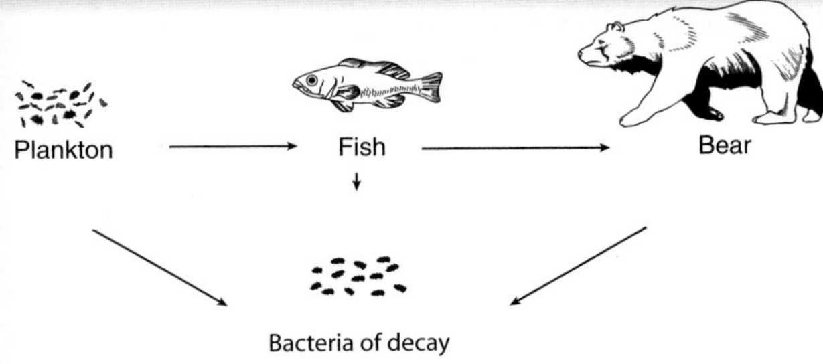


1. The diagram shows a food chain. If environmental pollution and overfishing were to decrease the number of fish in the ocean, which situation might occur? *(Section 2.2)*

**A.** The bear population would increase.
**B.** The plankton population would increase.
**C.** The plankton population would decrease.
**D.** The bacteria population would increase.

## Tuesday

2. Which best describes the role of RNA molecules that form in the nucleus? *(Section 12.3)*

**A.** RNA molecules carry the code from DNA to the ribosomes.
**B.** RNA molecules are responsible for the genetic code.
**C.** RNA molecules attach to ribosomes.
**D.** RNA molecules determine how an organism looks and acts.

## Wednesday

3. What happens after ribosomes pass into the cytoplasm? *(Section 12.3)*

**A.** They pass through the nuclear envelope.
**B.** They may attach to areas of endoplasmic reticulum.
**C.** They replicate the DNA.
**D.** They sort and distribute proteins to cell organelles.

## Thursday

4. Which organelle is most like a miniature stomach? *(Section 7.3)*

**A.** centriole
**B.** chloroplast
**C.** lysosome
**D.** vacuole

## Friday

5. Which is referred to as a cell's "powerhouse"? *(Section 7.3, 8.3)*

**A.** cytoskeleton
**B.** mitochondrion
**C.** flagellum
**D.** lysosome

# Standards Practice Countdown

## Week 3

### Monday

*Use the figure below to answer questions 1 and 2.*

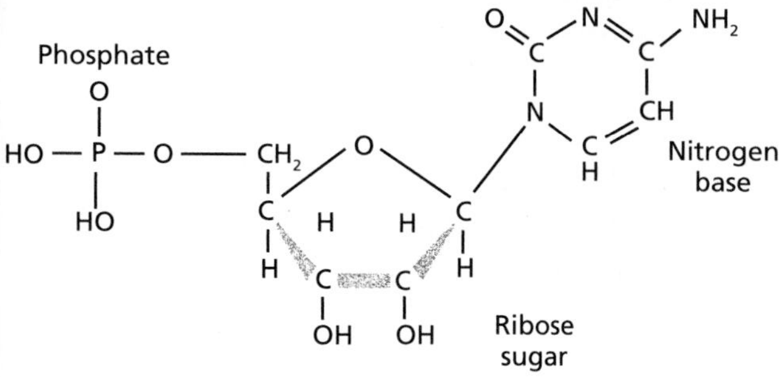

1. Which describes the nitrogen base in the nucleotide shown to the left? *(Sections 6.3, 12.1)*

**A.** a branched chain
**B.** a macromolecule
**C.** a ring structure
**D.** a straight chain

### Tuesday

2. How many carbon atoms are in this nucleotide? *(Section 6.3)*

**A.** 4
**B.** 5
**C.** 7
**D.** 9

### Wednesday

3. Which stage of meiosis begins with homologous chromosomes, each with its two chromatids, separating and moving to opposite ends of the cell? *(Section 10.1)*

**A.** anaphase I
**B.** metaphase I
**C.** prophase I
**D.** telophase I

### Thursday

4. When non-sister chromatids from homologous chromosomes break and exchange genetic material, what process has occurred? *(Section 10.1)*

**A.** trisomy
**B.** nondisjunction
**C.** crossing over
**D.** sexual reproduction

### Friday

5. What is nondisjunction? *(Section 11.3)*

**A.** failure of genes to be passed on to future generations
**B.** failure of chromosomes to separate properly during meiosis
**C.** A mutation most often caused by environmental factors.
**D.** A duplication of genes on a chromosome.

# Week 4

## Monday

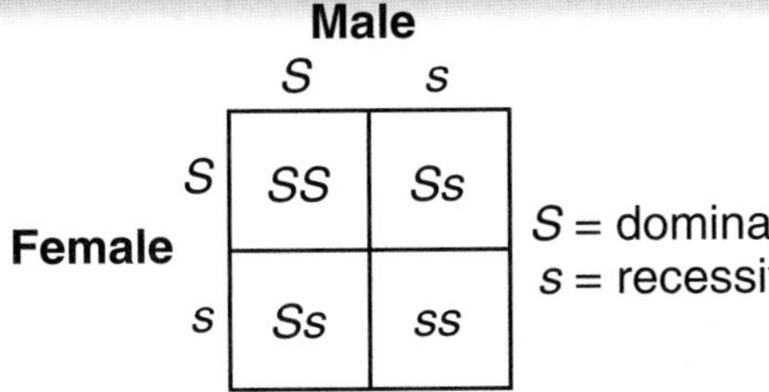


1. In a certain type of corn plant, the gene for smooth seeds is a dominant trait (*S*), while the gene for wrinkled seeds is recessive (*s*). Based on the Punnett square above, what kinds of seeds will the offspring of these two corn plants have? *(Section 10.2)*

**A.** One hundred percent will be smooth, and none will be wrinkled.
**B.** Fifty percent will be smooth, and fifty percent will be wrinkled.
**C.** Seventy-five percent will be smooth, and twenty-five percent will be wrinkled.
**D.** Twenty-five percent will be smooth, and seventy-five percent will be wrinkled.

## Tuesday

2. What is the type of cell division where one body cell produces four gametes, each containing half the number of chromosomes as a parent's body cell? *(Section 10.1)*

**A.** diploid
**B.** gametes
**C.** meiosis
**D.** mitosis

## Wednesday

3. In humans, what is the role of the 23rd pair of chromosomes? *(Section 11.2)*

**A.** It determines the sex of an individual.
**B.** It determines the eye and hair color of an individual.
**C.** It determines male pattern baldness in an individual.
**D.** It determines the blood type of an individual.

## Thursday

4. A purebred animal with brown fur is crossed with a purebred animal with tan fur. The only offspring has both tan and brown fur. What type of inheritance pattern is involved? *(Section 11.2)*

**A.** codominance
**B.** incomplete dominance
**C.** polygenic inheritance
**D.** simple inheritance

## Friday

5. A plant shows incomplete dominance. First generation offspring of a cross between plants with white flowers and plants with purple flowers will produce flowers with which color? *(Section 11.2)*

**A.** purple
**B.** white
**C.** deep purple
**D.** light blue

# Standards Practice Countdown

## Week 5

### Monday

1. Which correctly sequences the main steps involved in protein synthesis? *(Section 12.3)*

**A.** free RNA nucleotides form mRNA; mRNA attaches to a ribosome; tRNA molecules pair with mRNA codons as the mRNA slides along the ribosome; amino acids are joined by an enzyme
**B.** mRNA attaches to a ribosome; tRNA molecules pair with mRNA codons as the mRNA slides along the ribosome; amino acids are joined by an enzyme; free RNA nucleotides form mRNA
**C.** tRNA molecules pair with mRNA codons as the mRNA slides along the ribosome; amino acids are joined by an enzyme; free RNA nucleotides for mRNA; mRNA attaches to a ribosome
**D.** free RNA nucleotides form mRNA; tRNA molecules pair with mRNA codons as the mRNA slides along the ribosome; amino acids are joined by an enzyme; mRNA attaches to a ribosome

### Tuesday

2. Which describes Mendel's first law, the law of segregation? *(Section 10.2)*

**A.** Two organisms can have the same phenotype but different genotypes.
**B.** When gametes are produced, each gamete receives one of two possible alleles.
**C.** Genes for different traits are inherited independently of each other.
**D.** An organism's two alleles are located on different copies of a chromosome.

### Wednesday

*Use the figure below to answer questions 3–5.*

3. Which nitrogenous base sequence will complement the anticodon shown? *(Section 12.3)*

**A.** AUG
**B.** GUA
**C.** TCG
**D.** AUT

### Thursday

4. This molecule plays a major role in which process? *(Section 12.3)*

**A.** meiosis
**B.** mitosis
**C.** replication
**D.** translation

### Friday

5. What kind of molecule is shown? *(Section 12.3)*

**A.** replicated DNA
**B.** messenger RNA
**C.** transfer RNA
**D.** transfer DNA

# Week 6

## Monday

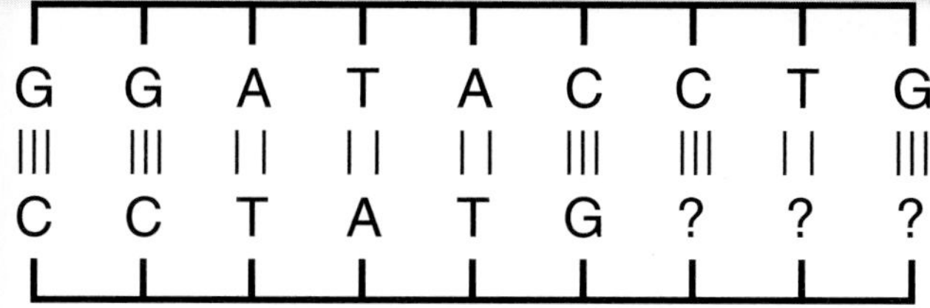


1. The diagram shows a portion of a DNA molecule. Which sequence of bases do the question marks represent? *(Section 12.1)*

**A.** CAC
**B.** GCA
**C.** GAC
**D.** TCA

## Tuesday

2. Which process does NOT require DNA replication? *(Section 9.1)*

**A.** mitosis
**B.** meiosis
**C.** cell division
**D.** cell growth

## Wednesday

3. Which base pairs with adenine in RNA? *(Section 12.1)*

**A.** cytosine
**B.** guanine
**C.** thymine
**D.** uracil

## Thursday

4. Why can the deletion of a single nitrogen base in DNA be harmful to an organism? *(Section 12.4)*

**A.** Deletion causes chromosomes to join backward or to join the wrong chromosomes.
**B.** Deletion causes nearly every amino acid in the protein to change.
**C.** Deletion causes a gamete to have an extra chromosome.
**D.** Deletion causes chromosomes to join with the wrong chromosome.

## Friday

5. What are the genotypes of a homozygous tall pea plant and a heterozygous tall pea plant, respectively? *(Section 10.2)*

**A.** *tt*, *Tt*
**B.** *TT*, *Tt*
**C.** *Tt*, *tt*
**D.** *Tt*, *TT*

# Standards Practice Countdown

## Week 7

### Monday

1. Which process does NOT involve ribonucleic acid? *(Section 10.1)*

A. replication
B. translation
C. transcription
D. codon attachment to a ribosome

### Tuesday

2. Which analogy is TRUE? *(Section 12.1)*

A. A copy of DNA is like a blueprint of the RNA code.
B. DNA can be compared to workers on an assembly line.
C. Nucleotides are the building blocks of nitrogenous bases.
D. The structure of DNA can be compared to a twisted ladder.

### Wednesday

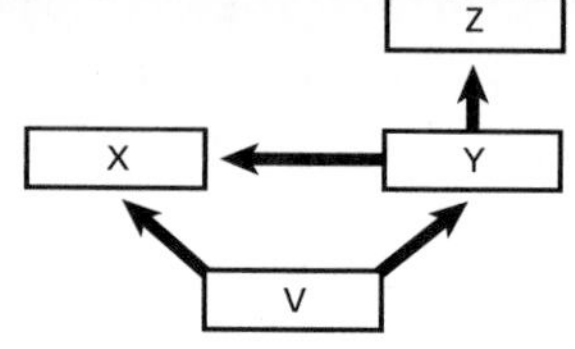


3. Which organism in the figure above is a first-order consumer? *(Section 2.2)*

A. V
B. X
C. both X and Y
D. both V and Z

### Thursday

4. Which process results in an RNA copy of a DNA strand? *(Section 12.3)*

A. translation
B. transcription
C. replication
D. mitosis

### Friday

5. Which does NOT describe restriction enzymes? *(Section 13.2)*

A. They are bacterial proteins.
B. They have the ability to cut double-stranded DNA.
C. They can carry DNA from one species into a host cell.
D. There are hundreds of restriction enzymes.

# Week 8

## Monday

A. 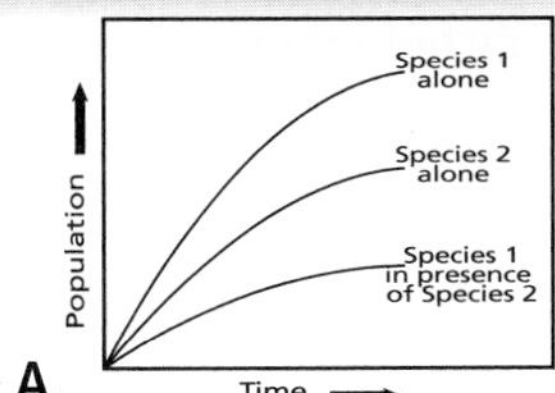


B. 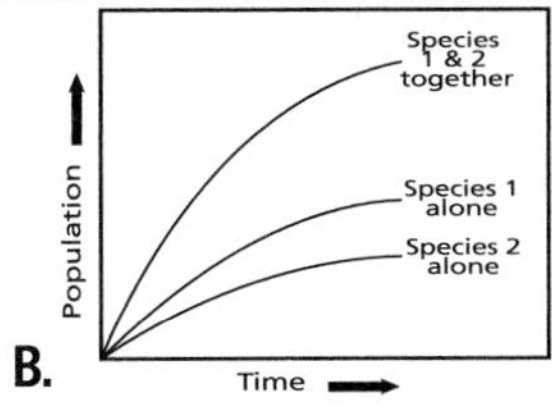


C. 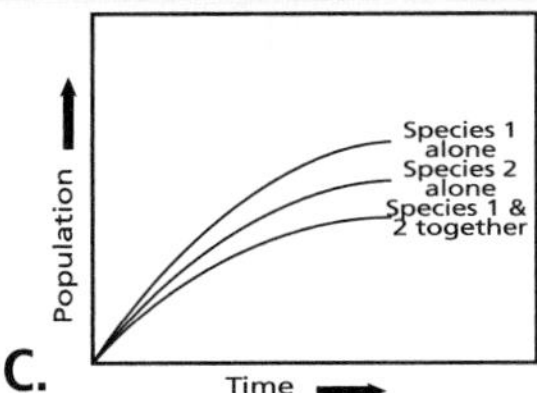


D. 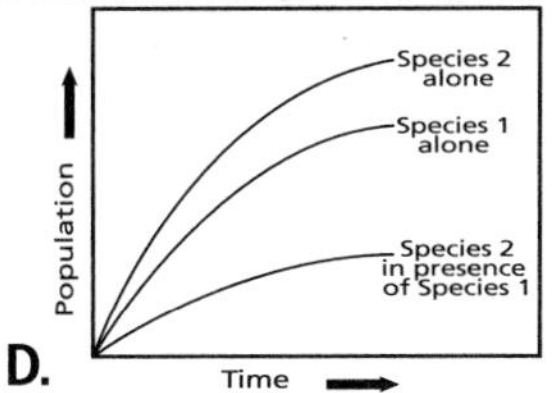


1. The graphs above illustrate the changing populations of two species in the same ecosystem over time. Which graph represents a mutualistic relationship? *(Section 2.1)*

## Tuesday

2. Which series correctly sequences interactions in nature from largest to smallest? *(Section 2.1)*

**A.** population, ecosystem, community
**B.** species, organism, community
**C.** ecosystem, community, population
**D.** community, population, ecosystem

## Wednesday

3. A manufacturing plant is located on the banks of a river. One day, toxic chemicals from the plant accidentally spilled into the river. Fish absorbed some of these chemicals into their bodies. Later, a hawk living near the river was found to have the same toxic chemicals in its system. Which statement best explains why? *(Section 2.2)*

**A.** The chemicals entered the air.
**B.** The chemicals entered the food chain.
**C.** The chemicals were contagious.
**D.** The chemicals are commonly found in the environment.

## Thursday

4. Which terms are NOT related? *(Section 2.3)*

**A.** water cycle—precipitation
**B.** phosphorus cycle—evaporation
**C.** nitrogen cycle—nitrogen fixation
**D.** carbon cycle—photosynthesis

## Friday

5. Based on what you've learned about the cycling of materials through ecosystems, which material would most likely be added to a chemical fertilizer to increase soil productivity? *(Section 2.3)*

**A.** $H_2O$
**B.** $CO_2$
**C.** $N_2$
**D.** $NO_3$

# Standards Practice Countdown

## Week 9

### Monday

1. Which best describes the bacteria shown in the figure? *(Section 18.1)*

**A.** streptococci
**B.** staphylococci
**C.** diplococci
**D.** diplobacilli

### Tuesday

2. How does parasitism differ from predation? *(Section 2.1)*

**A.** No organism is harmed in a parasitic relationship.
**B.** No organism is harmed in a predator-prey relationship.
**C.** Parasitism does not always result in the death of an organism.
**D.** Parasitism does not occur among mammals.

### Wednesday

3. Which model would an ecologist use to show the weight of living material in an ecosystem? *(Section 2.2)*

**A.** a food web
**B.** a pyramid of energy
**C.** a pyramid of numbers
**D.** a pyramid of biomass

### Thursday

4. How does camouflage aid in the evolutionary process? *(Section 15.2)*

**A.** Camouflage enables an organism to copy the appearance of another species.
**B.** This anatomical adaptation helps an organism mutate.
**C.** Organisms that are well camouflaged are more likely to escape predators and survive to reproduce.
**D.** The ability to camouflage is lost during embryonic development.

### Friday

5. Both parents carry a single recessive gene. What are the chances of their child inheriting the recessive disorder caused by the gene? *(Section 11.1)*

**A.** 2 percent
**B.** 25 percent
**C.** 50 percent
**D.** 100 percent

# Week 10

## Monday

1. What is a mutation in which a single base is added to or deleted from DNA? *(Section 12.4)*

**A.** chromosomal mutation
**B.** frameshift mutation
**C.** junction mutation
**D.** point mutation

## Tuesday

2. Industrialization in England in the early 1900s produced black soot that covered many tree trunks and branches. At about the same time, the number of light-colored moths in this part of the country decreased over time. Which is a possible explanation for this? *(Section 15.3)*

**A.** The soot killed only light-colored moths.
**B.** The light-colored moths became extinct.
**C.** The light-colored moths showed up against the dark tree bark and could be easily seen by the birds that fed on them.
**D.** Reproductive speciation occurred.

## Wednesday

3. What is an alteration of allelic frequencies by chance events that greatly affects small populations? *(Section 15.3)*

**A.** allelic frequency
**B.** genetic equilibrium
**C.** gene pool
**D.** genetic drift

## Thursday

4. Dolphins and fish are unrelated vertebrates with similar body shapes that are adapted for moving efficiently through water. What evolutionary process is shown by this example? *(Section 15.3)*

**A.** convergent evolution
**B.** divergent evolution
**C.** polyploid speciation
**D.** reproductive isolation

## Friday

| Chemicals Present | |
|---|---|
| **Bacteria 1** | A, G, T, C, L, E, S, H |
| **Bacteria 2** | A, G, T, C, L, D |
| **Bacteria 3** | A, G, T, C, L, D, P, U, S, R, I, V |
| **Bacteria 4** | A, G, T, C, L, D, H |

5. The table above shows chemicals found in certain bacteria. Each capital letter represents a different chemical. Which bacteria are most closely related? *(Section 15.2)*

**A.** bacteria 1 and 2
**B.** bacteria 1 and 3
**C.** bacteria 2 and 3
**D.** bacteria 2 and 4

# Standards Practice Countdown

## Week 11

### Monday

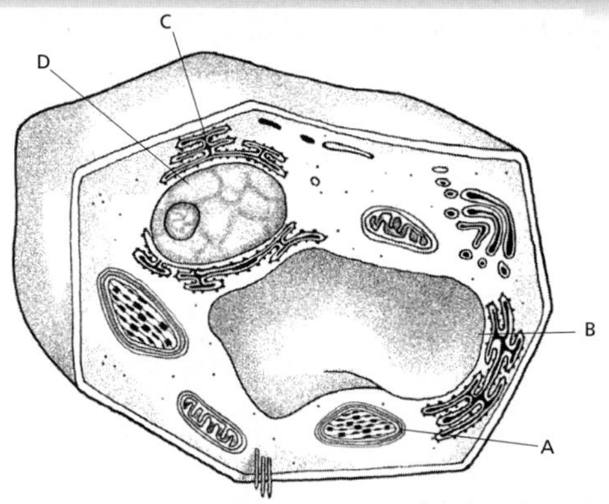


1. To which answer choice could the circular structures on membrane C be best compared? *(Sections 7.3, 12.3)*

**A.** workers on an assembly line
**B.** storage bins
**C.** scaffolding
**D.** delivery trucks

### Tuesday

2. Periods of drought (absence of rain) break up a forest into smaller patches of trees. Natural selection results in tree frog populations evolving distinct gene pools. Groups of frogs can no longer produce fertile offspring. Which process occurred in this situation? *(Section 15.3)*

**A.** convergent evolution
**B.** extinction
**C.** geographic isolation
**D.** phylogenetic classification

### Wednesday

3. The presence of gills and tails in the early stages of all vertebrates indicates common ancestry. Which evidence from the fossil record supports this statement? *(Section 15.2)*

**A.** Aquatic, gill-breathing vertebrates were the ancestors of air-breathing land species.
**B.** Fossils generally are older than the rocks in which they are found.
**C.** Similarities among DNA indicate a common ancestor.
**D.** Structural adaptations are not inherited from parents.

### Thursday

4. What is cellular respiration? *(Section 8.3)*

**A.** a process that uses oxygen to break down glucose and release energy
**B.** a process that rids the body of nitrogen gases
**C.** a process during which cilia constantly move to filter out foreign material
**D.** a process during which the muscles of the chest cavity contract and relax

### Friday

5. Which describes the parasympathetic nervous system? *(Section 33.2)*

**A.** It controls many of the body's internal functions when the body is at rest.
**B.** It relays information between the skin, the CNS, and skeletal muscles.
**C.** It carries impulses from the CNS to internal organs.
**D.** It controls internal functions during times of stress.

# Week 12

## Monday

1. Which is NOT a function of the endocrine system? *(Section 35.3)*

A. Released hormones convey information to other cells in the body, controlling metabolism, growth, development, and behavior.
B. The pituitary gland releases chemicals and stimulates other glands to release their chemicals.
C. A positive feedback system controls homeostasis.
D. The hypothalamus receives messages from the brain and internal organs.

## Tuesday

2. Which does NOT describe how an impulse is transmitted? *(Section 33.1)*

A. Depolarization moves like a wave down the axon.
B. Calcium diffuses across the membrane and releases synaptic chemicals.
C. Gated potassium channels open, letting $K^+$ ions out, repolarizing the cell.
D. Gated potassium channels close, allowing the $Na^+$/ $K^+$ pump to restore ion distribution.

## Wednesday

3. What do interneurons do? *(Section 33.1)*

A. carry impulses from the body to the spinal cord and brain
B. receive impulses and carry them toward the cell body
C. carry response impulses away from the brain and spinal cord to a muscle or gland
D. process incoming impulses and pass response impulses on to motor neurons

## Thursday

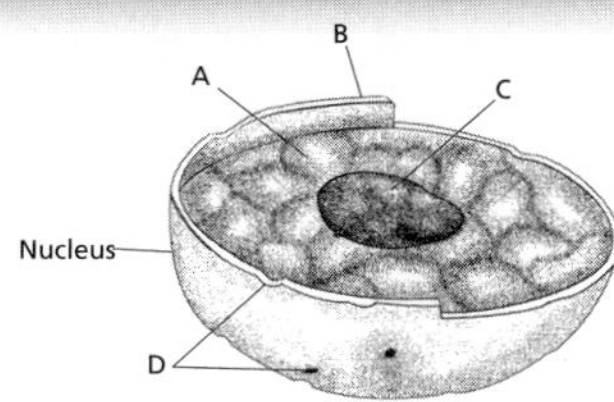


4. What is the function of the structure labeled C? *(Section 7.3)*

A. to suspend organelles
B. to produce ribosomes
C. to generate energy
D. to maintain homeostasis

## Friday

5. The epidermis contains which protein that helps protect living cell layers from exposure to bacteria, heat, and chemicals? *(Section 32.1)*

A. keratin
B. melanin
C. myosin
D. vitamin D

# Standards Practice Countdown

## Week 13

### Monday

1. As part of their job, a group of factory workers must handle certain chemicals every day. The workers are concerned that the chemicals are making them ill. The factory hires a researcher to investigate the situation. The researcher conducts a poll with factory workers at a different plant, and compares the results. In both cases, few people were hospitalized, so the researcher concludes there is no health problem. The workers charge that the study is biased. Which statement below does NOT reflect bias in the study? *(Section 1.3)*

**A.** The researcher was hired by the factory.
**B.** Polls are not valid.
**C.** Sick people do not always require hospitalization.
**D.** The factory workers might have handled different materials.

### Tuesday

2. What is a vaccine? *(Section 37.2)*

**A.** an injection of antibodies from animals or humans that have immunity
**B.** weakened, dead, or incomplete portions of pathogens or antigens
**C.** venom from the bite of a snake
**D.** antibodies that come from a mother's milk

### Wednesday

3. How does penicillin affect a bacterial cell? *(Section 37.1)*

**A.** It interferes with transcription.
**B.** It interferes with DNA replication.
**C.** It interferes with protein synthesis.
**D.** It interferes with the construction and repair of a bacterial cell wall.

### Thursday

4. What is a virus? *(Section 18.2)*

**A.** an infectious agent with a cell wall composed of only a single, circular strand of RNA
**B.** a disease-causing, nonliving particle composed of an inner core of nucleic acids surrounded by a capsid
**C.** an infectious agent with a sticky gelatinous capsule around the cell wall
**D.** a disease-causing plasmid with a few genes located in a small circular chromosome

### Friday

**Population of Unknown Organisms**

| Year | Spring | Summer | Autumn | Winter |
|---|---|---|---|---|
| 1995 | 564 | 14,598 | 25,762 | 127 |
| 1996 | 750 | 16,422 | 42,511 | 102 |
| 1997 | 365 | 14,106 | 36,562 | 136 |

5. Based on the data above, what can you conclude about the organism? *(Section 1.3)*

**A.** It has a short life span.
**B.** It has a long life span.
**C.** It thrives in even-numbered years.
**D.** It doesn't like hot or cold temperatures.

# Week 14

## Monday

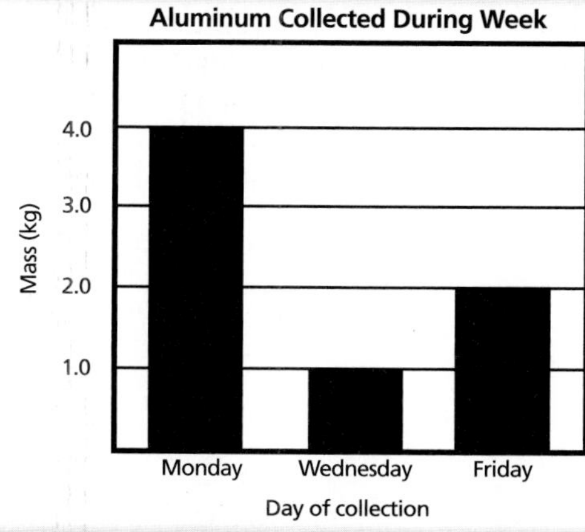


1. The graph shows the amount of aluminum collected during one week for recycling. Which of the following statements best describes the data shown? *(Section 1.3)*

   **A.** More aluminum was collected on Wednesday than Friday.
   **B.** Twice as much aluminum was collected on Monday than Friday.
   **C.** Less aluminum was collected on Monday than Friday.
   **D.** The most aluminum was collected on Friday.

## Tuesday

2. During an experiment to test the heat absorption rates of different-colored materials, a researcher placed a white cloth in direct sunlight and a black cloth under a lamp. He then placed a thermometer under each cloth and recorded the temperature changes every 5 min for 30 min. When he presented his results to a colleague, the colleague told him that the experiment contained a crucial flaw. What is the flaw? *(Section 1.3)*

   **A.** The researcher did not control variables.
   **B.** The researcher did not use the proper equipment.
   **C.** The researcher should have used cloths of the same color.
   **D.** The researcher should have recorded temperature changes each minute.

## Wednesday

3. Which distinguishes a hypothesis from a theory? *(Section 1.3)*

   **A.** A theory can be proven.
   **B.** A theory is testable.
   **C.** A theory explains a natural phenomenon.
   **D.** A theory is supported by repeated observations and tests.

## Thursday

4. Why should quantitative experiments be repeated? *(Section 1.3)*

   **A.** to publish results
   **B.** to communicate results
   **C.** to clearly display information
   **D.** to reduce the chance of error

## Friday

5. What type of data will a student need to collect to determine the speed of a toy car? *(Section 1.3)*

   **A.** qualitative
   **B.** quantitative
   **C.** subjective data
   **D.** inaccurate data

## Week 15

### Monday

1. Which pair of terms is NOT related? *(Section 7.3)*

**A.** nucleus—DNA
**B.** flagella—cilia
**C.** chloroplasts—chlorophyll
**D.** nucleus—cell wall

### Tuesday

2. What is the function of the leaves of a plant? *(Section 22.2)*

**A.** conserve gases
**B.** support the plant
**C.** obtain water
**D.** trap sunlight

### Wednesday

3. In which stage does one diploid cell produce four haploid cells, providing a way for offspring to have the same number of chromosomes as their parents? *(Section 10.1)*

**A.** meiosis
**B.** mitosis
**C.** prophase I of meiosis
**D.** telophase II of meiosis

### Thursday

4. What are the chances of being a carrier of a defective gene if both parents are carriers? *(Section 11.1)*

**A.** 2 percent
**B.** 25 percent
**C.** 50 percent
**D.** 100 percent

### Friday

5. If two heterozygous animals that have a single dominant trait mate, what is the phenotype ratio of their young? *(Section 10.3)*

**A.** 3:1
**B.** 1:2:1
**C.** 9:3:3:1
**D.** 1:6:9:1

# Week 16

## Monday

1. Plants or animals that contain functional recombinant DNA from an organism of a different genus are known as what? *(Section 13.2)*

A. recombinant organisms
B. heterozygous organisms
C. polygenic organisms
D. transgenic organisms

## Tuesday

2. Which food chain correctly shows the path of matter and energy through an ecosystem? *(Section 2.2)*

A. deer → bear → grass
B. grass → deer → bear
C. seeds → bear → chipmunk
D. chipmunk → seeds → deer

## Wednesday

3. Which is NOT a factor that contributes to natural selection? *(Section 15.1)*

A. overproduction of offspring
B. inheritance of unfavorable variations
C. inheritance of favorable variations
D. survival and reproduction of individuals with favorable variations

## Thursday

4. Which is NOT true about hemoglobin? *(Section 34.1)*

A. It carries $CO_2$.
B. It carries $O_2$.
C. It is an iron-containing protein molecule in RBCs.
D. It is involved in blood clotting.

## Friday

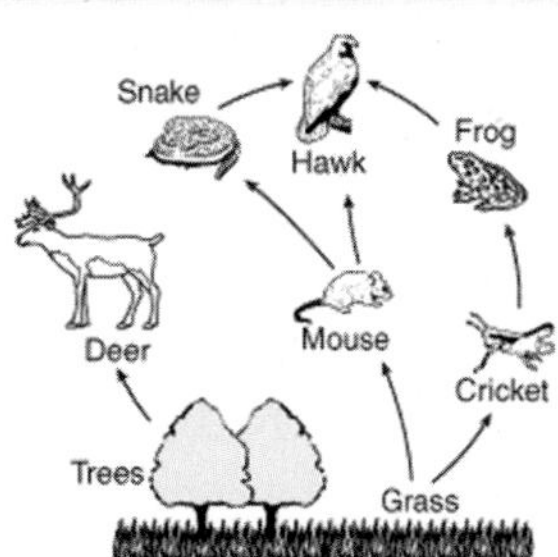


5. The food web above shows how many predators? *(Section 2.2)*

A. one
B. two
C. three
D. four

# Contents

## Unit 3



## Unit 4

## DATA ANALYSIS LAB

Build your analysis skills using actual data from real scientific sources.

## MiniLab

Practice scientific methods and hone your lab skills with these quick activities.

## MiniLab

Practice scientific methods and hone your lab skills with these quick activities.

# BIOLAB

**Apply the skills you developed in Launch Labs, MiniLabs, and Data Analysis Labs in these chapter-culminating, real-world labs.**

Chapter



Chapter

# Real-World Biology Features

**Explore today's world of biology. Discover the hot topics in biology, delve into new technologies, uncover the discoveries impacting biology, and investigate careers in biology.**

## BioDiscoveries

Discover pivotal advancements that have influenced the biological sciences.



## CUTTING-EDGE BIOLOGY

Challenge your brain with recent cutting edge developments in biology.



## Biology & Society

Examine biology in the news and sharpen your debating skills on complex issues in biology.



## In the Field

Get an inside look at careers in biology.

# Careers

## CAREERS IN BIOLOGY

Investigate a day in the life of people working in the field of biology.

# As You Read

**Within each section, you will find a tool to deepen your understanding and a tool to check your understanding.**

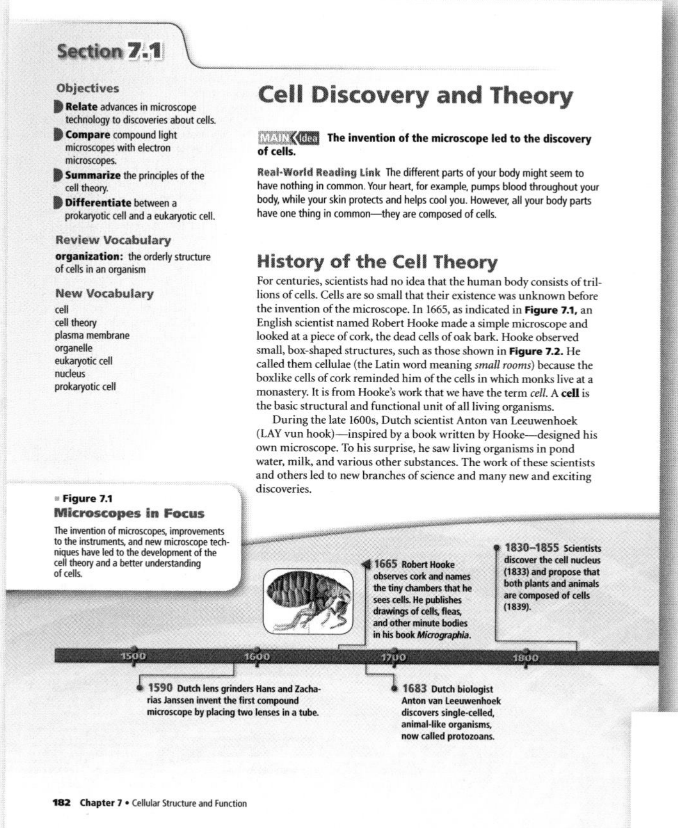

Section 7.1

**Objectives**

- **Relate** advances in microscope technology to discoveries about cells.
- **Compare** compound light microscopes with electron microscopes.
- **Summarize** the principles of the cell theory.
- **Differentiate** between a prokaryotic cell and a eukaryotic cell.

**Review Vocabulary**

**organization:** the orderly structure of cells in an organism

**New Vocabulary**

cell
cell theory
plasma membrane
organelle
eukaryotic cell
nucleus
prokaryotic cell

## Cell Discovery and Theory

MAIN Idea **The invention of the microscope led to the discovery of cells.**

**Real-World Reading Link** The different parts of your body might seem to have nothing in common. Your heart, for example, pumps blood throughout your body, while your skin protects and helps cool you. However, all your body parts have one thing in common—they are composed of cells.

### History of the Cell Theory

For centuries, scientists had no idea that the human body consists of trillions of cells. Cells are so small that their existence was unknown before the invention of the microscope. In 1665, as indicated in **Figure 7.1**, an English scientist named Robert Hooke made a simple microscope and looked at a piece of cork, the dead cells of oak bark. Hooke observed small, box-shaped structures, such as those shown in **Figure 7.2.** He called them cellulae (the Latin word meaning *small rooms*) because the boxlike cells of cork reminded him of the cells in which monks live at a monastery. It is from Hooke's work that we have the term *cell.* A **cell** is the basic structural and functional unit of all living organisms.

During the late 1600s, Dutch scientist Anton van Leeuwenhoek (LAY vun hook)—inspired by a book written by Hooke—designed his own microscope. To his surprise, he saw living organisms in pond water, milk, and various other substances. The work of these scientists and others led to new branches of science and many new and exciting discoveries.

**Figure 7.1**
**Microscopes in Focus**
The invention of microscopes, improvements to the instruments, and new microscope techniques have led to the development of the cell theory and a better understanding of cells.

1590 Dutch lens grinders Hans and Zacharias Janssen invent the first compound microscope by placing two lenses in a tube.

1665 Robert Hooke observes cork and names the tiny chambers that he sees cells. He publishes drawings of cells, fleas, and other minute bodies in his book *Micrographia*.

1683 Dutch biologist Anton van Leeuwenhoek discovers single-celled, animal-like organisms, now called protozoans.

1830–1855 Scientists discover the cell nucleus (1833) and propose that both plants and animals are composed of cells (1839).

1500 1600 1700 1800

182 Chapter 7 • Cellular Structure and Function

Source: Section 7.1, p.182

❮ **The Real-World Reading Link describes how the section's content might relate to you.**

Source: Section 7.1, p.183

**The cell theory** Naturalists and scientists continued observing the living microscopic world using glass lenses. In 1838, German scientist Matthias Schleiden carefully studied plant tissues and concluded that all plants are composed of cells. A year later, another German scientist, Theodor Schwann, reported that animal tissues also consisted of individual cells. Prussian physician Rudolph Virchow proposed in 1855 that all cells are produced from the division of existing cells. The observations and conclusions of these scientists and others are summarized as the cell theory. The **cell theory** is one of the fundamental ideas of modern biology and includes the following three principles:

1. All living organisms are composed of one or more cells.
2. Cells are the basic unit of structure and organization of all living organisms.
3. Cells arise only from previously existing cells, with cells passing copies of their genetic material on to their daughter cells.

**Reading Check** Can cells appear spontaneously without genetic material from previous cells?

### Microscope Technology

The discovery of cells and the development of the cell theory would not have been possible without microscopes. Improvements made to microscopes have enabled scientists to study cells in detail, as described in **Figure 7.1.**

Turn back to the opening pages of this chapter and compare the magnifications of the skin shown there. Note that the detail increases as the magnification and resolution—the ability of the microscope to make individual components visible—increase. Hooke and van Leeuwenhoek would not have been able to see the individual structures within human skin cells with their microscopes. Developments in microscope technology have given scientists the ability to study cells in greater detail than early scientists ever thought possible.

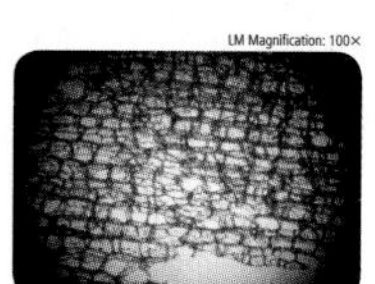


**Figure 7.2** Robert Hooke used a basic light microscope to see what looked like empty chambers in a cork sample.
**Infer** *What do you think Hooke would have seen if these were living cells?*

**LAUNCH Lab**
**Review** Based on what you've read about cells, how would you now answer the analysis questions?

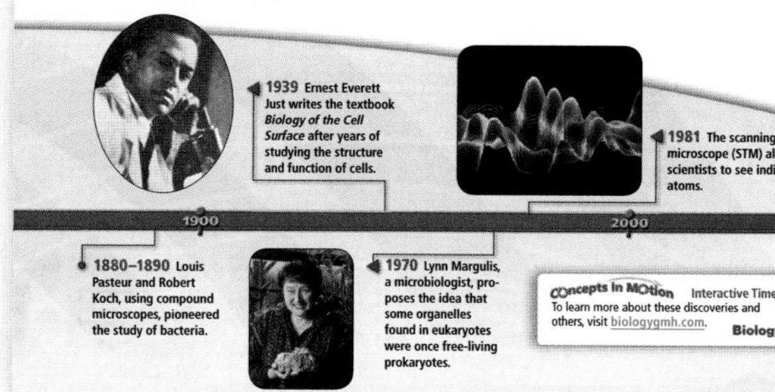

1939 Ernest Everett Just writes the textbook Biology of the Cell Surface after years of studying the structure and function of cells.
1981 The scanning tunneling microscope (STM) allows scientists to see individual atoms.
1900
2000
1880–1890 Louis Pasteur and Robert Koch, using compound microscopes, pioneered the study of bacteria.
1970 Lynn Margulis, a microbiologist, proposes the idea that some organelles found in eukaryotes were once free-living prokaryotes.


Concepts in Motion Interactive Time Line
To learn more about these discoveries and others, visit biologygmh.com.
Biology Online

Section 1 • Cell Discovery and Theory 183

**Reading Checks are questions that assess your understanding.** ❯

## OTHER READING SKILLS

- Ask yourself what is the BIG Idea? What is the MAIN Idea?
- Think about people, places, and situations that you've encountered. Are there any similarities with those mentioned in *Glencoe Biology?*
- Relate the information in *Glencoe Biology* to other areas you have studied.
- Predict events or outcomes by using clues and information that you already know.
- Change your predictions as you read and gather new information.

# After You Read

**Follow-up your reading with a summary and assessment of the material to evaluate if you understood the text.**

Look again at **Figure 7.4** and compare the types of cells. You can see why scientists place them into two broad categories that are based on internal structures. Both have a plasma membrane, but one cell contains many distinct internal structures called **organelles**—specialized structures that carry out specific cell functions.

**Eukaryotic cells** contain a nucleus and other organelles that are bound by membranes, also referred to as membrane-bound organelles. The **nucleus** is a distinct central organelle that contains the cell's genetic material in the form of DNA. Organelles enable cell functions to take place in different parts of the cell at the same time. Most organisms are made up of eukaryotic cells and are called eukaryotes. However, some unicellular organisms, such as some algae and yeast, are also eukaryotes.

**Prokaryotic cells** are defined as cells without a nucleus or other membrane-bound organelles. Most unicellular organisms, such as bacteria, are prokaryotic cells. Thus they are called prokaryotes. Many scientists think that prokaryotes are similar to the first organisms on Earth.

VOCABULARY
WORD ORIGIN
**Eukaryote**
**Prokaryote**
***eu–*** prefix; from Greek, meaning *true*
***pro–*** prefix; from Greek, meaning *before*
***–kary*** from Greek, meaning *nucleus*

**Origin of cell diversity** If you have ever wondered why a company makes two products that are similar, you can imagine that scientists have asked why there are two basic types of cells. The answer might be that eukaryotic cells evolved from prokaryotic cells millions of years ago. According to the endosymbiont theory, a symbiotic mutual relationship involved one prokaryotic cell living inside of another. The endosymbiont theory is discussed in greater detail in Chapter 14.

Imagine how organisms would be different if the eukaryotic form had not evolved. Because eukaryotic cells are larger and have distinct organelles, these cells have developed specific functions. Having specific functions has led to cell diversity, and thus more diverse organisms that can adapt better to their environments. Life-forms more complex than bacteria might not have evolved without eukaryotic cells.

**Section 7.1 Assessment**

**Section Summary**
- Microscopes have been used as a tool for scientific study since the late 1500s.
- Scientists use different types of microscopes to study cells.
- The cell theory summarizes three principles.
- There are two broad groups of cell types—prokaryotic cells and eukaryotic cells.
- Eukaryotic cells contain a nucleus and organelles.

**Understand Main Ideas**
1. MAIN Idea **Explain** how the development and improvement of microscopes changed the study of living organisms.
2. **Compare and contrast** a compound light microscope and an electron microscope.
3. **Summarize** the cell theory.
4. **Differentiate** the plasma membrane and the organelles.

**Think Scientifically**
5. *Describe* how you would determine if the cells of a newly discovered organism were prokaryotic or eukaryotic.
6. MATH in Biology If the overall magnification of a series of two lenses is 30×, and one lens magnified 5×, what is the magnification of the other lens? Calculate the total magnification if the 5× lens is replaced by a 7× lens.

186 Chapter 7 • Cellular Structure and Function     Biology Online Self-Check Quiz biologygmh.com

Source: Chapter 7, p.186

**Each section concludes with an assessment. The assessment contains a summary and questions. The summary reviews the section's key concepts while the questions test your understanding.**

CHAPTER 7 **Study Guide**

STUDY TO GO Download quizzes, key terms, and flash cards from biologygmh.com.

FOLDABLES **Apply** Use what you have learned about osmosis and cellular transport to design an apparatus that would enable a freshwater fish to survive in a saltwater habitat.

| Vocabulary | Key Concepts |
|---|---|
| **Section 7.1 Cell Discovery and Theory** | |
| • cell (p. 182)<br>• cell theory (p. 183)<br>• eukaryotic cell (p. 186)<br>• nucleus (p. 186)<br>• organelle (p. 186)<br>• plasma membrane (p. 185)<br>• prokaryotic cell (p. 186) | MAIN Idea The invention of the microscope led to the discovery of cells.<br>• Microscopes have been used as a tool for scientific study since the late 1500s.<br>• Scientists use different types of microscopes to study cells.<br>• The cell theory summarizes three principles.<br>• There are two broad groups of cell types—prokaryotic cells and eukaryotic cells.<br>• Eukaryotic cells contain a nucleus and organelles. |
| **Section 7.2 The Plasma Membrane** | |
| • fluid mosaic model (p. 190)<br>• phospholipid bilayer (p. 188)<br>• selective permeability (p. 187)<br>• transport protein (p. 189) | MAIN Idea The plasma membrane helps to maintain a cell's homeostasis.<br>• Selective permeability is the property of the plasma membrane that allows it to control what enters and leaves the cell.<br>• The plasma membrane is made up of two layers of phospholipid molecules.<br>• Cholesterol and transport proteins aid in the function of the plasma membrane.<br>• The fluid mosaic model describes the plasma membrane. |
| **Section 7.3 Structures and Organelles** | |
| • cell wall (p. 198)<br>• centriole (p. 196)<br>• chloroplast (p. 197)<br>• cilium (p. 198)<br>• cytoplasm (p. 191)<br>• cytoskeleton (p. 191)<br>• endoplasmic reticulum (p. 194)<br>• flagellum (p. 198)<br>• Golgi apparatus (p. 195)<br>• lysosome (p. 196)<br>• mitochondrion (p. 197)<br>• nucleolus (p. 193)<br>• ribosome (p. 193)<br>• vacuole (p. 195) | MAIN Idea Eukaryotic cells contain organelles that allow the specialization and the separation of functions within the cell.<br>• Eukaryotic cells contain membrane-bound organelles in the cytoplasm that perform cell functions.<br>• Ribosomes are the sites of protein synthesis.<br>• Mitochondria are the powerhouses of cells.<br>• Plant and animal cells contain many of the same organelles, while other organelles are unique to either plant cells or animal cells. |
| **Section 7.4 Cellular Transport** | |
| • active transport (p. 205)<br>• diffusion (p. 201)<br>• dynamic equilibrium (p. 202)<br>• endocytosis (p. 207)<br>• exocytosis (p. 207)<br>• facilitated diffusion (p. 202)<br>• hypertonic solution (p. 205)<br>• hypotonic solution (p. 204)<br>• isotonic solution (p. 204)<br>• osmosis (p. 203) | MAIN Idea Cellular transport moves substances within the cell and moves substances into and out of the cell.<br>• Cells maintain homeostasis using passive and active transport.<br>• Concentration, temperature, and pressure affect the rate of diffusion.<br>• Cells must maintain homeostasis in all types of solutions, including isotonic, hypotonic, and hypertonic.<br>• Some large molecules are moved into and out of the cell using endocytosis and exocytosis. |

210 Chapter 7 • Study Guide     Biology Online Vocabulary PuzzleMaker biologygmh.com

Source: Chapter 7, p.210

**At the end of each chapter you will find a Study Guide. The chapter's vocabulary words as well as key concepts are listed here. Use this guide for review and to check your comprehension.**

## OTHER WAYS TO REVIEW

- State the BIG Idea.
- Relate the MAIN Idea to the BIG Idea.
- Use your own words to explain what you read.
- Apply this new information in other school subjects or at home.
- Identify sources you could use to find out more information about the topic.

# Scavenger Hunt

*Glencoe Biology* contains a wealth of information. Complete this fun activity so you will know where to look to learn as much as you can.

**As you complete this scavenger hunt, either alone or with your teacher or family, you will learn quickly how *Glencoe Biology* is organized and how to get the most out of your reading and study time.**

1. How many units are in this book? How many chapters?
2. On what page does the glossary begin? What glossary is online?
3. In what two areas can you find a listing of Laboratory Safety Symbols?
4. Suppose you want to find a list of all the MiniLabs, Data Analysis Labs, and BioLabs. Where in the front do you look?
5. How can you quickly find the pages that have information about scientist Jewell Plummer Cobb?
6. What is the name of the table that summarizes the Key Concepts of a chapter?
7. In what special feature can you find information on unit conversion? What are the page numbers?
8. On what page can you find the BIG Idea for Unit 1? On what page can you find the MAIN Idea for Chapter 2?
9. What feature at the start of each unit provides insight into biologists in action?
10. Name four activities that are found at Biology Online.
11. What study tool shown at the beginning of a chapter can you make from notebook paper?
12. Where do you go to view the Concepts In Motion?
13. CUTTING-EDGE BIOLOGY and BioDiscoveries are two types of end-of-chapter features. What are the other two types?

# Investigation and Experimentation

The foundation of scientific knowledge is Investigation and Experimentation. In this section, you will read about lab safety, the proper way to take measurements, and some laboratory techniques. While not every situation you might encounter in the laboratory is covered here, you will gain practical and useful knowledge to make your investigation and experimentation a successful experience.

## Laboratory Safety

**Follow these safety guidelines and rules to help protect you and others during laboratory investigations.**

### Complete the Lab Safety Form

- Prior to each investigation your teacher will have you complete a lab safety form. This contract will inform your teacher that you have read the procedure and are prepared to perform the investigation.
- After your teacher reviews your comments, make any necessary corrections, and sign or initial the form.
- Use the lab safety form to help you prepare for each procedure and take responsibility for your own safety.

Teacher Approval Initials ________

Date of Approval ________

**Student Lab/Activity Safety Form**

Student Name: ____________________

Date: ____________________

Lab/Activity Title: ____________________

In order to show your teacher that you understand the safety concerns of this lab/activity, the following questions must be answered after the teacher explains the information to you. You must have your teacher initial this form before you can proceed with the activity/lab.

1. How would you describe what you will be doing during this lab/activity?

What are the safety concerns associated with this lab/activity (as explained by your teacher)?

- ____________________
- ____________________
- ____________________
- ____________________
- ____________________

What additional safety concerns or questions do you have?

Adapted from Gerlovich, et al. (2005). The Total Science Safety System CD, JaKel, Inc. Used with Permission.

### Prevent Accidents

- Always wear chemical splash safety goggles (not glasses) in the laboratory. Goggles should fit snugly against your face to prevent any liquid from entering the eyes. Put on your goggles before beginning the lab and wear them throughout the entire activity, cleanup, and hand washing.
- Wear protective aprons and the proper type of gloves as your teacher instructs.
- Keep your hands away from your face and mouth while working in the laboratory.
- Do not wear sandals or other open-toed shoes in the lab.
- Remove jewelry on hands and wrists before doing lab work. Remove loose jewelry, such as chains and long necklaces, to prevent them from getting caught in equipment.
- Do not wear clothing loose enough to catch on anything. If clothing is loose, tape or tie it down.
- Tie back long hair to keep it away from flames and equipment.
- Do not use hair spray or other flammable hair products just before or during laboratory work where an open flame is used. These products ignite easily.
- Eating, drinking, chewing gum, applying makeup, and smoking are prohibited in the laboratory.
- You are expected to behave properly in the laboratory. Practical jokes and fooling around can lead to accidents or injury.
- Notify your teacher about allergies or other health conditions that can affect participation in a lab.

## Follow Lab Procedures

- Study all procedures before you begin a laboratory investigation. Ask questions if you do not understand any part of the procedures.
- Review and understand all safety symbols associated with the investigation. A table of the safety symbols is found on page xxxi for your reference.
- Do not begin any activity until directed to do so by your teacher.
- Use all lab equipment for its intended purpose only.
- Collect and carry all equipment and materials to your work area before beginning the lab.
- When obtaining laboratory materials, dispense only the amount you will use.
- If you have materials left over after completing the investigation, check with your teacher to determine the best choice for recycling or disposing of the materials.
- Keep your work area uncluttered.
- Learn and follow procedures for using specific laboratory equipment, such as balances, microscopes, hot plates, and burners.
- When heating or rinsing a container such as a test tube or flask, point it away from yourself and others.
- Do not taste, touch or smell any chemical or substance in the lab.
- If instructed to smell a substance in a container, hold the container a short distance away and fan vapors toward your nose.
- Do not substitute other chemicals or substances for those in the materials list unless instructed to do so by your teacher.
- Do not take any chemical or material outside of the laboratory.

## Clean up the Lab

- Turn off all burners, gas valves, and water faucets before leaving the laboratory. Disconnect all electrical devices.
- Clean all equipment as instructed by your teacher. Return everything to the proper storage place.
- Dispose of all materials properly. Place disposable items in containers specifically marked for that type of item. Do not pour liquids down the drain unless instructed to do so by your teacher.
- **Wash your hands thoroughly with soap and warm water after each activity and before removing your goggles.**

## Know How to Handle Emergencies

- **Inform your teacher immediately of any mishap, such as fire, bodily injuries, burns, electrical shock, glassware breakage, and chemical or other spills.**
- Do not attempt to clean up spills unless you are given permission and instructions on how to do so. In most instances, your teacher will clean up spills.
- Know the location of the fire extinguisher, safety shower, eyewash, fire blanket, and first-aid kit. After receiving instructions, you can use the safety shower, eyewash, and fire blanket in an emergency without your teacher's permission. However, the fire extinguisher and first-aid kit should only be used by your teacher or, in an extreme emergency, with your teacher's permission.
- If chemicals come into contact with your eyes or skin, notify your teacher immediately and flush your skin or eyes with water.
- If someone is injured or becomes ill, only a professional medical provider or someone certified in first aid should perform first-aid procedures.

## Be Responsible

Because your teacher cannot anticipate every safety hazard that might occur and he or she cannot be everywhere in the room at the same time, you need to take some responsibility for your own safety. The general information below should apply to nearly every science lab.

You must:

- review any safety symbols in the labs and be certain you know what they mean;
- follow all teacher instructions for safety and make certain you understand all the hazards related to the lab you are about to perform;
- be able to explain the purpose of the lab;
- be able to explain, or demonstrate, all reasonable emergency procedures, such as:
  - how to evacuate the room during emergencies;
  - how to react to any chemical emergencies;
  - how to deal with fire emergencies;
  - how to perform a scientific investigation safely;
  - how to anticipate some safety concerns and be prepared to address them;
  - how to use equipment properly and safely.
- be able to locate and use all safety equipment as directed by your teacher, such as:
  - fire extinguishers;
  - fire blankets;
  - eye protective equipment (goggles, safety glasses, face shield);
  - eyewash;
  - drench shower.
- be sure to ask questions about any safety concerns that you might have BEFORE starting any investigation.

## Safety Symbols

These safety symbols are used in laboratory and field investigations in this book to indicate possible hazards. Learn the meaning of each symbol and refer to this page often. *Remember to wash your hands thoroughly after completing lab procedures.*

| SAFETY SYMBOLS | HAZARD | EXAMPLES | PRECAUTION | REMEDY |
|---|---|---|---|---|
| DISPOSAL | Special disposal procedures need to be followed. | certain chemicals, living organisms | Do not dispose of these materials in the sink or trash can. | Dispose of wastes as directed by your teacher. |
| BIOLOGICAL | Organisms or other biological materials that might be harmful to humans | bacteria, fungi, blood, unpreserved tissues, plant materials | Avoid skin contact with these materials. Wear mask or gloves. | Notify your teacher if you suspect contact with material. Wash hands thoroughly. |
| EXTREME TEMPERATURE | Objects that can burn skin by being too cold or too hot | boiling liquids, hot plates, dry ice, liquid nitrogen | Use proper protection when handling. | Go to your teacher for first aid. |
| SHARP OBJECT | Use of tools or glassware that can easily puncture or slice skin | razor blades, pins, scalpels, pointed tools, dissecting probes, broken glass | Practice common-sense behavior and follow guidelines for use of the tool. | Go to your teacher for first aid. |
| FUME | Possible danger to respiratory tract from fumes | ammonia, acetone, nail polish remover, heated sulfur, moth balls | Make sure there is good ventilation. Never smell fumes directly. Wear a mask. | Leave foul area and notify your teacher immediately. |
| ELECTRICAL | Possible danger from electrical shock or burn | improper grounding, liquid spills, short circuits, exposed wires | Double-check setup with teacher. Check condition of wires and apparatus. Use GFI-protected outlets. | Do not attempt to fix electrical problems. Notify your teacher immediately. |
| IRRITANT | Substances that can irritate the skin or mucous membranes of the respiratory tract | pollen, moth balls, steel wool, fiberglass, potassium permanganate | Wear dust mask and gloves. Practice extra care when handling these materials. | Go to your teacher for first aid. |
| CHEMICAL | Chemicals that can react with and destroy tissue and other materials | bleaches such as hydrogen peroxide; acids such as sulfuric acid, hydrochloric acid; bases such as ammonia, sodium hydroxide | Wear goggles, gloves, and an apron. | Immediately flush the affected area with water and notify your teacher. |
| TOXIC | Substance may be poisonous if touched, inhaled, or swallowed. | mercury, many metal compounds, iodine, poinsettia plant parts | Follow your teacher's instructions. | Always wash hands thoroughly after use. Go to your teacher for first aid. |
| FLAMMABLE | Open flame may ignite flammable chemicals, loose clothing, or hair. | alcohol, kerosene, potassium permanganate, hair, clothing | Avoid open flames and heat when using flammable chemicals. | Notify your teacher immediately. Use fire safety equipment if applicable. |
| OPEN FLAME | Open flame in use, may cause fire. | hair, clothing, paper, synthetic materials | Tie back hair and loose clothing. Follow teacher's instructions on lighting and extinguishing flames. | Always wash hands thoroughly after use. Go to your teacher for first aid. |

**Eye Safety**
Proper eye protection must be worn at all times by anyone performing or observing science activities.

**Clothing Protection**
This symbol appears when substances could stain or burn clothing.

**Animal Safety**
This symbol appears when safety of animals and students must be ensured.

**Radioactivity**
This symbol appears when radioactive materials are used.

**Handwashing**
After the lab, wash hands with soap and water before removing goggles.

## Field Investigation Safety

**On occasion your teacher might conduct a field investigation—an investigation on school grounds or off-campus. While many of the laboratory safety guidelines apply, the field has unique safety considerations.**

### Work Together

- Work with at least one other person.
- Never stray from the main group either alone or with a small group.
- Make sure each person in your group understands their task and how to perform it. Ask your teacher for clarification if necessary.
- Determine how members of your group will communicate in case of a loud environment or an emergency.
- Your teacher or chaperones should be equipped with either cell phones or walkie-talkies. They should be able to communicate with one another, the school, or emergency personnel if needed, so be sure to let your teacher know if you need help.

### Dress Appropriately

- Wear your safety goggles, aprons, and gloves as indicated by the procedure.
- Protect yourself from the Sun with sunblock and a hat.
- Long pants and shirts with long sleeves will protect you from the Sun, insects, and plants such as poison ivy or poison oak.

Poison ivy

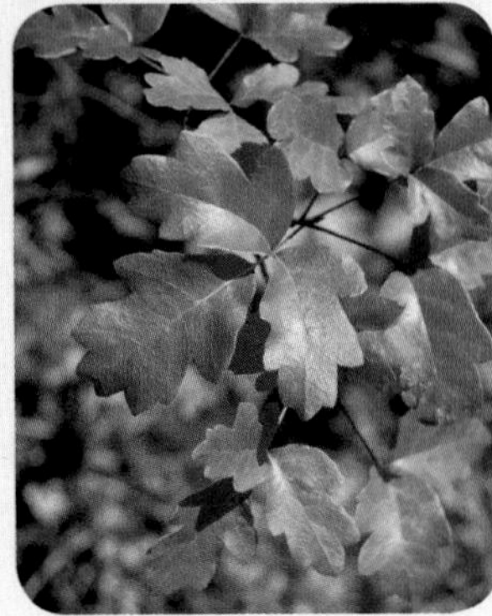

Poison oak

- Insect-repellent sprays or creams may be necessary to use.
- Be sure to wear shoes that have a closed toe and heel as well as a textured sole.
- If your investigation requires that you wade into a stream, river, lake, or other body of water, wear water-resistant clothing. Do not enter the water if you have any open sores.

### Consider Your Environment

- Never approach wildlife.
- Never drink water from a stream, river, lake, or other body of water.
- Do not remove the habitat. Create a sketch of organisms you are studying.
- Stay away from power lines.
- Stay away from the edge of cliffs or ledges.
- Stay on the marked trails.

### Follow General Guidelines

- Treat your field investigation like a laboratory investigation. There should be no horseplay.
- A first aid kit should be brought to the investigation site.
- Always wash your hands when you are finished. If soap and water are unavailable, use an alcohol-based hand sanitizer.

## Data Collection

**Biologists take measurements in many types of investigations.**
- **a population biologist might count tree frogs in a rain forest survey**
- **a physical therapist might observe range of motion of an injured knee**
- **microbiologist might measure the diameters of bacteria.**

**In this section, you will learn how biologists take careful measurements. When you plan and perform your biology labs, use this section as a guide.**

### Accuracy, Precision, and Error

In any measurement, there always will be some error—the difference between the measured value and the real or accepted value. Error comes from several sources, including the experimenter, the equipment, and even changes in experimental conditions. Errors can affect both the accuracy and precision of measurements.

- **Accuracy** refers to how close a measurement is to the real value or the accepted value.
- **Precision** refers to how close a series of measurements are to one another.

Examine the targets below while you consider a food scientist who measures the mass of a sample three times.

- Proper equipment set up and good technique—accurate and precise data
- Incorrect equipment set up but good technique—precise but inaccurate data
- Incorrect equipment set up and careless technique—inaccurate and imprecise data

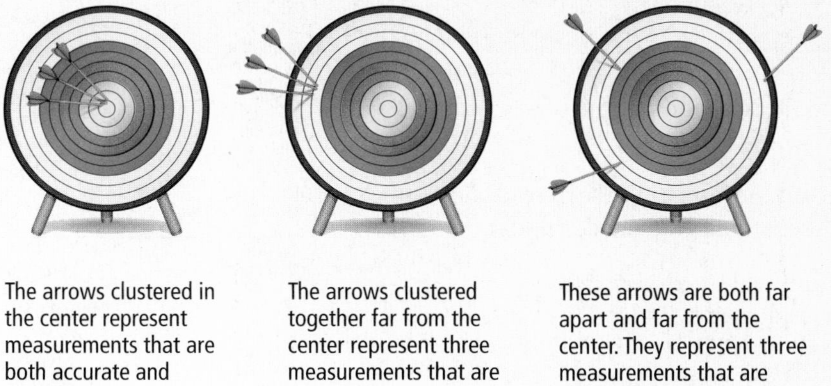

**Figure 1** The arrows clustered in the center represent measurements that are both accurate and precise. The arrows clustered together far from the center represent three measurements that are precise but inaccurate. These arrows are both far apart and far from the center. They represent three measurements that are inaccurate and imprecise.

### Error Analysis

Imagine that an epidemiologist (eh puh dee mee AHL uh just)—a biologist who studies epidemics—tested a hypothesis about the way avian flu might spread from chickens to humans. All data have been gathered. The epidemiologist must now perform an error analysis, which is a process to identify and describe possible sources of error in measurements.

In your biology investigations, you will need to think of possible sources of measurement errors. Ask yourself questions such as:
- Did I take more than one reading of each measurement?
- Did I use the equipment properly?
- Was I objective, or did I make the results turn out as I expected they might?

## Measure Mass

### Triple-Beam Balance

A triple-beam balance has a pan and three beams with sliding masses called riders. At one end of the beams is a pointer that indicates whether the mass on the pan is equal to the masses shown on the beams.

**To use:**

1. Make sure the balance is zeroed before measuring the mass of an object. The balance is zeroed if the pointer is at zero when nothing is on the pan and riders are at their zero points.
2. Place the object to be measured on the pan.
3. Move the riders one notch at a time away from the pan. Begin with the largest rider. If moving the largest rider one notch brings the pointer below zero, begin measuring the mass with the next smaller rider.
4. Change the positions of the riders until they balance the mass on the pan and the pointer is at zero. Then add the readings from the three beams to determine the mass of the object.

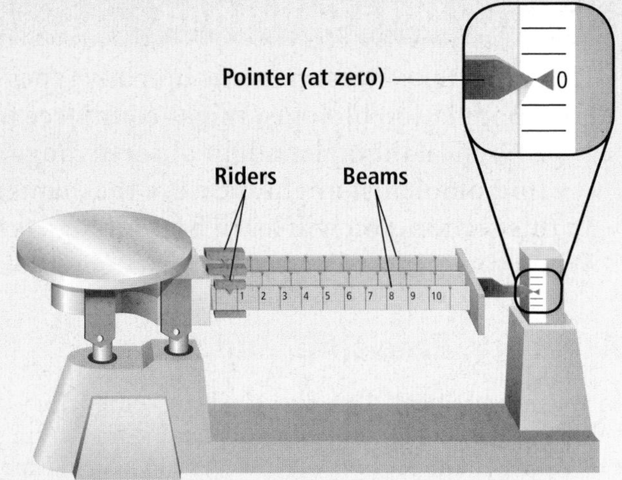


**Figure 2**

**TIP**

**When using a weighing boat or weighing paper, be sure to zero the balance after you've placed the boat or paper on the pan and before you add your substance to the boat or paper.**

## Measure Volume

### Graduated Cylinder

Use a graduated cylinder to measure the volume of a liquid.

**To use:**

1. Be sure to have your eyes at the level of the surface of the liquid when reading the scale on a graduated cylinder.
2. The surface of most liquids will be curved slightly down when they are held in a graduated cylinder. This curve is called the meniscus. Read the volume of the liquid at the bottom of the meniscus, as shown in **Figure 3.**
3. The volume will often be between two lines on the graduated cylinder. You should estimate the final digit in your measurement. For example, if the bottom of the meniscus appears to be exactly half way between the marks for 96 mL and 97 mL, you would read a volume of 96.5 mL.
4. To find the volume of a small solid object, record the volume of some water in a graduated cylinder. Then, measure the volume of the water after you add the object to the cylinder. The volume of the object is the difference between the first and second measurements.

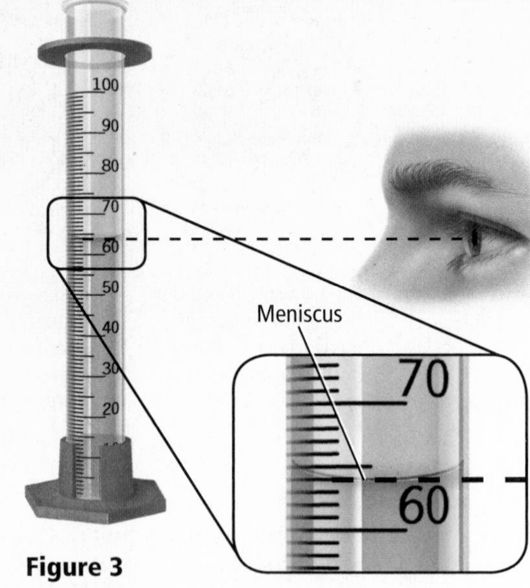


**Figure 3**

**TIP**

**Do not use a beaker to measure the volume of a liquid. Beakers are used for holding and pouring liquids. To avoid overflow, be sure to use a beaker that holds roughly twice as much liquid as you need.**

## Perform Chromatography

Paper chromatography is a commonly used technique in the biology laboratory for separating mixtures of substances. You will perform chromatography with a special chromatography paper or with filter paper and a liquid solvent. Separation occurs based on the ability of substances in the mixture to dissolve in the solvent. The general steps for this type of chromatography are:

1. a mixture is dissolved in a liquid and placed on the paper;

2. one end of the paper is placed in a solvent;

3. the substances separate based on their tendencies to move along the surface of the paper while in the solvent.

For example, chlorophyll from leaves can be separated by paper chromatography, as shown in **Figure 14.** A dot of the chlorophyll extract is placed near one end of the strip of paper. The end of the paper nearest the dot is placed in alcohol, which acts as the solvent. The alcohol should not touch the extract to be separated, but should be just below it.

The alcohol moves up the paper and picks up substances in the chlorophyll extract. Substances in the extract that are tightly held to the paper will move slowly up the paper, while extract substances that are not as tightly held move quickly up the paper. This results in bands of different substances on the chromatography paper.

**Figure 14**

## Use Indicators

Indicators are used to test for the presence of specific types of chemicals or substances. The table below lists commonly used indicators, what they test for, and how they react.

**Indicators**

| Indicator | What it indicates in a solution | Reaction |
|---|---|---|
| **Litmus paper** | acid or base | • red litmus turns blue if a base<br>• blue litmus turns red if an acid |
| **pH paper** | pH | • color change compared to a color chart to estimate the pH |
| **Bromthymol blue** | presence of carbon dioxide | • turns yellow if carbon dioxide is present<br>• change to blue from yellow when carbon dioxide is removed |
| **Phenolphthalein solution** | presence of carbon dioxide or a basic solution | • turns from clear to a bright pink in the presence of either substance |
| **Benedict's solution** | presence of simple sugars when heated | • high sugar concentration, change from blue to red<br>• low sugar concentration, change from blue to yellow |
| **Biuret solution** | presence of protein | • turns from light blue to purple |
| **Lugol's solution** | presence of starch | • turns from deep brown to bluish-black |

# The Study of Life

**Section 1**
**Introduction to Biology**
MAIN Idea All living things share the characteristics of life.

**Section 2**
**The Nature of Science**
MAIN Idea Science is a process based on inquiry that seeks to develop explanations.

**Section 3**
**Methods of Science**
MAIN Idea Biologists use specific methods when conducting research.

## BioFacts

- There are approximately 200 billion stars that make up the Milky Way galaxy.
- Humans are 1 out of an estimated 100 million species of life on Earth.
- The human brain is made up of 100 billion neurons.

Earth

Human population

**Human neurons**
Color-Enhanced SEM
Magnification: unavailable

# Start-Up Activities

## LAUNCH Lab

### Why is observation important in science?

Scientists use a planned, organized approach to solving problems. A key element of this approach is gathering information through detailed observations. Scientists extend their ability to observe by using scientific tools and techniques.

**Procedure**

1. Read and complete the lab safety form.
2. Pick an unshelled **peanut** from the **container of peanuts.** Carefully observe the peanut using your senses and available tools. Record your observations.
3. Do not change or mark the peanut. Return your peanut to the container.
4. After the peanuts are mixed, locate your peanut based on your recorded observations.

**Analysis**

1. **List** the observations that were the most helpful in identifying your peanut. Which were the least helpful?
2. **Classify** your observations into groups.
3. **Justify** why it was important to record detailed observations in this lab. Infer why observations are important in biology.

Visit biologygmh.com to:

- study the entire chapter online
- explore the Interactive Time Line, Concepts in Motion, Interactive Tables, Microscopy Links, Virtual Labs, and links to virtual dissections
- access Web links for more information, projects, and activities
- review content online with Interactive Tutor and take Self-Check Quizzes

**Biologists** Make the following Foldable to help you organize examples of things biologists do.

**STEP 1** Stack three sheets of notebook paper 2.5 cm apart as illustrated.

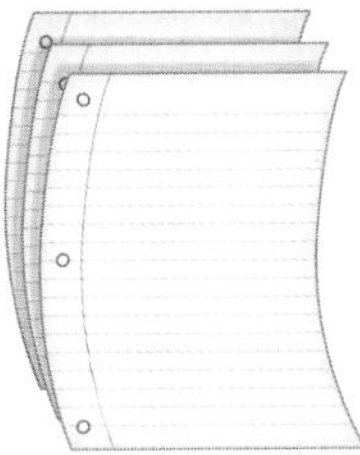

**STEP 2** Bring up the bottom edges and fold to form five tabs of equal size.

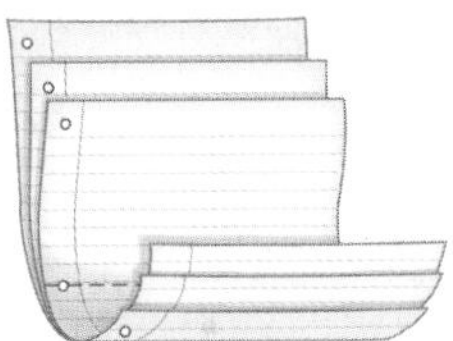

**STEP 3** Rotate your Foldable 180°. Staple along the folded edge to secure all sheets. Label the tabs *Some Roles of Biologists, Study the diversity of life, Research diseases, Develop technology, Improve agriculture*, and *Preserve the environment*.

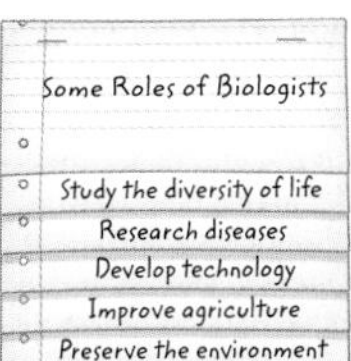


FOLDABLES **Use this Foldable with Section 1.1.** As you study the section, summarize these examples of the different roles of biologists.

Section 1.1

## Objectives

- **Define** biology.
- **Identify** possible benefits from studying biology.
- **Summarize** the characteristics of living things.

### Review Vocabulary

**environment:** the living and nonliving things that surround an organism and with which the organism interacts

### New Vocabulary

biology
organism
organization
growth
development
reproduction
species
stimulus
response
homeostasis
adaptation

# Introduction to Biology

MAIN Idea **All living things share the characteristics of life.**

**Real-World Reading Link** Think about several different living or once-living things. The bacteria that live in your small intestine, the great white sharks in the ocean, a field of corn, a skateboarder, and the extinct *Tyrannosaurus rex* differ in structure and function. Who discovered what all these things have in common?

## The Science of Life

Before Jane Goodall, pictured in **Figure 1.1,** arrived in Gombe Stream National Park in Tanzania in 1960 to study chimpanzees, the world of chimpanzees was a mystery. Jane's curiosity, determination, and patience over a long period of time resulted in the chimpanzee troop's acceptance of her presence so that she was able to observe their behavior closely.

When people study living things or pose questions about how living things interact with the environment, they are learning about **biology**—the science of life. Life flourishes on Earth, and a curiosity about life is a major reason why some people study biology.

In biology, you will study the origins and history of life and once-living things, the structures of living things, how living things interact with one another, and how living things function. This will help you understand how humans have a vital role in preserving the natural environment and sustaining life on Earth.

Have you ever hiked in a forest and wondered why different trees have leaves with different shapes? Maybe you have watched an ant quickly cross the sidewalk toward a breadcrumb and wondered how the ant knew that the breadcrumb was there. When you ask these questions, you are observing, and you are asking questions about life.

**Vocabulary**
**Word Origin**
**Biology**
***bio–*** prefix; from the Greek word *bios,* meaning *life.*
***–logy*** suffix; from the Greek word *logos,* meaning *study.*

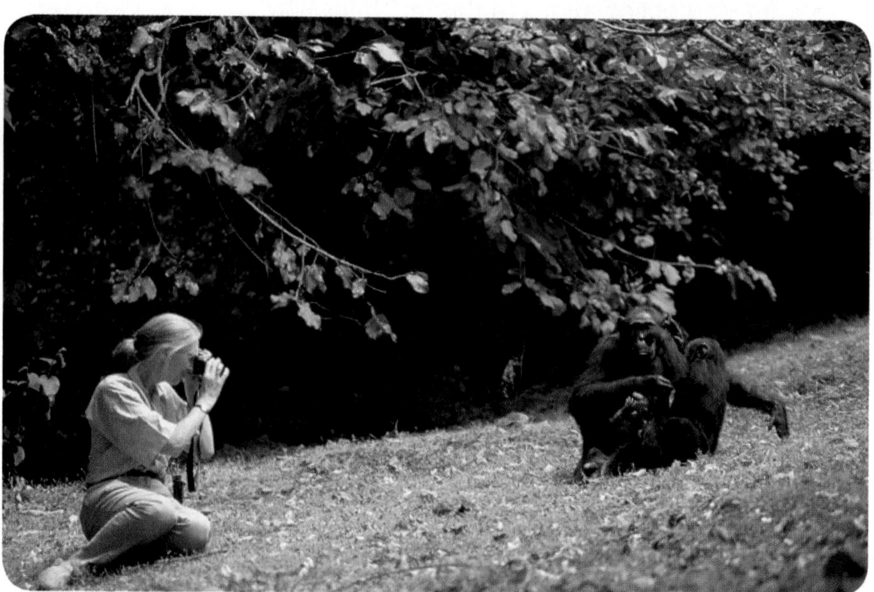

**Figure 1.1** Jane Goodall conducted field research for many years to observe chimpanzee behavior.
**Predict** *the types of questions you would ask if you observed chimpanzee behavior.*

## What do biologists do?

Imagine being the first person to look into a microscope and discover cells. What do you think it was like to find the first dinosaur fossils that indicated feathers? Who studies how organisms, including the marbled stargazer fish in **Figure 1.2,** obtain food? Will the AIDS virus be defeated? Is there life on other planets or anywhere else in the universe? The people who study biology—biologists—make discoveries and seek explanations by performing laboratory and field investigations. Throughout this textbook, you will discover what biologists in the real world do and you will learn about careers in biology.

**Figure 1.2** The marbled stargazer fish lives beneath the ocean floor off the coast of Indonesia. It explodes upward from beneath the sand to grab its food.
**Observe** ***How does this fish hide from its food?***

**Study the diversity of life** Jane Goodall, shown in **Figure 1.1,** studied chimpanzees in their natural environments. She asked questions such as, "How do chimpanzees behave in the wild?" and "How can chimpanzee behaviors be characterized?" From her recorded and detailed observations, sketches, and maps of chimpanzees' daily travels, Goodall learned how chimpanzees grow and develop and how they gather food. She studied and recorded chimpanzee reproductive habits and their aggressive nature. She learned that they use tools. Goodall's data provided a better understanding of chimpanzees, and as a result, scientists know how to best protect them.

**FOLDABLES**
Incorporate information from this section into your Foldable.

**Research diseases** Mary-Claire King also studied chimpanzees—not their behavior but their genetics. In 1973, she established that the genomes (genes) of chimpanzees and humans are 99 percent identical. Her work currently focuses on unraveling the genetic basis of breast cancer, a disease that affects one out of eight women.

Many biologists research diseases. Questions such as "What causes the disease?", "How does the body fight the disease?", and "How does the disease spread?" often guide biologists' research. Biologists have developed vaccines for smallpox, chicken pox, and diphtheria, and currently, some biologists are researching the development of a vaccine for HIV. Other biologists focus their research on diseases such as diabetes, avian flu, anorexia, and alcoholism, or on trauma such as spinal cord injuries that result in paralysis. Biologists worldwide are researching new medicines for such things as lowering cholesterol levels, fighting obesity, reducing the risk of heart attacks, and preventing Alzheimer's disease.

**Figure 1.3** A prosthetic "bionic" hand is new technology that can help extend human capabilities.

**Develop technologies** When you hear the word *technology,* you might think of high-speed computers, cell phones, and DVD players. However, technology is defined as the application of scientific knowledge to solve human needs and to extend human capabilities. **Figure 1.3** shows how new technology—a "bionic" hand—can help someone who has lost an arm.

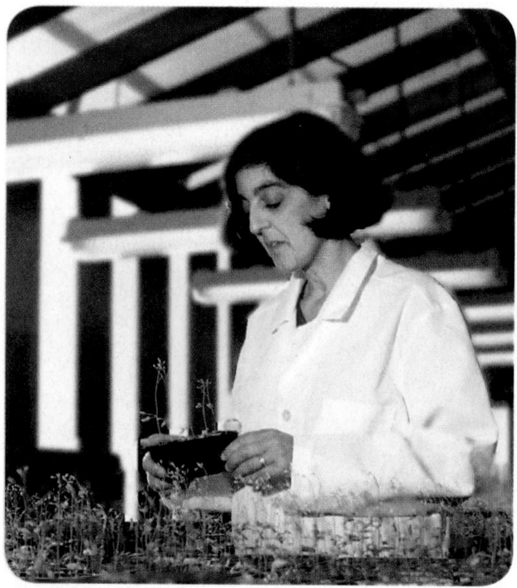

■ **Figure 1.4** Joanne Chory, a plant biologist, researches how plants respond to light.

For example, Charles Drew was a doctor who pioneered methods to separate blood plasma from blood cells and safely store and transport blood plasma for transfusions. His research led to blood banks that saved soldiers during World War II and helps countless patients today.

Biologists today continue to discover new ways to improve and save lives. For example, the field of bioengineering applies knowledge gained from studying the function of living systems to the design of mechanical devices such as artificial limbs. In addition, biologists in the field of biotechnology research cells, DNA, and living systems to discover new medicines and medical treatments.

**Improve agriculture** Some biologists study the possibilities of genetically engineering plants to grow in poor soils or to resist insects, fungal infections, or frost damage. Other biologists research agricultural issues to improve food production to feed the world's growing human population.

Joanne Chory, a plant biologist shown in **Figure 1.4,** studies mustard plants' sensitivity to light and their responses when exposed to different light sources, different times of exposure, and other conditions. Because of her work with plant growth hormones and light, agriculturists might be able to increase the amount of food produced from crops or to grow crops in areas where they normally would not grow.

**Preserve the environment** Environmental biologists seek to prevent the extinction of animals and plants by developing ways to protect them. Some biologists study the reproductive strategies of endangered species while they are in captivity. Other biologists work in nature preserves that provide safe places for endangered species to live, reproduce, and have protection against poachers.

Lee Anne Martinez is an ecologist who worked to protect the environment where outdoor toilets are common. She helped people in rural Africa construct composting toilets that use no water. The composted waste from the toilets can be added to soil to improve it for agricultural use.

■ **Figure 1.5** *Streptococcus pyogenes* is a unicellular organism. It can infect the throat, sinuses, or middle ear.

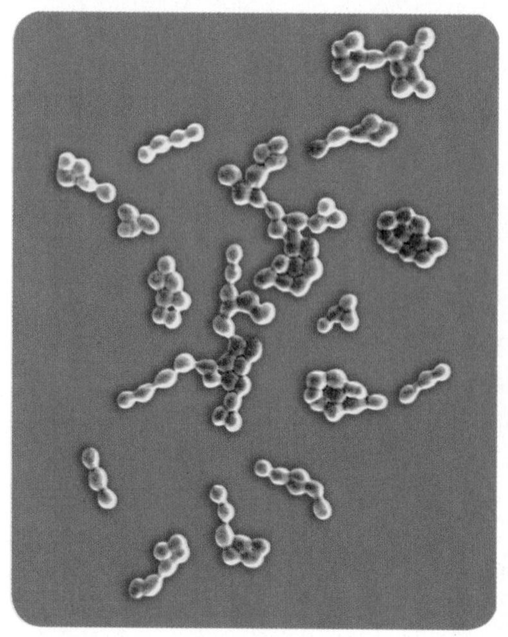

SEM Magnification: 7300×

## The Characteristics of Life

Have you ever tried to define the word *alive?* If you were to watch a grizzly bear catch a salmon from a river, you obviously would conclude that the bear and salmon are both alive. Is fire alive? Fire moves, increases in size, has energy, and seems to reproduce, but how does fire differ from the bear and salmon?

Over time and after many observations, biologists concluded that all living things have certain characteristics, as listed in **Table 1.1.** An **organism** is anything that has or once had all these characteristics.

**Made of one or more cells** Have you ever had strep throat? It probably was caused by a group A streptococcal bacteria, such as the *Streptococcus pyogenes* shown in **Figure 1.5.** A bacterium is unicellular—it has just one cell—yet it displays all the characteristics of life just like a skin cell on your body or a cell in a plant's leaf. Humans and plants are multicellular—they have many cells.

Concepts In Motion
Interactive Table To explore more about the characteristics of life, visit biologygmh.com.

**Table 1.1** **Characteristics of Living Organisms**

| Characteristic of Life | Example | Description |
|---|---|---|
| **Made of one or more cells** | Magnification: 160× | All organisms are made of one or more cells. The cell is the basic unit of life. Some organisms, such as the *Paramecium sp.*, are unicellular. |
| **Displays organization** | | The levels of organization in biological systems begin with atoms and molecules and increase in complexity. Each organized structure in an organism has a specific function. The structure of an anteater's snout relates to one of its functions—a container for the anteater's long tongue. |
| **Grows and develops** | | Growth results in an increase in mass. Development results in different abilities. A bullfrog tadpole grows and develops into an adult bullfrog. |
| **Reproduces** | | Organisms reproduce and pass along traits from one generation to the next. For a species like the koala to continue to exist, reproduction must occur. |
| **Responds to stimuli** | | Reactions to internal and external stimuli are called responses. This cheetah responds to the need for food by chasing a gazelle. The gazelle responds by running away. |
| **Requires energy** | | Energy is required for all life processes. Many organisms, like this squirrel, must take in food. Other organisms make their own food. |
| **Maintains homeostasis** | | All organisms keep internal conditions stable by a process called homeostasis. For example, humans perspire to prevent their body temperature from rising too high. |
| **Adaptations evolve over time** | | Adaptations are inherited changes that occur over time that help the species survive. Tropical orchids have roots that are adapted to life in a soil-less environment. |

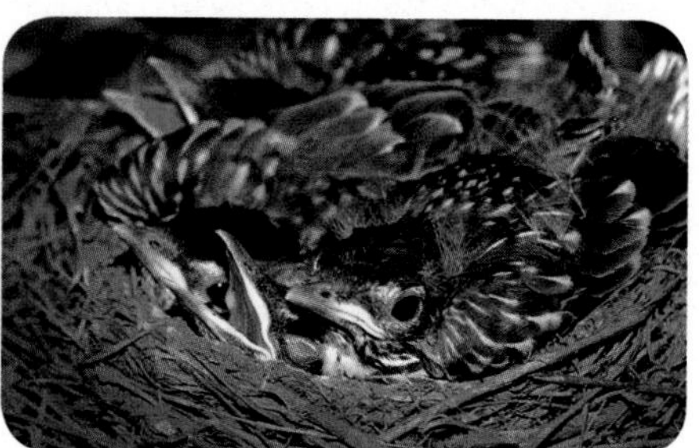

**Figure 1.6** In less than a month, these robin chicks grow and develop from helpless chicks to birds capable of flying.
**Infer** *how the robins have developed in other ways.*

Cells are the basic units of structure and function in all living things. For example, each heart cell has a structure that enables it to contribute to the heart's function—continually pumping blood throughout the body. Likewise, each cell in a tree's roots has a structure that enables it to help anchor the tree in the ground and to take in water and dissolved minerals from the surrounding soil.

**Displays organization** Think of all the people in your high school building each day. Students, faculty, counselors, administrators, building service personnel, and food service personnel are organized based on the different tasks they perform and the characteristics they share. For example, the students are designated freshmen, sophomores, juniors, and seniors based on age and coursework.

Living things also display **organization,** which means they are arranged in an orderly way. The *Paramecium* in **Table 1.1** is made up of one cell, yet that cell is a collection of organized structures that carries on life functions. Each of those structures is composed of atoms and molecules. The many cells that make up the robin chicks in **Figure 1.6** also contain structures made of atoms and molecules. However, in multicellular organisms, specialized cells are organized into groups that work together called tissues. These tissues are organized into organs, which carry on functions such as digestion and reproduction. Organ systems work together to support an organism. You will learn in Chapter 3 how individual organisms are organized and supported by the biosphere.

## MiniLab 1.1

### Observe Characteristics of Life

**Is it living or nonliving?** In this lab, you will observe several objects to determine if they are living or nonliving.

**Procedure**

1. Read and complete the lab safety form.
2. Create a data table with four columns titled *Object, Prediction, Characteristic of Life,* and *Evidence.*
3. Your teacher will provide several objects for observation. List each **object** in your table. Predict whether each object is living or nonliving.
4. Carefully observe each object. Discuss with your lab partner what characteristics of life it might exhibit.
5. Use **Table 1.1** to determine whether each object is living or nonliving. List the evidence in your data table.

**Analysis**

1. **Compare and contrast** your predictions and observations.
2. **Explain** why it was difficult to classify some objects as living or nonliving.

**Grows and develops** Most organisms begin as one cell. **Growth** results in the addition of mass to an organism and, in many organisms, the formation of new cells and new structures. Even a bacterium grows. Think about how you have grown throughout your life.

Robin chicks, like those in **Figure 1.6,** cannot fly for the first few weeks of their lives. Like most organisms, robins develop structures that give them specific abilities, such as flying. **Development** is the process of natural changes that take place during the life of an organism.

**Reproduces** Most living things are the result of **reproduction**—the production of offspring. Reproduction is not an essential characteristic for individual organisms. Many pets are spayed or neutered to prevent unwanted births. Obviously, these pets can still live even though they cannot reproduce. However, if a species is to continue to exist, then members of that species must reproduce. A **species** is a group of organisms that can breed with one another and produce fertile offspring. If the individuals of a species do not reproduce, then when the last individual of that species dies, the species becomes extinct.

**Responds to stimuli** An organism's external environment includes all things that surround it, such as air, water, soil, rocks, and other organisms. An organism's internal environment is all things inside it. Anything that is part of either environment and causes some sort of reaction by the organism is called a **stimulus** (plural, stimuli). The reaction to a stimulus is a **response.** For example, if a shark smells blood in the ocean, it will respond quickly by moving toward the blood and attacking any organism present. Plants also respond to their environments, but they do so more slowly than most other organisms. If you have a houseplant and you place it near a sunny window, it will grow toward the window in response to the light. How does the Venus flytrap in **Figure 1.7** respond to stimuli?

Being able to respond to the environment is critical for an organism's safety and survival. If an organism is unable to respond to danger or to react to potential enemies, it might not live long enough to reproduce.

**CAREERS IN BIOLOGY**

**Biology Teacher** An enthusiasm for biology is one of the many reasons people become biology teachers. Other than courses in biological sciences, prospective biology teachers might take classroom management, teaching methods, and other courses needed to develop teaching skills. For more information on biology careers, visit biologygmh.com.

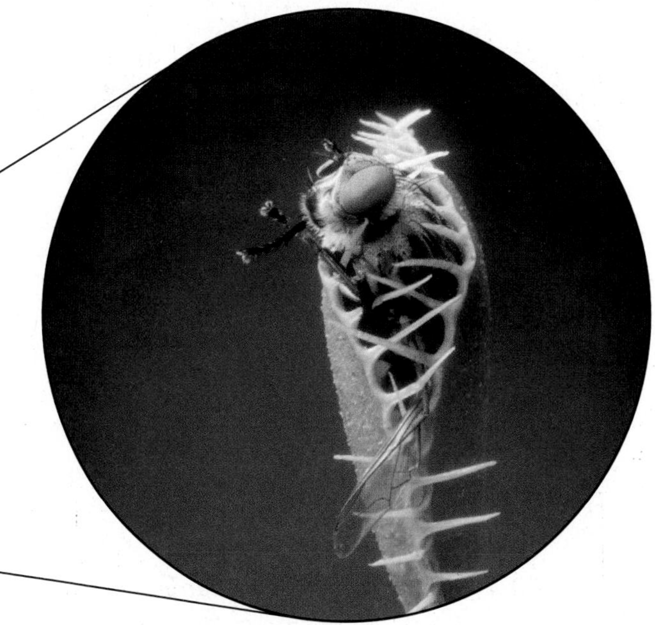

**Figure 1.7** In nature, this Venus flytrap grows in soils that lack certain nutrients. The plant captures and digests insects and takes in needed nutrients.
**Explain** ***How does this plant respond to stimuli to obtain food?***

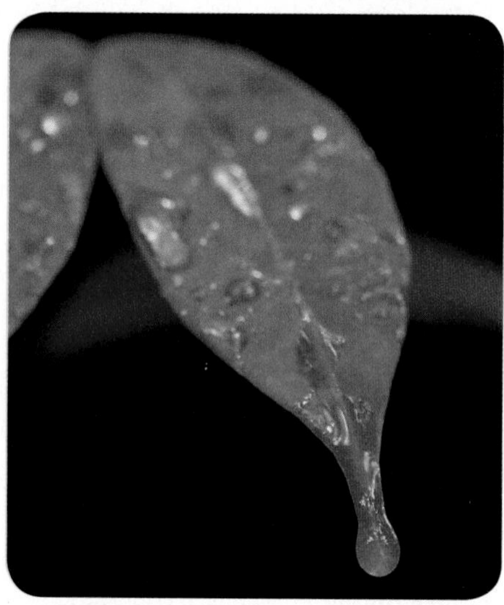

■ **Figure 1.8** The structure of a drip-tip leaf is an adaptation to rainy environments.

**Requires energy** Living things need sources of energy to fuel their life functions. Living things get their energy from food. Most plants and some unicellular organisms use light energy from the Sun to make their own food and fuel their activities. Other unicellular organisms can transform the energy in chemical compounds to make their food.

Organisms that cannot make their own food, such as animals and fungi, get energy by consuming other organisms. Some of the energy that an organism takes in is used for growth, development, and maintaining homeostasis. However, most of the energy is transformed into thermal energy and is radiated to the environment as heat.

**Maintains homeostasis** Regulation of an organism's internal conditions to maintain life is called **homeostasis** (hoh mee oh STAY sus). Homeostasis occurs in all living things. If anything happens within or to an organism that affects its normal state, processes to restore the normal state begin. If homeostasis is not restored, death might occur.

**Connection to Earth Science** When athletes travel to a location that is at a higher altitude than where they live, they generally arrive long before the competition so that their bodies have time to adjust to the thinner air. At higher altitudes, air has fewer molecules of gases, including oxygen, per unit of volume. Therefore, there is less oxygen available for an athlete's red blood cells to deliver to the cells and tissues, which disrupts his or her body's homeostasis. To restore homeostasis, the athlete's body produces more red blood cells. Having more red blood cells results in an adequate amount of oxygen delivered to the athlete's cells.

**Adaptations evolve over time** Many trees in rain forests have leaves with drip tips, like the one shown in **Figure 1.8.** Water runs off more easily and quickly from leaves with drip tips. Harmful molds and mildews will not grow on dry leaves. This means a plant with dry leaves is healthier and has a better chance to survive. Drip tips are an adaptation to the rain forest environment. An **adaptation** is any inherited characteristic that results from changes to a species over time. Adaptations like rain forest trees with drip tips enable species to survive and, therefore, they are better able to pass their genes to their offspring.

## Section 1.1 Assessment

### Section Summary

- Biology is the science of life.
- Biologists study the structure and function of living things, their history, their interactions with the environment, and many other aspects of life.
- All organisms have one or more cells, display organization, grow and develop, reproduce, respond to stimuli, use energy, maintain homeostasis, and have adaptations that evolve over time.

### Understand Main Ideas

1. MAIN Idea **Describe** four characteristics used to identify whether something is alive.
2. **Explain** why cells are considered the basic units of living things.
3. **List** some of the benefits of studying biology.
4. **Differentiate** between response and adaptation.

### Think Scientifically

5. MATH in Biology Survey students in your school—biology students and non-biology students—and adults. Have participants choose characteristics of life from a list of various characteristics and rank their choices from most important to least important. Record, tabulate, average, and graph your results. Prepare a report that summarizes your findings.

Biology Online Self-Check Quiz biologygmh.com

# Section 1.2

## Objectives

- **Explain** the characteristics of science.
- **Compare** something that is scientific with something that is pseudoscientific.
- **Describe** the importance of the metric system and SI.

## Review Vocabulary

**investigation:** a careful search or examination to uncover facts

## New Vocabulary

science
theory
peer review
metric system
SI
forensics
ethics

# The Nature of Science

**MAIN Idea Science is a process based on inquiry that seeks to develop explanations.**

**Real-World Reading Link** If you see a headline that reads "Alien baby found in campsite," how do you know whether you should believe it or not? How do you know when to trust claims made in an advertisement on television or the Internet, or in a newspaper or magazine? What makes something science-based?

## What is science?

Have you ever wondered how science is different from art, music, and writing? **Science** is a body of knowledge based on the study of nature. Biology is a science, as are chemistry, physics, and Earth science, which you might also study during high school. The nature, or essential characteristic, of science is scientific inquiry—the development of explanations. Scientific inquiry is both a creative process and a process rooted in unbiased observations and experimentation. Sometimes scientists go to extreme places to observe and experiment, as shown in **Figure 1.9.**

**Relies on evidence** Has anyone ever said to you, "I have a theory about that?" That person probably meant that he or she had a possible explanation about something. Scientific explanations combine what is already known with consistent evidence gathered from many observations and experiments.

When enough evidence from many related investigations supports an idea, scientists consider that idea a **theory**—an explanation of a natural phenomenon supported by many observations and experiments over time. For example, what happens when you throw a ball up in the air anywhere on Earth? The results are always the same. Scientists explain how the ball is attracted to Earth in the theory of universal gravitation. In biology, two of the most highly regarded theories are the cell theory and the theory of evolution. Both theories are based on countless observations and investigations, have extensive supporting evidence, and enable biologists to make accurate predictions.

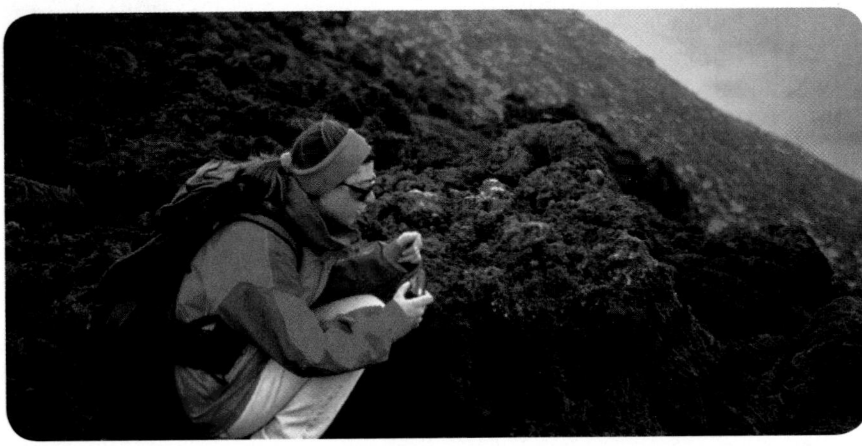

■ **Figure 1.9** This volcanologist is near molten lava flowing from Mount Etna. Lava temperatures can reach 750°C.

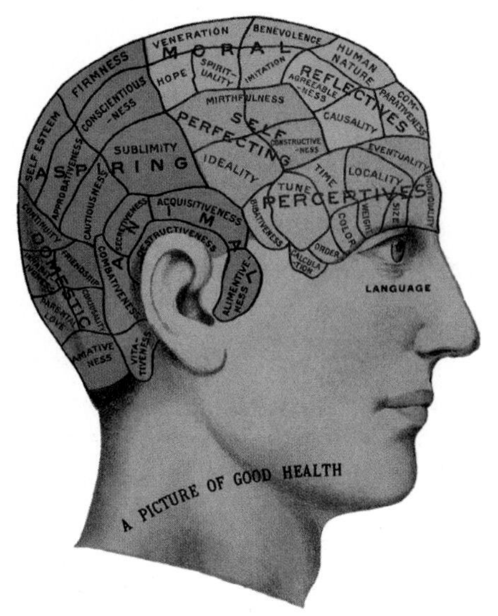


■ **Figure 1.10** Phrenology is based on observation—not scientific evidence.

**Connection to History** In the eighteenth and nineteenth centuries, many people practiced physiognomy (fih zee AHG nuh mee)—judging someone's character or personality based on physical features, especially facial features. Phrenology (frih NAH luh jee), the practice of reading the bumps on a person's head, illustrated in **Figure 1.10,** also is a type of physiognomy. Physiognomy often was used to determine whether individuals were appropriate for employment and other roles in society, or whether they had criminal tendencies. In fact, Charles Darwin almost did not get to take his famous voyage on the HMS *Beagle* because of the shape of his nose. Physiognomy was used and accepted even though there was no scientific evidence to support it.

Although physiognomy was based on observations and what was known at the time, it was not supported by scientific explanation. Physiognomy is considered a pseudoscience (soo doh SI uhnts). Pseudosciences are those areas of study that try to imitate science, often driven by cultural or commercial goals. Astrology, horoscopes, psychic reading, tarot card reading, face reading, and palmistry are pseudosciences. They do not provide science-based explanations about the natural world.

 **Reading Check** **Describe** one way that science and pseudoscience differ.

**Expands scientific knowledge** How can you know what information is science-based? Most scientific fields are guided by research that results in a constant reevaluation of what is known. This reevaluation often leads to new knowledge that scientists then evaluate. The search for new knowledge is the driving force that moves science forward. Nearly every new finding, like the discoveries shown in **Figure 1.11,** causes scientists to ask more questions that require additional research.

With pseudoscience, little research is done. If research is done, then often it is simply to justify existing knowledge rather than to extend the knowledge base. Pseudoscientific ideas generally do not ask new questions or welcome more research.

■ **Figure 1.11**

**Milestones in Biology**

Major events and discoveries in the past century greatly contributed to our understanding of biology today.

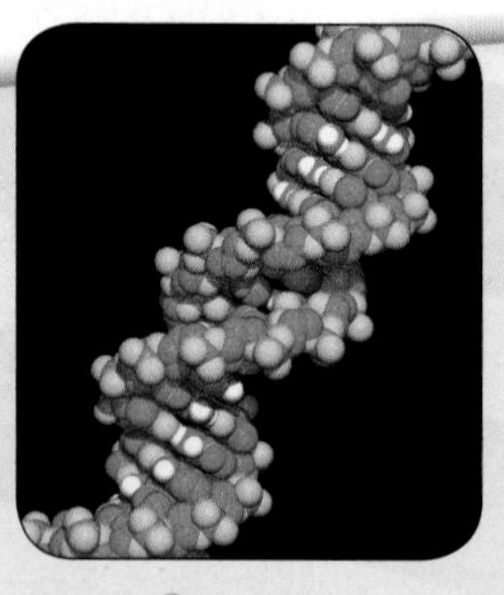

**1953** The structure of DNA is identified due to research by Rosalind Franklin, Maurice Wilkins, James Watson, and Francis Crick. **Chapter 12**

1915 — 1930 — 1945

**1912–1939** Writings on cell biology by Ernest Everett Just influence the use of scientific methods in biology. **Chapter 7**

**1962** Rachel Carson's book *Silent Spring,* about the environmental dangers of pollution and pesticide use, is published. **Chapter 2**

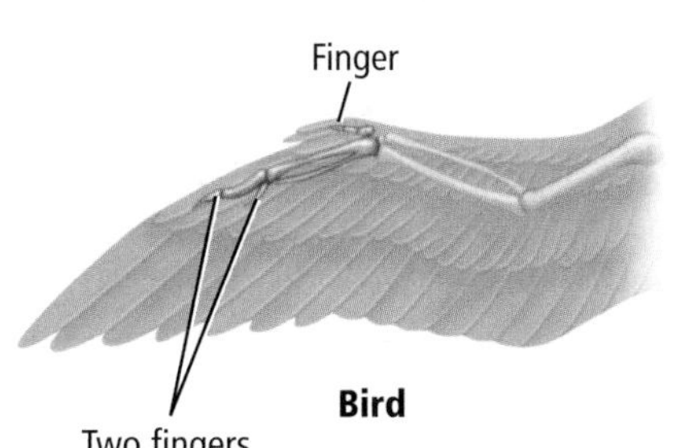


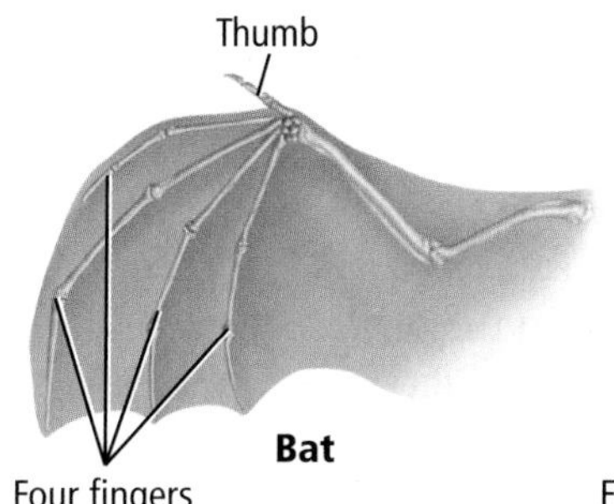


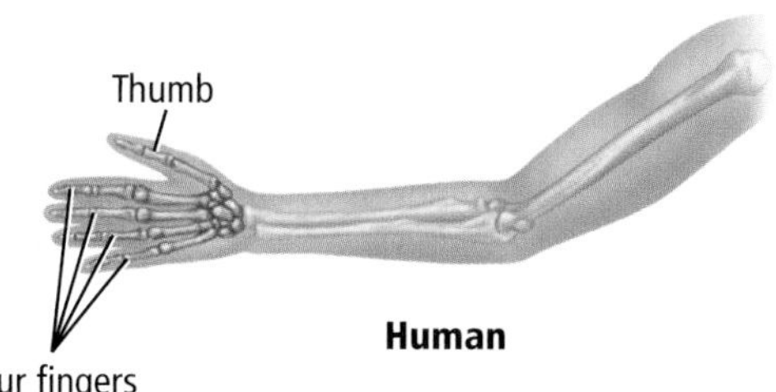


**Figure 1.12** The structure of a bat's wing is more like that of a human arm than a bird's wing.

**Challenges accepted theories** Scientists welcome debate about one another's ideas. They regularly attend conferences and meetings where they discuss new developments and findings. Often, disagreements occur among scientists. Then additional investigations and/or experiments are done to substantiate claims.

Sciences advance by accommodating new information as it is discovered. For example, since the emergence of AIDS in the 1980s, our understanding of HIV, our ideas about how HIV is transmitted, the manner in which we treat AIDS, and the ways in which we educate people about the disease have changed dramatically due to new information from many scientific studies.

**Questions results** Observations or data that are not consistent with current scientific understanding are of interest to scientists. These inconsistencies often lead to further investigations. For example, early biologists grouped bats with birds because both had wings. Further study showed that bat wings are more similar to mammalian limbs than they are to bird wings, as shown in **Figure 1.12.** This led to an examination of the anatomy, genes, and proteins of rats and bats. The relationship was confirmed, and scientists established that bats were more closely related to mammals than birds. With pseudoscience, observations or data that are not consistent with beliefs are discarded or ignored.

**CAREERS IN BIOLOGY**

**Science Writer** Communicating scientific information to the public is one of the goals of a science writer. He or she might write news stories, manuals, or press releases, or edit and summarize the written materials of scientists. For more information on biology careers, visit biologygmh.com.

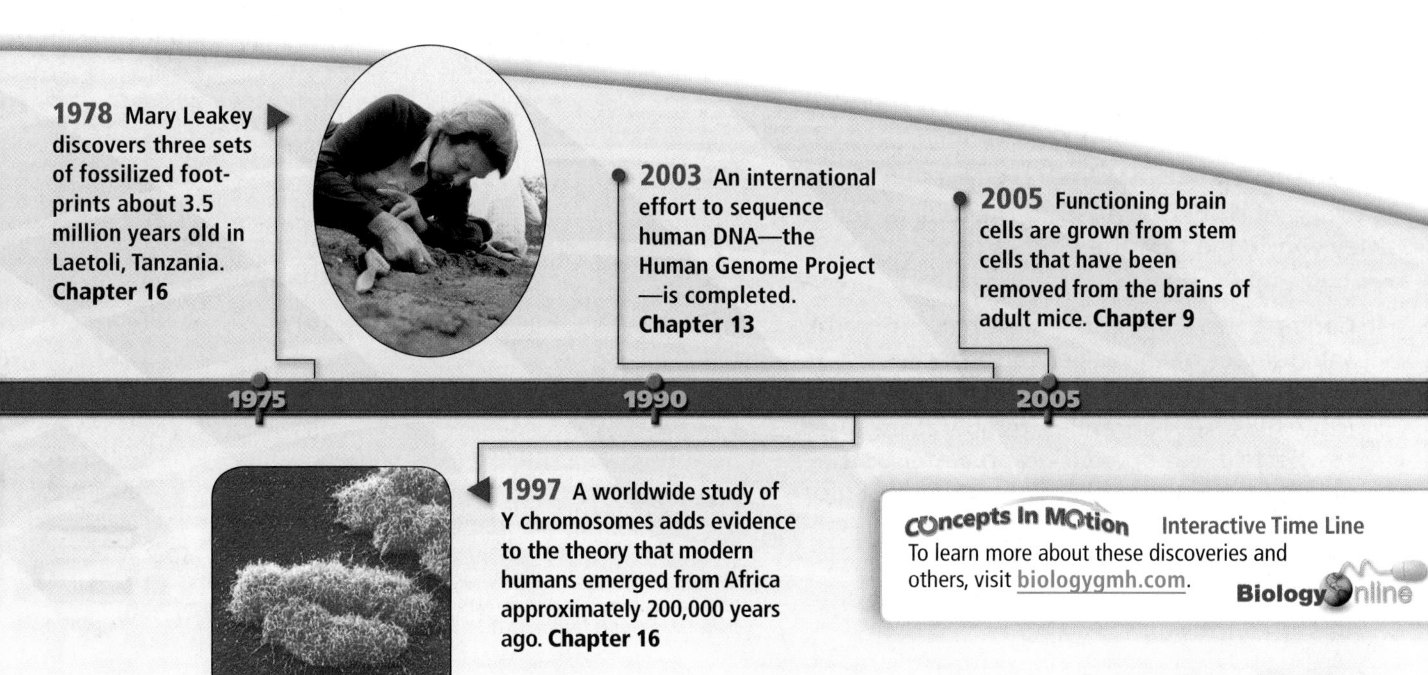


**1978** Mary Leakey discovers three sets of fossilized footprints about 3.5 million years old in Laetoli, Tanzania. Chapter 16

**1997** A worldwide study of Y chromosomes adds evidence to the theory that modern humans emerged from Africa approximately 200,000 years ago. Chapter 16

**2003** An international effort to sequence human DNA—the Human Genome Project —is completed. Chapter 13

**2005** Functioning brain cells are grown from stem cells that have been removed from the brains of adult mice. Chapter 9

Concepts In Motion Interactive Time Line
To learn more about these discoveries and others, visit biologygmh.com. Biology Online

**VOCABULARY**

**ACADEMIC VOCABULARY**

**Unbiased:**
To be objective, impartial, or fair.
*The judges were unbiased in choosing the winner.*

**Tests claims** Whenever biologists engage in research, they use standard experimental procedures. Science-based information makes claims based on a large amount of data and observations obtained from unbiased investigations and carefully controlled experimentation. Conclusions are reached from the evidence. However, pseudoscientists often make claims that cannot be tested. These claims often are mixtures of fact and opinion.

**Undergoes peer review** Before it is made public, science-based information is reviewed by scientists' peers—scientists who are working in the same field of study. **Peer review** is a process by which, in science, the procedures used during an experiment and the results are evaluated by other scientists who are in the same field or who are conducting similar research.

**Uses metric system** Scientists can repeat the work of others as part of a new experiment. Using the same system of measurements helps make this possible. Most scientists use the metric system when collecting data and performing experiments. The **metric system** uses units with divisions that are powers of ten. The General Conference of Weights and Measures established the unit standards of the metric system in 1960. The system is called the International System of Units, commonly known as **SI.** In biology, the SI units you will use most often are meter (to measure length), gram (to measure mass), liter (to measure volume), and second (to measure time).

## DATA ANALYSIS LAB 1.1

**Based on Real Data***

### Peer Review

**Can temperature be predicted by counting cricket chirps?** Many outdoors enthusiasts claim that air temperature (°F) can be estimated by adding the number 40 to the number of cricket chirps counted in 15 seconds. Is there scientific evidence to support this idea?

**Data and Observations**

A group of students collected the data at right. They concluded that the claim is correct.

**Effect of Temperature on Chirping**

| Temperature (°F) | Cricket Chirps (per min) |
|---|---|
| 68 | 121 |
| 75 | 140 |
| 80 | 160 |
| 81 | 166 |
| 84 | 181 |
| 88 | 189 |
| 91 | 200 |
| 94 | 227 |

**Think Critically**

1. **Convert** the number of chirps per minute to the number of chirps per 15 seconds.
2. **Plot** the number of chirps per 15-second interval versus Fahrenheit temperature. Draw the best-fit line on your graph. Refer to the Skillbuilder Handbook, pages 1115–1118, for help with graphs.
3. **Write** the equation for the best-fit line.
4. **Peer review** Do the results support the students' conclusion? Explain.

*Data obtained from: Horak, V. M. 2005. Biology as a source for algebra equations: insects. *Mathematics Teacher* 99(1): 55-59.

## Science in Everyday Life

There is widespread fascination with science. Popular television programs about crime are based on **forensics,** which is the field of study that applies science to matters of legal interest. The media is filled with information on flu epidemics, the latest medical advances, discoveries of new species, and technologies that improve or extend human lives. Clearly, science is not limited to the laboratory. The results of research go far beyond reports in scientific journals and meetings.

**Science literacy** In order to evaluate the vast amount of information available in print, online, and on television, and to participate in the fast-paced world of the twenty-first century, each of us must be scientifically literate. A person who is scientifically literate combines a basic understanding of science and its processes with reasoning and thinking skills.

Many of the issues that are faced every day relate to the world of biology. Drugs, alcohol, tobacco, AIDS, mental illness, cancer, heart disease, and eating disorders provide subjects for biological research worldwide. Environmental issues such as global warming, pollution, deforestation, the use of fossil fuels, nuclear power, genetically modified foods, and conserving biodiversity are issues that you and future generations will face. Also, genetic engineering, cloning—producing genetically identical individuals, genetic screening—searching for genetic disorders in people, euthanasia (yoo thuh NAY zhuh)—permitting a death for reasons of mercy, and cryonics (kri AH niks)—freezing a dead person or animal with the hope of reviving it in the future—all involve **ethics,** which is a set of moral principles or values. Ethical issues must be addressed by society based on the values it holds important.

Scientists provide information about the continued expansion of science and technology. As a scientifically literate adult, you will be an educated consumer who can participate in discussions about important issues and support policies that reflect your views. Who knows? You might serve on a jury where DNA evidence, like that shown in **Figure 1.13,** is presented. You will need to understand the evidence, comprehend its implications, and decide the outcome of the trial.

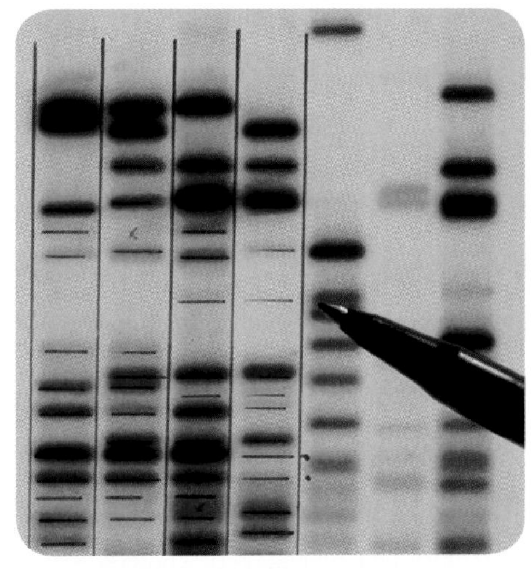

**Figure 1.13** DNA analysis might exclude an alleged thief because his or her DNA does not match the DNA from the crime scene.

## Section 1.2 Assessment

### Section Summary

- Science is the study of nature and is rooted in observation and experimentation.
- Pseudoscience is not based on standard scientific research; it does not deal with testable questions, welcome critical review, or change its ideas when new discoveries are made.
- Science and ethics affect issues in health, medicine, the environment, and technology.

### Understand Main Ideas

1. MAIN Idea **Describe** the characteristics of science.
2. **Define** scientific theory.
3. **Defend** the use of the metric system to a scientist who does not want to use it.
4. **Compare and contrast** science with pseudoscience.

### Think Scientifically

5. *WRITING in* **Biology** Predict what might happen to a population of people who do not understand the nature of science. Use examples of key issues facing our society.
6. **MATH in Biology** One kilogram equals 1000 grams. One milligram equals 0.001 grams. How many milligrams are in one kilogram?

## Section 1.3

### Objectives

- **Describe** the difference between an observation and an inference.
- **Differentiate** among control, independent variable, and dependent variable.
- **Identify** the scientific methods a biologist uses for research.

### Review Vocabulary

**theory:** an explanation of a natural phenomenon supported by many observations and experiments over time

### New Vocabulary

observation
inference
scientific method
hypothesis
serendipity
experiment
control group
experimental group
independent variable
dependent variable
constant
data
safety symbol

# Methods of Science

**MAIN Idea Biologists use specific methods when conducting research.**

**Real-World Reading Link** What do you do to find answers to questions? Do you ask other people, read, investigate, or observe? Are your methods haphazard or methodical? Over time, scientists have established standard procedures to find answers to questions.

## Ask a Question

Imagine that you saw an unfamiliar bird in your neighborhood. You might develop a plan to observe the bird for a period of time. Scientific inquiry begins with **observation,** a direct method of gathering information in an orderly way. Often, observation involves recording information. In the example of your newly discovered bird, you might take photographs or draw a picture of it. You might write detailed notes about its behavior, including when and what it ate.

Science inquiry involves asking questions and processing information from a variety of reliable sources. After observing the bird, you might combine what you know with what you have learned and begin a process of making logical conclusions. This process is called making **inferences**, or inferring. For instance, if you saw a photo of a bird similar to the unfamiliar bird in your neighborhood, you might infer that your bird and the bird in the photo are related. **Figure 1.14** illustrates how a field guide might be helpful in making inferences.

**Scientific methods** Biologists work in different places to answer their questions. For example, some biologists work in laboratories, perhaps developing new medicines, while others work outdoors in natural settings. No matter where they work, biologists all use similar methods to gather information and to answer questions. These methods sometimes are referred to as **scientific methods,** illustrated in **Figure 1.15.** Even though scientists do not use scientific methods in the same way each time they conduct an experiment, they observe and infer throughout the entire process.

■ **Figure 1.14** Scientists might use a field guide to help them identify or draw conclusions about things they observe in nature, such as this peregrine falcon.

# Visualizing Scientific Methods

**Figure 1.15**
The way that scientists answer questions is through an organized series of events called scientific methods. There are no wrong answers to questions, only answers that provide scientists with more information about those questions. Questions and collected information help scientists form hypotheses. As experiments are conducted, hypotheses might or might not be supported.

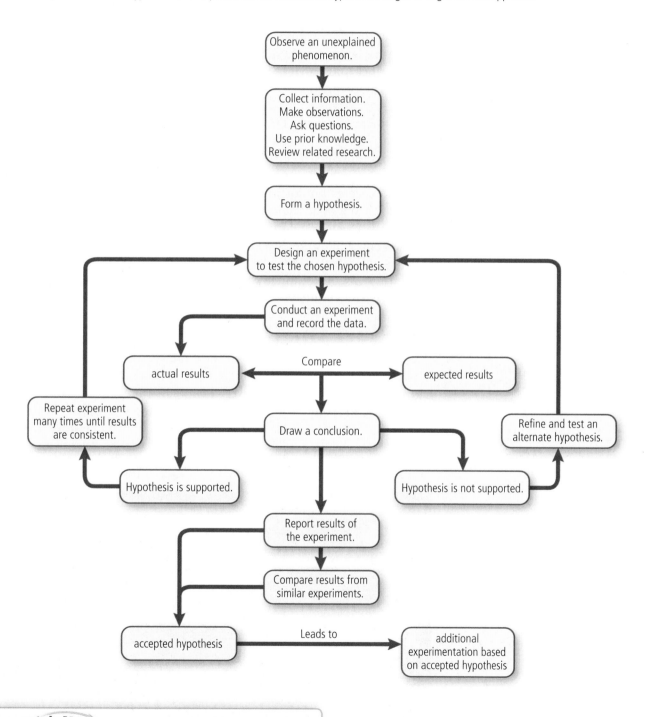



**Concepts In Motion** **Interactive Figure** To see an animation of scientific methods, visit biologygmh.com.

**Biology Online**

## Form a Hypothesis

Imagination, curiosity, creativity, and logic are key elements of the way biologists approach their research. In 1969, the U.S. Air Force asked Dr. Ron Wiley to investigate how to enhance a pilot's ability to endure the effects of an increase in gravity (*g*-force) while traveling at high speed in an F-16 aircraft. It was known that isometrics, which is a form of exercise in which muscles are held in a contracted position, raised blood pressure. Wiley formed the hypothesis that the use of isometric exercise to raise blood pressure during maneuvers might increase tolerance to *g*-force and prevent blackouts. A **hypothesis** (hi PAH thuh sus) is a testable explanation of a situation.

Before Wiley formed his hypothesis, he made inferences based on his experience as a physiologist, what he read, discussions with Air Force personnel, and previous investigations. He did find that increasing a pilot's blood pressure could help the pilot withstand *g*-forces. But he also made an unexpected discovery.

During his study, Dr. Wiley discovered that isometric exercise decreased the resting blood pressure of the pilots. As a result, weight lifting and muscle-strengthening exercises are recommended today to help people lower blood pressure. **Serendipity** is the occurrence of accidental or unexpected but fortunate results. There are other examples of serendipity throughout science. For example, the discovery of penicillin was partially due to serendipity.

When a hypothesis is supported by data from additional investigations, usually it is considered valid and is accepted by the scientific community. If not, the hypothesis is revised, and additional investigations are conducted.

*Study Tip*

**Clarification** Choose a concept from the text and write its definition in the middle of a piece of paper. Circle the most important word. Around the word, write ideas related to it or examples that support it.

## Collect the Data

Imagine that while in Alaska on vacation, you noticed various kinds of gulls. You saw them nesting high in the cliffs, and you wondered how they maintain their energy levels during their breeding season. A group of biologists wondered the same thing and did a controlled experiment using gulls known as black-legged kittiwakes shown in **Figure 1.16.** When a biologist conducts an **experiment,** he or she investigates a phenomenon in a controlled setting to test a hypothesis.

**LAUNCH Lab**

**Review Based on what you've read about observing and inferring, how would you now answer the analysis questions?**

■ **Figure 1.16** This colony of black-legged kittiwakes along the Alaskan coast includes nesting pairs.

# CHAPTER 1 Assessment

## Section 1.1

### Vocabulary Review

*Replace the underlined phrase with the correct vocabulary term from the Study Guide page.*

1. The production of offspring is a characteristic of life that enables the continuation of a species.
2. The internal control of mechanisms allows for an organism's systems to remain in balance.
3. The science of life involves learning about the natural world.

### Understand Key Concepts

*Use the graph below to answer question 4.*

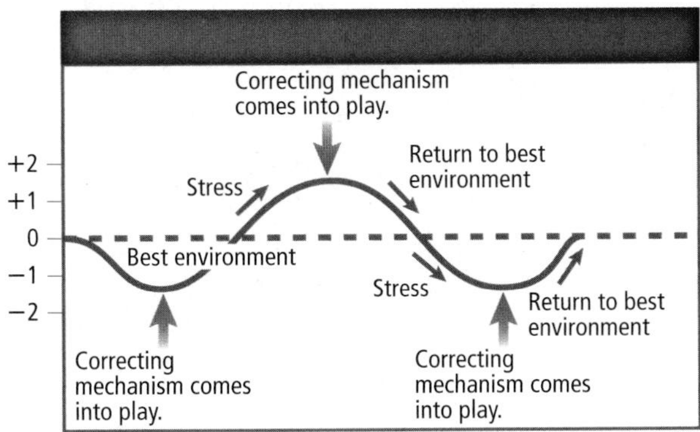


4. Which characteristic of life should be the title of this graph?
   **A.** Cellular Basis
   **B.** Growth
   **C.** Homeostasis
   **D.** Reproduction
5. Which best describes adaptation?
   **A.** reproducing as a species
   **B.** a short-term change in behavior in response to a stimuli
   **C.** inherited changes in response to environmental factors
   **D.** change in size as an organism ages

### Constructed Reponse

6. **Open Ended** What is the role of energy in living organisms? Is it a more or less important role than other characteristics of life? Defend your response.

### Think Critically

7. **Evaluate** how the contributions made by Goodall, Chory, and Drew reinforce our understanding of the characteristics of life.
8. **Compare and contrast** a response and an adaptation. Use examples from your everyday world in your answer.

## Section 1.2

### Vocabulary Review

*Replace the underlined phrase with the correct vocabulary term from the Study Guide page.*

9. the measurements based on powers of ten used by scientists when conducting research
10. a well-tested explanation that brings together many observations in science such as evolution, plate tectonics, biogenesis

### Understand Key Concepts

*Use the photo below to answer question 11.*

11. Which SI base unit would be used to describe the physical characteristics of dolphins?
    **A.** second
    **B.** kilogram
    **C.** inches
    **D.** gallon
12. Which is true about scientific inquiry?
    **A.** It poses questions about astrology.
    **B.** It can be done only by one person.
    **C.** It is resistant to change and not open to criticism.
    **D.** It is testable.

### Constructed Response

13. **Short Answer** Differentiate between pseudoscience and science.

### Think Critically

14. **Evaluate** how technology impacts society in a positive and negative way at the same time.

## Section 1.3

### Vocabulary Review

*Explain the differences between the terms in the following sets.*

15. observation, data
16. control group, experimental group
17. independent variable, dependent variable

### Understand Key Concepts

18. Which describes this statement, "The frog is 4 cm long"?
    **A.** quantitative data
    **B.** inference
    **C.** control group
    **D.** qualitative data

19. Which is a testable explanation?
    **A.** dependent variable
    **B.** independent variable
    **C.** hypothesis
    **D.** observation

### Constructed Response

*Use the table below to answer question 20.*

**Mean Body Mass and Field Metabolic Rate (FMR) of Black-Legged Kittiwakes**

| | Number | Mean body mass (g) | FMR |
|---|---|---|---|
| Fed females | 14 | 426.8 | 2.04 |
| Control females | 14 | 351.1 | 3.08 |
| Fed males | 16 | 475.4 | 2.31 |
| Control males | 18 | 397.6 | 2.85 |

20. **Short Answer** Examine the data shown above. Describe the effects of feedings on the energy expenditure, FMR, of male and female kittiwakes.

### Think Critically

21. **Design** a survey to investigate students' opinions about current movies. Use 10 questions and survey 50 students. Graph the data. Report the findings to the class.

## Additional Assessment

22. WRITING in **Biology** Prepare a letter to the editor of your school newspaper that encourages citizens to be scientifically literate about topics such as cancer, the environment, ethical issues, AIDS, smoking, lung diseases, cloning, genetic diseases, and eating disorders.

### DBQ Document Based Questions

*Use the data below to answer questions 23 and 24.*

Data obtained from: U.S. Geological Survey. *Seabirds, forage fish, and marine ecosystems.* http://www.absc.usgs.gov/research/seabird_foragefish/foragefish/index.html

**Relative Fish Biomass of Three Seabird Colonies in Lower Cook Inlet**

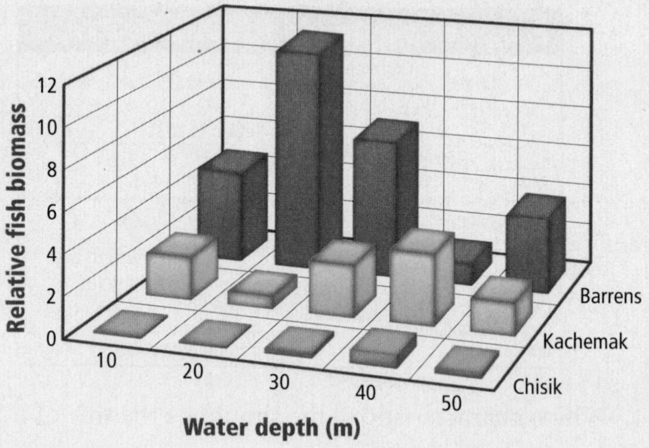


23. Identify the water depth with the highest relative fish biomass.
24. Determine which seabird colony has access to the highest fish biomass at a depth of 40 m.

### CUMULATIVE REVIEW

In Chapters 2–37, Cumulative Review questions will help you review and check your understanding of concepts discussed in previous chapters.

# Standardized Test Practice

## Multiple Choice

1. Many scientific discoveries begin with direct observations. Which could be a direct observation?
   **A.** Ants communicate by airborne chemicals.
   **B.** Birds navigate by using magnetic fields.
   **C.** Butterflies eat nectar from flowers.
   **D.** Fish feel vibrations through special sensors.

*Use this experimental description and data table to answer question 2.*

A student reads that some seeds must be exposed to cold before they germinate. She wants to test seeds from one kind of plant to see if they germinate better after freezing. The student put the seeds in the freezer, took samples out at certain times, and tried to germinate them. Then she recorded her results in the table.

**Germination Rate for Seeds Stored in a Freezer**

| Time in Freezer at −15°C | Germination Rate |
|---|---|
| 30 days | 48% |
| 60 days | 56% |
| 90 days | 66% |
| 120 days | 52% |

2. According to the results of this experiment, how many days should seeds be stored in the freezer before planting for best germination?
   **A.** 30
   **B.** 60
   **C.** 90
   **D.** 120

## Short Answer

3. Appraise one benefit to scientists of using SI units as standard units of measurement.

## Extended Response

*Use this drawing to answer question 4.*

4. Look at the drawing and write five specific questions about the organisms shown that a biologist might try to investigate.

5. Compare and contrast a scientific hypothesis and a scientific theory.

## Essay Question

A researcher experimented with adhesives and glues to find new and stronger adhesives. In 1968, he discovered an adhesive that was very weak rather than strong. The adhesive would stick to paper but it could be removed easily without leaving a trace of adhesive. Because he was trying to find stronger adhesives, the results of that experiment were considered a failure. Several years later, he had the idea of coating paper with the weak adhesive. This meant that notes could be stuck to paper and easily removed at a later time. Today, these removable notes are used by millions of people.

*Using the information in the paragraph above, answer the following question in essay format.*

6. The original adhesive experiment was considered a failure. Appraise the importance of evaluating the results of an experiment with an open mind.

| NEED EXTRA HELP? | | | | | | |
|---|---|---|---|---|---|---|
| If You Missed Question . . . | 1 | 2 | 3 | 4 | 5 | 6 |
| Review Section . . . | 1.3 | 1.3 | 1.2 | 1.1 | 1.3 | 1.2 |

# UNIT 1 Ecology

**Chapter 2**
Principles of Ecology
BIG Idea Energy is required to cycle materials through living and nonliving systems.

**Chapter 3**
Communities, Biomes, and Ecosystems
BIG Idea Limiting factors and ranges of tolerance are factors that determine where terrestrial biomes and aquatic ecosystems exist.

**Chapter 4**
Population Ecology
BIG Idea Population growth is a critical factor in a species' ability to maintain homeostasis within its environment.

**Chapter 5**
Biodiversity and Conservation
BIG Idea Community and ecosystem homeostasis depend on a complex set of interactions among biologically diverse individuals.

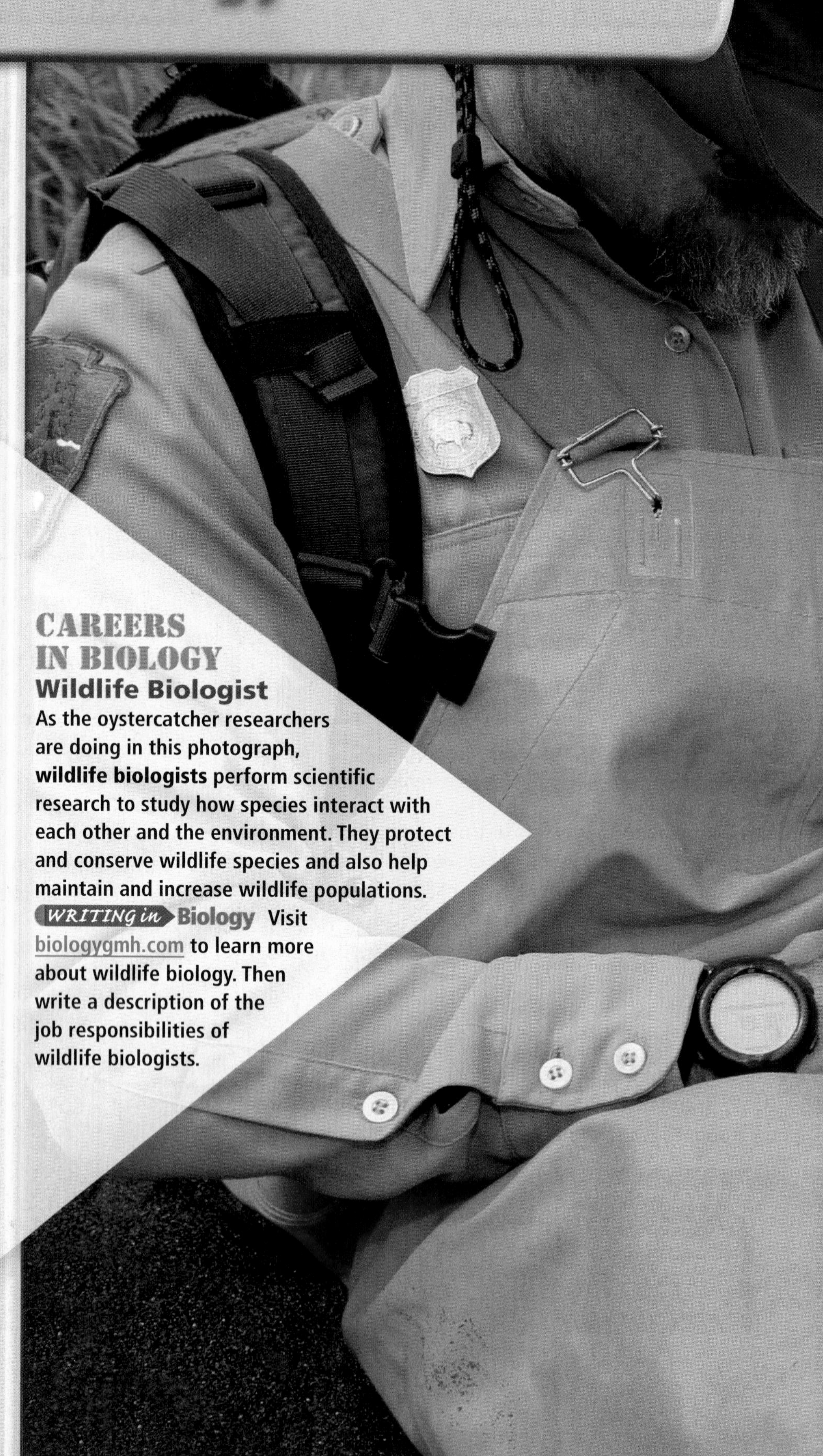

## CAREERS IN BIOLOGY

### Wildlife Biologist

As the oystercatcher researchers are doing in this photograph, **wildlife biologists** perform scientific research to study how species interact with each other and the environment. They protect and conserve wildlife species and also help maintain and increase wildlife populations.

WRITING in Biology Visit biologygmh.com to learn more about wildlife biology. Then write a description of the job responsibilities of wildlife biologists.

**Biology Online**

To read more about wildlife biologists in action, visit biologygmh.com.

CHAPTER 2

# Principles of Ecology

**Section 1**
**Organisms and Their Relationships**
MAIN Idea Biotic and abiotic factors interact in complex ways in communities and ecosystems.

**Section 2**
**Flow of Energy in an Ecosystem**
MAIN Idea Autotrophs capture energy, making it available for all members of a food web.

**Section 3**
**Cycling of Matter**
MAIN Idea Essential nutrients are cycled through biogeochemical processes.

## BioFacts

- The Pacific tree frog can change from light colored to dark colored quickly. This could be a response to changes in temperature and humidity.
- The spotted owl nests only in old growth forests and might be in danger of becoming extinct due to the loss of these forests.

# LAUNCH Lab

## Problems in *Drosophila* world?

As the photos on the left illustrate, what we understand to be the world is many smaller worlds combined to form one large world. Within the large world, there are populations of creatures interacting with each other and their environment. In this lab, you will observe an example of a small part of the world.

### Procedure

1. Read and complete the lab safety form.
2. Prepare a data table to record your observations.
3. Your teacher has prepared a **container housing several fruit flies** *(Drosophila melanogaster)* with food for the flies in the bottom. Observe how many fruit flies are present.
4. Observe the fruit flies over a period of one week and record any changes.

### Analysis

1. **Summarize** the results of your observations.
2. **Evaluate** whether or not this would be a reasonable way to study a real population.

Visit biologygmh.com to:

- study the entire chapter online
- explore the Interactive Time Line, Concepts in Motion, Microscopy Links, Virtual Labs, and links to virtual dissections
- access Web links for more information, projects, and activities
- review content online with the Interactive Tutor and take Self-Check Quizzes

**Natural Cycles** Make this Foldable to help you compare and contrast the water cycle and the carbon cycle.

**STEP 1** Fold a sheet of notebook paper in half lengthwise so that the side without holes is 2.5 cm shorter than the side with the holes. Then fold the paper into thirds as shown.

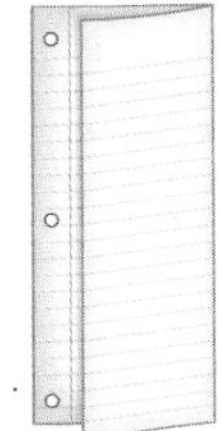

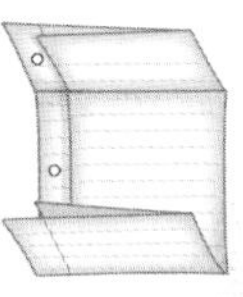

**STEP 2** Unfold the paper and draw the Venn diagram. Then cut along the two fold lines of the top layer only. This makes three tabs.

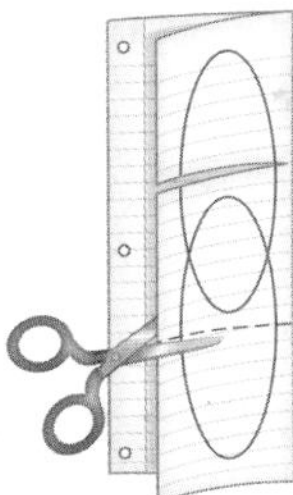

**STEP 3** Label the tabs as illustrated.

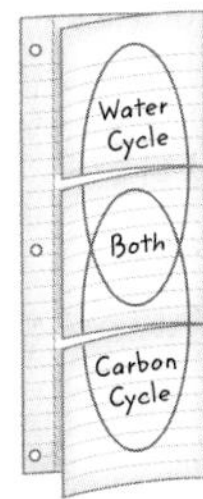


FOLDABLES **Use this Foldable with Section 2.3.** As you study the section, record what you learn about the two cycles under the appropriate tabs and determine what the cycles have in common.

Section 2.1

**Objectives**

- **Explain** the difference between abiotic factors and biotic factors.
- **Describe** the levels of biological organization.
- **Differentiate** between an organism's habitat and its niche.

**Review Vocabulary**

**species:** group of organisms that can interbreed and produce fertile offspring in nature

**New Vocabulary**

ecology
biosphere
biotic factor
abiotic factor
population
biological community
ecosystem
biome
habitat
niche
predation
symbiosis
mutualism
commensalism
parasitism

# Organisms and Their Relationships

**MAIN Idea** **Biotic and abiotic factors interact in complex ways in communities and ecosystems.**

**Real-World Reading Link** On whom do you depend for your basic needs such as food, shelter, and clothing? Humans are not the only organisms that depend on others for their needs. All living things are interdependent. Their relationships are important to their survival.

## Ecology

Scientists can gain valuable insight about the interactions between organisms and their environments and between different species of organisms by observing them in their natural environments. Each organism, regardless of where it lives, depends on nonliving factors found in its environment and on other organisms living in the same environment for survival. For example, green plants provide a source of food for many organisms as well as a place to live. The animals that eat the plants provide a source of food for other animals. The interactions and interdependence of organisms with each other and their environments are not unique. The same type of dependency occurs whether the environment is a barren desert, a tropical rain forest, or a grassy meadow. **Ecology** is the scientific discipline in which the relationships among living organisms and the interaction the organisms have with their environments are studied.

**Figure 2.1**
**Milestones in Ecology**

Ecologists have worked to preserve and protect natural resources.

**1872** Yellowstone becomes the first national park in the U.S.

1900

**1905** Theodore Roosevelt urges the U.S. Congress to set aside over 70 million hectares of land to protect the natural resources found on them.

**1962** Rachel Carson publishes a best-selling book warning of the environmental danger of pollution and pesticides.

1960

**1967** The government of Rwanda and international conservation groups begin efforts to protect mountain gorillas, due in a large part to the work of Dian Fossey.

1970

**1971** Marjorie Carr stops the construction of the Cross Florida Barge Canal because of the environmental damage the project would cause.

■ **Figure 2.2** Ecologists work in the field and in laboratories. This ecologist is enduring harsh conditions to examine a seal.

The study of organisms and their environments is not new. The word *ecology* was first introduced in 1866 by Ernst Haeckel, a German biologist. Since that time, there have been many significant milestones in ecology, as shown in **Figure 2.1.**

Scientists who study ecology are called ecologists. Ecologists observe, experiment, and model using a variety of tools and methods. For example, ecologists, like the one shown in **Figure 2.2,** perform tests in organisms' environments. Results from these tests might give clues as to why organisms are able to survive in the water, why organisms become ill or die from drinking the water, or what organisms could live in or near the water. Ecologists also observe organisms to understand the interactions between them. Some observations and analyses must be made over long periods of time in a process called longitudinal analysis.

A model allows a scientist to represent or simulate a process or system. Studying organisms in the field can be difficult because there often are too many variables to study at one time. Models allow ecologists to control the number of variables present and to slowly introduce new variables in order to fully understand the effect of each variable.

**Reading Check** **Describe** a collection of organisms and their environment that an ecologist might study in your community.

**VOCABULARY**

**WORD ORIGIN**

**Ecology**

comes from the Greek words *oikos,* meaning *house,* and *ology,* meaning *to study.*

**1990** The Indigenous Environmental Network (IEN), directed by Tom Goldtooth, is formed by Native Americans to protect their tribal lands and communities from environmental damage.

**2004** Wangari Maathai wins a Nobel Prize. She began the Green Belt Movement in Africa, which hires women to plant trees to slow the process of deforestation and desertification.

1980 — 1990 — 2000

**1987** The United States and other countries sign the Montreal Protocol, an agreement to phase out the use of chemical compounds that destroy atmospheric ozone.

**1996** Completing a phase-out that was begun in 1973, the U.S. Environmental Protection Agency bans the sale of leaded gasoline for vehicle use.

**Concepts In Motion** Interactive Time Line

To learn more about these milestones and others, visit biologygmh.com. Biology Online

■ **Figure 2.3** This color-enhanced satellite photo of Earth taken from space shows a large portion of the biosphere.

## The Biosphere

Because ecologists study organisms and their environments, their studies take place in the biosphere. The **biosphere** (BI uh sfihr) is the portion of Earth that supports life. The photo of Earth taken from space shown in **Figure 2.3** shows why the meaning of the term *biosphere* should be easy to remember. The term *bio* means "life," and a sphere is a geometric shape that looks like a ball. When you look at Earth from this vantage point, you can see how it is considered to be "a ball of life."

Although "ball of life" is the literal meaning of the word *biosphere,* this is somewhat misleading. The biosphere includes only the portion of Earth that includes life. The biosphere forms a thin layer around Earth. It extends several kilometers above the Earth's surface into the atmosphere and extends several kilometers below the ocean's surface to the deep-ocean vents. It includes landmasses, bodies of freshwater and saltwater, and all locations below Earth's surface that support life.

**Figure 2.4** shows a satellite image of Earth's biosphere on the surface of Earth. The photo is color-coded to represent the distribution of chlorophyll. Chlorophyll is a green pigment found in green plants and algae that you will learn about in later chapters. Because most organisms depend on green plants or algae for survival, green plants are a good indicator of the distribution of living organisms in an area. In the oceans, red represents areas with the highest density of chlorophyll followed by yellow, then blue, and then pink, representing the lowest density. On land, dark green represents the area with highest chlorophyll density and pale yellow represents the area with the lowest chlorophyll density.

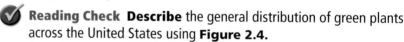

**Reading Check Describe** the general distribution of green plants across the United States using **Figure 2.4.**

The biosphere also includes areas such as the frozen polar regions, deserts, oceans, and rain forests. These diverse locations contain organisms that are able to survive in the unique conditions found in their particular environment. Ecologists study these organisms and the factors in their environment. These factors are divided into two large groups—the living factors and the nonliving factors.

■ **Figure 2.4** This color-coded satellite photo shows the relative distribution of life on Earth's biosphere based on the distribution of chlorophyll.

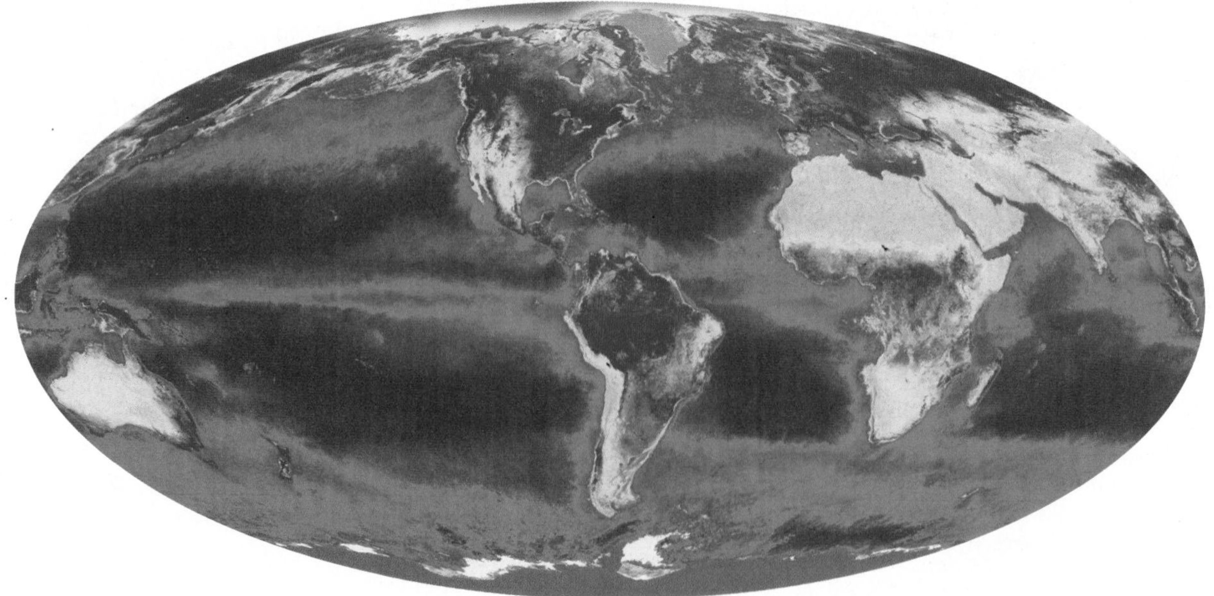

**Figure 2.5** The salmon swimming upstream are biotic factors in the stream community. Other organisms in the water, such as frogs and algae, also are biotic factors.
**Explain** ***How are organisms dependent on other organisms?***

**Biotic factors** The living factors in an organism's environment are called the **biotic** (by AH tihk) **factors.** Consider the biotic factors in the habitat of salmon shown in **Figure 2.5.** These biotic factors include all of the organisms that live in the water, such as other fish, algae, frogs, and microscopic organisms. In addition, organisms that live on the land adjacent to the water might be biotic factors for the salmon. Migratory animals, such as birds that pass through the area, also are biotic factors. The interactions among organisms are necessary for the health of all species in the same geographic location. For example, the salmon need other members of their species to reproduce. Salmon also depend on other organisms for food and, in turn, are a food source for other organisms.

**Abiotic factors** The nonliving factors in an organism's environment are called **abiotic** (ay bi AH tihk) **factors.** The abiotic factors for different organisms vary across the biosphere, but organisms that live in the same geographic area might share the same abiotic factors. These factors might include temperature, air or water currents, sunlight, soil type, rainfall, or available nutrients. Organisms depend on abiotic factors for survival. For example, the abiotic factors important to a particular plant might be the amount of rainfall, the amount of sunlight, the type of soil, the range of temperature, and the nutrients available in the soil. The abiotic factors for the salmon in **Figure 2.5** might be the temperature range of the water, the pH of the water, and the salt concentration of the water.

Organisms are adapted to surviving in the abiotic factors that are present in their natural environments. If an organism moves to another location with a different set of abiotic factors, the organism might die if it cannot adjust quickly to its new surroundings. For example, if a lush green plant that normally grows in a swampy area is transplanted to a dry desert, the plant likely will die because it cannot adjust to abiotic factors present in the desert.

**Reading Check** **Compare and contrast** abiotic and biotic factors for a plant or animal in your community.

**CAREERS IN BIOLOGY**

**Ecologist** The field of ecology is vast. Ecologists study the organisms in the world and the environments in which they live. Many ecologists specialize in a particular area such as marine ecology. For more information on biology careers, visit biologygmh.com.

## Levels of Organization

The biosphere is too large and complex for most ecological studies. To study relationships within the biosphere, ecologists look at different levels of organization or smaller pieces of the biosphere. The levels increase in complexity as the numbers and interactions between organisms increase. The levels of organization are

- organism;
- population;
- biological community;
- ecosystem;
- biome;
- biosphere.

Refer to **Figure 2.6** as you read about each level.

*Study Tip*

**Question Session** Study the levels of organization illustrated in **Figure 2.6** with a partner. Question each other about the topic to deepen your knowledge.

**Organisms, populations, and biological communities** The lowest level of organization is the individual organism itself. In **Figure 2.6,** the organism is represented by a single fish. Individual organisms of a single species that share the same geographic location at the same time make up a **population.** The school of fish represents a population of organisms. Individual organisms often compete for the same resources, and if resources are plentiful, the population can grow. However, usually there are factors that prevent populations from becoming extremely large. For example, when the population has grown beyond what the available resources can support, the population size begins to decline until it reaches the number of individuals that the available resources can support.

The next level of organization is the biological community. A **biological community** is a group of interacting populations that occupy the same geographic area at the same time. Organisms might or might not compete for the same resources in a biological community. The collection of plant and animal populations, including the school of fish, represents a biological community.

**LAUNCH Lab**

**Review** Based on what you've read about populations, how would you now answer the analysis questions?

**Ecosystems, biomes, and the biosphere** The next level of organization after a biological community is an ecosystem. An **ecosystem** is a biological community and all of the abiotic factors that affect it. As you can see in **Figure 2.6,** an ecosystem might contain an even larger collection of organisms than a biological community. In addition, it contains the abiotic factors present, such as water temperature and light availability. Although **Figure 2.6** represents an ecosystem as a large area, an ecosystem also can be small, such as an aquarium or tiny puddle. The boundaries of an ecosystem are somewhat flexible and can change, and ecosystems even might overlap.

The next level of organization is called the biome and is one that you will learn more about in Chapter 3. A **biome** is a large group of ecosystems that share the same climate and have similar types of communities. The biome shown in **Figure 2.6** is a marine biome. All of the biomes on Earth combine to form the highest level of organization—the biosphere.

**Reading Check Infer** what other types of biomes might be found in the biosphere if the one shown in **Figure 2.6** is called a marine biome.

Section 2.2

## Objectives

- **Describe** the flow of energy through an ecosystem.
- **Identify** the ultimate energy source for photosynthetic producers.
- **Describe** food chains, food webs, and pyramid models.

## Review Vocabulary

**energy:** the ability to cause change; energy cannot be created or destroyed, only transformed

## New Vocabulary

autotroph
heterotroph
herbivore
carnivore
omnivore
detritivore
trophic level
food chain
food web
biomass

# Flow of Energy in an Ecosystem

**MAIN Idea Autotrophs capture energy, making it available for all members of a food web.**

**Real-World Reading Link** When you eat a slice of pizza, you are supplying your body with energy from the Sun. You might be surprised to learn that the Sun is the original source of energy for your body. How did the Sun's energy get into the pizza?

## Energy in an Ecosystem

One way to study the interactions of organisms within an ecosystem is to follow the energy that flows through an ecosystem. Organisms differ in how they obtain energy, and they are classified as autotrophs or heterotrophs based on how they obtain their energy in an ecosystem.

**Autotrophs** All of the green plants and other organisms that produce their own food in an ecosystem are primary producers called autotrophs. An **autotroph** (AW tuh trohf) is an organism that collects energy from sunlight or inorganic substances to produce food. As you will learn in Chapter 8, organisms that have chlorophyll absorb energy during photosynthesis and use it to convert the inorganic substances carbon dioxide and water to organic molecules. In places where sunlight is unavailable, some bacteria use hydrogen sulfide and carbon dioxide to make organic molecules to use as food. Autotrophs are the foundation of all ecosystems because they make energy available for all other organisms in an ecosystem.

**VOCABULARY**
**ACADEMIC VOCABULARY**
**Foundation:**
a basis upon which something stands or is supported.
*Autotrophs provide the foundation of the food supply for other organisms.*

**Heterotrophs** A **heterotroph** (HE tuh roh trohf) is an organism that gets its energy requirements by consuming other organisms. Therefore, heterotrophs also are called consumers. A heterotroph that eats only plants is an **herbivore** (HUR buh vor) such as a cow, a rabbit, or grasshopper. Heterotrophs that prey on other heterotrophs, such as wolves, lions, and lynxes, shown in **Figure 2.11,** are called **carnivores** (KAR nuh vorz).

■ **Figure 2.11** This lynx is a heterotroph that is about to consume another heterotroph.
**Identify** *What is an additional classification for each of these animals?*

■ **Figure 2.12** This fungus is obtaining food energy from the dead log. Fungi are decomposers that recycle materials found in dead organisms.
**Explain** *why decomposers are important in an ecosystem.*

In addition to herbivores and carnivores, there are organisms that eat both plants and animals, called **omnivores** (AHM nih vorz). Bears, humans, and mockingbirds are examples of omnivores.

The **detritivores** (duh TRYD uh vorz), which eat fragments of dead matter in an ecosystem, return nutrients to the soil, air, and water where the nutrients can be reused by organisms. Detritivores include worms and many aquatic insects that live on stream bottoms. They feed on small pieces of dead plants and animals. Decomposers, similar to detritivores, break down dead organisms by releasing digestive enzymes. Fungi, such as those in **Figure 2.12,** and bacteria are decomposers.

All heterotrophs, including detritivores, perform some decomposition when they consume another organism and break down its body into organic compounds. However, it is primarily the decomposers that break down organic compounds and make nutrients available to producers for reuse. Without the detritivores and decomposers, the entire biosphere would be littered with dead organisms. Their bodies would contain nutrients that would no longer be available to other organisms. The detritivores are an important part of the cycle of life because they make nutrients available for all other organisms.

## Models of Energy Flow

Ecologists use food chains and food webs to model the energy flow through an ecosystem. Like any model, food chains and food webs are simplified representations of the flow of energy. Each step in a food chain or food web is called a **trophic** (TROH fihk) **level.** Autotrophs make up the first trophic level in all ecosystems. Heterotrophs make up the remaining levels. With the exception of the first trophic level, organisms at each trophic level get their energy from the trophic level before it.

## MiniLab 2.1

### Construct a Food Web

**How is energy passed from organism to organism in an ecosystem?** A food chain shows a single path for energy flow in an ecosystem. The overlapping relationships between food chains are shown in a food web.

**Procedure**

1. Read and complete the lab safety form.
2. Use the following information to construct a food web in a meadow ecosystem:
   - Red foxes feed on raccoons, crayfishes, grasshoppers, red clover, meadow voles, and gray squirrels.
   - Red clover is eaten by grasshoppers, muskrats, red foxes, and meadow voles.
   - Meadow voles, gray squirrels, and raccoons all eat parts of the white oak tree.
   - Crayfishes feed on green algae and detritus, and they are eaten by muskrats and red foxes.
   - Raccoons feed on muskrats, meadow voles, gray squirrels, and white oak trees.

**Analysis**

1. **Identify** all of the herbivores, carnivores, omnivores, and detritivores in the food web.
2. **Describe** how the muskrats would be affected if disease kills the white oak trees.

32. What are the two major life processes that involve carbon and oxygen?
 A. coal formation and photosynthesis
 B. photosynthesis and respiration
 C. fuel combustion and open burning
 D. death and decay

33. Which process locks phosphorus in a long-term cycle?
 A. organic materials buried at the bottom of oceans
 B. phosphates released into the soil
 C. animals and plants eliminating wastes
 D. rain eroding mountains

## Constructed Response

34. **Short Answer** Clarify what is meant by the following statement: Grass is just as important as mice in the diet of a carnivore such as a fox.

35. **Short Answer** The law of conservation of matter states that matter cannot be created or destroyed. How does this law relate to the cycling of carbon in an ecosystem?

36. **Short Answer** Explain the role of decomposers in the nitrogen cycle.

## Think Critically

*Use the illustration below to answer question 37 and 38.*

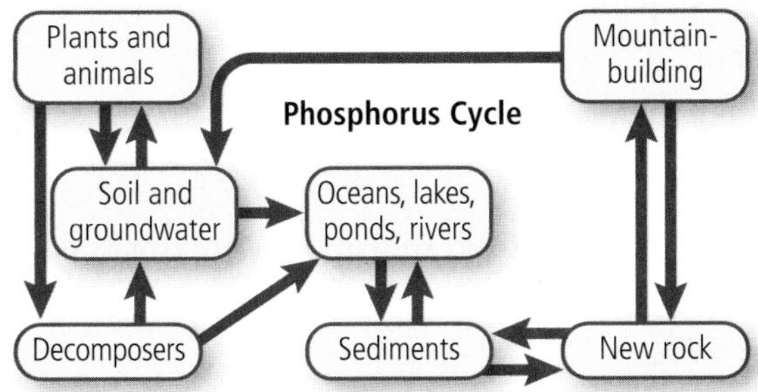


37. **Interpret Scientific Illustrations** Predict the effect of additional mountain building in the Rocky Mountains on the levels of phosphorus in the surrounding valleys.

38. **Explain** how decomposers supply phosphorus to soil, groundwater, oceans, lakes, ponds, and rivers.

## Additional Assessment

39. WRITING in Biology Write a poem that includes vocabulary terms and concepts from the chapter.

### DBQ Document-Based Questions

*The following information pertains to an ancient sand dune in Florida that is now landlocked—Lake Wales Ridge. Read the passage and answer the following questions.*

Data obtained from: Mohlenbrock, R. H. 2004–2005. Florida high. *Natural History* 113: 46–47.

*The federally listed animals that live on the ridge are the blue-tailed mole skink, the Florida scrub jay, and the sand skink (which seems to "swim" through loose sand of the scrub). Other animals on the ridge are the eastern indigo snake (which can grow to more than eight feet long, making it the longest nonvenomous snake species in North America), the Florida black bear, the Florida gopher frog, the Florida mouse, the Florida pine snake, the Florida sandhill crane, the Florida scrub lizard, the gopher tortoise, Sherman's fox squirrel, and the short-tailed snake.*

*The gopher tortoise is particularly important because its burrows, sometimes as long as thirty feet, serve as homes for several of the rare species as well as many other more common organisms. The burrows also provide temporary havens when fires sweep through the area, or when temperatures reach high or low extremes.*

40. Construct a simple food web using at least five of the organisms listed.

41. Explain how the burrows are used during fires and why they are effective.

### Cumulative Review

42. Distinguish between science and pseudoscience. **(Chapter 1)**

43. Describe conditions under which a controlled experiment occurs. **(Chapter 1)**

# Standardized Test Practice

**Cumulative**

## Multiple Choice

1. Which would be considered an ecosystem?
   A. bacteria living in a deep ocean vent
   B. biotic factors in a forest
   C. living and nonliving things in a pond
   D. populations of zebras and lions

*Use the illustration below to answer questions 2 and 3.*

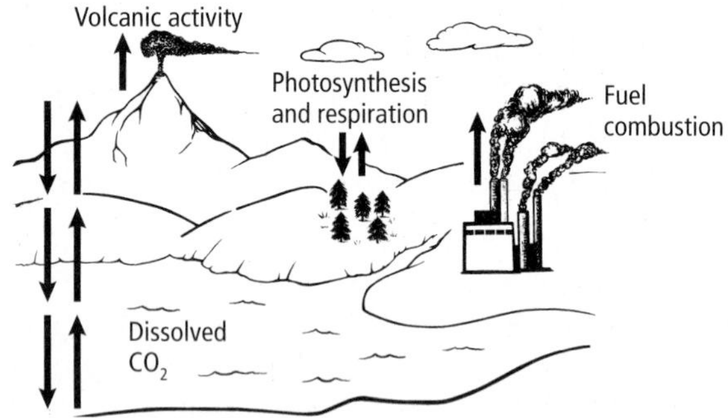


2. Which part of the diagram above relates to carbon leaving a long-term cycle?
   A. Dissolved $CO_2$
   B. Fuel combustion
   C. Photosynthesis and respiration
   D. Volcanic activity

3. Which part of the diagram above relates to carbon moving from an abiotic to a biotic part of the ecosystem?
   A. Dissolved $CO_2$
   B. Fuel combustion
   C. Photosynthesis and respiration
   D. Volcanic activity

4. Which is a scientific explanation of a natural phenomenon supported by many observations and experiments?
   A. factor
   B. hypothesis
   C. result
   D. theory

5. The mole is the SI unit for which quantity?
   A. number of particles in a substance
   B. compounds that make up a substance
   C. number of elements in a substance
   D. total mass of a substance

6. Suppose two leaf-eating species of animals live in a habitat where there is a severe drought, and many plants die as a result of the drought. Which term describes the kind of relationship the two species probably will have?
   A. commensalism
   B. competition
   C. mutualism
   D. predation

*Use the illustration below to answer questions 7–9.*

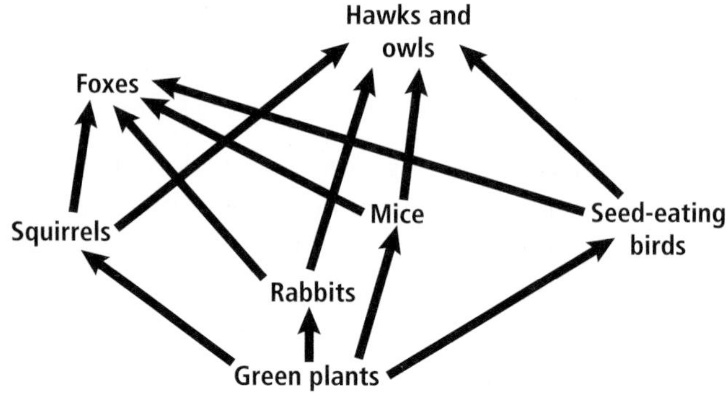


7. Which part of the food web above contains the greatest biomass?
   A. foxes
   B. green plants
   C. mice
   D. rabbits

8. Which part of the food web above contains the least biomass?
   A. foxes
   B. green plants
   C. mice
   D. rabbits

9. What happens to the energy that the fox uses for maintaining its body temperature?
   A. It is taken up by decomposers that consume the fox.
   B. It moves into the surrounding environment.
   C. It stays in the fox through the metabolism of food.
   D. It travels to the next trophic level when the fox is eaten.

## Short Answer

*Use the illustration below to answer questions 10 and 11.*

**10.** What are two biotic factors and two abiotic factors that affect a worm found in a situation similar to what is shown in the diagram?

**11.** Explain the portions of the following biogeochemical cycles that are related to the diagram above.
**A.** Nitrogen cycle
**B.** Oxygen cycle
**C.** Carbon cycle

**12.** Distinguish between the everyday use of the term *theory* and its true scientific meaning.

**13.** Evaluate how scientific knowledge changes and how the amount of scientific knowledge grows. Suggest a reason why it probably will continue to grow.

**14.** Describe how a forest ecosystem might be different without the presence of decomposers and detritivores.

**15.** Suppose that some unknown organisms are discovered in the deep underground of Earth. Give two examples of questions that biologists might try to answer by researching these organisms.

## Extended Response

*Use this drawing to answer questions 16 and 17.*

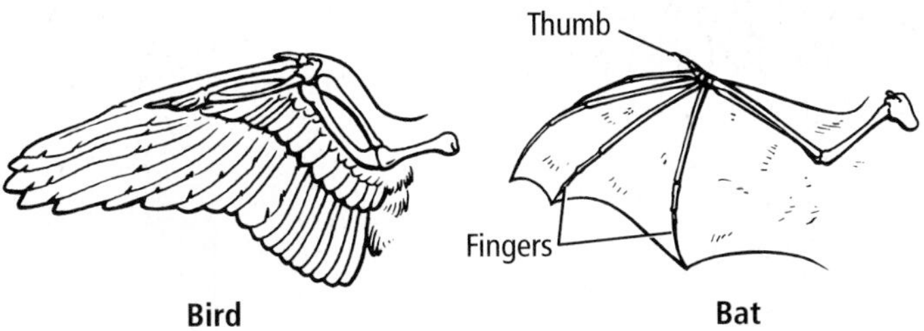


**16.** Someone tells you that bats and birds are closely related because they both have wings. Evaluate how this diagram could be used to critique the idea that bats and birds are not closely related.

**17.** Suppose you form a hypothesis that bats and birds are not closely related and you want to confirm this by comparing the way bats and birds fly. Design an experiment to test this hypothesis.

## Essay Question

Various substances or elements on Earth move through long-term and short-term biogeochemical cycles as they become part of different aspects of the biosphere. The amount of a substance that is involved in a long-term cycle has an effect on the availability of that substance for use by humans and other organisms on Earth.

*Using the information in the paragraph above, answer the following question in essay format.*

**18.** Choose a substance or element that you know is involved in both long-term and short-term biogeochemical cycles. In a well-organized essay, describe how it moves through both types of cycles, and how these cycles affect its availability to humans and other organisms.

| NEED EXTRA HELP? | | | | | | | | | | | | | | | | | | |
|---|---|---|---|---|---|---|---|---|---|---|---|---|---|---|---|---|---|---|
| **If You Missed Question . . .** | 1 | 2 | 3 | 4 | 5 | 6 | 7 | 8 | 9 | 10 | 11 | 12 | 13 | 14 | 15 | 16 | 17 | 18 |
| **Review Section . . .** | 2.2 | 2.3 | 2.3, 2.1 | 1.2 | 1.2 | 2.1 | 2.2 | 2.2 | 2.2 | 2.1 | 2.3 | 1.2 | 1.2 | 2.2 | 1.3 | 1.2 | 1.3 | 2.3 |

CHAPTER 3

# Communities, Biomes, and Ecosystems

**Section 1**
**Community Ecology**
**MAIN Idea** All living organisms are limited by factors in the environment.

**Section 2**
**Terrestrial Biomes**
**MAIN Idea** Ecosystems on land are grouped into biomes primarily based on the plant communities within them.

**Section 3**
**Aquatic Ecosystems**
**MAIN Idea** Aquatic ecosystems are grouped based on abiotic factors such as water flow, depth, distance from shore, salinity, and latitude.

## BioFacts

- The Great Barrier Reef off the coast of northeastern Australia, shown here, is the largest living structure on Earth and is visible from space. It extends over 2000 km.
- Coral reefs grow at a rate of only about 1.27 cm/y.
- Coral reefs located where the Indian and Pacific Oceans meet are the most diverse reefs; they can have as many as 400 species of coral.

# LAUNCH Lab

## What is my biological address?

Just as you have a postal address, you also have a biological "address." As a living organism, you are part of interwoven ecological units that vary in size from as large as the whole biosphere to the place you occupy right now.

### Procedure

1. Consider the following question: What do the terms *community* and *ecosystem* mean to you?
2. Describe the biological community and an ecosystem to which you belong.

### Analysis

1. **Compare** Did your classmates all identify the same community and ecosystem? How would you describe, in general, the plants and animals in your area to someone from another country?
2. **Examine** Communities and ecosystems are constantly changing through a process known as succession. What changes do you think your biological community has undergone in the last 100 to 150 years?

Visit biologygmh.com to:

- study the entire chapter online
- explore Concepts in Motion, Microscopy Links, and links to virtual dissections
- access Web links for more information, projects, and activities
- review content online with the Interactive Tutor and take Self-Check Quizzes

**Terrestrial Biomes** Make this Foldable to help you understand primary succession and secondary succession.

**STEP 1** Draw a line through the middle of a sheet of notebook paper as shown.

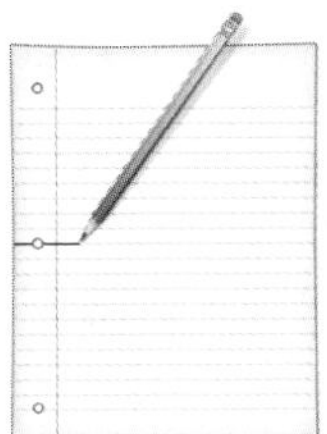

**STEP 2** Fold the paper from the top and bottom so the edges meet at the center line.

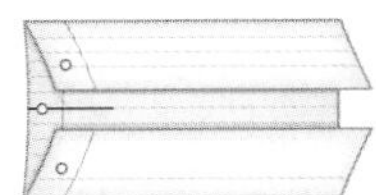

**STEP 3** Label the two tabs as illustrated.

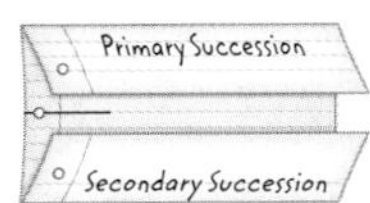


FOLDABLES **Use this Foldable with Section 3.1.** As you read the chapter, record what you learn about primary succession and secondary succession under the tabs. Use the front of the tabs to draw a visual representation of each.

Section 3.1

### Objectives

- **Recognize** how unfavorable abiotic and biotic factors affect a species.
- **Describe** how ranges of tolerance affect the distribution of organisms.
- **Sequence** the stages of primary and secondary succession.

### Review Vocabulary

**abiotic factor:** the nonliving part of an organism's environment

### New Vocabulary

community
limiting factor
tolerance
ecological succession
primary succession
climax community
secondary succession

# Community Ecology

MAIN Idea **All living organisms are limited by factors in the environment.**

**Real-World Reading Link** Wherever you live, you probably are used to the conditions of your environment. If it is cold outdoors, you might wear a coat, hat, and gloves. Other organisms also adapt to their environment, even when conditions are harsh and changing.

## Communities

When you describe your community, you probably include your family, the students in your school, and the people who live nearby. A biological **community** is a group of interacting populations that occupy the same area at the same time. Therefore, your community also includes plants, other animals, bacteria, and fungi. Not every community includes the same variety of organisms. An urban community is different from a rural community, and a desert community is different from an arctic community.

In Chapter 2, you learned that organisms depend on one another for survival. You also learned about abiotic factors and that abiotic factors affect individual organisms. How, then, might abiotic factors affect communities? Consider soil, which is an abiotic factor. If soil becomes too acidic, some species might die or become extinct. This might affect food sources for other organisms, resulting in a change in the community.

Organisms adapt to the conditions in which they live. For example, a wolf's heavy fur coat enables it to survive in harsh winter climates, and a cactus's ability to retain water enables it to tolerate the dry conditions of a desert. Depending on which factors are present, and in what quantities, organisms can survive in some ecosystems but not in others. As an example, the plants in the desert oasis shown in **Figure 3.1** decrease in abundance away from the water source.

**Figure 3.1** Notice that populations of organisms live within a relatively small area surrounding the oasis.

**Limiting factors** Any abiotic factor or biotic factor that restricts the numbers, reproduction, or distribution of organisms is called a **limiting factor.** Abiotic limiting factors include sunlight, climate, temperature, water, nutrients, fire, soil chemistry, and space. Biotic limiting factors include living things, such as other plant and animal species. Factors that restrict the growth of one population might enable another to thrive. For example, in the oasis shown in **Figure 3.1,** water is a limiting factor for all of the organisms. Temperature also might be a limiting factor. Desert species must be able to withstand the heat of the Sun and the cold temperatures of desert nights.

**Range of tolerance** For any environmental factor, there is an upper limit and lower limit that define the conditions in which an organism can survive. For example, steelhead trout live in cool, clear coastal rivers and streams from California to Alaska. The ideal range of water temperature for steelhead trout is between 13°C and 21°C, as illustrated in **Figure 3.2.** However, steelhead trout can survive water temperatures from 9°C to 25°C. At these temperatures, steelhead trout experience physiological stress, such as inability to grow or reproduce. They will die if the water temperature goes beyond the upper and lower limits.

Have you ever had to tolerate a hot day or a boring activity? Similarly, the ability of any organism to survive when subjected to abiotic factors or biotic factors is called **tolerance.** Consider **Figure 3.2** again. Steelhead trout tolerate a specific range of temperatures. That is, the range of tolerance of water temperature for steelhead is 9°C to 25°C. Notice the greatest number of steelhead live in the optimum zone in which the temperature is best for survival. Between the optimum zone and the tolerance limits lies the zone of physiological stress. At these temperatures, there are fewer fish. Beyond the upper tolerance limit of 25°C and the lower tolerance limit of 9°C, there are no steelhead trout. Therefore, water temperature is a limiting factor for steelhead when water temperature is outside the range of tolerance.

 **Reading Check Describe** the relationship between a limiting factor and a range of tolerance.

**CAREERS IN BIOLOGY**

**Conservation Biologist** Among other duties, a conservation biologist might tag and track animals in a community. Understanding the biotic and abiotic factors of the community can help explain changes in populations. For more information on biology careers, visit biologygmh.com.

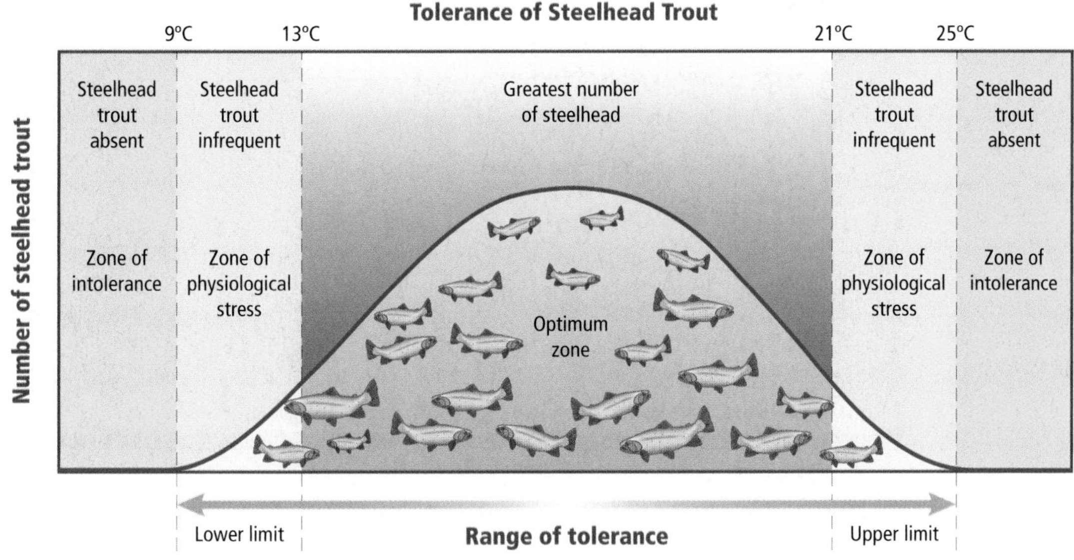


**Figure 3.2** Steelhead trout are limited by the temperature of the water in which they live.
**Infer** *which other abiotic factors might limit the survival of steelhead trout.*

**FOLDABLES** Incorporate information from this section into your Foldable.

# Ecological Succession

Ecosystems are constantly changing. They might be modified in small ways, such as a tree falling in the forest, or in large ways, such as a forest fire. They also might alter the communities that exist in the ecosystem. Forest fires can be good and even necessary for the forest community. Forest fires return nutrients to the soil. Some plants, such as fireweed, have seeds that will not sprout until they are heated by fire. Some ecosystems depend on fires to get rid of debris. If fires are prevented, debris builds up to the point where the next fire might burn the shrubs and trees completely. A forest fire might change the habitat so drastically that some species no longer can survive, but other species might thrive in the new, charred conditions.

The change in an ecosystem that happens when one community replaces another as a result of changing abiotic and biotic factors is **ecological succession.** There are two types of ecological succession—primary succession and secondary succession.

**VOCABULARY**

**SCIENCE USAGE V. COMMON USAGE**

**Primary**

***Science usage:*** first in rank, importance, value, or order.
*A doctor's primary concern should be the patient.*

***Common usage:*** the early years of formal education.
*Elementary grades, up to high school, are considered to comprise a student's primary education.*

**Primary succession** On a solidified lava flow or exposed rocks on a cliff, no soil is present. If you took samples of each and looked at them under a microscope, the only biological organisms you would observe would be bacteria and perhaps fungal spores or pollen grains that drifted there on air currents. The establishment of a community in an area of exposed rock that does not have any topsoil is **primary succession,** as illustrated in **Figure 3.3.** Primary succession usually occurs very slowly at first.

Most plants require soil for growth. How is soil formed? Usually lichens, a combination of a fungus and algae that you will learn more about in Chapter 20, begin to grow on the rock. Because lichens, along with some mosses, are among the first organisms to appear, they are called pioneer species. Pioneer species help to create soil by secreting acids that help to break down rocks.

**Figure 3.3** The formation of soil is the first step in primary succession. Once soil formation starts, there is succession toward a climax community.

**Concepts In Motion**

**Interactive Figure** To see an animation of how a climax community forms, visit biologygmh.com.

# Visualizing Global Effects on Climate

**Figure 3.7**
Some parts of Earth receive more heat from the Sun. Earth's winds and ocean currents contribute to climate and balance the heat on Earth. Many scientists think human impacts on the atmosphere upset this balance.

### Winds on Earth

60°N
30°N
0°
30°S
60°S
Equator
Westerlies
Northeast trade winds
Southeast trade winds
Westerlies

Winds are created as warm air rises and cool air sinks. Distinct global wind systems transport cold air to warm areas and warm air to cold areas.

### Earth's Ocean Currents

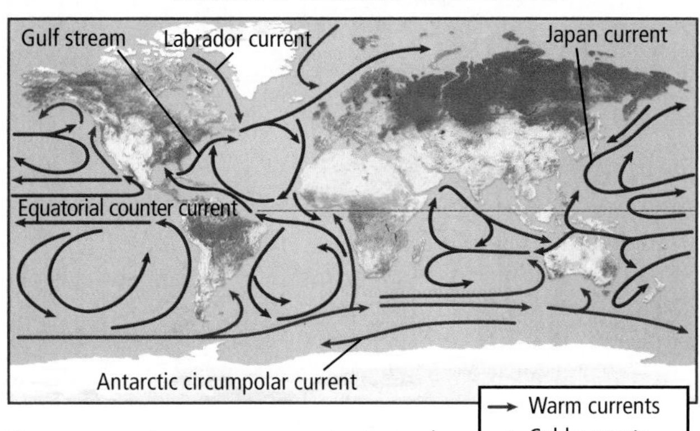


Ocean currents carry warm water toward the poles. As the water cools, it sinks toward the ocean floor and moves toward tropical regions.

### Greenhouse Effect

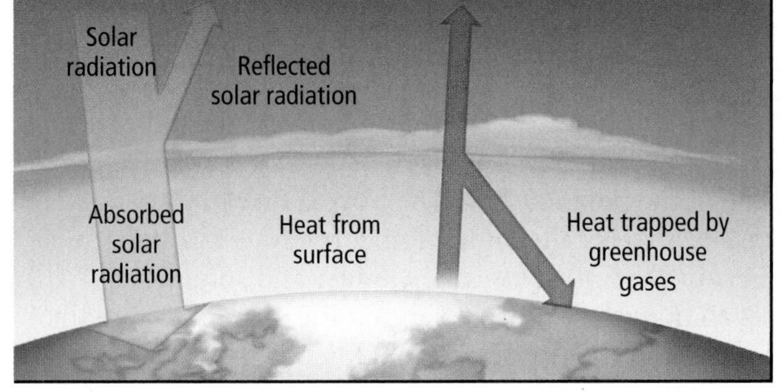


Earth's surface is warmed by the greenhouse effect. Certain gases in Earth's atmosphere, primarily water vapor, reduce the amount of energy Earth radiates into space. Other important greenhouse gases are carbon dioxide and methane.

### Human Impact on the Atmosphere

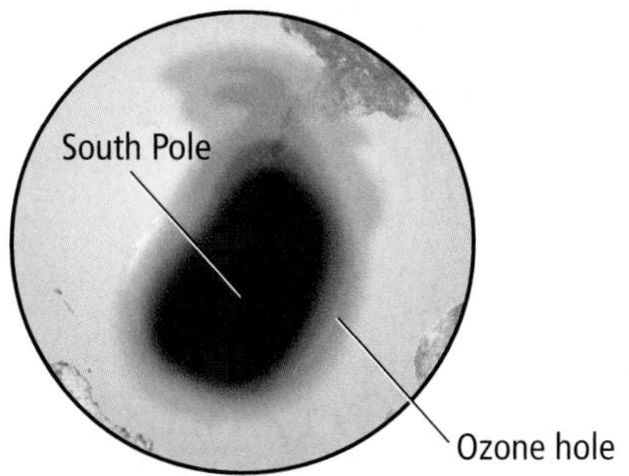


The ozone layer is a protective layer in the atmosphere that absorbs most of the harmful UV radiation from the Sun. Atmospheric studies have indicated that chlorofluorocarbons (CFCs) contribute to a seasonal reduction in ozone concentration over Antarctica, forming the Antarctic ozone hole.

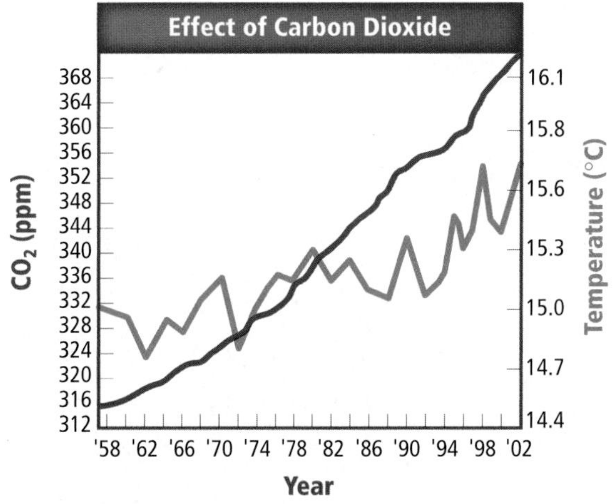


The measured increase of carbon dioxide ($CO_2$) in the atmosphere is mainly due to the burning of fossil fuels. As carbon dioxide levels have increased, the average global temperature has increased.

**Concepts In Motion** **Interactive Figure** To see an animation of the global effects on climate, visit biologygmh.com.

**Biology Online**

**Figure 3.8** Tundra
**Average precipitation:** 15–25 cm per year
**Temperature range:** −34°C–12°C
**Plant species:** short grasses, shrubs
**Animal species:** Caribou, polar bears, birds, insects, wolves, salmon, trout
**Geographic location:** South of the polar ice caps in the Northern Hemisphere
**Abiotic factors:** soggy summers; permafrost; cold and dark much of the year

**Tundra** Extending in a band below the polar ice caps across northern North America, Europe, and Siberia in Asia is the tundra. The **tundra** is a treeless biome with a layer of permanently frozen soil below the surface called permafrost. Although the ground thaws to a depth of a few centimeters in the summer, its constant cycles of freezing and thawing do not allow tree roots to grow. Some animals and shallow-rooted plants that have adapted to tundra conditions are illustrated in **Figure 3.8.**

**Boreal forest** South of the tundra is a broad band of dense evergreen forest extending across North America, Europe, and Asia, called the boreal forest. The **boreal forest,** illustrated in **Figure 3.9,** also is called northern coniferous forest, or taiga. Summers in the boreal forest are longer and somewhat warmer than in the tundra, enabling the ground to remain warmer than in the tundra. Boreal forests, therefore, lack a permafrost layer.

**Figure 3.9** Boreal forest
**Average precipitation:** 30–84 cm per year
**Temperature range:** −54°C–21°C
**Plant species:** spruce and fir trees, deciduous trees, small shrubs
**Animal species:** birds, moose, beavers, deer, wolverines, mountain lions
**Geographic location:** northern part of North America, Europe, and Asia
**Abiotic factors:** summers are short and moist; winters are long, cold, and dry

**Figure 3.10** Temperate forest
**Average precipitation:** 75–150 cm per year
**Temperature range:** −30°C–30°C
**Plant species:** oak, beech, and maple trees, shrubs
**Animal species:** squirrels, rabbits, skunks, birds, deer, foxes, black bears
**Geographic location:** south of the boreal forests in eastern North America, eastern Asia, Australia, and Europe
**Abiotic factors:** well-defined seasons; summers are hot, winters are cold

**Temperate forest** Temperate forests cover much of southeastern Canada, the eastern United States, most of Europe, and parts of Asia and Australia. As shown in **Figure 3.10,** the **temperate forest** is composed mostly of broad-leaved, deciduous (dih SIH juh wus) trees—trees that shed their leaves in autumn. The falling red, orange, and gold leaves return nutrients to the soil. Winters are cold. In spring, warm temperature and precipitation restart the growth cycles of plants and trees. Summers are hot.

**Temperate woodland and shrubland** Open **woodlands** and mixed shrub communities are found in areas with less annual rainfall than in temperate forests. The woodland biome occurs in areas surrounding the Mediterranean Sea, on the western coasts of North and South America, and in South Africa and Australia. Areas that are dominated by shrubs, such as in California, are called the chaparral. **Figure 3.11** illustrates woodland and shrub communities.

**Figure 3.11** Temperate woodland and shrubland
**Average precipitation:** 38–100 cm per year
**Temperature range:** 10°C–40°C
**Plant species:** evergreen shrubs, corn oak
**Animal species:** foxes, jackrabbits, birds, bobcats, coyotes, lizards, snakes, butterflies
**Geographic location:** surrounds the Mediterranean Sea, western coasts of North and South America, South Africa, and Australia
**Abiotic factors:** summers are very hot and dry; winters are cool and wet

**Figure 3.12** Temperate grassland
**Average precipitation:** 50–89 cm per year
**Temperature range:** −40°C–38°C
**Plant species:** grasses and herbs
**Animal species:** gazelles, bison, horses, lions, deer, mice, coyotes, foxes, wolves, birds, quail, snakes, grasshoppers, spiders
**Geographic location:** North America, South America, Asia, Africa, and Australia
**Abiotic factors:** summers are hot, winters are cold, moderate rainfall, fires possible

**Temperate grassland** A biome that is characterized by fertile soils that are able to support a thick cover of grasses is called **grassland,** illustrated in **Figure 3.12.** Drought, grazing animals, and fires keep grasslands from becoming forests. Due to their underground stems and buds, perennial grasses and herbs are not eliminated by the fires that destroy most shrubs and trees. Temperate grasslands are found in North America, South America, Asia, Africa, and Australia. Grasslands are called steppes in Asia; prairies in North America; pampas, llanos, and cerrados in South America; savannahs and velds in Africa; and rangelands in Australia.

**Desert** Deserts exist on every continent except Europe. A **desert** is any area in which the annual rate of evaporation exceeds the rate of precipitation. You might imagine a desert as a desolate place full of sand dunes, but many deserts do not match that description. As shown in **Figure 3.13,** deserts can be home to a wide variety of plants and animals.

**Figure 3.13** Desert
**Average precipitation:** 2–26 cm per year
**Temperature range:** high: 20°C–49°C, low: −18°C–10°C
**Plant species:** cacti, Joshua trees, succulents
**Animal species:** lizards, bobcats, birds, tortoises, rats, antelope, desert toads
**Geographic location:** every continent except Europe
**Abiotic factors:** varying temperatures, low rainfall

**Figure 3.14** Tropical savanna
**Average precipitation:** 50–130 cm per year
**Temperature range:** 20°C–30°C
**Plant species:** grasses and scattered trees
**Animal species:** lions, hyenas, cheetahs, elephants, giraffes, zebras, birds, insects
**Geographic location:** Africa, South America, and Australia
**Abiotic factors:** summers are hot and rainy, winters are cool and dry

**Tropical savanna** A **tropical savanna** is characterized by grasses and scattered trees in climates that receive less precipitation than some other tropical areas. Tropical savanna biomes occur in Africa, South America, and Australia. The plants and animals shown in **Figure 3.14** are common to tropical savannas.

**Tropical seasonal forest** **Figure 3.15** illustrates a tropical seasonal forest. **Tropical seasonal forests,** also called tropical dry forests, grow in areas of Africa, Asia, Australia, and South and Central America. In one way, the tropical seasonal forest resembles the temperate deciduous forest because during the dry season, almost all of the trees drop their leaves to conserve water.

**Reading Check** **Compare and contrast** tropical savannas and tropical seasonal forests.

**Figure 3.15** Tropical seasonal forest
**Average precipitation:** >200 cm per year
**Temperature range:** 20°C–25°C
**Plant species:** deciduous and evergreen trees, orchids, mosses
**Animal species:** elephants, tigers, monkeys, koalas, rabbits, frogs, spiders
**Geographic location:** Africa, Asia, Australia, and South and Central America
**Abiotic factors:** rainfall is seasonal

**Figure 3.16** Tropical rain forest
**Average precipitation:** 200–1000 cm per year
**Temperature range:** 24°C–27°C
**Plant species:** broadleaf evergreens, bamboo, sugar cane
**Animal species:** chimpanzees, Bengal tigers, elephants, orangutans, bats, toucans, sloth, cobra snakes
**Geographic location:** Central and South America, southern Asia, western Africa, and northeastern Australia
**Abiotic factors:** humid all year, hot and wet

**Tropical rain forest** Warm temperatures and large amounts of rainfall throughout the year characterize the **tropical rain forest** biome illustrated in **Figure 3.16.** Tropical rain forests are found in much of Central and South America, southern Asia, western Africa, and northeastern Australia. The tropical rain forest is the most diverse of all land biomes. Tall, broad-leaved trees with branches heavy with mosses, ferns, and orchids make up the canopy of the tropical rain forest. Shorter trees, shrubs, and plants, such as ferns and creeping plants, make up another layer, or understory, of tropical rain forests.

## Other Terrestrial Areas

You might have noticed that the list of terrestrial biomes does not include some important areas. Many ecologists omit mountains from the list. Mountains are found throughout the world and do not fit the definition of a biome because their climate characteristics and plant and animal life vary depending on elevation. Polar regions also are not considered true biomes because they are ice masses and not true land areas with soil.

**Mountains** If you go up a mountain, you might notice that abiotic conditions, such as temperature and precipitation, change with increasing elevation. These variations allow many communities to exist on a mountain. As **Figure 3.17** illustrates, biotic communities also change with increasing altitude, and the tops of tall mountains may support communities that resemble those of the tundra.

*Study Tip*

**Summaries** Review the terrestrial biomes featured in this section. Choose one or two biomes and write two sentences that summarize the information.

**Figure 3.17** As you climb a mountain or increase in latitude, the temperature drops and the climate changes.
**Describe** *the relationship between altitude and latitude.*

■ **Figure 3.18** A surprising number of species inhabit the polar regions, including these penguins in Antarctica.

**Polar regions** Polar regions border the tundra at high latitudes. These polar regions are cold all year. In the northern polar region lies the ice-covered Arctic Ocean and Greenland. Antarctica is the continent that lies in the southern polar region. Covered by a thick layer of ice, the polar regions might seem incapable of sustaining life. The coldest temperature, −89°C, was recorded in the Antarctica. However, as shown in **Figure 3.18,** colonies of penguins live in Antarctica. Additionally, whales and seals patrol the coasts, preying on penguins, fish, or shrimplike invertebrates called krill. The arctic polar region supports even more species, including polar bears and arctic foxes. Human societies have also inhabited this region throughout history. Although average winter temperature is about −30°C, the Arctic summer in some areas is warm enough for vegetables to be grown.

**CAREERS IN BIOLOGY**

**Climatologist** Unlike meteorologists, who study current weather conditions, climatologists study long-term climate patterns and determine how climate changes affect ecosystems. For more information on biology careers, visit biologygmh.com.

## Section 3.2 Assessment

### Section Summary

- Latitude affects terrestrial biomes according to the angle at which sunlight strikes Earth.
- Latitude, elevation, ocean currents, and other abiotic factors determine climate.
- Two major abiotic factors define terrestrial biomes.
- Terrestrial biomes include tundra, boreal forests, temperate forests, temperate woodlands and shrublands, temperate grasslands, deserts, tropical savannas, tropical seasonal forests, and tropical rain forests.

### Understand Main Ideas

1. MAIN Idea **Describe** nine major biomes.
2. **Describe** the abiotic factors that determine a terrestrial biome.
3. **Summarize** variations in climate among three major zones as you travel south from the equator toward the south pole.
4. **Indicate** the differences between temperate grasslands and tropical savannas.
5. **Compare and contrast** the climate and biotic factors of tropical seasonal forests and temperate forests.

### Think Scientifically

6. *Hypothesize* why the tropical rain forests have the greatest diversity of living things.
7. WRITING in **Biology** Tropical forests are being felled at a rate of 17 million hectares per year, which represents almost two percent of the forest area. Use this information to write a pamphlet decribing how much rain forest area exists and when it might be gone.

Section 3.3

## Objectives

- **Identify** the major abiotic factors that determine the aquatic ecosystems.
- **Recognize** that freshwater ecosystems are characterized by depth and water flow.
- **Identify** transitional aquatic ecosystems and their importance.
- **Distinguish** the zones of marine ecosystems.

## Review Vocabulary

**salinity:** a measure of the amount of salt in a body of water

## New Vocabulary

sediment
littoral zone
limnetic zone
plankton
profundal zone
wetlands
estuary
intertidal zone
photic zone
aphotic zone
benthic zone
abyssal zone

# Aquatic Ecosystems

MAIN Idea **Aquatic ecosystems are grouped based on abiotic factors such as water flow, depth, distance from shore, salinity, and latitude.**

**Real-World Reading Link** Think about the body of water that is closest to where you live. What are its characteristics? How deep is it? Is it freshwater or salty? For centuries, bodies of water have been central to cultures around the world.

## The Water on Earth

When you think about water on Earth, you might recall a vacation at the ocean or a geography lesson in which you located Earth's oceans and seas. You probably have heard about other large bodies of water, such as the Amazon river and the Great Salt Lake. A globe of Earth is mainly blue in color because the planet is largely covered with water. Ecologists recognize the importance of water because of the biological communities that water supports. In this section, you will read about freshwater, transitional, and marine aquatic ecosystems. You also will read about the abiotic factors that affect these ecosystems.

## Freshwater Ecosystems

The major freshwater ecosystems include ponds, lakes, streams, rivers, and wetlands. Plants and animals in these ecosystems are adapted to the low salt content in freshwater and are unable to survive in areas of high salt concentration. Only about 2.5 percent of the water on Earth is freshwater, as illustrated by the circle graph on the left in **Figure 3.19.** The graph on the right in **Figure 3.19** shows that of that 2.5 percent, 68.9 percent is contained in glaciers, 30.8 percent is groundwater, and only 0.3 percent is found in lakes, ponds, rivers, streams, and wetlands. Interestingly, almost all of the freshwater species live in this 0.3 percent.

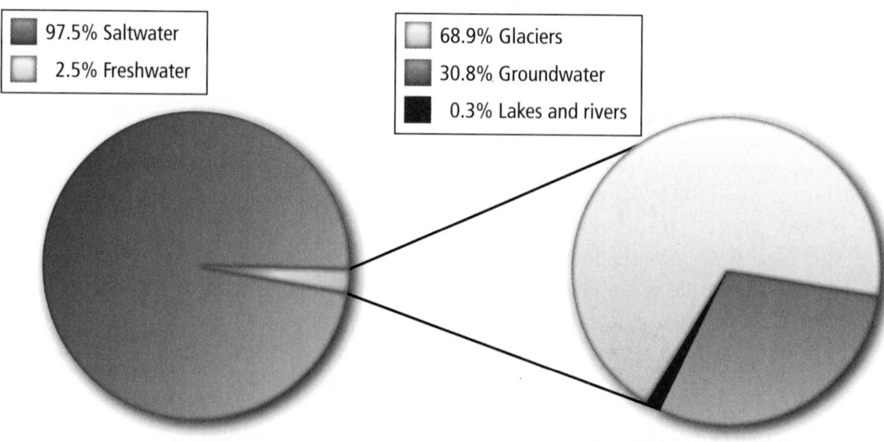


**Figure 3.19** The vast majority of Earth's water is salt water. Most of the freshwater supply is locked in glaciers.

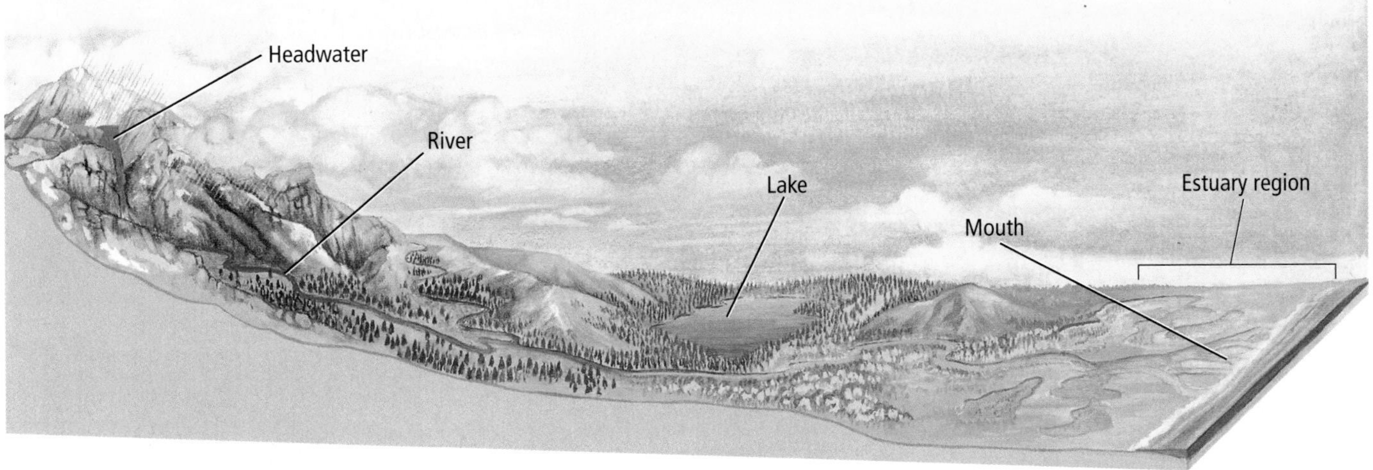


■ **Figure 3.20** Mountain streams have clear, cold water that is highly oxygenated and supports the larvae of many insects and the coldwater fish that feed on them. Rivers become increasingly wider, deeper, and slower. At the mouth, many rivers divide into many channels where wetlands or estuaries form.

**Rivers and streams** The water in rivers and streams flows in one direction, beginning at a source called a headwater and traveling to the mouth, where the flowing water empties into a larger body of water, as illustrated in **Figure 3.20.** Rivers and streams also might start from underground springs or from snowmelt. The slope of the landscape determines the direction and speed of the water flow. When the slope is steep, water flows quickly, causing a lot of sediment to be picked up and carried by the water. **Sediment** is material that is deposited by water, wind, or glaciers. As the slope levels, the speed of the water flow decreases and sediments are deposited in the form of silt, mud, and sand.

The characteristics of rivers and streams change during the journey from the source to the mouth. Interactions between wind and the water stir up the water's surface, which adds a significant amount of oxygen to the water. Interactions between land and water result in erosion, changes in nutrient availability, and changes to the path of the river or stream.

The currents and turbulence of fast-moving rivers and streams prevent much accumulation of organic materials and sediment. For this reason, there usually are fewer species living in the rapid waters shown in **Figure 3.21.** An important characteristic of all life in rivers and streams is the ability to withstand the constant water current. Plants that can root themselves into the streambed are common in areas where water is slowed by rocks or sand bars. Young fish hide in these plants and feed on the drifting microscopic organisms and aquatic insects.

In slow-moving water, insect larvae are the primary food source for many fish, including American eel, brown bullhead catfish, and trout. Other organisms, such as crabs and worms, are sometimes present in calm water. Animals that live in slow-moving water include newts, tadpoles, and frogs.

 **Reading Check** **Describe** key abiotic factors that define rivers and streams.

■ **Figure 3.21** The turbulent churning action of fast-moving rivers and streams does not allow for many plants to take root or for other species to inhabit these waters.

■ **Figure 3.22** The temperature of lakes and ponds varies depending on the season. During spring and autumn, deep water receives oxygen from the surface water and surface water receives inorganic nutrients from the deep water.

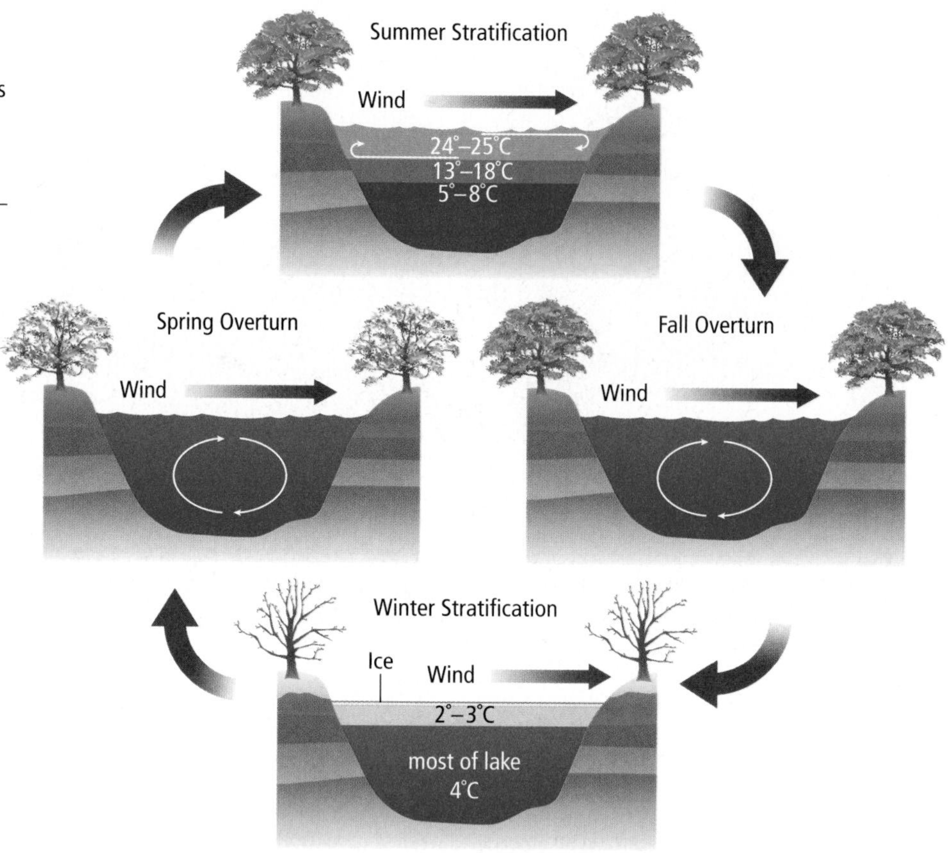


**Lakes and ponds** An inland body of standing water is called a lake or a pond. It can be as small as a few square meters or as large as thousands of square meters. Some ponds might be filled with water for only a few weeks or months each year, whereas some lakes have existed for hundreds of years. **Figure 3.22** illustrates how in temperate regions the temperature of lakes and ponds varies depending on the season.

During the winter, most of the water in a lake or pond is the same temperature. In the summer, the warmer water on top is less dense than the colder water at the bottom. During the spring and fall, as the water warms or cools, turnover occurs. The top and bottom layers of water mix, often due to winds, and this results in a uniform water temperature. This mixing circulates oxygen and brings nutrients from the bottom to the surface.

Nutrient-poor lakes, called oligotrophic (uh lih goh TROH fihk) lakes, often are found high in the mountains. Few plant and animal species are present as a result of small amounts of organic matter and nutrients. Nutrient-rich lakes, called eutrophic (yoo TROH fihk) lakes, usually are found at lower altitudes. Many plant and animal species are present as a result of organic matter and plentiful nutrients, some of which come from agricultural and urban activities.

Lakes and ponds are divided into three zones based on the amount of sunlight that penetrates the water. The area closest to the shore is the **littoral** *(LIH tuh rul)* **zone.** The water in this zone is shallow, which allows sunlight to reach the bottom. Many producers, such as aquatic plants and algae, live in these shallow waters. The abundance of light and producers make the littoral zone an area of high photosynthesis. Many consumers also inhabit this zone, including frogs, turtles, worms, crustaceans, insect larvae, and fish.

**VOCABULARY**

**WORD ORIGIN**

**Eutrophic/oligotrophic**

***eu–*** prefix; from Greek, meaning *well*
***oligo–*** prefix; from Greek, meaning *few*
***–trophic;*** from Greek, meaning *nourish.*

### Understand Key Concepts

29. Where is the largest percentage of water located?
   A. groundwater
   B. rivers
   C. oceans
   D. glaciers

*Use the diagram below to answer question 30.*

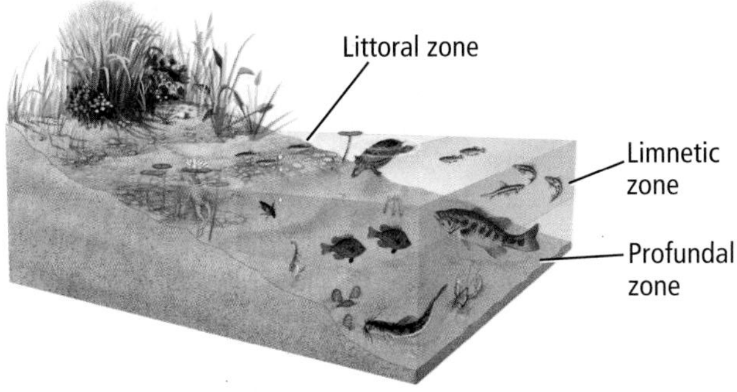


30. In which area of the lake is there likely to be the greatest diversity of plankton?
   A. littoral zone
   B. limnetic zone
   C. profundal zone
   D. aphotic zone

31. Which best describes the intertidal zone on a rocky shore?
   A. The dominant low-energy community is likely to be an estuary.
   B. The communities are adapted to shifting sands due to incoming waves.
   C. The communities are stratified from the high-tide line to the low-tide line.
   D. The organisms in the community constantly require dissolved oxygen.

### Constructed Response

32. **Short Answer** How is light a limiting factor in oceans?

33. **Short Answer** Describe characteristics of an estuary.

34. **Open Ended** Describe adaptations of an organism living in the abyssal zone of the ocean.

### Think Critically

35. **Predict** the consequences a drought would have on a river such as the Mississippi River.

36. **Compare** the intertidal zone with the photic zone in terms of tidal effect.

## Additional Assessment

37. *WRITING in* **Biology** Choose a biome other than the one in which you live. Write an essay explaining what you think you would like and what you think you would dislike about living in your chosen biome.

### DBQ Document-Based Questions

*"Leaf mass per area (LMA) measures the leaf dry-mass investment per unit of light-intercepting leaf area deployed. Species with high LMA have a thicker leaf blade or denser tissue, or both."*

*"Plant ecologists have emphasized broad relationships between leaf traits and climate for at least a century. In particular, a general tendency for species inhabiting arid and semi-arid regions to have leathery, high-LMA leaves has been reported. Building high-LMA leaves needs more investment per unit leaf area. Construction cost per unit leaf mass varies relatively little between species: leaves with high protein content (typically low-LMA leaves) tend to have low concentrations of other expensive compounds such as lipids or lignin, and high concentrations of cheap constituents such as minerals. Leaf traits associated with high LMA (for example, thick leaf blade; small, thick-walled cells) have been interpreted as adaptations that allow continued leaf function (or at least postpone leaf death) under very dry conditions, at least in evergreen species."*

Data obtained from: Wright, I.J. et al. The worldwide leaf economics spectrum. *Nature* 428:821–828.

38. From the information presented, would you expect leaves on trees in the tropical rain forest to contain large quantities of lipids? Explain your answer in terms of energy investment.

39. Hypothesize how high-LMA leaves are adapted for dry conditions.

### Cumulative Review

40. Explain the difference between autotrophs and heterotrophs. **(Chapter 2)**

# Standardized Test Practice

**Cumulative**

## Multiple Choice

1. If science can be characterized as discovery, then technology can be characterized as which?
   A. application
   B. information
   C. manufacturing
   D. reasoning

*Use the illustration below to answer questions 2 and 3.*

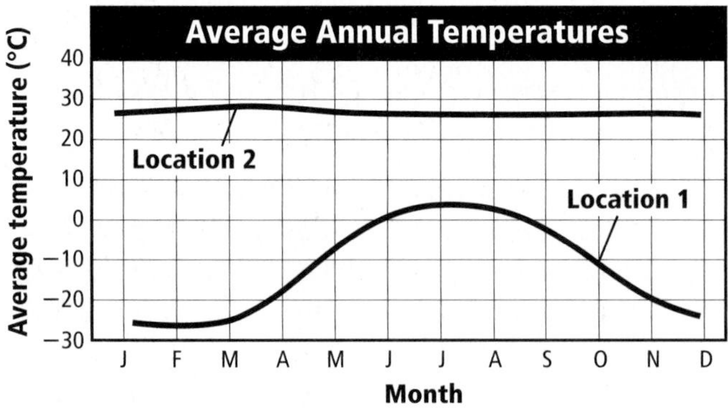


2. Based on the graph above, which term describes Location 2?
   A. oceanic
   B. polar
   C. temperate
   D. tropical

3. Suppose that in Location 2 there is very little rainfall during the year. What would be the name of that biome in this region?
   A. desert
   B. tundra
   C. temperate forest
   D. tropical rain forest

4. Which process is associated with long-term cycling of matter through the biosphere?
   A. breakdown of organic material by decomposers
   B. formation and weathering of minerals in rocks
   C. formation of compounds used for food by living organisms
   D. movement of fresh water from the land into bodies of water through run-off

*Use the illustration below to answer question 5.*

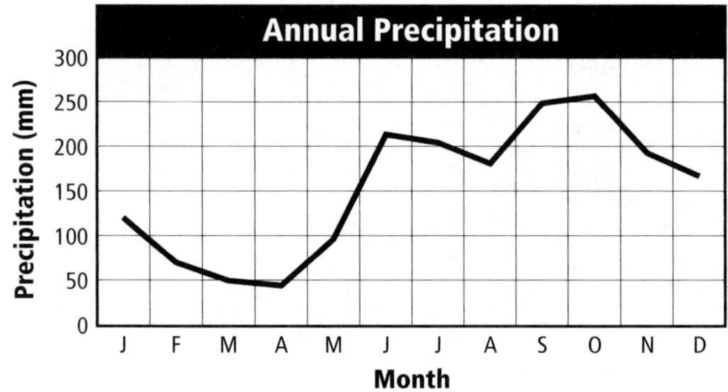


5. Look at the information in the graph. From what kind of biome are these data probably taken?
   A. desert
   B. tundra
   C. temperate forest
   D. tropical rain forest

6. Which system of measurement is the basis for many of the SI units?
   A. binary
   B. English
   C. metric
   D. number

7. Which of these organisms is a decomposer?
   A. a bacterium that makes food from inorganic compounds
   B. a clam that takes in water and filters food
   C. a fungus that gets nutrients from dead logs
   D. a plant that makes food using sunlight

8. Which distinguishes scientific ideas from popular opinions?
   A. Popular opinions are always rational and logical.
   B. Popular opinions depend on research and evidence.
   C. Scientific ideas are always testable and repeatable.
   D. Scientific ideas depend on anecdotes and hearsay.

## Short Answer

9. How is a tundra similar to and different from a boreal forest? Use a Venn diagram to organize information about the similarities and differences of these biomes.

10. What is the role of a pioneer species in primary succession?

11. Give two examples of how the human body shows the living characteristic of organization.

12. Suppose a certain insect species lives only in a specific species of tree. It feeds off the sap of the tree and produces a chemical that protects the tree from certain fungi. What kind of relationship is this?

13. Why would you expect to find different animals in the photic and aphotic zones of the ocean?

14. Suppose a gardener learns that the soil in a garden has low nitrogen content. Describe two ways to increase the nitrogen available for plants in the garden.

15. Explain how the establishment of a climax community through primary succession differs from the establishment of a climax community that occurs through secondary succession.

16. Why is the ability to adapt an important characteristic of living things?

## Extended Response

*Use the illustration below to answer question 17.*

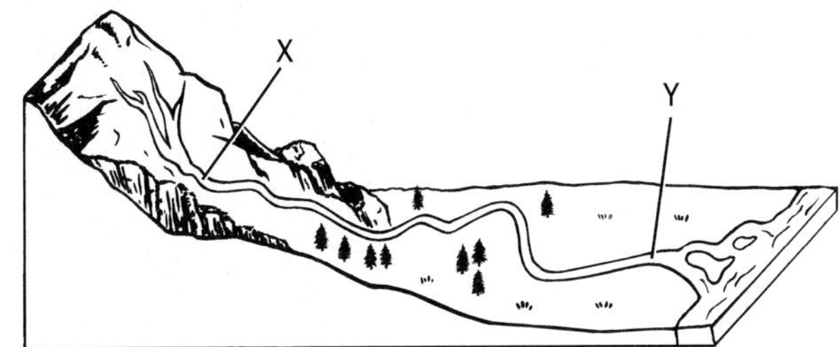


17. Based on the information in the illustration above, what can you infer about the major differences between the freshwater ecosystems at Point X and Point Y?

18. Suppose a nonnative species is introduced into an ecosystem. What is one kind of community interaction you might expect from the other organisms in that ecosystem?

## Essay Question

Suppose there is a dense temperate forest where people do not live. After a few hot, dry months, forest fires have started to spread through the forest area. There is no threat of the fires reaching areas inhabited by humans. Some people are trying to get the government to intervene to control the fires, while others say the fires should be allowed to run their natural course.

*Using the information in the paragraph above, answer the following question in essay format.*

19. Explain which side of this debate you would support. Be sure to provide evidence based on what you know about change in ecosystems.

| NEED EXTRA HELP? | | | | | | | | | | | | | | | | | | | |
|---|---|---|---|---|---|---|---|---|---|---|---|---|---|---|---|---|---|---|---|
| **If You Missed Question . . .** | 1 | 2 | 3 | 4 | 5 | 6 | 7 | 8 | 9 | 10 | 11 | 12 | 13 | 14 | 15 | 16 | 17 | 18 | 19 |
| **Review Section . . .** | 3.2 | 3.2 | 3.2 | 2.3 | 3.3 | 1.2 | 2.2 | 1.3 | 3.2 | 3.1 | 1.1 | 2.1 | 3.3 | 2.3 | 3.1 | 1.1 | 3.3 | 3.3 | 3.1, 3.2 |

CHAPTER 4

# Population Ecology

**Section 1**
**Population Dynamics**
**MAIN Idea** Populations of species are described by density, spatial distribution, and growth rate.

**Section 2**
**Human Population**
**MAIN Idea** Human population growth changes over time.

## BioFacts

- Deer can be found in most parts of the United States except the southwest, Alaska, and Hawaii.
- Parasites that attack deer include fleas, ticks, lice, mites, and tapeworms.
- Diseases such as Lyme disease, chronic wasting disease, and hemorrhagic disease can kill deer.

**Lyme disease bacteria**
Color-Enhanced SEM
Magnification: 2850×

**Deer tick**
Color-Enhanced SEM
Magnification: 22×

# LAUNCH Lab

## A population of one?

Ecologists study populations of living things. They also study how populations interact with each other and with the abiotic factors in the environment. But what exactly is a population? Are the deer shown on the previous page a population?
Is a single deer a population?

### Procedure

1. Read and complete the lab safety form.
2. In your assigned group, brainstorm and predict the meaning of the following terms: *population, population density, natality, mortality, emigration, immigration,* and *carrying capacity.*

### Analysis

1. **Infer** whether it is possible to have a population of one. Explain your answer.
2. **Analyze** your definitions and determine whether a relationship exists between the terms. Explain.

Visit biologygmh.com to:

- study the entire chapter online
- explore the Interactive Time Line, Concepts in Motion, the Interactive Table, Microscopy Links, Virtual Labs, and links to virtual dissections
- access Web links for more information, projects, and activities
- review content online with the Interactive Tutor and take Self-Check Quizzes

**Population Characteristics** Make this Foldable to help you learn the characteristics used to describe populations.

**STEP 1** Fold a sheet of paper vertically with the edges about 2 cm apart.

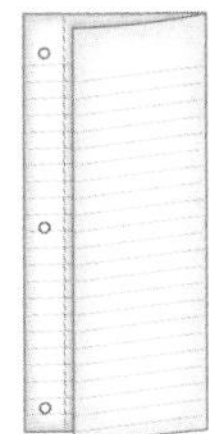

**STEP 2** Fold the paper into thirds.

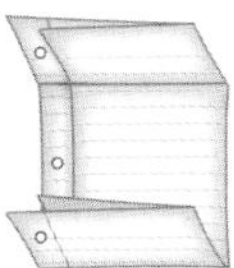

**STEP 3** Unfold and cut the top layer of both folds to make three tabs.

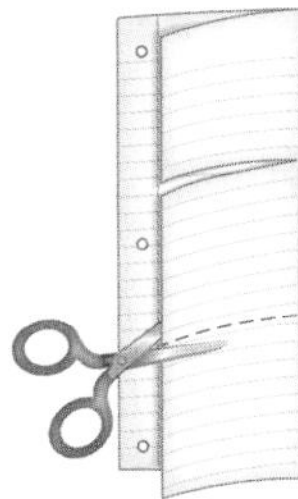

**STEP 4** Label each tab as shown: *Population Density, Spatial Distribution, Growth Rate.*

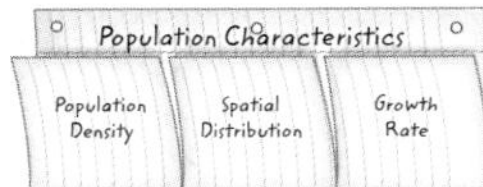


FOLDABLES **Use this Foldable with Section 4.1.** As you study this section, write what you learn about each characteristic under the correct tab.

Section 4.1

# Population Dynamics

### Objectives

- **Describe** characteristics of populations.
- **Understand** the concepts of carrying capacity and limiting factors.
- **Describe** the ways in which populations are distributed.

### Review Vocabulary

**population:** the members of a single species that share the same geographic location at the same time

### New Vocabulary

population density
dispersion
density-independent factor
density-dependent factor
population growth rate
emigration
immigration
carrying capacity

**MAIN Idea** **Populations of species are described by density, spatial distribution, and growth rate.**

**Real-World Reading Link** Have you ever observed a beehive or an ant farm? The population had certain characteristics that could be used to describe it. Ecologists study population characteristics that are used to describe all populations of organisms.

## Population Characteristics

All species occur in groups called populations. There are certain characteristics that all populations have, such as population density, spatial distribution, and growth rate. These characteristics are used to classify all populations of organisms, including bacteria, animals, and plants.

**Population density** One characteristic of a population is its **population density,** which is the number of organisms per unit area. For example, the population density of cattle egrets, shown with the water buffalo in **Figure 4.1,** is greater near the buffalo than farther away. Near the water buffalo, there might be three birds per square meter. Fifty meters from the water buffalo, the density of birds might be zero.

**Spatial distribution** Another characteristic of a population is called **dispersion**—the pattern of spacing of a population within an area. **Figure 4.2** shows the three main types of dispersion—uniform, clumped groups, and random. Black bears are typically dispersed in a uniform arrangement. American bison are dispersed in clumped groups or herds. White-tailed deer are dispersed randomly with unpredictable spacing. One of the primary factors in the pattern of dispersion for all organisms is the availability of resources such as food.

**Figure 4.1** The population density of the cattle egrets is greater near the water buffalo. **Identify** *What type of dispersion do these birds appear to have?*

# Visualizing Population Characteristics

**Figure 4.2**
Population density describes how many individual organisms live in a given area. Dispersion describes how the individuals are spaced within that area. Population range describes a species' distribution.

**Black Bear**

**Dispersion:** American black bear males usually are dispersed uniformly within territories as large as several hundred square kilometers. Females have smaller territories that overlap those of males.

**Density:** one bear per several hundred square kilometers

**Black Bear Distribution (in purple)**

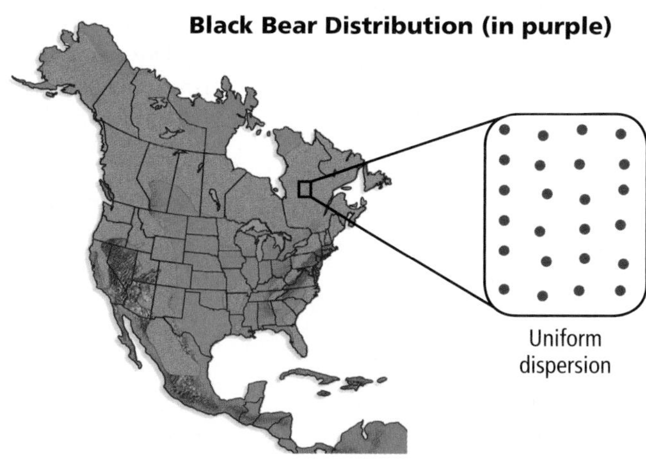


**American Bison**

**Dispersion:** American bison are found in clumped groups called herds.

**Density:** four bison/km$^2$ in Northern Yellowstone in 2000

**Bison Distribution (historic range prior to 1865 in orange)**

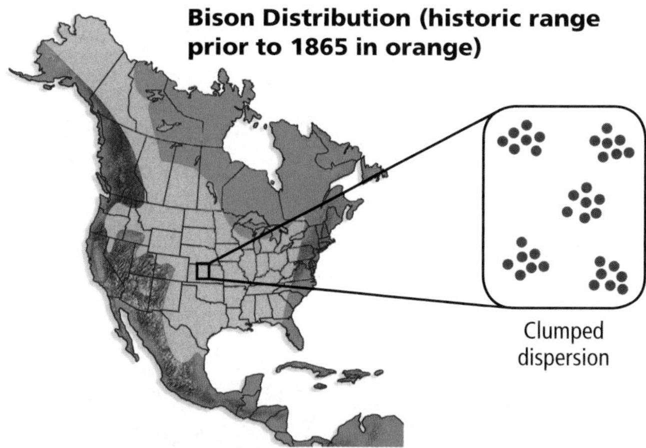


**White-tailed Deer**

**Dispersion:** White-tailed deer are dispersed randomly throughout appropriate habitats.

**Density:** 10 deer/km$^2$ in some areas of the northeastern United States

**White-tailed Deer Distribution (in blue)**

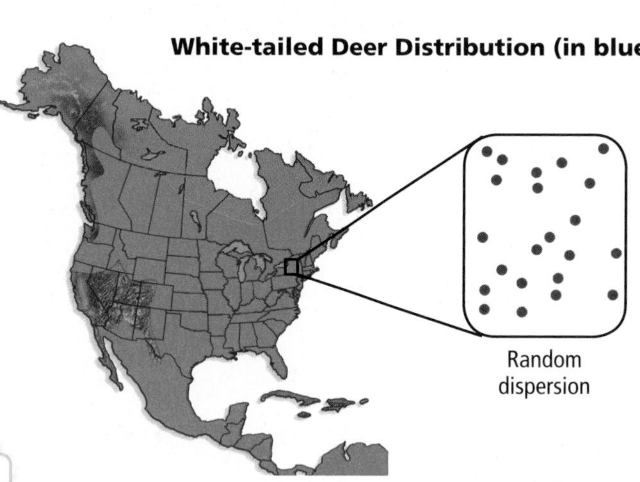


Concepts In Motion **Interactive Figure** To see an animation of population distribution, visit biologygmh.com.

**VOCABULARY**

**SCIENCE USAGE V. COMMON USAGE**

**Distribution**

***Science usage:*** the area where something is located or where a species lives and reproduces

*The white-tailed deer has a wide distribution that covers much of the United States.*

***Common usage:*** the handing out or delivery of items to a number of people

*The distribution of report cards to students occurred today.*

**Population ranges** No population, not even the human population, occupies all habitats in the biosphere. Some species, such as the iiwi (EE ee wee) shown in **Figure 4.3,** have a very limited population range. This songbird is found only on some of the islands of Hawaii. Other species, such as the peregrine falcon shown in **Figure 4.3,** have a vast distribution. Peregrine falcons are found on all continents except Antarctica. Note the distribution of the animals in **Figure 4.2.**

Recall from Chapter 2 that organisms adapt to the biotic and abiotic factors in their environment. A species might not be able to expand its population range because it cannot survive the abiotic conditions found in the expanded region. A change in temperature range, humidity level, annual rainfall, or sunlight might make a new geographic area uninhabitable for the species. In addition, biotic factors, such as predators, competitors, and parasites, present threats that might make the new location difficult for survival.

 **Reading Check** **Describe** two different types of population ranges.

## Population-Limiting Factors

In Chapter 3, you learned that all species have limiting factors. Limiting factors keep a population from continuing to increase indefinitely. Decreasing a limiting factor, such as the available food supply, often changes the number of individuals that are able to survive in a given area. In other words, if the food supply increases a larger population might result, and if the food supply decreases a smaller population might result.

**Density-independent factors** There are two categories of limiting factors—density-independent factors and density-dependent factors. Any factor in the environment that does not depend on the number of members in a population per unit area is a **density-independent factor.** These factors usually are abiotic and include natural phenomena such as weather events. Weather events that limit populations include drought or flooding, extreme heat or cold, tornadoes, and hurricanes.

■ **Figure 4.3** The iiwi lives only on some of the Hawaiian islands. The peregrine falcon is found worldwide.

**Iiwi**

**Peregrine falcon**

**Crown fire damage**

**Managed ground fire damage**

■ **Figure 4.4** A crown fire is a density-independent factor that can limit population growth. However, small ground fires can promote growth of pines in a pine forest community.
**Explain** ***Why do these two situations involving fire have different results on the pine tree populations?***

**Figure 4.4** shows an example of the effects that fire can have on a population. Fire has damaged this ponderosa pine forest community. Sometimes the extreme heat from a crown fire, which is a fire that advances to the tops of the trees, can destroy many mature ponderosa pine trees—a dominant species in forests of the western United States. In this example, the fire limits the population of ponderosa trees by killing many of the trees. However, smaller but more frequent ground fires have the opposite effect on the population. By thinning lower growing plants that use up nutrients, a healthier population of mature ponderosa pines is produced.

Populations can be limited by the unintended results of human alterations of the landscape. For example, over the last 100 years, human activities on the Colorado River, such as building dams, water diversions, and water barriers, have significantly reduced the amount of water flow and changed the water temperature of the river. In addition, the introduction of nonnative fish species altered the biotic factors in the river. Because of the changes in the river, the number of small fish called humpback chub was reduced. During the 1960s, the number of humpback chub dropped so low that they were in danger of disappearing from the Colorado River altogether.

Air, land, and water pollution are the result of human activities that also can limit populations. Pollution reduces the available resources by making some of the resources toxic.

**CAREERS IN BIOLOGY**

**Population Biologist** A population biologist studies the characteristics of populations, such as growth, size, distribution, or genetics. For more information on biology careers, visit biologygmh.com.

**Density-dependent factors** Any factor in the environment that depends on the number of members in a population per unit area is a **density-dependent factor.** Density-dependent factors are often biotic factors such as predation, disease, parasites, and competition. A study of density-dependent factors was done on the wolf–moose populations in northern Michigan on Isle Royale, located in Lake Superior.

**Figure 4.5** The long-term study of the wolf and moose populations on Isle Royale shows the relationship between the number of predators and prey over time.
**Infer** ***What might have caused the increase in the number of moose in 1995?***

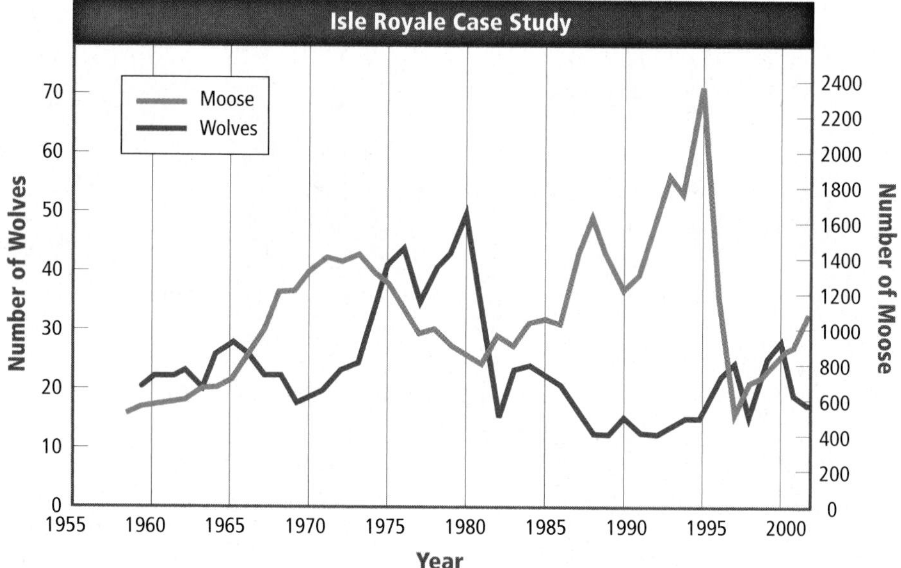


FOLDABLES
Incorporate information from this section into your Foldable.

Prior to the winter of 1947–48, apparently there were no wolves on Isle Royale. During that winter, a single pair of wolves crossed the ice on Lake Superior, reaching the island. During the next ten years, the population of wolves reached about twenty individuals. **Figure 4.5** shows some of the results from the long-term study conducted by population biologists. Notice that the rise and fall of the numbers of each group was dependent on the other group. For example, follow the wolves' line on the graph. As the number of wolves decreased, the number of moose increased.

**Disease** Another density-dependent factor is disease. Outbreaks of disease tend to occur when population size has increased and population density is high. When population density is high, disease is transmitted easily from one individual to another because contact between individuals is more frequent. Therefore, the disease spreads easily and quickly through a population. This is just as true for human populations as it is for populations of protists, plants, and other species of animals.

**Competition** Competition between organisms also increases when density increases. When the population increases to a size so that resources such as food or space become limited, individuals in the population must compete for the available resources. Competition can occur within a species or between two different species that use the same resources. Competition for insufficient resources might result in a decrease in population density in an area due to starvation or to individuals leaving the area in search of additional resources. As the population size decreases, competition becomes less severe.

The lemmings shown in **Figure 4.6** are an example of a population that often undergoes competition for resources. Lemmings are small mammals that live in the tundra biome. When food is plentiful, their population increases exponentially. As food becomes limited, many lemmings begin to starve and their population size decreases significantly.

**Figure 4.6** Lemmings are mammals that produce offspring in large numbers when food is plentiful. When the food supply diminishes, lemmings starve and many die.

**Parasites** Populations also can be limited by parasites, in a way similar to disease, as population density increases. The presence of parasites is a density-dependent factor that can negatively affect population growth at higher densities.

**Population growth rate** An important characteristic of any population is its growth rate. The **population growth rate** (PGR) explains how fast a given population grows. One of the characteristics of the population ecologists must know, or at least estimate, is natality. The natality of a population is the birthrate, or the number of individuals born in a given time period. Ecologists also must know the mortality—the number of deaths that occur in the population during a given time period.

The number of individuals emigrating or immigrating also is important. **Emigration** (em uh GRAY shun) is the term ecologists use to describe the number of individuals moving away from a population. **Immigration** (ih muh GRAY shun) is the term ecologists use to describe the number of individuals moving into a population. In most instances, emigration is about equal to immigration. Therefore, natality and mortality usually are most important in determining the population growth rate.

Some populations tend to remain approximately the same size from year to year. Other populations vary in size depending on conditions within their habitats. To better understand why populations grow in different ways, you should understand two mathematical models for population growth—the exponential growth model and the logistic growth model.

**Exponential growth model** Look at **Figure 4.7** to see how a population of mice would grow if there were no limits placed on it by the environment. Assume that two adult mice breed and produce a litter of young. Also assume the two offspring are able to reproduce in one month. If all of the offspring survive to breed, the population grows slowly at first. This slow growth period is defined as the lag phase. The rate of population growth soon begins to increase rapidly because the total number of organisms that are able to reproduce has increased. After only two years, the experimental mouse population would reach more than three million mice.

**Connection to Math** Notice in **Figure 4.7** that once the mice begin to reproduce rapidly, the graph becomes J-shaped. A J-shaped growth curve illustrates exponential growth. Exponential growth, also called geometric growth, occurs when the growth rate is proportional to the size of the population. All populations grow exponentially until some limiting factor slows the population's growth. It is important to recognize that even in the lag phase, the use of available resources is exponential. Because of this, the resources soon become limited and population growth slows.

**Logistic growth model** Many populations grow like the model shown in **Figure 4.8** rather than the model shown in **Figure 4.7.** Notice that the graphs look exactly the same through some of the time period. However, the second graph curves into an S-shape. An S-shaped curve is typical of logistic growth. Logistic growth occurs when the population's growth slows or stops following exponential growth, at the population's carrying capacity. A population stops increasing when the number of births is less than the number of deaths or when emigration exceeds immigration.

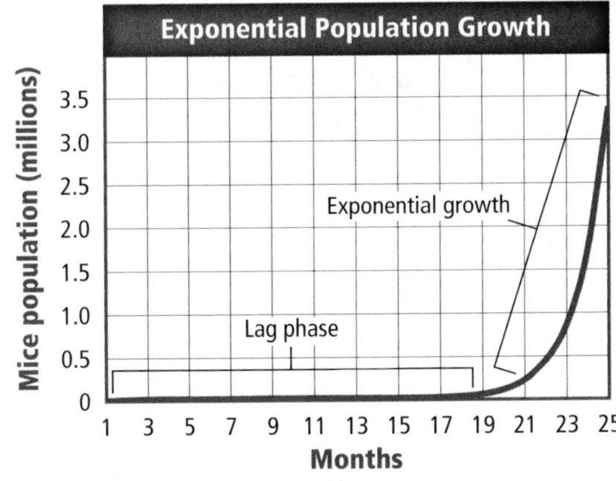


**Figure 4.7** If two mice were allowed to reproduce unhindered, the population would grow slowly at first but would accelerate quickly.

**Infer** ***Why don't mice or other populations continue to grow exponentially?***

**Figure 4.8** When a population exhibits growth that results in an S-shaped graph, it exhibits logistic growth. The population levels off at a limit called the carrying capacity.

**Concepts In Motion**

Interactive Figure To see an animation of population growth, visit biologygmh.com.

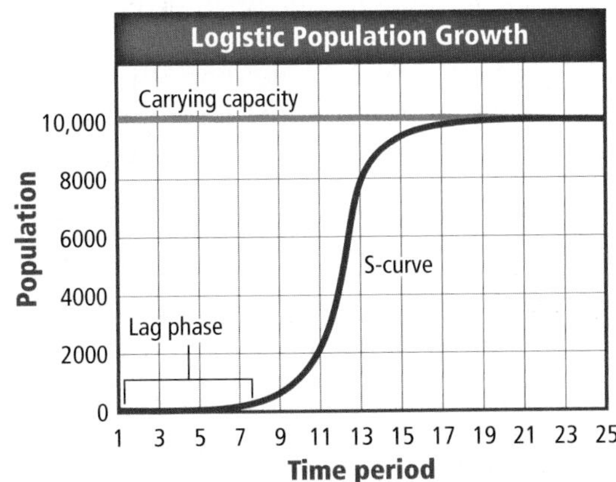

■ **Figure 4.9** Locusts, which are *r*-strategists, usually have a short life span and produce many offspring.
**Infer** *What specific factors might fluctuate in a locust's environment?*

**Carrying capacity** In **Figure 4.8** on the previous page, notice that logistic growth levels off at the line on the graph identified as the carrying capacity. The maximum number of individuals in a species that an environment can support for the long term is the **carrying capacity.** Carrying capacity is limited by the energy, water, oxygen, and nutrients available. When populations develop in an environment with plentiful resources, there are more births than deaths. The population soon reaches or passes the carrying capacity. As a population nears the carrying capacity, resources become limited. If a population exceeds the carrying capacity, deaths outnumber births because adequate resources are not available to support all of the individuals. The population then falls below the carrying capacity as individuals die. The concept of carrying capacity is used to explain why many populations tend to stabilize.

**Reproductive patterns** The graph in **Figure 4.8** shows the number of individuals increasing until the the carrying capacity is reached. However, there are several additional factors that must be considered for real populations. Species of organisms vary in the number of births per reproduction cycle, in the age that reproduction begins, and in the life span of the organism. Both plants and animals are placed into groups based on their reproductive factors.

Members of one of the groups are called the *r*-strategists. The rate strategy, or *r*-strategy, is an adaptation for living in an environment where fluctuation in biotic or abiotic factors occur. Fluctuating factors might be availability of food or changing temperatures. An *r*-strategist is generally a small organism such as a fruit fly, a mouse, or the locusts shown in **Figure 4.9.** *R*-strategists usually have short life spans and produce many offspring.

## DATA ANALYSIS LAB 4.1

**Based on Real Data***

### Recognize Cause and Effect

**Do parasites affect the size of a host population?** In 1994, the first signs of a serious eye disease caused by the bacterium *Mycoplasma gallisepticum* were observed in house finches that were eating in backyard bird feeders. Volunteers collected data beginning three different years on the number of finches infected with the parasite and the total number of finches present. The graph shows the abundance of house finches in areas where the infection rate was at least 20 percent of the house finch population.

**Think Critically**

1. **Compare** the data from the three areas.
2. **Hypothesize** Why did the house finch abundance stabilize in 1995 and 1996?

*Data obtained from: Gregory, R., et al. 2000. Parasites take control. *Nature* 406: 33–34.

**Data and Observations**

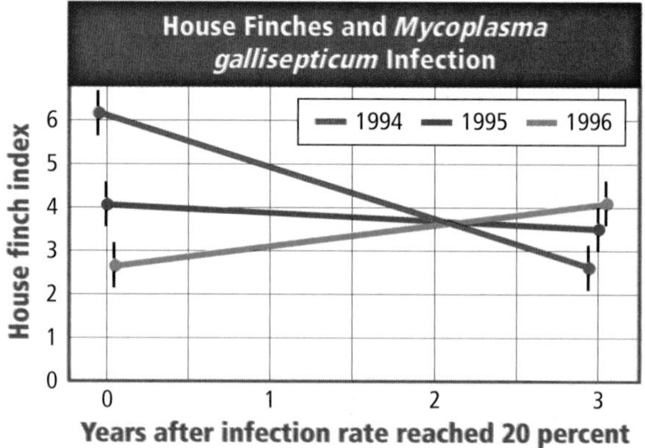


3. **Infer** Is the parasite, *Mycoplasma gallisepthicum,* effective in limiting the size of house finch populations? Explain.

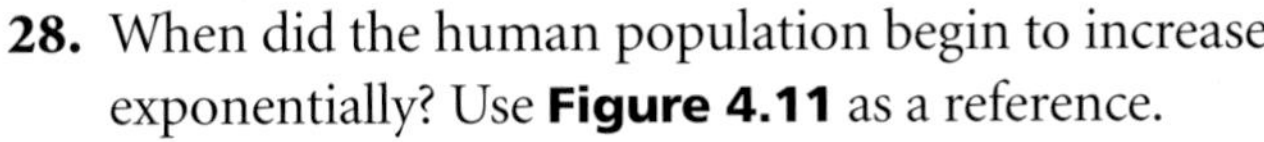

28. When did the human population begin to increase exponentially? Use **Figure 4.11** as a reference.
    **A.** 2 million years ago **C.** 1800 B.C.
    **B.** 6500 B.C. **D.** 1500 A.D.

29. Asia (excluding China) had a birthrate of 24 and a death rate of eight in 2004. What was the PGR?
    **A.** 0.16 percent **C.** 16 percent
    **B.** 1.6 percent **D.** 160 percent

30. Georgia, a country in Western Asia, had a birthrate of 11 and a death rate of 11 in 2004. What was the PGR of Georgia in that year?
    **A.** 0 percent **C.** 1.1 percent
    **B.** 0.11 percent **D.** 11 percent

## Constructed Response

31. **Open Ended** Do you think the birthrate or the death rate is more important to human populations? Explain your answer.

32. **Short Answer** Why won't the population stop growing immediately when ZPG is reached?

33. **Short Answer** Study **Figure 4.11** and identify which phase of growth occurred between the Old Stone Age and the Middle Ages.

## Think Critically

34. Hypothesize the shape of the age diagram for Switzerland, a developed country in Europe.

*Use the graph below to answer question 35.*

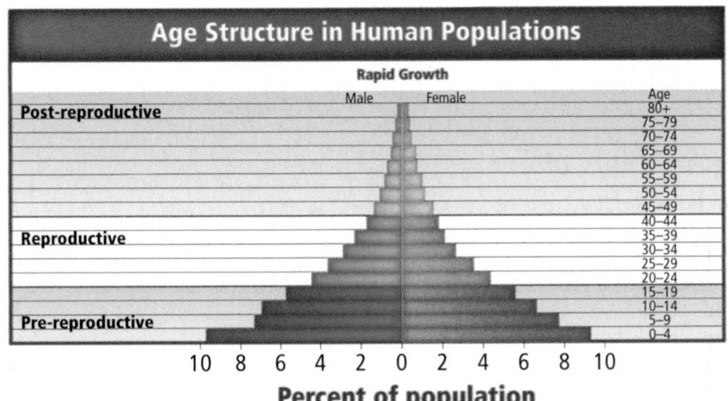


35. Describe the advantages and disadvantages of a population that has this type of age structure.

## Additional Assessment

36. **WRITING in Biology** Write a letter to the editor of your student newspaper expressing your views on the effect of human activities on a population of animals in your area.

### Document-Based Questions

*Northern right whales were once abundant in the northwestern Atlantic Ocean. By 1900, their numbers were almost depleted. Today, there are an estimated 300 individuals remaining.*

*Use the graph below to answer the following questions.*

Data obtained from: Fujiwara, M., et al. 2001. Demography of the endangered North Atlantic right whale. *Nature* 414: 537-540.

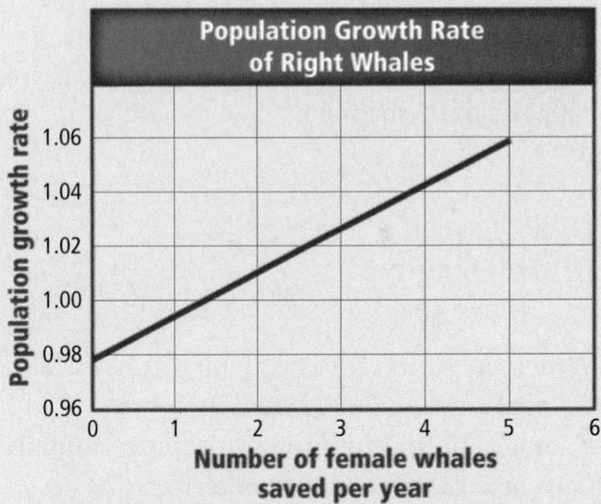


37. Predict the population growth rate if six female North Atlantic right whales were saved each year.

38. Saving females isn't the only factor to take into consideration when trying to restore the whale population. Write a hypothetical plan of action that takes into account two other factors that you think might help.

### Cumulative Review

39. Predict the probable results to a community if all of the top predators were removed by hunting. **(Chapter 2)**

40. Describe three types of symbiosis. **(Chapter 2)**

# Standardized Test Practice

**Cumulative**

## Multiple Choice

1. Which is the main benefit of scientific debate for scientists?
   A. challenging accepted theories
   B. creating controversy
   C. gaining research funding
   D. publishing results

*Use the graph below to answer question 2.*

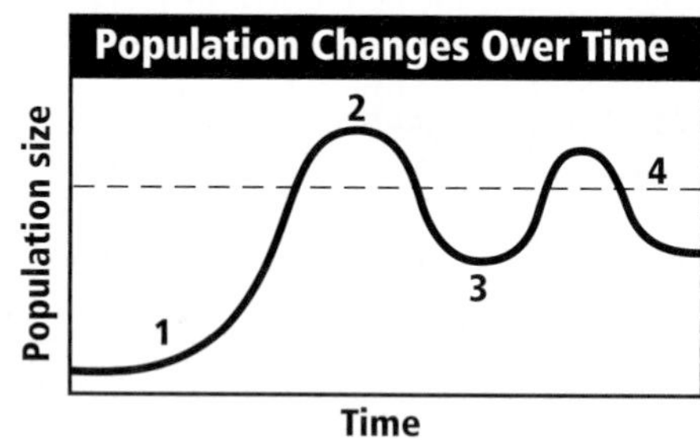


2. Which part of the graph indicates the carrying capacity of the habitat?
   A. 1
   B. 2
   C. 3
   D. 4

3. Which one is likely to be an oligotrophic lake?
   A. a lake formed by a winding river
   B. a lake in the crater of a volcanic mountain
   C. a lake near the mouth of a river
   D. a lake where algae blooms kill the fish

4. Which characteristic of a plant would NOT be studied by biologists?
   A. beauty
   B. chemical processes
   C. growth rate
   D. reproduction

5. Which statement describes the first changes in a forest that would follow a forest fire?
   A. A climax community is established.
   B. New plants grow from seeds that the wind carries to the area.
   C. New soil forms.
   D. Pioneer species are established.

*Use this graph to answer question 6.*

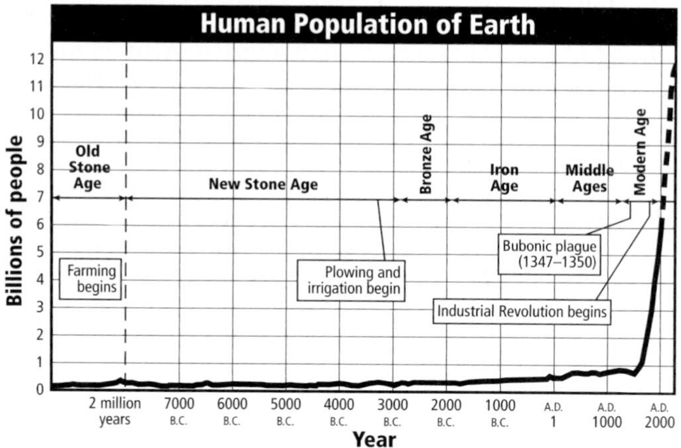


6. Which event appears to coincide with a gradual increase in human population?
   A. Bubonic plague
   B. farming
   C. Industrial Revolution
   D. plowing and irrigation

7. Suppose an organism is host to a parasitic tapeworm. Which would be beneficial to the tapeworm?
   A. death of the host from disease caused by the tapeworm
   B. absorbing enough nutrients to sustain the tapeworm without harming the host
   C. treatment of the host with antitapeworm drugs
   D. weakening of the host by the tapeworm

8. Which adaptation would you expect to find in an organism living in an intertidal zone?
   A. ability to live in total darkness
   B. ability to live in very cold water
   C. ability to survive in moving water
   D. ability to survive without water for 24 h

9. Which limiting factor is dependent on the density of the population?
   A. contagious fatal virus
   B. dumping toxic waste in a river
   C. heavy rains and flooding
   D. widespread forest fires


Biology Online Standardized Test Practice biologygmh.com

**Biology Online**

To read more about forensic pathologists in action, visit biologygmh.com.

# Chemistry in Biology

**Section 1**
**Atoms, Elements, and Compounds**
**MAIN Idea** Matter is composed of tiny particles called atoms.

**Section 2**
**Chemical Reactions**
**MAIN Idea** Chemical reactions allow living things to grow, develop, reproduce, and adapt.

**Section 3**
**Water and Solutions**
**MAIN Idea** The properties of water make it well suited to help maintain homeostasis in an organism.

**Section 4**
**The Building Blocks of Life**
**MAIN Idea** Organisms are made up of carbon-based molecules.

## BioFacts

- Collagen is the most abundant protein in mammals.
- Collagen can be found in muscle, bone, teeth, skin, and the cornea of the eye.
- Wrinkles that become visible as people age are the result of collagen breaking down.

**Multiple collagen fibers**
SEM Magnification: 8000×

**Single collagen fiber**
SEM Magnification: Unavailable

# LAUNCH Lab

## How does the nutrient content of foods compare?

Your body's structure and function depends on chemical elements including those found in proteins, carbohydrates, fats, vitamins, minerals, and water. In this lab, you will investigate nutrients that provide those elements.

### Procedure

1. Read and complete the lab safety form.
2. Construct a data chart to record grams or percent of each nutrient listed above. Include columns for Serving Size, Calories, and Calories from Fat.
3. Study and record data from the Nutrition Facts label on a **cereal box.**
4. Choose three additional **labeled food items.** Predict how the nutrients in these items compare with the nutrients in the cereal. Use the Nutrition Facts labels to record data.

### Analysis

1. **Evaluate** What factors influenced your predictions of the nutrient contents? Were your predictions correct?
2. **Analyze** Which food item has the greatest amount of proteins per serving? The least?

Visit biologygmh.com to:

- study the entire chapter online
- explore Concepts in Motion, the Interactive Table, Microscopy Links, Virtual Labs, and links to virtual dissections
- access Web links for more information, projects, and activities
- review content online with the Interactive Tutor and take Self-Check Quizzes

**Enzymes** Make this Foldable to help you organize information about enzyme structure and function.

**STEP 1** Draw a line across the middle of a piece of paper.

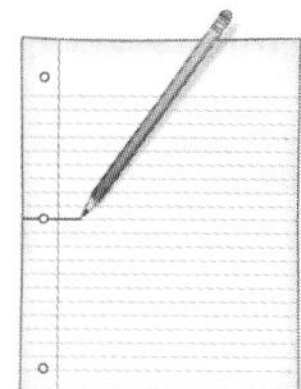

**STEP 2** Fold the top and bottom edges to meet at the middle of the paper.

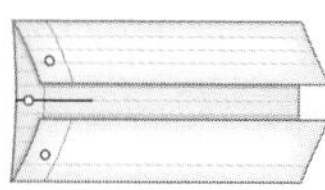

**STEP 3** Fold in half to make four sections as shown.

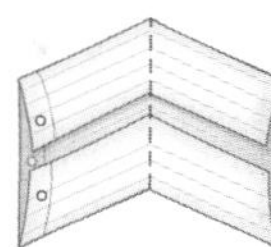

**STEP 4** Cut along the fold lines of the top and bottom flaps to form four tabs of equal size. Label the tabs *A*, *B*, *C*, and *D* as shown.

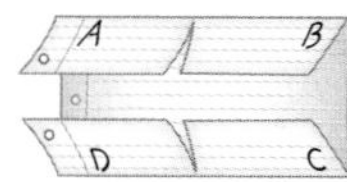


FOLDABLES **Use this Foldable with Section 6.2.** As you study the section, record what you learn about enzymes. On the front tabs, draw the four general steps of enzyme activity.

# Section 6.1

### Objectives

- **Identify** the particles that make up atoms.
- **Diagram** the particles that make up an atom.
- **Compare** covalent bonds and ionic bonds.
- **Describe** van der Waals forces.

### Review Vocabulary

**substance:** a form of matter that has a uniform and unchanging composition

### New Vocabulary

atom
nucleus
proton
neutron
electron
element
isotope
compound
covalent bond
molecule
ion
ionic bond
van der Waals force

# Atoms, Elements, and Compounds

**MAIN Idea Matter is composed of tiny particles called atoms.**

**Real-World Reading Link** Many scientists think that the universe began with a huge explosion billions of years ago. They think that the building blocks that make up the amazing diversity of life we see today are a result of that explosion. The study of those building blocks is the science of chemistry.

## Atoms

Chemistry is the study of matter—its composition and properties. Matter is anything that has mass and takes up space. All of the organisms you study in biology are made up of matter. **Atoms** are the building blocks of matter.

**Connection to History** In the fifth century B.C., the Greek philosophers Leucippus and Democritus first proposed the idea that all matter is made up of tiny, indivisible particles. It wasn't until the 1800s that scientists began to collect experimental evidence to support the existence of atoms. As technology improved over the next two centuries, scientists proved not only that atoms exist but also that they are made up of even smaller particles.

**The structure of atoms** An atom is so small that billions of them fit on the head of a pin. Yet, atoms are made up of even smaller particles called neutrons, protons, and electrons, as illustrated in **Figure 6.1.** Neutrons and protons are located at the center of the atom, which is called the **nucleus. Protons** are positively charged particles ($p^+$), and **neutrons** are particles that have no charge ($n^0$). **Electrons** are negatively charged particles that are located outside the nucleus ($e^-$). Electrons constantly move around an atom's nucleus in energy levels. The basic structure of an atom is the result of the attraction between protons and electrons. Atoms contain an equal number of protons and electrons, so the overall charge of an atom is zero.

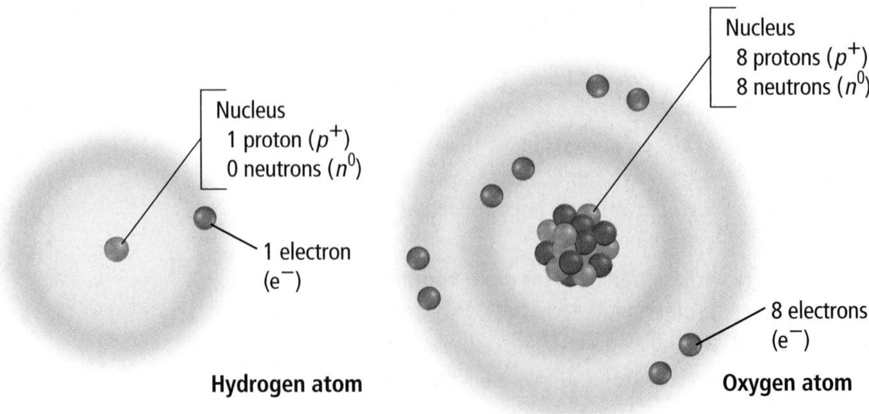


**Figure 6.1** Hydrogen has only one proton and one electron. Oxygen has eight protons, eight neutrons, and eight electrons. The electrons move around the nucleus in two energy levels (shown as the darker shaded rings).

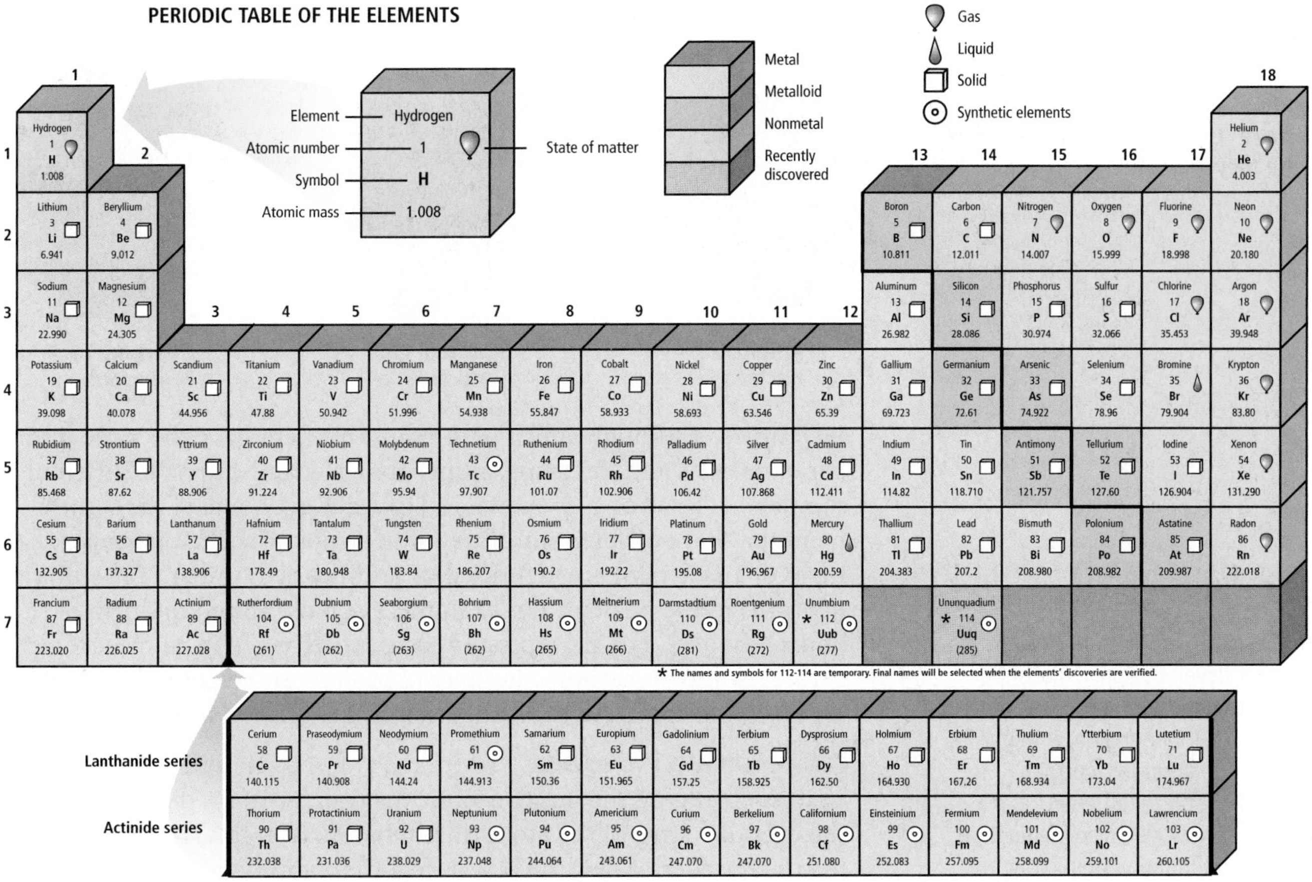

**PERIODIC TABLE OF THE ELEMENTS**

Element — Hydrogen; Atomic number — 1; Symbol — H; Atomic mass — 1.008; State of matter

Metal | Metalloid | Nonmetal | Recently discovered

Gas | Liquid | Solid | Synthetic elements

| | 1 | 2 | 3 | 4 | 5 | 6 | 7 | 8 | 9 | 10 | 11 | 12 | 13 | 14 | 15 | 16 | 17 | 18 |
|---|---|---|---|---|---|---|---|---|---|---|---|---|---|---|---|---|---|---|
| 1 | Hydrogen 1 H 1.008 | | | | | | | | | | | | | | | | | Helium 2 He 4.003 |
| 2 | Lithium 3 Li 6.941 | Beryllium 4 Be 9.012 | | | | | | | | | | | Boron 5 B 10.811 | Carbon 6 C 12.011 | Nitrogen 7 N 14.007 | Oxygen 8 O 15.999 | Fluorine 9 F 18.998 | Neon 10 Ne 20.180 |
| 3 | Sodium 11 Na 22.990 | Magnesium 12 Mg 24.305 | | | | | | | | | | | Aluminum 13 Al 26.982 | Silicon 14 Si 28.086 | Phosphorus 15 P 30.974 | Sulfur 16 S 32.066 | Chlorine 17 Cl 35.453 | Argon 18 Ar 39.948 |
| 4 | Potassium 19 K 39.098 | Calcium 20 Ca 40.078 | Scandium 21 Sc 44.956 | Titanium 22 Ti 47.88 | Vanadium 23 V 50.942 | Chromium 24 Cr 51.996 | Manganese 25 Mn 54.938 | Iron 26 Fe 55.847 | Cobalt 27 Co 58.933 | Nickel 28 Ni 58.693 | Copper 29 Cu 63.546 | Zinc 30 Zn 65.39 | Gallium 31 Ga 69.723 | Germanium 32 Ge 72.61 | Arsenic 33 As 74.922 | Selenium 34 Se 78.96 | Bromine 35 Br 79.904 | Krypton 36 Kr 83.80 |
| 5 | Rubidium 37 Rb 85.468 | Strontium 38 Sr 87.62 | Yttrium 39 Y 88.906 | Zirconium 40 Zr 91.224 | Niobium 41 Nb 92.906 | Molybdenum 42 Mo 95.94 | Technetium 43 Tc 97.907 | Ruthenium 44 Ru 101.07 | Rhodium 45 Rh 102.906 | Palladium 46 Pd 106.42 | Silver 47 Ag 107.868 | Cadmium 48 Cd 112.411 | Indium 49 In 114.82 | Tin 50 Sn 118.710 | Antimony 51 Sb 121.757 | Tellurium 52 Te 127.60 | Iodine 53 I 126.904 | Xenon 54 Xe 131.290 |
| 6 | Cesium 55 Cs 132.905 | Barium 56 Ba 137.327 | Lanthanum 57 La 138.906 | Hafnium 72 Hf 178.49 | Tantalum 73 Ta 180.948 | Tungsten 74 W 183.84 | Rhenium 75 Re 186.207 | Osmium 76 Os 190.2 | Iridium 77 Ir 192.22 | Platinum 78 Pt 195.08 | Gold 79 Au 196.967 | Mercury 80 Hg 200.59 | Thallium 81 Tl 204.383 | Lead 82 Pb 207.2 | Bismuth 83 Bi 208.980 | Polonium 84 Po 208.982 | Astatine 85 At 209.987 | Radon 86 Rn 222.018 |
| 7 | Francium 87 Fr 223.020 | Radium 88 Ra 226.025 | Actinium 89 Ac 227.028 | Rutherfordium 104 Rf (261) | Dubnium 105 Db (262) | Seaborgium 106 Sg (263) | Bohrium 107 Bh (262) | Hassium 108 Hs (265) | Meitnerium 109 Mt (266) | Darmstadtium 110 Ds (281) | Roentgenium 111 Rg (272) | Ununbium * 112 Uub (277) | | Ununquadium * 114 Uuq (285) | | | | |

* The names and symbols for 112-114 are temporary. Final names will be selected when the elements' discoveries are verified.

| Lanthanide series | Cerium 58 Ce 140.115 | Praseodymium 59 Pr 140.908 | Neodymium 60 Nd 144.24 | Promethium 61 Pm 144.913 | Samarium 62 Sm 150.36 | Europium 63 Eu 151.965 | Gadolinium 64 Gd 157.25 | Terbium 65 Tb 158.925 | Dysprosium 66 Dy 162.50 | Holmium 67 Ho 164.930 | Erbium 68 Er 167.26 | Thulium 69 Tm 168.934 | Ytterbium 70 Yb 173.04 | Lutetium 71 Lu 174.967 |
|---|---|---|---|---|---|---|---|---|---|---|---|---|---|---|
| Actinide series | Thorium 90 Th 232.038 | Protactinium 91 Pa 231.036 | Uranium 92 U 238.029 | Neptunium 93 Np 237.048 | Plutonium 94 Pu 244.064 | Americium 95 Am 243.061 | Curium 96 Cm 247.070 | Berkelium 97 Bk 247.070 | Californium 98 Cf 251.080 | Einsteinium 99 Es 252.083 | Fermium 100 Fm 257.095 | Mendelevium 101 Md 258.099 | Nobelium 102 No 259.101 | Lawrencium 103 Lr 260.105 |

■ **Figure 6.2** The periodic table of the elements organizes all of the known elements. Examine the biologists' guide to the periodic table on the back cover of this book.

# Elements

An **element** is a pure substance that cannot be broken down into other substances by physical or chemical means. Elements are made of only one type of atom. There are over 100 known elements, 92 of which occur naturally. Scientists have collected a large amount of information about the elements, such as the number of protons and electrons each element has and the atomic mass of each element. Also, each element has a unique name and symbol. All of these data, and more, are collected in an organized table called the periodic table of elements.

**The periodic table of elements** As shown in **Figure 6.2,** the periodic table is organized into horizontal rows, called periods, and vertical columns, called groups. Each individual block in the grid represents an element. The table is called periodic because elements in the same group have similar chemical and physical properties. This organization even allows scientists to predict elements that have not yet been discovered or isolated. As shown in **Figure 6.3,** elements found in living organisms also are found in Earth's crust.

■ **Figure 6.3** The elements in Earth's crust and living organisms vary in their abundance. Living things are composed primarily of three elements—carbon, hydrogen, and oxygen.
**Interpret** ***What is the most abundant element that exists in living things?***

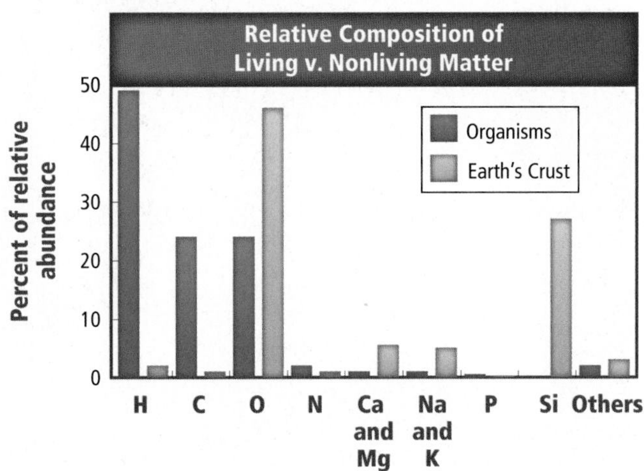

■ **Figure 6.4** Carbon-12 and carbon-13 occur naturally in living and nonliving things. All living things also contain a small amount of carbon-14.
**Compare** *How do the isotopes differ? How are they the same?*

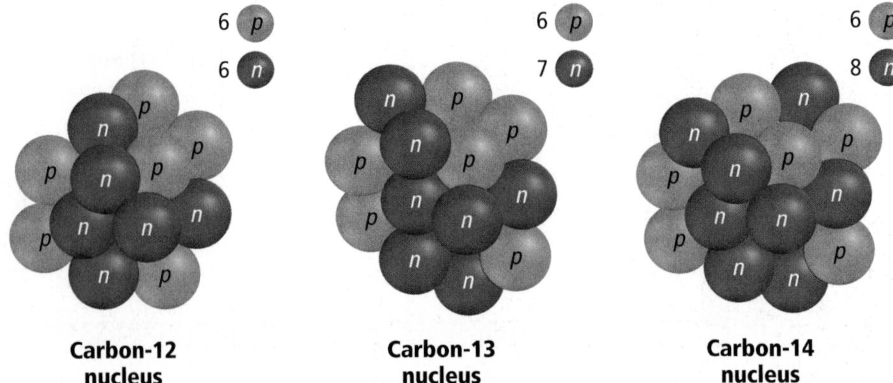


**Isotopes** Although atoms of the same element have the same number of protons and electrons, atoms of an element can have different numbers of neutrons, as shown in **Figure 6.4.** Atoms of the same element that have different numbers of neutrons are called **isotopes.** Isotopes of an element are identified by adding the number of protons and neutrons in the nucleus. For example, the most abundant form of carbon, carbon-12, has six protons and six neutrons in its nucleus. One carbon isotope—carbon-14—has six protons and eight neutrons. Isotopes of elements have the same chemical characteristics.

**CAREERS IN BIOLOGY**

**Nuclear Engineer** A nuclear engineer develops applications that use the radioactive properties of elements. Nuclear engineers might focus on radiation for medical diagnostics and treatments, food preservation, or electricity generation. For more information on biology careers, visit biologygmh.com.

**Radioactive isotopes** Previously, you read that neutrons have no charge. Changing the number of neutrons in an atom does not change the overall charge of the atom (it still has no charge). However, changing the number of neutrons can affect the stability of the nucleus, in some cases causing the nucleus to decay, or break apart. When a nucleus breaks apart, it gives off radiation that can be detected and used for many applications. Isotopes that give off radiation are called radioactive isotopes.

Carbon-14 is a radioactive isotope that is found in all living things. Scientists know the half-life, or the amount of time it takes for half of carbon-14 to decay, so they can calculate the age of an object by finding how much carbon-14 remains in the sample. Other radioactive isotopes have medical uses, such as in radiation therapy to treat cancers, as shown in **Figure 6.5.**

■ **Figure 6.5** Radioactive isotopes are used to help doctors diagnose disease and locate and treat certain types of cancer.

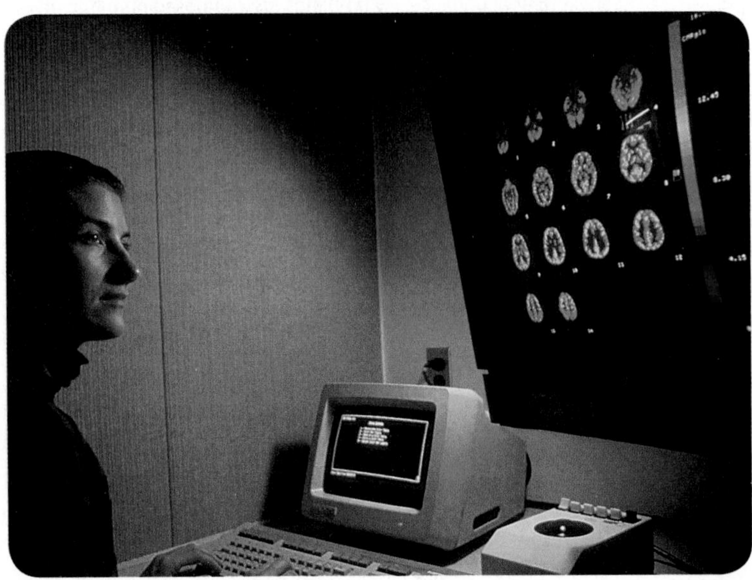

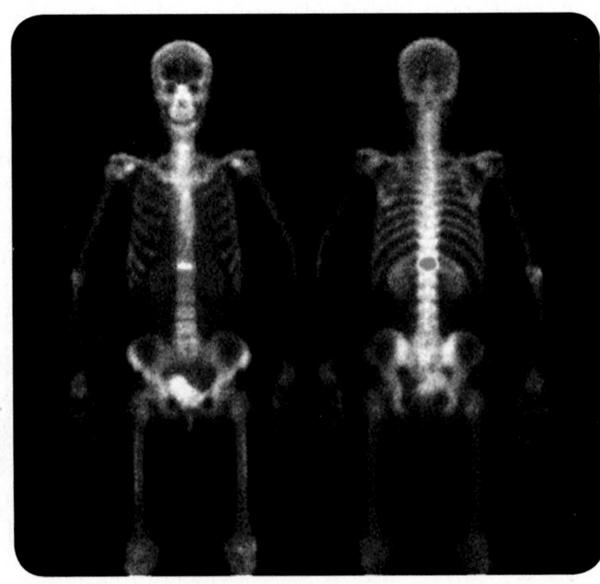

Brilliant fireworks displays depend on compounds containing the metal strontium.

Table salt is the compound NaCl.

Wetlands are sources of living things made of complex compounds and the simple compound methane ($CH_4$).

■ **Figure 6.6** You and your world are made of compounds.

## Compounds

Elements can combine to form more complex substances. A **compound** is a pure substance formed when two or more different elements combine. There are millions of known compounds and thousands more discovered each year. **Figure 6.6** shows you a few. Each compound has a chemical formula made up of the chemical symbols from the periodic table. You might know that water is the compound $H_2O$. Sodium chloride (NaCl) is the compound commonly called table salt. The fuel people use in cars is a mixture of hydrocarbon compounds. Hydrocarbons only have hydrogen and carbon atoms. Methane ($CH_4$) is the simplest hydrocarbon. Bacteria in areas such as the wetlands shown in **Figure 6.6** release 76 percent of global methane from natural sources by decomposing plants and other organisms. They are made of compounds, too.

Compounds have several unique characteristics. First, compounds are always formed from a specific combination of elements in a fixed ratio. Water always is formed in a ratio of two hydrogen atoms and one oxygen atom, and each water molecule has the same structure. Second, compounds are chemically and physically different than the elements that comprise them. For example, water has different properties than hydrogen and oxygen.

Another characteristic of compounds is that they cannot be broken down into simpler compounds or elements by physical means, such as tearing or crushing. Compounds, however, can be broken down by chemical means into simpler compounds or into their original elements. Consider again the example of water. You cannot pass water through a filter and separate the hydrogen from the oxygen, but a process called electrolysis, illustrated in **Figure 6.7,** can break water down into hydrogen gas and oxygen gas.

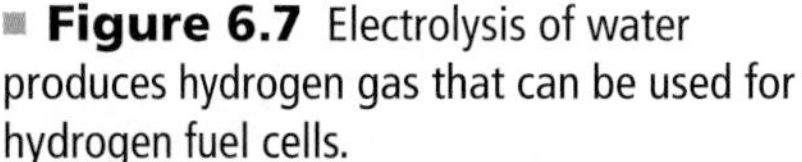

■ **Figure 6.7** Electrolysis of water produces hydrogen gas that can be used for hydrogen fuel cells.

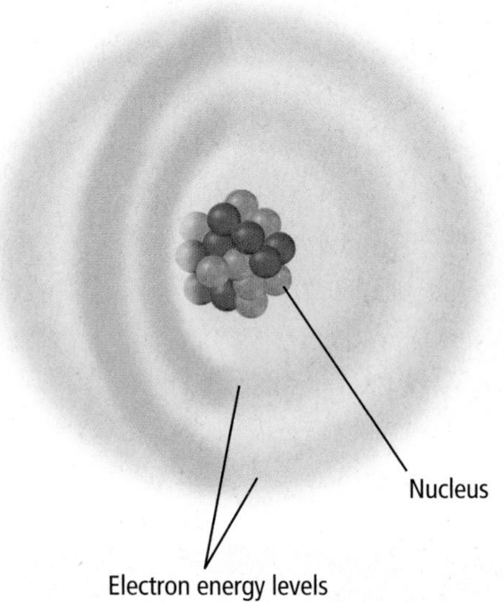


**Figure 6.8** Electrons are moving constantly within the energy levels surrounding the nucleus.

## Chemical Bonds

Compounds such as water, salt, and methane are formed when two or more substances combine. The force that holds the substances together is called a chemical bond. Think back to the protons, neutrons, and electrons that make up an atom. The nucleus determines the chemical identity of an atom, and the electrons are involved directly in forming chemical bonds. Electrons travel around the nucleus of an atom in areas called energy levels, as illustrated in **Figure 6.8.** Each energy level has a specific number of electrons that it can hold at any time. The first energy level, which is the level closest to the nucleus, can hold up to two electrons. The second can hold up to eight electrons.

A partially-filled energy level is not as stable as an energy level that is empty or completely filled. Atoms become more stable by losing electrons or attracting electrons from other atoms. This results in the formation of chemical bonds between atoms. It is the forming of chemical bonds that stores energy and the breaking of chemical bonds that provides energy for processes of growth, development, adaptation, and reproduction in living things. There are two main types of chemical bonds—covalent bonds and ionic bonds.

**Covalent bonds** When you were younger, you probably learned to share. If you had a book that your friend wanted to read as well, you could enjoy the story together. In this way, you both benefited from the book. Similarly, one type of chemical bond happens when atoms share electrons in their outer energy levels.

The chemical bond that forms when electrons are shared is called a **covalent bond. Figure 6.9** illustrates the covalent bonds between oxygen and hydrogen to form water. Each hydrogen (H) atom has one electron in its outermost energy level and oxygen (O) has six. Because the outermost energy level of oxygen is the second level, which can hold up to eight electrons, oxygen has a strong tendency to fill the energy level by sharing the electrons from the two nearby hydrogen atoms. Hydrogen does not completely give up the electrons, but also has a strong tendency to share electrons with oxygen to fill its outermost energy level. Two covalent bonds form, which creates water.

Most compounds in living organisms have covalent bonds holding them together. Water and other substances with covalent bonds are called molecules. A **molecule** is a compound in which the atoms are held together by covalent bonds. Depending on the number of pairs of electrons that are shared, covalent bonds can be single, double, or triple, as shown in **Figure 6.10.**

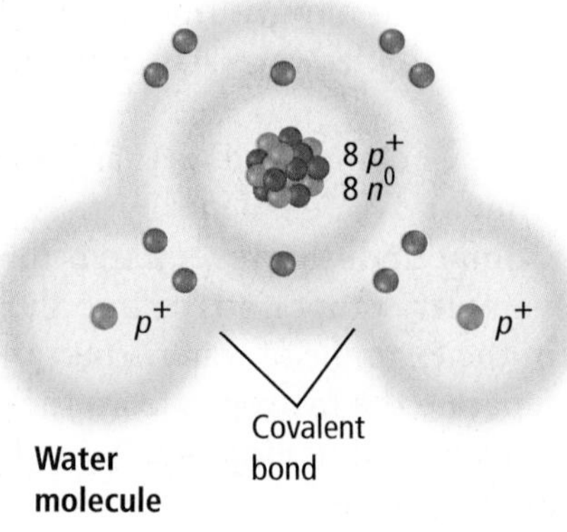


**Figure 6.9** In water ($H_2O$), two hydrogen atoms each share one electron with one oxygen atom. Because the oxygen atom needs two electrons to fill its outer energy level, it forms two covalent bonds, one with each hydrogen atom.

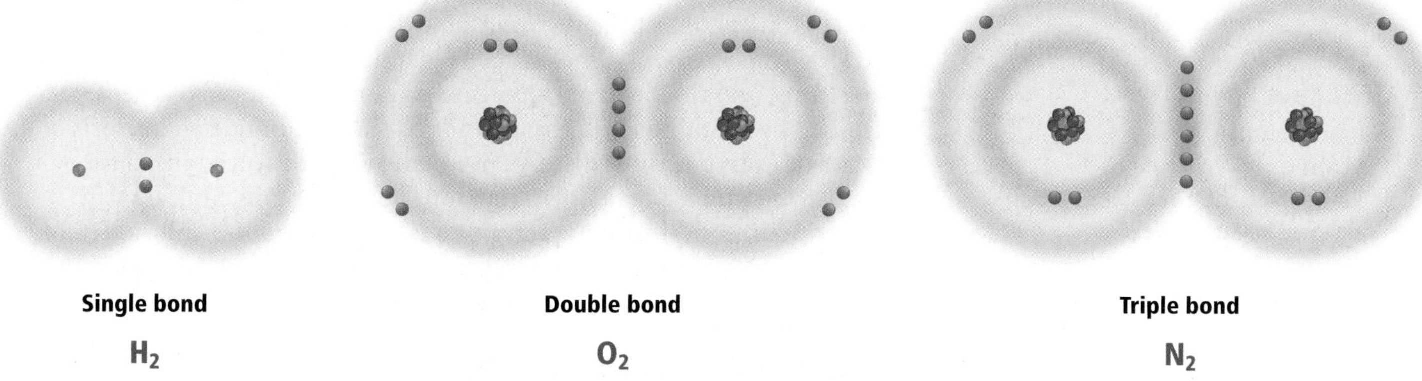


■ **Figure 6.10** A single bond has one pair of shared electrons, a double bond has two pairs, and a triple bond has three pairs.

**Ionic bonds** Recall that atoms are neutral—they do not have an electric charge. Also recall that for an atom to be most stable, the outermost energy level should be either empty or completely filled. Some atoms tend to give up (donate) or obtain (accept) electrons to empty or fill the outer energy level in order to be stable. An atom that has lost or gained one or more electrons becomes an **ion** and carries an electric charge. For example, sodium has one electron in its outermost energy level. Sodium can become more stable if it gives up this one electron, leaving its outer energy level empty. When it gives away this one negative charge, the neutral sodium atom becomes a positively charged sodium ion ($Na^+$). Similarly, chlorine has seven electrons in its outer energy level and needs just one electron to fill it. When chlorine accepts an electron from a donor atom, such as sodium, chlorine becomes a negatively charged ion ($Cl^-$).

An **ionic bond** is an electrical attraction between two oppositely charged atoms or groups of atoms called ions. **Figure 6.11** shows how an ionic bond forms as a result of the electrical attraction between $Na^+$ and $Cl^-$ to produce NaCl (sodium chloride). Substances formed by ionic bonds are called ionic compounds.

Ions in living things include sodium, potassium, calcium, chloride, and carbonate ions. They help maintain homeostasis as they travel in and out of cells. In addition, ions help transmit signals among cells that allow you to see, taste, hear, feel, and smell.

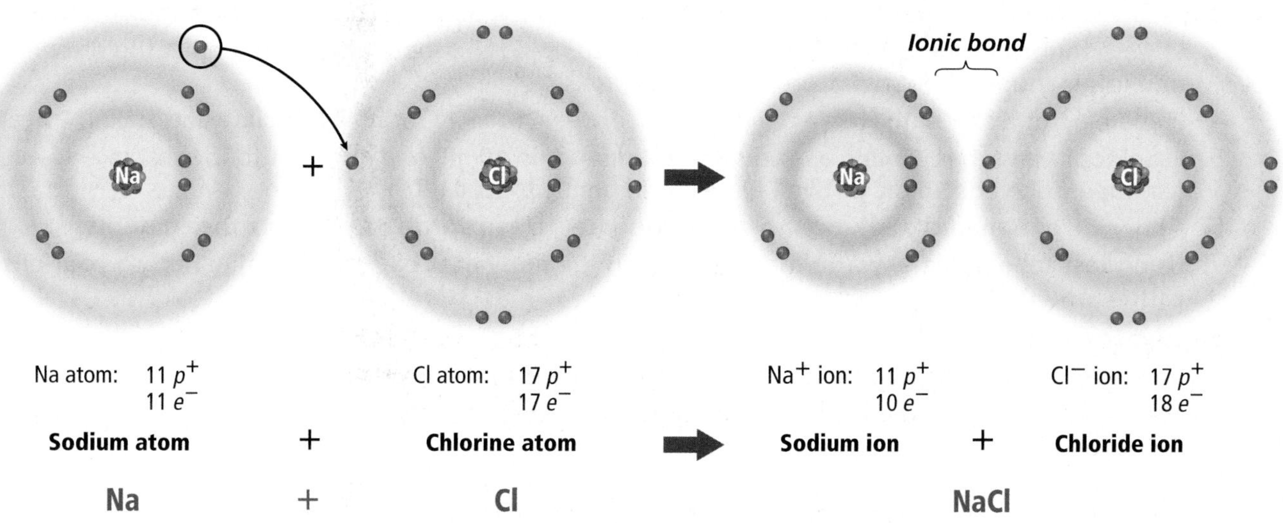


■ **Figure 6.11** To form ions, sodium donates an electron and chlorine gains an electron. An ionic bond forms when the oppositely charged ions come close together.

Concepts In Motion

**Interactive Figure** To see an animation of how ionic bonds form, visit biologygmh.com.

**Vocabulary**

**Word origin**

**Atom**
comes from the Greek word *atomos*, meaning *not divisible.*

Some atoms tend to donate or accept electrons more easily than other atoms. Look at the periodic table of elements inside the back cover of this textbook. The elements identified as metals tend to donate electrons, and the elements identified as nonmetals tend to accept electrons. The resulting ionic compounds have some unique characteristics. For example, most dissolve in water. When dissolved in solution, ionic compounds break down into ions and these ions can carry an electric current. Most ionic compounds, such as sodium chloride (table salt), are crystalline at room temperature. Ionic compounds generally have higher melting points than molecular compounds formed by covalent bonds.

**Connection to Earth Science** Although most ionic compounds are solid at room temperature, other ionic compounds are liquid at room temperature. Like their solid counterparts, ionic liquids are made up of positively and negatively charged ions. Ionic liquids have important potential in real-world applications as safe and environmentally friendly solvents that can possibly replace other harmful solvents. The key characteristic of ionic liquid solvents is that they typically do not evaporate and release chemicals into the atmosphere. Most ionic liquids are safe to handle and store, and they can be recycled after use. For these reasons, ionic liquids are attractive to industries that are dedicated to environmental responsibility.

**Reading Check** **Compare** ionic solids and liquids.

## MiniLab 6.1

### Test for Simple Sugars

**What common foods contain glucose?** Glucose is a simple sugar that provides energy for cells. In this lab, you will use an reagent called Benedict's solution, which indicates the presence of –CHO (carbon, hydrogen, oxygen) groups. A color change determines the presence of glucose and other simple sugars in common foods.

**Procedure**

1. Read and complete the lab safety form.
2. Create a data table with columns labeled *Food Substance, Sugar Prediction, Observations,* and *Results.*
3. Choose four **food substances** from those provided. Read the food labels and predict the presence of simple sugar in each food. Record your prediction.
4. Prepare a **hot water bath** with a temperature between 40°–50°C using a **hot plate** and **1000-mL beaker.**
5. Label four **test tubes.** Obtain a **graduated cylinder.** Add 10 mL of a different food substance to each test tube. Then add 10 mL **distilled water.** Swirl gently to mix.
6. Add 5 mL of **Benedict's solution** to each tube. Use a clean **stirring rod** to mix the contents.
7. Using **test tube holders,** warm the test tubes in the hot water bath for 2–3 min. Record your observations and results.

**Analysis**

1. **Interpret Data** Did any of the foods contain simple sugars? Explain.
2. **Think Critically** Could a food labeled "sugar free" test positive using Benedict's solution as an indicator? Explain.

## Macromolecules

Carbon atoms can be joined to form carbon molecules. Similarly, most cells store small carbon compounds that serve as building blocks for large molecules. **Macromolecules** are large molecules that are formed by joining smaller organic molecules together. These large molecules are also called polymers. **Polymers** are molecules made from repeating units of identical or nearly identical compounds called monomers that are linked together by a series of covalent bonds. As shown in **Table 6.1,** biological macromolecules are organized into four major categories: carbohydrates, lipids, proteins, and nucleic acids.

**Reading Check** **Use an analogy** to describe macromolecules.

**VOCABULARY**
**WORD ORIGIN**
**Polymer**
***poly–*** prefix; from Greek, meaning *many.*
***–meros*** from Greek, meaning *part.*

**Concepts In Motion**
**Interactive Table** To explore more about biological macromolecules, visit biologygmh.com.

**Table 6.1 Biological Macromolecules**

| Group | Example | Function |
|---|---|---|
| **Carbohydrates** | | • Store energy<br>• Provide structural support |
| **Lipids** | | • Store energy<br>• Provide barriers |
| **Proteins** | **Hemoglobin** | • Transport substances<br>• Speed reactions<br>• Provide structural support<br>• Make hormones |
| **Nucleic acids** | DNA stores genetic information in the cell's nucleus. | • Store and communicate genetic information |

*Study Tip*

**Double-Entry Notes** Fold a piece of paper in half lengthwise and write the boldfaced headings that appear under the *Biological Macromolecules* label on the left side. As you read the text, make a bulleted list of notes about the important ideas and terms.

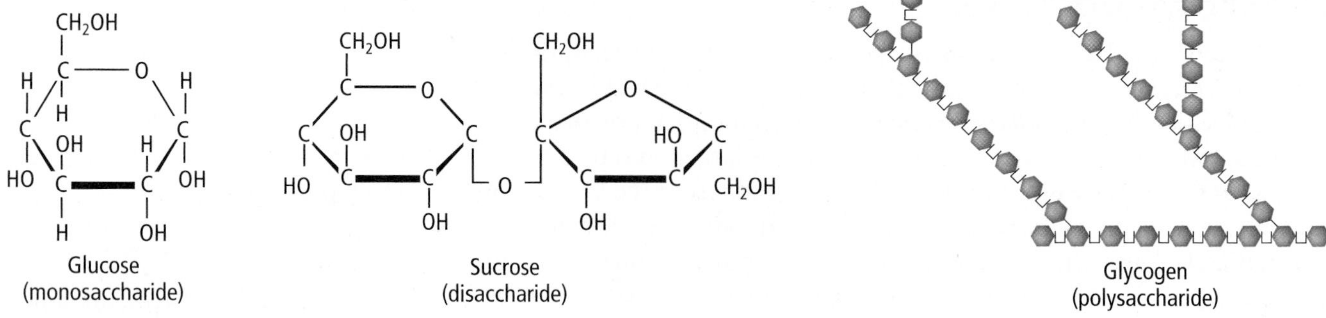


**Figure 6.26** Glucose is a monosaccharide. Sucrose is a disaccharide composed of glucose and fructose monosaccharides. Glycogen is a branched polysaccharide made from glucose monomers.

**Carbohydrates** Compounds composed of carbon, hydrogen, and oxygen in a ratio of one oxygen and two hydrogen atoms for each carbon atom are called **carbohydrates.** A general formula for carbohydrates is written as $(CH_2O)_n$. Here the subscript $n$ indicates the number of $CH_2O$ units in a chain. Biologically important carbohydrates that have values of $n$ ranging from three to seven are called simple sugars, or monosaccharides (mah nuh SA kuh rid). The monosaccharide glucose, shown in **Figure 6.26,** plays a central role as an energy source for organisms.

Monosaccharides can be linked to form larger molecules. Two monosaccharides joined together form a disaccharide (di SA kuh rid). Like glucose, disaccharides serve as energy sources. Sucrose, also shown in **Figure 6.26,** which is table sugar, and lactose, which is a component of milk, are both disaccharides. Longer carbohydrate molecules are called polysaccharides. One important polysaccharide is glycogen, which is shown in **Figure 6.26.** Glycogen is an energy storage form of glucose that is found in the liver and skeletal muscle. When the body needs energy between meals or during physical activity, glycogen is broken down into glucose.

In addition to their roles as energy sources, carbohydrates have other important functions in biology. In plants, a carbohydrate called cellulose provides structural support in cell walls. As shown in **Figure 6.27,** cellulose is made of chains of glucose linked together into tough fibers that are well-suited for their structural role. Chitin (KI tun) is a nitrogen-containing polysaccharide that is the main component in the hard outer shell of shrimp, lobsters, and some insects, as well as the cell wall of some fungi.

**Figure 6.27** The cellulose in plant cells provides the structural support for trees to stand in a forest.

**Lipids** Another important group of biological macromolecules is the lipid group. **Lipids** are molecules made mostly of carbon and hydrogen that make up the fats, oils, and waxes. Lipids are composed of fatty acids, glycerol, and other components. The primary function of lipids is to store energy. A lipid called a triglyceride (tri GLIH suh rid) is a fat if it is solid at room temperature and an oil if it is liquid at room temperature. In addition, triglycerides are stored in the fat cells of your body. Plant leaves are coated with lipids called waxes to prevent water loss, and the honeycomb in a beehive is made of beeswax.

**Saturated and unsaturated fats** Organisms need lipids in order to function properly. The basic structure of a lipid includes fatty acid tails as shown in **Figure 6.28.** Each tail is a chain of carbon atoms bonded to hydrogen and other carbon atoms by single or double bonds. Lipids that have tail chains with only single bonds between the carbon atoms are called saturated fats because no more hydrogens can bond to the tail. Lipids that have at least one double bond between carbon atoms in the tail chain can accommodate at least one more hydrogen and are called unsaturated fats. Fats with more than one double bond in the tail are called polyunsaturated fats.

**Phospholipids** A special lipid shown in **Figure 6.28,** called a phospholipid, is responsible for the structure and function of the cell membrane. Lipids are hydrophobic, which means they do not dissolve in water. This characteristic is important because it allows lipids to serve as barriers in biological membranes.

**Steroids** Another important category of lipids is the steroid group. Steroids include substances such as cholesterol and hormones. Despite its reputation as a "bad" lipid, cholesterol provides the starting point for other necessary lipids such as vitamin D and the hormones estrogen and testosterone.

## DATA ANALYSIS LAB 6.2

**Based on Real Data***

### Interpret the Data

**Does soluble fiber affect cholesterol levels?** High amounts of a steroid called cholesterol in the blood are associated with the development of heart disease. Researchers study the effects of soluble fiber in the diet on cholesterol.

#### Data and Observations

This experiment evaluated the effects of three soluble fibers on cholesterol levels in the blood: pectin (PE), guar gum (GG), and psyllium (PSY). Cellulose was the control (CNT).

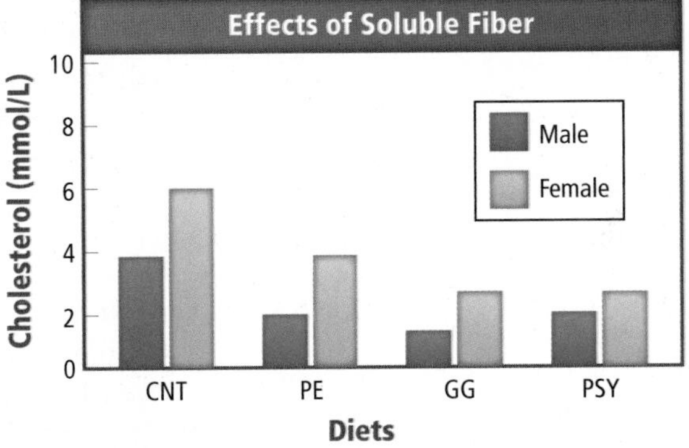


#### Think Critically

1. **Calculate** the percentage of change in cholesterol levels as compared to the control.
2. **Describe** the effects soluble fiber appears to have on cholesterol levels in the blood.

*Data obtained from: Shen, et al. 1998. Dietary soluble fiber lowers plasma LDL cholesterol concentrations by altering lipoprotein metabaolism in female Guinea pigs. *Journal of Nutrition* 128: 1434-1441.

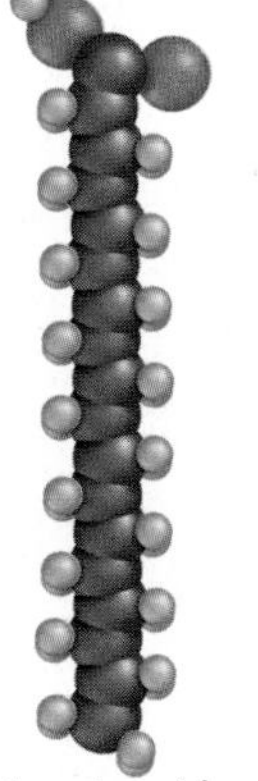


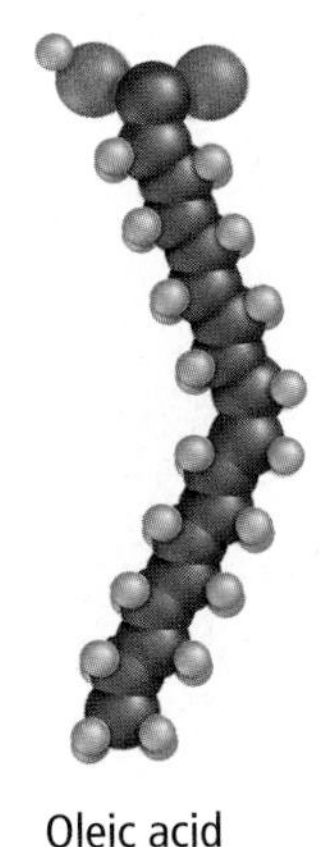


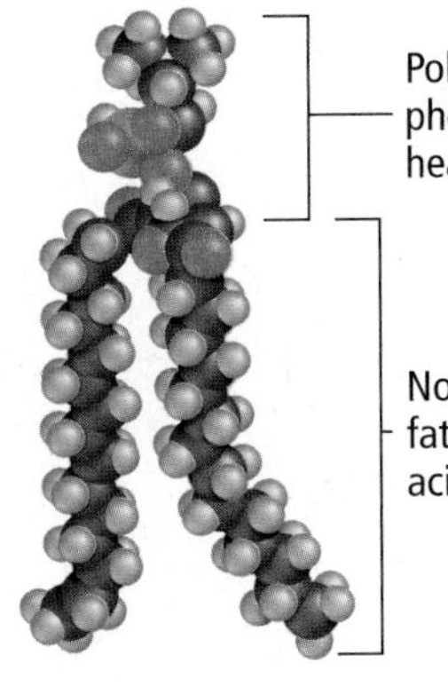


**Figure 6.28** Stearic acid has no double bonds between carbon atoms; oleic acid has one double bond. Phospholipids have a polar head and two nonpolar tails.

R Variable side chain

Amino group $H_2N-C-C-OH$ Carboxyl group

Hydrogen atom H O

Peptide bond

$H_2N-C(R_1)(H)-C(=O)-N(H)-C(R_2)(H)-C(=O)-OH$

Dipeptide

**Figure 6.29**
**Left:** The general structure of an amino acid has four groups around a central carbon.
**Right:** The peptide bond in a protein happens as a result of a chemical reaction.
**Interpret** ***What other molecule is a product when a peptide bond forms?***

**Concepts In Motion**

**Interactive Figure** To see an animation of peptide bond, visit biologygmh.com.

**Proteins** Another primary building block of living things is protein. A **protein** is a compound made of small carbon compounds called amino acids. **Amino acids** are small compounds that are made of carbon, nitrogen, oxygen, hydrogen, and sometimes sulfur. All amino acids share the same general structure.

**Amino acid structure** Amino acids have a central carbon atom like the one shown in **Figure 6.29.** Recall that carbon can form four covalent bonds. One of those bonds is with hydrogen. The other three bonds are with an amino group ($-NH_2$), a carboxyl group ($-COOH$), and a variable group ($-R$). The variable group makes each amino acid different. There are 20 different variable groups, and proteins are made of different combinations of all 20 different amino acids. Several covalent bonds called peptide bonds join amino acids together to form proteins, which is also shown in **Figure 6.29.** A peptide forms between the amino group of one amino acid and the carboxyl group of another.

**Three-dimensional protein structure** Based on the variable groups contained in the different amino acids, proteins can have up to four levels of structure. The number of amino acids in a chain and the order in which the amino acids are joined define the protein's primary structure. After an amino acid chain is formed, it folds into a unique three-dimensional shape, which is the protein's secondary structure. **Figure 6.30** shows two basic secondary structures—the helix and the pleat. A protein might contain many helices, pleats, and folds. The tertiary structure of many proteins is globular, such as the hemoglobin protein shown in **Table 6.1,** but some proteins form long fibers. Some proteins form a fourth level of structure by combining with other proteins.

**Protein function** Proteins make up about 15 percent of your total body mass and are involved in nearly every function of your body. For example, your muscles, skin, and hair all are made of proteins. Your cells contain about 10,000 different proteins that provide structural support, transport substances inside the cell and between cells, communicate signals within the cell and between cells, speed up chemical reactions, and control cell growth.

**Figure 6.30** The shape of a protein depends on the interactions among the amino acids. Hydrogen bonds help the protein hold its shape.

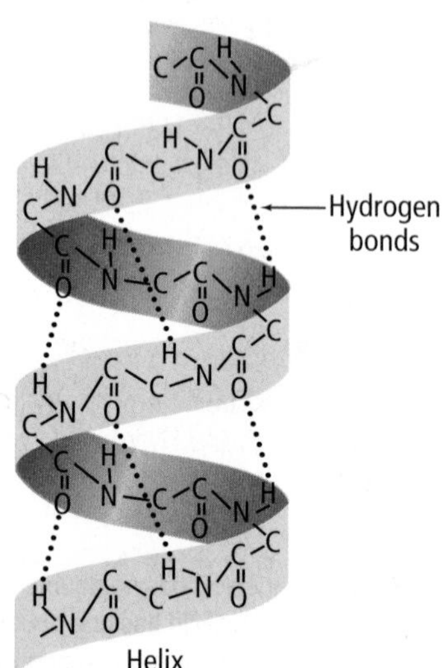


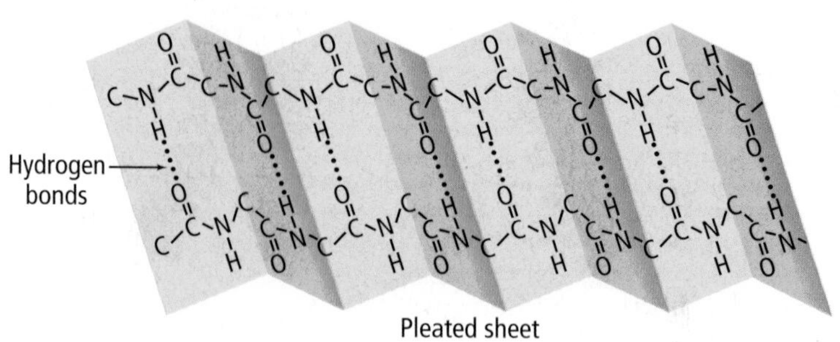

Phosphate group

Sugar

Nitrogen-containing base

**Nucleotide**

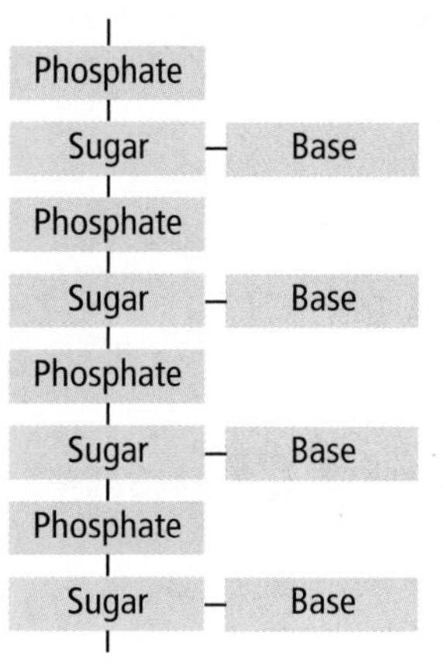


**Nucleic acid**

**Figure 6.31**
**Left:** DNA nucleotides contain the sugar deoxyribose. RNA nucleotides contain the sugar ribose.
**Right:** Nucleotides are joined together by bonds between their sugar group and phosphate group.

**Nucleic acids** The fourth group of biological macromolecules are nucleic acids. **Nucleic acids** are complex macromolecules that store and transmit genetic information. Nucleic acids are made of smaller repeating subunits called **nucleotides.** Nucleotides are composed of carbon, nitrogen, oxygen, phosphorus, and hydrogen atoms arranged as shown in **Figure 6.31.** There are six major nucleotides, all of which have three units—a phosphate, a nitrogenous base, and a ribose sugar.

There are two types of nucleic acids found in living organisms: deoxyribonucleic (dee AHK sih rib oh noo klay ihk) acid (DNA) and ribonucleic (rib oh noo KLAY ihk) acid (RNA). In nucleic acids such as DNA and RNA, the sugar of one nucleotide bonds to the phosphate of another nucleotide. The nitrogenous base that sticks out from the chain is available for hydrogen bonding with other bases in other nucleic acids. You will learn more about the structure and function of DNA and RNA in Chapter 12.

A nucleotide with three phosphate groups is adenosine triphosphate (ATP). ATP is a storehouse of chemical energy that can be used by cells in a variety of reactions. It releases energy when the bond between the second and third phosphate group is broken.

## Section 6.4 Assessment

### Section Summary

- Carbon compounds are the basic building blocks of living organisms.
- Biological macromolecules are formed by joining small carbon compounds into polymers.
- There are four types of biological macromolecules.
- Peptide bonds join amino acids in proteins.
- Chains of nucleotides form nucleic acids.

### Understand Main Ideas

1. MAIN Idea **Explain** If an unknown substance found on a meteorite is determined to contain no trace of carbon, can scientists conclude that there is life at the metorite's origin?
2. **List** and compare the four types of biological macromolecules.
3. **Identify** the components of carbohydrates and proteins.
4. **Discuss** the importance of amino acid order to a protein's function.

### Think Scientifically

5. *Summarize* Given the large number of proteins in the body, explain why the shape of an enzyme is important to its function.
6. *Draw* two structures (one straight chain and one ring) of a carbohydrate with the chemical formula $(CH_2O)_6$.

# In the Field

## Career: Field Chemist

### pH and Alkalinity

Water is one of the most important abiotic factors in any ecosystem. Whether in the desert or the rainforest, the availability of water as rain, surface water, and ground water affects every living thing. It isn't surprising that the task of monitoring and testing water is an important aspect of biological field work.

**Effects of pH** Several factors can affect the chemistry of available water in an ecosystem, including dissolved oxygen content, salinity, and pH. Factors such as agricultural runoff and acid rain can cause the pH of a body of water to change.

**Acidity** Acidic conditions, which indicate high levels of $H^+$, can disrupt biological processes in many water-dwelling organisms, such as snails, clams, and fish. Disrupting these processes can hamper reproduction and can eventually kill the organisms. Although organisms exhibit various degrees of resistance to changes in pH, a resistant organism that is dependent on a susceptible one will feel the effects of pH through that relationship. In addition, pH also affects the solubility of certain substances. For example, the concentration dissolved aluminum in a stream or lake increases at lower pH. Aluminum in water is toxic to many living things.

**Alkalinity** Despite the fact that water quality is affected by pH, a body of water also has the ability to resist pH changes that are associated with increasing acidity. The ability of a body of water to neutralize acid is referred to as its alkalinity. Carbonate and bicarbonate compounds are important acid-neutralizing compounds found in lakes and streams. pH can be controlled as long as carbonates are present. If the carbonates are used up, additional acid in the water will lower the pH and possibly endanger the inhabitants.

**Assessing pH** Biologists who perform field testing can assess the pH and alkalinity of a stream or lake by testing the water. When monitoring water, the location of the body of water, the depth of the sample, and the speed of the current where the sample is taken are all important considerations. In general, most freshwater has a pH between 6.5 and 8.0, but there can be some variation. If the pH strays from the optimal range for the water source, local communities can take action to preserve the environment and restore the pH to normal levels.

**WRITING in Biology**

Research water quality and testing issues for the Gulf Coast in the wake of hurricanes Katrina and Rita. Prepare a report that explains the water-quality problems caused by the hurricanes and what solutions were developed by the crisis management teams. For more information about water quality, visit biologygmh.com.

Design Your Own

# BIOLAB

## WHAT FACTORS AFFECT AN ENZYME REACTION?

**Background: The compound hydrogen peroxide, $H_2O_2$, is produced when organisms metabolize food, but hydrogen peroxide damages cell parts. Organisms combat the buildup of $H_2O_2$ by producing the enzyme peroxidase. Peroxidase speeds up the breakdown of hydrogen peroxide into water and oxygen.**

**Question:** *What factors affect peroxidase activity?*

### Possible Materials

| | |
|---|---|
| 400-mL beaker | 50-mL graduated cylinder |
| kitchen knife | 10-mL graduated cylinder |
| hot plate | tongs or large forceps |
| test tube rack | square or rectangular pan |
| ice | stopwatch or timer |
| beef liver | nonmercury thermometer |
| dropper | 3% hydrogen peroxide |
| distilled water | potato slices |

18-mm × 150-mm test tubes
buffer solutions (pH 5, pH 6, pH 7, pH 8)

### Safety Precautions

CAUTION: *Use only GFCI-protected circuits for electrical devices.*

### Plan and Perform the Experiment

1. Read and complete the lab safety form.
2. Choose a factor to test. Possible factors include temperature, pH, and substrate ($H_2O_2$) concentration.
3. Form a hypothesis about how the factor will affect the reaction rate of peroxidase.
4. Design an experiment to test your hypothesis. Create a procedure and identify the controls and variables.
5. Create a data table for recording your observations and measurements.
6. Make sure your teacher approves your plan before you proceed.
7. Conduct your approved experiment.
8. **Cleanup and Disposal** Clean up all equipment as instructed by your teacher and return everything to its proper place. Wash your hands thoroughly with soap and water.

### Analyze and Conclude

1. **Describe** how the factor you tested affected the enzyme activity of peroxidase.
2. **Graph** your data, then analyze and interpret your graph.
3. **Discuss** whether or not your data supported your hypothesis.
4. **Infer** why hydrogen peroxide is not the best choice for cleaning an open wound.
5. **Error Analysis** Identify any experimental errors or other errors in your data that might have affected the accuracy of your results.

### SHARE YOUR DATA

**Compare** your data with the data collected by other groups in the class that are testing the same factor. Infer reasons why your group's data might have differed from the data collected by other groups. To learn more about enzymes, visit Biolabs at biologygmh.com.

CHAPTER 6

# Study Guide

Download quizzes, key terms, and flash cards from biologygmh.com.

FOLDABLES **Examine** and report on the role of carbon in organisms and explain why so many carbon structures exist.

| Vocabulary | Key Concepts |
|---|---|
| **Section 6.1 Atoms, Elements, and Compounds** | |
| • atom (p. 148)<br>• compound (p. 151)<br>• covalent bond (p. 152)<br>• electron (p. 148)<br>• element (p. 149)<br>• ion (p. 153)<br>• ionic bond (p. 153)<br>• isotope (p. 150)<br>• molecule (p. 152)<br>• neutron (p. 148)<br>• nucleus (p. 148)<br>• proton (p. 148)<br>• van der Waals force (p. 155) | MAIN Idea Matter is composed of tiny particles called atoms.<br>• Atoms consist of protons, neutrons, and electrons.<br>• Elements are pure substances made up of only one kind of atom.<br>• Isotopes are forms of the same element that have a different number of neutrons.<br>• Compounds are substances with unique properties that are formed when elements combine.<br>• Elements can form covalent and ionic bonds. |
| **Section 6.2 Chemical Reactions** | |
| • activation energy (p. 158)<br>• active site (p. 160)<br>• catalyst (p. 159)<br>• chemical reaction (p. 156)<br>• enzyme (p. 159)<br>• product (p. 157)<br>• reactant (p. 157)<br>• substrate (p. 160) | MAIN Idea Chemical reactions allow living things to grow, develop, reproduce, and adapt.<br>• Balanced chemical equations must show an equal number of atoms for each element on both sides.<br>• Activation energy is the energy required to begin a reaction.<br>• Catalysts are substances that alter chemical reactions.<br>• Enzymes are biological catalysts. |
| **Section 6.3 Water and Solutions** | |
| • acid (p. 164)<br>• base (p. 164)<br>• buffer (p. 165)<br>• hydrogen bond (p. 161)<br>• mixture (p. 163)<br>• pH (p. 165)<br>• polar molecule (p. 161)<br>• solute (p. 163)<br>• solution (p. 163)<br>• solvent (p. 163) | MAIN Idea The properties of water make it well suited to help maintain homeostasis in an organism.<br>• Water is a polar molecule.<br>• Solutions are homogeneous mixtures formed when a solute is dissolved in a solvent.<br>• Acids are substances that release hydrogen ions into solutions. Bases are substances that release hydroxide ions into solutions.<br>• pH is a measure of the concentration of hydrogen ions in a solution. |
| **Section 6.4 The Building Blocks of Life** | |
| • amino acid (p. 170)<br>• carbohydrate (p. 168)<br>• lipid (p. 169)<br>• macromolecule (p. 167)<br>• nucleic acid (p. 171)<br>• nucleotide (p. 171)<br>• polymer (p. 167)<br>• protein (p. 170) | MAIN Idea Organisms are made up of carbon-based molecules.<br>• Carbon compounds are the basic building blocks of living organisms.<br>• Biological macromolecules are formed by joining small carbon compounds into polymers.<br>• There are four types of biological macromolecules.<br>• Peptide bonds join amino acids in proteins.<br>• Chains of nucleotides form nucleic acids. |

**Vocabulary PuzzleMaker** biologygmh.com

# Assessment

## Section 6.1

### Vocabulary Review

*Describe the difference between the terms in each set.*

1. electron—proton
2. ionic bond—covalent bond
3. isotope—element
4. atom—ion

### Understand Key Concepts

*Use the photo below to answer question 5.*

5. What does the image above show?
   A. a covalent bond
   B. a physical property
   C. a chemical reaction
   D. van der Waals forces

6. Which process changes a chlorine atom into a chloride ion?
   A. electron gain
   B. electron loss
   C. proton gain
   D. proton loss

7. Which of the following is a pure substance that cannot be broken down by a chemical reaction?
   A. a compound
   B. a mixture
   C. an element
   D. a neutron

8. How do the isotopes of hydrogen differ?
   A. the number of protons
   B. the number of electrons
   C. the number of energy levels
   D. the number of neutrons

### Constructed Response

9. **Short Answer** What is a radioactive isotope? List uses of radioactive isotopes.

10. **Short Answer** What factor determines that an oxygen atom can form two covalent bonds while a carbon atom can form four?

11. **Open Ended** Why is it important for living organisms to have both strong bonds (covalent and ionic) and weak bonds (hydrogen and van der Waals forces)?

### Think Critically

*Use the graph below to answer question 12.*

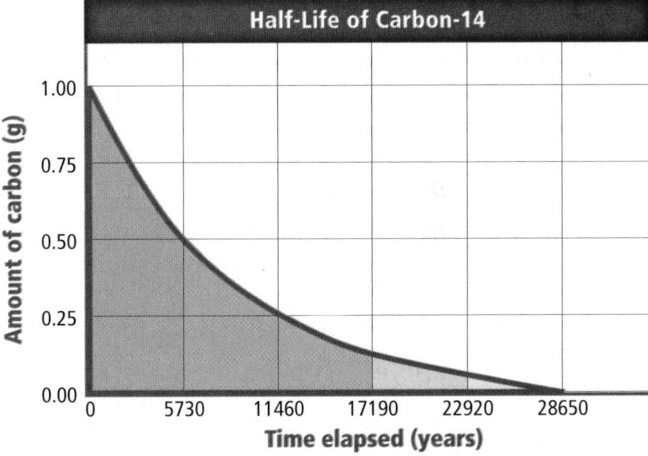


12. **Analyze** According to the data, what is the half-life of carbon-14? How can this information be used by scientists?

13. **Explain** The gecko is a reptile that climbs on smooth surfaces such as glass using van der Waals forces to adhere to the surface. How is this method of adhesion more advantageous than covalent interactions?

## Section 6.2

### Vocabulary Review

*Match the term on the left with the correct definition on the right.*

14. activation energy
15. substrate
16. enzyme
17. product

A. a protein that speeds up a reaction
B. a substance formed by a chemical reaction
C. the energy required to start a reaction
D. a substance that binds to an enzyme

### Understand Key Concepts

18. Which of the following is a substance that lowers the activation energy?
    A. an ion
    B. a reactant
    C. a catalyst
    D. a substrate

19. In which of the following are bonds broken and new bonds are formed?
    A. chemical reactions
    B. elements
    C. isotopes
    D. polar molecules

20. Which statement is true of chemical equations?
    A. Reactants are on the right.
    B. Products are on the right.
    C. Products have fewer atoms than reactants.
    D. Reactants have fewer atoms than products.

### Constructed Response

21. **Short Answer** What features do all reactions involving enzymes have in common?

22. **Open Ended** Identify and describe factors that can influence enzyme activity.

### Think Critically

*Use the graph to answer questions 23 and 24.*

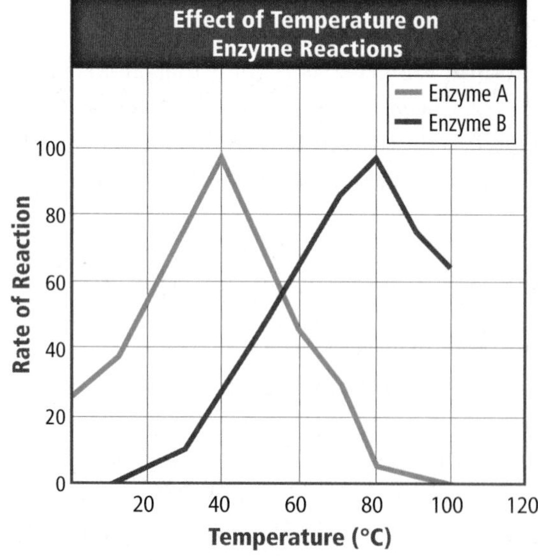


23. **Describe** the effect temperature has on the rate of the reactions using the graph above.

24. **Infer** Which enzyme is more active in a human cell? Why?

## Section 6.3

### Vocabulary Review

*State the relationship between the terms in each set.*

25. solution—mixture
26. pH—buffer
27. acid—base
28. solvent—solute
29. polar molecule—hydrogen bond

### Understand Key Concepts

*Use the figure below to answer question 30.*

30. What does the image above show?
    A. a heterogeneous mixture
    B. a homogeneous mixtrure
    C. a solution
    D. a suspension

31. Which statement is not true about pure water?
    A. It has a pH of 7.0.
    B. It is composed of polar molecules.
    C. It is composed of ionic bonds.
    D. It is a good solvent.

32. Which is a substance that produces $OH^-$ ions when dissolved in water?
    A. a base
    B. an acid
    C. a buffer
    D. salt

### Constructed Response

33. **Open Ended** Why are hydrogen bonds so important for living organisms?

34. **Short Answer** Hydrochloric acid (HCl) is a strong acid. What ions are formed when HCl dissolves in water? What is the effect of HCl on the pH of water?

35. **Open Ended** Explain the importance of buffers to living organisms.



Biology Online Chapter Test biologygmh.com

### Think Critically

36. **Predict** two places in the body where buffers are used to limit sharp changes in pH.

37. **Draw** a diagram of table salt (NaCl) dissolved in water.

## Section 6.4

### Vocabulary Review

*Complete the following sentences with vocabulary terms from the Study Guide page.*

38. Carbohydrates, lipids, proteins, and nucleic acids are __________.

39. Proteins are made from __________ that are joined by __________.

40. __________ make up fats, oils, and waxes.

41. DNA and RNA are examples of __________.

### Understand Key Concepts

42. Which two elements are always found in amino acids?
    **A.** nitrogen and sulfur
    **B.** carbon and oxygen
    **C.** hydrogen and phosphorus
    **D.** sulfur and oxygen

43. Which joins amino acids together?
    **A.** peptide bonds
    **B.** hydrogen bonds
    **C.** van der Waals forces
    **D.** ionic bonds

44. Which substance is not part of a nucleotide?
    **A.** a phosphate
    **B.** a base
    **C.** a sugar
    **D.** water

### Constructed Response

45. **Open Ended** Why do cells contain both macromolecules and small carbon compounds?

46. **Open Ended** Why can't humans digest all carbohydrates?

### Think Critically

47. **Create** a table for the four main biological macromolecules that lists their components and functions.

## Additional Assessment

48. WRITING in **Biology** Research and write a job description for a biochemist. Include the types of tasks biochemists perform and materials that are used in their research.

### DBQ Document-Based Questions

*Starch is the major carbon storehouse in plants. Experiments were performed to determine if trehalose might regulate starch production in plants. Leaf discs were incubated for three hours in sorbitol (the control), sucrose, and trelahose solutions. Then, levels of starch and sucrose in the leaves were measured. Use the data to answer the questions below.*

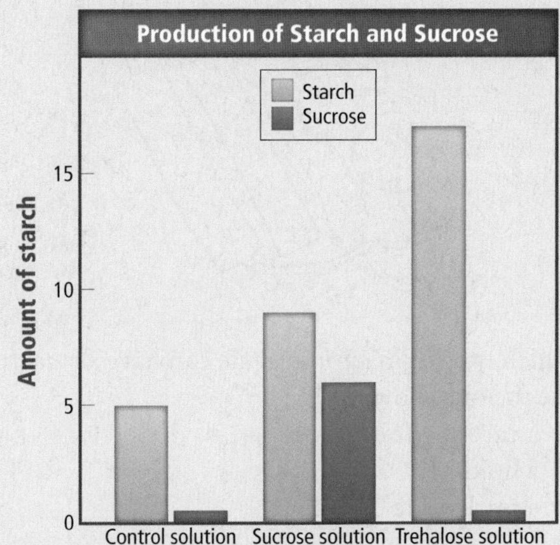


Data obtained from: Kolbe, et al. Trehalose 6-phosphate regulates starch synthesis via post translational redox activation of ADP-glucose pyrophophorylase. *Proceedings of the National Academy of Sciences of the USA* 102(31): 11118–11123.

49. Summarize the production of starch and sucrose in the three solutions.

50. What conclusion might the researchers have reached based on this data?

### Cumulative Review

51. How do reproductive strategies differ? **(Chapter 4)**

52. Describe three broad categories of biodiversity value. **(Chapter 5)**

# Standardized Test Practice

**Cumulative**

## Multiple Choice

1. If a population of parrots has greater genetic diversity than a hummingbird population in the same region, which outcome could result?
   A. The parrot population could have a greater resistance to disease than the hummingbird population.
   B. Other parrot populations in different regions could become genetically similar to this one.
   C. The parrot population could have a greater variety of abiotic factors with which to interact.
   D. The parrot population could interact with a greater variety of other populations.

*Use the diagram below to answer questions 2 and 3.*

2. Which type of macromolecule can have a structure like the one shown?
   A. a carbohydrate
   B. a lipid
   C. a nucleotide
   D. a protein

3. Which molecular activity requires a folded structure?
   A. behavior as a nonpolar compound
   B. function of an active site
   C. movement through cell membranes
   D. role as energy store for the cell

4. Which describes the effects of population increase and resource depletion?
   A. increased competition
   B. increased emigration
   C. exponential population growth
   D. straight-line population growth

5. Which property of populations might be described as random, clumped, or uniform?
   A. density
   B. dispersion
   C. growth
   D. size

6. Which is an example of biodiversity with direct economic value?
   A. sparrow populations that have great genetic diversity
   B. species of a water plant that makes a useful antibiotic
   C. trees that create a barrier against hurricane winds
   D. villagers who all use the same rice species for crops

*Use the illustration below to answer question 7.*

7. Which term describes the part of the cycle labeled 1?
   A. condensation
   B. evaporation
   C. run off
   D. precipitation

8. Which is a characteristic of exponential growth?
   A. the graphical representation goes up and down
   B. the graphical representaion has a flat line
   C. a growth rate that increases with time
   D. a growth rate that stays constant in time

## Short Answer

9. Assess what might happen if there were no buffers in human cells.

10. Choose an example of an element and a compound and then contrast them.

*Use the chart below to answer question 11.*

| Factors Affecting Coral Survival | |
|---|---|
| **Factor** | **Optimal Range** |
| Water Temperature | 23 to 25°C |
| Salinity | 30 to 40 parts per million |
| Sedimentation | Little or no sedimentation |
| Depth | Up to 48 m |

11. Using the data in the chart, describe which region of the world would be optimal for coral growth.

12. Provide a hypothesis to explain the increase in species diversity as you move from the polar regions to the tropics.

13. In a country with a very slow growth rate, predict which age groups are the largest in the population.

14. Why is it important that enzymes can bind only to specific substrates?

## Extended Response

15. Suddenly, after very heavy rains, many fish in a local lake begin to die, yet algae in the water seem to be doing very well. You know that the lake receives runoff from local fields and roads. Form a hypothesis about why the fish are dying, and suggest how to stop the deaths.

16. When scientists first discovered atoms, they thought they were the smallest parts into which matter could be divided. Relate how later discoveries led scientists to revise this definition.

17. Identify and describe three types of symbiotic relationships and provide an example of each.

## Essay Question

Many kinds of molecules found in living organisms are made of smaller monomers that are put together in different sequences, or in different patterns. For example, organisms use a small number of nucleotides to make nucleic acids. Thousands of different sequences of nucleotides in nucleic acids provide the basic coding for all the genetic information in living things.

*Using the information in the paragraph above, answer the following question in essay format.*

18. Describe how it is beneficial for organisms to use monomers to create complex macromolecules.

| NEED EXTRA HELP? | | | | | | | | | | | | | | | | | | |
|---|---|---|---|---|---|---|---|---|---|---|---|---|---|---|---|---|---|---|
| **If You Missed Question . . .** | 1 | 2 | 3 | 4 | 5 | 6 | 7 | 8 | 9 | 10 | 11 | 12 | 13 | 14 | 15 | 16 | 17 | 18 |
| **Review Section . . .** | 5.1 | 6.4 | 6.4 | 4.1 | 5.1 | 2.3 | 4.1 | 4.1 | 6.3 | 5.3 | 3.1, 3.3 | 5.1 | 4.2 | 6.2 | 5.2 | 6.1 | 2.1 | 6.4 |

# Cellular Structure and Function

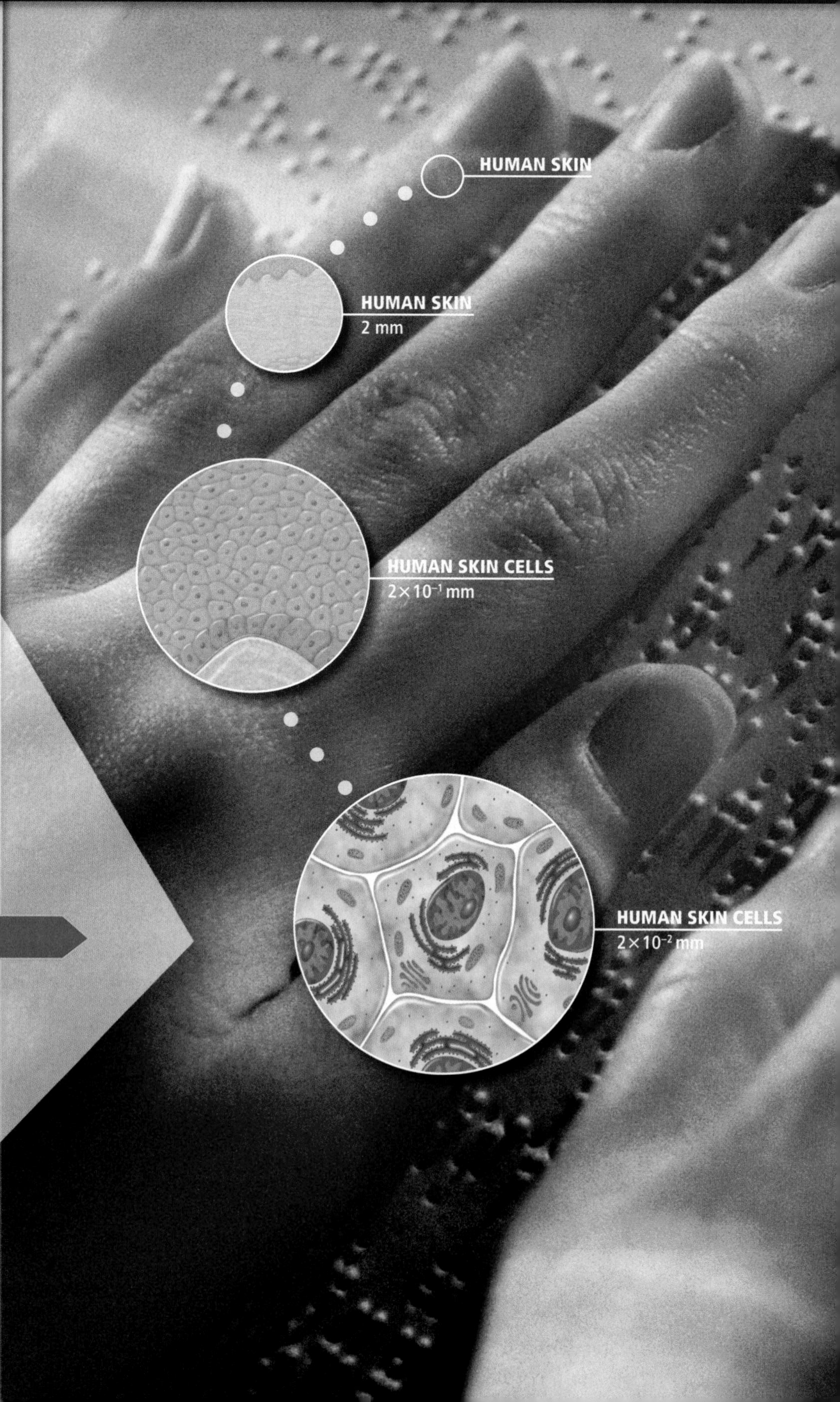

**Section 1**
**Cell Discovery and Theory**
**MAIN Idea** The invention of the microscope led to the discovery of cells.

**Section 2**
**The Plasma Membrane**
**MAIN Idea** The plasma membrane helps to maintain a cell's homeostasis.

**Section 3**
**Structures and Organelles**
**MAIN Idea** Eukaryotic cells contain organelles that allow the specialization and the separation of functions within the cell.

**Section 4**
**Cellular Transport**
**MAIN Idea** Cellular transport moves substances within the cell and moves substances into and out of the cell.

## BioFacts

- About ten trillion cells make up the human body.
- The largest human cells are about the diameter of a human hair.
- The 200 different types of cells in the human body come from just one cell.

# LAUNCH Lab

## What is a cell?

All things are made of atoms and molecules, but only in living things are the atoms and molecules organized into cells. In this lab, you will use a compound microscope to view slides of living things and nonliving things.

### Procedure

1. Read and complete the lab safety form.
2. Construct a data table for recording your observations.
3. Obtain **slides of the various specimens.**
4. View the slides through a **microscope** at the power designated by your teacher.
5. As you view the slides, fill out the data table you constructed.

### Analysis

1. **Describe** some of the ways to distinguish between the living things and the nonliving things.
2. **Write** a definition of a cell based on your observations.

Visit biologygmh.com to:

- study the entire chapter online
- explore the Interactive Time Line, Concepts in Motion, the Interactive Table, Microscopy Links, Virtual Labs, and links to virtual dissections
- access Web links for more information, projects, and activities
- review content online with the Interactive Tutor, and take Self-Check Quizzes

**Cellular Transport** Make this Foldable to help you characterize the various methods of cellular transport.

**STEP 1** Place two sheets of notebook paper 1.5 cm apart as illustrated.

**STEP 2** Roll up the bottom edges making all tabs 1.5 cm in size. Crease to form four tabs of equal size.

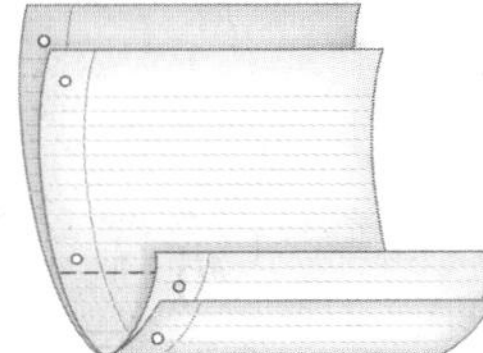

**STEP 3** Staple along the folded edge to secure all sheets. Label the tabs as illustrated.

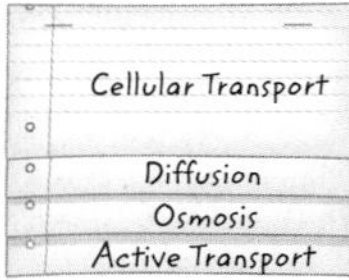


FOLDABLES **Use this Foldable with Section 7.4.** As you study the section, consider the role of energy in each of the cellular transport methods discussed.

Section 7.1

## Objectives

- **Relate** advances in microscope technology to discoveries about cells.
- **Compare** compound light microscopes with electron microscopes.
- **Summarize** the principles of the cell theory.
- **Differentiate** between a prokaryotic cell and a eukaryotic cell.

## Review Vocabulary

**organization:** the orderly structure of cells in an organism

## New Vocabulary

cell
cell theory
plasma membrane
organelle
eukaryotic cell
nucleus
prokaryotic cell

# Cell Discovery and Theory

**MAIN Idea The invention of the microscope led to the discovery of cells.**

**Real-World Reading Link** The different parts of your body might seem to have nothing in common. Your heart, for example, pumps blood throughout your body, while your skin protects and helps cool you. However, all your body parts have one thing in common—they are composed of cells.

## History of the Cell Theory

For centuries, scientists had no idea that the human body consists of trillions of cells. Cells are so small that their existence was unknown before the invention of the microscope. In 1665, as indicated in **Figure 7.1,** an English scientist named Robert Hooke made a simple microscope and looked at a piece of cork, the dead cells of oak bark. Hooke observed small, box-shaped structures, such as those shown in **Figure 7.2.** He called them cellulae (the Latin word meaning *small rooms*) because the boxlike cells of cork reminded him of the cells in which monks live at a monastery. It is from Hooke's work that we have the term *cell.* A **cell** is the basic structural and functional unit of all living organisms.

During the late 1600s, Dutch scientist Anton van Leeuwenhoek (LAY vun hook)—inspired by a book written by Hooke—designed his own microscope. To his surprise, he saw living organisms in pond water, milk, and various other substances. The work of these scientists and others led to new branches of science and many new and exciting discoveries.

**Figure 7.1**
**Microscopes in Focus**
The invention of microscopes, improvements to the instruments, and new microscope techniques have led to the development of the cell theory and a better understanding of cells.

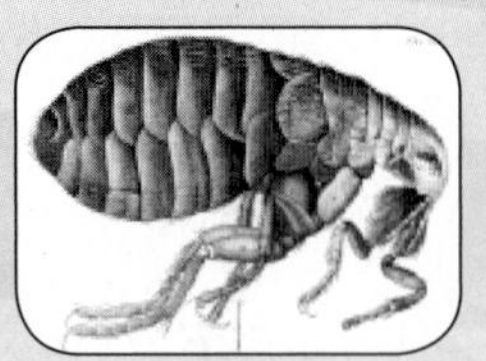

**1590** Dutch lens grinders Hans and Zacharias Janssen invent the first compound microscope by placing two lenses in a tube.

**1665** Robert Hooke observes cork and names the tiny chambers that he sees cells. He publishes drawings of cells, fleas, and other minute bodies in his book *Micrographia*.

**1683** Dutch biologist Anton van Leeuwenhoek discovers single-celled, animal-like organisms, now called protozoans.

**1830–1855** Scientists discover the cell nucleus (1833) and propose that both plants and animals are composed of cells (1839).

1500 1600 1700 1800

**The cell theory** Naturalists and scientists continued observing the living microscopic world using glass lenses. In 1838, German scientist Matthias Schleiden carefully studied plant tissues and concluded that all plants are composed of cells. A year later, another German scientist, Theodor Schwann, reported that animal tissues also consisted of individual cells. Prussian physician Rudolph Virchow proposed in 1855 that all cells are produced from the division of existing cells. The observations and conclusions of these scientists and others are summarized as the cell theory. The **cell theory** is one of the fundamental ideas of modern biology and includes the following three principles:

1. All living organisms are composed of one or more cells.
2. Cells are the basic unit of structure and organization of all living organisms.
3. Cells arise only from previously existing cells, with cells passing copies of their genetic material on to their daughter cells.

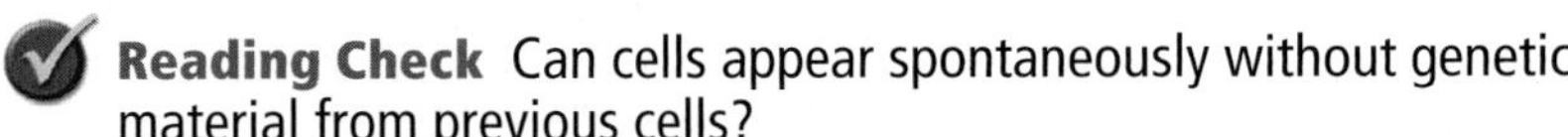

**Reading Check** Can cells appear spontaneously without genetic material from previous cells?

LM Magnification: 100×

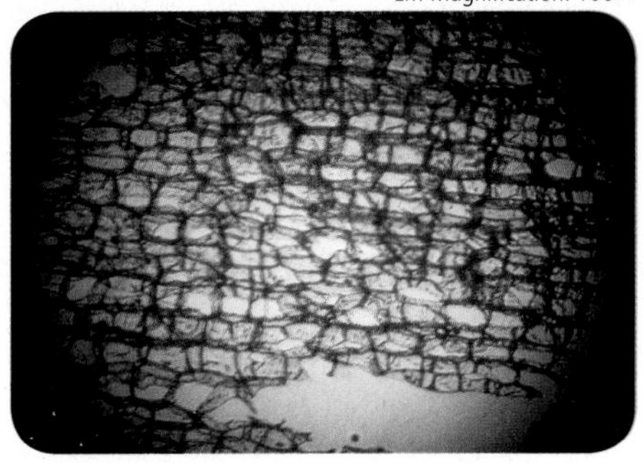

**Figure 7.2** Robert Hooke used a basic light microscope to see what looked like empty chambers in a cork sample.
**Infer** ***What do you think Hooke would have seen if these were living cells?***

**LAUNCH Lab**

**Review** Based on what you've read about cells, how would you now answer the analysis questions?

## Microscope Technology

The discovery of cells and the development of the cell theory would not have been possible without microscopes. Improvements made to microscopes have enabled scientists to study cells in detail, as described in **Figure 7.1.**

Turn back to the opening pages of this chapter and compare the magnifications of the skin shown there. Note that the detail increases as the magnification and resolution—the ability of the microscope to make individual components visible—increase. Hooke and van Leewenhoek would not have been able to see the individual structures within human skin cells with their microscopes. Developments in microscope technology have given scientists the ability to study cells in greater detail than early scientists ever thought possible.

**1880–1890** Louis Pasteur and Robert Koch, using compound microscopes, pioneered the study of bacteria.

1900

**1939** Ernest Everett Just writes the textbook *Biology of the Cell Surface* after years of studying the structure and function of cells.

**1970** Lynn Margulis, a microbiologist, proposes the idea that some organelles found in eukaryotes were once free-living prokaryotes.

**1981** The scanning tunneling microscope (STM) allows scientists to see individual atoms.

2000

**Concepts In Motion** Interactive Time Line
To learn more about these discoveries and others, visit biologygmh.com. **Biology Online**

**Compound light microscopes** The modern compound light microscope consists of a series of glass lenses and uses visible light to produce a magnified image. Each lens in the series magnifies the image of the previous lens. For example, when two lenses each individually magnify 10 times, the total magnification would be 100 times ($10 \times 10$). Scientists often stain cells with dyes to see them better when using a light microscope because cells are so tiny, thin, and translucent. Over the years, scientists have developed various techniques and modifications for light microscopes, but the properties of visible light will always limit resolution with these microscopes. Objects cause light to scatter, which blurs images. The maximum magnification without blurring is around 1000×.

**Electron microscopes** As they began to study cells, scientists needed greater magnification to see the details of tiny parts of the cell. During the second World War, in the 1940s, they developed the electron microscope. Instead of lenses, the electron microscope uses magnets to aim a beam of electrons at thin slices of cells. This type of electron microscope is called a transmission electron microscope (TEM) because electrons are passed, or transmitted, through a specimen to a fluorescent screen. Thick parts of the specimen absorb more electrons than thin parts, forming a black-and-white shaded image of the specimen. Transmission electron microscopes can magnify up to 500,000×, but the specimen must be dead, sliced very thin, and stained with heavy metals.

Over the past 65 years, many modifications have been made to the original electron microscopes. For example, the scanning electron microscope (SEM) is one modification that directs electrons over the surface of the specimen, producing a three-dimensional image. One disadvantage of using a TEM and an SEM is that only nonliving cells and tissues can be observed. To see photomicrographs made with electron microscopes, visit biologygmh.com and click on *Microscopy Links.*

**CAREERS IN BIOLOGY**

**Technology Representative** Companies that manufacture scientific equipment employ representatives to demonstrate and explain their products to the scientific community. A technology representative is an expert in these new technology products and brings this expertise to scientists who might use the products in the laboratory. For more information on biology careers, visit biologygmh.com.

## MiniLab 7.1

### Discover Cells

**How can you describe a new discovery?** Imagine you are a scientist looking through the eyepiece of some new-fangled instrument called a microscope and you see a field of similarly shaped objects. You might recognize that the shapes you see are not merely coincidence and random objects. Your whole idea of the nature of matter is changing as you view these objects.

**Procedure**

1. Read and complete the lab safety form.
2. Prepare a data table in which you will record observations and drawings for three slides.
3. View the **slide images** your teacher projects for the class.
4. Describe and draw what you see. Be sure to include enough detail in your drawings to convey the information to other scientists who have not observed cells.

**Analysis**

1. **Describe** What analogies or terms could explain the images in your drawings?
2. **Explain** How could you show Hooke, with twenty-first-century technology, that his findings were valid?

## Cell Structures

In a factory, there are separate areas set up for performing different tasks. Eukaryotic cells also have separate areas for tasks. Membrane-bound organelles make it possible for different chemical processes to take place at the same time in different parts of the cytoplasm. Organelles carry out essential cell processes, such as protein synthesis, energy transformation, digestion of food, excretion of wastes, and cell division. Each organelle has a unique structure and function. You can compare organelles to a factory's offices, assembly lines, and other important areas that keep the factory running. As you read about the different organelles, refer to the diagrams of plant and animal cells in **Figure 7.9** to see the organelles of each type.

**The nucleus** Just as a factory needs a manager, a cell needs an organelle to direct the cell processes. The nucleus, shown in **Figure 7.10,** is the cell's managing structure. It contains most of the cell's DNA, which stores information used to make proteins for cell growth, function, and reproduction.

The nucleus is surrounded by a double membrane called the nuclear envelope. The nuclear envelope is similar to the plasma membrane, except the nuclear membrane has nuclear pores that allow larger-sized substances to move in and out of the nucleus. Chromatin, which is a complex DNA attached to protein, is spread throughout the nucleus.

**Reading Check** **Describe** the role of the nucleus.

**Ribosomes** One of the functions of a cell is to produce proteins. The organelles that help manufacture proteins are called **ribosomes.** Ribosomes are made of two components—RNA and protein—and are not bound by a membrane like other organelles. Within the nucleus is the site of ribosome production called the **nucleolus,** shown in **Figure 7.10.**

Cells have many ribosomes that produce a variety of proteins that are used by the cell or are moved out and used by other cells. Some ribosomes float freely in the cytoplasm, while others are bound to another organelle called the endoplasmic reticulum. Free-floating ribosomes produce proteins for use within the cytoplasm of the cell. Bound ribosomes produce proteins that will be bound within membranes or used by other cells.

**VOCABULARY**

**WORD ORIGIN**

**Cytoplasm**
**Cytoskeleton**
*cyte–* prefix; from Greek, meaning *cell.*

**Figure 7.10** The nucleus of a cell is a three-dimensional shape. The photomicrograph shows a cross-section of a nucleus.
**Infer** ***Explain why all the cross-sections of a nucleus are not identical.***

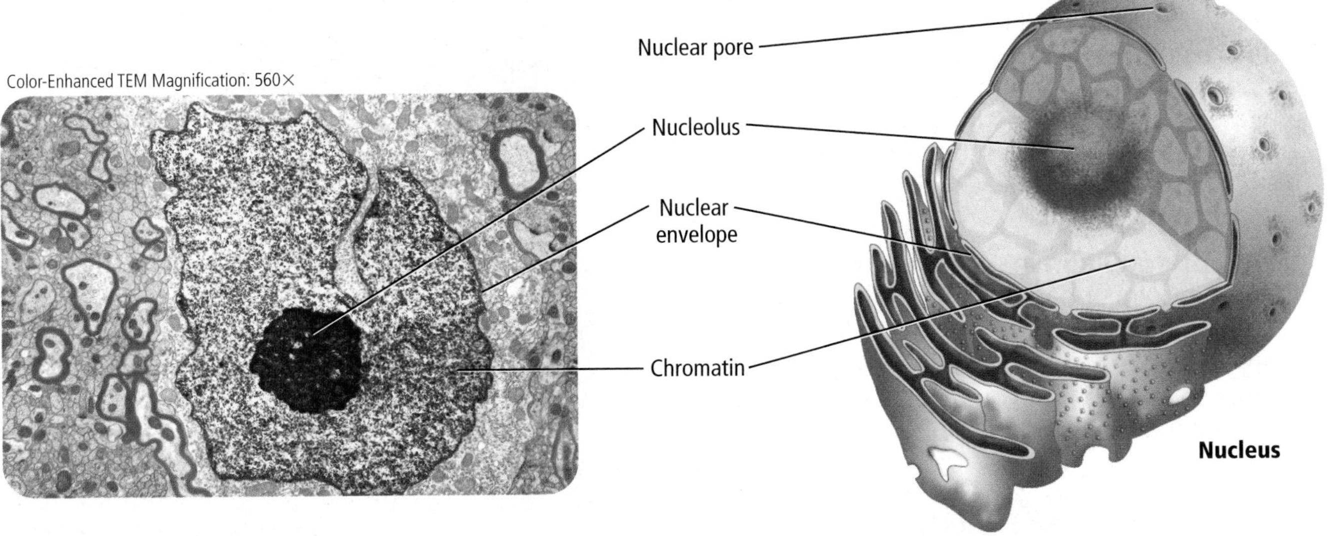

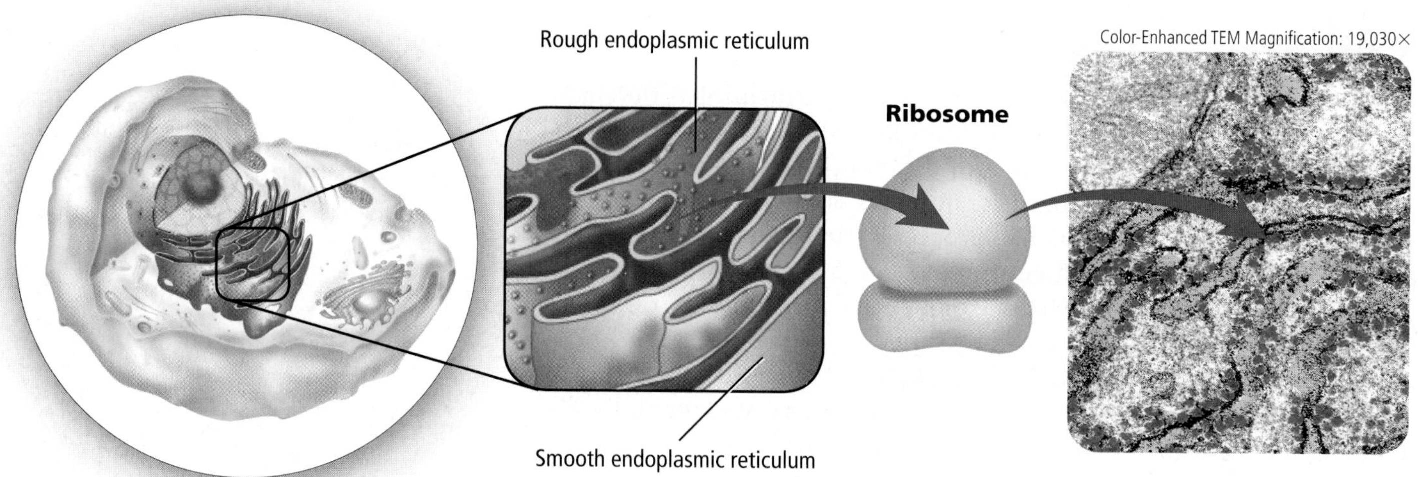


■ **Figure 7.11** Ribosomes are simple structures made of RNA and protein that may be attached to the surface of the rough endoplasmic reticulum. They look like bumps on the endoplasmic reticulum.

**Endoplasmic reticulum** The **endoplasmic reticulum** (en duh PLAZ mihk • rih TIHK yuh lum), also called ER, is a membrane system of folded sacs and interconnected channels that serves as the site for protein and lipid synthesis. The pleats and folds of the ER provide a large amount of surface area where cellular functions can take place. The area of ER where ribosomes are attached is called rough endoplasmic reticulum. Notice in **Figure 7.11** that the rough ER appears to have bumps on it. These bumps are the attached ribosomes that will produce proteins for export to other cells.

**Figure 7.11** also shows that there are areas of the ER that do not have ribosomes attached. The area of ER where no ribosomes are attached is called smooth endoplasmic reticulum. Although the smooth ER has no ribosomes, it does perform important functions for the cell. For example, the smooth ER provides a membrane surface where a variety of complex carbohydrates and lipids, including phospholipids, are synthesized. Smooth ER in the liver detoxifies harmful substances.

## DATA ANALYSIS LAB 7.2

**Based on Real Lab Data***

### Interpret the Data

**How is vesicle traffic from the ER to the Golgi apparatus regulated?** Some proteins are synthesized by ribosomes on the endoplasmic reticulum (ER). The proteins are processed in the ER, and vesicles containing these proteins pinch off and migrate to the Golgi apparatus. Scientists currently are studying the molecules that are involved in fusing these vesicles to the Golgi apparatus.

**Think Critically**

1. **Interpret a Diagram** Name two complexes on the Golgi apparatus that might be involved in vesicle fusion.
2. **Hypothesize** an explanation for vesicle transport based on what you have read about cytoplasm and the cytoskeleton.

**Data and Observations**

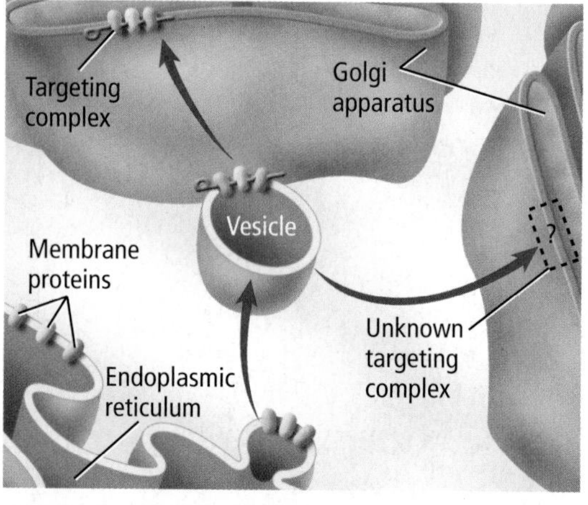


*Data obtained from: Brittle, E. E., and Waters, M. G. 2000. ER-to-golgi traffic—this bud's for you. *Science* 289: 403–404.

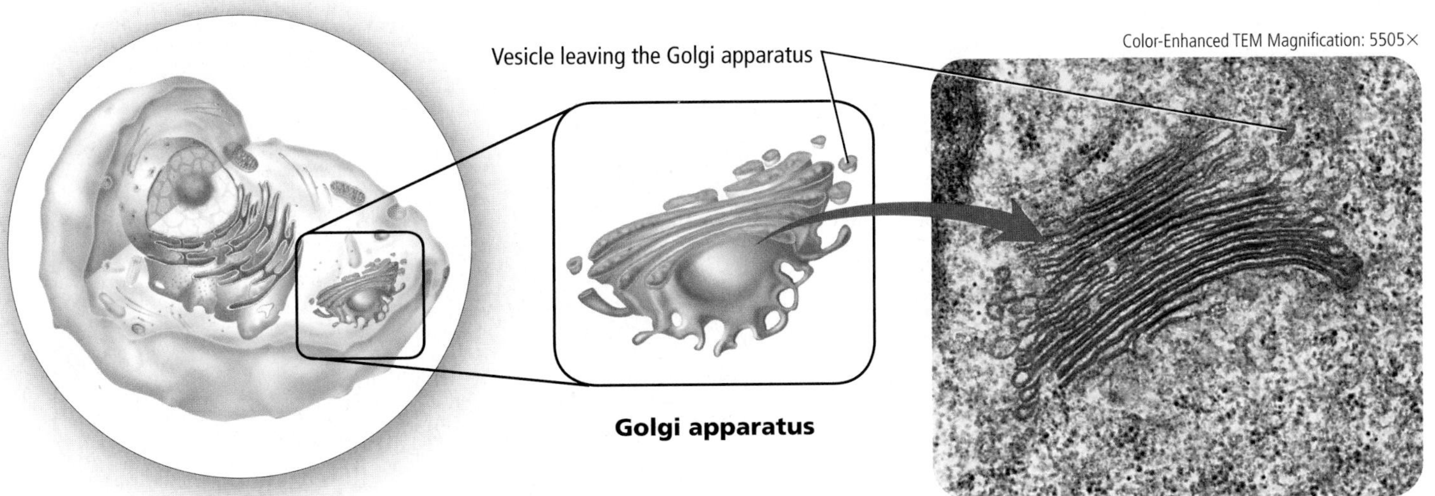


■ **Figure 7.12** Flattened stacks of membranes make up the Golgi apparatus.

**Golgi apparatus** After the hiking boots are made in the factory, they must be organized into pairs, boxed, and shipped. Similarly, after proteins are made in the endoplasmic reticulum, some might be transferred to the Golgi (GAWL jee) apparatus, illustrated in **Figure 7.12.** The **Golgi apparatus** is a flattened stack of membranes that modifies, sorts, and packages proteins into sacs called vesicles. Vesicles then can fuse with the cell's plasma membrane to release proteins to the environment outside the cell. Observe the vesicle in **Figure 7.12.**

**Vacuoles** A factory needs a place to store materials and waste products. Similarly, cells have membrane-bound vesicles called vacuoles for temporary storage of materials within the cytoplasm. A **vacuole,** such as the plant vacuole shown in **Figure 7.13,** is a sac used to store food, enzymes, and other materials needed by a cell. Some vacuoles store waste products. Interestingly, animal cells usually do not contain vacuoles. If animal cells do have vacuoles, they are much smaller than those in plant cells.

■ **Figure 7.13** Plant cells have large membrane-bound storage compartments called vacuoles.

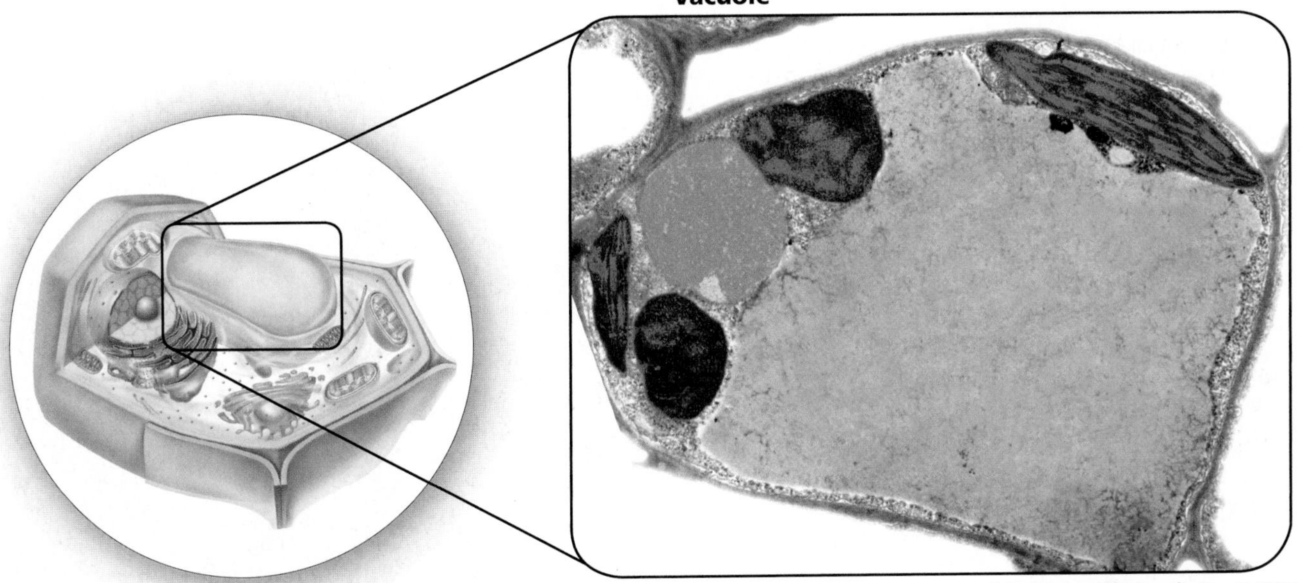

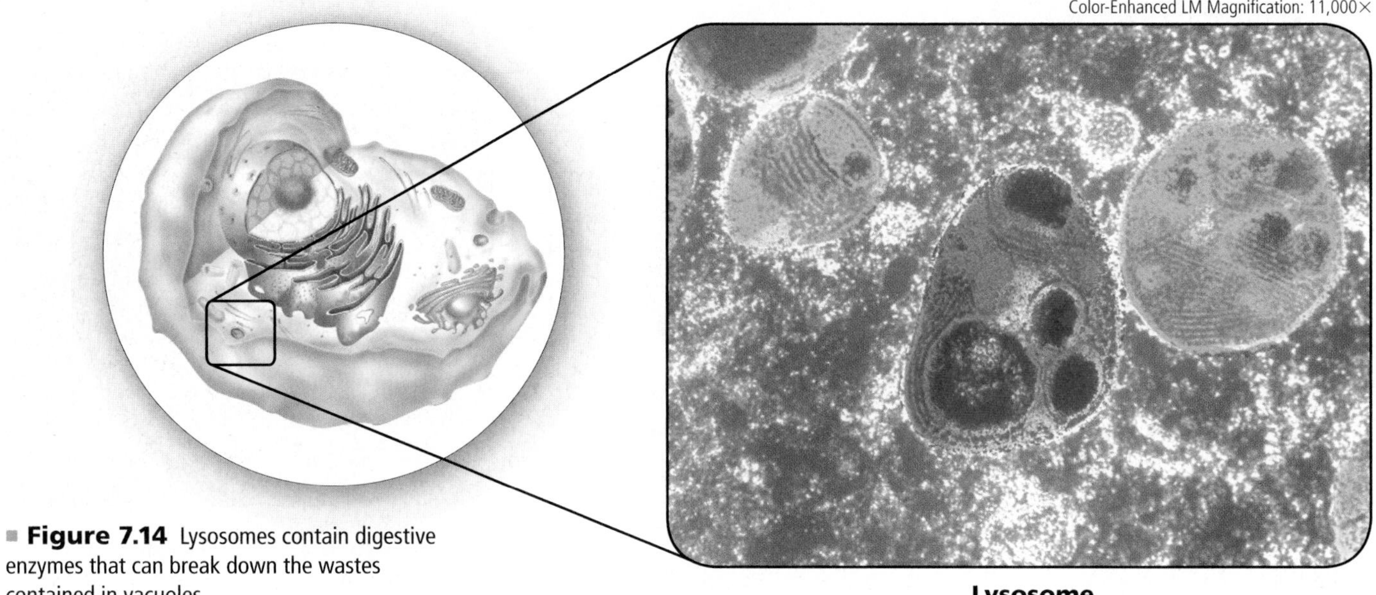


**Figure 7.14** Lysosomes contain digestive enzymes that can break down the wastes contained in vacuoles.

**Lysosomes** Factories and cells also need clean-up crews. In the cell, **lysosomes,** shown in **Figure 7.14,** are vesicles that contain substances that digest excess or worn-out organelles and food particles. Lysosomes also digest bacteria and viruses that have entered the cell. The membrane surrounding a lysosome prevents the digestive enzymes inside from destroying the cell. Lysosomes can fuse with vacuoles and dispense their enzymes into the vacuole, digesting the wastes inside.

**Centrioles** Previously in this section you read about microtubules and the cytoskeleton. Groups of microtubules form another structure called a centriole (SEN tree ol). **Centrioles,** shown in **Figure 7.15,** are organelles made of microtubules that function during cell division. Centrioles are located in the cytoplasm of animal cells and most protists and usually are near the nucleus. You will learn about cell division and the role of centrioles in Chapter 9.

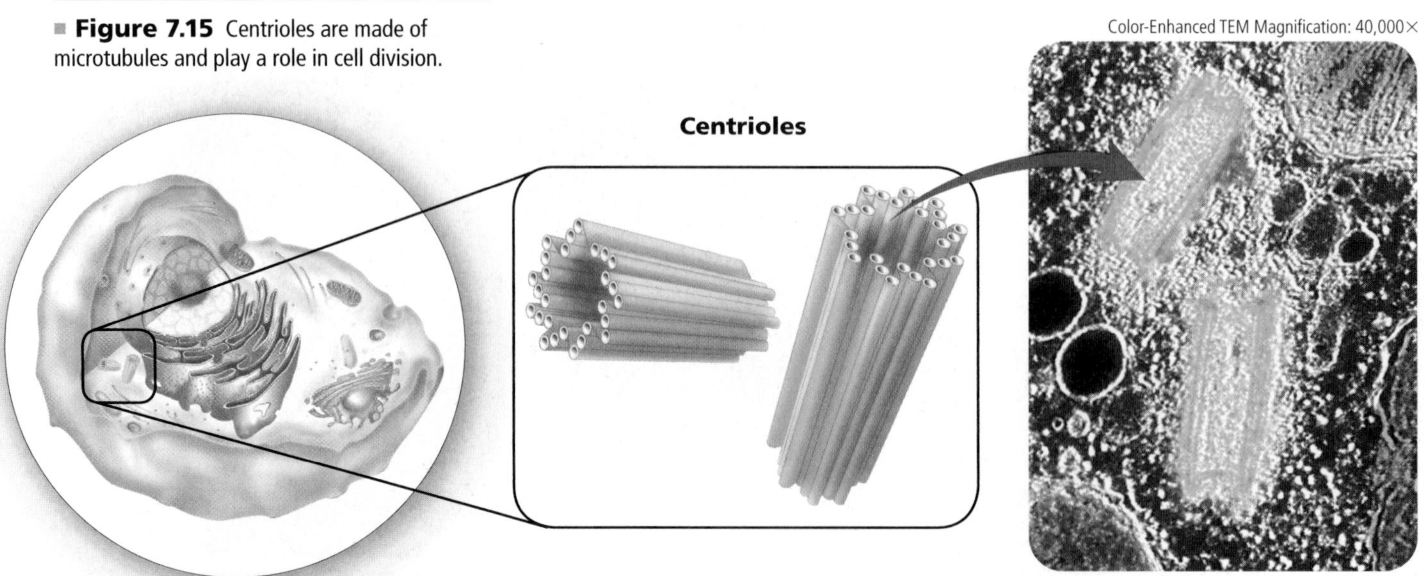


**Figure 7.15** Centrioles are made of microtubules and play a role in cell division.

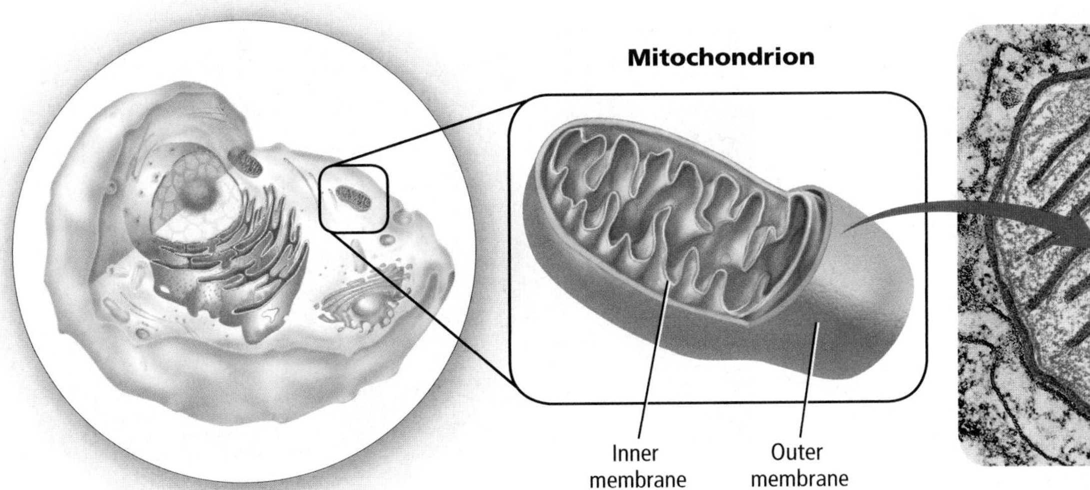


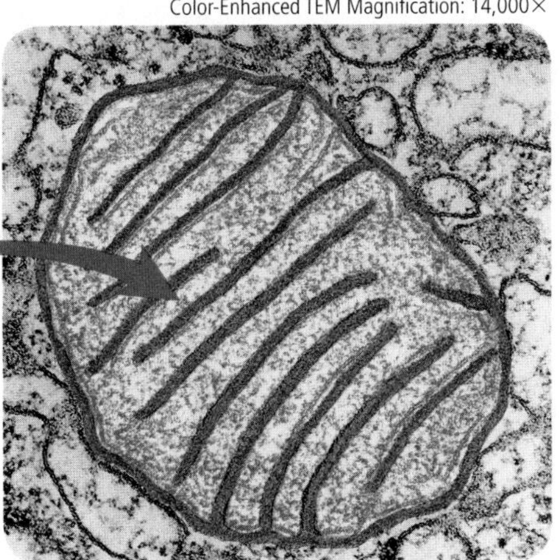


■ **Figure 7.16** Mitochondria make energy available to the cell.
**Describe** ***the membrane structure of a mitochondrion.***

**Mitochondria** Imagine now that the boot factory has its own generator that produces the electricity it needs. Cells also have energy generators called **mitochondria** (mi tuh KAHN dree uh; singular, mitochondrion) that convert fuel particles (mainly sugars), into usable energy. **Figure 7.16** shows that a mitochondrion has an outer membrane and a highly folded inner membrane that provides a large surface area for breaking the bonds in sugar molecules. The energy produced from that breakage is stored in the bonds of other molecules and later used by the cell. For this reason, mitochondria often are referred to as the "powerhouses" of cells.

**Chloroplasts** Factory machines need electricity that is generated by burning fossil fuels or by collecting energy from alternative sources, such as the Sun. Plant cells have their own way of using solar energy. In addition to mitochondria, plants and some other eukaryotic cells contain **chloroplasts,** which are organelles that capture light energy and convert it to chemical energy through a process called photosynthesis. Examine **Figure 7.17** and notice that inside the inner membrane are many small, disk-shaped compartments called thylakoids. It is here that the energy from sunlight is trapped by a pigment called chlorophyll. Chlorophyll gives leaves and stems their green color.

Chloroplasts belong to a group of plant organelles called plastids, some of which are used for storage. Some plastids store starches or lipids. Others, such as chromoplasts, contain red, orange, or yellow pigments that trap light energy and give color to plant structures such as flowers or leaves.

■ **Figure 7.17** In plants, chloroplasts capture and convert light energy to chemical energy.

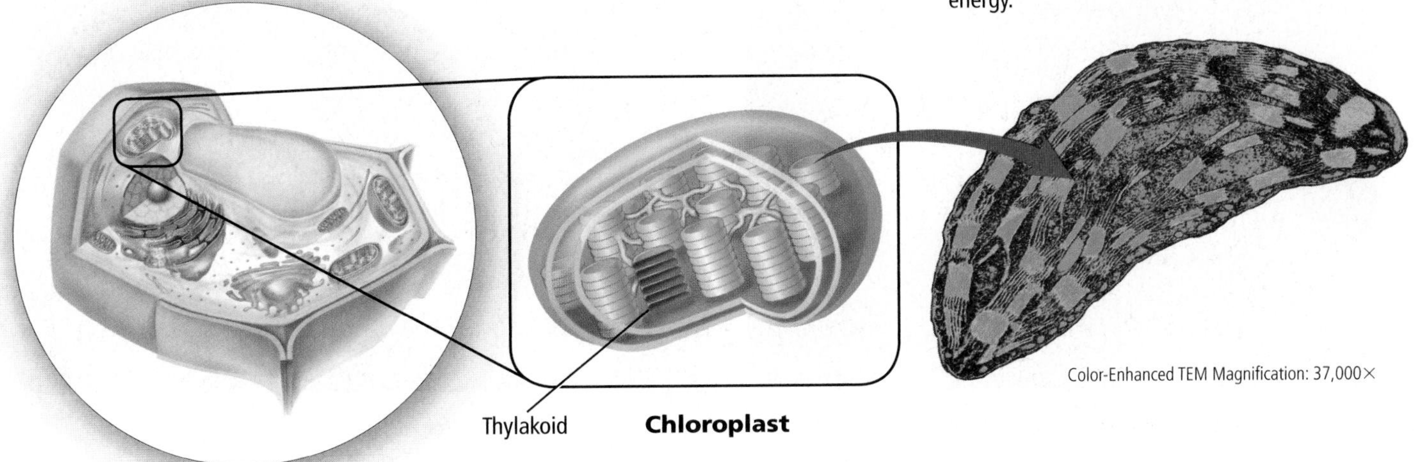

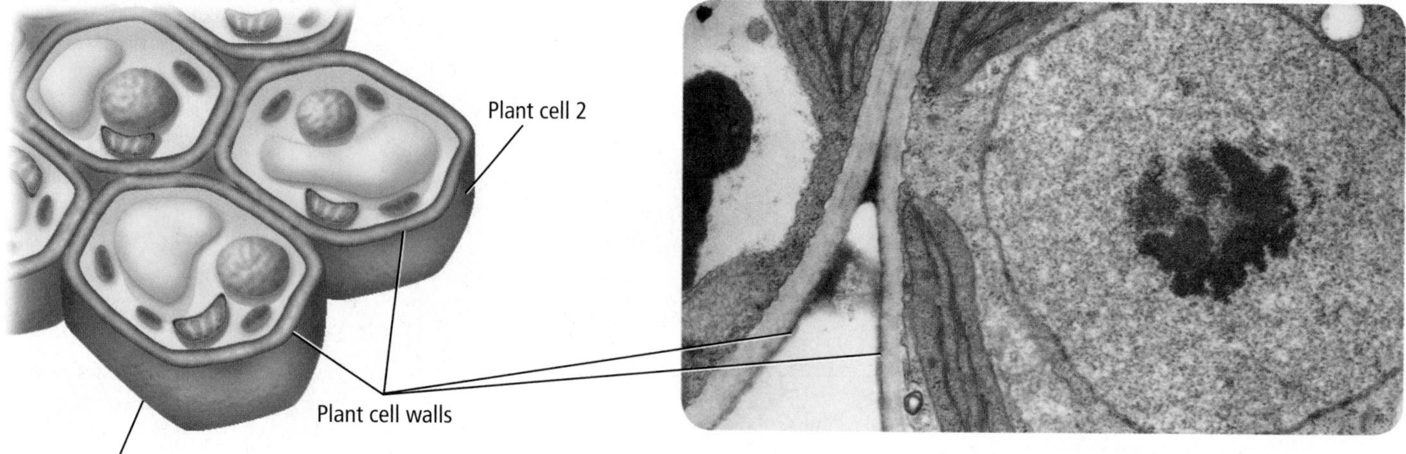


**Figure 7.18** The illustration shows plant cells and their cell walls. Compare this to the transmission electron micrograph showing the cell walls of adjacent plant cells.

**Cell wall** Another structure associated with plant cells is the cell wall, shown in **Figure 7.18.** The **cell wall** is a thick, rigid, mesh of fibers that surrounds the outside of the plasma membrane, protecting the cell and giving it support. Rigid cell walls allow plants to stand at various heights—from blades of grass to California redwoods. Plant cell walls are made of a carbohydrate called cellulose, which gives the wall its inflexible characteristics. **Table 7.1** lists cell walls and various other cell structures.

**Cilia and flagella** Some eukaryotic cell surfaces have structures called cilia and flagella that project outside the plasma membrane. As shown in **Figure 7.19, cilia** (singular, cilium) are short, numerous projections that look like hairs. The motion of cilia is similar to the motion of oars in a rowboat. **Flagella** (singular, flagellum) are longer and less numerous than cilia. These projections move with a whiplike motion. Cilia and flagella are composed of microtubules arranged in a 9 + 2 configuration, in which nine pairs of microtubules surround two single microtubules. Typically, a cell has one or two flagella.

Prokaryotic cilia and flagella contain cytoplasm and are enclosed by the plasma membrane. They consist of protein building blocks. While both structures are used for cell movement, cilia are also found on stationary cells.

**Figure 7.19** The hairlike structures in the photomicrograph are cilia, and the tail-like structures are flagella. Both structures function in cell movement.
**Infer** ***Where in the body of an animal would you predict cilia might be found?***

**Cilia on the surface of a *Paramecium***

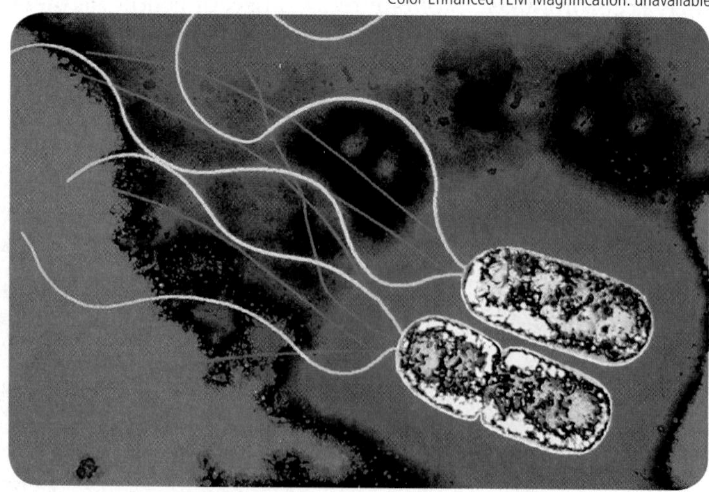


**Bacteria with flagella**

Concepts In Motion
Interactive Table To explore more about cell structures, visit biologygmh.com.

## Table 7.1 Summary of Cell Structures

| Cell Structure | Example | Function | Cell Type |
|---|---|---|---|
| **Cell wall** | | An inflexible barrier that provides support and protects the plant cell | Plant cells, fungi cells, and some prokaryotes |
| **Centrioles** | | Organelles that occur in pairs and are important for cell division | Animal cells and most protist cells |
| **Chloroplast** | | A double-membrane organelle with thylakoids containing chlorophyll where photosynthesis takes place | Plant cells only |
| **Cilia** | | Projections from cell surfaces that aid in locomotion and feeding; also used to sweep substances along surfaces | Some animal cells, protist cells, and prokaryotes |
| **Cytoskeleton** | | A framework for the cell within the cytoplasm | All eukaryotic cells |
| **Endoplasmic reticulum** | | A highly folded membrane that is the site of protein synthesis | All eukaryotic cells |
| **Flagella** | | Projections that aid in locomotion and feeding | Some animal cells, prokaryotes, and some plant cells |
| **Golgi apparatus** | | A flattened stack of tubular membranes that modifies proteins and packages them for distribution outside the cell | All eukaryotic cells |
| **Lysosome** | | A vesicle that contains digestive enzymes for the breakdown of excess or worn-out cellular substances | Animal cells only |
| **Mitochondrion** | | A membrane-bound organelle that makes energy available to the rest of the cell | All eukaryotic cells |
| **Nucleus** | | Control center of the cell that contains coded directions for the production of proteins and cell division | All eukaryotic cells |
| **Plasma membrane** | | A flexible boundary that controls the movement of substances into and out of the cell | All eukaryotic cells |
| **Ribosome** | | Organelle that is the site of protein synthesis | All cells |
| **Vacuole** | | A membrane-bound vesicle for the temporary storage of materials | Plant cells–one large; animal cells–a few small |

CAREERS IN BIOLOGY

**Science Communications Specialist** Many publishers of scientific material hire communications specialists to write about research and its importance to the general public. This often is accomplished through press releases, ads, pamphlets, and targeted mailings. For more information on biology careers, visit biologygmh.com.

## Comparing Cells

**Table 7.1** summarizes the structures of eukaryotic plant cells and animal cells. Notice that plant cells contain chlorophyll—they can capture and transform energy from the Sun into a usable form of chemical energy. This is one of the main characteristics that distinguishes plants from animals. In addition, remember that animal cells usually do not contain vacuoles. If they do, vacuoles in animal cells are much smaller than vacuoles in plant cells. Also, animal cells do not have cell walls. Cell walls give plant cells protection and support.

## Organelles at Work

With a basic understanding of the structures found within a cell, it becomes easier to envision how those structures work together to perform cell functions. Take, for example, the synthesis of proteins.

Protein synthesis begins in the nucleus with the information contained in the DNA. Genetic information is copied and transferred to another genetic molecule called RNA. Then RNA and ribosomes, which have been manufactured in the nucleolus, leave the nucleus through the pores of the nuclear membrane. Together, RNA and ribosomes manufacture proteins. Each protein made on the rough ER has a particular function; it might become a protein that forms a part of the plasma membrane, a protein that is released from the cell, or a protein transported to other organelles. Other ribosomes will float freely in the cytoplasm and make proteins as well.

Most of the proteins made on the surface of the ER are sent to the Golgi apparatus. The Golgi apparatus packages the proteins in vesicles and transports them to other organelles or out of the cell. Other organelles use the proteins to carry out cell processes. For example, lysosomes use proteins, enzymes in particular, to digest food and waste. Mitochondria use enzymes to produce a usable form of energy for the cell.

After reading about the organelles in a cell, it becomes clearer why people equate the cell to a factory. Each organelle has its job to do, and the health of the cell depends on all of the components working together.

## Section 7.3 Assessment

### Section Summary

- Eukaryotic cells contain membrane-bound organelles in the cytoplasm that perform cell functions.
- Ribosomes are the sites of protein synthesis.
- Mitochondria are the powerhouses of cells.
- Plant and animal cells contain many of the same organelles, while other organelles are unique to either plant cells or animal cells.

### Understand Main Ideas

1. MAIN Idea **Identify** the role of the nucleus in a eukaryotic cell.
2. **Summarize** the role of the endoplasmic reticulum.
3. **Analogy** Make a flowchart comparing the parts of a cell to an automobile production line.
4. **Infer** why some scientists do not consider ribosomes to be cell organelles.

### Think Scientifically

5. *Hypothesize* how lysosomes would be involved in changing a caterpillar into a butterfly.
6. *WRITING in* **Biology** Categorize the structures and organelles in **Table 7.1** into lists based on cell type, then draw a concept map illustrating your organization.

# Section 7.4

## Objectives

- **Explain** the processes of diffusion, facilitated diffusion, and active transport.
- **Predict** the effect of a hypotonic, hypertonic, or isotonic solution on a cell.
- **Discuss** how large particles enter and exit cells.

## Review Vocabulary

**homeostasis:** regulation of the internal environment of a cell or organism to maintain conditions suitable for life

## New Vocabulary

diffusion
dynamic equilibrium
facilitated diffusion
osmosis
isotonic solution
hypotonic solution
hypertonic solution
active transport
endocytosis
exocytosis

# Cellular Transport

**MAIN Idea Cellular transport moves substances within the cell and moves substances into and out of the cell.**

**Real-World Reading Link** Imagine studying in your room while cookies are baking in the kitchen. You probably didn't notice when the cookies were put into the oven because you couldn't smell them. But, as the cookies baked, the movement of the aroma from the kitchen to your room happened through a process called diffusion.

## Diffusion

**Connection to Chemistry** As the aroma of baking cookies makes its way to you, the particles are moving and colliding with each other in the air. This happens because the particles in gases, liquids, and solids are in random motion. Similarly, substances dissolved in water move constantly in random motion called Brownian motion. This random motion causes **diffusion,** which is the net movement of particles from an area where there are many particles of the substance to an area where there are fewer particles of the substance. The amount of a substance in a particular area is called concentration. Therefore, substances diffuse from areas of high concentration to low concentration. **Figure 7.20** illustrates the process of diffusion. Additional energy input is not required for diffusion because the particles already are in motion.

For example, if you drop red and blue ink into a container of water at opposite ends the container, which is similar to the watery environment of a cell, the process of diffusion begins, as shown in **Figure 7.20(A).** In a short period of time, the ink particles have mixed as a result of diffusion to the point where a purple color blend area is visible. **Figure 7.20(B)** shows the initial result of this diffusion.

**Figure 7.20** Diffusion causes the inks to move from high-ink concentration to low-ink concentration until the colors become evenly blended in the water.

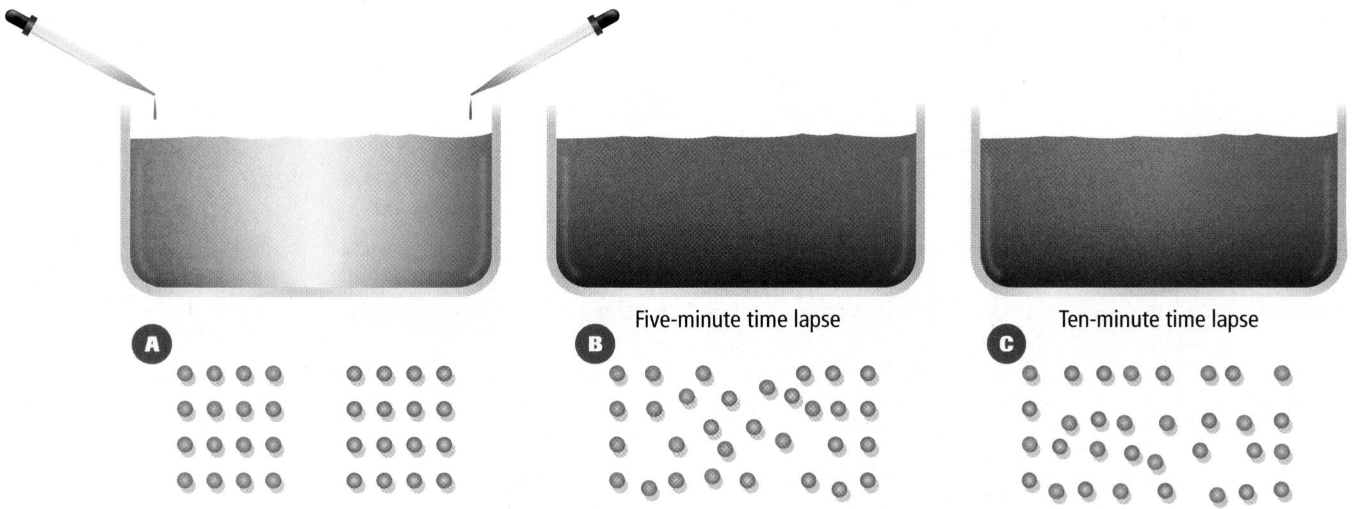

Given more time, the ink particles continue to mix and, in this case, continue to form the uniform purple mixture shown in **Figure 7.20(C).** Mixing continues until the concentrations of red ink and blue ink are the same in all areas. The final result is the purple solution. After this point, the particles continue to move randomly, but no further change in concentration will occur. This condition, in which there is continuous movement but no overall change, is called **dynamic equilibrium.**

**VOCABULARY**

**ACADEMIC VOCABULARY**

**Concentration:**
the amount of component in a given area or volume.
*The concentration of salt in the aquarium was too high, causing the fishes to die.*

One of the key characteristics of diffusion is the rate at which diffusion takes place. Three main factors affect the rate of diffusion: concentration, temperature, and pressure. When concentration is high, diffusion occurs more quickly because there are more particles that collide. Similarly, when the temperature or pressure increases, the number of collisions increases, thus increasing the rate of diffusion. Recall that at higher temperatures particles move faster, and at higher pressure the particles are closer together. In both cases, more collisions occur and diffusion is faster. The size and charge of a substance also affects the rate of diffusion.

**FOLDABLES**
Incorporate information from this section into your Foldable.

**Diffusion across the plasma membrane** In addition to water, cells need certain ions and small molecules, such as chloride ions and sugars, to perform cellular functions. Water can diffuse across the plasma membrane, as shown in **Figure 7.21(A),** but most other substances cannot. Another form of transport, called **facilitated diffusion,** uses transport proteins to move other ions and small molecules across the plasma membrane. By this method, substances move into the cell through a water-filled transport protein called a channel protein that opens and closes to allow the substance to diffuse through the plasma membrane, as shown in **Figure 7.21(B).** Another type of transport protein called a carrier protein also can help substances diffuse across the plasma membrane. Carrier proteins change shape as the diffusion process continues to help move the particle through the membrane, as illustrated in **Figure 7.21(C).**

Diffusion of water and facilitated diffusion of other substances require no additional input of energy because the particles are moving from an area of high concentration to an area of lower concentration. This is also known as passive transport. You will learn later in this section about a form of cellular transport that does require energy input.

**Reading Check** **Describe** how sodium ($Na^+$) ions get into cells.

**Figure 7.21** Although water moves freely through the plasma membrane, other substances cannot pass through the phospholipid bilayer on their own. Such substances enter the cell by facilitated transport.

**Concepts In Motion**
**Interactive Figure** To see an animation of how molecules can be passively transported through a plasma membrane, visit biologygmh.com.

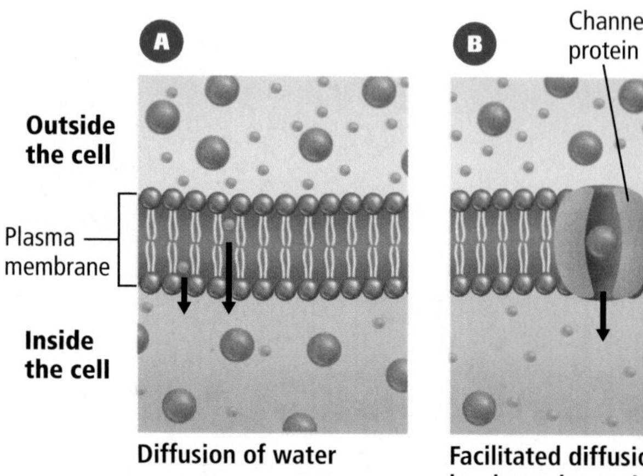


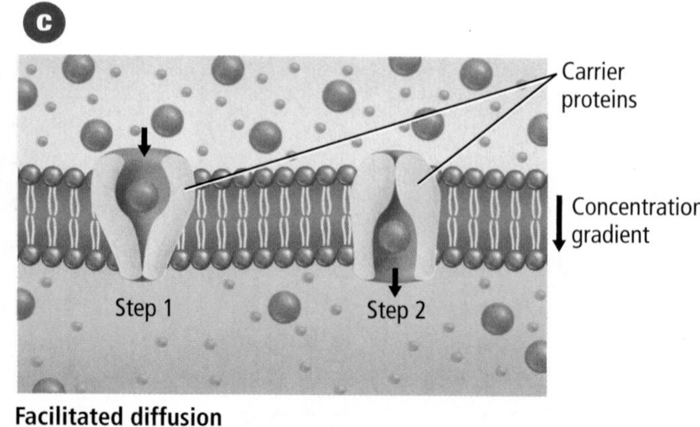

## Osmosis: Diffusion of Water

Water is a substance that passes freely into and out of the cell through the plasma membrane. The diffusion of water across a selectively permeable membrane is called **osmosis** (ahs MOH sus). Regulating the movement of water across the plasma membrane is an important factor in maintaining homeostasis within the cell.

**How osmosis works** Recall that in a solution, a substance called the solute is dissolved in a solvent. Water is the solvent in a cell and its environment. Concentration is a measure of the amount of solute dissolved in a solvent. The concentration of a solution decreases when the amount of solvent increases.

Examine **Figure 7.22** showing a U-shaped tube containing solutions with different sugar concentrations separated by a selectively permeable membrane. What will happen if the solvent (water) can pass through the membrane but the solute (sugar) cannot?

Water molecules diffuse toward the side with the greater sugar concentration—the right side. As water moves to the right, the concentration of the sugar solution decreases. The water continues to diffuse until dynamic equilibrium occurs—the concentration of the solutions is the same on both sides. Notice in **Figure 7.22** that the result is an increase in solution level on the right side. During dynamic equilibrium, water molecules continue to diffuse back and forth across the membrane. But, the concentrations on each side no longer change.

**Reading Check** **Compare and contrast** diffusion and osmosis.

### MiniLab 7.2

### Investigate Osmosis

**What will happen to cells placed in a strong salt solution?** Regulating flow and amount of water into and out of the cell is critical to the survival of that cell. Osmosis is one method used to regulate a cell's water content.

**Procedure**

1. Read and complete the lab safety form.
2. Prepare a control **slide** using **onion epidermis, water,** and **iodine stain** as directed by your teacher.
3. Prepare a test slide using onion epidermis, **salt water,** and iodine stain as directed by your teacher.
4. Predict the effect, if any, that the salt solution will have on the onion cells in the test slide.
5. View the control slide using a **compound microscope** under low power and sketch several onion cells.
6. View the test slide under the same magnification and sketch your observations.

**Analysis**

1. **Analyze and Conclude** Was your prediction correct or incorrect? Explain.
2. **Explain** Use the process of osmosis to explain what you observe.

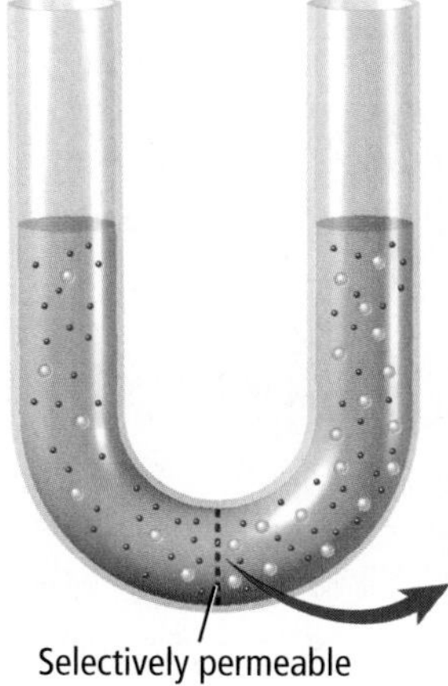


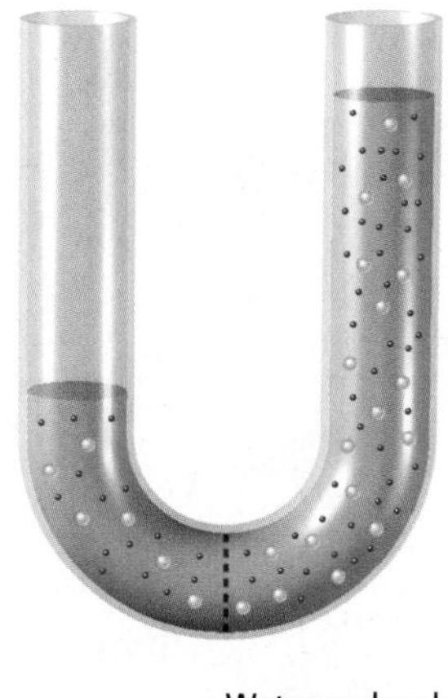


■ **Figure 7.22** Before osmosis, the sugar concentration is greater on the right side. After osmosis, the concentrations are the same on both sides.
**Name** *the term for this phenomenon.*

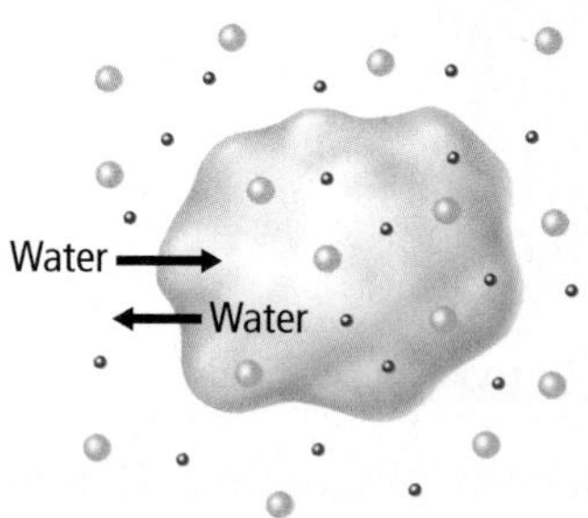


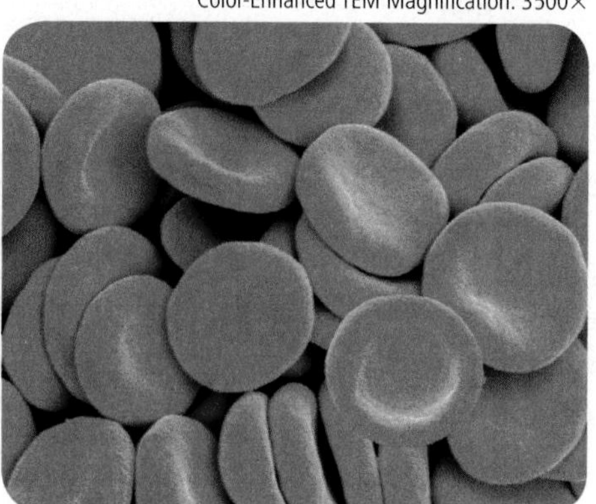


Animal cells

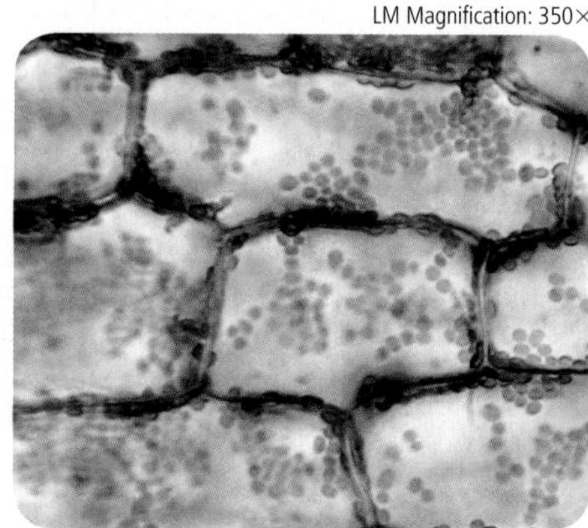


Plant cells

■ **Figure 7.23** In an isotonic solution, water molecules move into and out of the cell at the same rate, and cells retain their normal shape. The animal cell and the plant cell have their normal shape in an isotonic solution.

**Concepts In Motion**

**Interactive Figure** To see an animation of osmosis in an isotonic, hypotonic, or hypertonic solution, visit biologygmh.com.

**Cells in an isotonic solution** When a cell is in a solution that has the same concentration of water and solutes—ions, sugars, proteins, and other substances—as its cytoplasm, the cell is said to be in an **isotonic solution.** *Iso-* comes from the Greek word meaning *equal.* Water still moves through the plasma membrane, but water enters and leaves the cell at the same rate. The cell is at equilibrium with the solution, and there is no net movement of water. The cells retain their normal shape, as shown in **Figure 7.23.** Most cells in organisms are in isotonic solutions, such as blood.

**Cells in a hypotonic solution** If a cell is in a solution that has a lower concentration of solute, the cell is said to be in a **hypotonic solution.** *Hypo-* comes from the Greek word meaning *under.* There is more water outside of the cell than inside. Due to osmosis, the net movement of water through the plasma membrane is into the cell, as illustrated in **Figure 7.24.** Pressure generated as water flows through the plasma membrane is called osmotic pressure. In an animal cell, as water moves into the cell, the pressure increases and the plasma membrane swells. If the solution is extremely hypotonic, the plasma membrane might be unable to withstand this pressure and the cell might burst.

Because they have a rigid cell wall that supports the cell, plant cells do not burst when in a hypotonic solution. As the pressure inside the cell increases, the plant's central vacuole fills with water, pushing the plasma membrane against the cell wall, shown in the plant cell in **Figure 7.24.** Instead of bursting, the plant cell becomes firmer. Grocers use this process to keep produce looking fresh by misting fruits and vegetables with water.

■ **Figure 7.24** In a hypotonic solution, water enters a cell by osmosis, causing the cell to swell. Animal cells may continue to swell until they burst. Plant cells swell beyond their normal size as internal pressure increases.

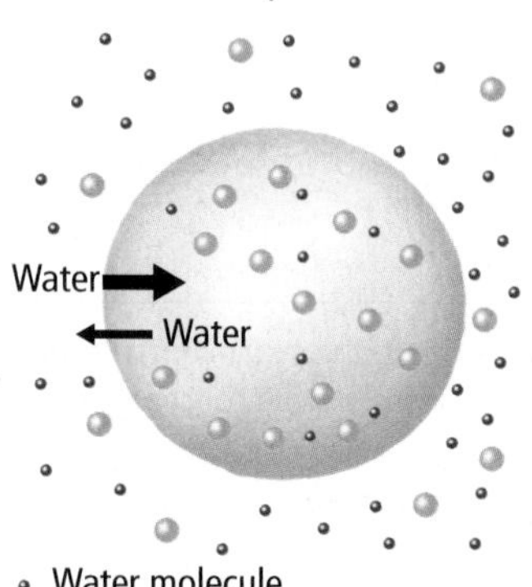

Animal cells

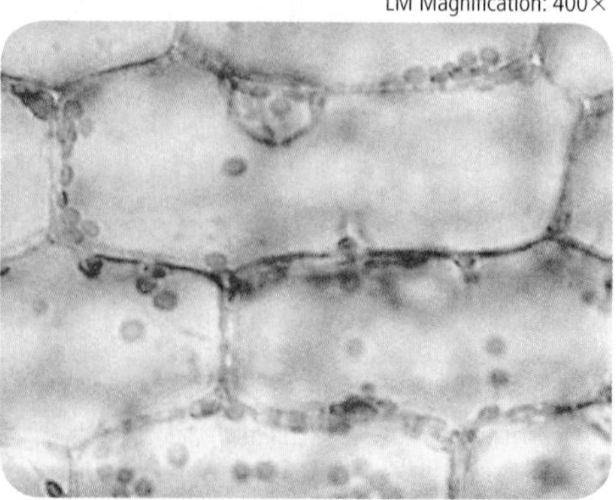


Plant cells

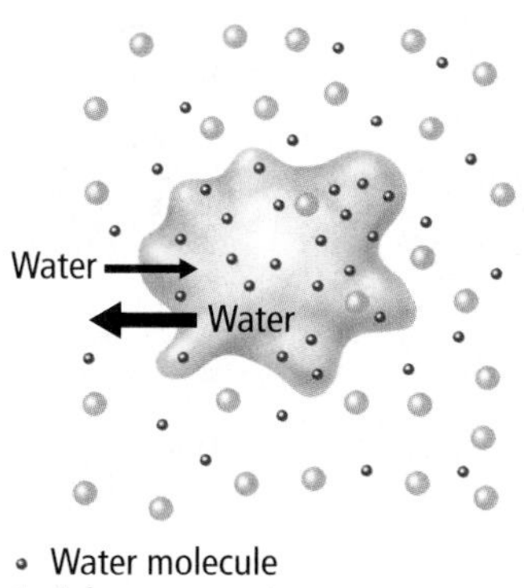


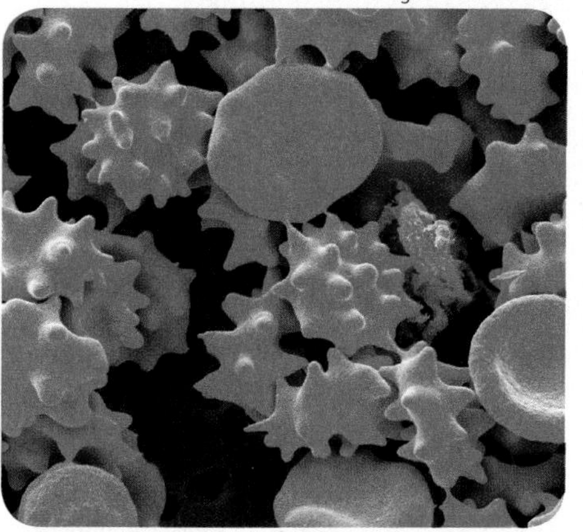


**Animal cells**

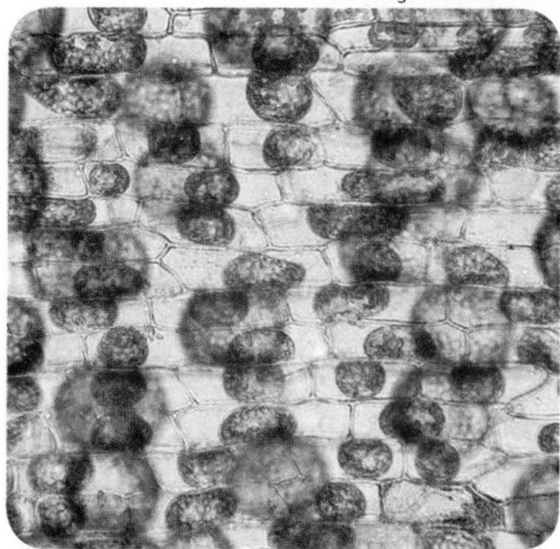


**Plant cells**

**Figure 7.25** In a hypertonic solution, water leaves a cell by osmosis, causing the cell to shrink. Animal cells shrivel up as they lose water. As plant cells lose internal pressure, the plasma membrane shrinks away from the cell wall.

**Cells in a hypertonic solution** When a cell is placed in a **hypertonic solution,** the concentration of the solute outside of the cell is higher than inside. *Hyper-* comes from the Greek word meaning *above.* During osmosis, the net movement of water is out of the cell, as illustrated in **Figure 7.25.** Animal cells in a hypertonic solution shrivel because of decreased pressure in the cells. Plant cells in a hypertonic solution lose water, mainly from the central vacuole. The plasma membrane shrinks away from the cell wall. Loss of water in a plant cell causes wilting.

## Active Transport

Sometimes substances must move from a region of lower concentration to a region of higher concentration against the passive movement from higher to lower concentration. This movement of substances across the plasma membrane against a concentration gradient requires energy, therefore, it is called **active transport. Figure 7.26** illustrates how active transport occurs with the aid of carrier proteins, commonly called pumps. Some pumps move one type of substance in only one direction, while others move two substances either across the membrane in the same direction or in opposite directions. Due to active transport, the cell maintains the proper balance of substances it needs. Active transport helps maintain homeostasis.

**Figure 7.26** Carrier proteins pick up and move substances across the plasma membrane against the concentration gradient and into the cell.
**Explain** ***Why does active transport require energy?***

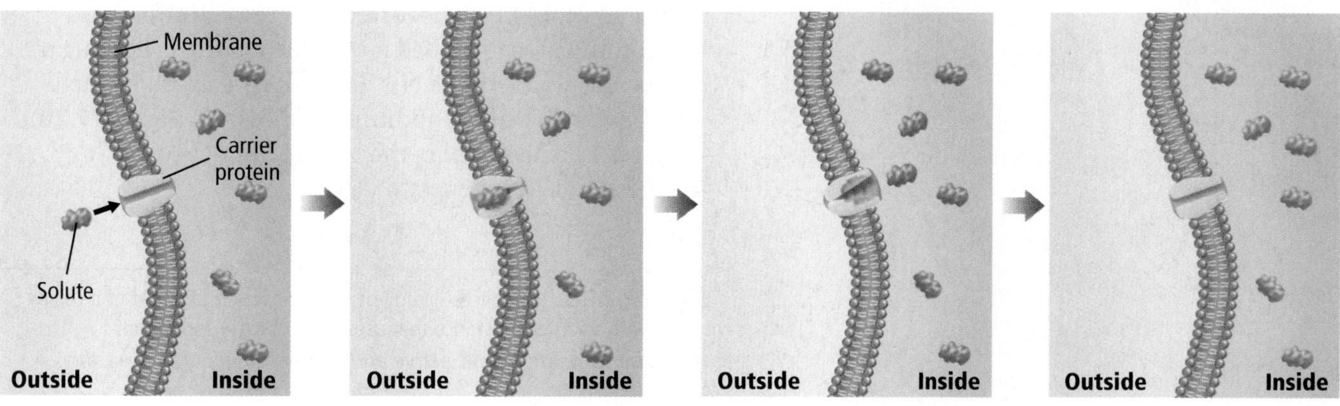

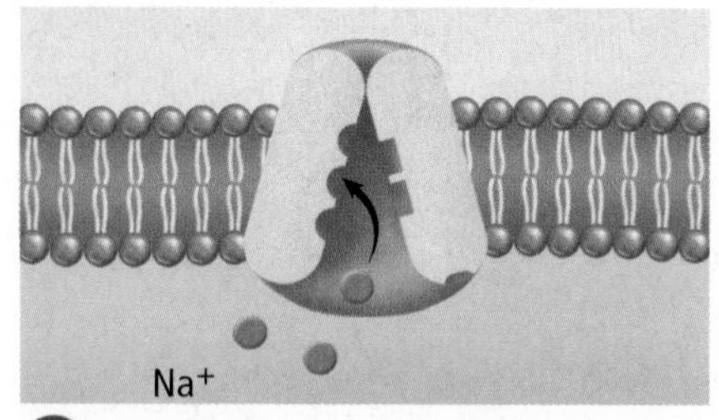


**A** Protein in the membrane binds intracellular sodium ions.

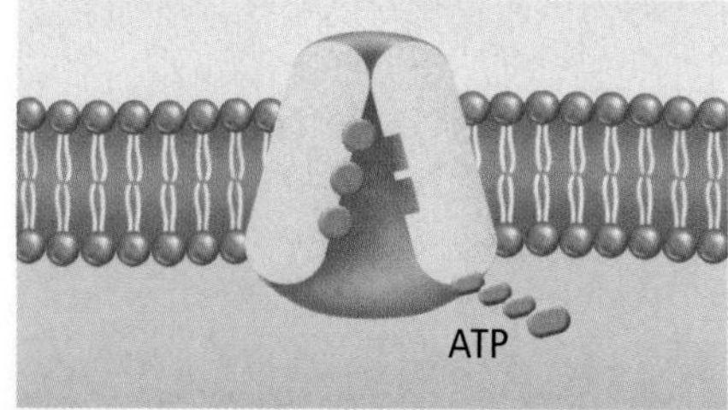


**B** ATP attaches to protein with bound sodium ions.

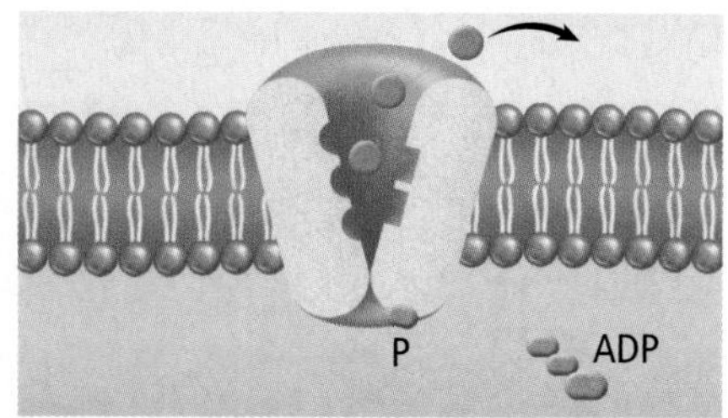


**C** The breakdown of ATP causes shape change in protein, allowing sodium ions to leave.

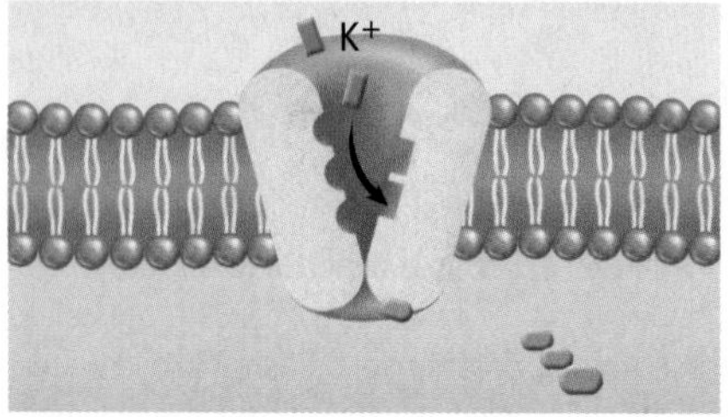


**D** Extracellular potassium ions bind to exposed sites.

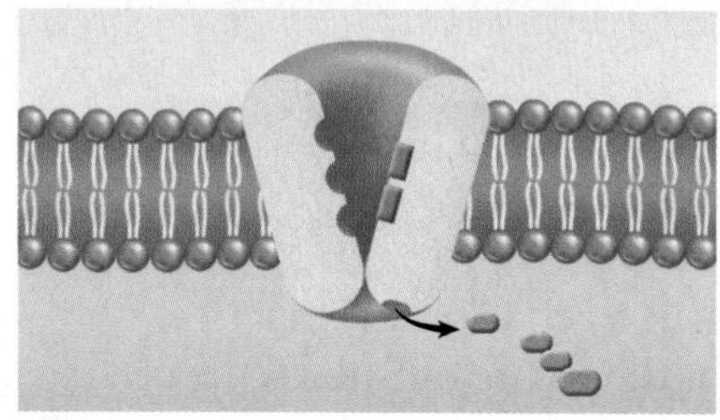

**E** Binding of potassium causes release of phosphate from protein.

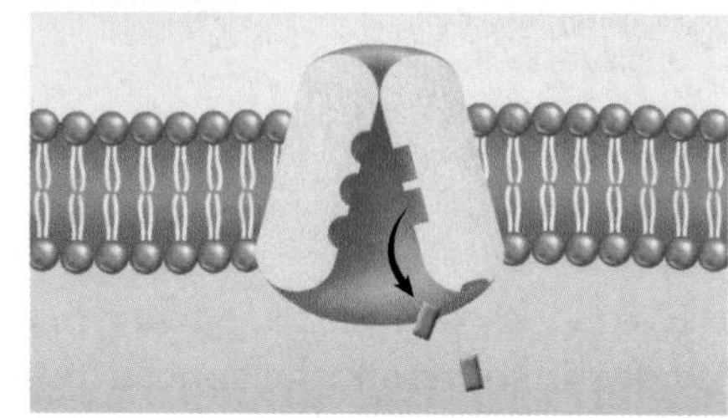

**F** Phospate release changes protein back to its original shape, and potassium ions move into the cell.

**Figure 7.27** Some cells use elaborate pumping systems, such as the $Na^+/K^+$ ATPase pump shown here, to help move substances through the plasma membrane.

**Concepts In Motion**

**Interactive Figure** To see an animation of how a $Na^+/K^+$ ATPase pump can actively transport molecules against a concentration gradient, visit biologygmh.com.

**$Na^+/K^+$ ATPase pump** One common active transport pump is called the sodium-potassium ATPase pump. This pump is found in the plasma membrane of animal cells. The pump maintains the level of sodium ions ($Na^+$) and potassium ions ($K^+$) inside and outside the cell. This protein pump is an enzyme that catalyzes the breakdown of an energy-storing molecule. The pump uses the energy in order to transport three sodium ions out of the cell while moving two potassium ions into the cell. The high level of sodium on the outside of the cell creates a concentration gradient. Follow the steps in **Figure 7.27** to see the action of the $Na^+/K^+$ ATPase pump.

The activity of the $Na^+/K^+$ ATPase pump can result in yet another form of cellular transport. Substances, such as sugar molecules, must come into the cell from the outside, where the concentration of the substance is lower than inside. This requires energy. Recall, however, that the $Na^+/K^+$ ATPase pump moves $Na^+$ out of the cell, which creates a low concentration of $Na^+$ inside the cell. In a process called coupled transport, the $Na^+$ ions that have been pumped out of the cell can couple with sugar molecules and be transported into the cell through a membrane protein called a coupled channel. The sugar molecule, coupled to a $Na^+$ ion, enters the cell by facilitated diffusion of the sodium, as shown in **Figure 7.28.** As a result, sugar enters the cell without spending any additional cellular energy.

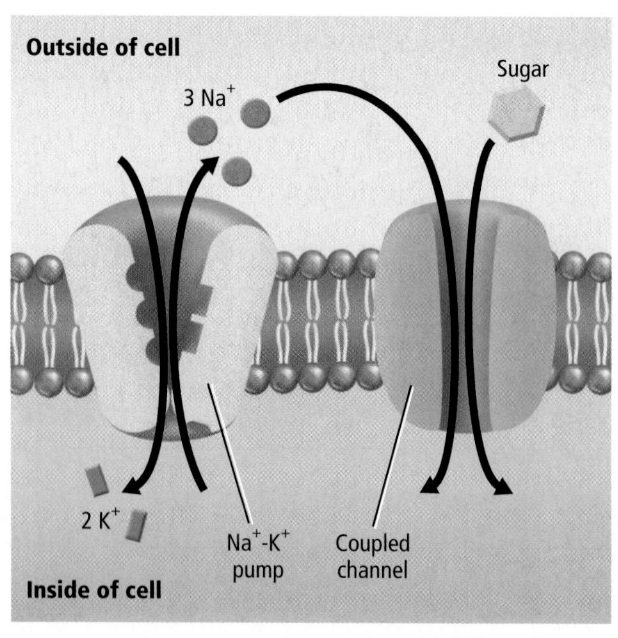


**Figure 7.28** Substances "piggy-back" their way into or out of a cell by coupling with another substance that uses an active transport pump.
**Compare and contrast** *active and passive transport across the plasma membrane.*

# Assessment

## Section 7.1

### Vocabulary Review

*Each of the following sentences is false. Make the sentence true by replacing the italicized word with a vocabulary term from the Study Guide page.*

1. The *nucleus* is a structure that surrounds a cell and helps control what enters and exits the cell.
2. A(n) *prokaryote* has membrane-bound organelles.
3. *Organelles* are basic units of all organisms.

### Understand Key Concepts

4. If a microscope has a series of three lenses that magnify individually 5×, 5×, and 7×, what is the total magnification when looking through the microscope?
   **A.** 25× **C.** 17×
   **B.** 35× **D.** 175×
5. Which is not part of the cell theory?
   **A.** The basic unit of life is the cell.
   **B.** Cells came from preexisting cells.
   **C.** All living organisms are composed of cells.
   **D.** Cells contain membrane-bound organelles.

*Use the photo to answer question 6.*

Color-Enhanced TEM Magnification: 8000×

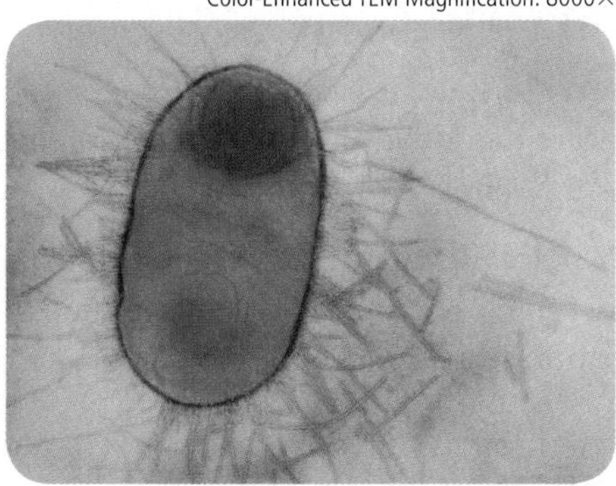

6. The photomicrograph shows which kind of cell?
   **A.** prokaryotic cell **C.** animal cell
   **B.** eukaryotic cell **D.** plant cell

### Constructed Response

7. **Open Ended** Explain how the development of the microscope changed how scientists studied living organisms.
8. **Short Answer** Compare and contrast prokaryotic cells and eukaryotic cells.

### Think Critically

9. **CAREERS IN BIOLOGY** Why might a microscopist, who specializes in the use of microscopes to examine specimens, use a light microscope instead of an electron microscope?
10. **Analyze** A material is found in an asteroid that might be a cell. What criteria must the material meet to be considered a cell?

## Section 7.2

### Vocabulary Review

*Complete the sentences below using vocabulary terms from the Study Guide page.*

11. A __________ is the basic structure molecule making up the plasma membrane.
12. The __________ is the component that surrounds all cells.
13. __________ is the property that allows only some substances in and out of a cell.

### Understand Key Concepts

14. Which of the following orientations of phospholipids best represents the phospholipid bilayer of the plasma membrane?

**A.** 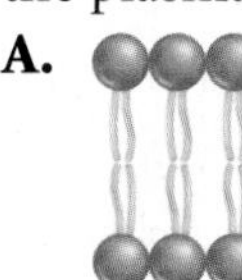 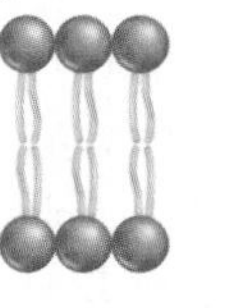

**C.** 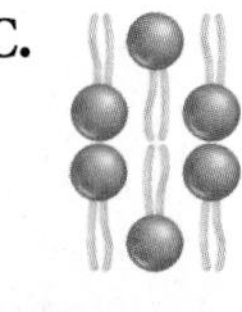

**B.** 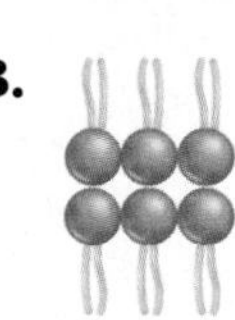

**D.** 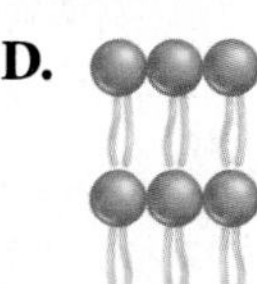

15. Which situation would increase the fluidity of a phospholipid bilayer?
    **A.** decreasing the temperature
    **B.** increasing the number of proteins
    **C.** increasing the number of cholesterol molecules
    **D.** increasing the number of unsaturated fatty acids

### Constructed Response

16. **Short Answer** Explain how the plasma membrane maintains homeostasis within a cell.

17. **Open Ended** Explain what a mosaic is and then explain why the term *fluid mosaic model* is used to describe the plasma membrane.

18. **Short Answer** How does the orientation of the phospholipids in the bilayer allow a cell to interact with its internal and external environments?

### Think Critically

19. **Hypothesize** how a cell would be affected if it lost the ability to be selectively permeable.

20. **Predict** What might happen to a cell if it no longer could produce cholesterol?

## Section 7.3

### Vocabulary Review

*Fill in the blank with the vocabulary term from the Study Guide page that matches the function definition.*

21. __________ stores wastes

22. __________ produces ribosomes

23. __________ generates energy for a cell

24. __________ sorts proteins into vesicles

### Understand Key Concepts

*Use the diagram below to answer questions 25 and 26.*

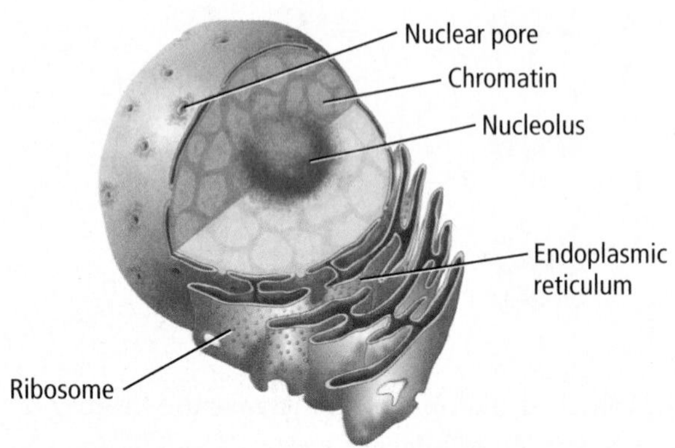


25. Which structure synthesizes proteins that will be used by the cell?
    **A.** chromatin
    **B.** nucleolus
    **C.** ribosome
    **D.** endoplasmic reticulum

26. Where are the ribosomes produced?
    **A.** nuclear pore
    **B.** nucleolus
    **C.** chromatin
    **D.** endoplasmic reticulum

27. In which structure would you expect to find a cell wall?
    **A.** a human skin cell
    **B.** a cell from an oak tree
    **C.** a blood cell from a cat
    **D.** a liver cell from a mouse

### Constructed Response

28. **Short Answer** Describe why the cytoskeleton within the cytoplasm was a recent discovery.

29. **Short Answer** Compare the structures and functions of the mitochondrion and chloroplast below.

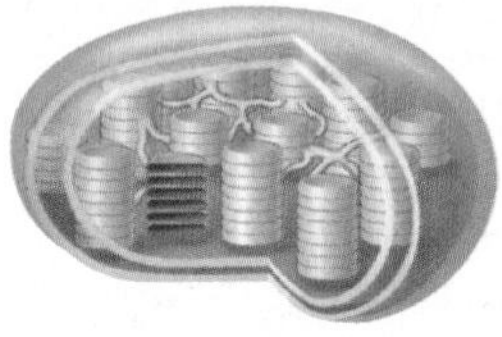

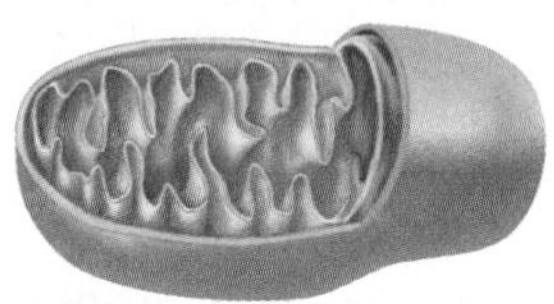

30. **Open Ended** Suggest a reason why packets of proteins collected in a vacuole might merge with lysosomes.

### Think Critically

31. **Identify** a specific example where the cell wall structure has aided the survival of a plant in its natural habitat.

32. **Infer** Explain why plant cells that transport water against the force of gravity contain many more mitochondria than other plant cells.

## Section 7.4

### Vocabulary Review

*Explain the difference in the terms given below. Then explain how the terms are related.*

33. active transport, facilitated diffusion

34. endocytosis, exocytosis

35. hypertonic solution, hypotonic solution

## Understand Key Concepts

36. Which is not a factor that affects the rate of diffusion?
   A. conductivity
   B. concentration
   C. pressure
   D. temperature

37. Which type of transport requires energy input from the cell?
   A. active transport
   B. facilitated diffusion
   C. osmosis
   D. simple diffusion

## Constructed Response

38. **Short Answer** Why is active transport an energy-utilizing process?

39. **Short Answer** Some protists that live in a hypotonic pond environment have cell membrane adaptations that slow water uptake. What adaptations might this protist living in the hypertonic Great Salt Lake have?

LM Magnification: 75×

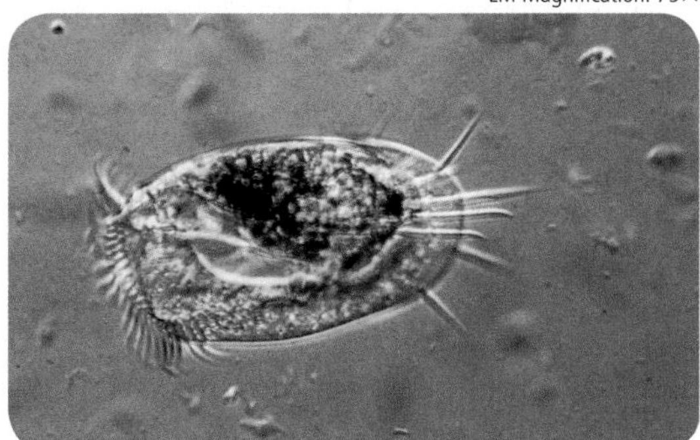

40. **Short Answer:** Summarize how cellular transport helps maintain homeostasis within a cell.

## Think Critically

41. **Hypothesize** how oxygen crosses the plasma membrane if the concentration of oxygen is lower inside the cell than it is outside the cell.

42. **Analyze** Farming and watering that is done in very dry regions of the world leaves salts that accumulate in the soil as water evaporates. Based on what you know about concentration gradients, why does increasing soil salinity have adverse effects on plant cells?

## Additional Assessment

43. WRITING in Biology Create a poem that decribes the functions of at least five cell organelles.

### Document-Based Questions

*The graph below describes the relationship between the amount of glucose entering a cell and the rate at which the glucose enters the cell with the help of carrier proteins. Use this graph to answer questions 44 and 45.*

Data obtained from: Raven, P.H., and Johnson, G.B. 2002. *Biology*, 6th ed.: 99.

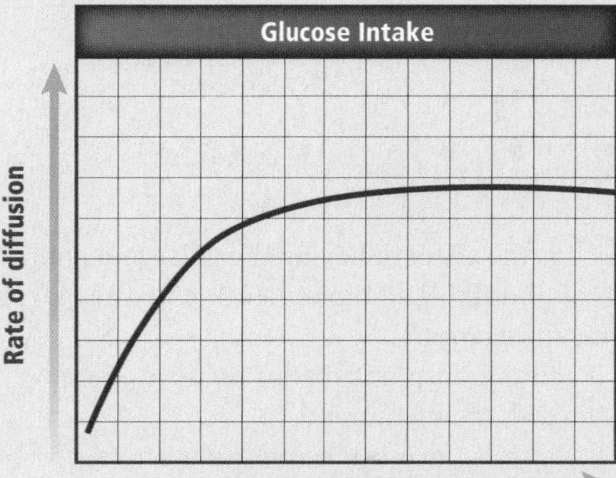


44. Summarize the relationship between the amount of glucose and the rate of diffusion.

45. Infer why the rate of diffusion tapers off with higher amounts of glucose. Make an illustration to explain your answer.

## Cumulative Review

46. Rabbits were introduced into Australia in the 1800s. The population of rabbits grew unchecked. Explain why this occurred and how this could adversely affect an ecosystem. **(Chapter 3)**

47. Algae are a group of plantlike organisms. Many of these organisms produce their own food by photosynthesis. Are these organisms autotrophs or heterotrophs? Explain. **(Chapter 2)**

# Standardized Test Practice

**Cumulative**

## Multiple Choice

*Use the illustration below to answer questions 1 and 2.*

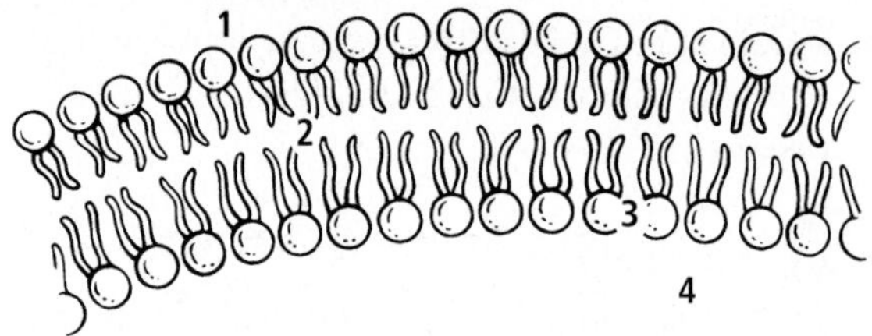


1. Which number in the illustration represents the location where you would expect to find water-insoluble substances?
   A. 1
   B. 2
   C. 3
   D. 4

2. Which is the effect of having the polar and nonpolar ends of phospholipid molecules oriented as they are in this illustration?
   A. It allows transport proteins to move easily through the membrane.
   B. It controls the movement of substances across the membrane.
   C. It helps the cell to maintain its characteristic shape.
   D. It makes more room inside the phospholipid bilayer.

3. Which of these habitats would be best suited for a population of *r*-strategists?
   A. desert
   B. grassland
   C. deciduous forest
   D. tropical rain forest

4. Which adaptation helps plants survive in a tundra biome?
   A. deciduous leaves that fall off as winter approaches
   B. leaves that store water
   C. roots that grow only a few centimeters deep
   D. underground stems that are protected from grazing animals

5. Which is a nonrenewable resource?
   A. clean water from freshwater sources
   B. energy provided by the Sun
   C. an animal species that has become extinct
   D. a type of fish that is caught in the ocean

*Use this incomplete equation to answer questions 6 and 7.*

$$CH_4 + 4Cl_2 \rightarrow \_\_HCl + \_\_CCl_4$$

6. The chemical equation above shows what can happen in a reaction between methane and chlorine gas. The coefficients have been left out in the product side of the equation. Which is the correct coefficient for HCl?
   A. 1
   B. 2
   C. 4
   D. 8

7. Which is the minimum number of chlorine (Cl) atoms needed for the reaction shown in the equation?
   A. 1
   B. 2
   C. 4
   D. 8

8. Why is *Caulerpa taxifolia* considered an invasive species in some coastal areas of North America?
   A. It is dangerous to humans.
   B. It is nonnative to the area.
   C. It grows slowly and invades over time.
   D. It outcompetes native species for resources.

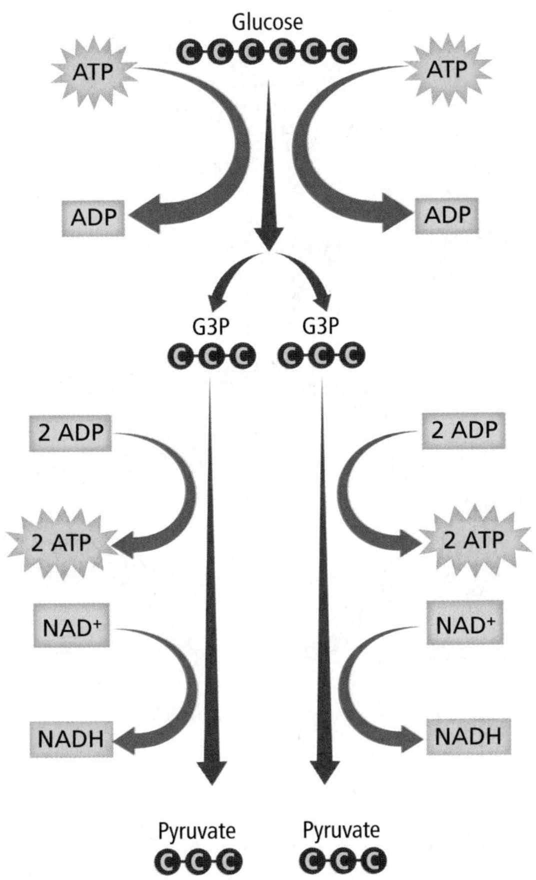

**Figure 8.12** Glucose is broken down during glycolysis inside the cytoplasm of cells.
**Summarize** *the reactants and products of glycolysis.*

## Glycolysis

Glucose is broken down in the cytoplasm through the process of **glycolysis.** Two molecules of ATP and two molecules of NADH are formed for each molecule of glucose that is broken down. Follow along with **Figure 8.12** as you read about the steps of glycolysis.

First, two phosphate groups, derived from two molecules of ATP, are joined to glucose. Notice that some energy, two ATP, is required to start the reactions that will produce energy for the cell. The 6-carbon molecule is then broken down into two 3-carbon compounds. Next, two phosphates are added and electrons and hydrogen ions ($H^+$) combine with two $NAD^+$ molecules to form two NADH molecules. $NAD^+$ is similar to NADP, an electron carrier used during photosynthesis. Last, the two 3-carbon compounds are converted into two molecules of pyruvate. At the same time, four molecules of ATP are produced.

**Reading Check** **Explain** why there is a net yield of two, not four, ATP molecules in glycolysis.

## Krebs Cycle

Glycolysis has a net result of two ATP and two pyruvate. Most of the energy from the glucose is still contained in the pyruvate. In the presence of oxygen, pyruvate is transported into the mitochondrial matrix, where it is eventually converted to carbon dioxide. The series of reactions in which pyruvate is broken down into carbon dioxide is called the **Krebs cycle** or tricarboxylic acid (TCA) cycle. This cycle also is referred to as the citric acid cycle.

**VOCABULARY**

**WORD ORIGIN**

**Glycolysis**
comes from the Greek words *glykys,* meaning *sweet*
and *lysis,* meaning *to rupture or break.*

**FOLDABLES**
Incorporate information from this section into your Foldable.

■ **Figure 8.13** Pyruvate is broken down into carbon dioxide during the Krebs cycle inside the mitochondria of cells.
**Trace** ***Follow the path of carbon molecules that enter and leave the Krebs cycle.***

**Concepts In Motion**
**Interactive Figure** To see an animation of the Krebs cycle, visit biologygmh.com.

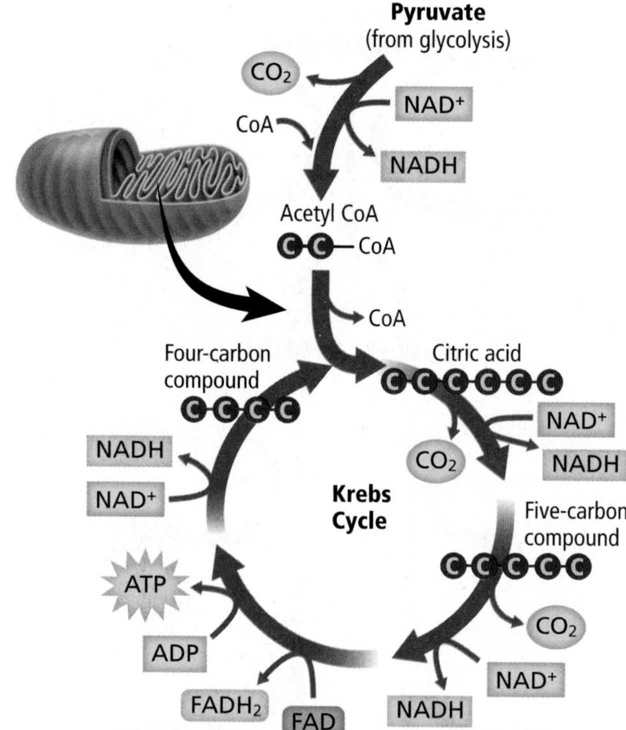


*Study Tip*

**Clarifying Statement** Work with a partner to read the text and discuss unfamiliar words and difficult concepts. Write a clarifying statement to summarize the Krebs cycle.

**Steps of the Krebs cycle** Prior to the Krebs cycle, pyruvate first reacts with coenzyme A (CoA) to form a 2-carbon intermediate called acetyl CoA. At the same time, carbon dioxide is released and $NAD^+$ is converted to NADH. Acetyl CoA then moves to the mitochondrial matrix. The reaction results in the production of two carbon dioxide molecules and two NADH. Follow along in **Figure 8.13** as you continue reading about the steps of the Krebs cycle.

- The Krebs cycle begins with acetyl CoA combining with a 4-carbon compound to form a 6-carbon compound known as citric acid.
- Citric acid is then broken down in the next series of steps, releasing two molecules of carbon dioxide and generating one ATP, three NADH, and one $FADH_2$. FAD is another electron carrier similar to $NAD^+$ and $NADP^+$.
- Finally, acetyl CoA and citric acid are generated and the cycle continues.

Recall that two molecules of pyruvate are formed during glycolysis, resulting in two "turns" of the Krebs cycle for each glucose molecule. The net yield from the Krebs cycle is six carbon dioxide molecules, two ATP, eight NADH, and two $FADH_2$. NADH and $FADH_2$ move on to play a significant role in the next stage of aerobic respiration.

**CAREERS IN BIOLOGY**

**Bioenergeticist** A researcher who studies energy transfers in cells is a bioenergeticist. Some bioenergeticists study mitochondria and their relationship to aging and disease. To learn more about biology careers, visit biologygmh.com.

## Electron Transport

In aerobic respiration, electron transport is the final step in the breakdown of glucose. It also is the point at which most of the ATP is produced. High-energy electrons and hydrogen ions from NADH and $FADH_2$ produced in the Krebs cycle are used to convert ADP to ATP.

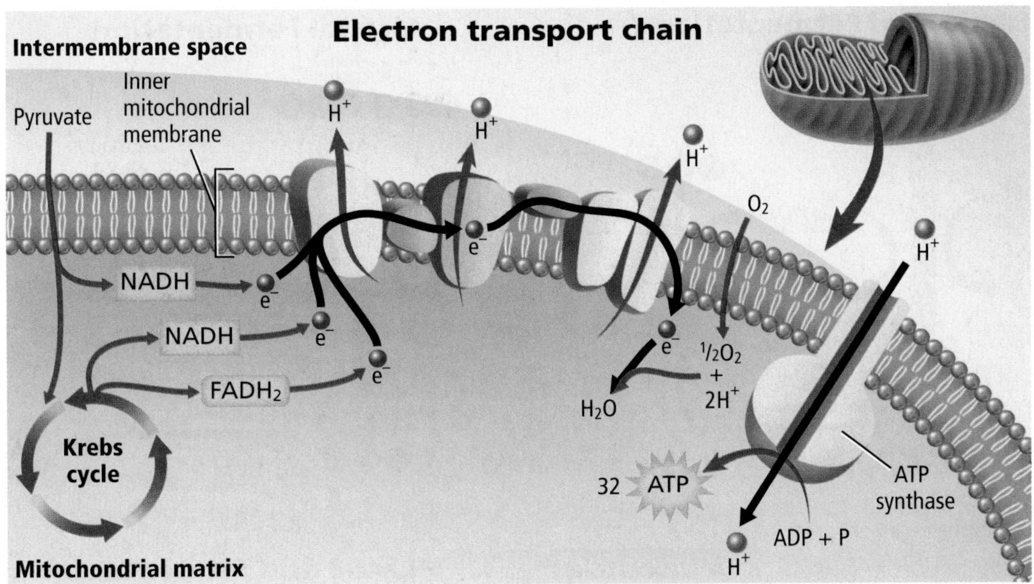


■ **Figure 8.14** Electron transport occurs along the mitochondrial membrane.
**Compare and contrast** ***electron transport in cellular respiration and photosynthesis.***

As shown in **Figure 8.14,** electrons move along the mitochondrial membrane from one protein to another. As NADH and $FADH_2$ release electrons, the energy carriers are converted to $NAD^+$ and FAD, and $H^+$ ions are released into the mitochondrial matrix. The $H^+$ ions are pumped into the mitochondrial matrix across the inner mitochondrial membrane. $H^+$ ions then diffuse down their concentration gradient back across the membrane and into the matrix through ATP synthase molecules in chemiosmosis. Electron transport and chemiosmosis in cellular respiration are similar to these processes in photosynthesis. Oxygen is the final electron acceptor in the electron transport system in cellular respiration. Protons and electrons are transferred to oxygen to form water.

Overall, electron transport produces 24 ATP. Each NADH molecule produces three ATP and each group of three $FADH_2$ produces two ATP. In eukaryotes, one molecule of glucose yields 36 ATP.

**Prokaryotic cellular respiration** Some prokaryotes also undergo aerobic respiration. Because prokaryotes do not have mitochondria, there are a few differences in the process. The main difference involves the use of the prokaryotic cellular membrane as the location of electron transport. In eukaryotic cells, pyruvate is transported to the mitochondria. In prokaryotes, this movement is unnecessary, saving the prokaryotic cell two ATP, and increasing the net total of ATP produced to 38.

**Vocabulary**

**Science usage v. Common usage**

**Concentration**

***Science usage:*** the relative amount of a substance dissolved in another substance.
*The concentration of hydrogen ions is greater on one side of the membrane than the other.*

***Common usage:*** the directing of close, undivided attention.
*The student's concentration was focused on the exam.*

## Anaerobic Respiration

Some cells can function for a short time when oxygen levels are low. Some prokaryotes are anaerobic organisms—they grow and reproduce without oxygen. In some cases these cells continue to produce ATP through glycolysis. However, there are problems with solely relying on glycolysis for energy. Glycolysis only provides two net ATP for each molecule of glucose, and a cell has a limited amount of $NAD^+$. Glycolysis will stop when all the $NAD^+$ is used up if there is not a process to replenish $NAD^+$. The anaerobic pathway that follows glycolysis is anaerobic respiration, or fermentation. **Fermentation** occurs in the cytoplasm and regenerates the cell's supply of $NAD^+$ while producing a small amount of ATP. The two main types of fermentation are lactic acid fermentation and alcohol fermentation.

**Lactic Acid Fermentation**

Glucose

GLYCOLYSIS

2 ADP

ATP

$NAD^+$

NADH

2 Lactic acid

2 Pyruvate

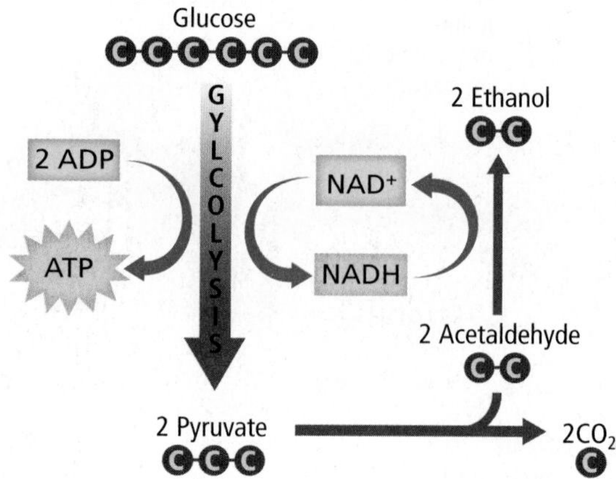


**Figure 8.15** When oxygen is absent or in limited supply, fermentation can occur. **Compare and contrast** *lactic acid fermentation and alcohol fermentation.*

**Connection to Health** **Lactic acid fermentation** In lactic acid fermentation, enzymes convert the pyruvate made during glycolysis to lactic acid, as shown in **Figure 8.15.** This involves the transfer of high-energy electrons and protons from NADH. Skeletal muscle produces lactic acid when the body cannot supply enough oxygen, such as during periods of strenuous exercise. When lactic acid builds up in muscle cells, muscles become fatigued and might feel sore. Lactic acid also is produced by several microorganisms that often are used to produce many foods, including cheese, yogurt, and sour cream.

**Alcohol fermentation** Alcohol fermentation occurs in yeast and some bacteria. **Figure 8.15** shows the chemical reaction that occurs during alcohol fermentation when pyruvate is converted to ethyl alcohol and carbon dioxide. Similar to lactic acid fermentation, NADH donates electrons during this reaction and $NAD^+$ is regenerated.

## DATA ANALYSIS LAB 8.1

**Based On Real Data***

### Interpret the Data

**How does viral infection affect cellular respiration?** Infection by viruses can significantly affect cellular respiration and the ability of cells to produce ATP. To test the effect of viral infection on the stages of cellular respiration, cells were infected with a virus, and the amount of lactic acid and ATP produced were measured.

**Data and Observations**

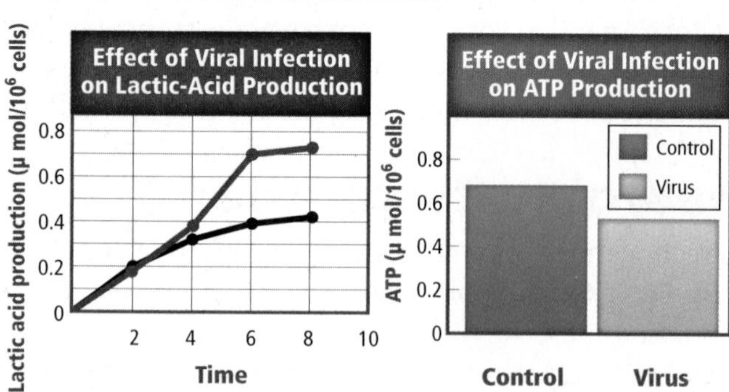


**Think Critically**

1. **Analyze** How did the virus affect lactic acid production in the cells?
2. **Calculate** After 8 h, by what percentage was the lactic acid higher in the virus group than in the control group? By what percentage was ATP production decreased?
3. **Infer** why having a virus like the flu might make a person feel tired.

Data obtained from: El-Bacha, T., et al. 2004. Mayaro virus infection alters glucose metabolism in cultured cells through activation of the enzyme 6-phosphofructo 1-kinase. *Molecular and Cellular Biochemistry* 266: 191–198.

## Short Answer

*Use the illustration below to answer question 10.*

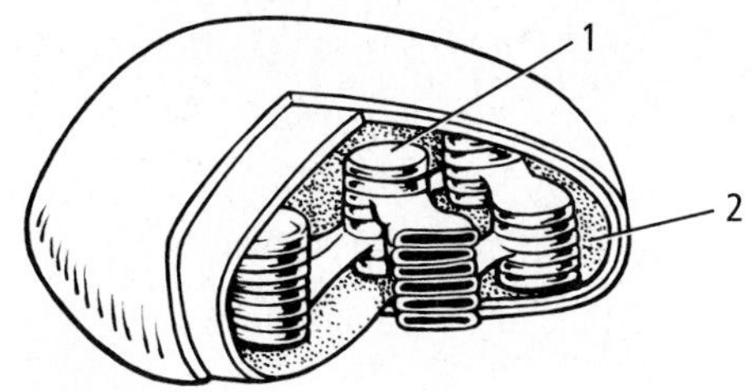


10. The diagram above shows a chloroplast. Name the two parts shown in the diagram and state which phase of photosynthesis occurs in each part.

11. Compare and contrast the structure of a cell wall and the structure of a cell membrane.

12. Relate the bonds between phosphate groups in ATP to the release of energy when a molecule of ATP is changed to ADP.

13. Name three components of a cell's plasma membrane and explain why each component is important for the function of the cell.

14. What kind of mixture is formed by stirring a small amount of table salt into water until the salt all dissolves? Identify the components of this mixture.

15. In which parts of a plant would you expect to find cells with the most chloroplasts? Explain your answer.

16. Long-distance runners often talk about training to raise their anaerobic threshold. The anaerobic threshold is the point at which certain muscles do not have enough oxygen to perform aerobic respiration and begin to perform anaerobic respiration. Hypothesize why you think it is important for competitive runners to raise their anaerobic threshold.

## Extended Response

*Use the graph below to answer question 17.*

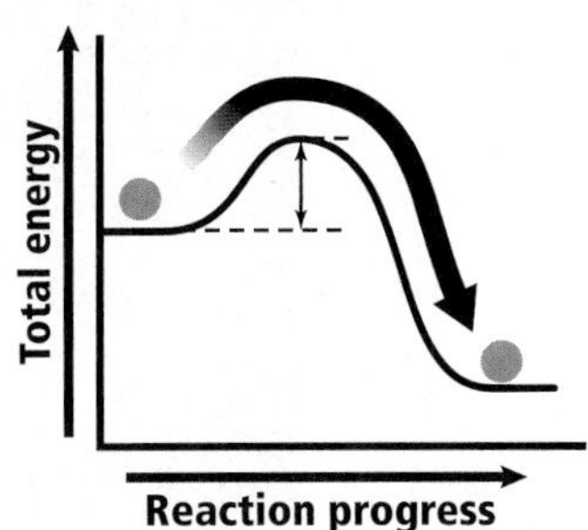


17. The graph shows the effect of an enzyme involved in the breakdown of proteins in the digestive system. Hypothesize how protein digestion would be different in a person who does not have this enzyme.

18. Which organelle would you expect to find in large numbers in cells that pump stomach acid out against a concentration gradient? Give a reason for your answer.

## Essay Question

The human body constantly interacts with the environment, taking in some substances and releasing others. Many substances humans take in have a specific role in maintaining basic cellular processes such as respiration, ion transport, and synthesis of various macromolecules. Likewise, many of the substances released by the body are waste products of cellular processes.

*Using the information in the paragraph above, answer the following question in essay format.*

19. Write an essay that explains how humans take in substances that are important for cellular respiration, and how they release the waste products from this process.

| NEED EXTRA HELP? | | | | | | | | | | | | | | | | | | | |
|---|---|---|---|---|---|---|---|---|---|---|---|---|---|---|---|---|---|---|---|
| If You Missed Question . . . | 1 | 2 | 3 | 4 | 5 | 6 | 7 | 8 | 9 | 10 | 11 | 12 | 13 | 14 | 15 | 16 | 17 | 18 | 19 |
| Review Section . . . | 6.1 | 4.1 | 7.4 | 8.2 | 5.2 | 6.4 | 8.1 | 7.1 | 1.3 | 8.2 | 7.3 | 8.1 | 7.2 | 6.3 | 7.3 | 8.3 | 6.2 | 7.2, 7.4 | 8.3 |

# CHAPTER 9 Cellular Reproduction

### Section 1
**Cellular Growth**

MAIN Idea Cells grow until they reach their size limit, then they either stop growing or divide.

### Section 2
**Mitosis and Cytokinesis**

MAIN Idea Eukaryotic cells reproduce by mitosis, the process of nuclear division, and cytokinesis, the process of cytoplasm division.

### Section 3
**Cell Cycle Regulation**

MAIN Idea The normal cell cycle is regulated by cyclin proteins.

## BioFacts

- Most animals stop growing once they reach a certain size, while most plants continue growing as long as they are alive.
- Plant roots contain regions where, at any given time, large numbers of cells undergo mitosis.
- Chemical treatments or changes in environmental conditions inhibit mitosis in onions, which prevents sprouting and extends storage times.

Root tip cells undergoing mitosis
Stained LM Magnification: 160×

Onion root tip
Stained LM Magnification: 50×

# Start-Up Activities

## LAUNCH Lab

### From where do healthy cells come?

All living things are composed of cells. The only way an organism can grow or heal itself is by cellular reproduction. Healthy cells perform vital life functions, and they reproduce to form more cells. In this lab you will investigate the appearance of different cell types.

**Procedure**

1. Read and complete the lab safety form.
2. Observe prepared **slides of human cells** under high magnification using a **light microscope.**
3. Observe **onion root tip cells** under the microscope.
4. Observe other cells on the **prepared slides** your teacher will give you.
5. Draw diagrams of the sample cells you observed. Identify and label any of the structures you recognize.

**Analysis**

1. **Compare and contrast** the different cells you observed.
2. **Hypothesize** why the cells you observed had different appearances and structures. How could you identify diseased cells?

**Biology Online**

Visit biologygmh.com to:

- study the entire chapter online
- explore the Concepts in Motion, Microscopy Links, Virtual Labs, and links to virtual dissections
- access Web links for more information, projects, and activities
- review content online with the Interactive Tutor and take Self-Check Quizzes

**Mitosis and Cytokinesis** Make this Foldable to help you understand how cells reproduce by a process called mitosis, resulting in two genetically identical cells.

**STEP 1** Stack three sheets of notebook paper approximately 1.5 cm apart vertically as illustrated.

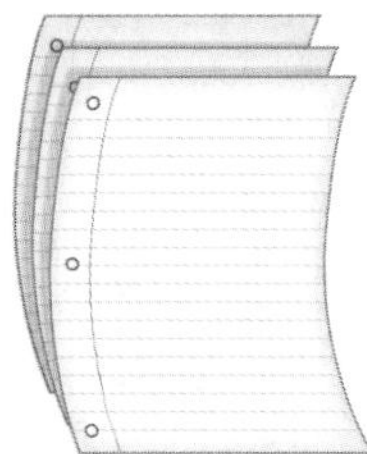

**STEP 2** Roll up the bottom edges and fold to form six tabs.

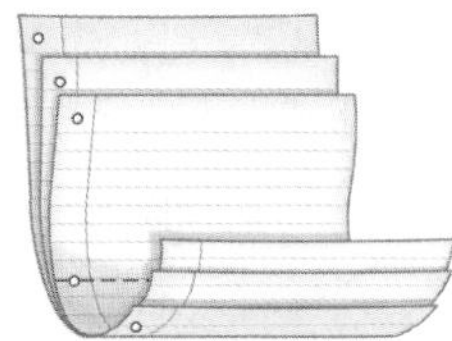

**STEP 3** Staple along the folded edge to secure all sheets. Rotate the Foldable and, with the stapled end at the top, label the tabs as illustrated.

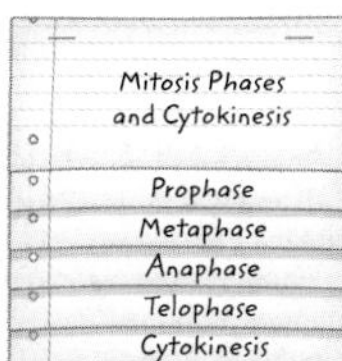


**FOLDABLES Use this Foldable with Section 9.2.** As you study the section, record what you learn about each of the four phases of mitosis. In the tab labeled *Cytokinesis,* write a brief description of cytokinesis, the division of cytoplasm.

Section 9.1

## Objectives

- **Explain** why cells are relatively small.
- **Summarize** the primary stages of the cell cycle.
- **Describe** the stages of interphase.

## Review Vocabulary

**selective permeability:** process in which a membrane allows some substances to pass through while keeping others out

## New Vocabulary

cell cycle
interphase
mitosis
cytokinesis
chromosome
chromatin

# Cellular Growth

MAIN Idea **Cells grow until they reach their size limit, then they either stop growing or divide.**

**Real-World Reading Link** If you've ever played a doubles match in tennis, you probably felt that you and your partner could effectively cover your half of the court. However, if the court were much larger, perhaps you could no longer reach your shots. For the best game, the tennis court must be kept at regulation size. Cell size also must be limited to ensure that the needs of the cell are met.

## Cell Size Limitations

Most cells are less than 100 μm ($100 \times 10^{-6}$ m) in diameter, which is smaller than the period at the end of this sentence. Why are most cells so small? This section investigates several factors that influence cell size.

**Ratio of surface area to volume** The key factor that limits the size of a cell is the ratio of its surface area to its volume. The surface area of the cell refers to the area covered by the plasma membrane. Recall from Chapter 7 that the plasma membrane is the structure through which all nutrients and waste products must pass. The volume refers to the space taken by the inner contents of the cell, including the organelles in the cytoplasm and the nucleus.

Connection to Math To illustrate the ratio of surface area to volume, consider the small cube in **Figure 9.1,** which has sides of one micrometer (μm) in length. This is approximately the size of a bacterial cell. To calculate the surface area of the cube, multiply length times width times the number of sides (1 μm × 1 μm × 6 sides), which equals 6 $\mu m^2$. To calculate the volume of the cell, multiply length times width times height (1 μm × 1 μm × 1 μm), which equals 1 $\mu m^3$. The ratio of surface area to volume is 6:1.

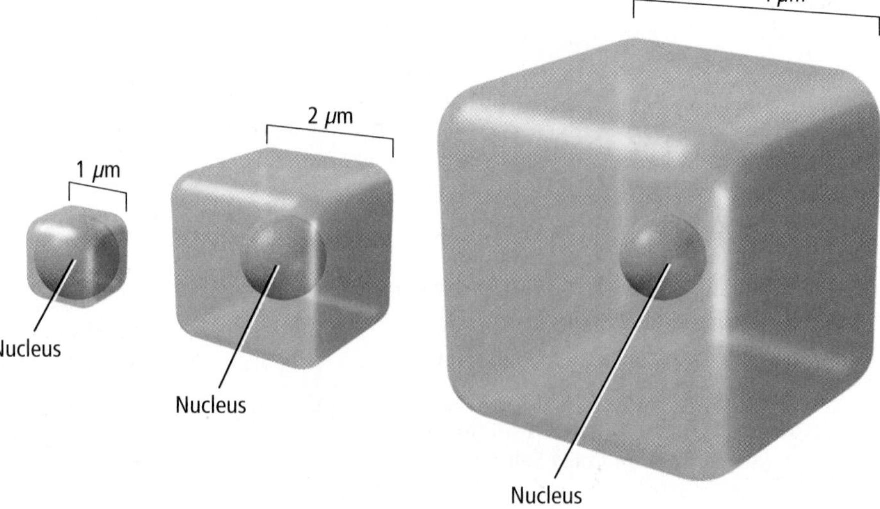


■ **Figure 9.1** Note how the ratio of surface area to volume changes as the size of the cell increases, and note the amount of contents the nucleus must control as cell size increases.
**Infer** ***How does the amount of surface area change as the cell's volume increases?***

If the cubic cell grows to 2 µm per side, as represented in **Figure 9.1,** the surface area becomes 24 $\mu m^2$ and the volume is 8 $\mu m^3$. The ratio of surface area to volume is now 3:1, which is less than it was when the cell was smaller. If the cell continues to grow, the ratio of surface area to volume will continue to decrease, as shown by the third cube in **Figure 9.1.** As the cell grows, its volume increases much more rapidly than the surface area. This means that the cell might have difficulty supplying nutrients and expelling enough waste products. By remaining small, cells have a higher ratio of surface area to volume and can sustain themselves more easily.

 **Reading Check** **Explain** why a high ratio of surface area to volume benefits a cell.

**Transport of substances** Another task that can be managed more easily in a small cell than in a large cell is the movement of substances. Recall that the plasma membrane controls cellular transport because it is selectively permeable. Once inside the cell, substances move by diffusion or by motor proteins pulling them along the cytoskeleton. Diffusion over large distances is slow and inefficient because it relies on random movement of molecules and ions. Similarly, the cytoskeleton transportation network, shown in **Figure 9.2,** becomes less efficient for a cell if the distance to travel becomes too large. Therefore, cells remain small to maximize the ability of diffusion and motor proteins to transport nutrients and waste products. Small cells maintain more efficient transport systems.

LM Magnification: 150×

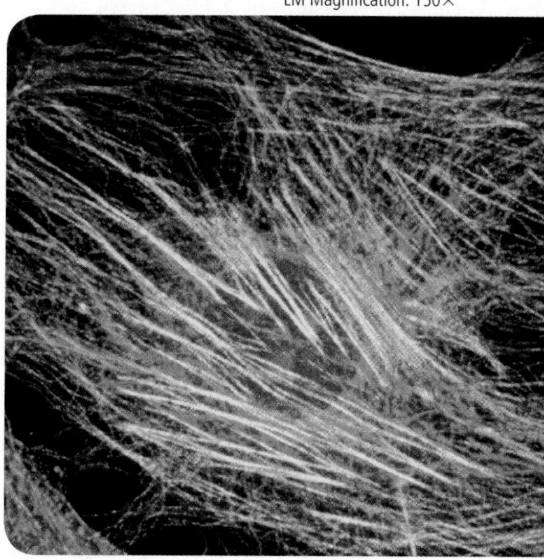

**Figure 9.2** In order for the cytoskeleton to be an efficient transportation railway, the distances substances must travel within a cell must be limited.

## MiniLab 9.1

### Investigate Cell Size

**Could a cell grow large enough to engulf your school?** What would happen if the size of an elephant were doubled? At the organism level, an elephant cannot grow significantly larger, because its legs would not support the increase in mass. Do the same principles and limitations apply at the cellular level? Do the math!

**Procedure**

1. Read and complete the lab safety form.
2. Prepare a data table for surface area and volume data calculated for five hypothetical cells. Assume the cell is a cube. (Dimensions given are for one face of a cube.)
   Cell 1: 0.00002 m (the average diameter of most eukaryotic cells)
   Cell 2: 0.001 m (the diameter of a squid's giant nerve cell)
   Cell 3: 2.5 cm
   Cell 4: 30 cm
   Cell 5: 15 m
3. Calculate the surface area for each cell using the formula: length × width × number of sides (6).
4. Calculate the volume for each cell using the formula: length × width × height.

**Analysis**

1. **Cause and Effect** Based on your calculations, confirm why cells don't become very large.
2. **Infer** Are large organisms, such as redwood trees and elephants, large because they contain extra large cells or just more standard-sized cells? Explain.

■ **Figure 9.3** The cell cycle involves three stages—interphase, mitosis, and cytokinesis. Interphase is divided into three substages.
**Hypothesize** ***Why does cytokinesis represent the smallest amount of time a cell spends in the cell cycle?***

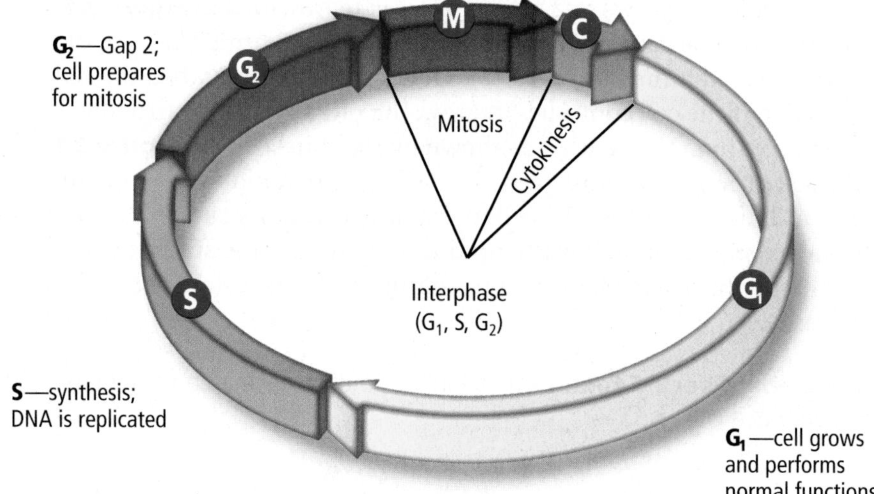


*Study Tip*

**Diagram** Draw your own version of the cell cycle, including the terms *interphase, mitosis,* and *cytokinesis* as you read the text.

**Cellular communications** The need for signaling proteins to move throughout the cell also limits cell size. In other words, cell size affects the ability of the cell to communicate instructions for cellular functions. If the cell becomes too large, it becomes almost impossible for cellular communications, many of which involve movement of substances and signals to various organelles, to take place efficiently. For example, the signals that trigger protein synthesis might not reach the ribosome fast enough for protein synthesis to occur to sustain the cell.

## The Cell Cycle

Once a cell reaches its size limit, something must happen—either it will stop growing or it will divide. Most cells will eventually divide. Cell division not only prevents the cell from becoming too large, but it also is the way the cell reproduces so that you grow and heal certain injuries. Cells reproduce by a cycle of growing and dividing called the **cell cycle.** Each time a cell goes through one complete cycle, it becomes two cells. When the cell cycle is repeated continuously, the result is a continuous production of new cells. A general overview of the cell cycle is presented in **Figure 9.3.**

There are three main stages of the cell cycle. **Interphase** is the stage during which the cell grows, carries out cellular functions, and replicates, or makes copies of its DNA in preparation for the next stage of the cycle. Interphase is divided into three substages, as indicated by the segment arrows in **Figure 9.3. Mitosis** (mi TOH sus) is the stage of the cell cycle during which the cell's nucleus and nuclear material divide. Mitosis is divided into four substages. Near the end of mitosis, a process called cytokinesis begins. **Cytokinesis** (si toh kih NEE sis) is the method by which a cell's cytoplasm divides, creating a new cell. You will read more about mitosis and cytokinesis in Section 9.2.

**Vocabulary**
**Word origin**
**Cytokinesis**
***cyto–*** prefix; from the Greek word *kytos,* meaning *hollow vessel*
***–kinesis*** from the Greek word *kinetikos,* meaning *putting in motion.*

The duration of the cell cycle varies, depending on the cell that is dividing. Some eukaryotic cells might complete the cycle in as few as eight minutes, while other cells might take up to one year. For most normal, actively dividing animal cells, the cell cycle takes approximately 12–24 hours. When you consider all that takes place during the cell cycle, you might find it amazing that most of your cells complete the cell cycle in about a day.

**The stages of interphase** During interphase, the cell grows, develops into a mature, functioning cell, duplicates its DNA, and prepares for division. Interphase is divided into three stages, as shown in **Figure 9.3:** $G_1$, S, and $G_2$, also called Gap 1, synthesis, and Gap 2.

The first stage of interphase, $G_1$, is the period immediately after a cell divides. During $G_1$, a cell is growing, carrying out normal cell functions, and preparing to replicate DNA. Some cells, such as muscle and nerve cells, exit the cell cycle at this point and do not divide again.

The second stage of interphase, S, is the period when a cell copies its DNA in preparation for cell division. **Chromosomes** (KROH muh sohmz) are the structures that contain the genetic material that is passed from generation to generation of cells. **Chromatin** (KROH muh tun) is the relaxed form of DNA in the cell's nucleus. As shown in **Figure 9.4,** when a specific dye is applied to a cell in interphase, the nucleus stains with a speckled appearance. This speckled appearance is due to individual strands of chromatin that are not visible under a light microscope without the dye.

The $G_2$ stage follows the S stage and is the period when the cell prepares for the division of its nucleus. A protein that makes microtubules for cell division is synthesized at this time. During $G_2$, the cell also takes inventory and makes sure it is ready to continue with mitosis. When these activities are completed, the cell begins the next stage of the cell cycle—mitosis.

**Mitosis and cytokinesis** The stages of mitosis and cytokinesis follow interphase. In mitosis, the cell's nuclear material divides and separates into opposite ends of the cell. In cytokinesis, the cell divides into two daughter cells with identical nuclei. These important stages of the cell cycle are described in Section 9.2.

**Prokaryotic cell division** The cell cycle is the method by which eukaryotic cells reproduce themselves. Prokaryotic cells, which you have learned are simpler cells, reproduce by a method called binary fission. You will learn more about binary fission in Chapter 18.

Stained LM Magnification: 400×

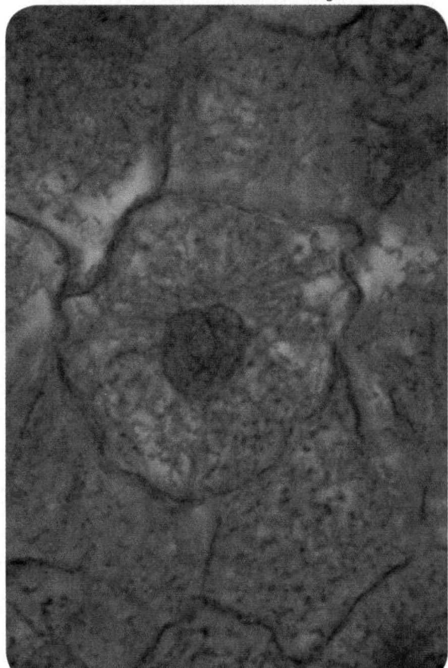

**Figure 9.4** The grainy appearance of this nucleus from a rat liver cell is due to chromatin, the relaxed material that condenses to form chromosomes.

## Section 9.1 Assessment

### Section Summary

- The ratio of surface area to volume describes the size of the plasma membrane relative to the volume of the cell.
- Cell size is limited by the cell's ability to transport materials and communicate instructions from the nucleus.
- The cell cycle is the process of cellular reproduction.
- A cell spends the majority of its lifetime in interphase.

### Understand Main Ideas

1. MAIN Idea **Relate** cell size to cell functions, and explain why cell size is limited.
2. **Summarize** the primary stages of the cell cycle.
3. **Describe** what happens to DNA during the S stage of interphase.
4. **Make a diagram** of the stages of the cell cycle and describe what happens in each.

### Think Scientifically

5. *Hypothesize* what the result would be if a large cell managed to divide, despite the fact that it had grown beyond an optimum size.
6. MATH in Biology If a cube representing a cell is 5 μm on a side, calculate the surface area-to-volume ratio, and explain why this is or is not a good size for a cell.

Section 9.2

### Section Objectives

- **Describe** the events of each stage of mitosis.
- **Explain** the process of cytokinesis.

### Review Vocabulary

**life cycle:** the sequence of growth and development stages that an organism goes through during its life

### New Vocabulary

prophase
sister chromatid
centromere
spindle apparatus
metaphase
anaphase
telophase

# Mitosis and Cytokinesis

MAIN Idea **Eukaryotic cells reproduce by mitosis, the process of nuclear division, and cytokinesis, the process of cytoplasm division.**

**Real-World Reading Link** Many familiar events are cyclic in nature. The course of a day, the changing of seasons year after year, and the passing of comets in space are some examples of cyclic events. Cells also have a cycle of growth and reproduction.

## Mitosis

You learned in the last section that cells cycle through interphase, mitosis, and cytokinesis. During mitosis, the cell's replicated genetic material separates and the cell prepares to split into two cells. The key activity of mitosis is the accurate separation of the cell's replicated DNA. This enables the cell's genetic information to pass into the new cells intact, resulting in two daughter cells that are genetically identical. In multicellular organisms, the process of mitosis increases the number of cells as a young organism grows to its adult size. Organisms also use mitosis to replace damaged cells. Recall the last time you accidently got cut. Under the scab, the existing skin cells divided by mitosis and cytokinesis to create new skin cells that filled the gap in the skin caused by the injury.

## The Stages of Mitosis

Like interphase, mitosis is divided into stages: prophase, metaphase, anaphase, and telophase.

**Prophase** The first stage of mitosis—the stage of mitosis during which a dividing cell spends the most time—is called **prophase.** In this stage, the cell's chromatin tightens, or condenses, into chromosomes. In prophase, the chromosomes are shaped like an X, as shown in **Figure 9.5.** At this point, each chromosome is a single structure that contains the genetic material that was replicated in interphase. Each half of this X is called a sister chromatid. **Sister chromatids** are structures that contain identical copies of DNA. The structure at the center of the chromosome where the sister chromatids are attached is called the **centromere.** This structure is important because it ensures that a complete copy of the replicated DNA will become part of the daughter cells at the end of the cell cycle. Locate prophase in the cell cycle illustrated in **Figure 9.6,** and note the position of the sister chromatids. As you continue to read about the stages of mitosis, refer back to **Figure 9.6** to follow the chromatids through the cell cycle.

**Reading Check** **Compare** the key activity of interphase with the key activity of mitosis.

**Figure 9.5** Chromosomes in prophase are actually sister chromatids that are attached at the centromere.

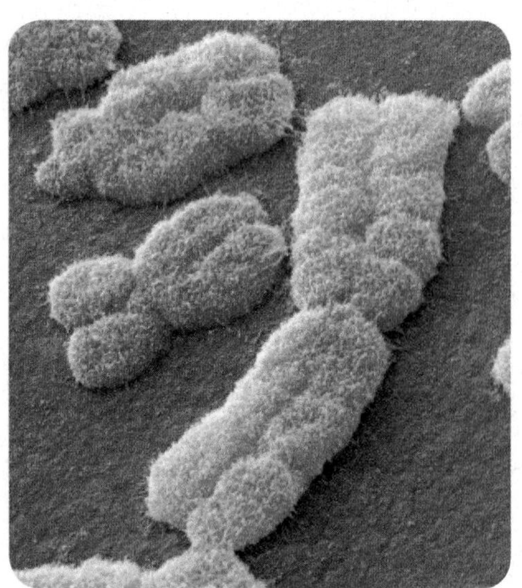

Color-Enhanced SEM magnification: 6875×

**Haploid and diploid cells** In order to maintain the same chromosome number from generation to generation, an organism produces **gametes,** which are sex cells that have half the number of chromosomes. Although the number of chromosomes varies from one species to another, in humans each gamete contains 23 chromosomes. The symbol $n$ can be used to represent the number of chromosomes in a gamete. A cell with $n$ number of chromosomes is called a **haploid** cell. Haploid comes from the Greek word *haploos,* meaning *single.*

The process by which one haploid gamete combines with another haploid gamete is called **fertilization.** As a result of fertilization, the cell now will contain a total of $2n$ chromosomes—$n$ chromosomes from the female parent plus $n$ chromosomes from the male parent. A cell that contains $2n$ number of chromosomes is called a **diploid** cell.

Notice that $n$ also describes the number of pairs of chromosomes in an organism. When two human gametes combine, 23 pairs of homologous chromosomes are formed.

**VOCABULARY**

**ACADEMIC VOCABULARY**

**Equator:**
a circle or circular band dividing the surface of a body into two usually equal and symmetrical parts.
*The chromosomes line up at the equator of the cell.*

# Meiosis I

Gametes are formed during a process called **meiosis,** which is a type of cell division that reduces the number of chromosomes; therefore, it is referred to as a reduction division. Meiosis occurs in the reproductive structures of organisms that reproduce sexually. While mitosis maintains the chromosome number, meiosis reduces the chromosome number by half through the separation of homologous chromosomes. A cell with $2n$ number of chromosomes will have gametes with $n$ number of chromosomes after meiosis, as illustrated in **Figure 10.2.** Meiosis involves two consecutive cell divisions called meiosis I and meiosis II.

**FOLDABLES** Incorporate information from this section into your Foldable.

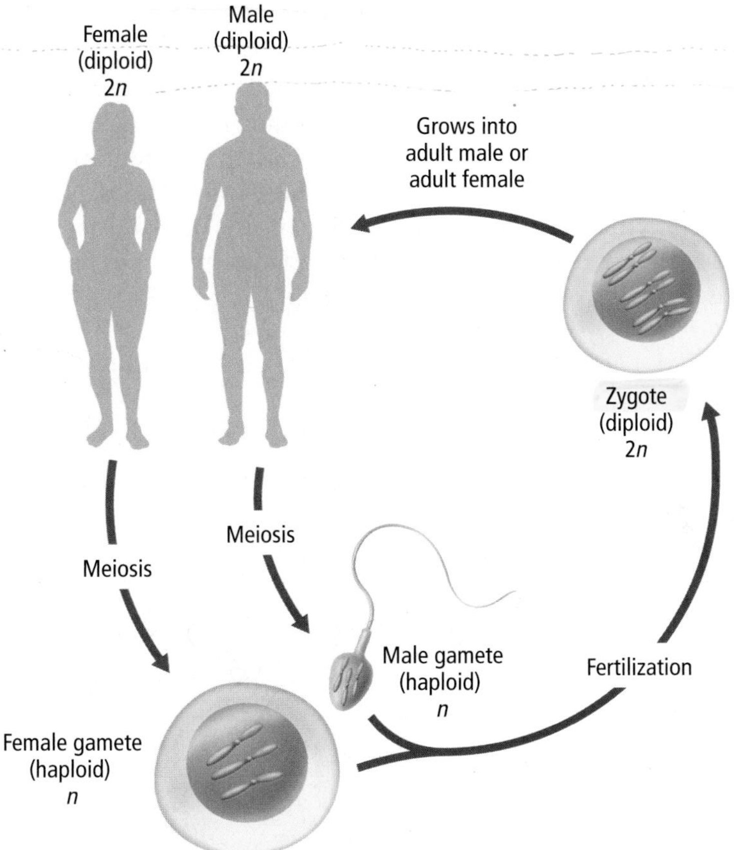


**Figure 10.2** The sexual life cycle in animals involves meiosis, which produces gametes. When gametes combine in fertilization, the number of chromosomes is restored.
**Describe** ***What happens to the number of chromosomes during meiosis?***

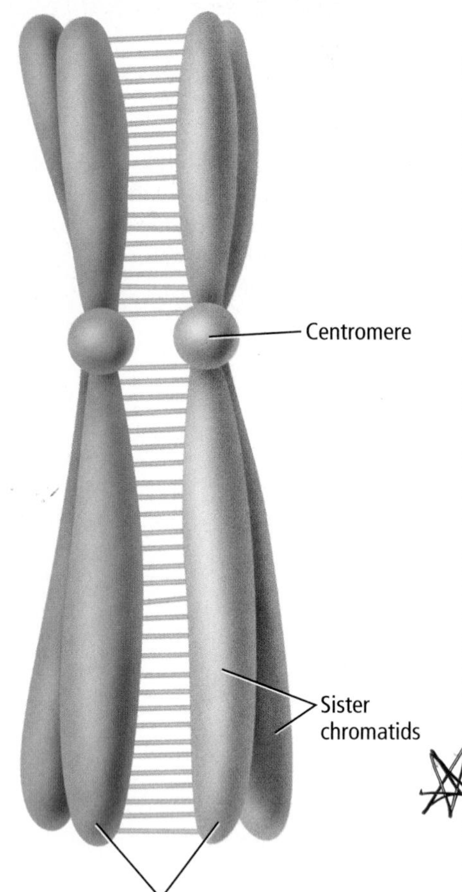


■ **Figure 10.3** The homologous chromosomes are physically bound together during synapsis in prophase I.

**Interphase** Recall that the cell cycle includes interphase prior to mitosis. Cells that undergo meiosis also go through interphase as part of the cell cycle. Cells in interphase carry out various metabolic processes, including the replication of DNA and the synthesis of proteins.

**Prophase I** As a cell enters prophase I, the replicated chromosomes become visible. As in mitosis, the replicated chromosomes consist of two sister chromatids. As the homologous chromosomes condense, they begin to form pairs in a process called synapsis. The homologous chromosomes are held tightly together along their lengths, as illustrated in **Figure 10.3.** Notice that in **Figure 10.4** the purple and green chromosomes have exchanged segments. This exchange occurs during synapsis. **Crossing over** is a process during which chromosomal segments are exchanged between a pair of homologous chromosomes.

As prophase I continues, centrioles move to the cell's opposite poles. Spindle fibers form and bind to the sister chromatids at the centromere.

**Metaphase I** In the next phase of meiosis, the pairs of homologous chromosomes line up at the equator of the cell, as illustrated in **Figure 10.5.** In meiosis, the spindle fibers attach to the centromere of each homologous chromosome. Recall that during metaphase in mitosis, the individual chromosomes, which consist of two sister chromatids, line up at the cell's equator. During metaphase I of meiosis, the homologous chromosomes line up as pairs at the cell's equator. This is an important distinction between mitosis and meiosis.

**Anaphase I** During anaphase I, the homologous chromosomes separate, which is also illustrated in **Figure 10.5.** Each member of the pair is guided by spindle fibers and moves toward opposite poles of the cell. The chromosome number is reduced from $2n$ to $n$ when the homologous chromosomes separate. Recall that in mitosis, the sister chromatids split during anaphase. During anaphase I of meiosis, however, each homologous chromosome still consists of two sister chromatids.

**Telophase I** The homologous chromosomes, consisting of two sister chromatids, reach the cell's opposite poles. Each pole contains only one member of the original pair of homologous chromosomes. Notice in **Figure 10.5** that each chromosome still consists of two sister chromatids joined at the centromere. The sister chromatids might not be identical because crossing over might have occurred during synapsis in prophase I.

■ **Figure 10.4** The results of crossing over are new combinations of genes.
**Determine** *Which chromatids exchanged genetic material?*

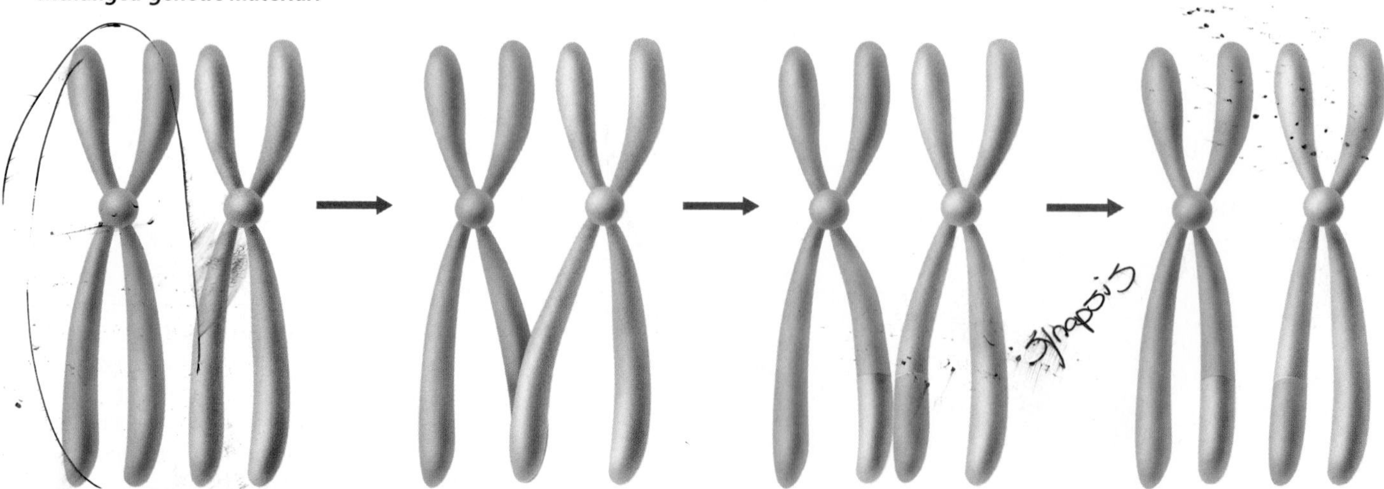

# Visualizing Meiosis

**Figure 10.5**
Follow along the stages of meiosis I and meiosis II, beginning with interphase at the left.

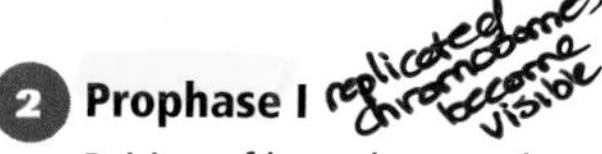

**2 Prophase I**
- Pairing of homologous chromosomes occurs, each chromosome consists of two chromatids.
- Crossing over produces exchange of genetic information.
- The nuclear envelope breaks down.
- Spindles form.

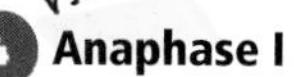

**3 Metaphase I**
- Chromosome centromeres attach to spindle fibers.
- Homologous chromosomes line up at the equator.

**4 Anaphase I**
- Homologous chromosomes separate and move to opposite poles of the cell.

**5 Telophase I**
- The spindles break down.
- Chromosomes uncoil and form two nuclei.
- The cell divides.

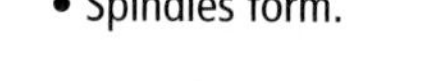

**1 Interphase**
- Chromosomes replicate.
- Chromatin condenses.

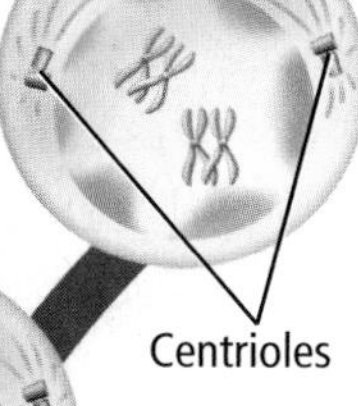

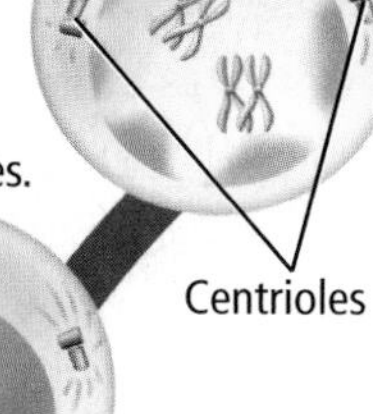

**6 Prophase II**
- Chromosomes condense.
- Spindles form in each new cell.
- Spindle fibers attach to chromosomes.

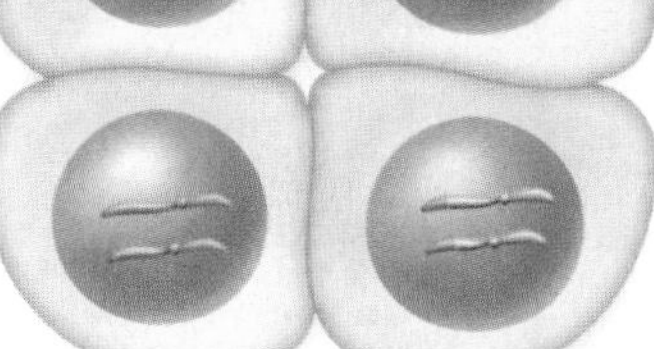

**10 Products**
- Four cells have formed.
- Each nucleus contains a haploid number of chromosomes.

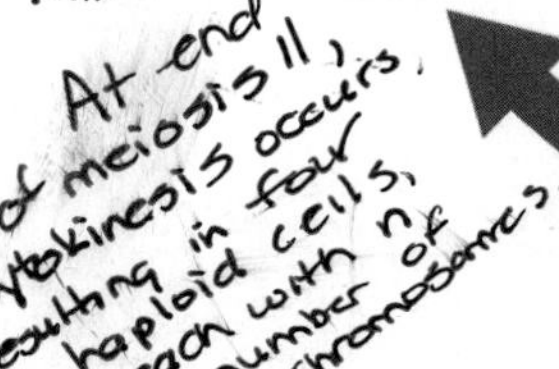

**7 Metaphase II**
- Centromeres of chromosomes line up randomly at the equator of each cell.

**9 Telophase II**
- Four nuclei form around chromosomes.
- Spindles break down.
- Cells divide.

**8 Anaphase II**
- Centromeres split.
- Sister chromatids separate and move to opposite poles.

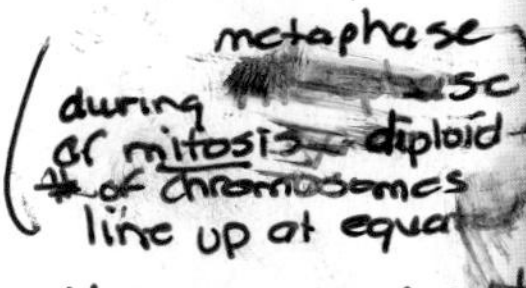

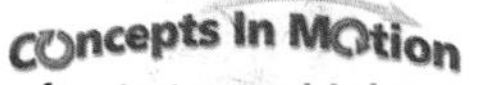

**Concepts In Motion** **Interactive Figure** To see an animation of meiosis, visit biologygmh.com.

## CAREERS IN BIOLOGY

**Medical Geneticist** A medical geneticist researches how diseases are inherited, how to diagnose genetic conditions, and treatments for genetic diseases. For more information on biology careers, visit biologygmh.com.

## LAUNCH Lab

**Review** Based on what you have read about meiosis, how would you now answer the analysis questions?

During telophase I, cytokinesis usually occurs, forming a furrow by pinching in animal cells and by forming a cell plate in plant cells. Following cytokinesis, the cells may go into interphase again before the second set of divisions. However, the DNA is not replicated again during this interphase. In some species, the chromosomes uncoil, the nuclear membrane reappears, and nuclei re-form during telophase I.

# Meiosis II

Meiosis is only halfway completed at the end of meiosis I. During prophase II, a second set of phases begins as the spindle apparatus forms and the chromosomes condense. During metaphase II, the chromosomes are positioned at the equator by the spindle fibers, as shown in **Figure 10.5.** During metaphase of mitosis, a diploid number of chromosomes line up at the equator. During metaphase II of meiosis, however, a haploid number of chromosomes line up at the equator. During anaphase II, the sister chromatids are pulled apart at the centromere by the spindle fibers, and the sister chromatids move toward the opposite poles of the cell. The chromosomes reach the poles during telophase II, and the nuclear membrane and nuclei reform. At the end of meiosis II, cytokinesis occurs, resulting in four haploid cells, each with $n$ number of chromosomes, as illustrated in **Figure 10.5.**

**Reading Check Infer** Why are the two phases of meiosis important for gamete formation?

## DATA ANALYSIS LAB 10.1

**Based on Real Data***

### Draw Conclusions

**How do motor proteins affect cell division?** Many scientists think that motor proteins play an important role in the movement of chromosomes in both mitosis and meiosis. To test this hypothesis, researchers have produced yeast that cannot make the motor protein called Kar3p. They also have produced yeast that cannot make the motor protein called Cik1p, which many think moderates the function of Kar3p. The results of their experiment are shown in the graph to the right.

**Think Critically**

1. **Evaluate** Does Cik1p seem to be important for yeast meiosis? Explain.
2. **Assess** Does Kar3p seem to be necessary for yeast meiosis? Explain.
3. **Conclude** Do all motor proteins seem to play a vital role in meiosis? Explain.

**Data and Observations**

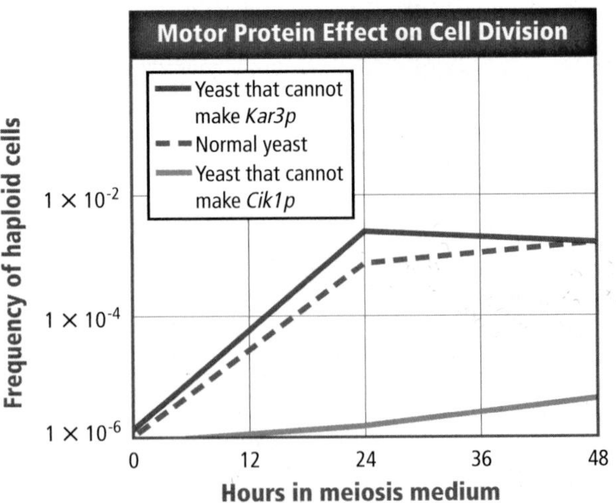


*Data obtained from: Shanks, et al. 2001. The Kar3-Interacting protein Cik1p plays a critical role in passage through meiosis I in *Saccharomyces cerevisiae*. *Genetics* 159: 939-951.

## The Importance of Meiosis

**Table 10.1** shows a comparison of mitosis and meiosis. Recall that mitosis consists of only one set of division phases and produces two identical diploid daughter cells. Meiosis, however, consists of two sets of divisions and produces four haploid daughter cells that are not identical. Meiosis is important because it results in genetic variation.

**Concepts In Motion** Interactive Table To explore more about mitosis and meiosis, visit biologygmh.com.

**Table 10.1 Mitosis and Meiosis**

| Mitosis | Meiosis |
|---|---|
| One division occurs during mitosis. | Two sets of divisions occur during meiosis: meiosis I and meiosis II. |
| DNA replication occurs during interphase. | DNA replication occurs once before meiosis I. |
| Synapsis of homologous chromosomes does not occur. | Synapsis of homologous chromosomes occurs during prophase I. |
| Two identical cells are formed per cell cycle. | Four haploid cells (*n*) are formed per cell cycle. |
| The daughter cells are genetically identical. | The daughter cells are not genetically identical because of crossing over. |
| Mitosis occurs only in body cells. | Meiosis occurs in reproductive cells. |
| Mitosis is involved in growth and repair. | Meiosis is involved in the production of gametes and providing genetic variation in organisms. |

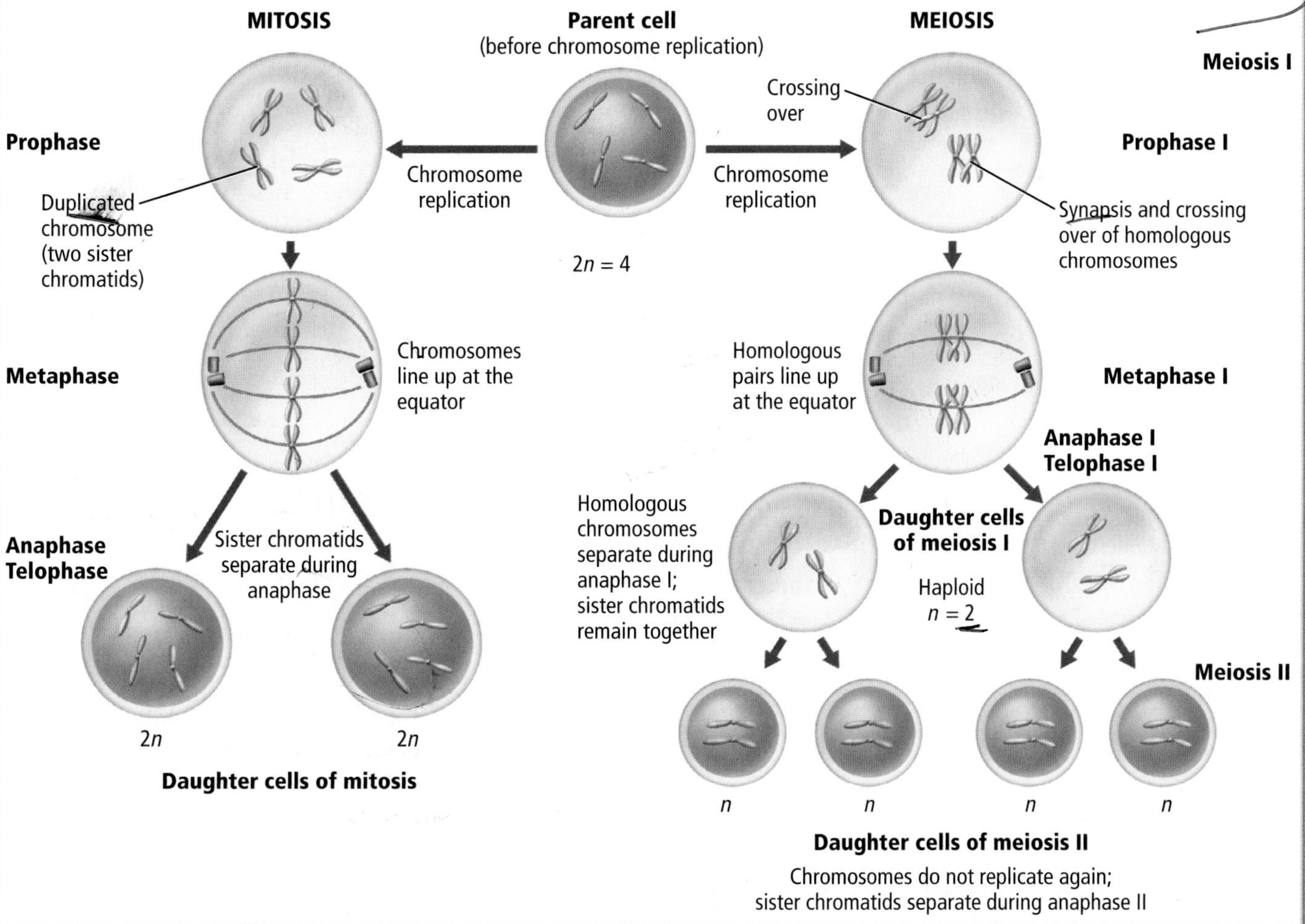

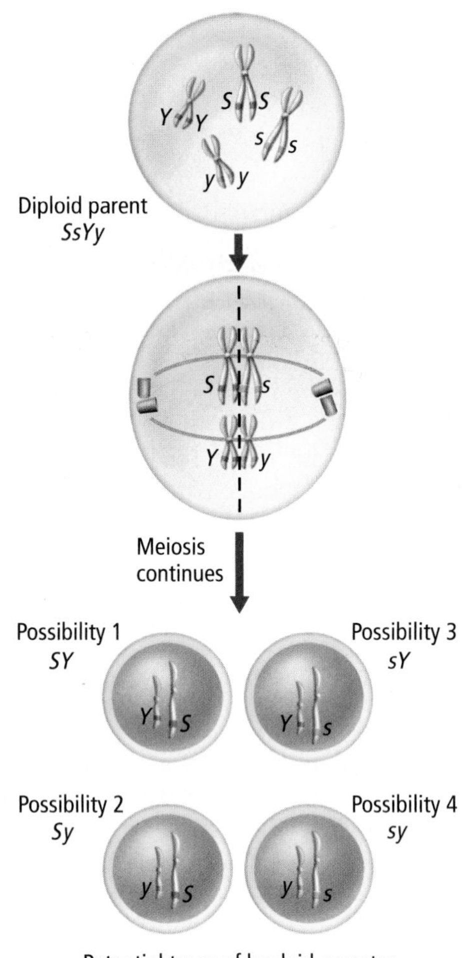


**Figure 10.6** The order in which the homologous pairs line up (*Y* with *S* or *Y* with *s*) explains how a variety of sex cells can be produced.

**Meiosis provides variation** Recall that pairs of homologous chromosomes line up at the equator during prophase I. How the chromosomes line up at the equator is a random process that results in gametes with different combinations of chromosomes, such as the ones in **Figure 10.6.** Depending on how the chromosomes line up at the equator, four gametes with four different combinations of chromosomes can result.

Notice that the first possibility shows which chromosomes were on the same side of the equator and therefore traveled together. Different combinations of chromosomes were lined up on the same side of the equator to produce the gametes in the second possibility. Genetic variation also is produced during crossing over and during fertilization, when gametes randomly combine.

## Sexual Reproduction v. Asexual Reproduction

Some organisms reproduce by asexual reproduction, while others reproduce by sexual reproduction. The life cycles of still other organisms might involve both asexual and sexual reproduction. During asexual reproduction, the organism inherits all of its chromosomes from a single parent. Therefore, the new individual is genetically identical to its parent. Bacteria reproduce asexually, whereas most protists reproduce both asexually and sexually, depending on environmental conditions. Most plants and many of the more simple animals can reproduce both asexually and sexually, compared to more advanced animals that reproduce only sexually.

Why do some species reproduce sexually while others reproduce asexually? Recent studies with fruit flies have shown that the rate of accumulation of beneficial mutations is faster when species reproduce sexually than when they reproduce asexually. In other words, when reproduction occurs sexually, the beneficial genes multiply faster over time than they do when reproduction is asexual.

## Section 10.1 Assessment

### Section Summary

- DNA replication takes place only once during meiosis, and it results in four haploid gametes.
- Meiosis consists of two sets of divisions.
- Meiosis produces genetic variation in gametes.

### Understand Main Ideas

1. MAIN Idea **Analyze** how meiosis produces haploid gametes.
2. **Indicate** how metaphase I is different from metaphase in mitosis.
3. **Describe** how synapsis occurs.
4. **Diagram** a cell with four chromosomes going through meiosis.
5. **Assess** how meiosis contributes to genetic variation, while mitosis does not.

### Think Scientifically

6. *Compare and contrast* mitosis and meiosis, using **Figure 10.5** and **Table 10.1,** by creating a Venn diagram.
7. WRITING in **Biology** Write a play or activity involving your classmates, to explain the various processes that occur during meiosis.



Biology Online **Self-Check Quiz** biologygmh.com

### Objectives

- **Explain** the significance of Mendel's experiments to the study of genetics.
- **Summarize** the law of segregation and law of independent assortment.
- **Predict** the possible offspring from a cross using a Punnett square.

### Review Vocabulary

**segregation:** the separation of allelic genes that typically occurs during meiosis

### New Vocabulary

genetics
allele
dominant
recessive
homozygous
heterozygous
genotype
phenotype
law of segregation
hybrid
law of independent assortment

■ **Figure 10.7** Gregor Mendel is known as the father of genetics.

# Mendelian Genetics

MAIN Idea **Mendel explained how a dominant allele can mask the presence of a recessive allele.**

**Real-World Reading Link** There are many different breeds of dogs, such as Labrador retrievers, dachshunds, German shepherds, and poodles. You might like a certain breed of dog because of its height, coat color, and general appearance. These traits are passed from generation to generation. The work of an Austrian monk led to a greater understanding of how genetic traits are passed on to the next generation.

## How Genetics Began

In 1866, Gregor Mendel, an Austrian monk and a plant breeder, published his findings on the method and the mathematics of inheritance in garden pea plants. The passing of traits to the next generation is called inheritance, or heredity. Mendel, shown in **Figure 10.7,** was successful in sorting out the mystery of inheritance because of the organism he chose for his study—the pea plant. Pea plants are easy to grow and many are true-breeding, meaning that they consistently produce offspring with only one form of a trait.

Pea plants usually reproduce by self-fertilization. A common occurrence in many flowering plants, self-fertilization occurs when a male gamete within a flower combines with a female gamete in the same flower. Mendel also discovered that pea plants could easily be cross-pollinated by hand. Mendel performed cross-pollination by transferring a male gamete from the flower of one pea plant to the female reproductive organ in a flower of another pea plant.

Connection to History Mendel rigorously followed various traits in the pea plants he bred. He analyzed the results of his experiments and formed hypotheses concerning how the traits were inherited. The study of **genetics,** which is the science of heredity, began with Mendel, who is regarded as the father of genetics.

## The Inheritance of Traits

Mendel noticed that certain varieties of garden pea plants produced specific forms of a trait, generation after generation. For instance, he noticed that some varieties always produced green seeds and others always produced yellow seeds. In order to understand how these traits are inherited, Mendel performed cross pollination by transferring male gametes from the flower of a true-breeding green-seed plant to the female organ of a flower from a true-breeding yellow-seed plant. To prevent self-fertilization, Mendel removed the male organs from the flower of the yellow-seed plant. Mendel called the green-seed plant and the yellow-seed plant the parent generation—also known as the P generation.

■ **Figure 10.8** The results of Mendel's cross involving true-breeding pea plants with yellow seeds and green seeds are shown here. **Explain** ***why the seeds in the $F_1$ generation were all yellow.***

**Concepts In Motion**

Interactive Figure To see an animation of the allele frequencies of three generations of flowers, visit biologygmh.com.

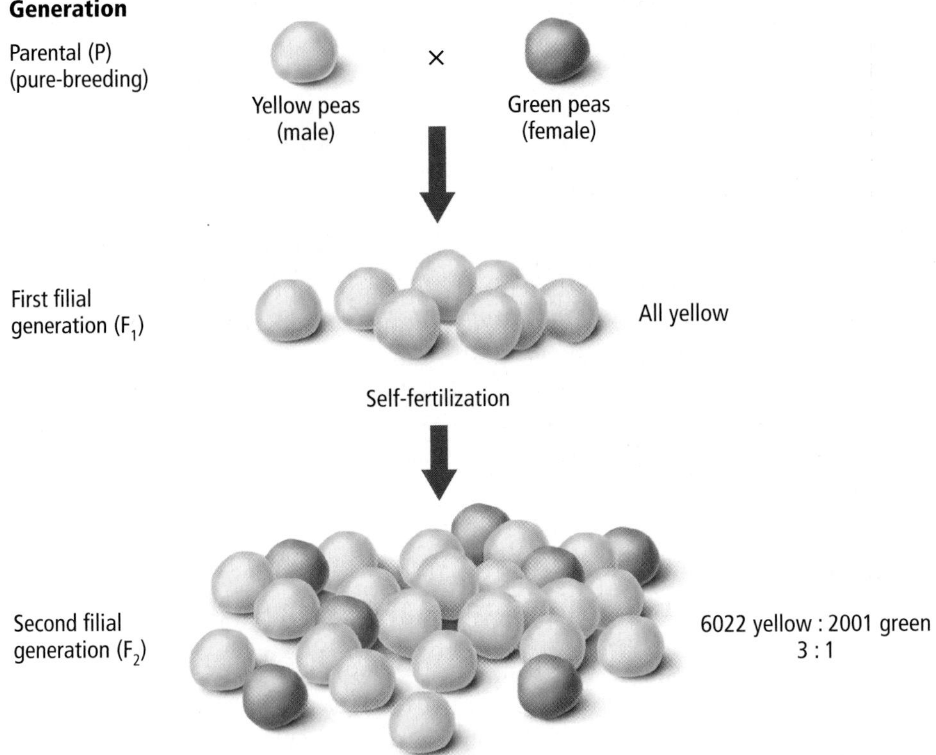


**$F_1$ and $F_2$ generations** When Mendel grew the seeds from the cross between the green-seed and yellow-seed plants, all of the resulting offspring had yellow seeds. The offspring of this P cross are called the first filial ($F_1$) generation. The green-seed trait seemed to have disappeared in the $F_1$ generation, and Mendel decided to investigate whether the trait was no longer present or whether it was hidden, or masked.

Mendel planted the $F_1$ generation of yellow seeds, allowed the plants to grow and self-fertilize, and then examined the seeds from this cross. The results of the second filial ($F_2$) generation—the offspring from the $F_1$ cross—are shown in **Figure 10.8.** Of the seeds Mendel collected, 6022 were yellow and 2001 were green, which almost is a perfect 3:1 ratio of yellow to green seeds.

Mendel studied seven different traits—seed or pea color, flower color, seed pod color, seed shape or texture, seed pod shape, stem length, and flower position—and found that the $F_1$ generation plants from these crosses also showed a 3:1 ratio.

**Genes in pairs** Mendel concluded that there must be two forms of the seed trait in the pea plants—yellow-seed and green-seed—and that each was controlled by a factor, which now is called an allele. An **allele** is defined as an alternative form of a single gene passed from generation to generation. Therefore, the gene for yellow seeds and the gene for green seeds are each different forms of a single gene.

Mendel concluded that the 3:1 ratio observed during his experiments could be explained if the alleles were paired in each of the plants. He called the form of the trait that appeared in the $F_1$ generation **dominant** and the form of the trait that was masked in the $F_1$ generation **recessive.** In the cross between yellow-seed plants and green-seed plants, the yellow seed was the dominant form of the trait and the green seed was the recessive form of the trait.

**CAREERS IN BIOLOGY**

**Genetics Laboratory Technician**
A technician in a genetics laboratory assists a researcher by conducting experiments and helping to maintain the lab. For more information on biology careers, visit biologygmh.com.

**Dominance** When he allowed the $F_1$ generation to self-fertilize, Mendel showed that the recessive allele for green seeds had not disappeared but was masked. Mendel concluded that the green-seed form of the trait did not show up in the $F_1$ generation because the yellow-seed form of the trait is dominant and masks the allele for the green-seed form of the trait.

Because the yellow-seed form of the trait is dominant, the allele for the yellow-seed form of the trait is represented by a capital *Y*. The allele for the green-seed form of the trait is represented by a lowercase *y* because it is recessive. An organism with two of the same alleles for a particular trait is **homozygous** (ho muh ZI gus) for that trait. Homozygous, yellow-seed plants are *YY* and green-seed plants are *yy*. An organism with two different alleles for a particular trait is **heterozygous** (heh tuh roh ZY gus) for that trait, in this case *Yy*. When alleles are present in the heterozygous state, the dominant trait will be observed.

**Genotype and phenotype** A yellow-seed plant could be homozygous or heterozygous for the trait form. The outward appearance of an organism does not always indicate which pair of alleles is present. The organism's allele pairs are called its **genotype.** In the case of plants with yellow seeds, their genotypes could be *YY* or *Yy*. The observable characteristic or outward expression of an allele pair is called the **phenotype.** The phenotype of pea plants with the genotype *yy* will be green seeds.

**Mendel's law of segregation** Mendel used homozygous yellow-seed and green-seed plants in his P cross. In **Figure 10.9,** the first drawing shows that each gamete from the yellow-seed plant contains one *Y*. Recall that the chromosome number is divided in half during meiosis. The resulting gametes contain only one of the pair of seed-color alleles.

The second drawing in **Figure 10.9** shows that each gamete from the green-seed plant contains one *y* allele. Mendel's **law of segregation** states that the two alleles for each trait separate during meiosis. During fertilization, two alleles for that trait unite.

The third drawing in **Figure 10.9** shows the alleles uniting to produce the genotype *Yy* during fertilization. All resulting $F_1$ generation plants will have the genotype *Yy* and will have yellow seeds because yellow is dominant to green. These heterozygous organisms are called **hybrids**.

**VOCABULARY**

**WORD ORIGIN**

**Homozygous** and **Heterozygous** come from the Greek words *homos*, meaning *the same; hetero*, meaning *other* or *different;* and *zygon*, meaning *yoke*.

**Study Tip**

**BioJournal** While you are reading, find more information and further clarification on different aspects of genetics at biologygmh.com. Add the information that you find to your BioJournal.

**Figure 10.9** During gamete formation in the *YY* or *yy* plant, the two alleles separate, resulting in *Y* or *y* in the gametes. Gametes from each parent unite during fertilization.

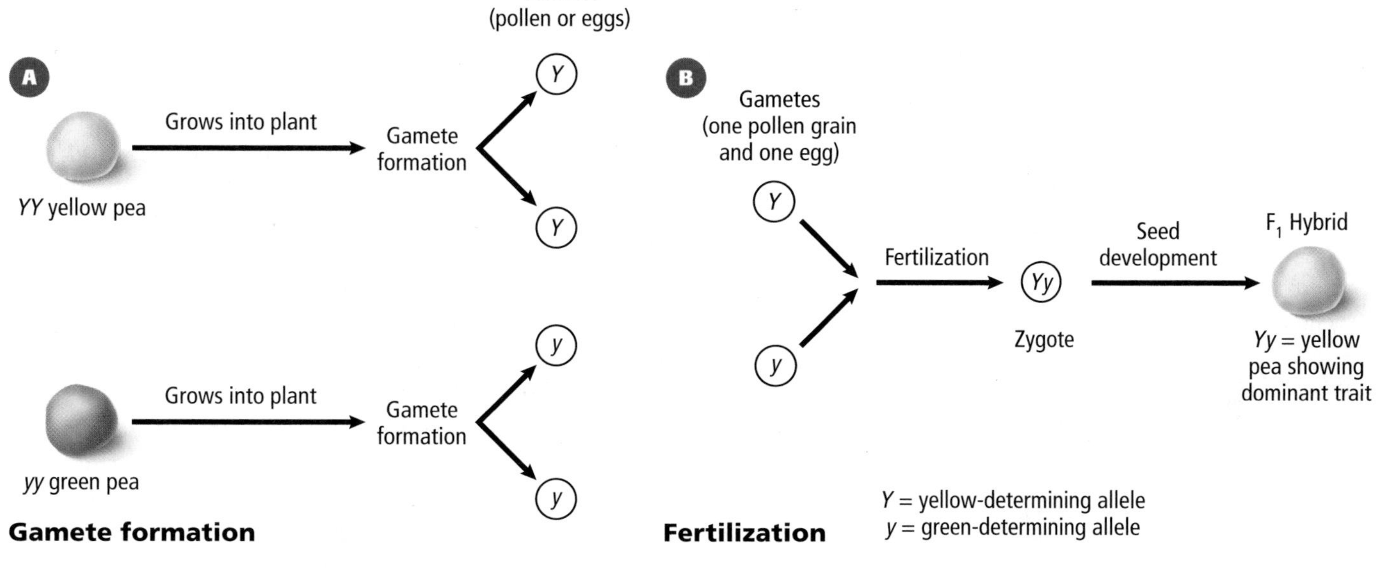

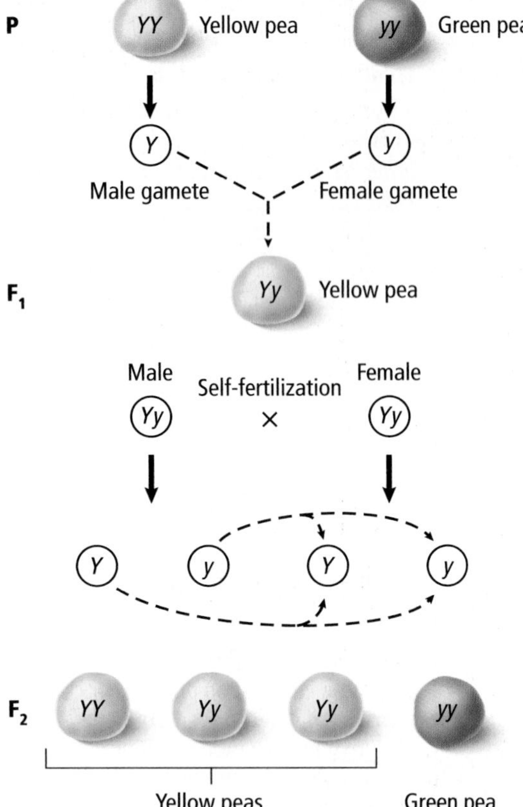


■ **Figure 10.10** During the $F_1$ generation self-fertilization, the male gametes randomly fertilize the female gametes.

■ **Figure 10.11** The law of independent assortment is demonstrated in the dihybrid cross by the equal chance that each pair of alleles (*Yy* and *Rr*) can randomly combine with each other.

**Predict** ***How many possible gamete types are produced?***

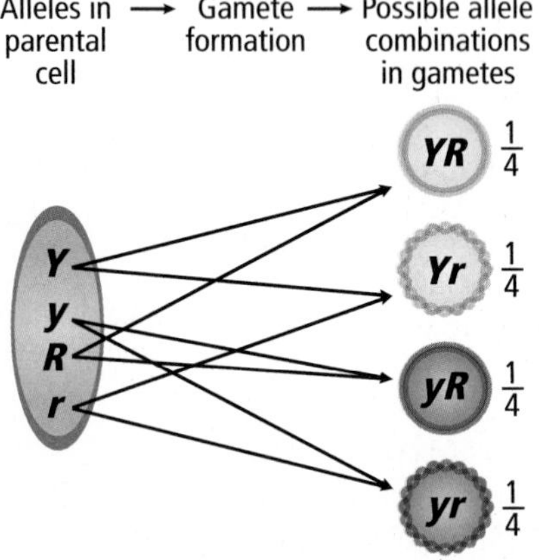


**Monohybrid cross** The diagram in **Figure 10.10** shows how Mendel continued his experiments by allowing the *Yy* plants to self-fertilize. A cross such as this one that involves hybrids for a single trait is called a monohybrid cross. The *Yy* plants produce two types of gametes—male and female—each with either the *Y* or *y* allele. The combining of these gametes is a random event. This random fertilization of male and female gametes results in the following genotypes—*YY, Yy, Yy,* or *yy,* as shown in **Figure 10.10.** Notice that the dominant *Y* allele is written first, whether it came from the male or female gamete. In Mendel's $F_1$ cross, there are three possible genotypes: *YY, Yy,* and *yy;* and the genotypic ratio is 1:2:1. The phenotypic ratio is 3:1—yellow seeds to green seeds.

**Dihybrid cross** Once Mendel established inheritance patterns of a single trait, he began to examine simultaneous inheritance of two or more traits in the same plant. In garden peas, round seeds *(R)* are dominant to wrinkled seeds *(r),* and yellow seeds *(Y)* are dominant to green seeds *(y).* If Mendel crossed homozygous yellow, round-seed pea plants with homozygous green, wrinkle-seed pea plants, the P cross could be represented by *YYRR* × *yyrr.* The $F_1$ generation genotype would be *YyRr*—yellow, round-seed plants. These $F_1$-generation plants are called dihybrids because they are heterozygous for both traits.

**Law of independent assortment** Mendel allowed $F_1$ pea plants with the genotype *YyRr* to self-fertilize in a dihybrid cross. Mendel calculated the genotypic and phenotypic ratios of the offspring in both the $F_1$ and $F_2$ generations. From these results, he developed the **law of independent assortment,** which states that a random distribution of alleles occurs during gamete formation. Genes on separate chromosomes sort independently during meiosis.

As shown in **Figure 10.11,** the random assortment of alleles results in four possible gametes: *YR, Yr, yR* or *yr,* each of which is equally likely to occur. When a plant self-fertilizes, any of the four allele combinations could be present in the male gamete, and any of the four combinations could be present in the female gamete. The results of Mendel's dihybrid cross included nine different genotypes: *YYRR, YYRr, YYrr, YyRR, YyRr, Yyrr, yyRR, yyRr,* and *yyrr.* He counted and recorded four different phenotypes: 315 yellow round, 108 green round, 101 yellow wrinkled, and 32 green wrinkled. These results represent a phenotypic ratio of approximately 9:3:3:1.

**Reading Check** **Evaluate** How can the random distribution of alleles result in a predictable ratio?

## Punnett Squares

In the early 1900s, Dr. Reginald Punnett developed what is known as a Punnett square to predict the possible offspring of a cross between two known genotypes. Punnett squares make it easier to keep track of the possible genotypes involved in a cross.

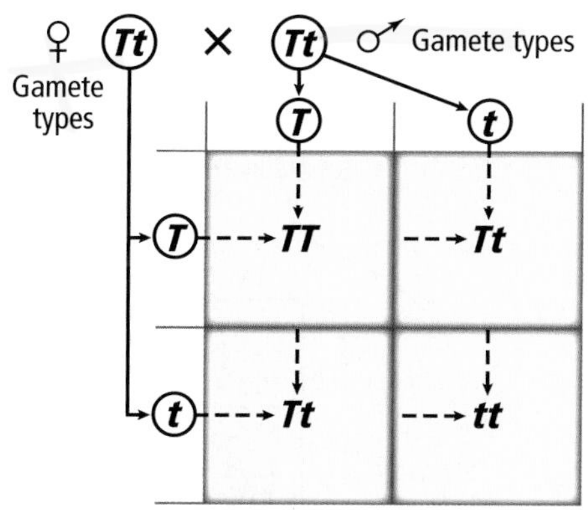


**Figure 10.12** The ability to roll one's tongue is a dominant trait. The Punnett square is a visual summary of the possible combinations of the alleles for the tongue-rolling trait.

**Punnett square—monohybrid cross** Can you roll your tongue like the person pictured in **Figure 10.12?** Tongue-rolling ability is a dominant trait, which can be represented by *T*. Suppose both parents can roll their tongues and are heterozygous (*Tt*) for the trait. What possible phenotypes could their children have?

Examine the Punnett square in **Figure 10.12.** The number of squares is determined by the number of different types of alleles—*T* or *t*—produced by each parent. In this case, the square is 2 squares × 2 squares because each parent produces two different types of gametes. Notice that the male gametes are written across the horizontal side and the female gametes are written on the vertical side of the Punnett square. The possible combinations of each male and female gamete are written on the inside of each corresponding square.

## MiniLab 10.1

### Predict Probability in Genetics

**How can an offspring's traits be predicted?** A Punnett square can help predict ratios of dominant traits to recessive traits in the genotype of offspring. This lab involves two parents who are both heterozygous for free earlobes (E), which is a dominant trait. The recessive trait is attached earlobes (e).

**Procedure**

1. Read and complete the lab safety form.
2. Determine the gamete genotype(s) for this trait that each parent contributes.
3. Draw a Punnett square that has the same number of columns and the same number of rows as the number of alleles contributed for this trait by the gametes of each parent.
4. Write the alphabetical letter for each allele from one parent just above each column, and write the alphabetical letter for each allele from the other parent just to the left of each row.
5. In the boxes within the table, write the genotype of the offspring resulting from each combination of male and female alleles.

**Analysis**

1. **Summarize** List the possible offspring phenotypes that could occur.
2. **Evaluate** What is the phenotypic ratio of the possible offspring? What is the genotypic ratio of the possible offspring?

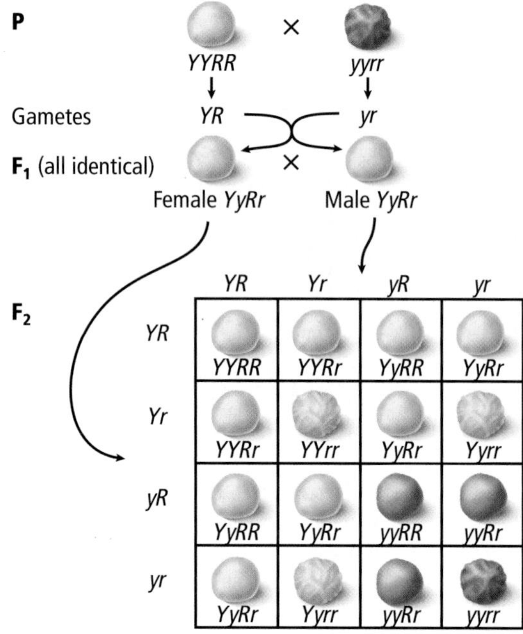


| Type | Genotype | Phenotype | Number | Phenotypic Ratio |
|---|---|---|---|---|
| Parental | Y_R_ | yellow round | 315 | 9:16 |
| Recombinant | yyR_ | green round | 108 | 3:16 |
| Recombinant | Y_rr | yellow wrinkled | 101 | 3:16 |
| Parental | yyrr | green wrinkled | 32 | 1:16 |

**Figure 10.13** The dihybrid Punnett square visually presents the possible combinations of the possible alleles from each parent.

How many different genotypes are found in the Punnett square? One square has *TT,* two squares have *Tt,* and one square has *tt.* Therefore, the genotypic ratio of the possible offspring is 1:2:1. The phenotypic ratio of tongue rollers to non-tongue rollers is 3:1.

**Punnett square—dihybrid cross** Now examine the Punnett square in **Figure 10.13.** Notice that in the P cross, only two types of alleles are produced. However, in the dihybrid cross—when the $F_1$ generation is crossed—four types of alleles from the male gametes and four types of alleles from the female gametes can be produced. The resulting phenotypic ratio is 9:3:3:1, yellow round to green round to yellow wrinkled to green wrinkled. Mendel's data closely matched the outcome predicted by the Punnett square.

## Probability

The inheritance of genes can be compared to the probability of flipping a coin. The probability of the coin landing on heads is 1 out of 2, or 1/2. If the same coin is flipped twice, the probability of it landing on heads is 1/2 each time or $1/2 \times 1/2$, or 1/4 both times.

Actual data might not perfectly match the predicted ratios. You know that if you flip a coin you might not get heads 1 out of 2 times. Mendel's results were not exactly a 9:3:3:1 ratio. However, the larger the number of offspring involved in a cross, the more likely it will match the results predicted by the Punnett square.

## Section 10.2 Assessment

### Section Summary

- The study of genetics began with Gregor Mendel, whose experiments with garden pea plants gave insight into the inheritance of traits.
- Mendel developed the law of segregation and the law of independent assortment.
- Punnett squares help predict the offspring of a cross.

### Understand Main Ideas

1. MAIN Idea **Diagram** Use a Punnett square to explain how a dominant allele masks the presence of a recessive allele.
2. **Apply** the law of segregation and the law of independent assortment by giving an example of each.
3. **Use a Punnett square** In fruit flies, red eyes (*R*) are dominant to pink eyes (*r*). What is the phenotypic ratio of a cross between a heterozygous male and a pink-eyed female?

### Think Scientifically

4. *Evaluate* Why would a large number of offspring in a cross be more likely to match Punnett-square ratios than a small number would?
5. MATH in Biology What is the probability of rolling a 2 on a six-sided die? What is the probability of rolling two 2s on two six-sided die? How is probability used in the study of genetics?



Biology Online Self-Check Quiz biologygmh.com

Section 10.3

# Gene Linkage and Polyploidy

**Objectives**

- **Summarize** how the process of meiosis produces genetic recombination.
- **Explain** how gene linkage can be used to create chromosome maps.
- **Analyze** why polyploidy is important to the field of agriculture.

**Review Vocabulary**

**protein:** large, complex polymer essential to all life that provides structure for tissues and organs and helps carry out cell metabolism

**New Vocabulary**

genetic recombination
polyploidy

MAIN Idea **The crossing over of linked genes is a source of genetic variation.**

**Real-World Reading Link** You might find many varieties of plants in a garden center that are not found in the wild. For example, you might have seen many varieties of roses that range in color from red to pink to white. Plant breeders use scientists' knowledge of genes to vary certain characteristics in an effort to make their roses unique.

## Genetic Recombination

Connection to Math The new combination of genes produced by crossing over and independent assortment is called **genetic recombination.** The possible combinations of genes due to independent assortment can be calculated using the formula $2^n$, where $n$ is the number of chromosome pairs. For example, pea plants have seven pairs of chromosomes. For seven pairs of chromosomes, the possible combinations are $2^7$, or 128 combinations. Because any possible male gamete can fertilize any possible female gamete, the number of possible combinations after fertilization is 16,384 ($128 \times 128$). In humans, the possible number of combinations after fertilization would be $2^{23} \times 2^{23}$, or more than 70 trillion. This number does not include the amount of genetic recombination produced by crossing over.

## Gene Linkage

Recall that chromosomes contain multiple genes that code for proteins. Genes that are located close to each other on the same chromosome are said to be linked and usually travel together during gamete formation. Study **Figure 10.14** and observe that genes *A* and *B* are located close to each other on the same chromosome and travel together during meiosis. The linkage of genes on a chromosome results in an exception to Mendel's law of independent assortment because linked genes usually do not segregate independently.

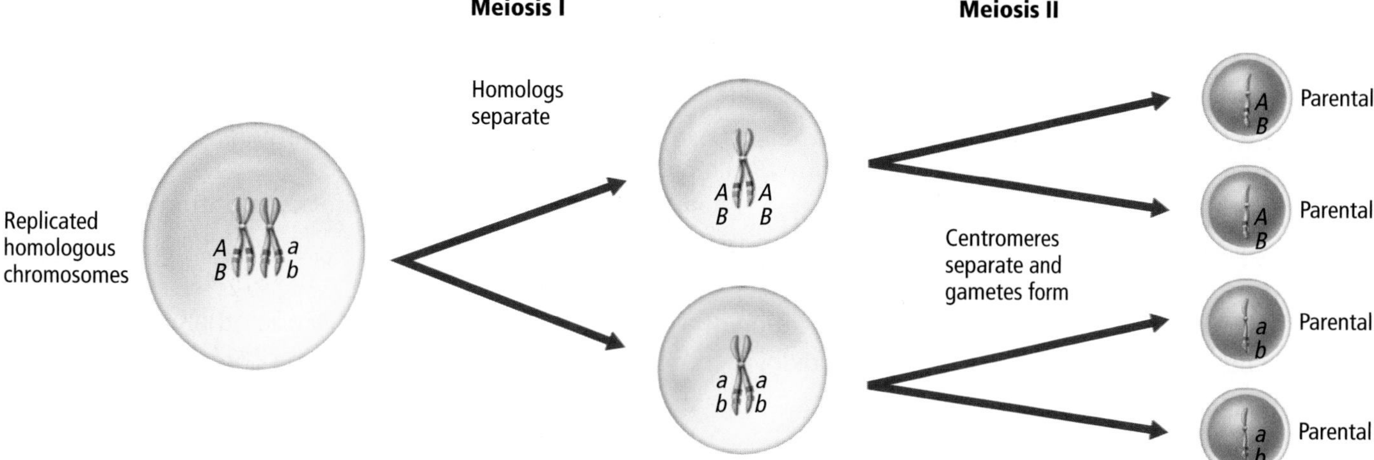


**Figure 10.14** Genes that are linked together on the same chromosome usually travel together in the gamete.
**Calculate** ***the number of possible combinations if two or three of these gametes were to combine.***

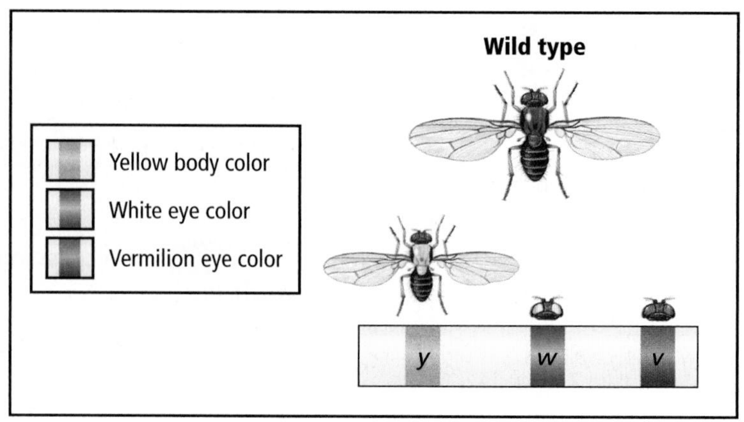


■ **Figure 10.15** This chromosome map of the X chromosome of the fruit fly *Drosophila melanogaster* was created in 1913.

Gene linkage was first studied using the fruit fly *Drosophila melanogaster.* Thousands of crosses confirmed that linked genes usually traveled together during meiosis. However, some results revealed that linked genes do not always travel together during meiosis. Scientists concluded that linked genes can separate during crossing over.

**Chromosome maps** Crossing over occurs more frequently between genes that are far apart than those that are close together. A drawing called a chromosome map shows the sequence of genes on a chromosome and can be created by using crossover data. The very first chromosome maps were published in 1913 using data from thousands of fruit fly crosses. Chromosome map percentages are not actual chromosome distances, but they represent relative positions of the genes. **Figure 10.15** shows the first chromosome map created using fruit fly data. Notice that the higher the crossover frequency, the farther apart the two genes are.

## MiniLab 10.2

### Map Chromosomes

**Where are genes located on a chromosome?** The distance between two genes on a chromosome is related to the crossover frequency between them. By comparing data for several gene pairs, a gene's relative location can be determined.

**Procedure**

1. Read and complete the lab safety form.
2. Obtain a table of the gene-pair crossover frequencies from your teacher.
3. Draw a line on a piece of paper and make marks every 1 cm. Each mark will represent a crossover frequency of 1 percent.
4. Label one mark near the middle of the line *A.* Find the crossover frequency between Genes A and B on the table, and use this data to label *B* the correct distance from A.
5. Use the crossover frequency between genes A and C and genes B and C to infer the position of gene C.
6. Repeat steps 4–5 for each gene, marking their positions on the line.

**Analysis**

1. **Evaluate** Is it possible to know the location of a gene on a chromosome if only one other gene is used?
2. **Consider** Why would using more crossover frequencies result in a more accurate chromosome map?

**Infering genotypes** Pedigrees are used to infer genotypes from the observation of phenotypes. By knowing physical traits, genealogists can determine what genes an individual is most likely to have. Phenotypes of entire families are analyzed in order to determine family genotypes, as symbolized in **Figure 11.3.**

Pedigrees help genetic counselors determine whether inheritance patterns are dominant or recessive. Once the inheritance pattern is determined, the genotypes of the individuals can largely be resolved through pedigree analysis. To analyze pedigrees, one particular trait is studied, and a determination is made as to whether that trait is dominant or recessive. Dominant traits are easier to recognize than recessive traits are, because dominant traits are exhibited in the phenotype.

A recessive trait will not be expressed unless the person is homozygous recessive for the trait. That means that a recessive allele is passed on by each parent. When recessive traits are expressed, the ancestry of the person expressing the trait is followed for several generations to determine which parents and grandparents were carriers of the recessive allele.

**Predicting disorders** If good records have been kept within families, disorders in future offspring can be predicted. However, more accuracy can be expected if several individuals within the family can be evaluated. The study of human genetics is difficult, because scientists are limited by time, ethics, and circumstances. For example, it takes decades for each generation to mature and then to have offspring when the study involves humans. Therefore, good record keeping, where it exists, helps scientists use pedigree analysis to study inheritance patterns, to determine phenotypes, and to ascertain genotypes within a family.

**CAREERS IN BIOLOGY**

**Genealogist** A genealogist studies or traces the descent of individuals or families. For more information on biology careers, visit biologygmh.com.

## Section 11.1 Assessment

### Section Summary

- Genetic disorders can be caused by dominant or recessive alleles.
- Cystic fibrosis is a genetic disorder that affects mucus and sweat secretions.
- Individuals with albinism do not have melanin in their skin, hair, and eyes.
- Huntington's disease affects the nervous system.
- Achondroplasia sometimes is called dwarfism.
- Pedigrees are used to study human inheritance patterns.

### Understand Main Ideas

1. MAIN Idea **Construct** a family pedigree of two unaffected parents with a child who suffers from cystic fibrosis.
2. **Explain** the type of inheritance associated with Huntington's disease and achondroplasia.
3. **Interpret** Can two parents with albinism have an unaffected child? Explain.
4. **Diagram** Suppose both parents can roll their tongues but their son cannot. Draw a pedigree showing this trait, and label each symbol with the appropriate genotype.

### Think Scientifically

5. MATH in Biology Phenylketonuria (PKU) is a recessive genetic disorder. If both parents are carriers, what is the probability of this couple having a child with PKU? What is the chance of this couple having two children with PKU?
6. *Determine* When a couple requests a test for cystic fibrosis, what types of questions might the physician ask before ordering the tests?

Section 11.2

**Objectives**

- **Distinguish** between various complex inheritance patterns.
- **Analyze** sex-linked and sex-limited inheritance patterns.
- **Explain** how the environment can influence the phenotype of an organism.

**Review Vocabulary**

**gamete:** a mature sex cell (sperm or egg) with a haploid number of chromosomes

**New Vocabulary**

incomplete dominance
codominance
multiple alleles
epistasis
sex chromosome
autosome
sex-linked trait
polygenic trait

# Complex Patterns of Inheritance

**MAIN Idea Complex inheritance of traits does not follow inheritance patterns described by Mendel.**

**Real-World Reading Link** Imagine that you have red-green color blindness. In bright light, red lights do not stand out against surroundings. At night, green lights look like white streetlights. To help those with red-green color blindness, traffic lights always follow the same pattern. Red-green color blindness, however, does not follow the same pattern of inheritance described by Mendel.

## Incomplete Dominance

Recall that when an organism is heterozygous for a trait, its phenotype will be that of the dominant trait. For example, if the genotype of a pea plant is *Tt* and *T* is the genotype for the dominant trait *tall*, then its phenotype will be tall. Examine **Figure 11.4.** However, when red-flowered snapdragons *(RR)* are crossed with white-flowered snapdragons *(rr)*, the heterozygous offspring have pink flowers *(Rr)*. This is an example of **incomplete dominance,** in which the heterozygous phenotype is an intermediate phenotype between the two homozygous phenotypes. When the heterozygous $F_1$ generation snapdragon plants are allowed to self-fertilize, as in **Figure 11.4,** the flowers are red, pink, and white in a 1: 2: 1 ratio, respectively.

## Codominance

Recall that when an organism is heterozygous for a particular trait the dominant phenotype is expressed. In a complex inheritance pattern called **codominance,** both alleles are expressed in the heterozygous condition. For example, sickle-cell disease follows codominant inheritance.

**Figure 11.4** The color of snapdragon flowers is a result of incomplete dominance. When a plant with white flowers is crossed with a plant with red flowers, the offspring have pink flowers. Red, pink, and white offspring will result from self fertilization of a plant with pink flowers.
**Predict** *What would happen if you crossed a pink flower with a white flower?*

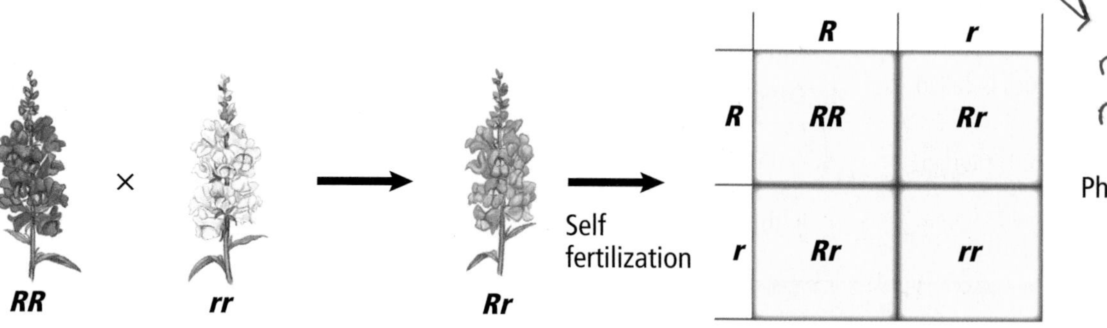

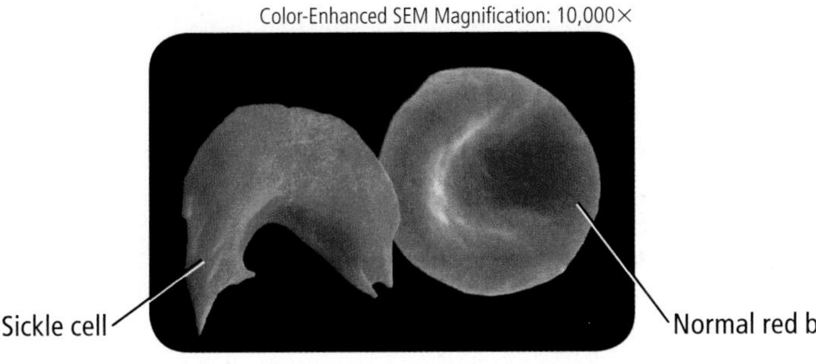


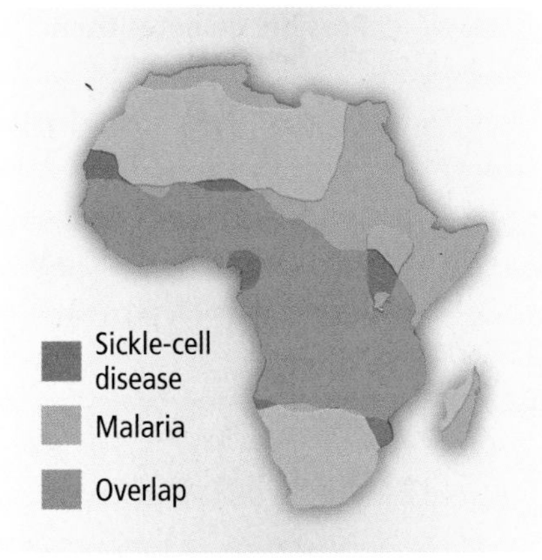


**Figure 11.5**
**Left:** Normal red blood cells are flat and disk-shaped. Sickle-shaped cells are elongated and "C" shaped. They can clump, blocking circulation in small vessels.
**Right:** The sickle-cell allele increases resistance to malaria.

**Sickle-cell disease** The allele responsible for sickle-cell disease is particularly common in people of African descent, with about nine percent of African Americans having one form of the trait. Sickle-cell disease affects red blood cells and their ability to transport oxygen. The photograph in **Figure 11.5** shows the blood cells of an individual who is heterozygous for the sickle-cell trait. Changes in hemoglobin—the protein in red blood cells—cause those blood cells to change to a sickle, or "C", shape. Sickle-shaped cells do not effectively transport oxygen because they block circulation in small blood vessels. Those who are heterozygous for the trait have both normal and sickle-shaped cells. These individuals can lead relatively normal lives, as the normal blood cells compensate for the sickle-shaped cells.

**Sickle-cell disease and malaria** Note in **Figure 11.5** the distribution of both sickle-cell disease and malaria in Africa. Some areas with sickle-cell disease overlap areas of widespread malaria. Why might such high levels of the sickle-cell allele exist in central Africa? Scientists have discovered that those who are heterozygous for the sickle-cell trait also have a higher resistance to malaria. The death rate due to malaria is lower where the sickle-cell trait is higher. Because less malaria exists in those areas, more people live to pass on the sickle-cell trait to offspring. Consequently, sickle-cell disease continues to increase in Africa.

## DATA ANALYSIS LAB 11.1

**Based On Real Data***

### Interpret the Graph

**What is the relationship between sickle-cell disease and other complications?** Patients who have been diagnosed with sickle-cell disease face many symptoms, including respiratory failure and neurological problems. The graph shows the relationship between age and two different symptoms—pain and fever—during the two weeks preceding an episode of acute chest syndrome and hospitalization.

**Think Critically**

1. **State** which age group has the highest level of pain before being hospitalized.
2. **Describe** the relationship between age and fever before hospitalization.

**Data and Observations**

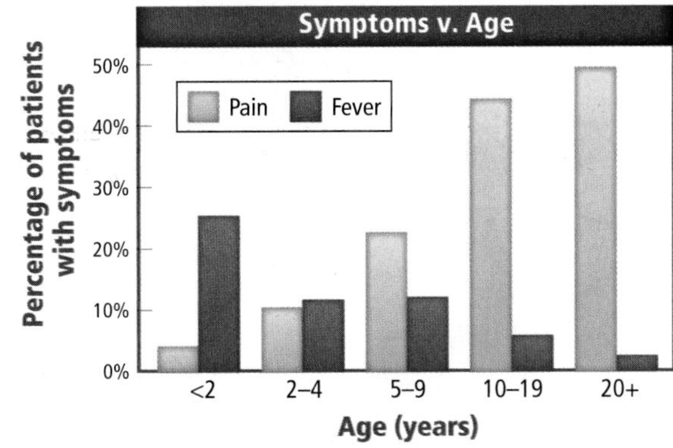


*Data obtained from: Walters, et al. 2002. Novel therapeutic approaches in sickle cell disease. *Hemotology* 17: 10-34.

|  | Possible gametes from female parent: $I^A$ | or $I^B$ | or $i$ |
|---|---|---|---|
| Possible gametes from male parent: $I^A$ | $I^AI^A$ | $I^AI^B$ | $I^Ai$ |
| or $I^B$ | $I^AI^B$ | $I^BI^B$ | $I^Bi$ |
| or $i$ | $I^Ai$ | $I^Bi$ | $ii$ |

Blood types: A, AB, B, O

■ **Figure 11.6** There are three forms of alleles in the ABO blood groups—$I^A$, $I^B$, and $i$.

# Multiple Alleles

So far, you have learned about inheritance involving two forms of alleles for a trait. Some forms of inheritance, such as blood groups in humans, are determined by **multiple alleles.**

**Blood groups in humans** ABO blood groups have three forms of alleles, sometimes called AB markers: $I^A$ is blood type A; $I^B$ is blood type B; and $i$ is blood type O. Type O is the absence of AB markers. Note that allele $i$ is recessive to $I^A$ and $I^B$. However, $I^A$ and $I^B$ are codominant; blood type AB results from both $I^A$ and $I^B$ alleles. Therefore, ABO blood groups are examples of both multiple alleles and codominance, as shown in **Figure 11.6.**

Blood also has Rh factors, inherited from each parent. Rh factors are either positive or negative (Rh+ or Rh–); Rh+ is dominant. The Rh factor is a blood protein named after the rhesus monkey, because studies of the rhesus monkey led to discovery of that blood protein.

**Coat color of rabbits** Multiple alleles can demonstrate a hierarchy of dominance. In rabbits, four alleles code for coat color: $C$, $c^{ch}$, $c^h$, and $c$. Allele $C$ is dominant to the other alleles and results in a full color coat. Allele $c$ is recessive and results in an albino phenotype when the genotype is homozygous recessive. Allele $c^{ch}$ is dominant to $c^h$, and allele $c^h$ is dominant to $c$ and the hierarchy of dominance can be written as $C > c^{ch} > c^h > c$. **Figure 11.7** shows the genotypes and phenotypes possible for rabbit-coat color. Full color is dominant over chinchilla, which is dominant over Himalayan, which is dominant over albino.

The presence of multiple alleles increases the possible number of genotypes and phenotypes. Without multiple-allele dominance, two alleles, such as $T$ and $t$, produce only three possible genotypes—in this example $TT$, $Tt$, and $tt$—and two possible phenotypes. However, the four alleles for rabbit-coat color produce ten possible genotypes and four phenotypes, as shown in **Figure 11.7.** More variation in rabbit coat color comes from the interaction of the color gene with other genes such as the agouti gene or the broken gene.

■ **Figure 11.7** Rabbits have multiple alleles for coat color. The four alleles provide four basic variations in coat color.

**No dark pigment present in fur** **Dark pigment present in fur**

■ **Figure 11.8** The results of epistasis in coat color in Labrador retrievers show an interaction of two genes, each with two alleles.

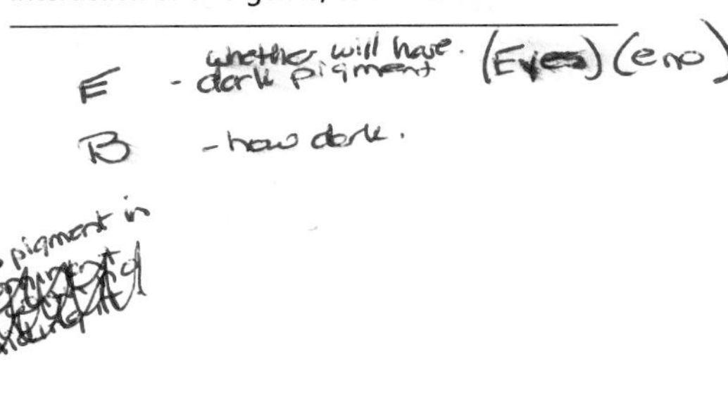

## Epistasis

Coat color in Labrador retrievers can vary from yellow to black. This variety is the result of one allele hiding the effects of another allele, an interaction called **epistasis** (ih PIHS tuh sus). A Labrador's coat color is controlled by two sets of alleles. The dominant allele *E* determines whether the fur will have dark pigment. The fur of a dog with genotype *ee* will not have any pigment. The dominant B allele determines how dark the pigment will be. Study **Figure 11.8.** If the dog's genotype is *EEbb* or *Eebb,* the dog's fur will be chocolate brown. Genotypes *eebb, eeBb,* and *eeBB* will produce a yellow coat, because the *e* allele masks the effects of the dominant *B* allele.

## Sex Determination

Each cell in your body, except for gametes, contains 46 chromosomes, or 23 pairs of chromosomes. One pair of these chromosomes, the **sex chromosomes,** determines an individual's gender. There are two types of sex chromosomes: X and Y. Individuals with two X chromosomes are female, and individuals with an X and a Y chromosome are male. The other 22 pairs of chromosomes are called **autosomes.** The offspring's gender is determined by the combination of sex chromosomes in the egg and sperm cell, as shown in **Figure 11.9.**

■ **Figure 11.9**
**Left:** The size and shape of the Y chromosome and the X chromosome are quite different from one another.
**Right:** The segregation of the sex chromosomes into gametes and the random combination of sperm and egg cells result in an approximately 1:1 ratio of males to females.

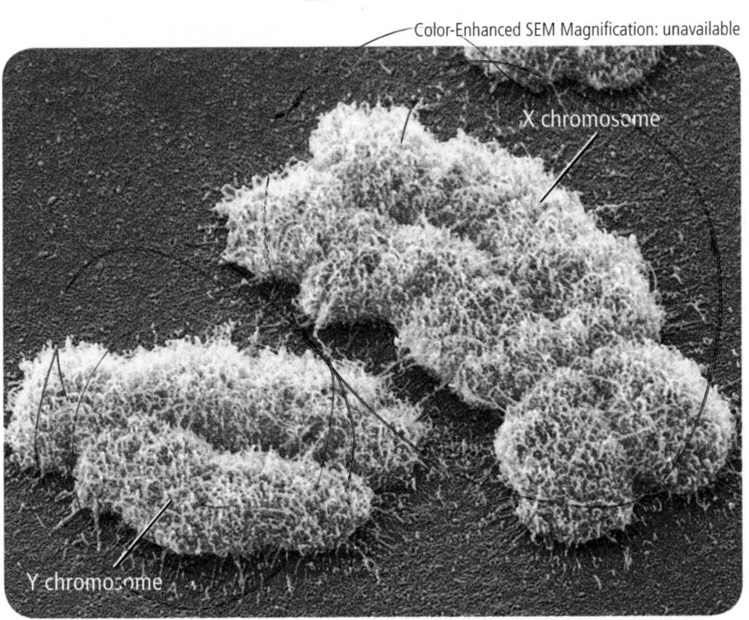


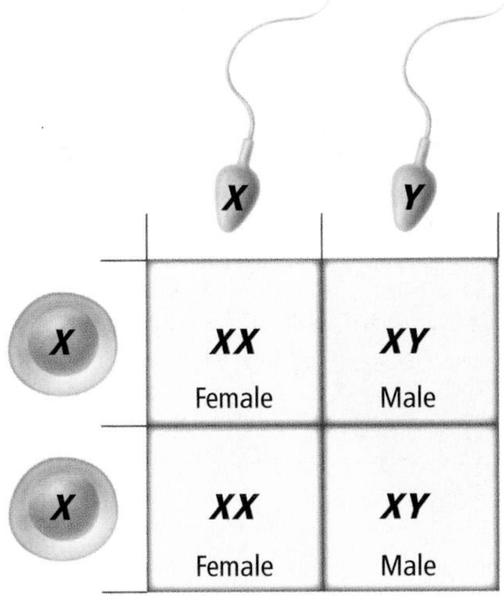


**XX** = 2/4 = 1/2
**XY** = 2/4 = 1/2

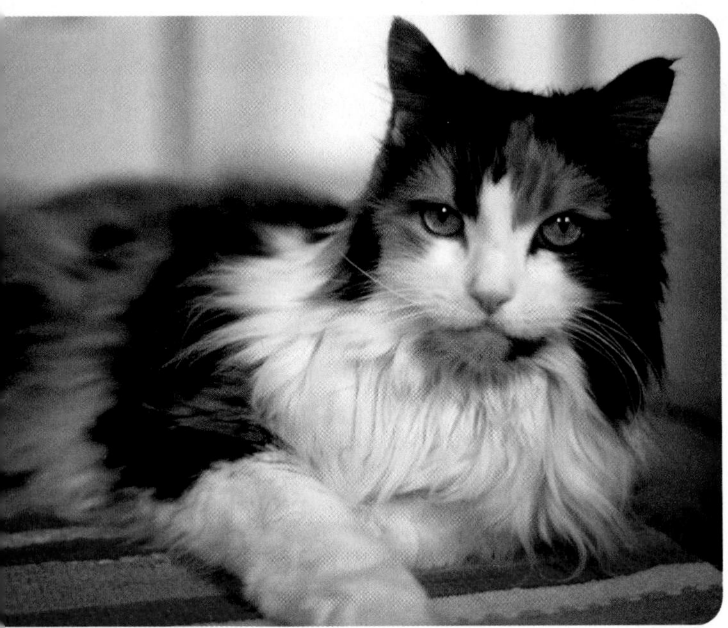

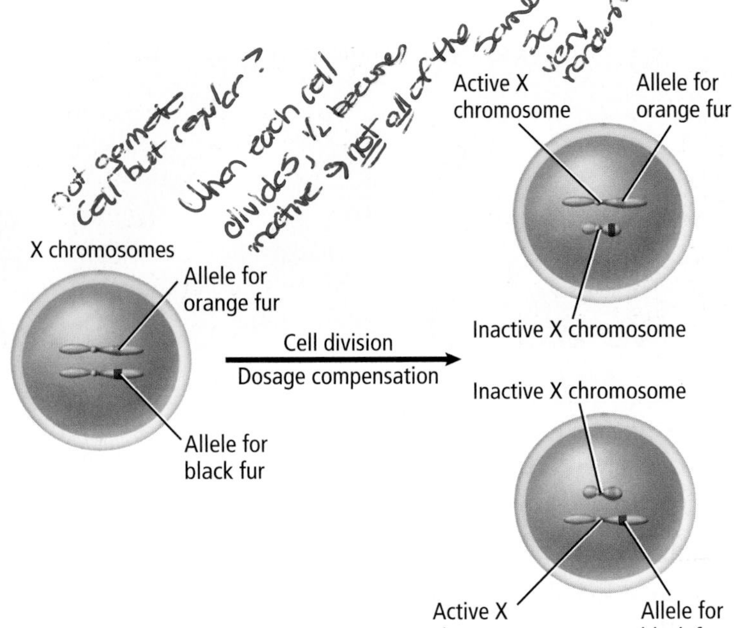


■ **Figure 11.10** The calico coat of this cat results from the random inactivation of the X chromosomes. One X chromosome codes for orange fur, and one X chromosome codes for black fur, as illustrated on the right.

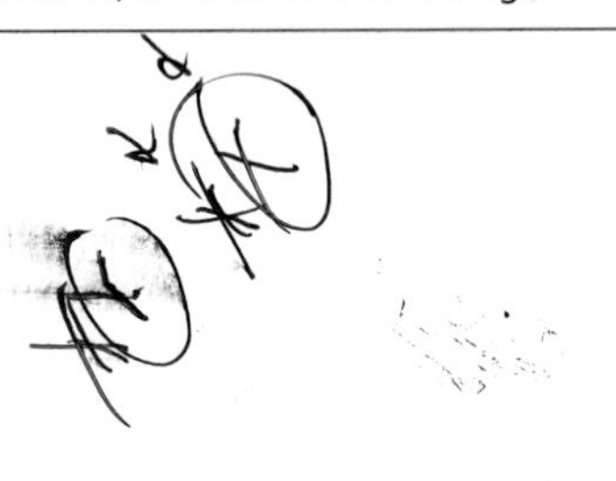

## Dosage Compensation

Human females have 22 pairs of autosomes and one pair of X chromosomes. Males have 22 pairs of autosomes along with one X and one Y chromosome. If you examine the X and Y chromosomes in **Figure 11.9,** you will notice that the X chromosome is larger than the Y chromosome. The X chromosome carries a variety of genes that are necessary for the development of both females and males. The Y chromosome mainly has genes that relate to the development of male characteristics.

Because females have two X chromosomes, it seems as though females get two doses of the X chromosome and males get only one dose. To balance the difference in the dose of X-related genes, one of the X chromosomes stops working in each of the female's body cells. This often is called dosage compensation or X-inactivation. Which X chromosome stops working in each body cell is a completely random event. Dosage compensation occurs in all mammals.

As a result of the Human Genome Project, the National Institutes of Health (NIH) has released new information on the sequence of the human X chromosome. Researchers now believe that some genes on the inactivated X chromosome are more active than previously thought.

**Chromosome inactivation** The coat colors of the calico cat shown in **Figure 11.10** are caused by the random inactivation of a particular X chromosome. The resulting colors depend on the X chromosome that is activated. The orange patches are formed by the inactivation of the X chromosome carrying the allele for black coat color. Similarly, the black patches are a result of the activation of the X chromosome carrying the allele for orange coat color.

**Barr bodies** The inactivated X chromosomes can be observed in cells. In 1949, Canadian scientist Murray Barr observed inactivated X chromosomes in female calico cats. He noticed a condensed, darkly stained structure in the nucleus. The darkly stained, inactivated X chromosomes, such as the one shown in **Figure 11.11,** are called Barr bodies. It was discovered later that only females, including human females, have Barr bodies in their cell nuclei.

■ **Figure 11.11** Inactivated X chromosomes in female body cells are called Barr bodies, a dark body usually found near the nucleus.

Phase contrast LM Magnification: 1000×

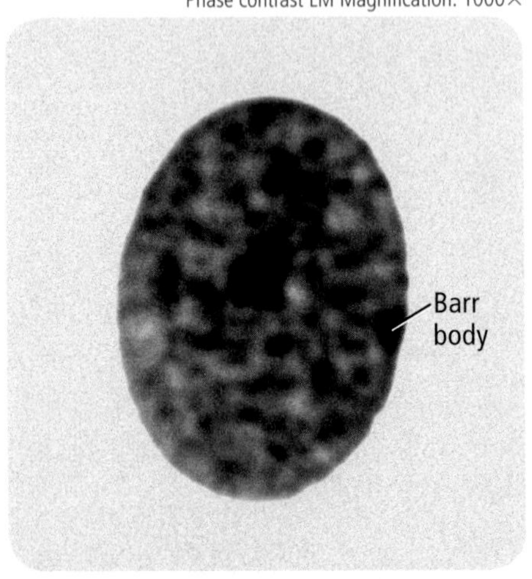

## Sex-Linked Traits

Recall that females have two X chromosomes and that males have one X and one Y chromosome. Traits controlled by genes located on the X chromosome are called **sex-linked traits**—also called X-linked traits. Since males have only one X chromosome, they are affected by recessive X-linked traits more often than are females. Females likely would not express a recessive X-linked trait because the other X chromosome will likely mask the effect of the recessive trait.

Some traits that are located on autosomes may appear to be sex-linked even though they are not. This occurs when an allele appears to be dominant in one gender but recessive in the other. For example, the allele for baldness is recessive in females but dominant in males, causing hair loss that follows a typical pattern called male-pattern baldness. A male would be bald if he were heterozygous for the trait, while the female would be bald only if she were homozygous recessive.

**Red-green color blindness** The trait for red-green color blindness is a recessive X-linked trait. About 8 percent of males in the United States have red-green color blindness. The photo in **Figure 11.12** shows how a person with red-green color blindness might view colors compared to a person who does not have red-green color blindness.

Study the Punnett square shown in **Figure 11.12.** The mother is a carrier for color blindness, because she has the recessive allele for color blindness on one of her X chromosomes. The father is not color blind, because he does not have the recessive allele. The sex-linked trait is represented by writing the allele on the X chromosome. Notice that the only child that can possibly have red-green color blindness is a male offspring. As a result of it being an X-linked trait, red-green color blindness is very rare in females.

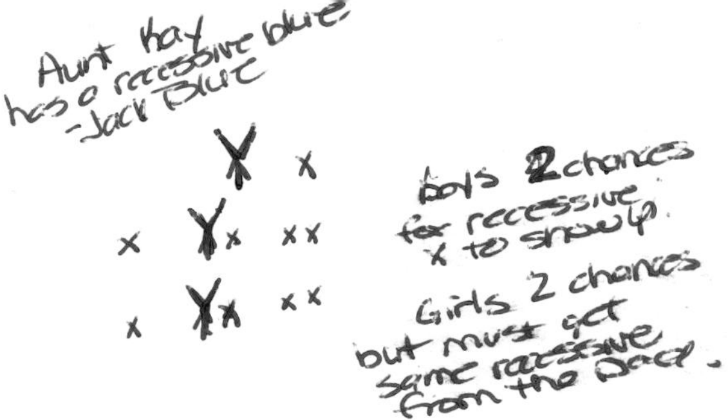

**Figure 11.12** People with red-green color blindness view red and green as shades of gray.

**Explain** *Why are there fewer females who have red-green color blindness than males?*

$X^B$ = Normal

$X^b$ = Red-green color blind

$Y$ = Y chromosome

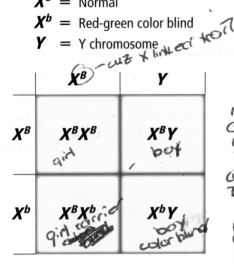

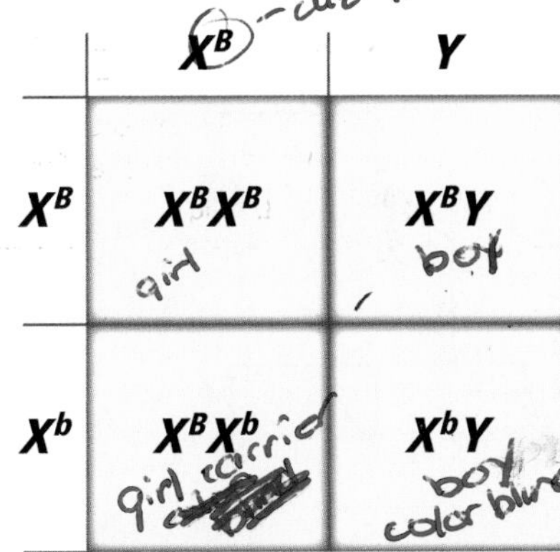


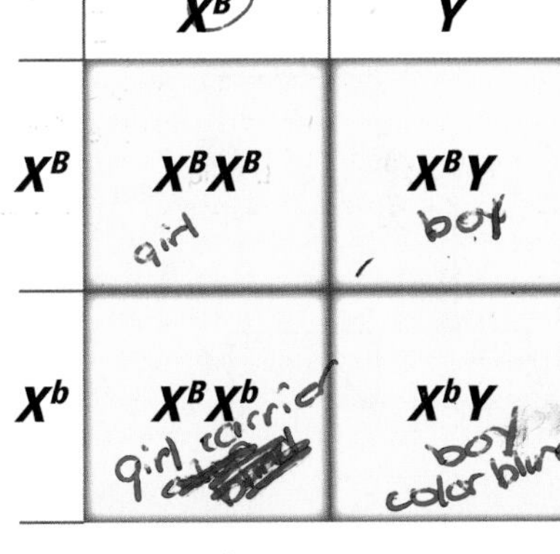

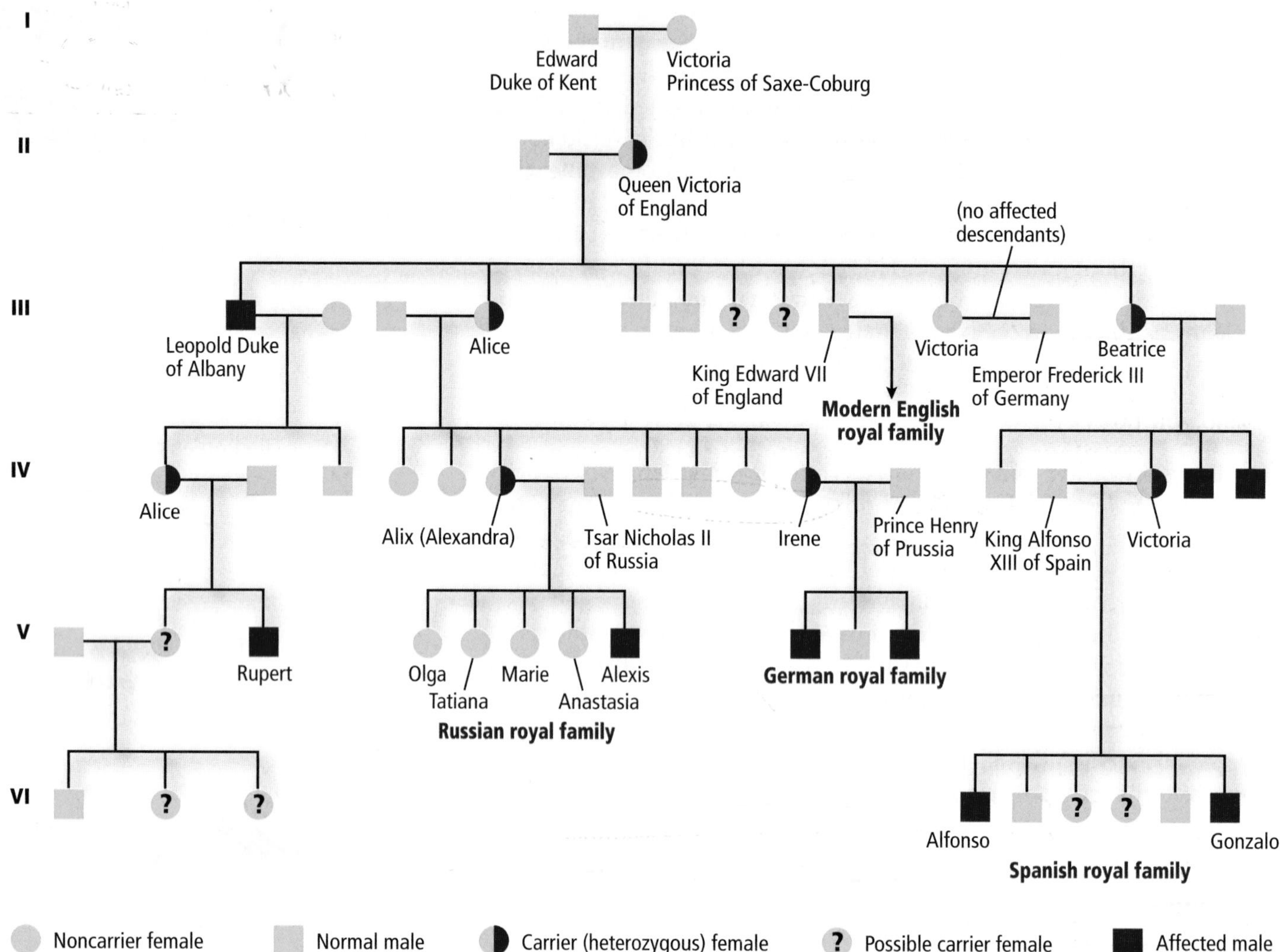


**Figure 11.13** The pedigree above shows the inheritance of hemophilia in the royal families of England, Germany, Spain, and Russia, starting with the children of Queen Victoria.

**Determine** ***Which of Alexandra's children inherited the disorder?***

**Hemophilia** Hemophilia, another recessive sex-linked disorder, is characterized by delayed clotting of the blood. Like red-green color blindness, this disorder is more common in males than in females.

A famous pedigree of hemophilia is one that arose in the family of Queen Victoria of England (1819-1901). Her son Leopold died of hemophilia, and her daughters Alice and Beatrice, illustrated in the pedigree in **Figure 11.13,** were carriers for the disease. Alice and Beatrice passed on the hemophilia trait to the Russian, German, and Spanish royal families. Follow the generations in this pedigree to see how this trait was passed through Queen Victoria's family. Queen Victoria's granddaughter Alexandra, who was a carrier for this trait, married Tsar Nicholas II of Russia. Irene, another granddaughter, passed the trait on to the German royal family. Hemophilia was passed to the Spanish royal family through a third granddaughter, whose name also was Victoria.

Men with hemophilia usually died at an early age until the twentieth century when clotting factors were discovered and given to hemophiliacs. However, blood-borne viruses such as Hepatitis C and HIV were often contracted by hemophiliacs until the 1990s, when safer methods of blood transfusion were discovered.

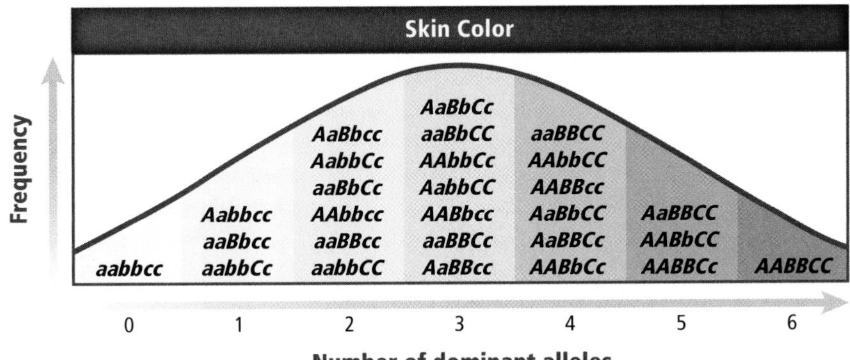


**Figure 11.14** This graph shows possible shades of skin color from three sets of alleles, although the trait is thought to involve more than three sets of alleles.

**Predict** ***Would more gene pairs increase or decrease the number of possible phenotypes?***

## Polygenic Traits

So far, you have examined traits determined by a pair of genes. Many phenotypic traits, however, arise from the interaction of multiple pairs of genes. Such traits are called **polygenic traits.** Traits such as skin color, height, eye color, and fingerprint pattern are polygenic traits. One characteristic of polygenic traits is that, when the frequency of the number of dominant alleles is graphed, as shown in **Figure 11.14,** the result is a bell-shaped curve. This shows that more of the intermediate phenotypes exist than do the extreme phenotypes.

**Reading Check Infer** Why would a graph showing the frequency of the number of dominant alleles for polygenic traits be a bell-shaped curve?

## Environmental Influences

The environment also has an effect on phenotype. For example, the tendency to develop heart disease can be inherited. However, environmental factors such as diet and exercise also can contribute to the occurrence and seriousness of the disease. Other ways in which environment influences phenotype are very familiar to you. You may not have thought of them in terms of phenotype, however. For example, sunlight, water, and temperature are environmental influences that affect an organism's phenotype.

**Sunlight and water** Without enough sunlight, most flowering plants do not bear flowers. Many plants lose their leaves in response to water deficiency. Most organisms experience phenotypic changes from extreme temperature changes. In extreme heat, for example, many plants suffer. Their leaves droop, flower buds shrivel, chlorophyll disappears, and roots stop growing. These are examples that probably do not surprise you, though you might never have thought of them as phenotypic changes. What other environmental factors affect the phenotypes of organisms?

**Temperature** Temperature also influences the expression of genes. Notice the fur of the Siamese cat shown in **Figure 11.15.** The cat's tail, feet, ears, and nose are dark. These areas of the cat's body are cooler than the rest. The gene that codes for production of the color pigment in the Siamese cat's body functions only under cooler conditions. Therefore, the cooler regions are darker; and the warmer regions, where pigment production is inhibited by temperature, are lighter.

**Figure 11.15** Temperature affects the expression of color pigment in the fur of Siamese cats.

**Figure 11.16** When a trait is found more often in both members of identical twins than in fraternal twins, the trait is presumed to have a significant inherited component.

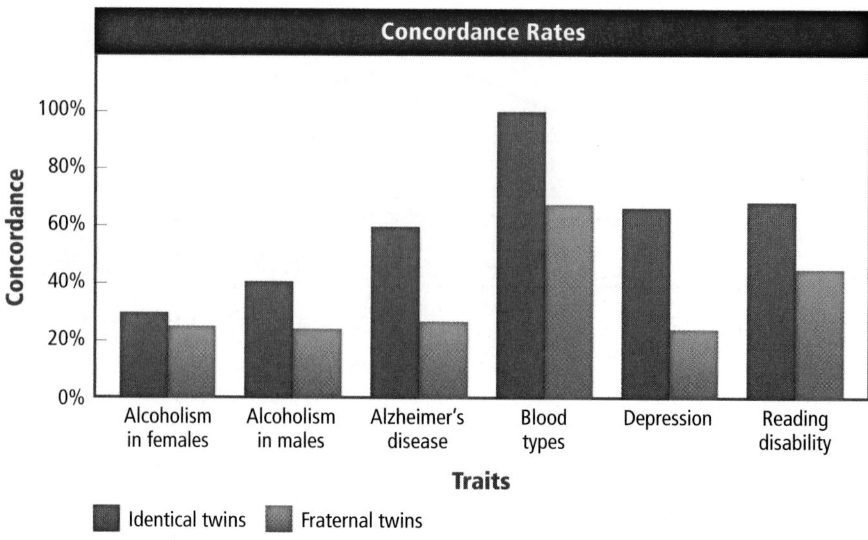


**LAUNCH Lab**

**Review** Based on what you've read about human inheritance, how would you now answer the analysis questions?

## Twin Studies

Another way to study inheritance patterns is to focus on identical twins, which helps scientists separate genetic contributions from environmental contributions. Identical twins are genetically the same. If a trait is inherited, both identical twins will have the trait. Scientists conclude that traits that appear frequently in identical twins are at least partially controlled by heredity. Also, scientists presume that traits expressed differently in identical twins are strongly influenced by environment. The percentage of twins who both express a given trait is called a concordance rate. Examine **Figure 11.16** for some traits and their concordance rates. A large difference between fraternal twins and identical twins shows a strong genetic influence.

## Section 11.2 Assessment

### Section Summary

- Some traits are inherited through complex inheritance patterns, such as incomplete dominance, codominance, and multiple alleles.
- Gender is determined by X and Y chromosomes. Some traits are linked to the X chromosome.
- Polygenic traits involve more than one pair of alleles.
- Both genes and environment influence an organism's phenotype.
- Studies of inheritance patterns of large families and twins give insight into complex human inheritance.

### Understand Main Ideas

1. MAIN Idea **Distinguish** between complex inheritance and inheritance patterns described in Chapter 10.
2. **Explain** What is epistasis, and how is it different from dominance?
3. **Determine** the genotypes of the parents if the father is blood type A, the mother is blood type B, the daughter is blood type O, one son is blood type AB, and the other son is blood type B.
4. **Analyze** how twin studies help to differentiate the effects of genetic and environmental influences.

### Think Scientifically

5. *Evaluate* whether having sickle-cell disease would be advantageous or disadvantageous to a person living in central Africa.
6. MATH in Biology What is the chance of producing a son with normal vision if the father is color-blind and the mother is homozygous normal for the trait? Explain.



Biology Online Self-Check Quiz biologygmh.com

Section 11.3

## Objectives

- **Distinguish** normal karyotypes from those with abnormal numbers of chromosomes.
- **Define and describe** the role of telomeres.
- **Relate** the effect of nondisjunction to Down syndrome and other abnormal chromosome numbers.
- **Assess** the benefits and risks of diagnostic fetal testing.

### Review Vocabulary

**mitosis:** a process in the nucleus of a dividing cell, including prophase, metaphase, anaphase, and telophase

### New Vocabulary

karyotype
telomere
nondisjunction

# Chromosomes and Human Heredity

**MAIN Idea** **Chromosomes can be studied using karyotypes.**

**Real-World Reading Link** Have you ever lost one of the playing pieces belonging to a game? You might not have been able to play the game because the missing piece was important. Just as a misplaced game piece affects a game, a missing chromosome has a significant impact on the organism.

## Karyotype Studies

The study of genetic material does not involve the study of genes alone. Scientists also study whole chromosomes by using images of chromosomes stained during metaphase. The staining bands identify or mark identical places on homologous chromosomes. Recall from Chapter 9 that during metaphase of mitosis, each chromosome has condensed greatly and consists of two sister chromatids. The pairs of homologous chromosomes are arranged in decreasing size to produce a micrograph called a **karyotype** (KER ee uh tipe). Karyotypes of a human male and a human female, each with 23 pairs of chromosomes, are shown in **Figure 11.17.** Notice that the 22 autosomes are matched together with one pair of nonmatching sex chromosomes.

## Telomeres

Scientists have found that chromosomes end in protective caps called **telomeres.** Telomere caps consist of DNA associated with proteins. The cap serves a protective function for the structure of the chromosome. Scientists have discovered that telomeres also might be involved in both aging and cancer.

**Figure 11.17** Karyotypes arrange the pairs of homologous chromosomes from increasing to decreasing size.
**Distinguish** *Which two chromosomes are arranged separately from the other pairs?*

False-Color LM Magnification: 1400×

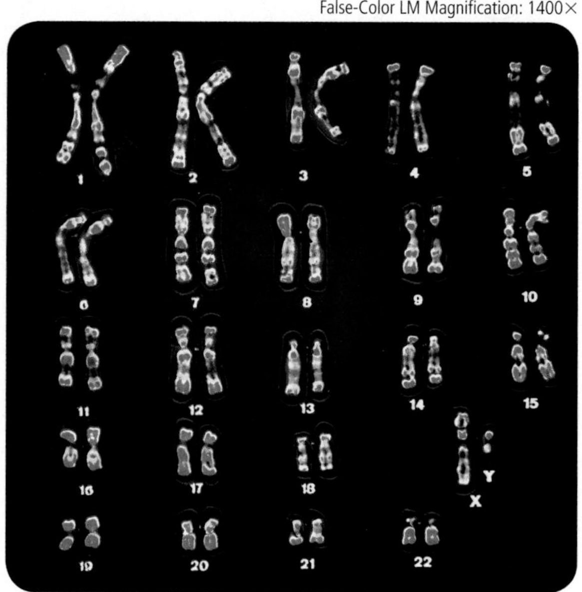


False-Color LM Magnification: 1400×

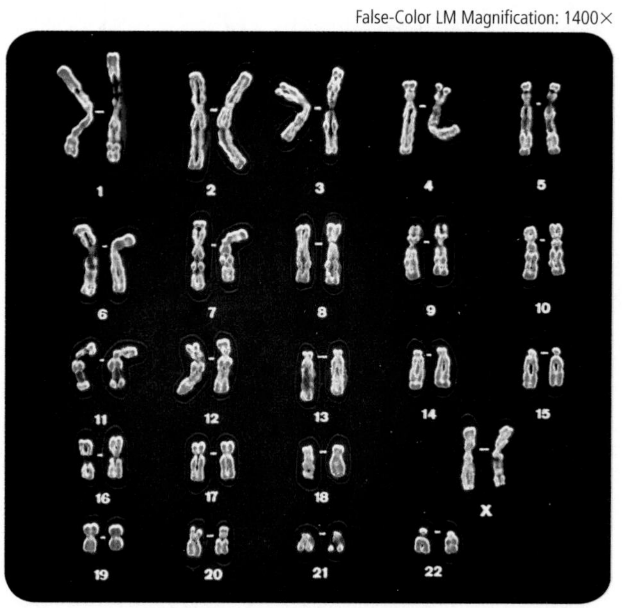

# Visualizing Nondisjunction

**Figure 11.18**
Gametes with abnormal numbers of chromosomes can result from nondisjunction during meiosis. The orange chromosomes come from one parent, and the blue chromosomes come from the other parent.

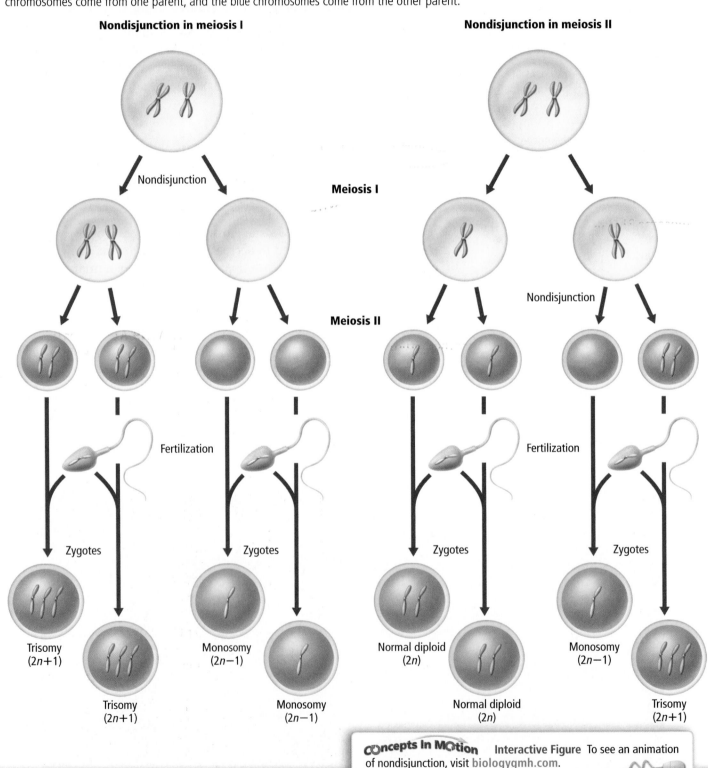



**Concepts In Motion** **Interactive Figure** To see an animation of nondisjunction, visit biologygmh.com.

**Biology Online**

27. Which statement concerning telomeres is not true?
    **A.** They are found on the ends of chromosomes.
    **B.** They consist of DNA and sugars.
    **C.** They protect chromosomes.
    **D.** Replication is a problem in most cells.

## Constructed Response

*Use the photo below to answer question 28.*

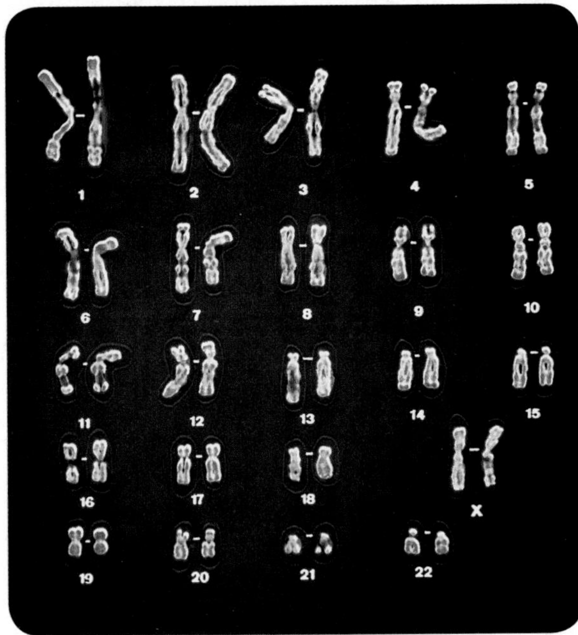


28. **Short Answer** Describe a fetal test that results in the karyotype shown above.

29. **Short Answer** What characteristics are associated with Down syndrome?

30. **Open Ended** Most cases of trisomy and monosomy in humans are fatal. Why might this be?

## Think Critically

31. **Hypothesize** why chromosomes need telomeres.

32. **Explain** why a girl who has Turner's syndrome has red-green color blindness even though both of her parents have normal vision.

33. **Illustrate** what might have occurred to result in an extra chromosome in the following example: A technician is constructing a karyotype from male fetal cells. The technician discovers that the cells have one extra X chromosome.

## Additional Assessment

34. WRITING in **Biology** Write a scenario for one of the genetic disorders described in **Table 11.2.** Then create a pedigree illustrating the scenario.

## DBQ Document-Based Questions

*Answer the questions below concerning the effect of environment on phenotype.*

Data obtained from: Harnly, M.H. 1936. Genetics. *Journal of Experimental Zoology* 56: 363-379.

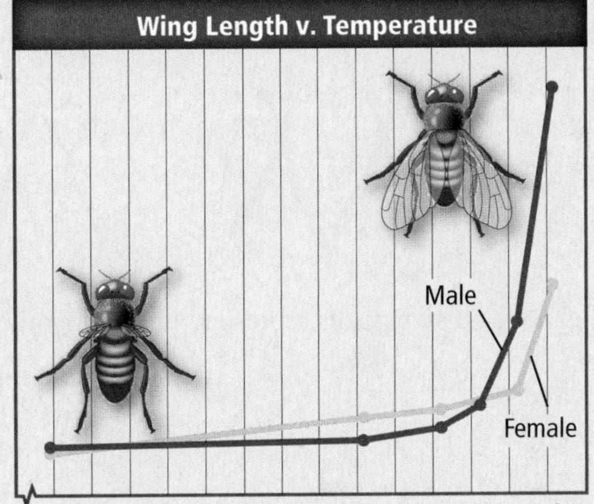


35. At which temperature is wing length the greatest?

36. Is male or female wing length more influenced by temperature? Explain.

37. Summarize the relationship between temperature and wing length for all flies.

## Cumulative Review

38. Describe the structure of an atom. Elaborate on the organization of protons, neutrons, and electrons. **(Chapter 6)**

39. Compare photosynthesis to cellular respiration, relating both to the body's energy needs. **(Chapter 8)**

# Standardized Test Practice

**Cumulative**

## Multiple Choice

1. Which is affected when a cell has a low surface-area-to-volume ratio?
   A. the ability of oxygen to diffuse into the cell
   B. the amount of energy produced in the cell
   C. the diffusion of proteins through the cells
   D. the rate of protein synthesis in the cell

*Use the diagram below to answer questions 2 to 4.*

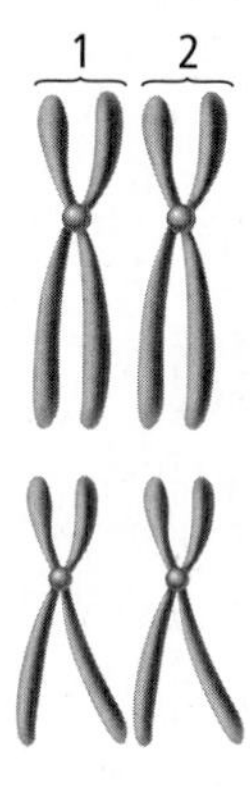

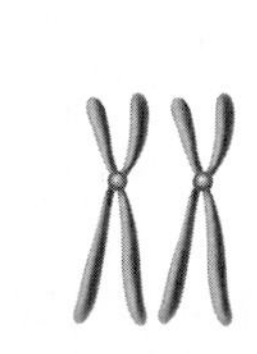
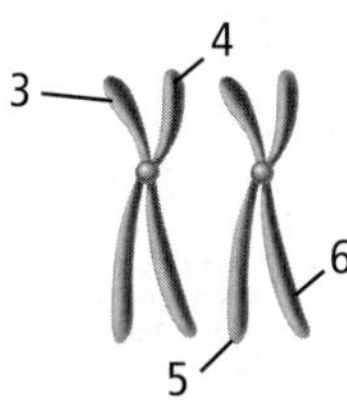

2. Which labeled structures represent a homologous pair?
   A. 1 and 2
   B. 3 and 4
   C. 3 and 6
   D. 7 and 8

3. Which parts of the chromosomes shown could appear together in a gamete of this organism?
   A. 1 and 2
   B. 3 and 6
   C. 3 and 7
   D. 5 and 6

4. If the diagram shows all the chromosomes from a body cell, how many chromosomes would be in a gamete of this organism at the end of meiosis I?
   A. 3
   B. 6
   C. 9
   D. 12

5. Which represents a polyploid organism?
   A. 1/2 $n$
   B. 1 1/2 $n$
   C. 2 $n$
   D. 3 $n$

*Use the pedigree below to answer questions 6 and 7.*

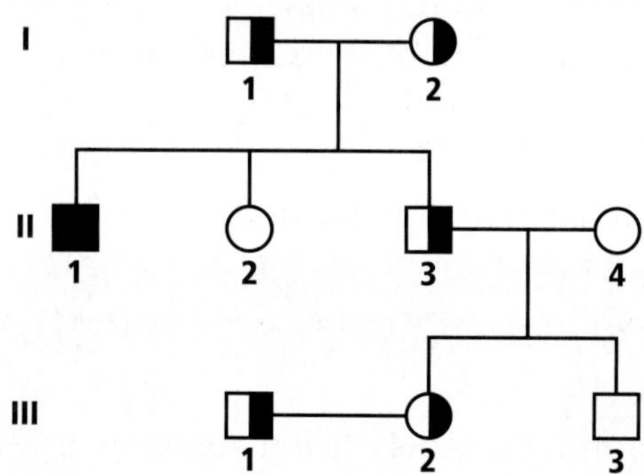


6. Which person could develop symptoms of the disease that is tracked in the pedigree?
   A. I1
   B. II1
   C. II2
   D. III2

7. According to the pedigree, who is a carrier and cannot have children with the disease?
   A. I1
   B. II1
   C. II3
   D. III1

8. Which condition would trigger mitosis?
   A. Cells touch each other.
   B. Cyclin builds up.
   C. Environmental conditions are poor.
   D. Growth factors are absent.

9. Shivering when you are cold raises your body temperature. This is an example of which characteristic of life?
   A. Your body adapts over time.
   B. Your body grows and develops.
   C. Your body has one or more cells.
   D. Your body maintains homeostasis.

## Short Answer

10. In pea plants, yellow seed color is the dominant trait, and green seed color is the recessive trait. Use a Punnett square to show the results of a cross between a heterozygous yellow-seed plant and a green-seed plant.

11. Based on your Punnett square from question 10, what percentage of the offspring would have a homozygous genotype? Explain your answer.

12. Because Huntington's disease is a dominant genetic disorder, it might seem that it would be selected out of a population naturally. Write a hypothesis that states why the disease continues to occur.

13. Explain how a cancerous tumor results from a disruption of the cell cycle.

14. Write, in order, the steps that must occur for cell division to result in an organism with trisomy.

15. Which function in metabolism is performed by both the thylakoid membrane and the mitochondrial membrane? Give a reason why this function might or might not be important.

16. Suppose two parents have a mild form of a genetic disease, but their child is born with a very severe form of the same disease. What kind of inheritance pattern took place for this disease?

17. Describe an example of each of the following: species diversity, genetic diversity, and ecosystem diversity.

## Extended Response

*Use the diagram below to answer question 18.*

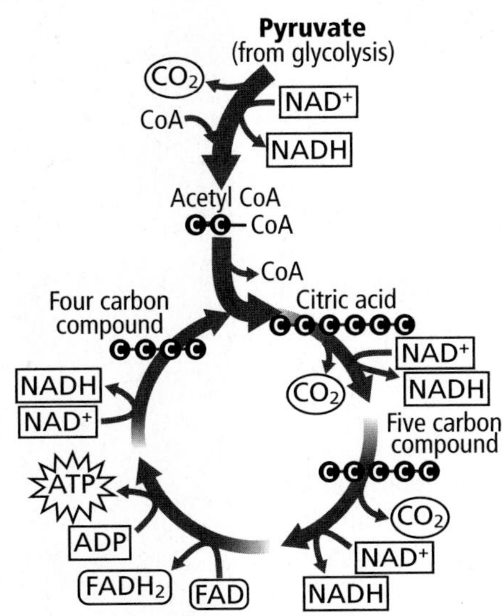


18. Identify the cycle in the figure and summarize the steps of the cycle.

19. Describe the function of microtubules, and predict what might happen if cells did NOT have microtubules.

## Essay Question

The type of pea plants that Mendel investigated had either purple flowers or white flowers. One flower-color trait is dominant, and the other is recessive.

*Using the information in the paragraph above, answer the following question in essay format.*

20. Explain what crosses Mendel would have performed to determine which color is the dominant trait.

| NEED EXTRA HELP? | | | | | | | | | | | | | | | | | | | | |
|---|---|---|---|---|---|---|---|---|---|---|---|---|---|---|---|---|---|---|---|---|
| If You Missed Question . . . | 1 | 2 | 3 | 4 | 5 | 6 | 7 | 8 | 9 | 10 | 11 | 12 | 13 | 14 | 15 | 16 | 17 | 18 | 19 | 20 |
| Review Section . . . | 9.1 | 10.1 | 10.1 | 10.1 | 10.1 | 11.1 | 11.1 | 9.2 | 1.1 | 10.2 | 10.2 | 11.1 | 9.3 | 11.3 | 8.2, 8.3 | 11.2 | 2.2 | 8.3 | 7.3 | 10.2 |

# CHAPTER 12 Molecular Genetics

**Section 1**
**DNA: The Genetic Material**
MAIN Idea The discovery that DNA is the genetic code involved many experiments.

**Section 2**
**Replication of DNA**
MAIN Idea DNA replicates by making a strand that is complementary to each original strand.

**Section 3**
**DNA, RNA, and Protein**
MAIN Idea DNA codes for RNA, which guides protein synthesis.

**Section 4**
**Gene Regulation and Mutation**
MAIN Idea Gene expression is regulated by the cell, and mutations can affect this expression.

## BioFacts

- The human body has about 100 trillion cells that contain the 46 chromosomes in which DNA is stored.
- If all of the DNA in a human cell were stretched end to end, it would form a line about 1.8 m long.
- The DNA that makes up a single human chromosome might be made up of more than 250 million nucleotides.

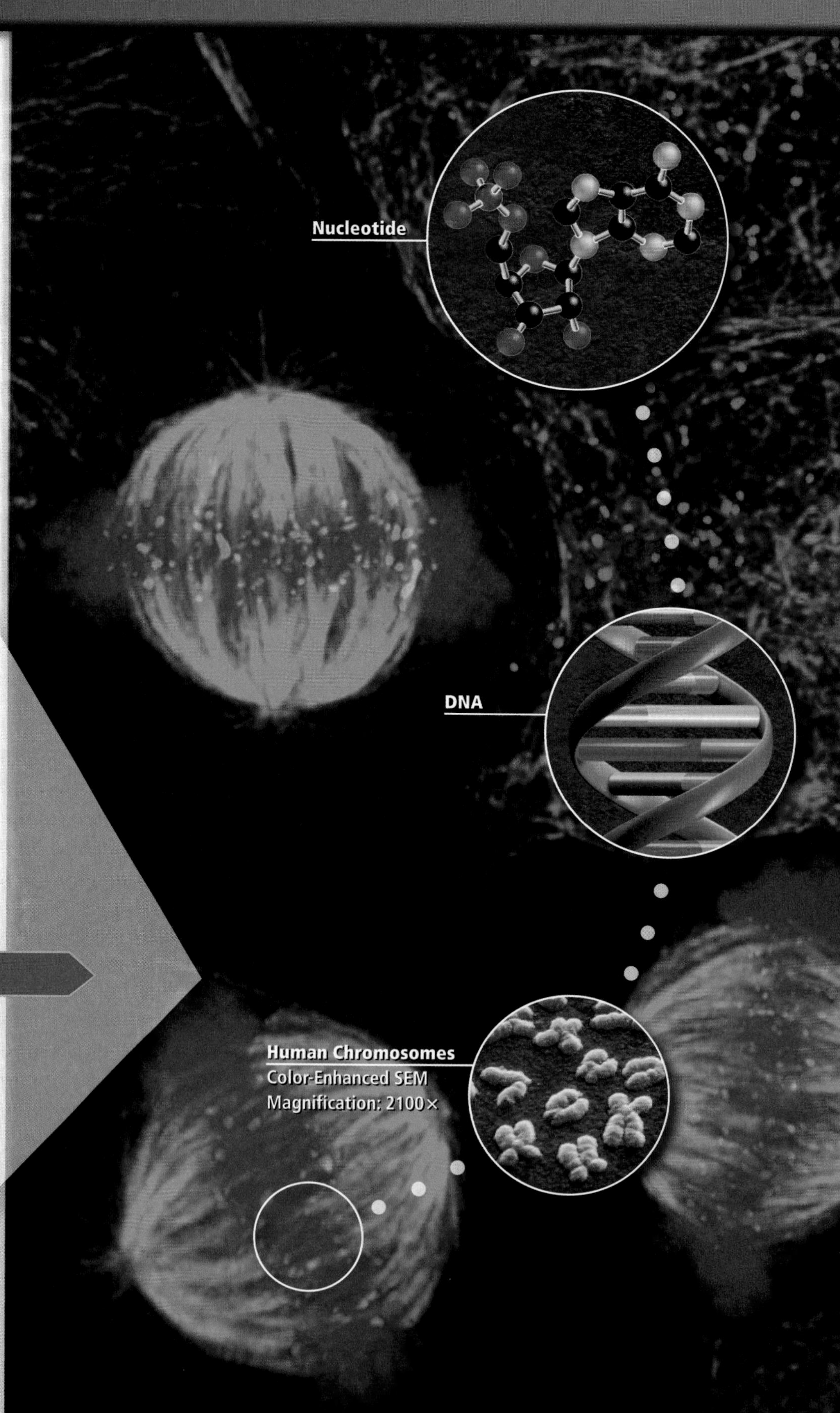

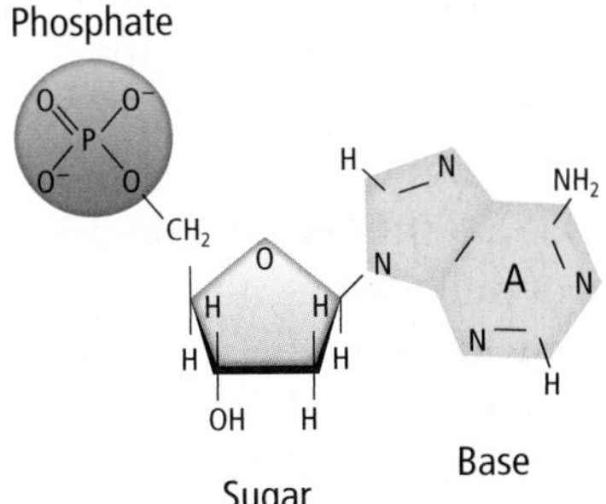


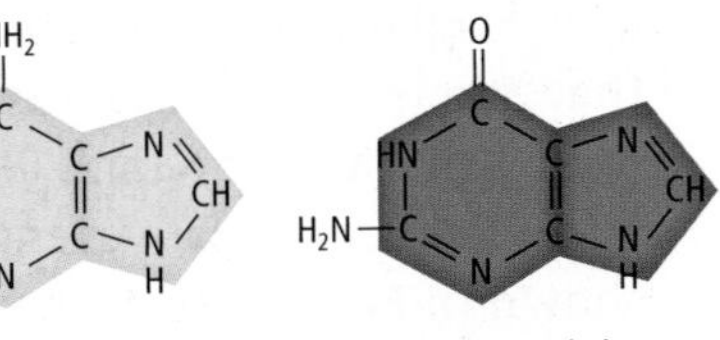


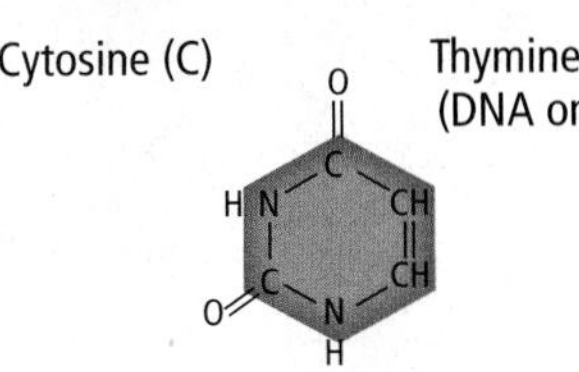


■ **Figure 12.4** Nucleotides are made of a phosphate, sugar, and a base. There are five different bases found in nucleotide subunits that make up DNA and RNA.
**Identify** ***What is the structural difference between purine and pyrimidine bases?***

## DNA Structure

After the Hershey-Chase experiment, scientists were more confident that DNA was the genetic material. The clues had led to the identification of the genetic material, but the questions of how nucleotides came together to form DNA and how DNA could communicate information remained.

**Nucleotides** In the 1920s, the biochemist P. A. Levene determined the basic structure of nucleotides that make up DNA. Nucleotides are the subunits of nucleic acids and consist of a five-carbon sugar, a phosphate group, and a nitrogenous base. The two nucleic acids found in living cells are DNA and RNA, which you learned about in Chapter 6. DNA nucleotides contain the sugar deoxyribose (dee ahk sih RI bos), a phosphate, and one of four nitrogenous bases: adenine (A duh neen), guanine (GWAH neen), cytosine (SI tuh seen), or thymine (THI meen). RNA nucleotides contain the sugar ribose, a phosphate, and one of four nitrogenous bases: adenine, guanine, cytosine, or uracil (YOO ruh sihl). Notice in **Figure 12.4** that guanine (G) and adenine (A) are double-ringed bases. This type of base is called a purine base. Thymine (T), cytosine (C), and uracil (U) are single-ringed bases called pyrimidine bases.

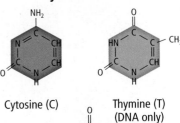

**Chargaff** Erwin Chargaff analyzed the amount of adenine, guanine, thymine, and cytosine in the DNA of various species. A portion of Chargaff's data, published in 1950, is shown in **Figure 12.5.** Chargaff found that the amount of guanine nearly equals the amount of cytosine, and the amount of adenine nearly equals the amount of thymine within a species. This finding is known as Chargaff's rule: C = G and T = A.

**The structure question** When four scientists joined the search for the DNA structure, the meaning and importance of Chargaff's data became clear. Rosalind Franklin, a British chemist; Maurice Wilkins, a British physicist; Francis Crick, a British physicist; and James Watson, an American biologist, provided information that was pivotal in answering the DNA structure question.

■ **Figure 12.5** Chargaff's data showed that though base composition varies from species to species, within a species C = G and A = T.

**Chargaff's Data**

| | Base Composition (Mole Percent) | | | |
|---|---|---|---|---|
| **Organism** | A | T | G | C |
| ***Escherichia coli*** | 26.0 | 23.9 | 24.9 | 25.2 |
| **Yeast** | 31.3 | 32.9 | 18.7 | 17.1 |
| **Herring** | 27.8 | 27.5 | 22.2 | 22.6 |
| **Rat** | 28.6 | 28.4 | 21.4 | 21.5 |
| **Human** | 30.9 | 29.4 | 19.9 | 19.8 |

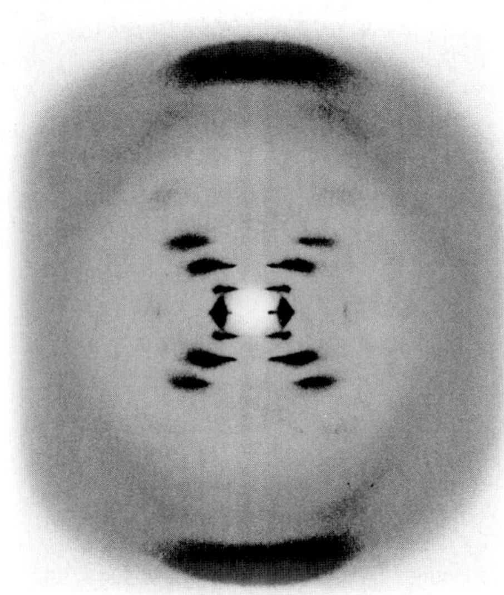

■ **Figure 12.6** Rosalind Franklin's Photo 51 and X-ray diffraction data helped Watson and Crick solve the structure of DNA. When analyzed and measured carefully, the pattern shows the characteristics of helix structure.

**X-ray diffraction** Wilkins was working at King's College in London, England, with a technique called X-ray diffraction, a technique that involved aiming X rays at the DNA molecule. In 1951, Franklin joined the staff at King's College. There she took the now famous Photo 51 and collected data eventually used by Watson and Crick. Photo 51, shown in **Figure 12.6,** indicated that DNA was a **double helix,** or twisted ladder shape, formed by two strands of nucleotides twisted around each other. The specific structure of the DNA double helix was determined later by Watson and Crick when they used Franklin's data and other mathematical data. DNA is the genetic material of all organisms, composed of two complementary, precisely paired strands of nucleotides wound in a double helix.

**Watson and Crick** Watson and Crick were working at Cambridge University in Cambridge, England, when they saw Franklin's X-ray diffraction picture. Using Chargaff's data and Franklin's data, Watson and Crick measured the width of the helix and the spacing of the bases. Together, they built a model of the double helix that conformed to the others' research. The model they built is shown in **Figure 12.7.** Some important features of their proposed molecule include the following:

1. two outside strands consist of alternating deoxyribose and phosphate
2. cytosine and guanine bases pair to each other by three hydrogen bonds
3. thymine and adenine bases pair to each other by two hydrogen bonds

**LAUNCH Lab**

**Review** Based on what you've read about the history of DNA experiments, how would you now answer the analysis questions?

**DNA structure** DNA often is compared to a twisted ladder, with the rails of the ladder represented by the alternating deoxyribose and phosphate. The pairs of bases (cytosine–guanine or thymine–adenine) form the steps, or rungs, of the ladder. A purine base always binds to a pyrimidine base, ensuring a consistent distance between the two rails of the ladder. This proposed bonding of the bases also explains Chargaff's data, which suggested that the number of purine bases equaled the number of pyrimidine bases in a sample of DNA. Remember, cytosine and thymine are pyrimidine bases, adenine and guanine are purines, and $C = G$ and $A = T$. Therefore, $C + T = G + A$, or purine bases equal pyrimidine bases. Complementary base pairing is used to describe the precise pairing of purine and pyrimidine bases between strands of nucleic acids. It is the characteristic of DNA replication through which the parent strand can determine the sequence of a new strand.

**Reading Check** **Explain** why Chargaff's data was an important clue for putting together the structure of DNA.

■ **Figure 12.7** Using Chargaff's and Franklin's data, Watson and Crick solved the puzzle of the structure of DNA.

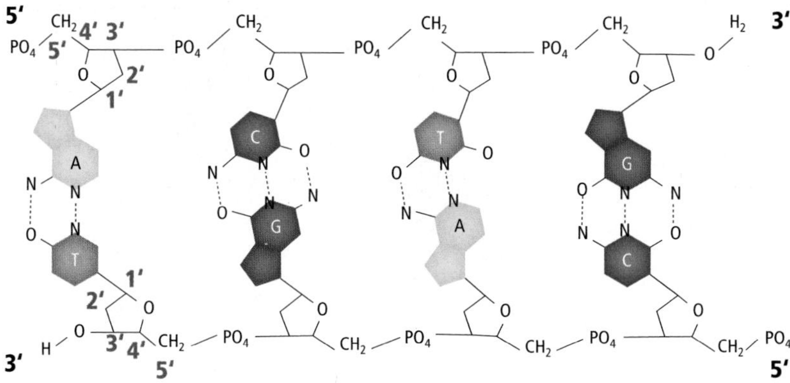

■ **Figure 12.8** Two strands of DNA running antiparallel make up the DNA helix.
**Explain** ***Why are the ends of the DNA strands labeled 3′ and 5′?***

**Concepts In Motion**

**Interactive Figure** To see an animation of the structure of DNA, visit biologygmh.com.

**Orientation** Another unique feature of the DNA molecule is the direction, or orientation, of the two strands. Carbon molecules can be numbered in organic molecules. **Figure 12.8** shows the orientation of the numbered carbons in the sugar molecules on each strand of DNA. On the top rail, the orientation of the sugar has the 5' (read "five-prime") carbon on the left, and on the end of that rail, the 3' (read "three-prime") carbon is on the right of the sugar-phosphate chain. The strand is said to be oriented 5' to 3'. The strand on the bottom runs in the opposite direction and is oriented 3' to 5'. This orientation of the two strands is called antiparallel. Another way to visualize antiparallel orientation is to take two pencils and position them so that the point of one pencil is next to the eraser of the other and vice versa.

**The announcement** In 1953, Watson and Crick surprised the scientific community by publishing a one-page letter in the journal *Nature* that suggested a structure for DNA and hypothesized a method of replication for the molecule deduced from the structure. In articles individually published in the same issue, Wilkins and Franklin presented evidence that supported the structure proposed by Watson and Crick. Still, the mysteries of how to prove DNA's replication and how it worked as a genetic code remained.

**VOCABULARY**

**SCIENCE USAGE V. COMMON USAGE**

**Prime**

***Science usage:*** a mark located above and to the right of a character, used to identify a number or variable.
*Carbon molecules in organic molecules are numbered and labeled with a prime.*

***Common usage:*** first in value, excellence, or quality.
*The student found the prime seats in the stadium for watching the game.*

## MiniLab 12.1

### Model DNA Structure

**What is the structure of the DNA molecule?** Construct a model to better understand the structure of the DNA molecule.

**Procedure**

1. Read and complete the lab safety form.
2. Construct a model of a short segment of DNA using the materials provided by your teacher.
3. Identify which parts of the model correspond to the different parts of a DNA molecule.

**Analysis**

1. **Describe** the structure of your DNA molecule.
2. **Identify** the characteristics of DNA that you focused on when constructing your model.
3. **Infer** In what way is your model different from your classmates' models? How does this relate to differences in DNA among organisms?

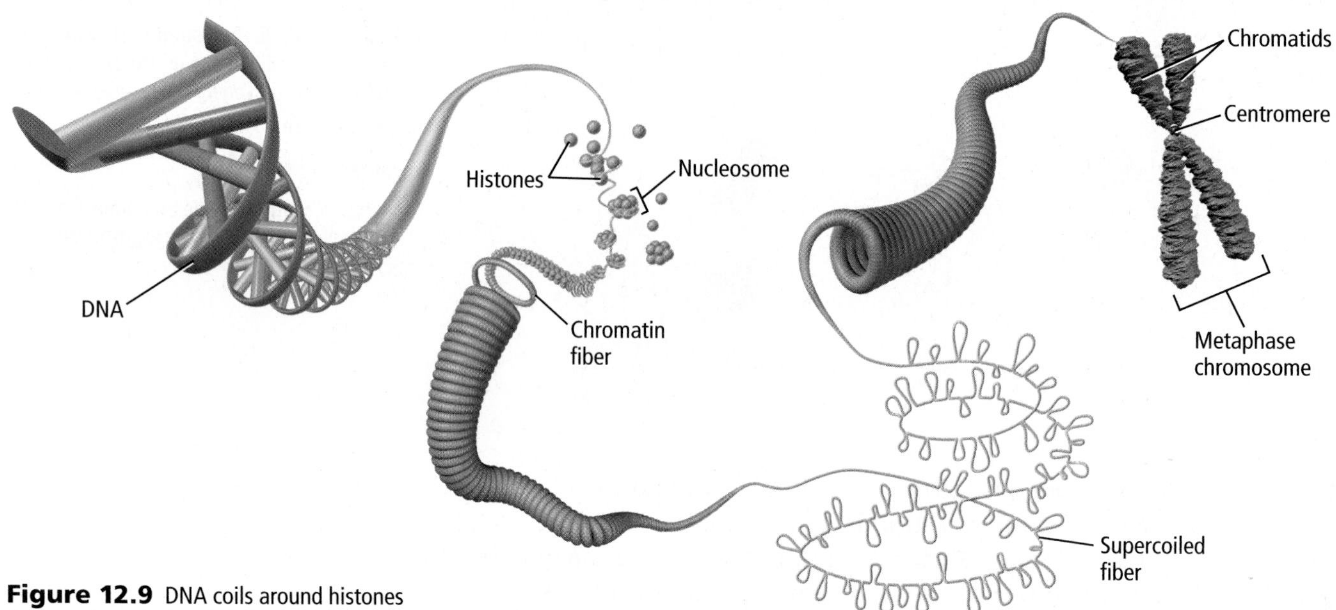


■ **Figure 12.9** DNA coils around histones to form nucleosomes, which coil to form chromatin fibers. The chromatin fibers supercoil to form chromosomes that are visible in the metaphase stage of mitosis.

## Chromosome Structure

In prokaryotes, the DNA molecule is contained in the cytoplasm and consists mainly of a ring of DNA and associated proteins. Eukaryotic DNA is organized into individual chromosomes. The length of a human chromosome ranges from 51 million to 245 million base pairs. If a DNA strand 140 million nucleotides long was laid out in a straight line, it would be about five centimeters long. How does all of this DNA fit into a microscopic cell? In order to fit into the nucleus of a eukaryotic cell, the DNA tightly coils around a group of beadlike proteins called histones, as shown in **Figure 12.9.** The phosphate groups in DNA create a negative charge, which attracts the DNA to the positively charged histone proteins and forms a **nucleosome.** The nucleosomes then group together into chromatin fibers, which supercoil to make up the DNA structure recognized as a chromosome.

## Section 12.1 Assessment

### Section Summary

- Griffith's bacterial experiment and Avery's explanation first indicated that DNA is the genetic material.
- The Hershey-Chase experiment provided evidence that DNA is the genetic material of viruses.
- Chargaff's rule states that, in DNA, the amount of cytosine equals the amount of guanine and the amount of thymine equals the amount of adenine.
- The work of Watson, Crick, Franklin, and Wilkins provided evidence of the double-helix structure of DNA.

### Understand Main Ideas

1. MAIN Idea **Summarize** the experiments of Griffith and Avery that indicated that DNA is the genetic material.
2. **Describe** the data used by Watson and Crick to determine the structure of DNA.
3. **Draw and label** a segment of DNA showing its helix and complementary base pairing.
4. **Describe** the structure of eukaryotic chromosomes.

### Think Scientifically

5. *Describe* two characteristics that DNA needs to fulfill its role as a genetic material.
6. *Evaluate* Hershey and Chase's decision to use radioactive phosphorus and sulfur for their experiments. Could they have used carbon or oxygen instead? Why or why not?



BiologyOnline Self-Check Quiz biologygmh.com

## Short Answer

*Use the figure below to answer question 9.*

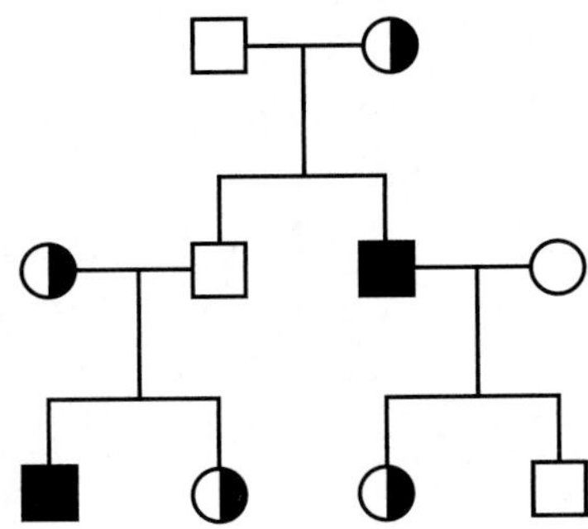

9. The pedigree in the figure tracks a dominant genetic disease. Explain the meaning of the symbols in the last generation.

10. Why are the protein-coding regions of most human genomes identical?

11. If hemophilia is a sex-linked recessive gene, what is the chance that a father with hemophilia and a mother who is a carrier for hemophilia will have a boy with hemophilia? Explain.

12. Compare and contrast the two major processes in protein synthesis.

13. List three genetic disorders; classify them as dominant or recessive; and name the affected organ systems.

14. Why might it take many generations to develop a purebred animal?

15. List the purine bases and the pyrimidine bases in DNA; explain their importance in DNA structure.

## Extended Response

16. Give the names of two DNA mutations, and illustrate how each one would change the following DNA sequence.

    CGATTGACGTTTTAGGAT

17. Chemosynthetic autotrophs might have evolved long before the photosynthetic ones that currently are more common on Earth. Propose an explanation for this difference in evolution.

18. Explain how the noncoding sequences in the human genome make it difficult to interpret the DNA code.

19. Even though chloroplasts and mitochondria perform different functions, their structures are similar. Relate the similarity of their structures to their functions.

## Essay Question

Suppose a scientist uses gel electrophoresis to separate the DNA extracted from a cell line. After performing the experiment, the scientist observes that several bands are missing and that other bands have traveled to the far end of the gel.

*Using the information in the paragraph above, answer the following question in essay format.*

20. Using what you know about DNA separation and gel electrophoresis, explain what might have gone wrong with the experiment. Then, describe how to adjust the experimental procedures to test your explanation.

**NEED EXTRA HELP?**

| If You Missed Question . . . | 1 | 2 | 3 | 4 | 5 | 6 | 7 | 8 | 9 | 10 | 11 | 12 | 13 | 14 | 15 | 16 | 17 | 18 | 19 | 20 |
|---|---|---|---|---|---|---|---|---|---|---|---|---|---|---|---|---|---|---|---|---|
| Review Section . . . | 9.2 | 13.2 | 13.3 | 10.3 | 12.1 | 11.1 | 12.3 | 10.3 | 11.1 | 13.3 | 11.3 | 12.3 | 11.2 | 13.1 | 12.1 | 12.4 | 2.2 | 13.3 | 7.3 | 13.2 |

# UNIT 4 History of Biological Diversity

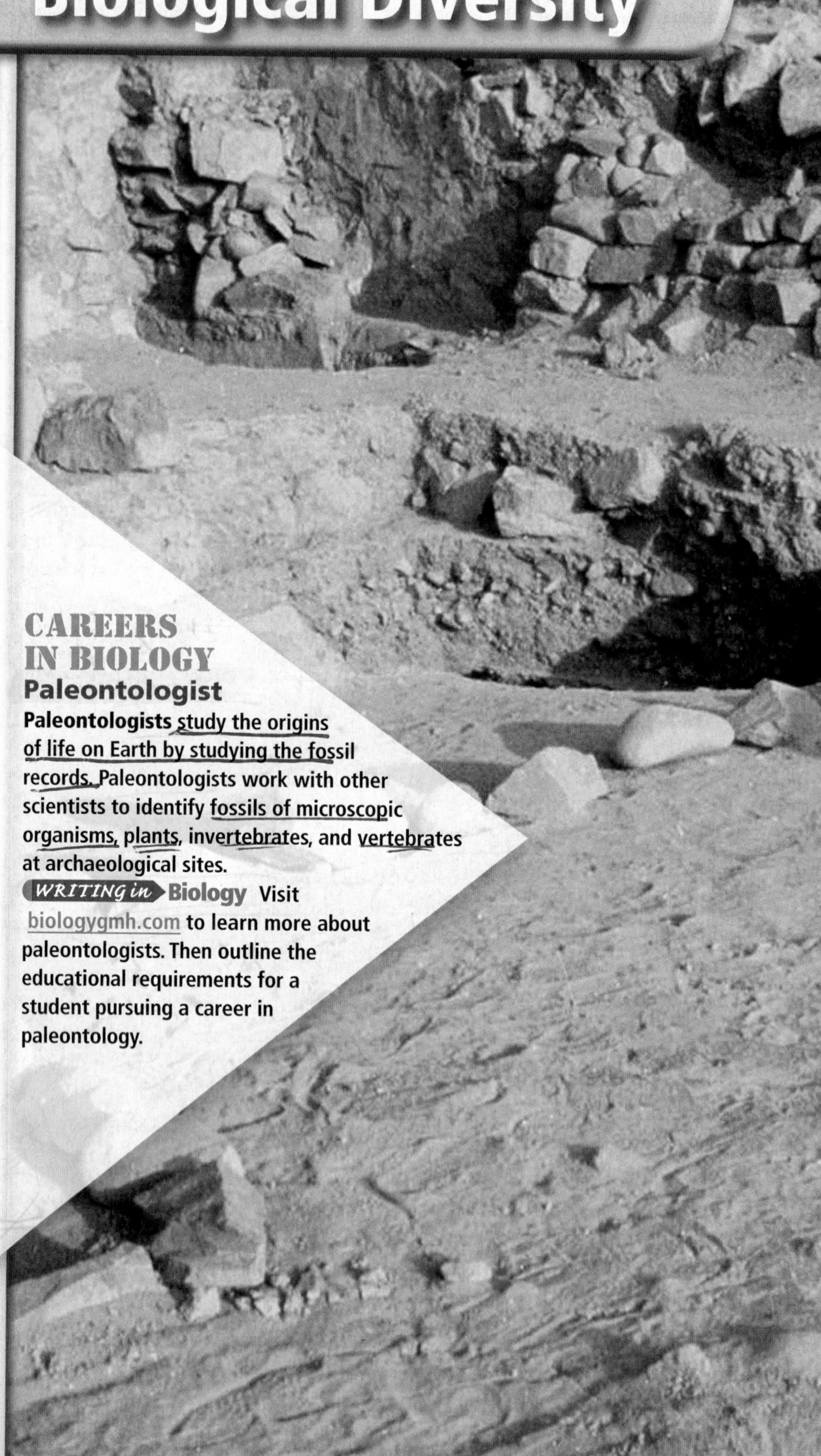

## CAREERS IN BIOLOGY

### Paleontologist

**Paleontologists** study the origins of life on Earth by studying the fossil records. Paleontologists work with other scientists to identify fossils of microscopic organisms, plants, invertebrates, and vertebrates at archaeological sites.

**WRITING in Biology** Visit biologygmh.com to learn more about paleontologists. Then outline the educational requirements for a student pursuing a career in paleontology.

**Chapter 14**
The History of Life
BIG Idea Fossils provide key evidence for understanding the origin and the history of life on Earth.

**Chapter 15**
Evolution
BIG Idea The theory of natural selection explains evolution and the diversity of life.

**Chapter 16**
Primate Evolution
BIG Idea Evolutionary change in a group of small, tree-living mammals eventually led to a diversity of species that includes modern humans.

**Chapter 17**
Organizing Life's Diversity
BIG Idea Evolution underlies the classification of life's diversity.

**Biology Online**

To read more about paleontologists in action, visit biologygmh.com.

# CHAPTER 14 The History of Life

**Section 1**
**Fossil Evidence of Change**
**MAIN Idea** Fossils provide evidence of change in organisms over time.

**Section 2**
**The Origin of Life**
**MAIN Idea** Evidence indicates that a sequence of chemical events preceded the origin of life on Earth and that life has evolved continuously since that time.

## BioFacts

- After laying their eggs, many dinosaurs remained on their nests to protect their young.
- A dinosaur fossil found in the 1920s atop an egg-containing nest was named *Oviraptor*, which means "egg thief."
- In the 1990s, similar *Oviraptor* fossils were found that contained fossilized *Oviraptor* embryos.

# LAUNCH Lab

## What can skeletal remains reveal?

Fossils are all that remain of extinct organisms. Paleontologists study fossils to understand how organisms looked and behaved when they lived on Earth. In this lab, you will infer an organism's characteristics based on skeletal remains.

### Procedure

1. Read and complete the lab safety form.
2. Choose an unidentified animal from the list provided by your teacher.
3. Imagine that the animal you selected has been extinct for millions of years. Study **skeletal parts, teeth, diagrams, and photos** provided.
4. Based on skeletal remains alone, list the animal's physical and behavioral characteristics.
5. Learn the identity of your animal from your teacher. Now make a new list of characteristics.

### Analysis

1. **Compare** the two lists. Do fossils limit what paleontologists can infer about an extinct organism? Explain.
2. **Conclude** Based on your observations, what general characteristics can be inferred about most animals based on fossilized remains?

**Visit biologygmh.com to:**

- study the entire chapter online
- explore Concepts in Motion, the Interactive Table, Microscopy Links, and links to virtual dissections
- access Web links for more information, projects, and activities
- review content online with the Interactive Tutor and take Self-Check Quizzes

**Origin of Life** Make this Foldable to help you understand some of the early experiments related to the origin of life.

**STEP 1** Fold a sheet of notebook paper in thirds lengthwise as shown.

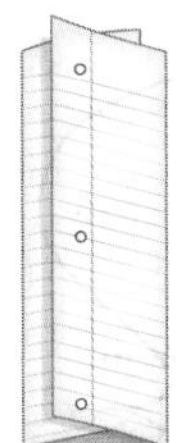

**STEP 2** Unfold the paper and make a fold a quarter of the way down the page.

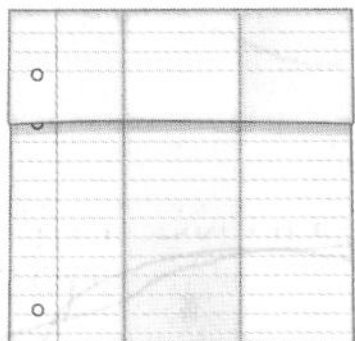

**STEP 3** With a pencil or pen, trace the fold lines to make a three-column chart.

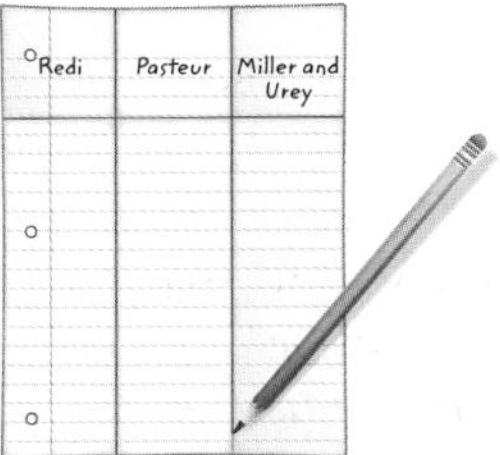


**STEP 4** Label the columns: *Redi, Pasteur,* and *Miller and Urey.*

**FOLDABLES Use this Foldable with Section 14.2.** As you study the chapter, record what you learn about each scientist and list the steps that helped him investigate spontaneous generation and biogenesis.

## Section 14.1

### Objectives

- **Describe** a typical sequence of events in fossilization.
- **Compare** techniques for dating fossils.
- **Identify** and describe major events using the geologic time scale.

### Review Vocabulary

**extinction:** the death of all individuals of a species

### New Vocabulary

fossil
paleontologist
relative dating
law of superposition
radiometric dating
half-life
geologic time scale
era
period
Cambrian explosion
K-T boundary
plate tectonics

# Fossil Evidence of Change

**MAIN Idea Fossils provide evidence of the change in organisms over time.**

**Real-World Reading Link** Did you know that when you look at the stars at night you are looking into the past? The stars are so far away that the light you see left the stars thousands and sometimes millions of years ago. You also are looking into the past when you look at rocks. The rocks formed thousands or even millions of years ago. Rocks can tell us what Earth was like in the distant past, and sometimes they can tell us what lived during that time.

## Earth's Early History

What were the conditions on Earth as it formed, and how did life arise on a lifeless planet? Because there were no people to witness Earth's earliest history, it might seem that this is a mystery. Like any good mystery, however, it left clues behind. Each clue to Earth's history and life's origin is open to investigation by the scientists who study the history of the Earth.

**Land environments** By studying other planets in the solar system and rocks on Earth, scientists conclude that Earth was a molten body when it formed about 4.6 billion years ago. Gravity pulled the densest elements to the center of the planet. After about 500 million years, a solid crust formed on the surface, much like the crust that forms on the top of molten iron, as shown in **Figure 14.1.** The surface was rich in lighter elements, such as silicon. From the oldest rocks remaining today, scientists infer that Earth's young surface included a number of volcanic features. In addition, the cooling interior radiated much more heat to the surface than it does today. Meteorites would have caused additional heating as they crashed into Earth's surface. If there had been any life on Earth, it most likely would have been consumed by the intense heat.

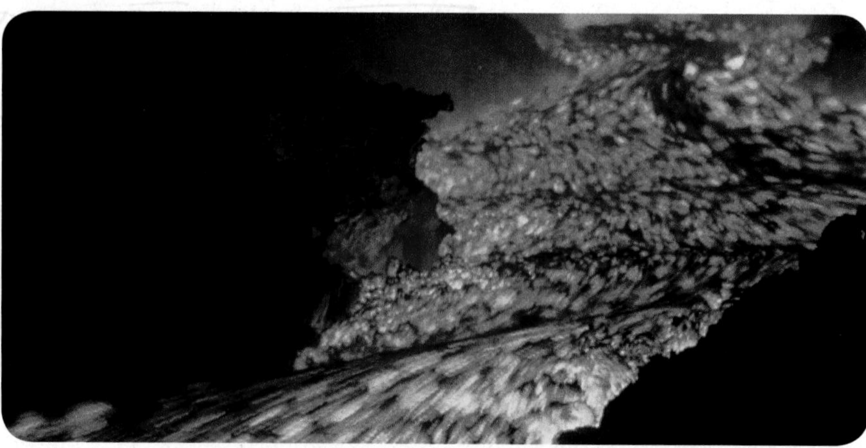

**Molten iron in lava flow**

**Figure 14.1** Just as a crust forms on top of cooling molten iron, a crust formed atop Earth's early surface.
**Infer** *the importance of the crust to the origin of life on Earth.*

**Atmosphere** Because of its gravitational field, Earth is a planet that is able to maintain an atmosphere. However, no one can be certain about the exact composition of Earth's early atmosphere. The gases that likely made up the atmosphere are those that were expelled by volcanoes. Volcanic gases today include water vapor ($H_2O$), carbon dioxide ($CO_2$), sulfur dioxide ($SO_2$), carbon monoxide ($CO$), hydrogen sulfide ($H_2S$), hydrogen cyanide ($HCN$), nitrogen ($N_2$), and hydrogen ($H_2$). Scientists infer that the same gases would have been present in Earth's early atmosphere. The minerals in the oldest known rocks suggest that the early atmosphere, unlike today's atmosphere, had little or no free oxygen.

**VOCABULARY**
**WORD ORIGIN**
**Fossil**
from the Latin word *fossilis,* meaning *dug up.*

## Clues in Rocks

Earth eventually cooled to the point where liquid water formed on its surface, which became the first oceans. It was a very short time after this—maybe as little as 500 million years—that life first appeared. The earliest clues about life on Earth date to about 3.5 billion years ago.

**The fossil record** A **fossil** is any preserved evidence of an organism. Six categories of fossils are shown in **Table 14.1.** Plants, animals, and even bacteria can form fossils. Although there is a rich diversity of fossils, the fossil record is like a book with many missing pages. Perhaps more than 99 percent of the species that ever have lived are now extinct, but only a tiny percentage of these organisms are preserved as fossils.

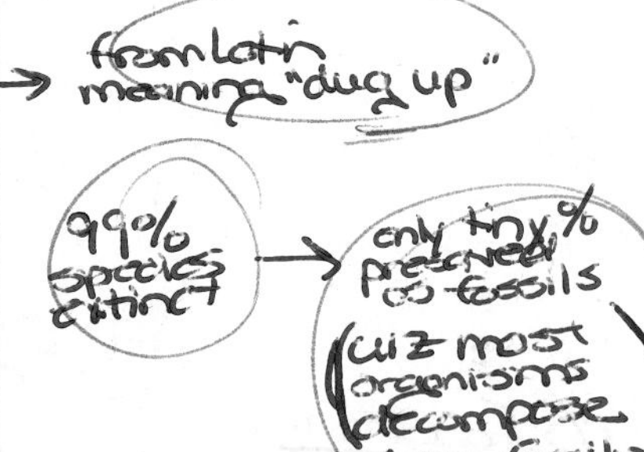

Most organisms decompose before they have a chance to become fossilized. Only those organisms that are buried rapidly in sediment are readily preserved. This occurs more frequently with organisms living in water because the sediment in aquatic environments is constantly settling, covering, and preserving the remains of organisms.

**Concepts In Motion**
Interactive Table To explore more about categories of fossil types, visit biologygmh.com.

**Table 14.1 Categories of Fossil Types**

| Category | Trace fossil | Molds and casts | Replacement | Petrified or permineralized | Amber | Original material |
|---|---|---|---|---|---|---|
| Example | | | | | | |
| Formation | A trace fossil is any indirect evidence left by an organism. Footprints, burrows, and fossilized feces are trace fossils. | A mold is an impression of an organism. A cast is a mold filled with sediment. | The original material of an organism is replaced with mineral crystals that can leave detailed replicas of hard or soft parts. | Empty pore spaces are filled in by minerals, such as in petrified wood. | Preserved tree sap traps an entire organism. The sap hardens into amber and preserves the trapped organism. | Mummification or freezing preserves original organisms. |

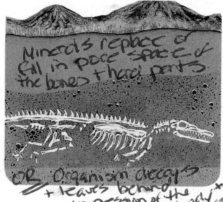

**Figure 14.2** (A) Organisms usually become fossilized after they die and are buried by sediment. (B) Sediments build up in layers, eventually encasing the remains in sedimentary rock. (C) Minerals replace, or fill in the pore space of, the bones and hard parts of the organism. (D) Erosion can expose the fossils.

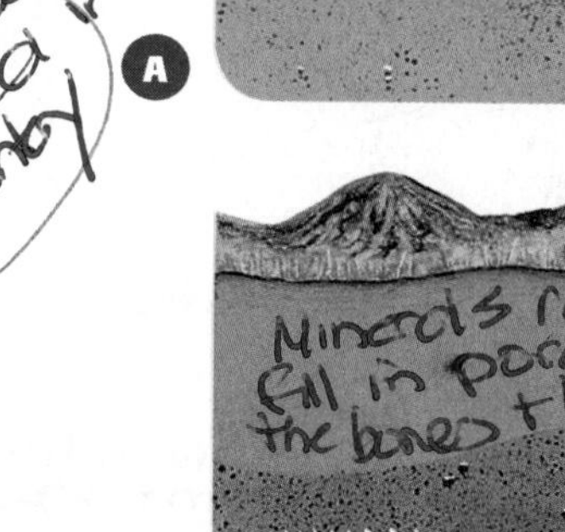

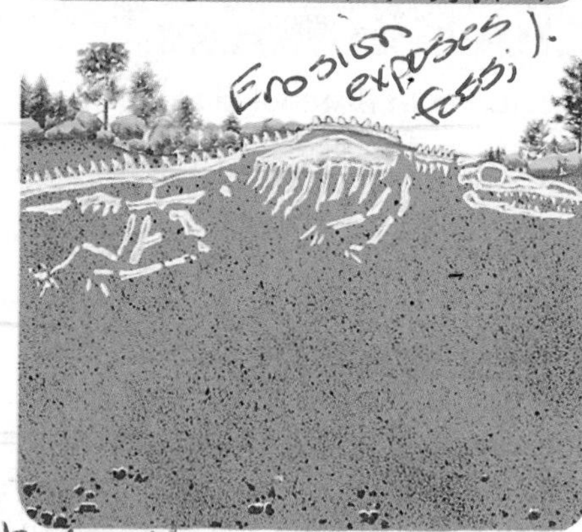

**Fossil formation** Fossils do not form in igneous (IHG nee us) or metamorphic (meh tuh MOR fihk) rocks. Igneous rocks form when magma from Earth's interior cools. Metamorphic rocks form when rocks are exposed to extreme heat and pressure. Fossils usually do not survive the heat or pressure involved in the formation of either of these kinds of rocks.

Nearly all fossils are formed in sedimentary rock through the process described in **Figure 14.2.** The organism dies and is buried in sediments. The sediments build up until they cover the organism's remains. In some cases, minerals replace the organic matter or fill the empty pore spaces of the organism. In other cases, the organism decays, leaving behind an impression of its body. The sediments eventually harden into rock.

A **paleontologist** (pay lee ahn TAH luh jist) is a scientist who studies fossils. He or she attempts to read the record of life left in rocks. From fossil evidence, paleontologists infer the diet of an organism and the environment in which it lived. In fact, paleontologists often can create images of extinct communities.

### Study Tip

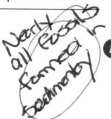

**Background Knowledge Check** Based on what you know, predict the meaning of each new vocabulary term before reading the section. As you read, check the actual meaning compared to your prediction.

**Connection to Earth Science** When geologists began to study rock layers, or strata, in different areas, they noticed that layers of the same age tended to have the same kinds of fossils no matter where the rocks were found. The geologists inferred that all strata of the same age contained similar collections of fossils. This led to the establishment of a relative age scale for rocks all over the world.

**Dating fossils** **Relative dating** is a method used to determine the age of rocks by comparing them with those in other layers. Relative dating is based on the **law of superposition,** illustrated in **Figure 14.3,** which states that younger layers of rock are deposited on top of older layers. The process is similar to stacking newspapers in a pile as you read them each day. Unless you disturb the newspapers, the oldest ones will be on the bottom.

■ **Figure 14.3** According to the law of superposition, rock layers are deposited with the youngest undisturbed layers on top.
**Infer** ***Which layer shows that an aquatic ecosystem replaced a land ecosystem?***

**Radiometric dating** uses the decay of radioactive isotopes to measure the age of a rock. Recall from Chapter 6 that an isotope is a form of an element that has the same atomic number but a different mass number. The method requires that the **half-life** of the isotope, which is the amount of time it takes for half of the original isotope to decay, is known. The relative amounts of the radioactive isotope and its decay product must also be known.

One radioactive isotope that is commonly used to determine the age of rocks is Uranium 238. Uranium 238 ($U^{238}$) decays to Lead 206 ($Pb^{206}$) with a half life of 4510 million years. When testing a rock sample, scientists calculate the ratio of the parent isotope to the daughter isotope to determine the age of the sample.

Radioactive isotopes that can be used for radiometric dating are found only in igneous or metamorphic rocks, not in sedimentary rocks, so isotopes cannot be used to date rocks that contain fossils. Igneous rocks that are found in layers closely associated with fossil-bearing sedimentary rocks often can be used for assigning relative dates to fossils.

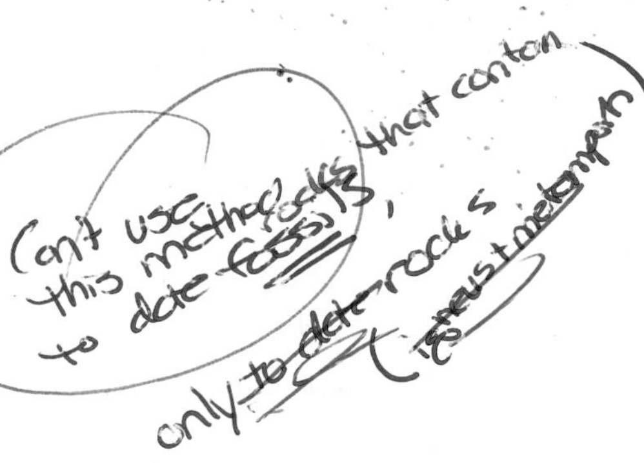

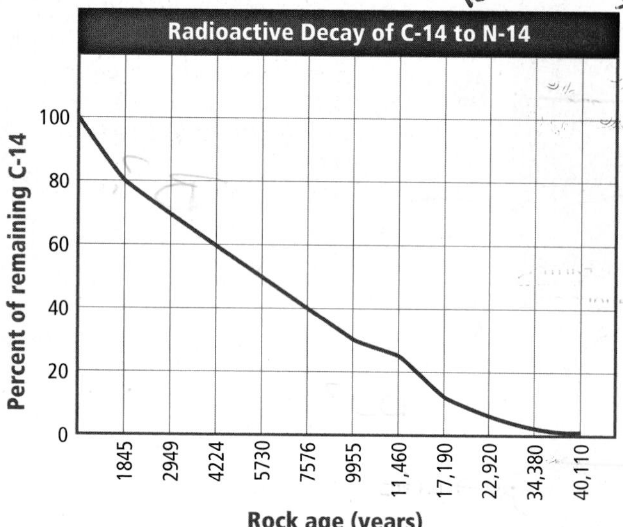


**Figure 14.4** The graph shows how the percent of carbon-14 indicates the age of a rock.

**Interpret the graph** ***What would the age of a rock be if it contained only 10 percent of C-14?***

Unaltered materials, such as mummies, can be dated directly using carbon-14. Carbon-14 is used to date organic substances, such as bones and tissues. Given the relatively short half-life of carbon-14, as shown in **Figure 14.4,** only materials less than 60,000 years old can be dated accurately with this isotope. Older materials don't have enough radioisotope left to date accurately.

## The Geologic Time Scale

Think of geologic time as a ribbon that is 4.6 m long. If each meter represents one billion years, each millimeter represents one million years. Earth was formed at one end of the ribbon, and humans appear at the very tip of the other end. This analogy of time as a ribbon will help you understand the long sequences of time represented by the geologic time scale.

The **geologic time scale,** shown in **Figure 14.5,** is a model that expresses the major geological and biological events in Earth's history. The geologic time scale is divided into the Precambrian time and the Phanerozoic (fan eh roh ZOH ihk) eon. An **era** is the next largest division of the geologic time scale. Notice in **Figure 14.5** that the eras of the Phanerozoic eon include the Paleozoic, Mesozoic, and Cenozoic eras. Each era is divided into one or more **periods.**

In 2004, geologists worldwide agreed on a revision of the names and dates in the geologic time scale based on a project coordinated by the International Commission on Stratigraphy. As in all fields of science, continuing research and discoveries might result in future revisions.

## MiniLab 14.1

### Correlate Rock Layers Using Fossils

**How can paleontologists establish relative age?** Scientists use fossils from many locations to piece together the sequence of Earth's rock layers. This is the process of correlation.

**Procedure**

1. Read and complete the lab safety form.
2. Your teacher will assign you to a group and will give your group a **container** with layers of material embedded with fossils.
3. Carefully remove each layer, noting any embedded materials.
4. Make a sketch of the cross section, and label each layer and any materials contained within it.
5. Collect copies of sketches from the other groups and use them to determine the sequence of all the layers the class has studied.

**Analysis**

1. **Describe** the materials in each cross section. What patterns did you observe?
2. **Explain** how your analysis would be different if different layers contained the same materials. What if some of the layers didn't overlap? Suggest a way to gather additional data that might resolve these issues.

# Visualizing the Geologic Time Scale

**Figure 14.5**
Eras, periods, and epochs are shown on this geologic time scale that begins with Earth's formation 4.6 billion years ago. Though not to scale, this diagram illustrates the approximate appearance of various organisms over time.

Cenozoic
Mesozoic
Paleozoic
Precambrian

| | Era | Period | Epoch | MYA | Biological events |
|---|---|---|---|---|---|
| Phanerozoic | Cenozoic | Neogene | Holocene | | • Humans form civilizations |
| | | | Pleistocene | 0.01 | • Ice ages occur<br>• Modern humans appear |
| | | | Pliocene | 1.8 | • Hominins appear<br>• Flowering plants are dominant |
| | | | Miocene | 5.3 | • Apes appear<br>• Climate is cooler |
| | | Paleogene | Oligocene | 23.0 | • Monkeys appear<br>• Climate is mild |
| | | | Eocene | 33.9 | • Flowering plants scattered<br>• Most mammal orders exist |
| | | | Paleocene | 55.8 | • Mammals, birds, and insects scatter<br>• Climate is tropical |
| | | | | Mass extinction | |
| | Mesozoic | Cretaceous | | 65.5 | • Flowering plants appear<br>• Dinosaur population peaks |
| | | Jurassic | | 145.5 | • First birds appear<br>• Dinosaurs scatter<br>• Forests are lush |
| | | Triassic | | 199.6 | • Gymnosperms are dominant<br>• Dinosaurs appear<br>• First mammals appear |
| | | | | Mass extinction | |
| | Paleozoic | Permian | | 251.0 | • Reptiles scatter |
| | | Carboniferous | | 299.0 | • Ferns and evergreens make up forests<br>• Amphibians appear<br>• Insects scatter |
| | | Devonian | Mass extinction | 359.2 | • Sharks and bony fishes appear |
| | | Silurian | | 416.0 | • Coral and other invertebrates are dominant<br>• Land plants and insects appear |
| | | | | Mass extinction | |
| | | Ordovician | | 443.7 | • First vertebrates appear<br>• First plants appear |
| | | Cambrian | | 488.3 | • Cambrian explosion<br>• All body plans arise |
| Precambrian | Proterozoic, Neoproterozoic | Ediacaran | | 542 | • Soft-bodied organisms appear |
| | | Cryogenian | | 630 | • Invertebrates and algae diversify |
| | | Tonian | | 850 | • Multicellular organisms appear |
| | | | | 1500 | • Oldest fossils of eukaryotes |
| | | | | 2500 | • Oldest fossils of prokaryotes |
| | | | | 4600 | • Earth forms |

**Concepts In Motion** Interactive Figure To see an animation of the geologic time scale, visit biologygmh.com.

Biology Online

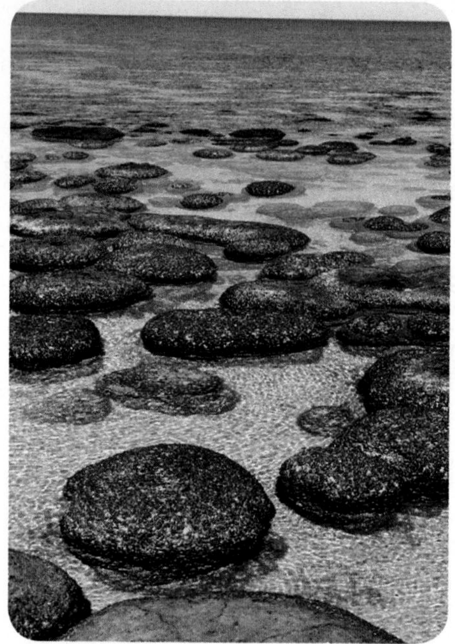

■ **Figure 14.6** Fossils much like these stromatolites are found in rocks almost 3.5 billion years old. Modern day stromatolites are formed by cyanobacteria.

**Precambrian** The first 4 m of the geologic time ribbon in **Figure 14.5** make up the Precambrian. This is nearly 90 percent of Earth's entire history, stretching from the formation of Earth to the beginning of the Paleozoic era about 542 million years ago. The Precambrian was an important time. Earth formed and life first appeared. Eventually, autotrophic prokaryotes, much like the cyanobacteria that made the stromatolites in **Figure 14.6,** enriched the atmosphere with oxygen. Eukaryotic cells also emerged, and by the end of the Precambrian, life was flourishing, and the first animals had appeared.

Extensive glaciation marked the second half of the Precambrian. This might have delayed the further evolution of life until the ice receded at the beginning of the Ediacaran (ee dee UH kur uhn) period. The Ediacaran period was added to the time scale in 2004. It is the first new period added to the time scale since 1891 and reflects new knowledge of Earth's history. The Ediacaran period lasted from about 630 million years ago to about 542 million years ago, representing about three quarters of a meter on the time ribbon at the end of the Precambrian. Simple organisms, such as the fossil in **Figure 14.7,** inhabited Ediacaran marine ecosystems. Food chains probably were short, and likely were dominated by animals that consumed tiny particles suspended in the water and by animals that ate debris on the bottom of the sea.

**Reading Check** **Infer** the process by which early autotrophic prokaryotes produced oxygen.

**The Paleozoic era** A drastic change in the history of animal life on Earth marked the start of the Paleozoic (pay lee uh ZOH ihk) era. In the space of just a few million years, the ancestors of most major animal groups diversified in what scientists call the **Cambrian explosion.** Not all major groups of organisms evolved rapidly at this time, and paleontologists still do not know when the rapid changes started or ended.

Although major changes in ocean life occurred during the Paleozoic, there is no evidence of life on land at the start of the Paleozoic. Life in the oceans continued to evolve at the end of the Cambrian period. Fish, land plants, and insects appeared during the Ordovician and Silurian periods. Organisms of many kinds, including huge insects, soon flourished in the swampy forests that dominated the land, as shown in **Figure 14.8.** The first tetrapods emerged in the Devonian period. Tetrapods were the first land vertebrates—animals with backbones. By the end of the Carboniferous period, the first reptiles were roaming the forests.

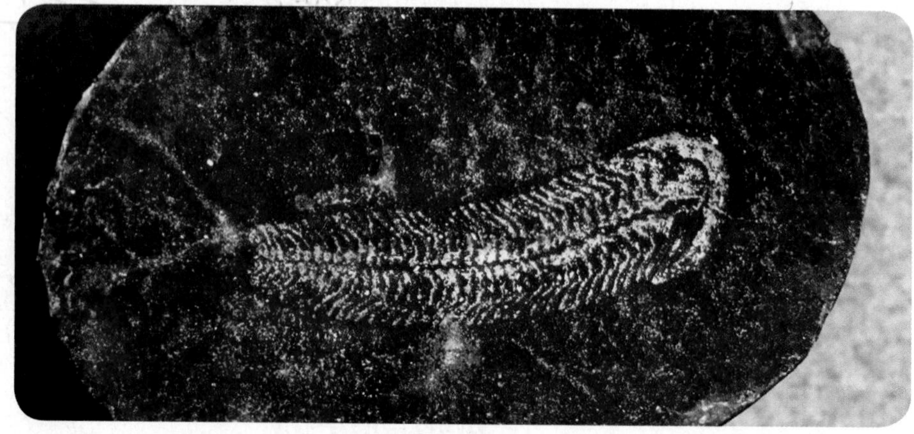

■ **Figure 14.7** Paleontologists disagree about scarce Ediacaran fossils such as this one. Some paleontologists suggest that they are relatives of today's living invertebrates such as segmented worms, while others think they represent an evolutionary dead end of giant protists or simple metazoans.

■ **Figure 14.8** During the Carboniferous period, swamp forests covered much of Earth's land surface. Insects dominated the air, and tetrapods flourished in freshwater pools.
**Infer** ***How were the plants of the Paleozoic era different from those of today?***

A mass extinction ended the Paleozoic era at the end of the Permian period. Recall from Chapter 5 that a mass extinction is an event in which many species become extinct in a short time. Mass extinctions have occurred every 26 to 30 million years on average, which is about 26 to 30 mm on your geologic time scale ribbon. Between 60 and 75 percent of the species alive went extinct in each of these events. Other mass extinctions have not been as severe as the one that ended the Permian period, during which 90 percent of marine organisms disappeared. Geologists disagree about the cause of the Permian extinction, but most agree that geological forces, including increased volcanic activity, would have disrupted ecosystems or changed the climate.

**CAREERS IN BIOLOGY**

**Paleobotanist** People who study plant fossils to understand what Earth's vegetation was in the past are paleobotanists. For more information on biology careers, visit biologygmh.com.

**The Mesozoic era** Biological change continued through the Mesozoic (mez uh ZOH ihk) era. At the beginning of the Triassic period, the ancestors of early mammals were the dominant land animals. Mammals and dinosaurs first appeared late in the Triassic period, and flowering plants evolved from nonflowering plants. Birds evolved from a group of predatory dinosaurs in the middle Jurassic period. For the rest of the Mesozoic, reptiles, particularly the dinosaurs, were the dominant organisms on the planet, as illustrated in **Figure 14.9.** Then, about 65 million years ago, a meteorite struck Earth.

The primary evidence for this meteorite impact is found in a layer of material between the rocks of the Cretaceous (krih TAY shus) period and the rocks of the Paleogene period, the first period of the Cenozoic era. Paleontologists call this layer the **K-T boundary.** Within this layer, scientists find unusually high levels of an element called iridium. Iridium is rare on Earth, but relatively common in meteorites. Therefore, the presence of iridium on Earth indicates a meteorite impact.

Many scientists think that this impact is related to the mass extinction at the end of the Mesozoic era, which eliminated all dinosaurs except birds, most marine reptiles, many marine invertebrates, and numerous plant species. The meteorite itself did not wipe out all of these species, but the debris from the impact probably stayed in the atmosphere for months or even years, affecting global climate. Those species that could not adjust to the changing climate disappeared.

■ **Figure 14.9** The dominant organisms during the Mesozoic era were dinosaurs. A mass extinction occurred at the end of the Mesozoic era that eliminated all dinosaurs, with the exception of their avian descendants.

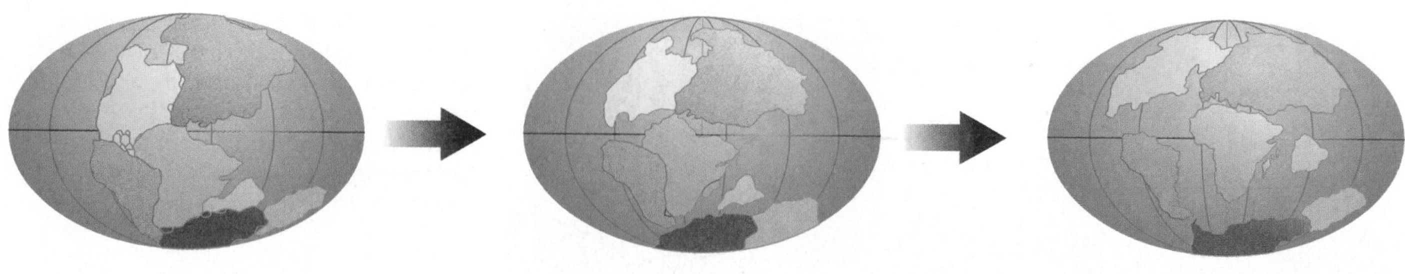


■ **Figure 14.10** These illustrations show the movement of Earth's major tectonic plates from about 225 million years ago, when all of the continents were joined into one land mass called Pangea.

**Concepts In Motion**

**Interactive Figure** To see an animation of continental drift, visit biologygmh.com.

Scientists also believe that the course of evolution in the Cenozoic era was shaped by the massive geological changes that characterized the Mesozoic era, as shown in **Figure 14.10.** While it might appear to us that continents are immobile, they actually have been moving since they formed. Alfred Wegener, a German scientist, presented the first evidence for continental drift in the 1920s. Continental drift has since become part of the theory of plate tectonics. **Plate tectonics** describes the movement of several large plates that make up the surface of Earth. These plates, some of which contain continents, move atop a partially molten layer of rock underneath them.

**The Cenozoic era** The most recent era is the one in which mammals became the dominant land animals. At the beginning of the Cenozoic (sen uh ZOH ihk) era, which means "recent life," most mammals were small and resembled shrews. After the mass extinction at the end of the Mesozoic era, mammals began to diversify into distinct groups, including primates—the group to which you belong. Humans appeared very recently, near the end of the geologic time scale, in the current Neogene period. Humans survived the last ice age, but many species of mammals did not. To get an idea of how recently modern humans have appeared, you need to remove about two threads at the end of your geologic time ribbon. These threads represent the time that humans have existed on Earth.

## Section 14.1 Assessment

### Section Summary

- Early Earth was lifeless for several hundred million years.
- Fossils provide evidence of past life.
- Relative dating and radiometric dating are two methods used to determine the age of fossils.
- The geologic time scale is divided into eras and periods.
- Major events in the geological time scale include both biological and geological changes.

### Understand Main Ideas

1. MAIN Idea **Discuss** how fossils provide evidence of change from the earliest life-forms to those alive today.
2. **Diagram** a typical sequence of events in fossilization.
3. **Discuss** two ways that radiometric dating can be used to establish the age of a fossil.
4. **Explain** major events in three periods of the geologic time scale.

### Think Scientifically

5. *Infer* what changes you might observe in the fossil record that would indicate the occurrence of a mass extinction.
6. **MATH in Biology** Out of the total of Earth's history (approximately 4.6 billion years), modern humans have existed for only 100,000 years. To put this in perspective, calculate the percentage of Earth's history that modern humans have existed.

## Section 14.2

### Objectives

- **Differentiate** between spontaneous generation and biogenesis.
- **Sequence** the events that might have led to cellular life.
- **Describe** the endosymbiont theory.

### Review Vocabulary

**amino acid:** building blocks for proteins

### New Vocabulary

spontaneous generation
theory of biogenesis
endosymbiont theory

# The Origin of Life

**MAIN Idea Evidence indicates that a sequence of chemical events preceded the origin of life on Earth and that life has evolved continuously since that time.**

**Real-World Reading Link** In a recipe, some steps can be out of order, but some steps have to occur earlier than others or the end result will be different from what was intended. In the same way, in order to arrive at the pattern of life that is seen today, events leading to the emergence of life had to occur in specific, well-ordered ways.

## Origins: Early Ideas

Perhaps one of the oldest ideas about the origin of life is spontaneous generation. **Spontaneous generation** is the idea that life arises from nonlife. For example, at one time people thought that mice could be created by placing damp hay and corn in a dark corner, or that mud could give rise to worms, insects, and fish. These ideas might seem humorous to us today, but before much was known about reproduction, it is easy to see how someone might form these conclusions.

One of the first recorded investigations of spontaneous generation came in 1668. Francesco Redi, an Italian scientist, tested the idea that flies arose spontaneously from rotting meat. He hypothesized that flies—not meat—produced other flies. In his experiment, illustrated using present-day equipment in **Figure 14.11,** Redi observed that maggots, the larvae of flies, appeared only in flasks that were open to flies. Closed flasks had no flies and no maggots. The results of his experiments failed to convince everyone, however. Although people were beginning to use the microscope during Redi's time and knew that organisms invisible to the naked eye could be found almost everywhere, some thought that these tiny organisms must arise spontaneously, even if flies did not.

**Figure 14.11** Francesco Redi showed that flies and maggots did not arise spontaneously from rotting meat.
**Infer** *the purpose of the covered flask in Redi's experiment.*

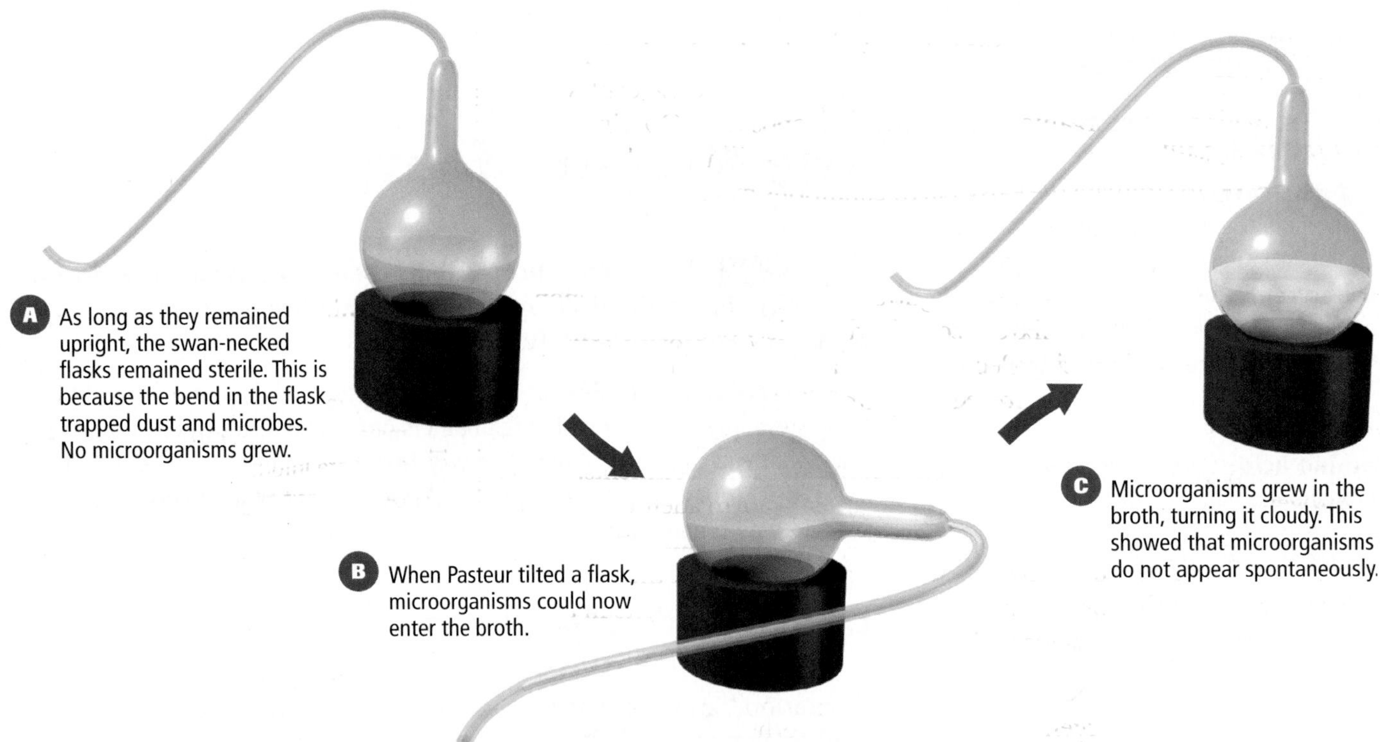

A As long as they remained upright, the swan-necked flasks remained sterile. This is because the bend in the flask trapped dust and microbes. No microorganisms grew.
B When Pasteur tilted a flask, microorganisms could now enter the broth.
C Microorganisms grew in the broth, turning it cloudy. This showed that microorganisms do not appear spontaneously.


■ **Figure 14.12** Pasteur's experiment showed that sterile broth remained free of microorganisms until exposed to air.

**FOLDABLES** Incorporate information from this section into your Foldable.

The idea of spontaneous generation was not completely rejected until the mid-1800s. It was replaced by the **theory of biogenesis** (bi oh JEN uh sus), which states that only living organisms can produce other living organisms. Louis Pasteur designed an experiment to show that biogenesis was true even for microorganisms. Pasteur's experiment is illustrated in **Figure 14.12.** In one flask, only air was allowed to contact a sterile nutrient broth. Nutrient broth supports the growth of microorganisms. In another flask, both air and microorganisms were allowed to contact the broth. No microorganisms grew in the first container. They did, however, grow in the second container.

## Origins: Modern Ideas

If life can arise only from pre-existing life, then how did the first life-form appear? Most biologists agree that life originated through a series of chemical events early in Earth's history. During these events, complex organic molecules were generated from simpler ones. Eventually, simple metabolic pathways developed. Such pathways allowed molecules to be synthesized or broken down more efficiently. These pathways might have led to the emergence of life as we know it. How this happened is a topic of ongoing research among scientists today.

**Simple organic molecule formation** The primordial soup hypothesis was an early hypothesis about the origin of life. Scientists Alexander Oparin and John Haldane suggested this hypothesis in the 1920s. They thought that if Earth's early atmosphere had a mix of certain gases, organic molecules could have been synthesized from simple reactions involving those gases in the early oceans. UV light from the Sun and electric discharge in lightning might have been the primary energy sources. They thought that these organic molecules would have eventually supplied the precursors to life.

**Connection to Chemistry** In 1953, American scientists Stanley Miller and Harold Urey were the first to show that simple organic molecules could be made from inorganic compounds, as proposed by Oparin and Haldane. Miller and Urey built a glass apparatus, illustrated in **Figure 14.13,** to simulate the early Earth conditions hypothesized by Oparin. They filled the apparatus with water and the gases that they thought had made up the early atmosphere. The water was boiled and electric discharges were used to simulate lightning as an energy source. Upon examination, the resulting mixture contained a variety of organic compounds including amino acids. Because amino acids are the building blocks of proteins, this discovery supported the primordial soup hypothesis.

Later, other scientists found that hydrogen cyanide could be formed from even simpler molecules in simulated early Earth environments. Hydrogen cyanide can react with itself to eventually form adenine, one of the nucleotide bases in the genetic code. Many other experiments have since been carried out under conditions that probably reflect the atmosphere of early Earth more accurately. The final reaction products in these experiments were amino acids and sugars as well as nucleotides.

**Deep-sea vents** Some scientists suggest that the organic reactions that preceded life's emergence began in the hydrothermal volcanic vents of the deep sea, where sulfur forms the base of a unique food chain. Still others believe that meteorites might have brought the first organic molecules to Earth.

CAREERS IN BIOLOGY

**Evolutionary Biochemist** Scientists who study chemistry and how it relates to life are biochemists. Evolution biochemists specifically study the structure and function of molecules from Earth's early history. For more information on biology careers, visit biologygmh.com.

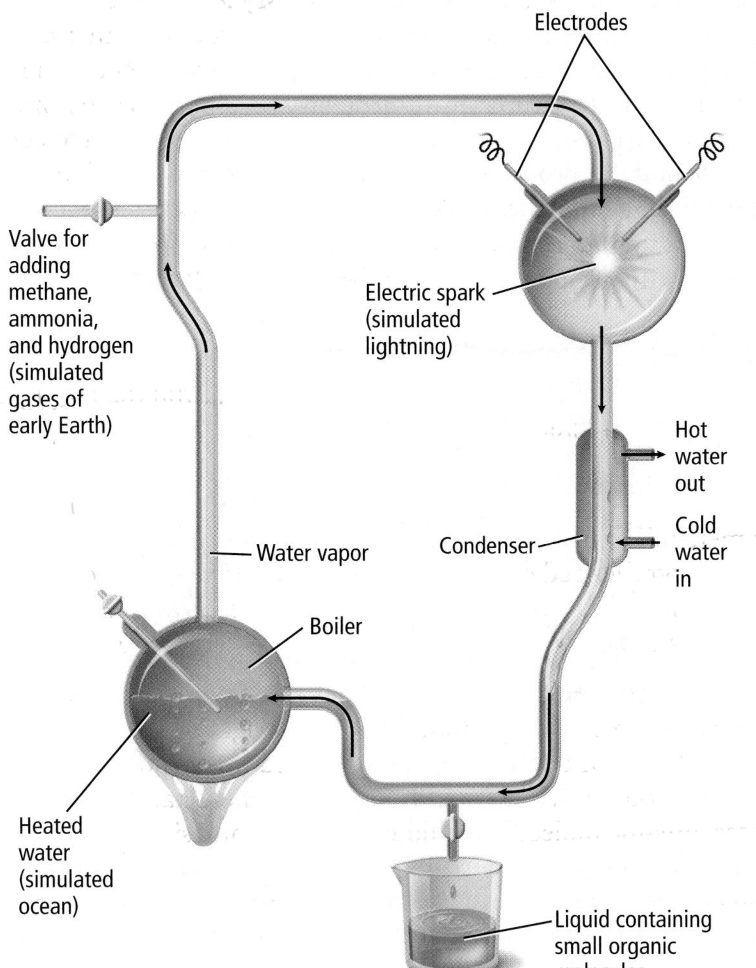


Concepts In Motion

Interactive Figure To see an animation of the Miller-Urey experiment, visit biologygmh.com.

**Figure 14.13** The Miller-Urey experiment showed for the first time that organic molecules could be produced from gases proposed to have made up the atmosphere of early Earth.

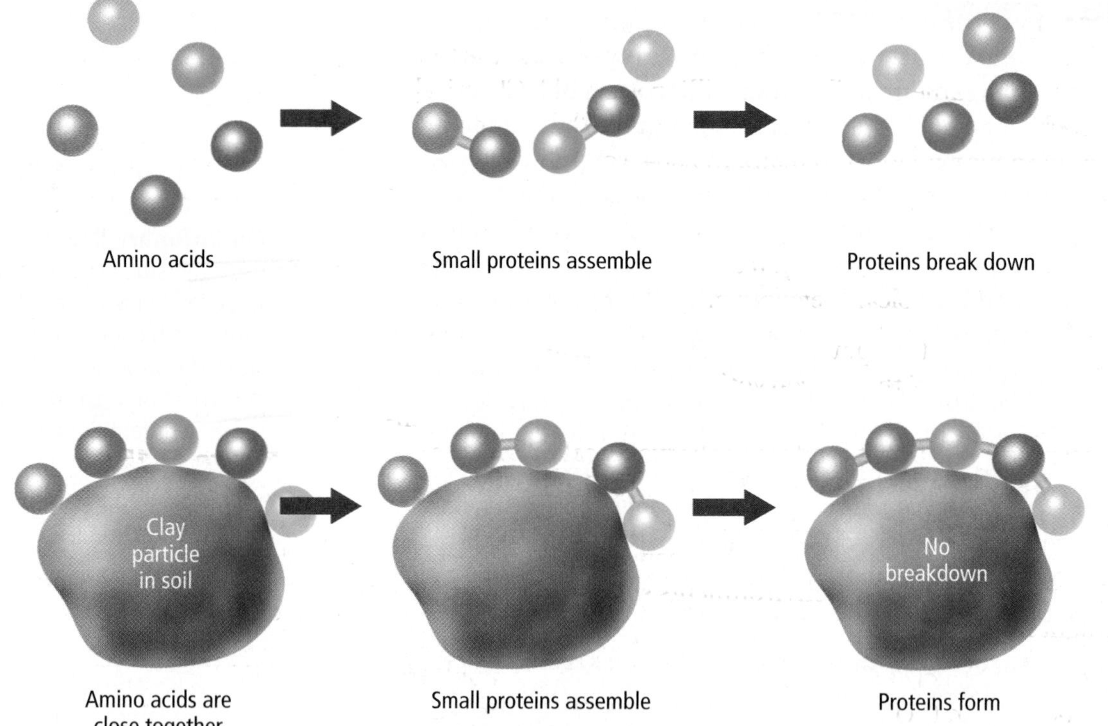


**Figure 14.14** Without clay, amino acids could have formed small, unstable proteins. In the presence of clay, amino acids might have come together in a more stable manner.

**Making proteins** Wherever the first organic molecules originated, it is clear that the next critical step was the formation of proteins. Amino acids alone are not sufficient for life. Life requires proteins, which, as you might recall from Chapter 6, are chains of amino acids. In the Miller-Urey experiment, amino acids could bond to one another, but they could separate just as quickly, as illustrated in **Figure 14.14.** One possible mechanism for the formation of proteins would be if amino acids were bound to a clay particle. Clay would have been a common sediment in early oceans, and it could have provided a framework for protein assembly.

**VOCABULARY**

**ACADEMIC VOCABULARY**

**Mechanism:**
an instrument or process by which something is done or comes into being.
*The mechanism for protein synthesis was unknown for a long time.*

**Genetic code** Another requirement for life is a coding system for protein production. All modern life has such a system, based on either RNA or DNA. Because all DNA-based life-forms also contain RNA, and because some RNA sequences appear to have changed very little through time, many biologists consider RNA to have been life's first coding system. Researchers have been able to demonstrate that RNA systems are capable of evolution by natural selection. Some RNAs also can behave like enzymes. These RNA molecules, called ribozymes, could have carried out some early life processes. Other researchers have proposed that clay crystals could have provided an initial template for RNA replication, and that eventually the resulting molecules developed their own replication mechanism.

**Molecules to cells** Another important step in the evolution of life was the formation of membranes. Researchers have tested ways of enclosing molecules in membranes, allowing early metabolic and replication pathways to develop. In this work, as in other origin-of-life research, the connection between the various chemical events and the overall path from molecules to cells remains unresolved.

## Cellular Evolution

What were the earliest cells like? Scientists don't know because the first life left no fossils. The earliest fossils are 3.5 billion years old. Chemical markings in rocks as old as 3.8 billion years suggest that life was present at that time even though no fossils remain. In 2004, scientists announced the discovery of what appeared to be fossilized microbes in volcanic rock that is 3.5 billion years old. This suggests that cellular activity had become established very early in Earth's history. It also suggests that early life might have been linked to volcanic environments.

**The first cells** Scientists hypothesize that the first cells were prokaryotes. Recall from Chapter 7 that prokaryotic cells are much smaller than eukaryotic cells, and they lack a defined nucleus and most other organelles. Many scientists think that modern prokaryotes called archaea (ar KEE uh) are the closest relatives of Earth's first cells. These organisms often live in extreme environments, such as the hot springs of Yellowstone Park or the volcanic vents in the deep sea, such as the one shown in **Figure 14.15.** These are environments similar to the environment that might have existed on early Earth.

**Figure 14.15** Some archaebacteria live near deep-sea hydrothermal vents. They use energy from inorganic molecules to form the base of the vent food web.
**Infer** ***Why do some scientists think these microorganisms most resemble the first cells?***

**Photosynthesizing prokaryotes** Although archaea are autotrophic, they do not obtain their energy from the Sun. Instead, they extract energy from inorganic compounds such as sulfur. Archaea also do not need or produce oxygen.

Scientists think that oxygen was absent from Earth's earliest atmosphere until about 1.8 billion years ago. Any oxygen that appeared earlier than 1.8 billion years ago likely bonded with free ions of iron as oxygen does today. Evidence that iron oxide was formed by oxygen generated by early life is found in unique sedimentary rock formations, such as those shown in **Figure 14.16,** that are between about 1.8 billion and 2.5 billion years old. Scientists hypothesize that after 1.8 billion years ago, the early Earth's free iron was saturated with oxygen, and oxygen instead began accumulating in the atmosphere.

Many scientists think that photosynthesizing prokaryotes evolved not long after the archaea—very early in life's history. Fossil evidence of these primitive prokaryotes, called cyanobacteria, has been found in rocks as old as 3.5 billion years. Cyanobacteria eventually produced enough oxygen to support the formation of an ozone layer. Once an ozone shield was established, conditions would be right for the appearance of eukaryotic cells.

**Figure 14.16** These sedimentary rock formations appear as banded layers. Scientists believe that banding is a result of cyclic peaks in oxygen production.

**The endosymbiont theory** Eukaryotic cells appeared in the fossil record about 1.8 billion years ago, around two billion years after life first formed. Eukaryotic cells have complex internal membranes, which enclose various organelles, including mitochondria and, in plant cells, chloroplasts. Mitochondria metabolize food through cellular respiration, and chloroplasts are the site of photosynthesis. Both mitochondria and chloroplasts are about the size of prokaryotic cells and contain similar prokaryote features. This lead some scientists to speculate that prokaryotic cells were involved in the evolution of eukaryotic cells.

In 1966, biologist Lynn Margulis proposed the endosymbiont theory. According to the **endosymbiont theory,** the ancestors of eukaryotic cells lived in association with prokaryotic cells. In some cases, prokaryotes even might have lived inside eukaryotes. Prokaryotes could have entered a host cell as undigested prey, or they could have been internal parasites. Eventually, the relationship between the cells became mutually beneficial, and the prokaryotic symbionts became organelles in eukaryotic cells. This theory explains the origin of chloroplasts and mitochondria, as illustrated in **Figure 14.17.**

**Evidence for the endosymbiont theory** When Margulis first proposed the endosymbiont theory, many scientists were hesitant to accept it. There is evidence, however, that at least mitochondria and chloroplasts formed by endosymbiosis. For example, mitochondria and chloroplasts contain their own DNA. It is arranged in a circular pattern, just as it is in prokaryotic cells. Mitochondria and chloroplasts also have ribosomes that more closely resemble those in prokaryotic cells than those in eukaryotic cells. Finally, like prokaryotic cells, mitochondria and chloroplasts reproduce by fission, independent from the rest of the cell.

## DATA ANALYSIS LAB 14.1

**Based on Real Data***

### Analyze Scientific Illustrations

**How did plastids evolve?**
Chloroplasts belong to a group of organelles called plastids, which are found in plants and algae. Chloroplasts perform photosynthesis. Other plastids store starch and make substances needed as cellular building blocks or for plant function.

**Think Critically**

1. **Summarize** the process described in the diagram. Include the definition of phagocytosis in your description.
2. **Compare** secondary endosymbiosis to the endosymbiont theory described in **Figure 14.17.**

**Data and Observations**

The illustration shows a way these plastids might have evolved.

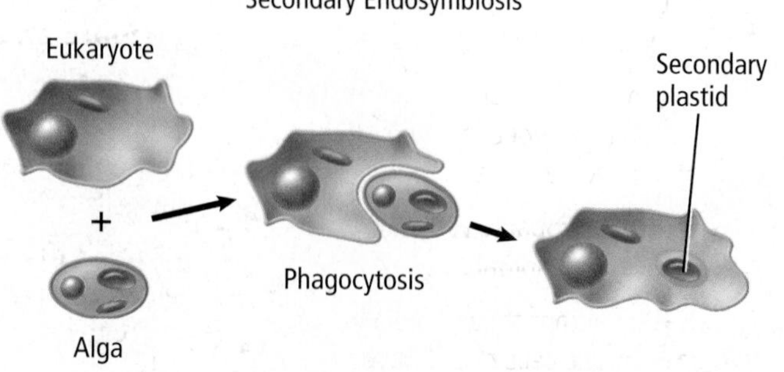


*Data obtained from: Dyall, S.D., et al. 2004. Ancient invasions: from endosymbionts to organelles. *Science* 304: 253–257.

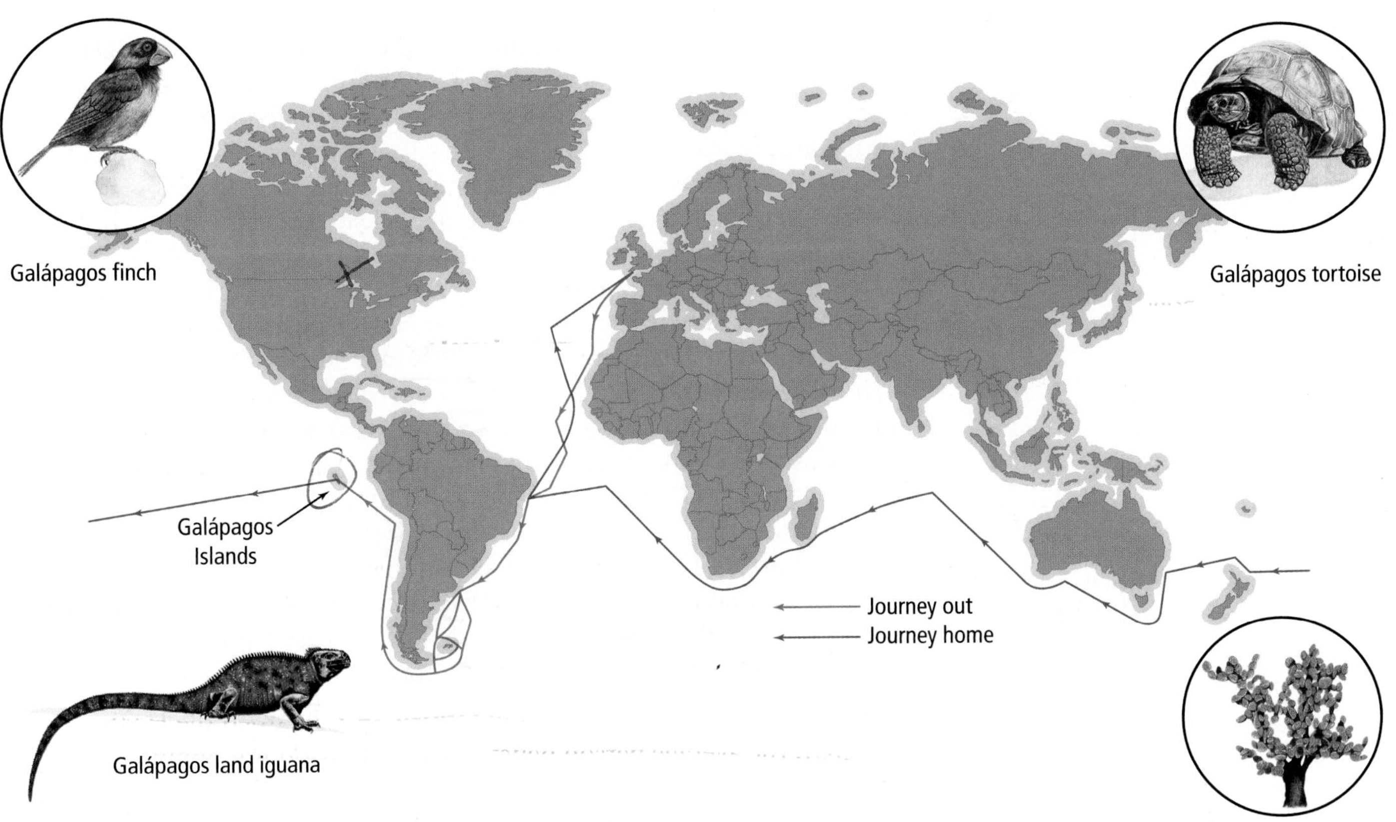


■ **Figure 15.2** The map shows the route of the *Beagle's* voyage. The species shown are all unique to the Galápagos Islands.
**Infer** ***How did the first organisms reach the Galápagos?***

A few years after Darwin returned to England, he began reconsidering his observations. He took note of the work of John Gould, an ornithologist who was classifying the birds Darwin brought back from the Galápagos. Gould discovered that the Galápagos mockingbirds were separate species and determined that the finches of the Galápagos did not live anywhere else in South America. In fact, almost every specimen that Darwin had collected on the islands was new to European scientists. These new species most closely resembled species from mainland South America, although the Galápagos and the mainland had different environments. Island and mainland species should not have resembled one another so closely unless, as Darwin began to suspect, populations from the mainland changed after reaching the Galápagos.

**Darwin continued his studies** Darwin hypothesized that new species could appear gradually through small changes in ancestral species, but he could not see how such a process would work. To understand it better, he turned to animal breeders—pigeon breeders in particular.

Different breeds of pigeons have certain distinctive traits that also are present in that breed's offspring. A breeder can promote these traits by selecting and breeding pigeons that have the most exaggerated expressions of those traits. For example, to produce pigeons with fan-shaped tails, the breeder will breed pigeons with the most fan-shaped tails. Their offspring will tend to have the fantail of their parents. Recall from Chapter 13 that this process is called selective breeding. Darwin called it **artificial selection.**

Artificial selection also occurs when developing new breeds of dogs or new strains of crop plants. Darwin inferred that if humans could change species by artificial selection, then perhaps the same process could work in nature. Further, Darwin thought that, given enough time, perhaps this process could produce new species.

**CAREERS IN BIOLOGY**

**Ornithologist** A scientist who studies birds is called an ornithologist. Such studies can range from bird behavior to classification. For more information on biology careers, visit biologygmh.com.

**Natural selection** While thinking about artificial selection, Darwin read an essay by the economist Thomas Malthus. The essay suggested that the human population, if unchecked, eventually would outgrow its food supply, leading to a competitive struggle for existence. Darwin realized that Malthus's ideas could be applied to the natural world. He reasoned that some competitors in the struggle for existence would be better equipped for survival than others. Those less equipped would die. Here, finally, was the framework for a new theory about the origin of species.

Darwin's theory has four basic principles that explain how traits of a population can change over time. First, individuals in a population show differences, or variations. Second, variations can be inherited, meaning that they are passed down from parent to offspring. Third, organisms have more offspring than can survive on available resources. The average cardinal, for example, lays nine eggs each summer. If each baby cardinal survived and reproduced just once, it would take only seven years for the first pair to have produced one million birds. Finally, variations that increase reproductive success will have a greater chance of being passed on than those that do not increase reproductive success. If having a fantail helps a pigeon reproduce successfully, future generations would include more pigeons with fan-shaped tails.

**FOLDABLES** Incorporate information from this section into your Foldable.

Darwin called his theory **natural selection.** He reasoned that, given enough time, natural selection could modify a population enough to produce a new species. **Figure 15.3** shows how natural selection might modify a population of sunflowers.

**Reading Check** **Explain** the four principles of natural selection.

# DATA ANALYSIS LAB 15.1

**Based on Real Data***

## Interpret the Data

**How did artificial selection change corn?** Plant breeders have made many changes to crops. In one of the longest experiments ever conducted, scientists have selected maize (corn) for oil content in kernels.

### Data and Observations

Look at the graph and compare the selection in the different plant lines.

Line IHO was selected for high oil content, and line ILO was selected for low oil content. The direction of selection was reversed in lines RHO (started from IHO) and RLO (started from ILO) at generation 48. In line SHO (derived from RHO), selection was switched back to high oil content at generation 55.

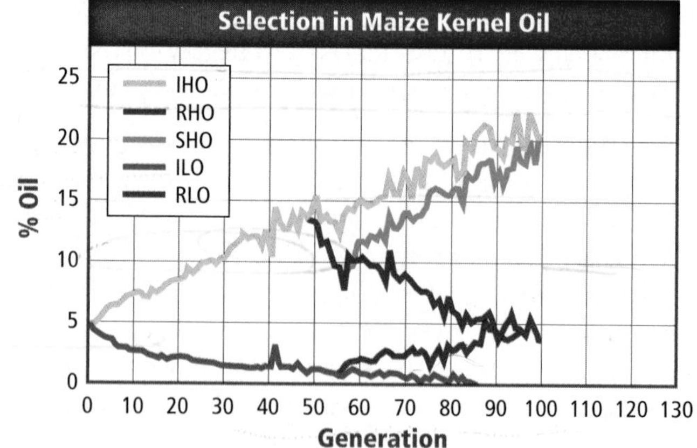


### Think Critically

1. **Measure** What were the highest and lowest percentages of oil seen in the experiment?
2. **Predict** If the trend continues for line RHO, after about how many generations will the oil content reach zero percent?

*Data obtained from: Hill, W. G. 2005. A century of corn selection. *Science* 307: 683-684.

# Visualizing Natural Selection

**Figure 15.3**
Darwin's theory of natural selection describes how, if given enough time, a population—in this case, a population of sunflowers—could be modified to produce a new species. The theory of natural selection describes four principles that explain how this can occur—variation, heritability, overproduction, and reproductive advantage.

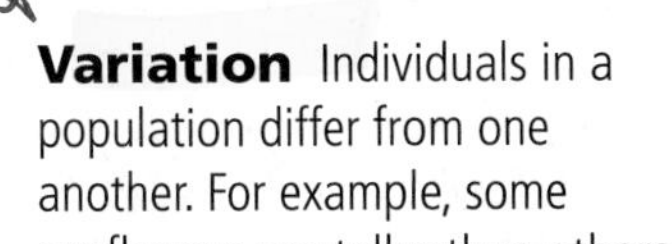

**Variation** Individuals in a population differ from one another. For example, some sunflowers are taller than others.

**Heritability** Variations are inherited from parents. Tall sunflowers produce tall sunflowers, and short sunflowers produce short sunflowers.

**Overproduction** Populations produce more offspring than can survive. Each sunflower has hundreds of seeds, most of which will not germinate.

**Reproductive Advantage** Some variations allow the organism that possesses them to have more offspring than the organism that does not possess them. For example, in this habitat, shorter sunflowers reproduce more successfully.

Over time, the average height of sunflower population is short if the short sunflowers continue to reproduce more successfully. After many generations, the short sunflowers may become a new species if they are unable to breed with the original sunflowers.

**Concepts In Motion** **Interactive Figure** To see an animation of natural selection, visit biologygmh.com.

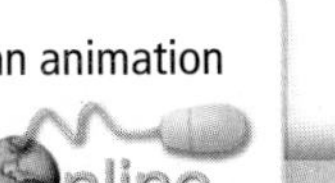

**Concepts In Motion** Interactive Table To explore more about the principles of natural selection, visit biologygmh.com.

**Table 15.1 Basic principles of natural selection**

| Principle | Example |
|---|---|
| Individuals in a population show variations among others of the same species. | The students in a classroom all look different. |
| Variations are inherited. | You look similar to your parents. |
| Animals have more young than can survive on the available resources. | The average cardinal lays nine eggs per summer. If each cardinal lived only one year, in seven years there would be a million cardinals if all offspring survived. |
| Variations that increase reproductive success will be more common in the next generation. | If having a fan-shaped tail increases reproductive success of pigeons, then more pigeons in the next generation will have fan-shaped tails. |

## The Origin of Species

Darwin had likely formulated his theory of natural selection by about 1840. Soon after, he began writing a multi-volume book compiling evidence for evolution and explaining how natural selection might provide a mechanism for the origin of species. **Table 15.1** summarizes the principles of natural selection. He continued to compile evidence in support of his theory for many years. For example, he spent eight years studying relationships among barnacles. In 1858, Alfred Russel Wallace, another English naturalist, proposed a theory that was almost identical to Darwin's theory of natural selection. Both men's ideas were presented to the Linnean Society of London. One year later, Darwin published *On the Origin of Species by Means of Natural Selection*—a condensed version of the book he had started many years before.

In his book, Darwin used the term *evolution* only on the last page. Today, biologists use the term **evolution** to define cumulative changes in groups of organisms through time. Darwin's theory of natural selection is not synonymous with evolution; it is a means of explaining how evolution works.

**Vocabulary**
**Word origin**
**Evolve**
comes from the Latin word *evolvere*, meaning *unroll* or *unfold*.

## Section 15.1 Assessment

### Section Summary

- Darwin drew from his observations on the HMS *Beagle* and later studies to develop his theory of natural selection.
- Natural selection is based on ideas of excess reproduction, variation, inheritance, and advantages of certain traits in certain environments.
- Darwin reasoned that the process of natural selection eventually could result in the appearance of new species.

### Understand Main Ideas

1. MAIN Idea **Describe** the evidence Charles Darwin gathered that led to his theory.
2. **Explain** how the idea of artificial selection contributed to Darwin's ideas on natural selection.
3. **Identify** the four principles of natural selection and provide examples not used in the section.
4. **Discuss** Wallace's contribution to the theory of natural selection.

### Think Scientifically

5. *Infer* the consequences for evolution if species did not vary.
6. WRITING in **Biology** Write a short story about what it might have been like to visit the Galápagos Islands with Darwin.



Biology Online Self-Check Quiz biologygmh.com

Section 15.2

**Objectives**

- **Describe** how fossils provide evidence of evolution.
- **Discuss** morphological evidence of evolution.
- **Explain** how biochemistry provides evidence of evolution.

**Review Vocabulary**

**fossil:** remains of an organism or its activities

**New Vocabulary**

derived trait
ancestral trait
homologous structure
vestigial structure
analogous structure
embryo
biogeography
fitness
mimicry
camouflage

# Evidence of Evolution

**MAIN Idea** **Multiple lines of evidence support the theory of evolution.**

**Real-World Reading Link** The evidence for evolution is like a set of building blocks. Just as you cannot build something with only one building block, one piece of evidence does not make a convincing theory. The evidence for evolution is more convincing when supported by many pieces of evidence, just as a structure is more sturdy when built with many blocks.

## Support for Evolution

Darwin's book *On the Origin of Species* demonstrated how natural selection might operate. The book also provided evidence that evolution has occurred on our planet. These are two different, though related, things. Darwin's theory of natural selection is part of the larger theory of evolution. In science, a theory provides an explanation for how some aspect of the natural world operates. Theories explain available data and suggest further areas for experimentation. The theory of evolution states that all organisms on Earth have descended from a common ancestor.

**The fossil record** Fossils offer some of the most significant evidence of evolutionary change. Fossils provide a record of species that lived long ago. They show that ancient species share similarities with species that now live on Earth, as illustrated in **Figure 15.4.** Not all extinct fossils have modern counterparts and some ancient species—such as the horseshoe crab—have remained virtually unchanged for millions of years. The fossil record is an important source of information for determining the ancestry of organisms and the patterns of evolution.

■ **Figure 15.4** The giant armadillo-like glyptodont, *Glyptodon,* is an extinct animal that Darwin thought must be related to the living armadillos that inhabit South America, Central America, and the southern United States.
**Observe** ***What features of the 2000-kg glyptodont are similar to those of the 4-kg armadillo?***

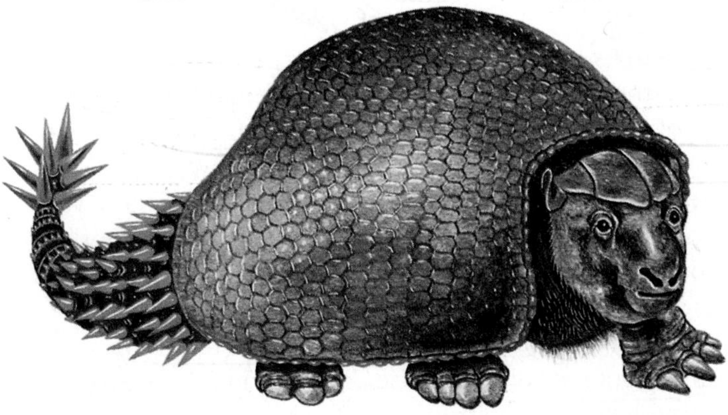

Glyptodont

Armadillo

■ **Figure 15.5** This artist's rendering of *Archaeopteryx* shows that it shares many features with modern birds while retaining ancestral dinosaur features.

**Connection to Earth Science** Though Darwin recognized the limitations of the fossil record, he predicted the existence of fossils intermediate in form between species. Today, scientists studying evolutionary relationships have found hundreds of thousands of transitional fossils that contain features shared by different species. For example, certain dinosaur fossils show feathers of modern birds and the teeth and bony tails of reptiles. **Figure 15.5** shows an artist's rendering of *Archaeopteryx*, one of the first birds. *Archaeopteryx* fossils provide evidence of characteristics that classify it as a bird, and also show that the bird retained several distinct dinosaur features.

Researchers consider two major classes of traits when studying transitional fossils: derived traits and ancestral traits. **Derived traits** are newly evolved features, such as feathers, that do not appear in the fossils of common ancestors. **Ancestral traits,** on the other hand, are more primitive features, such as teeth and tails, that do appear in ancestral forms. Transitional fossils provide detailed patterns of evolutionary change for the ancestors of many modern animals, including mollusks, horses, whales, and humans.

**VOCABULARY**
**WORD ORIGIN**
**Homologous**
from the Greek words *homos,* meaning *same,* and *logos,* meaning *relation* or *reasoning.*

**Comparative anatomy** Why do the vertebrate forelimbs shown in **Figure 15.6** have different functions but appear to be constructed of similar bones in similar ways? Evolutionary theory suggests that the answer lies in shared ancestry.

**Homologous structures** Anatomically similar structures inherited from a common ancestor are called **homologous structures.** Evolution predicts that an organism's body parts are more likely to be modifications of ancestral body parts than they are to be entirely new features. The limbs illustrated in **Figure 15.6** move animals in different ways, yet they share similar construction. Bird wings and reptile limbs are another example. Though birds use their wings to fly and reptiles use their limbs to walk, bird wings and reptile forelimbs are similar in shape and construction, which indicates that they were inherited from a common ancestor. While homologous structures alone are not evidence of evolution, they are an example for which evolution is the best available explanation for the biological data.

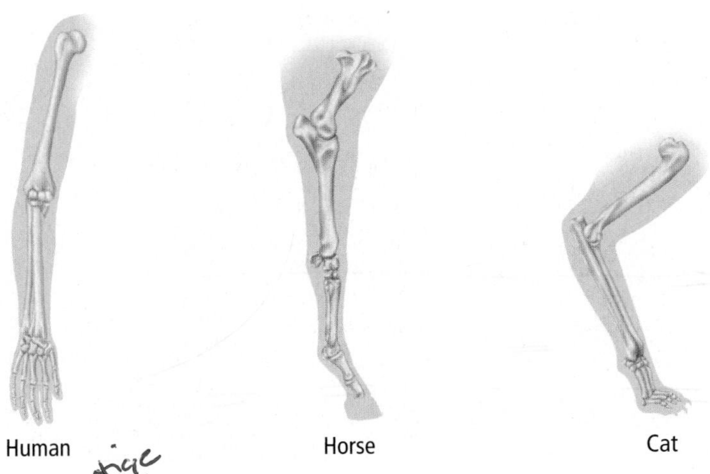


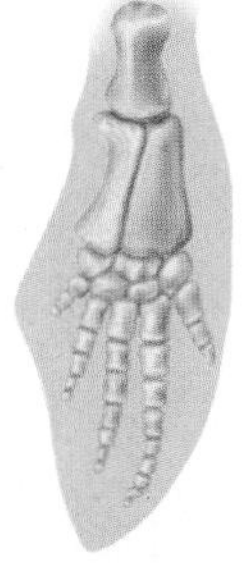


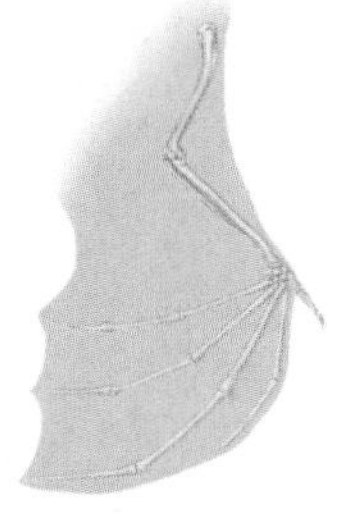


**Figure 15.6** The forelimbs of vertebrates illustrate homologous structures. Each limb is adapted for different uses, but they all have similar bones.

**Infer** ***Which of the forelimbs shown would most likely resemble a whale's fluke?***

**Vestigial structures** In some cases, a functioning structure in one species is smaller or less functional in a closely related species. For example, most birds have wings developed for flight. Kiwis, however, have very small wings that cannot be used for flying. The kiwi wing is a kind of homologous structure called a vestigial structure. **Vestigial structures** are structures that are the reduced forms of functional structures in other organisms. **Table 15.2** illustrates some vestigial structures in different species. Evolutionary theory predicts that features of ancestors that no longer have a function for that species will become smaller over time until they are lost.

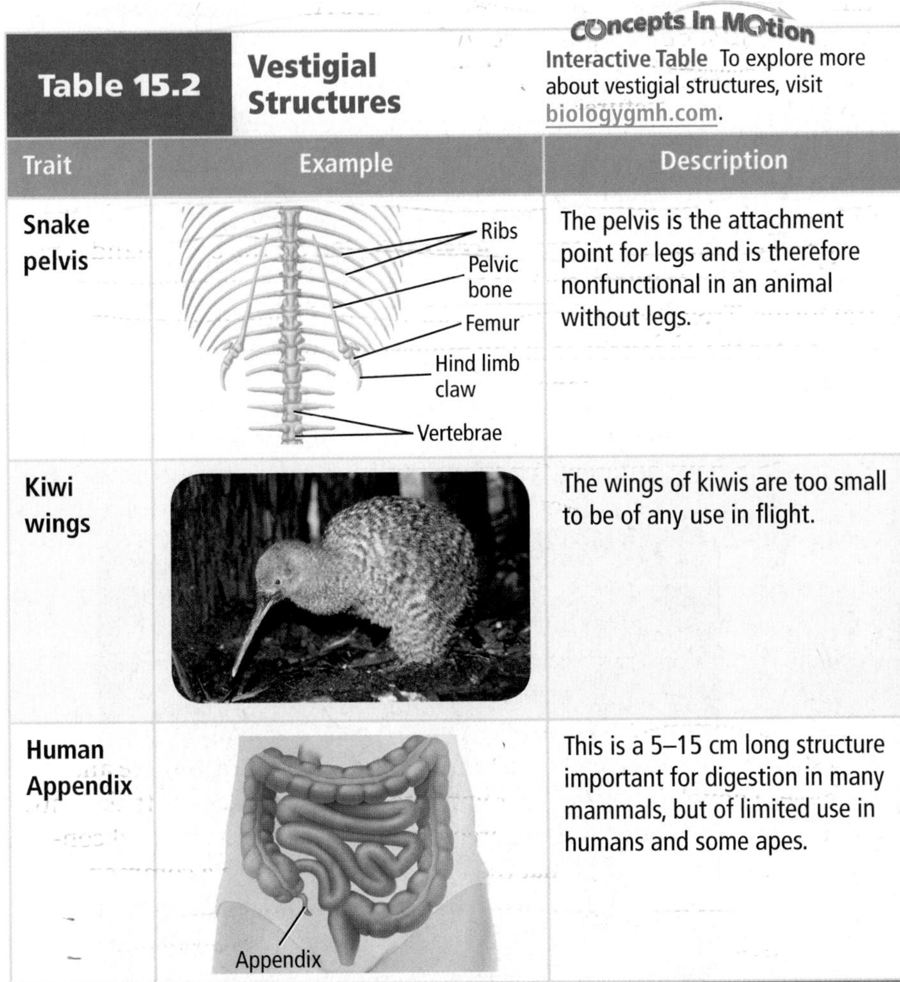

**Table 15.2 Vestigial Structures**

**Concepts In Motion** Interactive Table To explore more about vestigial structures, visit biologygmh.com.

| Trait | Example | Description |
|---|---|---|
| **Snake pelvis** | Ribs, Pelvic bone, Femur, Hind limb claw, Vertebrae | The pelvis is the attachment point for legs and is therefore nonfunctional in an animal without legs. |
| **Kiwi wings** | | The wings of kiwis are too small to be of any use in flight. |
| **Human Appendix** | Appendix | This is a 5–15 cm long structure important for digestion in many mammals, but of limited use in humans and some apes. |

**Figure 15.7** Eagles and beetles use their wings to fly, but their wing structures are different.

Bald Eagle

May Beetle

Not all anatomically similar features are evidence of common ancestry. **Analogous structures** can be used for the same purpose and can be superficially similar in construction, but are not inherited from a common ancestor. As shown in **Figure 15.7,** the wing of an eagle and the wing of a beetle have the same function—they both enable the organism to fly—but they are constructed in different ways from different materials. While analogous structures do not indicate close evolutionary relationships, they do show that functionally similar features can evolve independently in similar environments.

**Reading Check** **Explain** why vestigial structures are considered examples of homologous structures.

**Comparative embryology** Vertebrate embryos provide more glimpses into evolutionary relationships. An **embryo** is an early, prebirth stage of an organism's development. Scientists have found that vertebrate embryos exhibit homologous structures during certain phases of development but become totally different structures in the adult forms. The embryos shown in **Figure 15.8,** like all vertebrate embryos, have a tail and paired structures called pharyngeal pouches. In fish the pouches develop into gills. In reptiles, birds, and mammals, these structures become parts of the ears, jaws, and throats. Though the adult forms differ, the shared features in the embryos suggest that vertebrates evolved from a shared ancestor.

**Figure 15.8** Embryos reveal evolutionary history. Bird and mammal embryos share several developmental features.

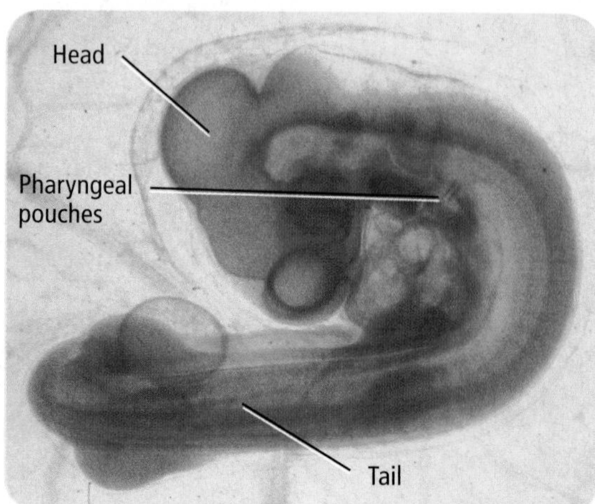


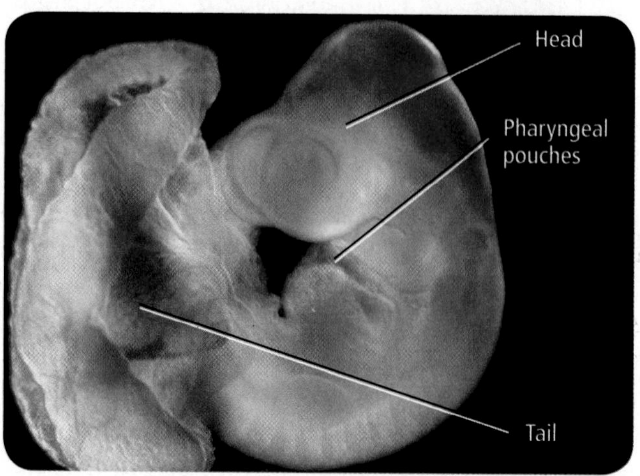

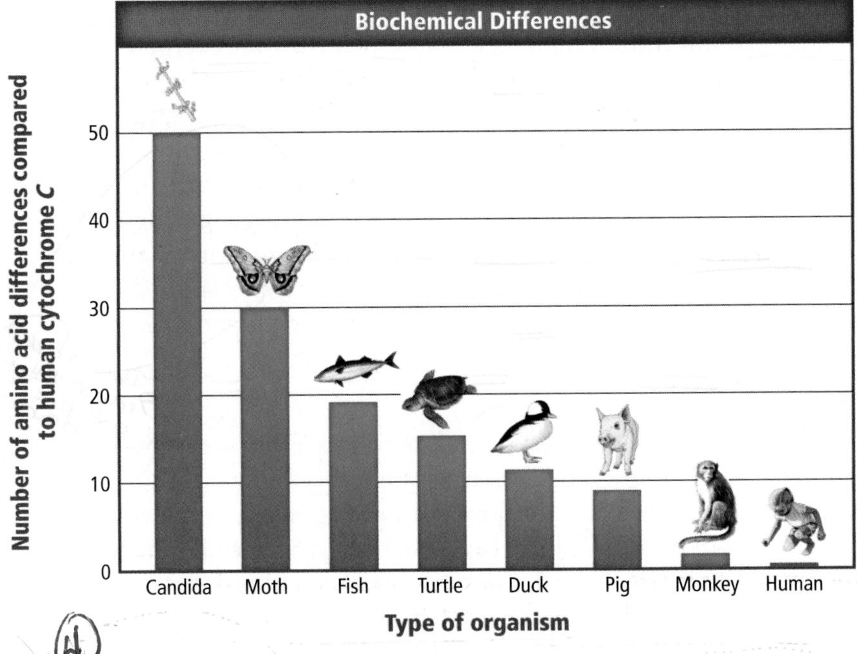

**Figure 15.9** This illustration compares amino acid sequences of cytochrome c in humans and other organisms.

**Infer** ***Would the cytochrome c of a reptile or a duck be expected to have more amino acid differences when compared with that of a human? Explain.***

**Comparative biochemistry** Scientific data also shows that common ancestry can be seen in the complex metabolic molecules that many different organisms share. Cytochrome *c* is an enzyme that is essential for respiration and is highly conserved in animals. This means that despite slight variations in its amino acid sequence, the molecule has changed very little over time.

Evolutionary theory predicts that molecules in species with a recent common ancestor should share certain ancient amino acid sequences. The more closely related the species are, the greater number of sequences will be shared. This predicted pattern is what scientists find to be true in cytochrome *c*. For example, as illustrated in **Figure 15.9,** the cytochrome *c* in the pig and in the monkey share more amino acid sequences with humans than the cytochrome *c* in birds shares with humans.

**Connection to Chemistry** Scientists have found similar biochemical patterns in other proteins, as well as in DNA and RNA. DNA and RNA form the molecular basis of heredity in all living organisms. The fact that many organisms have the same complex molecules suggests that these molecules evolved early in the history of life and were passed on through the life-forms that have lived on Earth. Comparisons of the similarities in these molecules across species reflect evolutionary patterns seen in comparative anatomy and in the fossil record. Organisms with closely related morphological features have more closely related molecular features.

**Geographic distribution** The distribution of plants and animals that Darwin saw during his South American travels first suggested evolution to Darwin. He observed that animals on the South American mainland were more similar to other South American animals than they were to animals living in similar environments in Europe. The South American mara, for example, inhabited a niche that was occupied by the rabbit in Europe. You can compare a mara and a rabbit in **Figure 15.10.** Darwin realized that the mara was more similar to other South American species than it was to the rabbit because it shared a closer ancestor with the South American animals.

**Figure 15.10** The mara *(Dolichotis patagonum)* exists in a niche similar to that of the English rabbit *(Oryctolagus cuniculus)*.

**Mara**

**English Rabbit**

Patterns of migration were critical to Darwin when he was developing his theory. Migration patterns explained why, for example, islands often have more plant diversity than animal diversity: the plants are more able to migrate from the closest mainland as seeds, either by wind or on the backs of birds. Since Darwin's time, scientists have confirmed and expanded Darwin's study of the distribution of plants and animals around the world in a field of study now called **biogeography.** Evolution is intimately linked with climate and geological forces, especially plate tectonics, which helps explain many ancestral relationships and geographic distributions seen in fossils and living organisms today.

## Adaptation

The five categories discussed in the previous section—the fossil record, comparative anatomy, comparative embryology, comparative biochemistry, and geographic distribution—offer evidence for evolution. Darwin drew on all of these except biochemistry—which was not well developed in his time—to develop his own theory of evolution by natural selection. At the heart of his theory lies the concept of adaptation.

**Types of adaptation** An adaptation is a trait shaped by natural selection that increases an organism's reproductive success. One way to determine how effectively a trait contributes to reproductive success is to measure fitness. **Fitness** is a measure of the relative contribution an individual trait makes to the next generation. It often is measured as the number of reproductively viable offspring that an organism produces in the next generation.

The better an organism is adapted to its environment, the greater its chances of survival and reproductive success. This concept explains the variations Darwin observed in the animals on the Galápagos Islands. Because the finches were each adapted to their individual islands, they had variations in their beaks.

**Camouflage** Some species have evolved morphological adaptations that allow them to blend in with their environments. This is called **camouflage** (KA muh flahj). Camouflage allows organisms to become almost invisible to predators, as shown in **Figure 15.11.** As a result, more of the camouflaged individuals survive and reproduce.

**VOCABULARY**
**SCIENCE USAGE V. COMMON USAGE**

**Adaptation**

***Science usage:*** a trait shaped by natural selection to increase the survival or reproductive success of an organism.
*The prehensile tail of monkeys is an adaptation for life in the trees.*

***Common usage:*** adjustment or change.
*The movie script is an adaptation of the original play.*

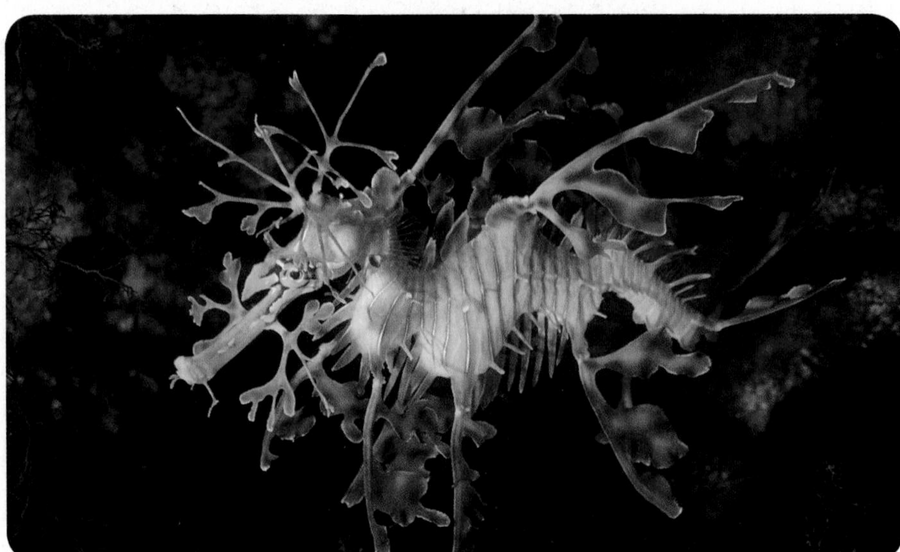

**Figure 15.11** It would be easy for a predator to overlook a leafy sea dragon, *Phycodurus eques*, in a sea grass habitat because of the animal's effective camouflage.

California Kingsnake

Western Coral Snake

■ **Figure 15.12** Predators avoid the harmless California kingsnake because it has color patterns similar to those of the poisonous western coral snake.

**Mimicry** Another type of morphological adaptation is mimicry. In **mimicry,** one species evolves to resemble another species. You might expect that mimicry would make it difficult for individuals in one species to find and breed with other members of their species, thus decreasing reproductive success. However, mimicry often increases an organism's fitness. Mimicry can occur in a harmless species that has evolved to resemble a harmful species, such as the example shown in **Figure 15.12.** Sometimes mimicry benefits two harmful species. In both cases, the mimics are protected because predators can't always tell the mimic from the animal it is mimicking, so they learn to avoid them both.

**Reading Check** **Compare** mimicry and camouflage.

**Antimicrobial resistance** Species of bacteria that originally were killed by penicillin and other antibiotics have developed drug resistance. For almost every antibiotic, at least one species of resistant bacteria exists. One unintended consequence of the continued development of antibiotics is that some diseases, which were once thought to be contained, such as tuberculosis, have reemerged in more harmful forms.

## MiniLab 15.1

### Investigate Mimicry

**Why do some species mimic the features of other species?** Mimicry is the process of natural selection shaping one species of organism to look similar to another species. Natural selection has shaped the nontoxic viceroy butterfly to look like the toxic monarch butterfly. Investigate the mimicry displayed during this lab.

**Procedure**

1. Read and complete the lab safety form.
2. Create a data table for recording your observations and measurements of the **monarch** and **viceroy butterflies.**
3. Observe the physical characteristics of both butterfly species and record your observations in your data table.

**Analysis**

1. **Compare and contrast** the physical characteristics of the two butterfly species.
2. **Hypothesize** why the viceroy butterflies have bright colors that are highly visible.

■ **Figure 15.13** Spaces between arches set in a square to support a dome are called spandrels and are often decorative. Some features might be like spandrels—a consequence of another adaptation.

**Consequences of adaptations** Not all features of an organism are necessarily adaptive. Some features might be consequences of other evolved characteristics. Biologists Stephen Jay Gould and Richard Lewontin made this point in 1979 in a paper claiming that biologists tended to overemphasize the importance of adaptations in evolution.

**Spandrel example** To illustrate this concept, they used an example from architecture. Building a set of four arches in a square to support a dome means that spaces called spandrels will appear between the arches, as illustrated in **Figure 15.13.** Because spandrels are often decorative, one might think that spandrels exist for decoration. In reality, they are an unavoidable consequence of arch construction. Gould and Lewontin argued that some features in organisms are like spandrels because even though they are prominent, they do not increase reproductive success. Instead, they likely arose as an unavoidable consequence of prior evolutionary change.

**Human example** A biological example is the helplessness of human babies. Humans give birth at a much earlier stage than other primates, leading to the need for increased care. While scientists thought at one time that early birth might serve an adaptive purpose—for instance, it might increase parental attention and encourage more learning, which might lead to increased fitness—many scientists now think that the helplessness of human babies is merely a consequence of the evolution of big brains and upright posture. To walk upright, humans need narrow pelvises, which means that babies' heads must be small enough to fit through the pelvic opening.

## Section 15.2 Assessment

### Section Summary

- Fossils provide strong direct evidence to support evolution.
- Homologous and vestigial structures indicate shared ancestry.
- Examples of embryological and biochemical traits provide insight into the evolution of species.
- Biogeography can explain why certain species live in certain locations.
- Natural selection gives rise to features that increase reproductive success.

### Understand Main Ideas

1. MAIN Idea **Describe** how fossils provide evidence of evolution.
2. **Explain** what natural selection predicts about mimicry, camouflage, homologous structures, and vestigial structures.
3. **Indicate** how biochemistry provides evidence of evolution.
4. **Compare** morphological and biochemical evidence supporting evolution.

### Think Scientifically

5. *Hypothesize* Evidence suggests that the bones in bird wings share a number of features with those of dinosaur arms. Based on this evidence, what hypothesis could you make about the evolutionary relationship between birds and dinosaurs?
6. *Think Critically* Research has shown that if a prescribed dose of antibiotic is not taken completely, some bacteria might not be killed and the disease might return. How does natural selection explain this phenomenon?



Biology Online Self-Check Quiz biologygmh.com

Section 15.3

**Objectives**

- **Discuss** patterns observed in evolution.
- **Describe** factors that influence speciation.
- **Compare** gradualism with punctuated equilibrium.

**Review Vocabulary**

**allele:** alternate forms of a character trait that can be inherited

**New Vocabulary**

Hardy-Weinberg Principle
genetic drift
founder effect
bottleneck
stabilizing selection
directional selection
disruptive selection
sexual selection
prezygotic isolating mechanism
allopatric speciation
postzygotic isolating mechanism
sympatric speciation
adaptive radiation
gradualism
punctuated equilibrium

# Shaping Evolutionary Theory

**MAIN Idea The theory of evolution continues to be refined as scientists learn new information.**

**Real-World Reading Link** The longer you operate a complicated piece of electronics, the better you understand how it works. The device does not change, but you become more familiar with its functions. Scientists have been studying evolution for almost 150 years, yet they are still learning new ways in which evolution leads to changes in species.

## Mechanisms of Evolution

Darwin's theory of natural selection remains a central theme in evolution. It explains how organisms adapt to their environments and how variations can give rise to adaptations within species. Scientists now know, however, that natural selection is not the only mechanism of evolution. Studies from population genetics and molecular biology have led to the development of evolutionary theory. At the center of this is the understanding that evolution occurs at the population level, with genes as the raw material.

**Population genetics** At the turn of the twentieth century, genes had not been discovered. However, the allele was understood to be one form of an inherited character trait, such as eye color, that gets passed down from parent to offspring. Scientists didn't understand why dominant alleles wouldn't simply swamp recessive alleles in a population.

In 1908, English mathematician Godfrey Hardy and German physician Wilhelm Weinberg independently came up with the same solution to this problem. They showed mathematically that evolution will not occur in a population unless allelic frequencies are acted upon by forces that cause change. In the absence of these forces, the allelic frequency remains the same and evolution doesn't occur. According to this idea, which is now known as the **Hardy-Weinberg principle,** when allelic frequencies remain constant, a population is in genetic equilibrium. This concept is illustrated in **Figure 15.14.**

**Figure 15.14** According to the Hardy-Weinberg principle, even though the number of owls doubled, the ratio of gray to red owls remained the same.

**CAREERS IN BIOLOGY**

**Biometrician** Almost all scientific research papers include some statistics. Many researchers consult biometricians—people who specialize in statistics related to biology—to help design studies and analyze study results. For more information on biology careers, visit biologygmh.com.

**Connection to Math** To illustrate the Hardy-Weinberg principle, consider a population of 100 humans. Forty of these people are homozygous dominant for earlobe attachment *(EE)*. Another 40 people are heterozygous for earlobe attachment *(Ee)*. Twenty people are homozygous recessive *(ee)*. In the 40 homozygous dominant people, there are 80 *E* alleles (2 *E* alleles × 40), and in the 20 homozygous recessive people there are 40 *e* alleles (2 *e* alleles × 20). The heterozygous people have 40 *E* alleles and 40 *e* alleles. Summing the alleles, we have 120 *E* alleles and 80 *e* alleles for a total of 200 alleles. The *E* allele frequency is 120/200, or 0.6. The *e* allele frequency is 80/200, or 0.4.

The Hardy-Weinberg principle states that the allele frequencies in populations should be constant. This often is expressed as $p + q = 1$. For our example, p can represent the *E* allele frequency and q can represent the *e* allele frequency.

Squaring both sides of the equation yields the new equation $p^2 + 2pq + q^2 = 1$. This equation allows us to determine the equilibrium frequency of each genotype in the population: homozygous dominant ($p^2$), heterozygous ($2pq$), and homozygous recessive ($q^2$). From the above example, $p = 0.6$, and $q = 0.4$, so $(0.6)(0.6) + 2(0.6)(0.4) + (0.4)(0.4) = 1$. In the example population, the equilibrium frequency for homozygous dominant will be 0.36, the equilibrium frequency of heterozygous will be 0.48, and the equilibrium frequency of homozygous recessive will be 0.16. Note that the sum of these frequencies equals one.

**Conditions** According to the Hardy-Weinberg principle, a population in genetic equilibrium must meet five conditions—there must be no genetic drift, no gene flow, no mutation, mating must be random, and there must be no natural selection. These are listed in **Table 15.3.** Populations in nature might meet some of these requirements, but hardly any population meets all five conditions for long periods of time. If a population is not in genetic equilibrium, at least one of the five conditions has been violated. These five conditions are known mechanisms of evolutionary change. Of these, only natural selection is thought to provide adaptive advantages to a population, and only natural selection acts on an organism's phenotype.

**Table 15.3 The Hardy-Weinberg Principle**

**Concepts In Motion** **Interactive Table** To explore more about the Hardy-Weinberg principle, visit biologygmh.com.

| Condition | Violation | Consequence |
|---|---|---|
| The population is very large. | Many populations are small. | Chance events can lead to changes in population traits. |
| There is no immigration or emigration. | Organisms move in and out of the population. | The population can lose or gain traits with movement of organisms. |
| Mating is random. | Mating is not random. | New traits do not pass as quickly to the rest of the population. |
| Mutations do not occur. | Mutations occur. | New variations appear in the population with each new generation. |
| Natural selection does not occur. | Natural selection occurs. | Traits in a population change from one generation to the next. |

**Genetic drift** Any change in the allelic frequencies in a population that is due to chance is called **genetic drift.** Recall from Chapter 10 that for simple traits only one of a parent's two alleles passes to the offspring, and that this allele is selected randomly through independent assortment. In large populations, enough alleles "drift" to ensure that the allelic frequency of the entire population remains relatively constant from one generation to the next. In smaller populations, however, the effects of genetic drift become more pronounced, and the chance of losing an allele becomes greater.

**Founder effect** The founder effect is an extreme example of genetic drift. The **founder effect** can occur when a small sample of a population settles in a location separated from the rest of the population. Because this sample is a random subset of the original population, the sample population carries a random subset of the population's genes. Alleles that were uncommon in the original population might be common in the new population, and the offspring in the new population will carry those alleles. Such an event can result in large genetic variations in the separated populations.

The founder effect is evident in the Amish and Mennonite communities in the United States in which the people rarely marry outside their own communities. The Old Order Amish have a high frequency of six-finger dwarfism. All affected individuals can trace their ancestry back to one of the founders of the Order.

**Bottleneck** Another extreme example of genetic drift is a **bottleneck,** which occurs when a population declines to a very low number and then rebounds. The gene pool of the rebound population often is genetically similar to that of the population at its lowest level, that is, it has reduced diversity. Researchers think that cheetahs in Africa experienced a bottleneck 10,000 years ago, and then another one about 100 years ago. Throughout their current range, shown in **Figure 15.15,** cheetahs are so genetically similar that they appear inbred. Inbreeding decreases fertility, and might be a factor in the potential extinction of this endangered species.

**Reading Check** **Explain** how genetic drift affects populations.

### Study Tip

**Concept Map** Make a concept map, placing the term *evolution* in the top oval. The second row of ovals should contain the following terms: *genetic drift, gene flow, nonrandom mating, mutation,* and *natural selection.* As you read the chapter, fill in definitions and write examples that illustrate each term.

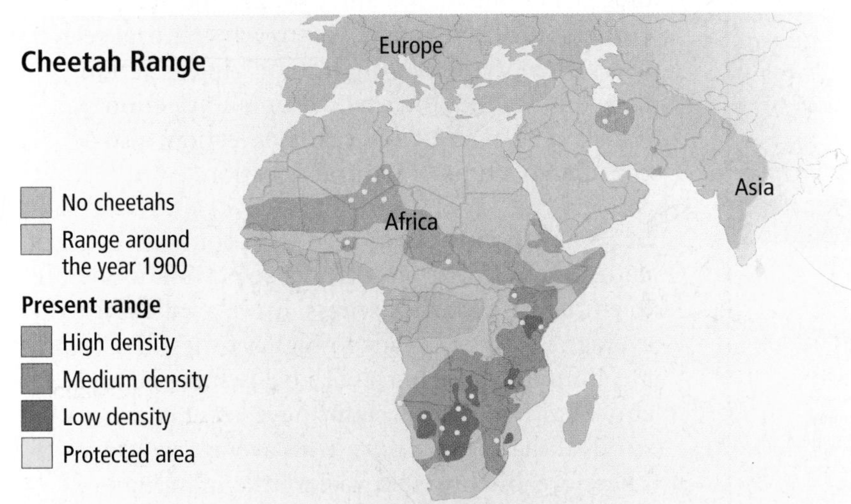


**Figure 15.15** The map shows the present range of cheetahs in Africa. It is believed that cheetahs had a much larger population until a bottleneck occurred.
**Apply Concepts** ***What effect has the bottleneck had on the reproductive rate of cheetahs?***

**Gene flow** A population in genetic equilibrium experiences no gene flow. It is a closed system, with no new genes entering the population and no genes leaving the population. In reality, few populations are isolated. The random movement of individuals between populations, or migration, increases genetic variation within a population and reduces differences between populations.

**Nonrandom mating** Rarely is mating completely random in a population. Usually, organisms mate with individuals in close proximity. This promotes inbreeding and could lead to a change in allelic proportions favoring individuals that are homozygous for particular traits.

**Mutation** Recall from Chapter 12 that a mutation is a random change in genetic material. The cumulative effect of mutations in a population might cause a change in allelic frequencies, and thus violate genetic equilibrium. Though many mutations cause harm or are lethal, occasionally a mutation provides an advantage to an organism. This mutation will then be selected for and become more common in subsequent generations. In this way, mutations provide the raw material upon which natural selection works.

**Reading Check** **Summarize** how mutation violates the Hardy-Weinberg principle.

**Figure 15.16** Natural selection can alter allele frequencies of a population in three ways. The bell-shaped curve shown as a dotted line in each graph indicates the trait's original variation in a population. The solid line indicates the outcome of each type of selection pressure.

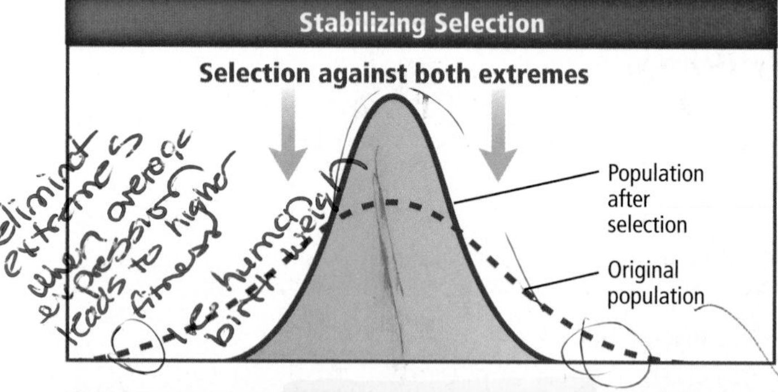


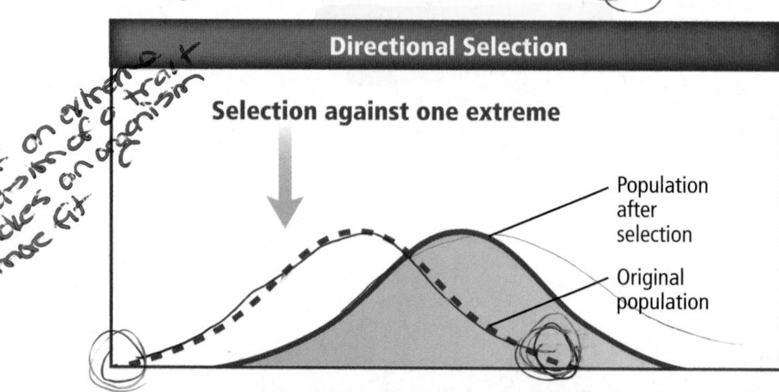


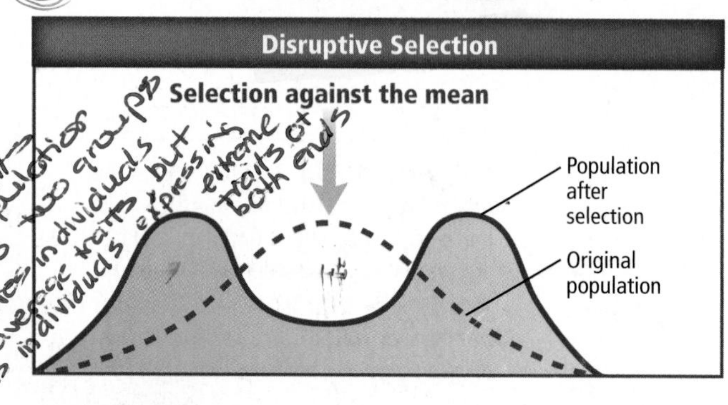


**Natural selection** The Hardy-Weinberg principle requires that all individuals in a population be equally adapted to their environment and thus contribute equally to the next generation. As you have learned, this rarely happens. Natural selection acts to select the individuals that are best adapted for survival and reproduction. Natural selection acts on an organism's phenotype and changes allelic frequencies. **Figure 15.16** shows three main ways natural selection alters phenotypes: through stabilizing selection, directional selection, and disruptive selection. A fourth type of selection, sexual selection, also is considered a type of natural selection.

**Stabilizing selection** The most common form of natural selection is **stabilizing selection.** It operates to eliminate extreme expressions of a trait when the average expression leads to higher fitness. For example, human babies born with below-normal and above-normal birth weights have lower chances of survival than babies born with average weights. Therefore, birth weight varies little in human populations.

**Directional selection** If an extreme version of a trait makes an organism more fit, **directional selection** might occur. This form of selection increases the expression of the extreme versions of a trait in a population. One example is the evolution of moths in industrial England. The peppered moth has two color forms, or morphs, as shown in **Figure 15.17.** Until the mid 1850s, nearly all peppered moths in England had light-colored wings. Beginning around 1850, however, dark moths began appearing. By the early 1900s, nearly all peppered moths were dark. Why? Industrial pollution favored the dark-colored moths at the expense of the light-colored moths. The darker the moth, the more it matched the sooty background of its tree habitat, and the harder it was for predators to see. Thus, more dark moths survived, adding more genes for dark color to the population. This conclusion was reinforced in the mid-1900s when the passage of air pollution laws led to the resurgence of light-colored moths. This phenomenon is called industrial melanism.

Directional selection also can be seen in Galápagos finches. For three decades in the latter part of the twentieth century, Peter and Rosemary Grant studied populations of these finches. The Grants found that during drought years, food supplies dwindled and the birds had to eat the hard seeds they normally ignored. Birds with the largest beaks were more successful in cracking the tough seed coating than were birds with smaller beaks. As a result, over the duration of the drought, birds with larger beaks came to dominate the population. In rainy years, however, the directional trend was reversed, and the population's average beak size decreased.

**Figure 15.17** The peppered moth exists in two forms.
**Infer** ***How might natural selection have caused a change in the frequencies of the two forms?***

# DATA ANALYSIS LAB 15.2

**Based on Real Data***

## Interpret the Graph

**How does pollution affect melanism in moths?** The changing frequencies of light-colored and dark-colored moths have been studied for decades in the United States. The percentage of the melanic, or dark, form of the moth was low prior to the industrial revolution. It increased until it made up nearly the entire population in the early 1900s. After antipollution laws were passed, the percentage of melanic moths declined, as shown in the graph.

### Think Critically

1. **Interpret** What was the percent decrease in Pennsylvania melanic moth population?
2. **Hypothesize** Why might the percentage of melanic moths have remained at a relatively low level in Virginia?

*Data obtained from: Grant, B. S. and L. L. Wiseman. 2002. Recent history of melanism in American peppered moths. *Journal of Heredity* 93: 86-90.

### Data and Observations

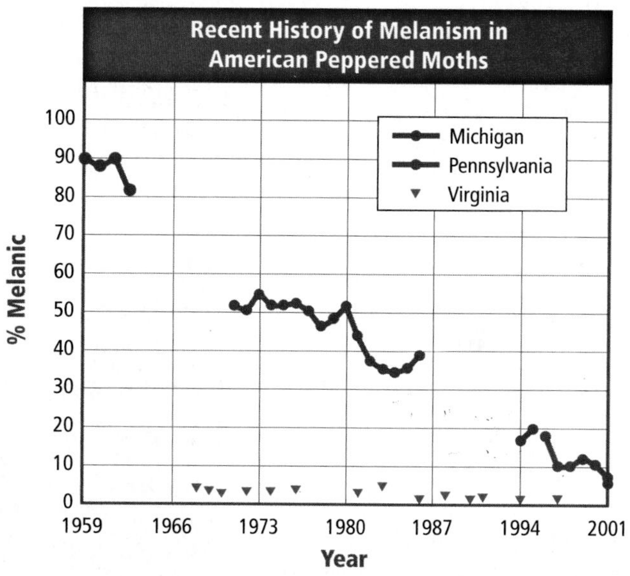

■ **Figure 15.18** Northern water snakes have two different color patterns depending on their habitat. Intermediate color patterns would make them more visible to predators.

**Disruptive selection** Another type of natural selection, **disruptive selection,** is a process that splits a population into two groups. It tends to remove individuals with average traits but retain individuals expressing extreme traits at both ends of a continuum. Northern water snakes, illustrated in **Figure 15.18,** are an example. Snakes living on the mainland shores inhabit grasslands and have mottled brown skin. Snakes inhabiting rocky island shores have gray skin. Each is adapted to its particular environment. A snake with intermediate coloring would be disadvantaged because it would be more visible to predators.

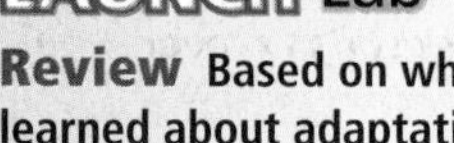

**LAUNCH Lab**

**Review** Based on what you have learned about adaptation, how would you now answer the analysis questions?

**Sexual selection** Charles Darwin recognized another type of natural selection that he called **sexual selection.** This type of selection often operates in populations where males and females differ significantly in appearance. Usually in these populations, males are the largest and most colorful of the group. The bigger the tail of a male peacock, as shown in **Figure 15.19,** the more attractive the bird is to females. Males also evolve threatening characteristics that intimidate other males; this is common in species, such as elk or deer, where the male keeps a harem of females.

Darwin was intrigued by sexual selection. He wondered why some qualities of sexual attractiveness appeared to be the opposite of qualities that might enhance survival. For example, the peacock's tail, while attracting females, is large and cumbersome, and it might make the peacock a more likely target for predators. Though some modern scientists think that sexual selection is not a form of natural selection, others think that sexual selection follows the same general principle: brighter colors and bigger bodies enhance reproductive success, whatever the chances are for long-term survival.

■ **Figure 15.19** Peacocks that have the largest tails tend to attract more peahens. The frequency of this trait increases because of sexual selection.

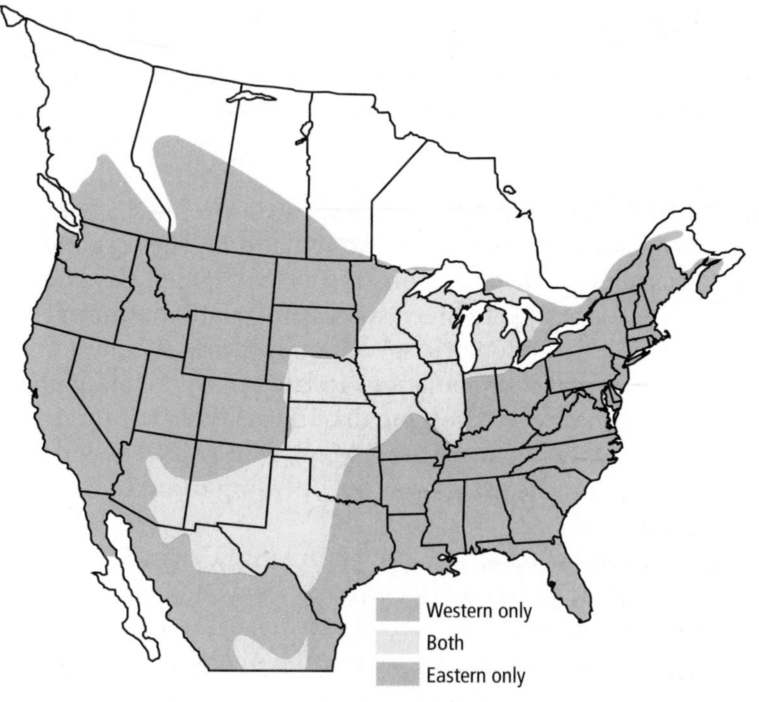

■ **Figure 15.20** The map shows the overlapping ranges of the Eastern meadowlark and Western meadowlark. While the two are similar in appearance, their songs separate them behaviorally.
**Infer** ***how different songs prevent the meadowlarks from breeding.***

## Reproductive Isolation

Mechanisms of evolution—genetic drift, gene flow, nonrandom mating, mutation, and natural selection—violate the Hardy-Weinberg principle. To what extent each mechanism contributes to the origin of new species is a major topic of debate in evolutionary science today. Most scientists define speciation as the process whereby some members of a sexually reproducing population change so much that they can no longer produce fertile offspring with members of the original population. Two types of reproductive isolating mechanisms prevent gene flow among populations. **Prezygotic isolating mechanisms** operate before fertilization occurs. **Postzygotic isolating mechanisms** operate after fertilization has occurred to ensure that the resulting hybrid remains infertile.

**Prezygotic isolation** Prezygotic isolating mechanisms prevent reproduction by making fertilization unlikely. These mechanisms prevent genotypes from entering a population's gene pool through geographic, ecological, behavioral, or other differences. For example, the eastern meadowlark and the western meadowlark, pictured in **Figure 15.20,** have overlapping ranges and are similar in appearance. These two species, however, use different mating songs and do not interbreed. Time is another factor in maintaining a reproductive barrier. Closely related species of fireflies mate at different times of night, just as different species of trout live in the same stream but breed at different times of the year.

**Postzygotic isolation** When fertilization has occurred but a hybrid offspring cannot develop or reproduce, postzygotic isolation has occurred. Postzygotic isolating mechanisms prevent offspring survival or reproduction. A lion and a tiger are considered separate species because even though they can mate, the offspring—a liger, shown in **Figure 15.21**—is sterile.

■ **Figure 15.21** The offspring of a male lion and a female tiger is a liger. Ligers are sterile.

## Speciation

For speciation to occur, a population must diverge and then be reproductively isolated. Biologists usually recognize two types of speciation: allopatric and sympatric.

**Allopatric speciation** In **allopatric speciation,** a physical barrier divides one population into two or more populations. The separate populations eventually will contain organisms that, if enough time has passed, will no longer be able to breed successfully with one another. Most scientists think that allopatric speciation is the most common form of speciation. Small subpopulations isolated from the main population have a better chance of diverging than those living within it. This was the conclusion of the biologist Ernst Mayr, who argued as early as the 1940s that geographic isolation was not only important but required for speciation.

**VOCABULARY**

**ACADEMIC VOCABULARY**

**Isolation:**
the condition of being separated from others.
*After infection, a patient is kept in isolation from other patients to prevent the infection from spreading.*

Geographic barriers can include mountain ranges, channels between islands, wide rivers, and lava flows. The Grand Canyon, pictured in **Figure 15.22,** is an example of a geographic barrier. The Kaibab squirrel is found on the canyon's north rim, while the Abert squirrel lives on the south rim. Scientists think that the two types of squirrels diverged from an ancestral species and today are reproductively isolated by the width of the canyon. While these animals officially belong to the same species, they demonstrate distinct differences and, in time, they might diverge enough to be classified as separate species.

**Sympatric speciation** In **sympatric speciation,** a species evolves into a new species without a physical barrier. The ancestor species and the new species live side by side during the speciation process. Evidence of sympatric evolution can be seen in several insect species, including apple maggot flies, which appear to be diverging based on the type of fruit they eat. Scientists think that sympatric speciation happens fairly frequently in plants, especially through polyploidy. Recall from Chapter 10 that polyploidy is a mutation that increases a plant's chromosome number. As a result, the plant is no longer able to interbreed with the main population.

■ **Figure 15.22** The Grand Canyon is a geographic barrier separating the Abert and Kaibab squirrels.

Abert Squirrel

Kaibab Squirrel

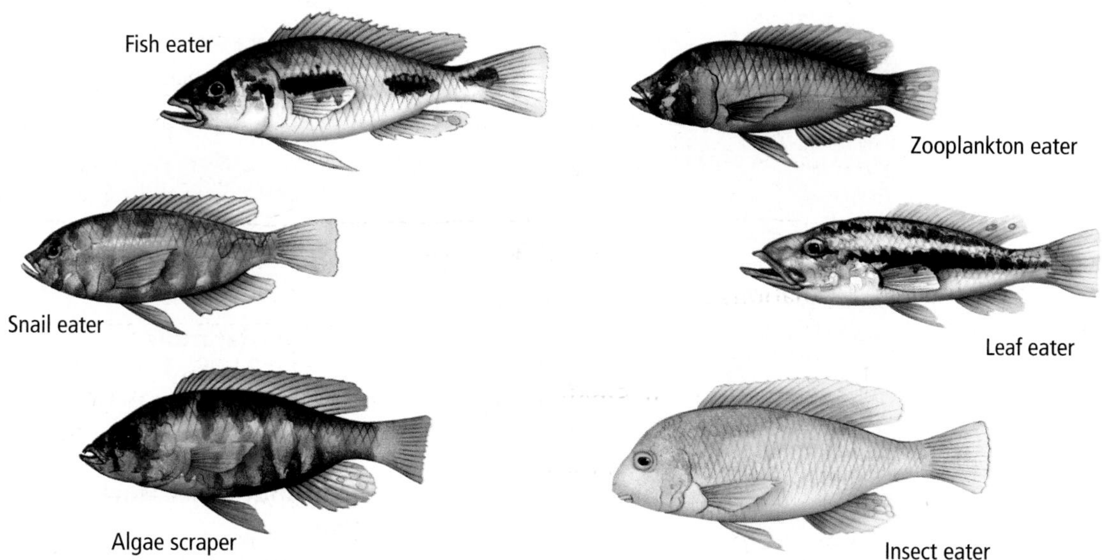


■ **Figure 15.23** More than 300 species of cichlid fishes once lived in Lake Victoria. Their adaptive radiation is remarkable because it is thought to have occurred in less than 14,000 years.

## Patterns of evolution

Many details of the speciation process remain unresolved. Relative to the human life span, speciation is a long process, and first-hand accounts of speciation are expected to be rare. However, evidence of speciation is visible in patterns of evolution.

**Adaptive radiation** More than 300 species of cichlid fish, six of which are illustrated in **Figure 15.23,** once lived in Africa's Lake Victoria. Data shows that these species diverged from a single ancestor within the last 14,000 years. This is a dramatic example of a type of speciation called **adaptive radiation.** Adaptive radiation, also called divergent evolution, can occur in a relatively short time when one species gives rise to many species in response to the creation of new habitat or another ecological opportunity. Likely, a combination of factors caused the explosive radiation of the cichlids, including the appearance of a unique double jaw, which allowed these fish to exploit various food sources. Adaptive radiation often follows large-scale extinctions. Adaptive radiation of mammals at the beginning of the Cenozoic following the extinction of dinosaurs likely produced the diversity of mammals visible today.

**Coevolution** Many species evolve in close relationship with other species. The relationship might be so close that the evolution of one species affects the evolution of other species. This is called coevolution. Mutualism is one form of coevolution. Recall from Chapter 2 that mutualism occurs when two species benefit each other. For example, comet orchids and the moths that pollinate them have coevolved an intimate dependency: the foot-long flowers of this plant perfectly match the foot-long tongue of the moth, shown in **Figure 15.24.**

In another form of coevolution, one species can evolve a parasitic dependency on another species. This type of relationship is often called a coevolutionary arms race. The classic example is a plant and an insect pathogen that is dependent on the plant for food. The plant population evolves a chemical defense against the insect population. The insects, in turn, evolve the biochemistry to resist the defense. The plant then steps up the race by evolving new defenses, the insect escalates its response, and the race goes on. Complex coevolutionary relationships like these might reflect thousands of years of evolutionary interaction.

■ **Figure 15.24** By coevolving, this moth and the comet orchid it pollinates exist in a mutualistic relationship.

| Table 15.4 | Convergent Evolution | Concepts In Motion: Interactive Table To explore more about convergent evolution, visit biologygmh.com. |
|---|---|---|
| Niche | Placental Mammals | Australian Marsupials |
| Burrower | Mole | Marsupial mole |
| Anteater | Lesser anteater | Numbat (anteater) |
| Mouse | Mouse | Marsupial mouse |
| Glider | Flying squirrel | Flying phalanger |
| Wolf | Wolf | Tasmanian wolf |

**Convergent evolution** Sometimes unrelated species evolve similar traits even though they live in different parts of the world. This is called convergent evolution. Convergent evolution occurs in environments that are geographically far apart but that have similar ecology and climate. The mara and rabbit discussed in Section 15.2 provide an example of convergent evolution. The mara and the rabbit are unrelated, but because they inhabit similar niches, they have evolved similarities in morphology, physiology, and behavior. **Table 15.4** shows examples of convergent evolution between Australian marsupials and the placental mammals on other continents.

**Rate of speciation** Evolution is a dynamic process. In some cases, as in a coevolutionary arms race, traits might change rapidly. In other cases, traits might remain unchanged for millions of years. Most scientists think that evolution proceeds in small, gradual steps. This is a theory called **gradualism.** A great deal of evidence favors this theory. However, the fossil record contains instances of abrupt transitions. For example, certain species of fossil snails looked the same for millions of years, then the shell shape changed dramatically in only a few thousand years. The theory of **punctuated equilibrium** attempts to explain such abrupt transitions in the fossil record. According to this theory, rapid spurts of genetic change cause species to diverge quickly; these periods punctuate much longer periods when the species exhibit little change.

# CHAPTER 15 Assessment

## Section 15.1

### Vocabulary Review

*Replace the underlined portions of the sentences below with words from the Study Guide to make each sentence correct.*

1. Natural selection is a mechanism for species change over time.
2. Selective breeding was used to produce purebred Chihuahuas and cocker spaniels.
3. Differential survival by members of a population with favorable adaptations is a mechanism for a theory developed by Charles Darwin.

### Understand Key Concepts

4. Which best describes the prevailing view about the age of Earth and evolution before Darwin's voyage on the HMS *Beagle?*
   **A.** Earth and life are recent and have remained unchanged.
   **B.** Species evolved rapidly during the first six thousand to a few hundred thousand years.
   **C.** Earth is billions of years old, but species have not evolved.
   **D.** Species have evolved on Earth for billions of years.

*Use the photo below to answer question 5.*

5. Which statement about the tortoise above would be part of an explanation for tortoise evolution based on natural selection?
   **A.** All tortoises look like the above tortoise.
   **B.** Tortoises with domed shells have more young than tortoises with flat shells.
   **C.** All the tortoises born on the island survive.
   **D.** The tortoise shell looks nothing like the shell of either parent.

### Constructed Response

6. **Open Ended** Summarize Darwin's theory of evolution by using an example.
7. **Short Answer** How is artificial selection similar to natural selection?

### Think Critically

8. **Sequence** Sequence events leading to evolution by natural selection.
9. **Recognize Cause and Effect** What is the likely evolutionary effect on a species of an increase in global temperatures over time?

## Section 15.2

### Vocabulary Review

*The sentences below include terms that have been used incorrectly. Make the sentences true by replacing the italicized word with a vocabulary term from the Study Guide page.*

10. Anatomical parts that have a reduced function in an organism are *analogous structures.*
11. *Biogeography* is a measure of the relative contribution an individual trait makes to the next generation.
12. *Camouflage* occurs when two or more species evolve adaptations to resemble each other.

### Understand Key Concepts

*Use the photos below to answer question 13.*

13. These organisms have similar features that are considered what kind of structures?
    **A.** vestigial
    **B.** homologous
    **C.** analogous
    **D.** comparative

*Use the photo below to answer question 14.*

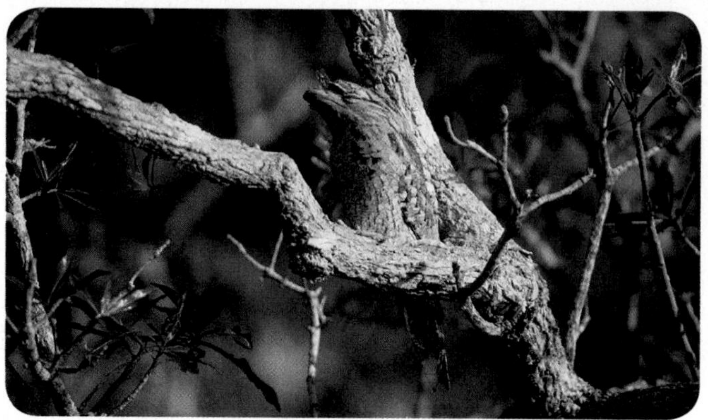

14. The photo of the bird above shows what kind of morphological adaptation?
    **A.** vestigial organ
    **B.** camouflage
    **C.** mimicry
    **D.** analogous structure

15. Which is not an example of a morphological adaptation?
    **A.** Cytochrome *c* is similar in monkeys and humans.
    **B.** Butterflies evolve similar color patterns.
    **C.** A harmless species of snake resembles a harmful species.
    **D.** Young birds have adaptations for blending into the environment.

16. Industrial melanism could be considered a special case of which of the following?
    **A.** embryological adaptation
    **B.** mimicry
    **C.** physiological adaptation
    **D.** structural adaptation

17. Which sets of structures are homologous?
    **A.** a butterfly's wing and a bat's wing
    **B.** a moth's eyes and a cow's eyes
    **C.** a beetle's leg and a horse's leg
    **D.** a whale's flipper and a bird's wing

## Constructed Response

18. **Short Answer** Describe how cytochrome *c* provides evidence of evolution.

19. **Short Answer** What can be concluded from the fact that many insects no longer are resistant to certain pesticides?

20. **Short Answer** Why are fossils considered to provide the strongest evidence supporting evolution?

## Think Critically

21. **Design an Experiment** How could you design an experiment to show that a species of small fish has the ability to evolve a camouflage color pattern?

22. **CAREERS IN BIOLOGY** An evolutionary biologist is studying several species of closely related lizards found on Cuba and surrounding islands. Each species occupies a somewhat different niche, but in some ways they all look similar to the green anole lizard found in Florida. Suggest the pattern of lizard evolution.

# Section 15.3

## Vocabulary Review

*Choose the vocabulary term from the Study Guide page that best matches each of the following descriptions.*

23. one species evolves over millions of years to become two different but closely related species

24. a species evolves into a new species without a physical barrier.

25. the random changes in gene frequency found in small populations

## Understand Key Concepts

*Use the figure below to answer question 26.*

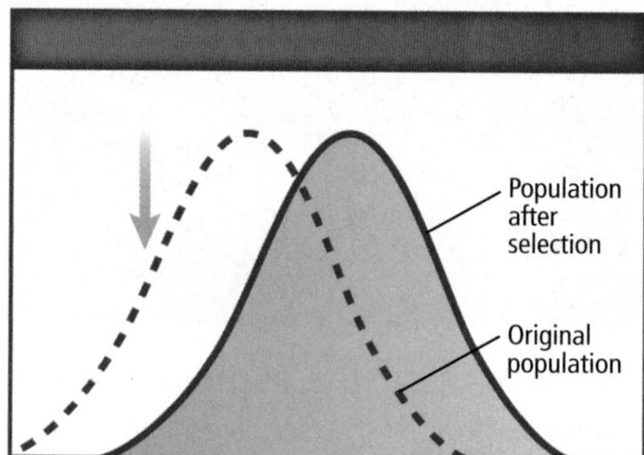


26. The graph above best represents which kind of selection?
    **A.** directional
    **B.** disruptive
    **C.** sexual
    **D.** stabilizing

*Use the photo below to answer question 27.*

27. The plant in the above illustration looks like a cactus, but is classified in a completely separate group of plants. This would be an example of which mechanism?
    **A.** adaptive radiation
    **B** disruptive selection
    **C.** convergent evolution
    **D.** punctuated equilibrium

## Constructed Response

**28. Open Ended** Discuss why the Hardy-Weinberg principle rarely is often violated in real populations.

**29. Open Ended** Sea stars eat clams by pulling apart the two halves of a clam's shell. Discuss how this could result in directional selection of clam muscle size.

**30. Short Answer** Compare and contrast genetic drift and natural selection as mechanisms of evolution.

## Think Critically

**31. Make and Use Graphs** Draw a graph that would illustrate a population that has a wide variation of color from light to dark brown. Then draw on the same graph what that population would look like after several years of stabilizing selection. Label your graph.

**32. Drawing a Conclusion** What would you conclude about the evolutionary process that produces two unrelated species that share similar niches on different continents?

## Additional Assessment

**33.**  WRITING in **Biology** Imagine that you are Charles Darwin and write a letter to your father detailing your observations aboard the *Beagle.*

**34.** WRITING in **Biology** Write a paragraph that explains why a genetic bottleneck can be an important evolutionary factor for a species.

## DBQ Document-Based Questions

Darwin, Charles. 1859. *On the Origin of Species by Means of Natural Selection, or the Preservation of Favoured Races in the Struggle for Life.*

*Naturalists continually refer to external conditions, such as climate, food, etc., as the only possible cause of variation. In one very limited sense, as we shall hereafter see, this may be true; but it is preposterous to attribute to mere external conditions, the structure, for instance, of the woodpecker, with its feet, tail, beak, and tongue, so admirably adapted to catch insects under the bark of trees.*

**35.** In Darwin's time, most naturalists considered only external conditions as causes of variation. What non-external mechanism did Darwin propose as a cause of variation?

**36.** How would modern scientists explain the non-external mechanisms that Darwin proposed?

**37.** Consider Darwin's example of the woodpecker. Explain the role of natural selection in producing a bird species with a woodpeckerlike beak.

## Cumulative Review

**38.** Explain the importance of radiometric dating to paleontologists. **(Chapter 14)**

**39.** Discuss two ways in which losses in biodiversity could affect humans. **(Chapter 5)**

**40.** In this chapter, you learned that mutations provide the new variations that are involved in natural selection. Explain how mutations occur, and discuss the consequences of a point mutation and a frameshift mutation. **(Chapter 12)**

# Standardized Test Practice

**Cumulative**

## Multiple Choice

1. Which experimental setup did Francesco Redi use to test the idea of spontaneous generation?
   A. a flask filled with all the chemicals present on early Earth
   B. mice sealed in jars with lit candles and jars with unlit candles
   C. rotten meat in covered jars and uncovered jars
   D. special flasks that were filled with broth

*Use the illustration below of tortoises on two different islands to answer questions 2 and 3.*

**Large Island**

**Small Island**

2. The above illustrates which principle of natural selection?
   A. inheritance
   B. variation
   C. differential reproduction
   D. overproduction of offspring

3. Tortoises that have shells with higher openings can eat taller plants. Others can only reach vegetation close to the ground. Judging from the differences in the tortoises' shells, what kind of vegetation would you expect to find on the large and small islands?
   A. Both islands have a dense ground cover of low-growing plants.
   B. Both islands have similar plants, but vegetation is more spread out on large islands.
   C. On the large island, the land is mostly dry, and only tall trees grow.
   D. The small island is less grassy, and plants grow with their leaves farther above ground.

4. A dinosaur footprint in rocks would be which kind of fossil?
   A. cast fossil
   B. petrified fossil
   C. replacement fossil
   D. trace fossil

5. Which concept is essential for the process of DNA fingerprinting?
   A. location of genes for related traits on different chromosomes
   B. organization of human DNA into 46 chromosomes
   C. provision by DNA of the codes for proteins in the body
   D. uniqueness of each person's pattern of noncoding DNA

6. Chargaff's rules led to the understanding of which aspect of DNA structure?
   A. base pairing
   B. helix formation
   C. alternation of deoxyribose and phosphate
   D. placement of 3' and 5' carbons

*Use the Punnett square below to answer question 7.*

| | B | ? |
|---|---|---|
| b | | |
| b | | |

7. A test cross, shown in the Punnett square above, is used to determine the genotype of an animal that is expressing a dominant gene (B) for a particular characteristic. If the animal is homozygous for the dominant trait, which percentage of its offspring will have the dominant gene?
   A. 25%
   B. 50%
   C. 75%
   D. 100%

8. What prevents the two strands of DNA from immediately coming back together after they unzip?
   A. addition of binding proteins
   B. connection of Okazaki fragments
   C. parting of leading and lagging strands
   D. use of multiple areas of replication



Biology Online Standardized Test Practice biologygmh.com

**Locomotion** Another characteristic of primates is their flexible bodies. Primates have limber shoulders and hips, and primarily rely on hind limbs for locomotion. Most primates live in trees and have developed an extraordinary ability to move easily from branch to branch. When on the ground, all primates except humans walk on all four limbs. Many primates can walk upright for short distances and many have a more upright posture compared to four-legged animals.

**Complex brain and behaviors** Primates tend to have large brains in relation to their body size. Their brains have fewer areas devoted to smell and more areas devoted to vision. They also tend to have larger areas devoted to memory and coordinating arm and leg movement. Along with larger brains, many primates have problem-solving abilities and well-developed social behaviors, such as grooming and communicating. Most diurnal primates spend a great deal of time socializing by spending time grooming each other. In addition, many primates have complex ways of communicating to each other, which include a wide range of facial expressions.

**Reproductive rate** Most primates have fewer offspring than other animals. Usually, primates give birth to one offspring at a time. Compared to other mammals, pregnancy is long, and newborns are dependent on their mothers for an extended period of time. For many primates, this time period allows for the increased learning of complex social interactions. A low reproductive rate, the loss of tropical habitats, and human predation has threatened some primate populations. Many are endangered. **Figure 16.2** illustrates the tropical areas of the world, such as Africa and Southeast Asia, where primates live.

**LAUNCH Lab**

**Review** Based on what you have read about primate characteristics, how would you now answer the analysis questions?

**Figure 16.2** Non-human primates live in a broad area spanning most of the world's tropical regions. Use this map as you read about the different primates.

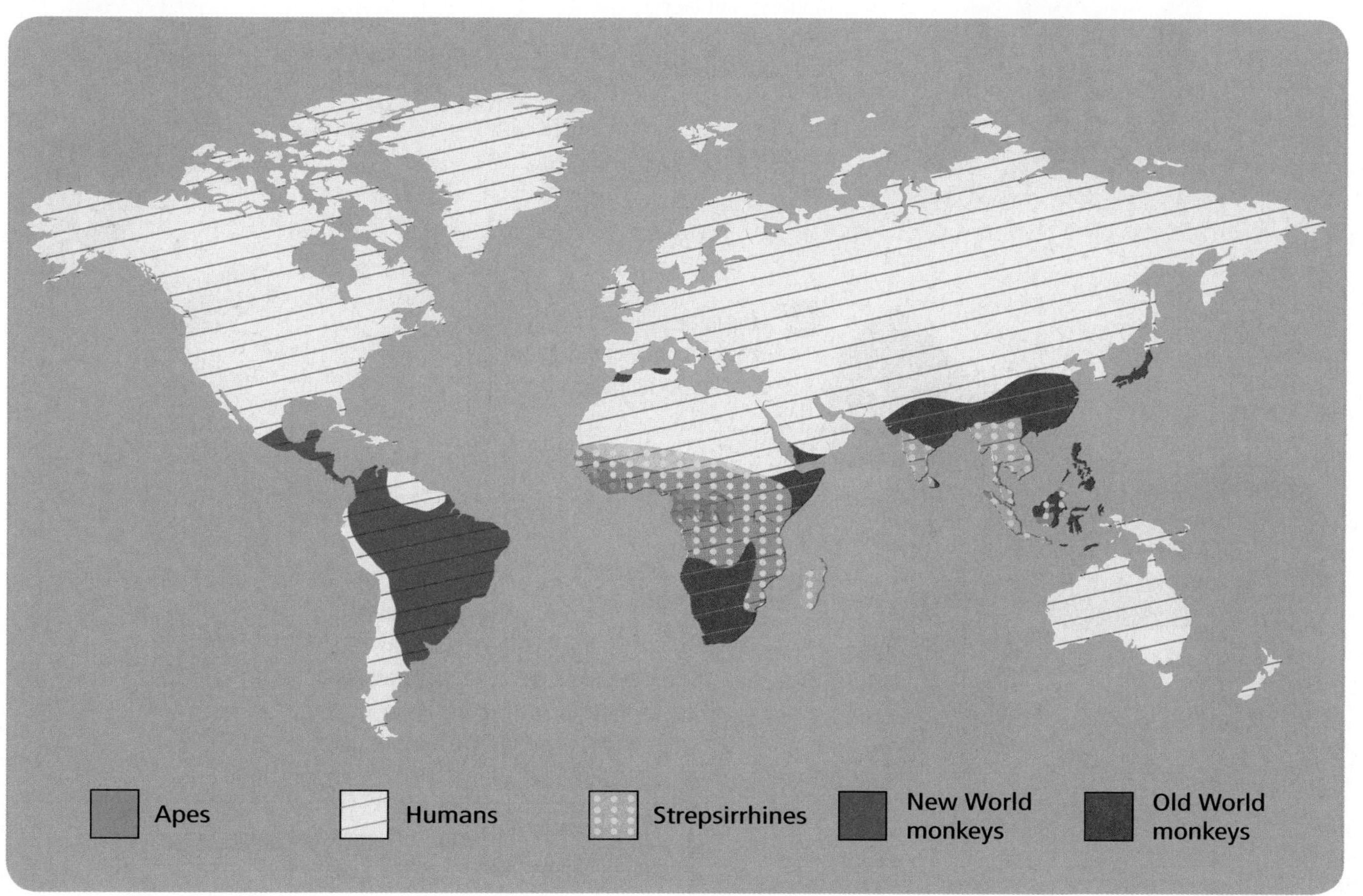

# Visualizing Primates

**Figure 16.3**
Primates are members of a highly diverse order of mammals. Most primates share common features such as binocular vision and opposable digits.

**A** The strepsirrhines are relatively small, have large eyes, and are nocturnal. They resemble the earliest primates.

**B** New World monkeys are characterized by a relatively long tail. Many have prehensile tails.

**C** Old World monkeys resemble New World monkeys, but lack a prehensile tail. Some have reduced tails.

**D** Asian apes are long-armed and inhabit tropical rain forests. Apes lack tails.

**E** African apes live in family groups or small bands and display complex social behavior.

**F** Humans, *Homo sapiens*, are the only living species in the hominin group. Hominins are unique because they possess the ability to walk for long distances on two legs.

**Concepts In Motion** **Interactive Figure** To explore more about primates, visit biologygmh.com.

**Biology Online**

## Primate Groups

Primates are a large, diverse group of more than 200 living species. Examine **Figure 16.3** as you read about this diverse group. Most primates are **arboreal** (ar BOHR ee uhl), or tree-dwelling. Arboreal primates live in the world's tropical and subtropical forests. Primates that lived on the ground are considered terrestrial.

Scientists generally classify primates into two subgroups based on characteristics of their noses, eyes, and teeth. The strepsirrhines (STREP sihr ines), or "wet-nosed" primates, are considered the earliest, most basic primates. The lemurs are the most numerous of this group. The second group consists of the haplorhines (HAP lohr ines), or "dry-nosed" primates. The haplorhines include the **anthropoids** (AN thruh poydz), or humanlike primates, as well as a unique primate called the tarsier (TAR see ur).

**CAREERS IN BIOLOGY**

**Primatologist** Researchers who study primates are called primatologists. Some primatologists study the behavior of the African apes to make inferences about human behavior. For more information on biology careers, visit biologygmh.com.

## Strepsirrhines

**Table 16.1** lists characteristics of some strepsirrhine groups. Strepsirrhines have large eyes and ears. They are the only primates that rely predominantly on smell for hunting and social interaction. They only live in tropical Africa and Asia. Most strepsirrhines, such as lemurs, sifakas (sih FA kas), indris (IN dreez), and aye-ayes (I iz) are only found in Madagascar and nearby islands. Madagascar drifted from the African mainland as these animals evolved, and scientists hypothesize that the ancestors of lemurs migrated to the island on rafts made of leaves. There they were reproductively isolated, which resulted in their diversification.

**VOCABULARY**
**WORD ORIGIN**
**Lemur**
comes from Latin, meaning *spirit of the night.*

**Concepts In Motion**
**Interactive Table** To explore more about strepsirrhines, visit biologygmh.com.

**Table 16.1 Characteristics of Strepsirrhines**

| Group | Lemurs | Aye-Ayes | Lorises | Galagos |
|---|---|---|---|---|
| Example | | | | |
| Active Period | Large—diurnal<br>Small—nocturnal | Nocturnal | Nocturnal | Mostly nocturnal |
| Range | Madagascar | Madagascar | Africa and Southeast Asia | Africa |
| Characteristics | • Vertical leaper<br>• Uses long bushy tail for balance<br>• Herbivores and omnivores | • Taps bark, listens, fishes out grubs with long third finger | • Small and slow climber, solitary<br>• Lack tails<br>• Some have toxic secretions | • Small and fast leaper<br>• No opposable digit<br>• Long tail |

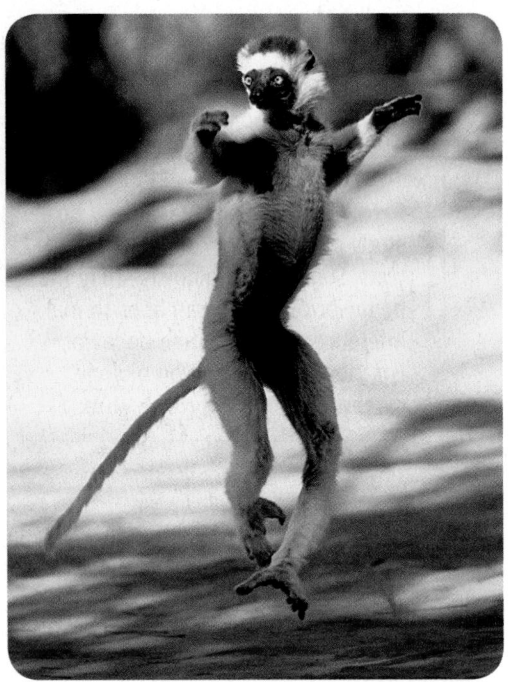

■ **Figure 16.4** Lemurs vary in their size and color. Some lemurs, like this sifaka, spend time on the ground.

Most small lemurs are nocturnal and solitary. Only a few large species, such as the sifaka shown in **Figure 16.4,** are diurnal and social. The indri is unique because it does not have a tail, unlike most lemurs that use their bushy tails for balance as they jump from branch to branch. Lorises are similar to lemurs but are found primarily in India and Southeast Asia. Galagos (ga LAY gohs), also called bushbabies, are found only in Africa.

## Haplorhines

The second group of primates is a much larger group. The haplorhines include tarsiers, monkeys, and apes. The apes, in turn, include gibbons, orangutans, gorillas, chimpanzees, and humans.

The tarsier is found only on Borneo and the Philippines. It is a small, nocturnal creature with large eyes. It has the ability to rotate its head 180 degrees like an owl. It lives in trees, where it climbs and leaps among the branches. The tarsier shares characteristics with both lemurs and monkeys. Scientists once classified it with the lemurs, but new evidence suggests that it is more closely related to anthropoids, which makes it part of the haplorhine group.

Anthropoids are generally larger than strepsirrhines, and they have large brains relative to their body size. They are more likely to be diurnal, with eyes adapted to daylight and sometimes to color. Anthropoids also have more complex social interactions. They tend to live longer than lemurs and other strepsirrhines. The anthropoids are split into the New World monkeys and the Old World monkeys. "New World" refers to the Americas; "Old World" refers to Africa, Asia, and Europe. New World monkeys are the only monkeys that live in the Americas.

**FOLDABLES** Incorporate information from this section into your Foldable.

**New World monkeys** The New World monkeys are a group of about 60 species of arboreal monkeys that inhabit the tropical forests of Mexico, Central America, and South America. New World monkeys include the marmosets and tamarins. These are among the smallest and most unique primates. Neither species has fingernails or opposable digits.

The New World monkeys also include the squirrel monkeys, spider monkeys, and capuchin monkeys. Some of these monkeys have opposable digits and most are diurnal and live together in social bands. Most are also distinguished by their prehensile (pree HEN sul) tails. A **prehensile tail** functions like a fifth limb. It can grasp tree branches or other objects and support a monkey's weight, like that shown in **Figure 16.5.**

■ **Figure 16.5** This spider monkey uses its prehensile tail as a fifth limb.

**Old World monkeys** Old World monkeys live in a wide variety of habitats throughout Asia and Africa, from snow-covered mountains in Japan to arid grasslands in Africa. Some Old World monkeys live in Gibraltar, which is located at the southern tip of Spain. There are about 80 species in this group, including macaques and baboons in one subgroup, and colobus and proboscis monkeys in another. Old World monkeys are similar to New World monkeys in many ways. They are diurnal and live in social groups. However, their noses tend to be narrower and their bodies are usually larger. They also spend more time on the ground. None have prehensile tails, and some have no tails. Most Old World monkeys have opposable digits.

Section 16.3

# Human Ancestry

### Objectives

- **Describe** species in the genus *Homo.*
- **Explain** the Out-of-Africa hypothesis.
- **Compare** Neanderthals and modern humans.

### Review Vocabulary

**mitochondrion:** an organelle found in eukaryotic cells containing genetic material and responsible for cellular energy

### New Vocabulary

*Homo*
Neanderthal
Cro-Magnon

MAIN Idea **Tracing the evolution of the genus *Homo* is important for understanding the ancestry of humans, the only living species of *Homo*.**

**Real-World Reading Link** Have you ever heard anyone use the term "cave man" in an insulting way? Unfortunately, this term is used sometimes to indicate brutish behavior. But the people who lived in caves 40,000 years ago were very much like you. Their art was beautiful and their tools were sophisticated.

## The Genus *Homo*

The African environment became considerably cooler between 3 and 2.5 mya. Forests became smaller in size, and the range of grasslands was extended. The genus ***Homo,*** which includes living and extinct humans, first appeared during these years and although the fossil record is lacking fossils, many scientists infer that they evolved from an ancestor of the australopithecines.

*Homo* species had bigger brains, lighter skeletons, flatter faces, and smaller teeth than their australopithecine ancestors. They also are the first species known to control fire and to modify stones for tool use. As they evolved, they developed language and culture.

***Homo habilis* used stone tools** The first undisputed member of the genus *Homo* for which fossils exist is *Homo habilis,* called "handy man" because of its association with primitive stone tools. This species lived in Africa between about 2.4 and 1.4 mya. **Figure 16.17** shows a scientific illustrator's idea of what *H. habilis* might have looked like.

*H. habilis* possessed a brain averaging 650 $cm^3$, about 20 percent larger than that of the australopithecines. It also had other traits of the *Homo* species, including a smaller brow, reduced jaw, a flatter face, and more humanlike teeth. Like australopithecines, it was small, long-armed, and it seems to have retained the ability to climb trees. Other *Homo* species might have coexisted with *H. habilis,* among them a species called *Homo rudolfensis.* Because few fossils of *H. rudolfensis* have been found, its exact relationship to the rest of the *Homo* line is uncertain.

**Figure 16.17** Scientific illustrators use fossils and their knowledge of anatomy to create drawings of what *H. habilis* might have looked like.

■ **Figure 16.18** Models of nonliving species also can be created from fossil remains. *H. ergaster* appeared in the fossil record about 1.8–1.3 mya.

***Homo ergaster* migrated** Within about 500,000 years of the appearance of *H. habilis,* another *Homo* species, *Homo ergaster,* emerged with an even larger brain. *H. ergaster,* illustrated in **Figure 16.18,** appeared only briefly in the fossil record, from about 1.8 to 1.3 mya. *H. ergaster* was taller and lighter than *H. habilis,* and had longer legs and shorter arms. Its brain averaged 1000 $cm^3$, and it had a rounded skull, reduced teeth, and what many scientists believe to be the first human nose (with the nostrils facing downward).

**Tools** Carefully made hand axes and other tools associated with *H. ergaster* fossils suggest to some scientists that *H. ergaster* was a hunter, but others think that *H. ergaster* was primarily a scavenger and used the tools to scrape the meat off of scavenged bones.

## MiniLab 16.2

### Explore Hominin Migration

**Where did early hominins live?** Scientists carefully record the locations where fossils are found. The latitude and longitude coordinates represent the known geographic points of each *Homo* species' range.

**Procedure**

1. Read and complete the lab safety form.
2. Plot the following fossil sites on the map your teacher gives you. Use a different color for each species. When you are finished, lightly shade in the approximate boundaries.
   *H. habilis* (2.4–1.4 million years ago): 37°E: 4°S, 36°E: 3°N, 36°E: 7°N, 43°E: 8°N
   *H. erectus* (2 million–400,000 years ago): 112°E: 38°N, 13°E: 47°N, 7°W: 34°N, 112°E: 8°S
   *H. neanderthalensis* (300,000–200,000 years ago): 8°E: 53°N, 66°E: 39°N, 5°W: 37°N, 36°E: 33°N
   *H. sapiens* (195,000 years ago–present): 70°E: 62°N, 24°E: 30°S, 138°E: 34°S, 112°E: 38°N, 99°W: 19°N, 102°W: 32°N

**Analysis**

1. **Hypothesize** According to the map you made, when was the earliest that hominins could have migrated out of Africa? Where did they go?
2. **Determine** what sets of fossils overlapped in geographic ranges. What does this suggest?

■ **Figure 16.19** *H. erectus* might have lived in caves, made tools, and used fire.

**Migration** Both scavenging and hunting are associated with a migratory lifestyle, and *H. ergaster* appears to have been the first African *Homo* species to migrate in large numbers to Asia and possibly Europe, perhaps following the trail of migrating animals. The Eurasian forms of *H. ergaster* are called *Homo erectus. H. ergaster* shares features with modern humans. Because of these shared features, scientists hypothesize that *H. ergaster* is an ancestor of modern humans.

***Homo erectus* used fire** *H. erectus,* illustrated in **Figure 16.19,** lived between 1.8 million and 400,000 years ago and appears to have evolved from *H. ergaster* as it migrated out of Africa. While some scientists consider *H. ergaster* and *H. erectus* a single species, *H. erectus* appears to have evolved traits that the early African *H. ergaster* species did not have. Members of this species seem to have been more versatile than their predecessors, and they adapted successfully to a variety of environments. *H. erectus* includes "Java Man," discovered in Indonesia in the 1890s, and "Peking Man," discovered in China in the 1920s.

In general, *H. erectus* was larger than *H. habilis* and had a bigger brain. It also had teeth that were more humanlike. Brain capacity ranged from about 900 $cm^3$ in early specimens to about 1100 $cm^3$ in later ones. It was as tall as *H. sapiens* but it had a longer skull, lower forehead, and thicker facial bones than either *H. ergaster* or *H. sapiens.* It also had a more prominent browridge. Evidence indicates that *H. erectus* made sophisticated tools, used fire, and sometimes lived in caves.

***Homo floresiensis*—"The Hobbit"** Most scientists believe that *H. erectus* went extinct about 400,000 years ago. However, a curious set of fossils were discovered in 2004 on the Indonesian island of Flores that suggest that descendants of *H. erectus*—or of some other ancient hominin species—remained on Earth until 12,000 years ago. These fossils, which are about 18,000 years old, represent a species called *Homo floresiensis* (flor eh see EN sus). *H. floresiensis,* nicknamed "The Hobbit," was only about 1 m tall when full grown. While it had brain and body proportions like all the australopithecines, primitive stone tools were found with its fossils. You can compare *H. floresiensis* and *H. sapiens* skulls in **Figure 16.20.**

 **Reading Check** What are the evolutionary relationships among *H. habilis, H. ergaster,* and *H. erectus?*

■ **Figure 16.20** Most scientists agree that unique *Homo* fossils represent a new species called *H. floresiensis.* The *H. floresiensis* skull on the left is smaller than the human skull on the right.
**Infer** ***what this skull comparison might predict about the evolutionary relationship between* H. floresiensis *and* H. sapiens.**

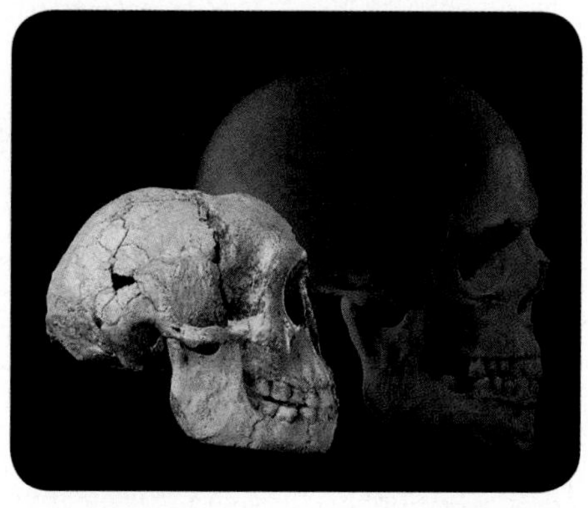

***Homo heidelbergensis*—"mosaic" traits** The transition from *H. ergaster* to modern humans appears to have occurred gradually. Numerous transitional fossils have been found that display a mixture, or mosaic, of *H. ergaster* and *H. sapiens* traits. These fossils are often categorized as *Homo heidelbergensis,* but others put them in a more generic category called *Homo sapiens.* These humans generally had larger brains and thinner bones than *H. ergaster,* but they still had browridges and receding chins.

***Homo neanderthalensis* built shelter** A distinct human species called *Homo neanderthalensis,* or the **Neanderthals,** evolved exclusively in Europe and Asia about 200,000 years ago, likely from *H. erectus* or a *Homo* intermediary. Neanderthals were shorter but had more muscle mass than most modern humans. Their brains were sometimes even larger than the brains of modern humans, though the brains might have been organized in different ways. Neanderthals had thick skulls, bony browridges, and large noses. They also had a heavily muscled, robust stature, as illustrated in **Figure 16.21.** Evidence of heavy musculature appears in the extremely large muscle attachments and the bowing of the long bones.

Neanderthals lived near the end of the Pleistocene ice age, a time of bitter cold, and their skeletons reflect lives of hardship; bone fractures and arthritis seem to have been common. There is evidence that they used fire and constructed complex shelters. They hunted and skinned animals, and it is possible that they had basic language. There is also some evidence that they cared for their sick and buried their dead.

**Are Neanderthals our ancestors?** In some areas of their range, particularly in the Middle East and southern Europe, Neanderthals and modern humans overlapped for as long as 10,000 years. Some scientists suggest that the two species interbred. A skeleton found in Portugal, for example, has features of both Neanderthals and modern humans. However, DNA tests on fossil bones suggest that Neanderthals were a distinct species that did not contribute to the modern human gene pool. Neanderthals went extinct about 30,000 years ago. The reasons why they went extinct are not known.

■ **Figure 16.21** *H. neanderthalensis* had much thicker bones than modern humans and a pronounced browridge. Neanderthals were hunters who used fire and tools.

## Emergence of Modern Humans

The species that displaced the Neanderthals, *Homo sapiens*, is characterized by a more slender appearance than all other *Homo* species. They have thinner skeletons, rounder skulls, and smaller faces with prominent chins. Their brain capacity averages 1350 $cm^3$. *H. sapiens* first appeared in the fossil record, in what is now Ethiopia, about 195,000 years ago. These early *H. sapiens* made chipped hand axes and other sophisticated stone tools. They appear to have had the ability to use a range of resources and environments, and at some point they began migrating out of Africa. **Table 16.2** compares modern humans with other *Homo* species.

**Concepts In Motion** **Interactive Table** To explore more about the *Homo* species, visit biologygmh.com.

**Table 16.2 Characteristics of the *Homo* species**

| Species | Skull | Time in fossil record | Characteristics |
|---|---|---|---|
| ***Homo habilis*** | | 2.4–1.4 million years ago | • Average brain had a capacity of 650 $cm^3$<br>• Used tools |
| ***Homo ergaster*** | | 1.8–1.2 million years ago | • Average brain had a capacity of 1000 $cm^3$<br>• Had thinner skull bones<br>• Had humanlike nose |
| ***Homo erectus*** | | 1.8 million–400,000 years ago | • Average brain had a capacity of 1000 $cm^3$<br>• Had thinner skull bones<br>• Used fire |
| ***Homo neanderthalensis*** | | 300,000–200,000 years ago | • Average brain had a capacity of 1500 $cm^3$<br>• Buried their dead<br>• Possibly had a language |
| ***Homo sapiens*** | | 195,000 years ago to present | • Average brain has a capacity of 1350 $cm^3$<br>• Does not have browridge<br>• Has a small chin<br>• Has language and culture |

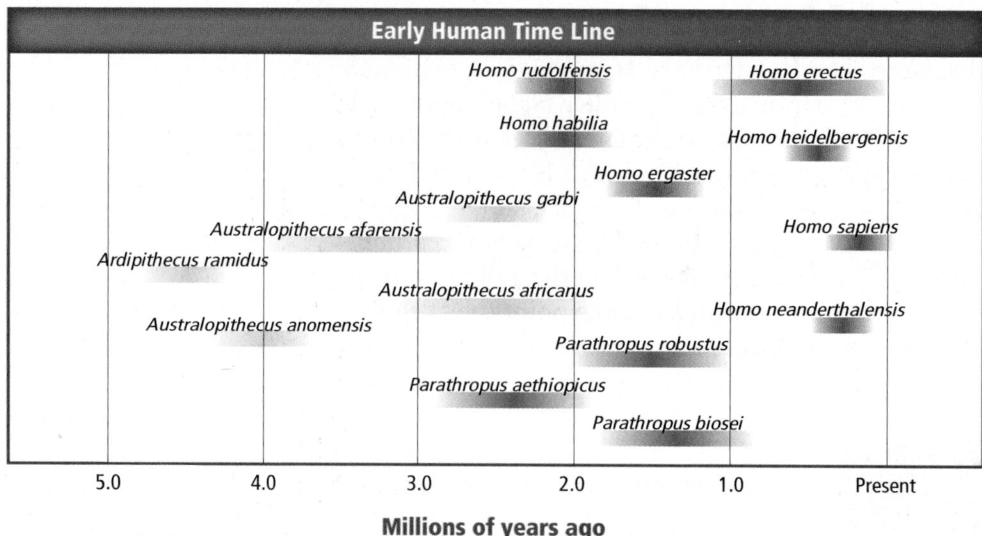


**Figure 16.22** The period of existence of several early hominins overlapped until about 30,000 years ago.

**Out-of-Africa hypothesis** The world's population 200,000 years ago looked significantly different than it does today. It was inhabited by a morphologically diverse genus of hominins, including primitive humans, Neanderthals, and modern humans, as illustrated in **Figure 16.22.** By 30,000 years ago, however, only modern humans remained. Some scientists propose that these modern humans evolved from several dispersed populations of early *Homo* species at the same time in different areas of the world. According to this multiregional evolution model, modern races of humans arose in isolated populations by convergent evolution.

Most scientists explain the global dominance of modern humans with the African Replacement model or, more commonly, the Out-of-Africa hypothesis. According to this hypothesis, which was first proposed by Christopher Stringer and Peter Andrews of the British Museum of Natural History in 1988, modern humans evolved only once, in Africa, and then migrated to all parts of the world, eventually displacing other hominins.

**"Mitochondrial Eve"** The Out-of-Africa hypothesis was supported by mitochondrial DNA analysis of contemporary humans in the early 1990s. Mitochondrial DNA changes very little over time, and humans living today have nearly identical mitochondrial DNA. Researchers Allan Wilson and Rebecca Cann of the University of California, Berkeley, reasoned that the population with the most variation should be the population that has had the longest time to accumulate diversity. This was exactly what they found in the mitochondrial DNA of Africans. Because mitochondrial DNA is inherited only from the mother, this analysis suggested that *H. sapiens* emerged in Africa about 200,000 years ago from a hypothetical "Mitochondrial Eve."

Later, work by other scientists studying DNA sequences in the male Y chromosome yielded similar results. While some scientists think that a single movement of only a few hundred modern humans ultimately gave rise to the world's current population, others think the process occurred in phases, with some interbreeding among the species that humans displaced.

**Study Tip**

**Discussion Group** Discuss with your classmates what you've learned about human evolution. What characteristics of early hominins have surprised you or your classmates?

**Reading Check** **Describe** evidence in support of the Out-of-Africa hypothesis.

**The beginning of culture** The first evidence of complex human culture appeared in Europe only about 40,000 years ago, shortly before the Neanderthals disappeared. Unlike the Neanderthals, early modern humans expressed themselves symbolically and artistically in decorative artifacts and cave drawings, as illustrated in **Figure 16.23.** They developed sophisticated tools and weapons, including spears and bows and arrows. They were the first to fish, the first to tailor clothing, and the first to domesticate animals. These and many other cultural expressions marked the appearance of fully modern humans, or *Homo sapiens sapiens*. Some people call them **Cro-Magnons,** and they represent the beginning of historic hunter-gatherer societies.

**Connection to History** Humans continued their migration throughout Europe and Asia. They probably reached Australia by boat and traveled to North America via a land bridge from Asia. From North America, they spread to South America. They adapted to new challenges along the way, leaving behind a trail of artifacts that we study today.

**Figure 16.23** Cro-Magnons were known for their sophisticated cave paintings, tools, and weapons. This painting was found in Lascaux Cave in France.

## Section 16.3 Assessment

### Section Summary

- The genus *Homo* is thought to have evolved from genus *Australopithecus*.
- Of the many species that have existed in the hominin group, only one species survives today.
- The first member of the genus *Homo* was *H. habilis*.
- The Out-of-Africa hypothesis suggests that humans evolved in Africa and migrated to Europe and Asia.
- *H. neanderthalensis* went extinct about 30,000 years ago and *H. sapiens* moved into those areas inhabited by *H. neanderthalensis* at about the same time.

### Understand Main Ideas

1. MAIN Idea **Hypothesize** why only one genus and species remains in the hominin group.
2. **Describe** how *H. habilis* might have lived.
3. **Apply** what you have learned about the Out-of-Africa hypothesis to what you know about the arrival of *H. sapiens* in North America.
4. **Compare and contrast** *H. neanderthalensis* and *H. sapiens* fossils.

### Think Scientifically

5. *Classify* How would you classify a fossil that was found in France and dated to about 150,000 years if the skull had a thick browridge, but in most other ways appeared human?
6. WRITING in Biology *Hypothesize* the importance of language to the early modern humans, and how it might have contributed to their success.

# BioDiscoveries

## One Family, One Amazing Contribution to Science

**Out of Africa** Growing up in Africa, Louis Leakey (1903–1972) believed, like Darwin, that humans evolved in Africa. After all, that is where our closest primate relatives—chimpanzees and gorillas—live. When Louis finished his education in England, he returned to the Olduvai Gorge in Tanzania, Africa. Hints of early man, such as stone tools, had been found in the gorge, and Louis was determined to find hominin bones.

Louis and Mary Leakey on an archaeological dig.

***Proconsul*** In 1948, while Louis and his wife, Mary (1913–1996), were living on an island in Africa's Lake Victoria, Mary found a hominoid skull that she and Louis named *Proconsul africanus.* By comparing the skull to other objects nearby, they determined that the skull was 20 million years old.

**"Zinj"** Shortly after discovering *Proconsul,* Mary and Louis returned to Olduvai Gorge. There, while walking her dogs one day in 1959, Mary saw a skull poking out of a rock. Further examination yielded a hominin skull with teeth still intact. The skull, which Mary named *Zinjanthropus boisei* (zihn JAN thruh pus • BOY see) (now called *Paranthropus boisei*), turned out to be 1.75 million years old—the oldest human-like ancestor then known.

**Renewed vigor** The Leakeys began spending more time at Olduvai and hired workers to help them find fossils. Louis, though often given credit, never found many hominin fossils. Mary, their three children, and their skilled fossil-hunting staff were the actual discoverers. The renewed vigor at Olduvai soon yielded many more discoveries, including the first *Homo habilis* fossil and, in 1976, fossilized australopithecine footprints.

**More skeletons** By the 1970s, the Leakeys' son Richard and his wife, Maeve, were making their own important discoveries at a camp in nearby Kenya. In 1984, Richard discovered "Turkana Boy," one of the most complete and oldest *H. ergaster* fossils yet found. In 1999, Maeve and her daughter Louise discovered *Kenyanthropus platyops* (ken yen THROH pus • plat ee ops), which lived about 3.5 mya. Some scientists think that *K. platyops* represents a new hominin genus.

**Enduring legacy** Over the course of six decades, three generations of the Leakey family have discovered pieces of the puzzle of the evolution of the *Homo* genus. Today, Louise heads the Koobi Fora Research Project on the shores of Lake Turkana.

### E-COMMUNICATION

**Travelogue** To learn more about the Leaky family, visit biologygmh.com. Imagine that you are accompanying the Leakeys on one of their digs. Write a travelogue to detail an amazing fossil they have just found, including potential implications it might have for human evolution. Share your travelogue with your classmates.

*Use the figure below to answer questions 31 and 32.*

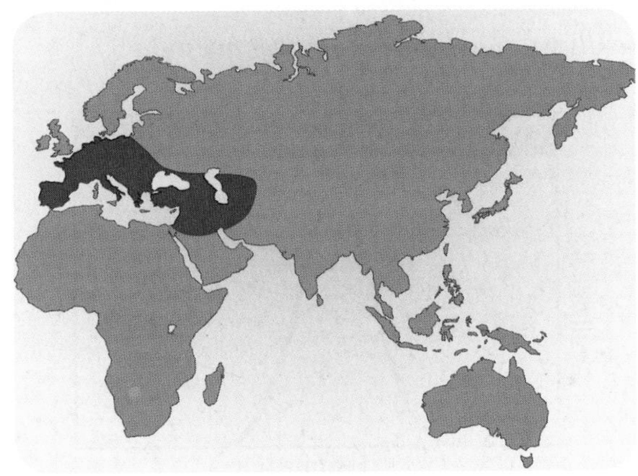

31. The map above represents the geographic range of which species?
    A. *Homo erectus*
    B. *Homo sapiens*
    C. *Homo neanderthalensis*
    D. *Homo heidelbergensis*

32. During what time did the species represented on the map live?
    A. 300,000–200,000 years ago
    B. 100,000–12,000 years ago
    C. 2.4–1.4 million years ago
    D. 1.8 and 1.2 million years ago

## Constructed Response

33. **Open Ended** Describe the importance of *H. habilis* in human evolution.

34. **Short Answer** Describe the importance of fire to the migration of early *Homo* species.

35. **Open Ended** From what you have learned about the evolution of primates, do you think *Homo sapiens,* our species, will continue to evolve? Why?

## Think Critically

36. **Apply Concepts** Explain why mitochondrial DNA instead of nuclear DNA is used to study the evolution of modern humans.

37. **Predict** If modern humans had not arrived in Europe, do you think Neanderthals would have persisted?

38. **Hypothesize** How might *H. floresiensis* have coexisted with modern humans?

## Additional Assessment

39. WRITING in Biology Write a paragraph to describe what you imagine a day in the life of *A. afarensis* to have been like.

### DBQ Document-Based Questions

*Scientists generally consider walking, but not running, to be a key trait in the evolution of humans. Like apes, humans are poor sprinters when compared to quadruped animals such as horses and dogs. Unlike apes, but like some quadrupeds, humans are capable of endurance running (ER), running long distances over extended time periods. The graph below compares speed during ER to length of an organism's stride (two steps for a human).*

Data obtained from: Bramble, D. and Lieberman, D. 2004. Endurance running and the evolution of *Homo. Nature* 432: 345–352.

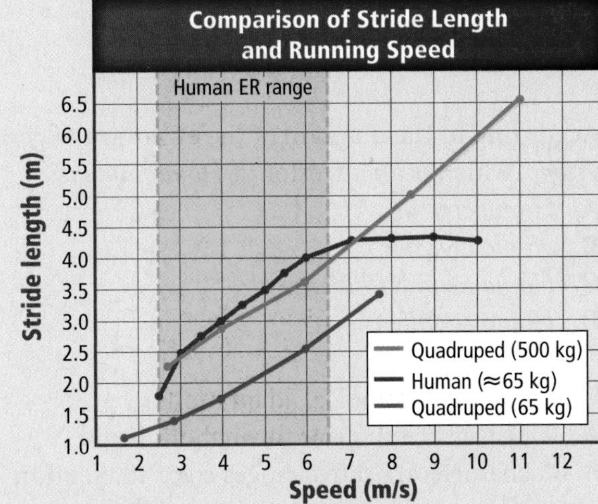


40. During ER, is the stride length of a human more like that of a 65-kg quadruped or a 500-kg quadruped?

41. Is a human more efficient at endurance running than a similar-size quadruped such as a cheetah or a leopard? Explain.

## Cumulative Review

42. Describe the role of mitochondria in eukaryotic cells. **(Chapter 7)**

43. Under what conditions would a population experience zero population growth? **(Chapter 4)**

# Standardized Test Practice

**Cumulative**

## Multiple Choice

1. A scientific understanding of which natural process helped Darwin formulate the concept of natural selection?
   **A.** artificial selection
   **B.** continental drift
   **C.** group selection
   **D.** plant genetics

*Use the diagram below to answer question 2.*

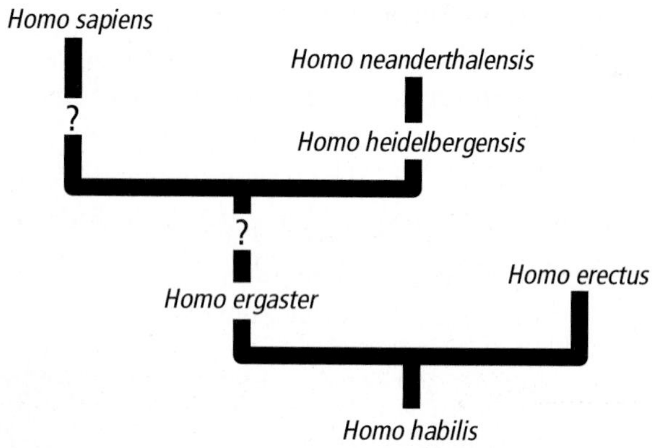


2. According to the diagram of the evolution of genus *Homo*, which is an ancestor of *Homo sapiens*?
   **A.** *Homo erectus*
   **B.** *Homo ergaster*
   **C.** *Homo neanderthalensis*
   **D.** *Homo rudolfensis*

3. Which is a physiological adaptation?
   **A.** A beaver's teeth grow throughout its life.
   **B.** A chameleon's skin changes color to blend in with its surroundings.
   **C.** A human sleeps during the day in order to work at night.
   **D.** An insect does not respond to a chemical used as an insecticide.

4. Which process can include the use of selective breeding?
   **A.** curing a tree of a disease
   **B.** finding the gene that makes a type of tree susceptible to disease
   **C.** mapping the genome of a fungus that causes disease in trees
   **D.** producing trees that resist certain diseases

*Use the illustration below to answer question 5.*

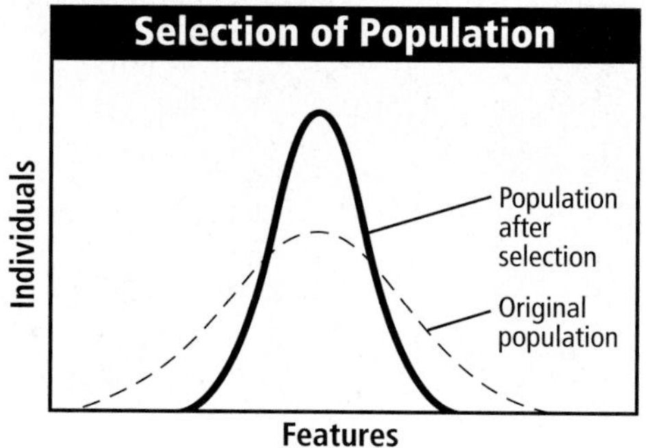


5. Which description fits the graph above?
   **A.** Average-sized features are selected for in population X.
   **B.** Larger features are selected for in population X.
   **C.** Smaller features are selected for in population X.
   **D.** Average-sized features are selected against in population X.

6. Which sequence correctly traces the order of hominin evolution?
   **A.** *Australopithecus afarensis* → *Australopithecus africanus* → *Proconsul* → *Homo*
   **B.** *Australopithecus africanus* ↦ *Australopithecus afarensis* → *Proconsul* → *Homo*
   **C.** *Homo* → *Australopithecus africanus* → *Australopithecus afarensis* → *Proconsul*
   **D.** *Proconsul* → *Australopithecus afarensis* → *Australopithecus africanus* → *Homo*

7. Which of the following is NOT a reason scientists support the endosymbiont theory?
   **A.** Mitochondria and chloroplasts are found living outside eukaryotic cells.
   **B.** Mitochondria and chloroplasts reproduce by fission.
   **C.** The size and structure of mitochondria and chloroplasts is similar to prokaryotic cells.
   **D.** The genetic material in mitochondria and chloroplasts is circular.



BiologyOnline Standardized Test Practice biologygmh.com

Aristotle's system was useful for organizing, but it had many limitations. Aristotle's system was based on his view that species are distinct, separate, and unchanging. The idea that species are unchanging was common until Darwin presented his theory of evolution. Because of his understanding of species, Aristotle's classification did not account for evolutionary relationships. Additionally, many organisms do not fit easily into Aristotle's system, such as birds that don't fly or frogs that live both on land and in water. Nevertheless, many centuries passed before Aristotle's system was replaced by a new system that was better suited to the increased knowledge of the natural world.

**Linnaeus's system** In the eighteenth century, Swedish naturalist Carolus Linnaeus (1707–1778) broadened Aristotle's classification method and formalized it into a scientific system. Like Aristotle, he based his system on observational studies of the morphology and the behavior of organisms. For example, he organized birds into three major groups depending on their behavior and habitat. The birds in **Figure 17.1** illustrate these categories. The eagle is classified as a bird of prey, the heron as a wading bird, and the cedar waxwing is grouped with the perching birds.

Linnaeus's system of classification was the first formal system of taxonomic organization. **Taxonomy** (tak SAH nuh mee) is a discipline of biology primarily concerned with identifying, naming, and classifying species based on natural relationships. Taxonomy is part of the larger branch of biology called systematics. Systematics is the study of biological diversity with an emphasis on evolutionary history.

**Binomial nomenclature** Linnaeus's method of naming organisms, called binomial nomenclature, set his system apart from Aristotle's system and remains valid today. **Binomial nomenclature** (bi NOH mee ul • NOH mun klay chur) gives each species a scientific name that has two parts. The first part is the genus (JEE nus) name, and the second part is the specific epithet (EP uh thet), or specific name, that identifies the species. Latin is the basis for binomial nomenclature because Latin is an unchanging language, and, historically, it has been the language of science and education.

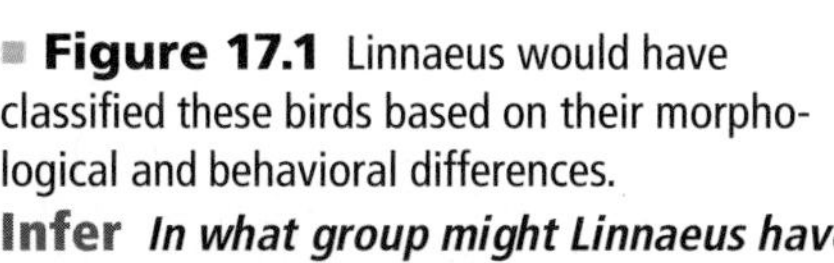

**Figure 17.1** Linnaeus would have classified these birds based on their morphological and behavioral differences.
**Infer** ***In what group might Linnaeus have placed a robin?***

**American bald eagle**
**Bird of prey**

**Great blue heron**
**Wading bird**

**Cedar waxwing**
**Perching bird**

■ **Figure 17.2** *Cardinalis cardinalis* is a bird with many common names and is seen throughout much of the United States. It is the state bird of Illinois, Indiana, Kentucky, North Carolina, and Ohio.
**Identify** ***some other animals that have multiple common names.***

Biologists use scientific names for species because common names vary in their use. Many times the bird shown in **Figure 17.2** is called a redbird, sometimes it is called a cardinal, and other times it is called a Northern cardinal. In 1758, Linnaeus gave this bird its scientific name, *Cardinalis cardinalis.* Biologists are never confused or mistaken about what is being referred to by this name. Binomial nomenclature also is useful because common names can be misleading. If you were doing a scientific study on fish, you would not include starfish in your studies. Starfish are not fish. In the same way, great horned owls do not have horns and sea cucumbers are not plants.

**VOCABULARY**
**WORD ORIGIN**
**Binomial nomenclature**
comes from the Latin words *bi,* meaning *two; nomen,* meaning *name;* and *calatus,* meaning *list.*

When writing a scientific name, scientists follow certain rules.

- The first letter of the genus name always is capitalized, but the rest of the genus name and all letters of the specific epithet are lowercase.
- If a scientific name is written in a printed book or magazine, it should be italicized.
- When a scientific name is written by hand, both parts of the name should be underlined.
- After the scientific name has been written completely, the genus name often will be abbreviated to the first letter in later appearances. For example, the scientific name of *Cardinalis cardinalis* can be written *C. cardinalis.*

**Reading Check** **Explain** why Latin is the basis for many scientific names.

**Modern classification systems** The study of evolution in the 1800s added a new dimension to Linnaeus's classification system. Many scientists at that time, including Charles Darwin, Jean-Baptiste Lamarck, and Ernst Haekel, began to classify organisms not only on the basis of morphological and behavioral characteristics. They also included evolutionary relationships in their classification systems. Today, while modern classification systems remain rooted in the Linnaeus tradition, they have been modified to reflect new knowledge about evolutionary ancestry.

## Taxonomic Categories

Think about how things are grouped in your favorite video store. How are the DVDs arranged on the shelves? They might be arranged according to genre—action, drama, or comedy—and then by title and year. Although taxonomists group organisms instead of DVDs, they also subdivide groups based on more specific criteria. The taxonomic categories used by scientists are part of a nested-hierarchal system—each category is contained within another, and they are arranged from broadest to most specific.

**Species and genus** A named group of organisms is called a **taxon** (plural, taxa). Taxa range from having broad diagnostic characteristics to having specific characteristics. The broader the characteristics, the more species the taxon contains. One way to think of taxa is to imagine nesting boxes—one fitting inside the other. You already have learned about two taxa used by Linnaeus—genus and species. Today, a **genus** (plural, genera) is defined as a group of species that are closely related and share a common ancestor.

Note the similarities and differences among the three species of bears in **Figure 17.3.** The scientific names of the American black bear *(Ursus americanus)* and Asiatic black bear *(Ursus thibetanus)* indicate that they belong to the same genus, *Ursus.* All species in the genus *Ursus* have massive skulls and similar tooth structures. Sloth bears *(Melursus ursinus),* despite their similarity to members of the genus *Ursus,* usually are classified in a different genus, *Melursus,* because they are smaller, have a different skull shape and size, and have two fewer incisor teeth than bears of the genus *Ursus.*

**Family** All bears, both living and extinct species, belong to the same family, Ursidae. A **family** is the next higher taxon, consisting of similar, related genera. In addition to the three species shown in **Figure 17.3,** the Ursidae family contains six other species: brown bears, polar bears, giant pandas, Sun bears, and Andean bears. All members of the bear family share certain characteristics. For example, they all walk flatfooted and have forearms that can rotate to grasp prey closely.

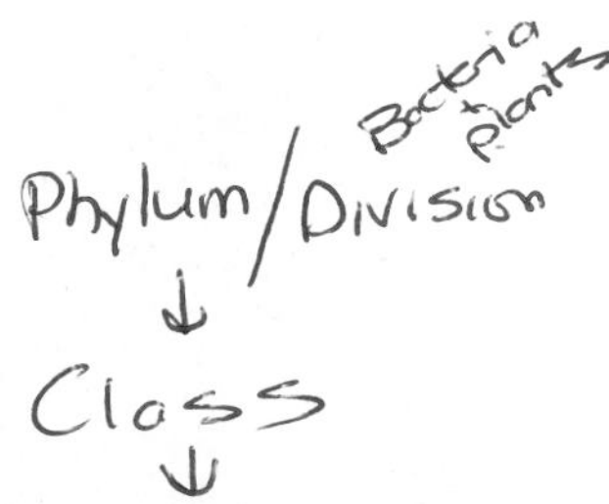

**CAREERS IN BIOLOGY**

**Wildlife Biologist** A scientist who studies organisms in the wild is called a wildlife biologist. Wildlife biologists might study populations of bears or work to educate the public about nature. For more information on biology careers, visit careers at biologygmh.com.

**Figure 17.3** All species in the genus *Ursus* have large body size and massive skulls. Sloth bears are classified in the genus *Melursus*.

***Ursus americanus***
**American black bear**

***Ursus thibetanus***
**Asiatic black bear**

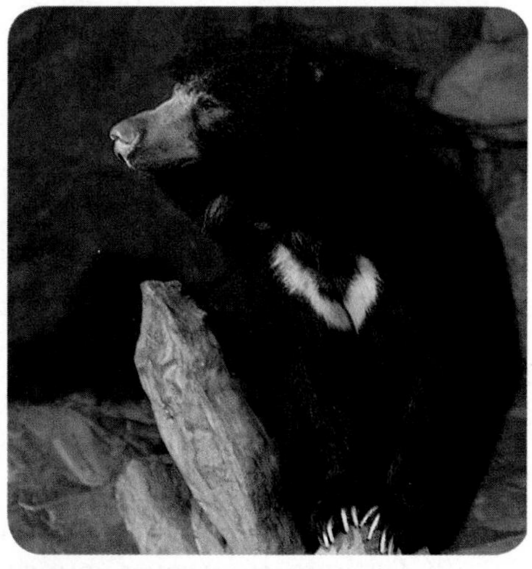

***Melursus ursinus***
**Sloth bear**

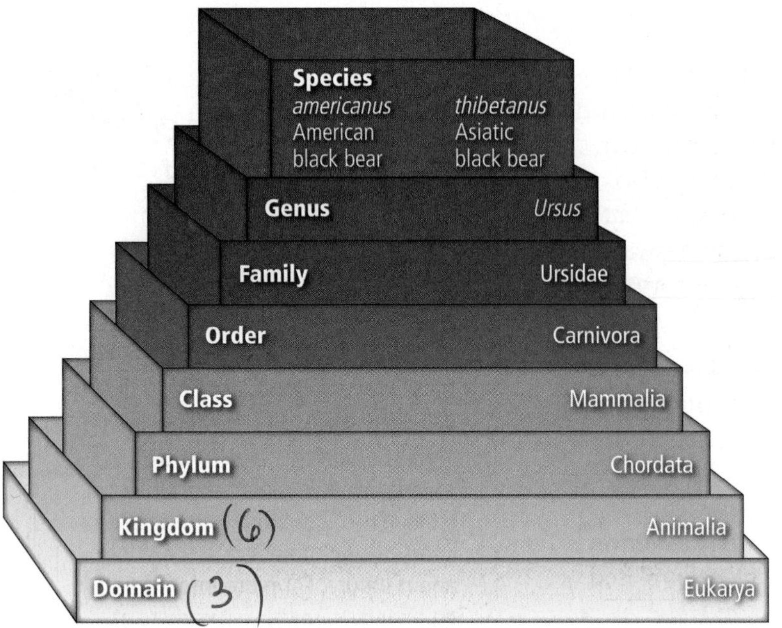


**Figure 17.4** Taxonomic categories are contained within one another like nesting boxes. Notice that the American black bear and Asiatic black bear are different species; however, their classification is the same for all other categories.

**Higher taxa** An **order** contains related families. A **class** contains related orders. The bears in **Figure 17.3** belong to the order Carnivora and class Mammalia. A **phylum** (FI lum) (plural, phyla) or **division** contains related classes. The term *division* is used instead of *phylum* for the classification of bacteria and plants. Sometimes scientists break the commonly used taxa into subcatagories, such as subspecies, subfamilies, infraorders, and subphyla.

The taxon composed of related phyla or divisions is a **kingdom**. Bears are classified in phylum Chordata, Kingdom Animalia, and Domain Eukarya. The **domain** is the broadest of all the taxa and contains one or more kingdoms. The basic characteristics of the three domains and six kingdoms are described later in this chapter.

**Figure 17.4** shows how the taxa are organized into a hierarchical system. The figure also shows the complete classification from domain to species for the American black bear and the Asiatic black bear. Notice that although these bears are classified as different species, the rest of their classification is the same.

## MiniLab 17.1

### Develop a Dichotomous Key

**How can you classify items?** Scientists group organisms based on their characteristics. These groups are the basis for classification tools called dichotomous keys. A dichotomous key consists of a series of choices that lead the user to the correct identification of an organism. In this lab, you will develop a dichotomous key as you group familiar objects.

**Procedure**

1. Read and complete the lab safety form.
2. Remove one **shoe** and make a shoe pile with other shoes from your group.
3. Write a question in your dichotomous key regarding whether the shoe has a characteristic of your choice. Divide the shoes into two groups based on that distinguishing characteristic.
4. Write another question for a different characteristic in your dichotomous key. Divide one of the subgroups into two smaller groups based on this distinguishing characteristic.
5. Continue dividing shoes into subgroups and adding questions to your key until there is only one shoe in each group. Make a branching diagram to identify each shoe with a distinctive name.
6. Use your diagram to classify your teacher's shoe.

**Analysis**

1. **Relate** taxa to the other groups you used to classify shoes. Which group relates to kingdom, phyla, and so on?
2. **Explain** how you were able to classify your teacher's shoe in Step 6.
3. **Critique** How could your classification system be modified to be more effective?

■ **Figure 17.5** This systematist is studying a cactus to determine if it is a new species.

## Systematics Applications

Scientists who study classification provide detailed guides that help people identify organisms. Many times a field guide will contain a dichotomous key, which is a key based on a series of choices between alternate characteristics. You can find out whether a plant or animal is poisonous by using a dichotomous (di KAHT uh mus) key to identify it.

**CAREERS IN BIOLOGY** Systematists, like the one shown in **Figure 17.5** also work to identify new species and relationships among known species. They incorporate information from taxonomy, paleontology, molecular biology, and comparative anatomy in their studies. While the discovery of new species is exciting and important, learning a new connection between species also impacts science and society. For example, if a biologist knows that a certain plant, such as the Madagascar periwinkle *Catharanthus roseus,* produces a chemical that can be used to treat cancer, he or she knows that it is possible related plants also might produce the same or similar chemicals.

## Section 17.1 Assessment

### Section Summary

- Aristotle developed the first widely accepted biological classification system.
- Linnaeus used morphology and behavior to classify plants and animals.
- Binomial nomenclature uses the Latin genus and specific epithet to give an organism a scientific name.
- Organisms are classified according to a nested hierarchical system.

### Understand Main Ideas

1. MAIN Idea **Explain** why it is important to have a biological classification system.
2. **Define and describe** binomial nomenclature.
3. **Compare and contrast** how modern classification systems differ from those used by Aristotle and Linnaeus.
4. **Classify** a giant panda, *Ailuropoda melanoleuca,* completely from domain to species level by referring to **Figure 17.4.**

### Think Scientifically

5. WRITING in **Biology** Write a short story describing an application of biological classification.
6. *Consider* Would you expect to see more biodiversity among members of a phyla or among members of a class? Why?
7. *Differentiate* between taxonomy and systematics.

Section 17.2

### Objectives

- **Compare and contrast** species concepts.
- **Describe** methods used to reveal phylogeny.
- **Explain** how a cladogram is constructed.

### Review Vocabulary

**evolution:** the historical development of a group of organisms

### New Vocabulary

phylogeny
character
molecular clock
cladistics
cladogram

# Modern Classification

MAIN Idea **Classification systems have changed over time as information has increased.**

**Real-World Reading Link** Did you ever try a new way of organizing your school notes? Just as you sometimes make changes in the way you do something based on a new idea or new information, scientists adjust systems and theories in science when new information becomes available.

## Determining Species

It isn't always easy to define a species. Organisms that are different species by one definition might be the same species by a different definition. As knowledge increases, definitions change. The concept of a species today is much different than it was 100 years ago.

**Typological species concept** Aristotle and Linnaeus thought of each species as a distinctly different group of organisms based on physical similarities. This definition of species is called the typological species concept. It is based on the idea that species are unchanging, distinct, and natural types, as defined earlier by Aristotle. The type specimen was an individual of the species that best displayed the characteristics of that species. When another specimen was found that varied significantly from the type specimen, it was classified as a different species. For example, in **Figure 17.6** the color patterns on the butterflies' wings are all slightly different. At one time, they would have been classified as three different species because of these differences, but now they are classified as the same species.

Because we now know that species change over time, and because we know that members of some species exhibit tremendous variation, the typological species concept has been replaced. However, some of its traditions, such as reference to type specimens, remain.

■ **Figure 17.6** Although these tropical butterflies vary in their color patterns, they are classified as different varieties of the same species, *Heliconius erato*.
**Describe** *Why might early taxonomists have classified them as separate species?*

**Biological species concept** Theodosius Dobzhansky and Ernst Mayr, two evolutionary biologists, redefined the term species in the 1930s and 1940s. They defined a species as a group of organisms that is able to interbreed and produce fertile offspring in a natural setting. This is called the biological species concept, and it is the definition for species used throughout this textbook. Though the butterflies in **Figure 17.6** have variable color patterns, they can interbreed to produce fertile offspring and therefore are classified as the same species.

There are limitations to the biological species concept. For example, wolves and dogs, as well as many plant species, are known to interbreed and produce fertile offspring even though they are classified as different species. The biological species concept also does not account for extinct species or species that reproduce asexually. However, because the biological species concept works in most everyday experiences of classification, it is used often.

**Phylogenetic species concept** In the 1940s, the evolutionary species concept was proposed as a companion to the biological species concept. The evolutionary species concept defines species in terms of populations and ancestry. According to this concept, two or more groups that evolve independently from an ancestral population are classified as different species. More recently, this concept has developed into the phylogenetic species concept. **Phylogeny** (fi LAH juh nee) is the evolutionary history of a species. The phylogenetic species concept defines a species as a cluster of organisms that is distinct from other clusters and shows evidence of a pattern of ancestry and descent. When a phylogenetic species branches, it becomes two different phylogenetic species. For example, recall from Chapter 15 that when organisms become isolated—geographically or otherwise—they often evolve different adaptations. Eventually they might become different enough to be classified as a new species.

This definition of a species solves some of the problems of earlier concepts because it applies to extinct species and species that reproduce asexually. It also incorporates molecular data. **Table 17.2** summarizes the three main species concepts.

*Study Tip*

**Note Discussions** While you read, use self-adhesive notes to mark passages that you do not understand. In addition, mark passages you do understand and can explain to others with your own explanations, examples, and ideas. Then, discuss them with your classmates.

**LAUNCH Lab**

**Review** Based on what you've read about classification systems, how would you now answer the analysis questions?

Concepts In Motion

**Interactive Table** To explore more about species concepts, visit biologygmh.com.

**Table 17.2 Species Concepts**

| Species Concept | Description | Limitation | Benefit |
|---|---|---|---|
| **Typological species concept** | Classification is determined by the comparison of physical characteristics with a type specimen. | Alleles produce a wide variety of features within a species. | Descriptions of type specimens provide detailed records of the physical characteristics of many organisms. |
| **Biological species concept** | Classification is determined by similar characteristics and the ability to interbreed and produce fertile offspring. | Some organisms, such as wolves and dogs that are different species, interbreed occasionally. It does not account for extinct species. | The working definition applies in most cases, so it is still used frequently. |
| **Phylogenetic species concept** | Classification is determined by evolutionary history. | Evolutionary histories are not known for all species. | Accounts for extinct species and considers molecular data. |

**VOCABULARY**

**SCIENCE USAGE V. COMMON USAGE**

**Character**

***Science usage:*** a feature that varies among species

*Organisms are compared based on similar characters*

***Common usage:*** imaginary person in a work of fiction—a play, novel, or film.

*The queen was my favorite character in the book.*

## Characters

To classify a species, scientists often construct patterns of descent, or phylogenies, by using **characters**—inherited features that vary among species. Characters can be morphological or biochemical. Shared morphological characters suggest that species are related closely and evolved from a recent common ancestor. For example, because hawks and eagles share many morphological characters that they do not share with other bird species, such as keen eyesight, hooked beaks, and taloned feet, they should share a more recent common ancestor with each other than with other bird groups.

**Morphological characters** When comparing morphological characters, it is important to remember that analogous characters do not indicate a close evolutionary relationship. Recall from Chapter 15 that analogous structures are those that have the same function but different underlying construction. Homologous characters, however, might perform different functions, but show an anatomical similarity inherited from a common ancestor.

**Birds and dinosaurs** Consider the oviraptor and the sparrow shown in **Figure 17.7.** At first you might think that dinosaurs and birds do not have much in common and do not share a close evolutionary relationship. A closer look at dinosaur fossils shows that they share many features with birds. Some fossil dinosaur bones, like those of the large, carnivorous theropod dinosaurs, show that their bones had large hollow spaces. Birds have bones with hollow spaces. In this respect, they are more like birds than most living reptiles, such as alligators, lizards, and turtles, which have dense bones. Also, theropods have hip, leg, wrist, and shoulder structures that are more similar to birds than to other reptiles. Recently, scientists have discovered some fossil dinosaur bones that suggest some theropods had feathers. The evidence provided by these morphological characters indicates that modern birds are related more closely to theropod dinosaurs than they are to other reptiles.

**Reading Check** **Explain** how morphological characters have influenced the classification of dinosaurs and birds.

■ **Figure 17.7** This artist's conception of *Oviraptor philoceratops* might not appear to be related to the sparrow *Zonotrichia leucophrys,* but these animals share many characteristics that indicate a shared evolutionary history.
**Deduce** *which similarities might prompt you to think that these species are more closely related than was commonly thought.*

***Oviraptor philoceratops***

***Zonotrichia leucophrys***

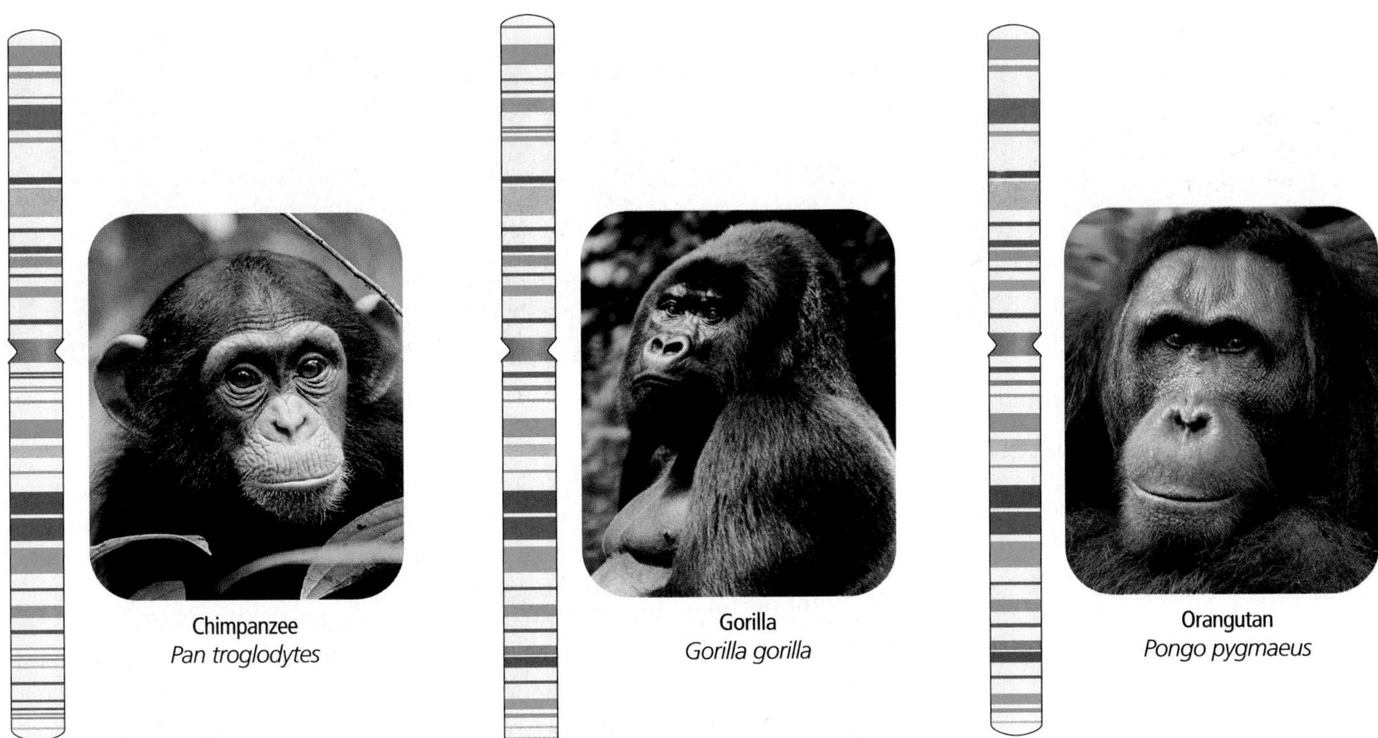


**Figure 17.8** The representation of chromosome-banding patterns for these homologous chromosomes illustrates the evidence of a close evolutionary relationship among the chimpanzee, gorilla, and orangutan.

**Biochemical characters** Scientists use biochemical characters, such as amino acids and nucleotides, to help them determine evolutionary relationships among species. Chromosome structure and number is also a powerful clue for determining species similarities. For example, members of the mustard family (Cruciferae)—including broccoli, cauliflower, and kale—all look different in the garden, but these plants have almost identical chromosome structures. This is strong evidence that they share a recent common ancestor. Likewise, the similar appearance of chromosomes among chimpanzees, gorillas, and orangutans suggests a shared ancestry. **Figure 17.8** shows the similar appearance of a chromosome-banding pattern in these three primates.

DNA and RNA analyses are powerful tools for reconstructing phylogenies. Remember that DNA and RNA are made up of four nucleotides. The nucleotide sequences in DNA define the genes that direct RNA to make proteins. The greater the number of shared DNA sequences between species, the greater the number of shared genes—and the greater the evidence that the species share a recent common ancestor.

Scientists use a variety of techniques to compare DNA sequences when assessing evolutionary relationships. They can sequence and compare whole genomes of different organisms. They can compare genome maps made by using restriction enzymes, like those you learned about in Chapter 13. They also use a technique called DNA-DNA hybridization, during which single strands of DNA from different species are melted together. The success of the hybridization depends on the similarity of the sequences—complementary sequences will bind to each other, while dissimilar sequences will not bind. Comparing the DNA sequences of different species is an objective, quantitative way to measure evolutionary relationships.

**VOCABULARY**

**ACADEMIC VOCABULARY**

**Corresponding:**
Being similar or equivalent in character, quantity, origin, structure, or function.
*The corresponding sequences matched perfectly.*

**African elephant (savannah)**

**African elephant (forest)**

**Asiatic elephant**

■ **Figure 17.9** The two populations of African elephants have been classified as the same species; however, DNA analysis shows that they might be separate species. The Asiatic elephant belongs to a separate genus.

**A species example** The classification of elephants is one example of how molecular data has changed traditional taxonomic organization. **Figure 17.9** shows pictures of elephants that live in the world today. Taxonomists have classified the Asiatic elephant *(Elephas maximus)* as one species and the African elephant *(Loxodonta africana)* as another for over 100 years. However, they have classified the two types of African elephant as the same species, even though the two populations look different. The forest-dwelling elephants are much smaller and have longer tusks and smaller ears than the savanna-dwelling elephants. Even so, scientists thought that the elephants interbred freely at the margins of their ranges. Recent DNA studies, however, show that the African elephants diverged from a common ancestor about 2.5 million years ago. Scientists have proposed renaming the forest-dwelling elephant *Loxodonta cyclotis.* Use **Data Analysis Lab 17.1** to explore molecular evidence for renaming the forest-dwelling elephant.

## DATA ANALYSIS LAB 17.1

**Based on Real Data***

### Draw a Conclusion

**Are African elephants separate species?**
Efforts to count and protect elephant populations in Africa were based on the assumption that all African elephants belong to the same species. Evidence from a project originally designed to trace ivory samples changed that assumption.

A group of scientists studied the DNA variation among 195 African elephants from 21 populations in 11 of the 37 nations in which African elephants range and from seven Asian elephants. They used biopsy darts to obtain plugs of skin from the African elephants. The researchers focused on a total of 1732 nucleotides from four nuclear genes that are not subject to natural selection. The following paragraph shows the results of the samples.

**Data and Observations**

*"Phylogenetic distinctions between African forest elephant and savannah elephant population corresponded to 58% of the difference in the same genes between elephant genera Loxodonta (African) and Elephas (Asian)."*

**Think Critically**

1. **Describe** the type of evidence used in the study.
2. **Explain** the evidence that there are two species of elephants in Africa.
3. **Propose** other kinds of data that could be used to support three different scientific names for elephants.
4. **Infer** Currently *Loxodonta africana* is protected from being hunted. How might reclassification affect the conservation of forest elephants?

*Data obtained from: Roca, A.L., et al. 2001. Genetic evidence for two species of elephant in Africa. *Science* 293(5534): 1473-1477.

**Molecular clocks** You know that mutations occur randomly in DNA. As time passes, mutations accumulate, or build up, in the chromosomes. Some of these mutations are neutral mutations that do not affect the way cells function, and they are passed down from parent to offspring. Systematists can use these mutations to help them determine the degree of relationship among species. A **molecular clock** is a model that is used to compare DNA sequences from two different species to estimate how long the species have been evolving since they diverged from a common ancestor. **Figure 17.10** illustrates how a molecular clock works.

Scientists use molecular clocks to compare the DNA sequences or amino acid sequences of genes that are shared by different species. The differences between the genes indicate the presence of mutations. The more mutations that have accumulated, the more time that has passed since divergence. When the molecular clock technique was first introduced in the 1960s, scientists thought the rate of mutation within specific genes was constant. Hence, they used the clock as an analogy. But while clocks measure time in predictable intervals, scientists now know that the speed by which mutations occur is not always the same in a single gene or amino acid sequence.

The rate of mutation is affected by many factors, including the type of mutation, where it is in the genome, the type of protein that the mutation affects, and the population in which the mutation occurs. In a single organism, different genes might mutate, or "tick," at different speeds. This inconsistency makes molecular clocks difficult to read. Researchers try to compare genes that accumulate mutations at a relatively constant rate in a wide range of organisms. One such gene is the gene for cytochrome *c* oxidase, which is found in the mitochondrial DNA of most organisms.

Despite their limitations, molecular clocks can be valuable tools for determining a relative time of divergence of a species. They are especially useful when used in conjunction with other data, such as the fossil record.

**CAREERS IN BIOLOGY**

**Molecular systematist** An evolutionary geneticist uses genetic analysis to establish evolutionary relationships. Often, they work at colleges and universities where they teach and perform research. For more information on biology careers, visit biologygmh.com.

■ **Figure 17.10** This molecular clock diagram shows how mutations might accumulate over time.

**Infer** ***Why is a clock not a good analogy for this process?***

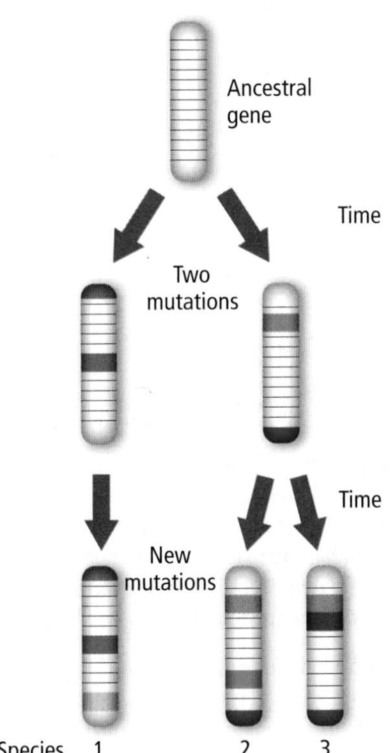


## Phylogenetic Reconstruction

The most common systems of classification today are based on a method of analysis called cladistics. **Cladistics** (kla DIHS tiks) is a method that classifies organisms according to the order that they diverged from a common ancestor. It reconstructs phylogenies based on shared characters.

**Character types** Scientists consider two main types of characters when doing cladistic analyses. An ancestral character is found within the entire line of descent of a group of organisms. Derived characters are present members of one group of the line but not in the common ancestor. For example, when considering the relationship between birds and mammals, a backbone is an ancestral character because both birds and mammals have a backbone and so did their shared ancestor. However, birds have feathers and mammals have hair. Therefore, having hair is a derived character for mammals because only mammals have an ancestor with hair. Likewise, having feathers is a derived character for birds.

**Vocabulary**
**Word origin**
**Cladistics**
comes from the Greek word *klados,* meaning *sprout* or *branch.*

**Cladograms** Sytematists use shared derived characters to make a cladogram. A **cladogram** (KLAD uh gram) is a branching diagram that represents the proposed phylogeny or evolutionary history of a species or group. A cladogram is a model similar to the pedigrees you studied in Chapter 11. Just as a pedigree's branches show direct ancestry, a cladogram's branches indicate phylogeny. The groups used in cladograms are called clades. A clade is one branch of the cladogram.

**Constructing a cladogram** **Figure 17.11** is a simplified cladogram for some major plant groups. This cladogram was constructed in the following way. First, two species were identified, conifers and ferns, to compare with the lily species. Then, another species was identified that is ancestral to conifers and ferns. This species is called the outgroup. The outgroup is the species or group of species on a cladogram that has more ancestral characters with respect to the other organisms being compared. In the diagram below, the outgroup is moss. Mosses are more distantly related to ferns, conifers, and lilies.

The cladogram is then constructed by sequencing the order in which derived characters evolved with respect to the outgroup. The closeness of clades in the cladogram indicate the number of characters shared. The group that is closest to the lily shares the most derived characters with lilies and thus shares a more recent common ancestor with lilies than with the groups farther away. The nodes where the branches originate represent a common ancestor. This common ancestor generally is not a known organism, species, or fossil. Scientists hypothesize its characters based on the traits of its descendants.

**The primary assumption** The primary assumption that systematists make when constructing cladograms is that the greater the number of derived characters shared by groups, the more recently the groups share a common ancestor. Thus, as shown in **Figure 17.11,** lilies and conifers have three derived characters in common and are presumed to share a more recent common ancestor than lilies and ferns, which share only two characters.

A cladogram also is called a phylogenetic tree. Detailed phylogenetic trees show relationships among many species and groups of organisms. **Figure 17.12** illustrates a phylogenetic tree that shows the relationships among the domains and kingdoms of the most commonly used classification system today.

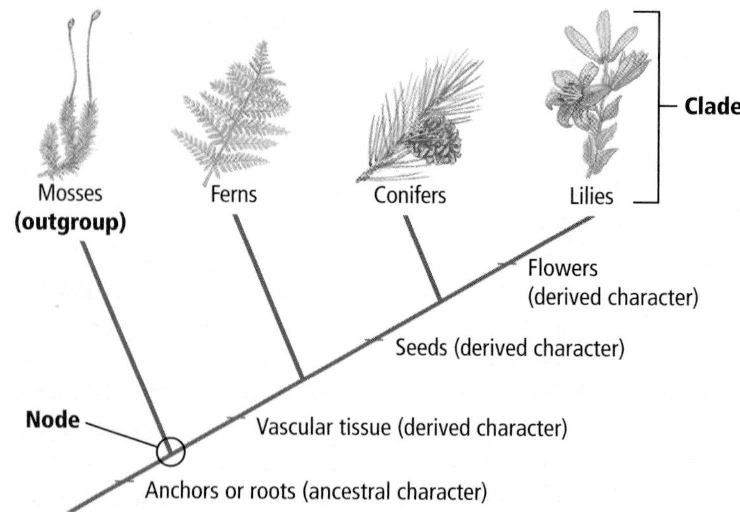


**Figure 17.11** This cladogram uses the derived characters of plant taxa to model its phylogeny. Groups that are closer to the lily on the cladogram share a recent common ancestor.
**Identify** ***which clades have chloroplasts but do not produce seeds.***

**Concepts In Motion**
**Interactive Figure** To see an animation of the cladistic method of classification, visit biologygmh.com.

# Visualizing the Tree of Life

**Figure 17.12**
This phylogenetic tree shows the main branches in the "tree of life." Notice the three domains and the four kingdoms of Domain Eukarya. All of the branches are connected at the trunk, which is labeled *Common Ancestor.*

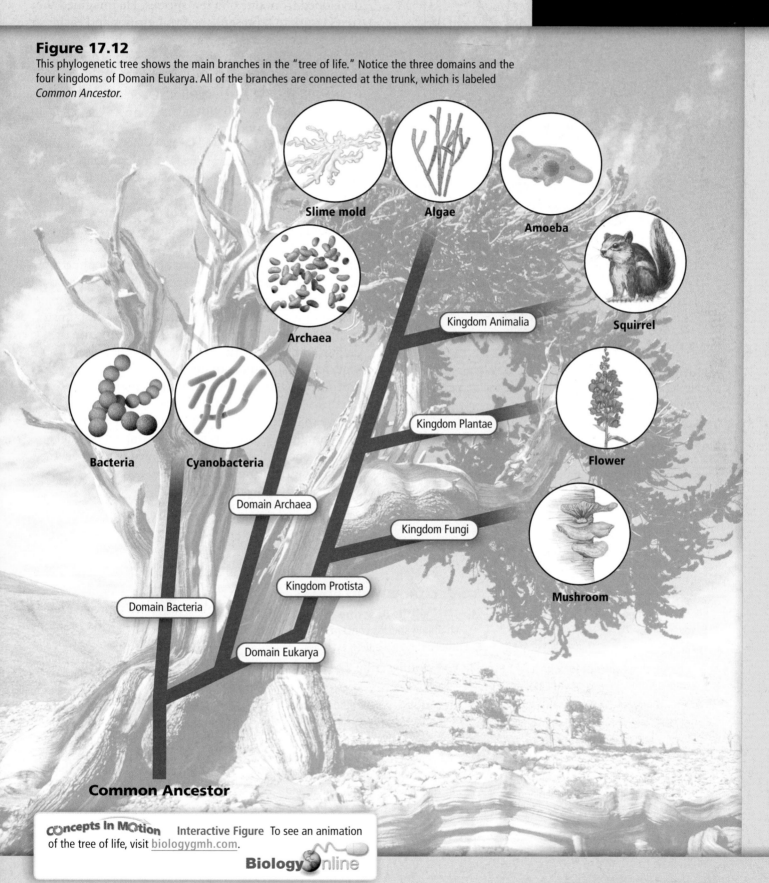

Slime mold
Algae
Amoeba
Squirrel
Archaea
Kingdom Animalia
Bacteria
Cyanobacteria
Kingdom Plantae
Flower
Domain Archaea
Kingdom Fungi
Mushroom
Kingdom Protista
Domain Bacteria
Domain Eukarya
**Common Ancestor**

**Concepts In Motion** Interactive Figure To see an animation of the tree of life, visit biologygmh.com.

Biology Online

Genealogical Tree of Humanity.

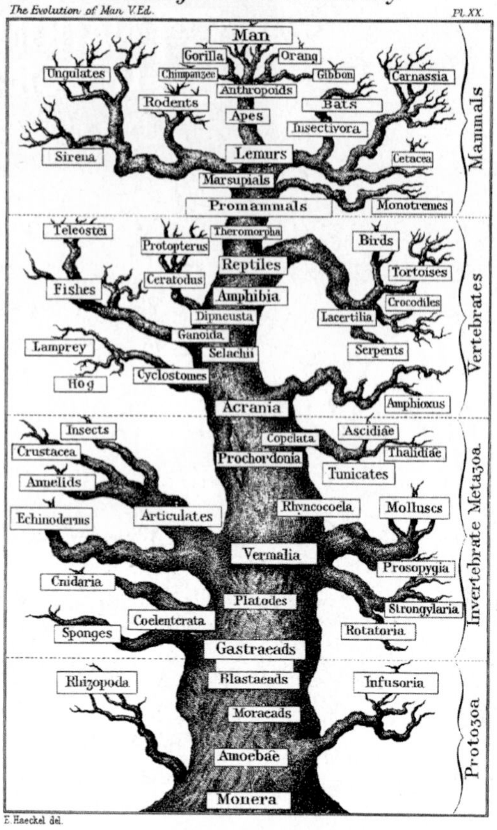

■ **Figure 17.13** This illustration, made by Ernst Haeckel in the nineteenth century, was one of the first graphic depictions of evolutionary relationships.

**Concepts In Motion**

**Interactive Figure** To see an animation of evolutionary trees, visit biologygmh.com.

**Connection to History** **The tree of life** In his book *On the Origin of Species*, Charles Darwin used the analogy of a tree to suggest that all of the species developed from one or a few species. He imagined the tree's trunk to represent ancestral groups and each of the branches to have similar species. From each branch, smaller and smaller branches grew. Finally, at the tips of the twigs of these branches were the leaves, consisting of individual living species. This concept was developed further, and the term *tree of life* was coined by German biologist Ernst Haeckel (1834–1919). **Figure 17.13** shows Haeckel's Genealogical Tree of Humanity. Haeckel was the first to represent phylogenies in the form of a tree, and while his phylogenies are no longer completely accurate, they represent the first step in the reconstruction of phylogenies.

The tree of life diagram in **Figure 17.13** is a representation of the diversity of living organisms. A tree of life that incorporates all known organisms is almost unimaginably large. Scientists have discovered and described nearly 1.75 million species, and they estimate that millions more remain unclassified. Assembling a comprehensive tree of life requires a convergence of data from phylogenetic and molecular analysis. It also requires collaboration among many scientists representing many disciplines, from molecular biology to Earth science to computer science. Many scientists believe that the construction of a comprehensive tree of life, though an enormous task, is an important goal. Knowing how all organisms are related would benefit industry, agriculture, medicine, and conservation.

## Section 17.2 Assessment

### Section Summary

- The definition of species has changed over time.
- Phylogeny is the evolutionary history of a species, evidence for which comes from a variety of studies.
- A molecular clock uses comparisons of DNA sequences to estimate phylogeny and rate of evolutionary change.
- Cladistic analysis models evolutionary relationships based on sequencing derived characters.

### Understand Main Ideas

1. MAIN Idea **Describe** how the changing species concept has affected classification systems.
2. **List and describe** the different concepts of a species.
3. **Describe** some methods used to determine phylogeny.
4. **Organize** the following derived characters on a cladogram in order of ascending complexity: multicellular, hair, backbone, unicellular, and four appendages.

### Think Scientifically

5. **MATH in Biology** Describe the mathematical challenges of counting the "ticks" of a molecular clock.
6. **WRITING in Biology** Evaluate the analogy of a tree for the organization of species based on phylogeny.
7. ***Indicate*** the hypothetical evolutionary relationship between two species if their DNA sequences share a 98 percent similarity.

*Use the photograph below to answer question 29.*

**29.** In which kingdom would this organism, which has chloroplasts, cell walls, but no organs, be classified?
**A.** Plantae
**B.** Animalia
**C.** Protista
**D.** Fungi

**30.** Which substance would most likely be in the cell walls of an organism with chloroplasts and tissues?
**A.** peptidoglycan
**B.** chitin
**C.** hyphae
**D.** cellulose

## Constructed Response

**31. Open Ended** Indicate the relationship between domains and kingdoms.

**32. Short Answer** Predict in which domain a taxonomist would place a newly discovered photosynthetic organism that has cells without membrane-bound organelles and no peptidoglycan.

**33. Open Ended** Write an argument for or against including Eubacteria and Archaea in the same domain. How would this affect the phylogenetic tree of life?

## Think Critically

**34. Analyze** Using the model in **Figure 17.13,** decide which three of the kingdoms in domain Eukarya evolved from the fourth.

**35. CAREERS IN BIOLOGY** A biologist studied two groups of frogs in the laboratory. The groups looked identical and produced fertile offspring when interbred. However in nature they don't interbreed because their reproductive calls are different and their territories do not overlap. Use your knowledge of species concepts and speciation to decide why they should or should not be placed in the same species.

## Additional Assessment

**36.** WRITING in Biology Suppose you found a cricket near your home. After a biologist from a local university studies your find, you learn that the cricket is a new species. Write a paragraph to explain how the biologist might have determined that the cricket is a new species.

## DBQ Document-Based Questions

Data obtained from: Blaxter, M. 2001. Sum of the arthropod parts. *Science* 413: 121-122.

*Scientists continue to debate about evolutionary relationships among organisms. Groups of arthropods were thought to be related in the way shown on the left, but new molecular evidence suggests that the grouping on the right is more accurate.*

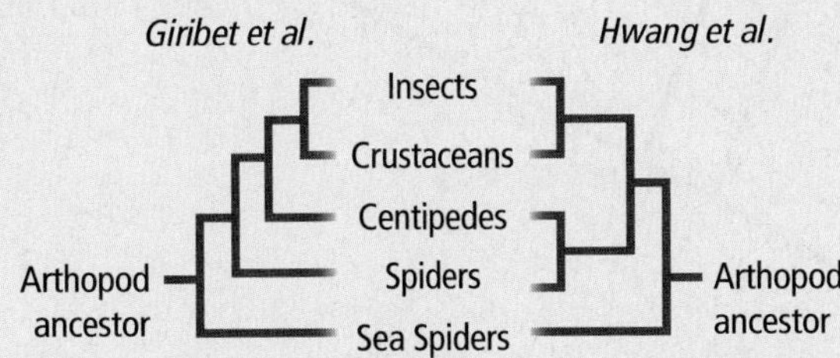


**37.** Compare and contrast the two cladograms. How did the molecular evidence change the relationship between centipedes and spiders?

**38.** To which group are crustaceans most closely related?

**39.** Which group in the cladogram appears to be the most ancestral?

## Cumulative Review

**40.** Describe how hemophilia is inherited. **(Chapter 11)**

**41.** Choose three lines of evidence that support evolution. Give an example of each. **(Chapter 15)**

# Standardized Test Practice

**Cumulative**

## Multiple Choice

1. Which data shows that Neanderthals are not the ancestors of modern humans?
   A. differences in Neanderthal and human DNA
   B. evidence from Neanderthal burial grounds
   C. muscular build of Neanderthals, as compared to humans
   D. patterns of Neanderthal extinction

*Use the illustration below to answer questions 2 and 3.*

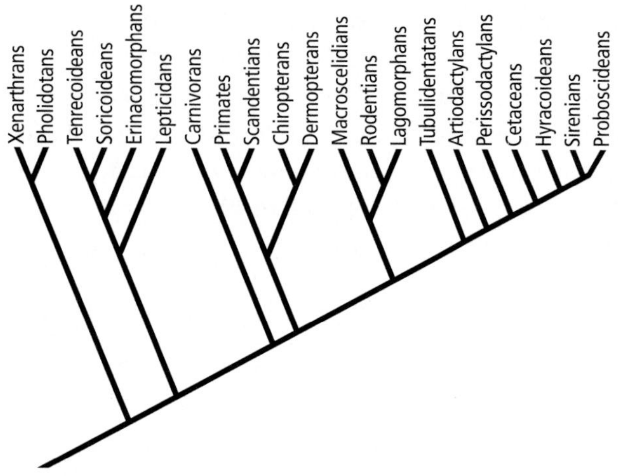


2. According to the cladogram of mammals, which two groups of animals have a more recent common ancestor?
   A. carnivorans and chiropterans
   B. cetaceans and hyracoideans
   C. dermopterans and carnivorans
   D. rodentians and lagomorphans

3. Which mammal is most closely related to bats (chiropterans)?
   A. carnivorans
   B. xenarthrans
   C. primates
   D. rodentians

4. Which radioactive isotope would be used to determine the specific age of a Paleozoic rock formation?
   A. Beryllium-10 (1.5 million years)
   B. Carbon-14 (5715 years)
   C. Thorium-232 (14 billion years)
   D. Uranium-235 (704 million years)

5. According to the Hardy-Weinberg principle, which situation would disrupt genetic equilibrium?
   A. A large population of deer inhabits a forest region.
   B. A particular population of flies mates randomly.
   C. A population of flowering plants always has the same group of natural predators.
   D. A small population of birds colonizes a new island.

*Use the diagram below to answer question 6.*

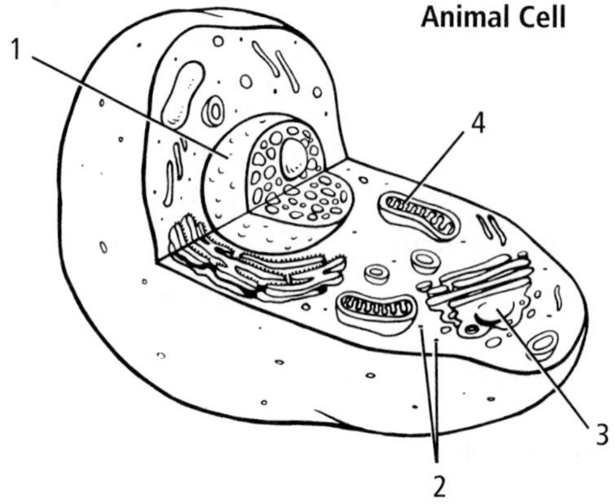


6. Which labeled structure contains the cell's genetic information?
   A. 1
   B. 2
   C. 3
   D. 4

7. Which structure is a vestigial structure?
   A. human appendix
   B. deer horns
   C. multiple cow stomachs
   D. snake tail

8. According to the endosymbiont theory, which part of the eukaryotic cell evolved from a prokaryotic cell?
   A. chloroplast
   B. golgi apparatus
   C. nucleus
   D. ribosome

## Short Answer

9. List three primate adaptations found in humans, and explain how each one relates to a tree-dwelling habitat.

10. Assess how molecular clocks are useful in investigating phylogeny in ways that morphological characteristics are not.

11. In terms of their evolution, how are homologous structures and analogous structures different?

12. Assess the advantage of bipedalism.

13. Infer why Aristotle only used two kingdoms to classify living things.

14. Assess the significance of the discovery of the Lucy fossil.

15. Contrast one of the characteristics of living things with the characteristics of nonliving things such as rocks.

*Use the figure below to answer question 16.*

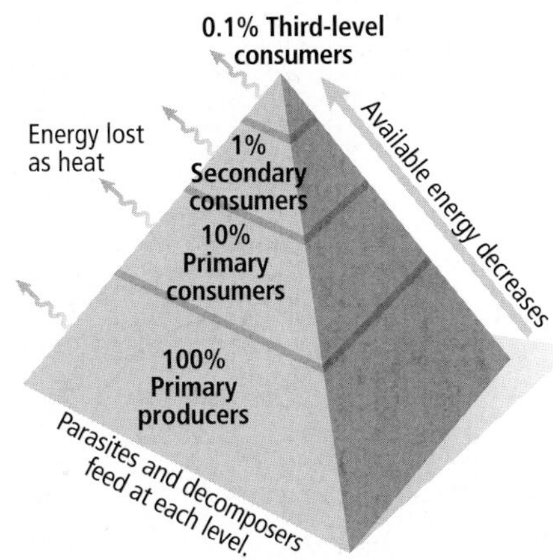


16. How much energy from one trophic level is available to organisms at the next higher trophic level?

## Extended Response

17. How could a mutagen cause a change in the protein for which a DNA strand is coding? Trace the effect of a specific mutation through the process of protein synthesis.

18. Assess the value of the binomial system of naming organisms.

19. Name two animals that you would expect to have similar chromosomal characters. Design an experiment to test whether they are similar.

## Essay Question

Scientists often use multiple types and sources of data in order to determine when different groups of organisms evolved. Taken together, the data can help construct an evolutionary history.

*Using the information in the paragraph above, answer the following question in essay format.*

20. What kind of evidence could help scientists determine whether eubacteria or archaebacteria evolved earlier on Earth? Write an essay that justifies what specific kinds of data would need to be collected to make this judgment.

| NEED EXTRA HELP? | | | | | | | | | | | | | | | | | | | | |
|---|---|---|---|---|---|---|---|---|---|---|---|---|---|---|---|---|---|---|---|---|
| **If You Missed Question . . .** | 1 | 2 | 3 | 4 | 5 | 6 | 7 | 8 | 9 | 10 | 11 | 12 | 13 | 14 | 15 | 16 | 17 | 18 | 19 | 20 |
| **Review Section . . .** | 16.3 | 17.2 | 17.2 | 14.1 | 15.3 | 16.2 | 15.2 | 14.2 | 16.1 | 7.2 | 15.2 | 16.2 | 17.1 | 16.2 | 1.1 | 2.2 | 12.3 | 17.1 | 17.2 | 17.2, 17.3 |

# UNIT 5 Bacteria, Viruses, Protists, and Fungi

**Chapter 18**
**Bacteria and Viruses**
**BIG Idea** Bacteria are microscopic organisms, and viruses are nonliving microscopic agents that invade cells.

**Chapter 19**
**Protists**
**BIG Idea** Protists are a diverse group of unicellular and multicellular organisms that do not necessarily share the same evolutionary history.

**Chapter 20**
**Fungi**
**BIG Idea** The Kingdom Fungi is made up of four phyla based on unique structures, methods of nutrition, and methods of reproduction.

## CAREERS IN BIOLOGY
### Microbiologist
**Microbiologists** study the growth and characteristics of microscopic organisms, including bacteria, viruses, protists, and fungi. Environmental microbiologists, like the one shown here, focus their research on biological and chemical pollutants in the environment.

**WRITING in Biology** Visit biologygmh.com to learn more about microbiologists. Compile a list of microbiology specialties associated with the food, agricultural, and pharmaceutical industries.

**Biology Online**

To read more about microbiologists in action, visit biologygmh.com.

CHAPTER 18

# Bacteria and Viruses

**Section 1**
**Bacteria**
MAIN Idea Bacteria are prokaryotic cells.

**Section 2**
**Viruses and Prions**
MAIN Idea Viruses and prions are smaller and less complex than bacteria; they invade cells and can alter cellular functions.

## BioFacts

- One spoonful of soil contains more than 100 million bacteria.
- A human has ten times more bacterial cells living on the body than body cells.
- More than 300 different viruses are known to infect humans.

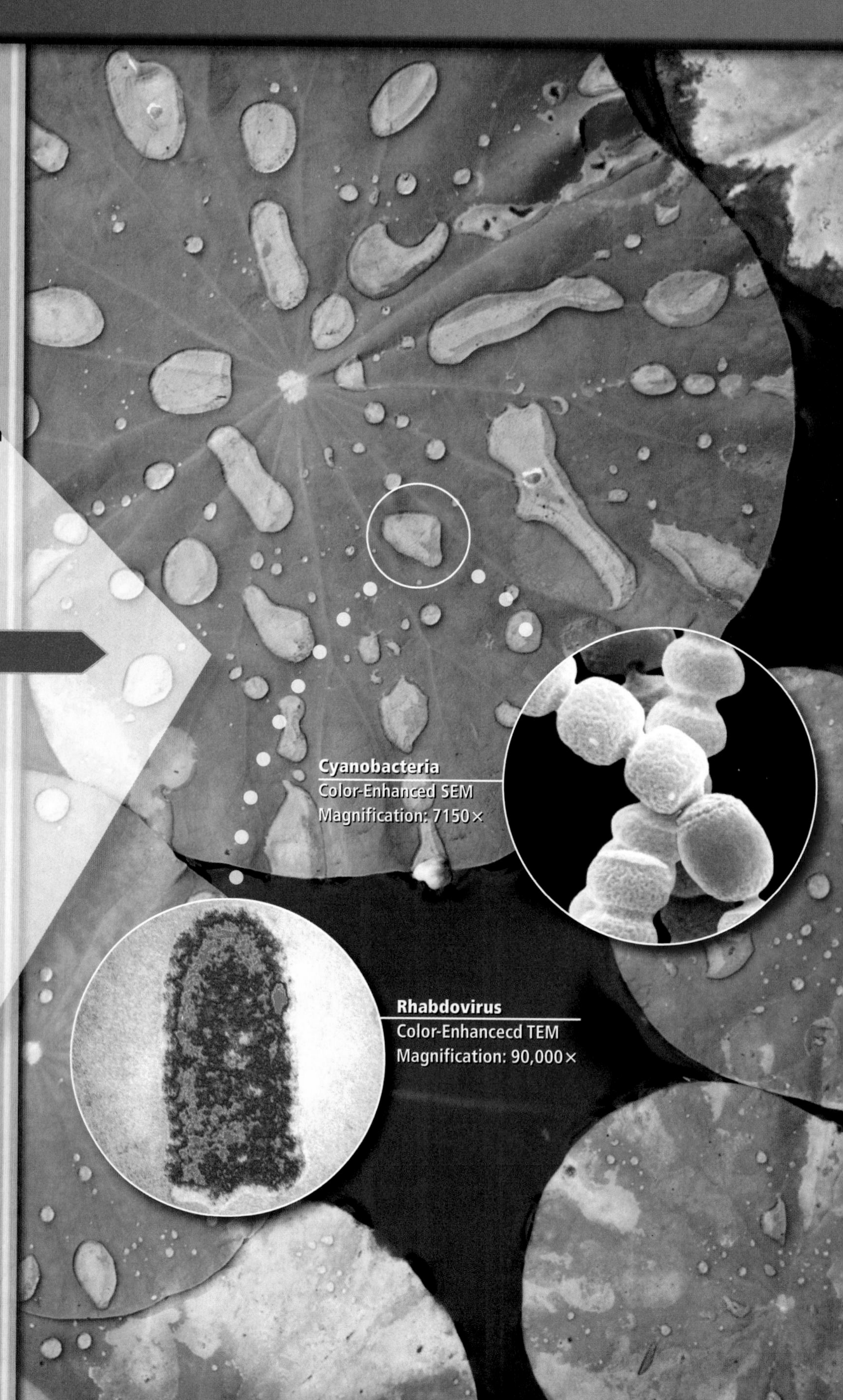

**Cyanobacteria**
Color-Enhanced SEM
Magnification: 7150×

**Rhabdovirus**
Color-Enhancecd TEM
Magnification: 90,000×

# LAUNCH Lab

## What are the differences between animal cells and bacterial cells?

You are already familiar with animal cells. How do animal cells compare to the cells of bacteria? Bacteria are the most common organisms in your environment. In fact, billions of bacteria live on and in your body. Many species of bacteria can cause diseases. What makes bacteria different from your own cells?

### Procedure

1. Read and complete the lab safety form.
2. Use a **compound light microscope** to observe the slides of **animal and bacterial cells.**
3. Complete a data table listing the similarities and differences between the two types of cells.

### Analysis

1. **Describe** the different cells you observed. What did you notice about each?
2. **Infer** whether they are living things. What leads you to these conclusions?

Visit biologygmh.com to:

- study the entire chapter online
- explore Concepts in Motion, Interactive Tables, Microscopy Links, links to virtual dissections, and the Interactive Time Line
- access Web links for more information, projects, and activities
- review content online with the Interactive Tutor and take Self-Check Quizzes

**Viral Replication** Make the following Foldable to help you organize the cycles of viral replication.

**STEP 1** Fold a sheet of paper in half vertically.

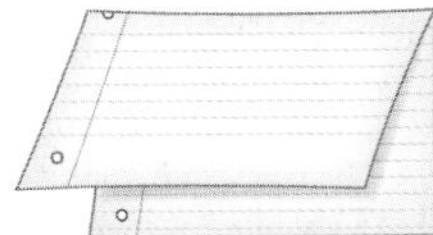

**STEP 2** Fold it in half again as shown.

**STEP 3** Cut along the middle fold of the top layer only.

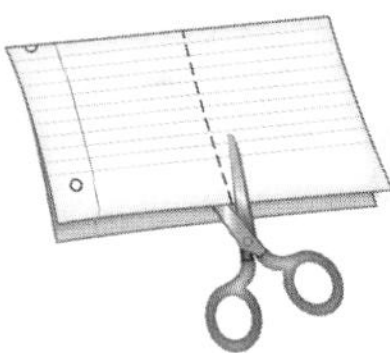

**STEP 4** Label the tabs as illustrated.

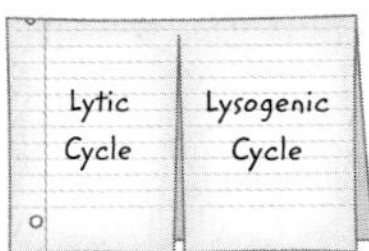


FOLDABLES **Use this Foldable as you study viral infection in Section 18.2.** Draw the stages of the two cycles under the flaps.

## Section 18.1

### Objectives

- **Differentiate** among archaebacteria and eubacteria and their subcategories.
- **Describe** survival mechanisms of bacteria at both the individual and population levels.
- **Describe** ways that bacteria are beneficial to humans.

### Review Vocabulary

**prokaryotic cell:** cell that does not contain any membrane-bound organelles

### New Vocabulary

bacteria
nucleoid
capsule
pilus
binary fission
conjugation
endospore

# Bacteria

**MAIN Idea** **Bacteria are prokaryotic cells.**

**Real-World Reading Link** What do yogurt, cheese, and strep throat have in common? You might wonder what food and disease have in common, but they each are the result of microscopic organisms called prokaryotes.

## Diversity of Prokaryotes

Recall from Chapter 7 that prokaryotic cells are simple cells with no organelles. **Bacteria** are microscopic organisms that are prokaryotes (proh KE ree ohts). You might wonder how something as small as a prokaryote could be important for human survival. Yet, prokaryotes are important in the human body, food production, industry, and the environment. Many scientists think the first organisms on Earth were microscopic unicellular organisms called prokaryotes. Today, prokaryotes are the most numerous organisms on Earth. These organisms are found everywhere from the deepest depths of the oceans to the air above the highest mountaintops. Some prokaryotic cells are the only organisms able to survive in hostile environments, such as the water in hot sulfur springs or the Great Salt Lake.

The word *prokaryote* is a Greek word that means *before a nucleus.* Prokaryotic cells do not have a nucleus. Instead, they have a specialized region of the cell containing DNA. All prokaryotes were previously classified into one group, the Kingdom Monera. Today, the prokaryotes are divided into two domains—the Domain Bacteria (eubacteria) and the Domain Archaea (archaebacteria). **Figure 18.1** shows representatives of these two domains.

**Figure 18.1** Prokaryotes are unicellular organisms. Archaebacteria are similar to the first life-forms on Earth. The middle photo shows cells of eubacteria. The right photo shows cyanobacteria, which are photosynthetic eubacteria.

Color-Enhanced SEM Magnification: unavailable

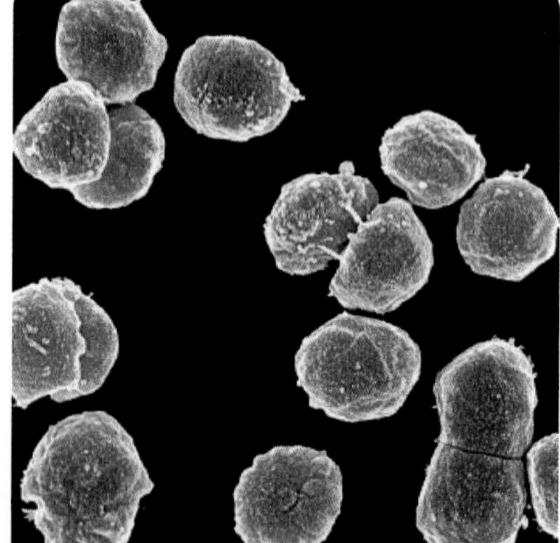

**Archaebacteria**

Color-Enhanced SEM Magnification: 23,000×

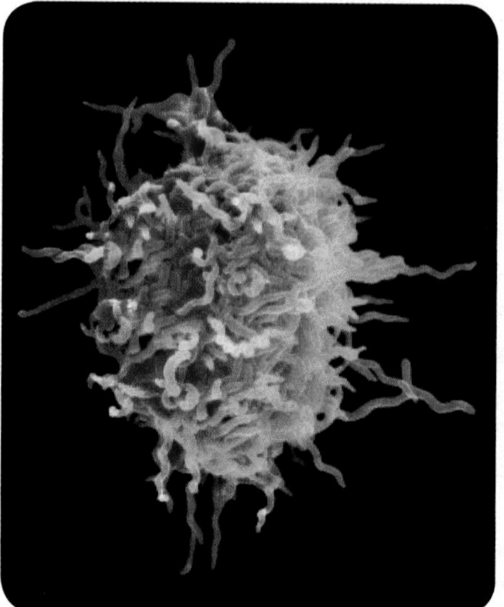

**Eubacteria**

Color-Enhanced SEM Magnification: 260×

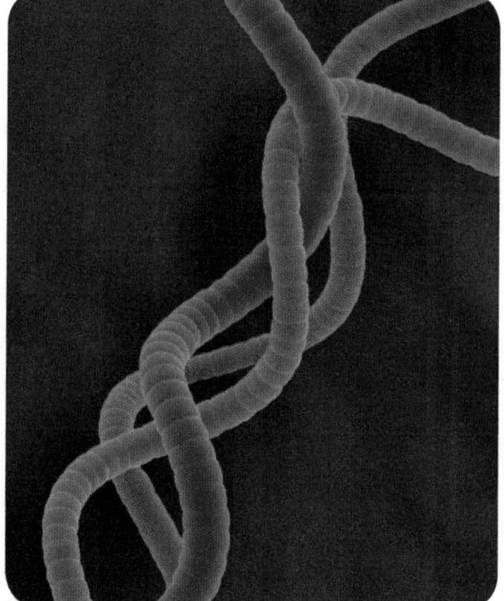

**Photosynthetic eubacteria**

**Hot springs**

**Great Salt Lake**

**Figure 18.2** Some members of the Domain Archaea can live in hostile environments such as the sulfur hot springs in Yellowstone National Park and the Great Salt Lake in Utah.
**Hypothesize** ***What other hostile places might you find archaebacteria?***

**Eubacteria** When most people read about or hear the word bacteria (singular, bacterium) they think of eubacteria. The eubacteria are the most-studied organisms and are found almost everywhere except in the extreme environments where mostly archaebacteria are found. Eubacteria have very strong cell walls that contain peptidogylcan. Some eubacteria have a second cell wall, a property which can be used to classsify them. Additionally, some eubacteria such as the cyanobacteria in **Figure 18.1,** are photosynthetic.

**Archaebacteria** In extreme environments that are hostile to most other forms of life, archaebacteria predominate. Some archaebacteria called thermoacidophiles (thur muh uh SIH duh filz) live in hot, acidic environments including sulfur hot springs shown in **Figure 18.2,** thermal vents on the ocean floor, and around volcanoes. These bacteria thrive in temperatures above 80°C and a pH of 1–2. Some of these bacteria cannot survive temperatures as low as 55°C. Many are strict anaerobes, which means that they die in the presence of oxygen.

Other archaebacteria called halophiles (HA luh filz) live in very salty environments. The salt concentration in your cells is 0.9 percent, oceans average 3.5 percent salt, and the salt concentrations in the Great Salt Lake shown in **Figure 18.2** and the Dead Sea can be greater than 15 percent. Halophiles have several adaptions that allow them to live in salty environments. Halophiles usually are aerobic, and some halophiles carry out a unique form of photosynthesis using a protein instead of the pigment chlorophyll.

The methanogens (meh THAHN oh jenz) are the third group of archaebacteria. These organisms are obligate anaerobes, which means they cannot live in the presence of oxygen. They use carbon dioxide during respiration and give off methane as a waste product. Methanogens are found in sewage treatment plants, swamps, bogs, and near volcanic vents. Methanogens even thrive in the gastrointestinal tract of humans and other animals and are responsible for the gases that are released from the lower digestive tract.

**Differences between eubacteria and archaebacteria** The cell walls of the eubacteria contain peptidoglycan, but the cell walls of archaebacteria do not. In addition, the two groups of organisms have different lipids in their plasma membranes and different ribosomal proteins and RNA. The ribosomal proteins in the achaebacteria are similar to those of eukaryotic cells.

**VOCABULARY**

**WORD ORIGIN**

**Halophile**
***halo-*** from the Greek word *hals,* meaning *salt.*
***-phile*** from the Greek word *phileo,* meaning *like.*

Figure 18.3 Prokaryotic cells have structures that are necessary for carrying out life processes.

**Compare and Contrast** ***How does a bacterial cell differ structurally from a eukaryotic cell?***

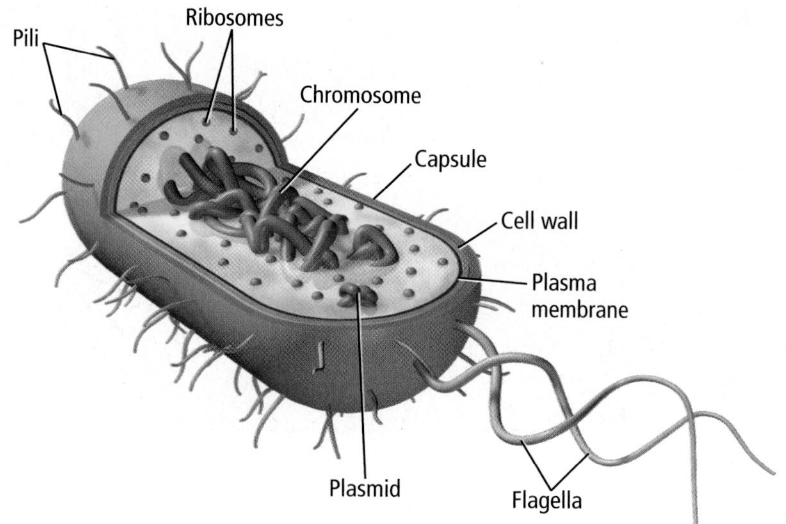


## Prokaryote Structure

Prokaryotes are microscopic, unicellular organisms. They have some characteristics of all cells, such as DNA and ribosomes, but they lack a nuclear membrane and other membrane-bound organelles, such as mitochondria and chloroplasts. Although a prokaryotic cell is very small and doesn't have membrane-bound organelles, it has all it needs to carry out life functions. Examine **Figure 18.3** as you read about the structure of prokaryotic cells.

**Chromosomes** The chromosomes in prokaryotes are arranged differently than the chromosomes found in eukaryotic cells. Their genes are found on a large, circular chromosome in an area of the cell called the **nucleoid.** Many prokaryotes also have at least one smaller piece of DNA, called a *plasmid,* which also has a circular arrangement.

**Capsule** Some prokaryotes secrete a layer of polysaccharides around the cell wall, forming a **capsule,** illustrated in **Figure 18.3.** The capsule has several important functions, including preventing the cell from drying out and helping the cell attach to surfaces in its environment. The capsule also helps prevent the bacteria from being engulfed by white blood cells and shelters the cell from the effects of antibiotics.

**LAUNCH Lab**

**Review** Based on what you've read about bacterial cells, how would you now answer the analysis questions?

**Pili** Structures called pili are found on the outer surface of some bacteria. **Pili** (singular, pilus) are submicroscopic, hairlike structures that are made of protein. Pili help bacterial cells attach to surfaces. Pili also can serve as a bridge between cells. Copies of plasmids can be sent across the bridge, thus providing some prokaryotes with new genetic characteristics. This is one way of transferring the resistance to antibiotics.

**Size** Even when using a typical light microscope, prokaryotes are small when magnified 400 times. Prokaryotes are typically only 1 to 10 micrometers long and 0.7 to 1.5 micrometers wide. Study **Figure 18.4,** which shows a bacterial cell and a human cell. Notice the relative size of bacterial cells found adjacent to a cheek cell.

Recall from Chapter 9 that small cells have a larger, more favorable surface area-to-volume ratio than large cells. Because prokaryotes are so small, nutrients and other substances the cells need can diffuse to all parts of the cell easily.

Figure 18.4 A size comparison shows how a human cheek cell is much larger than bacteria found in a human mouth.

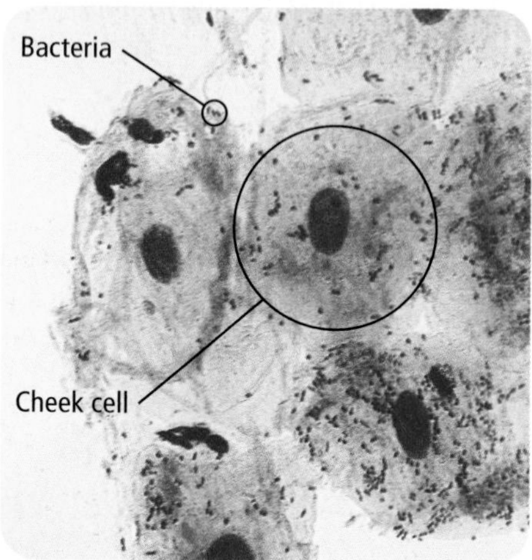


Stained LM Magnification: 400×

## Identifying Prokaryotes

As with other types of organisms, prokaryotes now can be identified using molecular techniques. By comparing DNA, evolutionary relationships can be determined. Historically, scientists identified bacteria using criteria such as shape, cell wall, and movement.

**Shape** There are three general shapes of prokaryotes, as shown in **Figure 18.5.** Spherical or round prokaryotes are called cocci (KAHK ki) (singular, coccus), rod-shaped prokaryotes are called bacilli (buh SIH li) (singular, bacillus), and spiral-shaped prokaryotes, or spirilli (spi RIH li) (singular, spirillium), are called spirochetes (SPI ruh keets).

**Cell walls** Scientists also classify eubacteria according to the composition of their cell walls. All eubacterial cells have peptidoglycan in their cell walls. Peptidoglycan is made of disaccarides and peptide fragments. Biologists add dyes to the bacteria to identify the two major types of bacteria—those with and those without an outer layer of lipid, in a technique called a Gram stain.

Bacteria with a large amount of peptidoglycan appear dark purple once they are stained, and are called gram positive. Bacteria with the lipid layer have less peptidoglycan and appear a light pink after staining. These bacteria are called gram negative. Because some antibiotics work by attacking the cell wall of bacteria, physicians need to know the type of cell wall that is present in the bacteria they suspect is causing illness in order to prescribe the proper antibiotic.

**Movement** Although some prokaryotes are stationary, other bacteria use flagella for movement. Prokaryotic flagella are made of filaments, unlike the flagella of eukaryotes that are made of microtubules . Flagella help prokaryotes to move toward light, higher oxygen concentration, or chemicals such as sugar or amino acids that they need to survive. Other prokaryotes move by gliding over a layer of secreted slime.

Color-Enhanced SEM Magnification: 6500×

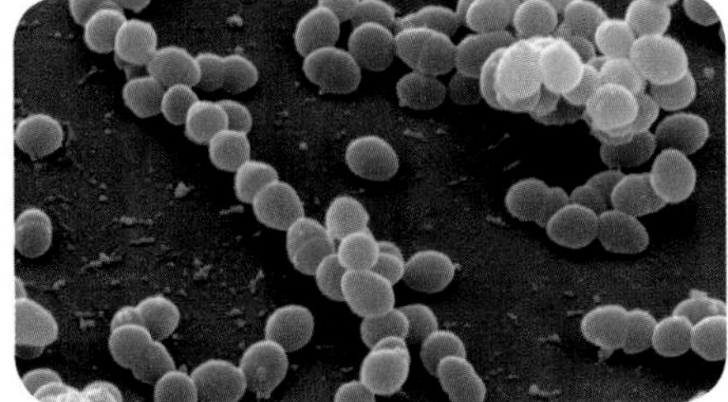

**Cocci**

Color-Enhanced SEM Magnification: 50,000×

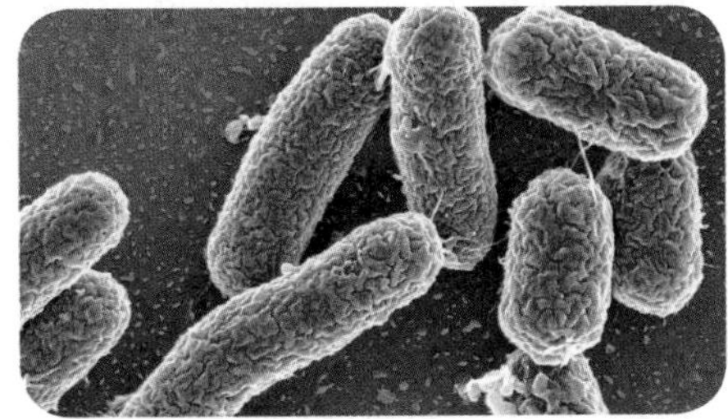

**Bacilli**

Color-Enhanced SEM Magnification: 2000×

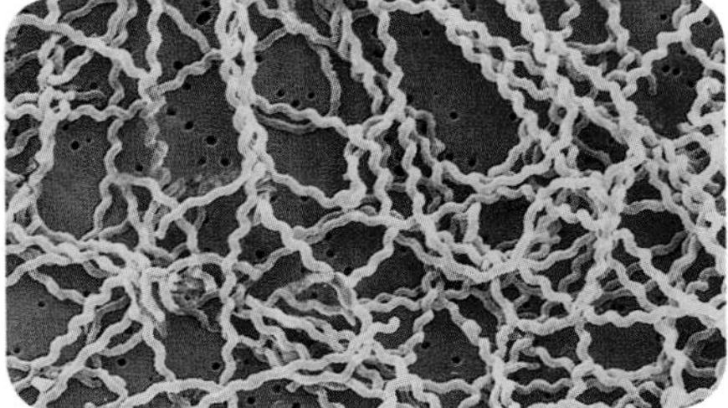

**Spirochetes**

■ **Figure 18.5** There are three shapes of prokaryotes: cocci, bacilli, and spirochetes.

## MiniLab 18.1

### Classify Bacteria

**What types of characteristics are used to divide bacteria into groups?** Bacteria can be stained to show the differences in peptidoglycan (PG) in their cell walls. Based on this difference in their cell walls, bacteria are divided into two main groups.

**Procedure**

1. Read and complete the lab safety form.
2. Choose four different **slides of bacteria** that have been stained to show cell wall differences. The slides will be labeled with the names of the bacteria and marked either thick PG layer or thin PG layer.
3. Use the oil immersion lens of your **microscope** to observe the four slides.
4. Record all of your observations, including those about the cell color, in a table.

**Analysis**

1. **Interpret Data** Based on your observations, make a hypothesis about how to differentiate between the two groups of bacteria.
2. **Describe** two different cell shapes you saw on the slides you observed.

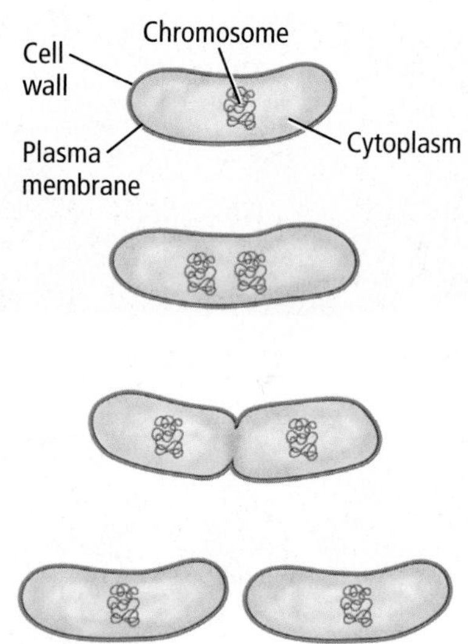


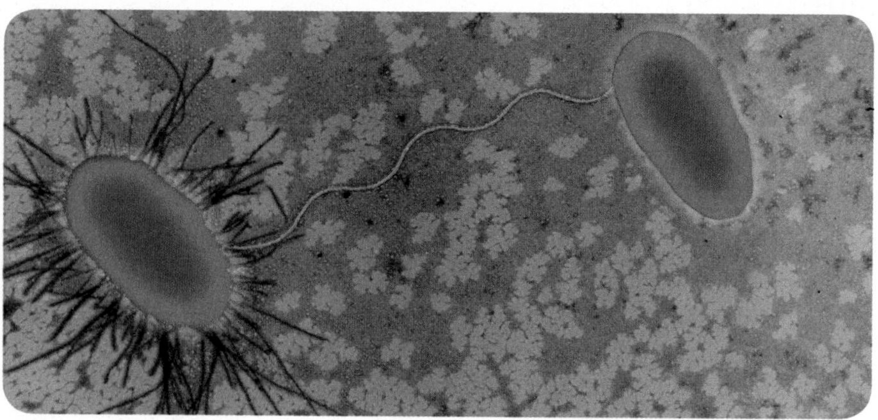


■ **Figure 18.6** Binary fission is an asexual form of reproduction used by some prokaryotes. Conjugation is also an asexual form of reproduction, but it does involve exchange of genetic material.
**Analyze** ***Which means of reproducing shown here exchanges genetic information?***

## Reproduction of Prokaryotes

Most prokaryotes reproduce by an asexual process called binary fission, illustrated in **Figure 18.6.** **Binary fission** is the division of a cell into two genetically identical cells. In this process, the prokaryotic chromosome replicates, and the original chromosome and the new copy separate. As this occurs, the cell gets larger by elongating. A new piece of plasma membrane and cell wall forms and separates the cell into two identical cells. Under ideal environmental conditions, this can occur quickly, as often as every 20 minutes. If conditions are just right, one bacterium could become one billion bacteria through binary fission in just ten hours.

Some prokaryotes exhibit a form of reproduction called **conjugation,** in which two prokaryotes attach to each other and exchange genetic information. As shown in **Figure 18.6,** the pilus is important for the attachment of the two cells so that there can be a transfer of genetic material from one cell to the other. In this way, new gene combinations are created and diversity of prokaryote populations is increased.

## Metabolism of Prokaryotes

Eubacteria and archaebacteria can be grouped based on how they obtain energy for cellular respiration, as shown in **Figure 18.7.** Some bacteria are heterotrophs, meaning they cannot synthesize their own food and must take in nutrients. Many heterotrophic eubacteria are saprotrophs, or saprobes. They obtain their energy by decomposing organic molecules associated with dead organisms or organic waste.

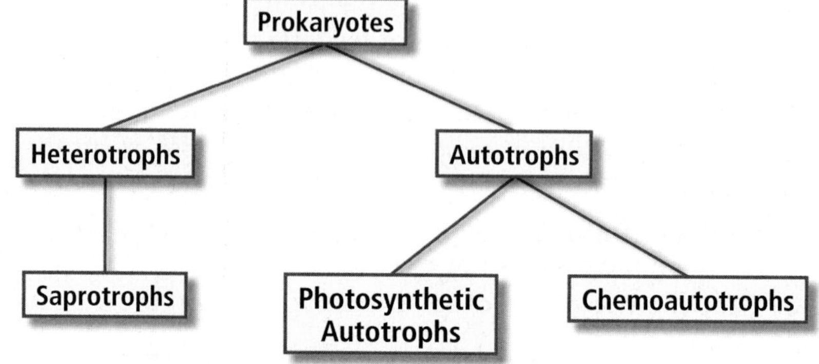


■ **Figure 18.7** Prokaryotes are grouped according to how they obtain nutrients for energy. Heterotrophic bacteria can also be saprotrophs; autotrophs can be photosynthetic or chemoautotrophic.

**Photoautotrophs** Some bacteria are photosynthetic autotrophs (AW tuh trohfs)—they carry out photosynthesis in a similar manner as plants. These bacteria must live in areas where there is light, such as shallow ponds and streams, in order to synthesize organic molecules to use as food.

Scientists once thought that these organisms were eukaryotes and called them blue-green algae. Later, it was discovered that they were prokaryotes and they were renamed cyanobacteria. These bacteria, like plants, are ecologically important because they are at the base of some food chains and release oxygen into the environment. Cyanobacteria are thought to have been the first group of organisms to release oxygen into Earth's early atmosphere, approximately three billion years ago.

*Study Tip*

**Summarization** Write a summary paragraph that addresses the diversity of prokaryotes, how they reproduce, and the importance of prokaryotes.

**Chemoautotrophs** A second type of bacteria that are autotrophs do not require light for energy. These organisms are called chemoautotrophs. They break down and release inorganic compounds that contain nitrogen or sulfur, such as ammonia and hydrogen sulfide, in a process called chemosynthesis. Some chemoautotrophs are important ecologically because they keep nitrogen and other inorganic compounds cycling through ecosystems.

**Aerobes and Anaerobes** Bacteria also vary in whether or not they can grow in the presence of oxygen. Obligate aerobes are bacteria that require oxygen to grow. Anaerobic bacteria do not use oxygen for growth or metabolism; these bacteria are called obligate anaerobes. Obligate anaerobes obtain energy through fermentation. Another group of bacteria, called facultative anaerobes, can grow either in the presence of oxygen or anaerobically by using fermentation.

## Survival of Bacteria

How can bacteria survive if their environment becomes unfavorable? They have several mechanisms that help them survive such environmental challenges as lack of water, extreme temperature change, and lack of nutrients.

**Endospores** When environmental conditions are harsh, some types of bacteria produce a structure called an **endospore.** The bacteria that cause anthrax, botulism, and tetanus are examples of endospore producers. An endospore can be thought of as a dormant cell. Endospores are resistant to harsh environments and might be able to survive extreme heat, extreme cold, dehydration, and large amounts of ultraviolet radiation. Any of these conditions would kill a typical bacterial cell.

As illustrated in **Figure 18.8,** when a bacterium is exposed to harsh environments, a spore coat surrounds a copy of the bacterial cell's chromosome and a small part of the cytoplasm. The bacterium itself might die, but the endospore remains. When environmental conditions become favorable again, the endospore grows, or germinates, into a new bacterial cell. Endospores are able to survive for long periods of time. Because a bacterial cell usually only produces one endospore, this is considered a survival mechanism rather than a type of reproduction.

**Figure 18.8** Endospores can survive extreme environmental conditions.

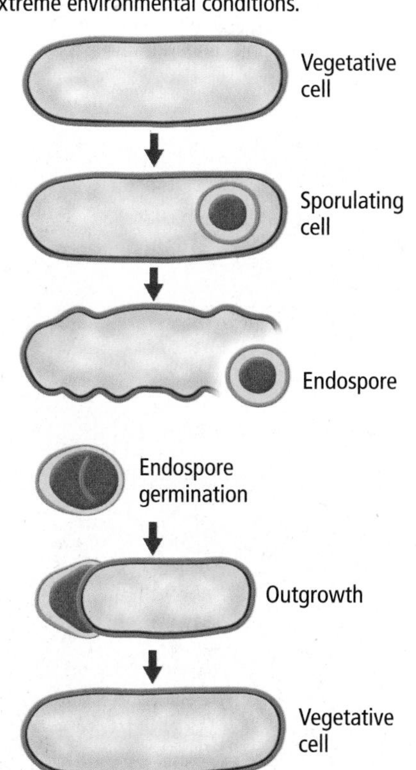

**Mutations** If the environment changes and bacteria are not well adapted to the new conditions, extinction of the bacteria is a possibility. Because bacteria reproduce quickly and their population grows rapidly, genetic mutations can help bacteria survive in changing environments. Mutations, which are changes or random errors in a DNA sequence, lead to new forms of genes, new gene combinations, new characteristics, and genetic diversity. If the environment happens to change, some bacteria in a population might have the right combination of genes to allow them to survive and reproduce. From the human point of view, this can lead to problems, such as antibiotic-resistant bacteria, as you will learn more about in Chapter 37.

**CAREERS IN BIOLOGY**

**Food Scientist** Food scientists help protect the flavor, color, texture, nutritional quality, and safety of our food. They test for amounts of nutrients and presence of harmful organisms such as bacteria. For more information on biology careers, visit biologygmh.com.

## Ecology of Bacteria

When many people think of bacteria, they immediately think of germs or disease. Most bacteria do not cause disease, and many are beneficial. In fact, it has been said that humans owe their lives to bacteria because they help fertilize fields, recycle nutrients, protect the body, and produce foods and medicines.

**Nutrient cycling and nitrogen fixation** In Chapter 2, you learned how nutrients are cycled in an ecosystem. Some organisms get their energy from the cells and tissues of dead organisms and are called decomposers or detrivores. Bacteria are decomposers, returning vital nutrients to the environment. Without nutrient recycling, all raw materials necessary for life would be used up. Without nitrogen fixation, far more fertilizer would be needed for growing plants.

**Connection to Chemistry** All forms of life require nitrogen. Nitrogen is a key component of amino acids, the building blocks of proteins. Nitrogen also is needed to make DNA and RNA. Most of Earth's nitrogen is found in the atmosphere in the form of nitrogen gas ($N_2$). Certain types of bacteria can use nitrogen gas directly. These bacteria have enzymes that can convert nitrogen gas into nitrogen compounds by a process called nitrogen fixation. Some of these bacteria live in the soil.

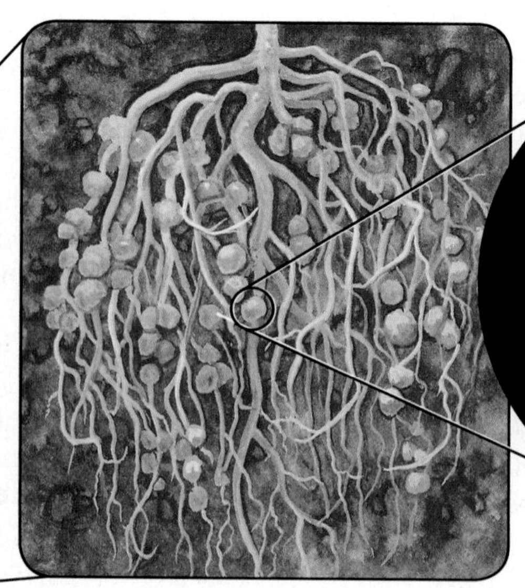

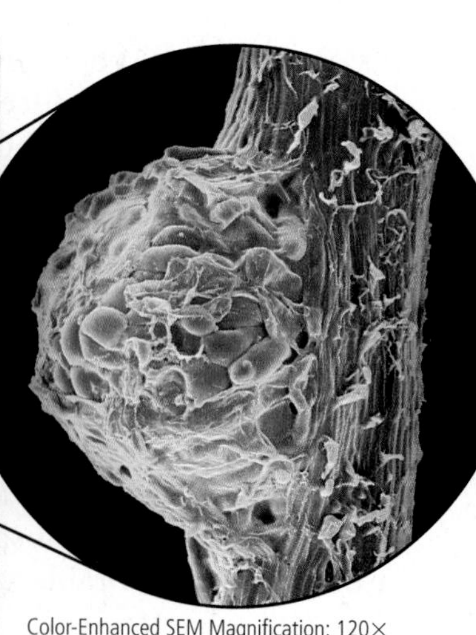

Color-Enhanced SEM Magnification: 120×

**Figure 18.9** Nitrogen-fixing bacteria on a plant root nodule are able to remove nitrogen from the air and convert it into a form the plant can use.

# CHAPTER 18 Assessment

## Section 18.1

### Vocabulary Review

*For each set of terms below, choose the one that does not belong and explain why it does not belong.*

1. capsule—pilus—endospore
2. binary fission—nitrogen fixation—conjugation
3. endospore—nucleoid—nitrogen fixation

### Understand Key Concepts

4. Which organism is not included in Domain Archaea?
   **A.** cyanobacteria
   **B.** methanogens
   **C.** halophilic bacteria
   **D.** thermoacidophilic bacteria

5. Why is an electron microscope useful when studying bacteria?
   **A.** Electrons can penetrate through the capsule surrounding bacteria.
   **B.** Bacteria are tiny.
   **C.** Bacteria move so quickly; the electrons stun the bacteria.
   **D.** Bacteria organelles are small and tightly packed together.

*Use the figure below to answer questions 6 and 7.*

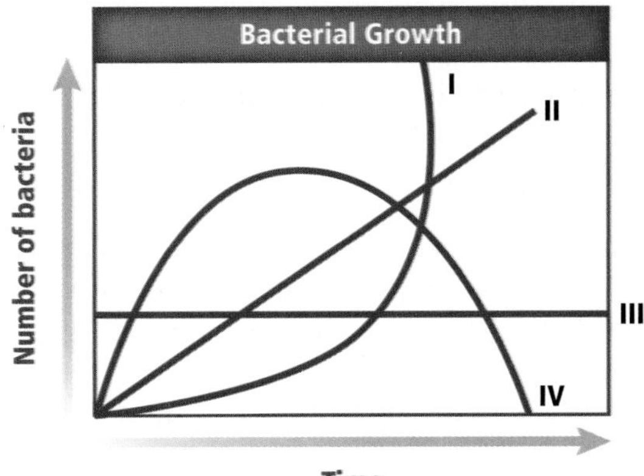


6. Which line on the graph best indicates the growth rate of a population of bacteria living in ideal conditions?
   **A.** line I  **C.** line III
   **B.** line II  **D.** line IV

7. Which line on the graph best indicates the growth rate of a population of bacteria exposed to an effective antibiotic?
   **A.** line I  **C.** line III
   **B.** line II  **D.** line IV

8. You have just been named a contestant on the reality show *Fear Factor.* Your first challenge is to swallow microbes. Which would be the most dangerous to swallow?
   **A.** thermoacidophilic bacteria
   **B.** halophilic bacteria
   **C.** *Escherichia coli*
   **D.** a bacteriophage

*Use the photos below to answer question 9.*

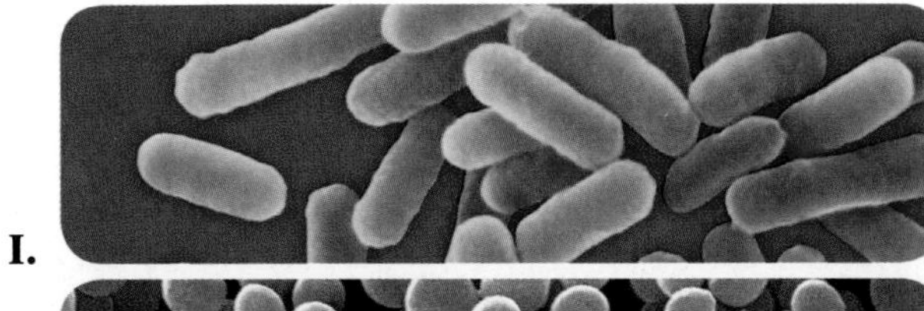
I.

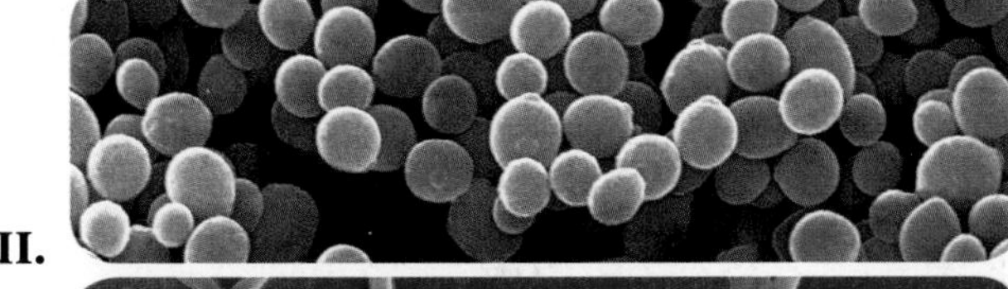
II.

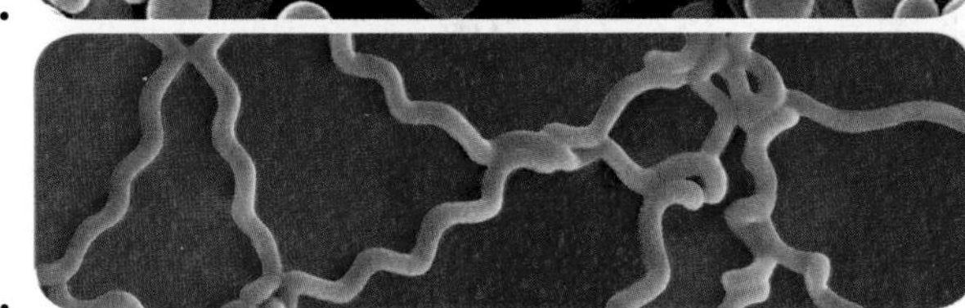
III.

9. Which is the correct identification for the bacteria shown above?
   **A.** I—cocci, II—bacilli, III—spirochetes
   **B.** I—bacilli, II—cocci, III—spirochetes
   **C.** I—spirochetes, II—cocci, III—bacilli
   **D.** I—bacilli, II—spirochetes, III—cocci

10. What is the likely cause of tooth decay?
   **A.** a lysogenic virus infecting the living cells of the tooth
   **B.** bacteria feeding on the sugar in the mouth and producing acid
   **C.** an excess of vitamin K production by mouth bacteria
   **D.** nitrogen-fixing bacteria releasing ammonia that is eroding the tooth enamel

### Constructed Response

11. **Open Ended** Make an argument for or against the following statement: Living organisms on Earth owe their lives to bacteria.
12. **Short Answer** Describe characteristics of bacteria (both at the individual and population level) that make them tough to destroy.
13. **Open Ended** What types of arguments do you think biologists use when they say bacteria were the first organisms on Earth?

### Think Critically

14. **Speculate** what life on Earth might be like if cyanobacteria had never evolved.
15. **Predict** any ecological consequences that would result if all types of nitrogen-fixing bacteria suddenly went extinct.
16. **Describe** some of the diverse characteristics of prokaryotes.

## Section 18.2

### Vocabulary Review

*Use what you know about the vocabulary terms on the Study Guide page to describe what the terms in each pair below have in common.*

17. lytic cycle—lysogenic cycle
18. prion—virus
19. capsid—prion
20. virus—retrovirus

### Understand Key Concepts

21. Viruses contain which substances?
    - **A.** genetic material and a capsid
    - **B.** a nucleus, genetic material, and a capsid
    - **C.** a nucleus, genetic material, a capsid, and ribosomes
    - **D.** a nucleus, genetic material, a capsid, ribosomes, and a plasma membrane

*Use the figure below to answer questions 22 and 23.*

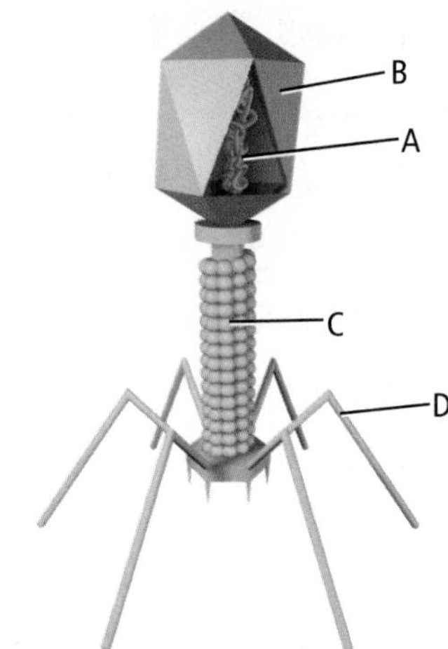


22. Which labeled structure represents the genetic material of a virus?
    - **A.** A
    - **B.** B
    - **C.** C
    - **D.** D
23. Which structure represents the capsid of a virus?
    - **A.** A
    - **B.** B
    - **C.** C
    - **D.** D
24. HIV is a retrovirus. What does this mean?
    - **A.** Viral RNA is used to make DNA.
    - **B.** Viral DNA is used to make RNA.
    - **C.** Protein is made directly from viral RNA.
    - **D.** Protein is made directly from viral DNA.
25. Which statement about prions is true?
    - **A.** Prions are renegade pieces of RNA that infect cells.
    - **B.** Prions are infectious proteins.
    - **C.** Prion-based diseases only affect cows.
    - **D.** Prions are a newly discovered type of genetic material.
26. Imagine that a patient in a hospital has died mysteriously. A doctor suspects the cause of death is Creutzfeldt-Jacob disease. How could this diagnosis be confirmed?
    - **A.** by examining the blood to see if there is a high viral count
    - **B.** by asking the patient's family and friends if the patient consumed a lot of meat
    - **C.** by examining the brain to see if there are a lot of spaces in the tissue
    - **D.** by examining nerve cells to see if they have been affected by a bacterial neurotoxin



Biology Online Chapter Test biologygmh.com

*Use the figure below to answer question 27.*

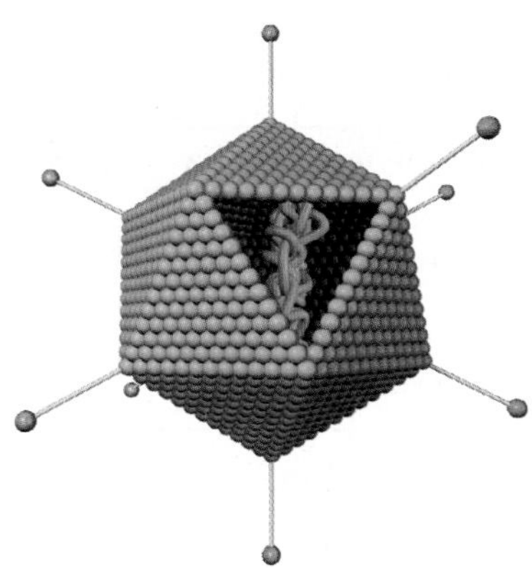

**27.** Which organisms does this virus infect?
  **A.** humans
  **B.** bacteria
  **C.** plants
  **D.** fungi

## Constructed Response

**28. Open Ended** Make an argument for or against the following statement: Viruses are living organisms.

**29. Open Ended** Should people with highly contagious, potentially deadly viruses be quarantined? Defend your response.

**30. Open Ended** Make an argument for or against the following statement: Prions are just viruses that lack a capsid.

## Think Critically

**31. Infer** why it is more difficult to make an antiviral drug that fights a virus that replicates through the lysogenic cycle than it is to make one that fights a virus that replicates through the lytic cycle.

**32. Evaluate** why it is easier to make drugs that fight bacteria than drugs that fight viruses, even though viruses are structurally less complex than bacteria.

**33. Hypothesize** and develop a technique to slow down or stop a viral replication cycle.

**34. Develop** a list of different careers that are associated with bacteria, viruses, and prions.

## Additional Assessment

**35.** *WRITING in* **Biology** Prepare a newspaper article that clearly explains the differences between disease-causing bacteria and viruses.

**36.** *WRITING in* **Biology** **Compose** a sentence that explains each step in the sequence of events in the replication of HIV.

### DBQ Document-Based Questions

U.S. Data: Centers for Disease Control http://www.cdc.gov/flu/avian/pdf/avianflufacts.pdf.
Global Data: Scotland Government http://www.scotland.gov.uk/library5/health/pfle-00.asp

*There were three worldwide influenza epidemics during the twentieth century. The number of deaths is presented in the table below.*

| | Spanish Flu | Asian Flu | Hong Kong Flu |
|---|---|---|---|
| Years | 1918–1919 | 1957–1958 | 1968–1969 |
| U.S. deaths | 500,000 | 70,000 | 34,000 |
| Global deaths | 20–40 million | 1 million | 1–4 million |

**37.** Which epidemic was the most deadly?

**38.** Why were deaths not as high in the United States with the Hong Kong flu compared to the Asian flu, but were higher worldwide?

**39.** Hypothesize why a flu epidemic eventually stops instead of eliminating all human life.

## Cumulative Review

**40.** Explain how the concepts of observation, inference, and skepticism differ. **(Chapter 1)**

**41.** Summarize the overall reactions of photosynthesis and cellular respiration. **(Chapter 8)**

**42.** Summarize how a cancer cell cycle is different than a normal cell cycle. **(Chapter 9)**

**43.** Describe the primate groups that comprise the anthropoids. **(Chapter 16)**

# Standardized Test Practice

**Cumulative**

## Multiple Choice

1. Which primate is an Asian ape?
   A. baboon
   B. gorilla
   C. lemur
   D. orangutan

*Use the chart below to answer questions 2 and 3.*

| Common Name | Scientific Name |
|---|---|
| Grey wolf | *Canis lupus* |
| Red wolf | *Canis rufus* |
| African hunting dog | *Lycaon pictus* |
| Pampas fox | *Pseudalopex gymnocercus* |

2. Which animal is related most closely to the Sechura fox *Pseudalopex sechurae*?
   A. African hunting dog
   B. Grey wolf
   C. Pampas fox
   D. Red wolf

3. Which kind of difference is a valid reason to classify the red wolf and pampas fox in separate genera?
   A. different prey
   B. different region of habitation
   C. different structure of skulls
   D. different age of evolutionary origin

4. Which describes the role of an endospore in bacteria?
   A. a dormant state of bacteria that can survive in unfavorable conditions
   B. a form of sexual reproduction in bacteria during which genetic information is exchanged
   C. a protective covering that bacteria secrete to protect them against harsh environments
   D. a tiny hairlike structure made of proteins that attaches the bacteria to a surface

5. Which information constitutes a scientific hypothesis?
   A. defined data
   B. proven explanation
   C. published conclusion
   D. reasonable guess

*Use the table below to answer questions 6 and 7.*

| Identifying Bacteria | | | |
|---|---|---|---|
| **Bacterial Strain** | **Gram Staining** | **Morphology** | **Related Disease** |
| *Bacillus cereus* | Gram-positive | Rods; arranged in chains | Meningitis |
| *Escherichia coli* | Gram-negative | Cocci | Traveler's diarrhea |
| *Pseudomonas aeruginosa* | Gram-negative | Rod-like; occur in pairs or short chains | Pneumonia |
| *Serratia mercescens* | Gram-negative | Rod-like | Pneumonia |

6. Which kind of bacteria stains Gram-negative and appears rodlike in short chains?
   A. *Bacillus cereus*
   B. *Escherichia coli*
   C. *Pseudomonas aeruginosa*
   D. *Serratia marcescens*

7. Which related disease would be associated with a bacterium that is Gram-negative and in paired rods?
   A. meningitis
   B. cystic fibrosis
   C. pneumonia
   D. traveler's diarrhea

8. Which taxon gives you the most general information about an organism?
   A. class
   B. domain
   C. family
   D. phylum

9. A population of rodents on an island makes up a distinct species that is similar to a species found on the mainland. Which process caused this speciation?
   A. behavioral isolation
   B. geographic isolation
   C. reproductive isolation
   D. temporal isolation

**Reproduction in ciliates** All known ciliates have two kinds of nuclei—the macronucleus and a smaller micronucleus. A cell might contain more than one of each of these nuclei. Both nuclei contain the genetic information for the cell. The macronuclei contain multiple copies of the cell's genome, which controls the everyday functions of the cell such as feeding, waste elimination, and maintaining water balance within the cell. The micronucleus is used for reproduction.

Ciliates reproduce asexually by binary fission. During this process, the macronucleus elongates and splits rather than undergoing mitotic division. Most ciliates maintain genetic variation by undergoing conjugation—a sexual process in which genetic information is exchanged. Conjugation is considered a sexual process, but it is not considered sexual reproduction because new organisms are not formed.

The process of conjugation for *Paramecium caudatum* is typical of most ciliates and is illustrated in **Figure 19.6.** During conjugation, two paramecia form a cytoplasmic bridge and their diploid micronuclei undergo meiosis. After three of the newly formed haploid micronuclei dissolve, the remaining micronucleus undergoes mitosis. One micronucleus from each connected cell is exchanged, and the two paramecia separate. The macronucleus disintegrates in each paramecium, and the micronuclei combine and form a new, diploid macronucleus. Each cell now contains a macronucleus, micronuclei, and a new combination of genetic information.

**Reading Check Explain** the purpose of the cytoplasmic bridge, shown in **Figure 19.6,** during conjugation.

**VOCABULARY**

**SCIENCE USAGE V. COMMON USAGE**

**Conjugation**

***Science usage:*** asexual reproduction in which there is an exchange of genetic information.

*Paramecia reproduce in a process called conjugation.*

***Common usage:*** in grammar an arrangement of the correct form of a verb.

*Victoria is practicing the conjugation of Spanish verbs.*

# DATA ANALYSIS LAB 19.2

**Based on Real Data***

## Recognize Cause and Effect

**How does solution concentration affect the contractile vacuole?** The contractile vacuole moves water from inside a paramecium back into its freshwater environment. Researchers have studied the effects of solution concentrations on paramecia.

### Data and Observations

Paramecia were allowed to adapt to various solutions for 12 h. Then, they were placed into hypertonic and hypotonic solutions. The graphs show the change in rate of water flow out of the contractile vacuole over time.

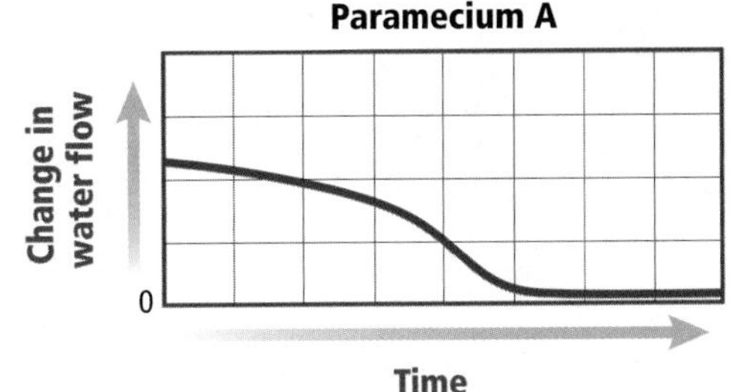


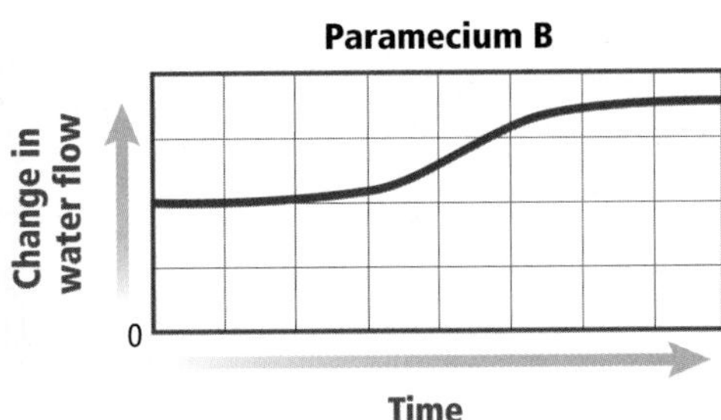


### Think Critically

1. **Analyze** What do the downward and upward slopes in the graphs indicate about the contractile vacuole?
2. **Infer** which paramecium was placed into a hypertonic solution. Explain.

*Data obtained from: Stock, et al. 2001. How external osmolarity affects the activity of the contractile vacuole complex, the cytosolic osmolarity and the water permeability of the plasma membrane in *Paramecium Multimicronucleatum. The Journal of Experimental Biology* 204: 291–304.

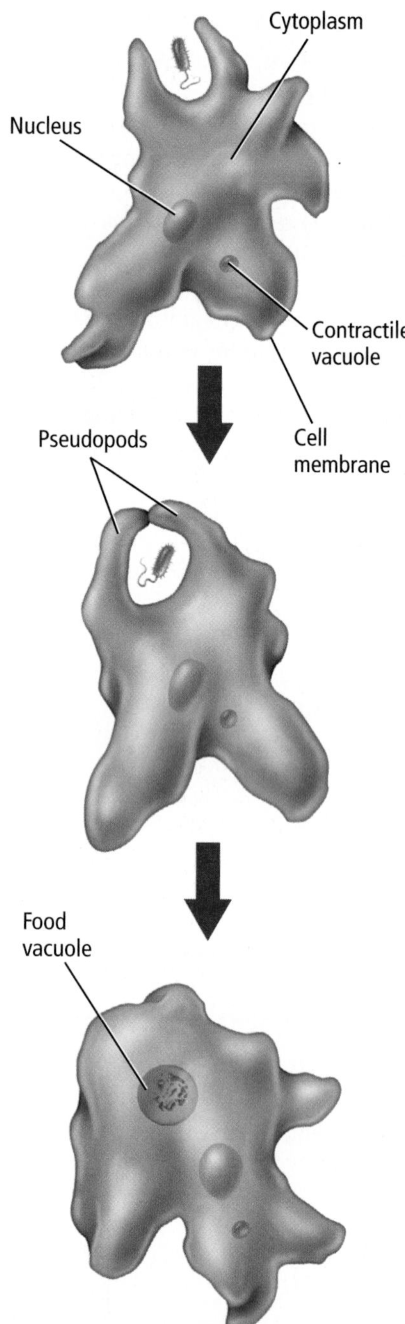


■ **Figure 19.7** Chemical stimuli from smaller organisms can cause the amoeba to form pseudopods from their cell membrane.

## Sarcodina

Members of the phylum Sarcodina (sar kuh DI nuh), also called sarcodines (SAR kuh dinez), are animal-like protists that use pseudopods for feeding and locomotion. A **pseudopod** (SEW duh pahd) is a temporary extension of cytoplasm and is shown in **Figure 19.7.** These extensions surround and envelop a smaller organism, forming a food vacuole. Digestive enzymes are secreted and break down the captured organism.

Some of the most commonly studied sarcodines are found in the genus *Amoeba.* Most amoebas are found in saltwater, although some freshwater species live in streams, in the muddy bottoms of ponds, and in damp patches of moss and leaves. Some amoebas are parasites that live inside an animal host.

**Amoeba structure** The structure of an amoeba is simple, as shown in **Figure 19.7.** Amoebas are enveloped in an outer cell membrane and an inner thickened cytoplasm called ectoplasm. Inside the ectoplasm, the cytoplasm contains a nucleus, food vacuoles, and occasionally a contractile vacuole. Notice that an amoeba does not have an anal pore like the paramecium. Waste products and undigested food particles are excreted by diffusion through the outer membrane into the surrounding water. The oxygen needed for cellular processes also diffuses into the cell from the surrounding water.

Foraminiferans (fuh rah muh NIH fur unz) and radiolarians (ray dee oh LER ee unz)are types of amoebas that have tests. A **test** is a hard, porous covering similar to a shell, which surrounds the cell membrane. Most of these amoebas live in marine environments, although there are some freshwater species.

**Connection to Earth Science** Foraminiferans have tests made of calcium carbonate ($CaCO_3$), grains of sand, and other particles cemented together. Geologists use the fossilized remains of foraminiferans to determine the age of some rocks and sediments, and to identify possible sites for oil drilling. Radiolarians, another amoeba with tests shown in **Figure 19.8,** have tests made mostly of silica ($SiO_2$).

**Amoeba reproduction** Amoebas reproduce by asexual reproduction during which a parent cell divides into two identical offspring. During harsh environmental conditions, some amoebas become cysts that help them survive until environmental conditions improve and survival is more likely.

SEM Magnification: 190×

■ **Figure 19.8**
Radiolarians have tests made of silica. Foraminiferans and radiolarians extend their pseudopods through openings in their tests.

## Apicomplexa

Animal-like protists that belong to the phylum Apicomplexa (ay puh KOM pleks uh) also are known as sporozoans (spo ruh ZOH unz). They are called sporozoans because they produce spores at some point in their life cycle. Spores are reproductive cells that form without fertilization and produce a new organism. Sporozoans lack contractile vacuoles and methods for locomotion. As in amoebas, respiration and excretion occur by diffusion through the plasma membrane.

All sporozoans are parasitic. Recall from Chapter 2 that parasites get their nutritional requirements from a host organism. Sporozoans infect vertebrates and invertebrates by living as internal parasites. Organelles at one end of the organism are specialized for penetrating host cells and tissues, allowing them to get their nutrients from their host.

The life cycle of sporozoans has both sexual and asexual stages. Often two or more hosts are required for an organism to complete a life cycle. The life cycle of *Plasmodium* is shown in **Figure 19.9.**

Sporozoans cause a variety of illnesses in humans, some of which are fatal. The sporozoans responsible for the greatest number of human deaths are found in the genus *Plasmodium.* These parasites cause malaria in humans and are transmitted to humans by female *Anopheles* mosquitoes. Malaria causes fever, chills, and other flu-like symptoms. Its greatest impact is in tropical and subtropical regions where factors such as high temperature, humidity, and rainfall favor the growth of mosquitoes and sporozoans, and preventative measures are too costly.

**VOCABULARY**

**WORD ORIGIN**

**Apicomplexa**

***apicalis*** from Latin; meaning *uppermost point or tip*

***complexus*** from Latin; meaning *comprised of multiple objects*

**Figure 19.9** Malaria is caused by a sporozoan transmitted by a mosquito.
**Identify** ***What are the two hosts that are required for this sporozoan to be successful?***

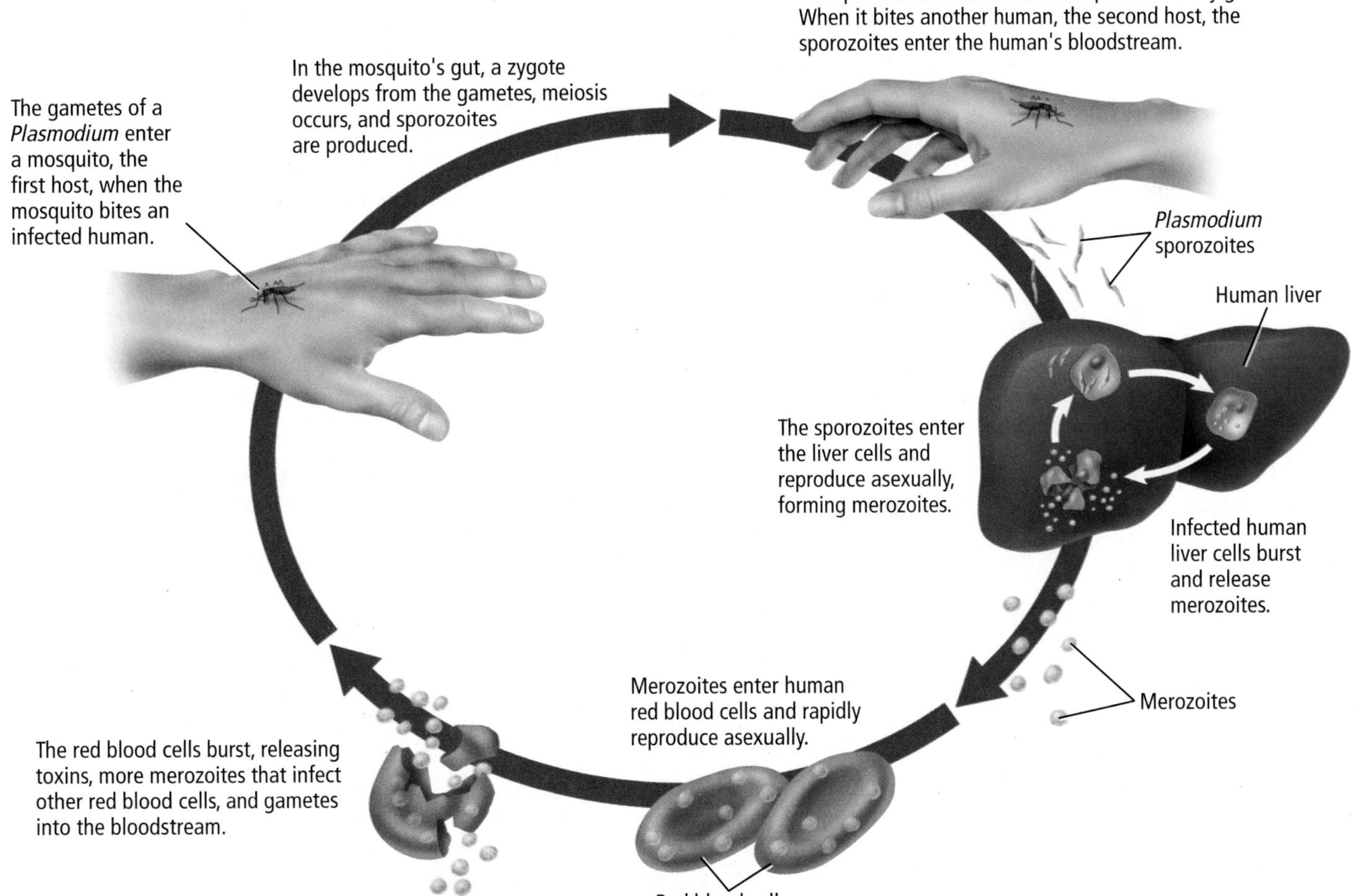

The gametes of a *Plasmodium* enter a mosquito, the first host, when the mosquito bites an infected human.
In the mosquito's gut, a zygote develops from the gametes, meiosis occurs, and sporozoites are produced.
The sporozoites travel to the mosquito's salivary glands. When it bites another human, the second host, the sporozoites enter the human's bloodstream.
*Plasmodium* sporozoites
Human liver
The sporozoites enter the liver cells and reproduce asexually, forming merozoites.
Infected human liver cells burst and release merozoites.
Merozoites
Merozoites enter human red blood cells and rapidly reproduce asexually.
Red blood cells
The red blood cells burst, releasing toxins, more merozoites that infect other red blood cells, and gametes into the bloodstream.

**Reduviid bug**

**Tsetse fly**

■ **Figure 19.10** The insects that carry protozoans from person to person are controlled by insecticides.

## Zoomastigina

Protozoans in the phylum Zoomastigina (zoh oh mast tuh JI nuh) are called zooflagellates. Zooflagellates (zoh oh FLA juh layts) are animal-like protozoans that use flagella for movement. Recall from Chapter 7 that flagella are long whiplike projections that protrude from the cell and are used for movement. Some zooflagellates are free living, but many are parasites inside other organisms.

At least three species of zooflagellates from the genus *Trypanosoma* (TRY pan uh zohm uh) cause infectious diseases in humans that often are fatal because of limited treatment options. One species found in Central and South America causes Chagas disease, sometimes called American sleeping sickness. The second species causes East African sleeping sickness. The third species causes West African sleeping sickness.

**American sleeping sickness** The zooflagellates that cause Chagas' disease are similar to the sporozoans that cause malaria because they have two hosts in their life cycle and insects spread the diseases through the human population. The reduviid bug (rih DEW vee id) bug, shown in **Figure 19.10,** serves as one host for the protist in Central and South America. The parasitic zooflagellates reproduce in the gut of this insect. The reduviid bug gets its nutrients by sucking blood from a human host. During the feeding process, the zooflagellates pass out of the reduviid body through its feces. The zooflagellates enter the human body through the wound site or mucus membranes. Once the zooflagellate enters the body, it multiplies in the bloodstream and can damage the heart, liver, and spleen.

**African sleeping sickness** The life cycles of the zooflagellates that cause both African sleeping sicknesses are similar to the one that causes American sleeping sickness. The insect host is the tsetse (SEET see) fly, shown in **Figure 19.10.** The blood-sucking tsetse fly becomes infected when it feeds on an infected human or other mammal. The zooflagellate reproduces in the gut of the fly and then migrates to its salivary glands. When the fly bites the human, the zooflagellate is transferred to the human host. The zooflagellates reproduce in the human host and cause fever, inflammation of the lymph nodes, and damage to the nervous system.

## Section 19.2 Assessment

### Section Summary

- Protozoans are single-celled protists that feed on other organisms to obtain nutrients.
- Protozoans live in a variety of aquatic environments.
- Protozoans reproduce in a variety of ways, including sexually and asexually.
- Protozoans have specialized methods for movement, feeding, and maintaining homeostasis.

### Understand Main Ideas

1. MAIN Idea **Compare** the methods of feeding, locomotion, and reproduction of three groups of protozoa.
2. **Explain** the function of three organelles found in protozoans.
3. **Diagram** and explain the life cycle of a member of the genus *Plasmodium*.
4. **Explain** why paramecium conjugation is not considered reproduction.

### Think Scientifically

5. *WRITING in* **Biology** Create an informational brochure about zooflagellates for people living in South America.
6. **MATH in Biology** There are approximately 50,000 species of protozoa, of which about 7000 are ciliates. What percentage of protozoans are ciliates?

Section 19.3

## Algae—Plantlike Protists

### Objectives

- **Describe** the characteristics of several phyla of algae.
- **Identify** secondary photosynthetic pigments that are characteristic of some algae.
- **Explain** how diatoms differ from most other types of algae.

### Review Vocabulary

**chloroplasts:** chlorophyll-containing organelles found in the cells of green plants and some protists that capture light energy and convert it to chemical energy

### New Vocabulary

bioluminescent
colony
alternation of generations

**MAIN Idea** **Algae are plantlike, autotrophic protists that are the producers for aquatic ecosystems.**

**Real-World Reading Link** Have you ever looked at a group of people and wondered what they had in common? You might discover that they all like the same type of music or they like the same type of sports. Most plantlike protists have something in common—they make their own food.

## Characteristics of Algae

The group of protists called algae (singular, alga) is considered plantlike because the members contain photosynthetic pigments. Recall from Chapter 8 that photosynthetic pigments enable organisms to produce their own food using energy from the Sun in a process called photosynthesis. Algae differ from plants because they do not have roots, leaves, or other structures typical of plants.

The light-absorbing pigments of algae are found in chloroplasts. In many algae, the primary pigment is chlorophyll—the same pigment that gives plants their characteristic green color. Many algae also have secondary pigments that allow them to absorb light energy in deep water. As water depth increases, much of the sunlight's energy is absorbed by the water. These secondary pigments allow algae to absorb light energy from wavelengths that are not absorbed by water. Because these secondary pigments reflect light at different wavelengths, algae are found in a variety of colors, as shown in **Figure 19.11.**

**Reading Check** **Explain** the function of chloroplasts and photosynthetic pigments in algae.

LM Magnification: 160×

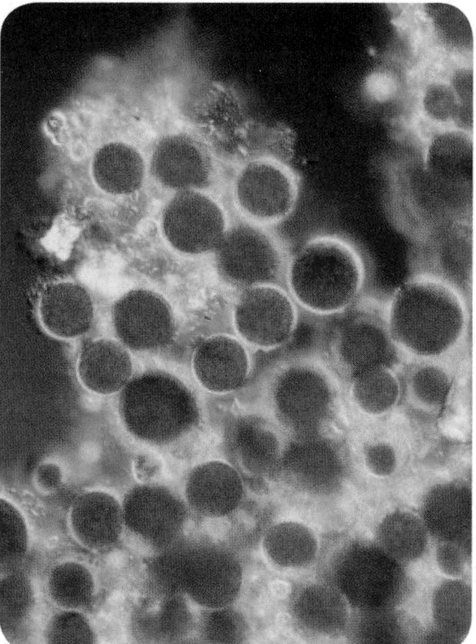

**Red algae**

LM Magnification: 250×

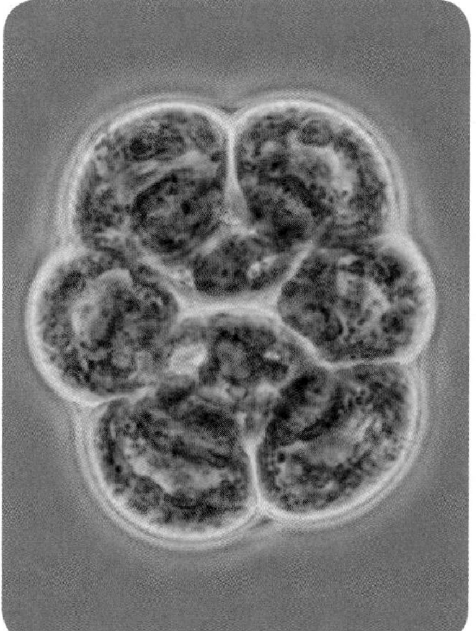

**Green algae**

■ **Figure 19.11** Algae vary in color because they contain different light-absorbing pigments.

LM Magnification: 30×

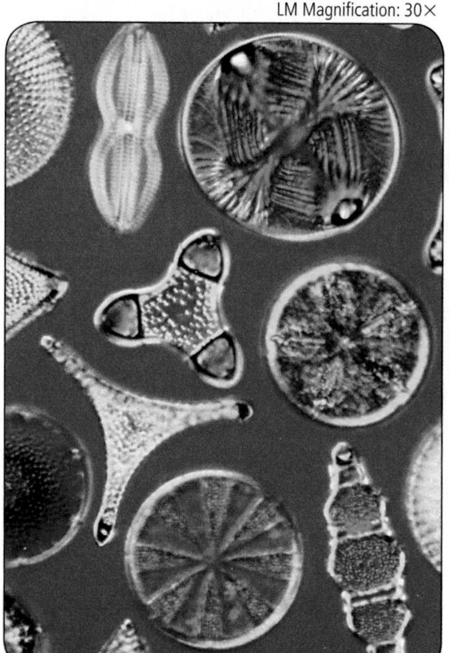

■ **Figure 19.12** The various species of diatoms have different shapes and sizes.

## Diversity of Algae

Algae have more differences than their color. For example, many algae exist as single cells, whereas others are huge multicellular organisms reaching 65 m in length. Some unicellular algae are referred to as phytoplankton—meaning "plant plankton." Phytoplankton is vital in aquatic ecosystems because it provides the base of the food web in these environments. As a by-product of photosynthesis, they also produce much of the oxygen found in Earth's atmosphere.

The great diversity of algae makes them a challenge to classify. Algologists usually use three criteria to classify algae: the type of chlorophyll and secondary pigments, the method of food storage, and the composition of the cell wall.

**Diatoms** The unicellular algae, shown in **Figure 19.12,** are members of the phylum Bacillariophyta (BAH sih LAYR ee oh FI tuh). These intricately shaped organisms are called diatoms. Look at **Figure 19.13** and notice that the diatom consists of two unequal halves—one fits neatly inside the other, forming a small box with a lid.

**Connection to Physics** Diatoms are photosynthetic autotrophs. They produce food by photosynthesis using chlorophyll and secondary pigments called carotenoids, which give diatoms their golden-yellow color. Diatoms store their food as oil instead of as a carbohydrate. The oil not only makes diatoms a nutritious food source for many marine animals, but it also provides buoyancy. Oil is less dense than water, so diatoms float closer to the surface of the water, where they can absorb energy from the Sun for photosynthesis.

Diatoms reproduce both sexually and asexually, as illustrated in **Figure 19.14.** Asexual reproduction occurs when the two separated halves each create a new half that can fit inside the old one. This process produces increasingly smaller diatoms. When a diatom is about one-quarter of the original size, sexual reproduction is triggered and gametes are produced. The gametes fuse to form a zygote that develops into a full-sized diatom. The reproduction cycle then repeats.

The hard silica walls of the diatom last long after the diatom has died. The silica walls accumulate on the ocean floor to form sediment known as diatomaceous earth. This sediment is collected and used as an abrasive and a filtering agent. The gritty texture of many tooth polishes and metal polishes is due to the presence of diatom shells.

**CAREERS IN BIOLOGY**

**Algologist** A biologist who specializes in the study of algae is an algologist. Algologists might work at fish hatcheries or conduct marine research. For more information on biology careers, visit biologygmh.com.

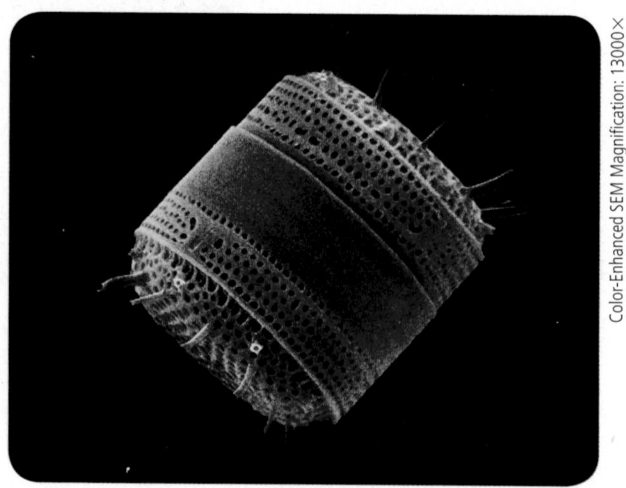

Color-Enhanced SEM Magnification: 13000×

■ **Figure 19.13** Diatoms are found in both marine and freshwater environments. A unique feature of the diatom is its cell wall made of silica.

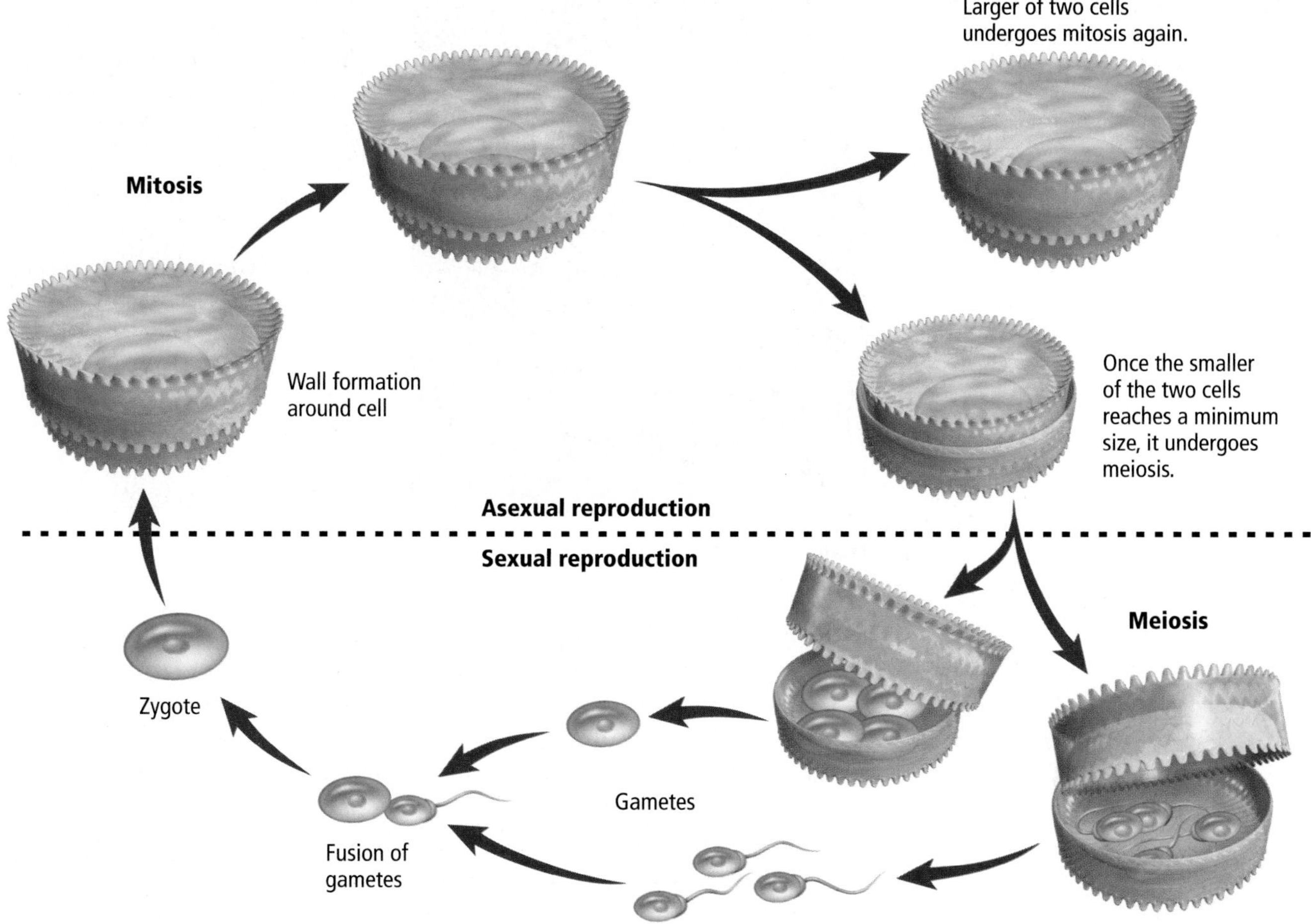
Larger of two cells
undergoes mitosis again.
Mitosis
Wall formation
around cell
Once the smaller
of the two cells
reaches a minimum
size, it undergoes
meiosis.
Asexual reproduction
Sexual reproduction
Meiosis
Zygote
Gametes
Fusion of
gametes

**Figure 19.14** Diatoms reproduce asexually for several generations before undergoing sexual reproduction.

**Dinoflagellates** Plantlike protists that are members of the phylum Pyrrophyta (puh RAH fuh tuh) are called dinoflagellates (di nuh FLA juh layts). Most members of the phylum are unicellular and have two flagella at right angles to one another. As these flagella beat, a spinning motion is created, so dinoflagellates spin as they move through the water. Some members in this group have cell walls made of thick cellulose plates that resemble helmets or suits of armor. Other members of this group are **bioluminescent,** which means they emit light. Although there are a few freshwater dinoflagellates, most are found in saltwater. Like diatoms, photosynthetic dinoflagellates are a major component of phytoplankton.

Dinoflagellates vary in how they get their nutritional requirements. Some dinoflagellates are photosynthetic autotrophs, and other species are heterotrophs. The heterotrophic dinoflagellates can be carnivorous, parasitic, or mutualistic. Mutualistic dinoflagellates have relationships with organisms such as jellyfishes, mollusks, and coral.

**Algal blooms** When food is plentiful and environmental conditions are favorable, dinoflagellates reproduce in great numbers. These population explosions are called blooms. Algal blooms can be harmful when they deplete the nutrients in the water. When the food supply diminishes, the dinoflagellates die in large numbers. As the dead algae decompose, the oxygen supply in the water is depleted, suffocating fish and other marine organisms. Additional fish suffocate when their gills become clogged with the dinoflagellates.

**VOCABULARY**

**WORD ORIGIN**

**Pyrrophyta**
***pyro–*** prefix; from Greek; meaning *fire*
***–phyton*** from Greek word *phyton*, meaning *plant.*

■ **Figure 19.15** The microscopic organism *Gonyaulax catanella* is one species of dinoflagellates that causes red tides. During red tides, many marine organisms die and shellfish can be too toxic for humans to eat.

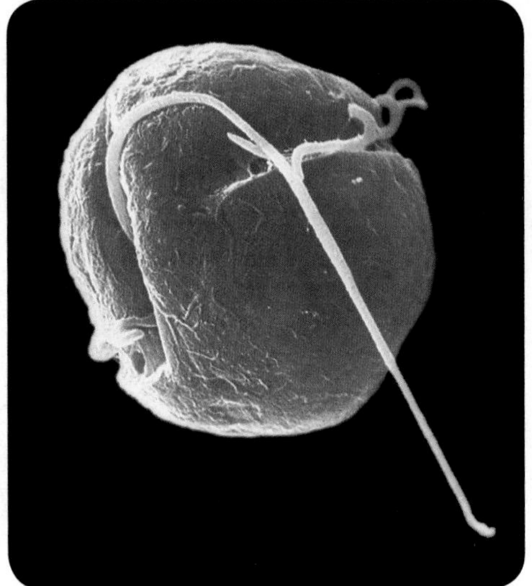


***Gonyaulax catanella***

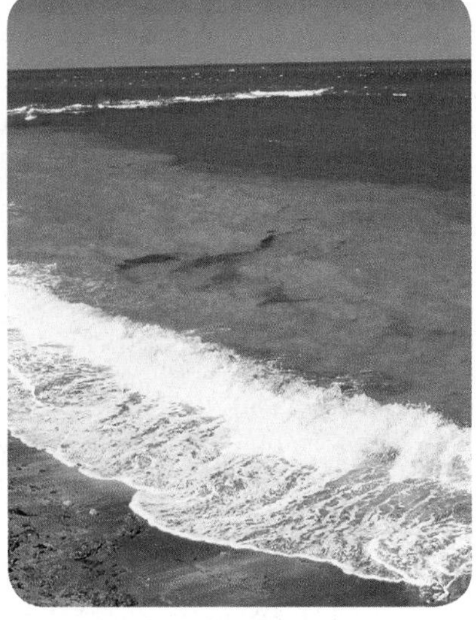

**Red tide**

**Red tides** Some dinoflagellates have red photosynthetic pigments, and when they bloom, the ocean is tinged red, as shown in **Figure 19.15.** These blooms are called red tides. Red tides can be a serious threat to humans because some species of dinoflagellates produce a potentially lethal nerve toxin. The toxins affect people primarily when people eat shellfish. Shellfish that feed by filtering particles ingest the toxic dinoflagellates from the water. The toxins become concentrated in tissues of the shellfish. People and other organisms can become seriously ill or die from consuming these toxic shellfish.

Red tides must be closely monitored. One method scientists use to track red tides is reviewing satellite images. However, floating robots are being developed that can constantly measure the concentration of red tide algae. If the concentration becomes too high, scientists can issue a warning to stop shellfish harvesting.

■ **Figure 19.16** *Euglena gracilis* are unicellular, plantlike algae that have characteristics of both plants and animals.

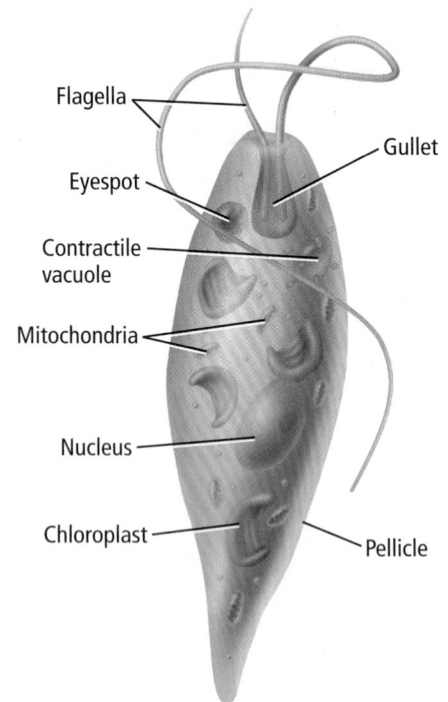


**Euglenoids** Members of the phylum Euglenophyta are unicellular, plantlike protists called euglenoids (yoo GLEE noydz). Most euglenoids are found in shallow freshwater, although some live in saltwater. Euglenoids are challenging to classify because they have characteristics of both plants and animals. Most euglenoids contain chloroplasts and photosynthesize, which is characteristic of plants, yet they lack a cell wall. Euglenoids also can be heterotrophs. When light is not available for photosynthesis, some can absorb dissolved nutrients from their environment. Others can ingest other organisms such as smaller euglenoids, which is a characteristic of animals. There even are a few species of euglenoids that are animal parasites.

The structure of a typical euglenoid is shown in **Figure 19.16.** Notice that instead of a cell wall, a flexible, tough outer membrane, called a pellicle, surrounds the cell membrane, which is similar to a paramecium. The pellicle allows euglenoids to crawl through mud when the water level is too low to swim. Note the flagella that are used to propel the euglenoid toward food or light. The eyespot is a light-sensitive receptor that helps orient the euglenoid toward light for photosynthesis. The contractile vacuole serves the same purpose in the euglenoid as it does in paramecia. It expels excess water from the cell to maintain homeostasis inside the cell.

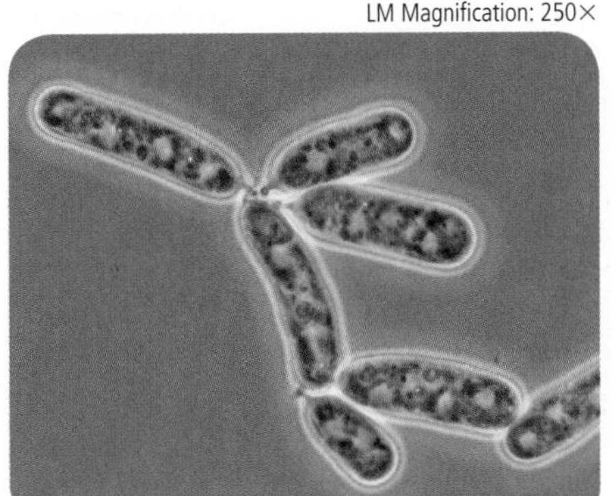


**Yellow-green algae**

**Golden-brown algae**

**Figure 19.17** Chrysophytes, like yellow-green and golden-brown algae, have carotenoids—secondary pigments used in photosynthesis.

**Chrysophytes** Yellow-green algae and golden-brown algae are in the phylum Chrysophyta (KRIS oh fyt uh) and are called chrysophytes (KRIS oh fytz). Like diatoms, these algae have yellow and brown carotenoids that give them their golden brown color. The algae in **Figure 19.17** are two examples of organisms from this phylum. Most members of this phylum are unicellular, but some species form colonies. A **colony** is a group of cells that join together to form a close association. The cells of chrysophytes usually contain two flagella attached at one end of the cell. All chrysophytes are photosynthetic, but some species also can absorb dissolved organic compounds through their cell walls or ingest food particles and prokaryotes. They reproduce both asexually and sexually, although sexual reproduction is rare. Chrysophytes are components of both freshwater and marine plankton.

 **Reading Check** **Identify** the substance that gives chrysophytes their golden-brown color.

*Study Tip*

**Shared Reading** Have a partner read two paragraphs aloud. Then, you summarize the key ideas in the paragraphs. Then, you read aloud and have your partner summarize the key ideas in your paragraphs.

**Brown algae** Brown algae are members of the phylum Phaeophyta (FAY oh FI tuh) and are some of the largest multicellular plantlike algae. These algae get their brown color from a secondary carotenoid pigment called fucoxanthin (fyew ko ZAN thun). Most of the 1500 species of brown algae live along rocky coasts in cool areas of the world. Look back at **Table 19.1** to see kelp, an example of a brown alga. The body of a kelp is called the thallus, as shown in **Figure 19.18.** The blades are the flattened portions, the stipe is the stalklike part, the holdfast is the rootlike structure, and the bladder is the bulging portion of the alga. The bladder is filled with air and keeps the alga floating near the surface of the water where light is available for photosynthesis.

**Green algae** The diverse group of algae from the phylum Chlorophyta (kloh RAH fy tuh) contains more than 7000 species. Green algae have several characteristics in common with plants. Green algae and plants both contain chlorophyll as a primary photosynthetic pigment, which gives both groups a green color. Both green algae and plant cells have cell walls, and both groups store their food as carbohydrates. These shared characteristics lead some scientists to think there is an evolutionary link between these two kingdoms. You will learn more about the plant kingdom in Chapter 21.

Most species of green algae are found in freshwater, but about ten percent are marine species. Green algae also are found on damp ground, tree trunks, and in snow. Green algae even are found in the fur of some animals, such as the sloth shown in **Figure 19.2.**

**Figure 19.18** Underwater kelp forests provide a habitat for many marine organisms, as well as provide algin—an additive used in many products.
**Explain** *What is the function of the bladder in kelp?*

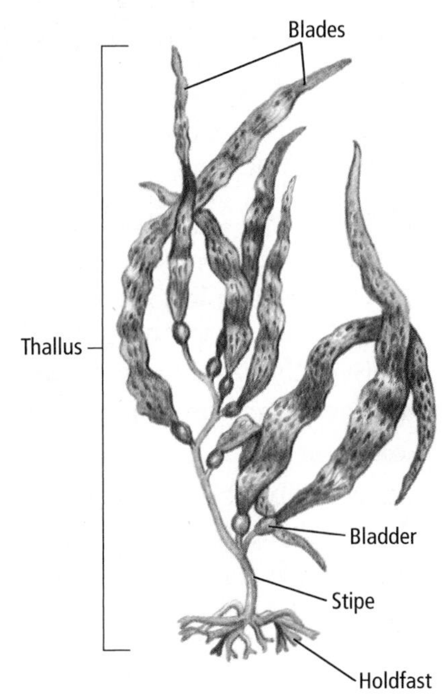

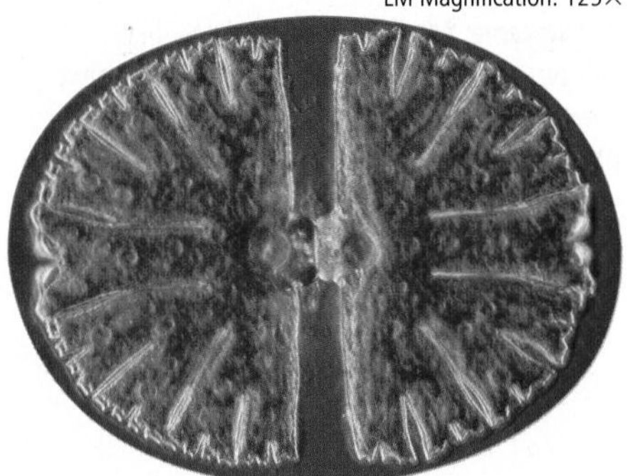


**Desmids**

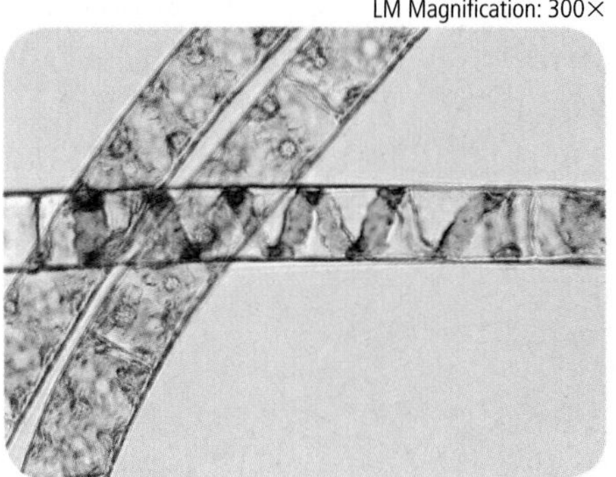


**Spirogyra**

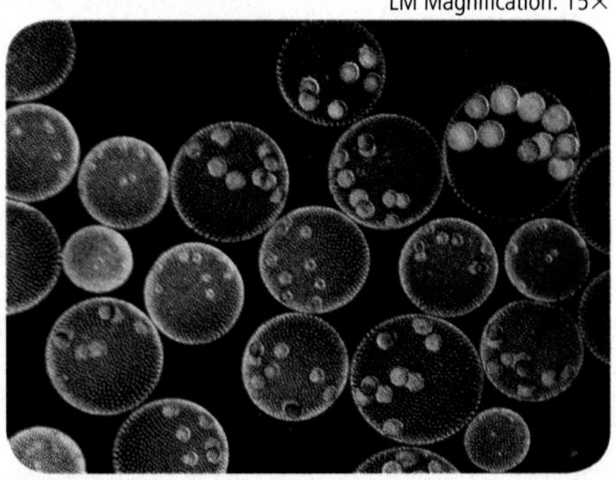


**Volvox**

■ **Figure 19.19** *Desmids* are unicellular green algae that have elaborate cell walls. The green alga *Spirogyra* is named for its spiraling chloroplasts. Many cells that make up the *Volvox* colony have daughter colonies within the larger colony.

There are a variety of growth patterns exhibited by green algae. The unicellular algae *Desmids,* shown in **Figure 19.19,** are characterized by their symmetrically divided cells. Notice how the cells have two identical sides that are connected by a bridge. Another growth pattern is found in Spirogyra, shown in **Figure 19.19.** *Spirogyra* is a multicellular green algae characterized by its long, thin filaments. The name Spirogyra comes from the spiral pattern of the chloroplasts. *Volvox,* shown in **Figure 19.19,** is an example of an alga that has a colonial growth pattern.

The single cells of the *Volvox* colony are held together by a gelatinlike secretion called cytoplasmic strands. Each cell has flagella that beat in unison to move the colony. *Volvox* colonies might include hundreds or even thousands of cells that form a hollow ball. Smaller colonies, called daughter colonies, form balls inside the larger colony. When the daughter cells have matured, they digest the parental cell and become free-swimming.

**Reading Check** **Identify** the growth patterns for the algae above.

## MiniLab 19.1

### Investigate Photosynthesis in Algae

**How much sunlight does green alga need to undergo photosynthesis?** Algae contain photosynthetic pigments that allow them to produce food by using energy from the Sun. Observe green algae to determine whether the amount of light affects photosynthesis.

**Procedure:**

1. Read and complete the lab safety form.
2. Obtain samples of **green algae** from your teacher. Place the sample of each type of algae in different locations in the classroom. Be sure one location is completely dark.
3. Hypothesize what will happen to the algae in each location.
4. Check each specimen every other day for a week. Record your observations.

**Analysis**

1. **Describe** the evidence you used to determine whether photosynthesis was occurring.
2. **Conclude** Was your hypothesis supported? Explain.
3. **Identify** What organelles would you expect to see if you looked at each type of algae under a microscope?

*Coralline*

■ **Figure 19.20** The red photosynthetic pigments allow the red algae to live in deep water and still use sunlight to photosynthesize.
**Explain** ***How do the red photosynthetic pigments make this possible?***

**Red Algae** Most red algae in phylum Rhodophyta (roh dah FI duh) are multicellular. Look at **Figure 19.20** to see how red algae got their name. These organisms contain red photosynthetic pigments called phycobilins that give them a red color. These pigments enable the red algae to absorb green, violet, and blue light that can penetrate water to a depth of 100 m or more. This allows red algae to live and photosynthesize in deeper water than other algae.

Some red algae also contribute to the formation of coral reefs. The cell walls of the red alga *Coralline* contain calcium carbonate. The calcium carbonate binds together the bodies of other organisms called stony coral to form coral reefs. You will learn more about the formation of coral reefs in Chapter 27.

**VOCABULARY**

**ACADEMIC VOCABULARY**

**Supplement:**
something that completes or makes an addition.
*Vitamins are taken to supplement one's diet.*

## Uses for Algae

Algae are used as a source of food for animals and people worldwide. In coastal areas of North America and Europe, algae are fed to farm animals as a food supplement. Algae are found in many dishes and processed foods, as described in **Table 19.2.** Algae are nutritious because of their high protein content and because they contain minerals, trace elements, and vitamins. Some of the substances found in algae also are used to stabilize or improve the texture of processed foods.

**Concepts In Motion**
**Interactive Table** To explore more about the uses for algae, visit biologygmh.com.

**Table 19.2 Some Uses for Algae**

| Type of Algae | Uses |
|---|---|
| Red algae | A species of red alga, *Porphyra,* is called nori, which is dried, pressed into sheets, and used in soups, sauces, sushi, and condiments. Some species of red algae provide agar and carrageenan, which are used in the preparation of scientific gels and cultures. Agar also is used in pie fillings and to preserve canned meat and fish. Carrageenan is used to thicken and stabilize puddings, syrups, and shampoos. |
| Brown algae | Brown algae are used to stabilize products, such as syrups, ice creams, and paints. The genus *Laminaria* is harvested and eaten with meat or fish and in soups. |
| Green algae | Species from the genera *Monostroma* and *Ulva,* also called sea lettuce, are eaten in salads, soups, relishes, and in meat or fish dishes. |
| Diatoms | Diatoms are used as a filtering material for processes such as the production of beverages, chemicals, industrial oils, cooking oils, sugars, water supplies, and the separation of wastes. They also are used as abrasives. |

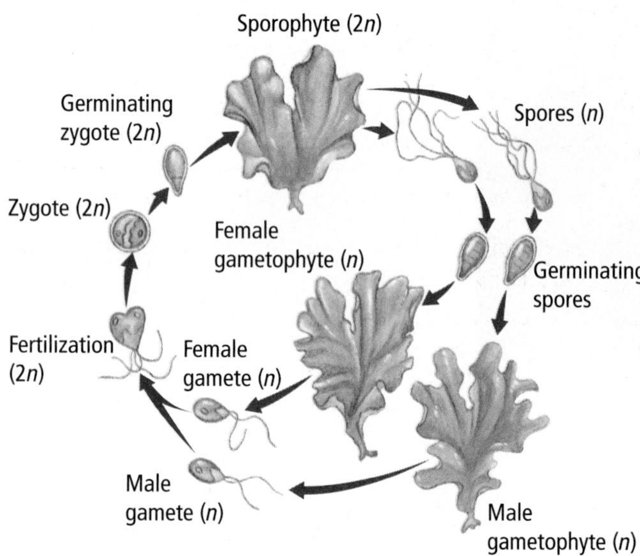


**Figure 19.21** The life cycle of many algae, including the sea lettuce *Ulva* shown here, includes an alternation between a diploid and haploid generation. Alternation of generations also is found in members of both the plant and fungi kingdoms.

## Life Cycle of Algae

The life cycles of many algae are complex. Algae can alternate between spore-producing forms and gamete-producing forms. They can reproduce sexually as well as asexually. Green algae also reproduce asexually through fragmentation—a process in which a multicellular individual breaks into separate pieces and each grows into an individual organism.

**Alternation of generations** The life cycles of many algae exhibit a pattern called alternation of generations, illustrated in **Figure 19.21** for the sea lettuce *Ulva*. **Alternation of generations** is a life cycle of algae that takes two generations—one that reproduces sexually and one that reproduces asexually—to complete a life cycle. Organisms alternate between a diploid *(2n)* form and a haploid *(n)* form in which each is considered a generation.

**Haploid and diploid generations** The haploid form of the organism is called the gametophyte generation because it produces gametes. This generation is represented by the red arrows in the diagram. Gametes from two different organisms combine to form a zygote with two complete sets of chromosomes. The diploid form of the organism is represented by blue arrows in the diagram. The zygote develops into the sporophyte *(2n)*. In the sporophyte, some cells divide by meiosis and become haploid spores *(n)*. Spores are reproductive cells that develop into gametophytes. The new gametophytes continue the cycle as shown in **Figure 19.21.**

## Section 19.3 Assessment

### Section Summary

- Plantlike protists produce their own food through photosynthesis.
- Algae are important producers of oxygen and food for aquatic ecosystems.
- Euglenoids, diatoms, and dinoflagellates are unicellular algae.
- Red, brown, and green algae have multicellular forms.
- The life cycles of algae include an alternation of generations.

### Understand Main Ideas

1. MAIN Idea **Explain** why algae are considered the primary producers for aquatic and marine ecosystems.
2. **Describe** the major characteristics of the three groups of algae.
3. **Explain** why you would expect to find more evidence of diatoms than green algae in a sample of ocean floor sediment.
4. **Apply** what you know about photosynthesis to explain why most algae live at or near the surface of the water.

### Think Scientifically

5. *Design an experiment* to determine the optimum color of light to grow green algae.
6. *Summarize* the role of secondary photosynthetic pigments in algae.
7. *WRITING in* **Biology** Write a brief public service announcement explaining the dangers of eating shellfish during a red tide.



Biology Online **Self-Check Quiz** biologygmh.com

Section 19.4

## Objectives

- **Describe** the characteristics of cellular and acellular slime molds.
- **Compare** the life cycle of cellular and acellular slime molds.
- **Explain** how water molds obtain their nutrition.

### Review Vocabulary

**cellulose:** a glucose polymer that forms the cell walls of plants and some funguslike potists

### New Vocabulary

plasmodium
acrasin

# Funguslike Protists

MAIN Idea **Funguslike protists obtain their nutrition by absorbing nutrients from dead or decaying organisms.**

**Real-World Reading Link** Have you ever heard the saying, "don't judge a book by its cover"? The same could be said of funguslike protists. Although at first glance they look like fungi, when they are examined more closely, many traits are revealed that are not true of fungi.

## Slime Molds

As you can imagine, funguslike protists are protists that have some characteristics of fungi. Fungi and slime molds use spores to reproduce. Slime molds, like fungi, feed on decaying organic matter and absorb nutrients through their cell walls. However, fungi and slime mold differ in the composition of their cell walls. Fungi cell walls are composed of a substance called chitin (KI tun). Chitin is a complex carbohydrate that is found in the cell walls of fungi, and in the external skeletons of insects, crabs, and centipedes. The cell walls of funguslike protists do not contain chitin as a true fungus does. The cell walls of these protists contain cellulose or celluloselike compounds.

Slime molds are found in a variety of colors, ranging from yellows and oranges to blue, black, and red as shown in **Figure 19.22.** They usually are found in damp, shady places where decaying organic matter is located, such as on a pile of decaying leaves or on rotting logs. Slime molds are divided into two groups—acellular slime molds and cellular slime molds.

 **Reading Check** **Compare and contrast** fungi and slime molds.

**Figure 19.22** Slime molds have a variety of colors and shapes, but they all have funguslike characteristics.
**Infer** *Where might these slime molds be obtaining their nutrition?*

**Myxamoebae slime mold**

**Red raspberry slime mold**

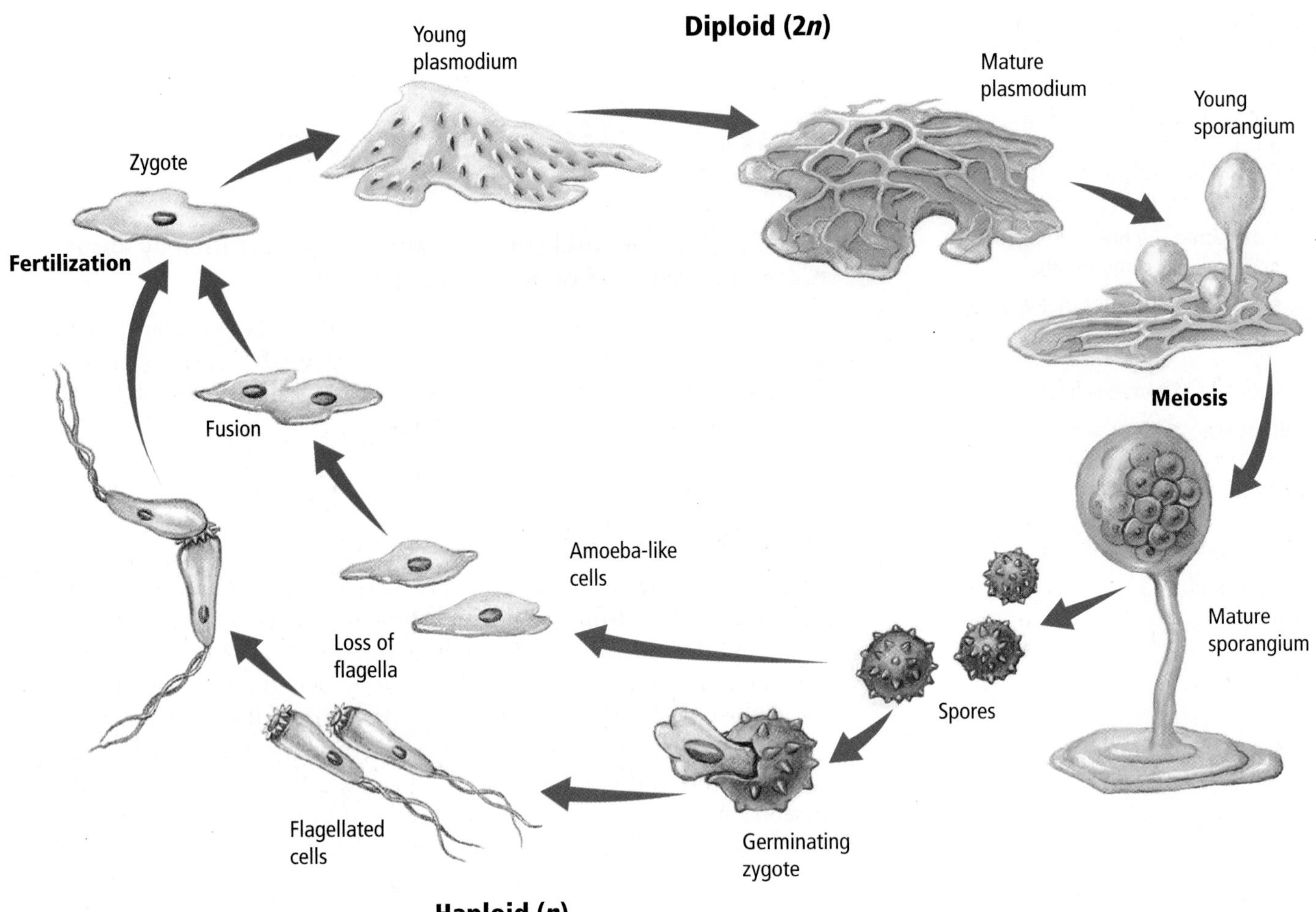


**Figure 19.23** Acellular slime mold goes through haploid and diploid phases during its life cycle.

**Acellular slime molds** Funguslike protists called acellular slime molds are found in the phylum Myxomycota (mihk soh mi COH tuh). They are acellular because they go through a phase in their life cycle in which the nucleus divides but no internal cell walls form, resulting in a mass of cytoplasm with multiple nuclei.

Follow the life cycle of a typical acellular slime mold shown in **Figure 19.23.** Acellular slime molds begin life as spores, usually when conditions are harsh—such as during a drought. In the presence of water, the spore produces a small mass of cytoplasm, or an amoeboid cell, or a cell with a flagella. The cell is propelled by the flagella until it comes in contact with a favorable surface. Then, the flagella permanently retract and the cell produces pseudopods that allow it to move like an amoeba. Both the flagellated cell and the amoeba-like cell are gametes and are haploid *(n).*

When two gametes unite, the next phase of the life cycle begins. The fertilized cells undergo repeated divisions of the nuclei, forming a plasmodium. A **plasmodium** (plaz MOH dee um)is a mobile mass of cytoplasm that contains many diploid nuclei but no separate cells. This is the feeding stage of the organism. It creeps over the surface of decaying leaves or wood like an amoeba and can grow as large as 30 cm in diameter. When food or moisture becomes limited, the slime mold develops spore-producing structures. Spores are produced through meiosis and dispersed by the wind. Once the spores are in the presence of water, the cycle repeats.

**VOCABULARY**

**ACADEMIC VOCABULARY**

**Phase:** a particular state in a regular cycle of changes.
*The phases of the moon are based on the positions of Earth, the Sun, and the moon.*

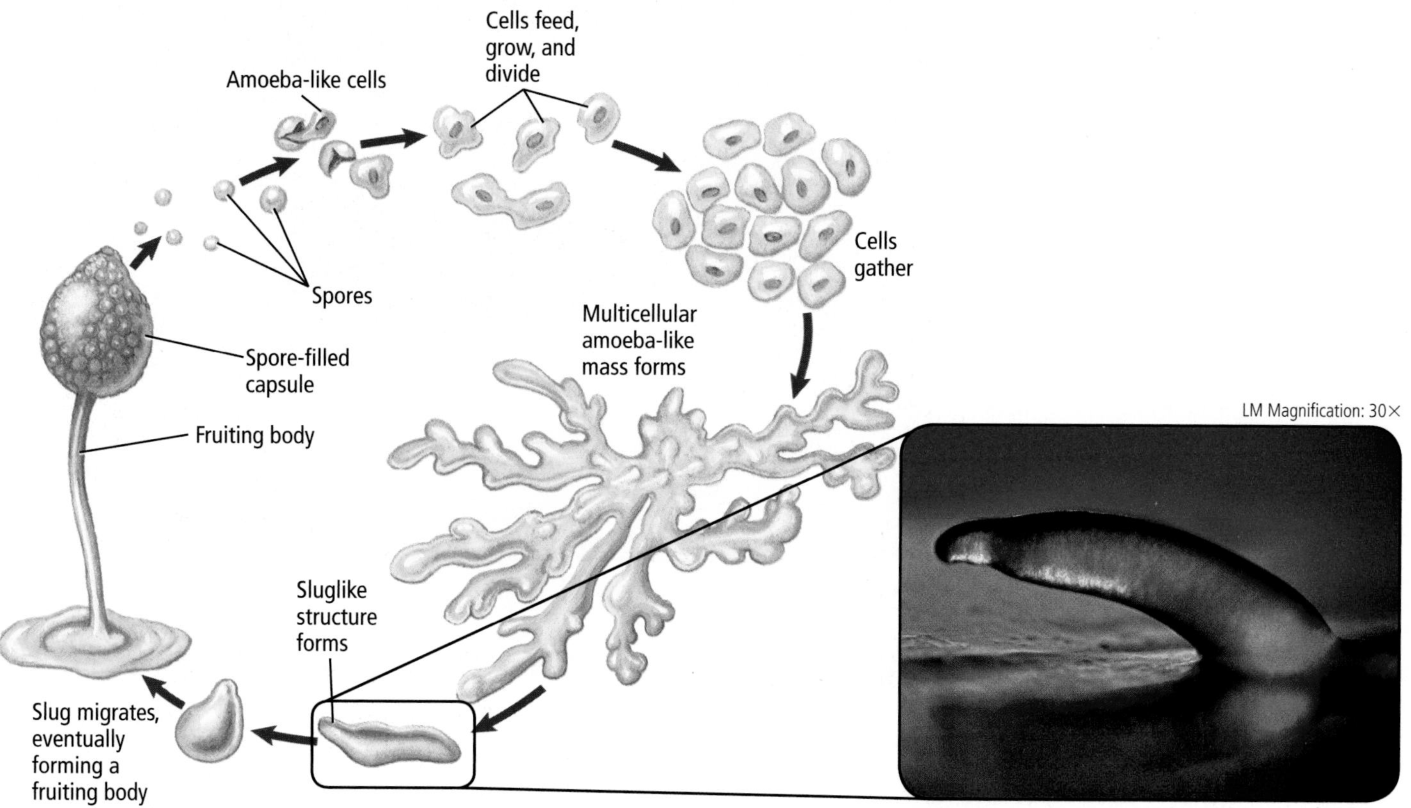


■ **Figure 19.24** Cellular slime molds reproduce both sexually and asexually. Amoeba-like cells congregate during asexual reproduction, shown above, to form a sluglike colony, which functions like a single organism.
**Explain** ***why the sluglike stage is considered a colony.***

**Cellular slime molds** Cellular slime molds are found in the phylum Acrasiomycota (uh kray see oh my COH tuh). These funguslike protists creep over rich, moist soil and engulf bacteria. Unlike acellular slime molds, they spend most of their life cycle as single amoeba-like cells and they have no flagella.

The life cycle of cellular slime molds is shown in **Figure 19.24.** When food is plentiful, the single amoeba-like cells reproduce rapidly by sexual reproduction. During sexual reproduction, two haploid amoebas unite and form a zygote. The zygote develops into a giant cell and undergoes meiosis followed by several divisions by mitosis. Eventually, the giant cell ruptures, releasing new haploid amoebas.

When food is scarce, the single amoeba-like cells reproduce asexually. The starving amoeba-like cells give off a chemical called **acrasin** (uh KRA sun). The amoeba-like cells begin to congregate in response to the chemical signal, forming a sluglike colony that begins to function like a single organism. The colony migrates for a while, eventually forming a fruiting body, like the one shown in **Figure 19.25.** The fruiting body produces spores. Once the spores are fully developed, they are released. The spores germinate, forming amoeba-like cells, and the cycle repeats.

**Reading Check** **Infer** why the stages in the life cycle of cellular slime molds contribute to their long-term survival.

■ **Figure 19.25** Cellular slime molds produce fruiting bodies that contain spores during part of their life cycle.

SEM Magnification: 2700×

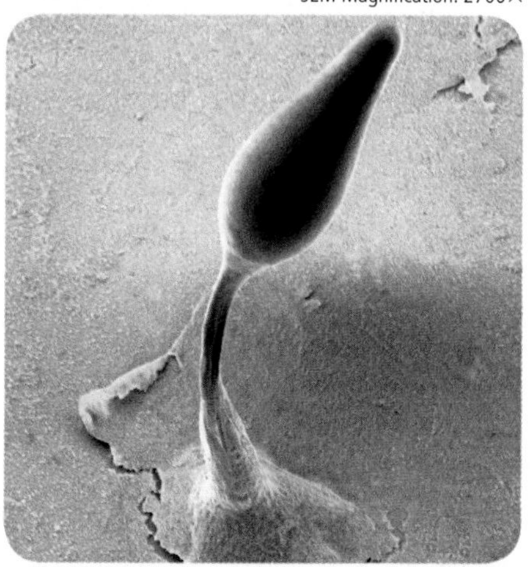

■ **Figure 19.26** This water mold is absorbing nutrients found in this dead insect.
**Explain** *What funguslike characteristic do water molds have?*

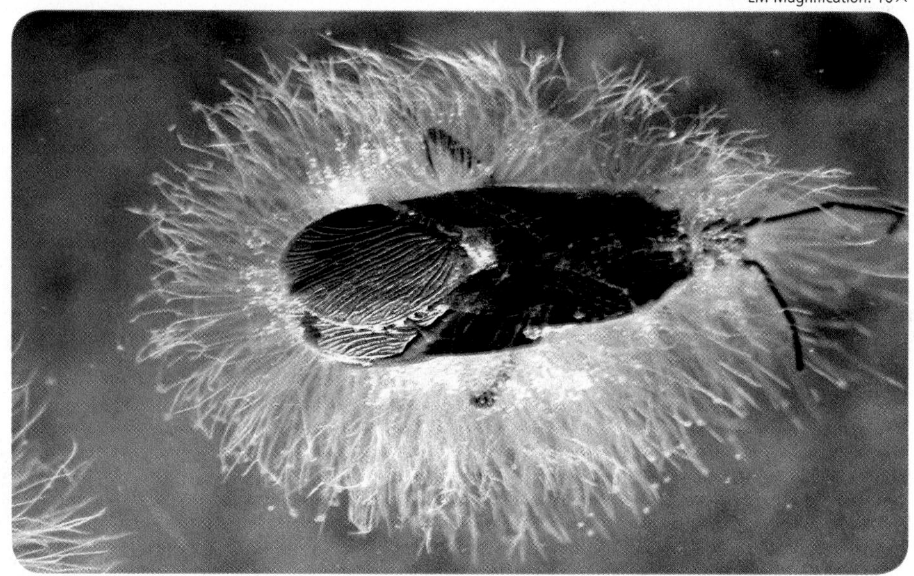

**Water mold**

## Water Molds and Downy Mildew

There are more than 500 species of water molds and downy mildews in the phylum Oomycota (oo oh my COH tuh). Most members of this group of funguslike protists live in water or damp places. Some absorb their nutrients from the surrounding water or soil, while others obtain their nutrients from other organisms, as shown in **Figure 19.26.**

Originally, water molds were considered fungi because of their method of obtaining nutrients. Like fungi, water molds envelope their food source with a mass of threads; they break down the tissue, and absorb the nutrients through their cell walls. Although this is characteristic of fungi, water molds differ from fungi in the composition of their cell walls and they produce flagellated reproductive cells. Recall that the cell walls of funguslike protists are composed of cellulose and celluloselike compounds.

**Reading Check** **Compare and contrast** water molds and fungi.

## MiniLab 19.2

### Investigate Slime Molds

**What is a slime mold?** In a kingdom of interesting creatures, slime molds perhaps are the most interesting. Observe different types of slime molds and observe the unusual nature of their bodies.

**Procedure** 

1. Read and complete the lab safety form.
2. Obtain **slides of different specimens of slime molds.** Examine the slides under a **microscope.**
3. Create a data table to record your information. Sketch and describe each specimen.

**Analysis**

1. **Compare and contrast** the specimens.
2. **Identify** specimens that have similar characteristics. Explain why the specimens are similar.
3. **Think Critically** How would you classify each specimen that you examined? Explain.

## CHAPTER 19

# Assessment

## Section 19.1

### Vocabulary Review

*Answer the following questions with complete sentences.*

1. What is another name for animal-like protists?
2. What are microscopic protozoans that are found in the gut of insects?

### Understand Key Concepts

3. Which process is most likely the way in which the first protists formed?
   **A.** aerobic respiration **C.** endosymbiosis
   **B.** decomposition **D.** photosynthesis
4. Which method below is used to divide protists into three groups?
   **A.** method of getting food
   **B.** method of movement
   **C.** type of reproduction
   **D.** type of respiration
5. Which is least likely to be a suitable environment for protists?
   **A.** decaying leaves **C.** damp soil
   **B.** the ocean **D.** dry sand

*Use the photo below to answer questions 6 and 7.*

LM Magnification: 125×

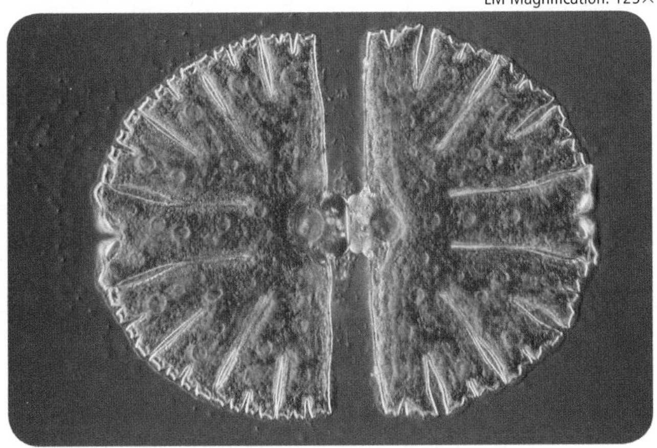

6. To which group does the protist belong?
   **A.** algae **C.** funguslike
   **B.** animal-like **D.** protozoan
7. Which term best describes this protist?
   **A.** acellular **C.** multicellular
   **B.** eukaryotic **D.** prokaryotic

### Constructed Response

8. **Open Ended** Describe three locations near your home or school where you might be able to find protists.
9. **CAREERS IN BIOLOGY** If you were a taxonomist given the task of organizing protists into groups, would you use the same method described in this book? Explain your answer.

### Think Critically

10. **Predict** changes in protist populations if an area had an above-average amount of rainfall.

## Section 19.2

### Vocabulary Review

*Define each of the structures below and provide an example of an organism where it could be found.*

11. pseudopod
12. contractile vacuole
13. test

### Understand Key Concepts

*Use the diagram below to answer question 14.*

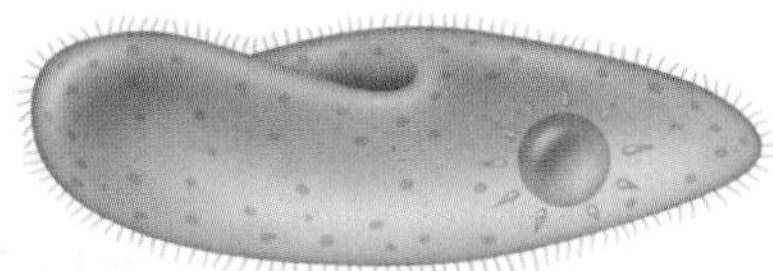

14. Which structure does this organism use for movement?
    **A.** cilia
    **B.** contractile vacuole
    **C.** flagella
    **D.** pseudopodia
15. What does the paramecium's contractile vacuole help regulate inside the cell?
    **A.** amount of food **C.** movement
    **B.** amount of water **D.** reproduction
16. Which are most likely to form fossils?
    **A.** apicomplexans **C.** foraminifera
    **B.** flagellates **D.** paramecia

### Constructed Response

17. **Open Ended** Explain why termites might die if their symbiotic flagellates died.

18. **Short Answer** Describe the process of conjugation in paramecia.

### Think Critically

19. **Apply Concepts** Recommend several options a village might consider to slow down the spread of malaria.

20. **Research Information** Research other diseases that are caused by protozoans. Use a map and plot locations where the diseases occur.

## Section 19.3

### Vocabulary Review

*Match each definition below with the correct vocabulary term from the Study Guide page.*

21. a life cycle of algae that requires two generations

22. a group of cells living together in close association

23. gives off light

### Understand Key Concepts

*Use the photo below to answer question 24.*

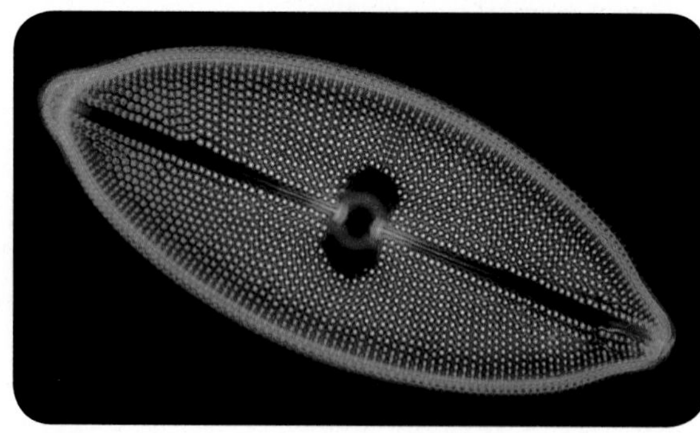

24. Which term best describes how this organism stores its excess food?
    - **A.** cellulose
    - **B.** oil
    - **C.** protein
    - **D.** carbohydrate

25. Which are used in the human food supply?
    - **A.** dinoflagellates
    - **B.** euglenoids
    - **C.** protozoans
    - **D.** red algae

26. Which organism has silica walls?
    - **A.** brown alga
    - **B.** diatom
    - **C.** dinoflagellate
    - **D.** euglenoid

*Use the illustration below to answer questions 27 and 28.*

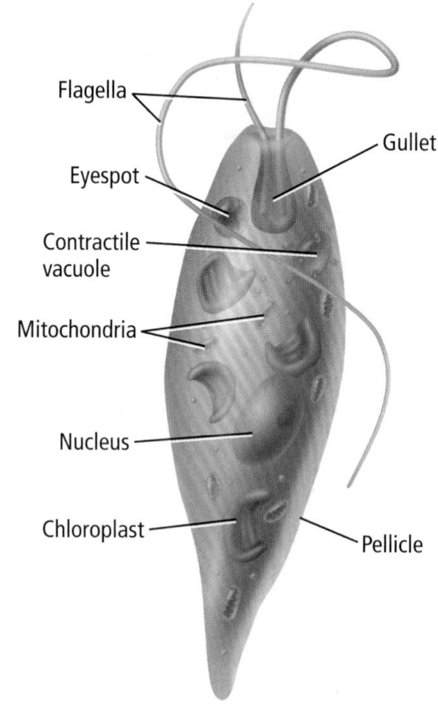


27. What is the name of the structure used by the organism above for movement?
    - **A.** cilia
    - **B.** contractile vacuole
    - **C.** flagella
    - **D.** pseudopod

28. Which structure is used to sense light?
    - **A.** chloroplast
    - **B.** eyespot
    - **C.** nucleus
    - **D.** pellicle

### Constructed Response

29. **Open Ended** Why are there more fossils of diatoms, foraminiferans, and radiolarians than of other algae?

30. **Short Answer** Explain why diatoms must reproduce sexually occasionally.

31. **Short Answer** Explain the relationship between the sporophyte and gametophyte in alternation of generations.

### Think Critically

32. **Analyze** the difference between freshwater algae and marine algae.



BiologyOnline Chapter Test biologygmh.com

33. **Recognize Cause and Effect** Explain the effects of a marine parasite that kills all phytoplankton.

## Section 19.4

### Vocabulary Review

*Replace the underlined words with the correct vocabulary term from the Study Guide page.*

34. A motile organism that consists of many diploid nuclei but no separate cells is a protoplasm.

35. Starving amoeboid cells give off a chemical called arsenic.

### Understand Key Concepts

36. Acellular slime molds have many nuclei, but what structure do they not have?
    **A.** chromosomes
    **B.** spores
    **C.** separate cells
    **D.** cilia

37. Which is present in the life cycle of water molds in a flagellated form?
    **A.** nuclei
    **B.** plasmodia
    **C.** pseudopods
    **D.** reproductive cells

### Constructed Response

38. **Short Answer** Compare and contrast a water mold and a cellular slime mold.

39. **Open Ended** Describe some environmental conditions that might lead to the production of spores by an acellular slime mold.

### Think Critically

40. **Analyze and Conclude** During the multinucleated plasmodial stage, could acellular slime molds be classified as multicellular organisms? Explain your reasoning.

## Additional Assessment

41. *WRITING in* **Biology** Choose one protist and help it "evolve" by determining a new organelle or structure that is going to develop. How will this new condition affect the protist? Will this change increase or decrease the chance of survival?

### DBQ Document-Based Questions

*The text below describes a new detection method for finding microscopic organisms in water sources.*

The protozoans *Giardia lamblia* and *Cryptosporidium parvom* are major causes of waterborne intestinal diseases throughout the world. A very sensitive detection method was developed using the DNA amplification procedure—polymerase chain reaction. This procedure can detect the presence of incredibly small amounts of these pathogens—as little as a single cell in two liters of water.

Data obtained from: Guy, et al. 2003. Real-time PCR for quantification of *Giarida* and *Cryptosporidium* in environmental water samples and sewage. *Applications of Environmental Biology* 2003 69(9): 5178-5185.

42. Explain how this detection method might be used by municipal water departments.

43. Analyze the significance of this research for global human health concerns especially in remote regions of the world.

44. Predict how this detection method might be used to monitor the level of organisms that cause red tides.

### Cumulative Review

45. Point out how meiosis provides genetic variety. **(Chapter 10)**

46. Sketch a branching diagram that explains evolution of hominoids from genus *Proconsul* to genus *Homo.* **(Chapter 16)**

47. Pick the traits you would use to make a key for classifying the kingdoms. Describe why you chose the characteristics on the list. **(Chapter 17)**

# Standardized Test Practice

**Cumulative**

## Multiple Choice

1. Which environment would likely have chemosynthetic autotrophic eubacteria?
   A. coral reef
   B. deep-ocean volcanic vent
   C. lake in the mountains
   D. soil near a spring

*Use the diagram below to answer questions 2 and 3.*

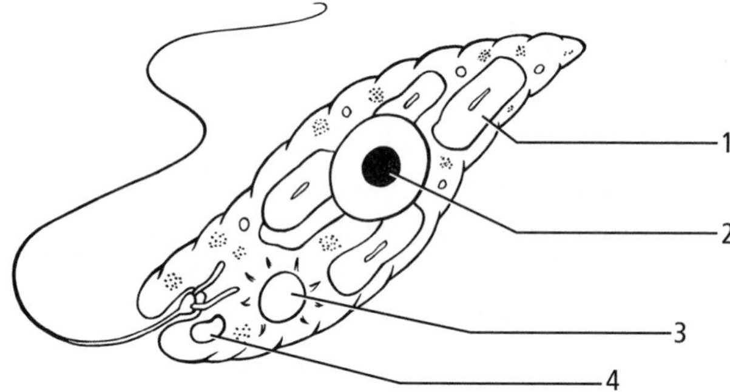


2. Which number represents the eyespot of the *Euglena?*
   A. 1
   B. 2
   C. 3
   D. 4

3. Which number represents an organelle that captures energy for the cell from sunlight?
   A. 1
   B. 2
   C. 3
   D. 4

4. Which do the two bats *Craseonycteris thonglongyai* and *Noctilio leporinus* have in common?
   A. division
   B. genus
   C. phylum
   D. species

5. Suppose you are investigating bone characteristics of two birds to determine how closely they are related in terms of phylogeny. Which type of evidence are you using?
   A. biochemical characters
   B. cellular characters
   C. chromosomal characters
   D. morphological characters

*Use the diagram below to answer question 6.*

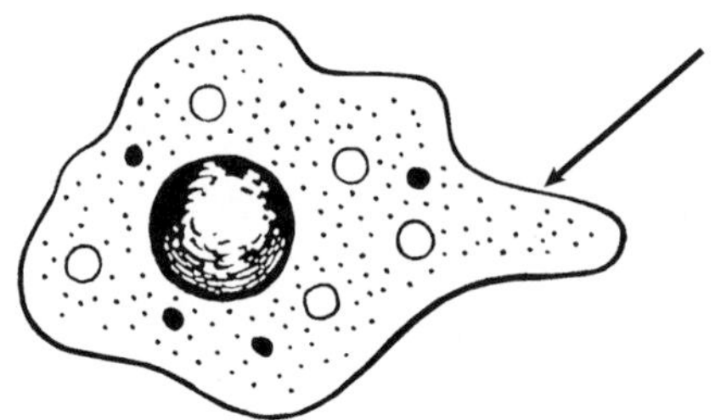

6. Members of the phylum Sarcodina use this structure for locomotion and which other activity?
   A. conjugation
   B. feeding
   C. protection
   D. reproduction

7. How do prions harm their host?
   A. by activating synthesis of viral RNA
   B. by causing normal proteins to mutate
   C. by deactivating part of the host's DNA
   D. by disrupting the way cells reproduce

8. Which could be a derived, rather than ancestral, character in one group of vertebrates?
   A. nervous system
   B. organized systems of tissues
   C. role of ATP in mitochondria
   D. wings used for flight

31. Why are lichens important bioindicators?
   A. They are susceptible to drought.
   B. They are unicellular.
   C. They are mutualistic.
   D. They are susceptible to air pollutants.

*Use the image below to answer question 32.*

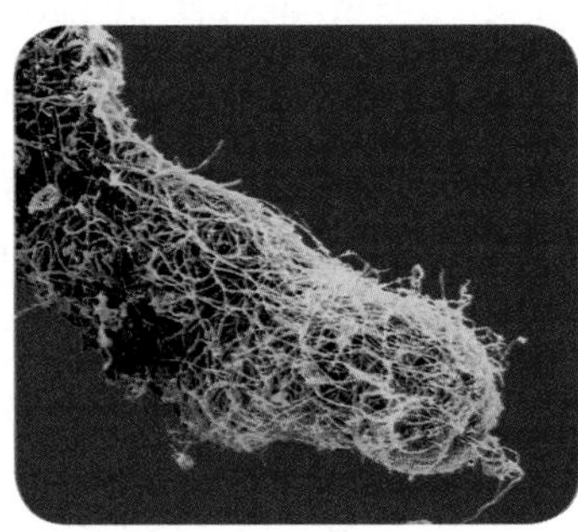

32. How is this lichen benefiting the plant?
   A. increases the surface area for gathering light
   B. decreases the need for water
   C. increases the surface area of the roots
   D. decreases the temperature

## Constructed Response

33. **Short Answer** In what ways are fungi beneficial to humans?

34. **Short Answer** Evaluate the role of lichens in the arctic environments.

## Think Critically

35. **Predict** how the availability of the antibiotic penicillin during World War II impacted the soldiers.

36. **Design an experiment** that will allow you to test the antibiotic effects of two or three common fungi.

37. **CAREERS IN BIOLOGY** Write a want ad for a mycologist in a research labratory.

38. **Design** an organism that cultivates its own food production using fungi. How might the fungi benefit from this relationship?

39. **Hypothesize** why mycorrhizae might have been important for the colonization of land by plants. What kind of evidence would you look for to support your hypothesis?

## Additional Assessment

40. *WRITING in* **Biology** Imagine yourself as a fungal spore landing near your home or school. Evaluate your chances of survival.

## DBQ Document-Based Questions

Data obtained from: Stokstad, E. 2004. Plant pathologists gear up for battle with dread fungus. *Science* 306: 1672–1673.

*This map shows where Asian soybean rust* Phakopsora pachyrhizi *is found in the United States. It is a recent arrival from Brazil and other parts of South America. Its presence in each state was officially diagnosed by the USDA. Soybean rust is a disease caused by the fungus* Phakopsora pachyrhiz *that recently has become a problem for soybean farmers in the United States. Losses from this infection can amount to 80 percent of the crop.*

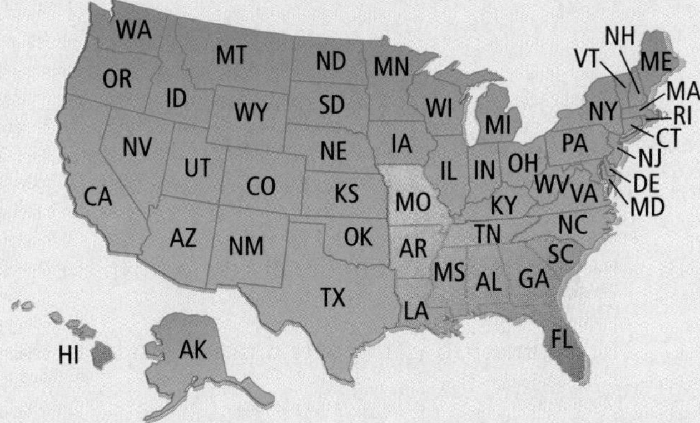


41. Evaluate the map and speculate about the factors affecting the distribution of soybean rust in the U.S. In which states is soybean rust most prevalent?

42. Apply what you know about fungi to recommend a course of action to eradicate this fungus.

43. Estimate the impact of this fungus on the future of soybean production in the U.S.

## Cumulative Review

44. Suppose the molecular clock technique indicates that two organisms have begun to evolve into separate species. Indicate the kinds of data or evidence you would expect to be able to find in the organisms. **(Chapter 17)**

# Standardized Test Practice

**Cumulative**

## Multiple Choice

1. Which are autotrophic protists commonly referred to as?
   A. algae
   B. protozoans
   C. slime molds
   D. water molds

*Use the diagram below to answer questions 2 and 3.*

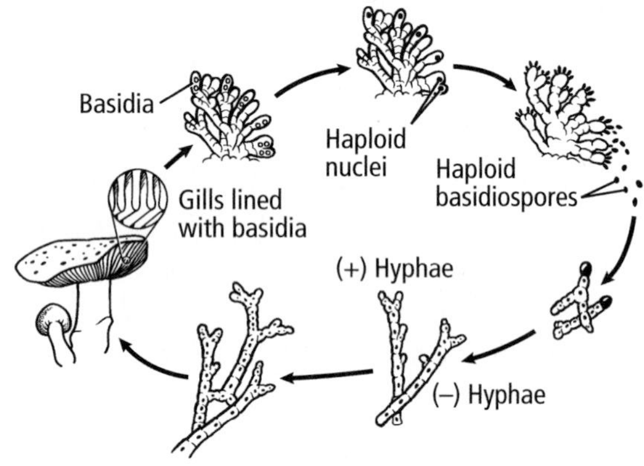


2. What part of this life cycle can be used to explain why many mushrooms grow quickly?
   A. The cap pulls in organic matter from the soil to fill the mushroom.
   B. The gills in the cap rapidly divide to form the mushroom.
   C. The hyphae grow and extend rapidly to form the mushroom.
   D. The basidia grow and lengthen the mushroom.

3. Which occurrence pictured in the diagram allows the mating types to fuse?
   A. basidia form
   B. hyphae unite
   C. mushroom forms
   D. spores release

4. A certain tree-dwelling primate has a prehensile tail and nails on its digits. To which group of primates would you expect this animal to belong?
   A. Asian apes
   B. New World monkeys
   C. Old World monkeys
   D. prosimians

5. Which occurs during the lytic cycle of a viral infection?
   A. The host cell becomes a factory that continually makes more copies of the virus.
   B. The host cell undergoes cell division that makes more copies of the virus.
   C. The virus incorporates its nucleic acid into the DNA of the host cell and lies dormant.
   D. The virus takes over the cell, makes copies of itself, and usually kills the host cell.

*Use the figure below to answer question 6.*

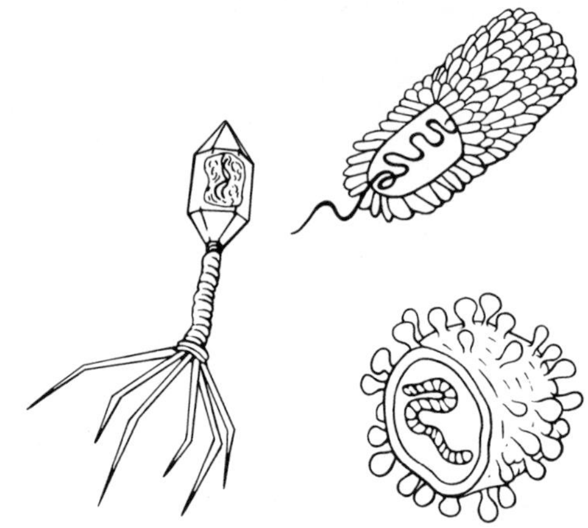

6. On what property do scientists base their classification of viruses?
   A. capsid proteins
   B. chromosome number
   C. host resistance
   D. type of genetic material

7. Which characteristic distinguishes australopithecines from earlier hominoids?
   A. binocular vision
   B. bipedalism
   C. fingernails
   D. opposable thumb

8. Which is a characteristic of an acellular slime mold?
   A. cytoplasm with many cells
   B. locomotion by means of cilia
   C. plasmodium with many nuclei
   D. reproduction by fragmentation

## Short Answer

*Use the diagram below to answer question 9.*

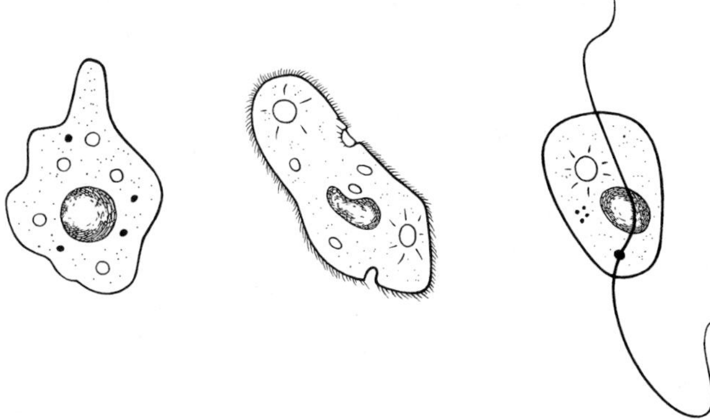

9. Identify the structure used for locomotion in each of these organisms and briefly describe how each structure functions.

10. Imagine that you found a unicellular organism living in the mud at the bottom of a pond. Write a plan to determine how you would classify it.

11. Some people think that technology can solve all human problems. Name and critique an example of a problem that technology might not be able to solve.

12. What characteristics are used to classify protists into three groups? Explain your answer.

13. Describe how sexual reproduction begins in Ascomycetes and assess its significance.

14. Give examples of three ways that fungi are important for human foods.

## Extended Response

15. Create a flowchart to show how isolation of a small population can lead to speciation.

16. Assess the value of mycorrhizae for plants.

17. Evaluate how viruses benefit from their small size and simple composition.

18. Imagine that you've noticed that mushrooms grow in one corner of a field every time it rains. Give a reason why picking the mushrooms immediately following a rainshower will not stop them from growing back.

## Essay Question

Light is needed for photosynthesis to take place. The algae depend on the energy from light to carry out photosynthesis. The main photosynthetic pigment of green algae is chlorophyll. Sunlight is made up of all the different wavelengths of visible light, but only blue and red are absorbed by chlorophyll. Other algae contain larger amounts of other pigments such as carotenoids. Carotenoids absorb energy from green light. Since algae live in water, this becomes important because water absorbs the different colors of light at different rates.

*Using the information in the paragraph above, answer the following question in essay format.*

19. Red light does not penetrate into water. Algae in water must be able to use light energy that is available underwater. Write an essay about why carotenoids are better than chlorophyll for algae living well below the surface.

| NEED EXTRA HELP? | | | | | | | | | | | | | | | | | | | |
|---|---|---|---|---|---|---|---|---|---|---|---|---|---|---|---|---|---|---|---|
| **If You Missed Question . . .** | 1 | 2 | 3 | 4 | 5 | 6 | 7 | 8 | 9 | 10 | 11 | 12 | 13 | 14 | 15 | 16 | 17 | 18 | 19 |
| **Review Section . . .** | 19.3 | 20.2 | 20.2 | 16.1 | 18.2 | 18.2 | 16.2 | 19.4 | 19.2 | 19.2 | 18.1 | 1.2 | 20.2 | 20.3 | 15.3 | 20.2 | 18.2 | 20.2 | 19.3 |

# UNIT 6 Plants

## Chapter 21
**Introduction to Plants**

**BIG Idea** Plants have changed over time and are now a diverse group of organisms.

## Chapter 22
**Plant Structure and Function**

**BIG Idea** The diverse nature of plants is due to the variety of their structures.

## Chapter 23
**Reproduction in Plants**

**BIG Idea** The life cycles of plants include various methods of reproduction.

### CAREERS IN BIOLOGY
### Botanist

**Botanists** are scientists who study plants. Botanists might specialize in many disciplines from bryology (the study of mosses and simple plants) to dendrology (the study of trees and woody plants). This giant sequoia researcher is a dendrologist.

**WRITING in Biology** Visit biologygmh.com to learn more about botany careers. Write a paragraph to briefly explain why the demand for botanists is increasing as the human population grows around the world.

**Biology Online**

To read more about botanists in action, visit biologygmh.com.

# CHAPTER 21 Introduction to Plants

**Section 1**
**Plant Evolution and Adaptations**
MAIN Idea Adaptations to environmental changes on Earth contributed to the evolution of plants.

**Section 2**
**Nonvascular Plants**
MAIN Idea Nonvascular plants are small and only grow in damp environments.

**Section 3**
**Seedless Vascular Plants**
MAIN Idea Because they have vascular tissues, seedless vascular plants generally are larger and better adapted to drier environments than nonvascular plants.

**Section 4**
**Vascular Seed Plants**
MAIN Idea Vascular seed plants are the most widely distributed plants on Earth.

## BioFacts

- The number of plant species is three times greater than the number of animal species.
- Nearly 98 percent of Earth's biomass consists of plants and plant products.
- Over 30 scientifically tested medicinal drugs, including three anti-cancer drugs, come from plants.

# Start-Up Activities

## LAUNCH Lab

### What characteristics differ among plants?

Scientists use specific characteristics to group plants within the plant kingdom. In this lab, you will examine some of the characteristics of plants.

**Procedure**

1. Read and complete the lab safety form.
2. Label **five plant specimens** using letters *A, B, C, D,* and *E.*
3. Study each plant carefully. Wash your hands thoroughly after handling plant material.
4. Based on your observations, list characteristics that describe the differences and similarities among these plants.
5. Rank your list of characteristics based on what you consider the most and least important.

**Analysis**

1. **Compare** your list to your classmates' lists.
2. **Describe** the diversity among the plants you studied.
3. **List** plant characteristics that you could not observe that might be useful in organizing these plants into groups.

Visit biologygmh.com to:

- study the entire chapter online
- explore Concepts in Motion, Microscopy Links, Virtual Labs, and links to virtual dissections
- access Web links for more information, projects, and activities
- review content online with the Interactive Tutor, and take Self-Check Quizzes

**Plant Adaptations** Make this Foldable to help you understand some adaptations that enabled plants to inhabit different land environments.

**STEP 1** Stack three sheets of notebook paper so that the top edges are 1.5 cm apart.

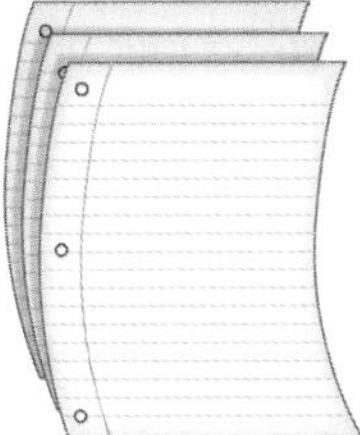

**STEP 2** Fold up the bottom edges to form five tabs of equal size.

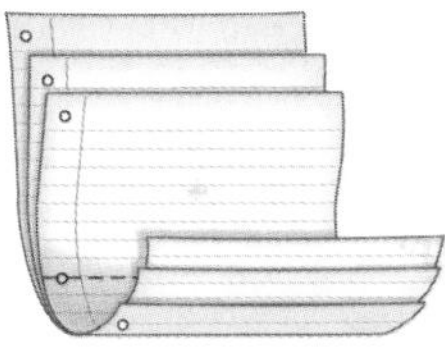

**STEP 3** Staple along the folded edge to secure all sheets, place the stapled edge at the top, and then label the tabs as shown.

FOLDABLES **Use the Foldable with Section 21.1.** As you study the section, record on your Foldable what you learn about the importance of each adaptation.

Section 21.1

## Objectives

- **Compare** the characteristics of plants and green algae.
- **Identify and evaluate** adaptations of plants to land environments.
- **Assess** the importance of vascular tissue to plant life on land.
- **Explain** alternation of generations of plants.
- **List** the divisions of the plant kingdom.

## Review Vocabulary

**limiting factor:** any abiotic or biotic factor that restricts the existence, numbers, reproduction, or distribution of organisms

## New Vocabulary

stomata
vascular tissue
vascular plant
nonvascular plant
seed

# Plant Evolution and Adaptations

**MAIN Idea** **Adaptations to environmental changes on Earth contributed to the evolution of plants.**

**Real-World Reading Link** Perhaps you have seen a photo of your ancestors and noticed that some of your living relatives resemble people in the photo. In a similar way, scientists who study evolution notice common characteristics between ancient groups of organisms and present-day groups.

## Plant Evolution

Plants are vital to our survival. The oxygen we breathe, the food we eat, and many of the things that make our lives comfortable, such as clothing, furniture, and our homes, come from or are parts of plants. If you were asked to describe a plant, would you describe a tree, a garden flower, or a houseplant? Biologists describe plants as multicellular eukaryotes with tissues and organs that have specialized structures and functions. For example, most plants have photosynthetic tissues, and organs that anchor them in soil or to an object or another plant. However, does this description apply to ancient plants?

**Connection to Earth Science** You read in Chapter 14 that Earth is about 4.6 billion years old. Can you imagine ancient Earth without land plants? That was the case until about 400 million years ago when primitive land plants appeared. However, fossil evidence from about 500 million years ago indicates that the shallow waters of ancient Earth were filled with a variety of organisms—bacteria, algae and other protists, and animals, such as sponges, corals, and worms.

There is strong evidence, including biochemical and fossil evidence, that multicellular land plants and present-day green algae share a common ancestor, as diagrammed in the evolutionary tree in **Figure 21.1.** This common ancestor might have been able to survive periods of drought. Through natural selection, drought-resistant adaptations in that ancestor, such as protected embryos and other survival characteristics, might have passed to future generations. When scientists compare present-day plants and present-day green algae, they find the following common characteristics:

- cell walls composed of cellulose
- cell division that includes the formation of a cell plate
- the same type of chlorophyll used in photosynthesis
- similar genes for ribosomal RNA
- food stored as starch
- the same types of enzymes in cellular vesicles

**Figure 21.1** This evolutionary tree shows the relationship of ancient freshwater green algae to present-day plants.

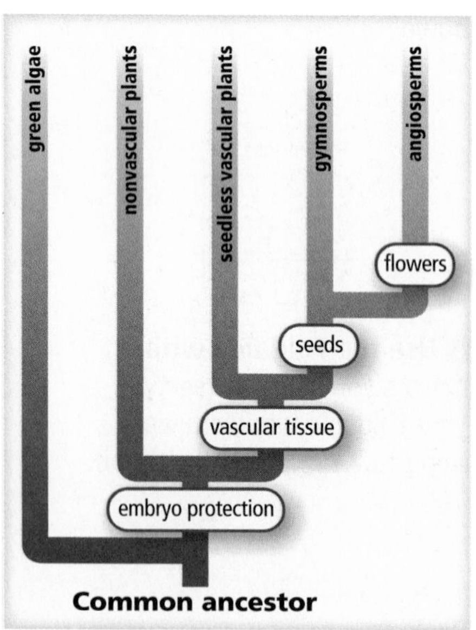

## Short Answer

9. Compare the sporophyte generation in nonvascular plants to the sporophyte generation in seedless vascular plants.

10. Describe the two membranes that make up an amoeba and suggest why it is beneficial for the amoeba to have two membranes.

11. What is the relationship between bat wings and monkey arms? Explain the importance of this relationship for the classification of organisms.

12. Describe how a multicellular fungus obtains nutrients from its environment and assess how that affects its role in the environment.

*Use the diagram of the lichen below to answer questions 13 and 14.*

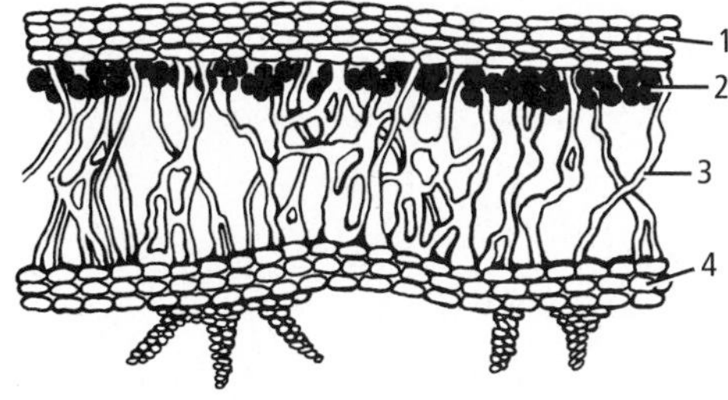


13. Identify and evaluate the importance of the layer of the lichen where photosynthesis takes place.

14. Analyze how the photosynthesizer and fungus benefit from being part of a lichen.

15. Evaluate how spore production gives fungi an advantage in an ecosystem.

## Extended Response

*Use the diagram below to answer question 16.*

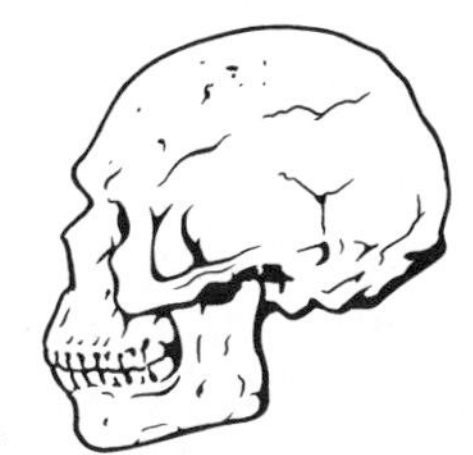


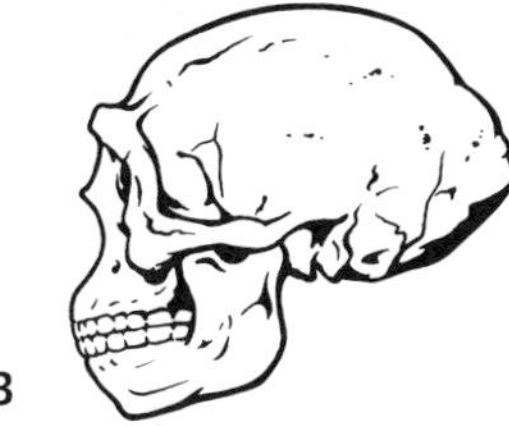


16. Look at the two skulls in the diagram. Infer which one you think is more closely related to *Homo sapiens.* Explain your inference.

17. Compare and contrast reproduction in paramecia and amoebas.

## Essay Question

During the 1840s, the potato was an extremely popular crop plant in Ireland. Many people in rural Ireland were completely dependent on potatoes for food. From 1845 to 1847, the potato blight—a funguslike disease—wiped out potato crops. The blight produces spores on the leaves of the potato plant. The spores can be transmitted by water or wind. They are carried into the soil by water, where they infect the potato tubers, and can survive through winter on the potatoes left buried in the fields. Close to one million people died from starvation and nearly as many left Ireland for America and other countries.

*Using the information in the paragraph above, answer the following question in essay format.*

18. Write an essay that indicates why potato blight spread so quickly through Ireland and how the spread of the fungus might have been slowed by different farming practices.

| NEED EXTRA HELP? | | | | | | | | | | | | | | | | | | |
|---|---|---|---|---|---|---|---|---|---|---|---|---|---|---|---|---|---|---|
| If You Missed Question . . . | 1 | 2 | 3 | 4 | 5 | 6 | 7 | 8 | 9 | 10 | 11 | 12 | 13 | 14 | 15 | 16 | 17 | 18 |
| Review Section . . . | 20.1 | 18.2 | 19.1 | 21.4 | 21.3 | 20.2 | 20.3 | 19.2 | 21.3 | 19.2 | 15.2 | 20.1 | 20.3 | 20.3 | 20.2 | 16.3 | 19.2 | 20.1 |

CHAPTER 22

# Plant Structure and Function

**Section 1**
**Plant Cells and Tissues**
**MAIN Idea** Different types of plant cells make up plant tissues.

**Section 2**
**Roots, Stems, and Leaves**
**MAIN Idea** The structures of plants are related to their functions.

**Section 3**
**Plant Hormones and Responses**
**MAIN Idea** Hormones can affect a plant's responses to its environment.

## BioFacts

- The pigment in coleus leaves that give them their reddish color serves as a Sun block—it protects the plant from harmful UV rays from the Sun.
- For over 2000 years, humans have grown plants for their stem fibers that are woven to make linen fabrics.
- With a few exceptions, 80–90 percent of a plant's roots grow in the top 30 cm of the soil.

**Cross section of coleus stem**
Stained LM Magnification: 47×

**Cross section of coleus leaf**
Stained LM Magnification: 75×

# LAUNCH Lab

## What structures do plants have?

Most plants have structures that absorb light and others that take in water and nutrients. In this lab, you will examine a plant and observe and describe structures that help the plant survive.

### Procedure

1. Read and complete the lab safety form.
2. Carefully examine a **potted plant** provided by your teacher. Use a **hand lens** to get a closer look. Make a list of each type of structure you observe.
3. Gently remove the plant from the pot and observe the plant structures in the soil. Do not break up the soil. Record your observations and place the plant back into the pot.
4. Sketch your plant and label each part.

### Analysis

1. **Compare** your list with those of other students. What structures were common to all plants?
2. **Infer** how each structure might be related to a function of the plant.
3. **Predict** the type of structural adaptations of plants living in dry environments.

Visit biologygmh.com to:

- study the entire chapter online
- explore the Concepts in Motion, Interactive Tables, Virtual Labs, Microscopy Links, and links to virtual dissections
- access Web links for more information, projects, and activities
- review content online with the Interactive Tutor, and take Self-Check Quizzes

**Leaf Structure and Function** Make this Foldable to help you investigate the structure and function of a typical leaf.

**STEP 1** Stack three sheets of paper, keeping all edges aligned.

**STEP 2** Fold the stack in half. Crease and staple the fold to make a six-page booklet.

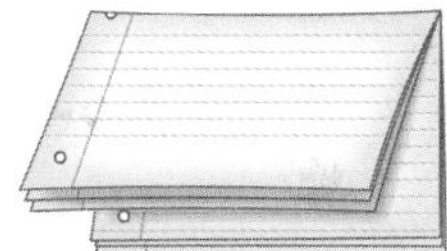

**STEP 3** Draw the outline of a large leaf on the front page and label the page *Cuticle*.

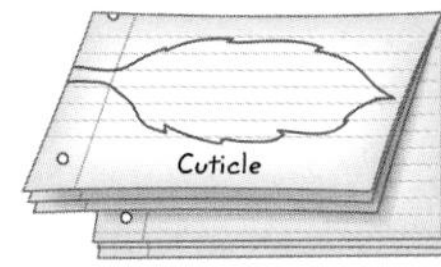


**STEP 4** Label the remaining five pages in the following order: *Epidermis*, *Palisade mesophyll*, *Spongy mesophyll*, *Epidermis*, and *Cuticle*.

FOLDABLES **Use this Foldable with Section 22.2.** As you read the section, write a description of each layer's structure and function on its page.

Section 22.1

## Objectives

- **Describe** the major types of plant cells.
- **Identify** the major types of plant tissues.
- **Distinguish** among the functions of plant cells and tissues.

### Review Vocabulary

**adaptation:** inherited characteristic that results from response to an environmental factor

### New Vocabulary

parenchyma cell
collenchyma cell
sclerenchyma cell
meristem
vascular cambium
cork cambium
epidermis
guard cell
xylem
vessel element
tracheid
phloem
sieve tube member
companion cell
ground tissue

# Plant Cells and Tissues

**MAIN Idea** **Different types of plant cells make up plant tissues.**

**Real-World Reading Link** Buildings are made of a variety of materials. Different materials are used for stairways, plumbing, doors, and the electrical system, because each of these has a different function. Similarly, different plant structures have cells and tissues that function efficiently for specific tasks.

## Plant Cells

Recall from Chapters 7 and 21 that you can identify a typical plant cell, like the one in **Figure 22.1,** by the presence of a cell wall and large central vacuole. Also, plant cells can have chloroplasts. However, there are many different types of plant cells—each with one or more adaptations that enable it to carry out a specific function. Three types of plant cells form most plant tissues. Together they provide storage and food production, strength, flexibility, and support.

**Parenchyma cells** Most flexible, thin-walled cells found throughout a plant are **parenchyma** (puh RENG kuh muh) **cells.** They are the basis for many plant structures and are capable of a wide range of functions, including storage, photosynthesis, gas exchange, and protection. These cells are spherical in shape and their cell walls flatten when they are packed tightly together, as shown in **Table 22.1.** An important trait of parenchyma cells is that they can undergo cell division when mature. When a plant is damaged, parenchyma cells divide to help repair it.

Depending on their function, parenchyma cells can have special features. Some parenchyma cells have many chloroplasts, also shown in **Table 22.1.** These cells often are found in leaves and green stems, and can carry on photosynthesis, producing glucose. Some parenchyma cells, such as those found in roots and fruits, have large central vacuoles that can store substances, such as starch, water, or oils.

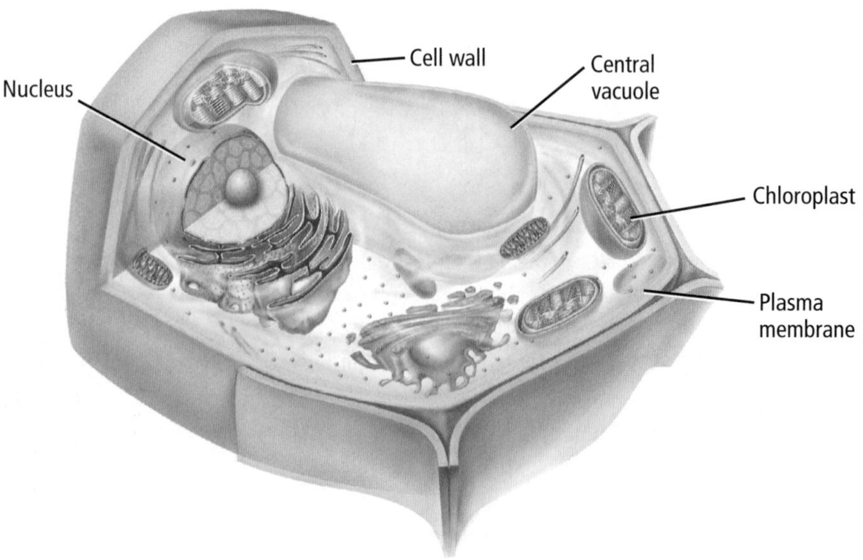


**Figure 22.1** Features unique to a plant cell include a cell wall and a large central vacuole. Plant cells also can contain chloroplasts where photosynthesis occurs.
**Infer** *why chloroplasts are not part of all plant cells.*

Concepts In Motion

Interactive Table To explore more about plant cells and their functions, visit biologygmh.com.

**Table 22.1 Plant Cells and Functions**

| Cell Type | Example | Functions |
|---|---|---|
| Parenchyma | Without chloroplasts (LM Magnification: 400×); With chloroplasts (Stained LM Magnification: 80×) | • Storage<br>• Photosynthesis<br>• Gas exchange<br>• Protection<br>• Tissue repair and replacement |
| Collenchyma | Collenchyma (Cell wall; LM Magnification: 100×) | • Support for surrounding tissues<br>• Provides flexibity for plant<br>• Tissue repair and replacement |
| Sclerenchyma | Sclereid (LM Magnification: 400×); Fibers (LM Magnification: 100×) | • Support<br>• Transport of materials |

**Collenchyma cells** If you have eaten celery, you might be familiar with collenchyma (coh LENG kuh muh) cells. These cells make up those long strings that you can pull from a celery stalk. **Collenchyma cells** are plant cells that often are elongated and occur in long strands or cylinders that provide support for the surrounding cells. As shown in **Table 22.1,** collenchyma cells can have unevenly thickened cell walls. As a collenchyma cell grows, the thinner portions of its cell wall can expand. Because of this growth pattern, collenchyma cells are flexible and can stretch, which enables plants to bend without breaking. Like parenchyma cells, collenchyma cells retain the ability to undergo cell division when mature.

**Sclerenchyma cells** Unlike parenchyma and collenchyma cells, **sclerenchyma** (skle RENG kuh muh) **cells** are plant cells that lack cytoplasm and other living components when they mature, but their thick, rigid cell walls remain. These cells provide support for a plant, and some are used for transporting materials within the plant. Sclerenchyma cells make up most of the wood we use for shelter, fuel, and paper products.

There are two types of sclerenchyma cells—sclereids and fibers—also shown in **Table 22.1.** You might have eaten sclereids—they create the gritty texture of pears. Sclereids, also called stone cells, can be distributed randomly throughout a plant, are shorter than fibers, and are somewhat irregularly shaped. The toughness of seed coats and nut shells results from the presence of sclereids. Sclereids also function in transport, which you will learn more about later in this section. A fiber cell is needle-shaped, has a thick cell wall, and has a small interior space. When stacked end-to-end, fibers form a tough, elastic tissue. Humans have used these fibers for making ropes and linen, canvas, and other textiles for centuries, as shown in **Figure 22.2.**

**Figure 22.2** Fiber cellls in plants have been used to make textiles such as these ancient Egyptian sandals.

## MiniLab 22.1

### Observe Plant Cells

**How can a microscope be used to distinguish plant cell types?** Investigate the three different types of plant cells by making and observing slides of some common plant parts.

**Procedure**

**WARNING:** ***Iodine is poisonous if swallowed and can stain skin and clothes.***

1. Read and complete the lab safety form.
2. Obtain a small, thin **slice of potato** and a thin **cross section of a celery stalk** from your teacher.
3. Place the potato slice on a **slide,** add a drop of **iodine,** and cover with a **coverslip.** Use a **microscope** to observe the potato slice. Record your observations.
4. Place the celery slice on a slide, add a drop of **water,** and cover with a coverslip.
5. Put a drop of **dye** at one end of the coverslip, and then touch a **paper towel** to the other end to draw the dye under the coverslip. Use a microscope to observe the celery slice. Record your observations.
6. Obtain a small amount of **pear tissue,** place it on a slide, and add a coverslip.
7. Using a **pencil eraser,** press gently but firmly on the coverslip until the pear tissue is a thin even layer. Use a microscope to observe the pear tissue. Record your observations.

**Analysis**

1. **Identify** the type of specialized plant cell observed on each slide.
2. **Infer** why there are different cell types in a potato, a celery stalk, and pear tissue.

# Plant Tissues

You learned in Chapter 9 that a tissue is a group of cells that work together to perform a function. Depending on its function, a plant tissue can be composed of one or many types of cells. There are four different tissue types found in plants—meristematic (mer uh stem AH tihk), dermal, vascular, and ground. These are illustrated in **Figure 22.3.**

**Meristematic tissue** Throughout their lives, plants can continue to produce new cells in their meristematic tissues. Meristematic tissues make up **meristems**—regions of rapidly dividing cells. Cells in meristems have large nuclei and small vacuoles or, in some cases, no vacuoles at all. As these cells mature, they can develop into many different kinds of plant cells. Meristematic tissues are located in different regions of a plant.

**Apical meristems** Meristematic tissues at the tips of roots and stems, which produce cells that result in an increase in length, are apical (AY pih kul) meristems, as shown in **Figure 22.3.** This growth is called primary growth. Since plants usually are stationary, it enables stems and roots to enter different environments or different areas of the same environments.

**Intercalary meristems** Another type of meristem, called intercalary (in TUR kuh LAYR ee) meristem, is related to a summer job you might have had—mowing grass. This meristem is found in one or more locations along the stems of many monocots. Intercalary meristem produces new cells that result in an increase in stem or leaf length. If grasses only had apical meristems, they would stop growing after the first mowing. They continue to grow because they have more than one type of meristematic tissue.

**Lateral meristems** Increases in root and stem diameters result from secondary growth produced by two types of lateral meristems. Only nonflowering seed plants, eudicots or dicots, and a few monocots have secondary growth.

The **vascular cambium,** also shown in **Figure 22.3,** is a thin cylinder of meristematic tissue that can run the entire length of roots and stems. It produces new transport cells in some roots and stems.

In some plants, another lateral meristem, the **cork cambium,** produces cells that develop tough cell walls. These cells form a protective outside layer on stems and roots. Cork tissues make up the outer bark on a woody plant like an oak tree. Recall that cells of cork tissue are what Robert Hooke observed when he looked through his microscope.

# Visualizing Meristematic Tissues

**Figure 22.3**
Most plant growth results from the production of cells by meristematic tissues. Stems and roots increase in length mostly due to the production of cells by apical meristems. A plant's vascular cambium produces cells that increase root and stem diameters.

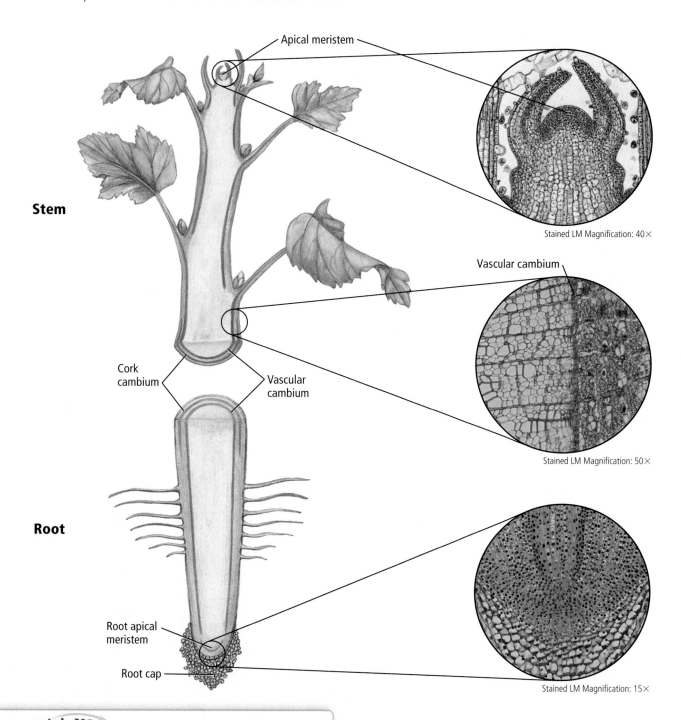

Apical meristem

**Stem**

Stained LM Magnification: 40×

Vascular cambium

Cork cambium

Vascular cambium

Stained LM Magnification: 50×

**Root**

Root apical meristem

Root cap

Stained LM Magnification: 15×

Concepts In Motion **Interactive Figure** To see an animation of plant tissues, visit biologygmh.com.

Biology Online

Stained LM Magnification: 200×

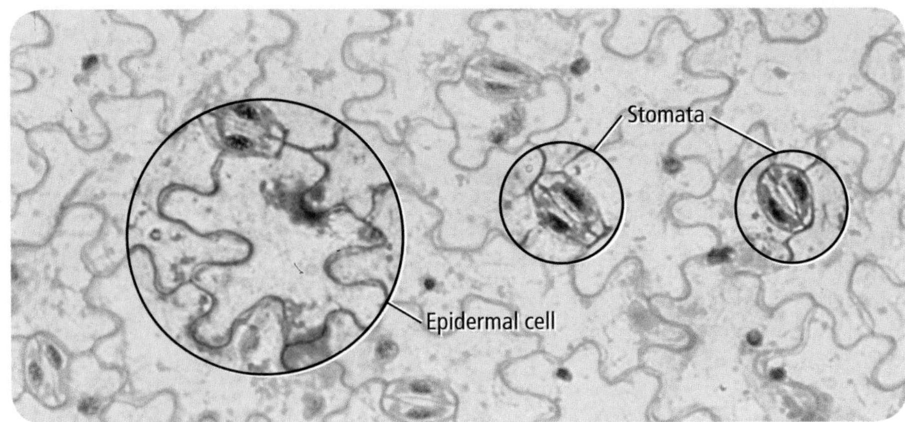


■ **Figure 22.4** The surface of a leaf is composed of tightly-packed epidermal cells that help protect the plant and prevent water loss. Stomata open and close to allow gases in and out.

**Dermal tissue—the epidermis** The layer of cells that makes up the outer covering on a plant is dermal tissue, also called the **epidermis.** Cells of the epidermis resemble pieces of a jigsaw puzzle with interlocking ridges and dips, as shown in **Figure 22.4.** Most epidermal cells can secrete a fatty substance that forms the cuticle. You might recall from Chapter 21 that the cuticle helps reduce water loss from plants by slowing evaporation. The cuticle also can help prevent bacteria and other disease-causing organisms from entering a plant.

**Stomata** Plants can have several adaptations of their epidermis. Recall from Chapter 21 that the epidermis of most leaves and some green stems have stomata—small openings through which carbon dioxide, water, oxygen, and other gases pass. The two cells that form a stoma are **guard cells.** Changes in the shapes of guard cells result in the opening and closing of stomata, as shown in **Figure 22.4.**

**VOCABULARY**

**WORD ORIGIN**

**Trichome**
from the Greek word *trickhma,* meaning *growth of hair.*

**Trichomes** Some epidermal cells on leaves and stems produce hairlike projections called trichomes (TRI kohmz), shown in **Figure 22.5.** Trichomes can give leaves a fuzzy appearance and can help protect the plant from insect and animal predators. Some trichomes even release toxic substances when touched. Trichomes help keep some plants cool by reflecting light.

Color-Enhanced SEM Magnification: 240×

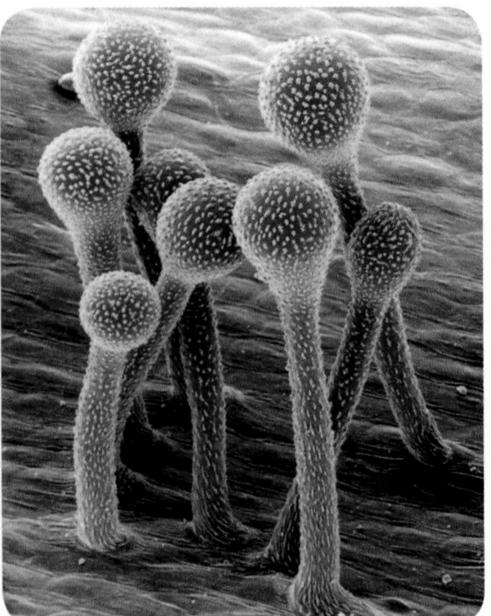

**Trichomes on a leaf**

Magnification: unavailable

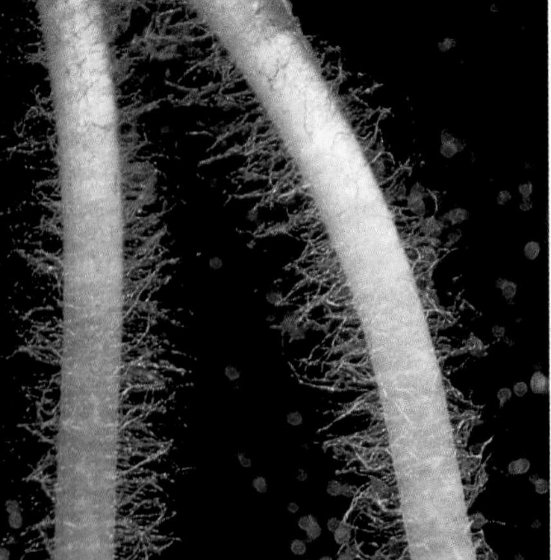

**Root hairs**

■ **Figure 22.5** Epidermal adaptations help plants survive. The tiny glands at the tip of a trichome can contain toxic substances. Root hairs increase the root's surface area.
**Infer** ***why it is important to water recently replanted plants.***

**Root hairs** Some roots have root hairs—fragile extensions of root epidermal cells. Root hairs, as shown in **Figure 22.5,** increase a root's surface area and enable the root to take in a greater volume of materials than it can without root hairs.

**Vascular tissues** Food, water, and other substances are carried throughout your body in your blood vessels. In a plant, the transportation of water, food, and dissolved substances is the main function of two types of vascular tissue—xylem and phloem.

**Xylem** Water that contains dissolved minerals enters a plant through its roots. Some of the water is used in photosynthesis. The dissolved minerals have many functions in cells. This water with dissolved minerals is transported throughout a plant within a system of xylem that flows continuously from the roots to the leaves. **Xylem** (ZI lum) is the water-carrying vascular tissue composed of specialized cells—vessel elements and tracheids (tray KEY ihdz). When mature, each vessel element and tracheid consists of just its cell wall. This lack of cytoplasm at maturity allows water to flow freely through these cells.

**Vessel elements** are tubular cells that are stacked end-to-end, forming strands of xylem called vessels. Vessel elements are open at each end with barlike strips across the openings. In some plants, mature vessel elements lose their end walls. This enables the free movement of water and dissolved substances from one vessel element to another.

**Tracheids** (tray KEY ihdz) are long, cylindrical cells with pitted ends. The cells are found end-to-end and form a tubelike strand. Unlike some mature vessel elements, mature tracheids have end walls. For this reason, tracheids are less efficient than vessel elements at transporting materials. Compare the structure of tracheids to vessel elements in **Figure 22.6.**

In gymnosperms or nonflowering seed plants, xylem is composed almost entirely of tracheids. However, in flowering seed plants, xylem consists of tracheids and vessels. Because vessels are more efficient at transporting water and materials, scientists propose that this might explain why flowering plants inhabit many different environments.

CAREERS IN BIOLOGY

**Turf Scientist** Parks, golf courses, and sports stadiums require the skills of a turf scientist to help maintain the grasses that grow there. He or she has an educational background that includes science, managerial, and business courses. For more information on biology careers, visit biologygmh.com.

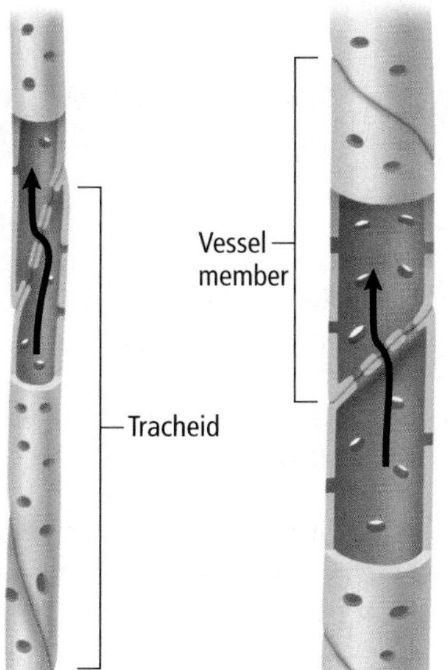


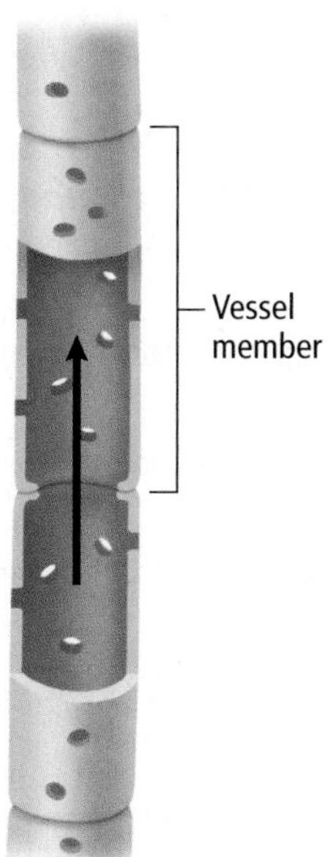


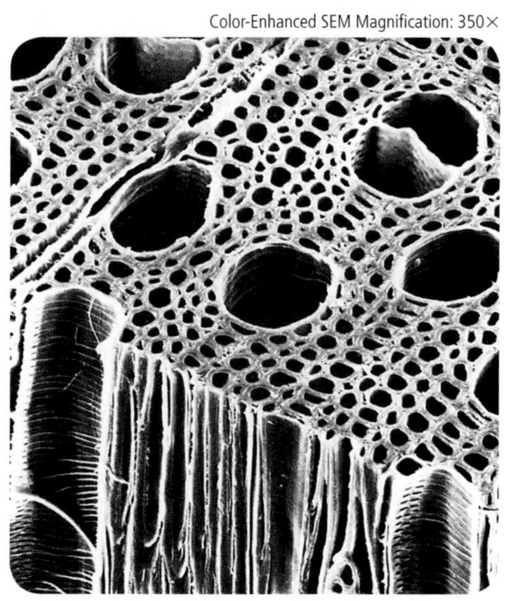


**Figure 22.6** Tracheids and vessel elements are the conducting cells of the xylem.

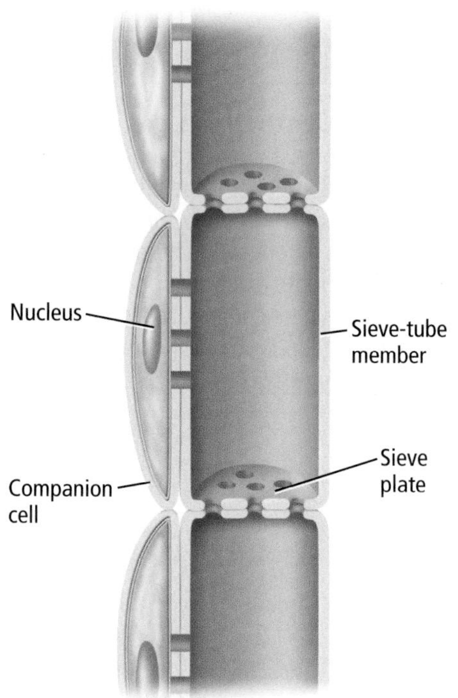


**Figure 22.7** Notice the openings in the sieve plates between the sieve-tube members.

**Phloem** The main food-carrying tissue is **phloem** (FLOH em). It transports dissolved sugars and other organic compounds throughout a plant. Recall that xylem only transports materials away from the roots. Phloem, however, transports substances from the leaves and stems to the roots and from the roots to the leaves and stems. Although not used for transport, there are sclereids and fibers associated with the phloem. These sturdy sclerenchyma cells provide support for the plant.

Phloem consists of two types of cells—sieve tube members and companion cells, shown in **Figure 22.7.** Each **sieve tube member** contains cytoplasm but lacks a nucleus and ribosomes when it is mature. Next to sieve tube members are **companion cells,** each with a nucleus. Scientists hypothesize that this nucleus functions for both the companion cell and the mature sieve tube member. In flowering plants, structures called cell plates are at the end of the sieve tube members. The cell plates have large pores through which dissolved substances can flow.

Some of the glucose produced in leaves and other photosynthetic tissue is metabolized by the plant. However, some is converted to other carbohydrates and transported and stored in regions of the plant called sinks. Examples of sinks are the parenchyma storage cells in the root cortex, which are described in the next section of this chapter. The transport in phloem of dissolved carbohydrates from sources to sinks and other dissolved substances is translocation.

**Vocabulary**
**Word origin**
**Phloem**
from the Greek word *phloios*, meaning *bark.*

**Ground tissue** The category for plant tissues that are not meristematic tissues, dermal tissues, or vascular tissues is ground tissue. **Ground tissues** consist of parenchyma, collenchyma, and sclerenchyma cells and have diverse functions, including photosynthesis, storage, and support. Most of a plant consists of ground tissue. The ground tissue of leaves and green stems contains cells with numerous chloroplasts that produce glucose for the plant. In some stems, roots, and seeds, cells of ground tissue have large vacuoles that store sugars, starch, oils, or other substances. Ground tissues also provide support when they grow between other types of tissue.

## Section 22.1 Assessment

### Section Summary

- There are three types of plant cells—parenchyma, collenchyma, and solerenchyma cells.
- The structure of a plant cell is related to its function.
- There are several different types of plant tissues—meristematic, dermal, vascular, and ground tissues.
- Xylem and phloem are vascular tissues.

### Understand Main Ideas

1. MAIN Idea **Describe** the different types of plant cells in plant tissues.
2. **Compare and contrast** the types of plant cells.
3. **Describe** a root hair and explain its function.
4. **Identify** the location and function of vascular cambium.
5. **Compare** the two types of specialized xylem cells.

### Think Scientifically

6. *Make a table,* using information in this section, that summarizes the structures and functions of the different plant tissues.
7. *Evaluate* the advantage of vessel elements without end walls.
8. WRITING in Biology
Compose a limerick about a type of plant tissue.

Self-Check Quiz biologygmh.com

# Roots, Stems, and Leaves

## Objectives

- **Relate** the structures of roots, stems, and leaves to their functions.
- **Compare and contrast** the structure and function of roots, stems, and leaves.

## Review Vocabulary

**apical meristem:** tissue at the tips of roots and stems that produces cells, which results in an increase in length

## New Vocabulary

root cap
cortex
endodermis
pericycle
petiole
palisade mesophyll
spongy mesophyll
transpiration

**MAIN Idea The structures of plants are related to their functions.**

**Real-World Reading Link** Using a fork to eat a lettuce salad usually is more effective than using a spoon. However, if you were eating tomato soup, a spoon would be more useful than a fork. These are examples of the common expression "the right tool for the right job." The same applies in nature. The variety of plant structures relates to the diversity of plant functions.

## Roots

If you ever have eaten a carrot, a radish, or a sweet potato, then you have eaten part of a plant root. The root usually is the first structure to grow out of the seed when it sprouts. For most plants, roots take in water and dissolved minerals that are transported to the rest of the plant. If you have tried to pull a weed, you experienced another function of roots—they anchor a plant in soil or to some other plant or object. Roots also support a plant against the effects of gravity, extreme wind, and moving water.

In some plants, the root system is so vast that it makes up more than half of the plant's mass. The roots of most plants grow 0.5 to 5 m down into the soil. However, some plants, such as the mesquite (mes KEET) that grows in the dry southwestern part of the United States, have roots that grow downward as deep as 50 m toward available water. Other plants, such as some cacti, have many, relatively shallow branching roots that grow out from the stem in all directions as far as 15 m. Both root types are adaptations to limited water resources.

**Figure 22.8** The root cap covers the root tip and loses cells as the root grows through soil.

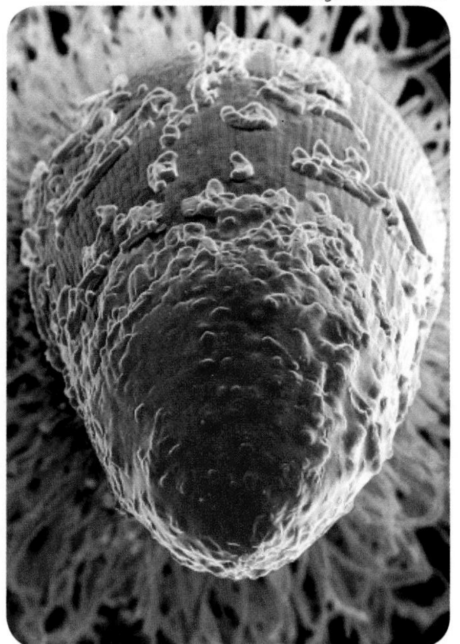

### Root structure and growth

The tip of a root is covered by the **root cap,** as shown in **Figure 22.8.** It consists of parenchyma cells that help protect root tissues as the root grows. The cells of the root cap produce a slimy substance that, together with the outside layer of cells, form a lubricant that reduces friction as the root grows through the soil, a crack in a sidewalk, or some other material. Cells of the root cap that are rubbed off as the root grows are replaced by new cells produced in the root's apical meristem. Recall from Section 22.1 that the root's apical meristem also produces cells that increase the root's length. These cells develop into the numerous types of root tissues that perform different functions.

You also learned in Section 22.1 that an epidermal layer covers the root. Some root epidermal cells produce root hairs that absorb water and dissolved minerals. The layer below this epidermal layer is the **cortex.** It is composed of ground tissues made of parenchyma cells that are involved in transport and storage of plant substances. The cortex is between the epidermis and the vascular tissues of the root. To reach vascular tissues, all water and nutrients that are taken in by the epidermal cells must move through the cortex.

 **Reading Check List** three functions of roots.

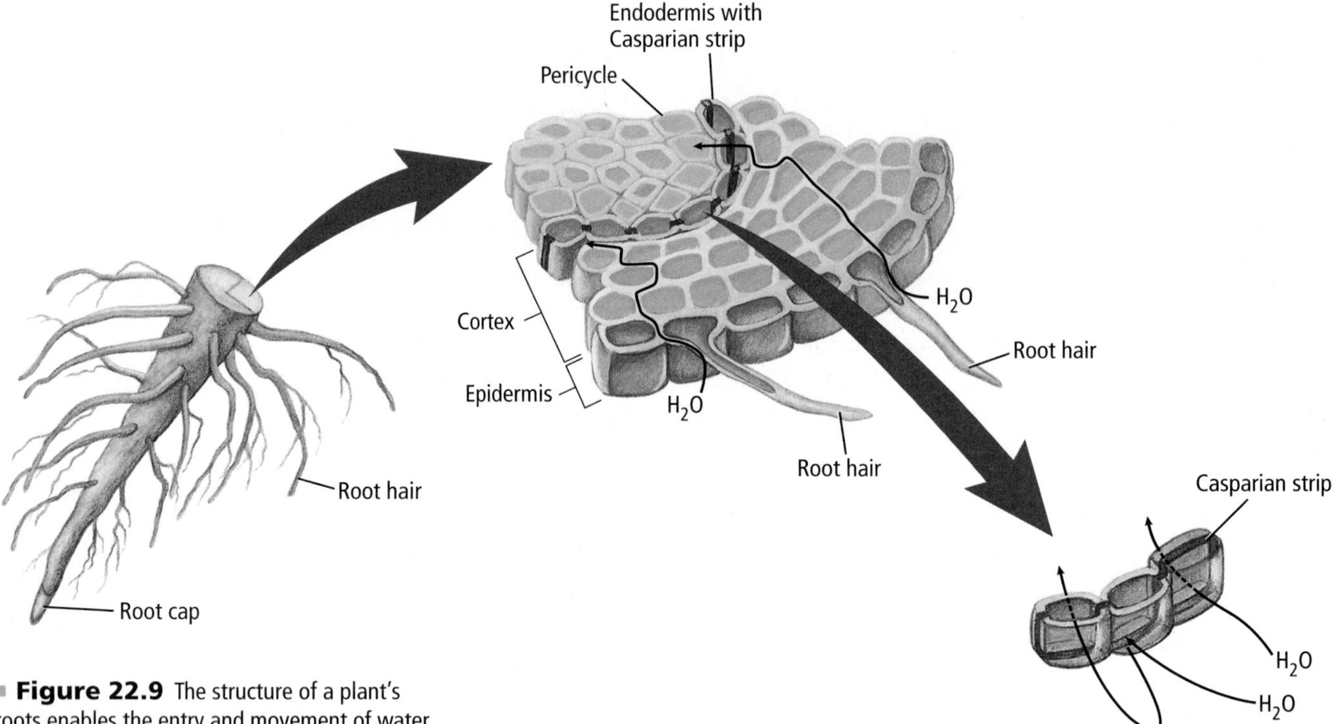


■ **Figure 22.9** The structure of a plant's roots enables the entry and movement of water and dissolved minerals into the plant.
**Sequence** ***the tissues through which water passes as it moves from a root hair to xylem tissue of a root.***

**Concepts In Motion**

**Interactive Figure** To see an animation showing ways that nutrients can enter the cells of roots, visit biologygmh.com.

At the inner boundary of the cortex is a layer of cells called the **endodermis,** as illustrated in **Figure 22.9.** Encircling each cell of the endodermis as part of the cell wall is a waterproof strip called a Casparian strip. Its location is similar to that of mortar that surrounds bricks in a wall. The Casparian strip creates a barrier that forces water and dissolved minerals to pass through endodermal cells rather than around them. Therefore, the plasma membranes of endodermal cells regulate the material that enters the vascular tissues.

The layer of cells directly next to the endodermis toward the center of the root is called the **pericycle.** It is the tissue that produces lateral roots. In dicots, most eudicots, and some monocots, a vascular cambium develops from part of the pericycle. Recall that the vascular cambium produces vascular tissues that contribute to an increase in the root's diameter. The vascular tissues—xylem and phloem—are in the center of a root. Monocots and eudicots or dicots can be distinguished by the pattern of the xylem and phloem in their roots, as shown in **Figure 22.10.**

Stained LM Magnification: 14×

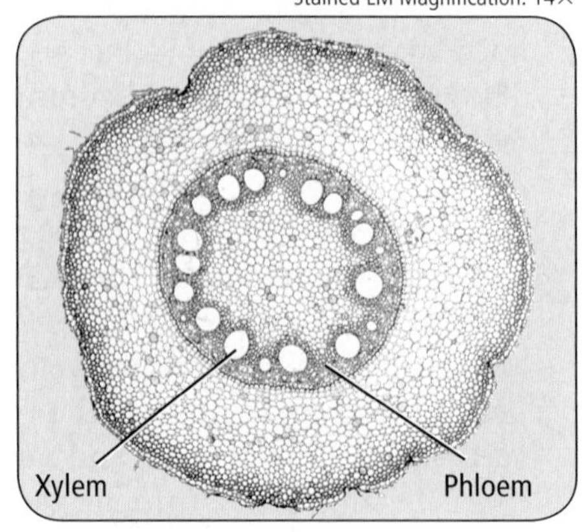


**Monocot**

Stained LM Magnification: 400×

Xylem

Phloem

**Eudicot or Dicot**

■ **Figure 22.10** In monocots, strands of xylem and phloem cells alternate, usually surrounding a central core of cells called pith. The xylem in eudicot and dicot roots is in the center and forms an X shape. Phloem cells are between the arms of the X.

**Poinsettias**

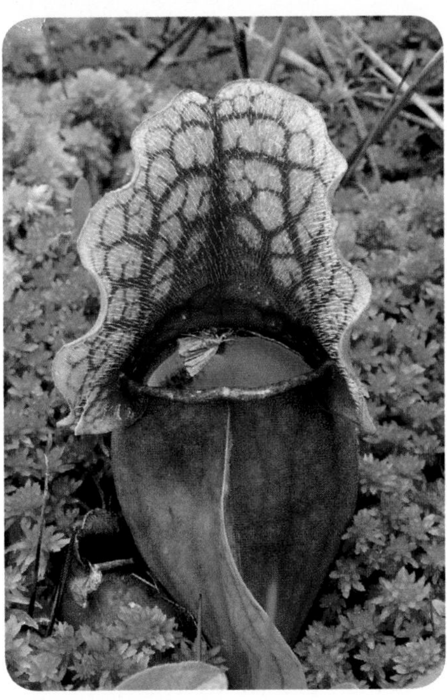

**Pitcher plant**

■ **Figure 22.16** Leaf modifications relate to different functions. Bracts grow below flowers and attract pollinators. The inside of the pitcher plant's modified leaf has hairs that grow downward. This prevents a trapped animal from crawling out.

In plants like poinsettias, leaves called bracts at the tips of stems change from green to another color in response to the number of hours of darkness in their environments. These plants usually have tiny flowers at the center of the colored leaves, shown in **Figure 22.16.** The leaves look like flower petals and attract pollinators.

The leaves of the sundew plant produce a sticky substance that traps insects. The pitcher plant, also shown in **Figure 22.16,** has cylinderlike modified leaves that fill with water and can trap and drown insects and small animals. Both of these adaptations enable the plants to get nutrients, especially nitrogen, from the insects they capture.

You might be familiar with poison ivy or poison oak that can cause severe skin irritation for some people. These are examples of leaves that contain toxic chemicals that deter organisms from touching them. Some leaves have modifications that deter herbivores from eating them. For example, the epidermis of tomato and squash leaves and stems have tiny hairs with glands at their tips. The glands contain substances that repel insects and other herbivores.

When you read about stems, you learned that bulbs were shortened stems with leaves. A bulb's leaves are modified food storage structures. They provide the dormant bulb with necessary energy resources when favorable growth conditions exist.

## Section 22.2 Assessment

### Section Summary

- Roots anchor plants and absorb water and nutrients.
- Stems support the plant and hold the leaves.
- Leaves are the sites of photosynthesis and transpiration.
- There are many different modifications of roots, stems, and leaves.
- Modifications help plants survive in different environments.

### Understand Main Ideas

1. MAIN Idea **Summarize** the functions of the root cap, cortex, and endodermis.
2. **Compare** a leaf's palisade mesophyll to its spongy mesophyll.
3. **Describe** two leaf modifications and their functions.
4. **Draw and label** the arrangement of vascular tissue in a monocot stem and root and in a eudicot stem and root.

### Think Scientifically

5. *Evaluate* why the role of stomata in a plant is important.
6. MATH in Biology A forest produces approximately 970 kg of oxygen for every metric ton of wood produced. If the average person breathes about 165 kg of oxygen per year, how many people does this forest support?

Biology Online Self-Check Quiz biologygmh.com

# Section 22.3

## Objectives

- **Identify** the major types of plant hormones.
- **Explain** how hormones affect the growth of plants.
- **Describe and analyze** the different types of plant responses.

## Review Vocabulary

**active transport:** the movement of materials across the plasma membrane against a concentration gradient; requires energy

## New Vocabulary

auxin
gibberellins
ethylene
cytokinin
nastic response
tropism

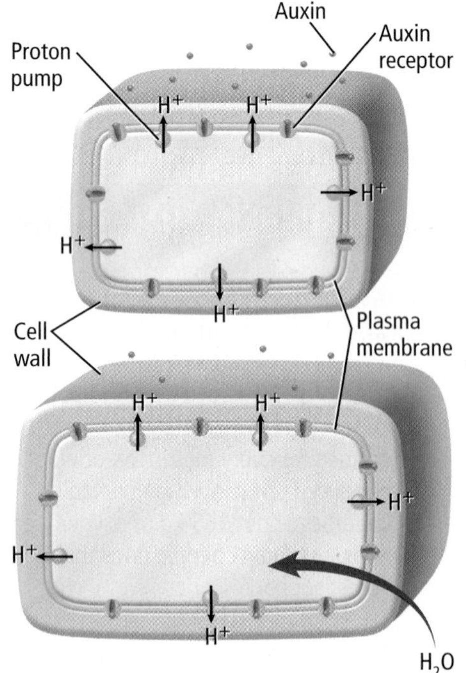


**Figure 22.17** Auxin promotes the flow of hydrogen ions into the cell wall, which weakens the cell wall. Water enters the cell and the cell lengthens.

# Plant Hormones and Responses

**MAIN Idea** **Hormones can affect a plant's responses to its environment.**

**Real-World Reading Link** As you might have learned in health class or another science course, various responses of your body are controlled by hormones. When you eat, hormones signal cells of your digestive system to release digestive enzymes. Although plants don't have digestive systems with enzymes, hormones do control many aspects of their growth and development.

## Plant Hormones

You read in Chapter 6 that hormones are organic compounds that are made in one part of an organism, and then are transported to another part where they have an effect. It takes only a tiny amount of a hormone to cause a change in an organism. Were you surprised to read that plants produce hormones? Plant hormones can affect cell division, growth, or differentiation. Research results indicate that plant hormones work by chemically binding to the plasma membrane at specific sites called receptor proteins. These receptors can affect the expression of a gene, the activity of enzymes, or the permeability of the plasma membrane. You will learn more about human hormones in Chapter 35.

**Auxin** One of the first plant hormones to be identified was **auxin.** There are different kinds of auxins, but indoleacetic (IHN doh luh see tihk) acid (IAA) is the most widely studied. IAA is produced in apical meristems, buds, young leaves, and other rapidly growing tissues. It moves throughout a plant from one parenchyma cell to the next by a type of active transport. The rate of this movement has been measured at 1 cm per hour. Some auxins also move in the phloem. Also, an auxin moves in only one direction—away from where it was produced.

**Connection to Chemistry** Auxin usually stimulates the lengthening, or elongation, of cells. Research indicates that in young cells this is an indirect process. Auxin promotes a flow of hydrogen ions through proton pumps from the cytoplasm into the cell wall. This creates a more acidic environment, which weakens the connections between the cellulose fibers in the cell wall. It also activates certain enzymes that help to break down the cell wall. Due to the loss of hydrogen ions in the cytoplasm, water enters the cell, as shown in **Figure 22.17.** The combination of weakened cell walls and increased internal pressure results in cell elongation.

The effect of auxin in a plant varies greatly depending on its concentration and location. For example, in some plants the concentration of auxin that promotes stem growth can inhibit root growth. Low concentrations of auxin usually stimulate cell elongation. However, at higher concentrations, auxin can have the reverse effect. The presence of other hormones can modify the effects of an auxin.

*Use the images below to answer question 33.*

**33.** Which stem shown above is exhibiting negative gravitropism?

**A.** A  **C.** C
**B.** B  **D.** D

## Constructed Response

**34. Open Ended** Discuss the pros and cons of the transport of auxin from one parenchyma cell to another instead of in the vascular tissue.

**35. Short Answer** Refer to **Figure 22.17** and explain how auxin can cause cell elongation.

**36. Short Answer** Explain why tropic responses are permanent while nastic responses are reversible.

## Think Critically

**37. Design** an experiment to determine if bean plants show apical dominance.

**38. Evaluate** the following statement: "Seeds soaked in gibberellins will germinate faster than seeds not soaked in gibberellins."

**39. CAREERS IN BIOLOGY** Farmers must evaluate the use of plant hormones to increase crop production. Do you think it is a good idea? Compare it to the use of growth hormones that are used to increase the milk production of cows.

## Additional Assessment

**40. WRITING in Biology** What if you could develop a new plant hormone? What would you have it do? How would it work and what would you name it?

## Document-Based Questions

*A team of biologists studied the effect of temperature and carbon dioxide on ponderosa pines. The graph below represents the amounts of tracheids with various diameters grown at different temperatures.*

*Use the graph to answer questions 41–42.*

Data obtained from: Maherali, H., and DeLucia, E. H. 2000. Interactive effects of elevated $CO_2$ and temperature on water transport in ponderosa pine. *Amer. Journal of Botany* 87: 243-249.

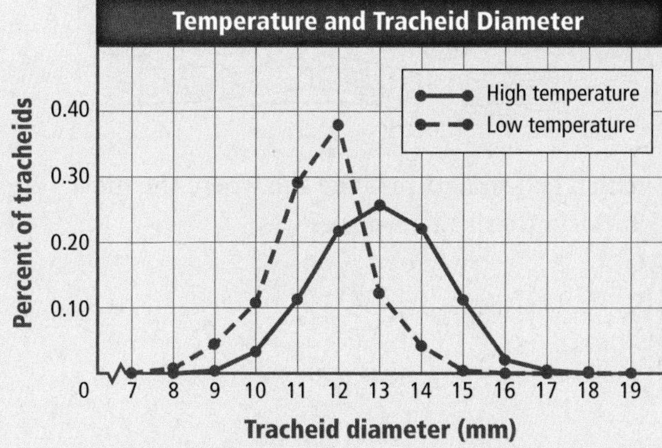


**41.** How does the temperature affect the diameter of developing tracheid cells?

**42.** How does the relationship between temperature and diameter relate to the tracheid function?

## Cumulative Review

**43.** In pigeons, the checker pattern of feathers (*P*) is dominant to the nonchecker pattern (*p*). Suppose a checker pigeon with the genotype *Pp* mates with a nonchecker pigeon. Use a Punnett square to predict the genotypic ratio of their offspring. **(Chapter 10)**

**44.** Create an analogy that illustrates why two species in the same family of organisms also must be in the same order. **(Chapter 17)**

# Standardized Test Practice

**Cumulative**

## Multiple Choice

1. The Miller-Urey experiment tested which hypothesis?
   A. Margulis's endosymbiont theory
   B. Miller's amino acid origin
   C. Oparin's primordial soup idea
   D. Pasteur's biogenesis theory

*Use the diagram below to answer question 2.*

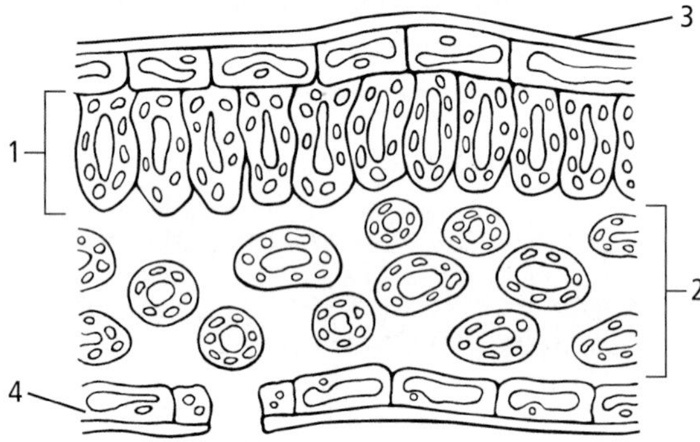


2. Which leaf structure is the site where the most photosynthesis takes place?
   A. 1
   B. 2
   C. 3
   D. 4

3. Lichens can be an indicator of environmental quality. If a coal-fired electric plant was built and then the lichens in the area decreased, which would be the most likely cause?
   A. air quality decreased
   B. annual temperatures decreased
   C. humidity patterns changed
   D. rainfall patterns changed

4. Which is one method of asexual reproduction that can occur in fungi?
   A. conjugation
   B. fragmentation
   C. segmentation
   D. transformation

5. Which development in plants contributed most to the evolution of large trees?
   A. alternation of generations
   B. flowers
   C. seeds
   D. vascular tissue

6. Which describes how funguslike protists obtain food?
   A. They absorb nutrients from decaying organisms.
   B. They obtain nutrients by feeding on unicellular organisms.
   C. They have a symbiotic relationship with an animal host, obtaining nutrients from it.
   D. They produce sugars as a nutrient source by using energy from sunlight.

7. Which is the function of a plant's root cap?
   A. generate new cells for root growth
   B. help the root tissues absorb water
   C. protect root tissue as the root grows
   D. provide support for the root tissues

*Use the diagram below to answer question 8.*

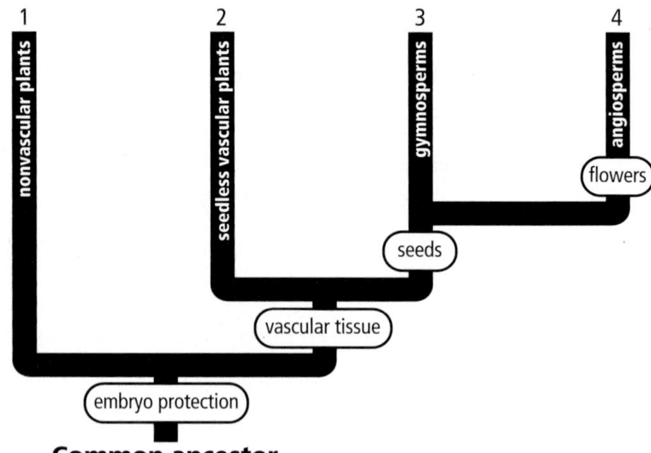


8. Which number represents where you would expect to find cycadophytes on this evolutionary tree?
   A. 1
   B. 2
   C. 3
   D. 4

**Pollination mechanisms** Different anthophyte species have flowers of distinctive sizes, shapes, colors, and petal arrangements. Many of these adaptations relate to pollination.

**Animal pollination** As shown in **Figure 23.9,** many animal-pollinated flowers are brightly colored, have strong scents, or produce a sweet liquid called nectar. When insects and other small animals move from flower to flower searching for nectar, they can carry pollen from one flower to another flower. Other insects collect pollen for food. The bright colors and sweet scents of peonies, roses, and lilacs attract insects such as bees, butterflies, beetles, and wasps. White or pale yellow flowers are more visible at dusk and at night, and attract nocturnal animals, such as moths and bats. The fruity smell of some flowers attracts fruit-eating bats that act as the flowers' pollinators. On the first page of this chapter, you read about *Rafflesia,* a flower. It gives off the odor of rotting meat. Flowers with this trait attract fly pollinators. Bird-pollinated flowers often give off little or no aroma. A bird generally has a poor sense of smell, so it usually locates flowers by sight.

**Wind pollination** Flowers that generally lack showy or fragrant floral parts, also shown in **Figure 23.9,** usually are wind-pollinated. They produce huge amounts of lightweight pollen. This helps to ensure that some pollen grains will land on the stigma of a flower of the same species. Also, the stamens of wind-pollinated flowers often hang below the petals, exposing them to the wind. The stigma of a wind-pollinated flower often is large, which helps to ensure that a pollen grain might land on it. Wind-pollinated plants include most trees and grasses.

**Self pollination** Connection to History Recall from Chapter 10 that Mendel chose to experiment with pea plants during his genetic experiments. He knew that pea flowers tend to self-pollinate, but also can be cross-pollinated. Self-pollinating flowers can pollinate themselves or another flower on the same plant. Cross-pollinated flowers receive pollen from another plant. Some flowers must be cross-pollinated. This is one reason that pollinators play important roles in anthophyte reproduction. Pollinators provide a way to transfer pollen for flowers that must be cross-pollinated. Pollinators also ensure that reproduction can occur for imperfect flowers, like squash blossoms, as shown in **Figure 23.10.**

**CAREERS IN BIOLOGY**

**Plant Breeder** Knowledge of flower structures, pollination mechanisms, and genetics are essential for a plant breeder. A plant breeder conducts selective breeding by choosing plants with desirable traits, breeding them together, and then recording results. For more information on biology careers, visit biologygmh.com.

■ **Figure 23.10** Honeybees or other insects must transfer pollen from the male squash flower to the female squash flower for the fruit—a squash—to form.
**Determine** ***Are squash flowers perfect or imperfect? Explain.***

**LAUNCH Lab**

**Review** Based on what you've read about plant reproduction, how would you now answer the analysis questions?

**Photoperiodism** After noticing that certain plants only flowered at certain times of the year, plant biologists conducted experiments to explain this observation. The research initially focused on the number of hours of daylight to which the plants were exposed. However, researchers discovered that the critical factor that influenced flowering was the number of hours of uninterrupted darkness, not the number of hours of daylight. This flowering response is known as **photoperiodism** (foh toh PIHR ee uh dih zum). Scientists also learned that the beginning of flower development for each plant species was a response to a range in the number of hours of darkness. This range of hours is called the plant's critical period.

Botanists classify flowering plants into one of four different groups—short-day plants, long-day plants, intermediate-day plants, or day-neutral plants. This classification is based on the critical period. The names reflect the researchers' original focus—the number of hours of daylight. It is important to remember that a more accurate term for a short-day plant, for example, would be a long-night plant. As you read the descriptions of these plants, refer to **Figure 23.11.**

**Short-day photoperiodism** A **short-day plant** flowers when exposed daily to a number of hours of darkness that is greater than its critical period. For example, a short-day plant could flower when exposed to 16 hours of darkness. Short-day plants flower during the winter, spring, or fall, when the number of hours of darkness is greater than the number of hours of light. Some short-day plants you might recognize are pansies, poinsettias, tulips, and chrysanthemums.

**Long-day photoperiodism** A **long-day plant** flowers when the number of hours of darkness is less than its critical period. These plants flower during the summer. Examples of long-day plants are lettuce, asters, coneflowers, spinach, and potatoes.

## MiniLab 23.2

### Compare Flower Structures

**How do the structures of flowers vary?** Just a quick browse through a flower garden or florist's shop reveals that there is great diversity among flowers. Investigate how flowers differ from species to species.

**Procedure**

1. Read and complete the lab safety form.
2. Create a data table to record your observations and measurements.
3. Obtain the **flowers** for this lab from your teacher.
4. Observe the differences in structure, color, size, and odor of the flowers. Do not damage the flowers in any way.
5. Make a sketch of each flower and record other observations in your data table.
6. Return the flowers to your teacher.

**Analysis**

1. **Compare and contrast** the flower structures you observed.
2. **Infer** why the flower petals that you observed were different colors.
3. **Propose** an explanation for the different sizes and shapes of flower structures.

As the endosperm matures, the outside layers of the ovule harden and form a protective tissue called the **seed coat.** You might notice the seed coats of beans or peas when you eat them. The seed coat is the thin, outer covering that often comes off or loosens as seeds are cooked.

Have you ever eaten a tomato or cucumber and noticed the number of seeds inside? Depending on the plant, the ovary can contain one ovule or hundreds. As the ovule develops into a seed, changes occur in the ovary that lead to the formation of a fruit.

Fruits form primarily from the ovary wall. In some cases, the fruit consists of the ovary wall and other flower organs. For example, the seeds of the apple are within the core that develops from the ovary. The juicy tissue that we eat develops from other flower parts.

Besides the apple, other fruits, such as peaches and oranges, are fleshy, while some are dry and hard, such as walnuts and grains. Study **Table 23.1** to learn about types of fruit.

**Reading Check** **Compare and contrast** the formation of a seed and a fruit.

**Concepts In Motion**

**Interactive Table** To explore more about types of fruit, visit Tables at biologygmh.com.

**Table 23.1 Types of Fruit**

| Fruit Type | Example of Flower and Fruit | Description |
|---|---|---|
| **Simple fleshy fruits** | **Peach** | Simple fleshy fruits can contain one or more seeds. Apples, peaches, grapes, oranges, tomatoes, and pumpkins are simple fleshy fruits. |
| **Aggregate fruits** | **Raspberry** | Aggregate fruits form from flowers with multiple female organs that fuse as the fruits ripen. Strawberries, raspberries, and blackberries are examples of aggregate fruits. |
| **Multiple fruits** | **Pineapple** | Multiple fruits form from many flowers that fuse as the fruits ripen. Figs, pineapples, mulberries, and osage oranges are examples of multiple fruits. |
| **Dry fruits** | **Redbud** | When mature, these fruits are dry. Examples of dry fruits include pods, nuts, and grains. |

**Seed dispersal** In addition to providing some protection for seeds, fruits also help disperse seeds. Dispersal of seeds away from the parent plant increases the survival rate of offspring. For example, when many plants are growing in one area, there is competition for light, water, and soil nutrients. Seeds sprouting next to parent plants and with other offspring compete for these resources.

Fruits that are attractive to animals can be transported great distances away from the parent plant. Animals that gather and bury or store fruits usually do not recover all of them, so the seeds might sprout. Some of the animals, such as deer, bears, and birds, consume fruits. The seeds pass through their digestive tracts undamaged and then are deposited on the ground along with the animals' wastes. Some seeds have structural modifications that enable them to be transported by water, animals, or wind. You can review seed dispersal in Chapter 21.

**Seed germination** When the embryo in a seed starts to grow, the process is called **germination.** There are a number of factors that affect germination, including the presence of water and/or oxygen, temperature, and those described in **Data Analysis Lab 23.1.** Most seeds have an optimum temperature for germination. For example, some seeds can germinate when soil is cool, but others need the warmer soils.

Germination begins when a seed absorbs water, either as a liquid or gas. As cells take in water, the seed swells; this can break the seed coat. Water also transports materials to the growing regions of the seed.

Within the seed, digestive enzymes help start the breakdown of stored food. This broken-down food and oxygen are the raw materials for cellular respiration, which results in the release of energy for growth.

## DATA ANALYSIS LAB 23.1

**Based on Real Data***

### Recognize Cause and Effect

**What is allelopathy?** In nature, some plants produce chemicals that affect nearby plants. This is called allelopathy (uh LEEL luh pa thee). Some scientists studied the connection between allelopathy and the spread of nonnative plants, such as garlic mustard *Alliaria petiolata*. They investigated the effect of garlic mustard on the seed germination of native plants *Geum urbanum* and *Geum laciniatum.*

**Think Critically**

1. **Describe** the effect of garlic mustard on seed germination.
2. **Design an experiment** Alfalfa is known to allelopathically inhibit germination of some seeds. Use alfalfa sprouts to investigate their effect on seeds of your choice.

**Data and Observations**

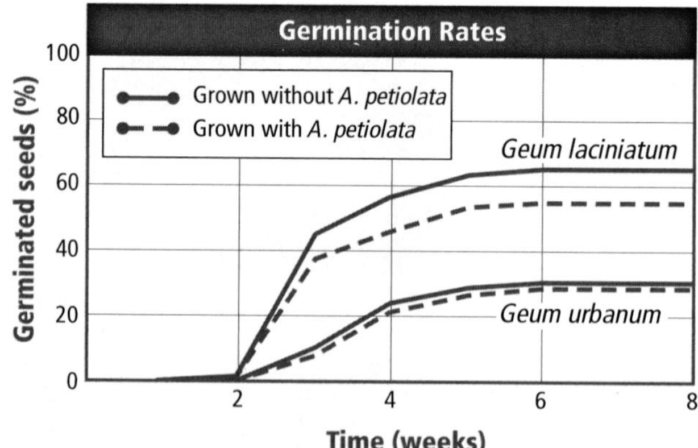


*Data obtained from: Prati, D. and O Bossdorf. 2004. Allelopathic inhibition of germination by *Alliaria petiolata* (Brassicaceae). *Amer. Journal of Bot.* 91(2): 285–288.

33. What is the inactive period of a seed?
    A. alternation of generations
    B. dormancy
    C. fertilization
    D. photoperiodism

## Constructed Response

34. **Short Answer** Explain why fruit and/or seed dispersal is so important.

35. **Open Ended** Hypothesize why an anthophyte's female gametophyte produces so many nuclei when only two are involved in fertilization.

36. **Open Ended** When a seed germinates, as shown in **Figure 23.16,** the radicle usually is the first structure to break through the seed coat. Why is this beneficial for the embryo?

## Think Critically

*Use the graph below to answer questions 37–38.*

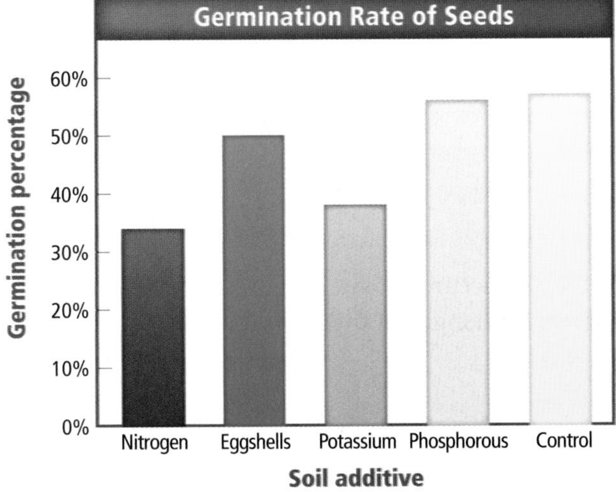


37. **Compare** the effects of each soil additive on the rate of germination to the control's rate of germination.

38. **Design** an experiment to test the effect on the rate of germination for various amounts of a soil additive. Choose one of the soil additives listed in the graph above.

39. **Analyze** the reduction in size of the gametophyte from mosses, to ferns, to anthophytes. What are the advantages or disadvantages of this trend?

## Additional Assessment

40.   Write a short story about the life of a pollen grain.

### DBQ Document-Based Questions

Data obtained from: Lang, A. et al. 1977. Promotion and inhibition of flower formation in a day-neutral plant in grafts with a short-day plant and a long-day plant. *Proc. Natl. Acad. Sci.* 74 (6): 2412-2416.

*The day-neutral plant flowered sooner when it was grafted to the short-day plant that was exposed to its critical period. The flowering of another day-neutral plant also was accelerated when it was grafted to a long-day plant that was exposed to its critical period.*

41. Examine the drawings. Form a hypothesis about why the grafted day-neutral plants flowered before the day-neutral plant that was not grafted.

42. Predict what might happen if a long-day plant was grafted to a short-day plant and they were exposed to the critical period of the short-day plant.

43. Design an experiment to determine the "longest day" under which a long-day plant flowers.

## Cumulative Review

44. Relate genetic engineering to agriculture. **(Chapter 13)**

45. Choose three lines of evidence that support evolution. Give an example of each. **(Chapter 15)**

46. Describe the types of environments where you would expect to find protists. **(Chapter 19)**

# Standardized Test Practice

**Cumulative**

## Multiple Choice

1. Which vascular tissue is composed of living tubular cells that carry sugars from the leaves to other parts of the plant?
   A. cambium
   B. parenchyma
   C. phloem
   D. xylem

*Use the diagram below to answer question 2.*

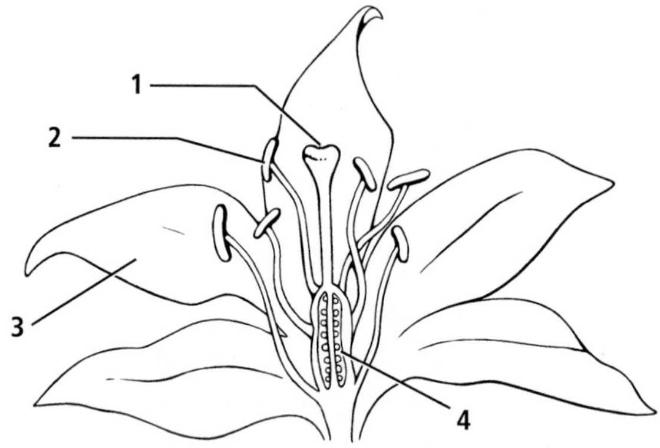


2. Which labeled structure is part of a flower's male reproductive organ?
   A. 1
   B. 2
   C. 3
   D. 4

3. Which statement provides evidence that anthophytes evolved after other seed plants?
   A. About 75 percent of all plants are anthophytes.
   B. Anthophytes do not require water to facilitate the fertilization of an egg.
   C. Prehistoric tree-like ferns were the main coal-forming plants.
   D. The seeds of anthophytes are more advanced than those of other seed plants.

4. Which precedes the haploid generation in seedless vascular plants?
   A. epiphytes
   B. gametophytes
   C. rhizomes
   D. spores

5. Which is the primary pollinator for conifers?
   A. birds
   B. insects
   C. water
   D. wind

*Use the diagram below to answer question 6.*

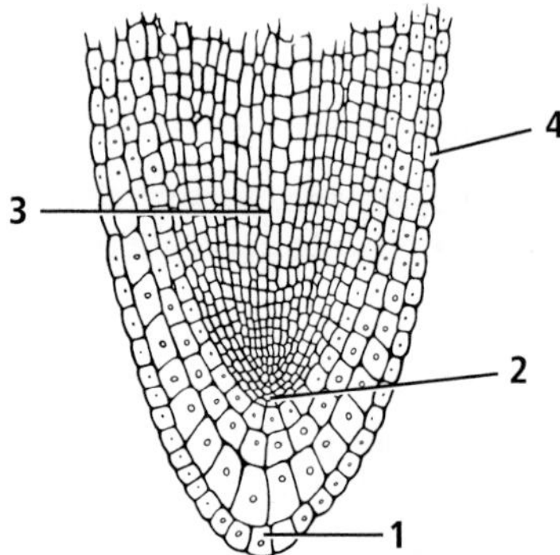


6. Which structure produces cells that result in an increase in length of the root?
   A. 1
   B. 2
   C. 3
   D. 4

7. Which statement is true of an aseptate fungus?
   A. Cell walls are made of cellulose.
   B. Cell walls are made of thin membranes.
   C. Hyphae are not divided by cross walls.
   D. Hyphae are not present except during reproduction.

8. A tuber is an adaptation of which structure?
   A. cell
   B. leaf
   C. root
   D. stem

## Short Answer

*Use the diagram below to answer question 9.*

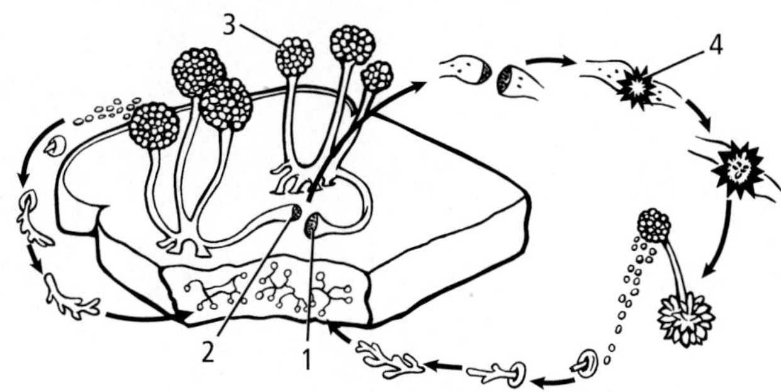


9. Describe two ways that bread mold could spread in a kitchen.

10. List two characteristics of nonvascular plants that compensate for their lack of transport tissues.

11. A certain type of fern has a chromosome number of 14. What would be the chromosome number of the prothallus? Explain why.

12. Explain the benefit to nonvascular plants of having very thin rhizoids and leaflike structures.

13. Name and describe the three types of plant cells and their functions.

14. Interpret how the actions of plate tectonics affected the evolution of primates.

15. Imagine that a friend who lives in Montana gives you some seeds from a plant. You plant the seeds in Florida but they do not grow. Predict why the seeds do not germinate in Florida.

## Extended Response

16. Infer how collenchyma cells support surrounding plant tissues.

17. Critique the idea that roots in the ground do not need oxygen to survive.

18. A forest near a city provides drainage for rainfall runoff. A group of citizens is protesting new housing developments in the forest because they believe flooding and property destruction will result. Analyze the value of biodiversity that describes their concern.

19. Suppose that a couple wants to have children and neither the man nor the woman has cystic fibrosis. However, some distant family members have cystic fibrosis. Could their child have the disease? Write an explanation summarizing the risk for this couple.

## Essay Question

Water is important for functions in plants. For example, it is one of the reactants in the chemical reactions of photosynthesis. Water enters a plant by diffusion. Most of the water that enters a plant diffuses into roots. Therefore, water must be in a higher concentration in the soil than in the roots. After water enters the roots, it moves through vascular tissue to tissues that contain chloroplasts. The water also diffuses into the plants' cells, making them rigid.

*Using the information in the paragraph above, answer the following question in essay format.*

20. When more water leaves a plant than enters it, the plant begins to wilt. Explain the role of guard cells in regulating the amount of water in a plant.

**NEED EXTRA HELP?**

| If You Missed Question . . . | 1 | 2 | 3 | 4 | 5 | 6 | 7 | 8 | 9 | 10 | 11 | 12 | 13 | 14 | 15 | 16 | 17 | 18 | 19 | 20 |
|---|---|---|---|---|---|---|---|---|---|---|---|---|---|---|---|---|---|---|---|---|
| Review Section . . . | 22.1 | 23.2 | 21.4 | 21.3 | 23.1 | 22.1 | 20.1 | 22.2 | 20.3 | 21.2 | 23.1 | 21.2 | 22.1 | 16.1 | 23.3 | 22.1 | 22.2 | 5.1 | 11.1 | 22.2 |

# UNIT 7 Invertebrates

**Chapter 24**
Introduction to Animals
**BIG Idea** Animal phylogeny is determined in part by animal body plans and adaptations.

**Chapter 25**
Worms and Mollusks
**BIG Idea** Worms and mollusks have evolved to have a variety of adaptations for living as parasites or for living in water or soil.

**Chapter 26**
Arthropods
**BIG Idea** Arthropods have evolved to have a variety of adaptations for successful diversity, population, and persistence.

**Chapter 27**
Echinoderms and Invertebrate Chordates
**BIG Idea** Echinoderms and invertebrate chordates have features that connect them to the chordates that evolved after them.

## CAREERS IN BIOLOGY

### Entomologist

**Entomologists** are scientists who study insects and their behavioral patterns. Entomologists who conduct research, such as this field entomologist is doing, contribute to a better understanding of the ecosystem's function as a whole.

**WRITING in Biology** Visit biologygmh.com to learn more about careers in entomology. Write two scenarios in which entomologists study insects that are directly beneficial to humans.

**Biology Online**

To read more about entomologists in action, visit biologygmh.com.

CHAPTER 24

# Introduction to Animals

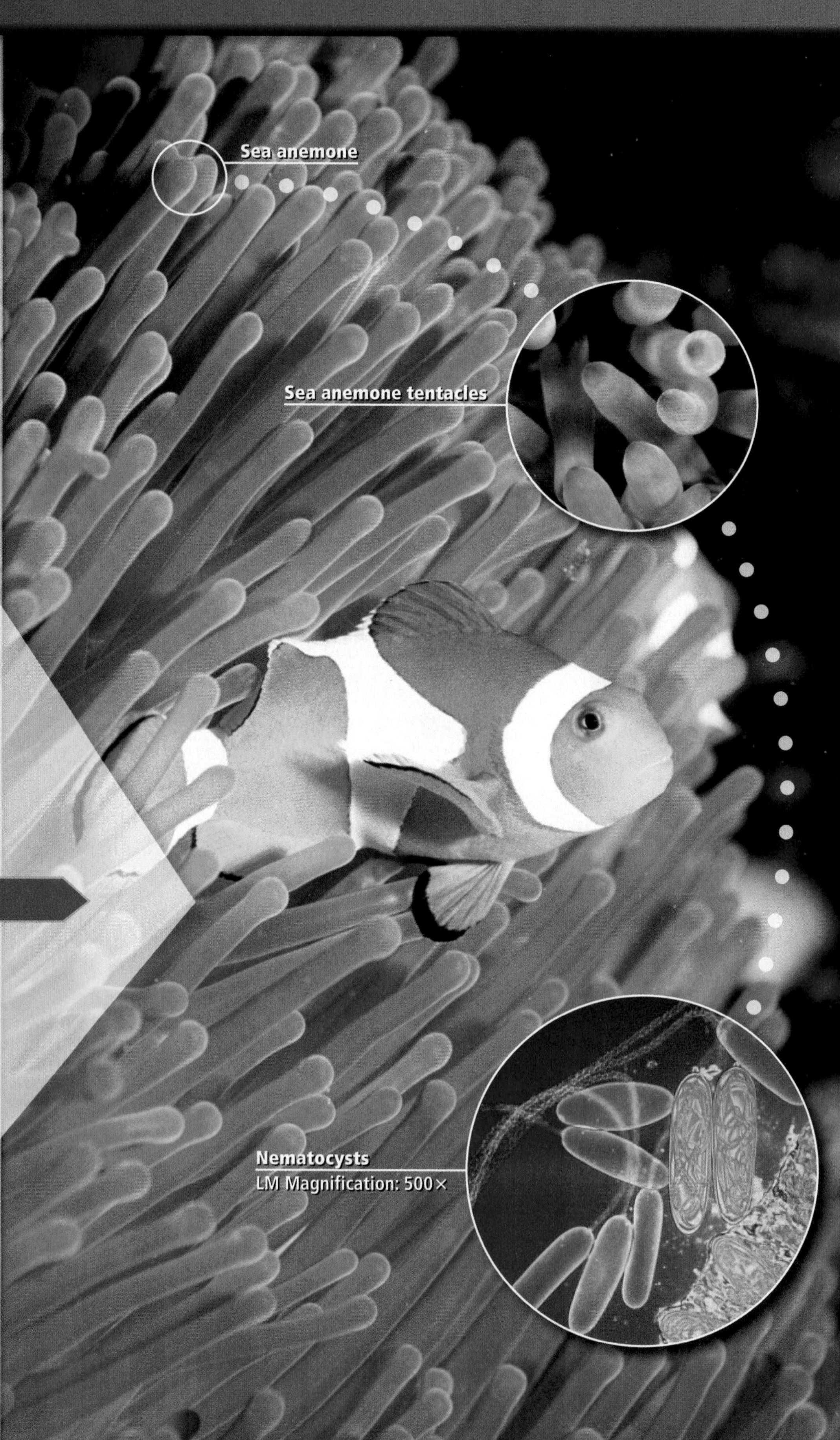


**Section 1**
**Animal Characteristics**
MAIN Idea Animals are multicellular, eukaryotic heterotrophs that have evolved to live in many different habitats.

**Section 2**
**Animal Body Plans**
MAIN Idea Animal phylogeny can be determined, in part, by body plans and the ways animals develop.

**Section 3**
**Sponges and Cnidarians**
MAIN Idea Sponges and cnidarians were the first animals to evolve from a multicellular ancestor.

## BioFacts

- Sea anemones protect clown fishes from predators, and clown fishes attract bigger fish prey to anemones.
- Sea anemone tentacles have stinging structures called nematocysts for stunning prey.
- A layer of mucus on their scales protects clown fish from anemone stings.

## LAUNCH Lab

### What is an animal?

Although animals share some characteristics with all other living organisms, they also have unique characteristics. In this lab, you will compare and contrast two organisms and determine which one is an animal.

**Procedure**

1. Read and complete the lab safety form.
2. Observe the **two organisms** you are given.
3. Compare and contrast the organisms using a **hand lens or stereomicroscope** if available.
4. Describe any specialized structures that you observe.
5. Based on your observations, predict how the form of each organism might be an adaptation to its habitat.

**Analysis**

1. **Identify** any structures that might be specific to animals.
2. **Predict** Based on your observations, can you predict which one of these organisms is more likely an animal? Explain.

Visit biologygmh.com to:

- study the entire chapter online
- explore the Interactive Time Line, Concepts in Motion, Interactive Tables, Microscopy Links, and links to virtual dissections
- access Web links for more information, projects, and activities
- review content online with the Interactive Tutor, and take Self-Check Quizzes

**Animal Body Plans** Make the following Foldable to help you identify the characteristics of acoelomate, pseudocoelomate, and coelomate body plans.

**STEP 1** Stack two sheets of paper about 1.5 cm apart vertically as illustrated.

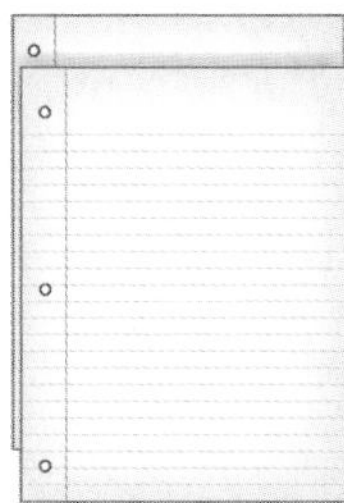

**STEP 2** Fold up the bottom edges of the paper to form four equal tabs.

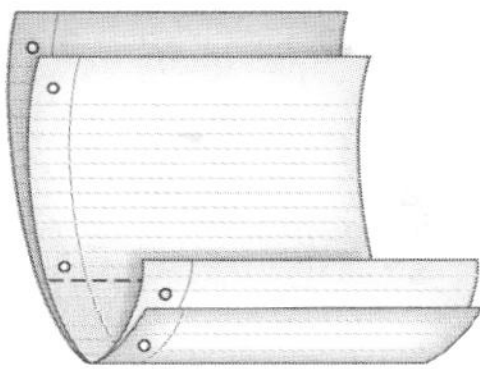

**STEP 3** Staple along the folded edge to secure all sheets. With the stapled edge at the top, label each tab as shown below.

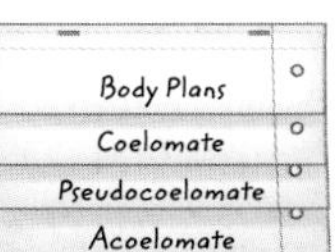


FOLDABLES **Use this Foldable with Section 24.2.** As you read the section, record information about each body plan under the tabs, and use what you learn to identify the body plans of animals around you.

## Section 24.1

### Objectives

- **Examine** adaptations that enable animals to live in different habitats.
- **Compare and contrast** animal structure and function.
- **Distinguish** among the stages of embryonic development in animals.

### Review Vocabulary

**protist:** diverse group of unicellular or multicellular eukaryotes that lack complex organ systems and live in moist environments

### New Vocabulary

invertebrate
exoskeleton
endoskeleton
vertebrate
hermaphrodite
zygote
internal fertilization
external fertilization
blastula
gastrula
endoderm
ectoderm
mesoderm

# Animal Characteristics

MAIN (Idea **Animals are multicellular, eukaryotic heterotrophs that have evolved to live in many different habitats.**

**Real-World Reading Link** When you think of animals, you might think of creatures that are furry and fuzzy. However, animals can have other outer coverings, such as feathers on birds and scales on fishes. Some animals even might be mistaken for plants.

## General Animal Features

Recall from Chapter 17 that biologists have created an evolutionary tree to organize the great diversity of living things. The ancestral animals at the beginning of the evolutionary tree are eukaryotic and multicellular—they are made up of many cells. The tiger in **Figure 24.1** and all other present-day animals might have evolved from choanoflagellates (KOH uh noh FLA juh layts), which are protists that formed colonies in the sea 570 million years ago. Choanoflagellates, such as the ones shown in **Figure 24.1,** might have been the earliest true animals. As animals evolved from this multicellular ancestor, they developed adaptations in structure that enabled them to function in numerous habitats. These features mark the branching points of the evolutionary tree and are discussed in the next section. In this section, you will learn about the characteristics that all animals have in common.

## Feeding and Digestion

Animals are heterotrophic, so they must feed on other organisms to obtain nutrients. A sea star obtains its food from a clam it has pried open, and a butterfly feeds on nectar from a flower. The structure or form of an animal's mouth parts determines how its mouth functions. You can investigate how some animals obtain food by performing **MiniLab 24.1.** After obtaining their food, animals must digest it. Some animals, such as sponges, digest their food inside specific cells. Others, such as earthworms and humans, digest their food in internal body cavities or organs.

**Figure 24.1** Present-day animals, such as this Bengal tiger, might have evolved from choanoflagellates such as this colony of *Zoothamnium*.

**Bengal tiger**

LM Magnification: 50×

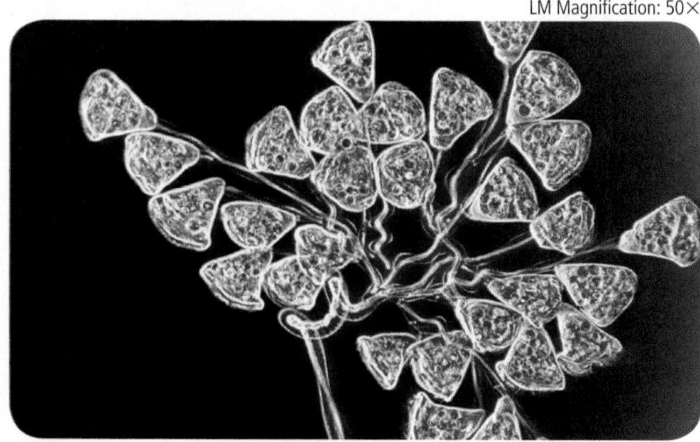

**Colony of *Zoothamnium***

29. Cnidarians evolved directly from which group?
  A. sponges
  B. multicellular choanoflagellates
  C. flatworms
  D. animals with bilateral symmetry

*Use the diagram below to answer question 30.*

30. How does the animal shown in the diagram reproduce?
  A. fragmentation
  B. external fertilization
  C. internal fertilization
  D. regeneration

31. Which is not a characteristic of sponges?
  A. filter feeding
  B. digestion inside cells
  C. asymmetry
  D. tissues

32. Which pair of words is mismatched?
  A. sponges—filter feeding
  B. cnidarians—nematocysts
  C. sponges—free swimming larva
  D. cnidarians—spicules

## Constructed Response

33. **Open Ended** Examine want ads in the paper to see how they are organized, and then use your knowledge of cnidarians to write a want ad that describes an ideal jellyfish homesite.

## Think Critically

34. **Calculate** Assume that a sponge filters 1.8 mL of water per second. How much water is filtered in one hour? In 12 hours?

35. **Create** Make a concept map using the following words: coral, polyp, cnidocyte, reef, calcium carbonate, zooxanthellae.

## Additional Assessment

36. *WRITING in* **Biology** Write an editorial for a newspaper advocating protection for coral reefs. Explain the dangers that corals are facing and make suggestions about what could be done to preserve and protect reefs.

### DBQ Document-Based Questions

*Transplantation experiments with early embryos of newts show that when tissue responsible for tail development was added into a different fluid-filled gastrula, it caused the effects shown below.*

Data obtained from: Niehrs, C. 2003. A tale of tails. *Nature* 424: 375–376.

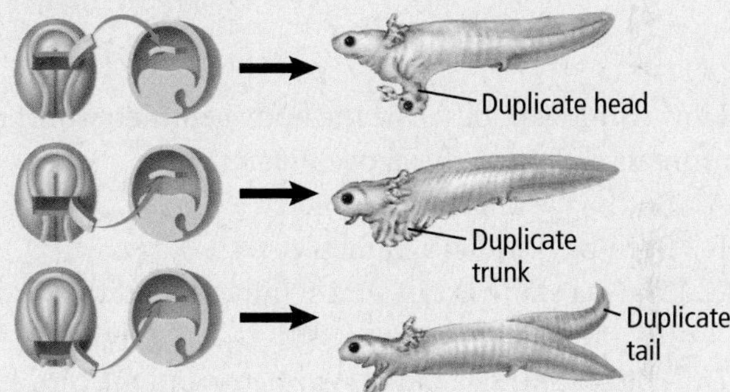


37. When a section from the top of the area was transplanted, where did the new tissue grow?

38. When a section from the bottom of the area was transplanted, where did the new tissue grow?

39. Make a summary statement that describes where new tissue grew when portions of the embryo responsible for tail development were transferred to fluid in the gastrula.

## Cumulative Review

40. Review what you learned about microscopic agents that cause disease. Which of these are considered living and which are not? Explain. **(Chapter 18)**

# Standardized Test Practice

**Cumulative**

## Multiple Choice

1. Which color of flower is most likely to attract nocturnal pollinators such as bats and moths?
   A. blue
   B. red
   C. violet
   D. white

*Use the illustration below to answer questions 2 and 3.*

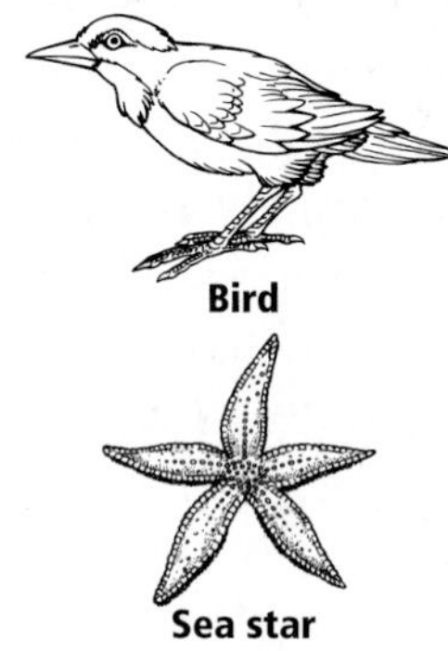


2. How would you describe the body symmetry of the animals shown in the above illustration?
   A. Both have bilateral symmetry.
   B. Both have radial symmetry.
   C. The sea star has bilateral symmetry and the bird has radial symmetry.
   D. The sea star has radial symmetry and the bird has bilateral symmetry.

3. How does the body shape of the sea star help with its survival?
   A. It enables the sea star to capture many kinds of prey.
   B. It enables the sea star to capture prey from many directions.
   C. It enables the sea star to move through the water quickly.
   D. It enables the sea star to move through the water feebly.

4. Which structure in nonvascular plants is similar to roots in vascular plants?
   A. chloroplast
   B. mucilage
   C. rhizoid
   D. sporophyte

5. Which hormone stimulates the ripening of fruit?
   A. auxin
   B. cytokinins
   C. ethylene
   D. gibberellins

*Use the diagram below to answer question 6.*

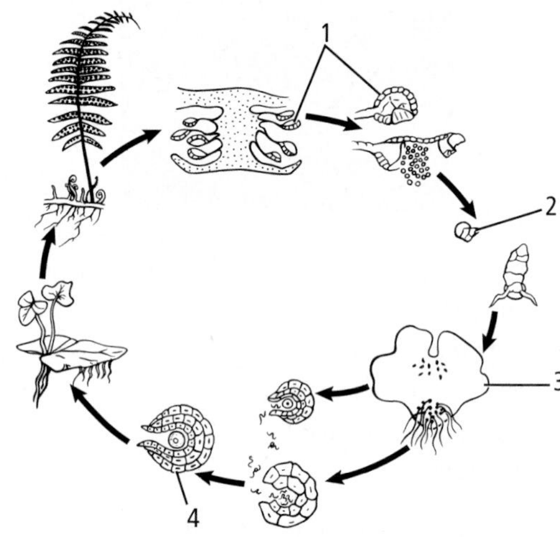


6. At which stage of the fern life cycle does the chromosome number change from haploid to diploid?
   A. 1
   B. 2
   C. 3
   D. 4

7. Which is the role of sclerenchyma cells in plants?
   A. gas exchange
   B. photosynthesis
   C. food storage
   D. support

8. What evidence would help scientists determine that colonial organisms were an early step in the evolution of multicellularity?
   A. similarities in DNA or RNA of early multicellular organisms and colonial unicellular organisms
   B. differences in DNA or RNA of early multicellular organisms and colonial unicellular organisms
   C. similarities of early multicellular organisms and present-day multicellular organisms
   D. differences between early multicellular organisms and present-day multicellular organisms

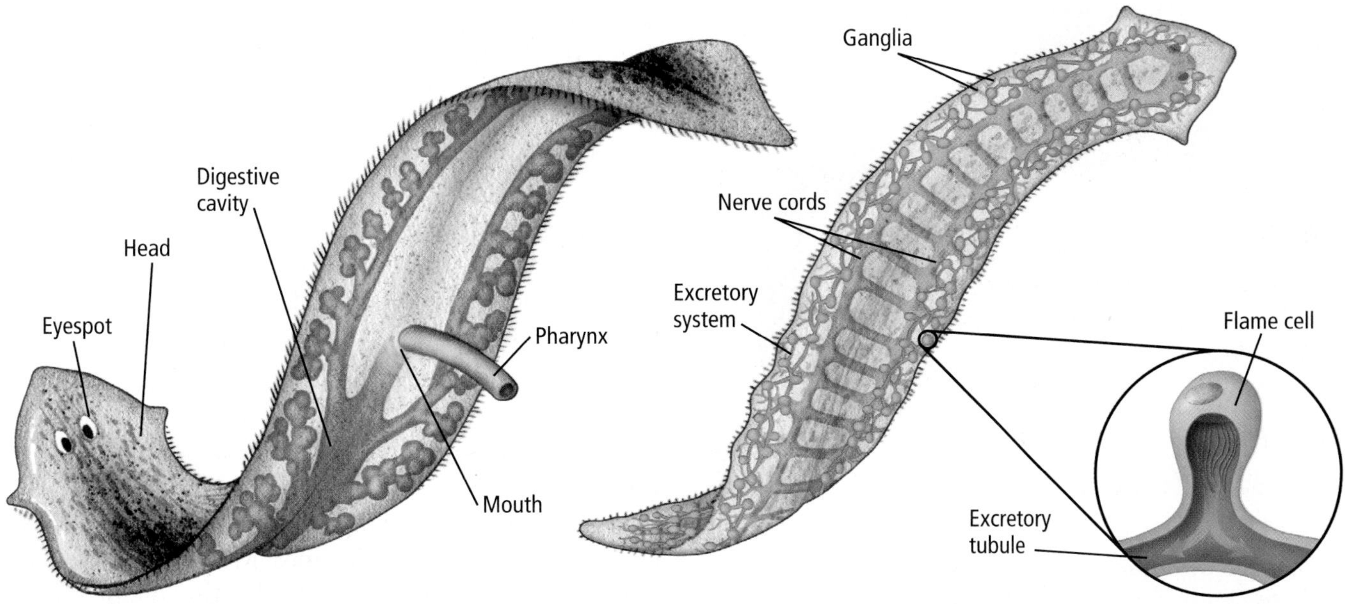


■ **Figure 25.2** Simple organ systems, such as the excretory and nervous systems, are found in flatworms.

**Concepts In Motion**

**Interactive Figure** To see an animation of the basic anatomy of a planarian, visit biologygmh.com.

**Feeding and digestion** Free-living flatworms feed on dead or slow-moving organisms. They extend a tubelike muscular organ, called the **pharynx** (FAHR ingks), out of their mouths. The pharynx, shown in **Figure 25.2,** releases enzymes that begin the digestion of prey. Then food particles are sucked into the digestive tract where digestion continues. Because flatworms have only one body opening, wastes are ejected through the mouth.

Parasitic flatworms have modified feeding structures called hooks and suckers, which enable them to stay attached to their hosts. Some parasitic flatworms have a reduced digestive system and feed on blood and other body tissues. Other parasitic flatworms lack a digestive system. Because they are so thin, like a single layer of cloth, and are surrounded by nutrients in their host's intestines, these parasites can absorb directly through their body walls partially or completely digested food eaten by the host.

 **Reading Check Compare** feeding and digestion in free-living flatworms and parasitic flatworms.

**Respiration, circulation, and excretion** Like sponges and cnidarians, flatworms do not have circulatory organs or respiratory organs. Because flatworms are so thin, their cells can use the process of diffusion to move dissolved oxygen and nutrients to all parts of their bodies. Carbon dioxide and other wastes also are removed from flatworm cells by diffusion.

Unlike sponges and cnidarians, flatworms have an excretory system that consists of a network of small tubes that run through the body. On side branches of the tubes, as shown in **Figure 25.2,** bulblike **flame cells** lined with cilia sweep water and excretory substances into tubules. These substances then exit through pores to the outside of the body. Flame cells were named because the flickering movements of the cilia inside the cells look like the light of a candle flame. Because flame cells move water out of the body, they keep flatworm cells from becoming waterlogged. In addition to the action of flame cells, flatworms also excrete waste products and maintain homeostatic water balance through their mouths.

**VOCABULARY**

**SCIENCE USAGE V. COMMON USAGE**

**Host**

***Science usage:*** an animal or plant on which or in which a parasite lives.
*Some parasitic worms live in the intestines of their hosts.*

***Common usage:*** a person who entertains guests.
*Tyler's dad was the host for the football party.*

# MiniLab 25.1

LM Magnification: 10×

Planarian

## Observe a Planarian

**How does a planarian behave?** Investigate the physical features and behavior of a planarian by observing this common flatworm.

### Procedure

1. Read and complete the lab safety form.
2. Observe the **planarian** in a **water-filled observation dish** by using a **magnifying glass.**
3. Create a data table to record your observations.
4. Record the physical characteristics and behaviors of the flatworm.
5. Place a small piece of **cooked egg white** into the dish, and observe the feeding behavior of the planarian.

### Analysis

1. **Compare and contrast** the physical features of the planarian with the features of the earthworm you observed in the Launch Lab.
2. **Analyze** how the body shape and movement of a planarian enables it to live in its environment.
3. **Infer** why scientists classify planaria into a group separate from other worms.

**Response to stimuli** The nervous system regulates the body's response to stimuli. In most flatworms, the nervous system consists of two nerve cords with connecting nerve tissue that run the length of the body. In most flatworms, the connecting nerve tissue looks like the rungs of a ladder, as illustrated in **Figure 25.2.** At the anterior end of the nerve cords is a small swelling composed of ganglia that send nerve signals to and from the rest of the body. A **ganglion** (plural, ganglia) is a group of nerve cell bodies that coordinates incoming and outgoing nerve signals.

**Movement** Some flatworms move by contracting muscles in the body wall. To escape predators and to find food, most free-living flatworms glide by using cilia located on their undersides. Mucus lubricates the worms and improves the gliding motion, while muscular action lets the animals twist and turn. If you ever have tried to loosen planaria worms from the bottoms of rocks, you know that their outer mucus covering enables them to stick tightly—an important adaptation in a swiftly moving stream. You can observe the features and behavior of a flatworm in **MiniLab 25.1.**

**Reproduction** Flatworms are hermaphrodites because they produce both eggs and sperm. During sexual reproduction, two different flatworms exchange sperm, and the eggs are fertilized internally. In marine flatworms, zygotes in cocoons are released into the water where they hatch within a few weeks.

Free-living flatworms can reproduce asexually by **regeneration**—a process in which body parts that are missing due to damage or predation can be regrown. A planarian that is cut in half horizontally can grow a new head on the tail end and a new tail on the head end, forming two new organisms, as shown in **Figure 25.3.**

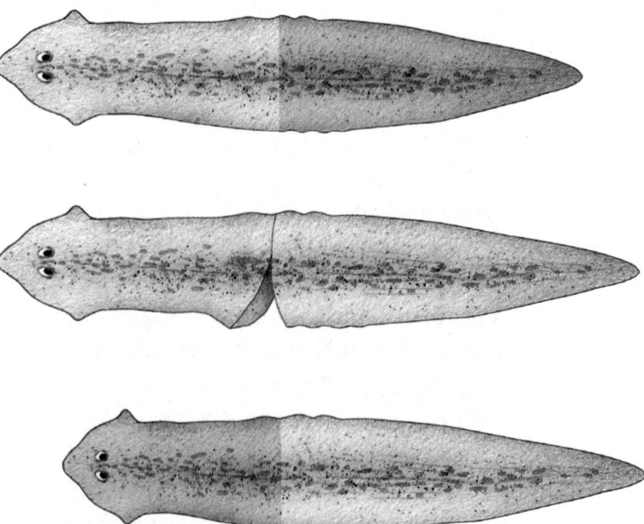

**Figure 25.3** Two new planaria form when one planarian is cut in half horizontally. Some planaria can regenerate from almost any piece of their bodies.

## Diversity of Flatworms

There are three main classes of flatworms: Turbellaria (tur buh LER ee uh), Trematoda (trem uh TOH duh), and Cestoda (ses TOH duh). Class Turbellaria consists of the free-living flatworms. Class Trematoda and class Cestoda consist of parasitic flatworms.

**Turbellarians** Members of the class Turbellaria are called turbellarians. Most turbellarians, like planarians, live in marine or freshwater habitats, while some live in moist soils. They vary in size, color, and body shape. As shown in **Figure 25.4,** turbellarians have eyespots that can detect the presence or absence of light. They also have sensory cells that help them identify chemicals and water movement.

The cells sensitive to chemicals are concentrated on small projections called auricles (OR ih kulz) at the anterior end of the worm. When a planarian hunts, it might wave its head back and forth as it crawls forward, exposing the auricles to chemical stimuli coming from food. At the same time, its eyespots might help it perceive light conditions that would protect it from predators.

**Trematodes** Flukes belong to class Trematoda—the trematodes. They are parasites that infect the blood or body organs of their hosts. The life cycle of the parasitic fluke *Schistosoma* is shown in **Figure 25.5.** Notice that this parasite requires two hosts to complete its life cycle.

When humans contract schistosomiasis (shihst tuh soh MI uh sis), the fluke eggs clog blood vessels, causing swelling and eventual tissue damage. Schistosomiasis can be prevented by proper sewage treatment and by wearing protective clothing when wading or swimming in infested water. Schistosomiasis infections are not common in the United States.

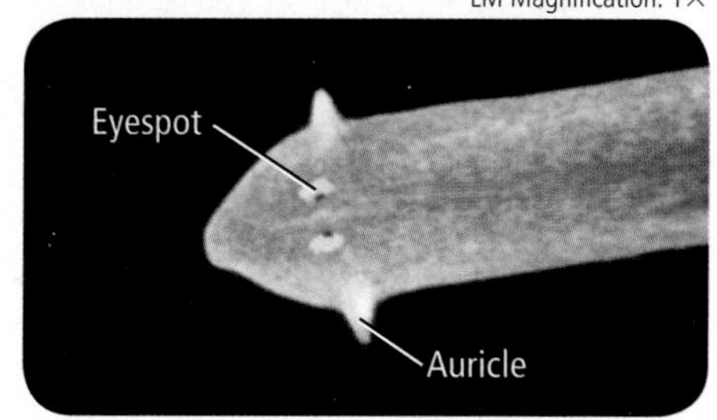


**Figure 25.4** Dark clusters of light-sensitive cells form the eyespots on this planarian. Note the auricles projecting from the same area.

**Figure 25.5** Two hosts—humans and snails—are needed to complete the life cycle of the fluke *Schistosoma*.
**Infer** ***Why are the two larval forms of the fluke different shapes?***

LM Magnification: 20×

**A** Fluke larvae can burrow into bare human skin. The larvae travel through the blood to the intestine where development continues.

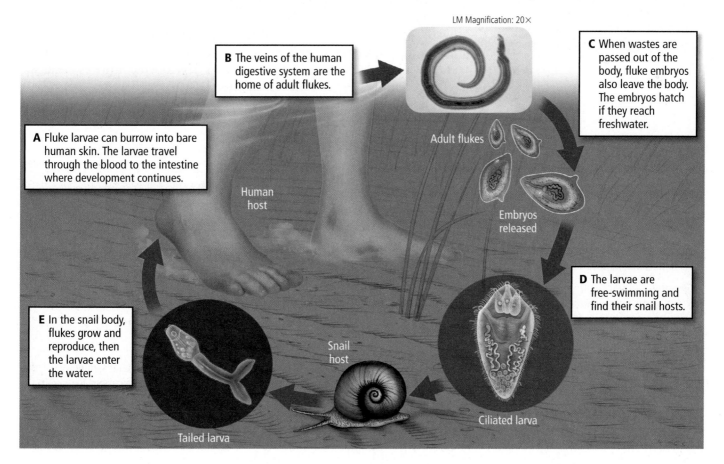

**B** The veins of the human digestive system are the home of adult flukes.

**C** When wastes are passed out of the body, fluke embryos also leave the body. The embryos hatch if they reach freshwater.

**D** The larvae are free-swimming and find their snail hosts.

**E** In the snail body, flukes grow and reproduce, then the larvae enter the water.

Human host
Adult flukes
Embryos released
Ciliated larva
Snail host
Tailed larva

■ **Figure 25.6** As the proglottids behind the scolex mature, new proglottids form.

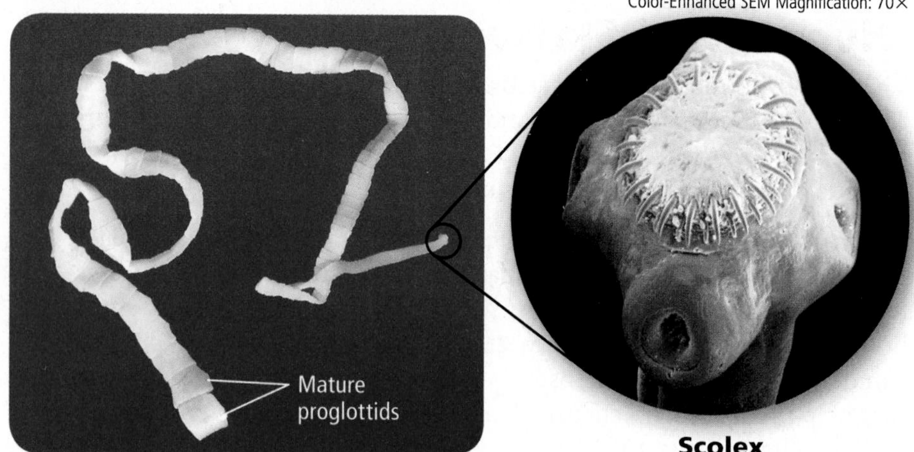


**Cestodes** All tapeworms are members of class Cestoda—the cestodes. They are parasites adapted to life in the intestines of their hosts. Look at the anterior end, or head, of the tapeworm in **Figure 25.6.** This is the **scolex** (SKOH leks), a knob-shaped structure with hooks and suckers that attach to the intestinal lining of a host such as a cow or a human.

Behind the scolex of the worm are a series of individual sections called **proglottids** (proh GLAH tihdz), each of which contains muscles, nerves, flame cells, and male and female reproductive organs. Proglottids form continuously; as new ones form near the scolex, older proglottids move farther back and mature. After eggs in the mature proglottids are fertilized, the last segments with developing embryos break off and pass out of the intestines of their hosts. Animals such as cattle might feed on vegetation or drink water contaminated by the tapeworm proglottids, and then the cycle of tapeworm growth is repeated.

When eaten by cattle, tapeworms can burrow through intestinal walls, entering blood and eventually muscle. If this infected beef is eaten rare or undercooked, human infection by tapeworms is likely. Tapeworm infections are uncommon in developed countries because these countries require beef inspections.

*Study Tip*

**Summarization** Develop a summary paragraph that addresses the body structure, reproduction, and life cycle of the tapeworm. Share your summary statement with the class.

## Section 25.1 Assessment

### Section Summary

- Flatworms were among the first animals to exhibit bilateral symmetry.
- Flatworms are acoelomates with limited numbers of organs and systems.
- Some flatworms are free-living, and others are parasitic.
- The three main classes of flatworms are Turbellaria, Trematoda, and Cestoda.
- Flatworms that are parasitic have specialized adaptations for parasitic life.

### Understand Main Ideas

1. MAIN Idea **Evaluate** the advantages of a flatworm's thin body.
2. **Compare and contrast** the adaptations of free-living flatworms and parasitic flatworms.
3. **Prepare** a chart that compares digestion, respiration, movement, and reproduction in the free-living and parasitic flatworms.
4. **Analyze** the importance of flame cells in a flatworm.

### Think Scientifically

5. *Design an experiment* to determine what habitat conditions planarians prefer.
6. *Evaluate* how the two classes of parasitic worms are adapted to their habitats.
7. *Diagram* bilateral symmetry using a planarian as an example. Explain the adaptive advantage of bilateral symmetry to a planarian.



Biology Online Self-Check Quiz biologygmh.com

Section 25.2

## Objectives

- **Compare** the features of roundworms to the features of flatworms.
- **Identify** roundworms based on movement.
- **Evaluate** the risk of contracting roundworm parasites.

### Review Vocabulary

**cilia:** short, numerous projections that look like hairs

### New Vocabulary

hydrostatic skeleton
trichinosis

# Roundworms and Rotifers

**MAIN Idea Roundworms and rotifers have a more highly evolved gut than flatworms derived from a pseudocoelomate body plan.**

**Real-World Reading Link** If you were to guess what animal is one of the most common in the world, what animal would you choose? Would you guess a roundworm? With 20,000 species of roundworms known, scientists estimate that there might be 100 times as many more kinds of roundworms still undiscovered.

## Body Structure of Roundworms

Roundworms are in phylum Nematoda (ne muh TOH duh) and often are called nematodes. Locate roundworms on the evolutionary tree in **Figure 25.7.** Notice that they have a body cavity in the form of a pseudocoelom. Roundworms have bilateral symmetry and are cylindrical, unsegmented worms that are tapered at both ends. Roundworms come in many sizes, as shown in **Figure 25.7.** Most are less than 1 mm long. However, the longest known roundworm, living in certain whales, can grow to 9 m in length.

Roundworms are found in both marine and freshwater habitats and on land. Some are parasites on plants and animals. A spadeful of garden soil might contain one million roundworms. One study revealed that a rotting apple contained 1074 roundworms! Dogs and cats can be plagued by roundworms if they are not wormed when they are young and at regular intervals during adulthood. Roundworms have adaptations that enable them to live in many places.

**Figure 25.7** Roundworms are pseudocoelomates with bilateral symmetry.

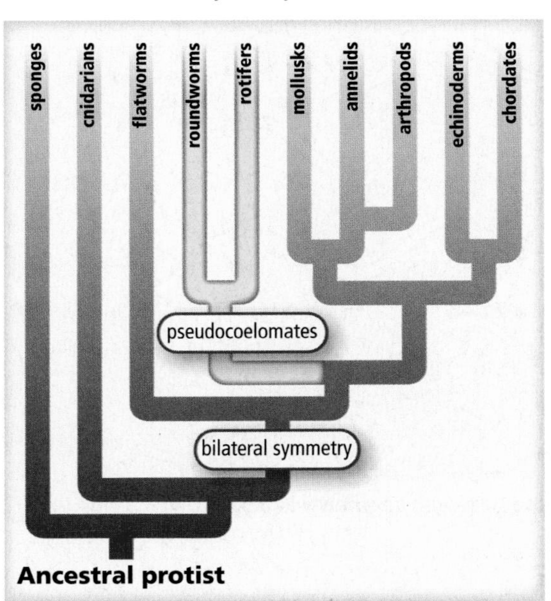


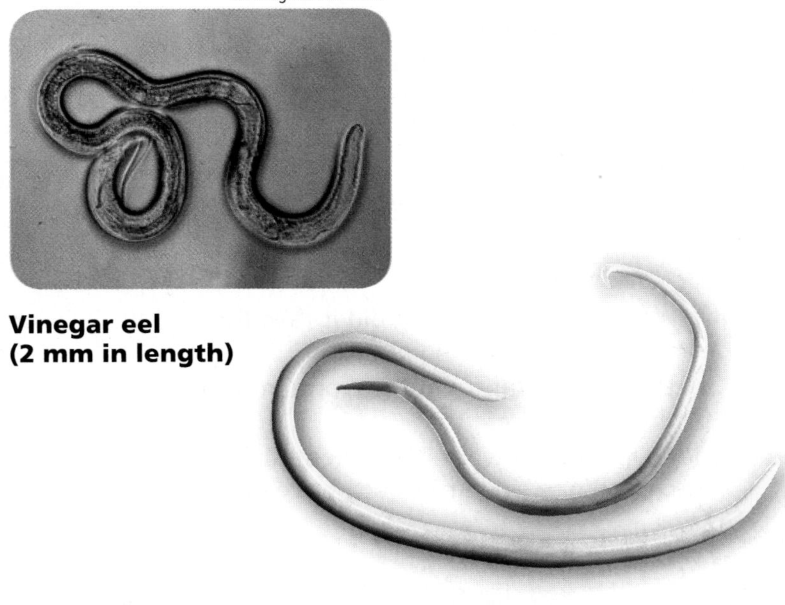


**Vinegar eel (2 mm in length)**

**Ascarid worms (10-35 cm in length)**

CAREERS IN BIOLOGY

**Veterinary Parasitologist** As scientists who keep parasites out of the food supply, veterinary parasitologists are responsible for the health of farm and domesticated animals. They determine ways to control and prevent parasites in animals such as cows, pigs, and chickens. For more information on biology careers, visit biologygmh.com.

**Feeding and digestion** Most roundworms are free-living, but some are parasites. Some free-living roundworms are predators of other tiny invertebrates, while others feed on decaying plant and animal matter. Free-living forms have a key evolutionary adaptation in their digestive systems. Recall from Chapter 24 that in the course of evolution, pseudocoelomate animals were the first to have a body cavity. The pseudocoelom of a nematode separates the endoderm-lined gut from the rest of the body. The movement of food through the gut, or digestive tract, is one-way—food enters through the mouth, and undigested food leaves through an opening at the end of the digestive tract called the anus.

**Respiration, circulation, excretion, and response to stimuli** Like flatworms, roundworms have no circulatory organs or respiratory organs, and they depend on diffusion to move nutrients and gases throughout their bodies. Most roundworms exchange gases and excrete metabolic wastes through their moist outer body coverings. More complex forms have excretory ducts that enable them to conserve water for living on land, while others have flame cells.

Ganglia and associated nerve cords coordinate nematode responses. Nematodes are sensitive to touch and to chemicals. Some have structures that might detect differences between light and dark.

**Movement** Roundworms have muscles that run the length of their bodies. These muscles cause their bodies to move in a thrashing manner as one muscle contracts and another relaxes. These muscles also pull against the outside body wall and the pseudocoelom. The pseudocoelom acts as a **hydrostatic skeleton**—fluid within a closed space that provides rigid support for muscles to work against. If you were to observe a roundworm moving, it might resemble a tiny piece of wriggling thread. Learn more about worm movement in **Data Analysis Lab 25.1.**

## DATA ANALYSIS LAB 25.1

**Based on Real Data***

### Interpret the Diagram

**How does a nematode move?** A nematode alternately contracts and relaxes muscles running lengthwise on each side of its body, which moves it forward in successive stages.

**Data and Observations**

Look at the diagram and observe how a nematode moves.

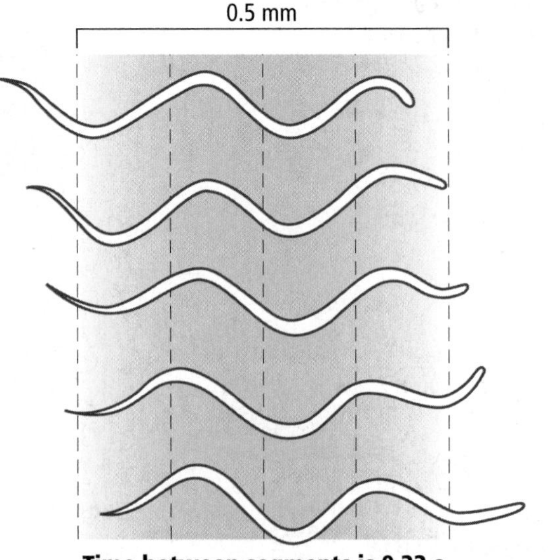

**Time between segments is 0.33 s**

**Think Critically**

1. **Interpret** About how long did it take the worm to move to its final location?
2. **Calculate** How far could the worm move in 10 min?
3. **Infer** How might worm movement differ if muscles on one side of its body were damaged?

*Data obtained from: Gray, J. and H.W. Lissmann. 1964. The locomotion of nematodes. *Journal of Experimental Biology* 41:135–154.

**Circulation** Unlike most mollusks, most annelids have a closed circulatory system. Oxygen and nutrients move to various parts of their bodies through their blood vessels. At the same time carbon dioxide and metabolic wastes are removed from the blood and excreted. Some of the vessels at the anterior end, or head, are large and muscular, as shown in **Figure 25.24,** and serve as hearts that pump the blood. The blood moves toward the anterior end of the worm in the dorsal blood vessel and toward the posterior end in the ventral blood vessel.

**Respiration and excretion** Earthworms take in oxygen and give off carbon dioxide through their moist skin. Some aquatic annelids have gills for the exchange of gases in the water. Segmented worms have two nephridia—similar to those in mollusks—in almost every segment. Cellular waste products are collected in the nephridia and are transported in tubes through the coelom and out of the body. Nephridia also function in maintaining homeostasis of the body fluids of annelids, ensuring that the volume and composition of body fluids are kept constant.

**Response to stimuli** In most annelids, such as the earthworm, the anterior segments are modified for sensing the environment. The brain and nerve cords composed of ganglia are shown in the earthworm in **Figure 25.23.** You might have seen an earthworm quickly withdraw into its burrow when you shine a flashlight on it or step close to it. These observations show that earthworms can detect both light and vibrations.

**Movement** When an earthworm moves, it contracts circular muscles running around each segment. This squeezes the segment and causes the fluid in the coelom to press outward like paste in a tube of toothpaste being squeezed. Because the fluid in the coelom is confined by the tissues between segments, the fluid pressure causes the segment to get longer and thinner. Next, the earthworm contracts the longitudinal muscles that run the length of its body. This causes the segment to shorten and return to its original shape, pulling its posterior end forward and resulting in movement.

Many annelids have setae on each segment. **Setae** (SEE tee) (singular, seta), as shown in **Figure 25.25,** are tiny bristles that push into the soil and anchor the worm during movement. By anchoring some segments and retracting others, earthworms can move their bodies forward and backward segment by segment.

**Reading Check** **Describe** how longitudinal and circular muscles work together to enable an earthworm to move.

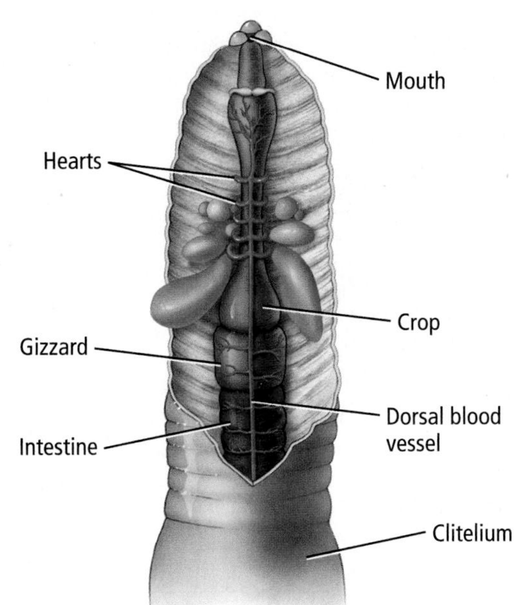


**Figure 25.24** An earthworm has five hearts that pump blood through its circulatory system.

**LAUNCH Lab**

**Review** Based on what you've read about earthworm movement, how would you now answer the analysis questions?

**Figure 25.25** This earthworm cross section shows how the setae extend from the body. Setae dig into soil and anchor the worm as it pushes forward.
**Evaluate** *whether an earthworm would move faster on a rough or a smooth surface.*

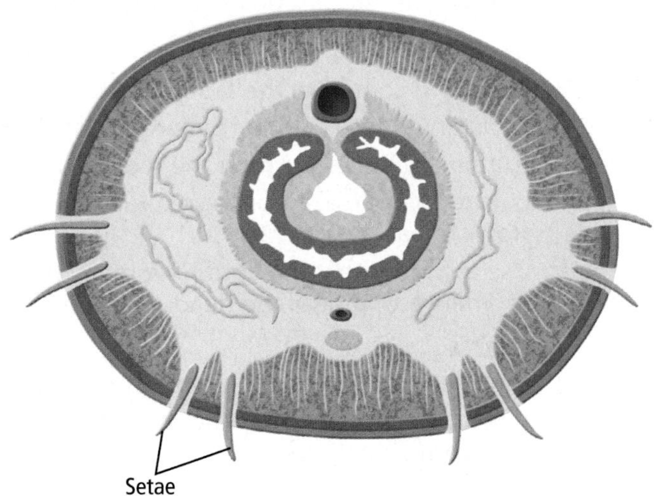

■ **Figure 25.26** After developing in the cocoon for two to three weeks, a young earthworm hatches.

FOLDABLES
Incorporate information from this section into your Foldable.

**Reproduction** Annelids can reproduce both sexually and asexually. Most annelids have separate sexes, but some, such as earthworms and leeches, are hermaphrodites. Sperm are passed between two worms near segments called the clitellum. Refer back to **Figure 25.23** and notice that the **clitellum** is a thickened band of segments. It produces a cocoon from which young earthworms hatch, as shown in **Figure 25.26.** Sperm and eggs pass into the cocoon as it slips forward off the body of the worm. After fertilization, the young are protected in the cocoon as they develop. Some annelids reproduce asexually by fragmentation. If a worm breaks apart, the missing parts can be regenerated.

## Diversity of Annelids

The phylum Annelida is divided into three classes: class Oligochaeta (ohl ih goh KEE tuh)—the earthworms and their relatives, class Polychaeta (pah lih KEE tuh)—the bristleworms and their relatives, and class Hirudinea (hur uh DIN ee uh)—the leeches.

**Earthworms and their relatives** Earthworms probably are the best-known annelids. They are used as bait for fishing and are found in garden soil. An earthworm can eat its own mass in soil every day. Earthworms ingest soil to extract nutrients. In this way, earthworms aerate the soil—they break up the soil to allow air and water to move through it.

In addition to earthworms, class Oligochaeta—the oligochaetes (AH lee goh keetz)—includes tubifex worms and lumbriculid worms. Tubifex worms are small, threadlike aquatic annelids that are common in areas of high pollution. Lumbriculid (lum BRIH kyuh lid) worms are freshwater oligochaetes that are about 6 cm long and live at the edges of lakes and ponds. You can observe a feature common to oligochaetes in **MiniLab 25.2.**

## MiniLab 25.2

### Observe Blood Flow in a Segmented Worm

**How does blood flow in a segmented worm?** The California blackworm has a closed circulatory system and a transparent body. Its blood can be viewed as it flows along the dorsal blood vessel.

**Procedure**

1. Read and complete the lab safety form.
2. Moisten a piece of **filter paper** with **spring water** and place it in a **Petri dish.**
3. Examine a **blackworm** on the moist paper using a **stereomicroscope.**
4. Locate the dorsal blood vessel in a segment near the midpoint of the worm. Observe how blood flows in each segment.
5. Use a **stopwatch** to record how many pulses of blood occur per minute. Repeat this for two more segments, one near the head and one near the tail of the worm. Record your data in a table.

**Analysis**

1. **Summarize** how blood moves through each segment, including the direction of blood flow.
2. **Compare and contrast** the rate of blood flow near the head, at the midpoint, and near the tail of the worm.

## Section 25.4

### Vocabulary Review

*An analogy is a comparison relationship between two pairs of words and can be written in the following manner: A is to B as C is to D. In the analogies that follow, one of the words is missing. Complete each analogy with a vocabulary term from the Study Guide page.*

**29.** Teeth are to human as __________ is to earthworm.

**30.** Cocoon is to butterfly as __________ is to earthworm.

**31.** Vacuole is to protist as __________ is to earthworm.

### Understand Key Concepts

*Use the diagram below to answer questions 32 and 33.*

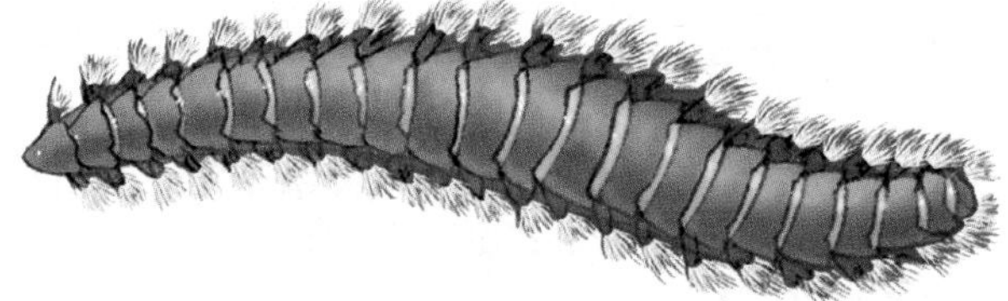

**32.** Which animal is illustrated in the diagram?
- **A.** roundworm
- **B.** leech
- **C.** polychaete
- **D.** earthworm

**33.** What feature is characteristic of this animal?
- **A.** foot
- **B.** parapodia
- **C.** sucker
- **D.** shell

### Constructed Response

**34. Open Ended** If global warming continues, predict how earthworms might change as a result of natural selection.

### Think Critically

**35. CAREERS IN BIOLOGY** Rheumatologists, doctors who treat arthritis, have observed that when leeches are applied for a short time to the skin near joints of people affected with arthritis, pain is relieved for up to six months. Design an experiment that would explain this phenomenon.

## Additional Assessment

**36.** WRITING in Biology Research mollusks that live in areas of hydrothermal vents. Write a report emphasizing the differences between hydrothermal vent mollusks and those that live in the habitats you studied in this chapter.

### DBQ Document-Based Questions

*The data below represent the percentages of the three main classes of flatworms.*

Data obtained from: Pechenik, J. 2005. *Biology of the Invertebrates.* New York: McGraw-Hill.

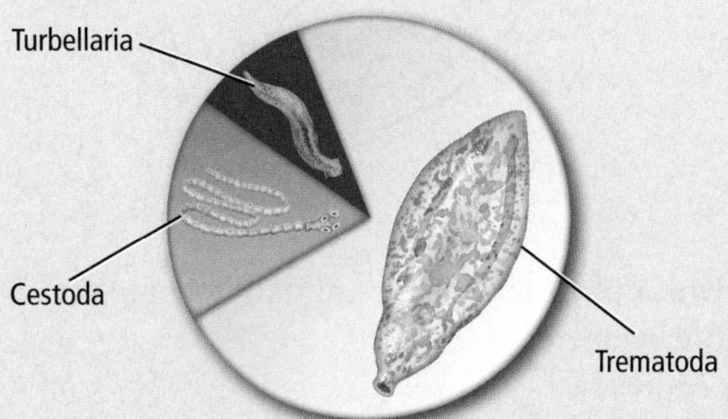


**37.** Approximately what percentage of flatworms are flukes?

**38.** Which group of flatworms has the least number of species?

**39.** Infer why there might be so many more of one kind of flatworm than any other kind.

### Cumulative Review

**40.** Place the following steps of DNA translation in the correct order. **(Chapter 12)**
1. tRNA carrying a methionine moves into the P site.
2. The mRNA attaches to the ribosome.
3. A tRNA brings the appropriate amino acid to the A site.
4. The tRNA is released to the E site.

- **A.** 2, 1, 3, 4
- **B.** 4, 3, 1, 2
- **C.** 3, 1, 2, 4
- **D.** 3, 2, 4, 1

# Standardized Test Practice

**Cumulative**

## Multiple Choice

1. During dry weather, pieces of a moss might be scattered by the wind. When it rains, these pieces can grow into new plants. Which process does this display?
   A. alternation of generations
   B. gametophyte reproduction
   C. sporophyte generation
   D. vegetative reproduction

*Use the diagram below to answer questions 2 and 3.*

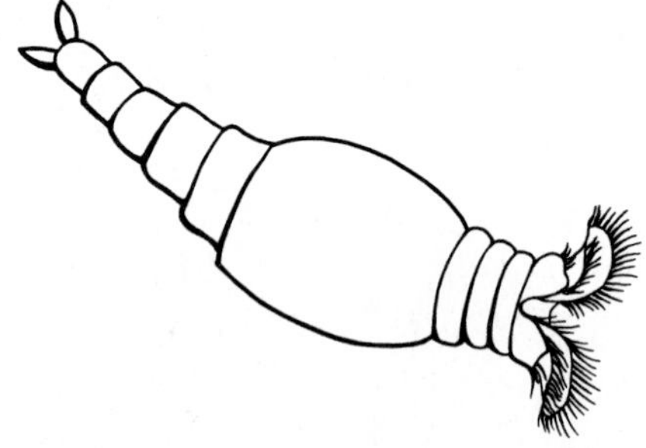

2. In which phylum does the animal shown in the figure belong?
   A. Annelida
   B. Nematoda
   C. Platyhelminthes
   D. Rotifera

3. Roundworms differ from the organism shown above because roundworms have which characteristic?
   A. a complete digestive tract
   B. inability to live in fresh water
   C. a smaller body size
   D. a body surface covered with cilia

4. Which is one characteristic of all cnidarians?
   A. Their tentacles contain cnidocytes.
   B. Their tentacles contain fibroblasts.
   C. They only live in freshwater environments.
   D. They spend some time as sessile animals.

5. Which is an example of a nastic response?
   A. bamboo plants growing toward a light
   B. corn plant roots growing downward
   C. sunflowers tracking the Sun
   D. vines growing up a tree

*Use the diagram below to answer question 6.*

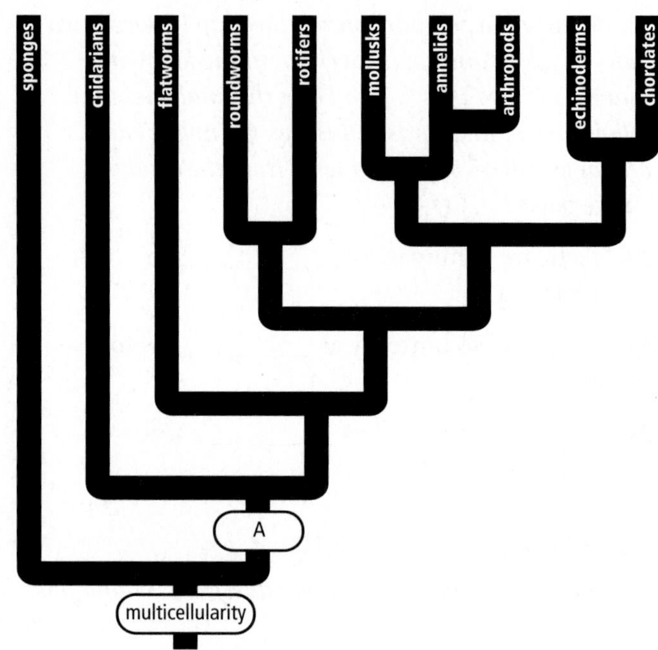


6. Which body structures are typical of all the animals above Point A on the evolutionary tree?
   A. cell walls
   B. coeloms
   C. tentacles
   D. tissues

7. How does an aggregate fruit, such as a blackberry or strawberry, form?
   A. when a flower has multiple female organs that fuse together
   B. when a fruit has multiple seeds that fuse together
   C. when multiple flowers from the same plant fuse together
   D. when multiple simple fruits fuse together

8. How do hornworts differ from other nonvascular plants?
   A. Their cells allow nutrients and water to move by diffusion and osmosis.
   B. Their cells can contain a type of cyanobacteria.
   C. They can be classified as either thallose or leafy.
   D. They have chloroplasts in some of their cells.



Biology Online Standardized Test Practice biologygmh.com

## Short Answer

*Use the diagram below to answer questions 9 and 10.*

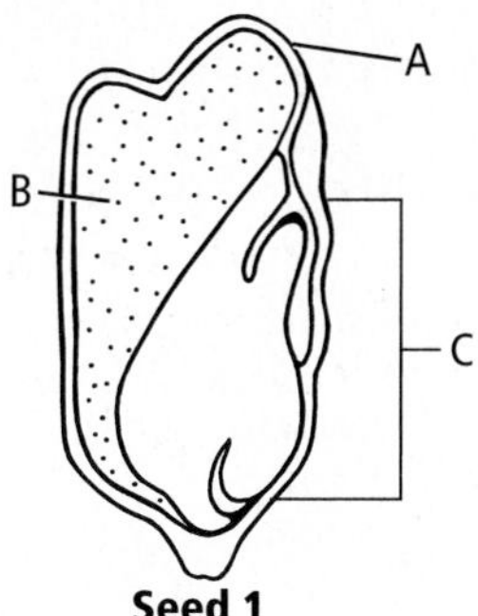

Seed 1

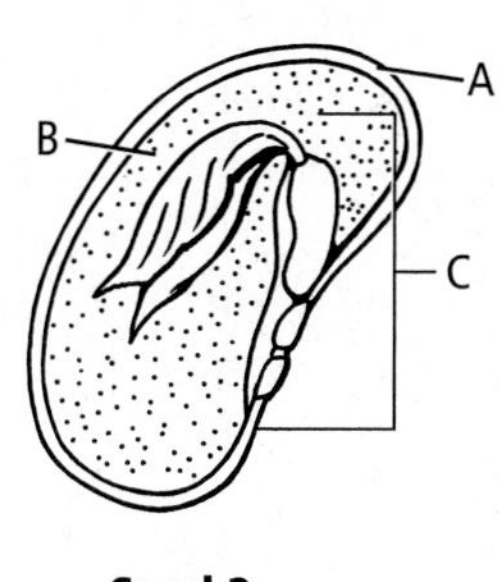

Seed 2

**9.** Name the parts of these seeds.

**10.** Which seed is a monocot and which is a eudicot? How do you know?

**11.** Explain why squids and clams are both included in Phylum Mollusca even though they appear to be very different kinds of animals.

**12.** What is one thing that humans can do to preserve reefs? Explain your reasoning.

**13.** Specify an example of an ancestral character and a derived character that angiosperms have.

**14.** Describe the alternation of generations in plants.

**15.** Describe how cellular slime molds reproduce and identify whether this process is sexual or asexual. Assess how this form of reproduction is beneficial for cellular slime molds.

## Extended Response

**16.** List two reasons why animals benefit from segmentation. Assess the importance of these benefits.

**17.** Suppose you are a scientist trying to determine the water quality of a river where mussels live. What data could you collect from the mussels in order to determine the quality of the river water?

## Essay Question

Schistosomiasis is caused by flukes, which have complex life cycles involving specific freshwater snail species as intermediate hosts. Infected snails release large numbers of minute, free-swimming larvae (cercariae) that are capable of penetrating the unbroken skin of a human host. Even brief exposure to contaminated freshwater, such as wading, swimming, or bathing, can result in infection. Human schistosomiasis cannot be acquired by wading or swimming in salt water (oceans or seas). The cercariae of birds and aquatic mammals can penetrate the skin of humans who enter infested fresh or salt water in many parts of the world, including cool temperate areas. The cercariae die in the skin but may elicit a puritic rash ("swimmer's itch" or "clam-digger's itch").

*Using the information in the paragraph above, answer the following question in essay format.*

**18.** Schistosomiasis is a disease that is most common in sub-Saharan Africa, the Philippines, southern China, and Brazil. Propose a plan to control this disease in a specific area. What steps would need to be taken to keep people from getting the disease? Develop a plan and explain it in a well-organized essay.

**NEED EXTRA HELP?**

| If You Missed Question . . . | 1 | 2 | 3 | 4 | 5 | 6 | 7 | 8 | 9 | 10 | 11 | 12 | 13 | 14 | 15 | 16 | 17 | 18 |
|---|---|---|---|---|---|---|---|---|---|---|---|---|---|---|---|---|---|---|
| Review Section . . . | 23.1 | 25.3 | 25.2 | 24.3 | 22.3 | 24.3 | 23.3 | 21.2 | 23.3 | 23.3 | 25.3 | 24.3 | 18.2 | 23.1 | 19.4 | 24.2 | 15.2 | 25.1 |

CHAPTER 26

# Arthropods

## Section 1
**Arthropod Characteristics**

MAIN Idea Arthropods have segmented bodies and tough exoskeletons with jointed appendages.

## Section 2
**Arthropod Diversity**

MAIN Idea Arthropods are classified based on the structure of their segments, types of appendages, and mouthparts.

## Section 3
**Insects and Their Relatives**

MAIN Idea Insects have structural and functional adaptations that have enabled them to become the most abundant and diverse group of arthropods.

## BioFacts

- Copepods are tiny, but they exist in such large numbers that they are a major source of protein in the oceans.
- A single copepod might eat 200,000 microscopic diatoms in one day.
- Copepod eggs can lie dormant for months or years until conditions are right for hatching.

Coepods
LM Magnification: 20×

Individual copepod
LM Magnification: unavailable

Jointed copepod antenna
LM Magnification: 100×

**Respiration** Arthropods obtain oxygen by using one of three structures—gills, tracheal tubes, or book lungs. Recall from Chapter 25 that maintaining a certain homeostatic balance of oxygen in body tissues enables animals to have energy for a variety of functions. Most aquatic arthropods have gills, like those shown in **Figure 26.6,** that function in the same way as the gills in mollusks. All terrestrial arthropod body tissues need to be near airways to obtain oxygen.

Terrestrial arthropods depend on respiratory systems rather than circulatory systems to carry oxygen to cells. Most terrestrial arthropods have a system of branching tubes called **tracheal** (TRAY kee ul) **tubes,** shown in **Figure 26.6,** that branch into smaller and smaller tubules. These tubules carry oxygen throughout the body.

Some arthropods, including spiders, have **book lungs,** saclike pockets with highly folded walls for respiration. In **Figure 26.6,** notice how the membranes in book lungs are like the pages in a book. The folded walls increase the surface area of the lungs and allow an efficient exchange of gases. You also can see how both tracheae and book lungs open to the outside of the body of the arthropod in openings called **spiracles** (SPIHR ih kulz).

**Circulation** Even though most arthropods do not rely on their circulatory systems to deliver oxygen, they do rely on their circulatory systems to transport nutrients and remove wastes. Arthropod blood is pumped by a heart into vessels that carry the blood to body tissues. The tissues are flooded with blood, which returns to the heart through open body spaces. The blood maintains homeostasis in tissues by delivering nutrients and removing wastes.

**Excretion** In most arthropods, cellular wastes are removed from the blood through **Malpighian** (mal PIH gee un) **tubules.** These tubules also help terrestrial arthropods preserve water in their bodies to maintain homeostatic water balance. In insects, the tubules, as shown in **Figure 26.7,** are located in the abdomen, unlike in segmented worms, where nephridia exist in each segment. Malpighian tubules are attached to and empty into the gut, which contains the undigested food wastes to be eliminated from the body. Crustaceans and some other arthropods do not have Malpighian tubules. They have modified nephridia, similar to those in annelids, to remove cellular wastes.

**FOLDABLES**
Incorporate information from this section into your Foldable.

**VOCABULARY**
**ACADEMIC VOCABULARY**
**Transport:**
To transfer from one place to another.
*Blood transports nutrients to cells throughout the body.*

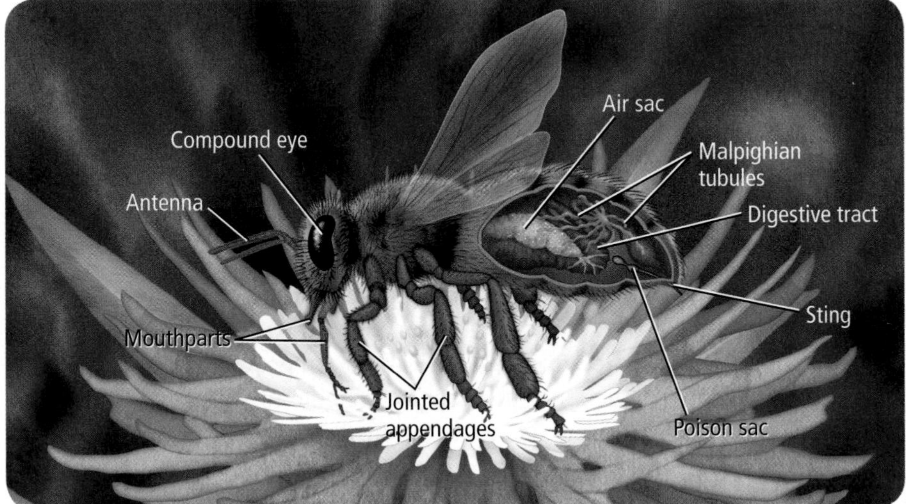


■ **Figure 26.7** Most arthropods get rid of cellular wastes through Malpighian tubules.
**Describe** ***another function of Malpighian tubules.***

■ **Figure 26.8** Compound eyes enable flying arthropods to see things in motion easily. The image the fly sees might not be as clear as that seen by a vertebrate. That blurry image is all the fly requires for its way of life.
**Infer** ***If a fly has blurry vision, how does it stay safe from predators?***

**Response to stimuli** Most arthropods have a double chain of ganglia throughout their bodies, on the ventral surface. Fused pairs of ganglia in the head make up the brain. Although most behaviors, such as feeding and locomotion, are controlled by the ganglia in each segment, the brain can inhibit these actions.

**Vision** Have you ever tried to swat a fly with a flyswatter? The fly's accurate vision allows the fly to spot even the slightest movement, and the fly often escapes. Most arthropods have one pair of large compound eyes. A compound eye, as shown in **Figure 26.8,** has many facets, which are hexagonal in shape. Each facet sees part of an image. The brain combines the images into a mosaic. The compound eyes of flying arthropods, such as dragonflies, enable them to analyze a fast-changing landscape during flight. Compound eyes can detect the movements of prey, mates, or predators, and also can detect colors. In addition, many arthropods have three to eight simple eyes. A simple eye has one lens and functions by distinguishing light from dark. In locusts and some other flying insects, simple eyes act as horizon detectors that help stabilize flight.

**Hearing** In addition to having eyes that detect movement and distinguish light from dark, many arthropods also have another sense organ called a tympanum (tihm PA num). A tympanum is a flat membrane used for hearing. It vibrates in response to sound waves. Arthropod tympanums can be located on the forelegs as in crickets, on the abdomen as in some grasshoppers, or on the thorax as in some moths.

**Chemicals** Imagine ants carrying off potato chip pieces, following each other like soldiers marching in formation. Ants communicate with each other by **pheromones** (FER uh mohnz), chemicals secreted by many animal species that influence the behavior of other animals of the same species. The ants use their antennae to sense the odor of pheromones and to follow the scent trail. Arthropods give off a variety of pheromones that signal behaviors such as mating and feeding.

**CAREERS IN BIOLOGY**

**Biochemist** As a scientist who determines how biological processes work, a biochemist might study the chemicals in pheromones to develop effective pest-management treatments. For more information on biology careers, visit biologygmh.com.

Tick

Color-Enhanced SEM Magnification: 75×

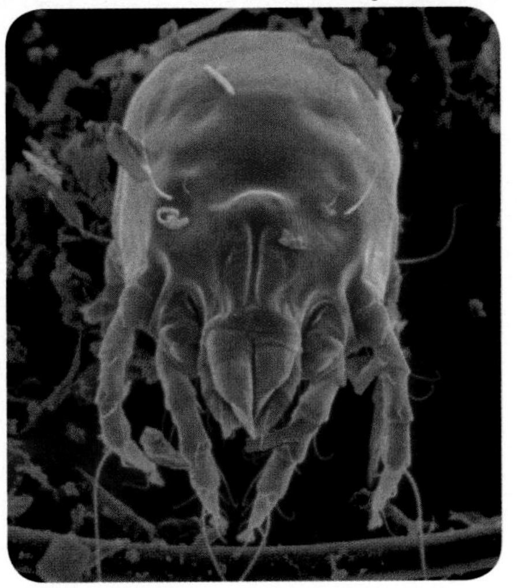
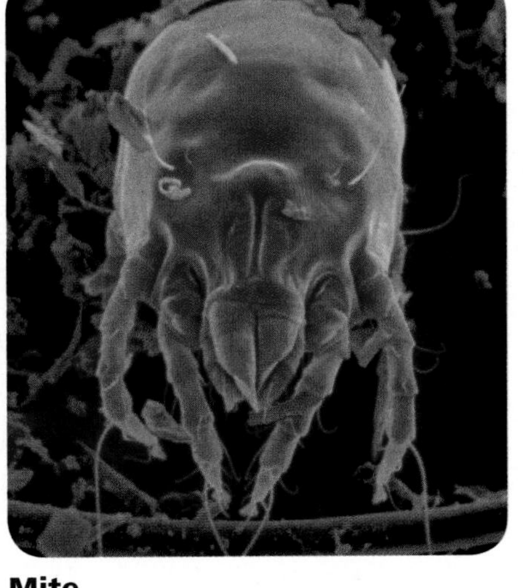

Mite

Scorpion

■ **Figure 26.13** Ticks, mites, and scorpions are in the same class as spiders.
**Describe** ***What characteristics of this class can you see in the photos?***

**Ticks, mites, and scorpions** Other members of class Arachnida—ticks, mites, and scorpions—are shown in **Figure 26.13.** Most mites are less than 1 mm long, with the cephalothorax and abdomen fused into one oval-shaped body section. They can be predators or parasites of other animals. Ticks are parasites that feed on blood after attaching themselves to the surface of their hosts. Ticks also harbor disease-causing agents, such as viruses, bacteria, and protozoa, and introduce them to their hosts when they bite. Some of these diseases, such as Lyme disease and Rocky Mountain spotted fever, affect humans.

Scorpions feed on insects, spiders, and small vertebrates that they capture with their pedipalps and tear apart with their chelicerae. They generally are nocturnal, hiding under logs or in burrows during the day. When you think of a scorpion, you might think of the stinger at the end of the abdomen. Most scorpions that live in the United States are not considered to be dangerous, but their sting can be quite painful. Compare different arthropod groups in **MiniLab 26.2.**

## MiniLab 26.2

### Compare Arthropod Characteristics

**How do the physical characteristics of arthropods differ?** Classify arthropods by observing specimens from the three major groups of arthropods.

**Procedure**

1. Read and complete the lab safety form.
2. Create a data table to record your observations of **live or preserved arthropod specimens.** **WARNING:** ***Treat live specimens in a humane manner at all times.***
3. Observe the arthropod specimens and record your observations about their physical characteristics in your data table.

**Analysis**

1. **Identify** the physical characteristics your arthropod specimens have in common.
2. **Classify** the arthropods into different taxonomic groups.

■ **Figure 26.14** Horseshoe crabs come to shore to lay eggs in the sand.

**Horseshoe crabs** Horseshoe crabs are an ancient group of marine animals, related to the arachnids, that have remained basically unchanged since the Triassic Period more than 200 million years ago. They have unsegmented heavy exoskeletons in the shape of a horseshoe. The chelicerae, pedipalps, and the next three pairs of legs are used for walking and getting food from the bottom of the sea. The animals feed on annelids, mollusks, and other invertebrates, which they capture with their chelicerae. The posterior appendages are modified with leaflike plates at their tips and can be used for digging or swimming.

Horseshoe crabs, shown in **Figure 26.14,** come to shore to reproduce at high tide. The female burrows into the sand to lay her eggs. A male follows behind and adds sperm before the female covers the eggs with sand. Young larvae hatch after a period of being warmed by the Sun and then return to the ocean during another high tide.

## Section 26.2 Assessment

### Section Summary

- Arthropods are divided into three major groups.
- Crustaceans have modified appendages for getting food, walking, and swimming.
- The first two pairs of arachnid appendages are modified as mouthparts, as reproductive structures, or as pincers.
- Spiders are carnivores that either hunt prey or trap it in webs that they spin out of silk.
- Horseshoe crabs are ancient arthropods that have remained unchanged for more than 200 million years.

### Understand Main Ideas

1. MAIN Idea **Classify** a small, quickly moving arthropod with two pairs of antennae, a segmented body, and mandibles that move from side to side.
2. **Compare and contrast** the ways of life of crustaceans and arachnids and explain how their body forms are adapted to their environments.
3. **Summarize** the differences in function among the various appendages of spiders.
4. **Identify** the common characteristics among ticks, scorpions, and horseshoe crabs.

### Think Scientifically

5. *Make a Hypothesis* Caribbean spiny lobsters have a navigation system that enables them to return to their original habitat after being moved to an unfamiliar location. Make a hypothesis about what signals the lobsters might use to orient themselves in the direction of their original habitat.
6. *Design an Experiment* A biologist wants to find out what brown recluse spiders eat. After some observation, she hypothesizes that the spiders prefer dead prey to live prey. Design an experiment that would test this hypothesis.



Biology Online Self-Check Quiz biologygmh.com

Section 26.3

## Objectives

- **Identify** characteristics of insects.
- **Analyze** how structure determines function in insects.
- **Compare and contrast** complete and incomplete metamorphosis.

## Review Vocabulary

**pollen:** a fine powder produced by certain plants when they reproduce

## New Vocabulary

metamorphosis
pupa
nymph
caste

# Insects and Their Relatives

MAIN Idea **Insects have structural and functional adaptations that have enabled them to become the most abundant and diverse group of arthropods.**

**Real-World Reading Link** Think about a time you were stung by a bee, admired a bright butterfly flitting from flower to flower, or heard the chirp of a cricket. It seems like insects are everywhere, and they affect your life in many ways.

## Diversity of Insects

Scientists estimate that there are as many as 30 million insect species, which is more species than all other animals combined. Recall that arthropods make up about three-fourths of all named animal species. About 80 percent of arthropods are insects. They are the most abundant and widespread of all terrestrial animals. You can find insects in soil, in forests and deserts, on mountaintops, and even in polar regions.

Insects live in many habitats because of their ability to fly and their ability to adapt. Their small size enables them to be moved easily by wind or water. Diversity of insects also is enhanced by the hard exoskeleton that protects them and keeps them from drying out in deserts and other dry areas. In addition, the reproductive capacity of insects ensures that they are successful in any areas they inhabit. Insects produce a large number of eggs, most of the eggs hatch, and the offspring have short life cycles, all of which can lead to huge insect populations.

## External Features

Insects have three body areas—the head, thorax, and abdomen, shown in **Figure 26.15.** Head structures include antennae, compound eyes, simple eyes, and mouthparts. Insects have three pairs of legs and generally two pairs of wings on the thorax. Some only have one pair of wings, and others do not have wings at all.

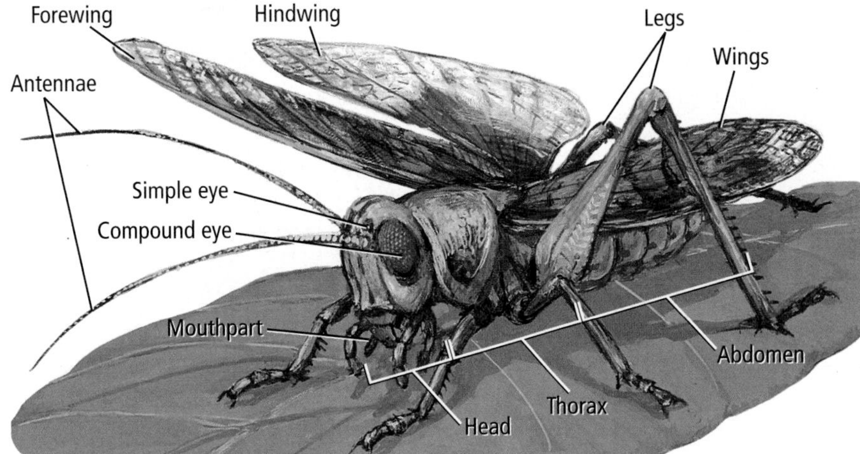


**Figure 26.15** The head, thorax, and abdomen regions of this cricket are characteristic of insects.
**Compare** *How do the body regions of insects differ from those of crustaceans?*

Concepts In Motion

**Interactive Figure** To see an animation of the basic anatomy of a grasshopper, visit biologygmh.com.

## Insect Adaptations

Structural adaptations to legs, mouthparts, wings, and sense organs have led to increased diversity in insects. These adaptations enable insects to utilize all kinds of food and to live in many different types of environments. Taking advantage of a variety of food sources, insects might be parasites, predators, or plant-sap suckers.

**Legs** Insect legs are adapted to a variety of functions. Beetles have walking legs with claws that enable them to dig in soil or crawl under bark. Flies have walking legs with sticky pads on the ends that enable them to walk upside down. Honeybee legs have adaptations for collecting pollen, while the hind legs of grasshoppers and crickets are adapted to jumping. Water striders have legs adapted to skimming over the surface of water. On its footpads, a water strider has water-repellent hairs that do not break the surface tension of the water. As it skates over the water, this insect propels itself with its back legs and steers with its front legs, like a rear-wheel-drive car.

**Mouthparts** Insects' mouthparts are adapted to the food they eat, as shown in **Table 26.2.** Butterflies and moths have a long tube through which they draw nectar from flowers in a motion similar to sipping through a straw. Different types of flies, such as houseflies and fruit flies, have sponging and lapping mouthparts that take up liquids. Some insects, such as leafhoppers and mosquitoes, have piercing mouthparts for feeding on plant juices or prey. Insects such as beetles and ants cut animal skin or plant tissue with their mandibles to reach the nutrients inside.

Concepts In Motion
Interactive Table To explore more about insect mouthparts, visit biologygmh.com.

**Table 26.2 Insect Mouthparts**

| Type of mouthpart | Siphoning | Sponging | Piercing/Sucking | Chewing |
|---|---|---|---|---|
| Example | | | | |
| Function | Feeding tube is uncoiled and extended to suck liquids into the mouth. | Fleshy end of mouthpart acts like a sponge to mop up food. | A thin, needlelike tube pierces the skin or plant wall to suck liquids into the mouth. | Mandible pierces or cuts animal or plant tissue, and other mouthparts bring food to the mouth. |
| Insects with adaptation | Butterflies, moths | Houseflies, fruit flies | Mosquitoes, leafhoppers, stink bugs, fleas | Grasshoppers, beetles, ants, bees, earwigs |

Trilobite fossil

Color-Enhanced SEM Magnification: 750×

Tardigrade

**Figure 26.21** Extinct trilobites are considered to be some of the first arthropods. They were abundant in Cambrian times. Tardigrades, belonging to a phylum that might be related to annelids and arthropods, are called water bears and can live in areas that are alternately wet and dry.

## Evolution of Arthropods

The relationships of tardigrades, trilobites, and arthropods have been under close scrutiny as new evidence is discovered. Fossil records show that trilobites, abundant in the mid-Cambrian but now extinct, were early arthropods. Trilobites, like the one shown in **Figure 26.21,** were oval, flattened, and divided into three body sections like some modern arthropods. The large number of identical segments of these ancestral arthropods evolved to more specialized appendages and fewer segments in modern arthropods.

Tardigrades also are related to arthropods, but they appear to be related less closely to arthropods than trilobites are. The tardigrade shown in **Figure 26.21** illustrates why these tiny animals are known commonly as water bears. The largest are 1.5 mm long with four pairs of stubby legs. They feed on algae, decaying matter, nematodes, and other soil animals. They inhabit freshwater, marine, and land habitats. During temperature extremes and drought, tardigrades can survive for years in a completely dry state with reduced metabolism until favorable conditions return.

## Section 26.3 Assessment

### Section Summary

- Insects make up approximately 80 percent of all arthropod species.
- A variety of adaptations have enabled insects to live in almost all habitats on Earth.
- Insect mouthparts reflect their diets.
- Most insects undergo metamorphosis.
- In some insects, social structure, including individual specializations, is necessary for the survival of the colony.

### Understand Main Ideas

1. MAIN Idea **Evaluate** three adaptations of insects in terms of the role they played in enabling insects to become so diverse and abundant.
2. **Identify** features common to all insects.
3. **List** adaptations of the mouthparts of insects that feed on three different food sources and explain each one.
4. **Identify** one reason most insects undergo complete metamorphosis.

### Think Scientifically

5. *Design an Experiment* Different species of firefly beetles flash their light in different sequences of short and long flashes. Design an experiment that would explain why fireflies flash their lights.
6. MATH in Biology There are approximately 1.75 million named animal species. About three-fourths of all known animal species are arthropods, and 80 percent of arthropods are insects. Approximately how many named species are insects?

# In the Field

## Career: Forensic Entomologist

### Insect Evidence

Insects often are the first to arrive at a crime scene. Blowflies can arrive within minutes. Over time, other insects arrive. As the insects feed, grow, and lay eggs, they follow predictable developmental cycles. For forensic entomologists—scientists who apply their knowledge of insects to help solve crimes—these cycles reveal information about the time and location of death.

**Time of death** Forensic entomologists use two methods to determine time of death. The first method is used when the victim has been dead for at least one month. While blowflies and houseflies arrive almost immediately, other species arrive later in the decomposition process. Some species arrive to feed on other insects already at the scene. The succession of insects provides information about the time that passed since death occurred.

When death has occurred within a few weeks, a second method used involves the developmental cycle of blowflies. Within a couple of days, the blowflies lay eggs. The next stages of development are determined in part by temperature, as shown in the graph. Based on the stage of insect development and area temperatures, entomologists can determine a range of days in which the first insects laid eggs in the body, establishing a time of death.

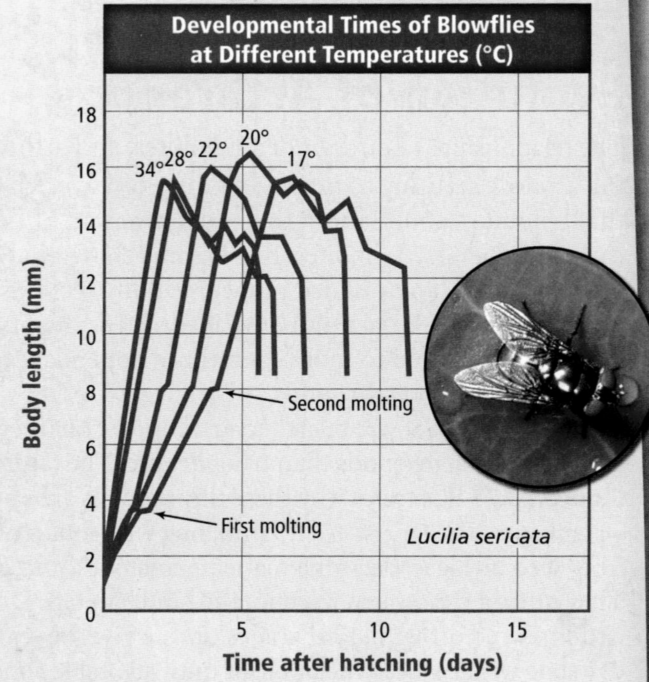


**Location of death** Insects help determine if a body was relocated after death. If insects found on the body are not native to the habitat where the body is found, investigators can assume that the body was moved. The species that are present also provide clues about the area where death took place.

**Limitations** In many locations, forensic entomology is less useful in winter, when insects are less active and less abundant. In addition, insects might be prevented from invading a body if it is frozen, buried deeply, or wrapped tightly. In many cases, however, insects can give crucial testimony about the details of a crime.

**MATH in Biology**

**Study the graph** to solve this problem: Blowfly larvae with a body length of about 6 mm are found on a corpse with a temperature of 22°C. How much time has passed since death? For more information about careers in biology, visit biologygmh.com.

# BIOLAB

## INTERNET: WHERE ARE MICROARTHROPODS FOUND?

**Background: Microarthropods range from 0.1 to 5 mm in size—barely visible to human eyes. Dozens of microarthropod species can be unearthed in one shovelful of soil. Discover these hidden animals during this investigation.**

**Question:** *What types of microarthropods can be found in your local environment?*

### Materials

soil sample
clear funnel
ring stand
gooseneck lamp
wire mesh
beaker
95% ethanol
plastic collection vials
magnifying lens
arthropod field guide
metric ruler

### Safety Precautions

### Procedure

1. Read and complete the lab safety form.
2. Obtain a sample of leaf litter and soil from your teacher.
3. Create a data table to record your observations.
4. Place the funnel in the ring stand.
5. Cut the mesh screen in a circle so it rests inside the funnel.
6. Pour ethanol into the beaker until the beaker is two-thirds full. Set the beaker under the funnel.
7. Remove your soil sample from the bag and place it carefully on the mesh screen in the funnel.
8. Place the lamp at least 10 cm above the sample. Switch on the light and leave it on for several hours. The heat from the lamp dries the soil. This forces the microarthropods downward until they fall through the screen and into the alcohol.
9. Use a magnifying lens to observe the physical characteristics of the microarthropods you collected.
10. **Cleanup and Disposal** Be certain to properly dispose of the alcohol and specimens you collected by following your teacher's instructions.

### Analyze and Conclude

1. **Classify** Place the microarthropods you collected into the three major groups of arthropods. Place unidentified specimens into a separate group.
2. **Graph** Use the data you collected to graph the abundances of each type of arthropod.
3. **Describe** Write a description of the physical characteristics of the microarthropod specimens that you could not classify into any of the three major groups.
4. **Hypothesize** How do microarthropods help create a healthy soil ecosystem?
5. **Error Analysis** Check your findings against those for the microarthropods collected by other classmates. Did you classify the microarthropods into the same group? If not, explain why.

### SHARE YOUR DATA

**Report** Use a field guide or dichotomous key to identify the microarthropods you collected. Visit Biolabs at biologygmh.com and post your findings in the table provided for this activity. Write a report comparing your findings to those of students in another area of the country.

CHAPTER 26

# Study Guide

Download quizzes, key terms, and flash cards from biologygmh.com.

FOLDABLES **Create** a scenario in which a species of terrestrial arthropod has been transferred from its native habitat to a nonnative habitat. Describe the possible short-term and long-term effects on the arthropod and on the habitat.

| Vocabulary | Key Concepts |
|---|---|
| **Section 26.1 Arthropod Characteristics** | |
| • abdomen (p. 763)<br>• appendage (p. 764)<br>• book lung (p. 767)<br>• cephalothorax (p. 763)<br>• Malpighian tubule (p. 767)<br>• mandible (p. 765)<br>• molting (p. 764)<br>• pheromone (p. 768)<br>• spiracle (p. 767)<br>• thorax (p. 763)<br>• tracheal tube (p. 767) | MAIN Idea Arthropods have segmented bodies and tough exoskeletons with jointed appendages.<br>• Arthropods can be identified by three main structural features.<br>• Arthropods have adaptations that make them the most successful animals on Earth.<br>• Arthropod mouthparts are adapted to a wide variety of food materials.<br>• In order to grow, arthropods must molt.<br>• Arthropods have organ system modifications that have enabled them to live in all types of habitats and to increase in variety and numbers. |
| **Section 26.2 Arthropod Diversity** | |
| • chelicera (p. 771)<br>• cheliped (p. 771)<br>• pedipalp (p. 772)<br>• spinneret (p. 772)<br>• swimmeret (p. 771) | MAIN Idea Arthropods are classified based on the structure of their segments, types of appendages, and mouthparts.<br>• Arthropods are divided into three major groups.<br>• Crustaceans have modified appendages for getting food, walking, and swimming.<br>• The first two pairs of arachnid appendages are modified as mouthparts, as reproductive structures, or as pincers.<br>• Spiders are carnivores that either hunt prey or trap it in webs that they spin out of silk.<br>• Horseshoe crabs are ancient arthropods that have remained unchanged for more than 200 million years. |
| **Section 26.3 Insects and Their Relatives** | |
| • caste (p. 779)<br>• metamorphosis (p. 778)<br>• nymph (p. 778)<br>• pupa (p. 778) | MAIN Idea Insects have structural and functional adaptations that have enabled them to become the most abundant and diverse group of arthropods.<br>• Insects make up approximately 80 percent of all arthropod species.<br>• A variety of adaptations have enabled insects to live in almost all habitats on Earth.<br>• Insect mouthparts reflect their diets.<br>• Most insects undergo metamorphosis.<br>• In some insects, social structure, including specializations, is necessary for the survival of the colony. |



Biology Online Vocabulary PuzzleMaker biologygmh.com

# CHAPTER 26 Assessment

## Section 26.1

### Vocabulary Review

*An analogy is a relationship between two pairs of words and can be written in the following manner:* A is to B as C is to D. *Complete each analogy by providing the missing vocabulary term from the Study Guide page.*

1. Spiracles are to breathing as __________ are to excreting wastes.
2. Compound eye is to sense organ as mandible is to __________.
3. Head is to thorax as __________ is to abdomen.

### Understand Key Concepts

*Use the diagram below to answer questions 4 and 5.*

4. Which labeled structure helps terrestrial arthropods maintain water balance?
   **A.** 1
   **B.** 2
   **C.** 3
   **D.** 4
5. Which labeled structure would an arthropod use to sense odors in its environment?
   **A.** 1
   **B.** 2
   **C.** 3
   **D.** 4
6. Which group of words has one that does not belong?
   **A.** exoskeleton, chitin, molting, growth
   **B.** mandible, antennae, appendage, leg
   **C.** cephalothorax, thorax, head, abdomen
   **D.** simple eye, compound eye, tympanum, thorax
7. The relationship between muscle size and exoskeleton thickness limits which in an arthropod?
   **A.** diet **C.** motion
   **B.** habitat **D.** size

### Constructed Response

8. **Open Ended** Make a table that lists arthropod structures, their functions, and an analogy of what each structure is like in a world of human-made devices. For example, a particular bird's bill that pulls insects out of bark might be compared to tweezers that can pull a sliver out of skin. Use the following structures in your table: antennae, exoskeleton, mandibles, tracheal tubes, and tympanum.
9. **Open Ended** Katydids are members of the grasshopper family. Most katydids are green, but occasionally both pink and yellow katydids appear. Make a hypothesis to explain why pink and yellow katydids sometimes appear.

### Think Critically

*Use the diagram below to answer question 10.*

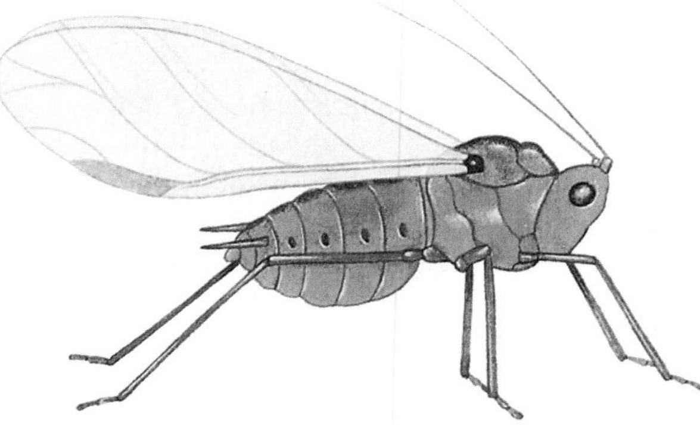

10. **CAREERS IN BIOLOGY** Arborists, people who specialize in caring for trees, sometimes spray horticultural oils on fruit trees to control aphids, the plant pest shown in the diagram. Based on your knowledge of insect anatomy, analyze why oils are an effective treatment to control plant pests.
11. **Infer** Some species of flowers produce heat that attracts certain beetles to live inside the bloom. Infer how the plant and the beetle both benefit from this relationship.

## Section 26.2

### Vocabulary Review

*For each set of vocabulary terms, explain the relationship that exists.*

**12.** cheliped, swimmeret

**13.** chelicera, pedipalp

**14.** cheliped, chelicera

### Understand Key Concepts

*Use the diagram below to answer question 15.*

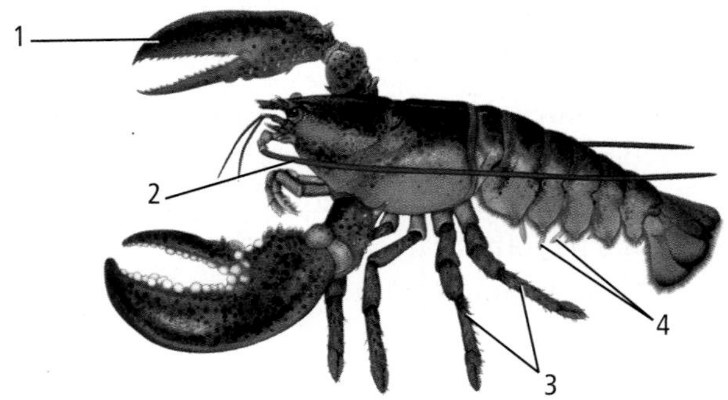


**15.** Which structure would a lobster use to catch and crush food?

**A.** 1 **C.** 3
**B.** 2 **D.** 4

**16.** Which is not a characteristic of arachnids?

**A.** chelicerae **C.** spinnerets
**B.** pedipalps **D.** antennae

**17.** An animal you found on the forest soil has two body sections, no antennae, and large pincers as the second pair of appendages. What type of animal is it?

**A.** tick **C.** spider
**B.** scorpion **D.** lobster

**18.** In spiders, the spinnerets are involved in which activity?

**A.** defense **C.** circulation
**B.** getting rid of waste **D.** spinning silk

**19.** Which is not a characteristic of mites?

**A.** one oval-shaped body section
**B.** carry lyme disease bacteria
**C.** less than 1 mm long
**D.** animal parasite

### Constructed Response

**20. Short Answer** Compare the body forms of aquatic crustaceans to those of terrestrial arachnids, showing how each is adapted to its environment.

**21. Open Ended** What would happen if crustaceans could not molt?

### Think Critically

**22. Formulate Models** Draw and describe a model of a spider that would be adapted to conditions in a hot, dry attic with only crawling insects as a food source.

**23. Interpret Scientific Illustrations** Based on the lobster diagram in **Figure 26.10** and your knowledge of crustaceans, what adaptations enable a lobster to survive in its aquatic enviroment?

## Section 26.3

### Vocabulary Review

*For each set of vocabulary terms, choose the one term that does not belong and explain why it does not belong.*

**24.** incomplete metamorphosis, pupa, larva, adult

**25.** complete metamorphosis, nymph, adult, molt

**26.** pupa, larva, nymph, caste, adult

### Understand Key Concepts

*Use the diagram below to answer question 27.*

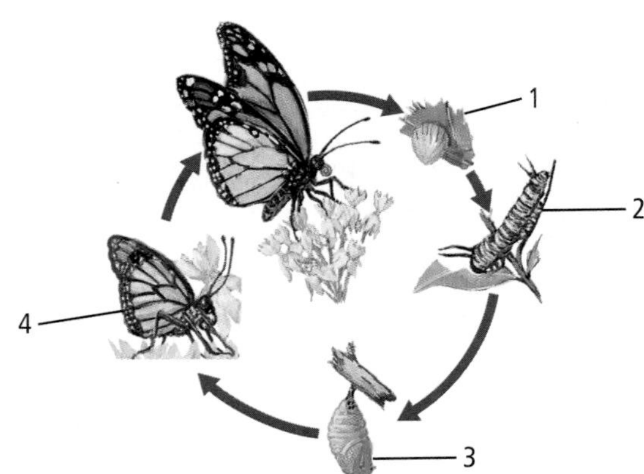


**27.** Which stage does not belong in the diagram of complete metamorphosis?

**A.** 1 **C.** 3
**B.** 2 **D.** 4

28. If the food is 40 degrees to the right of the Sun, what will be the angle of the straight line of the figure-eight waggle dance?
   A. 60 degrees to the right of vertical
   B. 40 degrees to the right of vertical
   C. 60 degrees to the right of horizontal
   D. 40 degrees to the right of horizontal

29. If a farm field has an infestation of insects, which method would the farmer use to manage it for the long-term?
   A. genetic engineering
   B. insecticides
   C. integrated pest management
   D. pesticide resistance

## Constructed Response

*Use the diagram below to answer questions 30 and 31.*

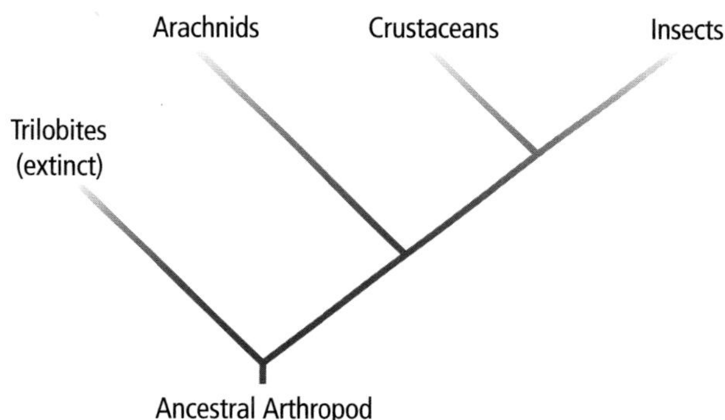


30. **Open Ended** Based on this interpretation of the phylogeny of arthropods, which group developed the earliest? Which group developed most recently?

31. **Open Ended** Examine the cladogram and sequence the order of appearance, from oldest to most modern, of the following features in the evolution of insects: chelicerae, mandibles, body divided into two regions, segmentation. Explain your reasoning.

## Think Critically

32. **Hypothesize** A certain species of beetle looks very much like an ant. Make a hypothesis about the advantage to the beetle of looking like a particular ant.

33. **Design an experiment** that would answer this question: Why do crickets chirp?

## Additional Assessment

34.  WRITING in Biology Malaria is spread by mosquitos and is one of the world's worst diseases in terms of numbers of people affected and the difficulties in treating and preventing it. Research and write an essay on how scientists are using fungi to prevent this disease.

### DBQ Document-Based Questions

*Desert locusts have two distinct phases in their lives: the solitary insect that stays in one area and the social phase in which locusts band together in swarms of billions and move kilometers in search of food. Biologists found that exposing individual insects to jostling by small paper balls induced swarming. Examine the locust below. Each color indicates the percentage of social behavior induced by touching the locust on various parts of the body.*

Data obtained from: Enserink, M. 2004. Can the war on locusts be won? *Science* 306 (5703): 1880–1882.

35. What percentage of social behavior resulted from touching the insect's thorax?

36. What part of the insect's body is the most sensitive for generating social activity when touched?

37. Draw a conclusion about what physical trigger causes locusts to swarm.

## Cumulative Review

38. Compare alternation of generations in plants and alternation of generations in jellyfishes. **(Chapter 24)**

# Standardized Test Practice

**Cumulative**

## Multiple Choice

1. Which common function do both the endoskeletons and exoskeletons of animals perform?
   A. growing along with the animal
   B. preventing water loss
   C. supporting the body
   D. providing protection from predators

*Use the diagram below to answer questions 2 and 3.*

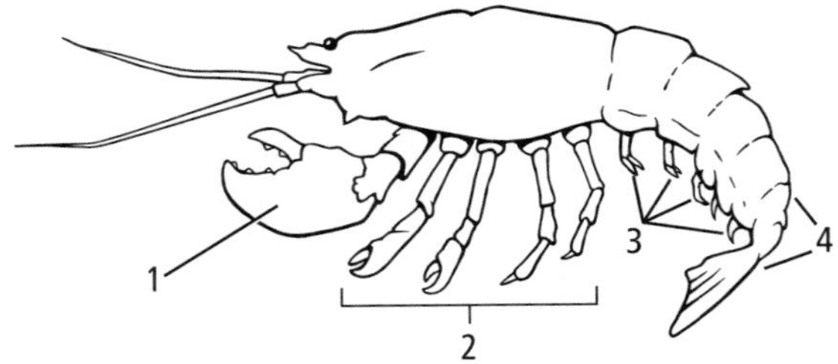


2. In which group does this animal belong?
   A. copepods
   B. crustaceans
   C. insects
   D. spiders

3. Which part of the body does this animal use for reproduction?
   A. 1
   B. 2
   C. 3
   D. 4

4. How are the organisms in Kingdom Protista different from animals?
   A. Some are multicellular.
   B. Some are prokaryotes.
   C. Some have cell walls.
   D. Some have tissues.

5. Which kind of asexual reproduction is possible in flatworms?
   A. budding
   B. fertilization
   C. parthenogenesis
   D. regeneration

*Use the drawing below to answer question 6.*

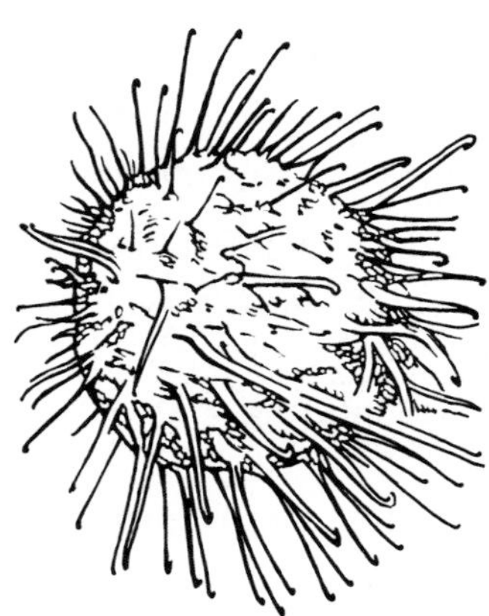

6. Which is the method of seed dispersal for this seed?
   A. animals
   B. gravity
   C. water
   D. wind

7. Which process is related to sexual reproduction in animals?
   A. budding
   B. fertilization
   C. fragmentation
   D. parthogenesis

8. Which is the role of an earthworm's clitellum in reproduction?
   A. It breaks off, allowing fragmentation to occur.
   B. It indicates whether or not an earthworm is hermaphroditic.
   C. It leaves the earthworm's body and forms a cocoon for developing earthworms.
   D. It produces sperm and eggs.

9. Which is used to classify protists?
   A. feeding
   B. habitat
   C. structure
   D. reproduction

## Short Answer

*Use the diagram below to answer question 10.*

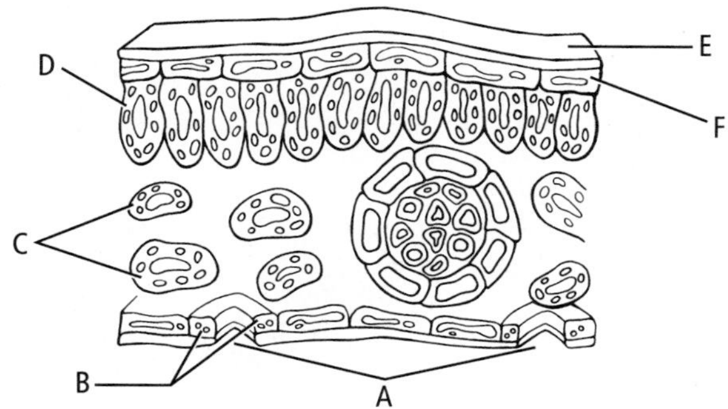


10. Identify the labeled parts of this leaf and state a function for each part.

11. Which characteristics differentiate arthropods from other invertebrates?

12. Describe embryonic development from a zygote to a gastrula. Provide the name of each stage, and explain how it is unique.

13. What characteristics do all mollusks share?

14. Compare and contrast how blood circulates through an insect with the circulation of blood in another kind of animal.

15. Explain the theory of endosymbiosis as it applies to protists. Assess the possible connection between certain organelles in eukaryotic protists and the structures of prokaryotic organisms.

16. Assess the importance of algae to all living things.

## Extended Response

*Use the illustrations below to answer question 17.*

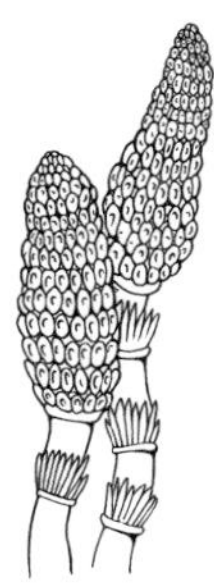

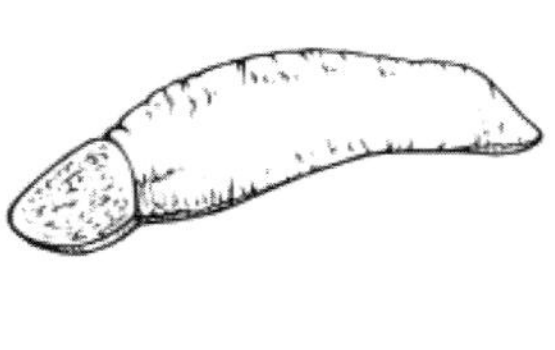

17. The figures above show spores and seeds from different kinds of plants. Explain why one of these structures would have an advantage and would be more likely to be naturally selected.

18. Evaluate the advantages and disadvantages of an exoskeleton.

## Essay Question

The world's coral reefs and associated ecosystems are threatened by an increasing array of pollution, habitat destruction, invasive species, disease, bleaching, and global climate change. The rapid decline of these complex and biologically diverse marine ecosystems has significant social, economic, and environmental impacts in the U.S. and around the world. The U.S. Coral Reef Task Force identified two basic themes for national action:

- understand coral reef ecosystems and the processes that determine their health and viability
- reduce the adverse impacts of human activities on coral reefs and associated ecosystems

*Using the information in the paragraph above, answer the following question in essay format.*

19. What steps do you think the U.S. should take to preserve coral reef ecosystems?

**NEED EXTRA HELP?**

| If You Missed Question . . . | 1 | 2 | 3 | 4 | 5 | 6 | 7 | 8 | 9 | 10 | 11 | 12 | 13 | 14 | 15 | 16 | 17 | 18 | 19 |
|---|---|---|---|---|---|---|---|---|---|---|---|---|---|---|---|---|---|---|---|
| Review Section . . . | 24.1 | 26.2 | 26.2 | 24.1 | 25.1 | 23.3 | 24.1 | 25.4 | 19.1 | 22.2 | 26.1 | 24.1 | 25.3 | 26.1 | 19.1 | 19.3 | 21.3 | 26.1 | 24.3 |

# CHAPTER 27 Echinoderms and Invertebrate Chordates

**Section 1**
**Echinoderm Characteristics**
MAIN Idea Echinoderms are marine animals with spiny endoskeletons, water-vascular systems, and tube feet; they have radial symmetry as adults.

**Section 2**
**Invertebrate Chordates**
MAIN Idea Invertebrate chordates have features linking them to vertebrate chordates.

## BioFacts

- A single crown-of-thorns sea star eats 2–6 $m^2$ of coral per year.
- Crown-of-thorns sea stars have spines that are covered with poison-filled skin.
- Another echinoderm, the sea cucumber, protects itself by changing the consistency of its skin from near liquid to solid and back again.

# Start-Up Activities

## LAUNCH Lab

### Why are tube feet important?

Like all echinoderms, the crown-of-thorns sea star in the opening photo has structures called tube feet. In this lab, you will observe tube feet and determine their function.

#### Procedure

1. Read and complete the lab safety form.
2. Place a **live sea star** in a **petri dish** filled with **water from a saltwater aquarium. WARNING:** ***Treat the sea star in a humane manner at all times.***
3. Observe the ventral side of the sea star under a **dissecting microscope.** Look for the rows of tube feet that run down the middle of each arm, and draw a diagram of the structures.
4. Gently touch the end of a tube foot with a **glass probe.** Record your observations.
5. Return the sea star and water to the aquarium.

#### Analysis

1. **Describe** the structure of the sea star's tube feet.
2. **Infer** Based on your observations, what is the function of an echinoderm's tube feet?

Visit biologygmh.com to:

- study the entire chapter online
- explore Concepts in Motion, the Interactive Table, Microscopy Links, and links to virtual dissections
- access Web links for more information, projects, and activities
- review content online with the Interactive Tutor and take Self-Check Quizzes

**Describing Invertebrate Chordates** Make the following Foldable to help you understand the physical features that link invertebrate chordates to vertebrate chordates.

**STEP 1** Collect three sheets of paper and layer them about 1.5 cm apart vertically. Keep the edges level.

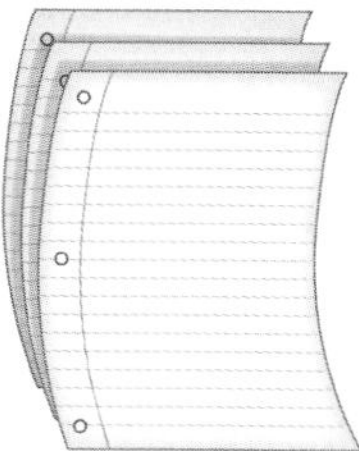

**STEP 2** Fold up the bottom edges of the paper to form six tabs.

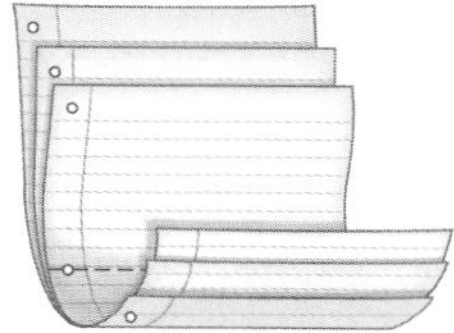

**STEP 3** Crease well along the fold to hold the tabs in place. Staple along the fold. Rotate the paper so the fold is at the top, and label each tab as shown.

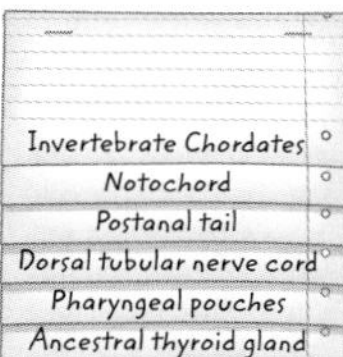


FOLDABLES **Use this Foldable with Section 27.2.** As you read the section, record information about the physical features of invertebrate chordates that link them to vertebrate chordates.

Section 27.1

## Objectives

- **Summarize** the characteristics common to echinoderms.
- **Evaluate** how the water-vascular system and tube feet are adaptations that enable echinoderms to be successful.
- **Distinguish** between the classes of echinoderms.

### Review Vocabulary

**endoskeleton:** an internal skeleton that provides support and protection and can act as a brace for muscles to pull against

### New Vocabulary

pedicellaria
water-vascular system
madreporite
tube foot
ampulla

# Echinoderm Characteristics

MAIN Idea **Echinoderms are marine animals with spiny endoskeletons, water-vascular systems, and tube feet; they have radial symmetry as adults.**

**Real-World Reading Link** To take a blood-pressure reading, a health care professional squeezes a bulb that forces air through a tube and into the blood-pressure cuff around your arm. The cuff remains tight around your arm until the pressure is released when the air is let out. Some animals use this same kind of system to obtain food and move.

## Echinoderms Are Deuterostomes

As shown in the evolutionary tree in **Figure 27.1,** echinoderms (ih KI nuh durmz) are deuterostomes—a major transition in the phylogeny of animals. Notice how the evolutionary tree branches at deuterostome development.

The mollusks, annelids, and arthropods you studied in previous chapters are protostomes. Recall that during development, a protostome's mouth develops from the opening on the gastrula, while a deuterostome's mouth develops from elsewhere on the gastrula. This might not seem important, but consider that only echinoderms and the chordates that evolved after echinoderms have this kind of development. Echinoderms and chordates are related more closely than groups that do not develop in this way. You are related more closely to the sea star in the opening photo than you are to a beetle or a clam.

The approximately 6000 living species of echinoderms are marine animals and include sea stars, sea urchins and sand dollars, sea cucumbers, brittle stars, sea lilies and feather stars, and sea daisies. Two echinoderms are shown in **Figure 27.1.**

**Figure 27.1** Echinoderms are marine animals and are the first animals in evolutionary history to have deuterostome development and an endoskeleton.

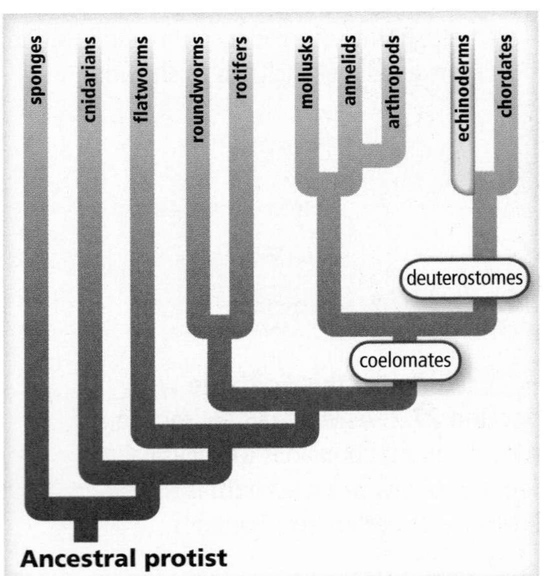

## Body Structure

The brittle star is an example of an echinoderm with the spiny endoskeleton that is characteristic of the organisms in this phylum. Echinoderms are the first group of animals in evolutionary history to have endoskeletons. In echinoderms, the endoskeleton consists of calcium carbonate plates, often with spines attached, and is covered by a thin layer of skin. On the skin are **pedicellariae** (PEH dih sih LAHR ee uh), small pincers that aid in catching food and in removing foreign materials from the skin.

All echinoderms have radial symmetry as adults. In **Figure 27.2,** you can see this feature in the five arms of the brittle star radiating out from a central disk. However, echinoderm larvae have bilateral symmetry, as shown in **Figure 27.2.** In the next chapter, you will learn how bilateral symmetry shows an embryonic link to the vertebrate animals that evolved later.

No other animals with the complex organ systems of echinoderms have radial symmetry. Scientists theorize that the ancestors of echinoderms did not have radial symmetry. Primitive echinoderms might have been sessile, and radial symmetry developed, to enable them to carry on a successful stationary existence. Free-moving echinoderms might have evolved from the sessile animals. Investigate the features of echinoderms in **MiniLab 27.1.**

 **Reading Check** **Infer** how radial symmetry is important to animals that cannot move quickly.

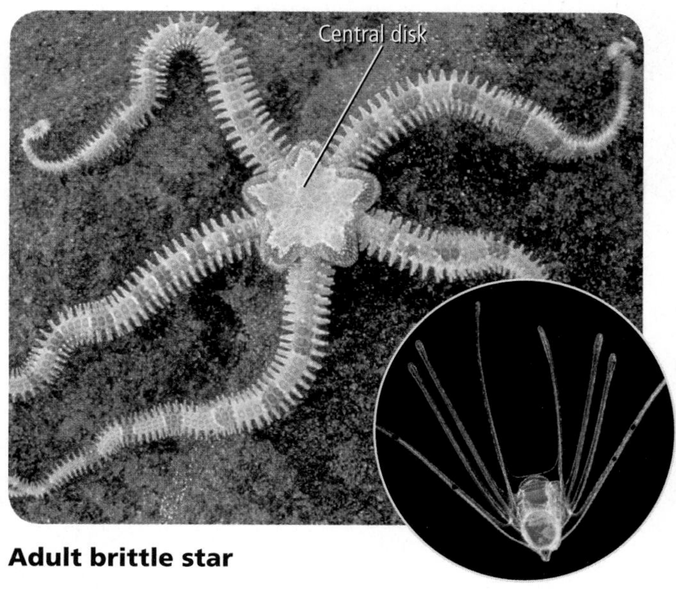


**Adult brittle star**

**Brittle star larva**

■ **Figure 27.2** Brittle star larvae have bilateral symmetry and can be divided along only one plane into mirror-image halves. Adult brittle stars have radial symmetry and can be divided through a central axis, along any plane, into equal halves.

## MiniLab 27.1

### Observe Echinoderm Anatomy

**What are the characteristics of echinoderms?** Although they have many shapes and sizes, all echinoderms have some features in common.

**Procedure**

1. Read and complete the lab safety form.
2. Study preserved specimens of **a sand dollar, a sea cucumber, a sea star,** and **a sea urchin.**
3. Create a data table to record your observations. Complete the table by describing the major features of each specimen. Include a sketch of each specimen.
4. Label any external features you can identify.
5. Clean all equipment and return it to the appropriate place. Wash your hands thoroughly after handling preserved specimens.

**Analysis**

1. **Compare** the external features of the echinoderms you studied. Can your observations completely justify why these four organisms are classified in the same phylum? Explain.
2. **Observe and Infer** What features are most important in helping echinoderms avoid being eaten by predators?

# Visualizing an Echinoderm

**Figure 27.3**
Sea urchins can be found in tidal areas of the sea. They burrow into crevices in rocks to hide, and they scrape algae with a hard five-plated structure, called Aristotle's lantern, in their mouths. Imagine that these plates are like teeth that move.

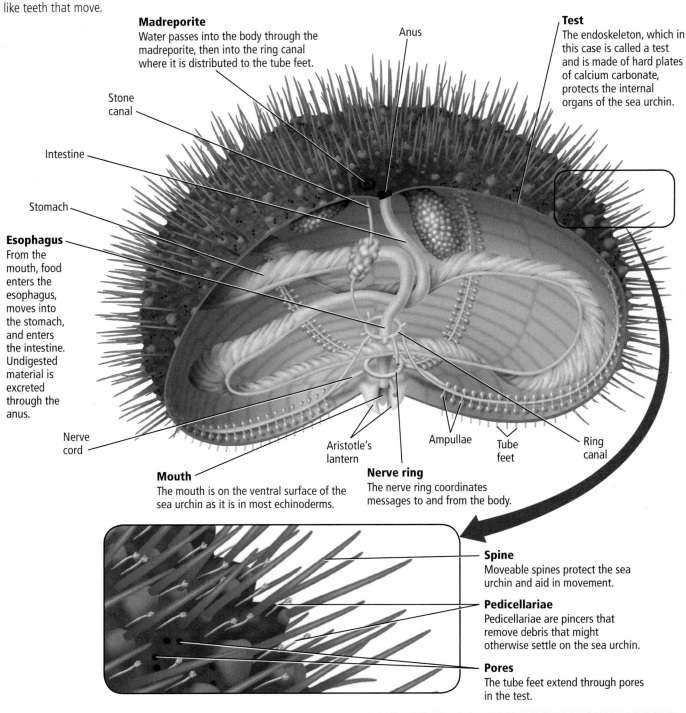



Madreporite
Water passes into the body through the madreporite, then into the ring canal where it is distributed to the tube feet.
Anus
Test
The endoskeleton, which in this case is called a test and is made of hard plates of calcium carbonate, protects the internal organs of the sea urchin.
Stone canal
Intestine
Stomach
Esophagus
From the mouth, food enters the esophagus, moves into the stomach, and enters the intestine. Undigested material is excreted through the anus.
Nerve cord

The mouth is on the ventral surface of the sea urchin as it is in most echinoderms.
Nerve ring
The nerve ring coordinates messages to and from the body.
Spine
Moveable spines protect the sea urchin and aid in movement.
Pedicellariae
Pedicellariae are pincers that remove debris that might otherwise settle on the sea urchin.
Pores
The tube feet extend through pores in the test.

**Concepts In Motion** **Interactive Figure** To see an animation of echinoderm features, visit biologygmh.com.

Ampullae
Tube feet
Ring canal

**Biology Online**

**Water-vascular system** Another feature of echinoderms is their **water-vascular system**—a system of fluid-filled, closed tubes that work together to enable echinoderms to move and get food. The strainerlike opening to the water-vascular system, shown in **Figure 27.3,** is called the **madreporite** (MA druh pohr it). Water is drawn into the madreporite, then moves through the stone canal to the ring canal. From there, the water moves to the radial canals and eventually to the tube feet.

**Tube feet** are small, muscular, fluid-filled tubes that end in suction-cup-like structures and are used in movement, food collection, and respiration. The opposite end of the tube foot is a muscular sac, called the **ampulla** (AM pyew luh). When muscles contract in the ampulla, water is forced into the tube foot and it extends. Imagine holding a small, partly inflated balloon in your hand and squeezing it. The balloon will extend from between your thumb and forefinger, which is similar to the way the tube foot extends. The suction-cup-like structure on the end of the tube foot attaches it to the surface. This hydraulic suction enables all echinoderms to move and some, such as sea stars, to apply a force strong enough to open the shells of mollusks, as illustrated in **Figure 27.4.**

**Figure 27.4** A sea star uses its tube feet to open the two shells of a clam.
**Describe** *the sea star's feeding method.*

**Feeding and digestion** Echinoderms use a great variety of feeding strategies in addition to tube feet. Sea lilies and feather stars extend their arms and trap food. Sea stars prey on a variety of mollusks, coral, and other invertebrates. Many species of sea stars can push their stomachs out of their mouths and onto their prey. They then spread digestive enzymes over the food and use cilia to bring the digested material to their mouths. Brittle stars can be active predators or scavengers, and they can trap organic materials in mucus on their arms. Most sea urchins use teethlike plates, shown in **Figure 27.3,** to scrape algae off surfaces or feed on other animals. Many sea cucumbers extend their branched, mucus-covered tentacles to trap floating food.

**LAUNCH Lab**

**Review** Based on what you've read about the water-vascular system, how would you now answer the analysis questions?

**Respiration, circulation, and excretion** Echinoderms also use their tube feet in respiration. Oxygen diffuses from the water through the thin membranes of the tube feet. Some echinoderms carry out diffusion of oxygen through all thin body membranes in contact with water. Others have thin-walled skin gills that are small pouches extending from the body. Many sea cucumbers have branched tubes, called respiratory trees, through which water passes and oxygen moves into the body.

Circulation takes place in the body coelom and the water-vascular system, while excretion of cellular wastes occurs by diffusion through thin body membranes. Cilia move water and body fluids throughout these systems aided by pumping action in some echinoderms. In spite of the simplicity of these organs and systems, echinoderms maintain homeostasis effectively with adaptations that are suited to their way of life.

**VOCABULARY**

**ACADEMIC VOCABULARY**

**Aid:**
To give assistance or to help.
*Echinoderms capture food aided by their tube feet.*

**Reading Check** **Summarize** the functions of an echinoderm's tube feet.

■ **Figure 27.5** A sea star lifts the end of an arm to sense light and movement.

**Response to stimuli** Echinoderms have both sensory and motor neurons with varying degrees of complexity in different species. In general, a nerve ring surrounds the mouth with branching nerve cords connecting to other body areas.

Sensory neurons respond to touch, chemicals dissolved in the water, water currents, and light. At the tips of the arms of sea stars are eyespots, clusters of light-sensitive cells, illustrated in **Figure 27.5.** Many echinoderms also sense the direction of gravity. For example, a sea star will return to an upright position after being overturned by a wave or current.

**Movement** Echinoderm locomotion is as varied as echinoderm body shapes. The structure of the endoskeleton is important for determining the type of movement an echinoderm can undertake. The movable bony plates in the endoskeletons of echinoderms enable them to move easily. Feather stars move by grasping the soft sediments of the ocean bottom with their cirri—long, thin appendages on their ventral sides—or by swimming with up-and-down movements of their arms. Brittle stars use their tube feet and their arms in snakelike movements for locomotion. Sea stars use their arms and tube feet for crawling. Sea urchins move by using tube feet and burrowing with their movable spines. Sea cucumbers crawl using their tube feet and body wall muscles.

 **Reading Check Summarize** In addition to using their tube feet, in what other ways do echinoderms move?

**VOCABULARY**

**SCIENCE USAGE V. COMMON USAGE**

**Structure**

***Science usage:*** the arrangement of parts of an organism.
*The structure of an insect's mouth determines how it functions.*

***Common usage:*** something that is constructed, such as a building.
*The workers built the structure in three months.*

**Reproduction and development** Most echinoderms reproduce sexually. The females shed eggs and the males shed sperm into the water where fertilization takes place. The fertilized eggs develop into free-swimming larvae with bilateral symmetry. After going through a series of changes, the larvae develop into adults with radial symmetry. Recall that echinoderms have deuterostome development, making them an important evolutionary connection to vertebrates.

The sea star in **Figure 27.6** illustrates an echinoderm regenerating a lost body part. Many echinoderms can drop off an arm when they are attacked, enabling them to flee while the predator is distracted. Others can expel part of their internal organ systems when threatened, an action that might surprise and deter predators. All of these body parts can be regenerated.

■ **Figure 27.6** This sea star is regenerating one of its arms, a process that can take up to one year.
**Explain** ***how regenerating body parts helps echinoderms survive.***

# CHAPTER 27 Assessment

## Section 27.1

### Vocabulary Review

*Distinguish between the terms in each of the following pairs.*

**1.** tube foot, ampulla

**2.** madreporite, water-vascular system

### Understand Key Concepts

**3.** Which is not an echinoderm?

**A.** 

**B.** 

**C.** 

**D.** 

**A.** A
**B.** B
**C.** C
**D.** D

**4.** Which echinoderm is sessile for part of its life?
**A.** sea cucumber
**B.** sea lily
**C.** brittle star
**D.** sea urchin

**5.** What three functions do tube feet perform?
**A.** reproduction, feeding, respiration
**B.** feeding, respiration, neural control
**C.** feeding, respiration, movement
**D.** development, reproduction, respiration

**6.** Which is not associated with deuterostomes?
**A.** a pattern of development
**B.** mouth develops from somewhere on the gastrula away from the opening
**C.** echinoderms
**D.** arthropods

**7.** Which are involved in protecting an echinoderm?
**A.** endoskeleton, pedicellariae, spines
**B.** madreporite, tentacles, endoskeleton
**C.** water-vascular system, ampulla, pedicellariae
**D.** exoskeleton, pedicellariae, spines

**8.** What is the main difference between echinoderm larvae and adults?
**A.** Larvae are protostomes and adults are deuterostomes.
**B.** Larvae are deuterostomes and adults are protostomes.
**C.** Larvae have bilateral symmetry and adults have radial symmetry.
**D.** Larvae have radial symmetry and adults have bilateral symmetry.

**9.** Which group of echinoderms has respiratory trees with many branches?
**A.** sea cucumbers
**B.** sea stars
**C.** sea lilies and feather stars
**D.** sea urchins and sand dollars

### Constructed Response

*Use the diagram below to answer questions 10 and 11.*

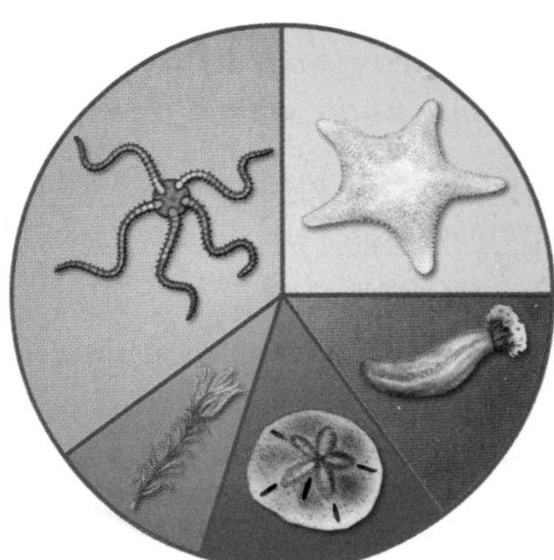

**10. Short Answer** Examine the circle graph and estimate the percentage of echinoderms that are sea cucumbers.

**11. Open Ended** Examine the circle graph and explain why class Concentricycloidea does not appear with the other classes of living echinoderms.

**12. Open Ended** Scientists have discovered a fossil that has the following characteristics: an endoskeleton similar to that of echinoderms, a tail-like structure with an anus at the end of the tail, a structure that might be a gill, and symmetry similar to echinoderms. How might scientists explain this animal in terms of echinoderm classification?

13. **Open Ended** Tidal animals suffer when water and air temperatures rise beyond the limits of tolerance of the animals. The temperature of sea stars remain about 18 degrees cooler than those of the surrounding mussels on a hot day. Make a hypothesis about why sea stars have a lower body temperature.

### Think Critically

14. **Observe and Infer** You are walking on the beach and find an animal that has many feathery arms and tube feet. What kind of animal might this be?

15. **Hypothesize** Some sea urchins seem to have relatively long lifespans. Make a hypothesis about why they live so long.

## Section 27.2

### Vocabulary Review

*Using the vocabulary terms from the Study Guide page, replace the underlined words with the correct term.*

16. Animals that have the features of chordates, but do not have backbones are the close relatives of chordates.

17. Located just below the nerve cord is a structure in chordates that enables invertebrate chordates to swim by moving their tails back and forth.

18. The connections between the muscular tube that links the mouth cavity and the esophagus develop slits and are used for filter feeding in some invertebrate chordates.

### Understand Key Concepts

19. Chordates have which features at some time in their lives?
    - **A.** water-vascular system, notochord, pharyngeal pouches, postanal tail
    - **B.** tunic, pharyngeal pouches, dorsal tubular nerve cord, postanal tail
    - **C.** tube feet, notochord, pharyngeal pouches, postanal tail
    - **D.** dorsal tubular nerve cord, notochord, pharyngeal pouches, postanal tail

20. Which is the main function of a postanal tail?
    - **A.** circulation
    - **B.** digestion
    - **C.** flexibility
    - **D.** locomotion

*Use the diagram below to answer questions 21 and 22.*

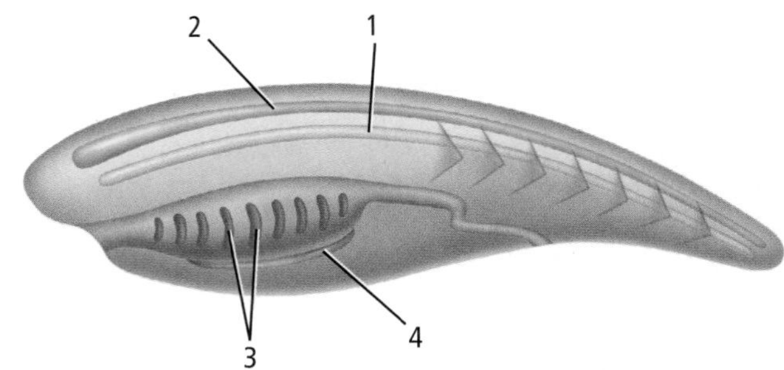


21. Fishlike swimming is made possible by which labeled structure above?
    - **A.** 1
    - **B.** 2
    - **C.** 3
    - **D.** 4

22. Which structure develops into the brain and spinal cord in most chordates?
    - **A.** 1
    - **B.** 2
    - **C.** 3
    - **D.** 4

23. Which describes adult sea squirts?
    - **A.** They are bilaterally symmetrical.
    - **B.** They have the same adult features as lancelets.
    - **C.** As adults, they have only one chordate feature.
    - **D.** They are actively swimming predators.

24. In invertebrate chordates, what does the endostyle secrete?
    - **A.** proteins similar to thyroid hormone
    - **B.** mucus
    - **C.** the notochord
    - **D.** pharyngeal pouches

25. The phylogeny of echinoderms indicates that echinoderms are related to chordates because they both have which feature?
    - **A.** pharyngeal pouches
    - **B.** deuterostome development
    - **C.** protostome development
    - **D.** pseudocoeloms



BiologyOnline Chapter Test biologygmh.com

26. Which structure might be an early form of the thyroid gland?
    **A.** dorsal tubular nerve cord
    **B.** endostyle
    **C.** notochord
    **D.** pharyngeal pouches

27. Which chordate feature enabled large animals to develop?
    **A.** dorsal tubular nerve cord
    **B.** notochord
    **C.** pharyngeal pouches
    **D.** postanal tail

## Constructed Response

28. **Open Ended** Infer why there are no freshwater invertebrate chordates.

29. **Open Ended** What would happen if all lancelets disappeared?

*Use the diagram below to answer questions 30 and 31.*

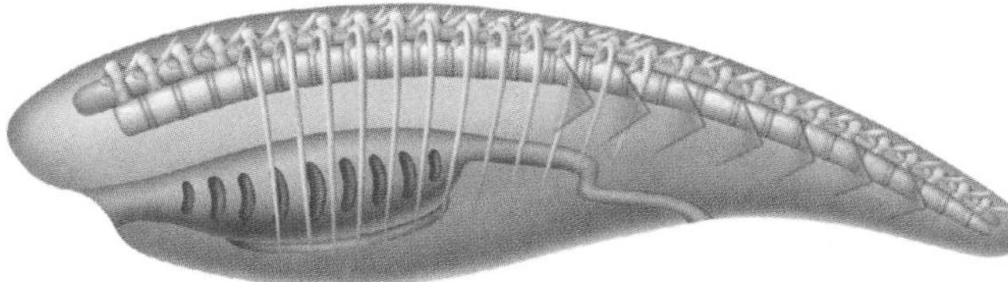

30. **Short Answer** Examine the diagram and explain why this animal could not be an invertebrate chordate.

31. **Short Answer** What features does this animal share with invertebrate chordates?

## Think Critically

32. **Analyze** How do the larvae of organisms help scientists classify and determine the phylogeny of animals?

33. **Use the Internet** Make a visual report of the newest information, both molecular and fossil evidence, gathered by scientists on the origins of chordates.

## Additional Assessment

34. WRITING in Biology **Create** a poem that describes your favorite echinoderm. Make sure you point out the actual features of the echinoderm.

### DBQ Document-Based Questions

*Study the illustration of the progression of development of arms in a specific sea star.*

Diagram based on examples from: Sumrall, Colin D., 2005. Unpublished research on the growth stages of *Neoisorophusella lanei*. The University of Tennessee. http://web.eps.utk.edu/Faculty/sumrall/research2.htm

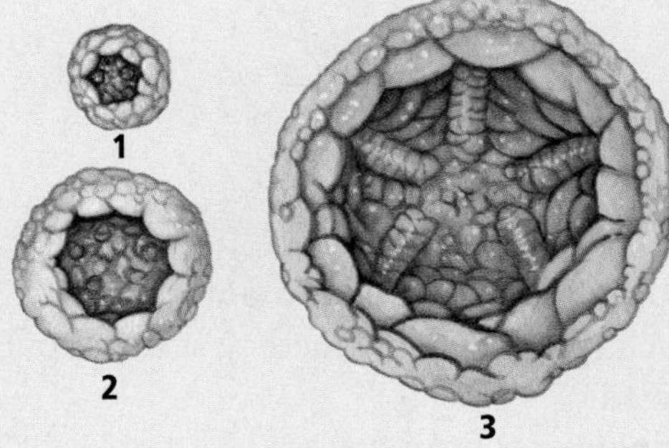


35. What kind of symmetry is shown in the diagram labeled 1?

36. Infer how additional arms might develop.

37. How does the number of arms in diagram 3 reflect the characteristics of all echinoderms?

## Cumulative Review

38. Compare Neanderthals and modern humans. **(Chapter 16)**

39. Compare and contrast the animal-like, plantlike, and funguslike protists. **(Chapter 19)**

40. Prepare a list of vocabulary words that describe general fungal structures, and sketch illustrations of each one. **(Chapter 20)**

41. Name three hormones and the effects they can have on plants. **(Chapter 22)**

42. Sequence the steps involved in the production of the pollen grain and egg in anthophytes. **(Chapter 23)**

# Standardized Test Practice

**Cumulative**

## Multiple Choice

1. In which structure of a flowering plant do eggs develop?
   A. anther
   B. ovule
   C. seed
   D. stigma

*Use the diagram below to answer question 2.*

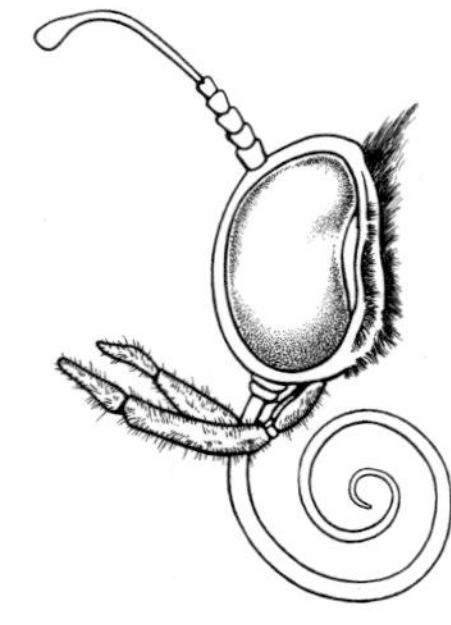

2. Arthropods have specialized mouthparts for feeding. For which type of feeding method is this mouthpart specialized?
   A. getting nectar from flowers
   B. sponging liquids from a surface
   C. sucking blood from a host
   D. tearing and shredding leaves

3. Which statement about a group of invertebrates is correct?
   A. Cnidarians have collar cells.
   B. Flatworms have flame cells.
   C. Flatworms have nematocysts.
   D. Sponges have a nervous system.

4. Echinoderms have which characteristic that is an evolutionary connection to vertebrates?
   A. bilateral symmetry as adults
   B. free-swimming larvae
   C. deuterostome development
   D. radial symmetry as larvae

5. Which special adaptation would be essential for an insect that swims in water?
   A. compound eyes
   B. modified legs
   C. sticky foot pads
   D. sharp mouth parts

*Use the diagram below to answer questions 6 and 7.*

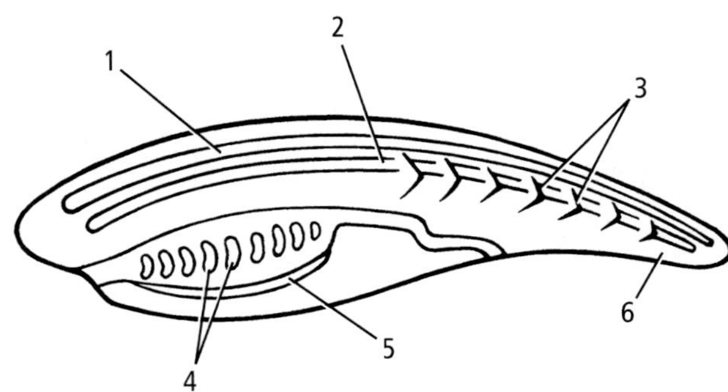


6. Which structure is replaced by bone or cartilage in vertebrate chordates?
   A. 1
   B. 2
   C. 4
   D. 5

7. Which structure is a bundle of nerves protected by fluid?
   A. 1
   B. 3
   C. 5
   D. 6

8. What kind of body organization or body structure first appeared with the evolution of flatworms?
   A. bilateral symmetry
   B. coelomic cavity
   C. nervous system
   D. radial symmetry

9. Suppose a cell from the frond of a fern contains 24 chromosomes. How many chromosomes would you expect to find in the spores?
   A. 6
   B. 12
   C. 24
   D. 48

## Short Answer

10. Use what you know about the body structure of a sponge to explain how it obtains food.

11. Sea stars are echinoderms that feed on oysters. Justify why oyster farmers should not cut up sea stars and toss the parts back into the water.

12. Evaluate the defense adaptations of the two groups of invertebrate chordates.

13. Contrast the main characteristics of echinoderms with the characteristics of the organisms in another phylum that you already know.

*Use the diagram below to answer questions 14 and 15.*

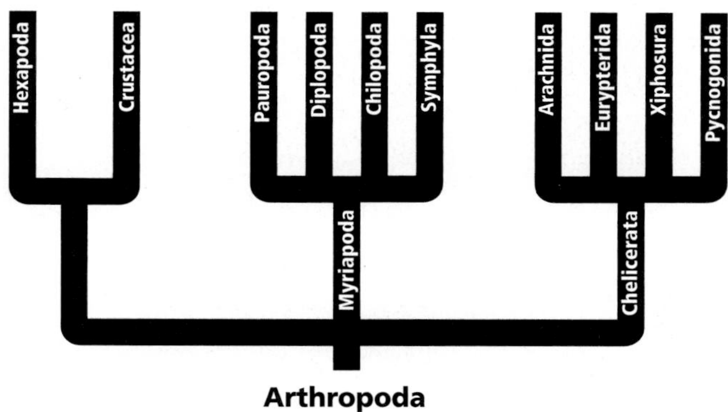


14. Write a hypothesis about why horseshoe crabs (in class Xiphosura) are more closely related to spiders than to regular crabs and lobsters.

15. Write a hypothesis about where trilobites would fit into this phylogenetic tree.

## Extended Response

16. Explain how echinoderms and annelids are similar, and how they are different.

17. In animals, how are mitosis and meiosis different?

18. Evaluate the idea that it was not a large evolutionary jump for aquatic arthropods to move onto land.

19. Suppose that one crow in an area's population is born with longer claws on its feet than other crows in the same population. According to Darwin's theory of natural selection, under what circumstances would this trait become common in the area's crow population?

## Essay Question

In the past, many horror movies have featured giant arthropods attacking major cities. These giant arthropods have included ants, grasshoppers, crabs, and spiders. Actually, the largest living insects are not very big. The longest insect, a walking stick, is about 40 cm long. Some marine arthropods grow larger. The largest arthropod is the Japanese spider crab that can grow up to 4 m wide. Some fossil marine arthropods are even larger. However, none of these are nearly as large as the size of the giant arthropod villains in the movies.

*Using the information in the paragraph above, answer the following question in essay format.*

20. Write an essay about why real-life arthropods cannot become as large as the giant arthropods shown in horror movies.

| NEED EXTRA HELP? | | | | | | | | | | | | | | | | | | | | |
|---|---|---|---|---|---|---|---|---|---|---|---|---|---|---|---|---|---|---|---|---|
| If You Missed Question . . . | 1 | 2 | 3 | 4 | 5 | 6 | 7 | 8 | 9 | 10 | 11 | 12 | 13 | 14 | 15 | 16 | 17 | 18 | 19 | 20 |
| Review Section . . . | 23.3 | 26.1 | 25.1 | 27.1 | 26.3 | 27.2 | 27.2 | 25.1 | 21.3 | 24.3 | 27.1 | 27.2 | 27.2 | 26.2 | 26.3 | 24.2 | 10.1 | 26.2 | 15.1 | 26.1 |

# UNIT 8 Vertebrates

**Chapter 28**
**Fishes and Amphibians**
**BIG Idea** Fishes have adaptations for living in aquatic environments. Most amphibians have adaptations for living part of their lives on land.

**Chapter 29**
**Reptiles and Birds**
**BIG Idea** Reptile and bird adaptations enable them to live and reproduce successfully in terrestrial habitats.

**Chapter 30**
**Mammals**
**BIG Idea** Mammals have evolved to have a variety of adaptations for maintaining homeostasis and living in a variety of habitats.

**Chapter 31**
**Animal Behavior**
**BIG Idea** Many animal behaviors are influenced by both genetics and environmental experiences.

## CAREERS IN BIOLOGY

### Veterinarian

**Veterinarians** are medical specialists trained to prevent, diagnose, and treat medical conditions in domestic, wildlife, zoo, and laboratory animals. Some veterinarians conduct research to expand knowledge of a particular species, much like this giant panda bear researcher is doing.

**WRITING in Biology** Visit biologygmh.com to learn more about veterinarians. Write a paragraph to compare and contrast the duties of veterinarians in private practices and in public institutions.

**Biology Online**

To read more about veterinarians in action, visit biologygmh.com.

# CHAPTER 28 Fishes and Amphibians

**Section 1**
**Fishes**
MAIN Idea Fishes are vertebrates that have characteristics allowing them to live and reproduce in water.

**Section 2**
**Diversity of Today's Fishes**
MAIN Idea Scientists classify fishes into three groups based on body structure.

**Section 3**
**Amphibians**
MAIN Idea Most amphibians begin life as aquatic organisms then live on land as adults.

## BioFacts

- Fish scales have growth rings similar to those of a tree trunk.
- Some types of scales contain enamel, the same material that makes up teeth.
- Fish scales do not have color. The apparent color comes from the skin just beneath the scales.

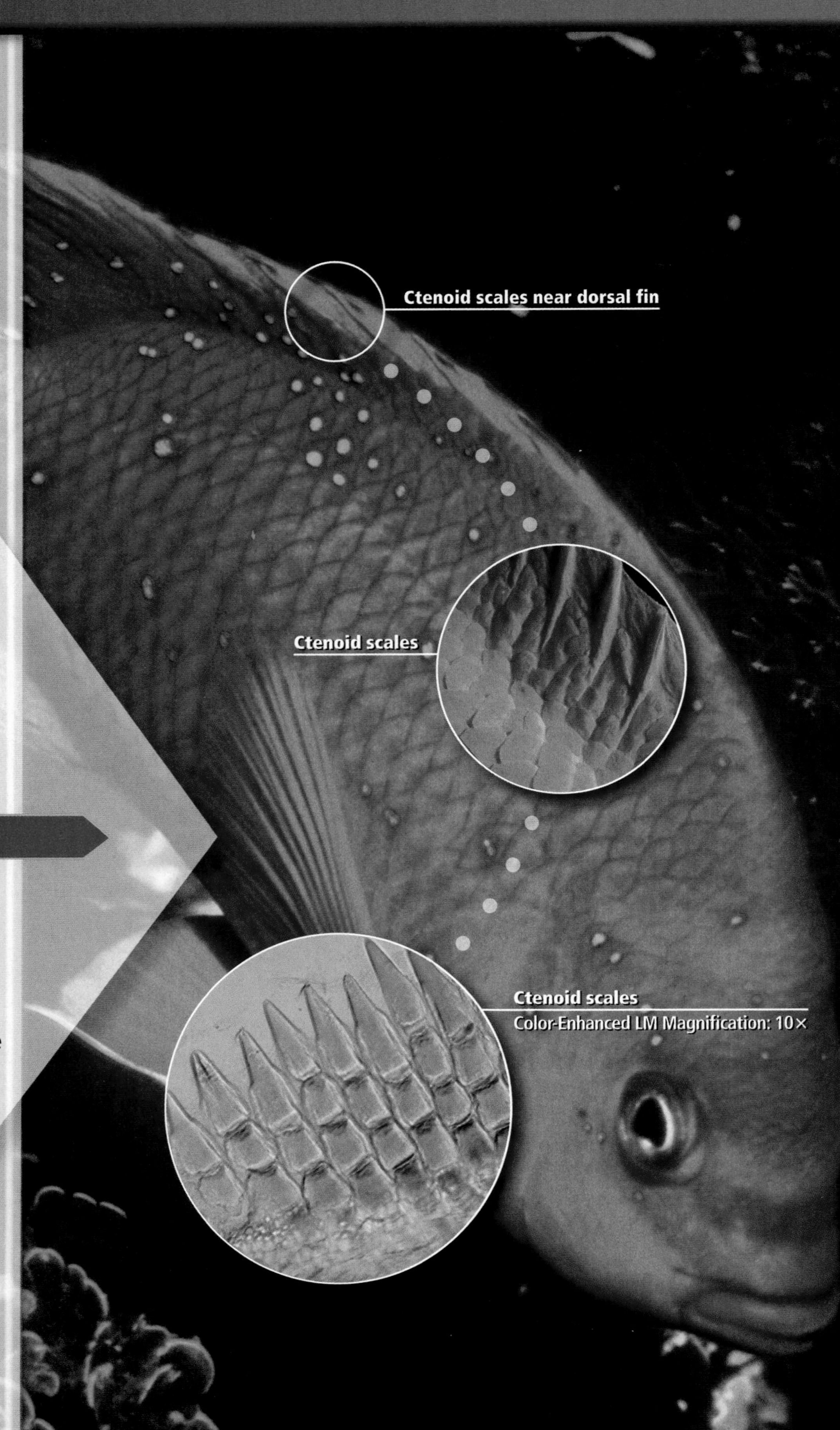

# LAUNCH Lab

## What are the characteristics of fishes in different groups?

Fishes are classified into three main groups—jawless fishes, cartilaginous fishes, and bony fishes. They are classified based on external and internal characteristics. In this lab, you will compare the external characteristics of fishes in the three groups.

### Procedure

1. Read and complete the lab safety form.
2. Examine **photos** of representatives from each of the three groups of fishes. Look at features such as skin/scales, fin position, fin shape, eyes, mouth shape and teeth, body shape, and tail shape.
3. Construct a table and record information about the external characteristics of the different groups of fishes.

### Analysis

1. **Summarize** What are the main external differences between these groups of fishes?
2. **Infer** Why is it important to examine and compare the internal structures and characteristics of organisms when trying to classify them?

Visit biologygmh.com to:

- study the entire chapter online
- explore Concepts in Motion, the Interactive Table, Microscopy Links, Virtual Labs, and links to virtual dissections
- access Web links for more information, projects, and activities
- review content online with the Interactive Tutor and take Self-Check Quizzes

**Fishes and Amphibians** Make the following Foldable to help you identify the characteristics of fishes, early tetrapods, and amphibians.

**STEP 1** Lay two sheets of paper about 1.5 cm apart vertically. Keep the edges level.

**STEP 2** Fold up the bottom edges of the paper to form four equal tabs.

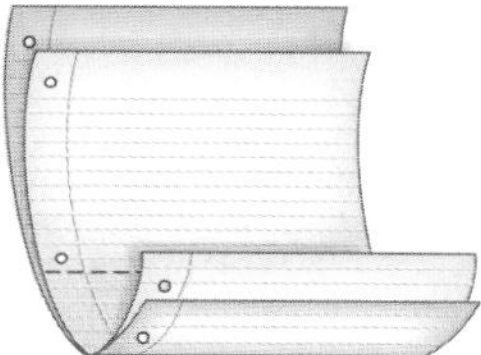

**STEP 3** Crease well to hold the tabs in place. Staple along the fold. Label each tab as shown.

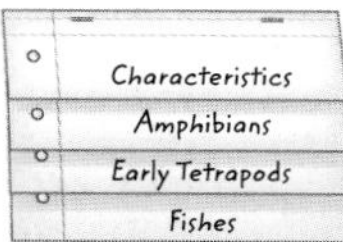


FOLDABLES **Use this Foldable with Section 28.3.** As you study the section, record and sketch what you learn about the characteristics of each group.

## Section 28.1

### Section Objectives

- **Identify** the features of vertebrates that make them different from invertebrates.
- **Describe** the characteristics that most fishes have in common.
- **Summarize** how the characteristics of fishes are adapted to aquatic life.

### Review Vocabulary

**notochord:** a flexible rodlike structure that extends the length of the body

### New Vocabulary

cartilage
neural crest
fin
scale
operculum
atrium
ventricle
nephron
lateral line system
spawning
swim bladder

# Fishes

**MAIN Idea Fishes are vertebrates that have characteristics allowing them to live and reproduce in water.**

**Real-World Reading Link** You might have seen an aquarium full of colorful fishes similar to those in the photo at the beginning of the chapter. What adaptations do fishes have for living in water? Fishes have unique characterisitics that allow them to live and reproduce in water.

## Characteristics of Vertebrates

Until now you have been studying sponges, worms, and sea stars, which are all invertebrates. Recall that the four main characteristics of chordates are that they have a dorsal nerve cord, a notochord, pharyngeal pouches, and a postanal tail. Animals belonging to subphylum Vertebrata are called vertebrates. Vertebrates have a vertebral column and specialized cells that develop from the nerve cord. The vertebral column, also called a spinal column, is the hallmark feature of vertebrates. Classes of vertebrates include fishes, amphibians, reptiles, birds, and mammals.

**Vertebral column** In most vertebrates, the notochord is replaced by a vertebral column that surrounds and protects the dorsal nerve cord. The replacement of the notochord happens during embryonic development. Cartilage or bone is the building material of most vertebrate endoskeletons. **Cartilage** (KAR tuh lihj) is a tough, flexible material making up the skeletons or parts of skeletons of vertebrates.

The vertebral columns, shown in **Figure 28.1,** are important structures in terms of the evolution of animals. The vertebral column functions as a strong, flexible rod that muscles can pull against during swimming or running. Separate vertebrae enhance an animal's ability to move quickly and easily. Bones enable forceful contraction of muscles, improving the strength of an animal.

**Figure 28.1** The vertebral column is present in most vertebrates, including bony fishes and reptiles as shown by the art.

**Triggerfish**

**Sidewinder**

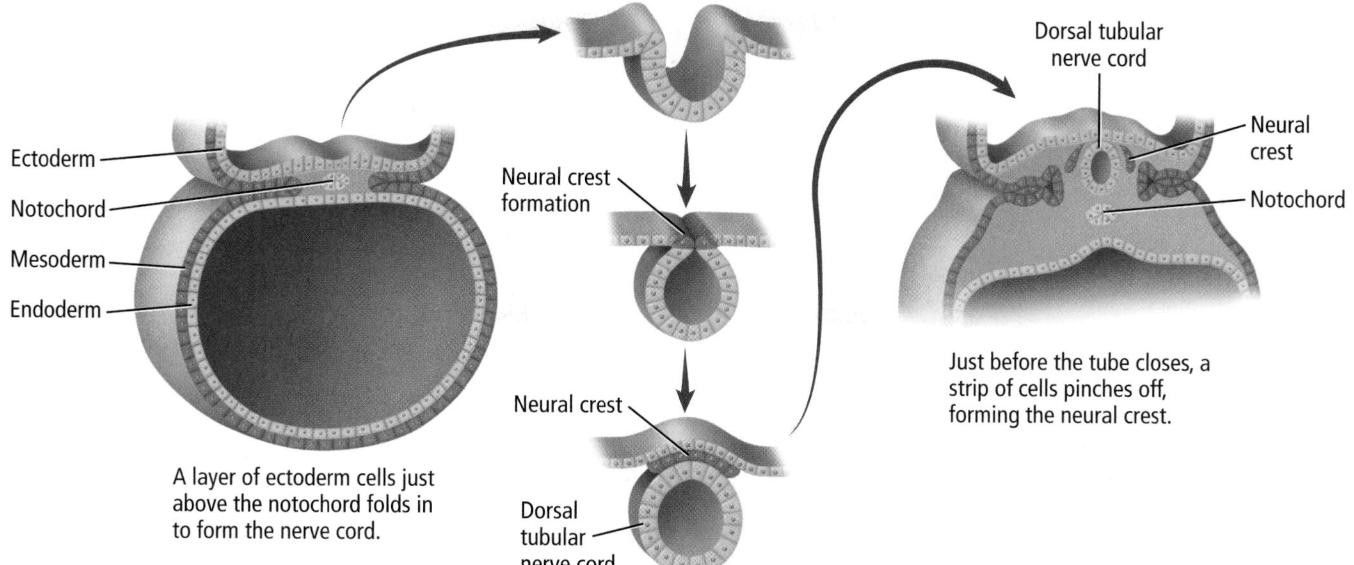


**Figure 28.2** The neural crest of vertebrates develops from the ectoderm of the embryo.

**Neural crest** As the nerve cord forms during embryonic development in vertebrates, another important process occurs: a neural (NOOR ul) crest forms. A **neural crest** is a group of cells that develop from the nerve cord in vertebrates. The process of neural crest formation is shown in **Figure 28.2.** Even though this group of cells is small, it is significant in the development of vertebrates because many important vertebrate features develop from the neural crest. These features include portions of the brain and skull, certain sense organs, parts of pharyngeal pouches, some nerve fibers, insulation for nerve fibers, and certain gland cells.

Other features that are characteristic of vertebrates include internal organs, such as kidneys and a liver. A heart and closed circulatory system also are features of all vertebrates.

**Reading Check** **Explain** why the neural crest is an important vertebrate feature.

## Characteristics of Fishes

Fishes live in most aquatic habitats on Earth—seas, lakes, ponds, streams, and marshes. Some fishes live in complete darkness at the bottom of the deep ocean. Others live in the freezing waters of the polar regions and have special proteins in their blood to keep the blood from freezing. There are about 24,600 species of living fishes, more than all other vertebrates combined. They range in size from whale sharks that can be 18 m long to tiny cichlids that are the size of a human fingernail.

The features of fishes provided the structural basis for the development of land animals during the course of evolution. Important characteristics of fishes include the development of jaws and, in some fishes, lungs. As shown in the evolutionary tree in **Figure 28.3,** there are three groups of fishes, all of which are vertebrates. Although fishes' body shapes and structures vary a great deal, they all have several characteristics in common. Most fishes have vertebral columns, jaws, paired fins, scales, gills, and single-loop blood circulation, and they are not able to synthesize certain amino acids.

**Figure 28.3** The branches of the different groups of fishes are highlighted in this evolutionary tree.

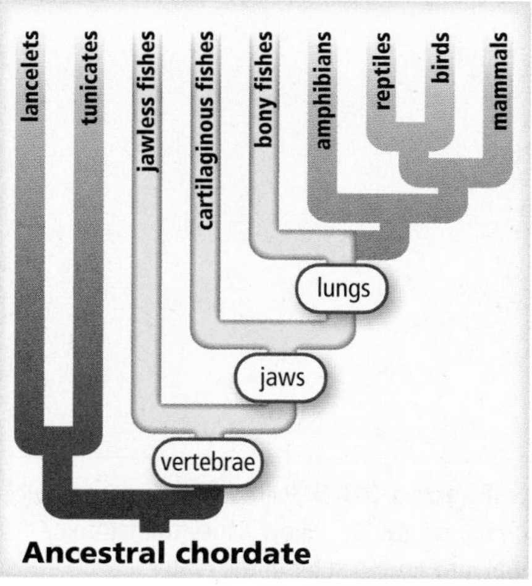

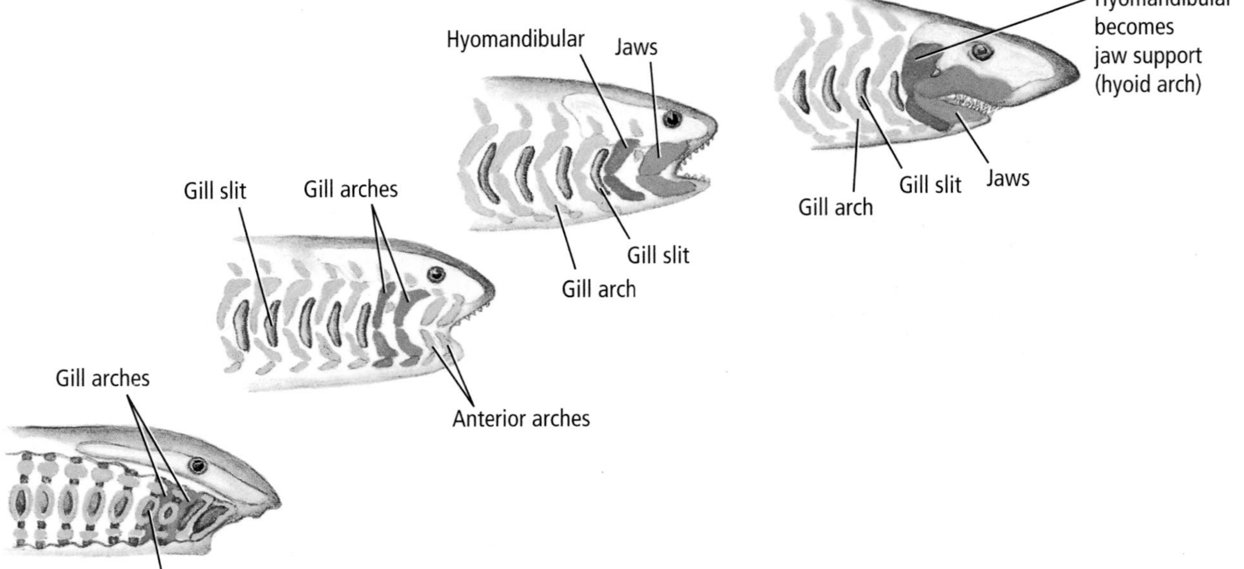


■ **Figure 28.4** Anterior gill arches evolved into jaws in ancient fishes.

**Jaws** Most fishes have jaws. The evolution of jaws is shown in **Figure 28.4,** where you can see that the anterior gill arches evolved to form jaws in ancient fishes. The development of jaws allowed ancient fishes to prey on a larger range of animals. This included being able to prey on fish that were larger in size and more active. Fishes grasp prey with their teeth and quickly crush them using powerful jaw muscles. Jaws also allow for a biting defense against predators.

 **Reading Check Describe** why the evolution of jaws in fishes was important.

**VOCABULARY**

**ACADEMIC VOCABULARY**

**Precision:**
characterized by accurate action.
*The basketball player shoots the ball with precision.*

**Paired fins** At the same time jaws were evolving, paired fins also were appearing in fishes. A **fin** is a paddle-shaped structure on a fish or other aquatic animal that is used for balance, steering, and propulsion. Pelvic fins and pectoral fins, like the ones shown in **Figure 28.5,** give fishes more stability. Most fishes have paired fins. Paired fins reduce the chance of rolling to the side and allow for better steering during swimming.

While fishes in ancient seas moved with precision and skill, they also were able to use their jaws in new ways. Both jaws and paired fins contributed to the evolution of a predatory way of life for some fishes and also enabled them to live in new habitats and produce more offspring.

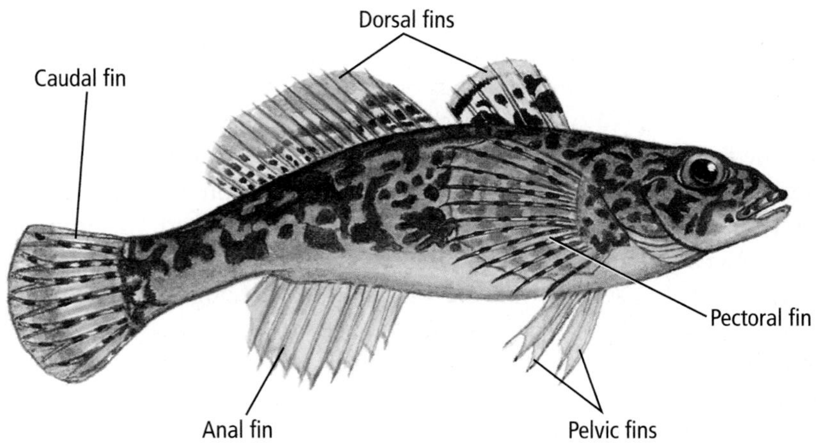


■ **Figure 28.5** Paired fins, such as pelvic and pectoral fins, allow fishes to maintain balance and to steer in the water.

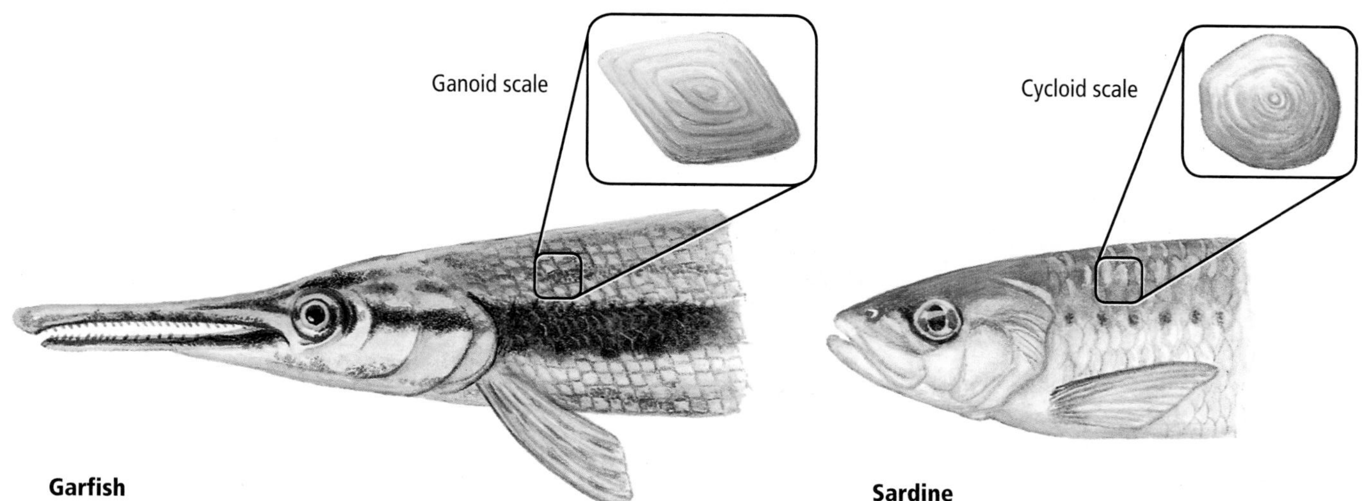


■ **Figure 28.6** Two types of fishes' scales are shown here—ganoid scales and cycloid scales.
**Describe** ***the difference in the appearance of cycloid and ganoid scales.***

**Scales** Most fishes have at least one of four different types of scales. A **scale** is small, flat, platelike structure near the surface of the skin of most fishes. There are four types of fish scales. Look again at one type, ctenoid (TEH noyd) scales, at the beginning of the chapter. Ctenoid scales and a second type of scale, cycloid (SY kloyd) scales, are made of bone and skin. Cycloid scales are shown in **Figure 28.6.** Ctenoid and cycloid scales are thin and flexible. The scales of a shark, called placoid (PLA koyd) scales, are made of toothlike materials and are rough and heavy. You can see a picture of placoid scales in **Figure 28.15** in the next section. The thick ganoid (GAN oyd) scales of a garfish, shown in **Figure 28.6,** are diamond-shaped and made of both enamel and bone.

## MiniLab 28.1

### Observe a Fish

**What inferences can you make about characteristics of fishes through observation?** In this lab, you will observe a fish in its aquatic environment.

**Procedure**

1. Read and complete the lab safety form.
2. Observe the **fish(es)** in an **aquarium.**
3. Make a diagram of a fish and label the following applicable structures: dorsal fin, caudal fin, anal fin, pectoral fins, pelvic fins, scales, mouth, eye, and gill covering.
4. Observe how the fish moves through the water. Illustrate how the fish moves its body and its fins as it moves forward in the water.

**Analysis**

1. **Infer** A fish's body is divided into three regions: head, trunk, and tail. Label these regions on your diagram of the fish you observed.
2. **Apply** Suppose a fish lost one of its pectoral fins when fighting off a predator. How might this affect its ability to move through the water?

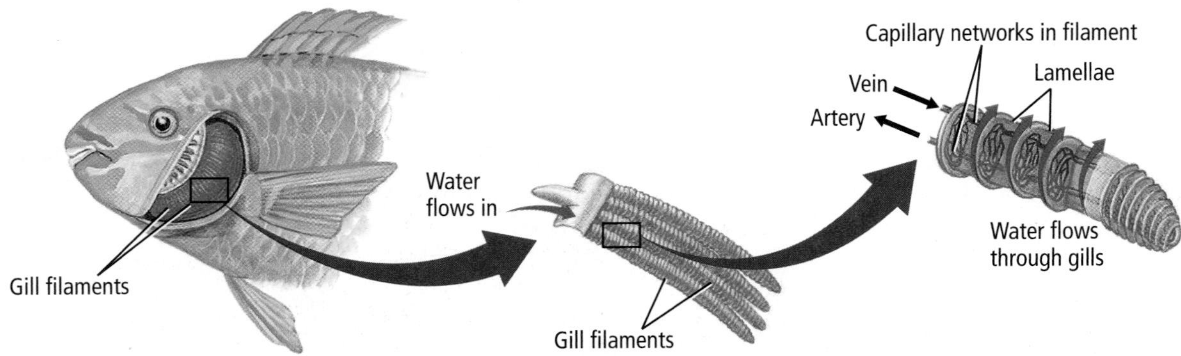


■ **Figure 28.7** The lamellae in a fish's gills have many blood vessels.
**Infer** ***Why are the gills of fishes made up of very thin tissue?***

**Gills** Another adaptation that allows fishes to live in aquatic environments is their ability to get oxygen from the water. Fishes get oxygen when water that enters their mouths flows across their gills, where oxygen from the water diffuses into the blood. Gills are composed of thin filaments that are covered with highly-folded, platelike lamellae (luh MEH lee). The gill structure of most fishes is shown in **Figure 28.7.** The lamellae have many blood vessels that can take in oxygen and give off carbon dioxide.

The flow of blood in the gill is opposite to the flow of water over the gill surface. This countercurrent flow is an efficient mechanism by which oxygen can be removed from water. Up to 85 percent of oxygen dissolved in water is removed as water flows over the gills in one direction and blood in the other. Some fishes have an **operculum** (oh PUR kyuh lum), a movable flap that covers the gills and protects them. An operculum also aids in pumping water coming in the mouth and over the gills. Some fishes, such as lungfishes, can live out of water for short times by using structures resembling lungs. Eels can breathe through their moist skin when they are out of water.

**VOCABULARY**
**WORD ORIGIN**
**Atrium**
from the Latin word *atrium*, meaning *central hallway.*

**Circulation** Vertebrates have a closed circulatory system in which the heart pumps blood through blood vessels. The circulatory system of fishes is shown in **Figure 28.8.** In most fishes, the blood is passed through the heart in a one-way loop. From the heart, the blood goes to the gills, and then through the body, delivering oxygenated blood to tissues. The blood then returns to the heart. From the heart, blood is pumped back to the gills and then to the body again. Because this system is a complete and uninterrupted circuit, it is called a single-loop circulatory system.

In most fishes, the heart consists of two main chambers that are analogous to parts of your own heart—an atrium and a ventricle. The **atrium** is the chamber of the heart that receives blood from the body. From there, blood is passed to the **ventricle,** a chamber of the heart that pumps blood from the heart to the gills. Once the blood passes over the gills, it travels to the rest of the body.

■ **Figure 28.8** A fish's heart pumps blood through a closed circulatory system.

**Concepts In Motion**
**Interactive Figure** To see an animation of how blood circulates through a fish, visit biologygmh.com.

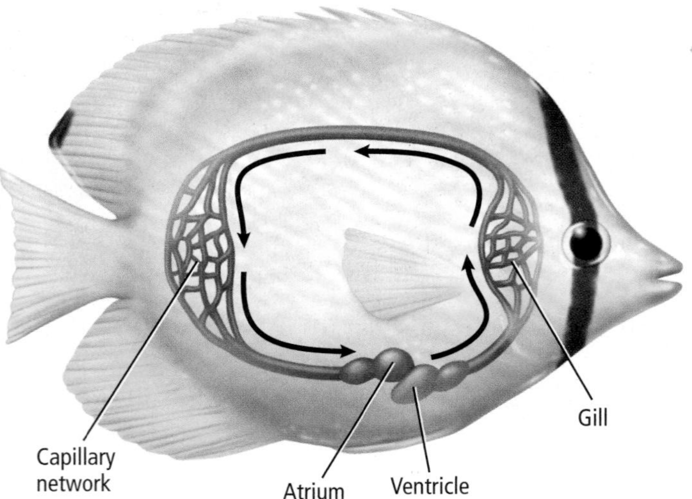

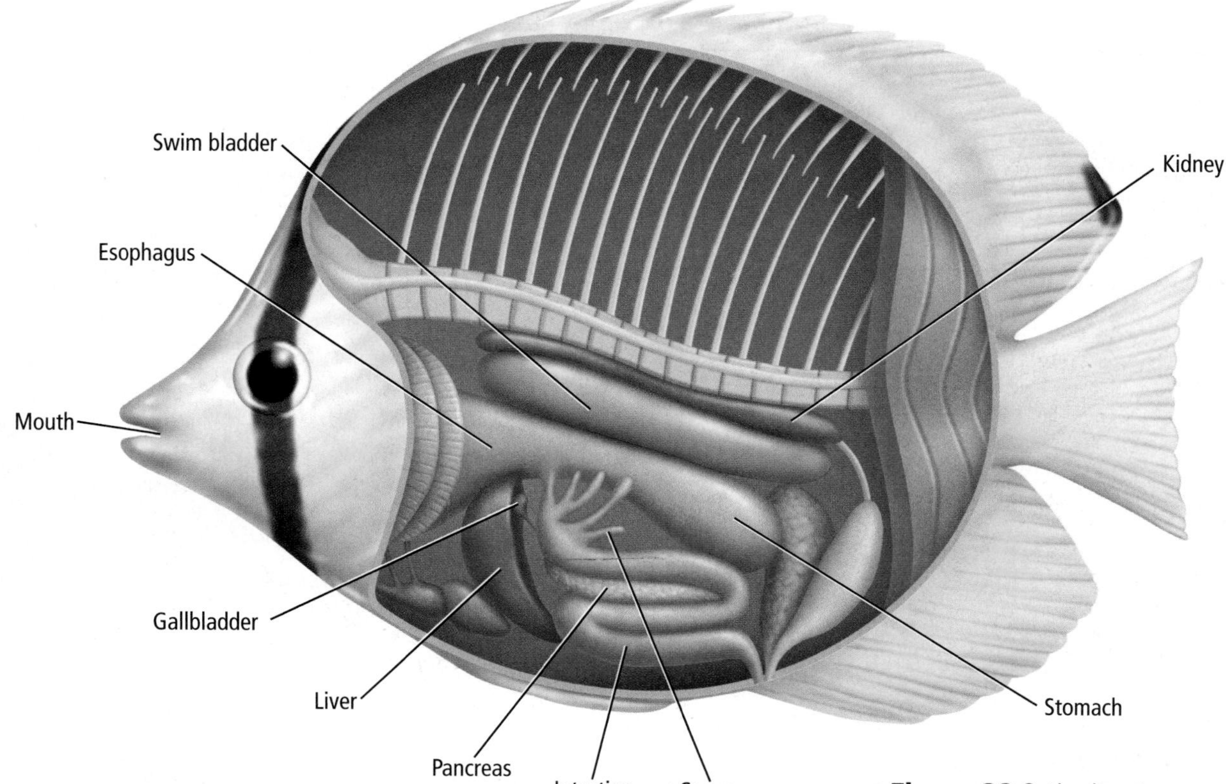


■ **Figure 28.9** The digestive organs of a fish are similar to those of other vertebrates. **List** ***the structures food passes through as it is being digested.***

**Feeding and digestion** Ancient fishes most likely were filter feeders or scavengers, sucking up organic debris on the ocean floor. With the evolution of jaws, fishes became efficient predators, and the diets of fishes changed dramatically. The digestive tract of fishes, illustrated in **Figure 28.9,** consists of organs similar to those of other vertebrates.

Most fishes swallow their food whole, passing it through a tube called the esophagus (ih SAH fuh gus) to the stomach, where digestion begins. Food then passes to the intestine, where most digestion occurs. Some fishes have pyloric (pi LOR ihk) ceca (SEE kuh) (singular, cecum), which are small pouches at the junction of the stomach and the intestine that secrete enzymes for digestion and absorb nutrients into the bloodstream. The liver, pancreas, and gallbladder add digestive juices that complete digestion.

Fishes are described not only by structures and their functions, but also by one important thing that they cannot do. They are not able to synthesize certain amino acids. Therefore, not only fishes, but all the vertebrates that evolved from them must get these same amino acids from the foods they eat.

**Excretion** Cellular wastes are filtered from fishes' blood by organs called kidneys. The main functional unit of the kidney is the nephron. A **nephron** is a filtering unit within the kidney that helps to maintain the salt and water balance of the body and to remove cellular waste products from the blood. Some cellular wastes are excreted by the gills.

**Connection to Chemistry** The bodies of freshwater fishes take in water by osmosis because the surrounding water is hypotonic—the water contains more water molecules than the fishes' tissues. The opposite occurs in saltwater bony fishes. Because the surrounding water is hypertonic—the water contains fewer water molecules than their tissues—their bodies tend to lose water. Kidneys, gills, and other internal mechanisms adjust the water and salt balance in the bodies of freshwater and saltwater fishes.

**CAREERS IN BIOLOGY**

**Ichthyologist** Researching information about the behavior, ecology, and anatomy and physiology of fishes, both in the field and in the lab, is just one of the jobs an ichthyologist (ihk thee AHL uh jist) might have. Ichthyologists also manage aquariums, organize museum collections, teach at universities, and work to conserve fish populations. For more information on biology careers, visit biologygmh.com.

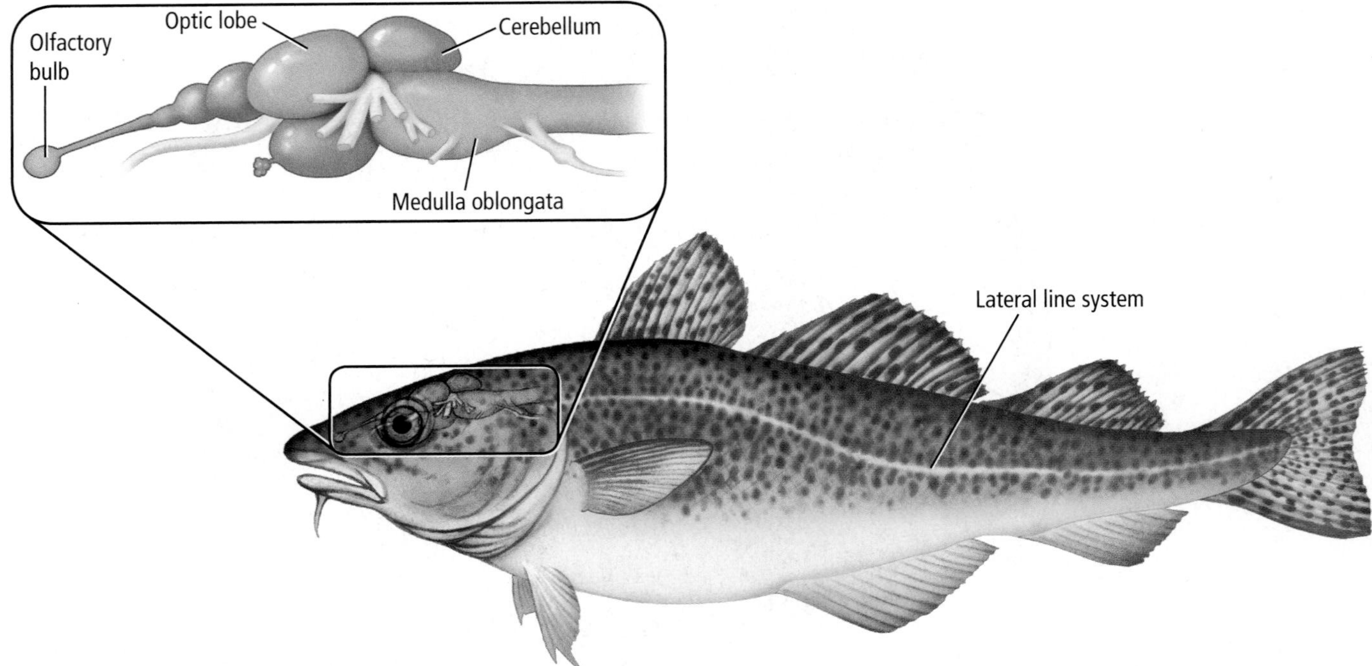


■ **Figure 28.10** Fishes have a brain that enables them to carry out their life functions.
**Infer** ***In what way would the brain of a fish that lived passively on the bottom of a pond feeding on organic debris be different from a predatory fish that had to swim swiftly after prey?***

**The brain and senses** As in other vertebrates, the nervous system of fishes consists of a spinal cord and a brain. A fish brain is shown in **Figure 28.10.** The cerebellum is involved in coordinating movement and controlling balance. Fishes have receptors for the sense of smell that enable them to detect chemicals in the water. The olfactory (ohl FAK tree) bulbs record and respond to incoming chemical input. Fishes also have color vision. The optic lobes are responsible for visual input. The cerebrum coordinates input from other parts of the brain. Internal organs are under the control of the medulla oblongata.

If you have spent any time fishing, you know that fishes can detect the slightest movement in the water. Fishes can do this because they have special receptors called the lateral line system. The **lateral line system** enables fishes to detect movement in the water and also helps to keep them upright and balanced. You can see the lateral line system of a fish in **Figure 28.10.**

**Reproduction** The majority of fishes reproduce through external fertilization. Male and female fishes release their gametes near each other in the water in a process called **spawning.** Developing embryos get nutrition from food stored in the yolk of the egg. Some fishes, such as sharks, reproduce through internal fertilization. Although fertilization takes place internally, development of the embryo of some fish species might occur outside of the female's body when fertilized eggs are laid. Some species of fishes have internal fertilization as well as internal development of offspring. In this case, the developing embryos get nutrition from the female's body.

Fishes that reproduce through external fertilization can produce millions of eggs in a single season. Most fishes do not protect or care for their eggs or offspring. As a result, many eggs and juvenile fishes are prey to other animals. The production of large numbers of eggs ensures that some offspring develop and survive to reproduce. One exception is the male sergeant major fish, shown in **Figure 28.11.** The male fish guards the fertilized eggs from predators until they hatch.

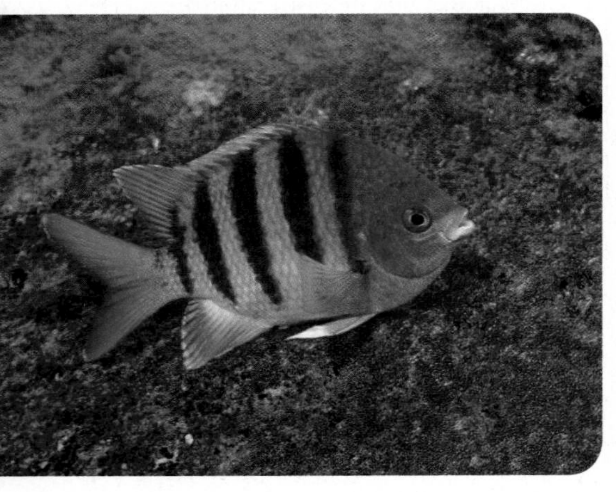

■ **Figure 28.11** Most fishes do not care for their young; however, male sergeant majors guard the eggs as the embryos develop.

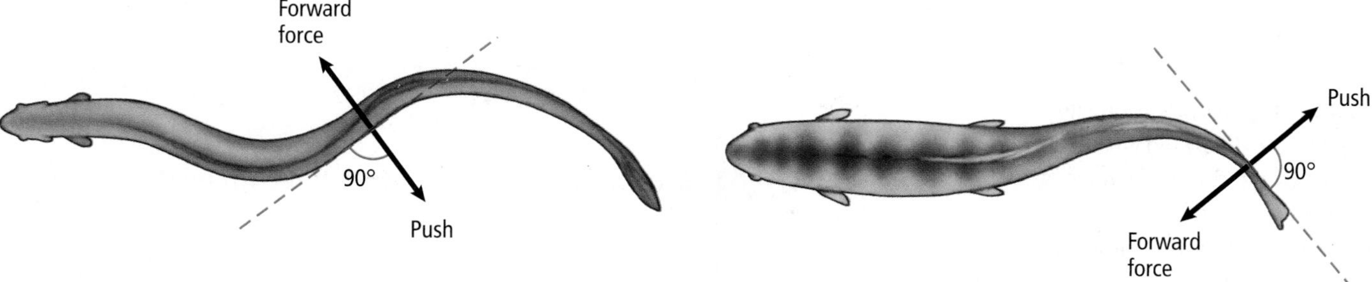


**Figure 28.12** An eel moves its whole body in an S-shaped pattern. Other, faster-moving fishes, such as trout, move only their tails as they push forward through the water.

**Movement** Fishes are well adapted to swimming in the water. Most fishes have a streamlined shape. Most also have mucus that lubricates their body surface and reduces friction between the fish and the water. Fins enable fishes to steer and maneuver in a variety of ways. The buoyant force of water reduces the effect of gravity on fishes. In addition, the **swim bladder,** which is shown in **Figure 28.9,** is a gas-filled space, like a balloon, found in bony fishes that allows a fish to control its depth. When gases diffuse out of the swim bladder, a fish can sink. When gases from the blood diffuse into the swim bladder, a fish can rise in the water column.

**Connection to Physics** Examine **Figure 28.12.** Fishes move through the water by contracting muscle groups on either side of their bodies. The arrangement of muscle in a fish allows muscle contraction to bend a large portion of the fish's body. As the body of a fish bends, it pushes against the water, creating an opposing force that moves the fish forward, but at an angle. Alternate contraction of muscles, first on one side of the body and then on the other, keep the fish moving in an S-shaped pattern.

## Section 28.1 Assessment

### Section Summary

- Vertebrates include fishes, amphibians, reptiles, birds, and mammals.
- All vertebrates have a notochord. In most vertebrates, the notochord is replaced by a vertebral column during embryonic development.
- Fishes share certain characteristics and, therefore, are classified together.
- The bodies of fishes have unique adaptations that enable them to live their entire lives in water.

### Understand Main Ideas

1. MAIN Idea **Describe** the characteristics fishes have that allow them to live and reproduce in water.
2. **Summarize** the features of vertebrates that make them different from invertebrates.
3. **Evaluate** the importance of the evolution of jaws in fishes.
4. **Identify** the characteristics most fishes have in common.
5. **Explain** why freshwater and saltwater bony fishes have to adjust the balance of salt and water in their bodies.

### Think Scientifically

6. *Hypothesize* Male three-spined stickleback fishes build nests using bright, shiny materials that are in limited supply and are chosen more frequently by females. Form a hypothesis about why this might ensure that a female is choosing a male that has strong traits of his species.
7. *Infer* How might an injury to a fish's lateral line system affect that fish's ability to escape predation?

Section 28.2

**Section Objectives**

- **Identify** the characteristics of different groups of fishes.
- **Compare** the key features of various types of fishes.
- **Explain** the evolution of fishes.

**Review Vocabulary**

**adaptive radiation:** the process of evolution that produces many species from an ancestral species

**New Vocabulary**

tetrapod

# Diversity of Today's Fishes

**MAIN Idea Scientists classify fishes into three groups based on body structure.**

**Real-World Reading Link** You already know that the basic structures and their functions in fishes are similar. Now think about all of the different types of fishes you have seen in aquariums, photos, or on television.

## Classes of Fishes

You have read about jellyfish, crayfish, and various shellfish, but none of these are true fishes. True fishes belong to three groups based on their body structure. Hagfishes and lampreys are jawless fishes; sharks, skates, and rays are cartilaginous (kar tuh LAJ uh nus) fishes; and the bony fishes include both ray-finned and lobe-finned fishes.

**Jawless fishes** Hagfishes, as shown in **Figure 28.13,** are jawless, eel-shaped fishes that do not have scales, paired fins, or a bony skeleton. Members of class Myxini (mik SEE nee), hagfishes have a notochord throughout life. Although they do not develop a vertebral column, they do have gills and many other characteristics of fishes. They live on the seafloor and feed on soft-bodied invertebrates and dead or dying fishes. Even though they are almost blind, their keen chemical sense enables them to locate food. They either enter the body of the fish through the mouth or they scrape an opening into the fish with toothlike structures on their tongues. After eating the internal parts of the fish, the hagfish leaves only a sac of skin and bones.

Hagfishes are known for their ability to produce slime. If threatened, they secrete fluid from glands in their skin. The fluid, when in contact with seawater, forms a slime that is slippery enough to prevent the hagfishes from being caught by predators.

■ **Figure 28.13** Hagfishes are jawless fishes that have toothlike structures on their tongues. Lampreys are parasites on other living fishes.
**Describe** ***What adaptations for life on the seafloor can you see in this hagfish photo?***

**Hagfish**

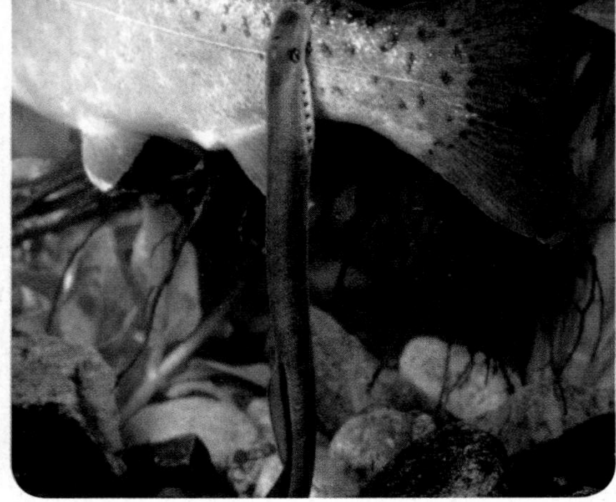

**Lamprey**

Lampreys, like hagfishes, also are jawless, eel-shaped fishes that lack scales, paired fins, or a bony skeleton. Lampreys, members of class Cephalaspidomorphi (ceh fah las pe doh MOR fee), retain a notochord throughout life, as do hagfishes. Lampreys have gills and other characteristics of fishes. Adult lamprey, shown in **Figure 28.13,** are parasites that feed by attaching themselves to other fishes. They use their sucker-like mouth and tongue with toothlike structures to feed on the blood and bodily fluids of their hosts.

**Reading Check** **List** the characteristics of jawless fishes.

**Cartilaginous fishes** When you hear the word *shark,* the first thing that might come to mind is a large fish with many sharp teeth. In spite of being famous for teeth, a shark's main distinguishing feature is its skeleton. All cartilaginous fishes have skeletons made of cartilage. The skeleton of a shark also is made of cartilage, which gives the skeleton flexibility, and calcium carbonate, which gives it strength.

Sharks belong to class Chondrichthyes (kon DRIK thees). Some species of sharks have several rows of sharp teeth as shown in **Figure 28.14.** As teeth are broken or lost, new ones move forward to replace them. Most sharks also have a streamlined shape, with a pointed head and a tail that turns up at the end, as shown in **Figure 28.15.**

These streamlining features, along with strong swimming muscles and sharp teeth, make sharks one of the top predators in the sea. They can sense chemicals in the water, allowing them to detect prey from a distance of one kilometer. As they move in closer, their lateral line systems can detect vibrations in the water. Finally, when they are in the last stages of pursuit, they use their vision and other receptors to detect the bioelectrical fields given off by all animals. An additional adaptation to a predatory life includes tough skin with placoid scales, shown in **Figure 28.15.**

Not all sharks have rows of teeth. Whale sharks, the largest living sharks, are filter-feeders with specialized straining structures in their mouths. Other sharks have mouths adapted to feeding on shelled mollusks.

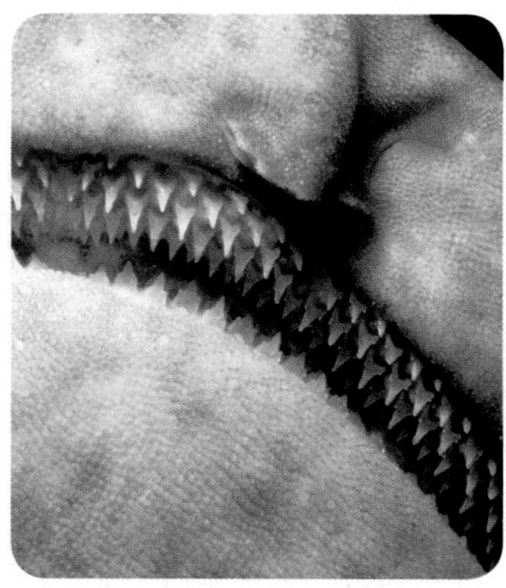

**Figure 28.14** Sharks have several rows of teeth. As teeth in the front row fall or are pulled out, teeth from the row behind them move up into their place.

**Figure 28.15** Great white sharks have streamlined bodies and are covered with tough placoid scales.

**Infer** ***What would a shark's skin feel like if you touched it?***

**Great white shark**

Color-Enhanced SEM Magnification: 40×

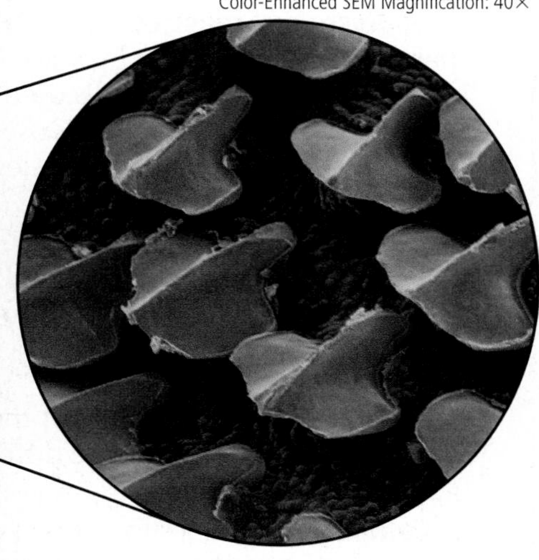

**Placoid scales**

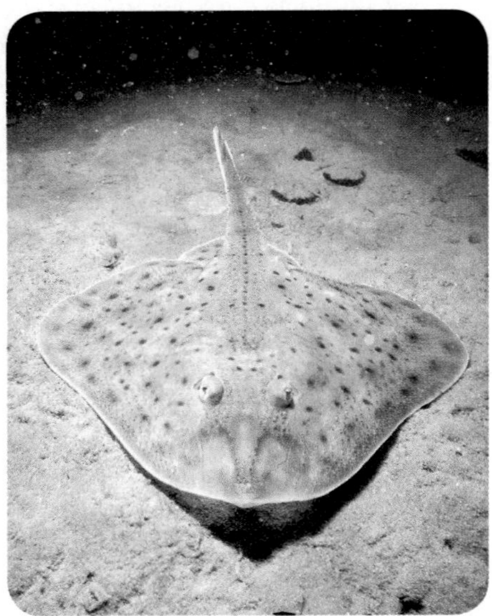

■ **Figure 28.16** Skates have flattened bodies that are adapted for living on the ocean floor.

Skates and rays are cartilaginous fishes adapted to life on the bottom of the sea. In addition to their flattened bodies, their pectoral fins, shown in **Figure 28.16,** are enlarged and attached to their heads. Their winglike fins flap slowly as they swim along the seafloor in search of mollusks and crustaceans, which they crush with their teeth.

**Bony fishes** Class Osteichthyes (ahs tee IHK theez) contains two groups of bony fishes: the ray-finned fishes, belonging to subclass Actinopterygii (AK tihn ahp TUR ee jee i), and the lobe-finned fishes, belonging to the subclass Sarcopterygii (SAR kahp TUR ee jee i). Modern ray-finned fishes have a bony skeleton, ctenoid or cycloid scales, an operculum covering the gills, and a swim bladder. The most distinguishing feature of ray-finned fishes is in their name. The thin membranes of these fishes' fins are supported by thin, spinelike rays, which are shown in **Figure 28.17.** Most fishes alive today, including salmon and trout, are ray-finned fishes.

There are only eight species of lobe-finned fishes living today. Their fins, shown in **Figure 28.17,** have muscular lobes and joints similar to those of land vertebrates. This makes the fins more flexible than those of ray-finned fishes. Lobe-finned fishes, such as the lungfish, usually have lungs for gas exchange. When drought occurs, a lungfish can burrow with its fleshy fins into the mud and breathe air. When rain returns, lungfishes come out of their burrows.

Coelacanths (SEE luh kanths) are another small group of lobe-finned fishes that many people thought had become extinct about 70 million years ago. However, in 1938, some people fishing off the coast of South Africa caught a coelacanth. Since that time, other coelacanths have been caught. A third group of lobe-finned fishes, now extinct, is thought to be the ancestor of tetrapods. A **tetrapod,** shown in **Figure 28.17,** is a four-footed animal with legs that have feet and toes that have joints.

## DATA ANALYSIS LAB 28.1

**Based on Real Data***

### Analyze Data

**How do sharks' muscles function?** Lamnid sharks have two types of muscles. Red muscle tissue does not tire easily and is used more during cruising. White muscle tissue is used more during short bursts of speed. Both muscles, however, are always used at the same time.

**Data and Observations**

The peaks of the graph represent when each muscle type contracts.

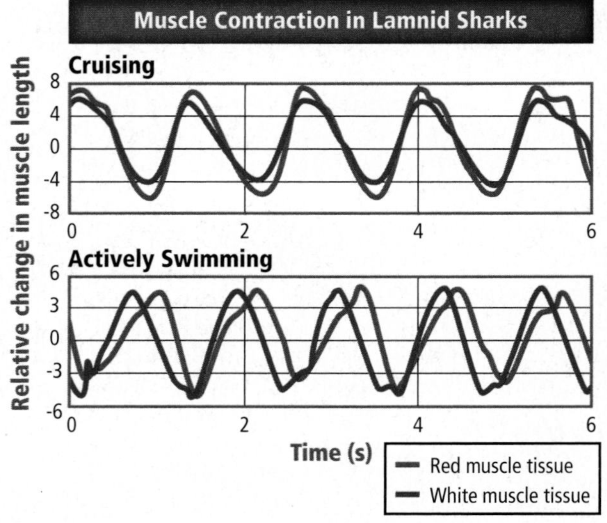


**Think Critically**

1. **Evaluate** Does the timing of the contractions of the two types of muscle differ when the sharks are cruising?
2. **Compare** How does the timing of the contractions between the two muscle types change when the sharks are actively swimming?

*Data obtained from: Donley, J., et al. 2004 Convergent evolution in mechanical design of lamnid sharks and tunas. *Nature* 429: 61-65.

# Visualizing Bony Fishes

**Figure 28.17**
Class Osteichthyes consists of the bony fishes, and it can be divided into two subclasses—ray-finned fishes and lobe-finned fishes. An extinct lobe-finned fish is thought to be the ancestor of modern tetrapods.

**Ray-finned fish**

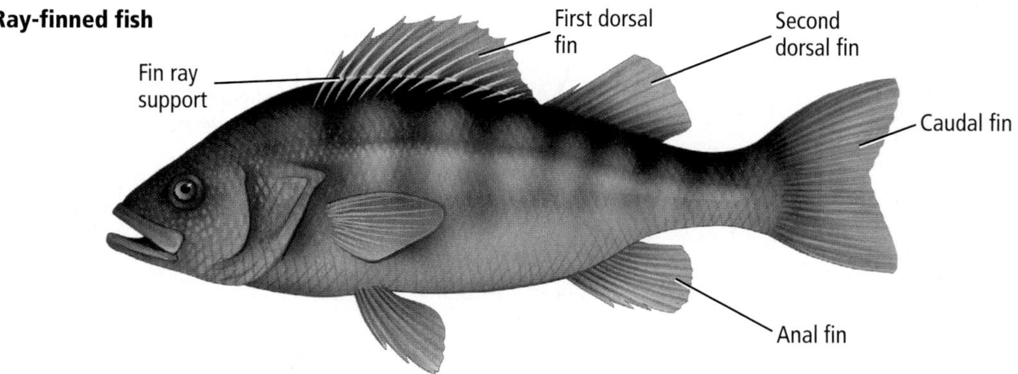


Ray-finned fishes have thin, spinelike rays that support the membranes of their fins.

**Lobe-finned fish**

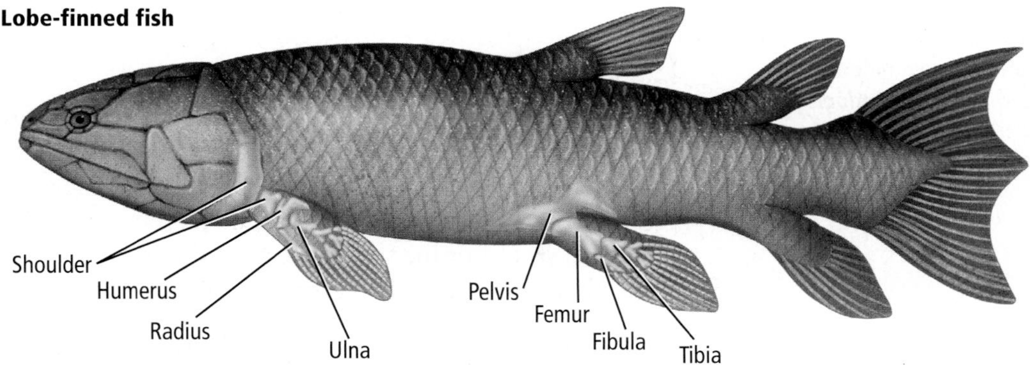


Lobe-finned fishes have muscular lobes and joints similar to those of tetrapods.

**Early tetrapod**

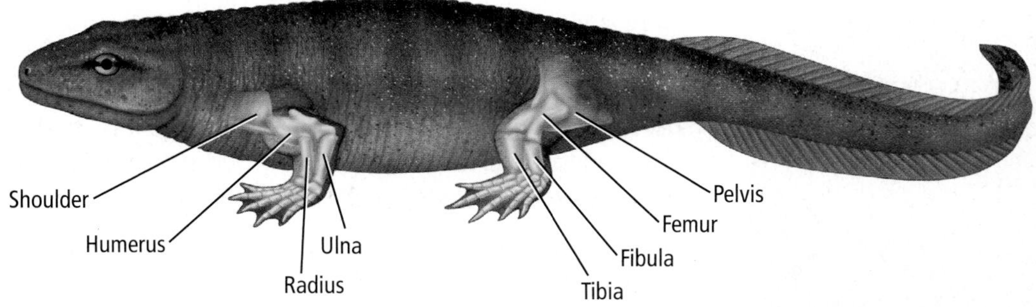


The limbs of tetrapods evolved from the fins of lobe-finned fishes. *Ichthyostega* was a tetrapod that lived about 325 million years ago, had fully formed limbs, and walked on land.

**Concepts In Motion** **Interactive Figure** To see an animation of bony fishes, visit biologygmh.com.

Biology Online

Bony fishes

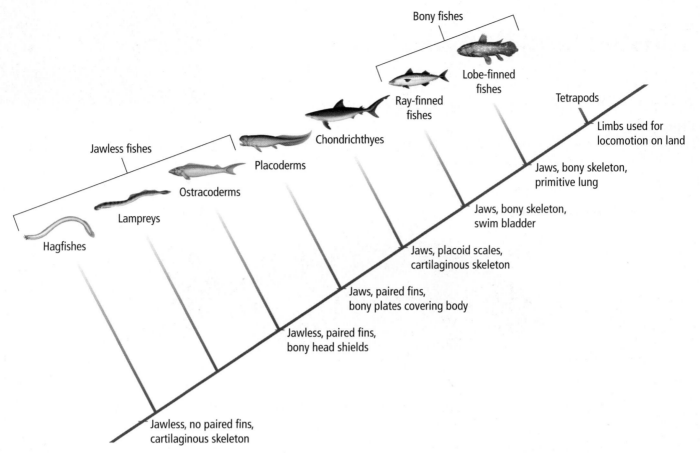

Lobe-finned fishes

Ray-finned fishes

Tetrapods

Limbs used for locomotion on land

Chondrichthyes

Jawless fishes

Placoderms

Ostracoderms

Lampreys

Hagfishes

Jaws, bony skeleton, primitive lung

Jaws, bony skeleton, swim bladder

Jaws, placoid scales, cartilaginous skeleton

Jaws, paired fins, bony plates covering body

Jawless, paired fins, bony head shields

Jawless, no paired fins, cartilaginous skeleton

■ **Figure 28.18** The cladogram shows one interpretation of the phylogeny of fishes.
**Identify** ***According to the cladogram, which fishes did not have jaws?***

■ **Figure 28.19** *Dinichthys,* also called *Dunkleosteus,* was a placoderm that had armor plating around its head.

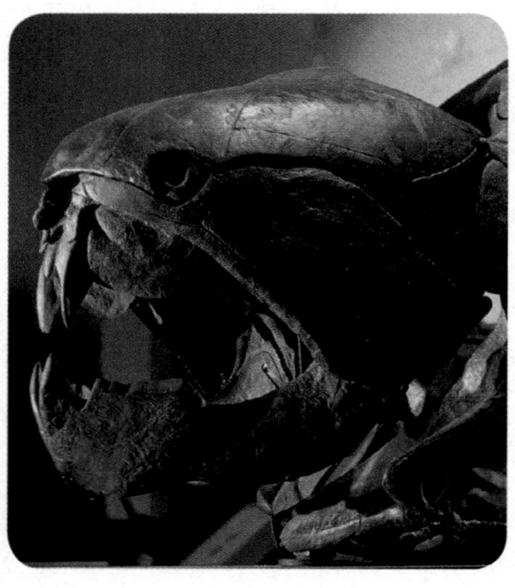

## Evolution of Fishes

In the ancient seas of the Cambrian, the first vertebrates wriggled through the water. They were jawless and toothless, but they did have gills, heads, and tails that moved them through the water. The cladogram shown in **Figure 28.18** is one interpretation of the phylogeny of fishes. As you examine the cladogram, notice the characteristics of fishes that developed during the course of their evolution.

**First fishes** These first jawless, toothless fishes sucked up organic materials from the ocean floor as if they were miniature vacuum cleaners. Ostracoderms (OS tra koh dermz) were the next group of fishes to appear in the fossil record of the Ordovician Period. Ostracoderms had head shields made of bone, a bony outer covering, and paired fins. They were jawless filter-feeders, many of which rested on the bottom of ancient seas.

The bony armor of ostracoderms was an evolutionary milestone in the development of vertebrates. Stronger movement is possible when muscle is attached to bone. Even though ostracoderms became extinct, scientists hypothesize that modern fishes share an ancestry with ostracoderms.

**Age of fishes** During the Devonian Period, modern fishes had their beginnings. Some were jawless, while some, such as the placoderms, had jaws, a covering of bony plates, paired fins, and an internal skeleton. A fossil of a placoderm fish is shown in **Figure 28.19.** Recall that three of these features are characteristics of the fishes that eventually replaced the placoderms as they became extinct. The Devonian Period often is referred to as the Age of Fishes because of the adaptive radiation of fishes that occurred at that time.

## Ecology of Fishes

Fishes are an important source of food in all aquatic ecosystems. Yet, their freshwater habitats and saltwater habitats are being changed by human activities, such as damming rivers or pollution. Fishes are good bioindicators of the environmental health of an aquatic system. When noncommercial fish populations decrease, the main cause often is habitat alteration. When fishes decline in numbers, not only are there negative human economic impacts, ecosystems also can become unbalanced as well.

**Habitat alteration** Some fishes, such as salmon, migrate. Salmon spend their adult lives in the ocean but return to freshwater to spawn in the streams where they hatched. In the Pacific Northwest, river and stream habitats have been changed by the construction of dams. Dams interfere with the upstream and downstream migration of salmon, as shown in **Figure 28.20.** The end result in the Pacific Northwest, for example, is that the number of salmon swimming upstream now is only about three percent of the 10 to 16 million salmon that swam up the rivers 150 years ago.

**Pollution** The habitats of fishes can be changed by pollution which can reduce the quality of water in lakes, rivers, and streams. This can result in a decline in both the number and diversity of fishes in an area. In some cases, when the cause of habitat alteration is stopped and suitable conditions return, fishes also return. For example, Atlantic salmon were not observed in the Penobscot River in Maine for ten years during a time when intense pollution altered water quality. When the pollution was stopped, the salmon returned.

**Figure 28.20** Not all salmon are able to get over the dams used to generate hydroelectricity. In order to spawn, salmon must return to the streams where they hatched.

**LAUNCH Lab**

**Review Based on what you've read about different fishes, how would you now answer the analysis questions?**

## Section 28.2 Assessment

### Section Summary

- Fishes can be placed into one of three main groups—jawless fishes, cartilaginous fishes, and bony fishes.
- Hagfishes and lampreys are examples of jawless fishes.
- Sharks, rays, and skates are examples of cartilaginous fishes.
- Bony fishes consist of two subclasses of fishes—ray-finned fishes and lobe-finned fishes.
- Ancient extinct fishes had features that enabled them to evolve into modern fishes.
- Habitat alteration and pollution can negatively affect fish populations.

### Understand Main Ideas

1. MAIN Idea **Compare and contrast** the structures of jawless fishes, cartilagenous fishes, and bony fishes.
2. **Identify** the characteristics of the two subclasses of bony fishes.
3. **Sketch** the basic shape that represents each of the three main groups of fishes.
4. **Describe** the evolutionary sequence of the different groups of fishes.
5. **Hypothesize** Bony fishes have either cycloid or ctenoid scales. Form a hypothesis that explains how scale type is related to diversity.

### Think Scientifically

6. MATH in Biology The number of fish species often decreases with latitude. In fact, the number of fish species in tropical lakes is much greater than the number of fish species in temperate lakes. Suggest a hypothesis that accounts for this mathematical phenomenon.

Section 28.3

### Section Objectives

- **Analyze** the kinds of adaptations that were important as animals moved to the land.
- **Summarize** the characteristics of amphibians.
- **Distinguish** among the orders of amphibians.

### Review Vocabulary

**metamorphosis:** a series of developmental changes in the form or structure of an organism

### New Vocabulary

cloaca
nictitating membrane
tympanic membrane
ectotherm

FOLDABLES Incorporate information from this section into your Foldable.

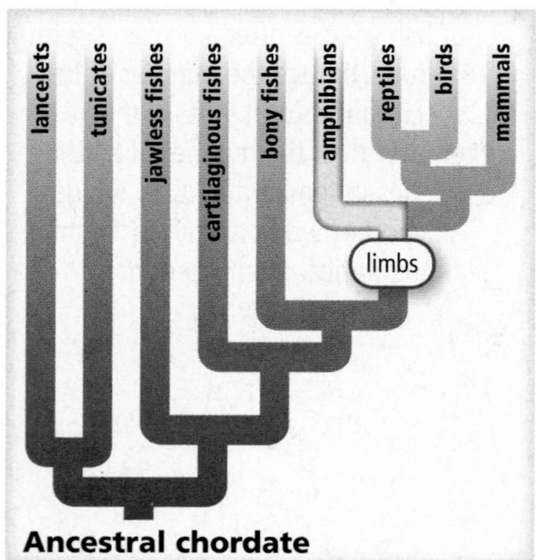


**Figure 28.21** The evolutionary tree shows how amphibians are related to other vertebrates.

# Amphibians

**MAIN Idea Most amphibians begin life as aquatic organisms then live on land as adults.**

**Real-World Reading Link** Think about the last time you went swimming. How is moving in water different from moving on land? Just as fishes have adaptations for living in water, tetrapods have adaptations for living on land.

## Evolution of Tetrapods

Tetrapods first appeared on Earth about 360 million years ago. The first amphibians to crawl onto land were different from today's amphibians. Examine the evolutionary tree in **Figure 28.21** to see how amphibians are related to other vertebrates. As millions of years passed, animals adapted to the conditions of life on land.

**The move to land** Animals faced several physical challenges in the move from water to land. **Table 28.1** lists some of the differences between conditions of life in the water and life on land. These differences include buoyancy, oxygen concentration, and temperature. **Table 28.1** also gives examples of how terrestrial vertebrates adapted to life on land.

**Table 28.1 Adaptations to Land**

Concepts In Motion — Interactive Table To explore more about adaptations for life on land, visit biologygmh.com.

| Conditions in Water | Conditions on Land | Terrestrial Vertebrate Adaptations |
|---|---|---|
| Water exerts a buoyant force that counters the force of gravity. | • Air is about 1000 times less buoyant than water.<br>• Animals must move against gravity. | Limbs develop and the skeletal and muscular systems of terrestrial animals become stronger. |
| Oxygen is dissolved in water and must be removed by gills through countercurrent circulation. | • Oxygen is at least 20 times more available in air than in water. | With lungs, terrestrial animals can get oxygen from air more efficiently than from water. |
| Water retains heat, so the temperature of water does not change quickly. | • Air temperature changes more easily than water temperature.<br>• Daily temperatures may change by 10°C between day and night. | Terrestrial animals develop behavioral and physical adaptations to protect themselves from extreme temperatures. |

In addition to the differences listed in **Table 28.1,** another difference between conditions in water and on land is that sound travels more quickly through water. Fishes use lateral line systems to sense vibrations, or sound waves, in water. A lateral line system is not effective in air. The ears of terrestrial vertebrates developed to sense sound waves traveling through air.

**Terrestrial habitats** In spite of the challenges associated with terrestrial life, there are many habitats available to animals on land. The different biomes on land, including tropical rain forests, temperate forests, grasslands, deserts, taiga, and tundra, provide suitable habitats for animals with appropriate adaptations.

## Characteristics of Amphibians

Have you ever watched a tadpole in a jar of pond water? Examine and describe the tadpole in **Figure 28.22.** A tadpole is the limbless, gill-breathing, fishlike larva of a frog. Day by day, the tadpole undergoes a metamorphosis (me tuh MOR fuh sihs)—hind legs form and grow longer, the tail shortens, gills are replaced by lungs, and forelimbs sprout. In just a few weeks or months, depending on the species, the tadpole becomes an adult frog. Most amphibians begin life as aquatic organisms. After metamorphosis, they are equipped to live life on land.

Modern amphibians include frogs, toads, salamanders, newts, and legless caecilians. Most amphibians are characterized by having four legs, moist skin with no scales, gas exchange through skin, lungs, a double-loop circulatory system, and aquatic larvae.

**Feeding and digestion** Most frog larvae are herbivores, whereas salamander larvae are carnivores. However, as adults their diets are similar as both groups become predators and feed on a variety of invertebrates and small vertebrates. Some salamanders and legless amphibians use just their jaws to catch prey. Others, such as frogs and toads, can flick out their long, sticky tongues with great speed and accuracy to catch flying prey.

Food moves from the mouth through the esophagus to the stomach, where digestion begins. From the stomach, food moves to the small intestine, which receives enzymes from the pancreas to digest food. From the intestine, food is absorbed into the bloodstream and delivered to body cells. Food moves from the small intestine into the large intestine before waste material is eliminated. At the end of the intestine is a chamber called the cloaca. The **cloaca** (kloh AY kuh) is a chamber that receives the digestive wastes, urinary waste, and eggs or sperm before they leave the body.

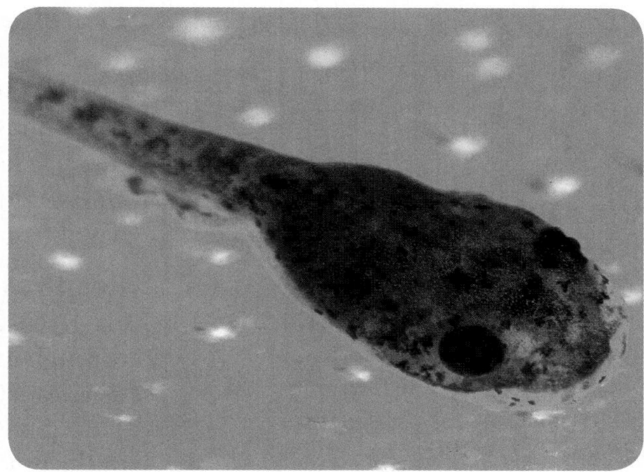

**Figure 28.22** The cayenne slender-legged tree frog is found in South America.
**Top:** A tadpole is limbless.
**Middle:** The frog is undergoing metamorphosis to become an adult frog. Notice the development of limbs.
**Bottom:** An adult frog has fully developed limbs and lacks a tail.

Concepts In Motion

**Interactive Figure** To see an animation of a frog's life cycle, visit biologygmh.com.

**Excretion** Amphibians filter wastes from the blood through their kidneys, and excrete either ammonia or urea as the waste product of cellular metabolism. Ammonia is the end product of protein metabolism and is excreted by amphibians that live in the water. Amphibians that live on land excrete urea that is made from ammonia in the liver. Unlike ammonia, urea is stored in the urinary bladder until it is eliminated from the body through the cloaca.

**VOCABULARY**

**SCIENCE USAGE V. COMMON USAGE**

**Amphibian**

***Science usage:*** organisms that are members of class Amphibia; most spend part of their lives in water and part on land.

*A frog is an amphibian.*

***Common usage:*** an airplane designed to take off from and land on either land or water.

*The amphibian landed smoothly in the lake water.*

**Respiration and circulation** As larvae, most amphibians exchange gases through their skin and gills. As adults, most breathe through lungs, their thin, moist skin, and the lining of the mouth cavities. Frogs can breathe through their skin either in or out of water. This ability enables them to spend the winter protected from the cold in the mud at the bottom of a pond.

The circulatory system of amphibians is shown in **Figure 28.23.** It consists of a double loop instead of the single loop you learned about in fishes. The first loop moves oxygen-poor blood from the heart to pick up oxygen in the lungs and skin, and then moves the oxygen-filled blood back to the heart. During circulation in the second loop, blood filled with oxygen moves from the heart through vessels to the body, where the oxygen diffuses into cells.

Amphibians have three-chambered hearts. The atrium is completely separated into two atria by tissue. The right atrium receives deoxygenated blood from the body, while the left atrium receives oxygenated blood from the lungs. The ventricle of amphibians remains undivided.

**Reading Check** **Describe** how the amphibian circulatory system is adapted to life on land.

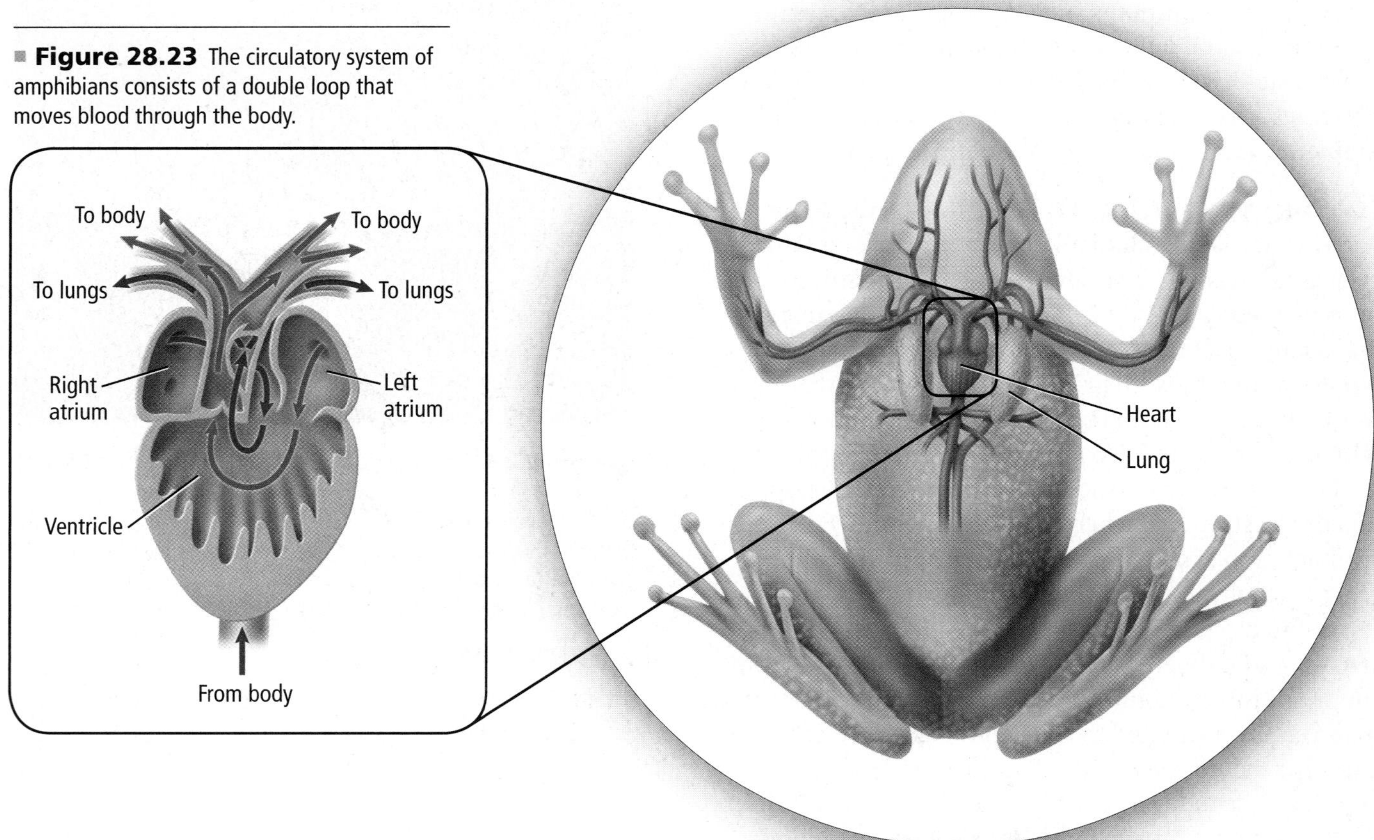


**Figure 28.23** The circulatory system of amphibians consists of a double loop that moves blood through the body.

**The brain and senses** Like fishes, the nervous systems of amphibians are well developed. The differences in conditions between life in the water and life on land are reflected in the differences between the brains of fishes and those of amphibians. For example, the forebrain of frogs contains an area that is involved with the detection of odors in the air. The cerebellum, which is important in maintaining balance in fishes, is not as well developed in terrestrial amphibians that stay close to the ground.

Vision is an important sense for most amphibians. They use sight to locate and capture prey that fly at high speeds and to escape predators. Frogs' eyes have structures called nictitating (NIK tuh tayt ing) membranes. The **nictitating membrane** is a transparent eyelid that can move across the eye to protect it underwater and keep it from drying out on land.

The amphibian ear also shows adaptation to life on land. The **tympanic** (tihm PA nihk) **membrane** is an eardrum. In frogs, it is a thin external membrane on the side of the head, as shown in **Figure 28.24.** Frogs use their tympanic membrane to hear high-pitched sounds and to amplify sounds from the vocal cords. Other senses in amphibians include touch, chemical receptors in skin, taste buds on the tongue, and sense of smell in the nasal cavity.

It is important for amphibians to sense the temperature of their environment because they are ectotherms. **Ectotherms** are animals that obtain their body heat from the external environment. Ectotherms cannot regulate their body temperatures through their metabolism, so they must be able to sense where they can go to get warm or to cool down. For example, if it is cold, a toad can find a warm, moist rock on which to bask and warm itself.

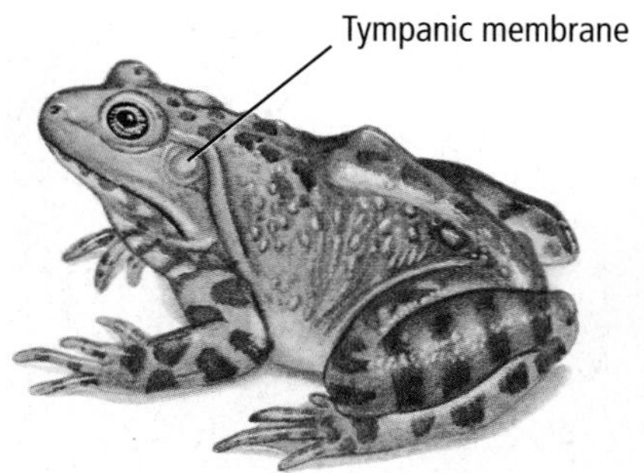


**Figure 28.24** The tympanic membrane is an adaptation for life on land.

Concepts In Motion

Interactive Figure To see an animation of the adaptations of a frog, visit biologygmh.com.

# DATA ANALYSIS LAB 28.2

Based on Real Data*

## Interpret a Graph

**How does temperature affect the pulse rate of calling in tree frogs?** Male tree frogs make calls that females can identify easily based on the rate of the sound pulses in the call.

### Data and Observations

The graph shows the pulse rate of two species of frogs versus temperature.

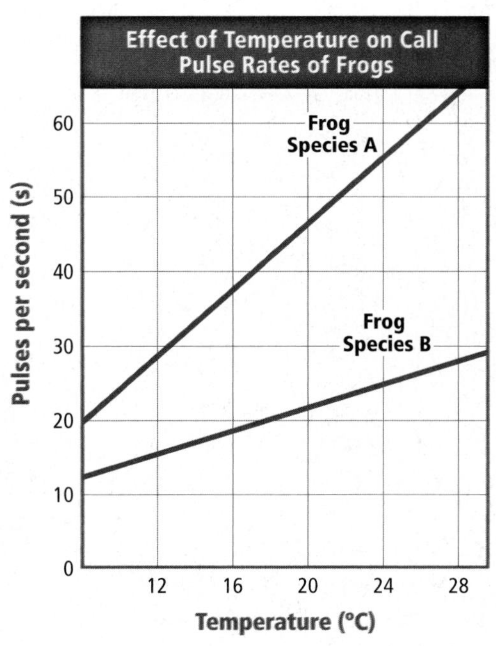


### Think Critically

1. **Interpret the Data** What is the relationship between sound pulses and temperature?
2. **Compare** How did temperature affect the rate of pulses in species A and in species B?
3. **Infer** Why is it important that the two species of frogs do not have the same pulse rate in their calls at the same temperature?

*Data obtained from: Gerhardt, H.C. 1978. Temperature coupling in the vocal communication system in the grey treefrog *Hyla versicolor*. *Science* 199: 992–994.

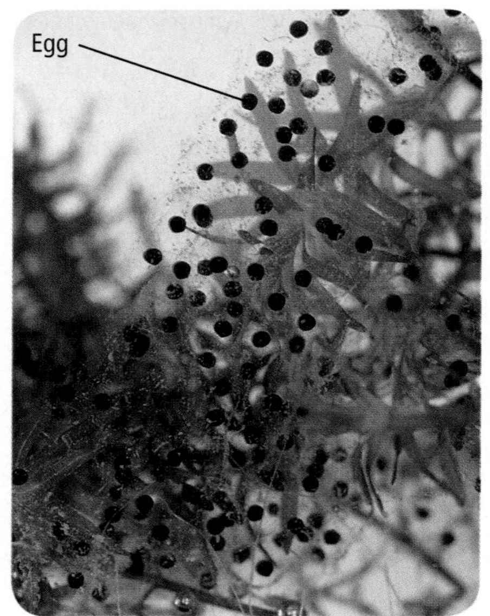


■ **Figure 28.25** Amphibian eggs do not have shells that would protect them from drying out.
**Infer** ***What adaptation ensures that amphibian eggs do not dry out?***

**Reproduction and development** Like many amphibians, female frogs lay eggs to be fertilized by males in the water. The eggs do not have shells or protective coverings to keep them from drying out. The eggs, like the ones shown in **Figure 28.25,** are covered with a sticky, jelly-like substance that helps them stay anchored to vegetation in the water. After fertilization, the developing embryo uses the yolk in the egg for nourishment until it hatches into a tadpole. A tadpole, like the one shown in **Figure 28.22,** changes from a gill-breathing, legless herbivore with fins and a two-chambered heart into a lung-breathing, four-legged carnivore with a three-chambered heart. The stages of metamorphosis are primarily under the control of chemicals released within the tadpole's body.

## Amphibian Diversity

Biologists classify modern amphibians into three orders. Order Anura (a NOOR ah) contains 4200 species of frogs and toads. Order Caudata (kaw DAY tah) has about 400 species of salamanders and newts. One hundred and fifty species of wormlike caecilians make up order Gymnophiona (JIHM noh fee oh nah). Frogs, toads, and salamanders live in moist areas in a variety of habitats, while newts are aquatic. Caecilians are tropical burrowing animals.

**Frogs and toads** Frogs and toads, shown in **Figure 28.26,** lack tails and have long legs enabling them to jump. Frogs have longer and more powerful legs than toads and are able to make more powerful jumps than the small hops of toads. Frogs have moist, smooth skin, while the skin of toads tends to be bumpy and dry. Though both need to be near water to carry out reproduction, toads generally live farther away from water than do frogs. Another difference between frogs and toads is that toads have kidney-bean-shaped glands near the back of their heads that release a bad-tasting poison. The poison discourages predators from eating them.

 **Reading Check** **Compare and contrast** the characteristics of frogs and toads.

■ **Figure 28.26** The bullfrog has moist, smooth skin compared to the skin of the American toad, which is dry and bumpy.

**Bullfrog**

**American toad**

Red salamander

Warty newt

■ **Figure 28.27** The red salamander is found in the eastern United States. The warty newt breeds in deep ponds that contain aquatic vegetation.

**Salamanders and Newts** Unlike frogs and toads, salamanders and newts have long, slim bodies with necks and tails, as shown in **Figure 28.27.** Most salamanders have four legs and thin, moist skin and cannot live far from water. Like frogs, most salamanders lay their eggs in water. The larvae look like miniature salamanders, except that they have gills. Newts, like the one in **Figure 28.27,** generally are aquatic throughout their lives, while most salamanders, as adults, live in moist areas such as under logs or in leaf litter. Salamanders range in size from about 15 cm long to the giant salamander that is 1.5 m long. An adult salamander's diet consists of worms, frog eggs, insects, and other invertebrates.

**Caecilians** Caecilians (si SILH yenz) are different from other amphibians because they are legless and wormlike, as shown in **Figure 28.28.** They burrow in the soil and feed on worms and other invertebrates. Skin covers the eyes of many caecilians, so they might be nearly blind. All caecilians have internal fertilization. They lay their eggs in moist soil located near water. Caecilians can be found in tropical forests of South America, Africa, and Asia.

**CAREERS IN BIOLOGY**

**Animal Curator** An animal curator works at a zoo, managing some part of the zoo's animal collection, such as the amphibian exhibit. Curators work together to decide the best way to maintain an animal's habitat in the zoo. For more information on biology careers, visit biologygmh.com.

■ **Figure 28.28** Caecilians do not have ear openings. It is not known if, or how, they can hear sounds.

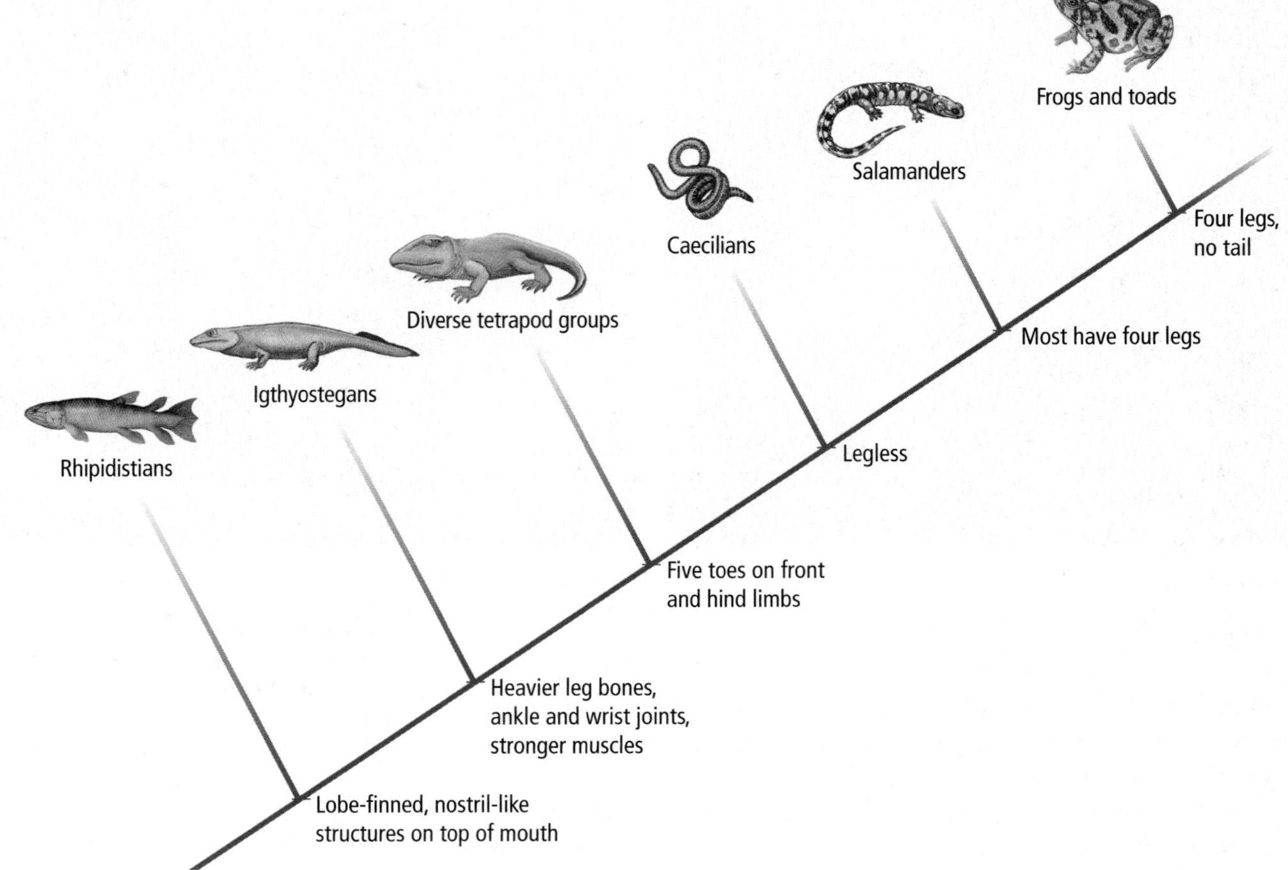


**Figure 28.29** The cladogram shows one interpretation of amphibian evolution.

## Evolution of Amphibians

Fossil evidence shows that the first tetrapods evolved limbs in water before they moved to land. Many adaptations that are useful on land first evolved in water. For example, legs with feet and toes could be helpful in moving through bottom vegetation. Ankles and wrists might have increased maneuverability. The attachment of hip bones to the vertebral column might have helped predators attack prey more easily.

The cladogram shown in **Figure 28.29** is one interpretation of the evolution of amphibians. Many scientists believe that early tetrapods are most closely related to a group of now extinct, lobe-finned fishes called rhipidistians (RI pih dihs tee unz). Characteristics that both early tetrapods and rhipidistians share include similar bone structure in the skull and limbs, nostril-like openings in the tops of their mouths, and a similar tooth structure.

Early tetrapods had defined legs with feet, but the construction of the legs was too weak for these animals to walk easily on land. Ichthyostegans, shown in **Figure 28.17,** had more support in the shoulder bones, heavier leg bones, and more muscular features that enabled them to pull themselves onto land and move a little more easily. The skull had the same general shape as the skulls of lobe-finned fishes. Tetrapod groups branched out to produce the three major groups of amphibians alive today, as well as reptiles, birds, and mammals.

 **Reading Check** **Explain** why scientists think that tetrapods evolved from rhipidistians.

### Study Tip

**Graphic Organizer** Make a Venn diagram comparing and contrasting fishes and amphibians. Draw two overlapping circles. List similarities in the overlapping section of the circles. List the differences on either side of the overlapping section.

**Vocabulary**

**Academic Vocabulary**

**Diversify:**
to produce variety.
*The bakery diversified the flavors of doughnuts it made, giving customers more choices.*

## Ecology of Amphibians

In recent decades, amphibian populations have been declining worldwide. Scientists have been collecting data to determine possible causes for the decline. The results have varied. In some cases, the cause can be isolated to a local condition. In other cases, the cause might be the result of several factors occurring on a large scale.

**Local factors** In some cases, such as that of the California red-legged frog, the decline is due to habitat destruction. When wetlands are drained and buildings are built in the areas instead, these areas of water are no longer available to amphibians that must lay eggs in or near water to reproduce successfully. In other areas, the introduction of exotic species—species that are not found in that area naturally—has affected amphibian populations. The exotic species compete with the amphibians for food and habitat space, or they are predators of amphibians. The introduction of trout, which prey on tadpoles, into the high-altitude lakes of California's Sierra Nevada Mountains is thought to have contributed to the near extinction of the mountain yellow-legged frog found in that region.

**Global factors** In addition to local factors, various global factors might be at work causing amphibian decline. Aspects of global climate change, such as increased temperature, decreased soil moisture, increased length of the dry season, and changes in rainfall can cause either death or stress to the bodies of amphibians, making them more susceptible to disease.

**Figure 28.30** compares healthy toad eggs versus those infected by a fungus. Some scientists believe that global climate changes that have led to a decreased amount of rainfall leave developing amphibians' eggs in shallow pond water. Because the depth of the water is reduced, the eggs are exposed to more ultraviolet light. Laboratory experiments have shown that increased exposure to UV light leads to an increased risk of fungal infection in amphibian eggs.

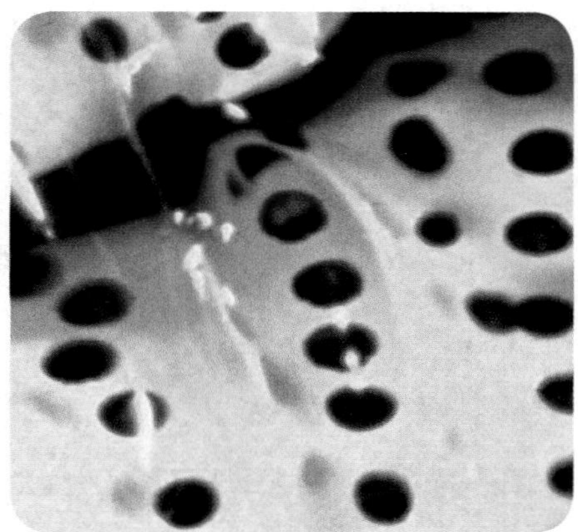

**Healthy toad eggs**

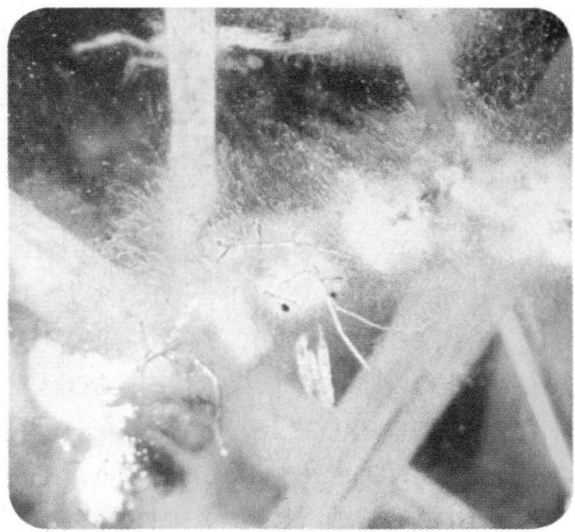

**Fungus-infected toad eggs**

■ **Figure 28.30** Healthy toad eggs are laid in single file in the water. Infected toad eggs are covered by fungus; fungus infection might account for a decrease in some toad populations.

## Section 28.3 Assessment

### Section Summary

- The transition of animals to land required a variety of adaptations.
- The bodies of amphibians have unique adaptations that enable them to live on land.
- Amphibians belong to three orders based on structural similarities.
- Ancient tetrapods evolved aquatic adaptations that eventually were used on land.
- Amphibian populations are declining worldwide for a variety of reasons.

### Understand Main Ideas

1. MAIN Idea **Summarize** the adaptations of amphibians that make them adapted to life on land.
2. **Compare** the conditions of a land environment to that of an aquatic environment.
3. **Analyze** the kinds of adaptations that were important as animals moved to land.
4. **Summarize** the characteristics of each order of amphibians.

### Think Scientifically

5. *Interpret Scientific Illustrations* Examine **Figure 28.29** and explain which of the three groups of amphibians is most recent and which is the most ancient.
6. WRITING in **Biology** On a hike in a marshy area near your home, you find a dead frog with deformed limbs. Hypothesize possible reasons why these deformities might have occurred.

# BioDiscoveries

## What is causing frog malformations?

**From classroom to newsroom** What began as a class field trip ended up alerting environmentalists to a potentially important problem. In August 1995, a class of students in LeSeuer, Minnesota, took a field trip to a wetland to learn about the ecosystem. While they were there, they noticed a large population of frogs—more than 50 percent of their catch—had malformations. In 1996, reports of frogs with malformations, including missing or extra legs, partially formed limbs, and missing eyes, were showing up elsewhere, including all across Minnesota and in several other states and countries.

**Leaping into the laboratory** Several studies are being conducted to determine the cause of the malformations. The results of one study indicate that poor water quality could be the cause. When frogs were grown in the laboratory in different samples of water, as many as 75 percent of the frogs were malformed when grown in the water from the Minnesota sites, compared to 0 percent when grown in purified water. The problem contaminant has not been identified yet. Scientists are testing other hypotheses as well, including that tadpoles are being infected by a parasitic worm or a fungus that could be causing the malformations. Another hypothesis being tested is whether or not increased exposure of frog eggs to UV light is causing the malformations.

Each of the studies has yielded data that support the hypotheses tested, but since the types and frequency of malformations are not the same from site to site, as shown in the graphs above, the real-world cause probably is a combination of factors.

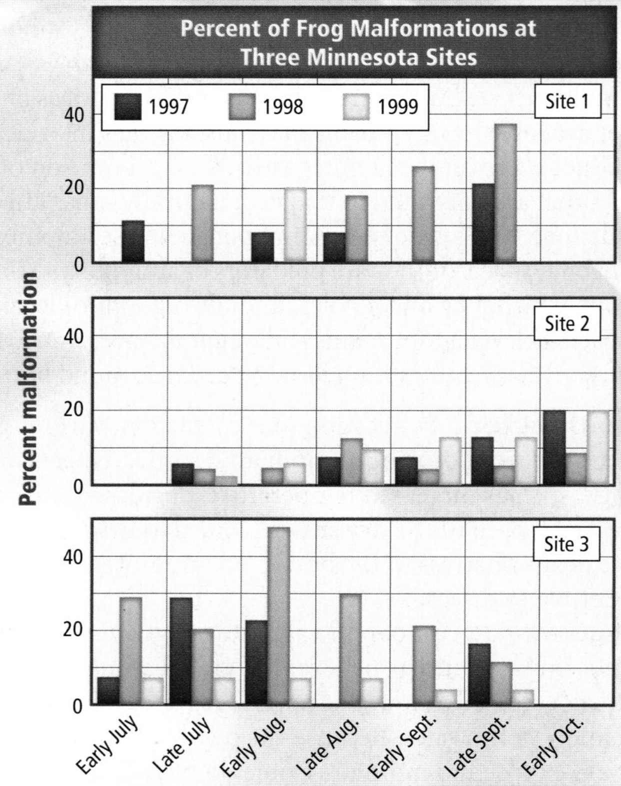


Malformation rates peak at different times from year to year and from site to site.

For instance, increased phosphorus and nitrogen in the water, caused by chemical use, can create an algal bloom. That algal bloom, in turn, increases the population of snails that carry the parasite that can cause malformations. Or, chemical mixtures, while harmless individually, might become toxic when mixed, or might change when exposed to sunlight.

### MATH in Biology

**Analyze Data** The graphs above show the differences in the percent of malformations in frogs at three sites in Minnesota over a three-year period. Find the average percent of malformations at each site for the three-year period. Which site had the largest percent of malformations? For more information about frog malformations, visit biologygmh.com.

24. Which is not associated with a tadpole?
   **A.** lungs
   **B.** tail
   **C.** gills
   **D.** herbivorous feeding

## Constructed Response

25. **Open Ended** Draw a picture that would illustrate how amphibians are affected by increased exposure to ultraviolet light.

26. **Open Ended** Describe how the structure and physiology of amphibians, presently adapted to temperate and tropical climates, might be modified to enable them to live in colder climates.

27. **Open Ended** Describe how the senses of amphibians are adapted to life on land.

## Think Critically

28. **Design an Experiment** Tadpole larvae of certain frogs gather in clusters so close together that the group looks like a moving football in the water. Design an experiment that would test a hypothesis about why the tadpoles exhibit this behavior.

29. **Create** Read the advertisements for homes in the newspaper to see how they are written, and write an ad for an amphibian home site based on what you know about the habitat, nutrition, and other needs of frogs.

*Use the diagram below to answer question 30.*

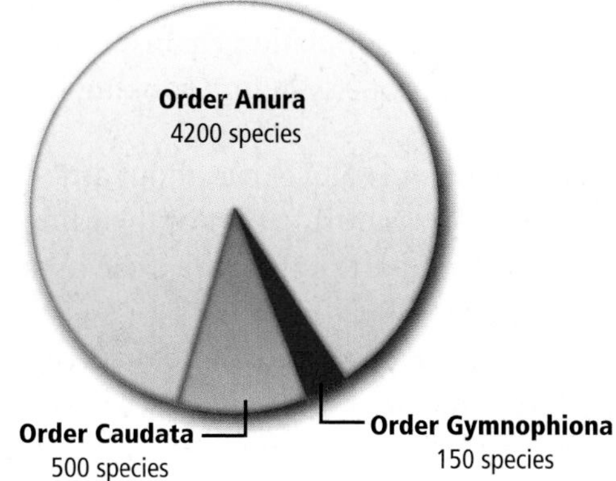


30. **Calculate** Determine the percent that each order of amphibians contributes to the total amount of amphibians.

## Additional Assessment

31. WRITING in **Biology** Research what efforts are being made by scientists to preserve amphibians. Write a newspaper article summarizing what you learned.

### DBQ Document-Based Questions

*Scientists are trying to determine the cause or causes for the decline in amphibian populations over the past few decades. The graph below shows the results of one study in which the survival rate of amphibian embryos was measured against the depth of the water in which they developed.*

Data obtained from: Kiesecker, J., et al. 2001. Complex causes of amphibian population declines. *Nature* 410: 681-683.

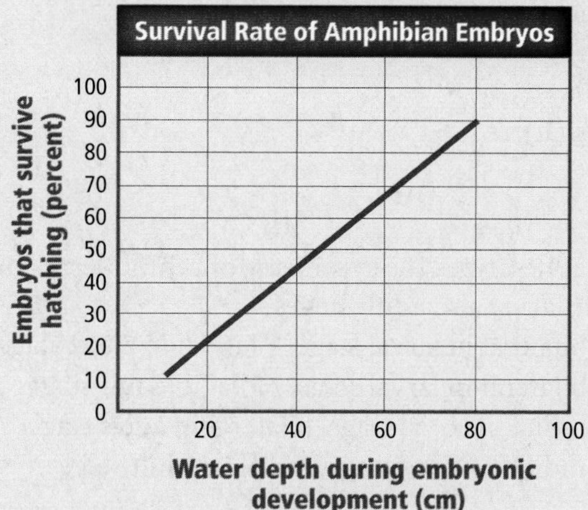


32. Describe the relationship between water depth during development and the survival rate of embryos.

33. Form a hypothesis about the decline of amphibian populations in relation to changes in climate.

## Cumulative Review

34. Explain the theory of evolution in terms of violating Hardy-Weinberg conditions. **(Chapter 15)**

35. Describe the adaptations that helped plants survive on land. **(Chapter 21)**

# Standardized Test Practice

**Cumulative**

## Multiple Choice

*Use the diagram below to answer question 1.*

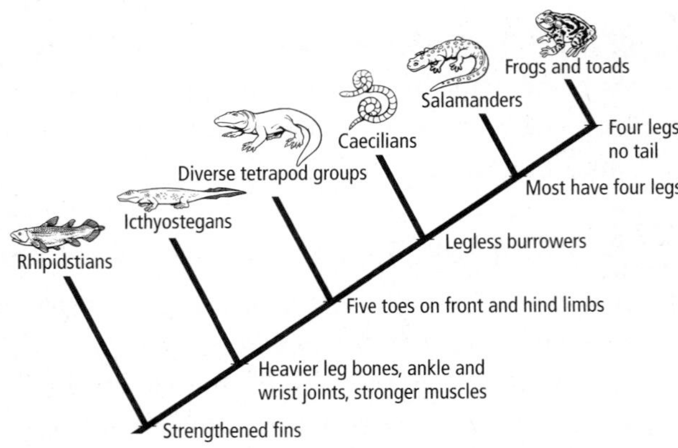


1. According to the cladogram, which is the earliest relative of the amphibians?
   - **A.** ichthyostegans
   - **B.** rhipidstians
   - **C.** rays
   - **D.** sharks

2. What describes the symmetry of echinoderms in their larval and adult stages?
   - **A.** bilateral in larval stage, bilateral in adult stage
   - **B.** bilateral in larval stage, radial in adult stage
   - **C.** radial in larval stage, bilateral in adult stage
   - **D.** radial in larval stage, radial in adult stage

3. Which is the role of the Malpighian tubules in arthropods?
   - **A.** adding digestive enzymes to the intestines
   - **B.** allowing oxygen into the body
   - **C.** maintaining homeostatic water balance
   - **D.** transporting blood to body tissues

4. Which method of communication does a honeybee use to tell others in the hive about the location of food?
   - **A.** chemical pheromones
   - **B.** complex dances
   - **C.** quiet buzzing sounds
   - **D.** rapid wing beating

5. What is the function of the simple eye in arthropods?
   - **A.** to analyze landscapes during flight
   - **B.** to detect colors
   - **C.** to distinguish light from dark
   - **D.** to see movement

*Use the chart below to answer question 6.*

| Row | Group | Characteristics |
|---|---|---|
| 1 | Invertebrate chordates | Lack a backbone |
| 2 | Jawless fishes | Lack a notochord |
| 3 | Bony fishes | Have a skeleton made of bone |
| 4 | Cartilaginous fishes | Have a skeleton made of cartilage |

6. Which row in the chart contains incorrect information?
   - **A.** 1
   - **B.** 2
   - **C.** 3
   - **D.** 4

7. Which statement describes the most reasonable way to prevent the disease of trichinosis in humans?
   - **A.** Cook pork thoroughly before eating it.
   - **B.** Treat infected pigs for trichinosis worm.
   - **C.** Vaccinate the population against trichinosis.
   - **D.** Wash pork properly before cooking it.

8. Which statement is NOT true about amphibians?
   - **A.** Many lack legs during part of their life cycle.
   - **B.** Many spend part of their life cycle in the water and part on land.
   - **C.** Most depend on outside water sources to keep their bodies moist.
   - **D.** They were the first animals to evolve lungs.

9. Which mutation is often caused by the addition or deletion of a single base pair?
   - **A.** frame shift
   - **B.** missense
   - **C.** substitution
   - **D.** tandem repeat

## Short Answer

*Use the diagrams below to answer question 10.*

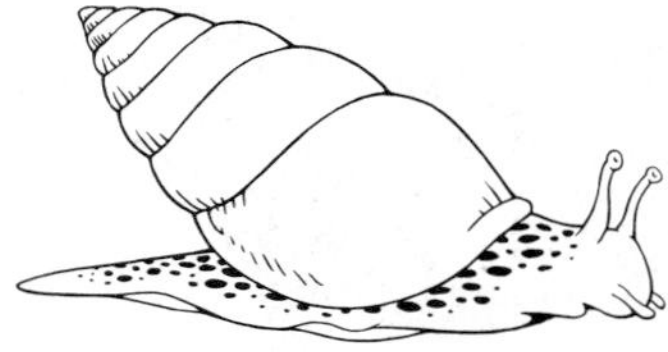

10. Describe a body structure from each of the mollusks shown above, and explain how these structures are related.

11. Sequence the energy transitions that have to take place in order for the Sun's energy to be used by a heterotroph.

12. Evaluate why the notochord is considered an evolutionary advancement.

13. Analyze which characteristics of a shark enabled it to be a fast swimmer. Explain your answer.

14. Name two groups of invertebrate chordates and describe how they feed. Relate their feeding patterns to their way of life.

15. Compare three characteristics of fishes to three characteristics of another group of animals that you already know.

## Extended Response

16. Create a Venn diagram to organize information about endoderm and ectoderm tissues that form during embryonic development. Then explain how endoderm and ectoderm tissues are similar and different.

17. Explain how the first photosynthetic prokaryotes changed life on Earth.

18. Contrast the circulatory systems of lancelets and tunicates and justify the classification of both kinds of organisms as invertebrate chordates.

19. Hypothesize whether incomplete metamorphosis or complete metamorphosis in insects is more primitive. Explain your reasoning.

## Essay Question

Most of the invertebrate animal groups living today trace their evolutionary history back more than 500 million years. Every other group of invertebrates living today expanded from the oceans to fresh water and, in many cases, to land. The fossil record for echinoderms shows that they have changed radically throughout their evolutionary history. Today, there are many diverse forms of echinoderms yet none have ever left the ocean.

*Using the information in the paragraph above, answer the following question in essay format.*

20. Hypothesize why echinoderms have continued living only in the ocean while other invertebrate groups have migrated to fresh water and land.

| NEED EXTRA HELP? | | | | | | | | | | | | | | | | | | | | |
|---|---|---|---|---|---|---|---|---|---|---|---|---|---|---|---|---|---|---|---|---|
| **If You Missed Question . . .** | 1 | 2 | 3 | 4 | 5 | 6 | 7 | 8 | 9 | 10 | 11 | 12 | 13 | 14 | 15 | 16 | 17 | 18 | 19 | 20 |
| **Review Section . . .** | 28.3 | 27.1 | 26.1 | 26.3 | 26.1 | 28.2 | 25.2 | 28.3 | 12.4 | 25.4 | 8.2, 8.3 | 27.2 | 28.2 | 27.2 | 28.1 | 24.1 | 14.2 | 27.2 | 26.3 | 27.1 |

CHAPTER 29 Reptiles and Birds

**Section 1**
**Reptiles**
MAIN Idea Reptiles are fully adapted to life on land.

**Section 2**
**Birds**
MAIN Idea Birds have feathers, wings, lightweight bones, and other adaptations that allow for flight.

## BioFacts

- The fangs of a rattlesnake lie flat on the roof of its mouth when its mouth is closed.
- When a rattlesnake's mouth is opened during a strike, its fangs rotate forward, ready to inject venom from the venom gland in the jaw through openings in the fangs.
- The speed of a rattlesnake strike is an amazing 2.4 m/s.

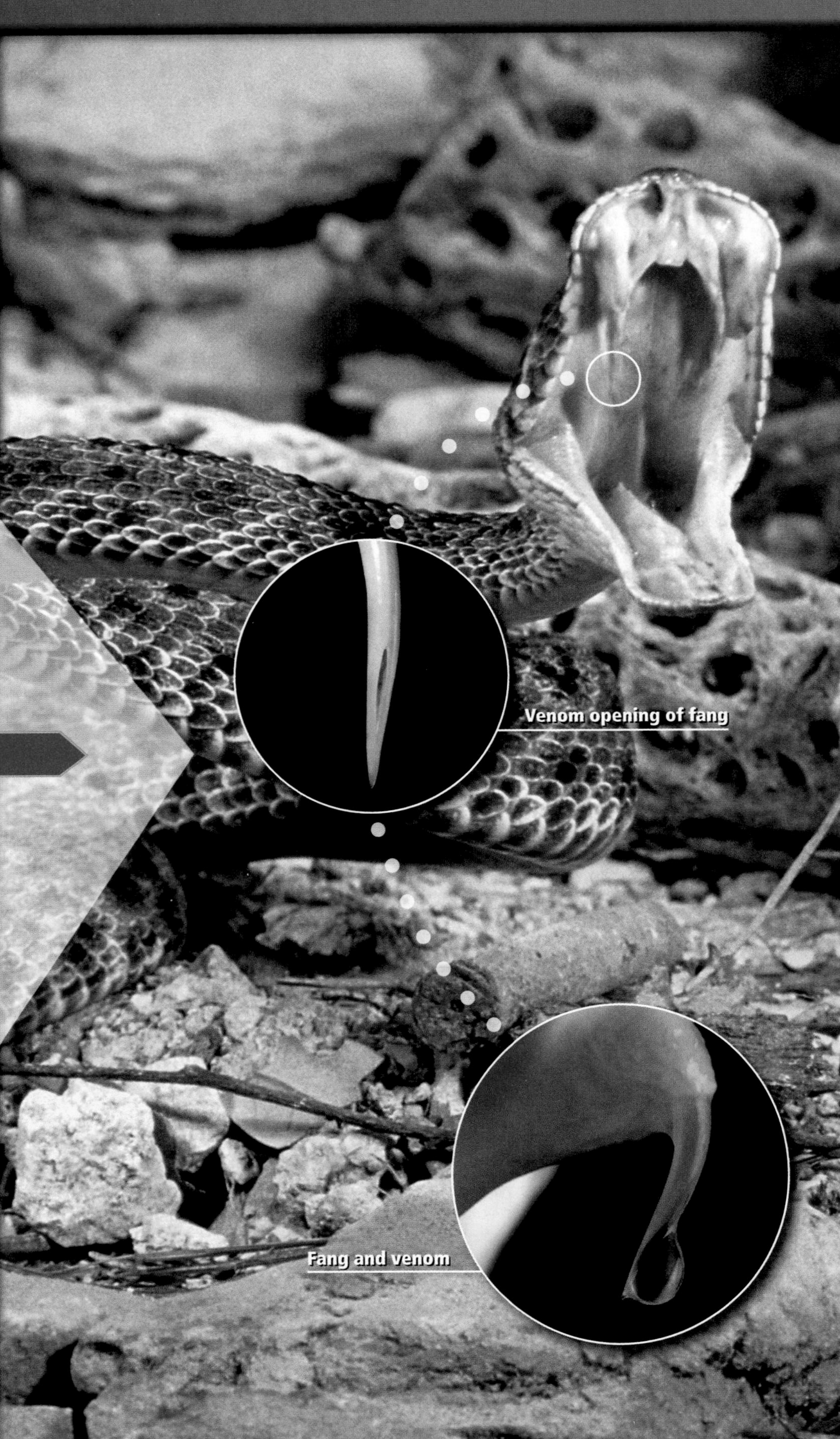

# LAUNCH Lab

## Are cultural symbols of reptiles and birds scientifically accurate?

Throughout history, reptiles and birds have been feared, revered, and symbolized. In this lab, you will review examples of symbolized reptiles and birds and determine if the representations are scientifically accurate.

### Procedure

1. Read and complete the lab safety form.
2. Research symbols, stories, or legends about reptiles or birds from different cultures.
3. Analyze the information in the materials you find from Step 2 for scientific accuracy. Hypothesize as to why a reptile or bird was used as a symbol or legend in each situation.

### Analysis

1. **Evaluate** How much of the information you analyzed was scientifically accurate? Why do you think some information was inaccurate?
2. **Synthesize** Choose one symbol or legend that contained inaccurate information and modify it so that it is scientifically accurate.

Visit biologygmh.com to:

- study the entire chapter online
- explore the Concepts in Motion, the Interactive Table, Virtual Labs, Microscopy Links, and links to virtual dissections
- access Web links for more information, projects, and activities
- review content online with the Interactive Tutor, and take Self-Check Quizzes

**Characteristics of Reptiles and Birds** Make the following Foldable to help you compare and contrast the characteristics of reptiles and birds.

**STEP 1** Fold one sheet of paper lengthwise, leaving the holes uncovered.

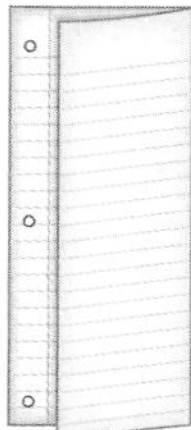

**STEP 2** Fold into thirds.

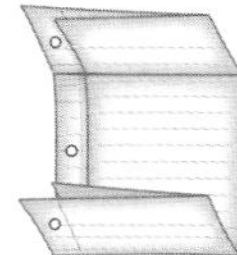

**STEP 3** Unfold and draw overlapping ovals. Cut the top sheet along the folds.

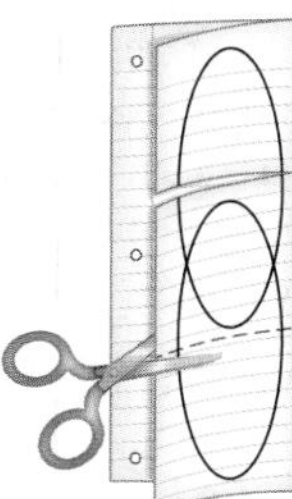

**STEP 4** Label the Venn diagram as shown.

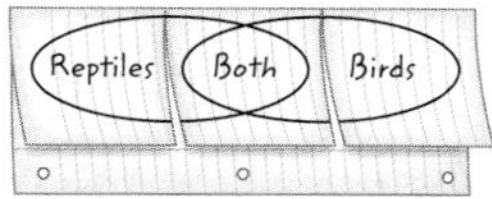


FOLDABLES **Use this Foldable with Sections 29.1 and 29.2.** As you read each section, record characteristics that are unique to reptiles and birds and those they have in common.

Section 29.1

**Objectives**

- **Analyze** how the amniotic egg made the move to land complete.
- **Summarize** the characteristics of reptiles.
- **Distinguish** between the orders of reptiles.

**Review Vocabulary**

**embryo:** the earliest stage of development of plants and animals after an egg has been fertilized

**New Vocabulary**

amnion
amniotic egg
Jacobson's organ
carapace
plastron

# Reptiles

**MAIN Idea Reptiles are fully adapted to life on land.**

**Real-World Reading Link** Think about the last time you saw a movie in which a reptile was a main character. Maybe it was a giant anaconda or a ferocious *Tyrannosaurus rex*. Maybe it was an animated character that was funny. As you read this section, think about whether the characteristics of the movie reptile were scientifically accurate.

## Characteristics of Reptiles

In Chapter 28, you learned that vertebrates with well-developed limbs, circulatory and respiratory systems, and other adaptations that equipped them for life on land moved from water to land. However, amphibians were left vulnerable to the drying effects of life on land with their shell-less eggs and larvae that breathed through gills. In contrast, reptiles, like the Western fence lizard shown in **Figure 29.1,** are fully adapted to life on land and were the first completely terrestrial vertebrates. Characteristics that allow reptiles to succeed on land include a shelled egg, scaly skin, and more efficient circulatory and respiratory systems.

**Amniotic eggs** As you can see in the evolutionary tree in **Figure 29.1,** reptiles have characteristics in common with other groups that have an amnion and other membranes that surround the embryo as it develops. An **amnion** (AM nee ahn) is a membrane that surrounds a developing embryo. It is filled with fluid that protects the embryo during development. Animals that undergo this type of development are called amniotes and include reptiles, birds, and mammals.

**Figure 29.1**
**Right:** This Western fence lizard is one of 7000 species of reptiles belonging to class Reptilia. Reptiles live in a variety of terrestrial and aquatic habitats.
**Left:** The phylogenetic tree shows that reptiles, along with birds and mammals, have an amnion.

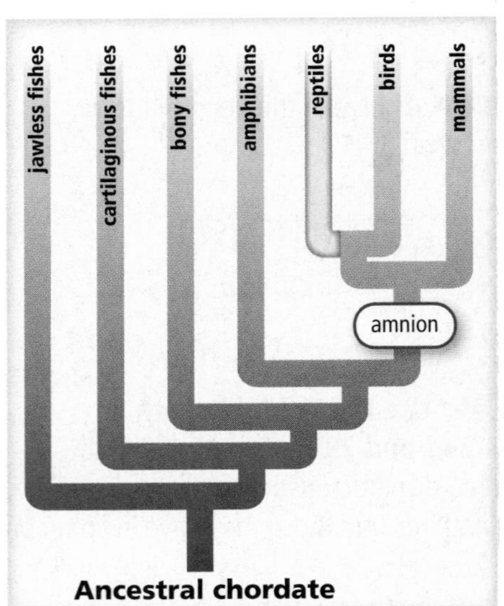


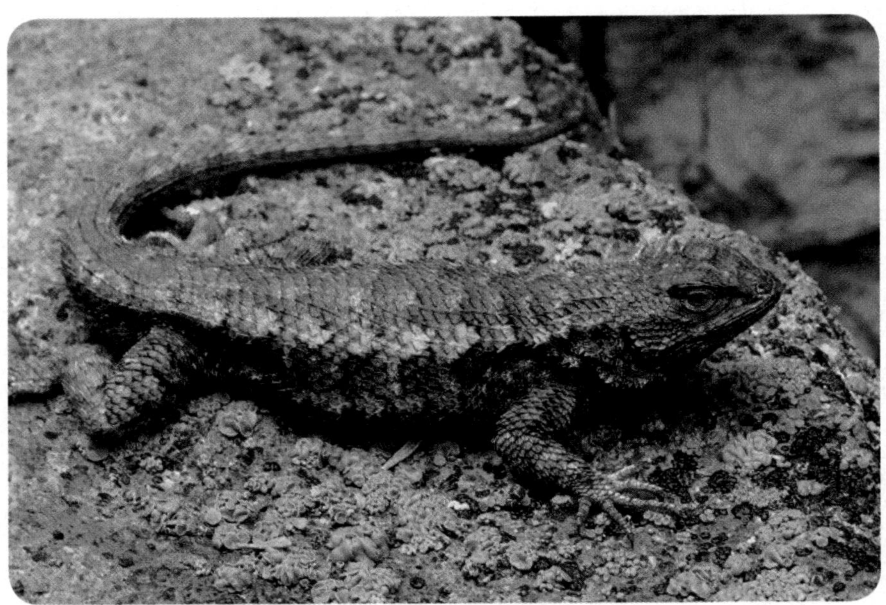

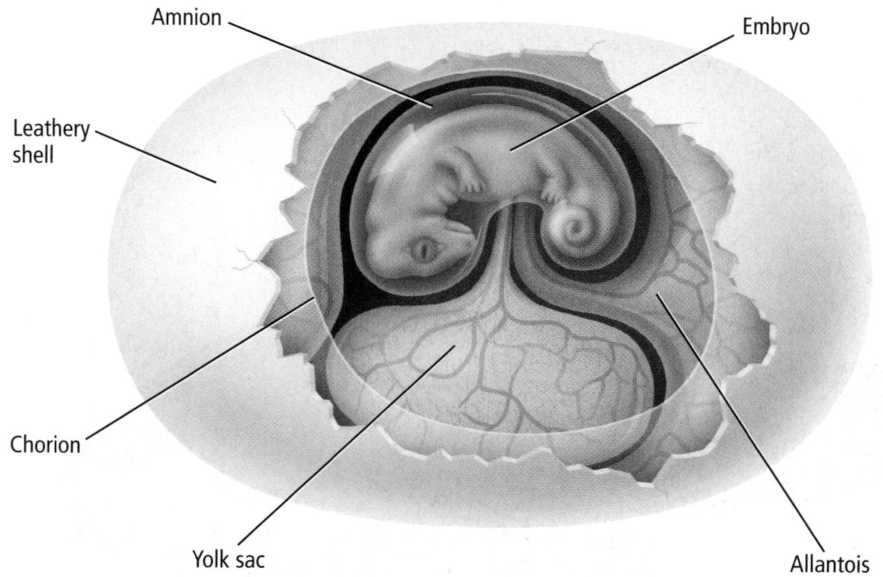


**Figure 29.2** The amniotic egg is protected by a shell and membranes with fluid that help to protect the embryo and keep it from drying out during development.

**Concepts In Motion**

**Interactive Figure** To see an animation of the form and function of an amniotic egg, visit biologygmh.com.

An **amniotic egg,** like the one shown in **Figure 29.2,** is covered with a protective shell and has several internal membranes with fluids contained between the membranes. Inside the egg, the embryo is self-sufficient because it gets its nutrition from food in the yolk sac inside the egg. Bathing the embryo within the amnion is amniotic fluid. Amniotic fluid mimics the aquatic environments of fish and amphibian embryos. The allantois (uh LAN tuh wus) is a membrane that forms a sac that contains wastes produced by the embryo. The outermost membrane of the egg is the chorion (KOR ee ahn), which allows oxygen to enter and keeps fluid inside the egg. In reptiles, the leathery shell protects the internal fluids and embryo, and prevents the egg from drying out on land. In birds, the shell is hard instead of leathery.

**Dry, scaly skin** In addition to keeping fluid in their eggs, reptiles also must keep fluids in their bodies. The dry skin of reptiles keeps them from losing internal fluids to the air. A layer of scales on the exterior of many reptiles also keeps them from drying out. However, one problem with having a tough outer covering is that an organism could have difficulty growing larger. In order to grow, some reptiles, like the snake in **Figure 29.3,** periodically must shed their skins in a process called molting. You might have seen the molt of a snake's skin while hiking a nature trail.

**Respiration** Most reptiles, except for some aquatic turtles, depend primarily on lungs for gas exchange. Recall that when amphibians breathe, they squeeze their throats to force air into their lungs. Reptiles are able to suck air into their lungs, or inhale, by contracting muscles of the rib cage and body wall to expand the upper part of the body cavity in which the lungs are held. They exhale by relaxing these same muscle groups. Reptiles exchange gases in lungs that have larger surface areas for gas exchange than the lungs of amphibians. With more oxygen, more energy can be released through metabolic reactions and made available for more complex movements.

**Reading Check** **Evaluate** why the amniotic egg is important for an animal to be able to live exclusively on land.

**Figure 29.3** Some reptiles molt as they grow larger.
**Compare** *molting in reptiles to molting in arthropods.*

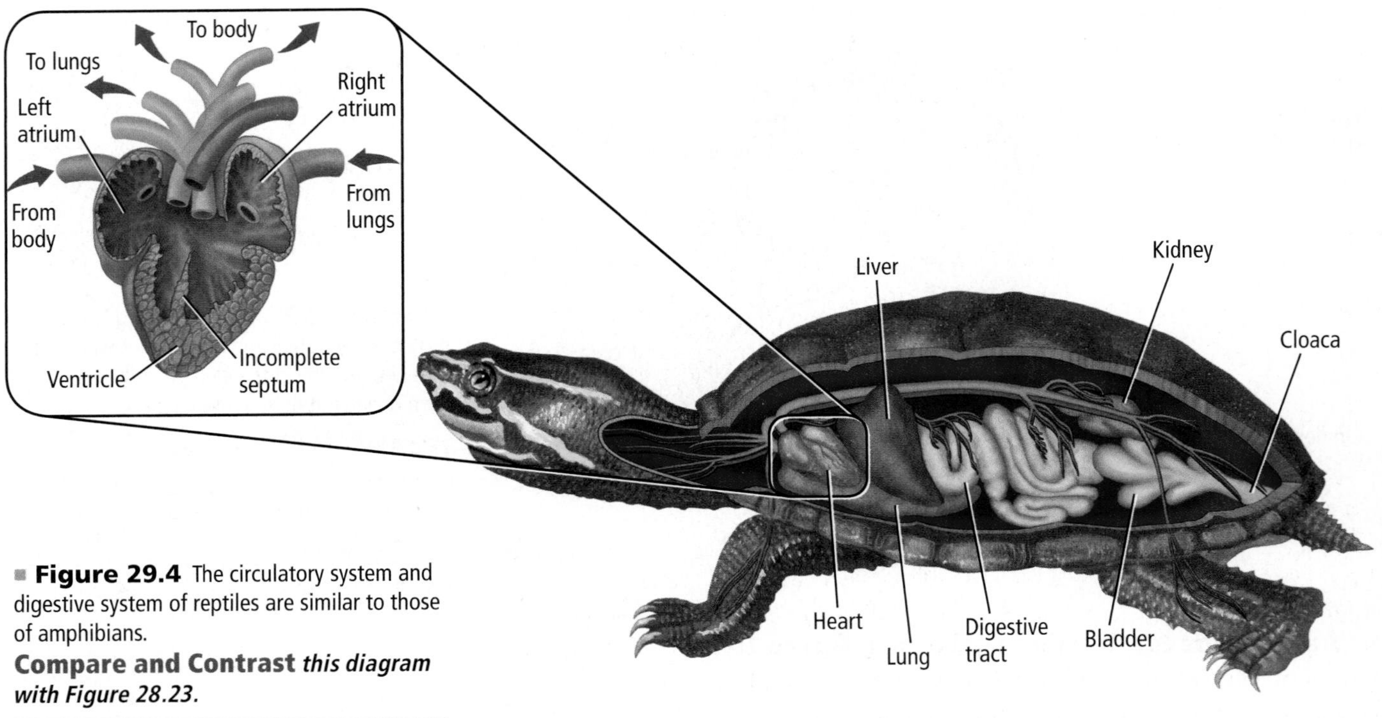


**Figure 29.4** The circulatory system and digestive system of reptiles are similar to those of amphibians.
**Compare and Contrast** ***this diagram with Figure 28.23.***

**Circulation** In most reptiles, oxygen from the lungs enters into a circulatory system that is similar to that of amphibians. Most reptiles have two separate atria and one ventricle that is partially divided by an incomplete septum, as shown in **Figure 29.4.** In crocodiles, however, the septum in the ventricles is complete, thereby resulting in a four-chambered heart. The separation into two ventricles keeps oxygen-rich blood separate from the oxygen-poor blood throughout the heart.

Because reptiles generally are larger than amphibians, they need to pump blood forcefully enough to reach parts of the body far away from the heart. In an example from the past, the dinosaur *Brachiosaurus* had to pump blood more than 6 m from the heart to the head!

**Feeding and digestion** The organs of the digestive system of reptiles, shown in **Figure 29.4,** are similar to those of fish and amphibians. Reptiles have a variety of feeding methods and diets. Most reptiles are carnivores, but some, such as iguanas and tortoises, are herbivores that feed on plants, and some turtles are omnivores. Turtles and crocodiles have tongues that help them swallow. Some lizards, such as the chameleon, have long, sticky tongues for catching insects.

Snakes have the ability to ingest prey much larger than themselves. The bones of the skull and jaws of snakes are joined loosely so that they can spread apart when taking in large food materials, as shown in **Figure 29.5.** To swallow, the opposite sides of the upper and lower jaws can alternately thrust forward and retract to draw in the food. Some snakes have venom that can paralyze and begin digestion of their prey.

**Figure 29.5** Snakes can consume a meal that is larger than their mouths because their jaws are loosely jointed, and upper and lower jaws can move independently of each other.

**Excretion** The excretory system of reptiles is adapted to life on land. The kidneys, such as the one shown in **Figure 29.4,** filter the blood to remove waste products. When urine enters the cloaca, water is reabsorbed to form uric acid, which is a semisolid excretion. This method of water reabsorption enables reptiles to conserve water and maintain homeostasis of water and minerals in their bodies.

**The brain and senses** Reptile brains are similar to amphibian brains, except that the cerebrum of reptiles is larger. Because vision and muscle function are more complex, the optic lobes and cerebellum portions in the brain of reptiles also are larger than those of amphibians. Vision is the main sense for most reptiles, and some reptiles even have color vision. Hearing varies in reptiles. Some reptiles have tympanic membranes similar to those of amphibians, while others, such as snakes, detect vibrations through their jaw bones.

The sense of smell is more highly evolved in reptiles than it is in amphibians. You might have seen video of snakes flicking their forked tongues. They do this to smell odors. The odor molecules stick to the tongue, which the snake places in its mouth. The odor molecules are transferred to a pair of saclike structures called **Jacobson's organs,** which are shown in **Figure 29.6.** These structures are on the roof of a snake's mouth and they sense odors. Experiments have shown that without Jacobson's organs, snakes have difficulty finding prey and mates.

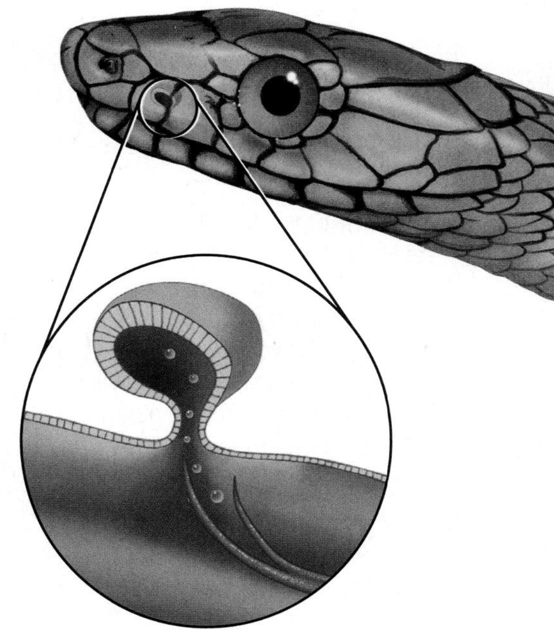

**Figure 29.6** In snakes, Jacobson's organs in the mouth are used to sense odors.

**Temperature control** Like amphibians, reptiles are ectotherms that cannot generate their own body heat. They regulate their body temperatures behaviorally. You might have seen turtles basking in the Sun on top of rocks. This raises body temperature. Body temperature can be lowered by moving into the shade or a cool burrow. Some reptiles in temperate regions survive winter by burrowing or going into a state of inactivity with lower body metabolism and lower body temperature. Others, such as some snakes, gather together in masses of hundreds during the winter. Heat loss is reduced when the snakes are covering each other.

**Movement** Compare the leg position of the salamander to the leg position of the crocodile shown in **Figure 29.7.** Note that the salamander's belly is on the ground, while the crocodile's belly is above the ground. Like amphibians, some reptiles move with limbs sprawled to their sides and push against the ground while swinging their bodies from side to side. Crocodiles, however, have their limbs rotated farther under the body and, as a result, can bear more weight and move faster. To bear more body weight on land, reptiles' skeletons are stronger with heavier bone structure. Reptiles also have claws on their toes which aid in digging, climbing, and gripping the ground for traction.

**Reading Check** **Compare and contrast** the brain and senses of reptiles to amphibians.

**Figure 29.7** Salamanders move with splayed legs pushing against the ground as their bodies drag along. Crocodiles have legs that are rotated underneath their bodies, which holds their bodies off the ground.

**Salamander**

**Crocodile**

**Reproduction** Reptiles have internal fertilization. In most reptiles, after fertilization, the egg develops to form the new embryo and all of the membranes associated with an amniotic egg to help ensure safe development. The female reproductive system produces a leathery shell around the eggs that will be laid. The developing embryo is nourished from the yolk of the egg. The female usually digs a hole and lays eggs in the ground or in plant debris. After laying their eggs, most females leave them alone to hatch. Alligators and crocodiles build a nest in which to lay eggs and tend to young after they hatch. Some snakes and lizards keep their eggs in their bodies until they hatch. In this way, the eggs are protected in the mother's body until they are fully developed young.

**CAREERS IN BIOLOGY**

**Herpetologist** Scientists that study reptiles and amphibians are called herpetologists. Herpetologists may specialize by studying the anatomy or ecology of one type of reptile, such as snakes or crocodiles. For more information on biology careers, visit biologygmh.com.

## Diversity of Modern Reptiles

From the ancient Age of Reptiles, in which an enormous variety of dinosaurs ruled Earth, four living orders of reptiles remain—snakes and lizards belonging to order Squamata (skwuh MAHD uh), crocodiles and alligators belonging to order Crocodilia, turtles and tortoises belonging to order Testudinata, and tuataras belonging to order Sphenodonta (sfee nuh DAHN tuh).

**VOCABULARY**
**WORD ORIGIN**
**Squamata**
***squama–*** from Latin, meaning *scale.*
***–ata*** from Latin, meaning *to bear.*

**Lizards and snakes** Lizards commonly have legs with clawed toes. Also, lizards usually have movable eyelids, a lower jaw with a movable hinge joint allowing for flexibility in jaw movement, and tympanic membranes. Common lizards include iguanas, chameleons, geckos, and anoles. An iguana is shown in **Figure 29.8.**

Snakes are legless and have shorter tails than lizards. Snakes lack movable eyelids and tympanic membranes. Like lizards, however, snakes have joints in their jaws enabling them to eat prey larger than their heads. Some snakes, such as the rattlesnake shown at the beginning of the chapter, have venom that can slow down or even kill their prey. Other snakes, such as the python shown in **Figure 29.8,** anacondas, and boas, are constrictors. Constrictors generally are very large snakes. They suffocate their prey by wrapping around the prey's body and tightening until the prey dies because it no longer can breathe.

**Reading Check** **Describe** the different methods by which snakes capture prey.

**Figure 29.8** The green iguana and the green tree python are both members of order Squamata.

**Green iguana**

**Green tree python**

**Eastern box turtle**

**American alligator**

■ **Figure 29.9** The shell of a turtle helps protect it from predators. An alligator has a broad snout and thick scales covering its body.

**Turtles** Observe the turtle shown in **Figure 29.9.** The protective shell in which a turtle's body is encased makes it different from other reptiles. The dorsal part of the shell is called the **carapace** (KAR ah pays) and the ventral part of the shell is called the **plastron** (PLAS trahn). The vertebrae and ribs of most turtles are fused to the inside of the carapace. Many turtles can pull their head and legs inside their shells to protect themselves against predators. Some turtles are aquatic, and some live on land. Turtles that live on land are called tortoises. Tortoises and turtles do not have teeth, but they have a sharp beak that can deliver a powerful bite.

**Crocodiles and alligators** Order Crocodilia includes crocodiles, alligators, and caimans. Crocodilians have a four-chambered heart, another adaptation which is also a characteristic of birds and mammals. Because a four-chambered heart can deliver oxygen more efficiently, powerful muscles enable crocodilians to move quickly and aggressively, both in and out of the water, attacking animals as large as cattle, deer, and humans.

Crocodiles have a long snout, sharp teeth, and powerful jaws. The teeth of crocodiles are similar to those of dinosaurs and the earliest birds. This type of tooth shows the close relationship between modern crocodilians and the dinosaurs that gave rise to living birds.

Alligators, like the one in **Figure 29.9,** generally have a broader snout than crocodiles. The upper jaw of an alligator is wider than the lower jaw. When an alligator closes its mouth, the upper jaw overlaps the lower jaw and its teeth are almost completely covered. The upper and lower jaws of a crocodile are about the same width. So when a crocodile closes its mouth, some teeth in the lower jaw are easily visible.

**Tuataras** Tuataras (tyew ah TAR ahz) look like large lizards, as shown in **Figure 29.10,** and are found only on islands off the coast of New Zealand. There are only two species of tuataras. Tuataras have a spiny crest that runs down the back and a "third eye" on top of the head. This structure is covered with scales but can sense sunlight. Biologists think that it might keep the tuatara from overheating in the Sun. One distinguishing feature of tuataras is that they have unique teeth compared to those of other reptiles. Two rows of teeth on the upper jaw shear against one row in the lower jaw, making them effective predators of small vertebrates.

*Study Tip*

**Reading Preview** *Endotherm* is a vocabulary term in Section 2. List other words that include the prefix *endo-*. List other words that contain the root word *therm.* Predict the meaning of the term *endotherm.*

■ **Figure 29.10** Tuataras reach a length of about 2 m and can live up to 80 years in the wild.

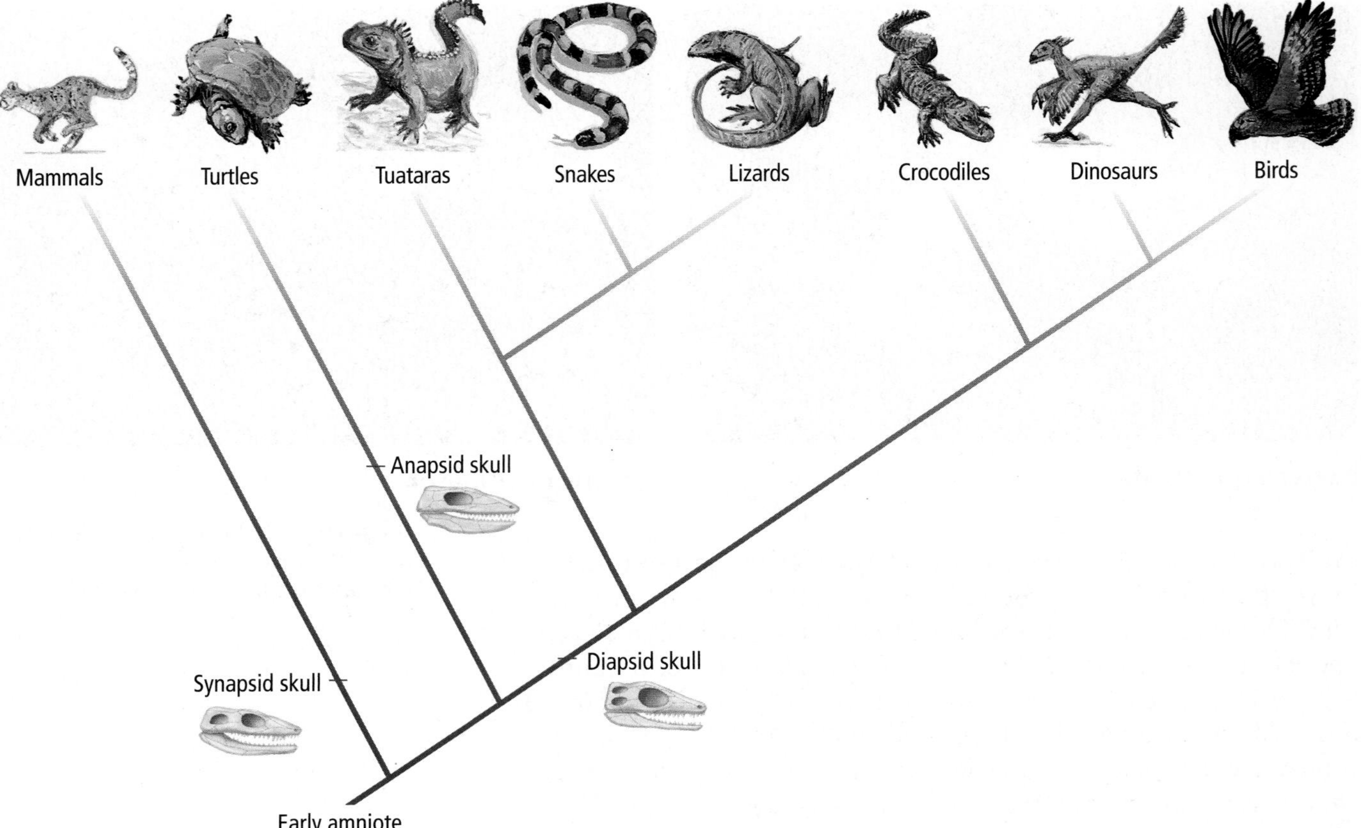


■ **Figure 29.11** The cladogram shows one interpretation of the relationships between amniotes.
**Interpret** ***Which modern reptiles evolved first? Which evolved most recently?***

## Evolution of Reptiles

The cladogram in **Figure 29.11** shows one interpretation of how early amniotes underwent adaptive radiation, giving rise to reptiles as well as modern birds and mammals. Recall that amniotes are vertebrates in which the embryo is encased in an amniotic membrane. As shown in the cladogram, early amniotes separated into three lines, each having a different skull structure. Anapsids, which might have given rise to turtles, have a skull that has no openings behind the eye sockets. Diapsids, which gave rise to crocodiles, dinosaurs, modern birds, tuataras, snakes, and lizards, have a skull with two pairs of openings behind each eye socket. Synapsids, which gave rise to modern mammals, have one opening behind each eye socket.

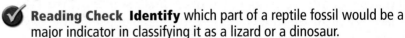

**VOCABULARY**
**ACADEMIC VOCABULARY**
**Interpretation:**
A particular adaptation or version of a work, method, or style.
*Scientists might make several interpretations of fossil evidence.*

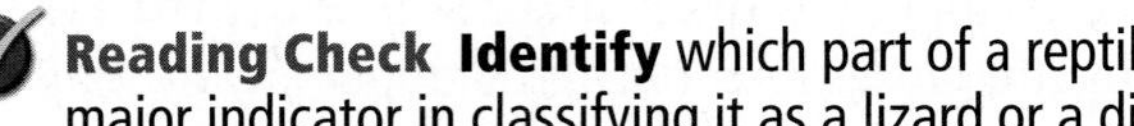
**Reading Check** **Identify** which part of a reptile fossil would be a major indicator in classifying it as a lizard or a dinosaur.

**Dinosaurs** For 165 million years, dinosaurs dominated Earth. Some, such as *Tyrannosaurus rex,* stood almost 6 m high, were 14.5 m long, weighed more than 7 tonnes, and were predatory. Others, such as *Triceratops,* had massive horns and were herbivores. Despite their diversity, dinosaurs can be divided into two groups based on the structure of their hips. A comparison of the two groups is shown in **Figure 29.12.** Saurischians (saw RISK ee unz) had hip bones that radiated out from the center of the hip area. In Ornithischians, some bones projected back toward the tail.

Like birds and crocodiles, some dinosaurs built nests and cared for eggs and young. Some dinosaurs might have had the ability to regulate their body temperatures. Fossil evidence shows that one group of dinosaurs had feathers and evolved into today's birds.

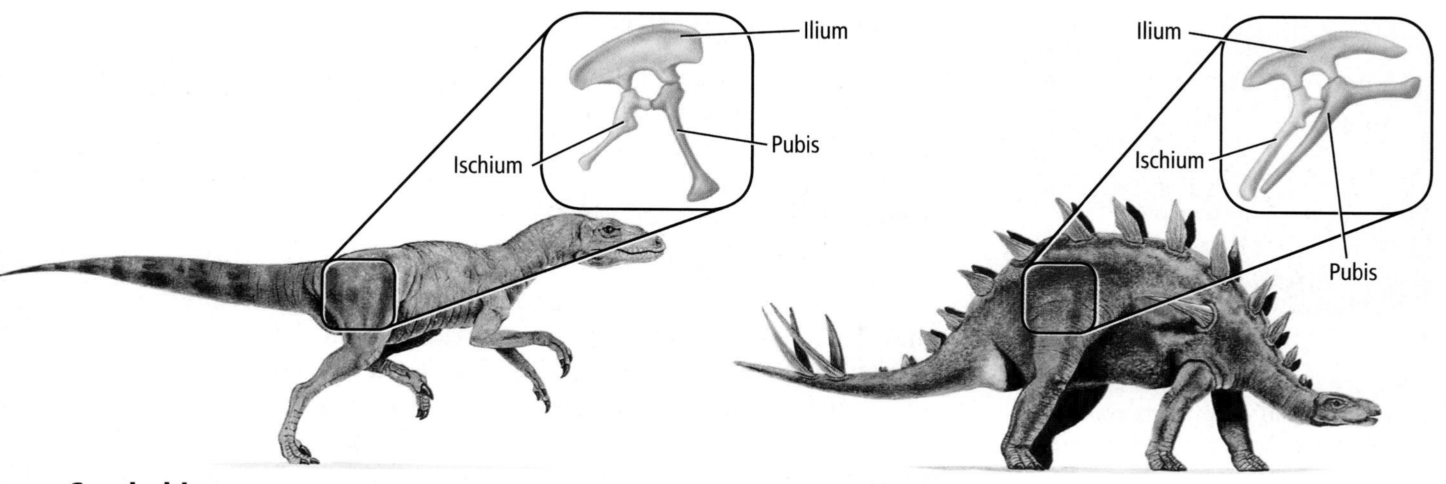


**Figure 29.12** Saurischians had a hip bone that pointed forward. Ornithischians had the same bone pointing back toward the tail end of the animal.

**Connection to Earth Science** The Cretaceous Period is known for worldwide mass extinction of many species, including all dinosaurs. Some scientists hypothesize that a meteorite crashed to Earth and caused this extinction. Clouds of dust might have blocked the Sun, causing a much cooler climate to develop. This change, along with fires, toxic dust, and gases, could have caused the death of many plants and animals at this time. When dinosaurs disappeared, the niches they had occupied were made available for other vertebrates to evolve.

## DATA ANALYSIS LAB 29.1

**Based on Real Data***

### Interpret the Data

**How fast did dinosaurs grow?** Scientists study thin sections of fossilized bone tissue to determine how rapidly bone grew. By studying how quickly dinosaurs grew, scientists can learn about their populations and ecology.

**Think Critically**

1. **Compare** During what age span did the dinosaurs experience the greatest growth? Explain.
2. **Analyze Data** Which dinosaur grew at the slowest rate? The fastest rate?
3. **Infer** Fast-growing bones have many blood vessels. How would the bones of *Tyrannosaurus* compare to those of *Daspletosaurus*?

**Data and Observations**

The graph shows bone-based growth curves comparing several dinosaurs.

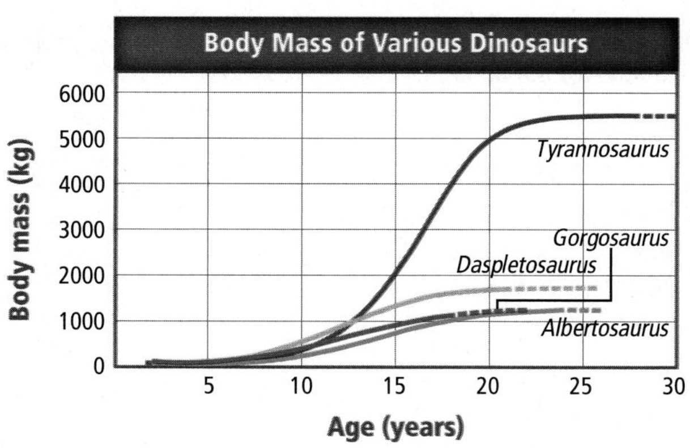


*Data obtained from: Stokstad, E. 2004. Dinosaurs under the knife. *Science* 306: 962-965.

■ **Figure 29.13** The San Francisco garter snake *(Thamnophis sirtalis tetrataenia)* lives in wetlands or grasslands near ponds and marshes.

## Ecology of Reptiles

Reptiles are important parts of food chains both as prey and as predators. The balance of an ecosystem can be disrupted when a reptile species is removed. For example, when certain snakes continually are removed from an environment, rodent populations can increase. Loss of habitat and the introduction of exotic species are factors that contribute to the decline in population of some reptile species.

**Habitat loss** Both the American alligator *(Alligator mississippiensis)* and the American crocodile *(Crocodylus acutus)* have been affected by habitat loss in the Florida Everglades. The destruction and fragmentation of wetlands for building development has led to reduced numbers of these reptiles. The American crocodile remains endangered, with only 500-1200 remaining in Florida. With the passage of laws to protect wetlands in certain areas, the American alligator population has rebounded enough so that its status has been changed from endangered to threatened.

**Introduction of exotic species** When species that are not naturally found in an area, exotic species, are introduced, the local animals might suffer due to predation or competition for resources. For example, when the mongoose, a small mammal, was introduced into Jamaica to kill rats in sugarcane fields, the mongoose fed mostly on several lizard species which are now endangered. This includes the Jamaican iguana, which was thought to have been extinct due to the introduction of the mongoose. In 1990, a small population was discovered in a remote area of Jamaica.

Some species, such as the San Francisco garter snake shown in **Figure 29.13,** have suffered a population decline due to both habitat loss and the introduction of exotic species. The use of land for building houses, other buildings, and agriculture has led to habitat loss for this snake. The introduction of the American bullfrog, which is not native to California, also has impacted the population number of this snake. The bullfrog eats both the garter snake as well as the red-legged frog, a food source of the garter snake.

## Section 29.1 Assessment

### Section Summary

- Reptiles have several types of adaptations for life on land.
- Eggs of reptiles are adapted to development on land.
- Reptiles belong to four living orders: snakes and lizards, crocodiles and alligators, turtles and tortoises, and tuataras.
- Modern reptiles evolved from early amniotes. Many ancient reptiles, including dinosaurs, became extinct.

### Understand Main Ideas

1. MAIN Idea **Identify** features that allow reptiles to live on land successfully.
2. **Describe** the parts of an amniotic egg. How did this structure allow the move to land?
3. **Compare and contrast** members of order Squamata with members of order Sphenodonta.
4. **Explain** the difference between anapsids, diapsids, and synapsids. Which gave rise to groups of reptiles?

### Think Scientifically

5. *Formulate Models* Make a model of the amniotic egg shown in **Figure 29.2.** Relate the function of each membrane.
6. MATH in Biology The biting force of alligators is directly proportional to their length. An alligator that is 1 m long has a biting force of 268 kg. What is the biting force of a larger alligator that is 3.6 m long?



Biology Online Self-Check Quiz biologygmh.com

Section 29.2

### Objectives

- **Summarize** the characteristics of birds.
- **Relate** the adaptations of birds to their ability to fly.
- **Describe** different orders of birds.

### Review Vocabulary

**terrestrial:** living on or in land

### New Vocabulary

endotherm
feather
contour feather
preen gland
down feather
sternum
air sac
incubate

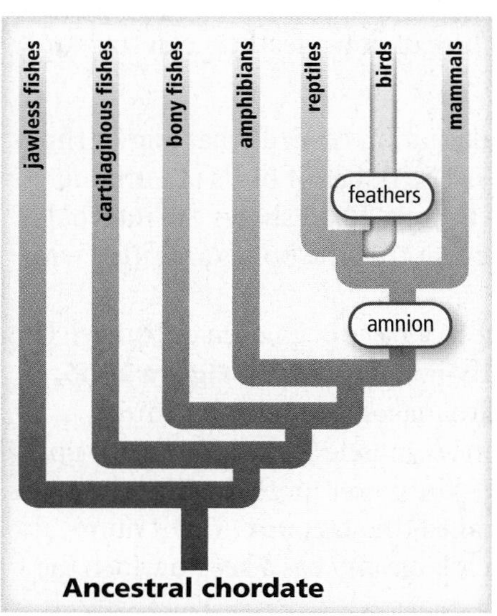


**Figure 29.14** The evolutionary tree shows that feathers are a unique characteristic of birds.

# Birds

**MAIN Idea Birds have feathers, wings, lightweight bones, and other adaptations that allow for flight.**

**Real-World Reading Link** Birds might be the most common wild vertebrates you see. You probably have heard the sayings: "Free as a bird," "Birds of a feather flock together," "Eat like a bird," or "Light as a feather." As people talk, listen for "bird words." As you read, see if these sayings refer to real science.

## Characteristics of Birds

Suppose your teacher asked you to describe a bird. You might respond that birds have feathers and that they fly—two characteristics that distinguish them from other vertebrates. Birds belong to class Aves and include about 8600 species, making them the most diverse of all terrestrial vertebrates. Birds range in size from tiny hummingbirds hovering over bright flowers to large flightless ostriches running across the African plains. Birds are found in deserts, forests, mountains, prairies, and on all seas.

As shown on the evolutionary tree in **Figure 29.14,** birds and reptiles have a common ancestor. Birds have many characteristics that demonstrate their reptilian roots. For example, birds lay amniotic eggs. In addition, scales similar to those of reptiles cover the legs of birds.

You can think of a bird as a collection of adaptations to a lifestyle that includes flight. The adaptations include being able to generate their own body heat internally, or endothermy, feathers, and lightweight bones. The respiratory and circulatory systems of birds also are adapted to provide more oxygen to working muscles to support flight.

**Endotherms** Unlike reptiles, birds are endotherms. An **endotherm** is an organism that generates its body heat internally by its own metabolism. The high metabolic rate associated with endothermy generates a large amount of ATP that can be used to power flight muscles or for other purposes. Endothermy might have evolved in dinosaurs and been passed along to birds. Endotherms generate heat due to their normal body metabolism. The body temperature of a bird is about 41°C. Your body temperature is about 37°C. A high body temperature enables the cells in a bird's flight muscles to use the large amounts of ATP needed for rapid muscle contraction during flight.

**Feathers** Birds are the only living animals to have feathers. **Feathers** are specialized outgrowths of the skin of birds. They are made of keratin (KER ah tihn), a protein in the skin that also makes up hair, nails, and horns of other animals. Feathers have two main functions: flight and insulation. Feathers keep heat generated during metabolism from escaping from the body of the bird. When a bird fluffs its feathers, it creates a dead air space that traps the heat. Similarly, if you are covered with a quilt while you sleep, the quilt creates dead air space between you and the cool air in the room so that you do not lose body heat.

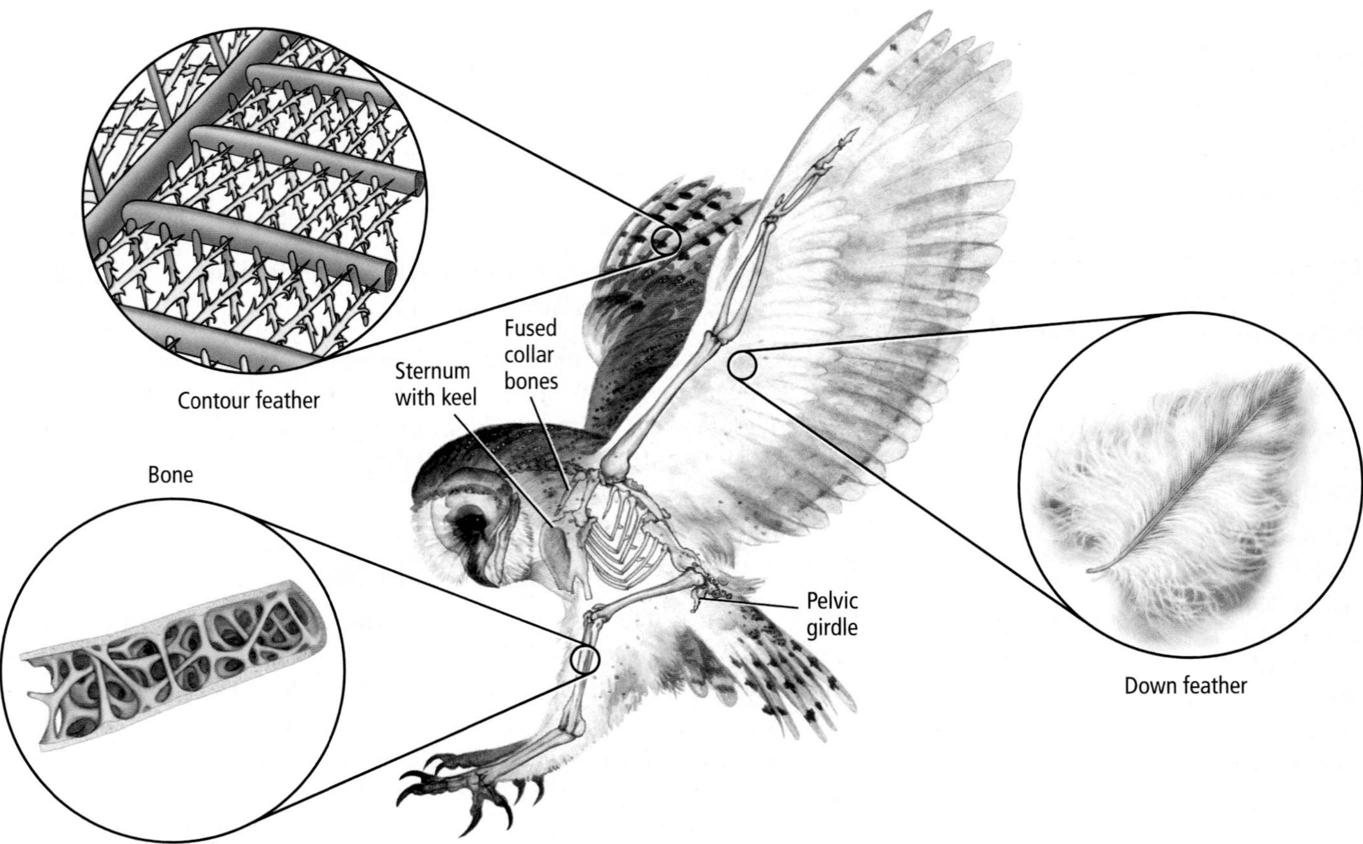


■ **Figure 29.15** Birds have contour feathers, down feathers, and lightweight bones.

**Concepts In Motion**

**Interactive Figure** To see an animation of the adaptations of a bird, visit biologygmh.com.

Feathers that cover the body, wings, and tail of a bird are called **contour feathers.** Examine the contour feathers shown in **Figure 29.15.** Contour feathers consist of a shaft with barbs that branch off. Barbules branch off barbs and are held together by hooks. If two adjoining barbs become separated, they can be rejoined like the teeth of a zipper. Birds repair broken links when they preen their feathers. They use their bills to preen their feathers, drawing the length of the feather through the bill to zip up broken links. Birds spend a large amount of time maintaining their feathers. Many birds have a **preen gland,** a gland located near the base of the tail that secretes oil. During preening, birds spread oil from the preen gland over their feathers, thereby adding a waterproofing coating. **Down feathers,** shown in **Figure 29.15,** are soft feathers located beneath contour feathers. Down feathers do not have hooks to hold barbs together. As a result, the looser structure of down feathers can trap air that acts as insulation.

**VOCABULARY**

**SCIENCE USAGE V. COMMON USAGE**

**Preen**

***Science usage:*** to maintain or repair using a bill (of a bird).

*The bluejay was preening its feathers before it flew away.*

***Common usage:*** to gloat or congratulate oneself on an achievement.

*Jim was preening over his victory at the track meet.*

**Lightweight bones** Another adaptation of birds that allows flight is their strong, lightweight skeletons. The bones of birds are unique because they contain cavities of air. **Figure 29.15** shows the internal structure of a bird bone. Despite the fact that the bones are filled with air, they are still strong.

Have you ever found the wishbone in a piece of chicken or turkey? The wishbone is formed from fused collarbones, as shown in **Figure 29.15.** Fusion of bones in the skeleton of a bird makes the skeleton sturdier, another adaptation for flight. Large breast muscles, which can make up 30 percent of a bird's total weight, provide the power for flight. These muscles connect the wing to the breastbone, called the **sternum** (STUR num), also shown in **Figure 29.15.** The sternum is large and has a keel to which the muscles attach.

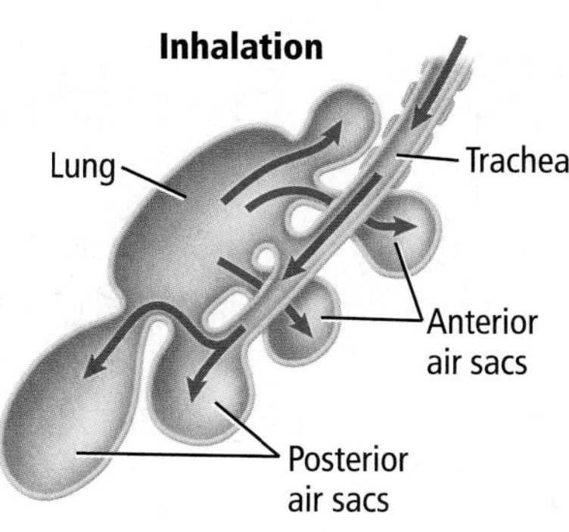


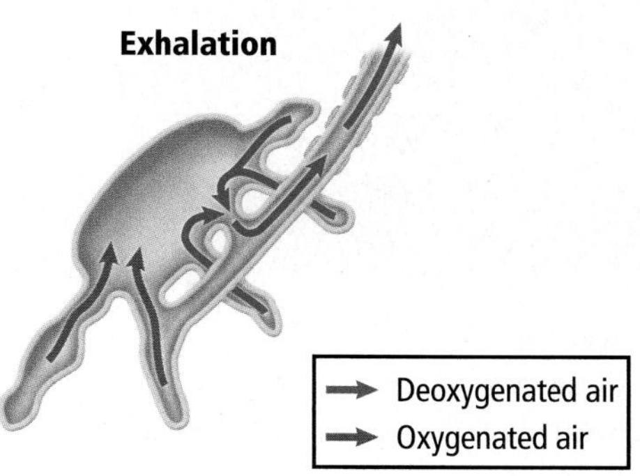


**Figure 29.16** When a bird breathes, air always flows in a single direction, and highly efficient gas exchange can be achieved.

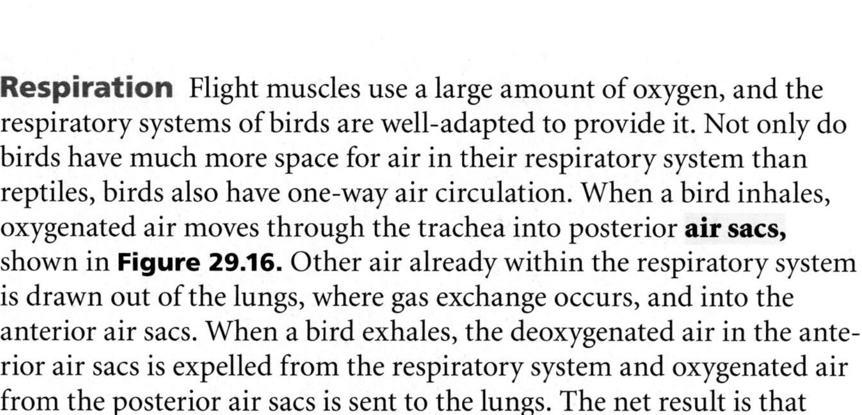

**Respiration** Flight muscles use a large amount of oxygen, and the respiratory systems of birds are well-adapted to provide it. Not only do birds have much more space for air in their respiratory system than reptiles, birds also have one-way air circulation. When a bird inhales, oxygenated air moves through the trachea into posterior **air sacs,** shown in **Figure 29.16.** Other air already within the respiratory system is drawn out of the lungs, where gas exchange occurs, and into the anterior air sacs. When a bird exhales, the deoxygenated air in the anterior air sacs is expelled from the respiratory system and oxygenated air from the posterior air sacs is sent to the lungs. The net result is that only oxygenated air is moved through the lungs, and it is moved in a single direction relative to blood flow.

**Circulation** A bird's circulatory system also helps it maintain high levels of energy by efficient delivery of oxygenated blood to the body. Recall that crocodiles are the only reptiles to have a heart ventricle completely divided by a septum. Birds also have a four-chambered heart, as shown in **Figure 29.17.** Having two ventricles keeps the oxygenated and deoxygenated blood separated and makes delivery of oxygenated blood more efficient. The left atrium receives blood from the lungs. This blood is pumped into the left ventricle and out to the body. Blood returning from the body is delivered to the right atrium, then moves into the right ventricle and on to the lungs where it will pick up more oxygen.

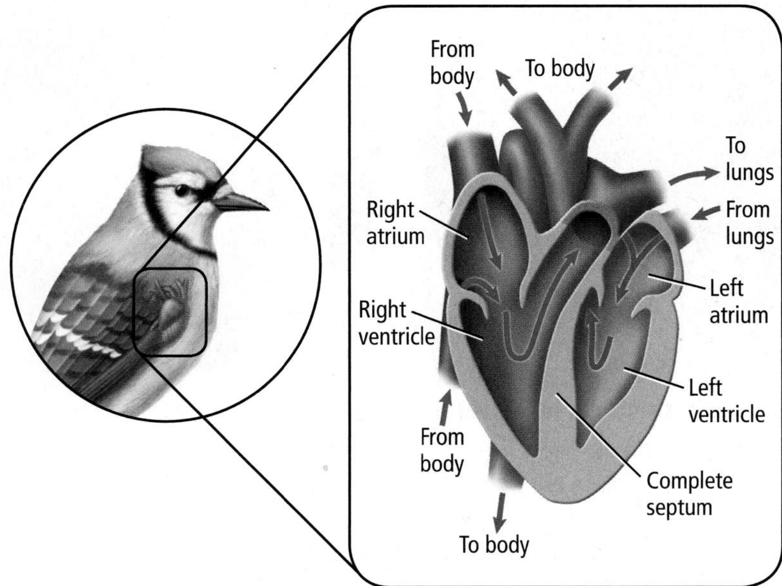


**Figure 29.17** Birds have a four-chambered heart that keeps oxygenated and deoxygenated blood separate.
**Compare** ***the heart of a bird to that of the reptile shown in Figure 29.4.***

# Visualizing Feeding and Digestion

**Figure 29.18**
Examine the organs in the digestive system of a bird. Aside from having unique adaptations to their digestive systems, birds have beaks that are adapted to the type of food they eat.

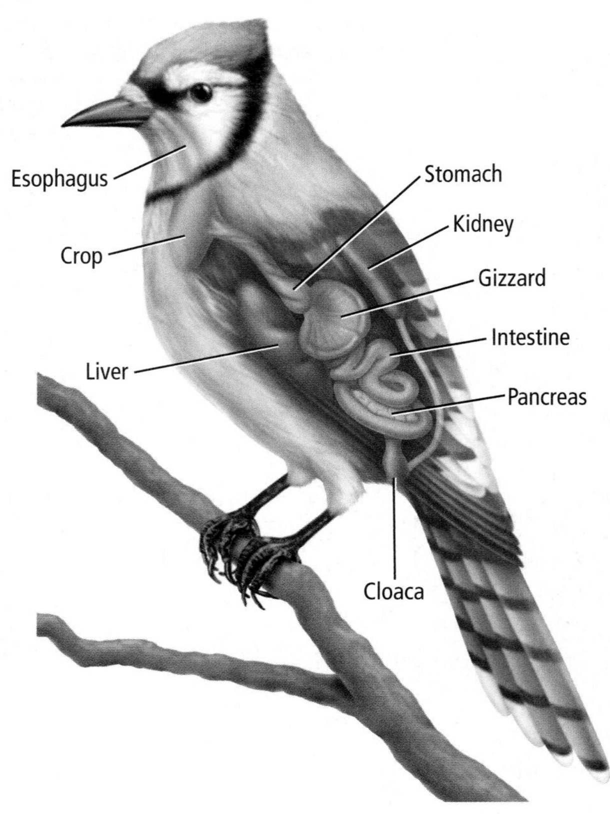

Herons use their long, thin, sharp bills to stab and capture fish and small amphibians as prey.

Hummingbirds have long, thin beaks shaped for drinking nectar from flowers.

An eagle uses its sharp beak to tear flesh from its prey.

A pelican uses its beak to scoop fish out of the water.

**Concepts In Motion** **Interactive Figure** To see an animation of feeding and digestion in birds, visit biologygmh.com.

**Biology Online**

**Feeding and digestion** Birds require large amounts of food to maintain their high metabolic rate. Once they have taken in food, birds process it with unique adaptations of their digestive systems, shown in **Figure 29.18.** Many birds have a storage chamber, called the crop, at the base of their esophagus. The crop stores food that the bird is ingesting. From the crop, food moves to the stomach. The posterior end of the stomach is a thick, muscular sac called the gizzard (GIH zurd). The gizzard often contains small stones that, together with the muscular action of the gizzard, crush food the birds have swallowed. The smaller food particles that result are easier to digest. Birds have no teeth and cannot chew their food. Digestion and absorption of food occurs primarily in the small intestine where secretions from the pancreas and liver aid the digestive process.

**Excretion** As in reptiles, bird kidneys filter wastes from the blood and convert it to uric acid. Birds also have a cloaca, shown in **Figure 29.18,** where the water is reabsorbed from the uric acid. Birds do not have urinary bladders where urine is stored. Stored urine would add weight during flight, so having no urinary bladder can be considered an adaptation for flight. Birds excrete uric acid in the form of a white, pasty substance.

**The brain and senses** The brains of birds, shown in **Figure 29.19,** are large compared to the body size of the bird. The cerebellum is large because birds need to coordinate movement and balance during flight. The optic lobes coordinate visual input. The core of the cerebrum also is large because it is the primary integrating center of the brain. This area of the brain controls eating, singing, flying, and instinctive behavior. The medulla oblongata controls automatic functions such as respiration and heartbeat.

Birds generally have excellent vision. Birds of prey, like the hawk shown in **Figure 29.19,** have a focusing system that instantaneously enables them to stay focused on moving prey as they make a dive for their food. The position of a bird's eyes on its head relates to its life habits. Birds of prey have eyes that are at the front of the head. This enables them to recognize the distance of an object because both eyes can focus on the same object. A pigeon has eyes on the sides of its head. This enables the bird to see nearly 360 degrees of the space nearby, with each eye focusing on different areas. A pigeon eats grain and seeds and does not pursue prey. Its eyesight is adapted to scout out predators that might be nearby. Birds also have a good sense of hearing. Owls can hear the faintest sound of a scurrying mouse in the night. Even as the mouse runs for cover, the owl can catch it by following just the sound.

FOLDABLES
Incorporate information from this section into your Foldable.

**LAUNCH Lab**
**Review** Based on what you've read about reptiles and birds, how would you now answer the analysis questions?

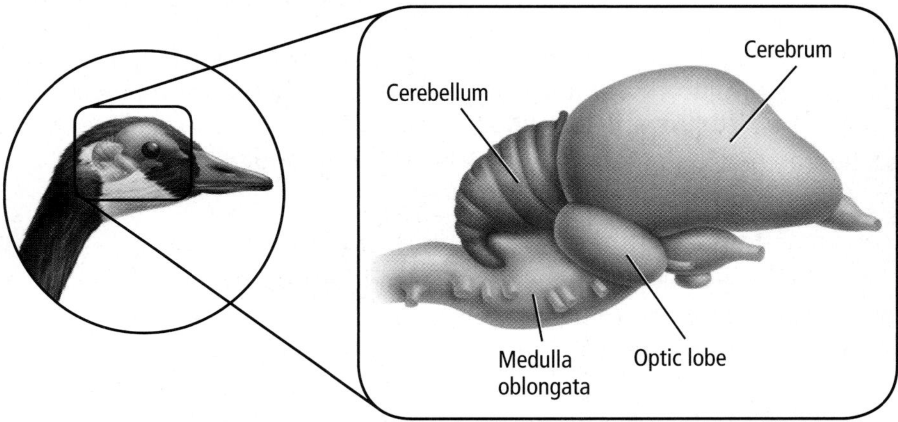

**Figure 29.19**
**Left:** Birds have large cerebellums that enable them to balance and coordinate movements. The medulla oblongata controls automatic processes.
**Right:** A hawk's eyes stay focused on moving prey as it dives.

**Reproduction** The reproductive activities of birds are complex. They include establishing territories, locating mates, courtship behavior, mating, constructing nests, incubating eggs, and feeding young. During breeding season, many birds gather in large colonies where they breed and take care of young. All birds have internal fertilization. Generally, after fertilization, the amniotic egg develops and is encased within a hard shell while still within the body of the female. After the shell forms, the egg or eggs are released through the cloaca to a nest, where the male or female or both birds incubate the egg or eggs and feed the young after hatching. To **incubate** means to maintain favorable conditions for hatching. Birds sit on their eggs to incubate them.

## Diversity of Modern Birds

Modern birds are divided into about 27 living orders, depending on the classification system used. Anatomical differences, specific behaviors, songs, and the habitats occupied distinguish the orders. In **Table 29.1,** you will study the most common orders of birds and their adaptations. The largest order of birds is the Passeriformes, which often are called perching birds or songbirds. There are more than 5000 species in order Passeriformes. Flightless birds, including ostriches, emus, and kiwis, have reduced or no wings. The kiwi, a bird about the size of a chicken found in New Zealand, lays an egg that is extremely large given the size of the bird. Some birds, such as penguins, geese, and ducks, have adaptations that allow them to swim. Penguins use their wings as paddles to swim through the water. Ducks and geese have webbed feet.

## MiniLab 29.1

### Survey Local Birds

**What birds live in your local area?** A variety of birds can be found in almost any environment. Explore the area around your school to survey the different birds that live there.

**Procedure**

1. Read and complete the lab safety form.
2. Predict the number of different kinds of birds you can observe in the area around your school. Make a data table to keep track of birds you observe.
3. Go for a 10-min walk in the area near your school. Be sure to follow your teacher's instructions about where you are allowed to go. Record information about the birds you observe. Use **binoculars** if necessary. If you cannot identify a bird, use a **field guide** for local birds.
4. Compile your findings as a class. Research information about the birds you observed.

**Analysis**

1. **Count** the number of bird species you observed. List the types of birds you observed.
2. **Identify** Were the birds you saw native to your area or have they been introduced?
3. **Analyze** Did any patterns emerge as you compiled the data?
4. **Predict** Would this list differ if you surveyed the area around your house? If so, how?

Concepts In Motion

Interactive Table To explore more about bird orders, visit biologygmh.com.

| Table 29.1 | Diversity of Bird Orders | | |
|---|---|---|---|
| **Order** | **Example** | **Members** | **Distinguishing Characteristics** |
| ***Passeriformes*** **Perching song-birds; about 5000 species** | | Thrushes, warblers, mockingbirds, crows, blue jays, nuthatches, finches | Members of this order have feet that are adapted for perching on thin stems and twigs. Many birds in this order sing. The vocal organ, called the syrinx, is well-developed in these birds. Other species, such as crows and ravens, do not sing. |
| ***Piciformes*** **Cavity-nesters; about 380 species** | | Woodpeckers, toucans, honeyguides, jacamars, puffbirds | Members of this order have highly specialized bills that are related to their feeding habits. They all build nests in cavities—for example, a hole in a dead tree. The feet have two toes that extend forward and two toes that extend backward, allowing them to cling to tree trunks. |
| ***Ciconiiformes*** **Wading birds and vultures; about 90 species** | | Herons, egrets, bitterns, storks, flamingoes, ibises, vultures | Members of this order are medium- to large-sized birds that have long necks and long legs. Most are wading birds that live in large colonies in wetlands. Vultures are closely related to storks but are detritovores. |
| ***Procellariiformes*** **Marine birds; about 100 species** | | Albatrosses, petrels, shearwaters, storm-petrels | All members of this order are marine birds. They have hooked beaks that aid in feeding on fish, squid, and small crustaceans. They all have tube-shaped nostrils located on the top of their beaks. Many have webbed feet. |
| ***Sphenisciformes*** **Penguins; about 17 species** | | Penguins | Penguins are marine birds that use their wings as flippers to swim through the water rather than fly. The bones of penguins are solid, lacking the air spaces of other birds. All species are found in the southern hemisphere. |
| ***Strigiformes*** **Owls; about 135 species** | | Owls | Owls are nocturnal birds with large eyes, strong, hooked beaks, and large, sharp talons on their feet. All of these adaptations aid in capturing prey. Many species have feathers on their legs. Owls are found worldwide except for Antarctica. |
| ***Struthioniformes*** **Flightless birds; 10 species** | | Ostriches, kiwis, cassowaries, emus, rheas | All members of this order have reduced wings and are flightless birds. The ostrich is the largest living bird, reaching a height of more than 2 m and a weight of 130 kg. All species are found in the southern hemisphere. |
| ***Anseriformes*** **Waterfowl; about 150 species** | | Swans, geese, ducks | Members of this order live in aquatic environments. They have webbed feet that aid in moving them through the water. Many have broad, round beaks. They feed on aquatic plants and sometimes crustaceans or small fish using broad, round beaks. |

■ **Figure 29.20** *Archaeopteryx* had a long, reptile-like tail, clawed fingers, teeth, and feathers. This artist's rendering of *Caudipteryx* has long feathers that might have been used for insulation and balance.

## Evolution of Birds

Fossil evidence shows that birds descended from archosaurs, the same line from which crocodiles and dinosaurs evolved, as you saw in **Figure 29.11.** Similarities between birds and reptiles are apparent. They have similar skeletal features, kidney and liver function, amniotic eggs, and behaviors such as nesting and caring for young. Discoveries of fossils of feathered dinosaurs in China support the idea that birds evolved from a group called theropod dinosaurs.

**Feathered dinosaurs** Three different species of birdlike dinosaurs from the Chinese fossil beds have been carefully studied. *Sinosauropteryx* had a coat of downy, featherlike fibers. *Protoarchaeopteryx* and *Caudipteryx,* illustrated in **Figure 29.20,** had long feathers on their front appendages and on their tails. The downy dinosaur feathers might have functioned as insulation, and the front appendage feathers might have served as balancing devices as the dinosaurs ran along the ground.

**Connection to History** In 1861, in southern Germany, paleontologist Hermann von Meyer discovered what is now known to be the oldest bird fossil—*Archaeopteryx. Archaeopteryx,* illustrated in **Figure 29.20,** lived about 150 million years ago. This ancient bird had a long reptile-like tail, clawed fingers in the wings, and teeth. These are features that modern birds do not have. Yet, like modern birds, its body was covered with feathers. The feathers were asymmetrical, like those found only in modern birds that fly. Recent fossil evidence also shows that the brain of *Archeopteryx* was much like that of modern birds.

**Recent discoveries** Two recent fossil discoveries of ancient birds, *Sinornis* and *Eoalulavis,* show that these birds had more features of modern birds. These birds lived between 135 and 115 million years ago. *Eoalulavis* had features that most likely enabled slow, hovering flight.

**CAREERS IN BIOLOGY**

**Paleontologist** Scientists who learn more about the history of life on Earth by studying fossils are paleontologists. Many paleontologists teach at colleges and conduct research in the field by uncovering fossils. Some work at museums, managing fossil exhibits. For more information on biology careers, visit biologygmh.com.

CHAPTER 29

# Assessment

## Section 29.1

### Vocabulary Review

*Each of the sentences below is false. Make the sentence true by replacing the italicized word with the correct vocabulary term from the Study Guide page.*

1. Several membranes are inside a(an) *carapace.*
2. The ventral part of a turtle's shell is called the *Jacobson's organ.*
3. The *plastron* is responsible for the sense of smell in snakes.
4. The dorsal part of a turtle's shell is the *amniotic egg.*

### Understand Key Concepts

5. Which is not a reptile?

**A.**

**C.**

**B.**

**D.**

6. Which is not true about respiration in reptiles?
   **A.** Most reptiles use lungs for gas exchange.
   **B.** As reptiles inhale, the muscles of the rib cage relax.
   **C.** As reptiles exhale, the muscle of the body wall relax.
   **D.** The lungs of reptiles have a larger surface area than those of amphibians.

7. In which structure in reptiles can uric acid be found?
   **A.** the lungs
   **B.** the cloaca
   **C.** the heart
   **D.** the stomach

8. Which statement best represents scientists' understanding of early reptiles?
   **A.** Dinosaurs evolved into modern-day reptiles such as lizards, snakes, and turtles.
   **B.** Birds and crocodiles are the closest relatives of dinosaurs.
   **C.** The earliest reptiles did not have amniotic eggs.
   **D.** Dinosaurs became extinct because they were too big.

### Constructed Response

9. **Open Ended** Make a table that lists the following structures, their functions, and an analogy of what that structure is like in the world of human-made devices: amnion, ventricle, bladder, Jacobson's organ, carapace and plastron, kidney.

10. **Open Ended** Make a dichotomous key that would allow a person to determine which order of reptile they are examining.

### Think Critically

11. **Apply Concepts** The feet of a gecko are covered by billions of tiny hairlike structures that stick to surfaces. When the hairs contact a surface, attractions between molecules bond the gecko's foot to the surface. These structures can support up to 400 times the body weight of the gecko. How could scientists use the way in which a gecko's foot sticks to surfaces to make a tool that would be useful to people?

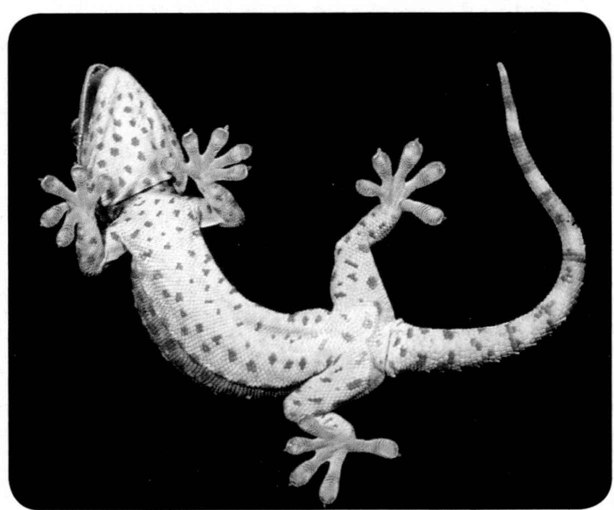

*Use the graph below to answer questions 12 and 13. The brown four-fingered skink was introduced to the Pacific island of Guam in the early 1950s.*

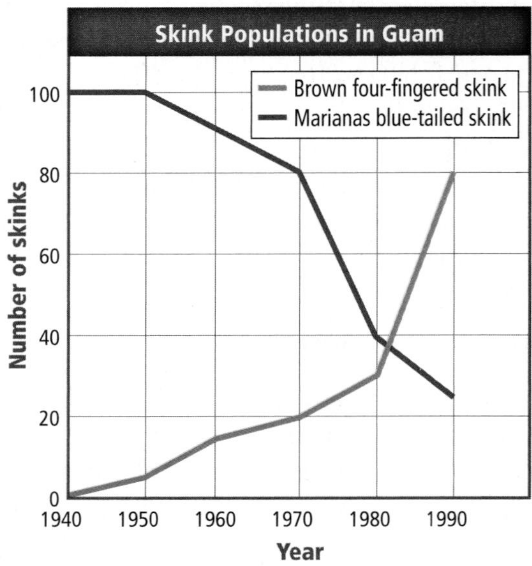


12. **Analyze Data** How have the populations of the brown four-fingered skink and the Marianas blue-tailed skink changed since the 1950s?

13. **Hypothesize** Form a detailed hypothesis that might explain the decline in population of the Marianas blue-tailed skink.

14. **Compare** How does circulation in reptiles compare to circulation in amphibians?

15. **Illustrate** Make a diagram, flowchart, concept map, or illustration that shows how the loss of habitat and the introduction of exotic species has affected the population of the San Francisco garter snake.

## Section 29.2

### Vocabulary Review

*Explain the relationship that exists between the vocabulary terms in each set.*

16. endotherm, down feather

17. contour feather, down feather

18. preen gland, contour feather

19. sternum, air sac

### Understand Key Concepts

20. Which group of words has a word that does not belong?
    - **A.** ventricle, atrium, oxygenated blood, deoxygenated blood
    - **B.** kidney, nitrogenous waste, uric acid, cloaca
    - **C.** cerebellum, cerebrum, optic lobes, medulla
    - **D.** amniotic egg, cloaca, kidney, amnion

*Use the figure below to answer question 21.*

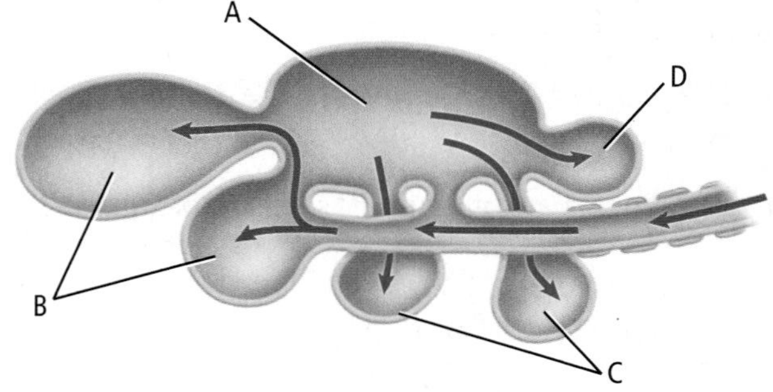


21. When a bird breathes in, oxygenated air goes into which structure(s)?
    - **A.** Structure A
    - **B.** Structure B
    - **C.** Structure C
    - **D.** Structure D

22. To which system do the kidney and cloaca belong?
    - **A.** excretory
    - **B.** nervous
    - **C.** digestive
    - **D.** reproductive

23. What type of beak would a bird need if it feeds on aquatic plants?
    - **A.** broad and flat
    - **B.** large and scooped
    - **C.** sharp and hooked
    - **D.** long, thin, and pointed

24. What does fossil evidence in dinosaurs show?
    - **A.** Dinosaurs were not related to birds.
    - **B.** Dinosaurs were not warm-blooded.
    - **C.** Dinosaurs were not flying animals.
    - **D.** Dinosaurs were not feathered.

### Constructed Response

**25. CAREERS IN BIOLOGY** Ornithologists hypothesized that the long-term memory of certain migratory birds would be better than that of nonmigrants. To test this hypothesis, two rooms were decorated—one with ivy and one with geraniums. Food was placed in only one room. Both migrant and nonmigrant birds were allowed to explore both of the rooms. One year later, the same birds were allowed to explore the rooms. Migrant birds spent significantly more time exploring the room that had contained food than the nonmigrants. Draw a conclusion about the long-term memories of these birds.

### Think Critically

**26. Hypothesize** Birds often sing at dawn. Biologists think that the birds are announcing their territories or letting potential mates know where they are. Biologists also have discovered that the larger a bird's eyes are, the earlier in the day it sings. Form a hypothesis about why eye size might be correlated to how early birds sing.

**27. Infer** Biologists know that the young of modern birds curl up their bodies in their nests to conserve body heat. Recently, fossils of dinosaurs' young have been found in a curled position in their nests. This particular line of dinosaurs is one with a direct lineage to birds. Infer what this curled-up position might mean about the bodies of these dinosaurs.

*Use the figure below to answer question 28.*

**28. Infer** What type of food does this bird eat? How does it use its beak during feeding?

## Additional Assessment

**29. WRITING in Biology** Write a summary for a yearbook page about the Ornithology Club, in which students went bird watching, recorded species, and conducted species counts.

### DBQ Document-Based Questions

*Sea snakes have highly toxic venom that they inject into prey. In many cases, the toxin paralyzes the muscles that pump water across the gills of fishes. The graph shows the rate of mortality of five species of fish when given different doses of venom from an olive sea snake.*

Data obtained from: Zimmerman, K.D., et al. 1992. Survival times and resistance to sea snake *(Aipysurus laevis)* venom by five species of prey fish. *Toxicon* 30: 259–264.

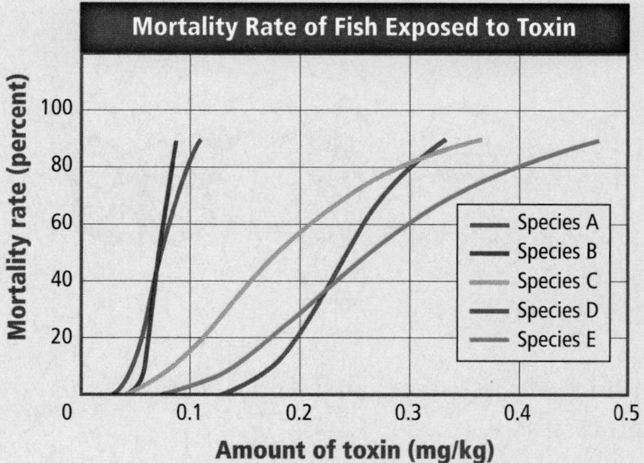


**30.** Which fish species is most affected by the venom? Which species is least affected? Explain how you know this.

**31.** The species of fish least affected by the venom have the ability to respire through their skin as well as through their gills. Why would this ability be important to surviving a bite by a sea snake?

### Cumulative Review

**32.** Sketch the four phases of mitosis in a cell with two chromosomes. **(Chapter 9)**

**33.** Explain the meaning of alternation of generations as it applies to plants. **(Chapter 21)**

# Standardized Test Practice

**Cumulative**

## Multiple Choice

1. The word *echinoderm* means "spiny skin." Which describes the skin of an echinoderm?
   - **A.** Calcium carbonate plates with spines covered with a thin skin.
   - **B.** Calcium carbonate spines that protrude through the skin.
   - **C.** Silicon plates with spines covering the entire surface.
   - **D.** Silicon spines that protrude through the skin.

*Use the figure below to answer questions 2 and 3.*

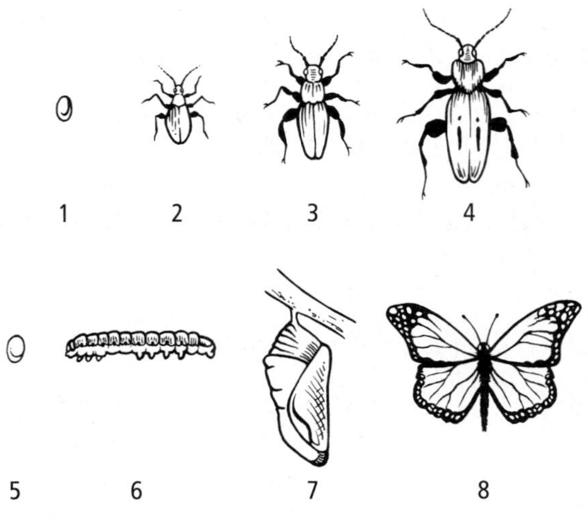


2. Which of these stages are identical between the processes?
   - **A.** 1, 5
   - **B.** 2, 7
   - **C.** 3, 8
   - **D.** 4, 7

3. During which stages do immature insects feed?
   - **A.** 1, 5
   - **B.** 1, 7
   - **C.** 2, 6
   - **D.** 4, 8

4. How do pseudocoelomates take in gases and excrete metabolic wastes?
   - **A.** Their digestive tract is used for gas exchange.
   - **B.** Gas exchange occurs through the endoderm tissue.
   - **C.** Materials diffuse through their body walls.
   - **D.** Materials exchange in the primitive respiratory system.

5. Which is a function of the lateral line system in fishes?
   - **A.** detecting chemicals in the water
   - **B.** detecting water pressure changes
   - **C.** keeping a fish upright and balanced
   - **D.** sending signals between fishes

*Use the diagram below to answer questions 6 and 7.*

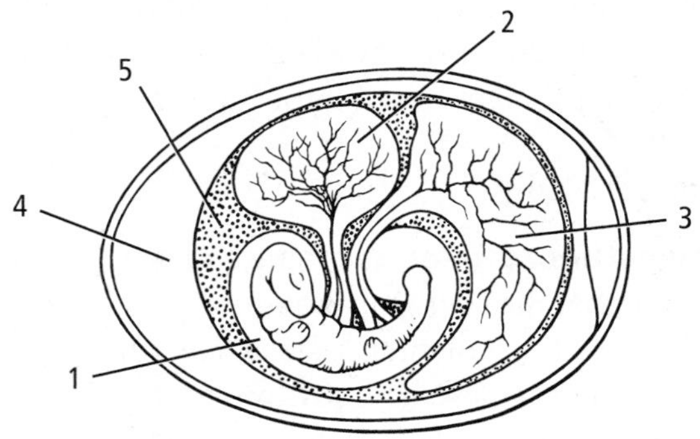


6. Which number represents the fluid-filled membrane that prevents dehydration and cushions the pictured embryo?
   - **A.** 1
   - **B.** 2
   - **C.** 4
   - **D.** 5

7. Which number represents the main food supply for the pictured developing reptile embryo?
   - **A.** 1
   - **B.** 2
   - **C.** 3
   - **D.** 4

8. Which structures are used in most adult amphibians to take in oxygen and transport it to body cells?
   - **A.** gills and a closed circulatory system
   - **B.** gills and an open circulatory system
   - **C.** lungs and a closed circulatory system
   - **D.** lungs and an open circulatory system



BiologyOnline Standardized Test Practice biologygmh.com

## Short Answer

*Use the diagram to answer questions 9 and 10.*

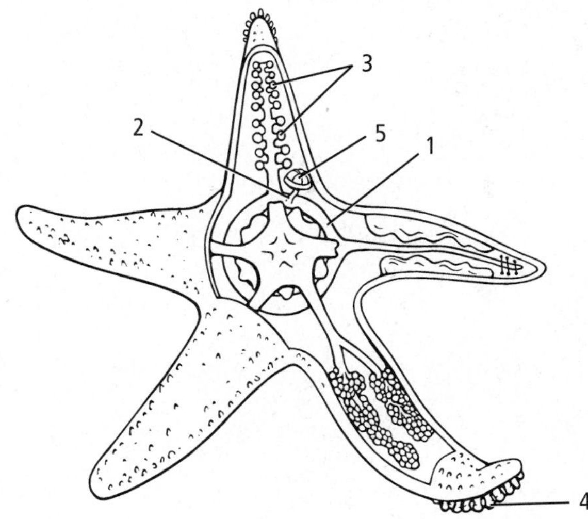


9. Name each of the numbered structures and describe how they enable a sea star to move.

10. Analyze how a sea star opens an oyster by relating the process to the above numbered structures.

11. Give a reason why most viruses are limited to attacking only a few types of cells and hypothesize why this might be important information for a medical researcher.

12. Relate evidence scientists use to propose that the lobe-finned fishes are the ancestors of the amphibians.

13. Describe how reptiles regulate their body temperature.

14. Explain why birds need an efficient respiratory system.

15. Generalize changes a tadpole goes through before becoming a frog.

## Extended Response

16. Contrast the circulatory system of a frog with the circulatory system of a fish and assess the importance of those differences.

17. Select a technology that has changed the way in which scientists learn about genetics, and describe how that technology has brought about the change.

## Essay Question

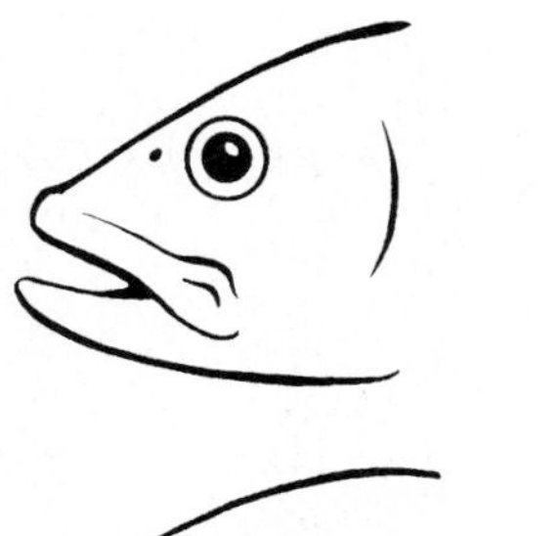

The evolution of a jaw was an important advancement in fish structure. The evolution of the jaw was a specialized adaptation for feeding. The jaw of fishes continued to evolve as fishes became more specialized in their feeding behaviors. The shape of the jaw gives important information about how a fish feeds and, in some cases, what it feeds on. By studying the different shapes of the jaw, scientists can understand how different species became adapted for their particular environments.

*Using the information in the paragraph above, answer the following question in essay format.*

18. Justify how each of these four types of jaws is suited for the food fishes eat.

| NEED EXTRA HELP? | | | | | | | | | | | | | | | | | | |
|---|---|---|---|---|---|---|---|---|---|---|---|---|---|---|---|---|---|---|
| **If You Missed Question . . .** | 1 | 2 | 3 | 4 | 5 | 6 | 7 | 8 | 9 | 10 | 11 | 12 | 13 | 14 | 15 | 16 | 17 | 18 |
| **Review Section . . .** | 27.1 | 26.3 | 26.3 | 25.1, 25.2 | 28.1 | 29.1 | 29.1 | 28.3 | 27.1 | 27.1 | 18.2 | 28.2 | 29.1 | 29.2 | 28.3 | 28.3 | 13.1 | 28.1 |

CHAPTER 30

# Mammals

### Section 1
**Mammalian Characteristics**

**MAIN Idea** Mammals have two distinct characteristics: hair and mammary glands.

### Section 2
**Diversity of Mammals**

**MAIN Idea** Class Mammalia is divided into three subgroups based on reproductive methods.

## BioFacts

- The hairs in a deer's winter coat are hollow. This helps insulate the deer against the cold and keep it afloat when moving through water.
- The hairs of a polar bear are transparent and have no color. The bears look white because the hollow hairs reflect and scatter light.
- Some red foxes actually have black fur, silver fur, or, in rare cases, both black and silver fur.

# LAUNCH Lab

## What is a mammal?

You see mammals every day—the neighborhood dog, a squirrel scampering across the grass, the people with whom you live. What characteristics do mammals share?

### Procedure

1. Read and complete the lab safety form.
2. Examine **specimens or photographs of mammals,** including the red fox shown on the opposite page.
3. Identify characteristics that the mammals in the photographs share.
4. Create a data table to record your observations.

### Analysis

1. **Infer** the function of each physical characteristic shared by mammals.
2. **Describe** the wide diversity of mammalian characteristics and behaviors using the photographs and your experiences with other mammals.
3. **Infer** how scientists would use different characteristics to classify mammals into specific groups.

Visit biologygmh.com to:

- study the entire chapter online
- explore Concepts in Motion, Interactive Tables, Microscopy Links, and links to virtual dissections
- access Web links for more information, projects, and activities
- review content online with the Interactive Tutor, and take Self-Check Quizzes

**Mammalian Subclasses** Make the following Foldable to help you compare the characteristics of mammals in each subgroup.

**STEP 1** Fold a sheet of notebook paper into thirds.

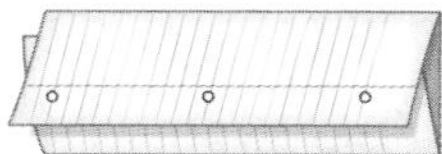

**STEP 2** Fold the paper down 2.5 cm from the top.

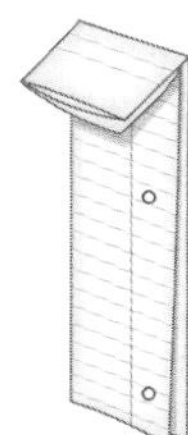

**STEP 3** Open and draw lines along the 2.5-cm fold. Write the following labels on the tabs: Monotremes, Marsupials, and Placentals.

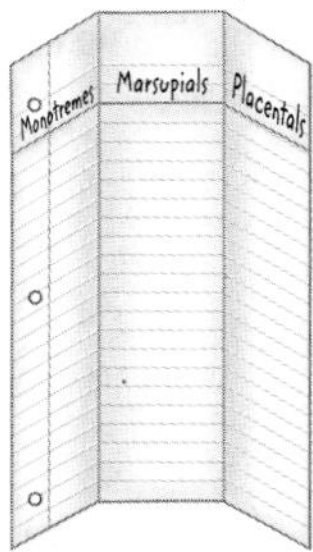


FOLDABLES **Use this Foldable with Section 30.2.** As you read the section, record what you learn about the characteristics of mammals in each subgroup, and use the information to compare and contrast each.

Section 30.1

# Mammalian Characteristics

**Objectives**

- **Identify** characteristics of mammals.
- **Describe** how mammals maintain a constant temperature to achieve homeostasis.
- **Distinguish** how respiration in mammals differs from that of other vertebrates.

**Review Vocabulary**

**metabolic rate:** the rate at which all the chemical reactions that occur within an organism take place

**New Vocabulary**

mammary gland
diaphragm
cerebral cortex
cerebellum
gland
uterus
placenta
gestation

MAIN Idea **Mammals have two distinct characteristics: hair and mammary glands.**

**Real-World Reading Link** Think about the characteristics of the other classes of vertebrates you have studied. Think about how you are different from the animals in the other classes. The characteristics you have as a mammal allow you to carry out your daily life functions and activities.

## Hair and Mammary Glands

Two characteristics that distinguish members of class Mammalia from other vertebrate animals are hair and mammary glands. **Mammary glands** produce and secrete milk that nourishes developing young. Recall that if an animal has feathers, it is a bird. In a similar way, if an animal has hair, it is a mammal. As you can see on the evolutionary tree in **Figure 30.1,** mammals have their own branch labeled *hair and mammary glands.*

**Functions of hair** Mammals' hair has several functions, including:

1. Insulation—One of the most important functions of hair is to insulate against the cold. Mammals benefit from having fur or hair that traps their body heat and prevents it from escaping.
2. Camouflage—The striped coat of a Bengal tiger allows it to blend into its natural habitat—the jungle.
3. Sensory devices—In some cases, hair has been modified into sensitive whiskers. Seals use the whiskers on their snouts to track prey in murky water by sensing changes in water movements when a fish is nearby.
4. Waterproofing—You might know how cool it feels when you come out of a swimming pool on a hot day. As the water evaporates from your skin, your body loses heat. Many aquatic mammals, such as the sea otter shown in **Figure 30.2,** have hair that keeps water from reaching their skin. This helps them maintain their body temperature.

■ **Figure 30.1** Hair and mammary glands are two characteristics that distinguish mammals from other vertebrates.

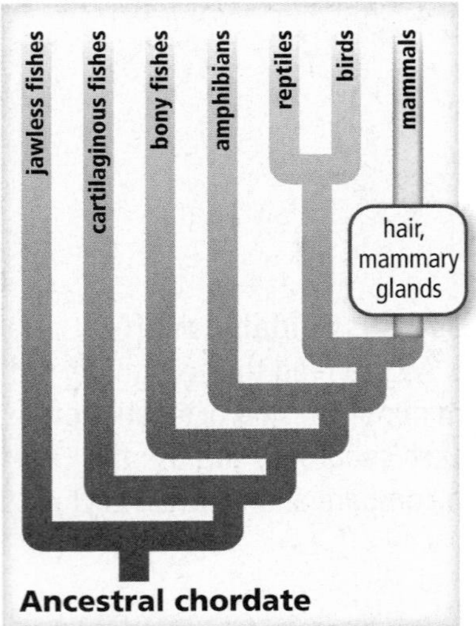


■ **Figure 30.2** The hair covering this sea otter helps keep water from reaching its skin.

Signaling

Defense

■ **Figure 30.3**
**Left:** The white hair on the tails of these deer signal them to follow each other as they run from predators.
**Right:** The quills of a porcupine are modified hairs that are used as protection from predation.

5. Signaling—Hair can function as a signaling device. The white-tailed deer in **Figure 30.3** raise their tails, the undersides of which are white, when they run so that other deer can follow.
6. Defense—Hair also can function as a defense against predators. The porcupine in **Figure 30.3** has sharp quills, which are modified hairs, that are easily detached when the animal is threatened by a predator. The quills stick to and stab predators that touch the porcupine.

**Structure of hair** The hair in a bushy fox tail and the hair on your head contains a tough, fibrous protein called keratin, which is a protein that also makes up nails, claws, and hooves. A coat of hair usually consists of two kinds of hair—long guard hairs that protect a dense layer of shorter insulating underhair. The air trapped in the thick underhair layer provides insulation against the cold and retains body heat.

 **Reading Check** **Explain** why hair is important to mammals.

## Other Characteristics

In addition to having hair and mammary glands, mammals share other characteristics. These include a high metabolic rate, which supports endothermy, specialized teeth and digestive systems, a diaphragm to aid in respiration, a four-chambered heart, and a highly developed brain.

**Endothermy** Mammals are endotherms, which means they produce their body heat internally. The source of body heat is internal—the result of heat produced by a high metabolic rate. Body temperature is regulated by internal feedback mechanisms that send signals between the brain and sensors throughout the body.

For example, when some mammals become warm as a result of exertion or because the air is warm, sweat glands in the skin are stimulated to secrete sweat that evaporates from the skin. As the sweat evaporates, it draws heat away from the body and cools it. When body temperature lowers, sweating stops. For other mammals that do not sweat, panting cools the body. You might have seen a dog panting in the summer's heat. During panting, water evaporates from the mouth and nose. Because mammals can regulate their body temperatures internally to maintain homeostasis, they can live in a range of ecosystems from the frigid temperatures of polar regions to the sweltering heat of deserts and the tropics.

*Study Tip*

**Prediction** Preview this section by looking at the bold titles and the photos. Predict the distinguishing characteristics of mammals. Use the titles and photos to help anticipate how to take notes on this section.

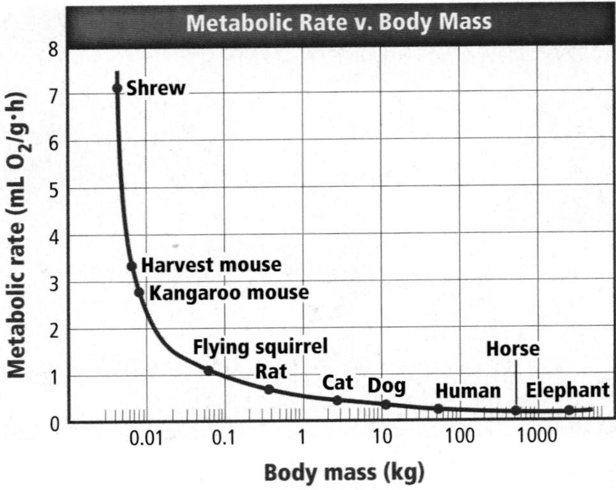


**Figure 30.4** Due to their high metabolic rates, some small mammals, such as mice and shrews, must eat food masses that are equivalent to their body masses each day in order to maintain temperature homeostasis.

**Analyze** ***Approximately how much food (in kg) does a shrew have to eat each day to survive?***

**CAREERS IN BIOLOGY**

**Mammalogist** The branch of biology that focuses on the study of mammals is mammalogy. A mammalogist might research the behavior, anatomy, or ecology of one or more species of mammal, or he or she can compare characteristics, such as digestion, in many species of mammals. For more information on biology careers, visit biologygmh.com.

**Feeding and digestion** Maintaining an endothermic metabolism requires large amounts of energy. Mammals get the energy they need from the breakdown of food. Much of an endotherm's daily intake of food is used to generate heat to maintain a constant body temperature.

Examine the graph in **Figure 30.4.** The graph shows the relationship of a mammal's metabolic rate to its body mass. Small mammals, including shrews, bats, and mice, have a high metabolic rate relative to their body mass. As a result, these small mammals must hunt and eat food almost constantly in order to fuel their metabolisms.

**Trophic categories** Mammalogists divide mammals into four trophic categories based on what they eat:

1. Insectivores, such as moles and shrews, eat insects and other small invertebrates.
2. Herbivores, such as rabbits and deer, feed on vegetation.
3. Carnivores, such as foxes and lions, mostly feed on herbivores.
4. Omnivores, such as raccoons and most primates, feed on both plants and animals.

A mammal's adaptations for finding, capturing, chewing, swallowing, and digesting food all influence the mammal's structure and life habits. The fibers of plants are more difficult to digest and take longer than the digestion of meat. As a result, mammals that eat plant material have a larger cecum and longer digestive tracts than those that eat meat, as shown in **Figure 30.5.**

**Ruminant herbivores** Cellulose, a component of the cell walls of plants, can be a source of nutrition and energy. However, the enzymes in the digestive system of mammals cannot digest cellulose. Instead, some herbivores have bacteria in the cecum—a pouch where the small intestine meets the large intestine. Other herbivores have bacteria in their stomachs that break down the cellulose and release nutrients the animals can use. These mammals, called ruminants, have large, four-chambered stomachs. Cattle, sheep, and buffalo are all ruminants. As a ruminant feeds, plant material passes into the first and second stomach chambers. Plants are partially digested by bacteria into a material called cud. The ruminant brings the cud back up into the mouth and chews the cud for a long period of time. This further crushes the grass fibers. Once the cud is swallowed, it eventually reaches the fourth chamber of the stomach where digestion continues.

**Reading Check** **Infer** the type of relationship that exists between a ruminant and the bacteria in its stomach.

# Visualizing the Digestive Systems of Mammals

**Figure 30.5**
The digestive systems of mammals are adapted to maximize the digestion and absorption of food. The protein consumed by carnivores and insectivores is readily digestible. Plant materials contain cellulose, which resists digestion, water, and some carbohydrates. Compare the structure of each digestive system below.

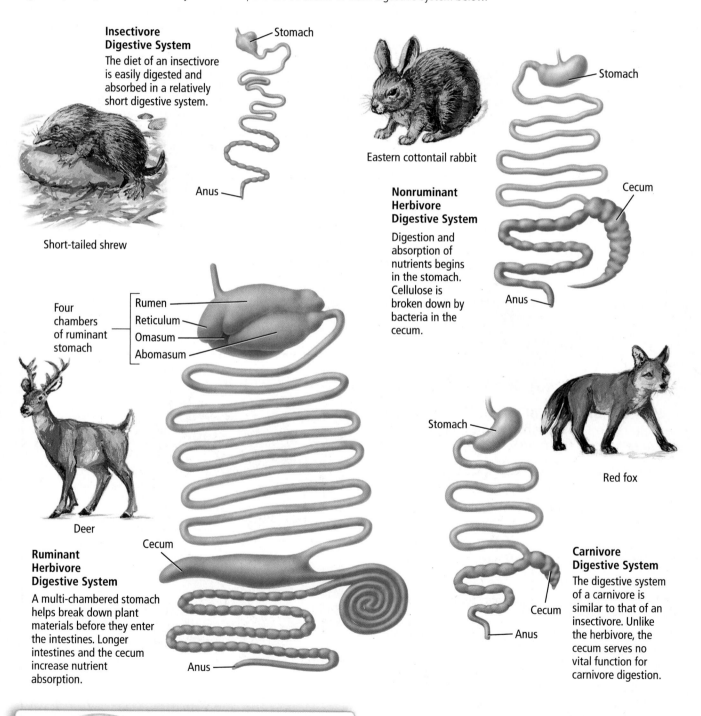

**Insectivore Digestive System**
The diet of an insectivore is easily digested and absorbed in a relatively short digestive system.

Stomach
Anus

Short-tailed shrew

Eastern cottontail rabbit

**Nonruminant Herbivore Digestive System**
Digestion and absorption of nutrients begins in the stomach. Cellulose is broken down by bacteria in the cecum.

Stomach
Cecum
Anus

Four chambers of ruminant stomach
Rumen
Reticulum
Omasum
Abomasum

Deer

Cecum
Anus

**Ruminant Herbivore Digestive System**
A multi-chambered stomach helps break down plant materials before they enter the intestines. Longer intestines and the cecum increase nutrient absorption.

Red fox

Stomach
Cecum
Anus

**Carnivore Digestive System**
The digestive system of a carnivore is similar to that of an insectivore. Unlike the herbivore, the cecum serves no vital function for carnivore digestion.

**Concepts In Motion** Interactive Figure To see an animation of mammal digestion, visit biologygmh.com.
**Biology Online**

**VOCABULARY**

**ACADEMIC VOCABULARY**

**Retain:**
to keep in possession or use.
*You can retain your teeth throughout adulthood by brushing and flossing.*

**Teeth** In addition to adaptations of the digestive system, teeth, perhaps more than any other physical characteristic, reveal the life habits of a mammal. Generally, in fish and reptile species, all teeth in the mouth look very much alike. This is because these animals use all their teeth in similar ways—for seizing prey or for tearing prey apart before swallowing. In contrast, mammals have different types of teeth that are specialized for various functions. Examine the four types of mammalian teeth—canines, incisors, premolars, and molars—illustrated in **MiniLab 30.1** below.

A fox's canines are long and sharp. Carnivores use canines to stab and pierce their prey. The canines of herbivores often are reduced in size. This is illustrated in the cow skull shown in **MiniLab 30.1.** The premolars and molars of carnivores are used to slice and shear meat from the bones of their prey, while crushing and grinding are the functions of premolars and molars in herbivores. The incisors of insectivores are long and curved, functioning as pincers in seizing insect prey. The chisel-like incisors of beavers are modified for gnawing. Because the teeth of mammals reflect their feeding habits, biologists can determine what a mammal eats by examining its teeth. Complete **MiniLab 30.1** to see what inferences you can make about a mammal's diet based on its teeth.

**Excretion** The kidneys of mammals excrete metabolic wastes and maintain the homeostatic balance of body fluids. Kidneys filter urea, an end product of cellular metabolism, from the blood. Mammalian kidneys excrete or retain the proper amount of water in body fluids as well. Kidneys enable mammals to live in extreme environments, such as deserts, because they can control the amount of water in body fluids and cells.

## MiniLab 30.1

### Compare Mammalian Teeth

**How are the teeth of mammals specialized?**
Explore how the teeth of different mammal species are related to their diets.

**Procedure**

1. Read and complete the lab safety form.
2. Observe **teeth from the skulls of different mammal species.**
3. List the similarities and differences among the teeth of the different mammal species.

**Analysis**

1. **Infer** the function of each type of tooth based on its shape.
2. **Identify** the type of tooth common to all of the mammals you studied.
3. **Describe** how each mammal you studied uses its teeth to obtain and ingest food.
4. **Explain** how scientists might use the differences in mammalian teeth to classify mammals into different groups.

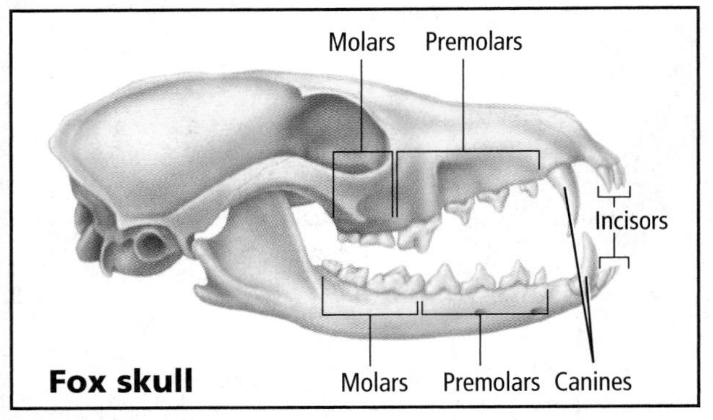

**Fox skull**

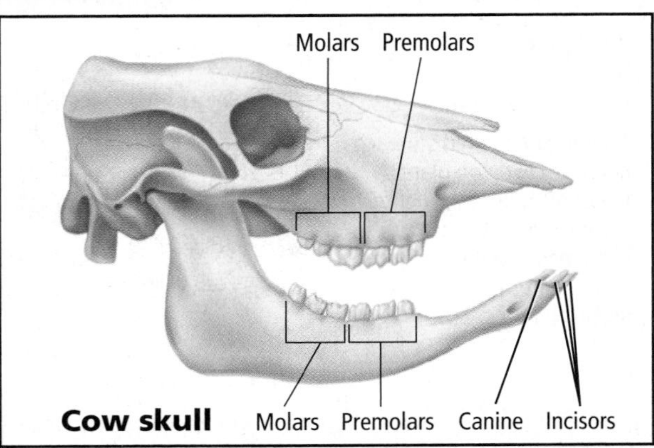

**Cow skull**

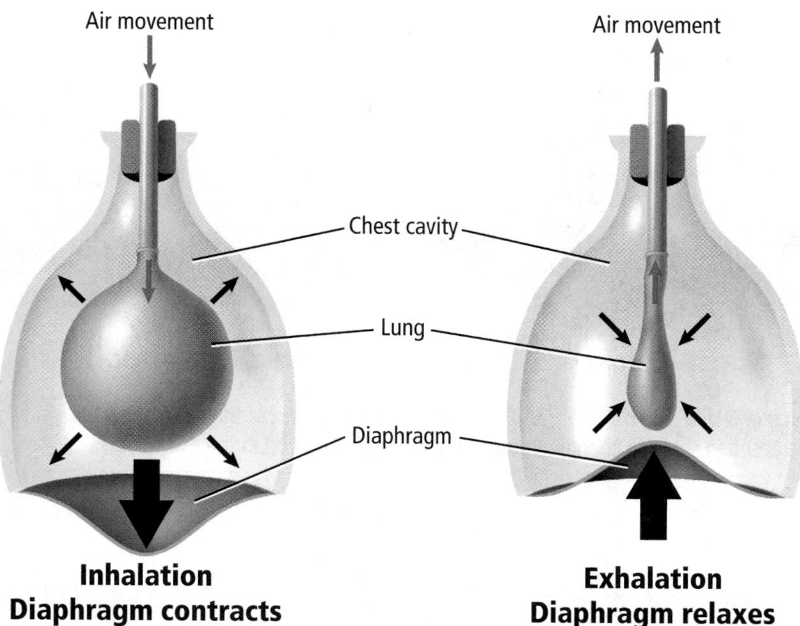


**Figure 30.6** The flask with the balloon is an analogy of how the diaphragm aids breathing in mammals.
**Describe** ***What happens to the chest cavity as the diaphragm contracts and relaxes?***

**Respiration** The food a mammal eats is used to maintain high energy levels. High levels of oxygen also are required to maintain a high level of metabolism. Oxygen is taken into the lungs of mammals during respiration. Although other animals, such as birds and reptiles, have lungs, mammals are the only animals that have a diaphragm. A **diaphragm** is a sheet of muscle located beneath the lungs that separates the chest cavity from the abdominal cavity where other organs are located. As the diaphragm contracts, it flattens, causing the chest cavity to enlarge, as shown in **Figure 30.6.** Once air enters the lungs, oxygen in the air moves by diffusion into blood vessels. When the diaphragm relaxes, the chest cavity becomes smaller and air is exhaled.

**Circulation** Once oxygen is in the blood, vessels carry it to the heart, which pumps it out to the body. Like birds, mammals have a four-chambered heart. Also as in birds, oxygenated blood is kept entirely separate from deoxygenated blood in mammals. This is illustrated in **Figure 30.7.** Because most mammals are physically active and all are endotherms—they require a consistent supply of nutrients and oxygen to maintain homeostasis. Keeping oxygenated and deoxygenated blood separate makes the delivery of nutrients and oxygen more efficient.

**Connection to Physics** The circulatory system of a mammal also functions to help maintain a constant internal temperature. When body temperature increases, the blood vessels near the surface of the skin dilate, or expand, and deliver more blood than usual. Heat moves from the blood to the surface of the skin by conduction. At the skin's surface, heat is lost from the body by radiation and the evaporation of sweat. When body temperature decreases, blood vessels near the surface of the skin contract and do not deliver as much blood as usual. This action reduces the loss of body heat.

**Reading Check** **Describe** how the respiratory system of mammals is different from other animals.

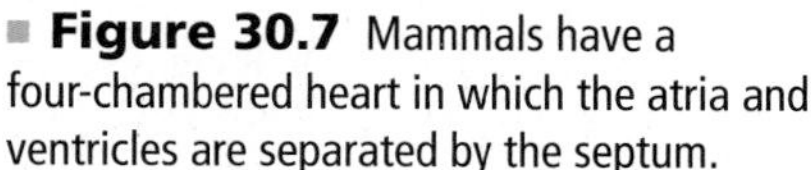

**Figure 30.7** Mammals have a four-chambered heart in which the atria and ventricles are separated by the septum.

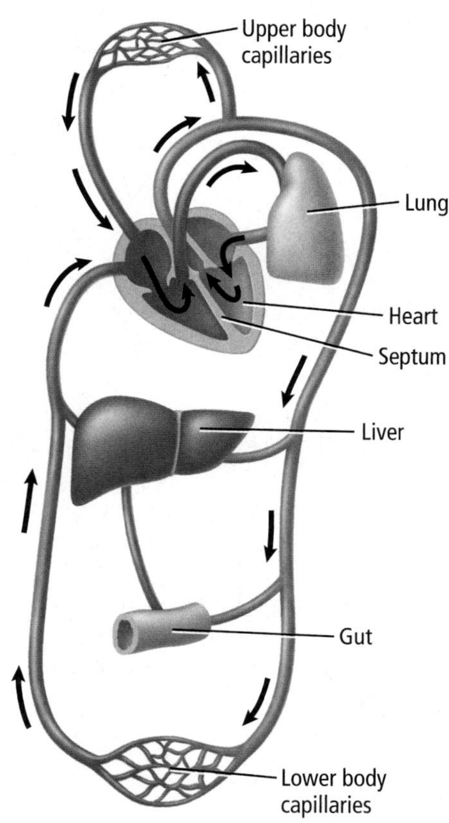

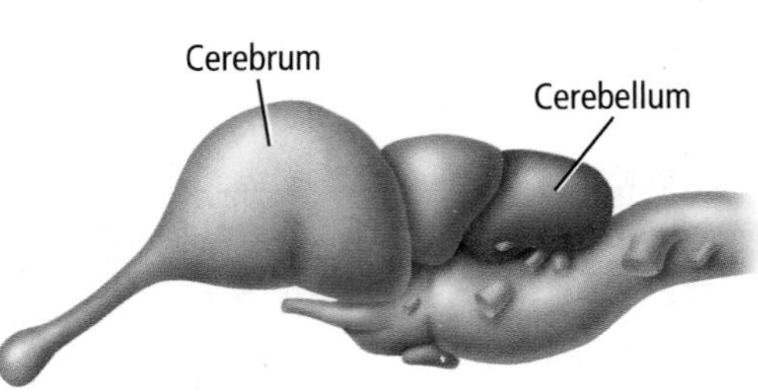

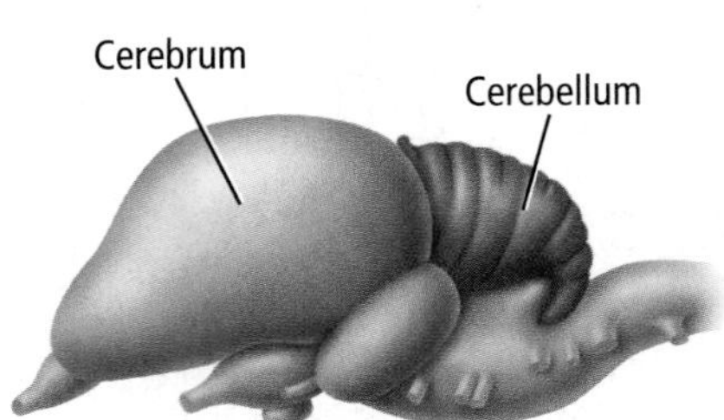

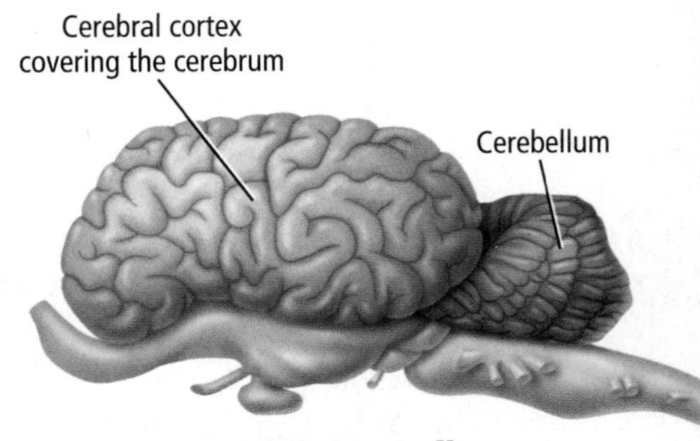


**Figure 30.8** The cerebral cortex is the most complex part of the brain and is the part that has increased in size and changed most during the course of vertebrate evolution.

**The brain and senses** Mammals have highly developed brains, especially the cerebrum. The **cerebral cortex,** shown in **Figure 30.8,** is the highly folded outer layer of the cerebrum. The foldings allow the brain to have a larger surface area for nerve connections while allowing it to still fit inside the skull. The cerebral cortex is responsible for coordinating conscious activities, memory, and the ability to learn.

Another area of the mammalian brain that is well developed is the cerebellum. The **cerebellum** is responsible for balance and coordinating movement. Compare the size and structure of the cerebellums of a reptile, a bird, and a mammal that are shown in **Figure 30.8.** A well-developed cerebellum allows an animal to have precise motor movements and to make complex movements in three dimensional space.

**Complex behavior** The mother fox referred to at the beginning of the chapter eventually will teach her young to hunt. Because mammals can learn and teach their young survival skills, they have an increased chance of survival. Mammals can carry out complex behaviors, such as learning and remembering what they have learned. Many mammals can get information about their environment and retain it. This information can then be used later. For example, mice that have had a chance to explore a habitat are able to avoid predators better than mice that have not had a chance to explore and learn about the same habitat.

**Senses** The importance of the senses varies from one group of mammals to the next. In some mammals, such as humans, vision is extremely important, while hearing is most important to mammals such as bats. Bats produce high-frequency sounds that bounce off objects and return to them. In this way a bat can detect objects in its path. This process is called echolocation. If you have seen how a dog sniffs people and objects in its surroundings, you recognize the importance of the sense of smell to this mammal. In some cases, a dog's sense of smell is one million times more sensitive than a human's sense of smell.

**VOCABULARY**

**SCIENCE USAGE V. COMMON USAGE**

**Sense**

***Science Usage:*** a specialized animal function that involves a sense organ and a stimulus.
*Dogs use their sense of smell to get information about their environments.*

***Common Usage:*** an intended meaning.
*As I read the paragraph, I tried to get a sense of the main idea.*

 **Reading Check** **Use an analogy** to describe the advantage of having folds in the outer layer of the cerebral cortex.

**Glands** A system of glands secretes a variety of fluids that helps to regulate a mammal's internal environment. A **gland** is a group of cells that secrete fluid to be used elsewhere in the body. Sweat glands help maintain body temperature. Mammary glands produce and secrete milk that nourishes developing young. Milk contains water, carbohydrates in the form of the sugar lactose, fat, and protein. The proportion of these nutrients differs according to species.

Examine **Table 30.1** to see the proportions of nutrients in the milk of various mammals. The proportion of nutrients is highly variable among different species of mammals. For example, fat amounts can range from one percent to 50 percent. Aquatic mammals, which use a layer of fat to help keep warm, usually have the highest percent of fat in their milk.

Scent glands produce substances that mammals use to mark their territories or attract mates. Oil glands in the skin maintain the quality of the animal's hair and skin. Other glands produce hormones that regulate internal processes, such as growth and release of eggs from ovaries.

**Reading Check** **Explain** why the fat content in milk would be higher in aquatic mammals.

**Reproduction** In mammals, the egg is fertilized internally. In most mammals, development of the embryo takes place in the female uterus. The **uterus** is a saclike muscular organ in which embryos develop. In most mammals, the developing embryo is nourished by the **placenta,** an organ that provides food and oxygen to and removes waste from the developing young. The gestation period is specific for particular species. **Gestation** is the amount of time the young stay in the uterus before they are born. Gestation periods in mammals can vary—the shortest being that of the Virginian opossum which can be only 12 days. The longest gestation period occurs in the African elephant, which is an average of 660 days and can be as long as 760 days. In general, the larger the mammal, the longer the gestation period. After birth, the offspring of mammals drink milk for nourishment from the mother's mammary glands.

**Vocabulary**

**Word Origin**

**Gestation**

***gest–*** from the Latin word *gestare,* meaning *to bear*

***–ation*** suffix; from Latin meaning *action* or *process.*

**Table 30.1** **Proportion of Nutrients in the Milk of Mammals**

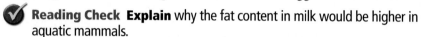

**Concepts In Motion** Interactive Table To explore more about nutrients in milk, visit biologygmh.com.

| Nutrient | Dog | Dolphin | Harp Seal | Rabbit | Zebra |
|---|---|---|---|---|---|
| Water | 76.3 | 44.9 | 43.8 | 71.3 | 86.2 |
| Protein | 9.3 | 10.6 | 11.9 | 12.3 | 3.0 |
| Fat | 9.5 | 34.9 | 42.8 | 13.1 | 4.8 |
| Sugar | 3.0 | 0.9 | 0.0 | 1.9 | 5.3 |

**Limbs used for digging and burrowing**

**Limbs used for flying**

**Figure 30.9**
**Left:** The mole has powerful, short forelimbs that are adapted for digging and burrowing in the ground.
**Right:** The bat can fly with thin membranes spread between the elongated arm and hand bones.

**Movement** Mammals must find food, shelter, and escape from predators. They have evolved a variety of limb types that enable them to carry out these essential behaviors. Some mammals, such as coyotes and foxes, run. The fastest land mammal—the cheetah—can reach speeds as fast as 110 km/h.

Other mammals, such as kangaroos, leap. Some mammals, including dolphins, swim. Bats are the only mammals that fly. The structure of the skeletal and muscular systems in animals reflects the type of movement that an animal uses. Examine **Figure 30.9,** which shows the forelimbs of a mole and those of a bat. How does the structure of these limbs reflect the habitat and behavior of these animals?

## Section 30.1 Assessment

### Section Summary

- Mammals are successful in a wide variety of habitats.
- Mammals have specialized teeth.
- Respiratory, circulatory, and nervous systems have complex adaptations that enable mammals to have the extra energy they need and to maintain homeostasis.
- Mammals have internal fertilization and, in most mammals, offspring develop within the female uterus.

### Understand Main Ideas

1. MAIN Idea **List** two characteristics unique to mammals.
2. **Explain** how mammals maintain a constant body temperature.
3. **Classify** the mammals that live in your area as herbivores, carnivores, omnivores, or insectivores.
4. **Summarize** how the respiratory and circulatory systems of mammals work together to enable mammals to have high energy levels.
5. **Compare and contrast** how respiration occurs in mammals to respiration in birds. Use **Figure 30.6** and **Figure 29.16** for reference.

### Think Scientifically

6. *Hypothesize* A sperm whale's clicking sound is one of the loudest sounds produced by any animal. The larger the whale, the louder the sound it can make. Form a hypothesis that explains why the whale might produce this sound.
7. **MATH in Biology** Suppose a hare spotted a coyote and tried to run away. Coyotes can run at a speed of 70 km/h. Hares can run at a speed of 65 km/h. How far could the hare run before the coyote catches up? Assume that the hare is 25 m from the coyote.



Biology Online **Self-Check Quiz** biologygmh.com

# Diversity of Mammals

### Objectives

- **Examine** the characteristics of mammals in each of the three subgroups of living mammals.
- **Distinguish** adaptations that contribute to the diversity of mammals and enable them to live in a variety of habitats.
- **Theorize** about the evolution of mammals.

### Review Vocabulary

**chromosome:** cell structure that carries genetic material that is copied and passed from generation to generation of cells

### New Vocabulary

monotreme
marsupial
placental mammal
therapsid

**MAIN Idea** **Class Mammalia is divided into three subgroups based on reproductive methods.**

**Real-World Reading Link** Think about the mammals you see every day, such as dogs or squirrels. They are only a small part of the 4500 living species of mammals found on Earth. Scientists have developed zoos and wild animal parks that offer opportunities to learn about and enjoy the great variety of mammal species found in the world today.

## Mammal Classification

Class Mammalia is divided into three subgroups based on methods of reproduction—monotremes, marsupials, and placental mammals.

**Monotremes** The animal shown in **Figure 30.10** with its duck bill and webbed feet might not look like any mammal you have seen. However, it has hair and mammary glands, which makes it a mammal. The duck-billed platypus is a monotreme that lays eggs similar to those of reptiles. **Monotremes** are mammals that reproduce by laying eggs. The only other living monotremes besides the duck-billed platypus are echidnas. An adult echidna and an echidna egg are shown in **Figure 30.10.** Both the duck-billed platypus and the echidna only live in Australia, Tasmania, and New Guinea. Besides laying eggs, other reptilian features of these mammals include similarities in bone structure in the shoulder area, lower body temperature than most mammals, and a unique mix of normal-sized chromosomes, mammal-sized chromosomes, and small, reptilelike chromosomes.

**Reading Check** **Identify** how monotremes are different from other subgroups of mammals.

**Figure 30.10** The echidna, like the duck-billed platypus, is an egg-laying mammal. Once an egg hatches, the offspring receive nourishment from the mother's mammary glands.

**Duck-billed platypus**

**Echidna**

**Echidna hatching from egg**

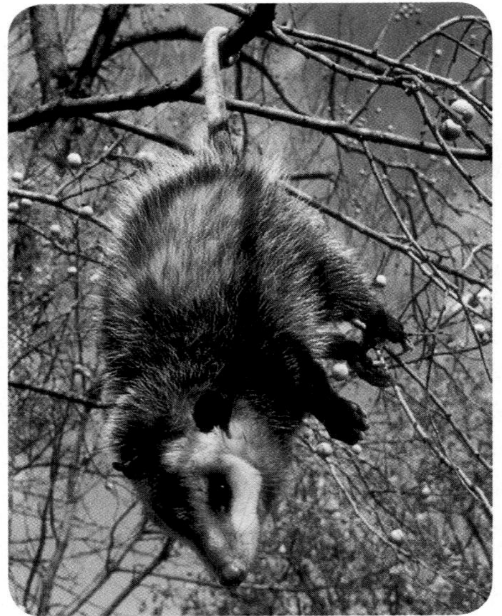

■ **Figure 30.11** Opossums are the only marsupials in North America. Most opossums spend much of their time in the trees.

**Marsupials** Pouched mammals that have a very short period of development in the uterus are **marsupials.** Immediately following birth, the offspring crawl into a pouch made of skin and hair on the outside of the mother's body. Within the pouch, the offspring continue development while being nourished by milk from the mother's mammary glands. In some species of marsupials, offspring are born and crawl into the mother's pouch only eight days after fertilization occurs.

The only North American marsupial is the opossum, shown hanging by its tail in **Figure 30.11.** Other marsupials include the koala, wallaby, kangaroo, and cuscus, some of which are shown in **Figure 30.12.** Australia and its nearby islands are home to most marsupials.

**Connection to Earth Science** Why marsupials are limited mostly to Australia is still a subject for debate among scientists. Based on fossil evidence, marsupials originated in North America, then spread to South America and Europe while the continents still were connected as one giant land mass. From South America, marsupials moved across Africa to Antarctica then to Australia. Then, about 200 million years ago, the continents separated due to the movement of Earth's plates. This isolated the ancestors of today's marsupials to Australia and nearby islands.

Australian marsupials thrived because they were isolated from competing placental mammals. In North and South America, however, placental mammals had competitive adaptive advantages. For example, placental mammals evolved highly social behavior, had more variety in food sources, and evolved greater diversity in form and function than marsupials.

Marsupials in Australia and New Guinea fill the niches occupied by placental mammals elsewhere in the world. For example, kangaroos are the grazers in Australia. They fill the niche that deer, antelope, and buffalo fill in other areas of the world.

■ **Figure 30.12** The cuscus is a nocturnal marsupial that is found in northern Australia and New Guinea. The red kangaroo has a development period of only 33 days, after which the newborn begins nursing in the pouch.

**Cuscus**

**Baby red kangaroo**

**Red kangaroo**

Humpback whale

Pygmy shrew

**Figure 30.13**
The humpback whale, weighing 100,000 kg, is one of the largest mammals. The pygmy shrew, weighing 1.5 g, is one of the smallest mammals. Notice the size of the pygmy shrew by comparing it to the size of the earthworm it is eating.

**Placental mammals** Most mammals living today, including humans, are placentals. The **placental mammals** are mammals that have a placenta, the organ that provides food and oxygen to and removes waste from developing young. Placental mammals give birth to young that do not need further development within a pouch.

Placental mammals are represented by 18 orders. Some orders are represented only by a few species. For example, there are only two species of flying lemurs in order Dermoptera. Flying lemurs can glide through the air because a flap of skin connects their arms and legs. The aardvark, a termite-eating mammal found in Africa, is the only species in its order. Other orders, such as Rodentia, which includes squirrels and rats, have almost 2000 species. Sizes of placental mammals range from 1.5-g pygmy shrews to 100,000-kg whales, both of which are shown in **Figure 30.13.** Their forms range from marine dolphins with adaptations for swimming to moles adapted for subterranean life and bats equipped with wings and ultrasonic echolocation for flying in the dark.

Scientists have hypothesized several reasons why there are greater numbers and kinds of placental mammals compared to marsupials. One hypothesis is that marsupial young must cling to their mother's fur at birth. Limbs, therefore, are limited in their ability to evolve into structures such as the flippers and wings of some placental mammals. Another hypothesis that explains the success of placental mammals points out that the cerebral cortex of placental mammals is larger and more complex than that of marsupials. This might be due to the more stable, oxygen-rich environment they experience inside the uterus. According to this hypothesis, this might have enabled placental mammals to develop more complex social behaviors that led to their success.

 **Reading Check** **Identify** how placental mammals differ from marsupials.

FOLDABLES
Incorporate information from this section into your Foldable.

LAUNCH Lab
**Review** Based on what you've read about mammal classification, how would you now answer the analysis questions?

**Order Insectivora—shrew**

**Order Chiroptera—flying fox**

■ **Figure 30.14** Shrews are members of order Insectivora. The flying fox is a bat that is a member of order Chiroptera.

**Order Insectivora** As the name implies, these mammals' main food source is insects. The shrew, shown in **Figure 30.14,** is an insectivore, as are hedgehogs and moles. Members of order Insectivora usually are small and have pointed snouts that allow them to capture insects easily. Shrews include the smallest of all mammals. Shrews can be found in almost all parts of the world and spend most of their lives underground.

**VOCABULARY**

**ACADEMIC VOCABULARY**

**Modify:**
to make changes that result in a new purpose
*The wings of a bat are modified forelimbs for flying.*

**Order Chiroptera** There are about 925 species in order Chiroptera (ky RAHP ter uh)—all of which are bats. As mentioned previously, bats are the only mammals that truly can fly. Their wings are thin membranes supported by modified forelimbs. Bats feed on a variety of foods. Some eat insects, some eat fruit, and others feed on blood. The most common North American bat is the little brown bat which you might have seen swooping and darting at dusk to catch insects. The flying fox, shown in **Figure 30.14,** is the largest of all bats. It lives in tropical regions worldwide and feeds on fruit.

**Order Primates** Monkeys, apes, and humans are all examples of primates. Primates' brains, with large cerebral hemispheres, are the most developed brains of all mammals. Most primates are tree dwellers. This leads scientists to hypothesize that the need to perform complex movements while in trees, such as those involved in capturing food and avoiding enemies, led to advances in the brain structure of primates. Primate forelimbs often are adapted for grasping, and most have nails instead of claws. The golden lion tamarin in **Figure 30.15** is grasping with its hands the branch on which it is sitting.

■ **Figure 30.15** Golden lion tamarins are omnivores that live in the coastal forests of Brazil.
**Identify** ***other animals that are members of order Primates.***

**Order Xenarthra** Animals in order Xenarthra (zen AR thra) either have no teeth or have simple, peglike teeth. Anteaters, like the one shown in **Figure 30.16,** are toothless. Anteaters have a spiny tongue and sticky saliva that allow them to easily capture ants and termites in their nests. Sloths and armadillos both have peglike teeth. Sloths mostly feed on leaves, and armadillos feed on insects. Most mammals in this order live in Central America and South America with the exception of the armadillo, which also can be found in the southern United States.

Giant anteater

Beaver

**Figure 30.16** The giant anteater, the largest anteater, is found throughout Central and South America. The largest rodent is the beaver, weighing as much as 80 kg.
**Describe** ***the characteristics of members of order Xenarthra.***

**Order Rodentia** These gnawing mammals in order Rodentia, called rodents, include the beaver, which is shown in **Figure 30.16,** rats, woodchucks, marmots, squirrels, hamsters, and gerbils. Rodents make up nearly 40 percent of all mammalian species. Two pairs of razor-sharp incisor teeth continue to grow throughout the life of a rodent. They use their sharp teeth to gnaw through wood, seed pods, or shells to get food. The ability of rodents to invade all land habitats and their successful reproductive behavior have made them ecologically important in all terrestrial ecosystems.

**Order Lagomorpha** Like rodents, members of the the order Lagomorpha—rabbits, pikas, and hares—have long sharp incisors that continue to grow. Lagomorphs also have a pair of peglike incisors that grow behind the first pair. These mammals are herbivores that eat grasses, herbs, fruits, and seeds. The pika shown in **Figure 30.17** lives in high latitude or high altitude environments in which the ground is covered with snow for parts of the year. The grasseaters adapt to these conditions by harvesting grass during the warm months and storing it. The pikas then eat the grass during the winter when no fresh vegetation is available.

**VOCABULARY**
**WORD ORIGIN**
**Lagomorpha**
***lago–*** from the Greek word *lagos,* meaning *hare.*
***–morph,*** from the Greek word *morphe,* meaning *form.*

**Order Carnivora** You might have a pet dog or cat. It, along with wolves, bears, seals, walruses, coyotes, skunks, otters, minks, and weasels, belongs to the order Carnivora. All of these carnivores are predators with teeth adapted to tearing flesh. The lioness, shown in **Figure 30.17,** feeds on antelope, giraffes, and even crocodiles. After she captures her prey, she uses her incisors to tear off chunks of meat.

**Figure 30.17** The American pika can be found in alpine regions of the western U.S. and southwestern Canada. The lioness uses her canines to stab and pierce her prey.

Pika

Lionness

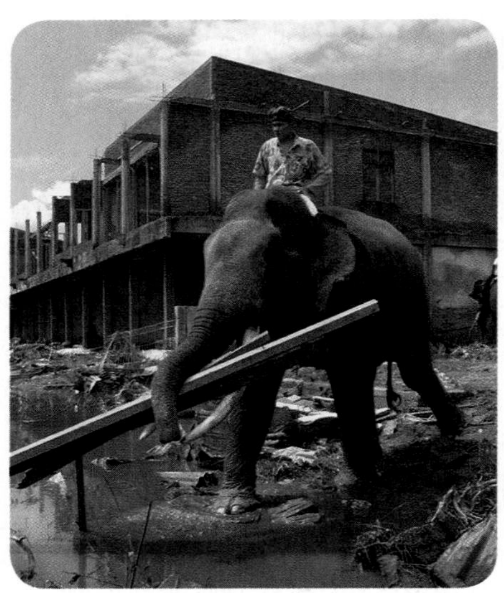

■ **Figure 30.18** The trunk of an elephant is called a proboscis. Trunks are unique to members of order Proboscidea.

**Order Proboscidea** Elephants are the largest living land mammals. They have flexible trunks adapted for gathering plants and taking in water. Two upper incisors are modified as tusks for digging up roots and tearing bark from trees. Some elephants are trained to help lift heavy objects. The elephant shown in **Figure 30.18** is helping remove debris that washed ashore during a tsunami in Indonesia on December 26, 2004. Ancient mastodons and mammoths are the extinct relatives of today's African and Asian elephants.

**Order Sirenia** Manatees and dugongs—members of the order Sirenia—are large, slow-moving mammals with big heads and no hind limbs. Their forelimbs are modified into flippers that aid in swimming. These animals are herbivores, feeding on seagrasses, algae, and other aquatic plants. Depending on their size, manatees can consume as much as 50 kg of vegetation per day. Sirenians can be found cruising the surface of warm tropical rivers and lagoons. Because they are so slow and prefer the surface of the water, they often are injured or killed by the propellers of speedboats. Notice the scars on the back of the manatee in **Figure 30.19.**

**Order Perissodactyla** These hoofed mammals include horses, zebras, and rhinoceroses. Members of this order have an odd number of toes, either one or three on each foot. These mammals are herbivores and have teeth that are adapted for grinding plant material. Perissodactyls can be found on all continents except Antarctica.

**Reading Check** **Compare** placental mammals using **Table 30.2.**

Concepts In Motion
**Interactive Table** To explore more about placental mammals, visit biologygmh.com.

**Table 30.2 Orders of Placental Mammals**

| Order | Example | Characteristics |
|---|---|---|
| **Insectivora** | Shrews, hedgehogs, moles | Pointed snouts, smallest mammals, live underground, insect-eaters |
| **Chiroptera** | Bats | Nocturnal, use sonar, adapted for flight, fruit and insect-eaters |
| **Primates** | Monkeys, apes, humans | Binocular vision, large brains, most are tree-dwellers, opposable thumb |
| **Xenarthra** | Anteaters, sloths, armadillos | Toothless or peg-like teeth, insect-eaters |
| **Rodentia** | Beavers, rats, woodchucks, marmots, squirrels, hamsters, and gerbils | Sharp incisor teeth, plant-eaters |
| **Lagomorpha** | Rabbits, pikas, hares | Back legs longer than front legs, adapted to jumping, incisors that continually grow |
| **Carnivora** | Dogs, cats, wolves, bears, seals, walruses, coyotes, skunks, otters, minks, and weasels | Teeth adapted to tear flesh, meat-eaters |
| **Proboscidea** | Elephants | Long trunks, incisors become long tusks, largest land animal |
| **Sirenia** | Manatees and dugongs | Slow moving, big heads, no hind limbs |
| **Perissodactyla** | Horses, zebras, rhinoceroses | Hoofed, odd number of toes, plant-eaters |
| **Artiodactyla** | Deer, antelopes, cattle, sheep, pigs, goats, hippopotamuses | Hoofed, even number of toes, plant-eaters that chew cud |
| **Cetacea** | Whales, dolphins, porpoises | Front limbs that are flippers, no hind limbs, nostril forms a blowhole |

Manatee

Humpback whale

■ **Figure 30.19** The West Indian manatee is endangered. Wildlife managers help rescue manatees that have been injured by boat propellers. The baleen of a whale is similar to a sieve.

**Order Artiodactyla** Members of the order Artiodactyla also are hoofed mammals. They differ from perissodactyls in that they have an even number of toes, either two or four, on each limb. Deer, antelopes, cattle, sheep, pigs, goats and hippopotamuses are all artiodactyls. Many cattle, sheep, and deer have horns or antlers. Mammals in this order are herbivorous and most chew their cud.

**Order Cetacea** Whales, dolphins, and porpoises have front limbs modified into flippers that aid in swimming. They have no hind limbs and the tail consists of fleshy flukes. Nostrils are modified into a single or double blowhole on top of the head. Except for a few muzzle hairs, their bodies are hairless. Some whales are predators. Others, like the blue whale, have a specialized structure inside their mouths called a baleen that is used to filter plankton for food. The baleen of a humpback whale is shown in **Figure 30.19.**

## DATA ANALYSIS LAB 30.1

Based on Real Data*

### Analyze and Conclude

**How does boat noise affect whales?** Killer whales might coordinate their cooperative hunting and other social behavior with certain calls that have meaning to the pod, or group, of whales with which they travel. The number of boats in the area of study increased by about five times from 1990–2000.

#### Data and Observations

Biologists examined the duration of whales' calls in three different pods for several years. Examine the graphs to the right.

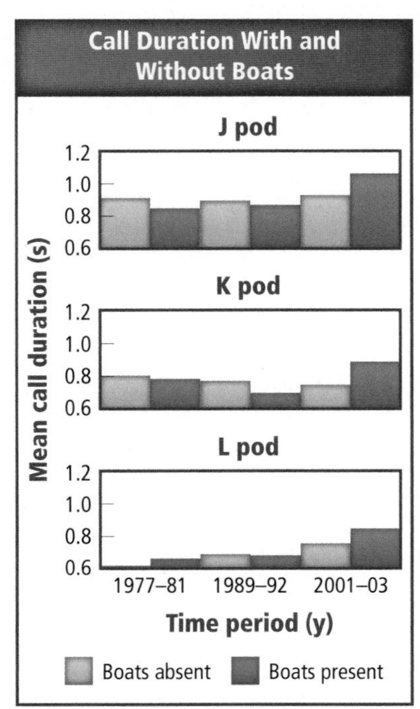


#### Think Critically

1. **Evaluate** the trend in call duration of whales in J, K, and L pods from 1977 to 2003. What might account for this trend?
2. **Hypothesis** Form a hypothesis that describes what the researchers were investigating in this study.

*Data obtained from: Foote, A., et al. 2004. Whale-call response to masking boat noise. *Nature* 428: 910.

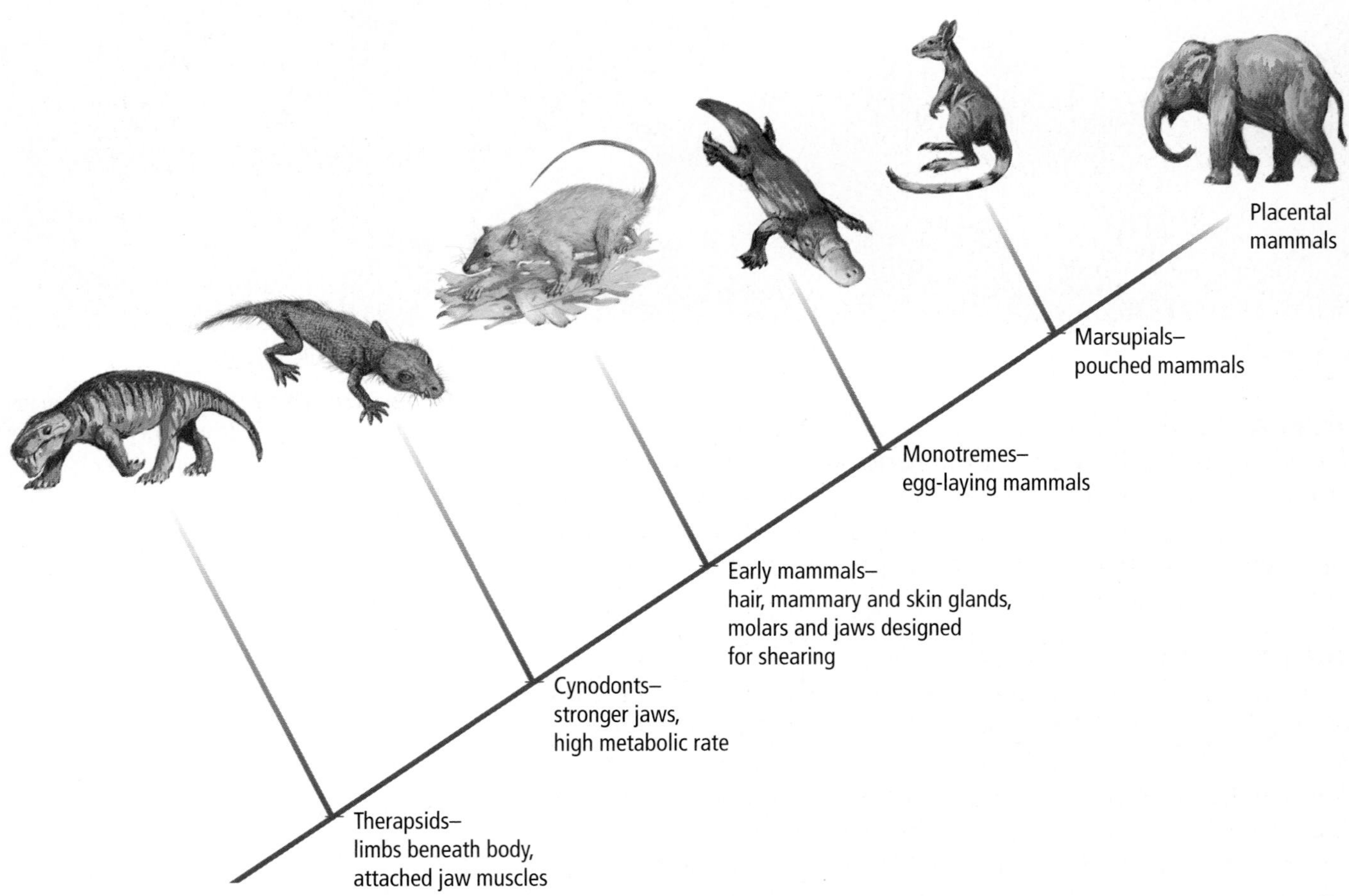


**Figure 30.20** Fossil evidence has enabled scientists to make this cladogram that reflects the phylogeny of the orders of living placental mammals.
**Interpret** ***Which present-day mammals have been on Earth longest?***

## Evolution of Mammals

The first mammals probably evolved from reptiles in the mid-Triassic period about 220 million years ago. A few lived side by side with the dinosaurs, but mammals did not become common until the dinosaurs disappeared. The cladogram in **Figure 30.20** shows one interpretation of the evolution of mammals.

**Therapsids** Fossil evidence indicates that the first mammals probably arose from a group of mammal-like reptiles called therapsids. A **therapsid** is an extinct vertebrate with both mammalian and reptilian features. Therapsids had some characteristics of mammals today, including a pair of holes in the roof of the skull that allowed for the attachment of jaw muscles. Therapsids also had limbs positioned beneath their bodies that allowed for more efficient movement.

Evidence shows that therapsids might have been endotherms. They ate more food than their ancestors, which might have provided them with the energy to produce their own body heat. Being endothermic would have given therapsids an advantage over other ectothermic vertebrates in that they would have been able to be more active during the winter. Therapsids went extinct about 170 million years ago. One group of therapsids called cynodonts continued to evolve more mammalian characteristics, including a high metabolic rate, stronger jaws, and a structure in the mouth that allowed them to breathe while holding food or nursing. A cynodont is shown in **Figure 30.21.**

**Cynodont**

***Eomaia***

**Figure 30.21** Cynodonts were animals that had some characteristics of mammals and were about the size of a weasel. *Eomaia* is the oldest placental mammal fossil discovered.

**The Age of Mammals** According to fossil evidence, the first placental mammals might have been mouse-sized animals such as *Eomaia*, shown in **Figure 30.21.** During the time when dinosaurs ruled Earth, mammals might have scurried about the forest floor at night and remained hidden during the day. When dinosaurs disappeared at the end of the Mesozoic Era, mammals underwent extraordinary adaptations to the environment. As flowering plants flourished, new sources of nutrition and new habitats became available. Mammals had new environments to fill. For example, fast-moving herbivores and their predators evolved to fill the niches in the drier prairies. The huge expansion in mammalian diversity and numbers led some scientists to call the Cenozoic Era the "Age of Mammals."

## Section 30.2 Assessment

### Section Summary

- Of the three subgroups of mammals, only the members of one lay eggs.
- The members of one of the mammalian subgroups have pouches in which the young spend most of their development time.
- Placental mammals have young that are nourished by the placenta as they develop in the uterus.
- Mammals might have evolved from reptilian ancestors called therapsids.
- There was a huge expansion in the diversity of mammals in the Cenozoic era.

### Understand Main Ideas

1. MAIN Idea **Name** the three subgroups of mammals and describe their features.
2. **Identify** the order or orders to which the following mammal might belong and explain your reasoning: it has reddish-brown fur, two pairs of incisors in the upper jaw (one pair behind the other), claws, a body that is a little smaller than a basketball, and it can jump easily.
3. **Compare and contrast** the characteristics of mammals in order Perissodactyla to those in order Artiodactyla.
4. **Explain** how mammals might have evolved from reptiles.

### Think Scientifically

5. *Hypothesize* The bill of a platypus can detect the electrical fields of muscle contraction of other animals. This is how the platypus searches for prey. Form a hypothesis about how this complicated adaptation developed in place of simply searching visually for prey.
6. WRITING in Biology Some people have the misconception that marsupials are inferior to placental mammals. Analyze and explain the faulty reasoning of this idea.

# Biology & Society

## Canine Helpers

Picture Trixie, a mixed-breed dog, who was alone with her owner who just had a stroke. The man was paralyzed and unable to leave his bed. Trixie went to the door, opened the door, and barked on the porch to get attention for her owner. The neighbors heard Trixie bark, came over and saw the owner needed medical attention. Trixie had saved her owner's life.

**Pack animals** Dogs were domesticated approximately 14,000 years ago and began to diverge from the wolf about 135,000 years ago. Because wolves are pack animals and dogs evolved from wolves, dogs behave like pack animals. When a dog becomes a member of a human family, it often interprets the family as part of its pack. Helping, protecting, and saving members of the pack from harm are part of a dog's behavior.

**The sense of smell** A dog's sense of smell is much more sensitive than a human's sense of smell. A dog has 200 million scent receptors compared to 5 million in humans. Dogs routinely are used to help locate drugs, explosives, and missing people. Certified avalanche dogs are used to help locate people who have been buried by avalanches. The dogs can locate people buried in up to 5 m of snow. An avalanche dog can cover an area the size of a football field and up to 36 m of snow depth in 30 min. It would take five people with probes 15 h to cover the same volume of space.

**Sensing cancer** Dogs also are used to detect the presence of cancerous tumors in a person. In a recent research study, dogs were able to recognize the presence of bladder cancer by sniffing patients' urine. In this experiment, the dogs were trained to lie down when they detected cancerous cells in a urine sample.

This dog, a member of the Transportation Security Administration Explosive Detection Canine Team, is sniffing luggage for explosives.

There is some evidence that dogs also can detect skin cancer by detecting odors given off by cancerous moles. Currently, studies are under way in which dogs are being tested to see if they can detect lung cancer and prostate cancer. Dogs may be able to provide an early detection system that medical science has yet to achieve.

**Sensing seizures** Some dogs also can sense when a person might be about to have a seizure. Seizure alert dogs are used to help warn people who have a seizure disorder of an impending seizure anywhere from 15 minutes to 12 h before the seizure. This can allow people time to take anti-seizure medication, call for help, or move to a safe place. Currently, the belief is that these dogs sense a change in the facial expression or sense that something is different about the rhythm of the person's personality.

### COMMUNITY SERVICE

**Contact** a retirement community near your school to see if it has a pet therapy program. Find out more about how the program works. Find out if your class could assist with the program to learn more about how pets assist senior citizens. For more information about pet therapy, visit biologygmh.com.

# BIOLAB

## INTERNET: HOW DO WE IDENTIFY MAMMALS?

**Background:** **The physical characteristics that all mammals share, such as fur and mammary glands, have enabled them to adapt to nearly every ecosystem in the biosphere. Mammals thrive in rain forests, deserts, and polar regions, and they have adapted to the environment near your home or school as well.**

**Question:** *What diversity of mammals can be found in your area?*

### Materials

North American mammal identification field guide
binoculars
field journal

### Safety Precautions

### Procedure

1. Read and complete the lab safety form.
2. List the mammals you have observed in your area of the country.
3. Predict how these species of mammals would be classified.
4. Design and construct a data table for recording the species; physical characteristics, such as size, body shape, and unique features; and taxonomic classifications of the mammals you have observed.
5. Research the mammals to fill in information in your data table. Either observe the animals in their natural habitat in your local area, such as a park or wetlands, or visit the zoo. If you cannot observe the animals in their natural habitats, obtain information about local mammals from a guide book.
6. Record your observations in your field journal and transfer the information to your data table.
7. Post your results at biologygmh.com.

### Analyze and Conclude

1. **Describe** basic characteristics shared by all mammals that you have observed.
2. **Compare and contrast** the mammals from your study to those of other students around the country.
3. **Compare and contrast** the physical characteristics scientists could use to separate the mammals into different taxonomic orders.
4. **Infer** how the mammals from your list have adapted to and survived in their environments.
5. **Describe** other observation strategies that could be used to conduct a more comprehensive mammal search of your chosen search area.
6. **Error Analysis** Compare your list of identified mammal species with the lists compiled by other students to determine possible identification errors.

### POSTER SESSION

**Make a Presentation** Collect photographs of the mammals from another area of the country and create a poster to present to your class. Include information about the specific characteristics and adaptations of each mammal. To find out more about mammals, visit biologygmh.com.

# CHAPTER 30 Study Guide

Download quizzes, key terms, and flash cards from biologygmh.com.

FOLDABLES **Hypothesize** Only three species of monotremes are living today—one species of duck-billed platypus, and two species of echidna. Form a hypothesis that explains why this subgroup of mammals has low diversity compared to the diversity of marsupials and placental mammals.

| Vocabulary | Key Concepts |
|---|---|
| **Section 30.1 Mammalian Characteristics** | |
| • cerebellum (p. 886)<br>• cerebral cortex (p. 886)<br>• diaphragm (p. 885)<br>• gestation (p. 887)<br>• gland (p. 887)<br>• mammary gland (p. 880)<br>• placenta (p. 887)<br>• uterus (p. 887) | **MAIN Idea** Mammals have two distinct characteristics: hair and mammary glands.<br>• Mammals are successful in a wide variety of habitats.<br>• Mammals have specialized teeth.<br>• Respiratory, circulatory, and nervous systems have complex adaptations that enable mammals to have the extra energy they need and to maintain homeostasis.<br>• Mammals have internal fertilization and, in most mammals, offspring develop within the female uterus.<br> |
| **Section 30.2 Diversity of Mammals** | |
| • marsupial (p. 890)<br>• monotreme (p. 889)<br>• placental mammal (p. 891)<br>• therapsid (p. 896) | **MAIN Idea** Class Mammalia is divided into three subgroups based on reproductive methods.<br>• Of the three subgroups of mammals, only the members of one lay eggs.<br>• The members of one of the mammalian subgroups have pouches in which the young spend most of their development time.<br>• Placental mammals have young that are nourished by the placenta as they develop in the uterus.<br>• Mammals might have evolved from reptilian ancestors called therapsids.<br>• There was a huge expansion in the diversity of mammals in the Cenozoic era.<br> |



Biology Online Vocabulary PuzzleMaker biologygmh.com

CHAPTER 30 # Assessment

## Section 30.1

### Vocabulary Review

*In the analogies that follow, one of the words is missing. Complete each analogy by filling in the blank with a vocabulary term from the Study Guide page.*

**1.** A yolk is to a bird as a __________ is to a mammal.

**2.** Incubation period is to a bird as a __________ period is to a mammal.

**3.** The nucleus is to the cell as the __________ is to the brain.

### Understand Key Concepts

*Use the diagram below to answer questions 4 and 5.*

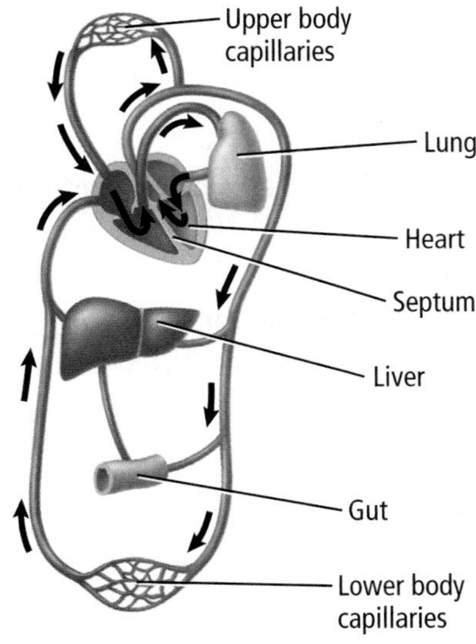


**4.** Which body system is illustrated in the diagram?
**A.** excretory system
**B.** skeletal system
**C.** circulatory system
**D.** reproductive system

**5.** Which best explains how this system supports endothermy in mammals?
**A.** Oxygenated blood is separated from deoxygenated blood.
**B.** The heart has three chambers and is able to pump more blood.
**C.** This system moves oxygenated blood to the lungs.
**D.** This system moves deoxygenated blood from the heart to the body.

**6.** Which is the least involved in maintaining homeostasis in mammals?
**A.** kidneys
**B.** heart
**C.** sweat glands
**D.** claws

**7.** Oil glands, sweat glands, and mammary glands are responsible for which functions?
**A.** hair and skin maintenance, temperature regulation, milk production
**B.** reproduction, hair and skin maintenance, temperature regulation
**C.** temperature regulation, milk production, reproduction
**D.** milk production, oxygen delivery, hair and skin maintenance

*Use the diagram below to answer questions 8 and 9.*

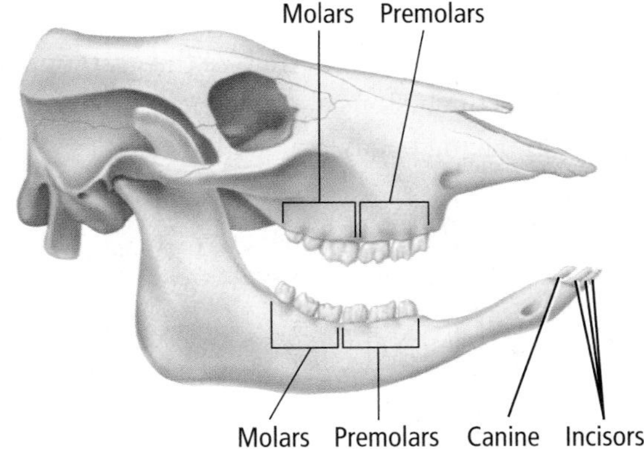


**8.** In what way did having a variety of tooth types contribute to the presence of mammals in all habitat types?
**A.** They could eat a variety of foods.
**B.** They could hunt effectively.
**C.** They could digest their food more easily.
**D.** Their digestive tracts were modified.

**9.** In which trophic category does this mammal belong?
**A.** herbivore
**B.** insectivore
**C.** carnivore
**D.** detritivore

### Constructed Response

**10. Open Ended** Examine **Table 30.1** and form a hypothesis that explains why there are such big differences in the fat content of seal milk, dolphin milk, and milk of other mammals.

11. **Open Ended** Many animals that live in the Arctic have large bodies with short extremities, such as ears and legs. Explain how this adaptation might help them keep warm.

### Think Critically

12. **Design an Experiment** Hippopotamuses secrete a fluid from glands deep in their skin that may function as sweat but can have other functions as well. Biologists hypothesize that this fluid might act as a sunscreen for the skin of the hippopotamus. Design an experiment using beads that absorb ultraviolet light that would test if the fluid on the skin of this mammal provides protection from the Sun.

13. **Analyze and Conclude** Biologists hypothesized that carnivores with large home range sizes, when in captivity in small spaces, had higher incidences of pacing behavior. They studied the arctic fox, the polar bear, and the lion. Analyze the graph below and make conclusions about the effect of confinement on pacing behavior.

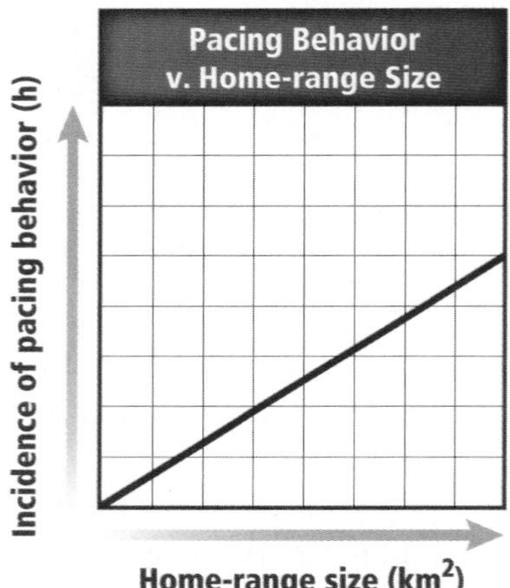


## Section 30.2

### Vocabulary Review

*Each of the following sentences is false. Make the sentence true by replacing the italicized word with a vocabulary term from the Study Guide page.*

14. An elephant is an example of a *marsupial.*

15. Mammals might have evolved from *monotremes.*

16. *Therapsids* are egg-laying mammals.

17. *Monotremes* are mammals that have a pouch.

### Understand Key Concepts

18. Which mammal is a member of order Cetacea?
    - **A.** beaver
    - **B.** whale
    - **C.** zebra
    - **D.** manatee

19. Which is a benefit of the development of young within a uterus?
    - **A.** Young are born alive.
    - **B.** Predation of the young is less likely.
    - **C.** Predation of the young is more likely.
    - **D.** Young are more fully developed at birth.

20. Which mammal is not a marsupial?
    - **A.** opossum
    - **B.** kangaroo
    - **C.** echidna
    - **D.** wallaby

21. Which is not a characteristic of the duck-billed platypus?
    - **A.** webbed feet
    - **B.** egg-laying ability
    - **C.** three-chambered heart
    - **D.** small, reptilelike chromosomes

22. Examine **Figure 30.20.** Which mammal evolved first?
    - **A.** elephant
    - **B.** opposum
    - **C.** echidna
    - **D.** blue whale

### Constructed Response

23. **Open Ended** Sketch and explain the ideal adaptations of a mammal that lives in 1-m deep marsh water, much underwater vegetation, and predatory snakes.

24. **Open Ended** Suggest reasons why you should study the orders of mammals.

25. **Open Ended** Arrange for a debate in your class about the use of animals for testing medicines and cosmetics. Visit biologygmh.com to do your research.

## Think Critically

26. **Infer** Fossil evidence indicates that mammals lived at the same time as dinosaurs for many millions of years. During this time, mammals were very small compared to the dinosaurs. Infer why it might have been an advantage for mammals to remain so small when dinosaurs roamed Earth.

27. **CAREERS IN BIOLOGY** Find out what mammals are endangered in your area. Assume that you will be the zookeeper responsible for providing and maintaining a space for a new animal that is locally endangered and will be kept on exhibit at the zoo. Design a space, feeding routine, and other care instructions for maintaining this animal in your local zoo. Prepare a sign for the space that will alert people of the importance of protecting this endangered species and ways in which individuals can participate in conservation measures.

28. **Research** Select your favorite group of mammals. Make a map that shows its world distribution. Reflect on ecological factors that might currently be limiting its potential range or might affect the group in the future. Make recommendations about what should be done to insure the success of your favorite mammal group.

*Use the table below to answer question 29.*

**Birth Weight and Protein Content of Milk**

| Mammal | Days Needed to Double Birth Weight | Protein Content of Milk (g/1000) |
|---|---|---|
| Human | 180 | 12 |
| Horse | 60 | 26 |
| Cow | 47 | 33 |
| Pig | 18 | 37 |
| Sheep | 10 | 51 |
| Cat | 9 | 101 |

29. **Analyze Data** Explain the relationship between the number of days it takes to double birth weight and the protein content of milk. Make a graph of this table.

## Additional Assessment

30. WRITING in **Biology** Visit biologygmh.com to research which mammal genomes have been sequenced. Write a summary paragraph describing what you learned.

### DBQ Document-Based Questions

*A specific type of ground squirrel was found to have the ability to produce ultrasonic calls that could not be heard by other mammals as well as calls that could be heard (audible). Biologists exposed ground squirrels to the ultrasonic call, background noise, a tone similar to the ultrasonic calls, and an audible call. Then they observed the portion of time the animals spent in vigilant behavior (looking for predators) during each sound. Use this graph to answer the questions below.*

Data obtained from: Wilson, D. and Hare, F. 2004. Ground squirrel uses ultrasonic alarms. *Nature* 430: 523.

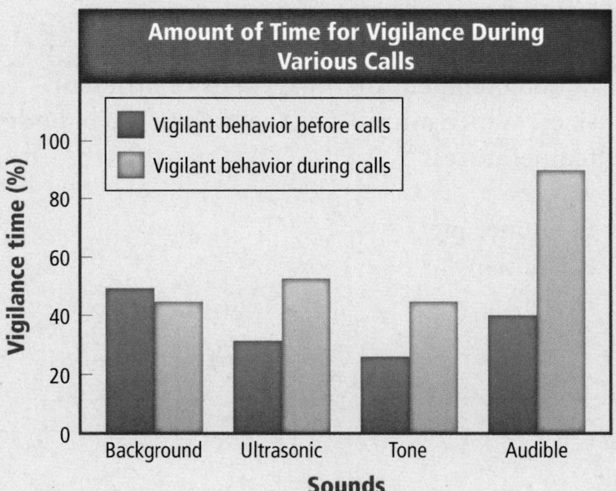


31. Under which conditions did ground squirrels exhibit the most vigilant behavior overall?

32. Under which conditions might an ultrasonic signal be more effective as a warning?

## Cumulative Review

33. Distinguish between vascular and nonvascular plants. **(Chapter 21)**

34. Suggest ways to avoid becoming the host of a flatworm. **(Chapter 25)**

# Standardized Test Practice

**Cumulative**

## Multiple Choice

*Use the graphs below to answer questions 1 and 2.*

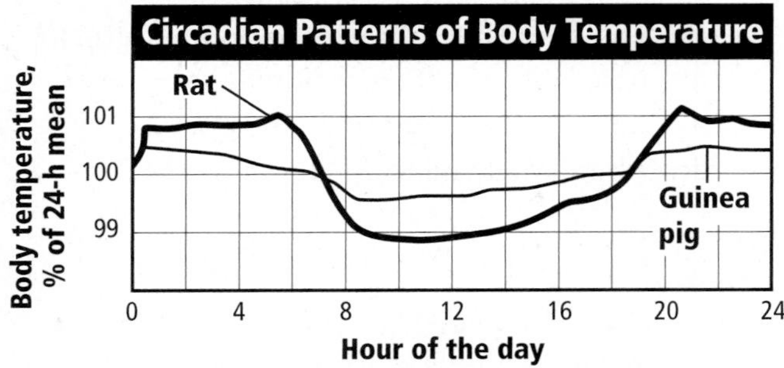


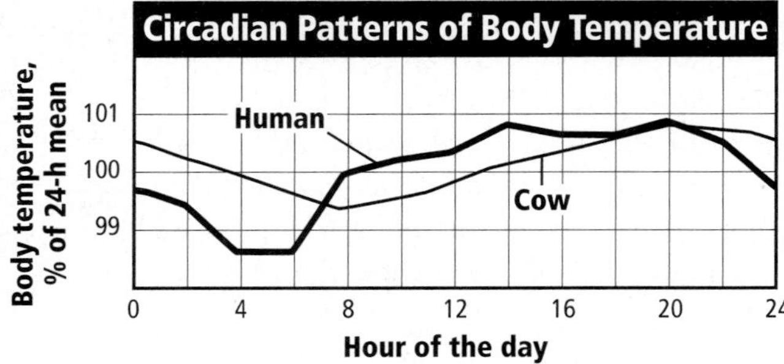


**1.** The graphs above show the circadian pattern of body temperature in animals of different sizes. Which animal has the highest mean body temperature?

**A.** cow
**B.** guinea pig
**C.** human
**D.** rat

**2.** The rat and guinea pig on the graph above are mainly nocturnal animals. What can you infer from this graph about the body temperatures of nocturnal animals?

**A.** They have higher body temperatures than animals that are active during the day.
**B.** They have more extreme temperature changes than animals that are active during the day.
**C.** They have lower body temperatures than animals that are active during the day.
**D.** They have less extreme temperature changes than animals that are active during the day.

**3.** Which statement describes the difference between invertebrate chordates and the rest of the phylum Chordata?

**A.** Invertebrate chordates lack a backbone.
**B.** Invertebrate chordates lack a notochord.
**C.** Other members of the phylum lack a backbone.
**D.** Other members of the phylum lack a notochord.

*Use the table below to answer question 4.*

| Row | Group | Some Components of the Digestive System |
|---|---|---|
| 1 | Amphibians | Has gizzard, stomach, intestines |
| 2 | Reptiles | Has crop, large and small intestines |
| 3 | Birds | Has crop, gizzard, intestines |
| 4 | Fishes | Has swim bladder, stomach, intestines |

**4.** Which row of information in the table contains correct information about the digestive system?

**A.** 1
**B.** 2
**C.** 3
**D.** 4

**5.** Pharyngeal pouches are defined as which of the following?

**A.** cavities that hold food as it is digested
**B.** sacs that hold the coiled digestive system in place
**C.** structures that link the mouth cavity and the esophagus
**D.** structures that regulate metabolism, growth, and development

**6.** How many pairs of jointed appendages do spiders have?

**A.** 3
**B.** 4
**C.** 5
**D.** 6

## Short Answer

*Use the diagram below to answer question 9.*

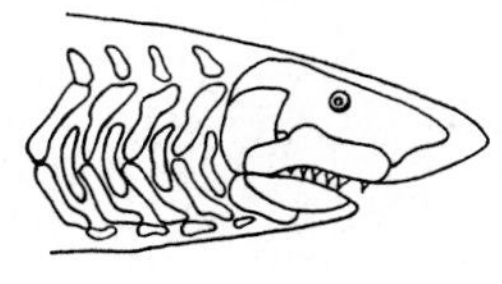

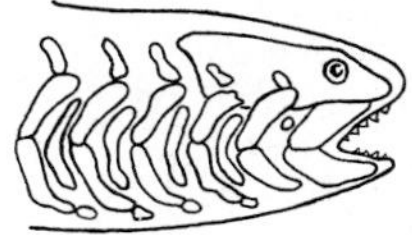

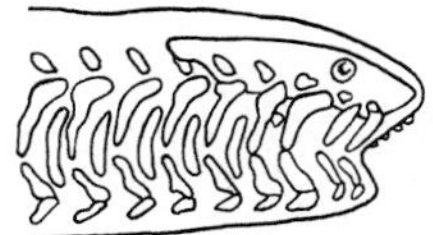

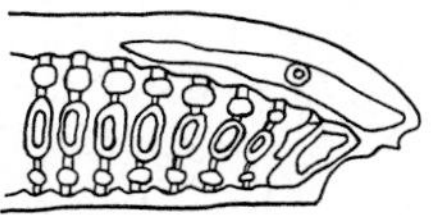

9. Describe the evolution of the jaw and explain how it was an important advancement for fishes.

10. Hypothesize why some birds migrate thousands of miles each year.

11. List three traits of mammals and explain why they are necessary for endotherms.

12. Compare and contrast an open circulatory system and a closed circulatory system.

13. Compare and contrast organisms in the order Rodentia with those in order Lagomorpha.

14. Hypothesize how an animal would benefit from a dominance hierarchy if it does not defend a territory.

## Extended Response

15. Suppose a plant with adaptations for survival in a tropical rain forest is transplanted to a tropical desert. What adaptations in the rain forest plant could cause it to have trouble surviving in the new environment?

16. A certain type of insect uses pheromones to attract mates. The insect is most active during the day. Propose the advantages and disadvantages of this type of behavior for attracting mates.

## Essay Question

The ring-tailed lemur is an herbivore. It eats a variety of plants and plant materials. Ring-trailed lemurs eat up to three dozen species of vegetation, but one of their favorites is the kily tree.

Groups of ring-tailed lemurs are led by a dominant female. A group usually contains between 15 and 30 lemurs. They can travel over a large area, some days more than 4 km. When the lemurs aren't eating, they often bathe in the Sun, groom each other, or play. Ring-tailed lemurs sleep under large trees. Settling down for the night is usually preceded by a loud whooplike call from all the lemurs.

*Using the information in the paragraph above answer the following question in essay format.*

17. The passage above describes the diet and behavior of ring-tailed lemurs. Suppose you want to do a study of lemur behavior. In an organized essay, explain what your research question would be and how you would study the behavior of ring-tailed lemurs.

| NEED EXTRA HELP? | | | | | | | | | | | | | | | | | |
|---|---|---|---|---|---|---|---|---|---|---|---|---|---|---|---|---|---|
| **If You Missed Question . . .** | 1 | 2 | 3 | 4 | 5 | 6 | 7 | 8 | 9 | 10 | 11 | 12 | 13 | 14 | 15 | 16 | 17 |
| **Review Section . . .** | 29.2 | 31.1 | 31.2 | 28.2 | 30.2 | 28.1 | 27.1 | 29.1 | 28.2 | 31.2 | 30.1 | 25.3 | 30.2 | 31.2 | 21.1 | 31.2 | 30.2 |

# UNIT 9 The Human Body

**Chapter 32**
Integumentary, Skeletal, and Muscular Systems
BIG Idea These systems work together to maintain homeostasis by protecting, supporting, and moving the body.

**Chapter 33**
Nervous System
BIG Idea The nervous system is essential for communication among cells, tissues, and organs.

**Chapter 34**
Circulatory, Respiratory, and Excretory Systems
BIG Idea These systems function together to maintain homeostasis by delivering important substances to the body's cells while removing wastes.

**Chapter 35**
Digestive and Endocrine Systems
BIG Idea The digestive system breaks down food to provide energy and nutrients for the body. Hormones regulate body functions.

**Chapter 36**
Human Reproduction and Development
BIG Idea Human reproduction involves the joining together of sperm and egg.

**Chapter 37**
Immune System
BIG Idea The immune system attempts to protect the body from contracting an infection through pathogens.

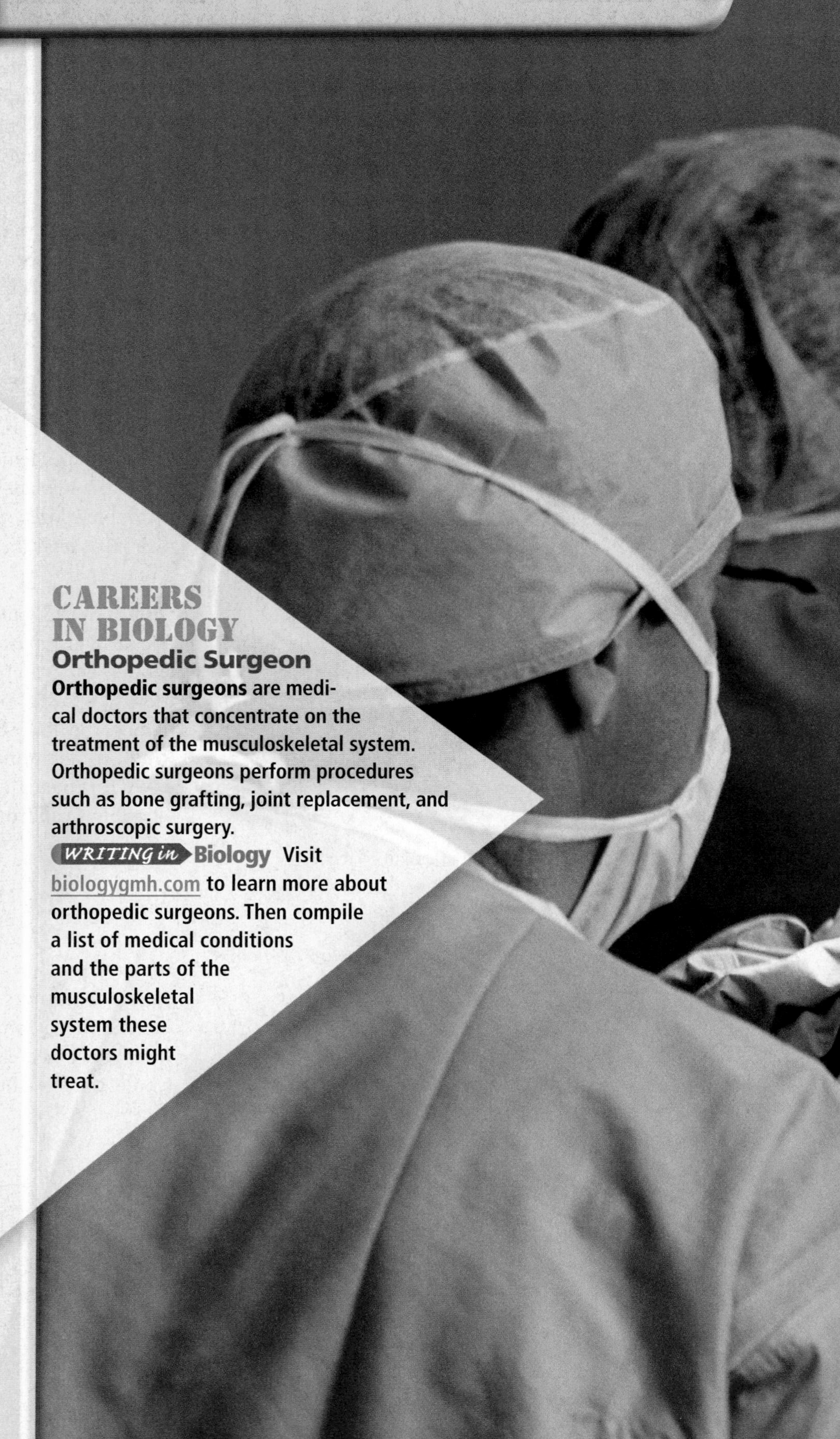

## CAREERS IN BIOLOGY

### Orthopedic Surgeon

**Orthopedic surgeons** are medical doctors that concentrate on the treatment of the musculoskeletal system. Orthopedic surgeons perform procedures such as bone grafting, joint replacement, and arthroscopic surgery.

WRITING in Biology Visit biologygmh.com to learn more about orthopedic surgeons. Then compile a list of medical conditions and the parts of the musculoskeletal system these doctors might treat.

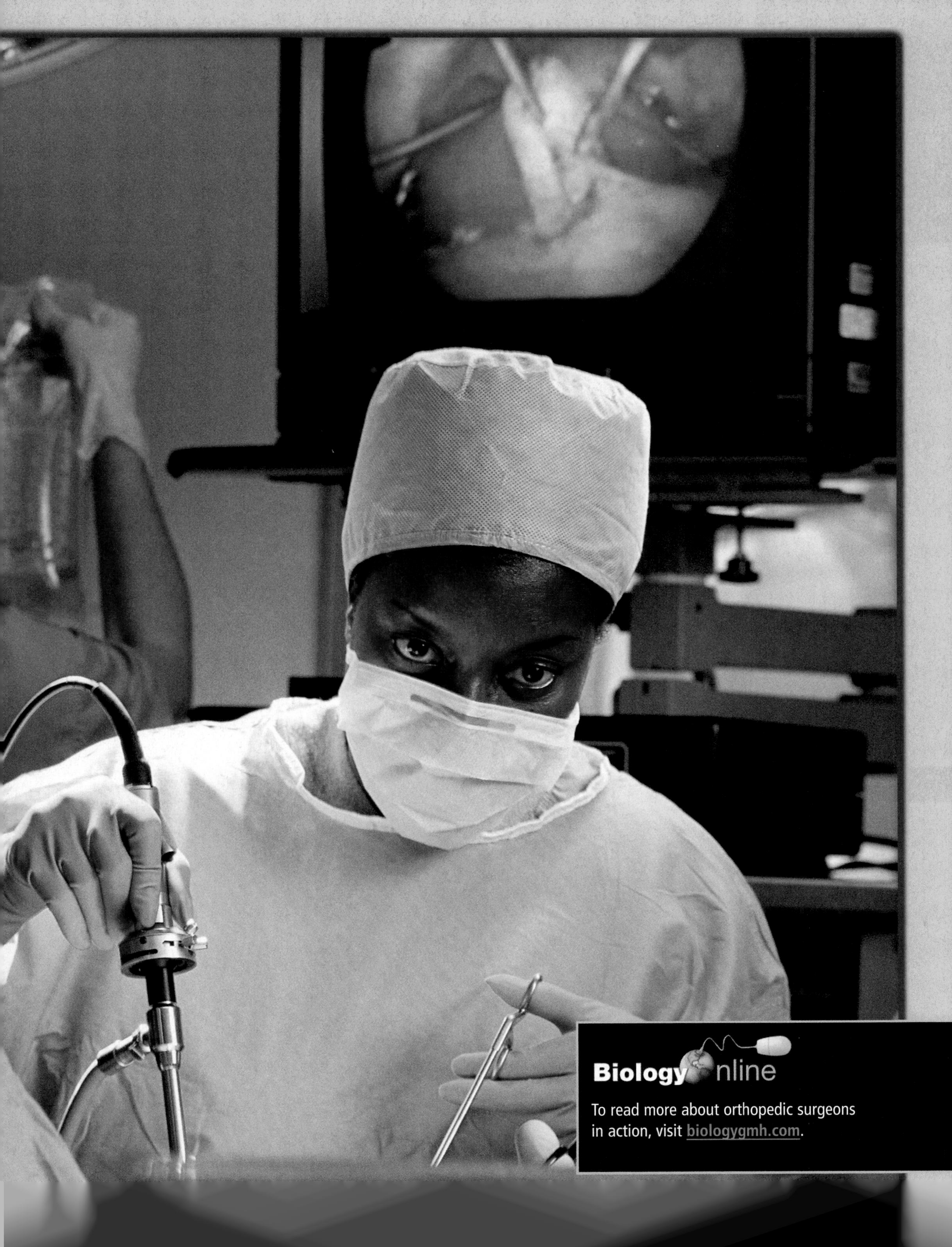
Biology Online
To read more about orthopedic surgeons in action, visit biologygmh.com.

CHAPTER 32

# Integumentary, Skeletal, and Muscular Systems

**Section 1**
**The Integumentary System**
MAIN Idea Skin is a multi-layered organ that covers and protects the body.

**Section 2**
**The Skeletal System**
MAIN Idea The skeleton provides a structural framework for the body and protects internal organs such as the heart, lungs, and brain.

**Section 3**
**The Muscular System**
MAIN Idea The three major types of muscle tissue differ in structure and function.

## BioFacts

- The skin of an adult can measure up to 18,580 $cm^2$ and can weigh as much as 3.5 kg.
- Adult humans have 206 bones in their bodies.
- Muscles work by contracting.

# Start-Up Activities

## LAUNCH Lab

### How is a chicken's wing like your arm?

Chickens have structures similar to ours. You will examine a chicken wing and begin to explore it.

**Procedure**

1. Read and complete the lab safety form.
2. Obtain a **treated chicken wing** in a **self-sealing sandwich bag.** Observe the skin of the wing.
3. Without removing the wing from the bag, manipulate the wing to determine how it moves and where the joints are located.
4. Lay the bag on a flat surface and gently press and massage the wing to determine where bones and muscles are located.
5. Based on your observations, draw the wing as you imagine it might look if the skin was removed. Show the bones and muscles.

**Analysis**

1. **Label** your drawing to show which parts correspond to your upper arm, elbow, wrist, and hand.
2. **Differentiate** How are the parts that make up your arm different from the chicken wing?

Visit biologygmh.com to:

- study the entire chapter online
- explore Concepts in Motion, the Interactive Table, Microscopy Links, Virtual Labs, and links to virtual dissections
- access Web links for more information, projects, and activities
- review content online with the Interactive Tutor and take Self-Check Quizzes

**Layers of Skin** Make this foldable to help you understand skin as a multilayered organ of the body.

**STEP 1** Place two sheets of notebook paper on top of each other with the top edges 1.5 cm apart.

**STEP 2** Roll up the bottom edges, making all tabs 1.5 cm in size. Crease to form four tabs of equal size.

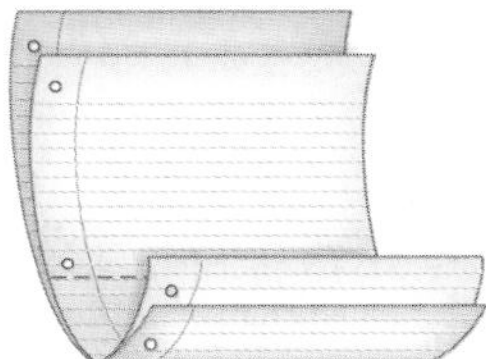

**STEP 3** Staple along the folded edge to secure all sheets. With the stapled end on the bottom, label the tabs as illustrated.

Subcutaneous
Dermis
Epidermis
SKIN

**FOLDABLES Use this Foldable with Section 32.1.** As you study the section, record what you learn about each layer of tissue, and explain how the layers work together to perform specific functions.

Section 32.1

### Objectives

- **List** the four tissue types that are found in the integumentary system.
- **Explain** the functions of the integumentary system.
- **Describe** the composition of the two layers of skin.
- **Summarize** events that occur when skin is repaired.

### Review Vocabulary

**integument:** an enveloping layer of an organism

### New Vocabulary

epidermis
keratin
melanin
dermis
hair follicle
sebaceous gland

# The Integumentary System

**MAIN Idea Skin is a multilayered organ that covers and protects the body.**

**Real-World Reading Link** The skin on the tips of fingers and toes is thick and is composed of curving ridges that form the basis of fingerprints. Fingerprints were first used in criminal investigations in 1860 by Henry Faulds, a Scottish medical missionary. Your skin is not just a simple covering that keeps your body together. It is complex and is essential for your survival. Your ridges are uniquely yours!

## The Structure of Skin

The integumentary (ihn TEG yuh MEN tuh ree) system is the organ system that covers and protects the body. Skin is the main organ of the integumentary system and is composed of four types of tissues: epithelial tissue, connective tissue, muscle tissue, and nerve tissue. Epithelial tissue covers body surfaces, and connective tissue provides support and protection. Muscle tissue is involved in body movement. Nerve tissue forms the body's communication network. You will learn more about muscle tissue in Section 32.3, and you will learn about nerve tissue in Chapter 33.

**The epidermis** Refer to **Figure 32.1,** which illustrates the two main layers of skin as seen through a microscope. The outer superficial layer of skin is the **epidermis.** The epidermis consists of epithelial cells and is about 10 to 30 cells thick, or about as thick as this page. The outer layers of epidermal cells contain **keratin** (KER uh tun), a protein which waterproofs and protects the cells and tissues that lie underneath. These dead, outer cells are constantly shed. **Figure 32.2** shows that some of the dust in a house actually is dead skin cells. As much as an entire layer of skin cells can be lost each month.

FOLDABLES
Incorporate information from this section into your Foldable.

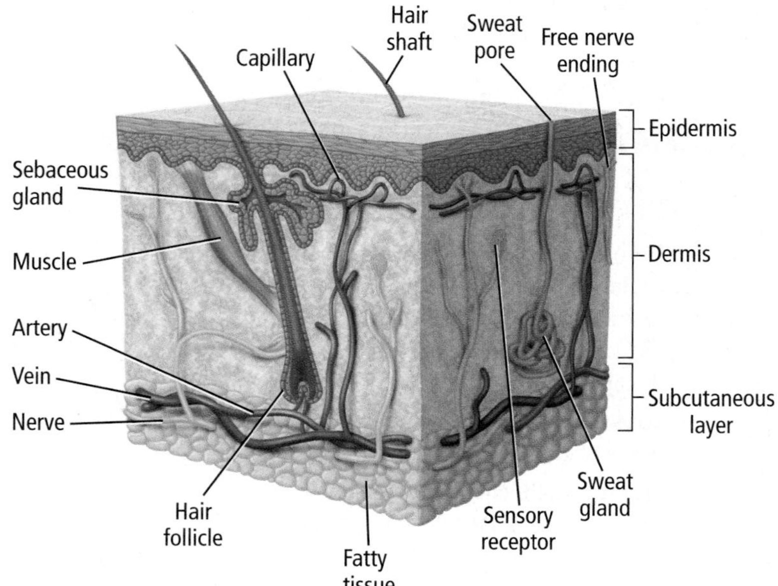


**Figure 32.1** Skin is an organ because it consists of different types of tissues joined together for specific purposes.
**Summarize** *What types of tissues make up the skin?*

The inner layer of the epidermis contains cells that continually are dividing by mitosis to replace cells that are lost or die. Some cells in the inner layer of the epidermis provide protection from harmful ultraviolet radiation by making a pigment called melanin. **Melanin** is a pigment that absorbs light energy, which protects deeper cells from the damaging effects of ultraviolet rays of sunlight. The amount of melanin that is produced also influences the color of a person's skin. A suntan results when melanin is produced in response to exposure to the ultraviolet radiation in sunlight.

**The dermis** Directly beneath the epidermis is the **dermis,** the second layer of skin. The thickness of the dermis varies but usually is 15–40 times thicker than the epidermis. The dermis consists of connective tissue, a type of tissue that prevents the skin from tearing and also enables the skin to return to its normal state after being stretched. This layer contains other structures including nerve cells, muscle fibers, sweat glands, oil glands, and hair follicles. Beneath the dermis is the subcutaneous layer, a layer of connective tissue that stores fat and helps the body retain heat.

**Hair and nails** Hair, fingernails, and toenails also are parts of the integumentary system. Both hair and nails contain keratin and develop from epithelial cells. Hair cells grow out of narrow cavities in the dermis called **hair follicles.** Cells at the base of a hair follicle divide and push cells away from the follicle, causing hair to grow.

Hair follicles usually have sebaceous or oil glands associated with them, as shown in **Figure 32.3. Sebaceous glands** lubricate skin and hair. When glands produce too much oil, the follicles can become blocked. The blockage can close the opening of a follicle, causing a whitehead, blackhead, or acne—an inflammation of the sebaceous glands.

**Reading Check** **Summarize** the differences in structure and function of the epidermis and the dermis.

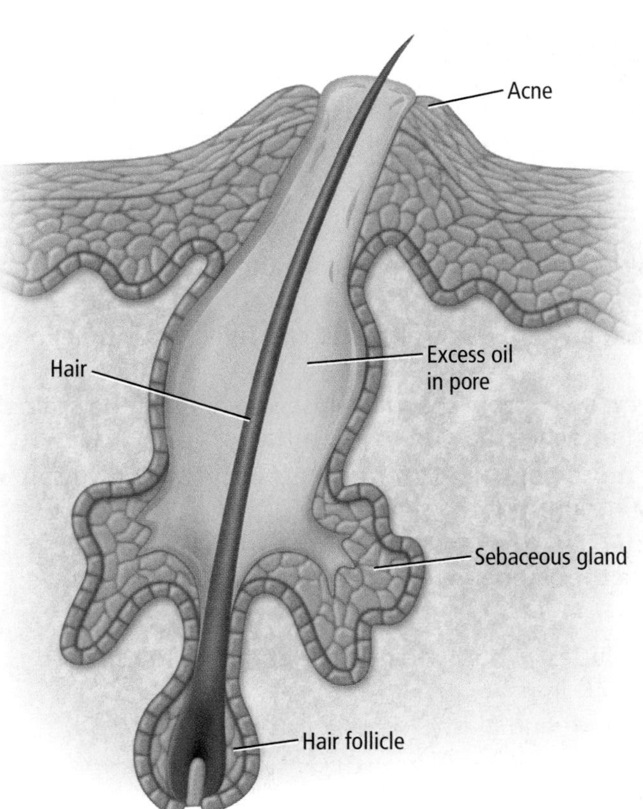


**Figure 32.3** Oil, dirt, and bacteria can become trapped in follicles and erupt and spread to the surrounding area, causing localized inflammation.

Color-Enhanced SEM Magnification: 187×

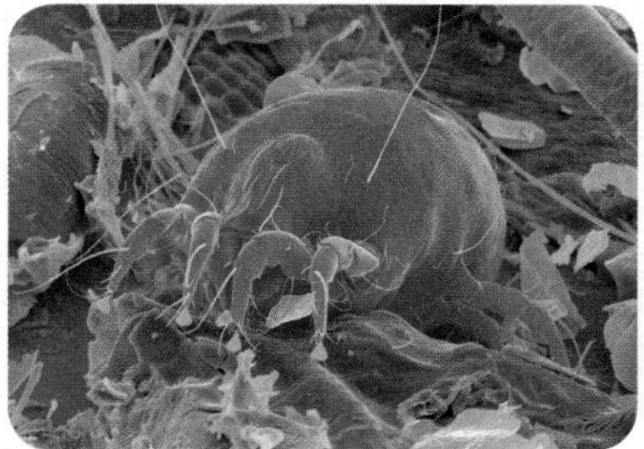

**Figure 32.2** The dust mite pictured here is feeding on dead skin cells—a major component of dust.

*Study Tip*

**Chart** Make a chart with *Skin, Bones,* and *Muscles* as row labels, and *Components and structure* and *Function and purpose* as the column labels. Work in small groups to complete your chart as you review the text.

■ **Figure 32.4** Muscles in the skin cause the hair of some mammals to stand on end, and cause "goose bumps" on human skin. **Relate** ***What environmental changes produce "goose bumps"?***

Fingernails and toenails grow from specialized epithelial cells at the base of each nail. As cells at the base of a nail divide, older dead cells are compacted and pushed out. Nails grow about 0.5 to 1.2 mm per day. You might have heard that nails and hair continue to grow for several days after death. This is a myth; cells surrounding the nail and hair cells dehydrate causing the cells to shrink and pull away from nails and hair. This makes both appear longer.

## Functions of the Integumentary System

Skin serves several important functions including regulation of body temperature, production of vitamin D, protection, and perception of one's surroundings.

**Temperature regulation** What happens when a person is working outside on a hot summer day? In order to regulate body temperature, the person sweats. As sweat evaporates it absorbs body heat, thereby cooling the body. What happens to skin when a person gets cold or frightened? "Goose bumps" are caused by the contraction of muscle cells in the dermis. In other mammals, when these muscles contract, the hair (fur) stands on end.

Notice the frightened cat in **Figure 32.4.** The cat appears larger, perhaps as a way to scare off enemies. This also is a mechanism for trapping air, which insulates or warms the mammal. Humans do not have as much hair as most other mammals, but "goose bumps" are caused by the same type of muscles that make a cat's fur stand on end. Humans rely on fat in the subcutaneous layer instead of hair to keep warm.

## MiniLab 32.1

### Examine Skin

**How is chicken skin similar to human skin?** The skin of chicken has characteristics similar to human skin. Using the chicken wing from the Launch Lab, you will further examine the characteristics of skin.

**Procedure**

1. Read and complete the lab safety form.
2. Wear disposable **lab gloves.** Remove the **chicken wing** from the **self-sealing bag** and place it in a **dissecting pan.**
3. Use a **dissecting kit** to remove the skin from the wing. Use **scissors** to carefully snip a hole in the skin that is loosely attached to the wing.
4. Make a cut about 6 cm in length. Pull the skin away from the wing. Use scissors and the **scalpel** to cut through the transparent membrane that attaches the skin to the muscles.
5. Try to remove the skin without making any more holes. Look for pockets of fat, blood vessels, and muscle fibers attached to the skin. Note the strength of the skin.
6. Dispose of the skin and used gloves as directed by your teacher. Clean your dissecting tools and dissecting pan with **warm, soapy water.** Save the skinned wing to use in the next MiniLab.

**Analysis**

1. **Think Critically** Human skin contains hair follicles. What type of follicles might you find on chicken skin?
2. **Explain** Why is it important for skin to be strong and elastic?

**Vitamin production** Skin also responds to exposure to ultraviolet light rays from the Sun by producing vitamin D. Vitamin D increases absorption of calcium into the bloodstream and is essential for proper bone formation. Many food products are now fortified with vitamin D.

**Protection and senses** Intact skin prevents the entry of microorganisms and other foreign substances. Skin helps maintain body temperature by preventing excessive water loss. Melanin in the skin protects against ultraviolet rays. Information about changes in the environment, such as pain, pressure, and temperature changes, is relayed to the brain.

VOCABULARY

ACADEMIC VOCABULARY

**Function:**
action, purpose.
*One function of the skin is to protect the body.*

## Damage to the Skin

Skin has remarkable abilities to repair itself. Without a repair mechanism, the body would be subject to invasion by microbes through breaks in the skin.

**Cuts and scrapes** Sometimes, as in the case of a minor scrape, only the epidermis is injured. Cells deep in the epidermis divide to replace the lost or injured cells. When the injury is deep, blood vessels might be injured, resulting in bleeding. Blood flows out of the wound and a clot is formed. Blood clots form a scab to close the wound, and cells beneath the scab multiply and fill in the wound. At the same time, infection-fighting white blood cells will help get rid of any bacteria that might have entered the wound.

**Effects of the Sun and burns** As people age, the elasticity of their skin decreases and they start to get wrinkles. Exposure to ultraviolet rays from the Sun might accelerate this process and can result in burning of the skin.

**Connection to Health** Burns, whether caused by the Sun, heat, or chemicals, usually are classified according to their severity. The types of burns are summarized in **Table 32.1**. First-degree burns generally are mild and involve only cells in the epidermis. A burn that blisters or leaves a scar is a second-degree burn and involves damage to both the epidermis and dermis. Third-degree burns are the most severe. Muscle tissue and nerve cells in both the epidermis and dermis might be destroyed, and skin function is lost. Healthy skin might have to be transplanted from another place on the body in order to restore the protective layer of the body.

CAREERS IN BIOLOGY

**Physical Therapist** A physical therapist helps injured or disabled people to improve or regain physical functions using techniques such as exercise and massage. For more information on biology careers, visit biologygmh.com.

**Table 32.1 Classification of Burns**

Concepts In Motion

Interactive Table To explore more about burns, visit biologygmh.com.

| Severity of burn | Damage | Effect |
|---|---|---|
| **First-degree** | Cells in the epidermis are injured and may die. | • Redness and swelling<br>• Mild pain |
| **Second-degree** | Cells deeper in the epidermis die. Cells in the dermis are injured and may die. | • Blisters<br>• Pain |
| **Third-degree** | Cells in the epidermis and dermis die. Nerve cells and muscles cells are injured. | • Skin function lost<br>• Healthy skin needs to be transplanted<br>• No pain because of nerve cell damage |

■ **Figure 32.5** Warning signs of skin cancer include any obvious change in a wart or mole, or moles that are irregularly shaped, varied in color, and/or are larger than the diameter of a pencil.

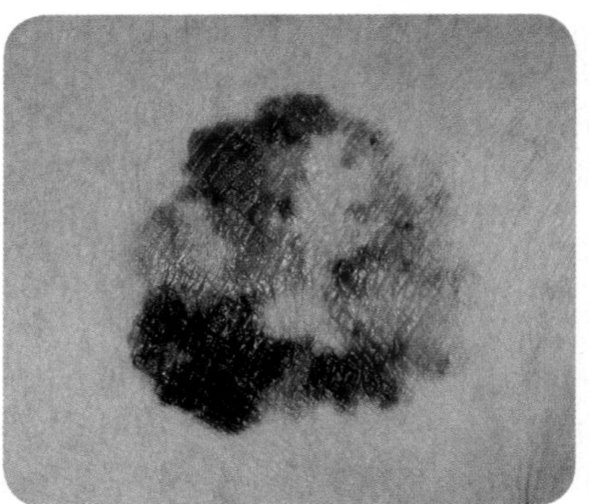

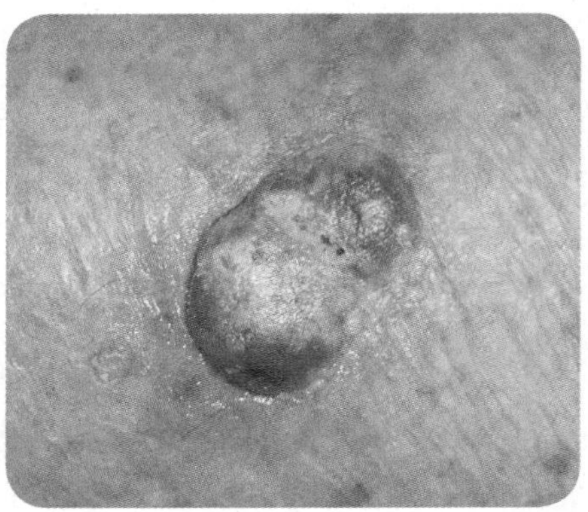

**Skin cancer** Exposure to ultraviolet radiation, whether it is from the Sun or from artificial sources such as tanning beds, is recognized as an important risk factor for the development of skin cancer. Ultraviolet radiation can damage the DNA in skin cells, causing those cells to grow and divide uncontrollably. When this happens, skin cancer results. Refer to **Figure 32.5** to see some warning signs of skin cancer.

Skin cancer is the most common cancer in the United States. There are two main categories of skin cancer: melanoma and nonmelanoma. Melanoma begins in melanocytes, the cells that produce the pigment melanin. Melanoma is the deadliest form of skin cancer. Melanoma can spread to internal organs and the lymphatic system. It is estimated that one person dies from melanoma every hour in the United States. Teens are at greater risk for melanoma because as they grow, their skin cells divide more rapidly than they will when they reach adulthood.

Anyone can get skin cancer. However, individuals with light skin, light-colored eyes, light hair color, and a tendency to burn or freckle are at the greatest risk. Everyone should try to avoid prolonged exposure to the Sun, especially between 10 A.M. and 4 P.M. when the Sun's rays are the strongest. Other preventative measures include wearing protective clothing or sunscreen with a Sun Protection Factor (SPF) of at least 15.

## Section 32.1 Assessment

### Section Summary

- The skin is the major organ of the integumentary system.
- Maintaining homeostasis is one function of the integumentary system.
- There are four types of tissues in the integumentary system.
- Hair, fingernails, and toenails develop from epithelial cells.
- Burns are classified according to the severity of the damage to skin tissues.

### Understand Main Ideas

1. MAIN Idea **Diagram** the two layers of the skin.
2. **Summarize** the types of tissues in the integumentary system and their functions.
3. **Generalize** different ways the integumentary system helps a human survive.
4. **Sequence** the process of skin repair in response to a cut.
5. **Compare** effects of first-degree, second-degree, and third-degree burns.

### Think Scientifically

6. *Evaluate* the labels of two name-brand skin creams to compare how the two products claim to benefit the skin.
7. MATH in Biology To determine how long an SPF will protect a person from burning in the Sun, multiply the amount of time the person can spend in the Sun before starting to burn by the SPF rating. If an individual who usually burns in 10 min uses a product with an SPF of 15, how long will the protection last?



Biology Online Self-Check Quiz biologygmh.com

Section 32.2

### Objectives

- **Distinguish** between the bones of the axial and appendicular skeletons.
- **Describe** how new bone is formed.
- **Summarize** the functions of the skeletal system.

### Review Vocabulary

**cartilage:** tough, flexible connective tissue that forms the skeletons of embryos and later covers the surface of bones that move against each other in joints

### New Vocabulary

axial skeleton
appendicular skeleton
compact bone
osteocyte
spongy bone
red bone marrow
yellow bone marrow
osteoblast
ossification
osteoclast
ligament

# The Skeletal System

MAIN Idea **The skeleton provides a structural framework for the body and protects internal organs such as the heart, lungs, and brain.**

**Real-World Reading Link** Framing is an early stage of building a house. A person can walk through a house at that stage and know the plan of the house because of the framework. The skeletal system can be compared to the framework of a house. The framework provides structure and protection.

## Structure of the Skeletal System

Notice all the bones in the adult skeleton pictured in **Figure 32.6.** If you counted them, you would find there are 206 bones. The human skeleton consists of two divisions—the axial skeleton and the appendicular skeleton. The **axial skeleton** includes the skull, the vertebral column, the ribs, and the sternum. The **appendicular skeleton** includes the bones of the shoulders, arms, hands, hips, legs, and feet.

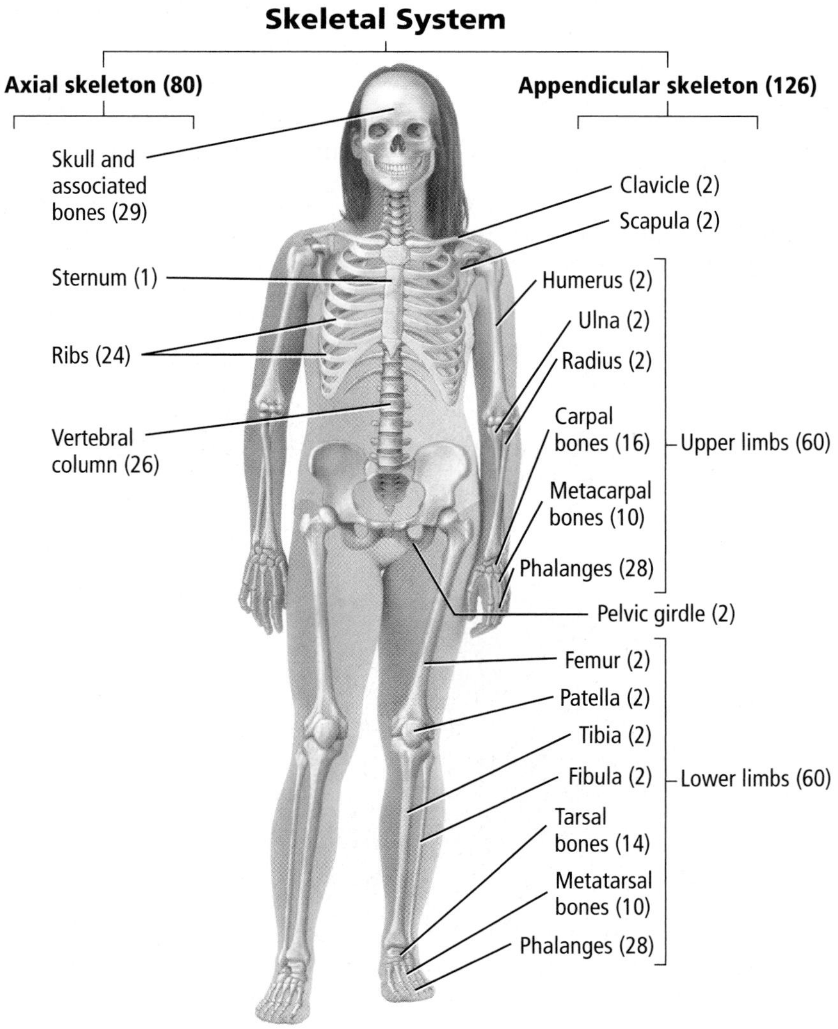

**Figure 32.6** The axial skeleton includes the bones of the head, back, and chest. Bones in the appendicular skeleton are related to movement of the limbs.

**CAREERS IN BIOLOGY**

**Medical Illustrator** A medical illustrator combines a talent in art with an interest in biology to illustrate procedures or to create teaching models. For more information on biology careers, visit biologygmh.com.

**VOCABULARY**

**WORD ORIGIN**

**Osteoblast**

***osteo–*** comes from the Greek word *osteon,* meaning *bone.*
***–blast*** from Greek, meaning *budding.*

**Compact and spongy bone** Bone is a connective tissue that has many shapes and sizes. Bones are classified as long, short, flat, or irregular. Refer back to **Figure 32.6.** Arm and leg bones are examples of long bones, and wrist bones are examples of short bones. Flat bones make up the skull. Facial bones and vertebrae are irregular bones. Regardless of their shape, all bones have the same basic structure.

The outer layers of all bones are composed of compact bone. **Compact bone** is dense and strong; it provides strength and protection. Running the length of compact bones are tubelike structures called osteons, or Haversian systems, which contain blood vessels and nerves. The blood vessels provide oxygen and nutrients to **osteocytes**—living bone cells. The centers of bones can differ greatly, as illustrated in **Figure 32.7.**

As the name suggests, **spongy bone** is less dense and has many cavities that contain bone marrow. Spongy bone is found in the center of short or flat bones and at the end of long bones. Spongy bone is surrounded by compact bone and does not contain Haversian systems.

There are two types of bone marrow—red and yellow. Red and white blood cells and platelets are produced in **red bone marrow.** Red bone marrow is found in the humerus bone of the arm, the femur bone of the leg, the sternum and ribs, the vertebrae, and the pelvis. The cavities of an infant's bones are composed of red marrow. Children's bones have more red marrow than adult bones. **Yellow bone marrow,** found in many other bones, consists of stored fat.

**Formation of bone** The skeletons of embryos are composed of cartilage. During fetal development, cells in fetal cartilage develop into bone-forming cells called **osteoblasts.** The formation of bone from osteoblasts is called **ossification.** Except for the tip of the nose, outer ears, discs between vertebrae, and the lining of movable joints, the human adult skeleton is all bone. Osteoblasts also are the cells responsible for the growth and repair of bones.

**Figure 32.7** Bone is either compact bone or spongy bone.
**Classify** ***How do spongy bone and compact bone differ in location and function?***

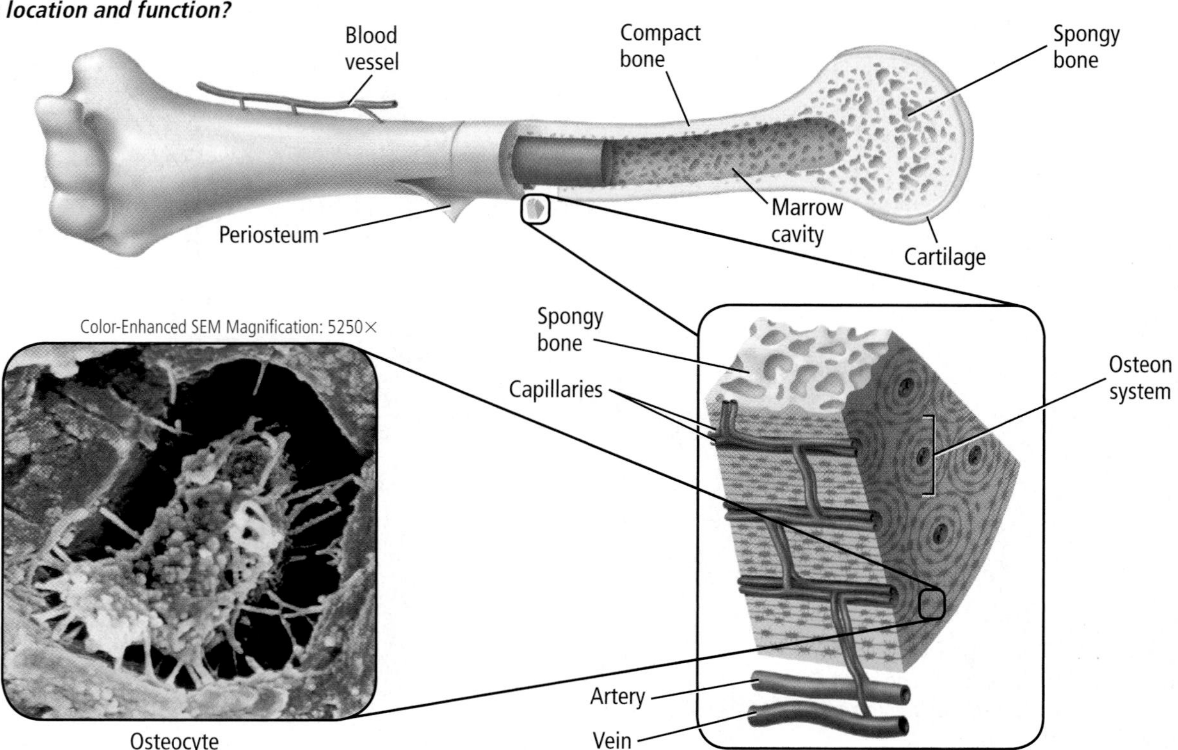

**Remodeling of bone** Bones constantly are being remodeled, which involves replacing old cells with new cells. This process is continual throughout life and is important in the growth of an individual. Cells called **osteoclasts** break down bone cells, which are then replaced by new bone tissue. Bone growth involves several factors, including nutrition and physical exercise. For example, a person with insufficient calcium can develop a condition known as osteoporosis that results in weak, fragile bones that break easily.

**Reading Check** **Compare** the roles of osteoblasts and osteoclasts.

**Repair of bone** Fractures are very common bone injuries. When a bone breaks but does not come through the skin, it is a simple fracture. A compound fracture is one in which the bone protrudes through the skin. A stress fracture is a thin crack in the bone. When a bone is fractured, repair begins immediately. Refer to **Figure 32.8,** which illustrates the steps in the repair of a broken bone.

**Fracture** Upon injury, endorphins, chemicals produced in the brain and sometimes called "the body's natural painkillers," flood the area of the injury to reduce the amount of pain temporarily. The injured area quickly becomes inflamed, or swollen. The swelling can last for two or three weeks.

Within about eight hours, a blood clot forms between the broken ends of the bone and new bone begins to form. First, a soft callus, or mass, of cartilage forms at the location of the break. This tissue is weak, so the broken bone must remain in place.

**Callus formation** About three weeks later, osteoblasts form a callus made of spongy bone that surrounds the fracture. The spongy bone is then replaced by compact bone. Osteoclasts remove the spongy bone while osteoblasts produce stronger, compact bone.

Splints, casts, and sometimes traction can ensure that the broken bone remains in place until new bone tissue has formed. Broken fingers often are kept in place by being taped to an adjacent finger.

**Remodeling** Bones require different amounts of time to heal. Age, nutrition, location, and severity of the break are all factors. A lack of calcium in a person's diet will slow down bone repair. Bones of younger people usually heal more quickly than bones of older people. For example, a fracture might take only four to six weeks to be repaired in a toddler, but it might take six months in an adult.

**Figure 32.8** Bone repair requires several steps. First, a mass of clotted blood forms in the space between the broken bones. Then connective tissue fills the space of the broken bone. Eventually, osteoblasts produce new bone tissue.

**Fracture**

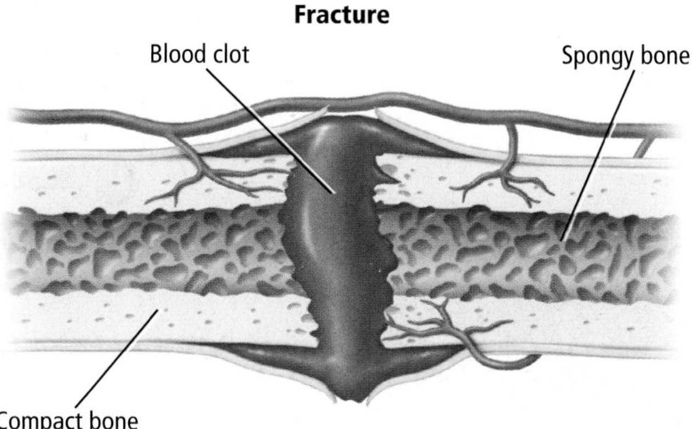


**Callus Formation**

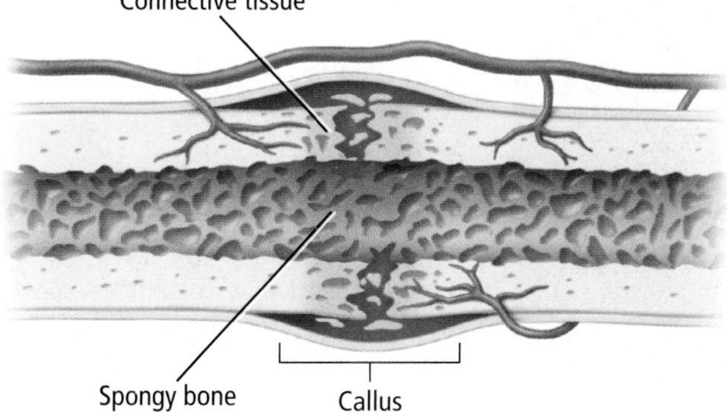


**Remodeling**

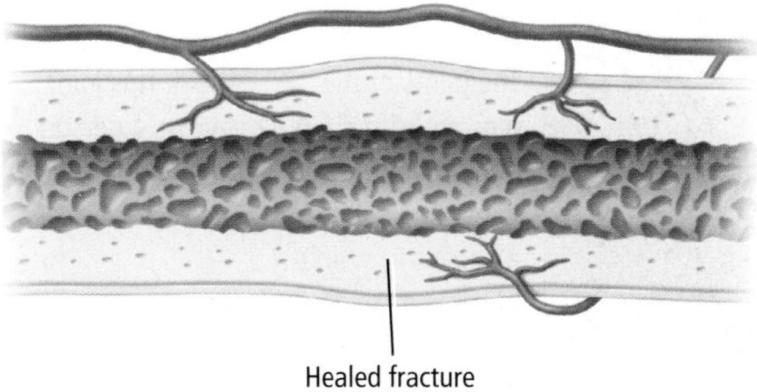

## Joints

Joints occur where two or more bones meet. Except for the joints in the skull, they can be classified according to the movement they allow and the shapes of their parts. **Table 32.2** identifies five kinds of joints—ball-and-socket, pivot, hinge, gliding, and sutures. Study **Table 32.2** to identify the type of movement that each kind of joint allows and also the bones involved in each example.

Not all joints are movable. The joints between some skull bones are fixed. At birth, however, skull bones are not all fused together. They become fused by the time a baby is about three months old. Gliding joints, like those found in the hand, have limited movement. Other joints, such as the hinge joint of the elbow and the pivot joint in the lower arm, allow back-and-forth movement and twisting. The ball-and-socket joints of the hips and shoulders have the widest range of motion.

The bones of joints are held together by ligaments. **Ligaments** are tough bands of connective tissue that attach one bone to another. You will learn more about ligaments and tendons, which attach muscle to bone, in the following section.

**Reading Check** **Review** the types of joints and how joints are classified.

**LAUNCH Lab**

**Review** Based on what you've read about joints, how would you now answer the analysis questions?

**Concepts In Motion**

**Interactive Table** To explore more about how joints move, visit biologygmh.com.

**Table 32.2 Some Joints of the Skeletal System**

| Name of Joint | Ball-and-Socket | Pivot | Hinge | Gliding | Sutures |
|---|---|---|---|---|---|
| Example | | | | | |
| Description | In a ball-and-socket joint, the ball-like surface of one bone fits into a cuplike depression of another bone and allows the widest range of motion of any kind of joint. The joints of the hips and shoulders are ball and socket joints. They allow a person to swing his or her arms and legs. | The primary movement at a pivot joint is rotation. One example of a pivot joint is the elbow joint where two bones of the lower arm, the radius, and the ulna meet. This joint allows a person to twist the lower arm. | In a hinge joint, the convex surface of one bone fits into the concave surface of another bone. Elbows and knees are hinge joints. They allow back-and-forth movement like that of a door hinge. | Gliding joints allow side-to-side and back-and-forth movement. The joints in wrists and ankles are gliding joints. The joints of vertebrae also are gliding joints. | Sutures are joints in the skull that are not movable. There are 22 bones in an adult skull. All skull bones except the lower jaw bone are joined at sutures. |

**Osteoarthritis** (ahs tee oh ar THRI tus) The ends of bones in movable joints, such as the knee, are covered by cartilage, which serves as a cushion and allows smooth movement of the joint. Osteoarthritis is a painful condition that affects joints and results from the deterioration of the cartilage. It is a very common condition in knees and hips and also affects the neck and back. Osteoarthritis affects about ten percent of Americans and the frequency increases with age. A young person who has a joint injury is at risk to develop osteoarthritis later in life.

**Rheumatoid arthritis** Rheumatoid (roo MAH toyd) arthritis is another form of arthritis that affects joints. Rheumatoid arthritis is not the result of cartilage deterioration or of wear and tear on the joint. Affected joints lose strength and function and are inflamed, swollen, and painful. Fingers can look deformed, as illustrated in **Figure 32.9.**

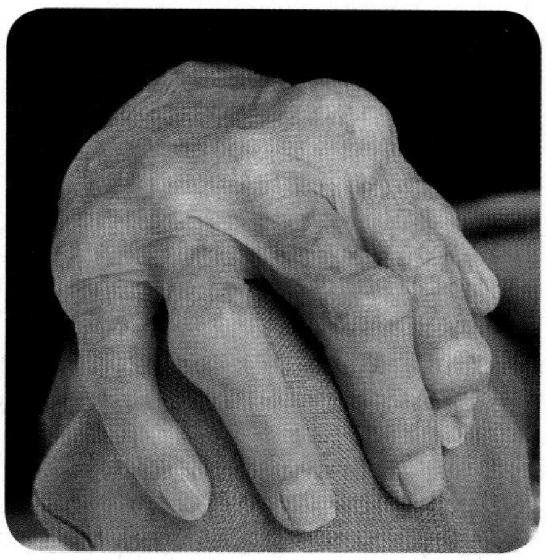

■ **Figure 32.9** Rheumatoid arthritis can cause loss of strength and function and involves severe pain.
**Compare** ***How does rheumatoid arthritis differ from the more common osteoarthritis?***

**Bursitis** Shoulders and knees also have fluid-filled sacs called bursae that surround these joints. Bursae decrease friction and act as a cushion between bones and tendons. Bursitis is an inflamation of the bursae and can reduce joint movement and cause pain and swelling. Perhaps you have heard of "tennis elbow" which is a form of bursitis. Treatment usually involves resting the joint involved.

**Sprains** A sprain involves damage to the ligaments that hold joints together. It is caused when a joint is twisted or overstretched and usually causes the joint to swell and be tender and painful.

## MiniLab 32.2

### Examine Bone Attachments

**How are bones attached to muscles and other bones?** Tendons attach muscle to bone, and ligaments attach bone to bone. You will examine these attachments using the skinned chicken wing from **MiniLab 32.1.**

**Procedure**

1. Read and complete the lab safety form.
2. Wear disposable **lab gloves.** Put the **skinned chicken wing** in a **dissection pan.**
3. Choose one muscle and use a pair of **dissection scissors** to cut the muscle away from the bone, leaving each end intact. Look for the long, white, tough tendons that connect the muscle to the bone.
4. Move the bones at the joint and notice how the tendon moves as the bones are pulled.
5. Carefully cut away all the muscles from the bones. The bones will still be attached to each other. Look for the white ligaments that hold them together. Examine the ends of each bone.
6. Draw a diagram of the wing without the muscles showing how the bones are attached to each other. Compare this drawing to the one you made in the Launch Lab.

**Analysis**

1. **Compare and Contrast** How is the drawing you made in the Launch Lab different from the drawing you made of the wing in this lab?
2. **Observe and Infer** Did you notice how a muscle is attached at one end to a bone and then how the ligament at the other end runs across a joint to attach that end of the muscle to the next bone? Explain why this is important. A diagram probably will help your explanation.
3. **Think Critically** At movable joints, what is the color of the ends of the bones? What do you think this material is?

Concepts In Motion

**Interactive Table** To explore more about the functions of the skeletal system, visit biologygmh.com.

**Table 32.3 Functions of the Skeletal System**

| Function | Description |
|---|---|
| **Support** | • Legs, pelvis, and vertebral column hold up the body<br>• Mandible supports the teeth<br>• Almost all bones support muscles |
| **Protection** | • Skull protects the brain<br>• Vertebrae protect the spinal column<br>• Rib cage protects the heart, lungs, and other organs |
| **Formation of blood cells** | • Red bone marrow produces red blood cells, white blood cells, and platelets |
| **Reservoir** | • Stores calcium and phosphorus |
| **Movement** | • Attached muscles pull on bones of arms and legs<br>• Diaphragm allows normal breathing |

## Functions of the Skeletal System

You might think that the only purpose of a skeleton is to serve as a framework to support the body. The bones of the legs, pelvis, and the vertebral column hold up the body. The mandible supports the teeth, and almost all bones support muscles. Many soft organs are directly or indirectly supported by nearby bones.

The skeletal system serves other functions besides support, as shown in **Table 32.3.** The skull protects the brain, vertebrae protect the spinal cord, and the rib cage protects the heart, lungs, and other organs.

The outer layers of bone tissue also protect the bone marrow found inside bones. In addition to forming red blood cells and white blood cells, red bone marrow forms platelets, which are involved in blood clotting. Red blood cells are produced at the rate of over two million per second.

Until a person reaches about seven years of age, all bone marrow is red bone marrow. Then, fat tissue replaces some red marrow and gives the marrow a yellowish appearance, which gives it its name. Fat is an important source of energy.

Bones are reservoirs for the storage of minerals such as calcium and phosphorus. When blood calcium levels are too low, calcium is released from bones. When blood calcium levels are high, excess calcium is stored in bone tissue. In this way, the skeletal system helps to maintain homeostasis.

Bones that have muscles attached to them allow movement of the body. For example, as muscles pull on the bones of the arms and legs, they cause movement. Muscles that are attached to your ribs allow you to breathe normally.

## Section 32.2 Assessment

### Section Summary

- The human skeleton consists of two divisions.
- Most bones are composed of two different types of tissue.
- Bones are being remodeled constantly.
- Bones work in conjunction with muscles.
- The skeleton has several important functions.

### Understand Main Ideas

1. MAIN Idea **List** and describe the functions of the axial skeleton and the appendicular skeleton.
2. **Compare** the compositions of red bone marrow and yellow bone marrow.
3. **Compare** the body's mechanism for repairing a fractured bone with the original development of bone.
4. **Construct** a classification scheme for all of the bones shown in **Figure 32.6.**

### Think Scientifically

5. *Consider* What might be the result if osteoblast and osteoclast cells did not function properly both in a developing fetus and in an adult?
6. *Distinguish* between compact and spongy bone based on their appearance, location, and function.



Biology Online **Self-Check Quiz** biologygmh.com

Section 32.3

# The Muscular System

### Objectives

- **Describe** the three types of muscle tissue.
- **Explain** at cellular and molecular levels the events involved in muscle contraction.
- **Distinguish** between slow-twitch and fast-twitch muscle fibers.

### Review Vocabulary

**anaerobic:** chemical reactions that do not require the presence of oxygen

### New Vocabulary

smooth muscle
involuntary muscle
cardiac muscle
skeletal muscle
voluntary muscle
tendon
myofibril
myosin
actin
sarcomere

MAIN Idea **The three major types of muscle tissue differ in structure and function.**

**Real-World Reading Link** Leonardo da Vinci contributed a great amount of knowledge to the scientific community. He studied the human body by examining cadavers. Da Vinci replaced muscles with string and learned that muscles shorten and pull on bones to make them move.

## Three Types of Muscle

A muscle consists of groups of fibers or muscle cells that are bound together. When the word muscle is used, many people immediately think of skeletal muscle. Examine **Figure 32.10** to see that there are three types of muscle: skeletal muscle, smooth muscle, and cardiac muscle. Muscles are classified according to their structure and function.

**Smooth muscle** Many hollow internal organs such as the stomach, intestines, bladder, and uterus are lined with **smooth muscle.** Smooth muscle is called **involuntary muscle** because it cannot be controlled consciously. For example, food moves through the digestive tract because of the action of smooth muscles that line the esophagus, stomach, and small and large intestines. Under a microscope, smooth muscle does not appear striated, or striped, and each cell has one nucleus.

**Cardiac muscle** The involuntary muscle present only in the heart is called **cardiac muscle.** Cardiac muscle cells are arranged in a network, or web, that allows the heart muscle to contract efficiently and rhythmically. This arrangement gives strength to the heart. Cardiac muscle is striped, or striated, with light and dark bands of cells with many nuclei. Cells usually have one nucleus and are connected by gap junctions.

■ **Figure 32.10** When magnified, differences in muscle shape and appearance can be seen. Smooth muscle fibers appear spindle-shaped; cardiac muscle appears striated or striped; skeletal muscle also appears striated.
**Explain** *In addition to their appearance, how else are muscles classified?*

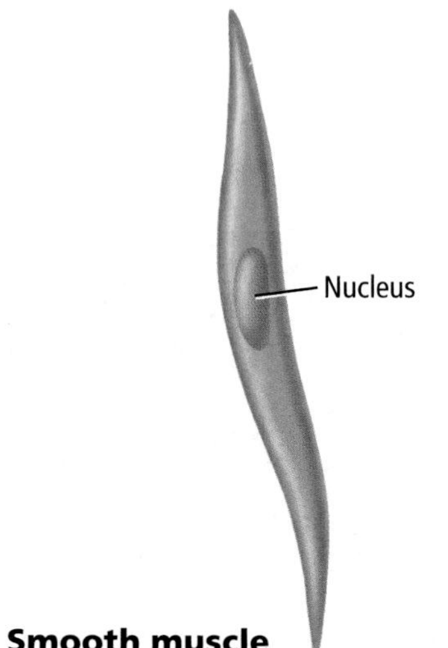


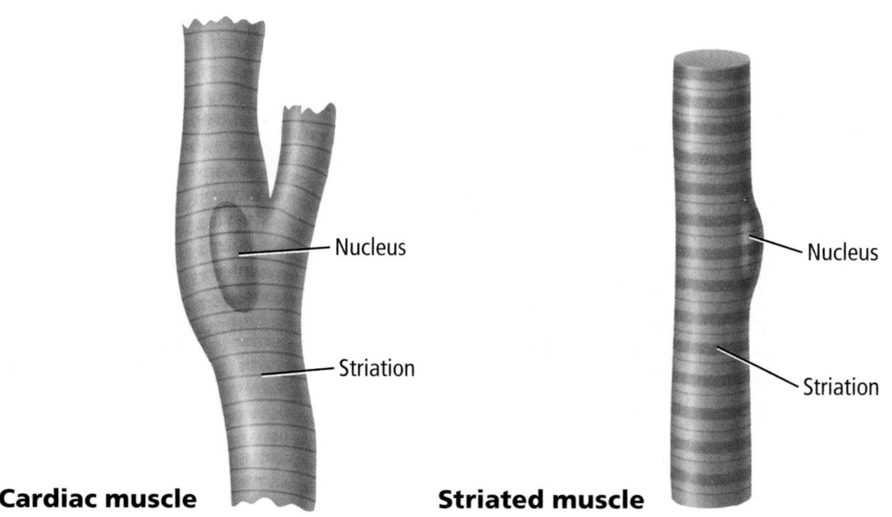

**VOCABULARY**

**SCIENCE USAGE V. COMMON USAGE**

**Contract**

***Science usage:*** to tighten or to shorten.

*Muscles contract and cause movement.*

***Common usage:*** to become affected with.

*If you are exposed to the flu, you may contract the illness.*

**Skeletal muscle** Most of the muscles in the body are skeletal muscles. **Skeletal muscles** are muscles attached to bones by tendons and when tightened, or contracted, cause movement. Skeletal muscles are **voluntary muscles** that are consciously controlled to move bones. **Tendons,** which are tough bands of connective tissue, connect muscles to bones. Under a microscope, skeletal muscles also appear striated.

## Skeletal Muscle Contraction

Most skeletal muscles are arranged in opposing, or antagonistic pairs. Refer to **Figure 32.11,** which illustrates muscles that you use to raise your arm and opposing muscles that you use to lower your arm. Skeletal muscle is arranged into fibers, which are fused muscle cells. Muscle fibers consist of many smaller units called **myofibrils.** Myofibrils consist of even smaller units, **myosin** and **actin,** which are protein filaments. Myofibrils are arranged in sections called sarcomeres. A **sarcomere** is the functional unit of a muscle and the part of the muscle that contracts as illustrated in **Figure 32.12.** The striations of skeletal muscles are a result of the sarcomeres, which run Z line to Z line. Z lines are where actin filaments attach within a myofibril. The overlap of actin and myosin filaments results in a dark band called the A band. The M line consists of only myosin filaments. The arrangement of the components of a sarcomere causes a muscle to shorten and then relax.

**Sliding filament theory** **Figure 32.12** also illustrates the sliding filament theory. This theory states that once a nerve signal reaches a muscle, the actin filaments slide toward one another, causing the muscle to contract. Notice that the myosin filaments do not move. There are many skeletal muscles involved in a simple motion, such as turning this page.

**Connection to Chemistry** When the nerve impulse reaches the muscle, calcium is released into the myofibrils. Calcium causes the myosin and actin to attach to each other. The actin filaments then are pulled toward the center of the sarcomere, which causes muscle contraction. ATP produced in the mitochondria is necessary for this step of muscle contraction. When the muscle relaxes, the filaments slide back into their original positions. You will learn more about nerve function in Chapter 33.

**Figure 32.11** Muscles are arranged in antagonistic pairs.

**Concepts In Motion**

**Interactive Figure** To see an animation of muscles contracting, visit biologygmh.com.

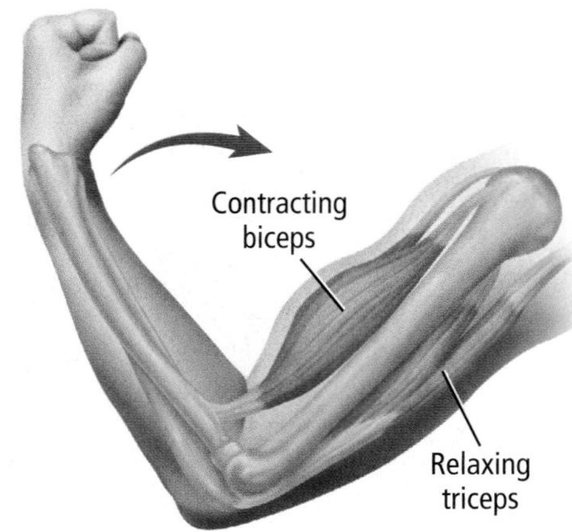


When the biceps muscle contracts, the lower arm is moved upward.

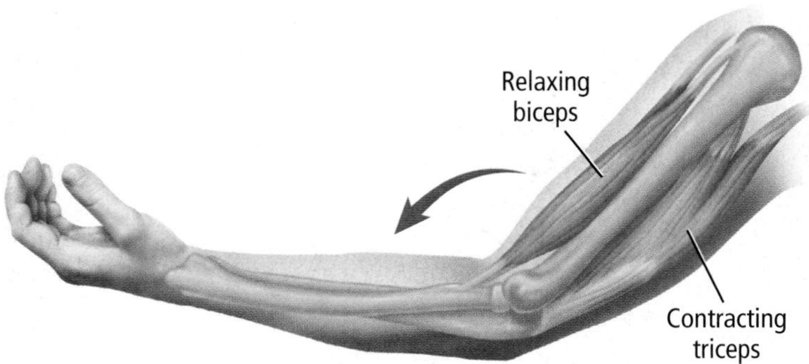


When the triceps muscle on the back of the upper arm contracts, the lower arm moves downward.

# Visualizing Muscle Contraction

**Figure 32.12**
A muscle fiber is made of myofibrils. The protein filaments actin and myosin form myofibrils.

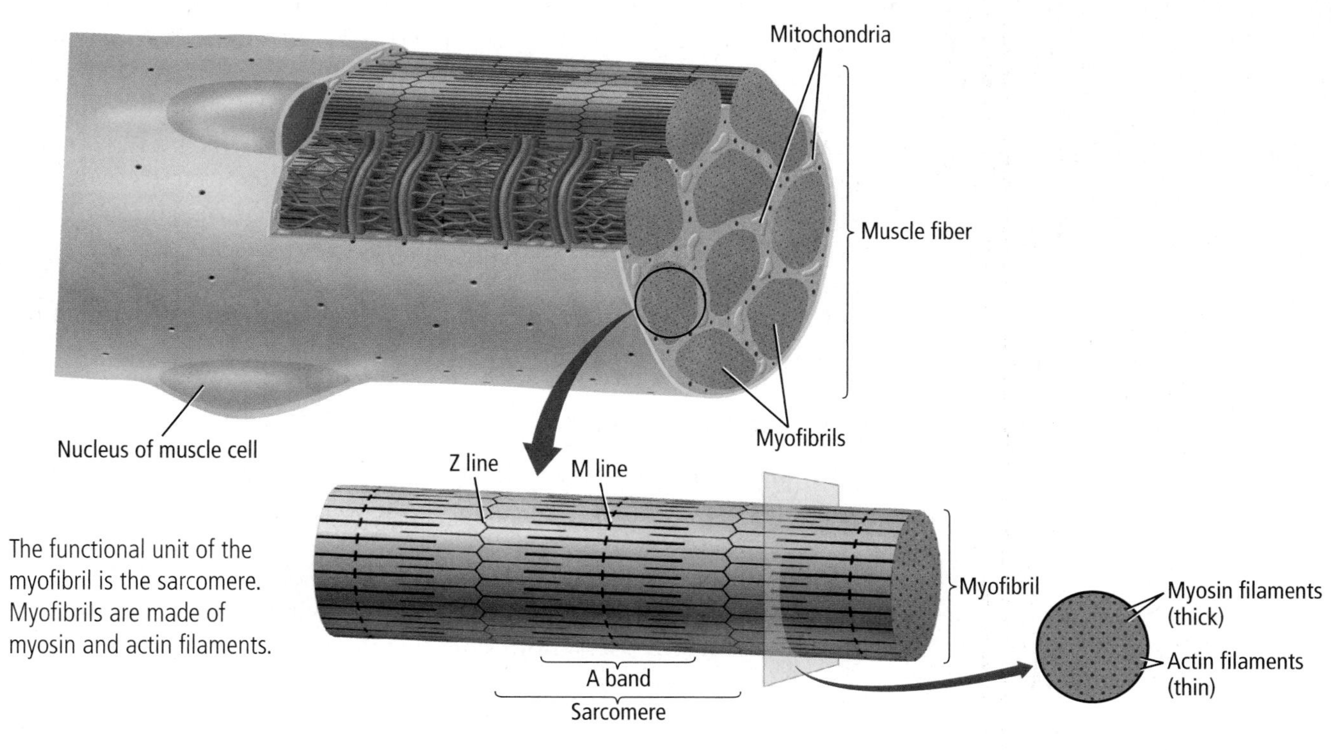


The functional unit of the myofibril is the sarcomere. Myofibrils are made of myosin and actin filaments.

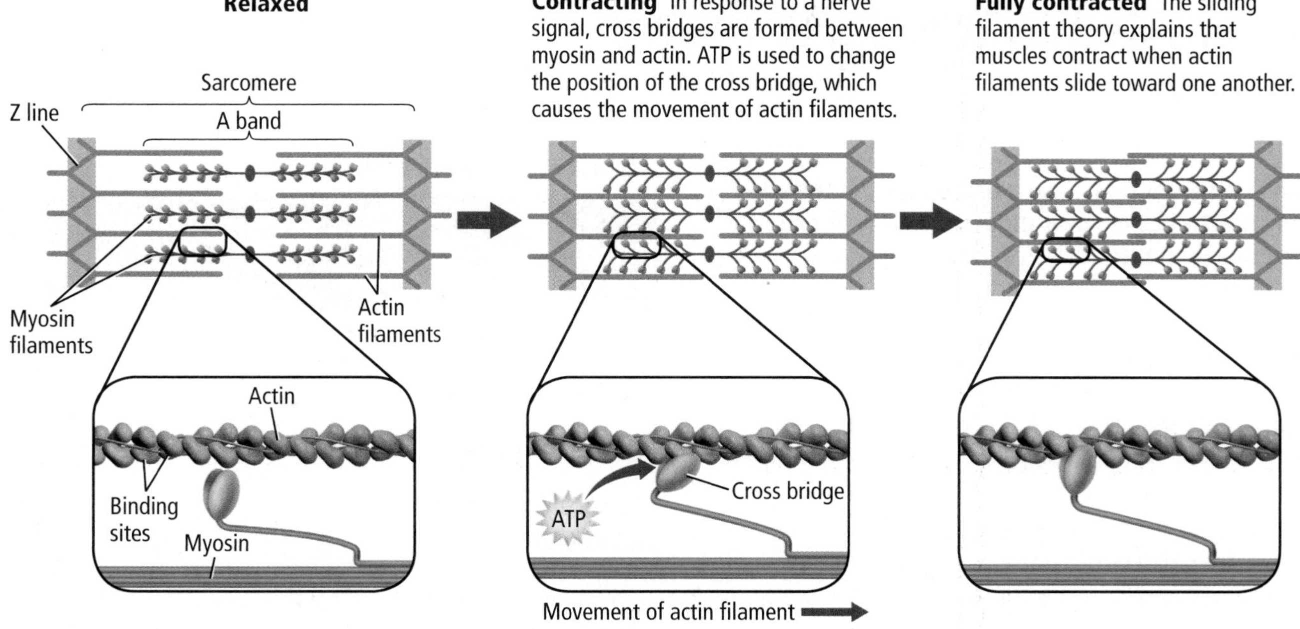


**Contracting** In response to a nerve signal, cross bridges are formed between myosin and actin. ATP is used to change the position of the cross bridge, which causes the movement of actin filaments.

**Fully contracted** The sliding filament theory explains that muscles contract when actin filaments slide toward one another.

**Concepts In Motion** Interactive Figure To see an animation of muscle contraction, visit biologygmh.com.

Biology Online

**Figure 32.13** Crossing the finish line is a moment of intense energy.
**Explain** *How is normal breathing restored after intense exercise?*

**Energy for muscle contraction** All muscle cells metabolize aerobically and anaerobically. When sufficient oxygen is available, aerobic cellular respiration occurs in muscle cells.

Recall from Chapter 8 that cellular respiration process provides ATP for energy. After a period of intense exercise, muscles might not get enough oxygen to sustain cellular respiration, limiting the amount of ATP that is available. Muscles, like those of the athlete in **Figure 32.13,** then must rely on the anaerobic process of lactic acid fermentation for energy.

During exercise, lactic acid builds up in muscle cells, causing fatigue. Excess lactic acid enters the bloodstream and this stimulates rapid breathing. After resting for a short time, adequate amounts of oxygen are restored and lactic acid is broken down.

You probably have seen a dead animal along the side of the road. When an animal dies, rigor mortis sets in. Rigor mortis is a state of prolonged muscular contraction. ATP is required to pump the calcium back out of the myofibrils, which causes the muscles to relax. In rigor mortis, the dead animal cannot produce ATP, so the calcium remains in the myofibrils and the muscle remains contracted. After 24 h, cells and tissues begin degrading and the muscle fibers cannot remain contracted.

## Skeletal Muscle Strength

Many people do not develop the physiques of champion bodybuilders, no matter how often they work out in the weight room. A person might be the fastest sprinter on the track team, but quickly becomes fatigued in a long-distance race. What might be the reason for these differences? The reason in both cases is the ratio of slow-twitch muscle fibers to fast-twitch muscle fibers. Both slow-twitch and fast-twitch fibers are present in every person's muscles.

## DATA ANALYSIS LAB 32.1

**Based on Real Data***

### Interpret the Data

**How is the percentage of slow-twitch muscle related to action of a muscle?** The proportion of slow-twitch to fast-twitch muscle fibers can be determined by removing a small piece of a muscle and staining the cells with a dye called *ATPase stain*. Fast-twitch muscle fibers with a high amount of ATP activity stain dark brown.

**Think Critically**

1. **Analyze** the data table. Hypothesize why a muscle such as the soleus has more slow-twitch muscle fibers than a muscle such as the orbicularis oculi.
2. **Classify** muscles by giving examples of muscles that have a high proportion of fast-twitch muscle fibers.

**Data and Observations**

| Muscle | Action | Percent Slow Twitch |
|---|---|---|
| **Soleus (leg)** | Elevates the foot | 87 |
| **Biceps femoris (leg)** | Flexes the leg | 67 |
| **Deltoid (shoulder)** | Lifts the arm | 52 |
| **Sternocleidomastoideus (neck)** | Moves the head | 35 |
| **Orbicularis oculi (face)** | Closes the eyelid | 15 |

*Data adapted from: Lamb, D.R. 1984. *Physiology of Exercise* New York: Macmillan Co.

# CHAPTER 32 Assessment

## Section 32.1

### Vocabulary Review

*Explain the difference between the terms in each set.*

**1.** epidermis, dermis

**2.** melanin, keratin

**3.** sebaceous glands, hair follicles

### Understand Key Concepts

*Use the diagram below to answer question 4.*

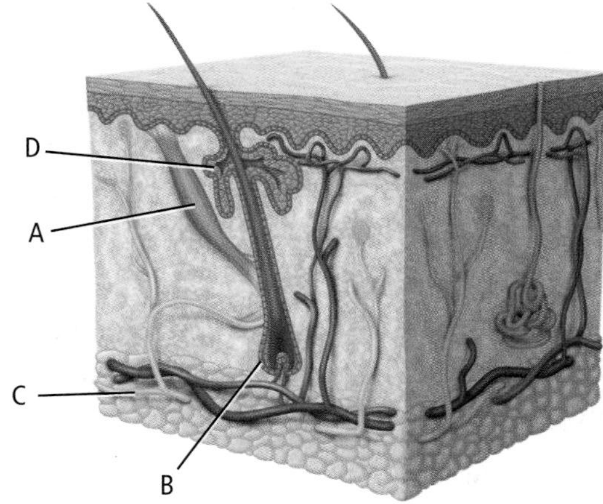


**4.** Which tissue type is responsible for the formation of "goose bumps"?
- **A.** A
- **B.** B
- **C.** C
- **D.** D

**5.** When are blackheads formed?
- **A.** when sebaceous glands become clogged
- **B.** when grooves in the epidermis gather dirt
- **C.** when hair follicles grow inward rather than outward
- **D.** when there is an excess of keratin produced

**6.** How does the skin regulate body temperature?
- **A.** by increasing sweat production
- **B.** by retaining water
- **C.** by producing vitamin D
- **D.** by regulating fat content in the epidermis

**7.** Which are not found in the dermis?
- **A.** muscles
- **B.** sweat and oil glands
- **C.** fat cells
- **D.** nerve cells

**8.** What could be inferred from suntans?
- **A.** Sunning for the purpose of tanning produces healthier skin.
- **B.** A tan might indicate sun damage to the skin.
- **C.** Tanning strengthens the elastic in the skin making the skin feel tight.
- **D.** Tanning promotes skin that has a more youthful appearance.

### Constructed Response

**9. Open Ended** What possible effects on the body might there be if the epidermis was absent?

**10. Open Ended** What possible effects on the body might there be if the dermis was absent?

**11. Short Answer** Describe how the integumentary system contributes to homeostasis.

### Think Critically

**12. Explain** why it does not hurt when you get a haircut.

**13. Assess** the reason why people with third degree burns might not feel pain at the site of the burn.

## Section 32.2

### Vocabulary Review

*Explain the difference between the terms in each set.*

**14.** spongy bone, compact bone

**15.** tendons, ligaments

**16.** osteoblasts, osteoclasts

### Understand Key Concepts

*Use the figure below to answer question 17.*

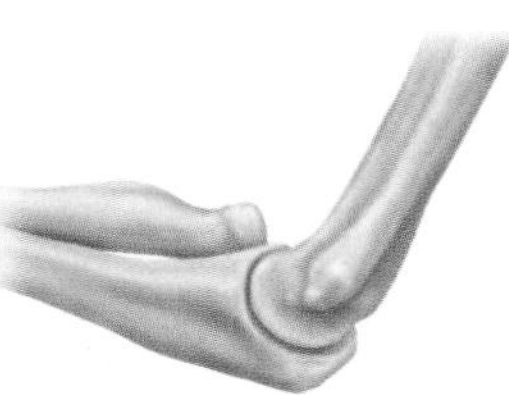

**17.** Where would you find the type of joint shown above?
- **A.** hip
- **B.** vertebrae
- **C.** elbow
- **D.** skull

**18.** Which is not a function of bone?
**A.** production of vitamin D
**B.** internal support
**C.** protection of internal organs
**D.** storage of calcium

*Use the diagram below to answer question 19.*

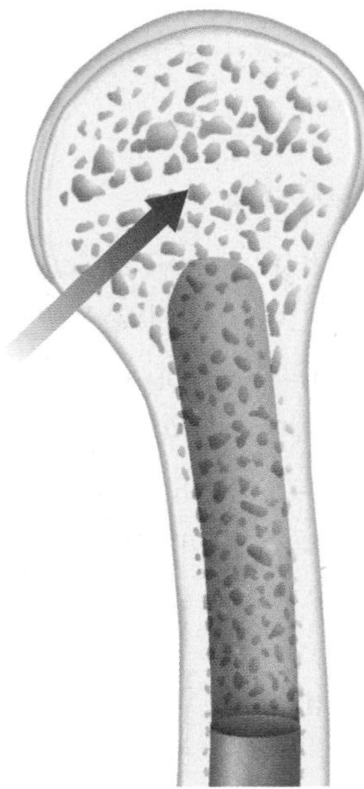

**19.** What is a characteristic of the portion of the bone indicated by the arrow?
**A.** It contains no living cells.
**B.** It contains bone marrow.
**C.** It is the only type of bone tissue in long bones.
**D.** It is made of overlapping osteon systems.

**20.** Which set of terms is mismatched?
**A.** cranium—sutures
**B.** wrist—pivot joint
**C.** shoulder—ball-and-socket joint
**D.** knee—hinge joint

**21.** What are the cells that remove old bone tissue called?
**A.** osteoblasts
**B.** osteocytes
**C.** osteoclasts
**D.** osteozymes

**22.** Which is not part of the axial skeleton?
**A.** skull
**B.** ribs
**C.** hip bone
**D.** vertebral column

**23.** Which is part of the appendicular skeleton?

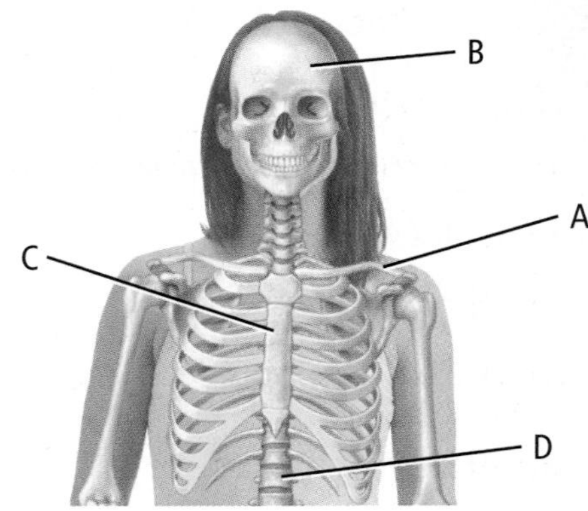


**A.** A
**B.** B
**C.** C
**D.** D

## Constructed Response

**24. Open Ended** Describe potential consequences if all bone tissue in humans was comprised of spongy bone and there was no compact bone.

**25. Open Ended** Describe potential consequences if all bone tissue in humans was comprised of compact bone and there was no spongy bone.

**26. Short Answer** Compare the function of osteoclasts and osteoblasts.

## Think Critically

**27. Analyze** the following scenario. A person enters the emergency room with an ankle injury. What structures of the patient's ankle need to be examined to determine the proper treatment?

**28. Hypothesize** what might happen to a woman's bones if she did not increase her intake of calcium during pregnancy?

# Section 32.3

## Vocabulary Review

*For each set of terms below, choose the one term that does not belong and explain why it does not belong.*

**29.** actin, melanin, myosin

**30.** cardiac muscle, smooth muscle, fast-twitch muscle

**31.** sarcomere, myofibril, myoglobin

### Understand Key Concepts

**32.** Which requires ATP?
**A.** muscle contraction
**B.** muscle relaxation
**C.** both muscle contraction and relaxation
**D.** neither muscle contraction nor relaxation

*Use the diagram below to answer question 33.*

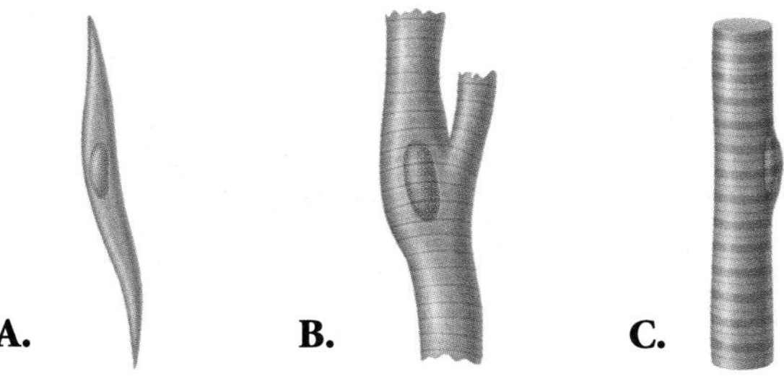


**33.** What muscles shown above are classified as voluntary muscles?
**A.** the muscle type shown in A
**B.** the muscle type shown in B
**C.** the muscle type shown in C
**D.** all muscles

**34.** Which is a characteristic of fast-twitch muscle fibers?
**A.** They contain more myoglobin than slow-twitch fibers.
**B.** They are resistant to fatigue.
**C.** They have fewer mitochondria than slow-twitch fibers.
**D.** They require high amounts of oxygen in order to function.

### Constructed Response

**35. Short Answer** Compare and contrast the structure of skeletal, smooth, and cardiac muscle.

**36. Short Answer** Explain, based on the structure of the muscle fibers, why skeletal muscles can contract but not lengthen.

### Think Critically

**37. Predict** any possible consequences if cardiac and smooth muscle had the same structure as skeletal muscle.

**38. Infer** why it is important that no muscle contains solely slow-twitch or fast-twitch fibers.

## Additional Assessment

**39.** WRITING in **Biology** Imagine you are a writer for a health magazine. Write a brief article about the need for calcium for the skeletal and muscular systems.

### DBQ Document-Based Questions

*Athletes burn fat at a maximum rate when they exercise at an intensity near the lactate threshold—the point at which lactic acid starts to build up in the muscles. In addition, athletes who consume the greatest amounts of oxygen during intense exercise* [$VO_{2peak}$] *burn the most fat. Researchers compared the lactate threshold and oxygen consumption of overweight subjects who did not exercise to those of highly-trained athletes.*

Data obtained from: Bircher, S. and Knechtle, B. 2004. Relationship between fat oxidation and lactate threshold in athletes and obese women and men. Journal of Sports Science and Medicine 3:174–181.

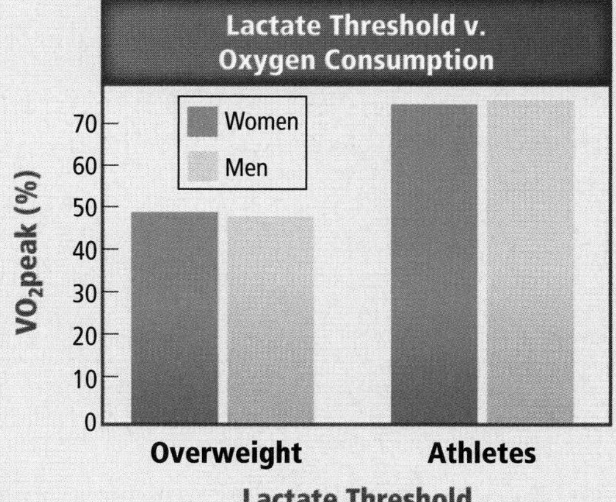


**40.** At what percent of $VO_{2\ peak}$ was the lactate threshold reached in overweight subjects?

**41.** How might an overweight person who does not exercise increase his or her $VO_{2\ peak}$ and, therefore, his or her lactate threshold?

### Cumulative Review

**42.** Make sketches of the distinctive parts of mammals that distinguish them from all other groups. **(Chapter 30)**

# Standardized Test Practice

**Cumulative**

## Multiple Choice

1. Which describes the circulatory system of most reptiles?
   **A.** double loop, four-chambered heart
   **B.** double loop, three-chambered heart
   **C.** single loop, three-chambered heart
   **D.** single loop, two-chambered heart

*Use the figure below to answer question 2.*

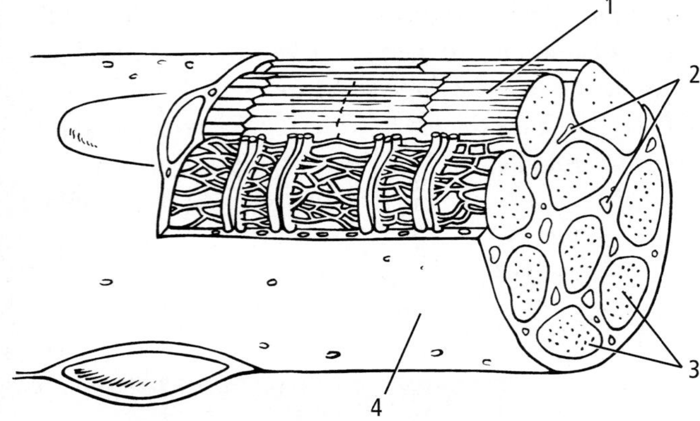


2. Which part of a muscle is used for cellular respiration?
   **A.** 1
   **B.** 2
   **C.** 3
   **D.** 4

3. Which characteristic makes bats unique among mammals?
   **A.** eyesight
   **B.** feathers
   **C.** flight
   **D.** teeth

4. Which learned behavior occurs only at a certain critical time in an animal's life?
   **A.** classical conditioning
   **B.** fixed action pattern
   **C.** habituation
   **D.** imprinting

*Use the figure of the joint below to answer question 5.*

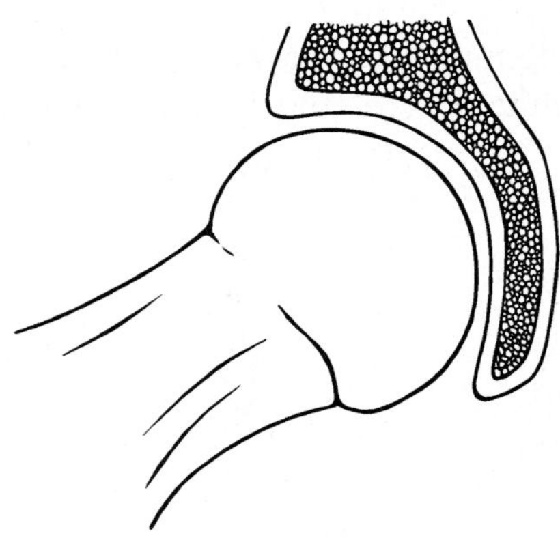

5. Where is the type of joint shown in the figure found?
   **A.** elbows and knees
   **B.** fingers and toes
   **C.** hips and shoulders
   **D.** wrists and ankles

6. Which describes the characteristics of a bird's brain?
   **A.** Birds have a large medulla to process their vision.
   **B.** Birds have a large cerebellum to control respiration and digestion.
   **C.** Birds have a large cerebrum to coordinate movement and balance.
   **D.** Birds have a large cerebral cortex to control flight.

7. Which type of bone is classified as irregular?
   **A.** leg bones
   **B.** skull
   **C.** vertebrae
   **D.** wrist bones

8. Which adaptation helps stop fishes from rolling side to side in the water?
   **A.** ctenoid scales
   **B.** paired fins
   **C.** placoid scales
   **D.** swim bladders

## Short Answer

*Use the diagram below to answer questions 9 and 10.*

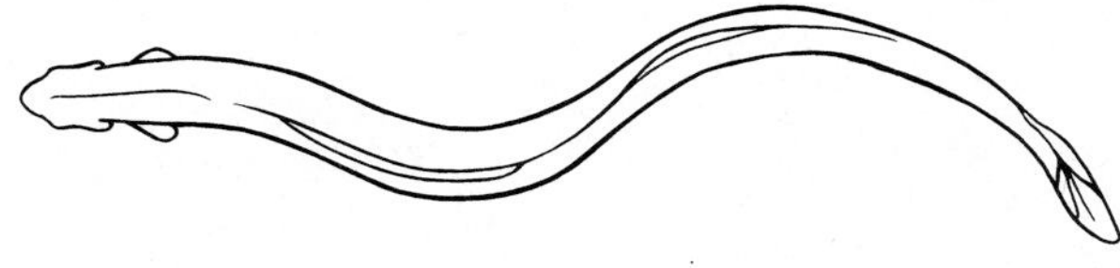

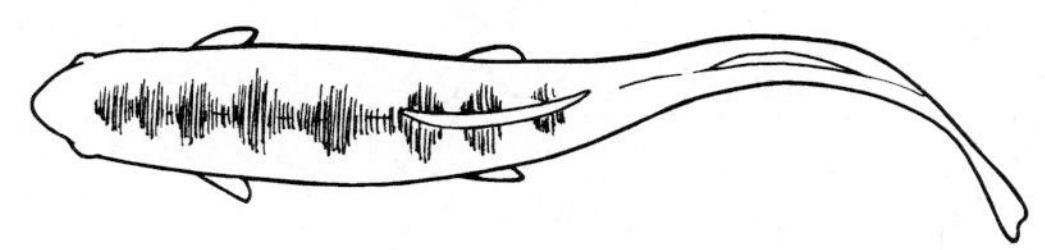

**9.** Describe the difference between how a fish with an S-shaped pattern swims and a fish that moves its tail only.

**10.** Decide where a fish with an S-shaped pattern would be likely found swimming.

**11.** Relate the key events in the life cycle of a butterfly to the key events in the life cycle of a grasshopper.

**12.** Howler monkeys are the loudest land animals. Their calls are heard for miles across the jungle. They use their calls to mark their territory. Assess this type of behavior.

**13.** Describe how fetal cartilage becomes bone.

**14.** A chimpanzee picks up a blade of grass and sticks it in an anthole. When it pulls the blade of grass out, it has ants on it. The chimpanzee eats the ants. The chimpanzee continues doing this because it is an easy way to get ants. Assess this activity as it relates to animal behaviors.

**15.** Describe two types of joint conditions.

## Extended Response

*Use the diagram to answer questions 16 and 17.*

Pigeon

Eagle

**16.** Evaluate what the location of the eyes on these two birds reveals about their behavior.

**17.** Explain how the beaks of these two birds give evidence of what they eat.

## Essay Question

Whooping cranes are an endangered species. One of the reasons for this is that they hatch in nesting areas and then migrate south for the winter. Humans can raise chicks, but teaching them to migrate is a different problem. Operation Migration solved this problem in 2001. Operation Migration used ultralight aircraft to lead a migration of human-raised whooping cranes on a 2000-km migration from Wisconsin to Florida. The whooping cranes followed the ultralight aircraft that used recorded calls to learn the migration route.

*Using the information in the paragraph above, answer the following question in essay format.*

**18.** Migratory behavior has been shown to be an innate behavior. Evaluate why it is necessary to use ultralight aircraft to guide the birds so they can learn the migration route.

**NEED EXTRA HELP?**

| If You Missed Question . . . | 1 | 2 | 3 | 4 | 5 | 6 | 7 | 8 | 9 | 10 | 11 | 12 | 13 | 14 | 15 | 16 | 17 | 18 |
|---|---|---|---|---|---|---|---|---|---|---|---|---|---|---|---|---|---|---|
| Review Section . . . | 29.1 | 32.3 | 30.1 | 31.1 | 32.2 | 29.2 | 32.2 | 28.1 | 28.1 | 28.1 | 26.3 | 31.2 | 32.2 | 31.1 | 32.2 | 29.2 | 29.2 | 31.2 |

# Chapter 33 Nervous System

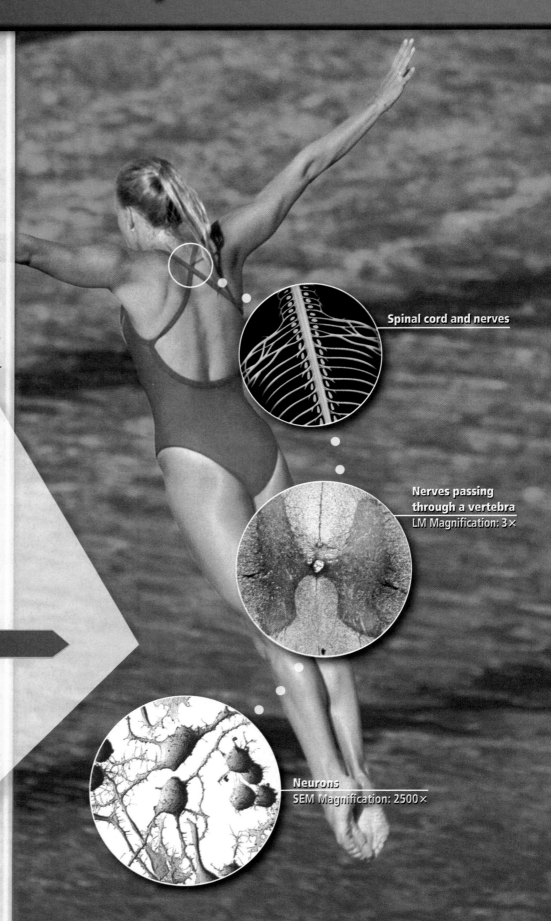

**Section 1**
**Structure of the Nervous System**
**MAIN Idea** Neurons conduct electrical impulses that allow cells, tissues, and organs to detect and respond to stimuli.

**Section 2**
**Organization of the Nervous System**
**MAIN Idea** The central nervous system and the peripheral nervous system are the two major divisions of the nervous system.

**Section 3**
**The Senses**
**MAIN Idea** Sensory receptors allow you to detect the world around you.

**Section 4**
**Effects of Drugs**
**MAIN Idea** Some drugs alter the function of the nervous system.

## BioFacts

- A nerve impulse can travel as fast as 402 km/h.
- There are over 100 billion neurons in the brain alone.
- A single neuron can connect with over 1000 other neurons.
- A human hand has approximately 2000 nerve endings per square centimeter.

Spinal cord and nerves

Nerves passing through a vertebra
LM Magnification: 3×

Neurons
SEM Magnification: 2500×

CHAPTER 33

# Assessment

## Section 33.1

### Vocabulary Review

*For each set of terms below, choose the one term that does not belong and explain why it does not belong.*

1. axon—dendrite—reflex arc
2. cell body—synapse—neurotransmitter
3. myelin—node—threshold

### Understand Key Concepts

*Use the diagram below to answer question 4.*

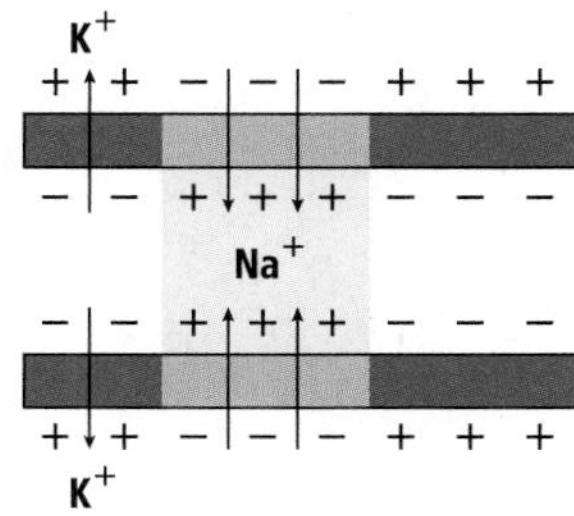


4. What is occurring in the diagram above?
   **A.** $K^+$ ions are entering the neuron.
   **B.** Negatively charged proteins are leaving the neuron.
   **C.** $Na^+$ ions are entering the neuron.
   **D.** The myelin coat has broken down, allowing ions to freely cross the plasma membrane.

5. Which is the correct path a nerve impulse will follow in a reflex arc?
   **A.** motor neuron → interneuron → sensory neuron
   **B.** interneuron → motor neuron → sensory neuron
   **C.** motor neuron → sensory neuron → interneuron
   **D.** sensory neuron → interneuron → motor neuron

### Constructed Response

6. **Short Answer** Hypothesize why it takes more energy for a nerve impulse to travel an axon that lacks myelin as opposed to an axon that has myelin.

7. **Short Answer** Explain the following analogy: A neuron is like a one-way street, while a nerve is like a two-way street.

### Think Critically

8. **Infer** In most animals, an action potential will travel only in one direction along a neuron. Infer what the result might be in humans if nerve impulses could travel in both directions on a single neuron.

## Section 33.2

### Vocabulary Review

*For each set of terms below, choose the one term that does not belong and explain why it does not belong.*

9. somatic system—parasympathetic system —sympathetic system
10. cerebrum—pons—medulla oblongata
11. autonomic nervous system—somatic nervous system—central nervous system

### Understand Key Concepts

12. Which is characteristic of the sympathetic division of the autonomic system?
    **A.** stimulates digestion
    **B.** dilates the bronchi
    **C.** slows the heart rate
    **D.** converts glucose to glycogen

*Use the diagram below to answer question 13.*

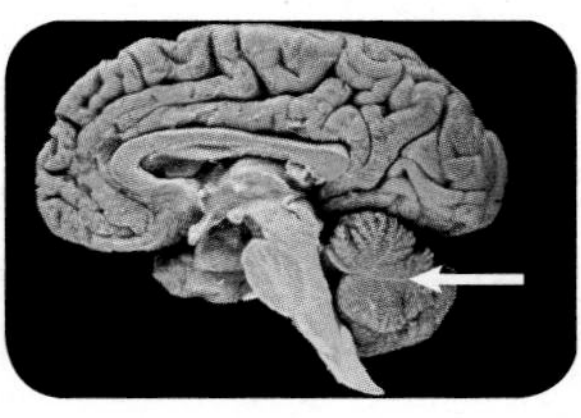

13. If the portion indicated by the arrow was damaged due to trauma, what effects would this person most likely experience?
    **A.** partial or complete memory loss
    **B.** body temperature fluctuations
    **C.** trouble maintaining balance
    **D.** rapid breathing

14. Which nervous system is the hypothalamus most involved in regulating?
    **A.** voluntary
    **B.** peripheral
    **C.** sensory
    **D.** autonomic

### Constructed Response

15. **Open Ended** Suppose you are on the debate team at school. You must support the following statement: The autonomic nervous system is more involved with homeostasis than the somatic nervous system. Build your case.

### Think Critically

16. **Critique** You might have heard the statement "humans use only ten percent of their brains." Use the Internet or other sources to compile evidence that either supports or refutes this idea.

17. **Analyze** The human cerebrum is disproportionately large compared to the cerebrum of other animals. What advantage does this give to humans?

## Section 33.3

### Vocabulary Review

*Distinguish between the terms in each of the following sets:*

18. rods—cones

19. cochlea—semicircular canals

20. retina—taste buds

### Understand Key Concepts

21. If there were a power outage in a movie theater and only a few dim emergency lights were lit, which cells of the retina would be most important for seeing your way to the exit?
   **A.** rods
   **B.** cones
   **C.** Rods and cones are equally important.

22. Which represents the correct sequence as sound waves travel in the ear to trigger an impulse?
   **A.** cochlea, incus, stape, eardrum
   **B.** tympanum, bones in the middle ear, cochlea, hair cells
   **C.** auditory canal, tympanum, hair cells, cochlea
   **D.** hair cells, auditory canal, cochlea, malleus

23. With which sense are free nerve endings associated?
   **A.** taste **C.** touch
   **B.** hearing **D.** sight

*Use the diagram below to answer question 24.*

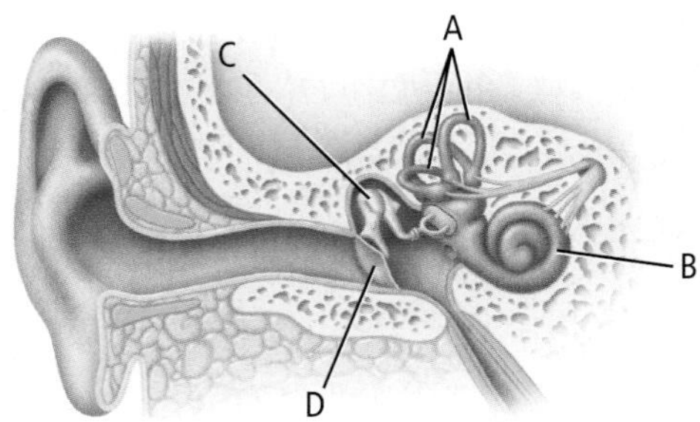


24. Some rides at amusement parks cause a person to become dizzy when the ride stops. Which structure in the diagram is most likely involved with the dizzy feeling?
   **A.** A **C.** C
   **B.** B **D.** D

### Constructed Response

25. **Open Ended** A rare condition exists in which a person cannot feel pain. Is this desirable or undesirable? Explain your response.

### Think Critically

26. **Explain** You have receptors for light (soft) touch all over your body. In terms of what you know about the nervous system, why are you not always conscious of things like wearing clothes or a wristwatch?

27. **Categorize** Rate the senses from 1 to 5 in order of importance (with 1 representing the most important.) Be prepared to debate this issue with other students in the class.

## Section 33.4

### Vocabulary Review

*Explain the difference between the terms in each set. Then explain how the terms are related.*

28. stimulants—depressants

29. tolerance—addiction

30. dopamine—drug

## Understand Key Concepts

**31.** Which of the following decreases brain activity?
**A.** nicotine
**B.** amphetamines
**C.** cocaine
**D.** alcohol

**32.** What is the most likely function of amphetamines?
**A.** to stimulate the sympathetic nervous system
**B.** to stimulate the parasympathetic nervous system
**C.** to stimulate the sympathetic and parasympathetic systems equally
**D.** do not affect either the sympathetic or parasympathetic nervous system

*Use the diagram below to answer question 33.*

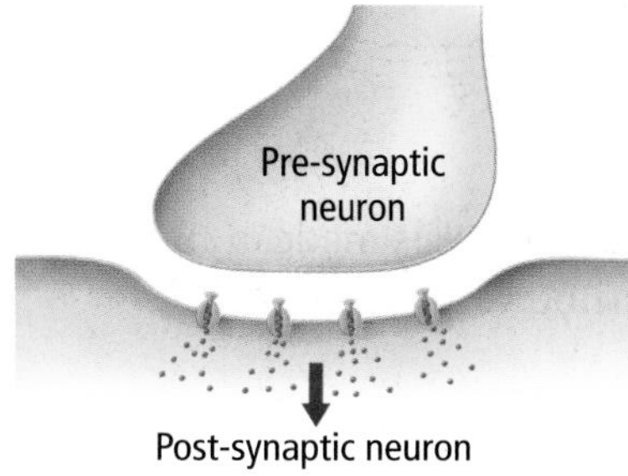


**33.** If a person is suffering from depression, which drug is one recommended treatment of the presynaptic neuron?
**A.** one that increases the re-uptake of dopamine.
**B.** one that increases the production of dopamine
**C.** one that decreases the receptors for dopamine
**D.** one that decreases the re-uptake of dopamine

## Constructed Response

**34. Short Answer** What does it mean when someone is addicted to a drug?

**35. Open Ended** Discuss what consequences might arise if a person's gene for the production of dopamine was defective.

## Think Critically

**36. Defend** Form a conclusion about the following statement: "It is more difficult for someone to get addicted to drugs than it is to stop using drugs." Defend your position.

## Additional Assessment

**37.**  WRITING in Biology Write a short story about a person who heard a loud noise and became afraid. Include in your story events that might occur in each division of the nervous system during such an experience.

### DBQ Document-Based Questions

Data obtained from: Blinkov, S.M., and Glezer, I.I. 1968. *The human brain in figures and tables: a quantitative handbook*. New York: Plenum Press.
Nieuwenhuys, R., Ten Donkelaar, H.J., and Nicholson, C. 1998. *The central nervous system of vertebrates*. Vol. 3. Berlin: Springer.
Berta, A., et al. 1999. *Marine mammals: evolutionary biology*. San Diego: Academic Press.

**Average Brain Weights (in grams)**

| Species | Weight (g) | Species | Weight (g) |
|---|---|---|---|
| Fin whale | 6930 | Dog (beagle) | 72 |
| Elephant | 6000 | Cat | 30 |
| Cow | 425–458 | Turtle | 0.3–0.7 |
| Adult human | 1300–1400 | Rat | 2 |

**38.** Does there appear to be a correlation between body size and brain weight?

**39.** Discuss possible explanations (in terms of adaptations) that would account for your response to question 38.

## Cumulative Review

**40.** Evaluate the role of fungi on Earth. **(Chapter 20)**

**41.** Examine the adaptations that have made arthropods the most evolutionarily successful animals. **(Chapter 26)**

**42.** Make an argument for or against the following statement: The skin should be considered an organ rather than a tissue. **(Chapter 32)**

# Standardized Test Practice

**Cumulative**

## Multiple Choice

1. Which characteristic is unique to mammals?
   A. hair
   B. endothermy
   C. four-chambered heart
   D. internal fertilization

*Use the diagram below to answer questions 2 and 3.*

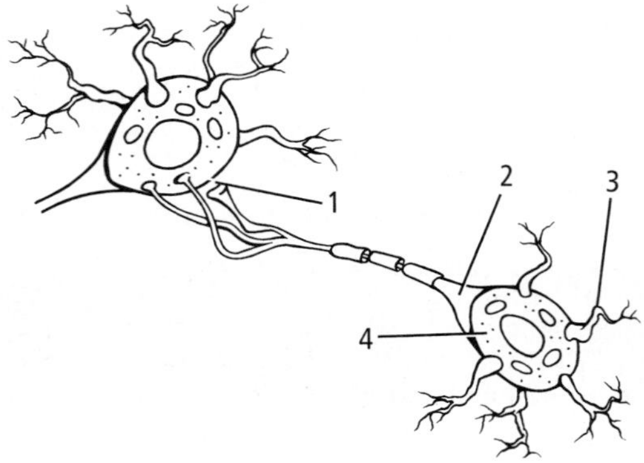


2. In which part of the diagram above would you expect to find myelin?
   A. 1
   B. 2
   C. 3
   D. 4

3. In which part of the diagram above would you expect to find neurotransmitters when an action potential reaches the end of the neuron?
   A. 1
   B. 2
   C. 3
   D. 4

4. What is the purpose of the epithelial tissue in the integumentary system?
   A. cover the body surface and protect its tissues
   B. move joints and bones
   C. provide a structural framework for the body
   D. transmit nerve signals

5. Which animal is a placental mammal?
   A. hummingbird
   B. kangaroo
   C. duck-billed platypus
   D. whale

*Use the diagram below to answer questions 6 and 7.*

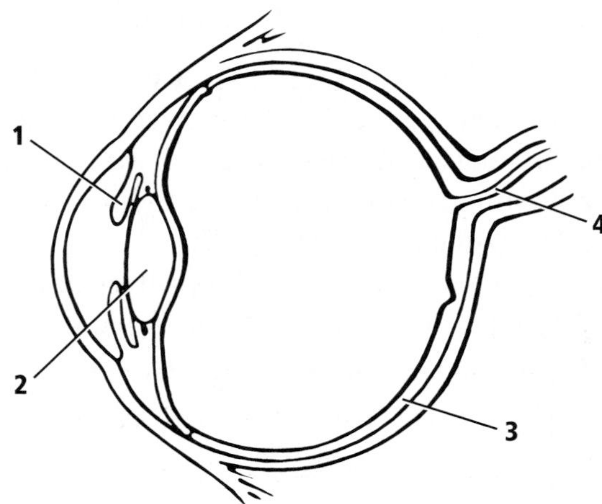


6. Which part of the eye is made of muscles that respond to stimuli?
   A. 1
   B. 2
   C. 3
   D. 4

7. If a person cannot see certain colors, what part of the eye might be damaged?
   A. 1
   B. 2
   C. 3
   D. 4

*Use the graph below to answer question 8.*

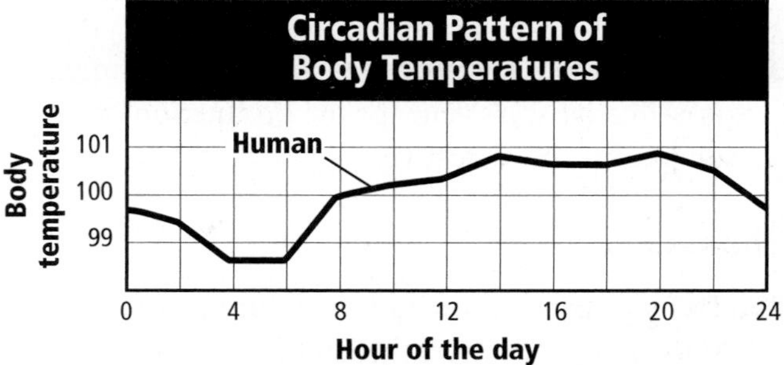


8. The graph above shows the circadian pattern of body temperature in humans. When does the body temperature of humans seem to be the lowest?
   A. after eating
   B. in the afternoon
   C. just before dawn
   D. late at night

## Short Answer

*Use the diagram below to answer questions 9 and 10.*

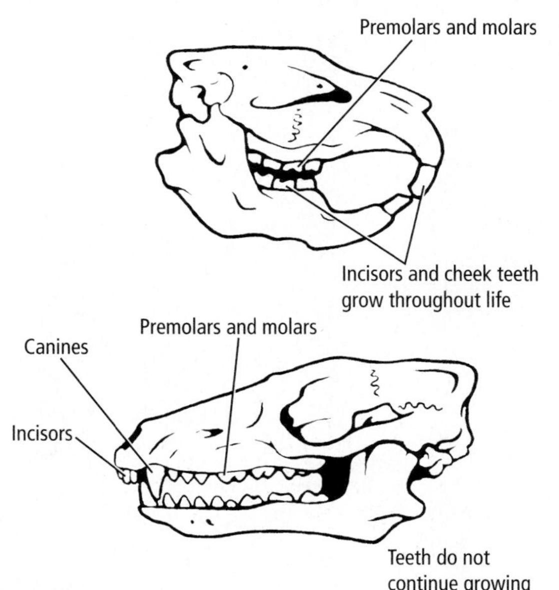


9. The figure above shows the teeth of two different types of mammals. From these teeth, what can you infer about the diets of these mammals?

10. Which animal's teeth most closely resemble those of humans? Explain your answer.

11. Explain how spiders predigest their food and compare this process to the digestion process of another animal with which you are familiar.

12. Suppose that a person who used to drink one cup of coffee to stay awake at night finds she needs to drink two cups. What is the name of this phenomenon and what causes it?

13. What is the role of the gametophyte generation in seed plants?

## Extended Response

14. Two abandoned whooping crane chicks are found several days after they had hatched. A scientist wants to raise the chicks. To make the chicks feel comfortable, the scientist uses a hand puppet that looks like a whooping crane. The scientist offers the chicks mealworms but they will not take them. Formulate a hypothesis that gives a possible explanation of the actions of the chicks.

15. How are the actions of myosin and actin fibers related to the contraction of a muscle?

16. What is the main difference between segmented worms and other worms? What is the importance of this difference?

## Essay Question

Each year doctors perform more than 450,000 joint repair and replacement surgeries. This surgery reduces pain and increases movement in the joints. Joint repair surgery involves removing any debris or excess bone growth from around the joint. This restores the functioning of the joint. Joint replacement surgery involves replacing the joint with a synthetic joint. The synthetic joint is made of polyethylene, ceramic, or metal. Joint replacement enables the joint to function in the same way as a natural joint. Joint replacements usually are performed on the knee, hip, or shoulder.

*Using the information in the paragraph above, answer the following question in essay format.*

17. Doctors usually only replace knee or hip joints on older patients who are less active than younger patients. Explain why doctors recommend this.

**NEED EXTRA HELP?**

| If You Missed Question . . . | 1 | 2 | 3 | 4 | 5 | 6 | 7 | 8 | 9 | 10 | 11 | 12 | 13 | 14 | 15 | 16 | 17 |
|---|---|---|---|---|---|---|---|---|---|---|---|---|---|---|---|---|---|
| Review Section . . . | 30.1 | 33.1 | 33.1 | 32.1 | 30.2 | 33.3 | 33.3 | 30.1 | 30.2 | 30.2 | 26.1 | 33.2 | 21.4 | 31.1 | 32.3 | 25.1 | 32.2 |

CHAPTER 34

# Circulatory, Respiratory, and Excretory Systems

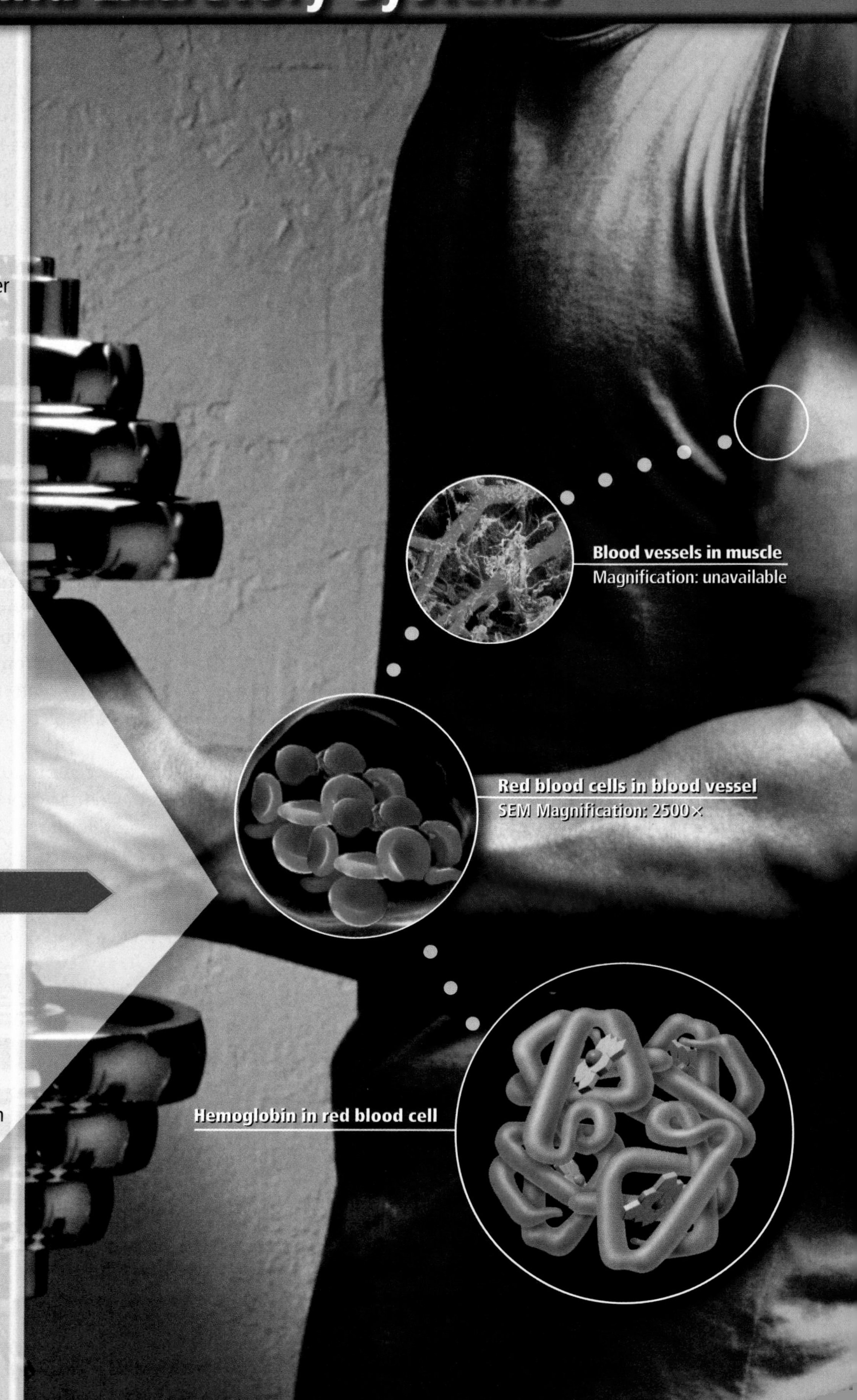


**Section 1**
**Circulatory System**
MAIN Idea The circulatory system transports blood to deliver important substances, such as oxygen, to cells and to remove wastes, such as carbon dioxide.

**Section 2**
**Respiratory System**
MAIN Idea The function of the respiratory system is the exchange of oxygen and carbon dioxide between the atmosphere and the blood and between the blood and the body's cells.

**Section 3**
**Excretory System**
MAIN Idea The kidneys maintain homeostasis by removing wastes and excess water from the body and by maintaining the pH of blood.

## BioFacts

- The only tissue in the human body that lacks blood vessels is the cornea of the eye.
- The heart beats more than two billion times in an average person's lifetime.
- Your lungs are made of 2414 km of airways and more than 300 million air sacs.
- The surface area of all of the air sacs surrounding the blood vessels in the lungs could cover a tennis court.

# LAUNCH Lab

## What changes take place in the body during exercise?

Body systems, including the respiratory and circulatory systems, function together to meet the demands of exercise and to maintain homeostasis. For example, red blood cells circulate throughout the body to deliver oxygen to cells, where it is used to help produce the energy required for exercise. In this lab, you will investigate how body system responses to exercise might be related to each other.

### Procedure

1. Read and complete the lab safety form.
2. Do a rhythmic exercise, such as jogging or marching in place, for two minutes. As you exercise, note how your body responds.
3. Make a list of the body system responses you identified as you exercised.

### Analysis

1. **Create** a flowchart showing how these body responses might be related to each other.
2. **Analyze** Propose how one of the body system responses on your list helps regulate the body's internal environment.

Visit biologygmh.com to:

- study the entire chapter online
- explore the Interactive Time Line, Concepts in Motion, Microscopy Links, Virtual Labs, and links to virtual dissections
- access Web links for more information, projects, and activities
- review content online with the Interactive Tutor, and take Self-Check Quizzes

**ABO Blood Types** Make the following Foldable to help you identify the four ABO blood groups: A, B, AB, and O.

**STEP 1** Fold a sheet of 11″ × 17″ paper into thirds lengthwise as shown.

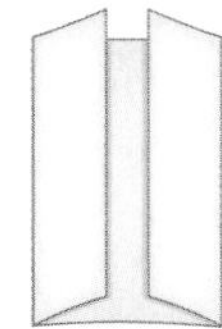

**STEP 2** Fold your paper in half. Crease the fold well.

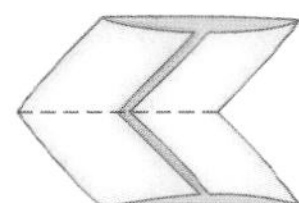

**STEP 3** Open the two vertical tabs and cut along the creases.

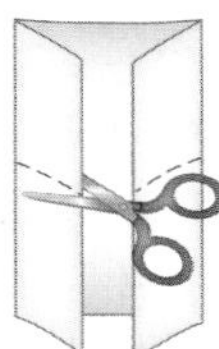

**STEP 4** Label the four tabs as shown.

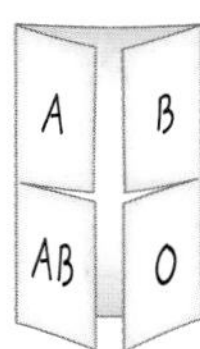


FOLDABLES **Use this Foldable with Section 34.1.** As you study the section, record what you learn about each of the four ABO blood groups.

## Section 34.1

### Objectives

- **Identify** the main functions of the circulatory system.
- **Diagram** the flow of blood through the heart and body.
- **Compare and contrast** the major components of the blood.

### Review Vocabulary

**muscle contraction:** muscle cells or fibers shorten in response to stimuli

### New Vocabulary

artery
capillary
vein
valve
heart
pacemaker
plasma
red blood cell
platelet
white blood cell
atherosclerosis

# Circulatory System

**MAIN Idea The circulatory system transports blood to deliver important substances, such as oxygen, to cells and to remove wastes, such as carbon dioxide.**

**Real-World Reading Link** Fast-moving highway traffic gets people to and from work quickly. Similarly, blood flowing in your body supplies nutrients and removes waste products quickly. When either traffic or blood flow is blocked, normal functions slow down or stop.

## Functions of the Circulatory System

Cells must have oxygen and nutrients and must get rid of waste products. This exchange is done by the circulatory system—the body's transport system. The circulatory system consists of blood, the heart, blood vessels, and the lymphatic system. Blood carries important substances to all parts of the body. The heart pumps blood through a vast network of tubes inside your body called blood vessels. The lymphatic system is considered part of the circulatory and immune systems. You will learn about the lymphatic system in Chapter 37. All of these components work together to maintain homeostasis in the body.

The circulatory system transports many important substances, such as oxygen and nutrients. The blood also carries disease-fighting materials produced by the immune system. The blood contains cell fragments and proteins for blood clotting. Finally, the circulatory system distributes heat throughout the body to help regulate body temperature.

**Figure 34.1**
**From Cadavers to Artificial Hearts**
The human circulatory system has been studied for thousands of years, leading to great advances in medical technology.

**350 B.C.** Greek physician Praxagoras recognizes that veins and arteries are two different kinds of vessels.

**1452–1519** Leonardo da Vinci conducts extensive research on human cadavers. It is believed that he dissected about 30 corpses in his lifetime.

**1628** The first accurate description is made of the human heart—a pump that circulates blood in a one-way system.

**1903** The first electrocardiograph records the electrical activity of the heart.

1500 1600 1900

## Blood Vessels

Highways have lanes that separate traffic. They also have access ramps that take vehicles to and from roads. Similarly, the body also has a network of channels—the blood vessels. Blood vessels circulate blood throughout the body and help keep the blood flowing to and from the heart. The fact that there are different kinds of blood vessels was first observed by Greek physician Praxagoras, as noted in **Figure 34.1.** The three major blood vessels are arteries, capillaries, and veins, as illustrated in **Figure 34.2.**

**Arteries** Oxygen-rich blood, or oxygenated blood, is carried away from the heart in large blood vessels called **arteries.** These strong, thick-walled vessels are elastic and durable. They are capable of withstanding high pressures exerted by blood as it is pumped by the heart.

As shown in **Figure 34.2,** arteries are composed of three layers: an outer layer of connective tissue, a middle layer of smooth muscle, and an inner layer of endothelial tissue. The endothelial layer of the artery is thicker than that of the other blood vessels. The endothelial layer of arteries needs to be thicker because blood is under higher pressure when it is pumped from the heart into the arteries.

**Capillaries** Arteries branch through the body like the branches of a tree, becoming smaller in diameter as they grow farther away from the main vessel. The smallest branches are capillaries. **Capillaries** are microscopic blood vessels where the exchange of important substances and wastes occurs. Capillary walls are only one cell thick, as illustrated in **Figure 34.2.** This permits easy exchange of materials between the blood and body cells, through the process of diffusion. These tubes are so small that red blood cells move single-file through these vessels.

The diameter of blood vessels changes in response to the needs of the body. For example, when you are exercising, muscle capillaries will expand, or dilate. This increases blood flow to working muscles, which brings more oxygen to cells and removes extra wastes from cells.

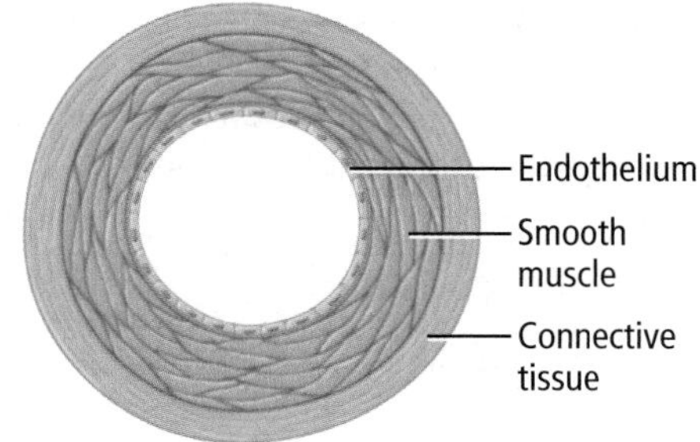


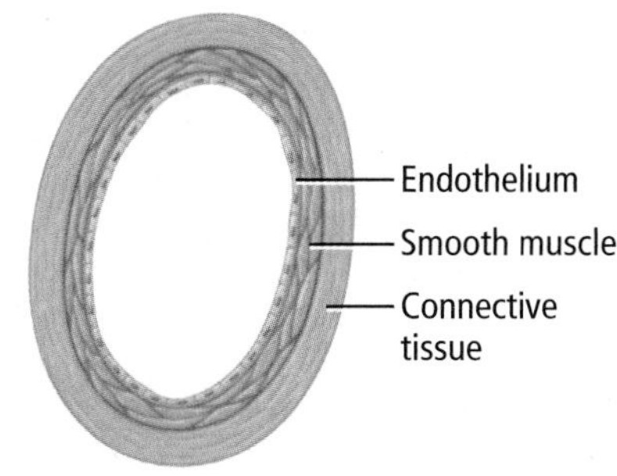

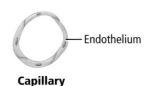

Endothelium

Capillary

■ **Figure 34.2** The three major blood vessels in the body are arteries, veins, and capillaries.

**Predict** ***By what process do you think materials cross the walls of capillaries?***

**Concepts In Motion**

Interactive Figure To see an animation of the structure of blood vessels, visit biologygmh.com.

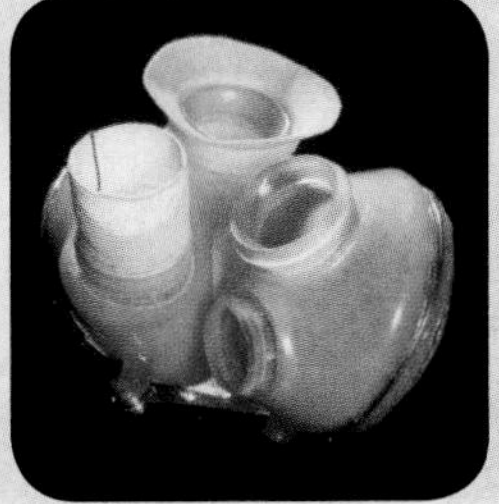

**1982** **The first artificial heart is implanted by William DeVries, a surgeon.**

**2004** **Research shows that cardiac stem cells can generate new muscle cells. This opens up new treatment possibilities for treating heart failure.**

1930 · 1965 · 2000

**1940–1941** **Dr. Charles R. Drew establishes the first blood banks for blood transfusions.**

**1967–1969** **Surgeons perform the first heart transplant. An artificial heart keeps the patient alive until a donated heart replaces it.**

**Concepts In Motion** Interactive Time Line

To learn more about these discoveries and others, visit biologygmh.com.

Biology Online

■ **Figure 34.3** Blood circulates throughout the body inside blood vessels.
**Hypothesize** ***How can body temperature be regulated by the diameter of blood vessels?***

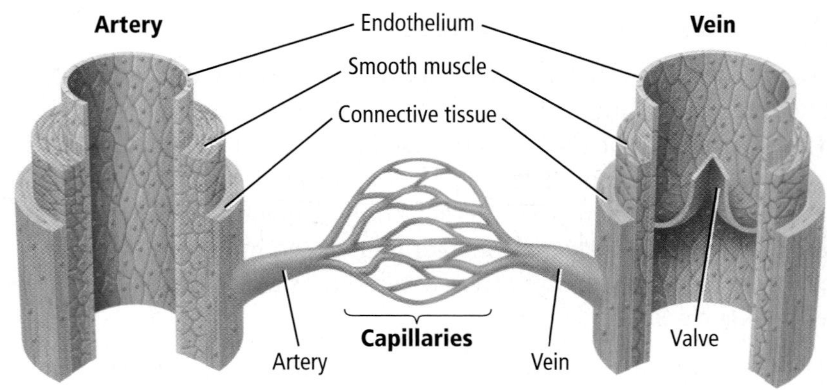


**Veins** After blood moves through the tiny capillaries, it enters the largest blood vessels, called veins. **Veins** carry oxygen-poor blood, or deoxygenated blood, back to the heart. The endothelial walls of veins are much thinner than the walls of arteries. Pressure of the blood decreases when the blood flows through capillaries before it enters the veins. By the time blood flows into the veins, the heart's original pushing force has less effect on making the blood move. So how does the blood keep moving? Because many veins are located near skeletal muscles, the contraction of these muscles helps keep the blood moving. Larger veins in your body also have flaps of tissue called **valves,** such as the one in **Figure 34.3,** that prevent blood from flowing backward. Lastly, breathing movements exert a squeezing pressure against veins in the chest, forcing blood back to the heart.

 **Reading Check** **Describe** the differences in structure among arteries, capillaries, and veins.

## The Heart

The **heart** is a muscular organ that is about as large as your fist and is located at the center of your chest. This hollow organ pumps blood throughout the body. The heart performs two pumping functions at the same time. The heart pumps oxygenated blood to the body, and it pumps deoxygenated blood to the lungs.

**Structure of the heart** Recall from Chapter 32 that the heart is made of cardiac muscle. It is capable of conducting electrical impulses for muscular contractions. The heart is divided into four compartments called chambers, as illustrated in **Figure 34.4.** The two chambers in the top half of the heart—the right atrium and the left atrium (plural, atria)—receive blood returning to the heart. Below the atria are the right and left ventricles, which pump blood away from the heart. A strong muscular wall separates the left side of the heart from the right side of the heart. The right and left atria have thinner muscular walls and do less work than the ventricles. Notice the valves in **Figure 34.4** that separate the atria from the ventricles and keep blood flowing in one direction. Valves also are found in between each ventricle and the large blood vessels that carry blood away from the heart, such as the aortic valve shown in a closed position in **Figure 34.4.**

**CAREERS IN BIOLOGY**

**Exercise Physiologist** Scientists who study the effects of exercise on the body are called exercise physiologists. They develop exercise programs and administer medical tests, such as stress tests. Their responsibilities might include monitoring heart activity and monitoring blood pressure levels. For more information on biology careers, visit biologygmh.com.

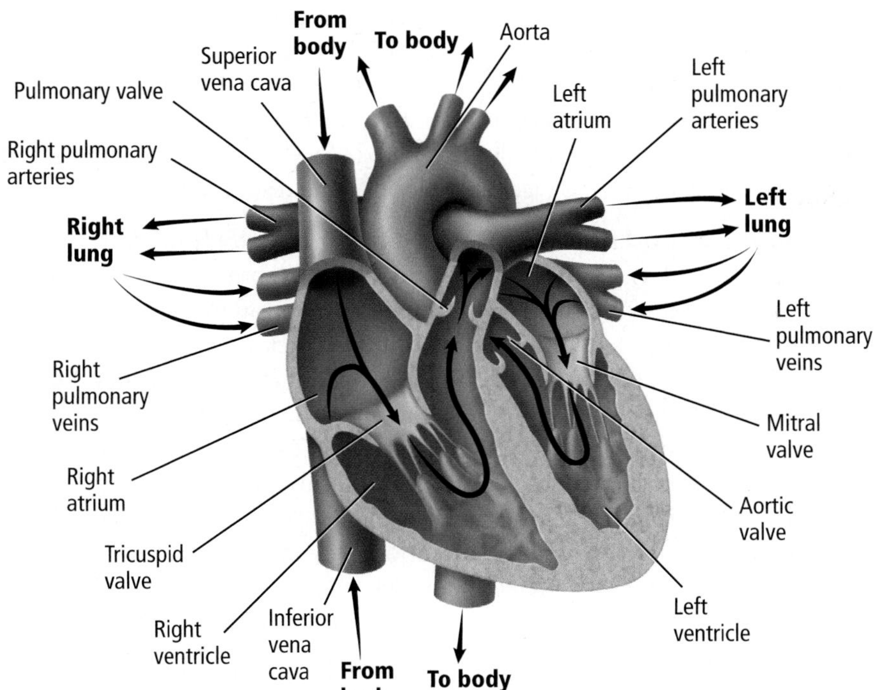


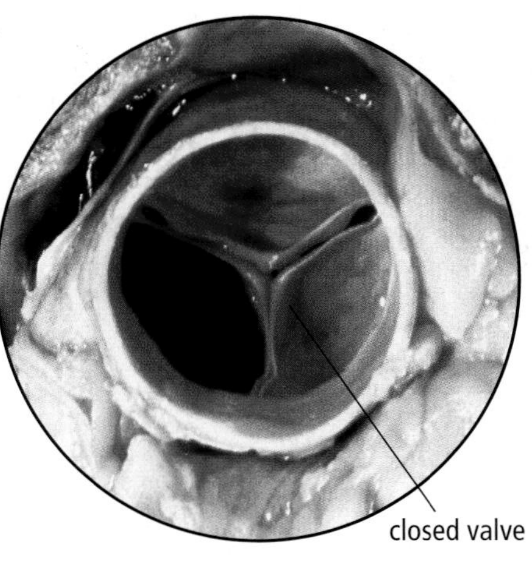


**Aortic valve—closed position**

■ **Figure 34.4** The arrows map out the path of blood as it circulates through the heart. **Diagram** ***Trace the path of blood through the heart.***

**How the heart beats** The heart acts in two main phases. In the first phase, the atria fill with blood. The atria contract, filling the ventricles with blood. In the second phase, the ventricles contract to pump blood out of the heart, into the lungs, and forward into the body.

The heart works in a regular rhythm. A group of cells found in the right atrium, called the **pacemaker** or sinoatrial (SA) node, send out signals that tell the heart muscle to contract. The SA node receives internal stimuli about the body's oxygen needs, and then responds by adjusting the heart rate. The signal initiated by the SA node causes both atria to contract. This signal then travels to another area in the heart called the atrioventricular (AV) node, illustrated in **Figure 34.5.** This signal travels through fibers, causing both ventricles to contract. This two-step contraction makes up one complete heartbeat.

**Pulse** The heart pulses about 70 times each minute. If you touch the inside of your wrist just below your thumb, you can feel a pulse in the artery in your wrist rise and fall. This pulse is the alternating expansion and relaxation of the artery wall caused by contraction of the left ventricle. The number of times the artery pulses is the number of times your heart beats.

**Blood pressure** Blood pressure is a measure of how much pressure is exerted against the vessel walls by the blood. Blood-pressure readings can provide information about the condition of arteries. The contraction of the heart, or systole (SIS tuh lee), causes the blood pressure to rise to its highest point, and the relaxation of the heart, or diastole (di AS tuh lee) brings the pressure down to its lowest point. A normal blood-pressure reading for a healthy adult is a reading below 120 (systolic pressure)/80 (diastolic pressure).

■ **Figure 34.5** The SA node initiates the contraction of the heart, which spreads through both atria to the AV node. The AV node transmits the signal through excitable fibers that stimulate both ventricles.

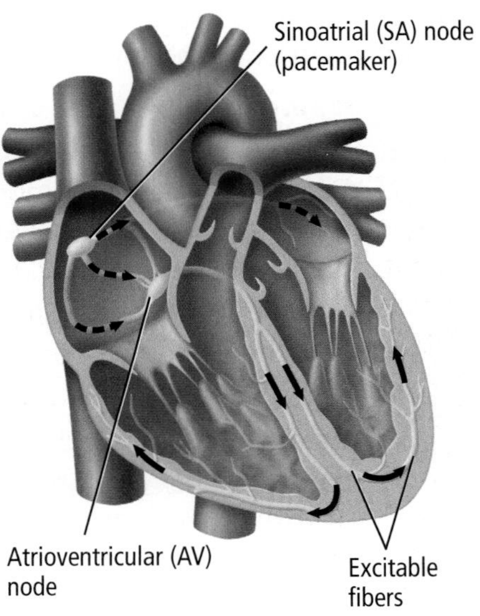

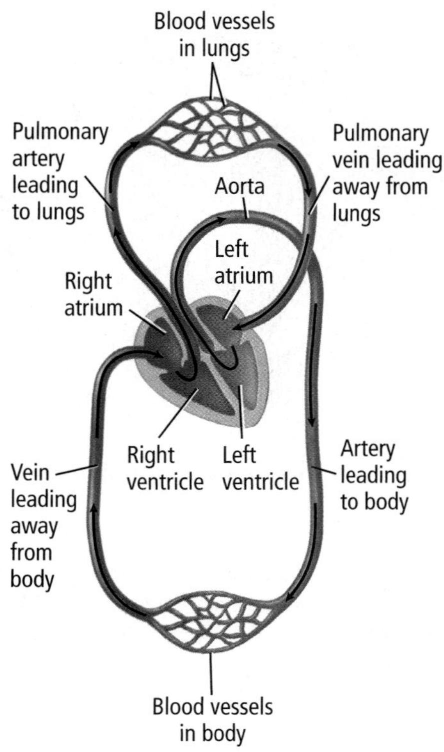


■ **Figure 34.6** Blood flow through the body consists of two different circulatory loops.

**Concepts In Motion**

**Interactive Figure** To see an animation of how blood flows through the circulatory system, visit biologygmh.com.

**Blood flow in the body** If you follow the flow of blood shown in **Figure 34.6,** you might notice that it flows in two loops. First, the blood travels from the heart to the lungs and back to the heart. Then, the blood is pumped in another loop from the heart through the body and back. The right side of the heart pumps deoxygenated blood to the lungs, and the left side of the heart pumps oxygenated blood to the rest of the body.

**To the lungs and back** When blood from the body flows into the right atrium, it has a low concentration of oxygen but a high concentration of carbon dioxide. This deoxygenated blood is dark red. The blood flows from the right atrium into the right ventricle and is pumped into the pulmonary arteries that lead to the lungs, as shown in **Figure 34.6.**

Eventually, blood flows into capillaries in the lungs that are in close contact with the air that comes into the lungs. The air in the lungs has a greater concentration of oxygen than the blood in the capillaries does, so oxygen diffuses from the lungs into the blood. At the same time, carbon dioxide diffuses in the opposite direction—from the blood into the air space in the lungs. Oxygenated blood, which is now bright red, flows to the left atrium of the heart to be pumped out to the body.

**To the body and back** The left atrium fills with oxygenated blood from the lungs, beginning the second loop of the figure eight. As shown in **Figure 34.6,** the blood then moves from the left atrium into the left ventricle. The left ventricle pumps the blood into the largest artery in the body called the aorta. Eventually, blood flows into the capillaries that branch throughout the body. Importantly, the capillaries are in close contact with body cells. Oxygen is released from the blood into the body cells by diffusion, and carbon dioxide moves from the cells to the blood by diffusion. The deoxygenated blood then flows back to the right atrium through veins.

## MiniLab 34.1

### Investigate Blood Pressure

**How does blood pressure change in response to physical activity?** Blood pressure changes from day to day, and throughout the day, and is affected by physical, psychological, behavioral, and inherited factors.

**Procedure**

1. Read and complete the lab safety form.
2. Watch the instructor demonstrate how to safely take a blood pressure. Practice using a **blood-pressure cuff** to measure a partner's blood pressure. Refer to a **blood-pressure chart** to interpret the reading.
3. Predict how exercise will affect systolic and diastolic blood pressure.
4. Take the resting blood-pressure reading of one member of your group.
5. Have the person whose blood pressure was taken do rhythmic exercise for one minute.
6. Take a second blood-pressure reading and compare it to the resting blood-pressure reading.

**Analysis**

1. **Identify** What are the experimental constants, the independent and dependent variables, and the control in your experiment?
2. **Conclude** Were your predictions supported? Explain.

# Blood Components

Blood is the fluid of life because it transports important substances throughout the body and contains living cells. Blood is made up of a liquid medium called plasma, red and white blood cells, and cell fragments called platelets.

**Plasma** The clear, yellowish fluid portion of blood is the **plasma**. Over fifty percent of blood is plasma. Ninety percent of plasma is water and nearly ten percent is dissolved materials. Plasma carries the breakdown products of digested food, such as glucose and fats. Plasma also transports vitamins, minerals, and chemical messengers such as hormones that signal body activities, such as the uptake of glucose by the cells. In addition, waste products from the cells are carried away by plasma.

There are three groups of plasma proteins that give plasma its yellow color. One group helps to regulate the amount of water in blood. The second group, produced by white blood cells, helps fight disease. The third group helps to form blood clots.

Color-Enhanced SEM Magnification: 1825×

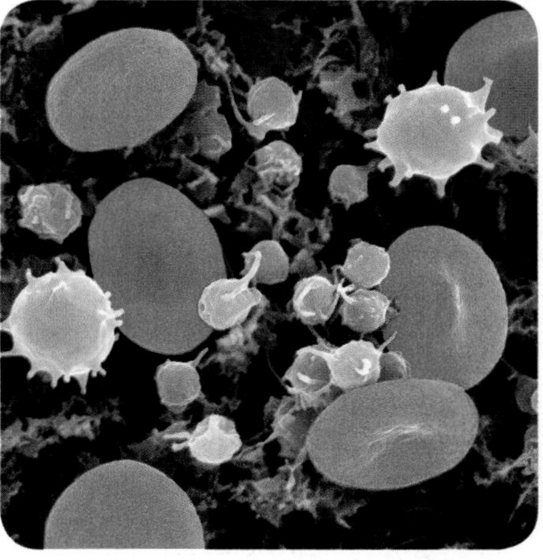

■ **Figure 34.7** Blood is composed of liquid plasma, red blood cells (dimpled discs), white blood cells (irregularly shaped cells), and platelets (flat fragments).
**Infer** ***What might be occurring if there were too many white blood cells?***

**Red blood cells** The **red blood cells** carry oxygen to all of the body's cells. Red blood cells resemble discs with pinched-in centers, as shown in **Figure 34.7.** Recall that red blood cells develop in the marrow—the center portion of large bones. Red blood cells have no nuclei and only live for about 120 days.

Red blood cells mostly consist of an iron-containing protein called hemoglobin. Hemoglobin chemically binds with oxygen molecules and carries oxygen to the body's cells. Some carbon dioxide is carried by the hemoglobin, but most carbon dioxide is carried in plasma.

**Platelets** Have you ever cut your finger? You probably have noticed that in a short while, the blood flowing from the cut slows and then stops as a blood clot forms a scab. **Platelets** are cell fragments that play an important part in forming blood clots.

When a blood vessel is cut, platelets collect and stick to the vessel at the site of the wound. The platelets then release chemicals that produce a protein called fibrin. Fibrin is a protein, also known as a clotting factor, which weaves a network of fibers across the cut that traps blood platelets and red blood cells, as shown in **Figure 34.8.** As more and more platelets and blood cells get trapped, a blood clot forms.

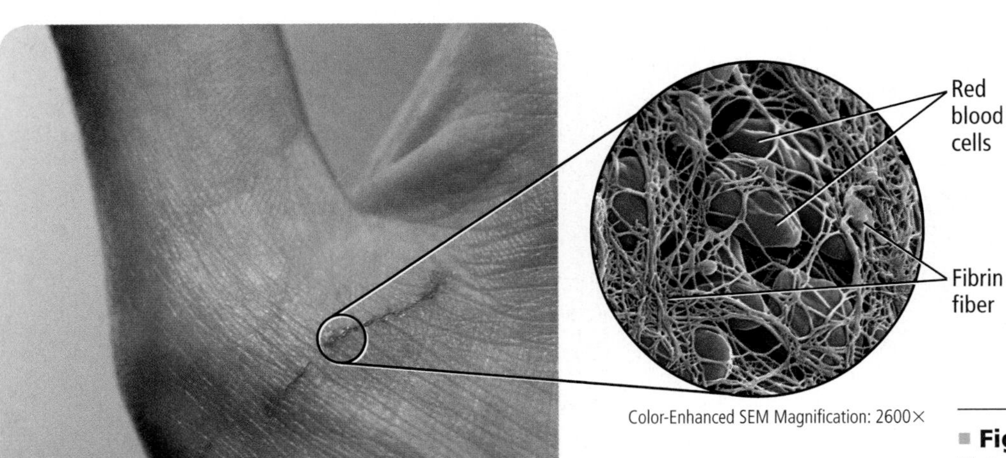


■ **Figure 34.8** A scab forms due to fibrin threads trapping blood cells and platelets.

## Study Tip

**Graphic Organizer** Make a word map with the word *blood* in a large circle in the middle. Place the words *components, blood groups, circulation,* and *heart* in smaller circles around the large circle. Find information you learned in the chapter and add it to the appropriate smaller circles.

**White blood cells** The body's disease fighters are the **white blood cells.** Like red blood cells, white blood cells are produced in bone marrow. Some white blood cells recognize disease-causing organisms, such as bacteria, and alert the body that it has been invaded. Other white blood cells produce chemicals to fight the invaders. Still, other white blood cells surround and kill the invaders. You will learn more about white blood cells in Chapter 37.

White blood cells are different from red blood cells in important ways. First, many white blood cells move from the marrow to other sites in the body to mature. Unlike red blood cells, there are fewer white blood cells—only about one white blood cell for every 500 to 1000 red blood cells. Also, white blood cells have nuclei. Finally, most white blood cells live for months or years.

# Blood Types

How do you know what type of blood you have? There are marker molecules attached to red blood cells. These markers determine blood type.

**FOLDABLES** Incorporate information from this section into your Foldable.

**ABO blood groups** There are four types of blood—A, B, AB, and O. If your blood type is A, you have A markers on your blood cells. If your blood type is B, you have B markers on your blood cells. People with blood type AB have both A and B markers. If your blood type is O, you do not have A or B markers.

**Importance of blood type** If you ever need a blood transfusion, you only will be able to receive certain blood types, as shown in **Table 34.1.** This is because plasma contains proteins called antibodies that recognize red blood cells with foreign markers and cause those cells to clump together. For example, if you have blood type B, your blood contains antibodies that cause cells with A markers to clump. If you received a transfusion of type-A blood, your clumping proteins would make the type-A cells clump together. Clumping of blood cells can be dangerous because it can block blood flow.

**Concepts In Motion** Interactive Table To explore more about blood groups, visit biologygmh.com.

| Table 34.1 | Blood Groups | | | |
|---|---|---|---|---|
| Blood type | A | B | AB | O |
| Marker molecule and antibody | Marker molecule: A<br>Antibody: anti-B | Marker molecules: B<br>Antibody: anti-A | Marker molecules: AB<br>Antibody: none | Marker molecules: none<br>Antibodies: anti-A, anti-B |
| Example | A A A A A A | B B B B B B | A B B A A B | |
| Can donate blood to: | A or AB | B or AB | AB | A, B, AB, or O |
| Can receive blood from: | A or O | B or O | A, B, AB, or O | O |

**Rh factor** Another marker found on the surface of red blood cells is called the Rh factor. The Rh marker can cause a problem when an Rh-negative person, someone without the Rh factor, receives a transfusion of Rh-positive blood that has the Rh marker. This can result in clumping of red blood cells because Rh-negative blood contains Rh antibodies against Rh-positive cells.

The Rh factor can cause complications during some pregnancies. If the Rh-positive blood of a fetus mixes with the mother's Rh-negative blood, the mother will make anti-Rh antibodies. If the mother becomes pregnant again, these antibodies can cross the placenta and can destroy red blood cells if the fetus has Rh-positive blood. Rh-negative mothers are given a substance that prevents the production of Rh antibodies in the blood, so these problems can be avoided.

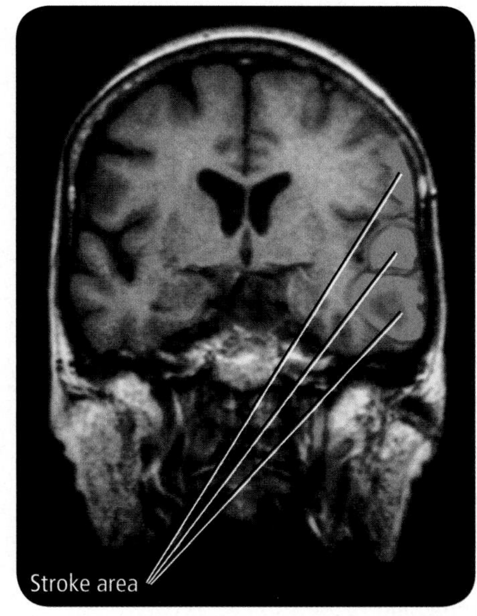


■ **Figure 34.9** Stroke is associated with ruptured blood vessels in the brain, as shown in red.

## Circulatory System Disorders

Several disorders of the blood vessels, heart, and brain are associated with the circulatory system. Blood clots and other matter, such as fat deposits, can reduce the flow of oxygen-rich and nutrient-rich blood traveling through arteries. Physicians refer to the condition of blocked arteries as **atherosclerosis** (a thuh roh skluh ROH sus). Signs of clogged arteries include high blood pressure and high cholesterol levels. When blood flow is reduced or blocked, the heart must work even harder to pump blood, and vessels can burst.

Atherosclerosis can lead to a heart attack or stroke. Heart attacks occur when blood does not reach the heart muscle. This can result in damage to the heart, or could even result in death if not treated. Strokes occur when clots form in blood vessels supplying oxygen to the brain. This can lead to ruptured blood vessels and internal bleeding, as shown in **Figure 34.9.** Parts of the brain die because brain cells are deprived of oxygen.

**VOCABULARY**

**WORD ORIGIN**

**Atherosclerosis**
comes from the Greek word *schlerosis*, meaning *hardening*.

## Section 34.1 Assessment

### Section Summary

- Blood vessels transport important substances throughout the body.
- The top half of the heart is made up of two atria, and the bottom half is made up of two ventricles.
- The heart pumps deoxygenated blood to the lungs, and it pumps oxygenated blood to the body.
- Blood is made up of plasma, red blood cells, white blood cells, and platelets.
- Blood can be classified into the following four blood types: A, B, AB, and O.

### Understand Main Ideas

1. MAIN Idea **Explain** the main functions of the circulatory system.
2. **Diagram** the path of blood through the heart and body.
3. **Compare and contrast** the structure of arteries with the structure of veins.
4. **Calculate** the average number of red blood cells for every 100 white blood cells in the human body.
5. **Summarize** the functions of the four components of blood.

### Think Scientifically

6. *Cause and Effect* If a pacemaker received faulty signals from the brain, what would happen?
7. *Hypothesize* why exercise is a way to maintain a healthy heart.
8. MATH in Biology Count the number of times your heart beats during 15 seconds. What is your heart rate per minute?

Section 34.2

## Objectives

- **Distinguish** between internal and external respiration.
- **Summarize** the path of air through the respiratory system.
- **Identify** what changes occur in the body during breathing.

## Review Vocabulary

**ATP:** biological molecule that provides the body's cells with chemical energy

## New Vocabulary

breathing
external respiration
internal respiration
trachea
bronchus
lung
alveolus

# Respiratory System

**MAIN Idea The function of the respiratory system is the exchange of oxygen and carbon dioxide between the atmosphere and the blood and between the blood and the body's cells.**

**Real-World Reading Link** Air filters separate out dust and other particles from the air before they enter your car's engine. This prevents engine problems and helps ensure good air flow. Similarly, your respiratory system has features that ensure enough clean air gets into your lungs.

## The Importance of Respiration

Your body's cells require oxygen. Recall from Chapter 8 that oxygen and glucose are used by cells to produce energy-rich ATP molecules needed to maintain cellular metabolism. This process is called cellular respiration. In addition to releasing energy, cellular respiration releases carbon dioxide and water.

**Breathing and respiration** The function of the respiratory system is to sustain cellular respiration by supplying oxygen to body cells and removing carbon dioxide waste from cells. The respiratory system can be divided into two processes: breathing and respiration. First, air must enter the body through breathing. **Breathing** is the mechanical movement of air into and out of your lungs. **Figure 34.10** illustrates air being released from the lungs into the air. Second, gases are exchanged in the body. **External respiration** is the exchange of gases between the atmosphere and the blood, which occurs in the lungs. **Internal respiration** is the exchange of gases between the blood and the body's cells.

■ **Figure 34.10** Exhaled air from your lungs can be seen on a chilly evening.
**Infer** *How is the air that you inhale different than the air you exhale?*

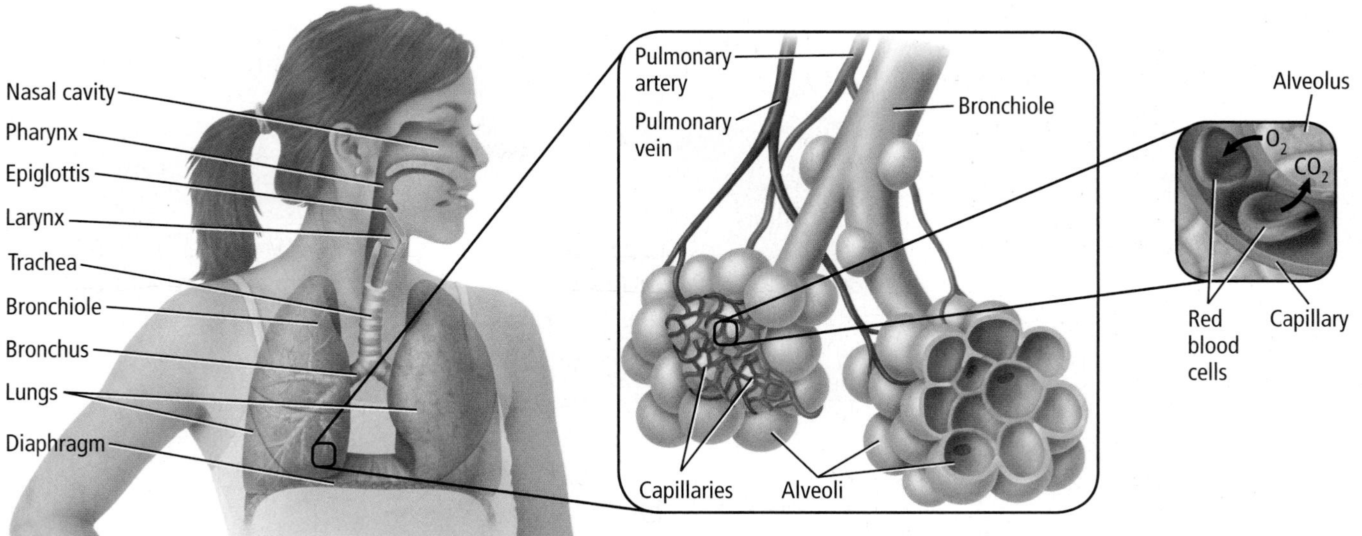


**Figure 34.11** Air travels into the alveoli of the lungs, where gases are exchanged across thin capillary walls.

**Diagram** ***Trace the path of oxygen from the atmosphere to the alveoli in the lungs.***

## The Path of Air

The respiratory system is made up of the nasal passages, pharynx (FER ingks), larynx (LER ingks), epiglottis, trachea, lungs, bronchi, bronchioles, alveoli (al VEE uh li), and diaphragm. Air travels from the outside environment to the lungs where it passes through the alveoli, as shown in **Figure 34.11.**

First, air enters your mouth or nose. Hairs in the nose filter out dust and other large particles in the air. Hairlike structures called cilia, shown in **Figure 34.12,** also line the nasal passages, as well as other respiratory tubes. Cilia trap foreign particles from the air and sweep them toward the throat so that they do not enter the lungs. Mucous membranes beneath the cilia in the nasal passages, also shown in **Figure 34.12,** warm and moisten the air while trapping foreign materials.

Filtered air then passes through the upper throat called the pharynx. A flap of tissue called the epiglottis, which covers the opening to the larynx, prevents food particles from entering the respiratory tubes. The epiglottis allows air to pass from the larynx to a long tube in the chest cavity called the **trachea,** or windpipe. The trachea branches into two large tubes, called **bronchi** (BRAHN ki) (singular, bronchus), which lead to the lungs. The **lungs** are the largest organs in the respiratory system, and gas exchange takes place in the lungs. Each bronchus branches into smaller tubes called bronchioles (BRAHN kee ohlz). Each of these small tubes continues to branch into even smaller passageways, each of which ends in an individual air sac called an **alveolus** (plural, alveoli). Each alveolus has a thin wall—only one cell thick—and is surrounded by very thin capillaries.

**Gas exchange in the lungs** Air travels to individual alveoli where oxygen diffuses across the moist, thin walls into capillaries and then into red blood cells, as shown in **Figure 34.11.** The oxygen is then transported by the blood to be released to tissue cells in the body during internal respiration. Meanwhile, carbon dioxide moves in the opposite direction in the alveoli. Carbon dioxide in the blood crosses capillary walls, and then diffuses into the alveoli to be returned to the atmosphere during external respiration.

**Reading Check** **Infer** why gas exchange is effective in alveoli.

**VOCABULARY**

**WORD ORIGIN**

**Alveolus**
comes from the Latin word *alveus,* meaning *belly* or *hollow space.*

**Figure 34.12** Hairlike cilia line the mucous membranes of the nasal cavity.

Color-Enhanced SEM Magnification: 2000×

**Figure 34.13** Rib and diaphragm muscles contract and relax during breathing.
**Analyze** *How do you think air pressure is involved in breathing?*

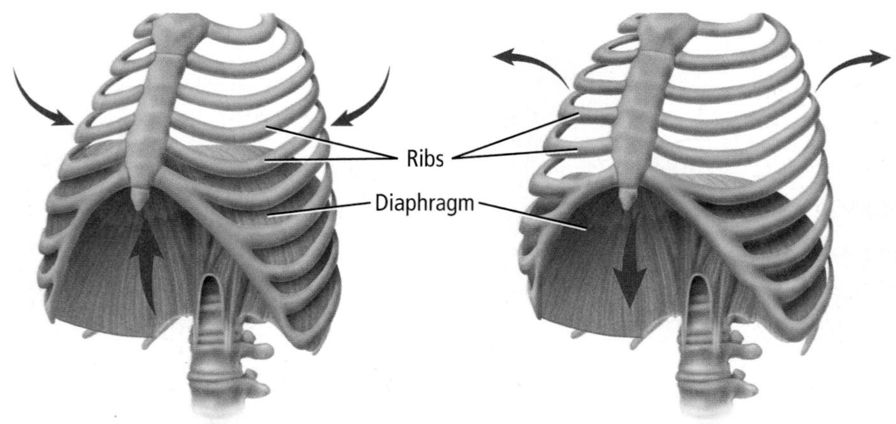


## Breathing

The brain directs the rate of breathing by responding to internal stimuli that indicate how much oxygen the body needs. When the concentration of carbon dioxide in the blood is high, the breathing rate increases because cells need more oxygen.

Inhalation is the act of taking air into the lungs. During inhalation, as shown in **Figure 34.13,** the diaphragm contracts. This causes the chest cavity to expand as the diaphragm moves down, allowing air to move into the lungs. During exhalation, the diaphragm relaxes and returns to its normal resting position. This reduces the size of the chest cavity as the diaphragm moves up. Air naturally flows out from the greater pressure of the lungs. Follow **Figure 34.14** to learn how circulation and respiration work together to supply the needed oxygen and to get rid of carbon dioxide.

**LAUNCH Lab**

**Review** Based on what you've read about respiration, how would you now answer the analysis questions?

## MiniLab 34.2

### Recognize Cause and Effect

**Does exercise affect metabolism?** All of the chemical reactions that occur in your cells make up your metabolism. In this lab, you will explore how exercise affects the circulatory and respiratory systems and infer how this affects metabolism.

**Procedure**

1. Read and complete the lab safety form.
2. Record the number of heartbeats and number of breaths per minute for ten classmates.
3. Instruct the same students to walk in place for five minutes. At the end of that time, record each person's heartbeat per minute and number of breaths per minute.
4. After students have rested for five minutes, intruct them to jog or walk briskly in place for five minutes. Then, record each person's heartbeat per minute and number of breaths per minute.
5. Plot your results on **graph paper.** Each coordinate point should indicate breaths per minute on the horizontal axis and heartbeats per minute on the vertical axis.

**Analysis**

1. **Interpret** What is the relationship between the two dependent variables of your experiment—heart rate and breathing rate?
2. **Conclude** Does exercise affect metabolism? Why?
3. **Hypothesize** Why might students have different numbers of heartbeats per minute and breaths per minute even though they all walked or jogged for the same amount of time?

# Visualizing Gas Exchange

**Figure 34.14**
Gases are exchanged in the lungs and in the tissue cells of the body.

In the lungs, oxygen ($O_2$) that is inhaled moves into capillaries and is transported to body cells. Carbon dioxide ($CO_2$) leaves the capillaries and is exhaled from the lungs.

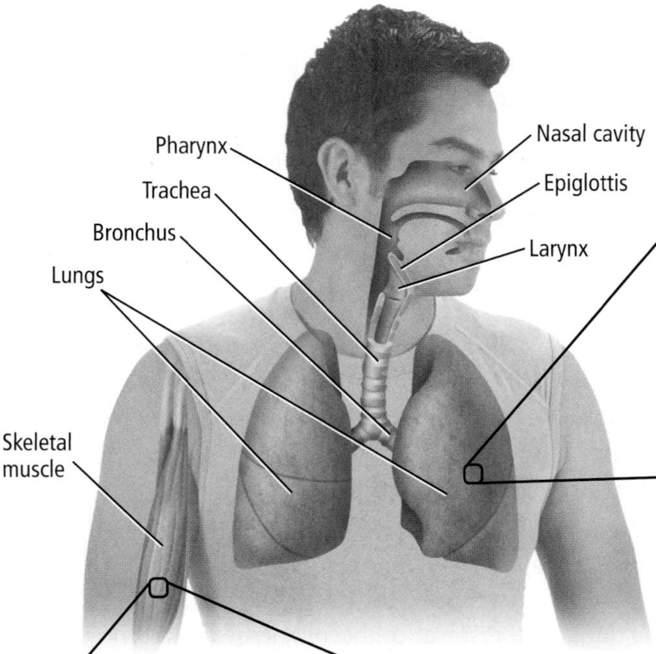

Color-Enhanced SEM Magnification: 300×

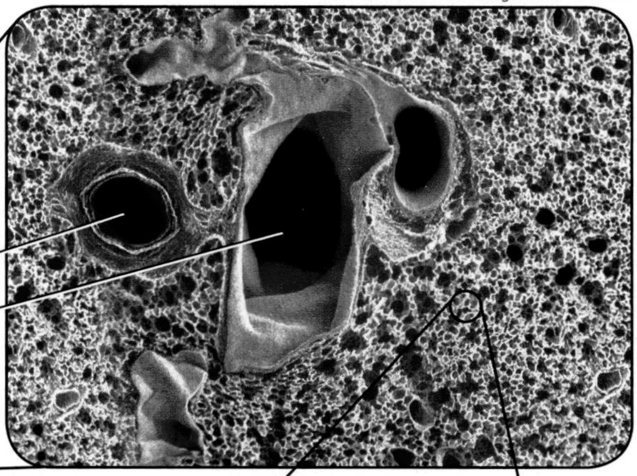

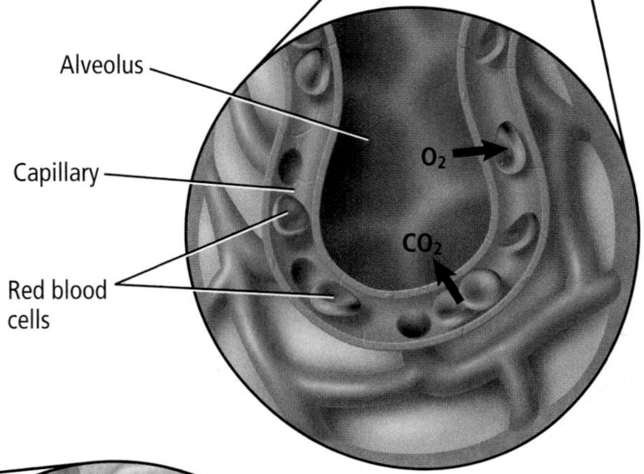

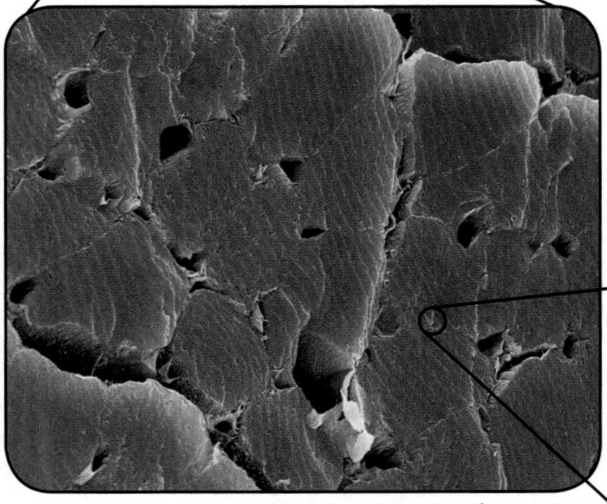

Pharynx
Nasal cavity
Trachea
Epiglottis
Bronchus
Larynx
Lungs
Skeletal muscle
Vein
Artery

Alveolus
Capillary
$O_2$
$CO_2$
Red blood cells

Color-Enhanced SEM Magnification: 1000×

In body tissues, such as muscle tissues, oxygen ($O_2$) moves from capillaries into tissue cells. Carbon dioxide ($CO_2$) produced by cellular respiration leaves tissue cells and moves into capillaries, and then is transported to the lungs.

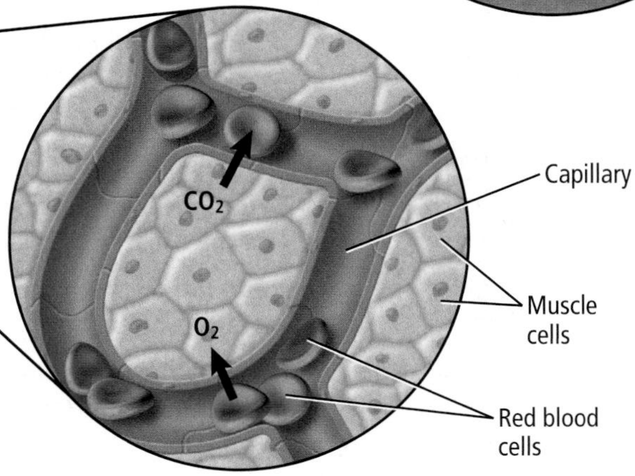

$CO_2$
$O_2$
Capillary
Muscle cells
Red blood cells

**Concepts In Motion** **Interactive Figure** To see an animation of gas exchange, visit biologygmh.com.

**Biology Online**

| Table 34.2 | Common Respiratory Disorders |
|---|---|
| Lung Disorder | Brief Description |
| **Asthma** | Respiratory pathways become irritated and bronchioles constrict. |
| **Bronchitis** | Respiratory pathways become infected, resulting in coughing and production of mucus. |
| **Emphysema** | Alveoli break down, resulting in reduced surface area needed for gas exchange with alveoli's blood capillaries. |
| **Pneumonia** | Infection of the lungs that causes alveoli to collect mucus material |
| **Pulmonary tuberculosis** | A specific bacterium infects the lungs, resulting in less elasticity of the blood capillaries surrounding alveoli, thus decreasing effective gas exchange between the air and blood. |
| **Lung cancer** | Uncontrolled cell growth in lung tissue can lead to a persistent cough, shortness of breath, bronchitis, or pneumonia, and can lead to death. |

Concepts In Motion
**Interactive Table** To explore more about respiratory disorders, visit biologygmh.com.

**VOCABULARY**
**SCIENCE USAGE V. COMMON USAGE**
**Inflame**
***Science usage:*** causing inflammation or swelling.
*Asthma can inflame the bronchioles.*

***Common usage:*** to make angry.
*Not doing your homework might inflame your teacher.*

## Respiratory Disorders

Some diseases and disorders irritate, inflame, or infect the respiratory system, as described in **Table 34.2.** These disorders can produce tissue damage that reduces the effectiveness of the bronchi and alveoli. When these tissues become damaged, respiration becomes difficult. Smoking also causes chronic irritation to respiratory tissues and inhibits cellular metabolism. Finally, exposure to airborne materials, such as pollen, can produce respiratory problems in some people due to allergic reactions.

# Section 34.2 Assessment

### Section Summary

- Alveoli in the lungs are the sites of gas exchange between the respiratory and circulatory systems.
- The pathway of air starts with the mouth or nose and ends at the alveoli located in the lungs.
- Inhalation and exhalation are the processes of taking in and expelling air.
- The respiratory and circulatory systems work together to help maintain homeostasis.
- Respiratory disorders can inhibit respiration.

### Understand Main Ideas

1. MAIN Idea **Identify** the main function of the respiratory system.
2. **Distinguish** between internal and external respiration.
3. **Sequence** the path of air from the nasal passages to the bloodstream.
4. **Describe** the mechanics of inhalation and exhalation.
5. **Infer** how the respiratory system would compensate for a circulatory disorder.
6. **Describe** three disorders of the respiratory system.

### Think Scientifically

7. ***Hypothesize*** an advantage of heating and moisturizing air before it reaches alveoli.
8. **MATH in Biology** The total surface area of the alveoli tissue in your lungs is approximately 70 $m^2$. This is more than 40 times the surface area of the skin. What is the surface area of your skin?



Biology Online **Self-Check Quiz** biologygmh.com

## Section 34.3

### Objectives

- **Summarize** the function of the kidney in the body.
- **Sequence** the steps of the excretion of wastes from the Bowman's capsule to the urethra.
- **Distinguish** between filtration and reabsorption in the kidney.

### Review Vocabulary

**pH:** measure of acidity and alkalinity of a solution

### New Vocabulary

kidney
urea

# Excretory System

**MAIN Idea The kidneys maintain homeostasis by removing wastes and excess water from the body and by maintaining the pH of blood.**

**Real-World Reading Link** Suppose that you cleaned your bedroom by first moving everything except large items into the hallway. You then return only the items you will keep to your bedroom and leave the items you want to get rid of in the hallway for later disposal. This is similar to how your kidneys filter materials in your blood.

## Parts of the Excretory System

The body collects wastes, such as toxins, waste products, and carbon dioxide, that result from metabolism in the body. The excretory system removes these toxins and wastes from the body. In addition, the excretory system regulates the amount of fluid and salts in the body, and maintains the pH of the blood. All of these functions help to maintain homeostasis.

The components that make up the excretory system include the lungs, skin, and kidneys, as illustrated in **Figure 34.15.** The lungs primarily excrete carbon dioxide. The skin primarily excretes water and salts contained in sweat. The kidneys, however, are the major excretory organ in the body.

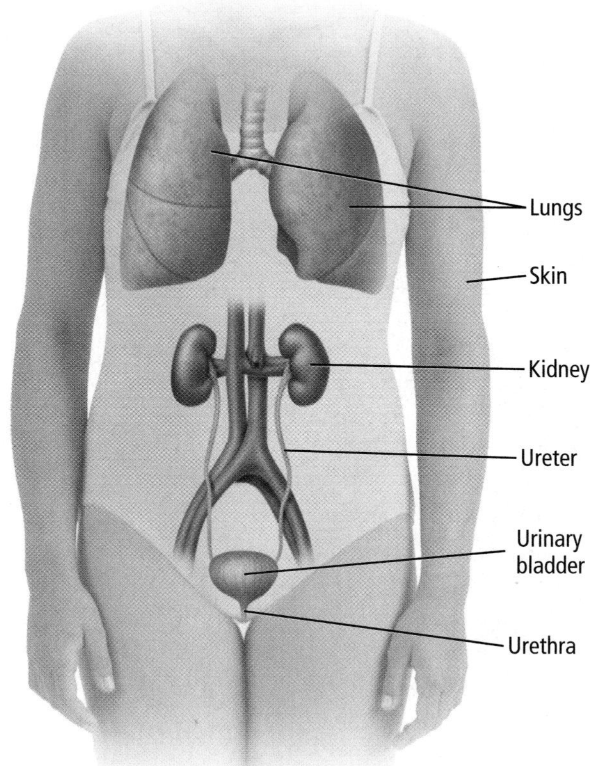


**Figure 34.15** The organs of excretion include the lungs, skin, and kidneys.

## The Kidneys

As shown in **Figure 34.16,** the **kidneys** are bean-shaped organs that filter out wastes, water, and salts from the blood. The kidneys are divided into two distinct regions, also illustrated in **Figure 34.16.** The outer portion is called the renal cortex and the inner region is called the renal medulla. Each of these regions contains microscopic tubes and blood vessels. In the center of the kidney is a region called the renal pelvis, where the body's filters are found. Follow **Figure 34.16** as you read about how the kidneys function.

**Nephron filtration** Each kidney contains approximately one million filtering units called nephrons. Blood enters each nephron through a long tube that is surrounded by a ball of capillaries called the glomerulus (gluh MER uh lus) (plural, glomeruli). The glomerulus is surrounded by a structure called the Bowman's capsule.

The renal artery transports nutrients and wastes to the kidney and branches into smaller and smaller blood vessels, eventually reaching the tiny capillaries in the glomerulus. The walls of the capillaries are very thin and the blood is under great pressure. As a result, water and substances dissolved in the water, such as the nitrogenous waste product called **urea,** are pushed through the capillary walls into the Bowman's capsule. Larger molecules, such as red blood cells and proteins, remain in the bloodstream.

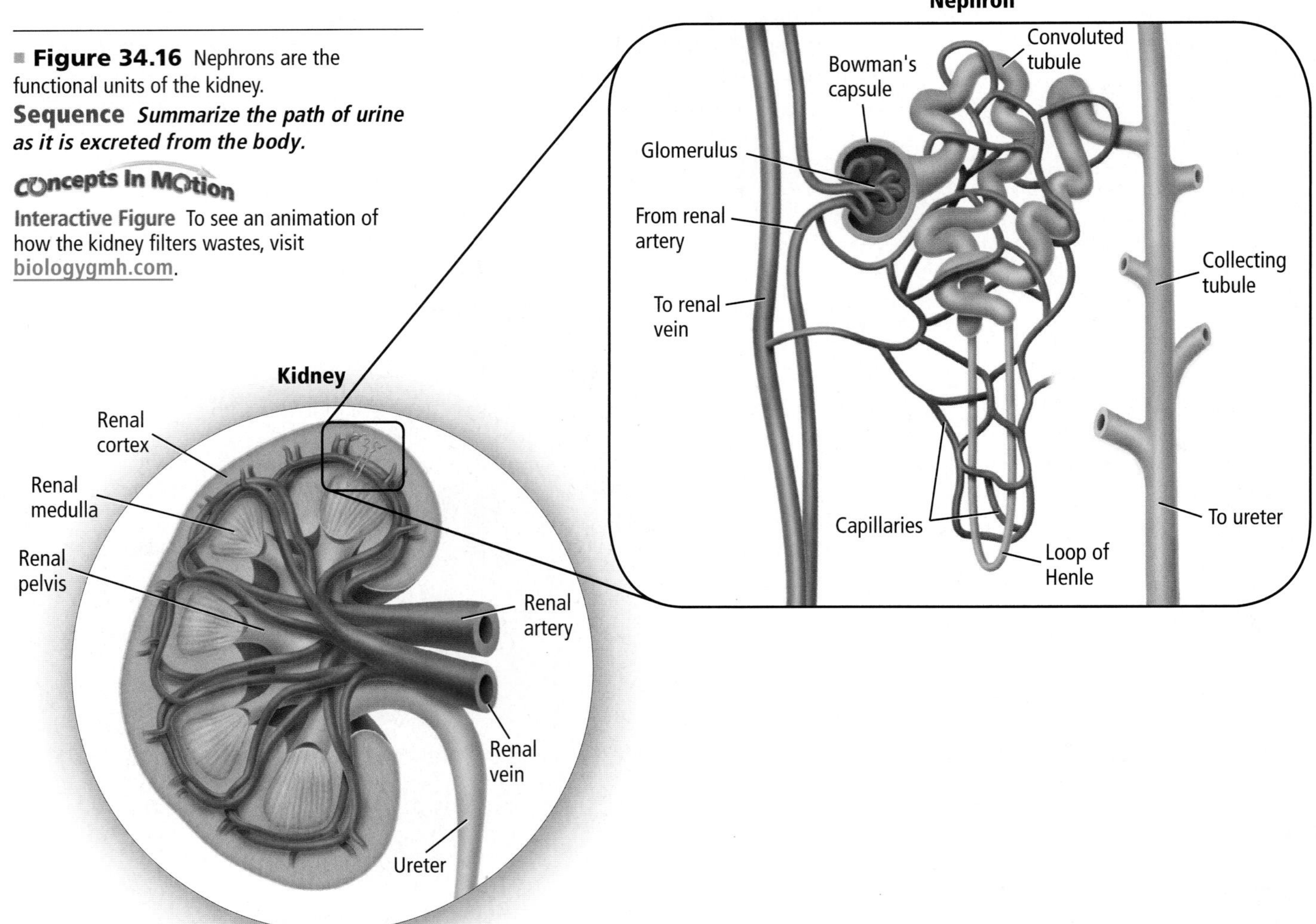


**Figure 34.16** Nephrons are the functional units of the kidney.
**Sequence** ***Summarize the path of urine as it is excreted from the body.***

**Concepts In Motion**
**Interactive Figure** To see an animation of how the kidney filters wastes, visit biologygmh.com.

**Reabsorption and the formation of urine** The filtrate collected in the Bowman's capsule flows through the renal tubule that consists of the convoluted tubule, the loop of Henle, and the collecting tubule, as illustrated in **Figure 34.16.** Much of the lost water and useful substances, such as glucose and minerals, are reabsorbed back into the capillaries surrounding the renal tubule. This process is called reabsorption. At the same time, excess fluids and toxic substances in the capillaries are passed to the collecting tubules. This waste product is called urine. Urine leaves the kidney through ducts called the ureters (YOO ruh turz), shown in **Figure 34.16.** Urine is then stored in the urinary bladder and exits the body through the urethra.

Each kidney filters about 180 L of blood each day in adults, but produces only about 1.5 L of urine. The process of filtration and reabsorption from the blood requires large amounts of energy. Although kidneys account for only one percent of body weight, they use 20 to 25 percent of the body's oxygen intake for their internal energy requirements.

**Connection to Chemistry** The kidney can help maintain a normal pH in the blood by adjusting the acid-base balance. Recall from Chapter 6 that low pH results when there is an abundance of $H^+$. When the blood pH is too low, the kidney can increase pH levels in the body by excreting hydrogen ($H^+$) ions and ammonia into the renal tubules. The kidney can decrease pH levels by reabsorbing buffers such as bicarbonate ($HCO_3^-$) and sodium ($Na^+$) ions. Because biological processes normally require pH between 6.5 and 7.5, the kidneys help to maintain homeostasis by keeping pH levels within the normal range.

**CAREERS IN BIOLOGY**

**Urologist** A urologist is a medical doctor who has specialized knowledge about problems of the male and female urinary systems. Responsibilities can include examining patients, performing laboratory tests, interpreting test results and examination findings, and treating injuries and disorders. For more information on biology careers, visit biologygmh.com.

## DATA ANALYSIS LAB 34.1

**Based On Real Data***

### Interpret the Data

**How do extreme conditions affect the average daily loss of water in the human body?** The body obtains water by absorbing it through the digestive tract. The body loses water primarily by excreting it in urine from the kidneys, through sweat, and through the lungs.

**Think Critically**

1. **Identify** What is the major source of water loss during normal weather?
2. **Hypothesize** Why is more water lost in sweat during rigorous exercise than in urine?
3. **Calculate** What is the percent of water loss for all three conditions?

**Data and Observations**

The table shows data collected in normal weather, hot weather, and during heavy exercise.

Average Daily Water Loss in Humans (in mL)

| Source | Normal Temperatures | High Temperatures | Rigorous Exercise |
|---|---|---|---|
| Kidneys | 1500 | 1400 | 750 |
| Skin | 450 | 1800 | 5000 |
| Lungs | 450 | 350 | 650 |

*Data obtained from: Beers, M. 2003. *The Merck Manual of Medical Information, Second Edition* West Point, PA.: Merck & Co. Inc.

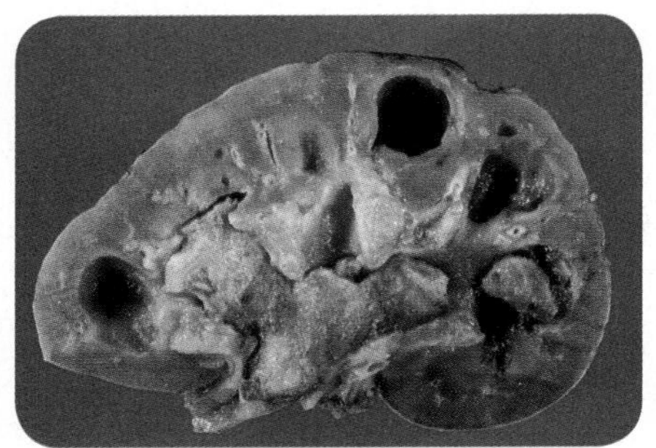

■ **Figure 34.17** Kidney stones form as minerals such as calcium become solid masses.

## Kidney Disorders

Sometimes kidney function can be inhibited or impaired by infections or disorders. When kidney function is impaired, the body cannot rid itself of wastes and homeostasis might be disrupted.

**Infections** Symptoms of a kidney infection include fever, chills, and mid- to low-back pain. Kidney infections often start as urinary bladder infections that spread to the kidney. Obstructions in the kidney also can cause an infection. If the infection is not treated, the kidneys can become scarred and their function might be permanently impaired. Antibiotics usually are effective in treating a bacterial infection.

**Nephritis** Another common kidney problem is nephritis (nih FRIH tus), which often is due to inflammation or painful swelling of some of the glomeruli, as listed in **Table 34.3.** This occurs for many reasons, such as when large particles in the bloodstream become lodged in some of the glomeruli. Symptoms of this condition include blood in the urine, swelling of body tissues, and protein in the urine. If this condition does not improve on its own, the patient may need a special diet or prescription drugs to treat the infection.

**Kidney stones** Kidney stones are another type of kidney disorder, as listed in **Table 34.3** and shown in **Figure 34.17.** A kidney stone is a crystallized solid, such as calcium compounds, that forms in the kidney. Small stones can pass out of the body in urine; this can be quite painful. Larger stones often are broken into small pieces by ultrasonic sound waves. The smaller stones then can pass out of the body. In some cases, surgery might be required to remove large stones.

Kidneys also can be damaged by other diseases present in the body. Diabetes and high blood pressure are the two most common reasons for reduced kidney function and kidney failure. In addition, kidneys can be damaged by prescription and illegal drug use.

**VOCABULARY**

**ACADEMIC VOCABULARY**

**Inhibit:**
To hold back, restrain, or block the action or function of something.
*The concentration of the protein in the blood inhibited the organ from producing more of the same protein.*

**Concepts In Motion**
**Interactive Table** To explore more about excretory disorders, visit biologygmh.com.

**Table 34.3 Common Excretory Disorders**

| Excretory Disorder | Brief Description |
|---|---|
| **Nephritis** | Inflammation of the glomeruli can lead to inflammation of the entire kidneys. This disorder can lead to kidney failure if left untreated. |
| **Kidney stones** | Hard deposits form in the kidney that might pass out of the body in urine. Larger kidney stones can block urine flow or irritate the lining of the urinary tract, leading to possible infection. |
| **Urinary tract blockage** | Malformations present at birth can lead to blockage of the normal flow of urine. If untreated, this blockage can lead to permanent damage of the kidneys. |
| **Polycystic (pah lee SIHS tihk) kidney disease** | This is a genetic disorder distinguished by the growth of many fluid-filled cysts in the kidneys. This disorder can reduce kidney function and lead to kidney failure. |
| **Kidney cancer** | Uncontrolled cell growth often begins in the cells that line the tubules within the kidneys. This can lead to blood in the urine, a mass in the kidneys, or affect other organs due to the cancer spreading, which can lead to death. |

# CHAPTER 34 Assessment

## Section 34.1

### Vocabulary Review

*Match the following definitions with the correct vocabulary term from the Study Guide page.*

**1.** a vessel carrying oxygen-rich blood

**2.** involved in blood vessel repair

**3.** stimulates the heart to contract

### Understand Key Concepts

**4.** When blood leaves the heart, where does it exit?
**A.** the aorta
**B.** the capillaries
**C.** the lungs
**D.** the pulmonary vein

*Use the diagram below to answer questions 5 and 6.*

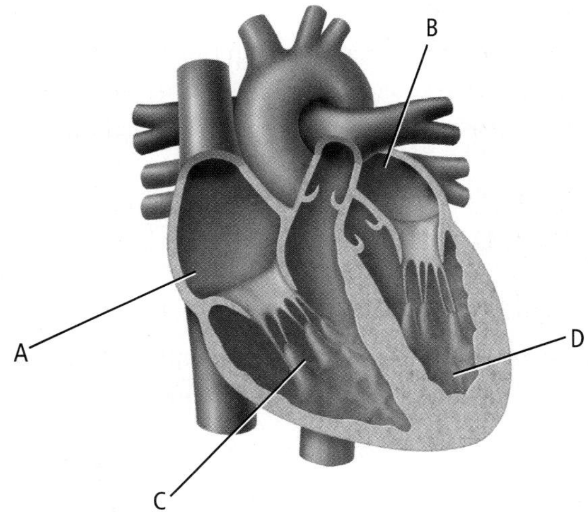


**5.** Which represents the right ventricle?
**A.** A
**B.** B
**C.** C
**D.** D

**6.** Into what part of the heart does oxygen-rich blood enter?
**A.** A
**B.** B
**C.** C
**D.** D

**7.** If a teenager with type A blood is injured in an auto accident and needs a blood transfusion, what type blood will he or she receive?
**A.** only type A
**B.** type A or type O
**C.** only type AB
**D.** only type O

**8.** Where are one-way valves in the circulatory system located?
**A.** arteries
**B.** capillaries
**C.** veins
**D.** white blood cells

**9.** When a small blood vessel in your hand is cut open, which plays an active defensive role against possible disease?
**A.** plasma
**B.** platelets
**C.** red blood cells
**D.** white blood cells

### Constructed Response

**10. Short Answer** Differentiate between the function of the atria and the function of the ventricles.

*Use the diagram to answer question 11.*

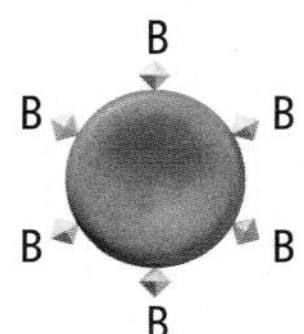


**11. Short Answer** A person has the blood type represented above. What type of blood can the person receive in a transfusion? Explain.

### Think Critically

**12. Hypothesize** an advantage of your heart containing two pumping systems rather than one pumping system within the same organ.

**13. Deduce** which ABO blood type—A, B, AB or O—is the most valuable to medical personnel in an extreme emergency situation and explain why.

## Section 34.2

### Vocabulary Review

*Use the vocabulary terms from the Study Guide page to answer the following questions.*

**14.** In what structure does external respiration take place?

**15.** Which term defines the exchange of gases between the blood and the body's cells?

**16.** Which part of the air pathway branches off the trachea?

### Understand Key Concepts

*Use the diagram below to answer questions 17 and 18.*

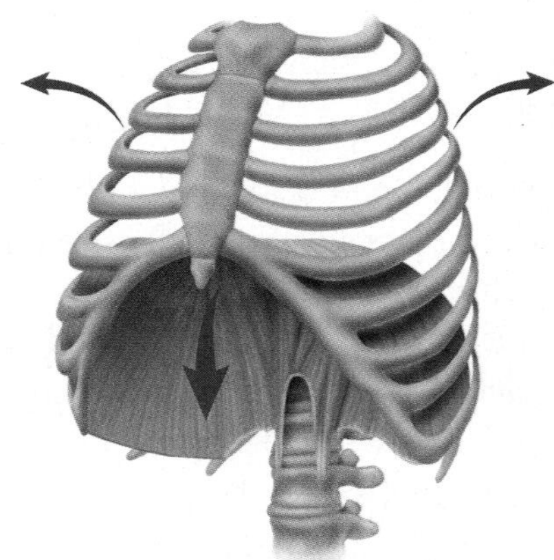

17. Which process is shown above?
    **A.** inhalation
    **B.** exhalation
    **C.** cellular respiration
    **D.** filtration

18. Which structure moves down as its muscles contract?
    **A.** trachea
    **B.** diaphragm
    **C.** pharynx
    **D.** ribs

19. Which process occurs inside the tissue cells in your legs?
    **A.** filtration
    **B.** breathing
    **C.** external respiration
    **D.** internal respiration

20. Which process causes the diaphragm to move back up?
    **A.** cellular respiration
    **B.** exhalation
    **C.** inspiration
    **D.** internal respiration

21. Which gas is needed by all cells?
    **A.** sulfur **C.** carbon dioxide
    **B.** hydrogen **D.** oxygen

22. How many breaths will a person take in one day if they take 12 breaths per minute?
    **A.** about 1000
    **B.** about 10,000
    **C.** about 17,000
    **D.** about 1,000,000

### Constructed Response

23. **Short Answer** Differentiate among asthma, bronchitis, and emphysema.

*Use the photo below to answer question 24.*

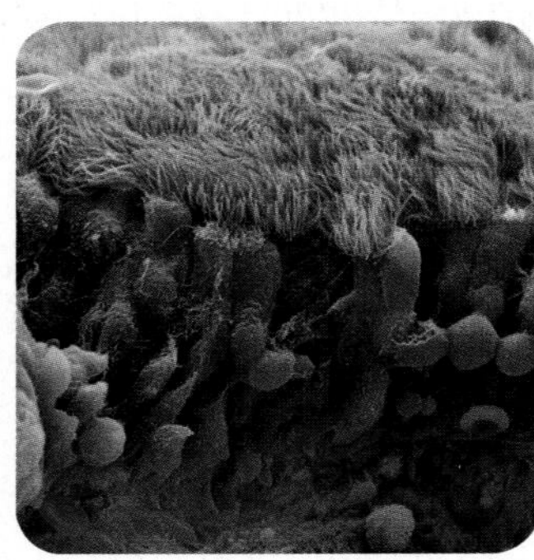

24. **Short Answer** Describe the function of the structures above. Where would these structures be found?

### Think Critically

25. **Hypothesize** an advantage in breathing more deeply during exercise compared to another person engaged in similar exercise breathing at a normal rate.

## Section 34.3

### Vocabulary Review

*Review the vocabulary terms found on the Study Guide page. Use the terms to answer the following questions.*

26. Where are nephrons located?

27. Which waste product is found in urine?

### Understand Key Concepts

28. Where is the loop of Henle?
    **A.** renal tubule
    **B.** glomerulus
    **C.** Bowman's capsule
    **D.** urethra

29. Which one of the kidney functions conserves water in the body?
    **A.** absorption **C.** reabsorption
    **B.** filtration **D.** breathing

30. Which process returns glucose to the blood?
    **A.** excretion **C.** reabsorption
    **B.** filtration **D.** exhalation



Biology Online Chapter Test biologygmh.com

*Use the table below to answer questions 31, 32, and 33.*

**Reabsorption of Some Substances in the Kidneys**

| Chemical substance | Amount Filtered by Kidneys (g/day) | Amount Excreted by Kidneys (g/day) | Percent of Filtered Chemical Reabsorbed (per day) |
|---|---|---|---|
| Glucose | 180 | 0 | 100 |
| Urea | 46.8 | 23.4 | 50 |
| Protein | 1.8 | 1.8 | 0 |

**31.** Based on the estimates from the table above, how much urea is absorbed by the kidneys?
**A.** 0.50 g/min
**B.** 23.4 g/day
**C.** 46.8 g/day
**D.** 50.0 g/day

**32.** Based on the table estimates above, what happens to glucose in the kidneys?
**A.** It is reabsorbed into the blood.
**B.** It is permanently filtered out of the blood.
**C.** It is treated in the kidney like creatinine.
**D.** It is treated in the kidney like urea.

**33.** Infer why proteins are not removed by nephrons.
**A.** Collecting ducts are too small.
**B.** Proteins cannot be filtered.
**C.** Proteins never enter the nephron.
**D.** Proteins are reabsorbed by nephrons.

## Constructed Response

**34. Short Answer** How many liters of blood flow through your kidneys in one hour?

**35. Short Answer** Explain the differences between filtration and reabsorption in the kidney.

**36. Open Ended** Infer why kidneys require so much energy to function.

## Think Critically

**37. CAREERS IN BIOLOGY** Formulate a list of questions one might ask a a urologist regarding urinary problems or keeping the male reproductive system healthy.

## Additional Assessment

**38.** *WRITING in* **Biology** Construct an analogy about the circulatory system that is based on your local highway system in your town, city, or rural area.

### DBQ Document-Based Questions

*The following data compare the state of five subjects whose circulation was monitored. (The weight, age, and sex of all five subjects were the same.) All of Subject A's data were within normal limits; the other four were not.*

Data obtained from: Macey, R. 1968. *Human Physiology.* Englewood Cliffs, NJ: Prentice Hall.

| Subject | Hemoglobin (Hb) content of blood (Hb/100 mL blood) | Oxygen contents of blood in arteries (mL $O_2$/100 mL blood) | Oxygen content of blood in veins (mL $O_2$/100 mL blood) |
|---|---|---|---|
| A | 15 | 19 | 15 |
| B | 15 | 15 | 12 |
| C | 8 | 9.5 | 6.5 |
| D | 16 | 20 | 13 |
| E | 15 | 19 | 18 |

**39.** Which subject might be suffering from a dietary iron deficiency? Explain your choice.

**40.** Which subject might have lived at a high altitude where the atmospheric oxygen is low? Explain your choice.

**41.** Which subject might have been poisoned by carbon monoxide that prevents tissue cells from using oxygen? Explain your choice.

## Cumulative Review

**42.** Draw diagrams of a typical example from each of the three classes of mollusks and label the distinctive characteristics. **(Chapter 25)**

# Standardized Test Practice

**Cumulative**

## Multiple Choice

1. What happens to a skeletal muscle when the actin fibers are pulled toward the center of the sarcomeres?
   **A.** It contracts.
   **B.** It grows.
   **C.** It relaxes.
   **D.** It stretches.

*Use the diagram to answer questions 2 and 3.*

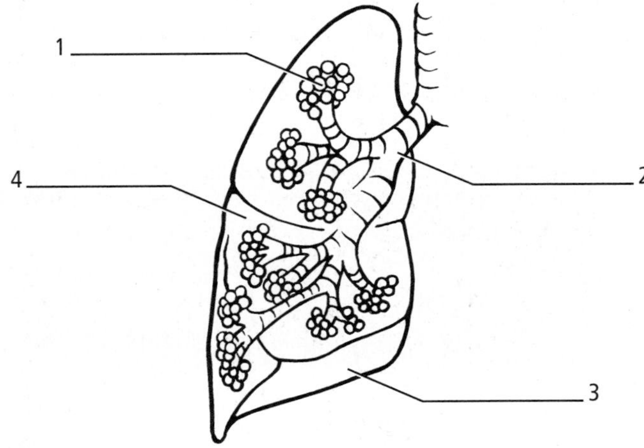


2. Which part of the respiratory system has hairs to filter particles from the air?
   **A.** 1
   **B.** 2
   **C.** 3
   **D.** 4

3. In which numbered location does gas exchange take place?
   **A.** 1
   **B.** 2
   **C.** 3
   **D.** 4

4. Which is an example of operant conditioning?
   **A.** A dog salivates when it hears a bell.
   **B.** A horse becomes accustomed to street noises.
   **C.** A newborn forms an attachment to the first animal seen after birth.
   **D.** A rat learns that it can get food by pulling a lever.

5. Which is an example of nurturing behavior?
   **A.** An animal in a colony spots a predator and warns the whole colony.
   **B.** A female chimpanzee takes care of her infant for three years.
   **C.** A male peacock displays its feathers in front of a female.
   **D.** A squirrel chatters at another squirrel to drive it away.

*Use the table below to answer question 6.*

| Muscle Type | Function |
|---|---|
| Skeletal muscles | attached to bones and tighten when contracted causing movement |
| Smooth muscles | line the hollow internal organs such as stomach, intestines, bladder, and uterus |
| Cardiac muscles | |

6. Where is the muscle type that is missing a description in the table located?
   **A.** in the heart
   **B.** in the kidneys
   **C.** lining the blood vessels
   **D.** lining the lymph vessels

7. Which answer choice is a result of parasympathetic stimulation?
   **A.** decreased heart rate
   **B.** decreased mucus production
   **C.** increased digestive activity
   **D.** increased pupil size

8. Which characteristic directly affects homeostatic temperature control in mammals?
   **A.** four-chambered heart
   **B.** high metabolic rate
   **C.** milk production
   **D.** signaling devices in fur

## Short Answer

*Use the diagram below to answer questions 9 and 10.*

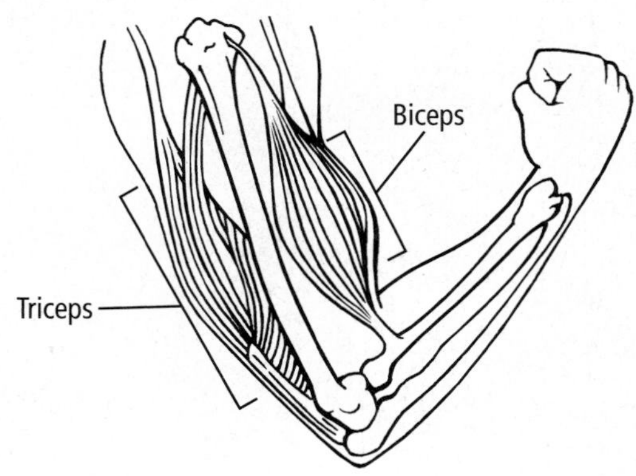


9. Describe how the biceps and triceps allow movement in the arm.

10. Explain why muscles are always in antagonistic pairs.

11. Some drugs cause an increased level of dopamine in nerve synapses. Name one of these drugs and relate the increased dopamine level to other effects that result from using the drug.

12. Use a table to organize information about the autonomic and somatic nervous systems. List the types of responses, systems affected, and include an example.

13. Monotremes are mammals that are similar to reptiles in some ways. Classify monotreme characteristics as similar to reptiles or similar to mammals.

14. A rare disease called amyotrophic lateral sclerosis (ALS) causes motor neurons in the body to lose myelin. What do you think would be the initial symptoms a person with ALS would have?

15. Explain how nephrons filter blood.

## Extended Response

*Use the illustration below to answer question 16.*

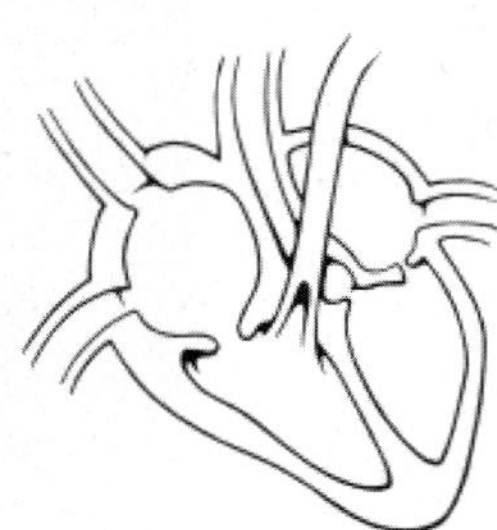

16. The illustration above shows a four-chambered mammalian heart. Write an explanation of the role of the four-chambered heart in circulating oxygenated blood throughout the body.

17. Compare and contrast apical meristems and lateral meristems in plants.

18. The invention of the microscope allowed scientists to discover hundreds of tiny living organisms that were never seen before. Distinguish, in a written statement, between an advance in technology and an advance in science using this historical example.

## Essay Question

The human nervous system consists of a complex arrangement of voluntary and involuntary responses and activities. The presence of these different types of responses has evolved in humans to help with survival.

*Using the information in the paragraph above, answer the following question in essay format.*

19. From what you know about different nervous system responses, write a well-organized essay explaining how different types of involuntary response systems in humans are helpful for survival.

**NEED EXTRA HELP?**

| If You Missed Question . . . | 1 | 2 | 3 | 4 | 5 | 6 | 7 | 8 | 9 | 10 | 11 | 12 | 13 | 14 | 15 | 16 | 17 | 18 | 19 |
|---|---|---|---|---|---|---|---|---|---|---|---|---|---|---|---|---|---|---|---|
| Review Section . . . | 32.3 | 34.2 | 34.2 | 31.1 | 31.2 | 32.3 | 33.2 | 30.1 | 32.3 | 32.3 | 33.4 | 33.2 | 22.1 | 33.1 | 34.3 | 30.2 | 22.1 | 1.2 | 33.2 |

# CHAPTER 35 Digestive and Endocrine Systems

**Section 1**
**The Digestive System**
**MAIN Idea** The digestive system breaks down food so nutrients can be absorbed by the body.

**Section 2**
**Nutrition**
**MAIN Idea** Certain nutrients are essential for the proper function of the body.

**Section 3**
**The Endocrine System**
**MAIN Idea** Systems of the human body are regulated by hormonal feedback mechanisms.

## BioFacts

- A person's stomach lining is replaced every few days.
- A person secretes almost one liter of saliva every day.
- The small intestine is about 6 m long, and the large intestine is about 1.5 m long.

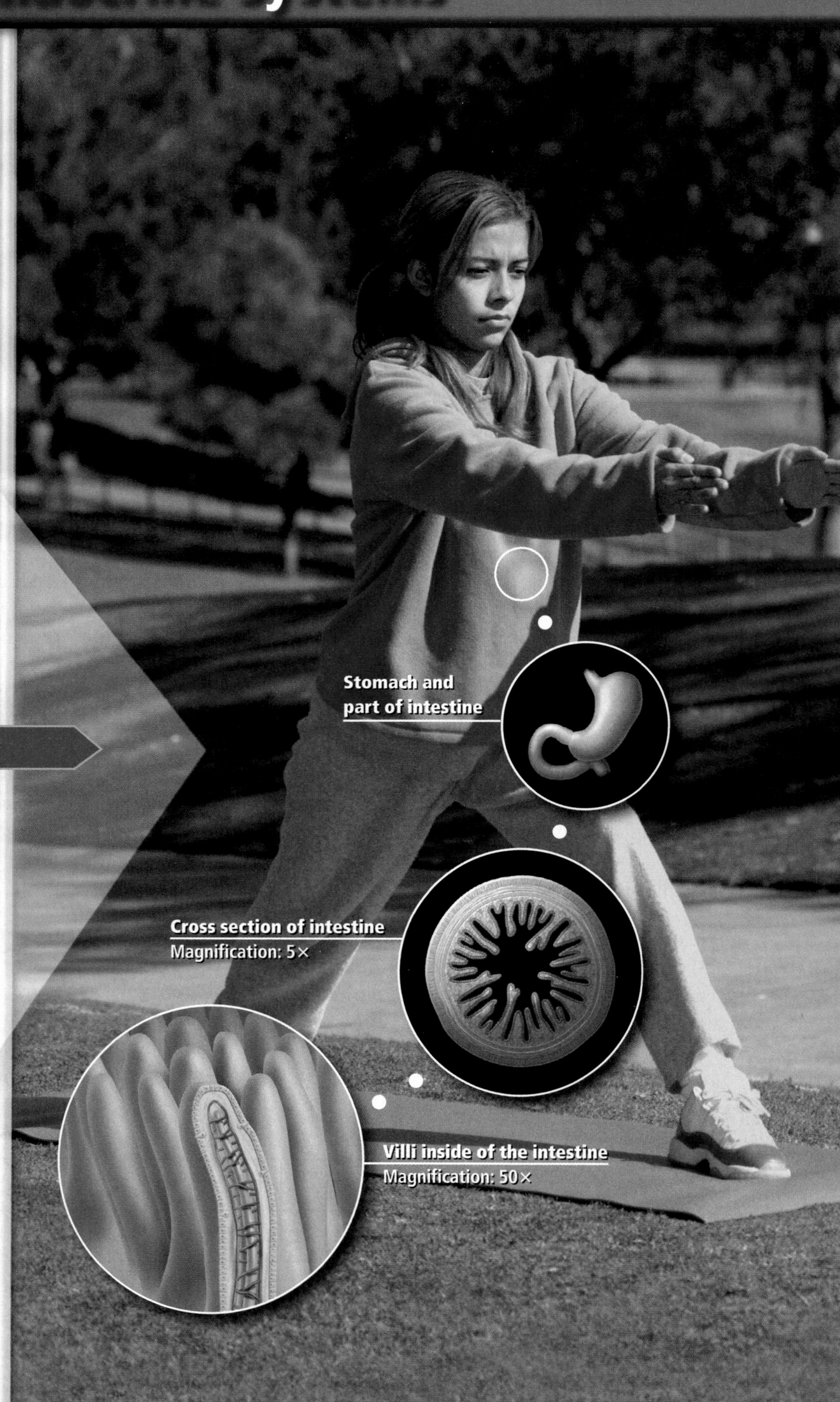

# Start-Up Activities

## LAUNCH Lab

### How does the enzyme pepsin aid digestion?

The acidic digestive juices in the stomach contain the enzyme pepsin. In this lab, you will investigate the role of pepsin in digestion.

**Procedure**

1. Read and complete the lab safety form.
2. Label and prepare **three test tubes.**
   A: 15 mL water
   B: 10 mL water, 5 mL **HCl solution**
   C: 5 mL each water, HCl solution, and **pepsin solution**
3. Cut **hard-boiled egg white** portions into pea-sized chunks with a **knife.**
4. Add equal amounts of egg white to each tube. Predict the relative amount of digestion in each test tube.
5. Place test tubes in an **incubator** overnight at 37°C. Record observations the next day.

**Analysis**

**Evaluate** Rank the test tubes based on the amount of digestion that occurred. Based on your results, describe the roles of pepsin and pH in digestion of proteins.

**Biology Online**

Visit biologygmh.com to:

- study the entire chapter online
- explore Concepts in Motion, Interactive Tables, Microscopy Links, and links to virtual dissections
- access Web links for more information, projects, and activities
- review content online with the Interactive Tutor and take Self-Check Quizzes

**Negative Feedback System** Make this Foldable to help you record what you learn about the role four hormones play in the negative feedback system.

**STEP 1** Fold a 5-cm tab along the short side of a sheet of 11"x 17" paper.

**STEP 2** Fold the same sheet of paper into fourths along the long axis to form a four-row chart.

**STEP 3** Draw lines along the creases.

**STEP 4** Label the rows as follows: *Parathyroid hormone, Antidiuretic hormone,* and *Human growth hormone,* then choose another hormone to include in your chart.

**FOLDABLES Use this Foldable with Section 35.3.** As you study the section, record what you learn about the importance of the negative feedback system to the production of each of the hormones listed in your chart.

Section 35.1

### Objectives

- **Summarize** the three main functions of the digestive system.
- **Identify** structures of the digestive system and their functions.
- **Describe** the process of chemical digestion.

### Review Vocabulary

**nutrient:** vital component of foods that provides energy and materials for growth and body functions

### New Vocabulary

mechanical digestion
chemical digestion
amylase
esophagus
peristalsis
pepsin
small intestine
liver
villus
large intestine

# The Digestive System

**MAIN Idea The digestive system breaks down food so nutrients can be absorbed by the body.**

**Real-World Reading Link** During a lifetime, as much as 45 tonnes of food can pass through a person's digestive system. The food will travel almost 3 m through the digestive tract. What happens as food passes through this long tube?

## Functions of the Digestive System

There are three main functions of the digestive system. The digestive system ingests food, breaks it down so nutrients can be absorbed, and eliminates what cannot be digested. Refer to **Figure 35.1** and **Figure 35.2** as you learn about the structure and function of the digestive system.

**Ingestion** On Friday night, you and your friends go out for pizza. When the pizza arrives at the table, you bite into a slice and begin to chew. Why do you need to chew each bite?

**Mechanical digestion** involves chewing food to break it down into smaller pieces. It also includes the action of smooth muscles in the stomach and small intestine that churn the food. Once a piece of pizza is chewed into smaller pieces, a digestive enzyme in saliva begins to break down carbohydrates. **Chemical digestion** is the action of enzymes—discussed in Chapter 6—in breaking down large molecules into smaller molecules that then can be absorbed by cells. **Amylase,** an enzyme found in saliva, begins the process of chemical digestion by breaking down starches into sugars.

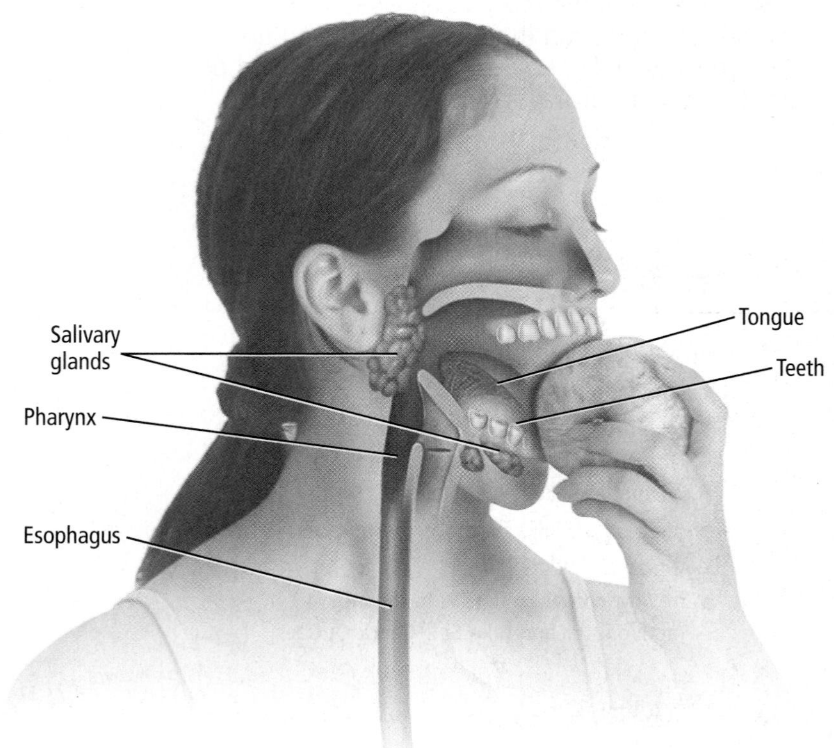


**Figure 35.1** Mechanical digestion starts in the mouth. Secretions from the salivary glands keep food moist and begin the process of chemical digestion. Food moves through the pharynx into the esophagus.

Concepts In Motion

**Interactive Figure** To see an animation of food moving through the esophagus, visit biologygmh.com.

**Esophagus** When the tongue pushes chewed food to the back of the mouth, the swallowing reflex is stimulated. The food is forced by the action of the tongue into the upper portion of the esophagus. The **esophagus** (ih SAH fuh gus) is a muscular tube that connects the pharynx, or throat, to the stomach, illustrated in **Figure 35.2.** The wall of the esophagus is lined with smooth muscles that contract rhythmically to move the food through the digestive system in a process called **peristalsis** (per uh STAHL sus). Peristalsis continues throughout the digestive tract. Even if a person were upside down, food would still move toward the stomach.

When a person swallows, the small plate of cartilage called the epiglottis covers the trachea. If this opening is not closed, food can enter the trachea and cause a person to choke. The body responds to this by initiating the coughing reflex in an attempt to expel the food to keep the food from entering the lungs.

**Stomach** When food leaves the esophagus, it passes through a circular muscle called a sphincter, and then it moves into the stomach. The sphincter between the esophagus and stomach is the cardiac sphincter. The walls of the stomach are composed of three overlapping layers of smooth muscle that are involved with mechanical digestion. As the muscles contract, they further break down the food and mix it with the secretions of glands that line the inner wall of the stomach.

**Connection to Chemistry** Recall from Chapter 6 that pH is a measure of a solution's acidity. The environment inside the stomach is very acidic. Stomach glands, called gastric glands, secrete an acidic solution, which lowers the pH in the stomach to a pH of about 2. This is about the same acidity as lemon juice. If the sphincter in the upper portion of the stomach allows any leakage, some of this acid might move back into the esophagus, causing what is commonly known as heartburn.

The acidic environment in the stomach is favorable to the action of **pepsin,** an enzyme involved in the process of the chemical digestion of proteins. Cells in the lining of the stomach secrete mucus to help prevent damage from pepsin and the acidic environment. Although most absorption occurs in the small intestine, some substances, such as alcohol and aspirin, are absorbed by cells that line the stomach. While empty, the capacity of the stomach is about 50 mL. When full, it can expand to 2–4 L.

The muscular walls of the stomach contract and push food farther along the digestive tract. The consistency of the food resembles tomato soup as it passes through the pyloric sphincter at the lower end of the stomach into the small intestine. **Figure 35.3** illustrates peristalsis in the small intestine.

**Reading Check** **Compare** digestion in the mouth with digestion in the stomach.

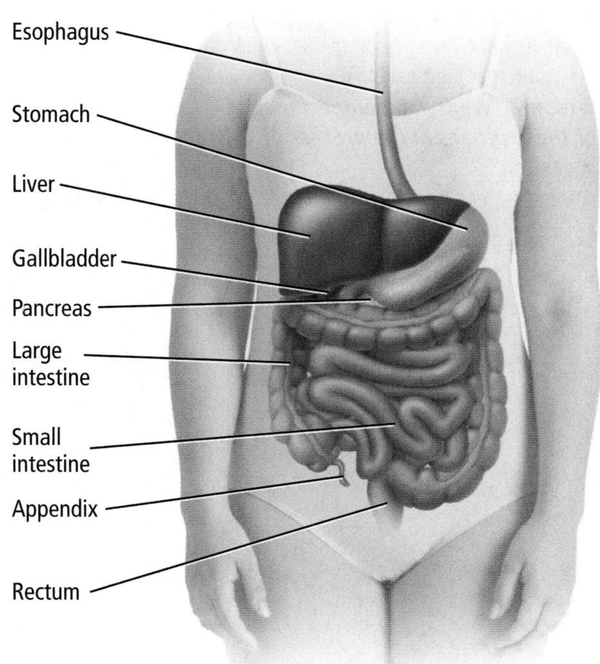


**Figure 35.2** The esophagus extends from the pharynx to the stomach and is approximately 25 cm long.
**Describe** ***What takes place as food moves through the digestive system?***

**Concepts In Motion**
**Interactive Figure** To see an animation of peristasis, visit biologygmh.com.

**Figure 35.3** The smooth muscles in the walls of the digestive tract contract in the process of peristalsis.

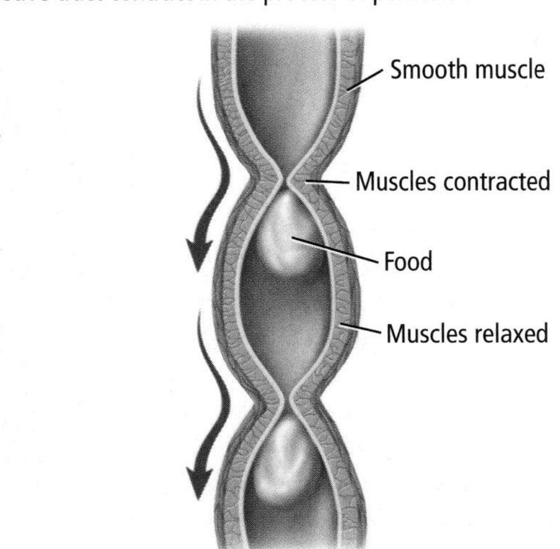

■ **Figure 35.4** Chemical digestion in the small intestine depends on the activities of the liver, pancreas, and gallbladder.
**Discuss** ***What is the importance of each of these organs in the process of chemical digestion?***

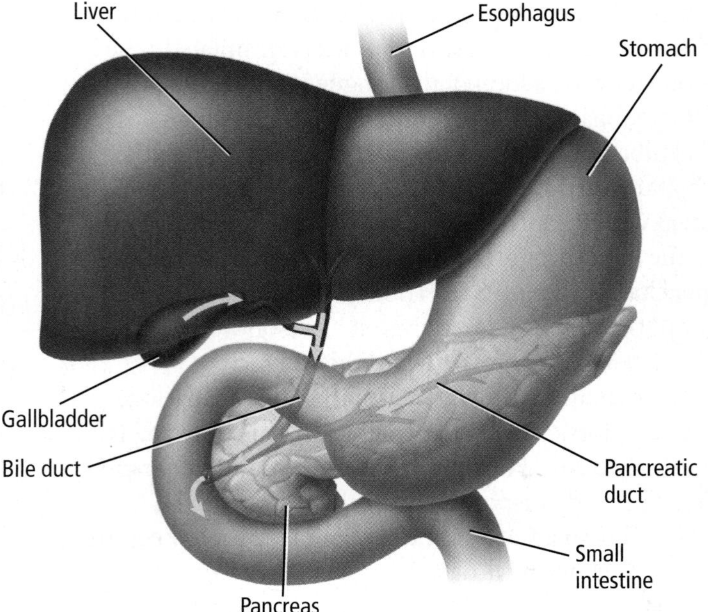


**Small intestine** The **small intestine** is approximately 7 m in length and is the longest part of the digestive tract. It is called small because it has a diameter of 2.5 cm compared to the 6.5 cm diameter of the large intestine. The smooth muscles in the wall of the small intestine continue the process of mechanical digestion and push the food farther through the digestive tract by peristalsis.

The completion of chemical digestion in the small intestine depends on three accessory organs—the pancreas, liver, and gallbladder, illustrated in **Figure 35.4.** The pancreas serves two main functions. One is to produce enzymes that digest carbohydrates, proteins, and fats. The other is to produce hormones, which will be discussed later in this chapter. The pancreas secretes an alkaline fluid to raise the pH in the small intestine to slightly above 7, which creates a favorable environment for the action of intestinal enzymes.

The **liver** is the largest internal organ of the body and produces bile, which helps to break down fats. About 1 L of bile is produced every day, and excess bile is stored in the gallbladder to be released into the small intestine when needed. **Figure 35.5** shows gallstones, which are cholesterol crystals that can form in the gallbladder.

*Study Tip*

**Sequence and Order** Using your notes, work with a partner to review the sequence of the organs in the digestive system. Then, practice retelling the sequence without your notes. Ask questions of one another for deeper learning.

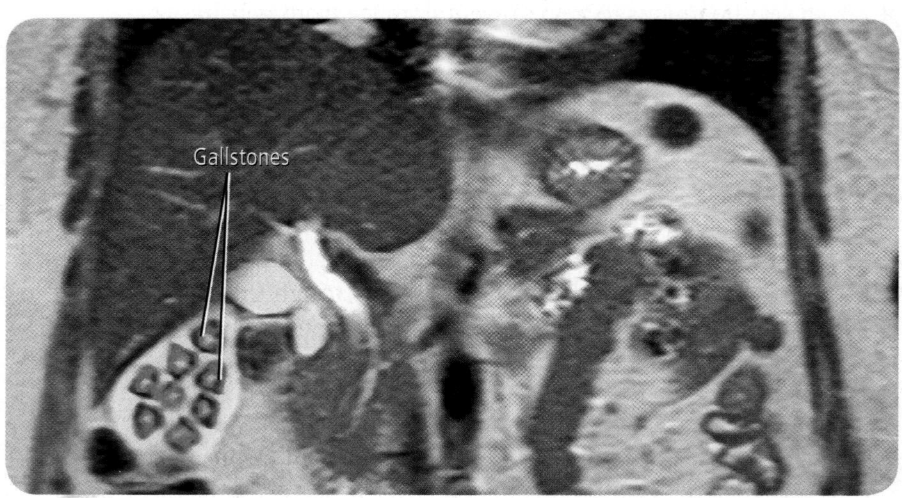


■ **Figure 35.5** Gallstones can obstruct the flow of bile from the gallbladder. Note the gallstones on this MRI film of a gallbladder.

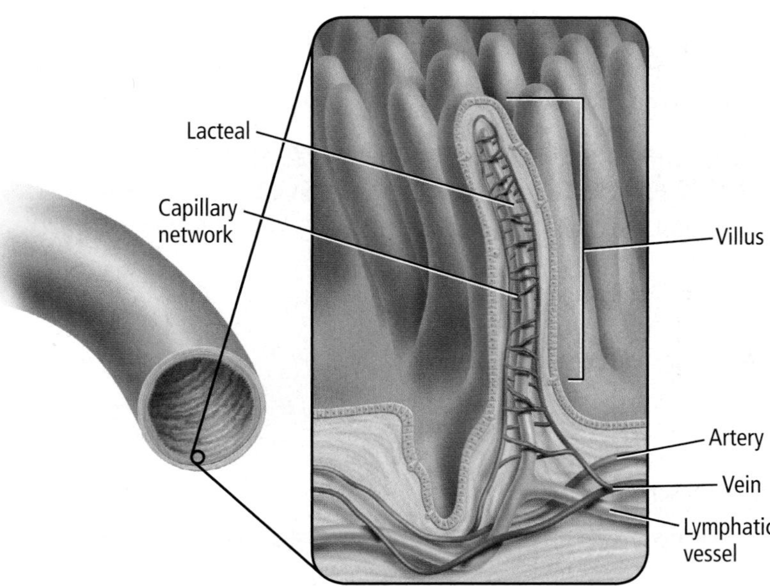


**Figure 35.6** A villus is a fingerlike extension of the lining of the small intestine. Nutrients diffuse into capillaries in the villi and reach body cells by means of circulating blood.

Chemical digestion is completed and most of the nutrients from food are absorbed from the small intestine into the bloodstream through fingerlike structures called **villi** (VIH li) (singular, villus). Villi, illustrated in **Figure 35.6,** increase the surface area of the small intestine, giving the small intestine approximately the same surface area as a tennis court.

Refer again to **Figure 35.1** and **Figure 35.2** to follow the movement of digested food through the digestive system. Once digestion is complete, the remaining food, now in a semiliquid form called chyme (KIME), moves into the large intestine. Chyme is made up of materials that cannot be digested or absorbed by villi in the small intestine.

## MiniLab 35.1

### Investigate Digestion of Lipids

**How do bile salts and pancreatic solution affect digestion?** Lipids, or fats, are not water soluble. The body compensates by producing bile, a chemical that breaks apart fat and helps the molecules mix with the watery solution in the small intestine. In this lab, you will investigate the breakdown of lipids.

**Procedure**

1. Read and complete the lab safety form.
2. Study the lab procedure and construct a data chart.
3. Label **three test tubes.** Add 5 mL **vegetable oil** and 8-10 drops **phenolphthalein** to each. Shake well. If the color is not pink, add **NaOH solution** one drop at a time until the solution turns pink.
4. Add 125 mL **water** to a **250-mL beaker.** Warm to about 40°C.
5. Prepare the test tubes as follows, then seal each with a **stopper.**
   Test Tube A: 5 mL **distilled water,** pinch of **bile salt**
   Test Tube B: 5 mL **pancreatic solution,** pinch of bile salt
   Test Tube C: 5 mL pancreatic solution
6. Shake each tube to mix the contents and gently place in the beaker. Record your observations.
7. Dispose of test tube contents in the designated container.

**Analysis**

1. **Analyze** What did a color change inside a test tube indicate? What caused the change?
2. **Draw Conclusions** Based on your results, describe the roles of bile and pancreatic solution in digestion.

CONCEPTS In MOtion
Interactive Table To explore more about digestion, visit biologygmh.com.

| Table 35.1 | Time for Digestion | |
|---|---|---|
| **Digestive Structure** | **Primary Function** | **Time Food in Structure** |
| **Mouth** | Mechanical and chemical digestion | 5–30 s |
| **Esophagus** | Transport (swallowing) | 10 s |
| **Stomach** | Mechanical and chemical digestion | 2–24 h |
| **Small intestine** | Mechanical and chemical digestion | 3–4 h |
| **Large intestine** | Water absorption | 18 h–2 days |

**Large intestine** The **large intestine** is the end portion of the digestive tract. It is about 1.5 m long and includes the colon, the rectum, and a small saclike appendage called the appendix. Although the appendix has no known function, it can become inflamed and swollen, resulting in appendicitis. If inflamed, the appendix likely will have to be removed surgically.

Some kinds of bacteria are normal in the colon. These bacteria produce vitamin K and some B vitamins that then become available to the body.

A primary function of the colon is to absorb water from the chyme. The indigestible material then becomes more solid and is called feces. Peristalsis continues to move feces toward the rectum, causing the walls of the rectum to stretch. This initiates a reflex that causes the final sphincter muscle to relax, and the feces are eliminated from the body through the anus. Refer to **Table 35.1** to review the primary function of each structure of the digestive system and how long food usually remains in each structure as it is being digested.

# Section 35.1 Assessment

## Section Summary

- The digestive system has three main functions.
- Digestion can be categorized as mechanical or chemical.
- Most nutrients are absorbed in the small intestine.
- Accessory organs provide enzymes and bile to aid digestion.
- Water is absorbed from chyme in the colon.

## Understand Main Ideas

1. MAIN Idea **Describe** the process that breaks down food so nutrients can be absorbed by the body.
2. **Analyze** the difference between mechanical digestion and chemical digestion, and explain why chemical digestion is necessary for the body.
3. **Summarize** the three main functions of the digestive system.
4. **Analyze** what the consequence might be if the lining of the small intestine were completely smooth instead of having villi.

## Think Scientifically

5. *Design* an experiment to gather data about the effect of pH on the digestion of different types of food.
6. MATH in Biology A can of soda pop typically holds about 354 mL of fluid. Compare this amount with the volume of an empty stomach. Give a ratio.
7. *Explain* The pH in the digestive system changes. Give examples and explain the importance of these changes.

Section 35.2

## Objectives

- **Correlate** activity level with the intake of Calories needed to maintain proper body weight.
- **Describe** how proteins, carbohydrates, and fats are broken down in the digestive tract.
- **Explain** the roles of vitamins and minerals in maintaining homeostasis.
- **Apply** the information in MyPyramid and on food labels as tools for establishing healthy eating habits.

## Review Vocabulary

**amino acid:** basic building block of proteins

## New Vocabulary

nutrition
Calorie
vitamin
mineral

# Nutrition

**MAIN Idea Certain nutrients are essential for the proper function of the body.**

**Real-World Reading Link** There is a saying, "You are what you eat." What do you think that means? Much of the time you have freedom to choose what you will eat. However, your choices have consequences. What you eat can affect your health now and in the future.

## Calories

**Nutrition** is the process by which a person takes in and uses food. Foods supply the building blocks and energy to maintain body mass. The daily input of energy from food should equal the amount of energy a person uses daily. A **Calorie** (with an uppercase C) is the unit used to measure the energy content of foods. A Calorie is equal to 1 kilocalorie, or 1000 calories (with a lowercase c). A calorie is the amount of heat needed to raise the temperature of 1 mL of water by 1°C.

The energy content of a food can be measured by burning the food and converting the stored energy to heat. Not all foods have the same energy content. The same mass of different foods does not always equal the same number of Calories. For example, one gram of carbohydrate or protein contains four Calories. One gram of fat contains nine Calories. Choosing foods wisely is important. To lose weight, more Calories must be used than consumed. The opposite is true to gain weight. In 2005, the United States Department of Agriculture released new guidelines for nutrition and suggested that people should become more active and use more Calories. **Table 35.2** compares Calorie usage with different activities.

**Table 35.2 Activities and Calories Used per Hour**

Concepts In Motion
Interactive Table To explore more about activities and Calories, visit biologygmh.com.

| Activity | Calories Used Per Hour | Activity | Calories Used Per Hour |
|---|---|---|---|
| Baseball | 282 | Hiking and backpacking | 564 |
| Basketball | 564 | Hockey (field and ice) | 546 |
| Bicycling | 240–410 | Jogging | 740–920 |
| Cross-country skiing | 700 | Skating | 300 |
| Football | 540 | Soccer | 540 |

■ **Figure 35.7** Your body needs carbohydrate-rich foods every day.
**Analyze** ***Which items in the photo are complex carbohydrates?***

**VOCABULARY**
**SCIENCE USAGE V. COMMON USAGE**
**Consume**
***Science usage:*** to eat or drink.
*We consume Calories when we eat food.*

***Common usage:*** to destroy.
*The fire consumed several buildings.*

## Carbohydrates

Cereal, pasta, potatoes, strawberries, and rice all contain a high proportion of carbohydrates. Recall from Chapter 6 that sugars, such as glucose, fructose, and sucrose, are simple carbohydrates that are found in fruits, soda pop, and candy. Complex carbohydrates are macromolecules such as starches, which are long chains of sugars. Foods such as those shown in **Figure 35.7** have a high starch content, as do some vegetables.

Complex carbohydrates are broken down into simple sugars in the digestive tract. Simple sugars are absorbed through villi in the small intestine into blood capillaries and circulated throughout the body to provide energy for cells. Excess glucose is stored in the liver in the form of glycogen. Cellulose, sometimes called dietary fiber, is another complex carbohydrate found in plant foods. Although humans cannot digest fiber, it is important because fiber helps keep food moving through the digestive tract and helps with the elimination of wastes. Bran, whole-grain breads, and beans are good sources of fiber.

 **Reading Check** **Compare** simple and complex carbohydrates.

## Fats

In proper amounts, fats are an essential part of a healthful diet. Fats are the most concentrated energy source available to the body, and they are building blocks for the body. Fats also protect some internal organs and help maintain homeostasis by providing energy, and storing and transporting certain vitamins. However, not all fats are beneficial.

**Connection to Health** Recall from Chapter 6 that fats are classified according to their chemical structure as saturated or unsaturated. Meats, cheeses, and other dairy products are sources of saturated fats. A diet high in saturated fats might result in high blood levels of cholesterol, which can lead to high blood pressure and other heart problems. Plants are the main source of unsaturated fats. They are not associated with heart disease, although excessive consumption of any type of fat can lead to weight gain.

A general rule is that saturated fats are solid and unsaturated fats are liquid at room temperature. The margarine in **Figure 35.8** contains less saturated fat than butter. Fats are digested in the small intestine and broken down into fatty acids and glycerol. Fatty acids can be absorbed through the villi and circulated in the blood throughout the body.

■ **Figure 35.8** Unprocessed fruits and vegetables have low fat content. The way in which naturally low-fat foods are cooked and served can increase fat content, such as when potatoes are fried in saturated fats.

## Proteins

You have learned that proteins are basic structural components of all cells, and that amino acids are the building blocks of proteins. Enzymes, hormones, neurotransmitters, and membrane receptors are just a few important proteins in the body.

During the process of digestion, proteins in foods are broken down to their subunit amino acids. The amino acids are absorbed into the bloodstream and carried to various body cells. These body cells, through the process of protein synthesis, assemble the amino acids into proteins needed for body structures and functions.

Humans require 20 different amino acids for protein synthesis. The human body can synthesize 12 of the 20 amino acids needed for cellular function. Essential amino acids are the eight amino acids that must be included in a person's diet. Animal products, such as meats, fish, poultry, eggs, and dairy products, are sources of all eight essential amino acids. Vegetables, fruits, and grains contain amino acids, but no single plant food source contains all eight essential amino acids. However, certain combinations, such as the beans and rice shown in **Figure 35.9,** provide all of the essential amino acids.

**Figure 35.9** Beans and rice can be combined to provide all the essential amino acids.
**Explain** ***Why is it important to eat foods that contain the essential amino acids?***

## Food Pyramid

In 2005, the United States Department of Agriculture published a new food pyramid, MyPyramid, which replaces the old pyramid that had been a symbol of good nutrition since 1992. **Figure 35.10** shows the new pyramid. Notice that the orange and green sections are wider than the purple and yellow sections. The message of the pyramid is that a person needs more nutrients from grains and vegetables than from meats and oils.

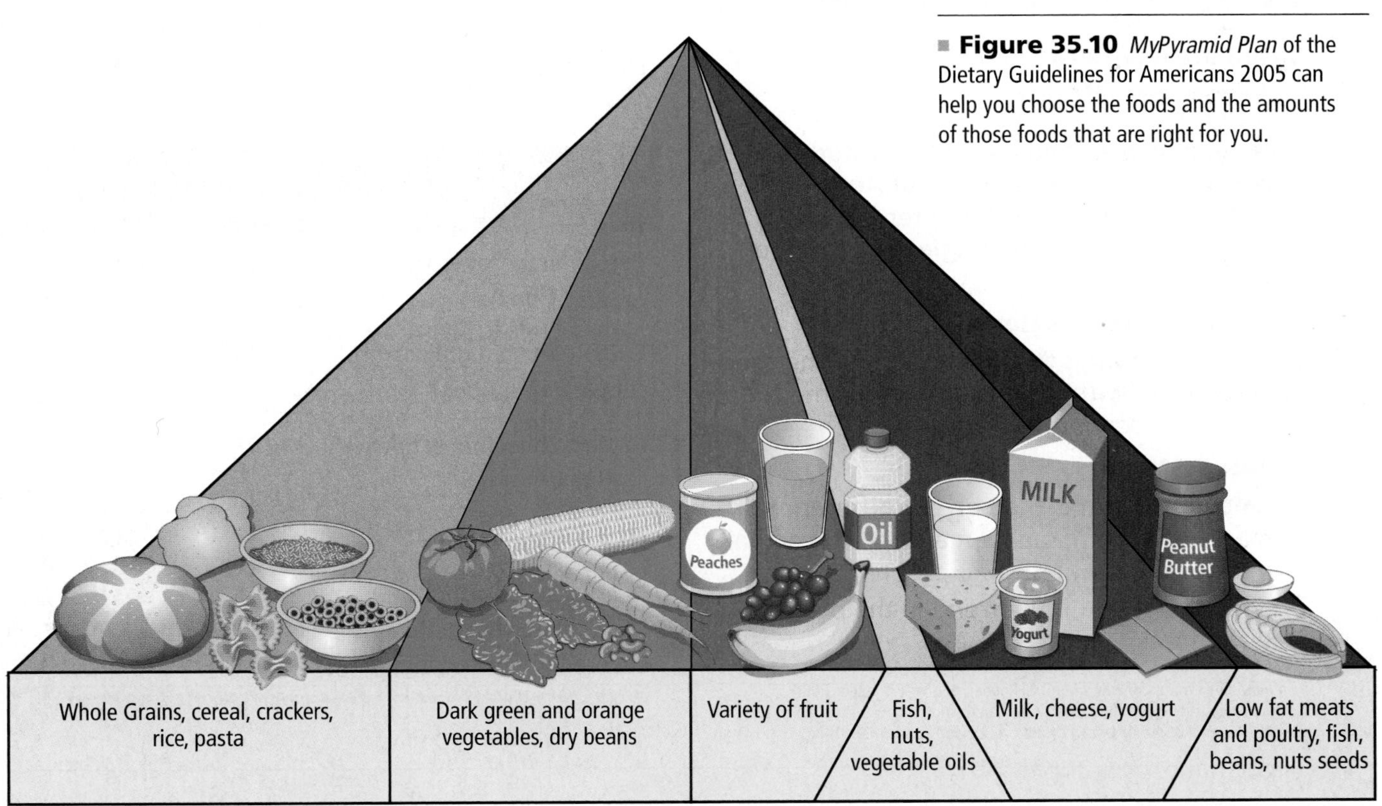


**Figure 35.10** *MyPyramid Plan* of the Dietary Guidelines for Americans 2005 can help you choose the foods and the amounts of those foods that are right for you.

## Vitamins and Minerals

In addition to carbohydrates, fats, and proteins, your body needs vitamins and minerals to function properly. **Vitamins** are organic compounds that are needed in small amounts for metabolic activities. Many vitamins help enzymes function well. Vitamin D is made by cells in your skin. Some B vitamins and vitamin K are produced by bacteria living in the large intestine. Sufficient quantities of most vitamins cannot be made by the body, but a well-balanced diet can provide the vitamins that are needed. Some vitamins that are fat-soluble can be stored in small quantities in the liver and fatty tissues of the body. Other vitamins are water-soluble and cannot be stored in the body. Foods providing an adequate level of these vitamins should be included in a person's diet on a regular basis.

**Minerals** are inorganic compounds used by the body as building material, and they are involved with metabolic functions. For example, the mineral iron is needed to make hemoglobin. Recall from Chapter 34 that oxygen binds to hemoglobin in red blood cells and is delivered to body cells as blood circulates in the body. Calcium, another mineral, is an important component of bones and is involved with muscle and nerve functions.

Vitamins and minerals are essential parts of a healthy diet. **Table 35.3** on the next page lists some important vitamins and minerals, their benefits, and some food sources that can provide these necessary nutrients. Over-the-counter vitamins also are available. Taking more than the recommended daily allowance, however, can be dangerous and should not be done without consulting a doctor.

**CAREERS IN BIOLOGY**

**Registered Dietician** A registered dietician helps people address a variety of health issues by showing them how to make healthful decisions about their diets. For more information on biology careers, visit biologygmh.com.

## DATA ANALYSIS LAB 35.1

**Based on Real Data***

### Compare Data

**How reliable are food labels?** In a study conducted at the U.S. Department of Agriculture Human Nutrition Research Center, scientists measured the mass of 99 single-serving food products.

**Data and Observations**

The table compares the mass listed on the food package label with the actual mass of the food in five single-serving packages.

| Food (1 serving) | Label Mass (g) | Actual Mass (g) |
|---|---|---|
| Cereal, bran flakes with raisins (1 box) | 39 | 54.2 |
| Cereal, toasted grains with supplement (1 box) | 23 | 39.6 |
| Cookie, chocolate sandwich (1 pkg) | 57 | 67.0 |
| Mini danish, apple (1 per serving) | 35 | 44.8 |
| Mini donut, chocolate covered (4 per serving) | 100 | 116.5 |

**Think Critically**

1. **Calculate** What is the percent difference in mass between the label mass and the actual mass of the cookies?
2. **Compare** What is the trend in the percent differences?

*Data obtained from: Conway, J.M., D.G. Rhodes, and W.V. Rumpler. 2004. Commercial portion-controlled foods in research studies: how accurate are label weights? *Journal of the American Dietetic Association* 104: 1420–1424.

Concepts In Motion
Interactive Table To explore more about vitamins and minerals, visit biologygmh.com.

## Table 35.3 Major Roles of Some Vitamins and Minerals

| Vitamin | Major Role in the Body | Possible Sources | Mineral | Major Role in the Body |
|---|---|---|---|---|
| A | • Vision<br>• Health of skin and bones | | Ca | • Strengthening of teeth and bone<br>• Nerve conduction<br>• Contraction of muscle |
| D | • Health of bones and teeth | | P | • Strengthening of teeth and bone |
| E | • Strengthening of red blood cell membrane | | Mg | • Synthesis of proteins |
| Riboflavin ($B_2$) | • Metabolism of energy | | Fe | • Synthesis of hemoglobin |
| Folic Acid | • Formation of red blood cells<br>• Formation of DNA and RNA | | Cu | • Synthesis of hemoglobin |
| Thiamine | • Metabolism of carbohydrates | | Zn | • Healing of wounds |
| Niacin ($B_3$) | • Metabolism of energy | | Cl | • Balance of water |
| Pyridoxine ($B_6$) | • Metabolism of amino acids | | I | • Synthesis of thyroid hormone |
| $B_{12}$ | • Formation of red blood cells | | Na | • Nerve conduction<br>• Balance of pH |
| C | • Formation of collagen | | K | • Nerve conduction<br>• Contraction of muscle |

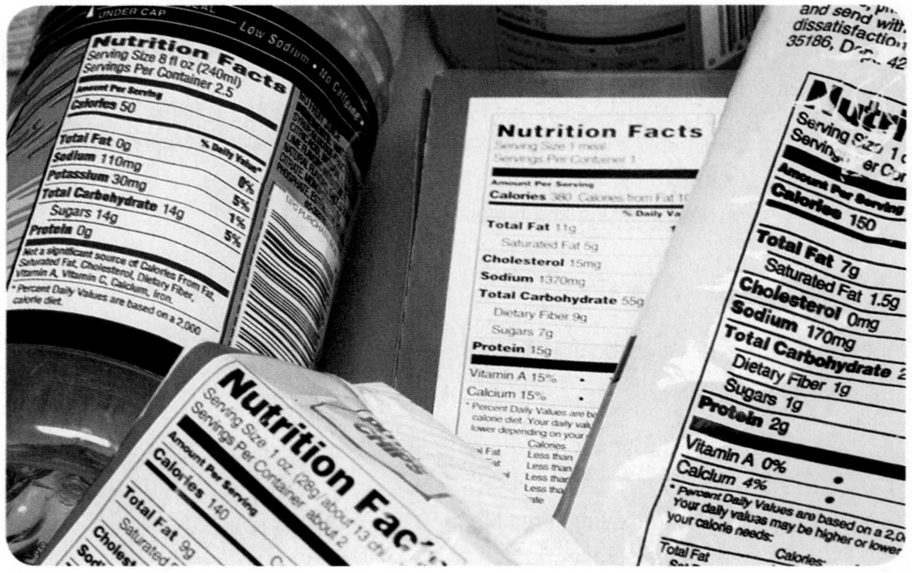


**Figure 35.11** Notice how many servings are in the food container. The percent daily values are based on an individual serving, not the entire package.

## Nutrition Labels

Nutrition labels are provided on commercially packaged foods like those shown in **Figure 35.11.** These labels are based on a 2000-Calorie per day diet. Labels can be especially useful for monitoring fat and sodium intake, two nutrients that need to be consumed in moderation. The FDA requires that food labels list the following information:

- name of the food
- net weight or volume
- name and address of manufacturer, distributor, or packager
- ingredients
- nutrient content

## Section 35.2 Assessment

### Section Summary

- The energy content of food is measured in Calories.
- Carbohydrates, fats, and proteins are three major groups of nutrients.
- Carbohydrates are a major source of energy for the body.
- Fats and proteins are important building blocks for the body and also provide energy.
- Vitamins and minerals are essential for proper metabolic functioning.
- The *MyPyramid Plan* and food labels are tools you can use to eat healthfully.

### Understand Main Ideas

1. MAIN Idea **Explain** why keeping a count of Calories consumed and Calories used is important in maintaining proper functioning of the body.
2. **Describe** how proteins, carbohydrates, and fats are changed in the process of digestion.
3. **Recommend** what nutrients a vegetarian should add to his or her diet.
4. **Explain** the roles of vitamins and minerals in the process of maintaining homeostasis.

### Think Scientifically

5. *Summarize* how many Calories you consume during one day. Record all the foods and beverages you eat and drink in one day. If possible, do the same for total fat and saturated fat.
6. *WRITING in* **Biology** Write a short article for your school newspaper describing what is needed for a well-balanced diet.



Biology Online Self-Check Quiz biologygmh.com

Section 35.3

## Objectives

- **Identify** and describe the function of glands that make up the endocrine system.
- **Explain** the role of the endocrine system in maintaining homeostasis.
- **Describe** feedback mechanisms that regulate hormone levels in the body.

## Review Vocabulary

**homeostasis:** regulation of an organism's internal environment conditions to maintain life

## New Vocabulary

endocrine gland
hormone
pituitary gland
thyroxine
calcitonin
parathyroid hormone
insulin
glucagon
aldosterone
cortisol
antidiuretic hormone

# The Endocrine System

**MAIN Idea Systems of the human body are regulated by hormonal feedback mechanisms.**

**Real-World Reading Link** A person who sends e-mails clicks "Send." The message travels electronically from the computer through a central computer system, which, within seconds, relays the message to a second computer. This is similar to the way your endocrine system works.

## Action of Hormones

The endocrine system is composed of glands and functions as a communication system. **Endocrine glands** produce hormones, which are released into the bloodstream and distributed to body cells. A **hormone** is a substance that acts on certain target cells and tissues to produce a specific response. Hormones are classified as steroid hormones and nonsteroid or amino acid hormones, based on their structure and mechanism of action.

**Steroid hormones** Estrogen and testosterone are two examples of steroid hormones. You will learn how each of these affect the human reproductive systems in Chapter 36. All steroid hormones work by causing the target cells to initiate protein synthesis, as illustrated in **Figure 35.12.**

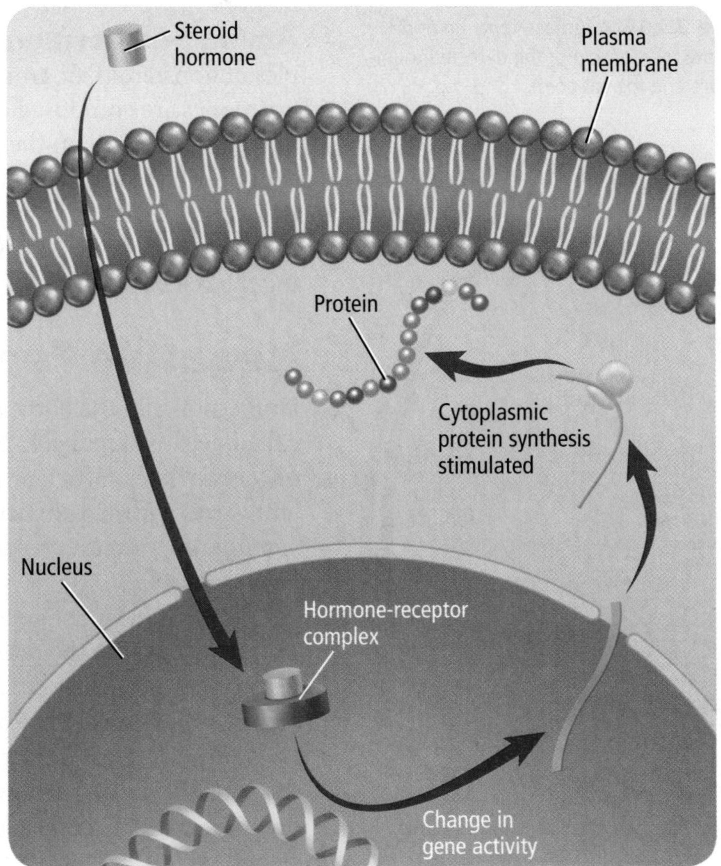


**Figure 35.12** A steroid hormone passes through a cell membrane, binds to a receptor within the cell, and stimulates protein synthesis.

Concepts In Motion

**Interactive Figure** To see an animation of how steroid hormones lead to the production of proteins in a cell, visit biologygmh.com.

■ **Figure 35.13** An amino acid hormone binds to a receptor on the plasma membrane before entering the cell.
**Explain** ***What is the difference between amino acid hormones and steroid hormones?***

**Concepts In Motion**

**Interactive Figure** To see an animation of the two ways an amino acid hormone can control what goes on in a target cell, visit biologygmh.com.

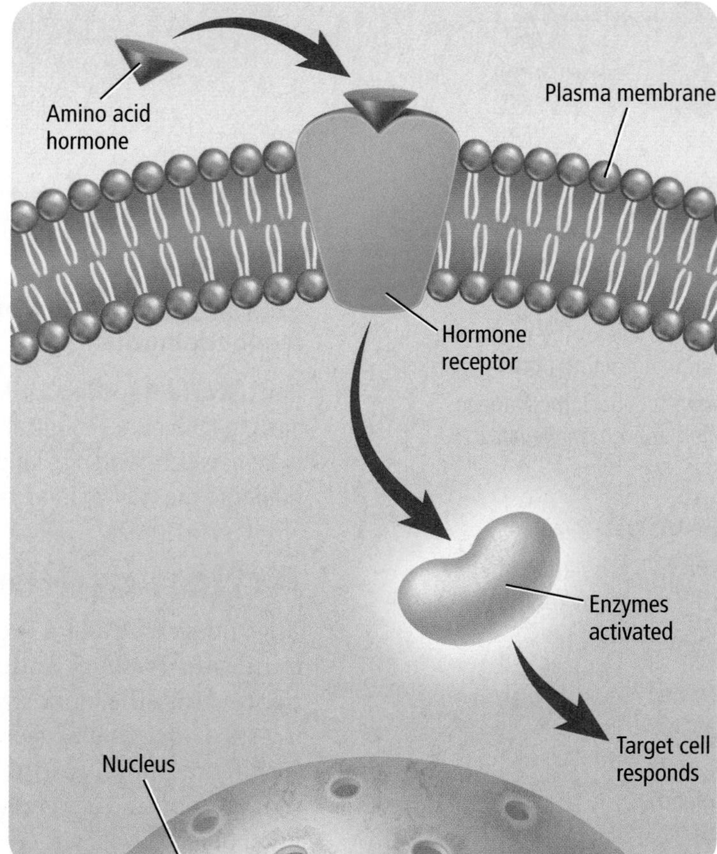


Steroid hormones are soluble in lipids and therefore can diffuse through the plasma membrane of a target cell. Once inside a target cell, they bind to a receptor in the cell. The hormone and the receptor that are bound together bind to DNA in the nucleus, which activates specific genes.

**Amino acid hormones** Insulin and growth hormones are two examples of nonsteroid, or amino acid, hormones. As the name implies, these hormones are composed of amino acids. Amino acid hormones must bind to receptors found on the plasma membrane of a target cell because they cannot diffuse through the plasma membrane. Once the hormone binds to the receptor, the receptor activates an enzyme found on the inside of the membrane. This usually initiates a biochemical pathway, eventually causing the cell to produce the desired response, as illustrated in **Figure 35.13.**

## Negative Feedback

Homeostasis in the body is maintained by internal feedback mechanisms called negative feedback. Negative feedback returns a system to a set point once it deviates sufficiently from that set point. As a consequence, the system varies within a particular range. You already might be familiar with an example of a negative feedback system in your own home, illustrated in **Figure 35.14.**

■ **Figure 35.14** A furnace turns on or off based on the relationship of the detected room temperature and the set point.

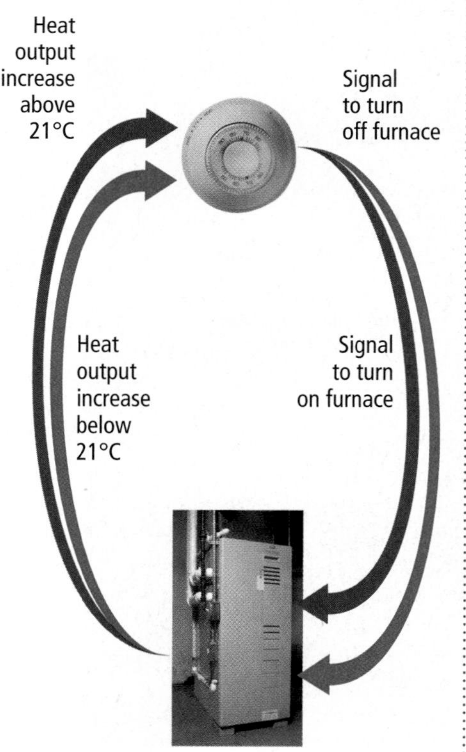


For example, the temperature in a house might be maintained at 21°C. The thermostat in the house detects the temperature, and when the temperature drops below 21°C, the thermostat sends a signal to the heat source, which turns it on and produces more heat. Soon the temperature rises above 21°C, and the thermostat sends a signal to the heat source to shut off. The heat source will not turn on again until the room temperature drops below 21°C and is detected by the thermostat. Because this process can go on indefinitely, negative feedback often is described as a "loop."

## Link to the Nervous System

The nervous and endocrine systems are similar in that they both are involved in regulating the activities of the body and maintaining homeostasis. Refer to **Figure 35.19** to study the role of the hypothalamus in homeostasis. Recall that this part of the brain, called the hypothalamus, is involved with many aspects of homeostasis. The hypothalamus produces two hormones, oxytocin (ahk sih TOH sun) and antidiuretic hormone (ADH). These hormones are transported through axons and stored in axon endings located in the pituitary gland. You will learn more about oxytocin in Chapter 36.

The **antidiuretic** (AN ti DY yuh REH tic) **hormone** (ADH) functions in homeostasis by regulating water balance. ADH affects portions of the kidneys called the collecting tubules. Think back to the last time you were working outside on a hot summer day. You produced a lot of sweat to help keep you cool and you might have become dehydrated. When this happens, cells in your hypothalamus detect that you are dehydrated—that the level of water in the blood is low—and respond by releasing ADH from axons in the pituitary gland that have been storing the hormone.

As illustrated in **Figure 35.20,** ADH travels in the blood to the kidney, where it binds to receptors on certain kidney cells. This causes the kidney to reabsorb more water and decrease the amount of water in the urine, increasing the water level in the blood. If there is too much water in a person's blood, the hypothalamus decreases ADH release, and the urine tends to be more dilute. ADH production is stimulated by nausea and vomiting, both of which cause dehydration. Blood loss of 15 or 20 percent by hemorrhage results in the release of ADH.

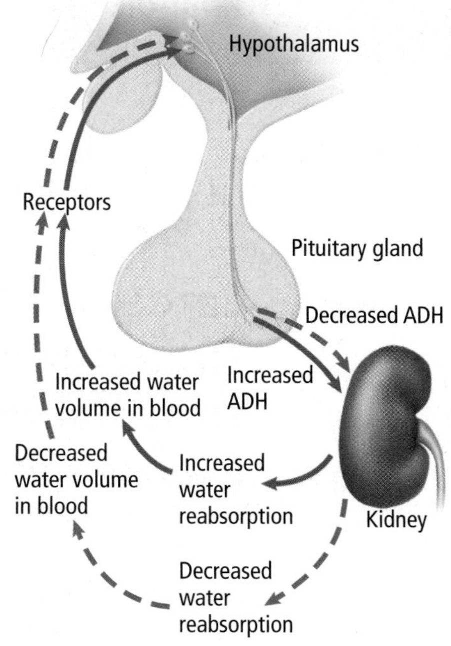


**Figure 35.20** Antidiuretic hormone (ADH) helps to control the concentration of water in the blood.

## Section 35.3 Assessment

### Section Summary

- Endocrine glands produce substances called hormones.
- Hormones travel throughout the body in the bloodstream.
- Hormones are classified as steroid hormones or amino acid hormones.
- Hormone levels are influenced by feedback systems.
- The endocrine system helps to maintain homeostasis with signals from internal mechanisms called negative feedback.

### Understand Main Ideas

1. MAIN Idea **Assess** the reasons why hormone feedback systems are referred to as "negative feedback."
2. **Predict** when you would expect to find high levels of insulin in a person's blood and when you would expect to find high levels of glucagon in a person's blood.
3. **Explain** how the endocrine and nervous systems work together to maintain homeostasis.
4. **Identify** and describe the function of pituitary, thyroid, parathyroid, pancreas, and adrenal glands.

### Think Scientifically

5. *Research* Iodine is essential for thyroid gland function. Fetal and childhood iodine deficiency is a major cause of mental retardation in the world, yet is easily preventable. Predict how iodine deficiency might lead to mental retardation or other health issues. Use your school library or the Internet to research what has been and is being done to alleviate this concern. Include possible sources of iodine in your response.
6. *Analyze* how a malfunction in a negative feedback mechanism can lead to the death of an organism.

# In the Field

## Careers: Forensic Pathologist and Forensic Toxicologist

### Tools and Techniques of Forensic Pathology

Can a dead person talk? In a way, yes. The condition of a dead body can speak volumes about the circumstances surrounding the death. Forensic pathologists gather data from a body, then analyze it to determine when and how a person died. The tools, techniques, and scientific methods that forensic pathologists use help investigators plot the last hours of a person's life, as well as the events that led to death.

**Clues from an autopsy** The purpose of an autopsy is to make a permanent legal record of a body's characteristics. A forensic pathologist is trained to examine victims of sudden, unexpected, or violent deaths. During an autopsy, the pathologist examines and weighs the lungs, brain, heart, liver, and stomach. He or she uses a scalpel to slice thin sections of the organs, such as the brain slice shown at the right. The slices are chemically preserved to prevent further decay.

**Digestion and time of death** During the autopsy, the pathologist examines the victim's stomach contents. Why is this important? At the moment of death, digestion stops. The pathologist can use the condition of the stomach to estimate a time line. If the stomach is entirely empty, the victim probably died at least three hours after he or she last ate. If the small intestine also is empty, death likely occurred at least ten hours after the last meal.

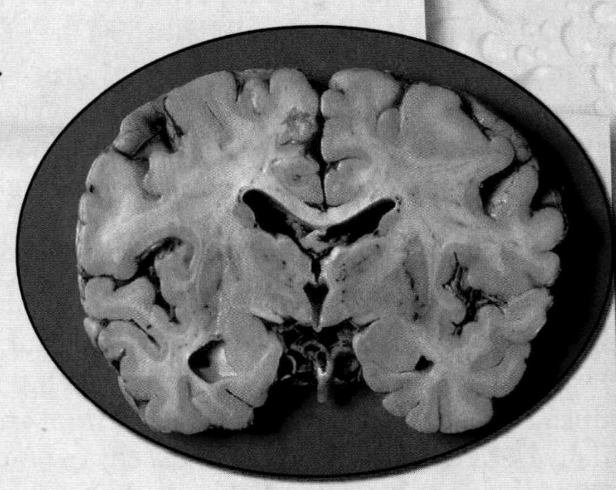

A brain slice might be used to determine a cause of death

Is it possible to identify the type of food in the stomach? In some cases, yes. A scanning electron microscope can be used to identify food particles. A stomach sample that matches the last known meal also can help investigators establish a time period.

**Stomach contents can reveal poisoning** Toxic substances such as household products, poisons, and drugs can be involved in a death. A forensic toxicologist, a specialist who can identify foreign chemicals that can lead to death, might be called.

While one piece of evidence rarely serves as conclusive proof, forensic pathologists are trained to note specific details. These details can add up and sometimes help tell the story of the final hours of a person's life.

**WRITING in Biology**

**Want Ad** Your city has a job opening for a forensic pathologist. Write an advertisement for the job. Be sure to include specific techniques and procedures with which applicants should be familiar, as well as general skills and characteristics applicants should have. For more information about forensic pathology, visit biologygmh.com.

# BIOLAB

Design Your Own

## HOW DOES THE RATE OF STARCH DIGESTION COMPARE AMONG CRACKERS?

**Background: Starch digestion begins in the mouth. The enzyme amylase, present in saliva, catalyzes the breakdown of starch into sugar molecules, the smallest of which is glucose, an important energy source. Foods, including crackers, vary in starch content. In this lab, you will compare how quickly starch is digested in several types of crackers to determine the relative amount in each.**

**Question:** *How does the amount of time required for starch digestion by amylase compare among various types of crackers?*

### Possible Materials

variety of crackers
mortar and pestle
test tubes and test tube rack
filter paper
funnels
balance
beaker
Bunsen burner or hot plate
graduated cylinder
iodine solution
droppers
watch glasses
amylase solution
glass markers or wax pencil

### Safety Precautions

WARNING: ***Iodine can irritate and will stain skin.***

### Plan and Perform the Experiment

1. Read and complete the lab safety form.
2. Examine three types of crackers. Design an experiment to compare the amount of time required to digest the starch in each. You will use the enzyme amylase to stimulate the digestion of starch. Iodine, a chemical indicator which turns blue-black when starch is present, will indicate when starch digestion is complete.
3. Construct a data chart to record your observations.
4. Consider these points with your group and modify the plan as necessary:
   - What factors will be held constant?
   - Have you established a control sample?
   - How will you know when starch digestion is complete in each sample?
   - How will you keep constant the amount of each type of cracker tested?
   - Will the chart accommodate your data?
5. Make sure your teacher approves your plan before you proceed.
6. Carry out your experiment.
7. **Cleanup and Disposal** Dispose of test tube contents as directed. Clean and return glassware and equipment. Wash hands thoroughly after handling chemicals and glassware.

### Analyze and Conclude

1. **Analyze** How did the amylase affect the starch in the crackers?
2. **Observe and Infer** In which cracker was starch digested most quickly? What does this indicate about the amount of starch in this cracker compared to the others?
3. **Think Critically** What variations among human mouths might affect the action of amylase on starch? Explain.
4. **Error Analysis** Did any steps in your procedure introduce uncontrolled variables into the experiment? Explain how the procedure could be redesigned to make these factors constant.

### APPLY YOUR SKILL

Redesign your experiment to determine how varying a condition like temperature or pH would affect the digestion of starch by amylase in one of the crackers. To learn more about amylase and digestion, visit BioLabs at biologygmh.com.

# Study Guide

Download quizzes, key terms, and flash cards from biologygmh.com.

FOLDABLES **Predict** what would happen if an organ in the endocrine system did not produce a specific hormone, and the receptive feedback system was either not "switched on" or not "turned off."

| Vocabulary | Key Concepts |
|---|---|
| **Section 35.1 The Digestive System** | |
| • amylase (p. 1020)<br>• chemical digestion (p. 1020)<br>• esophagus (p. 1021)<br>• large intestine (p. 1024)<br>• liver (p. 1022)<br>• mechanical digestion (p. 1020)<br>• pepsin (p. 1021)<br>• peristalsis (p. 1021)<br>• small intestine (p. 1022)<br>• villus (p. 1023) | MAIN Idea The digestive system breaks down food so nutrients can be absorbed by the body.<br>• The digestive system has three main functions.<br>• Digestion can be categorized as mechanical or chemical.<br>• Most nutrients are absorbed in the small intestine.<br>• Accessory organs provide enzymes and bile to aid digestion.<br>• Water is absorbed from chyme in the colon. |
| **Section 35.2 Nutrition** | |
| • Calorie (p. 1025)<br>• mineral (p. 1028)<br>• nutrition (p. 1025)<br>• vitamin (p. 1028) | MAIN Idea Certain nutrients are essential for the proper function of the body.<br>• The energy content of food is measured in Calories.<br>• Carbohydrates, fats, and proteins are three major groups of nutrients.<br>• Carbohydrates are a major source of energy for the body.<br>• Fats and proteins are important building blocks for the body and also provide energy.<br>• Vitamins and minerals are essential for proper metabolic functioning.<br>• The *MyPyramid Plan* and food labels are tools for establishing healthy eating habits. |
| **Section 35.3 The Endocrine System** | |
| • aldosterone (p. 1035)<br>• antidiuretic hormone (p. 1037)<br>• calcitonin (p. 1034)<br>• cortisol (p. 1035)<br>• endocrine gland (p. 1031)<br>• glucagon (p. 1034)<br>• hormone (p. 1031)<br>• insulin (p. 1034)<br>• parathyroid hormone (p. 1034)<br>• pituitary gland (p. 1033)<br>• thyroxine (p. 1034) | MAIN Idea Systems of the human body are regulated by hormonal feedback mechanisms.<br>• Endocrine glands produce substances called hormones.<br>• Hormones travel throughout the body in the bloodstream.<br>• Hormones are classified as steroid hormones or amino acid hormones.<br>• Hormone levels are influenced by feedback systems.<br>• The endocrine system helps to maintain homeostasis with signals from internal mechanisms called negative feedback. |

# CHAPTER 35 Assessment

## Section 35.1

### Vocabulary Review

*For each set of terms, choose the one term that does not belong and explain why it does not belong.*

1. esophagus—pancreas—large intestine
2. pepsin—glycogen—glucose
3. bile—amylase—peristalsis

### Understand Key Concepts

4. Which action takes place in the stomach?
   **A.** Large fat molecules are digested into smaller molecules.
   **B.** Proteins are broken down.
   **C.** Amylase breaks down starches into smaller sugar molecules.
   **D.** Insulin is secreted for use in the small intestine.

5. Which row in the chart contains the words that best complete this statement? The (1) produces (2), which is secreted into the (3).

| Row | 1 | 2 | 3 |
|---|---|---|---|
| A | liver | bile | small intestine |
| B | gallbladder | pepsin | stomach |
| C | pancreas | acid | large intestine |
| D | villi | amylase | mouth |

   **A.** Row A
   **B.** Row B
   **C.** Row C
   **D.** Row D

6. A person complaining of digestion problems is determined to be not digesting fats well. Which explains this condition?
   **A.** The sphincter at the bottom of the stomach is not allowing bile to pass into the small intestine.
   **B.** The duct leading from the liver and gallbladder is blocked.
   **C.** The person is secreting excess bile.
   **D.** The stomach is not acidic enough for the digestion of fats.

*Use the graph to answer question 7.*

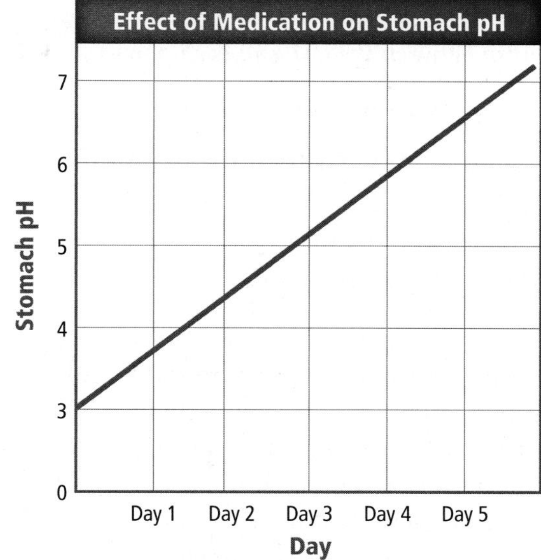


7. A person has been taking a medication for 5 days. Which of the following is likely to be a consequence of this medication?
   **A.** Pepsin would not be able to break down proteins.
   **B.** Amylase would not be able to break down starch.
   **C.** Bile would not be able to be produced.
   **D.** Enzymes secreted by the pancreas would not function well.

### Constructed Response

8. **Short Answer** Explain why the term *heartburn* is an inaccurate description of this condition.
9. **Short Answer** Refer to **Table 35.1** to summarize the digestive processes that occur in the following structures: mouth, large intestine, stomach, small intestine, and esophagus.
10. **Open Ended** Why can a person live without a gall bladder? Assess the effects (if any) that this would have on the person's ability to digest food.

### Think Critically

11. **Explain** why a drug manufacturer might add vitamin K to some antibiotics in tablet or pill form.
12. **Hypothesize** why humans have an appendix if it has no known useful function.

# Chapter 35 Assessment

## Section 35.2

### Vocabulary Review

*Distinguish between the terms in each pair.*

**13.** saturated fats—unsaturated fats

**14.** micronutrients—macronutrients

**15.** vitamins—minerals

### Understand Key Concepts

**16.** Which are characteristic of saturated fats?
- **A.** liquid at room temperature and found in vegetable oils
- **B.** mostly absorbed in the large intestine
- **C.** derived from animal sources and are solid at room temperature
- **D.** tend to lower blood cholesterol

**17.** Which carbohydrate is not digestible and provides fiber in your diet?
- **A.** sucrose
- **B.** starch
- **C.** glycogen
- **D.** cellulose

**18.** Which combinations in the stomach break down high-protein foods?
- **A.** a low pH and pepsin
- **B.** a high pH and bile
- **C.** a high pH and pepsin
- **D.** a low pH and bile

*Use the image below to answer question 19.*

**19.** If you ate the entire bag of chips, what percent of the recommended daily value of saturated fat would you consume?
- **A.** 14 percent
- **B.** 28 percent
- **C.** 5 percent
- **D.** 35 percent

### Constructed Response

**20.** **CAREERS IN BIOLOGY** According to dieticians, low carbohydrate diets are usually high-fat, high-protein diets. Evaluate what health risks might be associated with long-term intake of foods high in fats and proteins.

**21.** **Open Ended** Point out what factors, besides not having enough food, might cause an individual to be malnourished.

### Think Critically

**22.** **Explain** why a diet high in fiber might reduce the chance of colon cancer.

**23.** **Infer** the reasons why obesity rates in the United States have continued to rise steadily for at least the past 30 years.

## Section 35.3

### Vocabulary Review

*Explain the difference between each term. Then explain how the terms are related.*

**24.** insulin—glucagon

**25.** estrogen—growth hormone

**26.** cortisol—epinephrine

### Understand Key Concepts

*Use the graph below to answer question 27.*

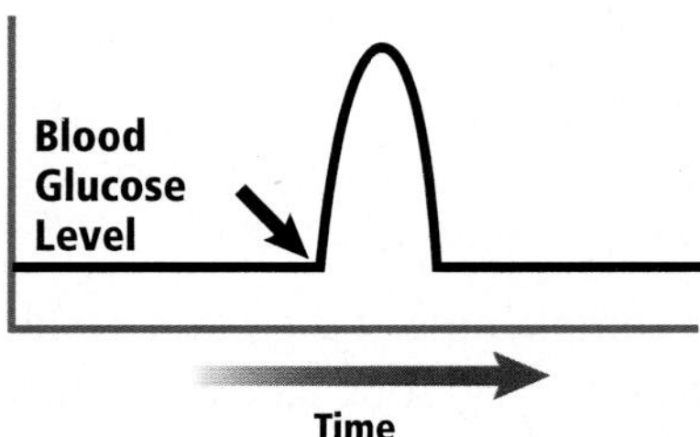


**27.** The graph shows blood glucose levels over a period of time. Which hormone might have caused a sudden surge as indicated by the arrow?
- **A.** antidiuretic hormone
- **B.** growth hormone
- **C.** glucagon
- **D.** insulin



BiologyOnline Chapter Test biologygmh.com

28. Which hormones are released from nerve cells rather than endocrine glands?
   **A.** antidiuretic hormone and oxytocin
   **B.** growth hormone and thyroxine
   **C.** insulin and glucagon
   **D.** norepinephrine and epinephrine

29. Which pairs of hormones have opposite effects?
   **A.** calcitonin and parathyroid hormone
   **B.** epinephrine and norepinephrine
   **C.** growth hormone and thyroxine
   **D.** aldosterone and cortisol

*Use the photo below to answer question 30.*

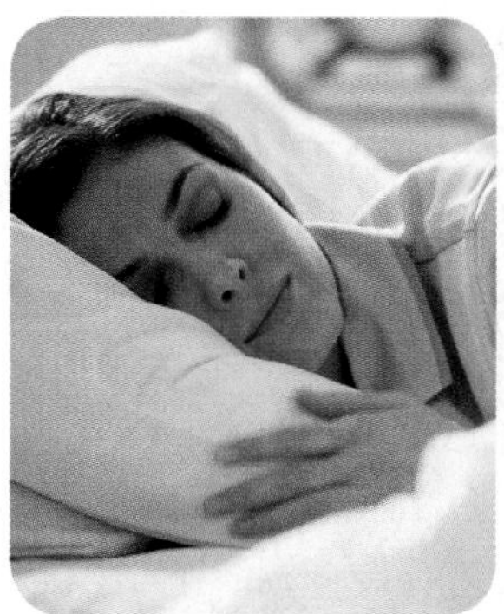

**A.**

**B.**

30. Which person is likely to have high levels of epinephrine?
   **A.** person A
   **B.** person B
   **C.** both persons
   **D.** neither person

## Constructed Response

31. **Open Ended** What would be the direct effect of overproduction of calcitonin? Analyze how this might disrupt homeostasis in systems other than the endocrine system.

32. **Short Answer** Assess how the long-term use of cortisol would impact one's ability to fight infection.

## Think Critically

33. **Create** an analogy using a balance describing the relationship between calcitonin and parathyroid hormone.

34. **Hypothesize** Why is insulin usually injected instead of taken orally?

## Additional Assessment

35.  **Biology** This chapter began with a situation in which you are eating a pizza. Write a short story describing the events that occur as the food moves through your digestive tract. *Hint: Be sure to include all major groups of nutrients.*

### DBQ Document-Based Questions

Source: *Dietary Guidelines for America 2005*

**Estimated Calorie Requirements in Gender and Age Groups**

| Gender | Age | Moderately Active | Active |
|---|---|---|---|
| Female | 9–13 | 1600–2000 | 1800–2200 |
| | 14–18 | 2000 | 2400 |
| | 19–30 | 2000–2200 | 2400 |
| | 31–50 | 2000 | 2200 |
| | 51+ | 1800 | 2000–2200 |
| Male | 9–13 | 1800–2200 | 2000–2600 |
| | 14–18 | 2400–2800 | 2800–3200 |
| | 19–30 | 2600–2800 | 3000 |
| | 31–50 | 2400–2600 | 2800–3000 |
| | 51+ | 2400 | 2400–2800 |

36. According to the chart, which gender needs more Calories?

37. Describe the general trend regarding the number of Calories needed to maintain energy balance in relation to age.

38. Why do individuals in the 19–30-year-old group need the most Calories?

## Cumulative Review

39. Describe the three different types of plant cells. **(Chapter 22)**

40. Apply your knowledge of radial symmetry to describe the feeding habits of cnidarians. **(Chapter 24)**

41. Sketch a typical arthropod and label its structures. **(Chapter 26)**

# Standardized Test Practice

**Cumulative**

## Multiple Choice

1. What is the function of melanin in the epidermis?
   A. to protect tissue from ultraviolet radiation
   B. to provide support for blood vessels
   C. to stimulate the growth of hair in the follicles
   D. to waterproof and protect the skin surface

*Use the diagram below to answer questions 2 and 3.*

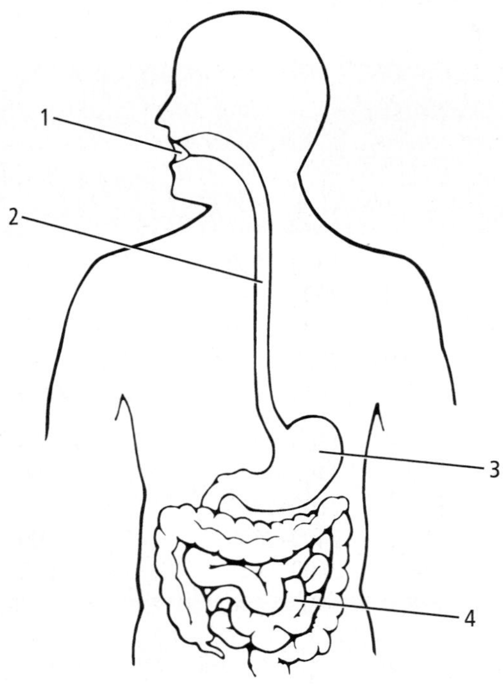


2. In which part of the digestive system does chemical and mechanical digestion first occur?
   A. 1
   B. 2
   C. 3
   D. 4

3. Which process happens first in a nerve cell when a stimulus reaches threshold?
   A. Potassium channels in the cell membrane open.
   B. Neurotransmitters are released into the synapse.
   C. Sodium ions move into the nerve cell.
   D. The cell becomes negatively charged.

4. Where would fat stored in bones be found?
   A. compact bone
   B. osteocytes
   C. red marrow
   D. yellow marrow

*Use the diagram below to answer question 5.*

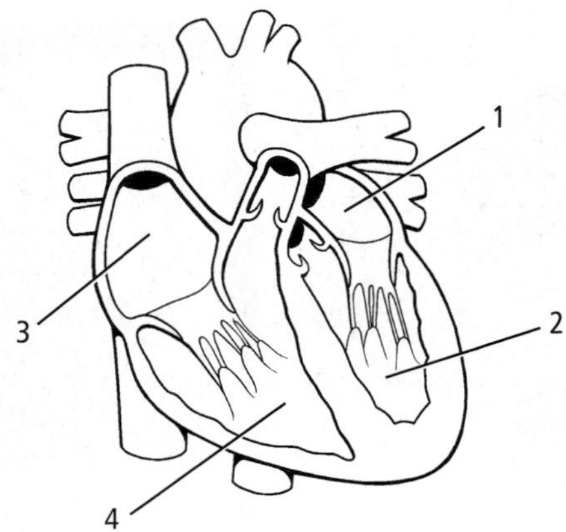


5. Which is the path that blood follows as it flows through the heart immediately after returning from the head and body?
   A. 1 → 2
   B. 2 → 1
   C. 3 → 4
   D. 4 → 3

6. Which describes how filtering occurs in the excretory system?
   A. Blood enters nephrons of the kidneys, and excess water and wastes are filtered from the blood.
   B. Urine leaves the kidneys through ureters.
   C. Water and nutrients are absorbed back into the blood.
   D. Water is added to excess nitrogenous wastes from the digestive system to form urine.

## Short Answer

*Use the graph below to answer questions 7 and 8.*

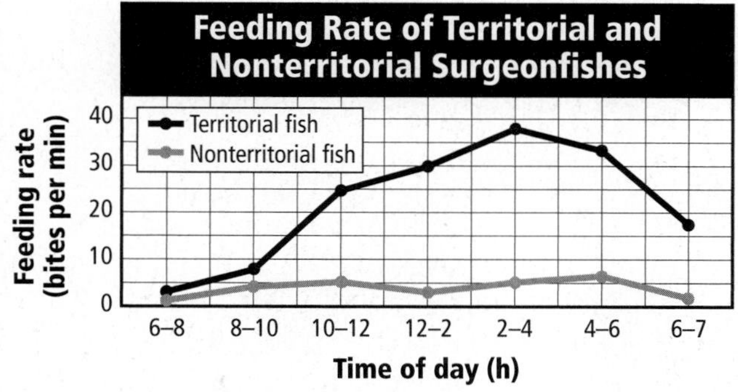


7. Compare and contrast the feeding behavior of the fishes shown in the graph.

8. Predict how the graph might appear if the territorial fish showed territorial behavior only during one season of the year.

9. Assess why a diet with no protein would be unhealthy.

10. What are two benefits to the young of mammals in receiving milk from their mothers?

11. Explain how the different body structures in roundworms and annelids enable them to move.

12. A person who exercises in extreme heat can lose salts that contain potassium and sodium through his or her sweat. What can you infer about the effect of overexertion on the nervous system?

13. Differentiate the three main vessels that blood flows through as it goes from the heart through the body, and returns to the heart.

## Extended Response

14. Evaluate how a swim bladder helps a fish maintain its depth.

15. Evaluate how high blood pressure and kidney damage could be related.

16. Name three components of sympathetic stimulation, and assess how they could be helpful to a human's survival.

## Essay Question

Humans need Vitamin C in their diet because it strengthens the function of the immune system and prevents a disease called scurvy. Vitamin C is water-soluble so it is not stored in the body. Vitamin C often is suggested for someone who is just getting sick or is already sick. Some people recommend taking very high doses of Vitamin C, sometimes even thousands of times higher than the recommended dose. Medical researchers disagree about the effectiveness of taking large doses of Vitamin C. Some researchers think that it does nothing while others think that it is helpful. Almost all medical researchers agree that taking large doses of Vitamin C for short periods of time is probably not harmful.

*Using the information in the paragraph above, answer the following question in essay format.*

17. Formulate a hypothesis about whether or not taking large doses of Vitamin C for a cold is helpful. Explain one way this hypothesis could be tested.

| NEED EXTRA HELP? | | | | | | | | | | | | | | | | | |
|---|---|---|---|---|---|---|---|---|---|---|---|---|---|---|---|---|---|
| If You Missed Question . . . | 1 | 2 | 3 | 4 | 5 | 6 | 7 | 8 | 9 | 10 | 11 | 12 | 13 | 14 | 15 | 16 | 17 |
| Review Section . . . | 32.1 | 35.1 | 33.1 | 32.2 | 34.1 | 34.3 | 31.1 | 31.1 | 35.2 | 30.1 | 25.3 | 33.1 | 34.1 | 28.2 | 34.3 | 33.2 | 35.2 |

CHAPTER 36

# Human Reproduction and Development

**Section 1**
**Reproductive Systems**
MAIN Idea Hormones regulate human reproductive systems, including the production of gametes.

**Section 2**
**Human Development Before Birth**
MAIN Idea A human develops from a single fertilized cell into trillions of cells with specialized functions.

**Section 3**
**Birth, Growth, and Aging**
MAIN Idea Developmental changes continue throughout the stages of life.

## BioFacts

- A human embryo increases in size 10,000 times in the first 30 days.
- The largest human newborn weighed 10.8 kg at birth.
- In 2002, 96.7 percent of all live births in the United States were single births and 3.3 percent were multiple births.

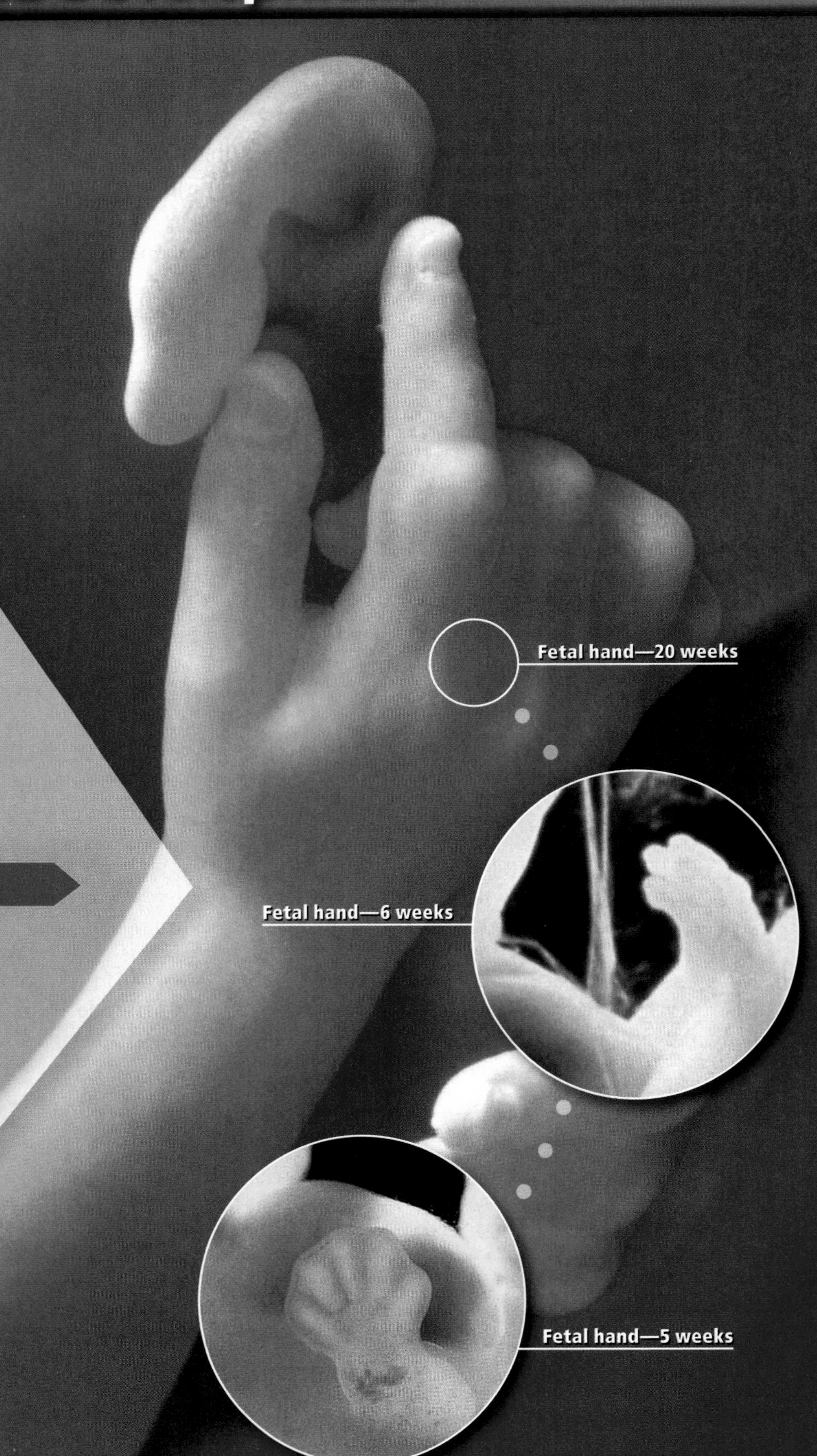

# Start-Up Activities

## LAUNCH Lab

### Sex Cell Characteristics

How are sex cells specialized for the formation of a zygote? Reproduction is a process which follows a predictable pattern. The production of sex cells is a crucial step in reproduction. Sperm and egg cells have specific characteristics that support their roles in reproduction. In this lab, you will investigate how the design of sex cells supports their function.

**Procedure**

1. Read and complete the lab safety form.
2. Observe the **slide of the egg cell** under the **microscope** and identify its characteristics. Make a sketch.
3. Observe the **slide of the sperm cell** under the microscope and identify its characteristics. Make a sketch.

**Analysis**

1. **Compare and contrast** the sperm and egg cells you studied. How do they differ?
2. **Identify** What structures and characteristics did you observe that might affect each cell's role in reproduction?

Visit biologygmh.com to:

- study the entire chapter online
- explore Concepts in Motion, Interactive Tables, Microscopy Links, and links to virtual dissections
- access Web links for more information, projects, and activities
- review content online with the Interactive Tutor, and take Self-Check Quizzes

**Reproductive System** Make this Foldable to help you compare and contrast the production of eggs and sperm.

**STEP 1** Draw a horizontal line along the middle of a sheet of notebook paper as shown.

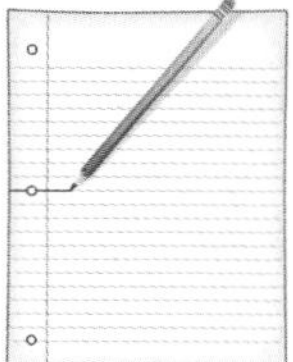

**STEP 2** Fold the paper from the top and bottom so the edges meet at the center line.

**STEP 3** Label the two tabs as shown.

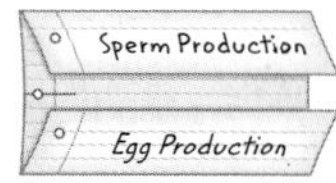


FOLDABLES **Use this Foldable with Section 36.1.** As you study the section, use the Foldable to record what you learn about the production of sperm in the testes and the production of eggs in the ovary.

Section 36.1

# Reproductive Systems

### Objectives

- **Summarize** the structures of the male and female reproductive systems and discuss the functions of each.
- **Explain** how hormones regulate the male and female reproductive systems.
- **Discuss** the events that take place during a menstrual cycle.

### Review Vocabulary

**hypothalamus:** portion of the brain that connects the endocrine and nervous systems, and controls the pituitary gland

### New Vocabulary

seminiferous tubule
epididymis
vas deferens
urethra
semen
puberty
oocyte
oviduct
menstrual cycle
polar body

MAIN Idea **Hormones regulate human reproductive systems, including the production of gametes.**

**Real-World Reading Link** You might have noticed how the temperature of a room affects the thermostat that controls furnace activity. If the room is warm, the thermostat will not allow the furnace to run. Similarly, male and female hormones in the human body have effects on body structures and influence human reproduction.

## Human Male Reproductive System

Reproduction is necessary to ensure continuation of a species. The result of the human reproductive process is the union of an egg cell and a sperm cell, development of the fetus, and the birth of an infant. The organs, glands, and hormones of the male and female reproductive systems are instrumental in meeting this goal.

**Figure 36.1** illustrates the male reproductive structures. The male reproductive glands are called the testes (tes TEEZ) (singular, testis) and are located outside of the body cavity in a pouch called the scrotum (SKROH tum). A temperature lower than 37°C—the average body temperature—is required for the development of sperm. Because the scrotum is located outside of the body cavity, it is several degrees cooler. This makes the environment suitable for the normal development of sperm.

**Figure 36.1** The male reproductive system produces gametes called sperm in the testes.

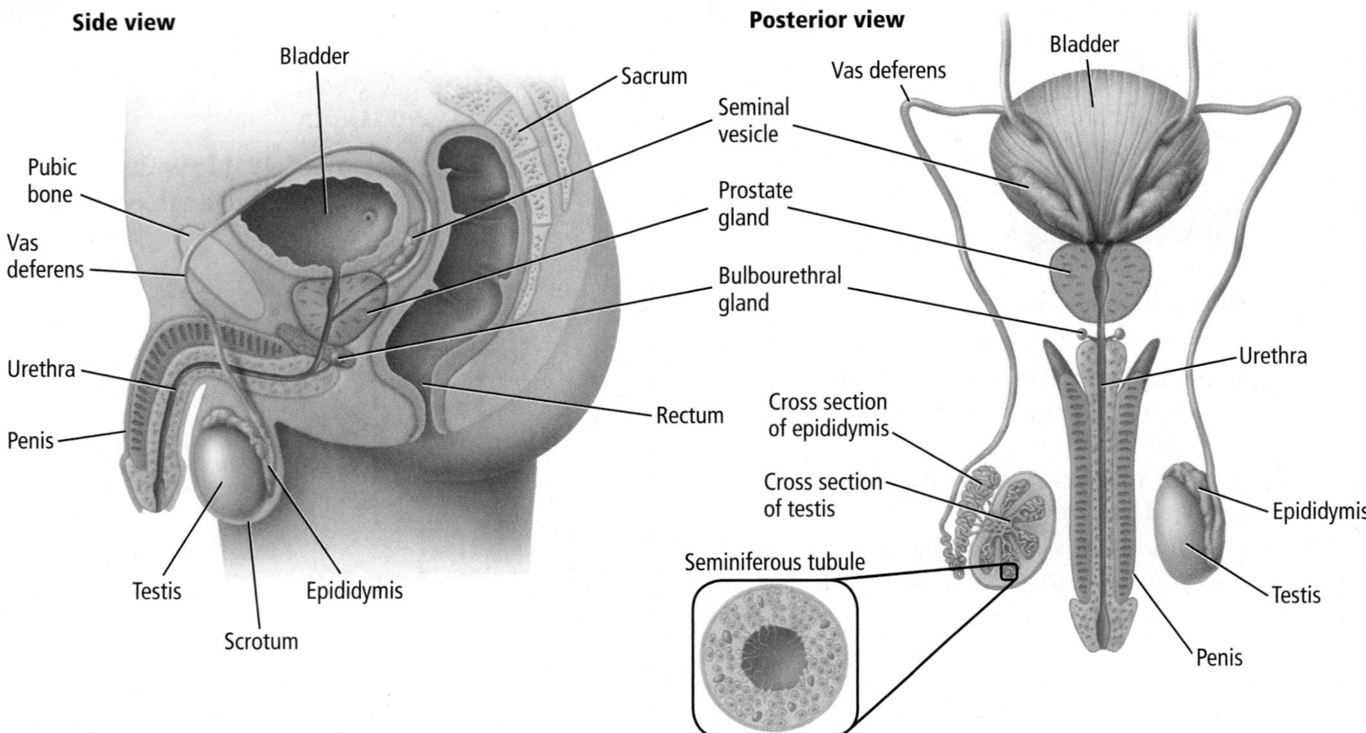

**Sperm cells** The male reproductive cells, called sperm cells, are produced in the testes. Follow the path that sperm travel in **Figure 36.1** as you read about the structures in the male reproductive system. Sperm, like the one shown in **Figure 36.2,** develop in the testes in the **seminiferous tubules** (se muh NIHF rus • TEW byulz). These tubules produce 100–200 million sperm each day. Next, sperm travel to the **epididymis** (eh puh DIH duh mus), a structure located on top of each testis where sperm mature and are stored. When the sperm are released from the body, they travel through the **vas deferens** (VAS • DEF uh runz), a duct leading away from the testis. There are two vas deferens, one leading away from each testis. The two vas deferens join together and enter the **urethra** (yoo REE thruh), the tube that carries both semen and urine outside of the body through the penis.

Sperm require a nourishing fluid to survive long enough to fertilize an egg. **Semen** (SEE mun) refers to the fluid that contains sperm, the nourishment, and other fluids from the male reproductive glands. The seminal vesicles contribute over half of the semen and secrete sugar into the fluid, which provides energy, other nutrients, proteins, and enzymes for the sperm. The prostate gland and bulbourethral glands contribute an alkaline solution to the fluid to neutralize acidic conditions sperm might encounter in the urethra and the female reproductive tract.

**Male hormones** Testosterone (tes TAHS tuh rohn), which is made in the testes, is a steroid hormone that is necessary for the production of sperm. It also influences the development of male secondary sex characteristics that begin to appear at **puberty,** the period of growth when sexual maturity is reached. These characteristics include hair on the face and chest, broad shoulders, increased muscle development, and a deeper voice. Recall from Chapter 34 that the larynx contains the vocal cords. Because the vocal cords are longer in males than in females, the male voice is deeper. Later in life, testosterone might lead to a receding hairline or baldness.

Three hormones influence testosterone production. **Figure 36.3** indicates that the hypothalamus, discussed in Chapter 33, produces gonadotropin-releasing hormone (GnRH) that acts on the anterior pituitary gland. GnRH increases the production of follicle-stimulating hormone (FSH) and luteinizing (LEW tee uh ni zing) hormone (LH). Both FSH and LH travel from the anterior pituitary gland through the bloodstream and to the testes. In the testes, FSH promotes the production of sperm, and LH stimulates the production and secretion of testosterone.

Levels of the male hormones are regulated by a negative feedback system that starts with the hypothalamus. Increased levels of testosterone in the blood are detected by cells in the hypothalamus and anterior pituitary, and the production of LH and FSH is decreased. When testosterone levels in the blood drop, the body responds by making more LH and FSH, as shown in **Figure 36.3.**

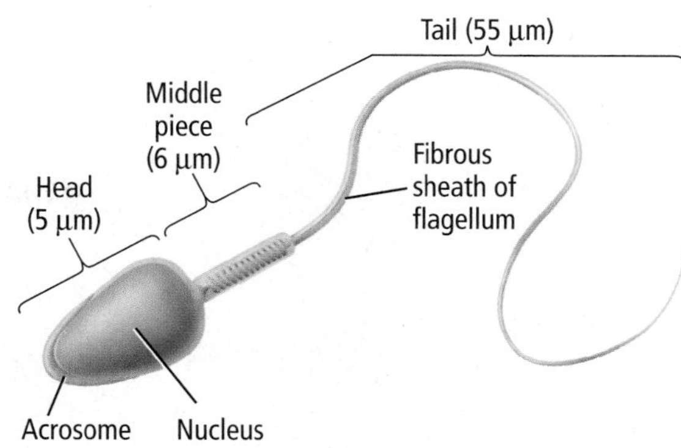


**Figure 36.2** A sperm is a flagellated cell composed of a head, midpiece, and tail.
***List,*** ***in correct sequence, the structures a sperm cell passes through or encounters as it makes its way out of the body.***

**Figure 36.3** The hypothalamus produces the releasing hormone GnRH that travels to the pituitary gland. GnRH influences the rate of LH and FSH production. The levels of LH and FSH are regulated by a negative feedback pathway.

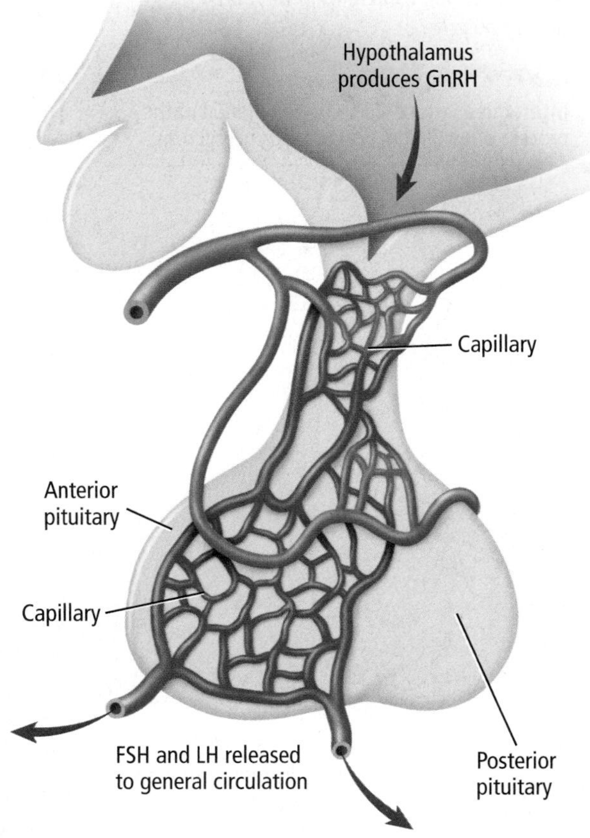

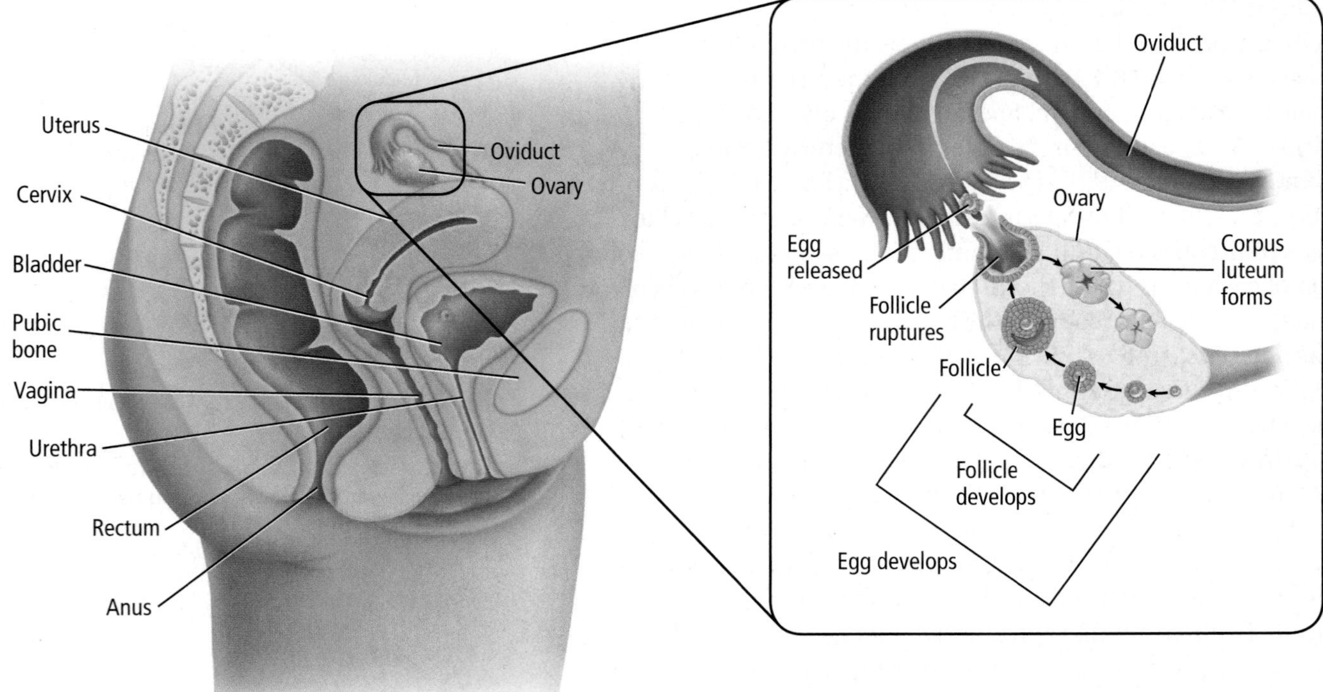


**Figure 36.4**
**Left:** The main structures of the female reproductive system are the vagina, uterus, and ovaries.
**Right:** During every menstrual cycle, one follicle fully matures and releases an egg. The follicle is then called the corpus luteum.
**Predict** ***What might be the result if more than one follicle fully develops during a cycle?***

**Concepts In Motion**

**Interactive Figure** To see an animation of the process of ovulation, visit biologygmh.com.

## Human Female Reproductive System

A female's reproductive system is specialized to produce egg cells, receive sperm, and provide an environment that is right for fertilization of an egg and the development of an embryo. Refer to **Figure 36.4** as you read about the structures of the female reproductive system.

**Egg cells** The female reproductive cells, called egg cells, are produced in the ovaries, also illustrated in **Figure 36.4.** Each ovary is about the size of an almond. Inside each ovary are **oocytes** (OH uh sites), which are immature eggs. Approximately once every 28 days, oocyte development is stimulated and an egg, called an ovum, is formed. The ovum is surrounded by follicle cells that provide protection and nourishment.

After the egg is released from the ovary, it travels through an **oviduct** (OH vuh duct), a tube that connects to the uterus. The uterus, or womb, is about the size of an average human fist and is where a baby develops before birth. The cervix at the lower end of the uterus has a narrow opening into the vagina, which leads to the outside of the female's body.

**Female hormones** Estrogen and progesterone (proh JES tuh rohn) are steroid hormones made by cells in the ovaries. A female's anterior pituitary gland also produces LH and FSH, which influence estrogen and progesterone levels in a negative feedback loop. Effects of LH and FSH are different in males and females. During puberty, an increase in estrogen levels causes a female's breasts to develop, her hips to widen, and her amount of fat tissue to increase. During puberty, a female also will experience her first **menstrual** (MEN stroo ul) **cycle**—the events that take place each month in the human female to help prepare the female body for pregnancy.

**FOLDABLES** Incorporate information from this section into your Foldable.

## Sex Cell Production

In Chapter 10, you learned that through meiosis, one cell in the male or female gonads—called testes and ovaries in humans—gives rise to four sex cells called gametes. In the human male, sperm are produced from primary spermatocytes daily beginning at puberty and continuing throughout a male's lifetime.

The production of eggs in the human female differs, as illustrated in **Figure 36.5.** A female is born with all of her eggs already beginning to develop. The genetic material has replicated in primary oocytes before birth, and the process of meiosis stops before the first meiotic division is completed. Then, once each menstrual cycle during the reproductive years, meiosis continues for a single developing oocyte. The resulting structures at the end of the first meiotic division of the oocyte are of unequal size. The smaller of the two structures is called a **polar body.** The chromosomes have segregated, but there is an unequal division of the cytoplasm. Most of the cytoplasm from the original cell goes to the cell that eventually will become the egg, and the polar body disintegrates.

During the second meiotic division, a similar process takes place. During metaphase of the second meiotic division, an egg ruptures through the ovary wall in a process called ovulation. The second meiotic division is completed only if fertilization takes place. Then, the zygote and the second polar body are formed, as shown in **Figure 36.5.** The second polar body also disintegrates.

Thus, the two meiotic divisions have yielded only one egg instead of four. If four eggs were formed and released midway through a female's menstrual cycle, more multiple births would be expected.

## The Menstrual Cycle

The length of the menstrual cycle can vary from 23 to 35 days, but it typically lasts around 28 days. The entire menstrual cycle can be divided into three phases: the flow phase, the follicular phase, and the luteal phase.

**Flow phase** Day one of the menstrual cycle is when menstrual flow begins. Menstrual flow is the shedding of blood, tissue fluid, mucus, and epithelial cells from the endometrium—the tissue that lines the uterus. The endometrium is where the embryo will implant if fertilization of the egg occurs. Because an embryo will need oxygen and nutrients, the endometrium has a good supply of blood. During menstruation, bleeding occurs because the outer layers of the endometrium tear away, and blood vessels that supply the endometrium are ruptured. Around day five, repair of the endometrial lining begins, and it becomes thicker as the cycle continues.

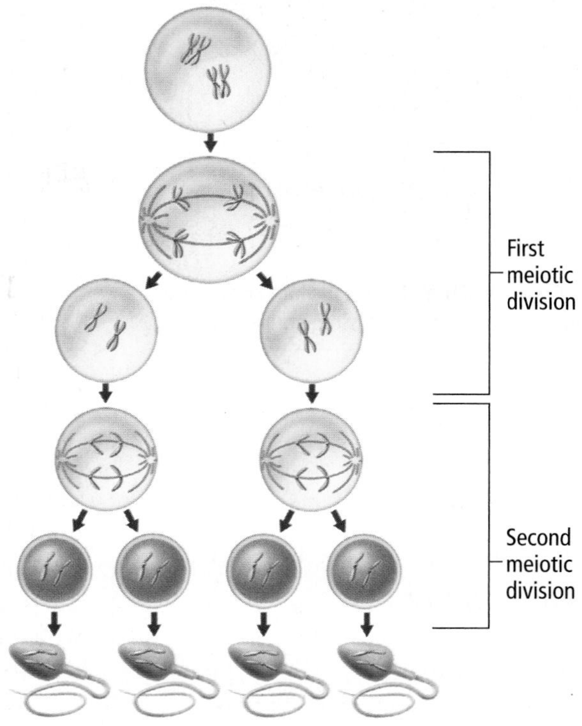


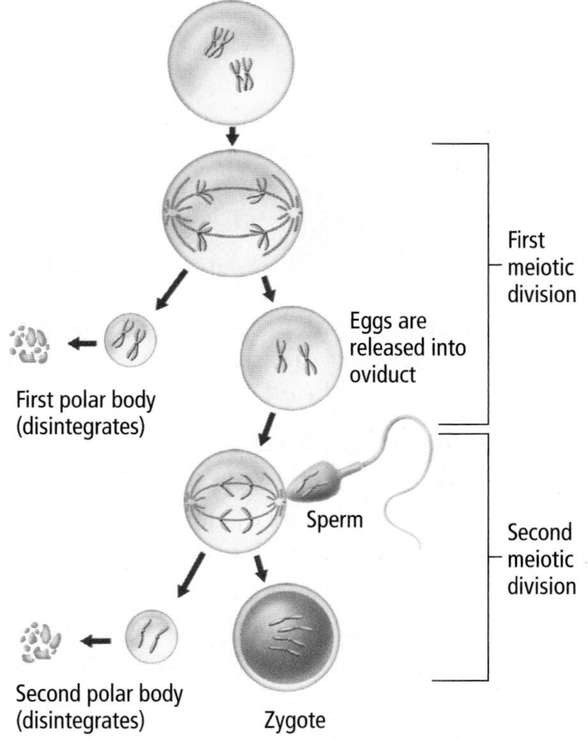


**Figure 36.5**
**Top:** The human male sex cell production follows the general pattern of meiosis and results in many sperms.
**Bottom:** Meiosis in the human female results in one egg. The second division in meiosis will not be completed in a human female unless the egg is fertilized.

LM Magnification: 10×

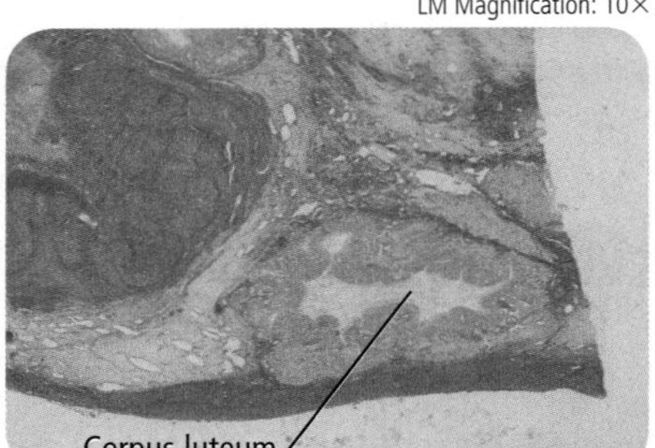


■ **Figure 36.6** The corpus luteum produces progesterone and some estrogen.

**Follicular phase** During the menstrual cycle, changes also occur in the ovaries as a result of changing hormone levels, as illustrated in **Table 36.1.** At the beginning of a menstrual cycle, when estrogen levels are low, the anterior pituitary begins to increase production of LH and FSH. This stimulates a few follicles to begin to mature in the ovary. Cells in the follicles then begin to produce estrogen and a small amount of progesterone. Inside each follicle is an immature egg—the oocyte. After about a week, usually only one of the growing follicles remains. This remaining follicle continues to grow and secrete estrogen, which keeps levels of LH and FSH low—an example of negative feedback.

On day 12, the high level of estrogen causes the anterior pituitary gland to release a surge of LH. This rapid release of a large quantity of LH causes the follicle to rupture, and ovulation occurs.

**Luteal phase** After ovulation, the cells of the follicle change, and the follicle is transformed into a structure called the corpus luteum (KOR pus • LEW tee um), illustrated in **Figure 36.6.** The corpus luteum slowly degenerates as the menstrual cycle continues. The corpus luteum produces high amounts of progesterone and some estrogen, which keep levels of LH and FSH low through negative feedback. Recall that FSH and LH stimulate new follicles to develop, but when these hormones are kept at low levels, new follicles are temporarily prevented from maturing. Toward the end of the cycle, the corpus luteum breaks down, no longer producing progesterone and estrogen. This results in a rapid decrease in progesterone and estrogen levels. A rapid decrease in hormones triggers detachment of the endometrium, and the flow phase of a new menstrual cycle will begin.

**VOCABULARY**

**WORD ORIGIN**

**Corpus luteum**
***corpus*** from Latin, meaning *body*
***luteum*** from Latin, meaning *yellow*.

## MiniLab 36.1

### Model Sex Cell Production

**Why does meiosis produce four sperm but only one egg?** The difference in the division of cytoplasm is the major reason meiosis is different in human males and females. Use clay to model how the sex cells are produced during meiosis.

**Procedure**

1. Read and complete the lab safety form.
2. Choose **two lumps of clay,** each of a different color. Choose one to represent a primary spermatocyte and the other a primary oocyte.
3. Use the primary spermatocyte to simulate the meiotic divisions as they occur in males.
4. Simulate maturation of the sperm by removing about half of the clay from each sperm and using a small part of it to add a flagellum to each cell.
5. Next simulate the first meiotic division in females.
6. Use one of the sperm and mold it to one side of the large cell. Now simulate the second meiotic division.

**Analysis**

1. **Use Models** Make drawings of each step above and label the following: primary spermatocyte and oocyte, egg, sperm, first polar body, second polar body, fertilized egg, and zygote.
2. **Explain** What is the benefit of meiosis concentrating most of the cytoplasm into one egg?

**Concepts In Motion**

**Interactive Table** To explore more about the menstrual cycle, visit biologygmh.com.

**Table 36.1 Menstrual Cycle Events**

| | Flow phase | Follicular phase | Luteal phase |
|---|---|---|---|
| Days | 1–5 | 6–14 | 15–28 |
| Ovarian activity | | | |
| Hormone levels (FSH, LH, Estrogen, Progesterone) | | | |
| Endometrium | | | |

If the egg is fertilized, a different chain of events occurs, and a new menstrual cycle does not begin. The progesterone levels remain high and increase the blood supply to the endometrium. The corpus luteum does not degenerate and hormone levels do not drop. The endometrium accumulates lipids and begins secreting a fluid rich in nutrients for the developing embryo.

## Section 36.1 Assessment

### Section Summary

- Levels of male and female hormones are regulated by negative feedback systems.
- The human male produces millions of sperm cells every day.
- The number of sex cells resulting from meiosis differs in males and females.
- The human female has a reproductive cycle called the menstrual cycle.
- The menstrual cycle has three phases: the flow phase, the follicular phase, and the luteal phase.

### Understand Main Ideas

1. MAIN Idea **Describe** how hormones help regulate the production of sperm and egg cells.
2. **Summarize** the structures of the male and female reproductive systems and their functions.
3. **Describe** the origin and importance of substances found in semen.
4. **Explain** the major events that take place in the endometrium and in the ovary during the menstrual cycle.

### Think Scientifically

5. *Infer* On Day 12, estrogen levels cause a sharp increase in the amount of LH that is released. According to a negative feedback model, what would you expect to happen?

6. MATH in Biology A woman began menstruating at age 12 and stopped menstruating at age 55. If she never became pregnant and her menstrual cycles averaged 28 days, how many eggs did she ovulate during her reproductive years?

Section 36.2

### Objectives

- **Discuss** the events that take place during the first week following fertilization.
- **Describe** the major changes that occur during each trimester of development.
- **Explain** how female hormone levels are altered during pregnancy.

### Review Vocabulary

**lysosome:** organelle that contains digestive enzymes

### New Vocabulary

morula
blastocyst
amniotic fluid

# Human Development Before Birth

**MAIN Idea A human develops from a single fertilized cell into trillions of cells with specialized functions.**

**Real-World Reading Link** Just as a single seed can grow into a plant with a beautiful flower, your complex body began as a single cell at the union of an egg and a sperm at fertilization.

## Fertilization

**Figure 36.7** shows the process of a sperm joining with an egg, which is called fertilization. Fertilization usually occurs in the upper portion of an oviduct near the ovary. In humans, sperm and eggs each are haploid, and each normally has 23 chromosomes. Fertilization brings these chromosomes together, restoring the diploid number of 46 chromosomes.

Sperm enter the vagina of the female's reproductive system when strong muscular contractions ejaculate semen from the male's penis during intercourse. Some sperm can exit through the penis before ejaculation without the male's knowledge. As a result, sexual activity that does not result in ejaculation can lead to the release of sperm, fertilization, and pregnancy.

Sperm can survive for 48 hours in the female reproductive tract, but an unfertilized egg can survive for only 24 hours. Fertilization can happen if intercourse occurs anytime from a few days before ovulation to a day after ovulation. Overall, there is a relatively short time when fertilization can occur sucessfully. But, it is important to remember that the length of the menstrual cycle can vary and ovulation can occur at any time.

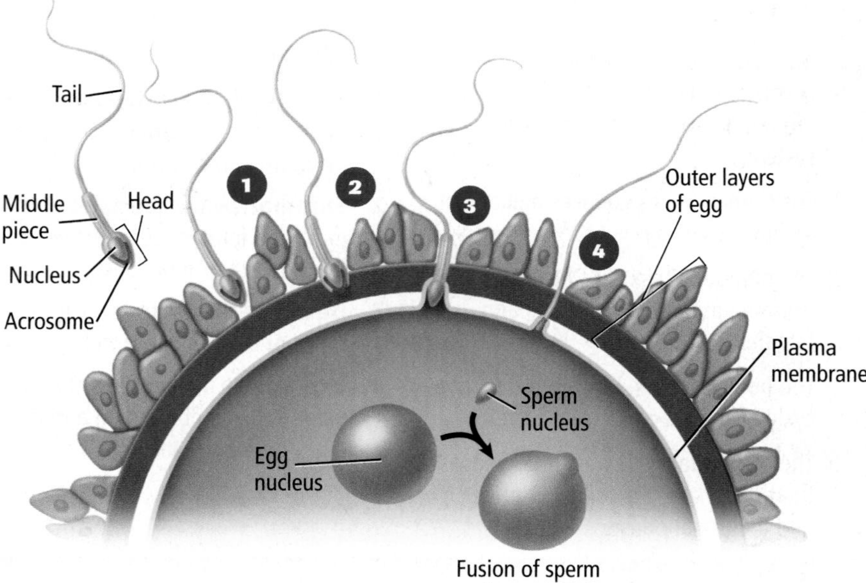


**Figure 36.7** Although many are needed to weaken the barrier that surrounds the egg, only one sperm fertilizes an egg (steps 1-4). Fertilization is complete when the sperm nucleus fuses with the egg nucleus.

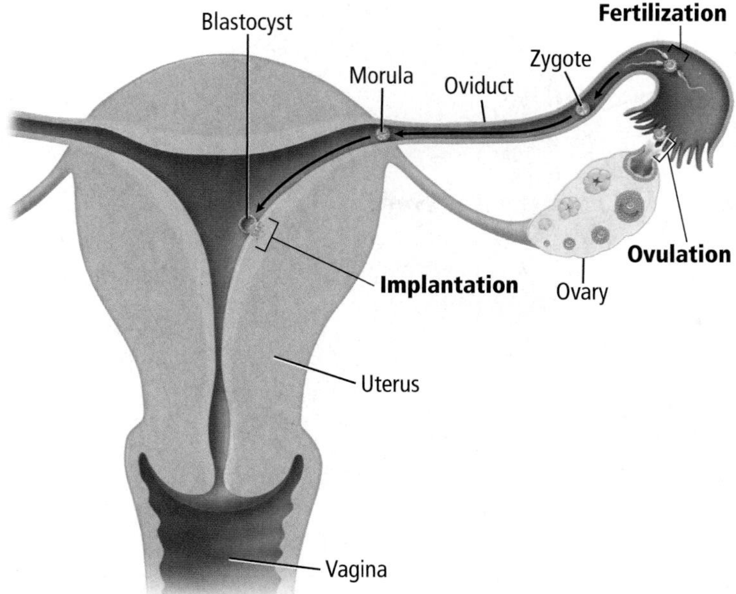


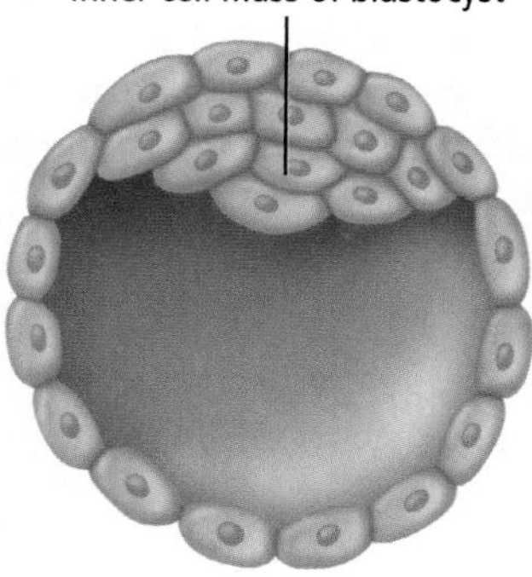


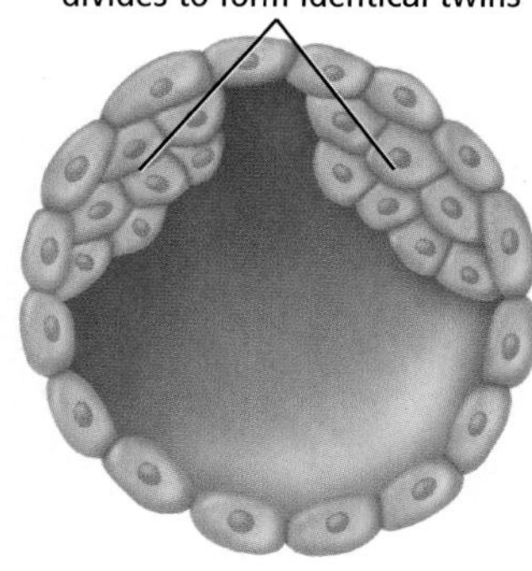


**Figure 36.8**
**Left:** During the first week of development, many developmental changes occur as the zygote travels through the oviduct.
**Right:** The inner cell mass of the blastocyst will develop into a fetus (top). If the inner cell mass divides, identical twins might form (bottom).

About 300 million sperm are released into the vagina during intercourse. Only several hundred of them will successfully complete the journey to the egg. Many never make it out of the vagina, some are attacked by white blood cells, and many simply die along the way. Only one sperm can fertilize an egg, but it takes several hundred to participate in the process.

**Connection to Chemistry** A single sperm cannot penetrate the plasma membrane that surrounds the human egg. Recall from Chapter 7 that lysosomes are organelles that contain digestive enzymes. Notice in **Figure 36.7** the tip of each sperm is a specialized lysosome called an acrosome. As each of several hundred sperm bombard the egg, the enzymes inside of the acrosome weaken the plasma membrane surrounding the egg. Eventually the plasma membrane becomes weak enough that one sperm can penetrate the egg. Immediately following this penetration, the egg forms a barrier to prevent other sperm from entering the now-fertilized egg.

 **Reading Check** **Explain** why hundreds of sperm are necessary for fertilization to take place.

## Early Development

**Figure 36.8** illustrates the first week of human development. The fertilized egg, which is called a zygote (ZI goht), moves through the oviduct propelled by involuntary smooth muscle contractions and by the cilia lining the oviduct. Around 30 hours after fertilization, the zygote undergoes its first mitosis and cell division. Cell division continues, and by the third day, the embryo leaves the oviduct and enters the uterus. At this point, the embryo is described as a **morula**—a solid ball of cells.

By the fifth day, the morula has developed into a **blastocyst,** which can be described as a hollow ball of cells. The blastocyst attaches to the endometrium around the sixth day and is fully implanted by Day 10. **Figure 36.8** shows that the blastocyst is not completely hollow. Inside the blastocyst is a group of cells called the inner cell mass. The inner cell mass eventually will become the embryo. Sometimes, the inner cell mass splits, and identical twins might form.

**CAREERS IN BIOLOGY**

**Reproductive Endocrinologist**
Physicians who have advanced training in the treatment of infertility and disorders involving the reproductive hormones are called reproductive endocrinologists. A reproductive endocrinologist also might conduct research or train medical students. For more information about biology careers, visit biologygmh.com.

■ **Figure 36.9** Four extraembryonic membranes—the amnion, chorion, yolk sac, and allantois—are important in development.
**Identify** ***What is the role of the yolk sac in humans?***

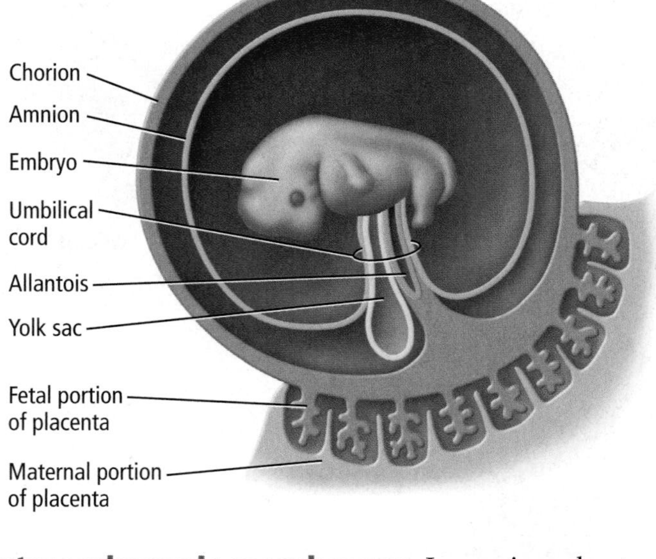


**Extraembryonic membranes** In previous chapters, you learned the importance of the membranes that extend beyond an embryo called the extraembryonic membranes. You also learned about the development of the amniotic egg, and how this enabled animals to reproduce on land. Developing humans have these membranes, shown in **Figure 36.9,** but because humans and most other mammals develop inside the mother's body, these membranes have somewhat different functions.

Early in human development, four extraembryonic membranes form. These membranes are the amnion, the chorion (KOR ee ahn), the yolk sac, and the allantois (uh LAN tuh wus), as illustrated in **Figure 36.9.** The amnion is a thin layer that forms a sac around the embryo. Inside this sac is the **amniotic fluid** (am nee AH tihk • FLU id), which protects, cushions, and insulates the embryo. Outside of the amnion is the chorion, which, together with the allantois, contributes to the formation of the placenta. The yolk sac in humans does not contain any yolk but serves as the first site of red blood cell formation for the embryo.

**VOCABULARY**

**ACADEMIC VOCABULARY**

**Enable:**
To make able or feasible.
*Amniotic eggs enable reproduction on land.*

**The placenta** About two weeks after fertilization, tiny fingerlike projections of the chorion, called chorionic villi (VIH li), begin to grow into the wall of the uterus. The placenta (pluh SEN tuh), the organ that provides food and oxygen and removes waste, begins to form and is fully formed by the tenth week. The placenta has two surfaces—a fetal side that forms from the chorion and faces the fetus, and a maternal side that forms from uterine tissue. When completely formed, the placenta is 15–20 cm in diameter, 2.5 cm thick, and has a mass of about 0.45 kg. The umbilical cord, a tube containing blood vessels, serves as the connection between the fetus and the mother. **Figure 36.10** illustrates the connection between the mother and fetus.

The placenta regulates what passes from the mother to the fetus and from the fetus to the mother. Oxygen and nutrients can travel from the mother to the fetus. Alcohol, drugs, various other substances, and the human immunodeficiency virus (HIV) also can pass through the placenta to the developing fetus.

Metabolic waste products and carbon dioxide travel from the fetus to the mother. Because the mother and the fetus have their own separate circulatory systems, blood cells do not pass through the placenta. However, the mother's antibodies pass to the fetus and help protect the newborn until its immune system is functioning.

*Study Tip*

**Time Line** Create a time line showing the development of a human being from fertilization to adulthood. Use average ages for various stages of development. Include major characteristics of each stage of development.

# Visualizing a Placenta

**Figure 36.10**
A growing fetus exchanges nutrients, oxygen, and wastes with the mother through the placenta. The placenta contains tissue from both mother and fetus.

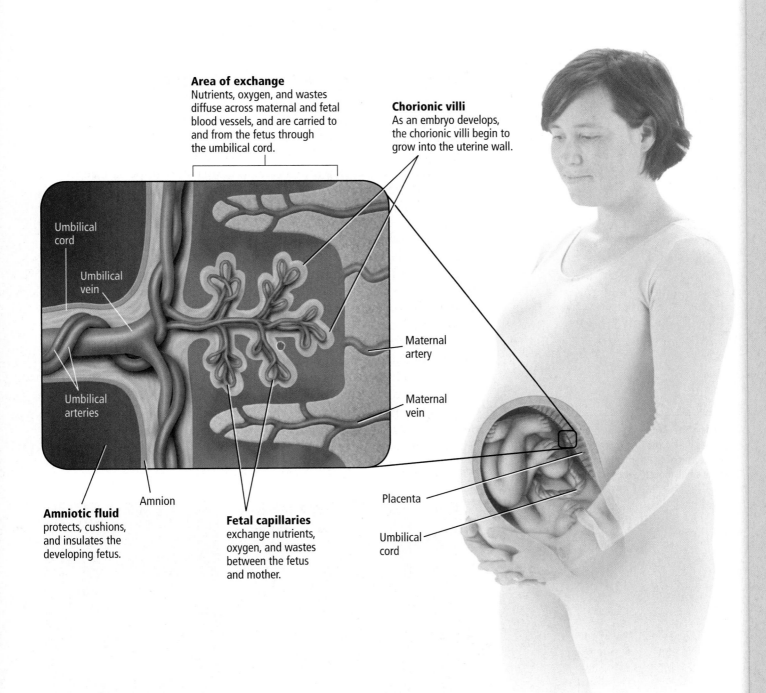

**Area of exchange**
Nutrients, oxygen, and wastes diffuse across maternal and fetal blood vessels, and are carried to and from the fetus through the umbilical cord.

**Chorionic villi**
As an embryo develops, the chorionic villi begin to grow into the uterine wall.

Umbilical cord

Umbilical vein

Umbilical arteries

Maternal artery

Maternal vein

Amnion

**Amniotic fluid**
protects, cushions, and insulates the developing fetus.

**Fetal capillaries**
exchange nutrients, oxygen, and wastes between the fetus and mother.

Placenta

Umbilical cord

Concepts In Motion **Interactive Figure** To see an animation of the placenta, visit biologygmh.com.

Biology Online

**Hormonal regulation during pregnancy** During the first week of development, the embryo begins to secrete a hormone, called human chorionic gonadotropin (hCG) (kor ee AH nihk • go na duh TROH pen), which keeps the corpus luteum from degenerating. If the corpus luteum remains active, progesterone levels, and to a lesser extent estrogen levels, remain high. Remember from the previous section that the decline of progesterone triggers a new menstrual cycle. If levels of these hormones remain high, a new menstrual cycle will not begin. Two to three months into development, the placenta secretes enough progesterone and estrogen to maintain the proper conditions for pregnancy.

**Reading Check** **Compare** two functions of the placenta.

## Three Trimesters of Development

On average, human development takes around 266 days from fertilization to birth. This time span is divided into three trimesters, each around three months long. During this time, many events take place. The zygote grows from a single cell into a baby that has trillions of cells. These cells develop into tissues and organs with specialized functions. Follow **Figure 36.11,** which shows different stages of human development during the first trimester.

**The first trimester** In the first trimester, all tissues, organs, and organ systems begin to develop. During this time of development, the embryo is especially vulnerable to the effects of alcohol, tobacco, drugs, and other environmental influences, such as environmental pollutants. During the first two weeks of development, the mother might not realize she is pregnant because she has not missed a menstrual period yet. A lack of certain essential nutrients during this time might cause irreversible damage to the developing embryo. A few of the major causes of preventable birth defects are listed in **Table 36.2.**

At the end of eight weeks, the embryo is called a fetus. All of the organ systems have begun to form. By the end of the first trimester, the fetus can move its arms, fingers, and toes and make facial expressions. Fingerprints also are present.

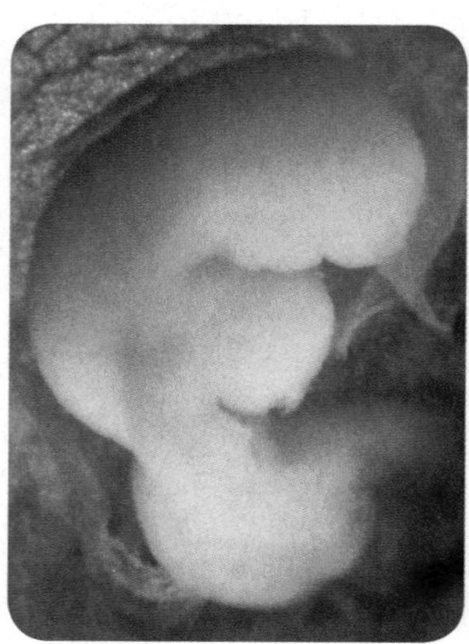

4 weeks

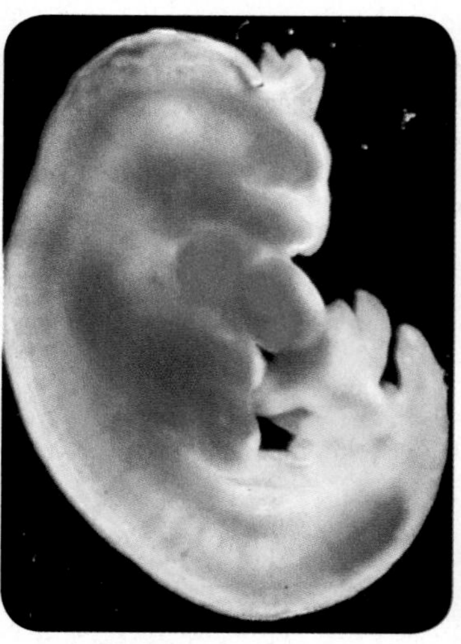

5–6 weeks

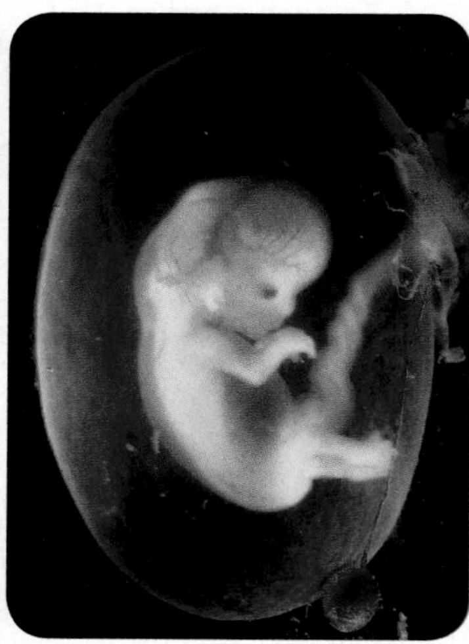

7–8 weeks

**Figure 36.11** The embryo develops into a fetus during the first trimester of pregnancy. By the end of the third month, the fetus can make small movements.

| Table 36.2 | Preventable Causes of Birth Defects |
|---|---|
| Cause | Defect |
| Alcohol consumption | • Mental retardation |
| Cigarette smoking | • Health problems related to premature births and underweight babies |
| Lack of folic acid in diet | • Anencephaly (head and brain do not completely form)<br>• Spina bifida (nerve cells from the spinal cord are exposed, leading to paralysis) |
| Cocaine | • Low birth weight<br>• Premature birth<br>• Possible permanent brain damage and behavioral disorders |
| Methamphetamine | • Premature birth<br>• Extreme irritability |

**Concepts In Motion**
**Interactive Table** To explore more about birth defects, visit biologygmh.com.

**The second trimester** The second trimester primarily is a period of growth. Around 18 to 20 weeks, the fetal heartbeat might be heard using a stethoscope. The developing fetus is capable of sucking its thumb and can develop the hiccups. The mother might feel a fluttering sensation or might even feel light kicks. Hair usually forms, and the fetal eyes will open during this period. At the end of this trimester, the fetus might be able to survive outside the mother's uterus with the aid of medical intervention, but the chances for survival are not very high. If born this early, the baby cannot maintain a constant body temperature. The baby's lungs have not developed fully, so respiratory failure is a great risk. Also, the baby is very likely to become seriously ill because its immune system is not fully functional.

**The third trimester** During the third trimester, the fetus continues to grow at a rapid rate. Fat accumulates under the skin to provide insulation for the fetus once it is born. Adequate protein intake by the mother is important during this time. Protein is essential for the rapid amount of brain growth that occurs. New nerve cells in the brain are forming at a rate of 250,000 cells per minute. The fetus now might respond to sounds in the environment, such as music or the sound of its mother's voice.

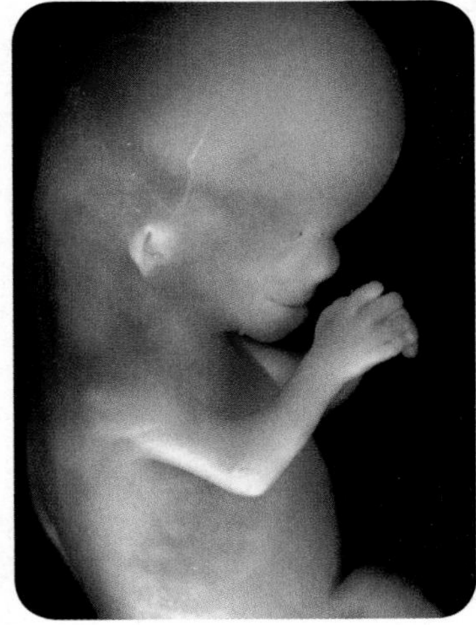

**9–10 weeks**

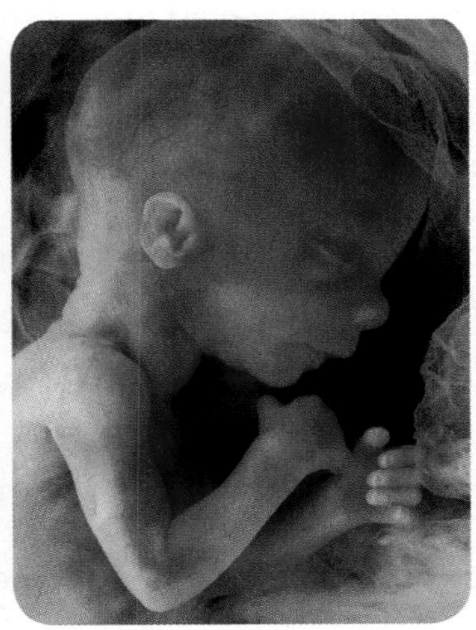

**12 weeks**

■ **Figure 36.12** In amniocentesis, fluid and cells lost from the fetus are removed from the amniotic fluid and analyzed.

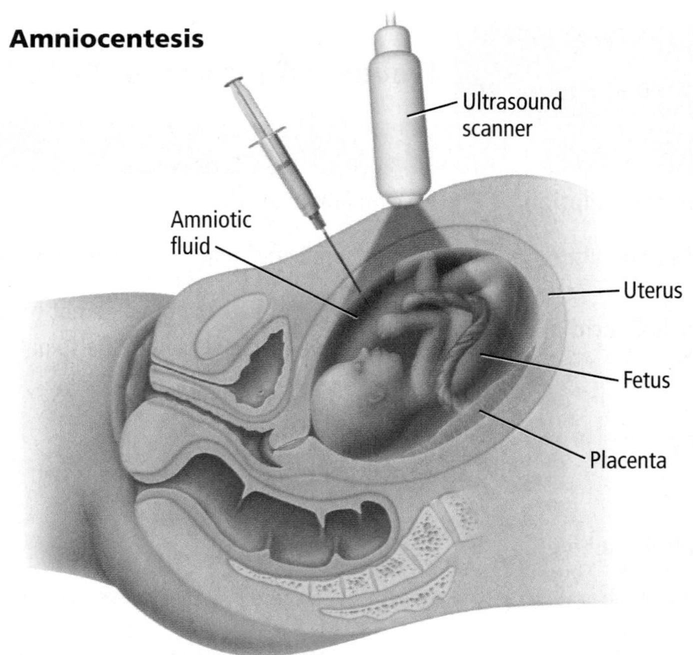


**CAREERS IN BIOLOGY**

**Ultrasound Technician**
Technical skills are needed in biology. An ultrasound technician obtains ultrasound images that are interpreted by a physician. For more information on biology careers, visit biologygmh.com.

## Diagnosis in the Fetus

Many conditions can be diagnosed before a baby is born. Identifying certain conditions as early as possible increases the chance for proper medical treatment to help a newborn baby have the highest quality of life possible.

**Ultrasound** One way to identify conditions in the fetus is by using ultrasound, a procedure in which sound waves are bounced off the fetus. These sound waves are converted into light images that can be seen on a video monitor. Ultrasound can be used to determine if the fetus is growing properly, the position of the fetus in the uterus, and the gender of the fetus.

## MiniLab 36.2

### Sequence Early Human Development

**What developmental changes occur during the first eight weeks of life?** Fertilization begins when a sperm penetrates the egg. The zygote undergoes predictable developmental changes. Cell division produces increasing numbers of cells. Cells move and arrange themselves to form specific organs, making it possible for cells to perform specific functions.

**Procedure**

1. Visit biologygmh.com to see **images of embryos.**
2. Study the images and information provided for Stage 1 through Stage 23, the first ten weeks after fertilization. Choose one factor to track through this developmental period. Factors might include embryonic size, cell differentiation, overall structural changes, specific organ or organ system development, or others.
3. Chart the development of this factor along a time line through the ten-week period.

**Analysis**

1. **Analyze** the time line you created. Identify developmental milestones related to this factor during the ten-week period.
2. **Summarize** the level of development of the factor you examined by the end of Stage 23.

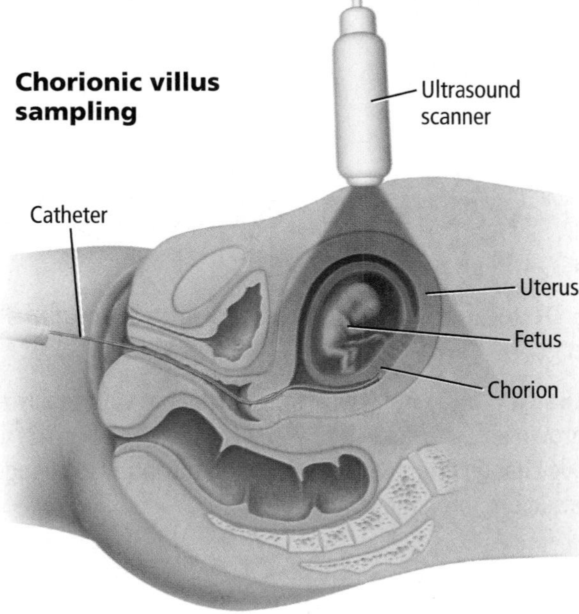


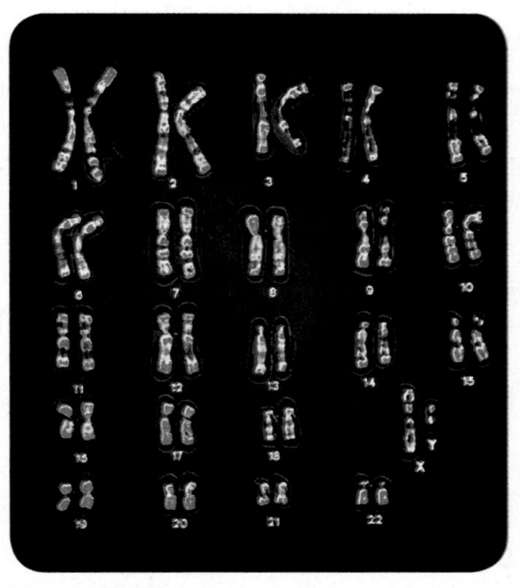

Karyotype

■ **Figure 36.13**
**Left:** Chorionic villus sampling involves removing cells from the chorion and analyzing them. Both procedures carry a small risk of a miscarriage. **Right:** Karyotypes can be analyzed to help with diagnosis.

**Amniocentesis and chorionic villus sampling** Amniocentesis (am nee oh sen TEE sus) and chorionic villus sampling are prenatal tests. During amniocentesis—usually performed in the second trimester—a needle is inserted through the abdomen of the pregnant female, illustrated in **Figure 36.12.** Fluid from the amniotic sac is removed and analyzed. Tests that measure enzyme levels associated with certain conditions can be performed. Fetal cells can be examined by a karyotype or even by DNA analysis. Recall from Chapter 11 that a karyotype is a chart of chromosome pairs that is valuable in identifying unusual chromosome numbers or the sex of the fetus.

In chorionic villus sampling—usually performed during the first trimester—a small tube, called a catheter, is inserted through the vagina and cervix of the mother, illustrated in **Figure 36.13.** Cells from the chorion are removed and analyzed by karyotyping. The chromosomes in the cells of the chorion are identical to those of the cells in the fetus.

## Section 36.2 Assessment

### Section Summary

- Fertilization is the joining of egg and sperm.
- Four extraembryonic membranes are associated with a human embryo.
- The placenta regulates what substances can be exchanged between a fetus and its mother.
- Hormone regulation during pregnancy is different from hormone regulation during the menstrual cycle.
- Some medical conditions of a baby can be detected before it is born.

### Understand Main Ideas

1. MAIN Idea **Describe** the changes that the zygote undergoes during the first week following fertilization.
2. **Describe** how defective acrosomes would affect the process of fertilization.
3. **Summarize** the major changes that occur during each trimester of development in a concept map.
4. **Compare and contrast** hormonal regulation during pregnancy with hormonal regulation during the menstrual cycle.

### Think Scientifically

5. WRITING in Biology Write a paragraph explaining the functions of the extraembryonic membrane in humans, and contrast those functions with the functions in other animals.
6. MATH in Biology Determine the due date (predicted birth date) of the baby if the egg was fertilized on January 1.

# Section 36.3

### Objectives

- **Discuss** the events that occur during the three stages of birth.
- **Describe** the stages of human development from infancy to adulthood.
- **Identify** hormones necessary for growth.

### Review Vocabulary

**growth:** increase in the amount of living material and formation of new structures in an organism

### New Vocabulary

labor
dilation
expulsion stage
placental stage
adolescence
infancy
adulthood

# Birth, Growth, and Aging

**MAIN Idea Developmental changes continue throughout the stages of life.**

**Real-World Reading Link** You know from looking at your family photo album that you have grown and changed since you were born. Your bones, teeth, eyes, and muscles have changed. You can look forward to continued changes in your face and body structure throughout your life.

## Birth

Birth occurs in three stages: dilation, expulsion, and the placental stage, as shown in **Figure 36.14.** Just before giving birth, the posterior pituitary gland releases the hormone oxytocin (ahk sih TOH sun), which stimulates involuntary muscles in the wall of the uterus to contract. This is the beginning of the birthing process called **labor.**

Another sign that the baby is going to be born is the **dilation** (di LAY shun), or opening, of the cervix. The cervix must open to allow the baby to leave the uterus. Contractions of the uterus become stronger and more frequent, and at some point the amniotic sac tears. The amniotic fluid flows out of the vagina, which is sometimes described as the "water breaking."

After a period of time that could be as short as a few hours or as long as a couple of days, the cervix fully dilates to around 10 cm. The uterine contractions are now very strong. The mother consciously will contract her abdominal muscles to help push the baby, usually head first, through the vagina in the **expulsion stage.** When the baby is out of the mother's body, the umbilical cord is clamped and cut. A small piece of the cord still attached to the baby soon will dry up and fall off, forming the navel, or belly button.

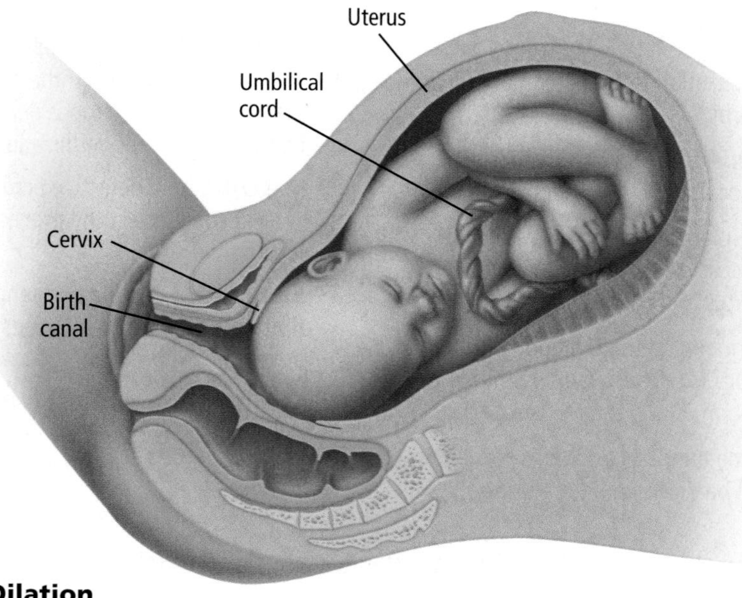


**Figure 36.14** Note the three stages of birth: Dilation: Labor contractions open the cervix. Expulsion stage: The baby rotates as it moves through the birth canal, making expulsion easier. Placental stage: The placenta and umbilical cord are expelled.
**Hypothesize** *What might happen if the placenta was not expelled quickly?*

Shortly after the baby is delivered, the placenta detaches from the uterus and leaves the mother's body along with extraembryonic membranes. This is the **placental stage** of the birthing process.

Sometimes, complications prevent the baby from being born through the vagina. In these cases, an incision is made through the muscles of the mother's abdomen and uterus, and the baby is removed from the mother's body. This process is called a cesarean section.

During the first four weeks of life, the baby is called a newborn. Human newborns vary in size. However, on average, a newborn human baby has a mass of 3300 g and is 51 cm long.

**Reading Check** **Describe** major events that occur during each stage of labor.

**VOCABULARY**
**SCIENCE USAGE V. COMMON USAGE**
**Labor**
***Science usage:*** the process of giving birth.
*There are three stages in labor: dilation, expulsion, and the placental stage.*

***Common usage:*** use of physical or mental effort.
*Lifting the heavy bags of soil requires labor.*

## Growth and Aging

Humans go through many stages of growth during their lives. After you were born, you were in your infancy, but soon you will enter adulthood. You now are in a major development phase called **adolescence** (a dul ES unts) that began with puberty and ends at adulthood.

Hormones, such as human growth hormone, thyroxine, and steroids, influence growth. Human growth hormone stimulates most areas of the body to grow as cells replicate by the process of mitosis. This hormone works by increasing the rates of protein synthesis and breakdown of fats. Thyroxine from the thyroid increases the overall metabolic rate, and is essential for growth to occur. Steroid hormones, such as estrogen and testosterone, also are important for growth. Recall from Chapter 35 that testosterone and estrogen pass through the plasma membrane and into the nucleus of a target cell. The hormones activate certain genes that promote the formation of proteins. In this way, testosterone, and to a lesser extent, estrogen, cause an increase in the size of cells.

**Reading Check** **Summarize** the roles of HGH and thyroxine.

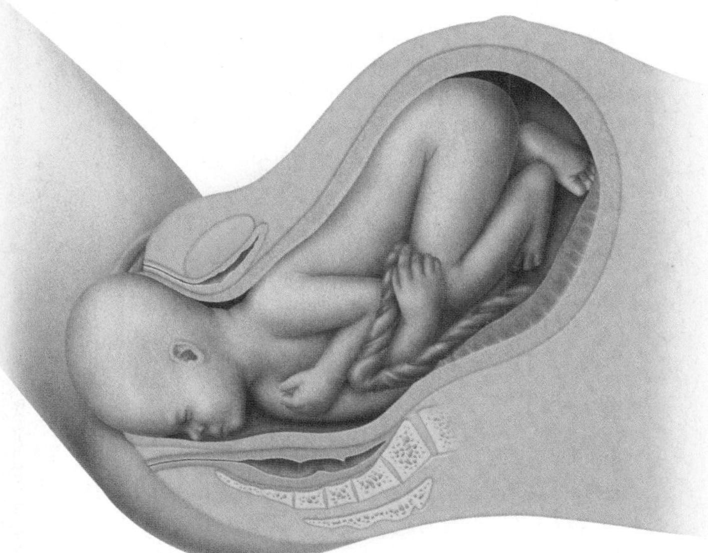
**Expulsion stage**

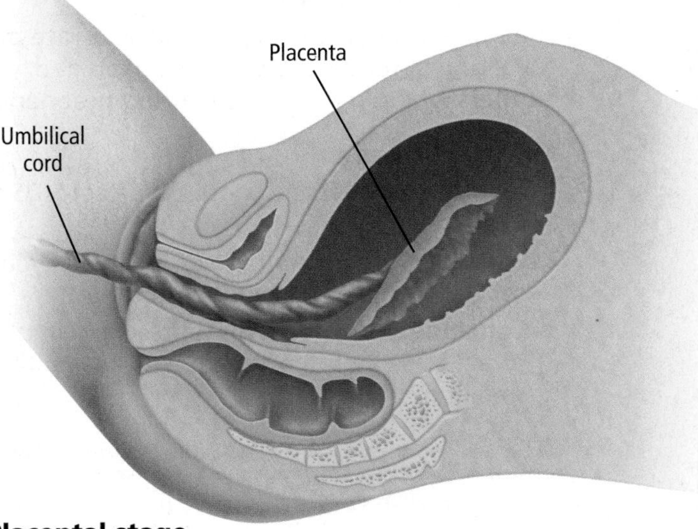

**Placental stage**

**Infancy** The first two years of life are known as **infancy.** Many changes take place during these years. An infant learns how to roll and crawl, grasp objects, and perform simple tasks. By the end of the first year, the infant likely is walking and might be uttering a few words. An enormous amount of mental development also occurs during these first two years.

In the first year, a baby typically grows about 25 cm in length and weighs three times more than when the baby was born. The child's growth slows during the second year; children grow at a rate of around 6 cm per year until the beginning of puberty.

**Childhood and adolescence** Childhood is the period of growth and development that extends from infancy to adolescence. The child's ability to reason and solve problems develops progressively during childhood. Puberty marks the beginning of adolescence, the period of growth between childhood and adulthood. Puberty usually begins between ages 8 to 13 in girls and ages 10 to 15 in boys.

In addition to the hormonal and sexual development that takes place during this time, other physical changes take place as well. An adolescent experiences a growth spurt—girls grow approximately 6–11 cm and boys grow approximately 7–13 cm—in one year. In girls, the hips become wider and the waist might become narrower. In boys, the shoulders usually become broader. At the end of adolescence, physical growth is complete, marking the beginning of **adulthood.** The transition between adolescence and adulthood can be hard to define because of physical, emotional, and behavioral changes.

## DATA ANALYSIS LAB 36.1

**Based on Real Data***

### Form a Conclusion

**Is SIDS linked to smoking?** In 1994, doctors began to recommend that babies sleep on their backs to reduce the risk of Sudden Infant Death Syndrome (SIDS).

#### Data and Observations

The table summarizes the annual SIDS rate per 1000 infants for mothers who smoked and mothers who did not smoke during pregnancy.

| SIDS Deaths | | |
|---|---|---|
| Year | Smoke Exposed | Unexposed |
| 1989 | 3.21 | 1.33 |
| 1990 | 2.96 | 1.34 |
| 1991 | 3.32 | 1.72 |
| 1992 | 2.93 | 1.41 |
| 1993 | 3.28 | 1.17 |
| 1994 | 1.65 | 0.79 |
| 1995 | 2.19 | 0.65 |
| 1996 | 1.61 | 0.82 |
| 1997 | 3.21 | 0.64 |
| 1998 | 1.80 | 0.37 |

#### Think Critically

1. **Analyze** Did sleeping position affect SIDS? Explain.
2. **Calculate** the percentage of SIDS each year for babies born to smoking mothers.
3. **Conclude** How does this data show that some SIDS cases might be linked to cigarette smoking?

*Data obtained from: Anderson, M.E., et al. 2005. Sudden Infant Death Syndrome and prenatal maternal smoking: rising attributed risk in the Back to Sleep era. *BMC Medicine* 3: 4.

31. During which stage of birth does structure *A* leave the female's body?
   **A.** first
   **B.** second
   **C.** third
   **D.** fourth

32. During which year of a person's life does the most rapid rate of growth occur?
   **A.** the first year of infancy
   **B.** the first year of puberty
   **C.** the second year of puberty
   **D.** the first year of adulthood

## Constructed Response

33. **Open Ended** What biological reasons can you think of to explain why women go through menopause and stop producing eggs while men can produce sperm all their lives?

34. **Short Answer** Compare puberty in females with puberty in males.

35. **CAREERS IN BIOLOGY** During rare occasions, a pediatrician examines a newborn baby who does not produce enough thyroxin. What are some possible results of this? Suggest a treatment for this condition.

## Think Critically

*Use the graph below to answer question 36.*

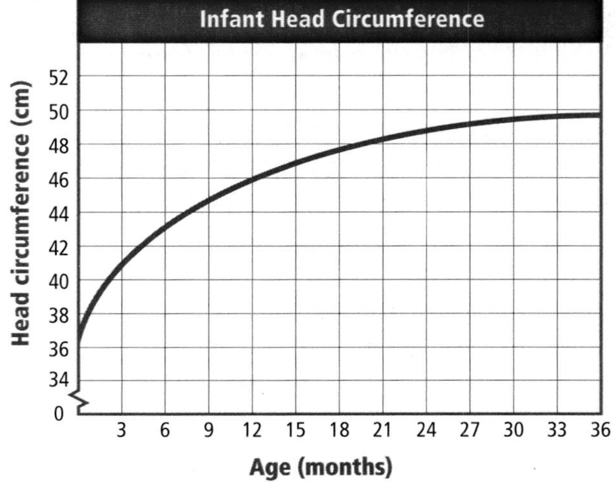


36. **Evaluate** During which period shown on the graph is the rate of change in head circumference greatest?

## Additional Assessment

37. WRITING in Biology Prepare a pamphlet for pregnant women on health and lifestyle issues during pregnancy. Include a chart on major events of fetal development.

### Document-Based Questions

*To reduce the chances of brain and spine birth defects, the U.S. Public Health Service recommended in 1992 that women of childbearing age increase folic acid in their diets. The U.S. Food and Drug Administration required all cereal products be enriched with folic acid beginning in January 1998 (an optional period began in March 1996).*

*Below is a table showing the rate per 100,000 births of anencephaly—incomplete head and brain development—from 1991–2002.*

| Year | Rate | Year | Rate |
|---|---|---|---|
| **1991** | 18.38 | **1997** | 12.51 |
| **1992** | 12.79 | **1998** | 9.92 |
| **1993** | 13.50 | **1999** | 10.81 |
| **1994** | 10.97 | **2000** | 10.33 |
| **1995** | 11.71 | **2001** | 9.42 |
| **1996** | 11.96 | **2002** | 9.55 |

Data obtained from: Mathews, T.J. Trends in Spina Bifida and Anencephalus in the United States, 1991–2002. National Center for Health Statistics/Centers for Disease Control and Prevention/Department of Health and Human Services.

38. Construct a graph to represent this data and describe the relationship between the variables that you observe.

39. Explain the overall trend in the number of cases of anencephaly during this time period.

## Cumulative Review

40. How do the concepts of population growth, natality, and birth rate differ? **(Chapter 4)**

41. What are the three main differences between DNA and RNA? **(Chapter 12)**

# Standardized Test Practice

**Cumulative**

## Multiple Choice

1. Which is the role of arteries in the circulatory system?
   A. to carry blood away from the heart
   B. to carry blood back to the heart
   C. to provide individual cells with nutrients
   D. to prevent blood from flowing backward

*Use the diagram below to answer question 2.*

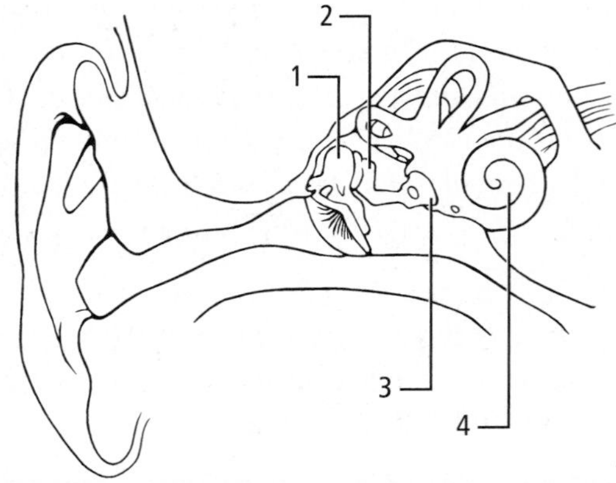


2. Which contains sensors for the auditory nerve?
   A. 1
   B. 2
   C. 3
   D. 4

3. What is the role of hormones in the body?
   A. They act as reaction catalysts.
   B. They control the breathing process.
   C. They help synthesize proteins.
   D. They regulate many body functions.

4. Which is the sequence of human development during the first week?
   A. egg → morula → blastocyst → zygote
   B. egg → zygote → morula → blastocyst
   C. morula → blastocyst → egg → zygote
   D. morula → egg → zygote → blastocyst

5. Which is the function of the kidneys?
   A. deplete carbon dioxide from the blood
   B. eliminate undigested foods from the body
   C. remove excess water and wastes from the blood
   D. rid excess proteins from the blood

*Use the diagram below to answer question 6.*

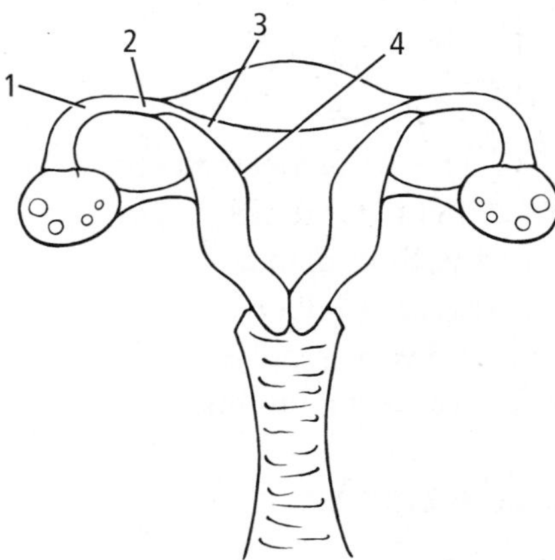


6. Where does fertilization take place?
   A. 1
   B. 2
   C. 3
   D. 4

7. When blood glucose levels are very high, what does the pancreas secrete?
   A. glycogen
   B. insulin
   C. insulin and glycogen
   D. neither insulin nor glycogen

8. Which describes the human circulatory system?
   A. four-chambered heart, one circulatory loop
   B. four-chambered heart, two circulatory loops
   C. two-chambered heart, one circulatory loop
   D. two-chambered heart, two circulatory loops

9. Which statement describes what happens during internal respiration?
   A. Carbon dioxide is used to derive energy from glucose.
   B. Gases are exchanged between the atmosphere and the blood.
   C. Gases are exchanged between the blood and the body's cells.
   D. Oxygen is used to derive energy from glucose.



Biology Online **Standardized Test Practice** biologygmh.com

## Short Answer

*Use the diagram below to answer questions 10 and 11.*

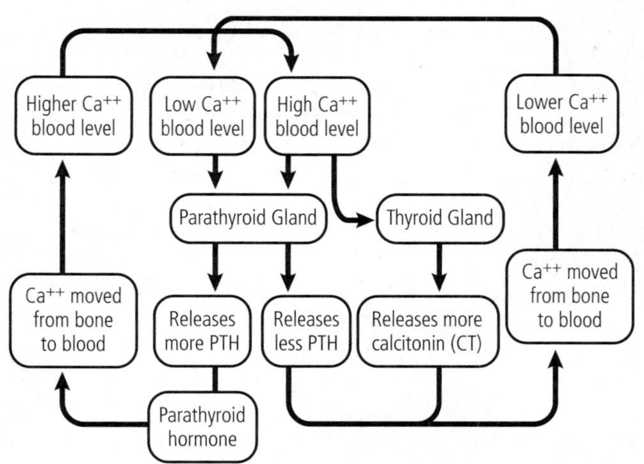


**10.** Assess how the parathyroid hormone affects bone tissue.

**11.** Evaluate how a person's blood calcium levels would be affected if his or her thyroid gland stopped working.

**12.** Analyze how Ivan Pavlov conditioned dogs to salivate when they heard a bell.

**13.** Assess how emphysema would cause difficulty for a person when climbing stairs.

**14.** Name and describe the two divisions of the human skeleton. Critique this division of the skeleton.

**15.** Think about the structure of the middle and inner ear. Infer why people might experience a temporary hearing loss after attending a loud concert.

**16.** Explain how the villi in the small intestine affect the rate of absorption.

## Extended Response

**17.** A student did an experiment in a sunny room using unripe bananas. He found that bananas ripened faster in a paper bag than on top of a plate. Based on these results, what conclusion could the student make about the ripening of the bananas? Give one example of a way to improve the experiment.

**18.** Muscles in the legs tend to store large amounts of glycogen and fat. Muscles in the arms do not. When the muscles are used repeatedly, why will the muscles in the arm fatigue the quickest?

**19.** Different kinds of mammals have different digestive systems. Explain how the digestive systems of ruminant herbivores differ from other herbivores.

## Essay Question

As elevation increases, air pressure decreases. At sea level, air pressure is about 760 mmHg. The percentage of oxygen in the atmosphere is about 21 percent. At 3200 m in elevation, the air pressure is 30 percent less than at sea level, however, the percentage of oxygen is the same. The difference in pressure occurs because the molecules of gas are spread farther apart. As altitude continues to increase, the pressure continues to decrease. Mountain climbers face the problems of decreased pressure when they climb a mountain. When climbers go to the summit of the highest mountains, they carry oxygen tanks with them to help them breathe.

*Using the information in the paragraph above, answer the following question in essay format.*

**20.** Evaluate why breathing oxygen would enable a mountain climber to reach a higher altitude.

**NEED EXTRA HELP?**

| If You Missed Question . . . | 1 | 2 | 3 | 4 | 5 | 6 | 7 | 8 | 9 | 10 | 11 | 12 | 13 | 14 | 15 | 16 | 17 | 18 | 19 | 20 |
|---|---|---|---|---|---|---|---|---|---|---|---|---|---|---|---|---|---|---|---|---|
| Review Section . . . | 34.1 | 33.3 | 35.1 | 36.2 | 34.3 | 36.2 | 35.3 | 34.3 | 34.2 | 35.3 | 35.3 | 31.1 | 34.2 | 32.2 | 33.3 | 35.1 | 1.3 | 32.3 | 30.2 | 34.2 |

CHAPTER 37

# Immune System

**Section 1**
**Infectious Diseases**
MAIN Idea Pathogens are dispersed by people, other animals, and objects.

**Section 2**
**The Immune System**
MAIN Idea The immune system has two main components: nonspecific immunity and specific immunity.

**Section 3**
**Noninfectious Disorders**
MAIN Idea Noninfectious disorders include genetic disorders, degenerative diseases, metabolic diseases, cancer, and inflammatory diseases.

## BioFacts

- There are more than 600 lymph nodes, such as the tonsil, in the human body.
- Macrophages have cytoplasm that is in constant motion. The cytoplasm may have ruffles or pseudopodia.
- Millions of viruses could fit on the head of a pin.

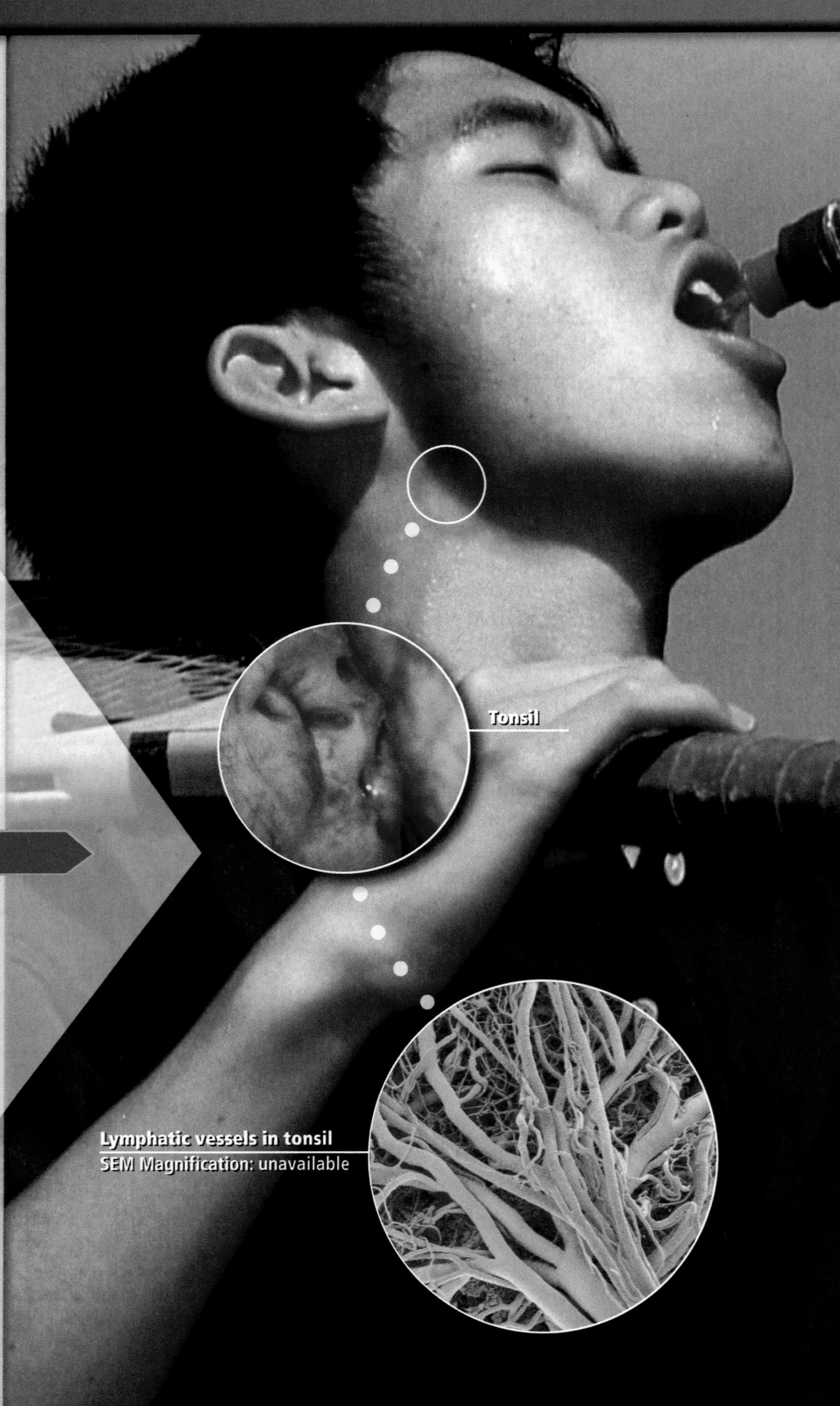

# LAUNCH Lab

## How do you track a cold?

Colds and many other illnesses are caused by pathogens that can pass from person to person. In this lab, you will trace the path of a cold.

### Procedure

1. Read and complete the lab safety form.
2. Create a series of questions you can ask your classmates about the last time they had a cold: their symptoms, other family members and friends who had the same symptoms, and the hygiene precautions they used to avoid illnesses.
3. Interview your classmates using your list.
4. Design a concept map that organizes the data you have collected to trace the paths the colds in your classmates took as they passed from person to person.

### Analysis

1. **Describe** how your concept map distinguishes between different cold symptoms present in your classmates.
2. **Infer** what paths the different colds might have taken as they passed from person to person among your classmates and their friends and family.

**Visit** biologygmh.com **to:**

- **study the entire chapter online**
- **explore the Interactive Time Line, Interactive Tables, Concepts in Motion, Microscopy Links, Virtual Labs, and links to virtual dissections**
- **access Web links for more information, projects, and activities**
- **review content online with the Interactive Tutor and take Self-Check Quizzes**

**Describing Immunity** Make the following Foldable to help you organize the ideas of immunity.

**STEP 1** Stack three sheets of notebook paper, each 2.5 cm apart.

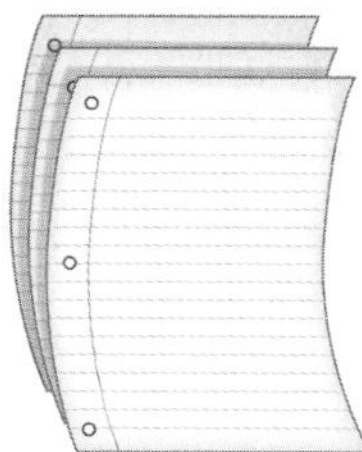

**STEP 2** Fold the sheets in half so that all the layers are the same distance apart.

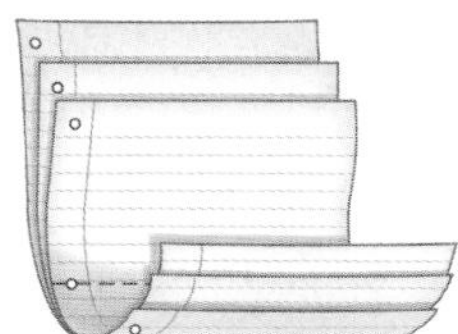

**STEP 3** Staple the Foldable at the bottom and label each tab as shown with the following titles: *Immunity from Disease, Innate Immunity, Antibody Immunity, Cellular Immunity, Passive Immunity,* and *Acquired Immunity.*

FOLDABLES **Use this Foldable with Section 37.2.** As you study the section, describe each type of immunity on the page opposite the title. Use the Foldable to review what you have learned about immunity.

## Section 37.1

### Objectives

- **Construct** a flow chart demonstrating Koch's postulates.
- **Explain** how diseases are transmitted and how reservoirs play a role in disease dispersal.
- **Describe** symptoms of bacterial infectious disease.

### Review Vocabulary

**protozoan:** unicellular, heterotrophic, animal-like protist

### New Vocabulary

infectious disease
pathogen
Koch's postulates
reservoir
endemic disease
epidemic
pandemic
antibiotic

**Figure 37.1** These rodlike bacteria cause the disease anthrax.

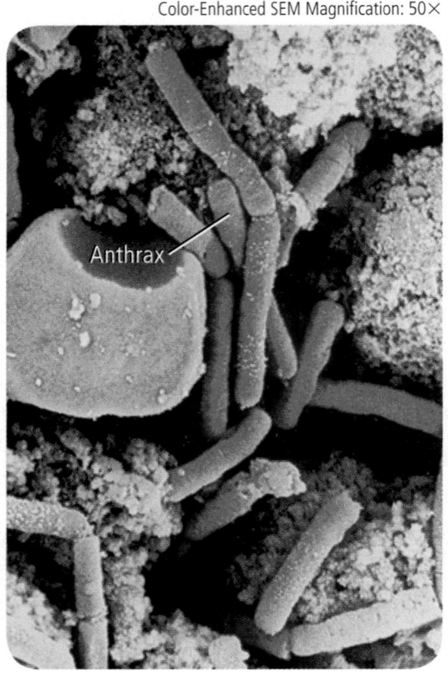


# Infectious Diseases

**MAIN Idea Pathogens are dispersed by people, other animals, and objects.**

**Real-World Reading Link** Have you ever gotten something sticky on your hands? As you touched other objects, they too became sticky. In a similar manner, the virus that caused your last cold can be transferred to objects that you touched, such as money, pencils, desktops, and doorknobs. When these objects are touched by someone else, the cold virus can be picked up by another person.

## Pathogens Cause Infectious Disease

What do a cold and athlete's foot have in common? They are both examples of an infectious disease. An **infectious disease** is a disease that is caused when a pathogen is passed from one organism to another, disrupting homeostasis in the organism's body. Agents called **pathogens** are the cause of infectious disease. Some but not all types of bacteria, viruses, protozoans, fungi, and parasites are included in this group.

Recall from Chapter 18 that many types of these organisms are present in the world around us without causing infectious diseases. Your body benefits from organisms, such as certain types of bacteria and protozoans, that normally live in your intestinal and reproductive tracts. Other bacteria live on your skin, especially in the shafts of your hair follicles. These organisms keep pathogens from thriving and multiplying on your body.

## Germ Theory and Koch's Experiments

Before the invention of the microscope, people thought "something" passed from a sick person to a well person to cause an illness. Then, scientists discovered microorganisms and Louis Pasteur demonstrated that microorganisms from the air are able to grow in nutrient solutions, as discussed in Chapter 14. With the knowledge gained from these and other discoveries, doctors and scientists began to develop the germ theory. The germ theory states that some microorganisms are pathogens. However, scientists were not able to prove this theory until Robert Koch developed his postulates.

**Identification of the first disease pathogen** In the late 1800s Robert Koch, a German physician, was studying anthrax (AN thraks)—a deadly disease that affects cattle and sheep and can also affect people. Koch isolated bacteria, like those in **Figure 37.1,** from the blood of cattle that had died from anthrax. After growing the bacteria in the laboratory, Koch injected the bacteria into healthy cattle. These animals developed the disease anthrax. He then isolated bacteria from the blood of newly infected cattle and grew the bacteria in the laboratory. The characteristics of the two sets of cultures were identical indicating that the same type of bacteria caused the illness in both sets of cattle. Thus, Koch demonstrated that the bacteria he originally isolated were the cause of anthrax.

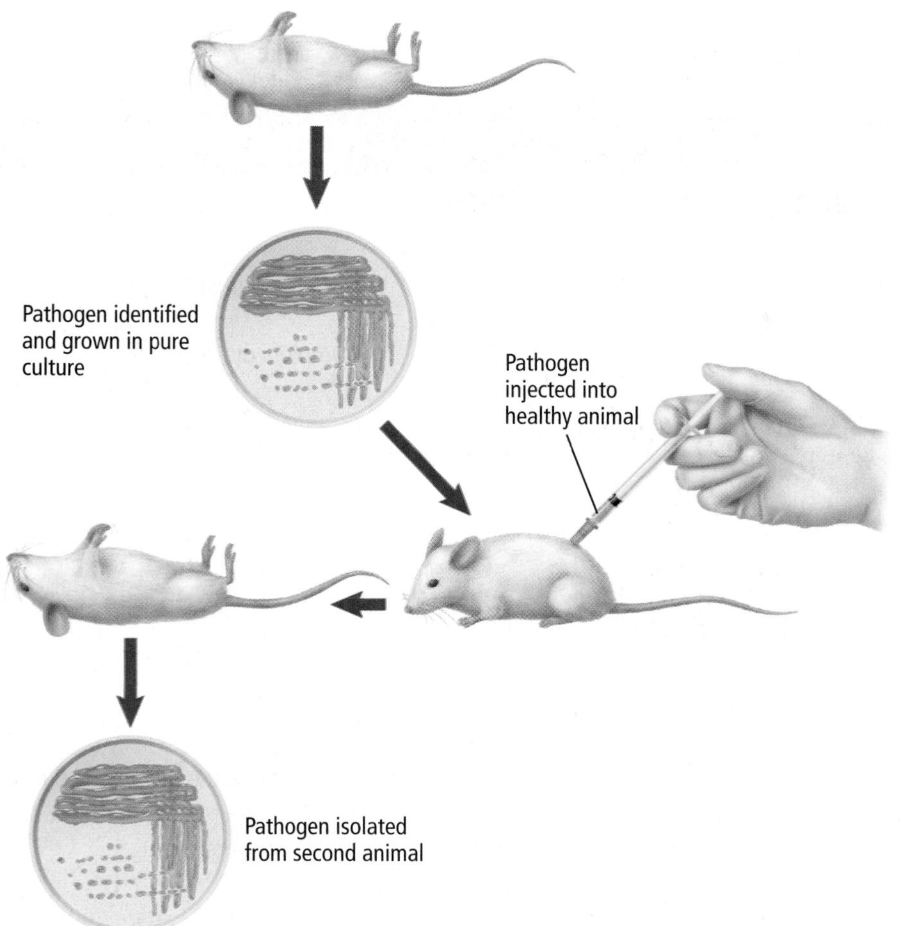
Pathogen identified and grown in pure culture
Pathogen injected into healthy animal
Pathogen isolated from second animal

**Postulate 1**

The suspected pathogen must be isolated from the diseased host in every case of the disease.

**Postulate 2**

The suspected pathogen must be grown in pure culture on artificial media in the laboratory.

**Postulate 3**

The suspected pathogen from the pure culture must cause the same disease when placed in a healthy new host.

**Postulate 4**

The suspected pathogen must be isolated from the new host, grown again in pure culture, and shown to have the same characteristics as the original pathogen.

■ **Figure 37.2** Koch's postulates demonstrate that a specific pathogen causes a specific disease.

**Think Critically** ***What did Koch demonstrate when he isolated the same bacteria from the cattle the second time?***

**Koch's postulates** Koch established and published experimental steps known as **Koch's postulates,** which are rules for demonstrating that an organism causes a disease. These steps are followed today to identify a specific pathogen as the agent of a specific disease. Follow the steps in **Figure 37.2** as you read each of the four postulates.

**Postulate 1:** The suspected pathogen must be isolated from the diseased host in every case of the disease.

**Postulate 2:** The suspected pathogen must be grown in pure culture on artificial media in the laboratory. A pure culture is a culture that contains no other types of microorganisms—only the suspected pathogen.

**Postulate 3:** The suspected pathogen from the pure culture must cause the disease when placed in a healthy new host.

**Postulate 4:** The suspected pathogen must be isolated from the new host, grown again in pure culture, and shown to have the same characteristics as the original pathogen.

Some exceptions to Koch's postulates do exist. Some pathogens, such as the pathogen that is believed to cause syphilis (SIH fuh lus), cannot be grown in pure culture on artificial media. Artificial media are the nutrients that the bacteria need to survive and reproduce. Pathogens are grown on this media in the laboratory. Also, in the case of viruses, cultured cells are needed because viruses cannot be grown on artificial media.

*Study Tip*

**Purposeful Reading** Before reading, predict how the information you learn about diseases can be applied to your daily life. Scan the chapter and focus on the boldfaced headings to get an idea about what you will study. Record your ideas. Refer to the list as you study the chapter.

Concepts In Motion

**Interactive Table** To explore more about infectious diseases, visit biologygmh.com.

**Table 37.1 Human Infectious Diseases**

| Disease | Cause | Affected Organ System | How Disease is Spread |
|---|---|---|---|
| **Tetanus** | Bacteria | Nervous system | Soil in deep puncture wound |
| **Strep throat** | Bacteria | Respiratory system | Droplets/direct contact |
| **Meningitis** | Bacteria | Nervous system | Droplets/direct contact |
| **Lyme disease** | Bacteria | Skeletal and nervous system | Vector (tick) |
| **Chicken pox** | Virus | Skin | Droplets/direct contact |
| **Rabies** | Virus | Nervous system | Animal bite |
| **Common cold** | Virus | Respiratory system | Droplets/direct contact |
| **Influenza** | Virus | Respiratory system | Droplets/direct contact |
| **Hepatitis B** | Virus | Liver | Direct contact with exchange of body fluids |
| **West Nile** | Virus | Nervous system | Vector (mosquito) |
| **Giardia** | Protozoan | Digestive tract | Contaminated water |
| **Malaria** | Protozoan | Blood and liver | Vector (mosquito) |
| **Athlete's foot** | Fungus | Skin | Direct contact or contaminated objects |

## Spread of Disease

Of the large number of microorganisms that coexist with humans, only a few cause disease. The pathogens vary as much as the diseases themselves. Some might cause mild diseases, such as the common cold. Others cause serious diseases, such as meningitis (men in JI tus), an infection of the coverings of the brain and spinal cord. **Table 37.1** lists some of the human infectious diseases you might know.

For a pathogen to spread, it must have both a reservoir and a way to spread. A disease **reservoir** is a source of the pathogen in the environment. Reservoirs might be animals, people, or inanimate objects, such as soil.

**Human reservoirs** Humans are the main reservoir for pathogens that affect humans. They might pass the pathogen directly or indirectly to other humans. Many pathogens might be passed on to other hosts before the person even knows he or she has the disease. An individual that is symptom-free but capable of passing the pathogen is called a carrier. Pathogens that cause colds, influenza (commonly referred to as the flu), and sexually transmitted diseases, such as human immunodeficiency (ih MYEWN noh dih fih shun see) virus (HIV), can be passed on without the person knowing he or she is infected.

**VOCABULARY**

**SCIENCE USAGE V. COMMON USAGE**

**Carrier**

***Science usage:*** person who spreads germs while remaining well.
*Typhoid fever was spread by a carrier known as "Typhoid Mary."*

***Common usage:*** a person or corporation in the transportation business.
*Freight is shipped by carriers.*

**Animal reservoirs** Other animals also are reservoirs of pathogens that can be passed to humans. Influenza and rabies are examples of human diseases listed in **Table 37.1** that are caused by pathogens passed to humans from other animals. Influenza can infect pigs and various types of birds. Rabies is found in domestic dogs and many wild animals, such as bats, foxes, skunks, and raccoons.

**Other reservoirs** Some bacteria normally found in the soil, such as tetanus bacteria, can cause disease in humans. The tetanus bacteria can cause a serious infection if it contaminates a deep wound in the body. Contamination of wounds by bacteria was a major cause of death during wars before the development of antibiotics and vaccinations.

Contaminated water or food is another reservoir of pathogens for human disease. One of the main purposes of sewage treatment plants is the safe disposal of human feces, which prevents contamination of the water supply by pathogens. Contaminated water used in growing or preparing food can transfer pathogens. Food also can become contaminated through contact with humans or insects such as flies.

**Transmission of pathogens** Pathogens mainly are transmitted to humans in four ways: direct contact, indirectly through the air, indirectly through touching contaminated objects, or by organisms called vectors that carry pathogens. Study **Figure 37.3,** which illustrates some of the ways pathogens can be transmitted to humans.

**Direct Contact** Direct contact with other humans is one of the major modes of transmission of pathogens. Diseases such as colds, infectious mononucleosis (mah noh new klee OH sus)(commonly referred to as mono, or the "kissing disease"), herpes (HUR peez), and sexually transmitted diseases are caused by pathogens passed through direct contact.

**CAREERS IN BIOLOGY**

**Epidemiologist** An epidemiologist studies disease patterns to help prevent and control the spread of diseases. For more information on biology careers, visit biologygmh.com.

■ **Figure 37.3** Diseases can be transmitted to humans in various ways.
**Think Critically** ***Identify ways to prevent contracting diseases if contact cannot be avoided.***

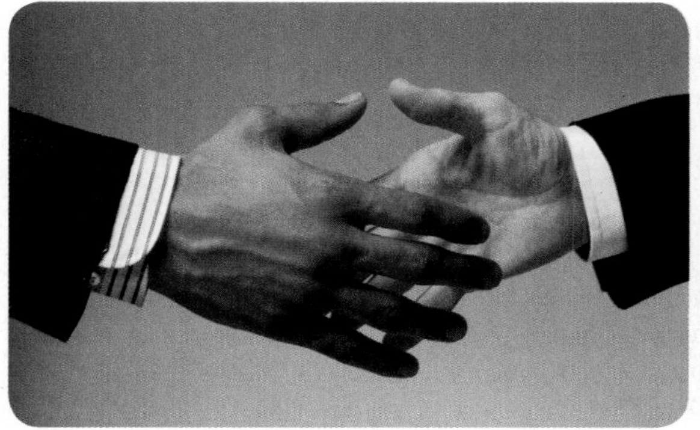

**Direct contact**

**Indirect contact through air**

**Indirect contact by objects**

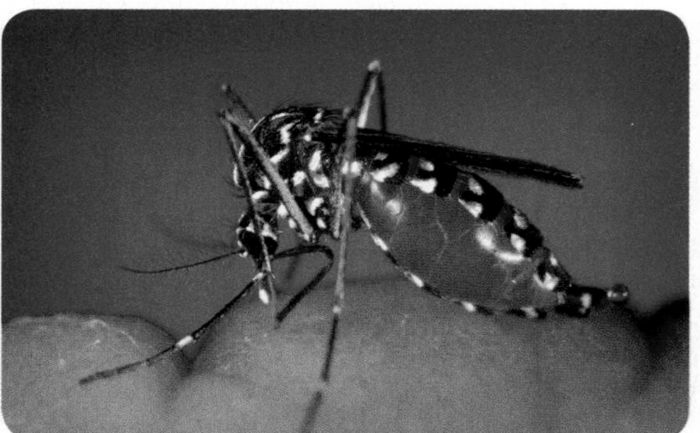

**Vectors**

**Indirect contact** Some pathogens can be passed through the air. When a person with an infectious disease sneezes or coughs, pathogens can be passed along with the tiny mucus droplets. These droplets then can spread pathogens to another person or to an object.

Many organisms can survive on objects handled by humans. Cleansing of dishes, utensils, and countertops with detergents as well as careful hand-washing help prevent the spread of diseases that are passed in this manner. As a result, there are various food rules that restaurants must abide by that are based on preventing the spread of disease.

**Vectors** Certain diseases can be transmitted by vectors. The most common vectors are arthropods, which include biting insects such as mosquitoes and ticks. Recall from **Table 37.1** that Lyme disease, malaria, and West Nile virus are diseases that are passed to humans by vectors. The West Nile virus, which is currently spreading across the United States, is transmitted from horses and other mammals to humans by mosquitoes. Flies can transmit pathogens by landing on infected materials, such as feces, and then landing on materials handled or eaten by humans.

**Reading Check** **Describe** how diseases are spread to humans.

**LAUNCH Lab**

**Review** Based on what you have read about spread of disease, how would you now answer the analysis questions?

## Symptoms of Disease

When you become ill with a disease such as the flu, why do you feel aches and pains, and why do you cough and sneeze? The pathogen, such as an influenza virus or bacteria, has invaded some of the cells of your body. The virus multiplies in the cells and leaves the cells either by exocytosis or by causing the cell to burst. Thus, the virus damages tissues and even kills some cells. When pathogenic bacteria invade the body, harmful chemicals or toxins might be produced. The toxins can be carried throughout the body via the bloodstream and damage various parts of the body.

**Figure 37.4**

### Immunology Through Time

For centuries, scientists have struggled to learn about the human immune system. Today, scientists are working to stop a virus that has attacked the immune system of over 40 million people worldwide—HIV.

**1908** Elie Metchnikoff observes phagocytosis, and Paul Erlich describes antibodies. They share a Nobel Prize for their discoveries.

**1981** The first clinical description of acquired immunodeficiency syndrome (AIDS) is established.

1800 1900 1970

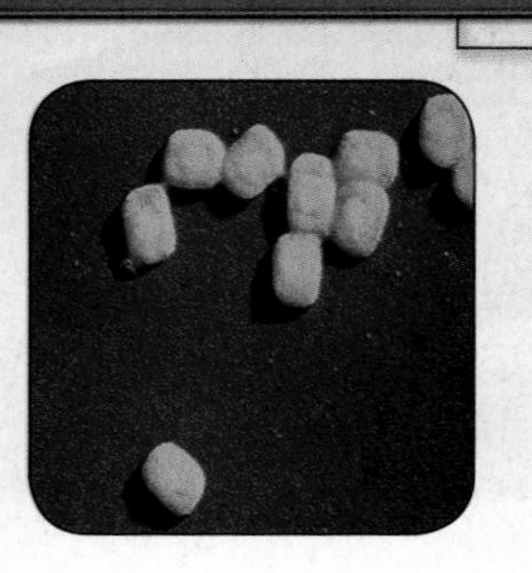

**1796** Edward Jenner discovers that a patient vaccinated with the cowpox virus is immune to smallpox.

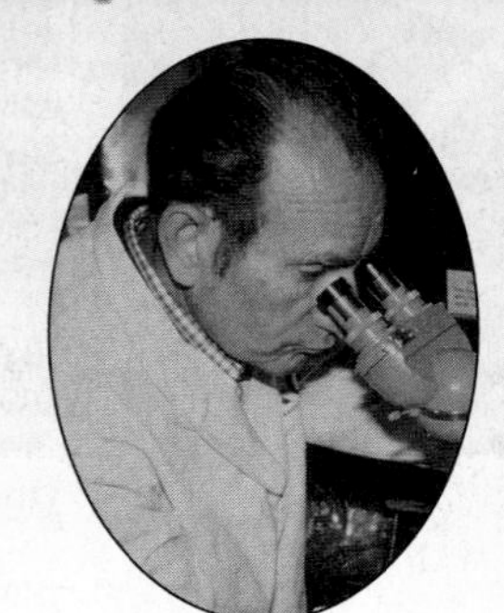

**1975** César Milstein and his research team develop a technique to clone a specific antibody.

Toxins produced by pathogens can affect specific organ systems. The tetanus bacteria produce a potent toxin that causes spasms in the voluntary muscles. The disease botulism (BAH chuh lih zum) usually is caused when a person consumes food in which the botulism bacteria have grown and produced a toxin. This toxin paralyzes nerves. The toxin from the botulism bacteria can cause disease in humans even when no bacteria are present.

Some types of bacteria, some protozoans, and all viruses invade and live inside cells, causing damage. Because the cells are damaged, they might die, causing symptoms in the host. Some disease symptoms, such as coughing and sneezing, are triggered by the immune system, as discussed later in this chapter. For a closer look at research on the immune system, examine **Figure 37.4.**

## Disease Patterns

As outbreaks of diseases spread, certain patterns are observed. Agencies such as the community health departments, the Centers for Disease Control and Prevention (CDC), and the World Health Organization (WHO) continually monitor disease patterns to help control the spread of diseases. The CDC, with headquarters in Atlanta, Georgia, receives information from doctors and medical clinics and publishes a weekly report about the incidence of specific diseases, as shown in **Figure 37.5.** The WHO similarly watches disease incidence throughout the world.

Some diseases, such as the common cold, are known as **endemic diseases** because they continually are found in small amounts within the population. Sometimes, a particular disease will have a large outbreak in an area and afflict many people, causing an **epidemic.** If an epidemic is widespread throughout a large region, such as a country, continent, or the entire globe, it is described as **pandemic.**

TABLE 2. Reported cases of notifiable diseases,* by geographic division and area — United States, 2003

| Area | Total resident population (in thousands) | AIDS† |
|---|---|---|
| UNITED STATES | 287,974 | 44,232** |
| NEW ENGLAND | 14,134 | 1,697 |
| Maine | 1,295 | 52 |
| N.H. | 1,274 | 37 |
| Vt. | 616 | 16 |
| Mass. | 6,422 | 757 |
| R.I. | 1,068 | 102 |
| Conn. | 3,459 | 733 |
| MID. ATLANTIC | 40,038 | 10,142 |
| Upstate N.Y. | 11,385 | 1,589 |
| N.Y. City | 7,749 | 5,133 |
| N.J. | 8,575 | 1,514 |
| Pa. | 12,329 | 1,906 |
| E.N. CENTRAL | 45,635 | 3,875 |
| Ohio | 11,409 | 775 |
| Ind. | 6,157 | 506 |
| Ill. | 12,586 | 1,734 |
| Mich. | 10,043 | 676 |
| Wis. | 5,440 | 184 |
| W.N. CENTRAL | 19,464 | 844 |
| Minn. | 5,025 | 179 |
| Iowa | 2,936 | 75 |
| Mo. | 5,670 | 404 |
| N. Dak. | 634 | 2 |
| S. Dak. | 760 | 13 |
| Nebr. | 1,728 | 60 |
| Kans. | 2,712 | 111 |
| S. ATLANTIC | 53,564 | 12,191 |
| Del. | 806 | 216 |
| Md. | 5,451 | 1,572 |
| D.C. | 569 | 961 |

**Figure 37.5** The Centers for Disease Control and Prevention publish reports on the incidence of certain diseases.
**Infer** *how these reports are helpful in understanding disease patterns.*

**1985** Flossie Wong-Staal and her team clone HIV, enabling scientists to create a test to determine whether or not a person has HIV.

**2004** HIV infection is pandemic in sub-Saharan Africa, where 10 percent of the world's population has 60 percent of the world's HIV infections.

1980 1990 2000

**1984** Luc Montagnier and Robert Gallo independently announce the discovery of the virus that causes AIDS.

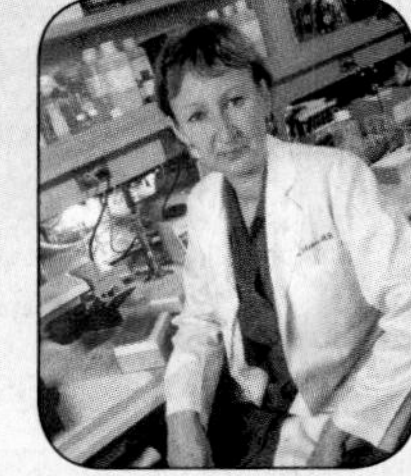

**1999** Dr. Beatrice Hahn hypothesizes that humans most likely were exposed to HIV from a chimp species found in west equatorial Africa.

**Concepts In Motion** Interactive Time Line
To learn more about these discoveries and others, visit biologygmh.com.
Biology Online

■ **Figure 37.6** Penicillin is secreted by the mold called *Penicillium,* shown growing on this orange.
**Hypothesize** ***Why are there so many antibiotics available?***

## Treating and Fighting Diseases

A medical professional may prescribe a drug to help the body fight a disease. One type of prescription drug is an **antibiotic** (an ti bi AH tihk), which is a substance that can kill or inhibit the growth of other microorganisms. Recall from Chapter 20 that penicillin is secreted by the fungus *Penicillium,* which is shown in **Figure 37.6.** This fungus secretes the chemical penicillin to kill competing bacteria that grow on the fungal food source. Penicillin was isolated, purified, and first used in humans during World War II. Many other fungal secretions are used as antibiotics, such as erythromycin, neomycin, and gentamicin. Synthetic antibiotics also have been developed by pharmaceutical companies.

Chemical agents also are used in the treatment of protozoan and fungal diseases. Some antiviral drugs are used to treat herpes infections, influenza in the elderly, and HIV infections. Most viral diseases are handled by the body's built-in defense system—the immune system.

**Connection to Health** Over the last 60 years, the widespread use of antibiotics has caused many bacteria to become resistant to particular antibiotics. Recall from Chapter 15 that natural selection occurs when organisms with favorable variations survive, reproduce, and pass their variations to the next generation. Bacteria in a population might have a trait that enables them to survive when a particular antibiotic is present. These bacteria can reproduce quickly and pass on the variation. Because reproduction can occur so rapidly in bacteria, the number of antibiotic-resistant bacteria in a population can increase quickly, too.

## Mini Lab 37.1

### Evaluate the Spread of Pathogens

**How can you evaluate the spread of disease?** Investigate what possible diseases might be transmitted by common items.

**Procedure**

1. Read and complete the lab safety form
2. Observe all the items given to you by your teacher.
3. Infer the types of diseases each item could pass on to a human (if any).
4. Evaluate the likelihood of each item transmitting a disease to a human and devise a scale for assessing each item's probability for transmitting an infectious disease.

**Analysis**

1. **Identify** the types of pathogens that might be transmitted by the items you were given and the methods of transmission of each pathogen.
2. **Infer** the items most likely to be disease reservoirs.
3. **Describe** possible disease patterns of each pathogen.
4. **Infer** how you could prevent getting diseases from these possible pathogens.

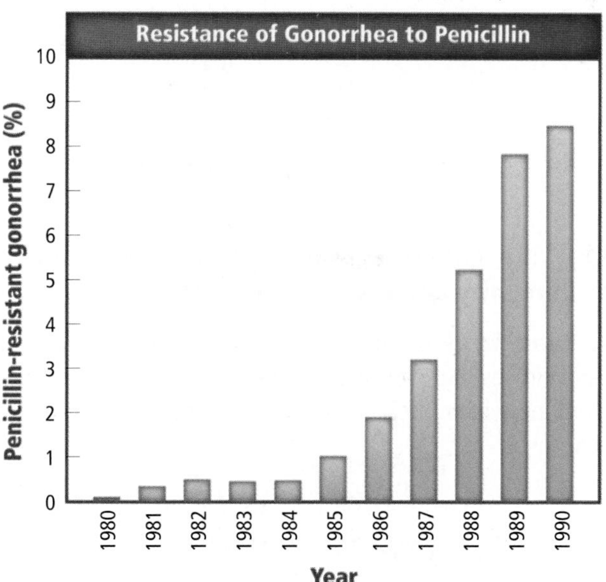


**Figure 37.7** The graph shows the reported incidence of penicillin-resistant gonorrhea in the United States from 1980–1990.

**Analyze** ***What is the percentage increase from 1980 to 1990?***

Antibiotic resistance of bacteria has presented the medical community with some problems with treating certain diseases. For example, penicillin was used effectively for many years to treat gonorrhea (gah nuh REE uh), a sexually transmitted disease, but now most strains of gonorrhea bacteria are resistant to penicillin. As a result, new drug therapies are needed to treat gonorrhea. **Figure 37.7** shows the increase in gonorrhea resistance as the bacteria have gained resistance to treatment with antibiotics.

Another treatment problem is with staphylococcal disease: it is acquired in a hospital, which can result in skin infections, pneumonia (noo MOH nyuh), or meningitis. These staphylococci often are strains of bacteria that are resistant to many current antibiotics and can be difficult to treat.

## Section 37.1 Assessment

### Section Summary

- Pathogens, such as bacteria, viruses, protozoans, and fungi, cause infectious diseases.
- Koch's postulates demonstrate how to show that a particular pathogen causes a certain disease.
- Pathogens are found in disease reservoirs and are transmitted to humans by direct and indirect methods.
- The symptoms of disease are caused by invasion of the pathogen and the response of the host immune system.
- Treatment of infectious disease includes the use of antibiotics and antiviral drugs.

### Understand Main Ideas

1. MAIN Idea **Compare** the mode of transmission of the common cold with that of malaria.
2. **Explain** how bacteria cause symptoms of bacterial infectious disease.
3. **Define** *infectious disease* and give three examples of infectious diseases.
4. **Application** Draw a graphic organizer or concept map illustrating Koch's postulates for a bacterial infectious disease in a rabbit.
5. **Infer** why a person might be exposed to tetanus bacteria after stepping on a dirty nail.

### Think Scientifically

6. *Evaluate* the following scenario: Two days after visiting a pet shop and observing green parrots in a display cage and fish in an aquarium, a student developed a fever, became quite ill, and was diagnosed with parrot fever. What might be the disease reservoir and possible transmission method?

7. *Evaluate* Animal feed often is medicated with a low level of antibiotics. Evaluate how this might play a role in the development of antibiotic-resistant bacteria.

## Section 37.2

### Objectives

- **Compare and contrast** nonspecific and specific immunity.
- **Summarize** the structure and function of the lymphatic system.
- **Distinguish** between passive and active immunity.

### Review Vocabulary

**white blood cells:** large, nucleated blood cells that play a major role in protecting the body from foreign substances and microorganisms

### New Vocabulary

complement protein
interferon
lymphocyte
antibody
B cell
helper T cell
cytotoxic T cell
memory cell
immunization

# The Immune System

**MAIN Idea** **The immune system has two main components: nonspecific immunity and specific immunity.**

**Real-World Reading Link** We live with a number of potential pathogens such as bacteria and viruses that can cause disease. Like a fort protecting a city from attack, the immune system protects the body against these and other disease-causing organisms.

## Nonspecific Immunity

At the time of birth, the body has a number of defenses in the immune system that fight off pathogens. These defenses are nonspecific because they are not aimed at a specific pathogen. They protect the body from any pathogen that the body encounters.

The nonspecific immunity provided by the body helps to prevent disease. Nonspecific immunity also helps to slow the progression of the disease while the specific immunity begins to develop its defenses. Specific immunity is the most effective immune response, but nonspecific immunity is the first line of defense.

**Barriers** Like the strong walls of a fort, barriers are used by the body to protect against pathogens. These barriers are found in areas of the body where pathogens might enter.

**FOLDABLES** Incorporate information from this section into your Foldable.

**Skin barrier** One of the simplest ways that the body avoids infectious disease is by preventing foreign organisms from entering the body. This major line of defense is the unbroken skin and its secretions. Recall that the skin contains layers of living cells covered by many layers of dead skin cells. By forming a barrier, the layers of dead skin cells help protect against invasion by microorganisms. Many of the bacteria that live symbiotically on the skin digest skin oils to produce acids that inhibit many pathogens. **Figure 37.8** shows some normal bacteria found on the skin that protect the skin from attack.

■ **Figure 37.8** These bacteria normally are found on human skin.

Color-Enhanced SEM Magnification: 14,000×

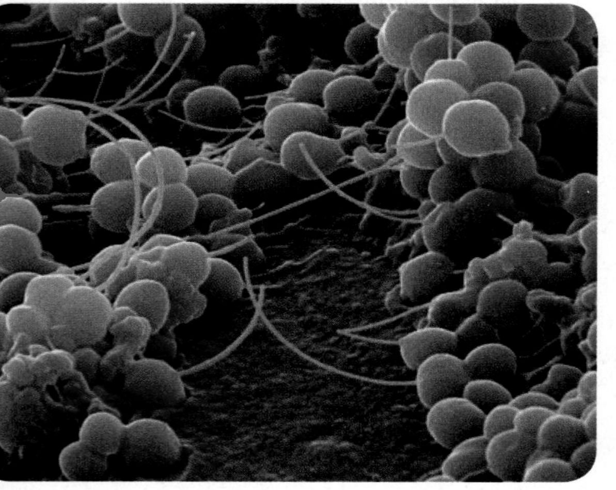

**Chemical barriers** Saliva, tears, and nasal secretions contain the enzyme lysozyme. Lysozyme breaks down bacterial cell walls, which kills pathogens.

Another chemical defense is mucus, which is secreted by many inner surfaces of the body. It acts as a protective barrier, blocking bacteria from sticking to the inner epithelial cells. Cilia, discussed in Chapter 7, also line the airway. Their beating motion sends any bacteria caught in the mucus away from the lungs. When the airway becomes infected, extra mucus is secreted, which triggers coughing and sneezing to help move the infected mucus out of the body.

A third chemical defense is the hydrochloric acid secreted in your stomach. In addition to its purpose in digestion, stomach acid kills many microorganisms found in food that could cause disease.

**Nonspecific responses to invasion** Even if an enemy gets through the walls of a town's fort, defense doesn't end. Similarly, the body has nonspecific immune responses to pathogens that get beyond its barriers.

**Cellular defense** If foreign microorganisms enter the body, the cells of the immune system, shown in **Table 37.2,** defend the body. One method of defense is phagocytosis. White blood cells, especially neutrophils and macrophages, are phagocytic. Recall from Chapter 7 and Chapter 34 that phagocytosis is the process by which phagocytic cells surround and internalize the foreign microorganisms. The phagocytes then release digestive enzymes and other harmful chemicals from their lysosomes, destroying the microorganism.

A series of about 20 proteins that are found in the blood plasma are involved in phagocytosis. These proteins are called complement proteins. **Complement proteins** enhance phagocytosis by helping the phagocytic cells bind better to pathogens, activating the phagocytes and enhancing the destruction of the pathogen's membrane, as illustrated in **Figure 37.9.** They are activated by materials that are in the cell wall of bacteria.

**Interferon** When a virus enters the body, another cellular defense helps prevent the virus from spreading. Virus-infected cells secrete a protein called **interferon.** Interferon binds to neighboring cells and stimulates these cells to produce antiviral proteins which can prevent viral replication in these cells.

**Inflammatory response** Another nonspecific response—the inflammatory response—is a complex series of events that involves many chemicals and immune cells that help enhance the overall immune response. When pathogens damage tissue, chemicals are released by both the invader and cells of the body. These chemicals attract phagocytes to the area, increase blood flow to the infected area, and make blood vessels more permeable to allow white blood cells to escape into the infected area. This response aids in the accumulation of white blood cells in the area. Some of the pain, heat, and redness experienced in an infectious disease are the result of the inflammatory response.

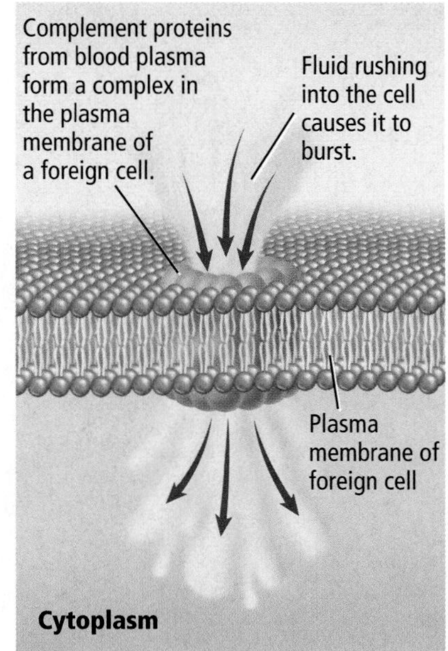

Complement proteins from blood plasma form a complex in the plasma membrane of a foreign cell.
Fluid rushing into the cell causes it to burst.
Plasma membrane of foreign cell
Cytoplasm

**Figure 37.9** Complement proteins form a hole in the plasma membrane of the invading cell.

**Concepts In Motion**
**Interactive Figure** To see an animation of how the complement system can destroy a pathogen, visit biologygmh.com.

**Concepts In Motion**
**Interactive Table** To explore more about cells of the immune system, visit biologygmh.com.

**Table 37.2 Cells of the Immune System**

| Type of Cell | Example | Function |
|---|---|---|
| Neutrophils | Stained LM Magnification: 2150× | Phagocytosis: blood cells that ingest bacteria |
| Macrophages | Stained LM Magnification: 380× | Phagocytosis: blood cells that ingest bacteria and remove dead neutrophils and other debris |
| Lymphocytes | Stained LM Magnification: 1800× | Specific immunity (antibodies and killing of pathogens): blood cells that produce antibodies and other chemicals |

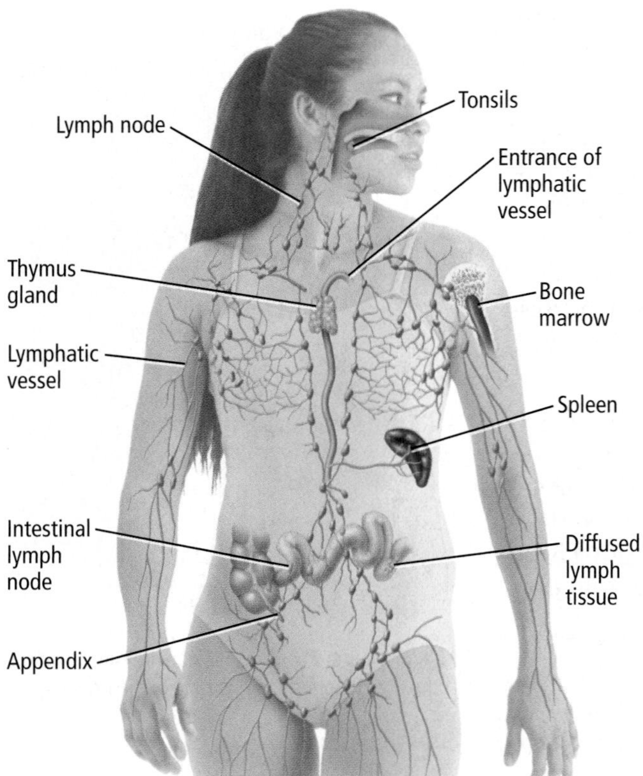


■ **Figure 37.10** The lymphatic system contains the organs involved in the specific immune response.
**Identify** ***Locate the lymphatic organ that is important for T cell development.***

**VOCABULARY**
**WORD ORIGIN**
**Thymus**
Comes from the Greek word *thymos,* meaning *warty excrescence.*

# Specific Immunity

Pathogens sometimes get past the nonspecific defense mechanisms. The body has a second line of defense that attacks these pathogens. Specific immunity is more effective, but takes time to develop. This specific response involves the tissues and organs found in the lymphatic system.

**Lymphatic system** The lymphatic (lim FA tihk) system, illustrated in **Figure 37.10,** includes organs and cells that filter lymph and blood and destroy foreign microorganisms. The lymphatic system also absorbs fat. Lymph is the fluid that leaks out of capillaries to bathe body cells. This fluid circulates among the tissue cells, is collected by lymphatic vessels, and is returned to the veins near the heart.

**Lymphatic organs** The organs of the lymphatic system contain lymphatic tissue, lymphocytes, a few other cell types, and connective tissue. **Lymphocytes** are a type of white blood cell that is produced in red bone marrow. These lymphatic organs include the lymph nodes, tonsils, spleen, thymus (THI mus) gland, and diffused lymphatic tissue found in mucous membranes of the intestinal, respiratory, urinary, and genital tracts.

The lymph nodes filter the lymph and remove foreign materials from the lymph. The tonsils form a protective ring of lymphatic tissue between the nasal and oral cavities. This helps protect against bacteria and other harmful materials in the nose and mouth. The spleen stores blood and destroys damaged red blood cells. It also contains lymphatic tissue that responds to foreign substances in the blood. The thymus gland, which is located above the heart, plays a role in activating a special kind of lymphocyte called T cells. T cells are produced in the bone marrow, but they mature in the thymus gland.

# B Cell Response

**Antibodies** are proteins produced by B lymphocytes that specifically react with a foreign antigen. An antigen is a substance foreign to the body that causes an imune response; it can bind to an antibody or T cell. B lymphocytes, often called **B cells,** are located in all lymphatic tissues and can be thought of as antibody factories. When a portion of a pathogen is presented by a macrophage, B cells produce antibodies. Follow along in **Figure 37.11,** as you learn about how B cells are activated to produce antibodies.

# Visualizing Specific Immune Responses

**Figure 37.11**

Specific immune responses involve antigens, phagocytes, B cells, helper T cells, and cytotoxic T cells. The antibody-mediated response involves antibodies produced by B cells and memory B cells. The cytotoxic T cell response results in cytotoxic T cell activation.

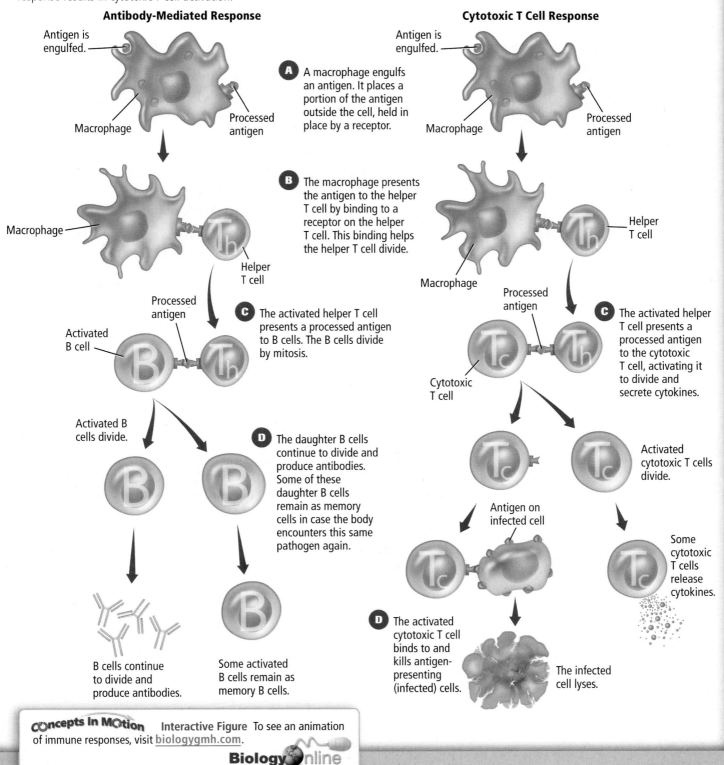

**Antibody-Mediated Response**

Antigen is engulfed.

Macrophage

Processed antigen

**A** A macrophage engulfs an antigen. It places a portion of the antigen outside the cell, held in place by a receptor.

Macrophage

Helper T cell

**B** The macrophage presents the antigen to the helper T cell by binding to a receptor on the helper T cell. This binding helps the helper T cell divide.

Processed antigen

Activated B cell

**C** The activated helper T cell presents a processed antigen to B cells. The B cells divide by mitosis.

Activated B cells divide.

**D** The daughter B cells continue to divide and produce antibodies. Some of these daughter B cells remain as memory cells in case the body encounters this same pathogen again.

B cells continue to divide and produce antibodies.

Some activated B cells remain as memory B cells.

**Cytotoxic T Cell Response**

Antigen is engulfed.

Macrophage

Processed antigen

Helper T cell

Macrophage

Processed antigen

Cytotoxic T cell

**C** The activated helper T cell presents a processed antigen to the cytotoxic T cell, activating it to divide and secrete cytokines.

Activated cytotoxic T cells divide.

Antigen on infected cell

Some cytotoxic T cells release cytokines.

**D** The activated cytotoxic T cell binds to and kills antigen-presenting (infected) cells.

The infected cell lyses.

Concepts In Motion **Interactive Figure** To see an animation of immune responses, visit biologygmh.com.

Biology Online

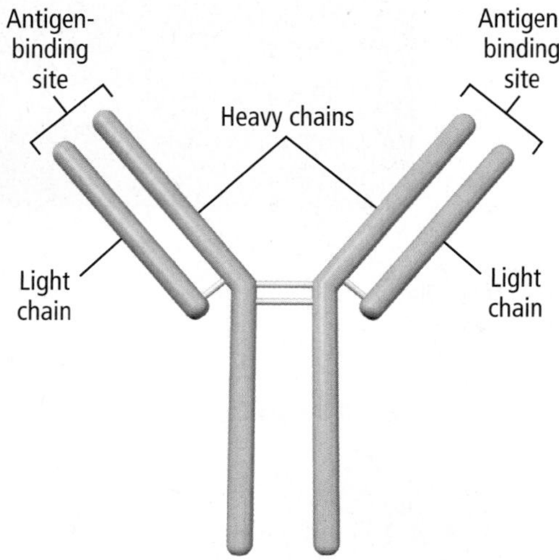


■ **Figure 37.12** Antibodies are made up of two types of protein chains—heavy and light chains.
**Summarize** *What cells produce antibodies?*

When a macrophage surrounds, internalizes, and digests a pathogen, it takes a piece of the pathogen, which is called a processed antigen, and displays it on its membrane, as illustrated in **Figure 37.11.** In the lymphatic tissues, such as the lymph nodes, the macrophage, with the processed antigen on its surface, binds to a type of lymphocyte called a **helper T cell.** This process activates the helper T cell. This lymphocyte is called a "helper" because it activates antibody secretion in B cells and another type of T cell, which will be discussed later, that aids in killing microorganisms:

- The activated helper T cell reproduces, binds processed antigens, and attaches to a B cell.
- The new helper T cells continue the process of binding antigens, attaching to B cells, and reproducing.
- Once an activated helper T cell binds to a B cell holding an antigen, the B cell begins to manufacture antibodies that specifically bind to the antigen.
- The antibodies can enhance the immune response by binding to microorganisms, making them more susceptible to phagocytosis and by initiating the inflammatory response, helping promote the nonspecific response.

B cells make many combinations of antibodies by using DNA that codes for the production of various heavy and light protein chains that make up antibodies as shown in **Figure 37.12.** Any heavy chain can combine with any light chain. If a B cell can make 16,000 different kinds of heavy chains and 1200 kinds of light chains, it can make 19,200,000 different types of antibodies (1200 × 16,000).

## T Cell Response

Once helper T cells are activated by the presentation of an antigen by macrophages, helper T cells can also bind to and activate a group of lymphocytes called cytotoxic T cells. Activated **cytotoxic T cells** destroy pathogens and release chemicals called cytokines. Cytokines stimulate the cells of the immune system to divide and recruit immune cells to an area of infection. Cytotoxic T cells bind to pathogens, release a chemical attack, and destroy the pathogens. Multiple target cells can be destroyed by a single cytotoxic T cell. **Figure 37.11** summarizes the activation of cytotoxic T cells.

**Reading Check** **Summarize** the role that lymphocytes play in immunity.

## Passive and Active Immunity

The body's first response to an invasion by a pathogen is called the primary response. For example, if the viral pathogen that causes chicken pox enters the body, nonspecific and specific immune responses eventually defeat the foreign virus and the body is cleared of the pathogen.

One result of the specific immune response is the production of memory B and T cells. **Memory cells** are long-living cells that are exposed to the antigen during the primary immune response. These cells are ready to respond rapidly if the body encounters the same pathogen later. Memory cells protect the body by reducing the likelihood of developing the disease if exposed again to the same pathogen.

**Passive immunity** Sometimes temporary protection against an infectious disease is needed. This type of temporary protection occurs when antibodies are made by other people or animals and are transferred or injected into the body. For example, passive immunity occurs between a mother and her child. Antibodies produced by the mother are passed through the placenta to the developing fetus and through breast milk to the infant child. These antibodies can protect the child until the infant's immune system matures.

Antibodies developed in humans and animals that are already immune to a specific infectious disease are used to treat some infectious diseases in others. These antibodies are injected into people who have been exposed to that particular infectious disease. Passive immune therapy is available for people who have been exposed to hepatitis A and B, tetanus, and rabies. Antibodies also are available to inactivate snake and scorpion venoms.

**Active immunity** Active immunity occurs after the immune system is exposed to disease antigens and memory cells are produced. Active immunity can result from having an infectious disease or immunization. **Immunization,** also called vaccination, is the deliberate exposure of the body to an antigen so that a primary response and immune memory cells will develop. **Table 37.3** lists some of the common immunizations offered in the United States. Immunizations contain killed or weakened pathogens, which are incapable of causing the disease.

Most immunizations include more than one stimulus to the immune system, given after the first immunization. These booster shots increase the immune response, providing further protection from the disease-causing organism.

**VOCABULARY**

**ACADEMIC VOCABULARY**

**Passive:**
not active; acted upon.
*The passive monkey stared lazily at the zoo visitors.*

**Concepts In Motion**

**Interactive Table** To explore more about immunizations, visit biologygmh.com.

**Table 37.3 Common Immunizations**

| Immunization | Disease | Contents |
|---|---|---|
| DPT | Diphtheria (D), tetanus (T), pertussis (P) (whooping cough) | D: inactivated toxin, T: inactivated toxin, P: inactivated bacteria |
| Inactivated polio | Poliomyelitis | Inactivated virus |
| MMR | Measles, mumps, rubella | All three inactivated viruses |
| Varicella | Chicken pox | Inactivated virus |
| HIB | Haemophilus influenzae (flu) type b | Portions of bacteria cell wall covering |
| HBV | Hepatitis B | Subunit of virus |

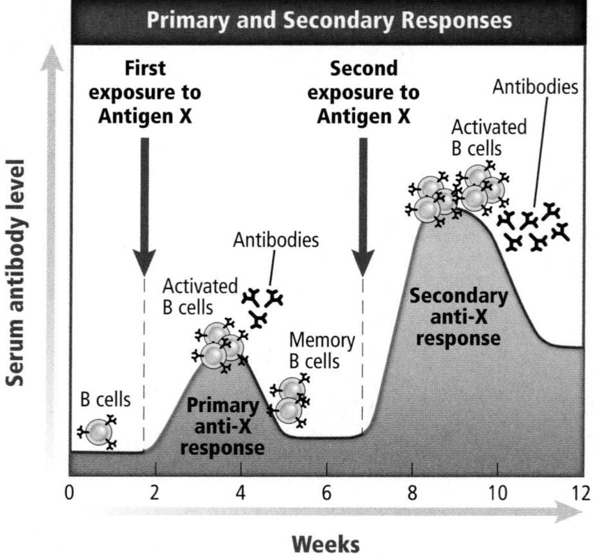


■ **Figure 37.13** This graph shows the difference between the primary and secondary immune responses to exposure to an antigen.

**Analyze** ***What are the differences between the primary and secondary immune responses?***

Why are immunizations effective in preventing disease? The characteristics of the secondary immune response, which is the response to a second exposure to an antigen, enable immunizations to be effective in preventing disease. Study the graph in **Figure 37.13.** Note that the secondary response to the antigen has a number of different characteristics. First, the response is more rapid than the primary response, as shown by the greater steepness in the portion of the curves plotted in red. Second, the overall response, both B and T cell response, is greater during the second exposure. Lastly, the overall memory lasts longer after the second exposure.

## Immune System Failure

Defects in the immune system can result in an increased likelihood of developing infectious diseases as well as certain types of cancers. Some diseases can affect the immune system's effectiveness. One such disease called acquired immunodeficiency syndrome (AIDS) results from an infection by human immunodeficiency virus (HIV). AIDS is a serious health problem worldwide.

In 2003, approximately 43,171 AIDS cases were diagnosed in the U.S. In 2003, 18,017 people died of AIDS in the U.S. In 2004, an estimated 40 million people globally were living with HIV infection.

## DATA ANALYSIS LAB 37.1

### Based on Real Data*

### Draw a Conclusion

**Is passive immune therapy effective for HIV infection?** The standard treatment for a patient with an HIV infection is antiviral drug therapy. Unfortunately, the side effects and increasing prevalence of drug-resistant viruses create a need for additional therapies. One area being studied is passive immune therapy.

#### Data and Observations

The graph shows HIV patient responses to passive immune therapy. The number of viral copies/mL is a measure of the amount of virus in the patient's blood.

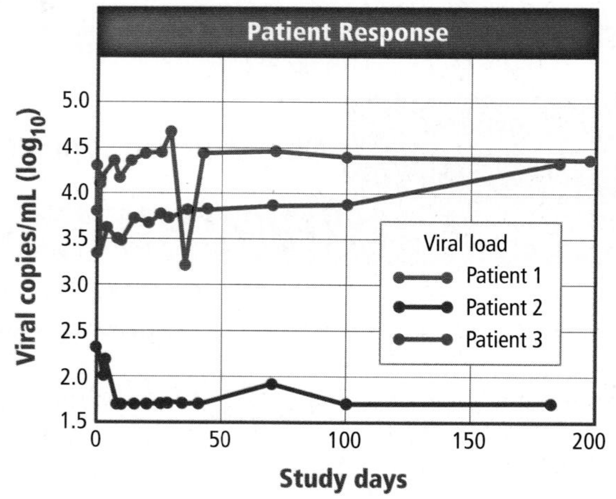


#### Think Critically

1. **Compare** the patient responses to passive immune therapy.
2. **Draw a conclusion** Can the researchers conclude passive immune therapy is effective? Explain.

*Data obtained from: Stiegler G., et al. 2002. Antiviral activity of the neutralizing antibodies 2FS and 2F12 in asymptomatic HIV-1-infected humans: a phase I evaluation. *AIDS* 16: 2019-2025.

Recall the important role that helper T cells play in specific immunity. HIV infects mainly helper T cells, also called $CD4^+$ cells because these cells have a receptor on the outside of their plasma membrane. This $CD4^+$ receptor is used by medical professionals to identify these cells, as illustrated in **Figure 37.14.**

In Chapter 18, you learned that HIV is an RNA virus that infects helper T cells. The helper T cells become HIV factories, producing new viruses that are released and infect other helper T cells. Over time, the number of helper T cells in an infected person decreases, making the person less able to fight disease. HIV infection usually has an early phase during the first six to twelve weeks while viruses are replicating in helper T cells.

The patient suffers symptoms such as night sweats and fever, but these symptoms are reduced after about eight to ten weeks. Then, the patient exhibits few symptoms for a period of time as long as ten years, but is capable of passing the infection through sexual intercourse or blood products. HIV is a secondary immunodeficiency disease, which means that the immune system of a previously healthy person fails. Without antiviral drug therapy, the patient usually dies from a secondary infection from another pathogen after about ten years of being infected with HIV. Current antiviral drug therapy is aimed at controlling the replication of HIV in the body. The therapy is expensive and its long-term results are not known.

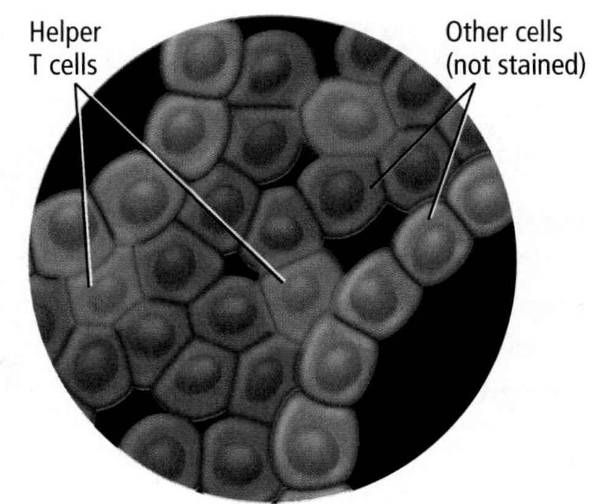


**Figure 37.14** Helper T cells have receptors on the surface that are used to identifiy them in the laboratory.

## Section 37.2 Assessment

### Section Summary

- The nonspecific immune response includes the skin barrier, secreted chemicals, and cellular pathways that activate phagocytosis.
- The specific immune response involves the activation of B cells, which produce antibodies, and T cells, which include helper T cells and cytotoxic T cells.
- Passive immunity involves receiving antibodies against a disease.
- Active immunity results in immune memory against a disease.
- HIV attacks helper T cells, causing an immune system failure.

### Understand Main Ideas

1. MAIN Idea **Identify** the cells that are involved in the nonspecific and specific immune responses.
2. **Describe** the steps involved in activating an antibody response to an antigen.
3. **Make** an illustration demonstrating passive and active immunity.
4. **Describe** the structure and function of the lymphatic system.
5. **Infer** Why is the destruction of helper T cells in HIV infection so devastating to specific immunity?

### Think Scientifically

6. *Hypothesize* what will happen if the HIV virus mutates such that viral-replication drugs are no longer effective.
7. *Evaluate* In the disease called severe combined immune deficiency, a child is born without T cell immunity. Evaluate the effects of this disease.
8. **MATH in Biology** Antibodies are made of two light protein chains and two heavy protein chains. If the molecular weight of a light chain is 25,000 and the molecular weight of a heavy chain is 50,000, what is the molecular weight of an antibody?

# Noninfectious Disorders

**Objectives**

- **Describe** five categories of noninfectious diseases.
- **Summarize** the role of allergens in allergies.
- **Distinguish** between allergies and anaphylactic shock.

**Review Vocabulary**

**cancer:** uncontrolled cell division that can be caused by environmental factors and/or changes in enzyme production in the cell cycle

**New Vocabulary**

degenerative disease
metabolic disease
allergy
anaphylactic shock

**MAIN Idea Noninfectious disorders include genetic disorders, degenerative diseases, metabolic diseases, cancer, and inflammatory diseases.**

**Real-World Reading Link** Maybe you have heard your parents or grandparents complain about their arthritis, which causes achy bones and joints. Perhaps some of your relatives have survived cancer or have diabetes. You or a friend may have an allergy to dust, plant pollens, or other environmental substances. These disorders are different from infectious diseases caused by pathogens.

## Genetic Disorders

Not all diseases or body disorders are caused by pathogens. In Chapter 11 you read about some diseases caused by the inheritance of genes that do not function properly in the body, such as albinism, sickle cell anemia, Huntington disease, and hemophilia. There also are chromosomal disorders that result from abnormal chromosome numbers, such as Down syndrome. Many diseases are complex and have both an environmental and a genetic cause.

Coronary artery disease (CAD) is an example of a condition with environmental and genetic origin. This cardiovascular disease can result in blockage of arteries, as shown in **Figure 37.15,** that deliver oxygenated blood to the heart muscle. There is a genetic component that increases a person's risk of developing CAD. Environmental factors such as diet contribute to the development of this complex disease. Families with a history of CAD have a two to seven times greater risk of having CAD than families without a history of CAD. The exact genetic factors, however, are not known.

**Figure 37.15** When blood cannot flow through a coronary artery, such as the one shown here, a heart attack or sudden death can result.

Stained LM Magnification: 5×

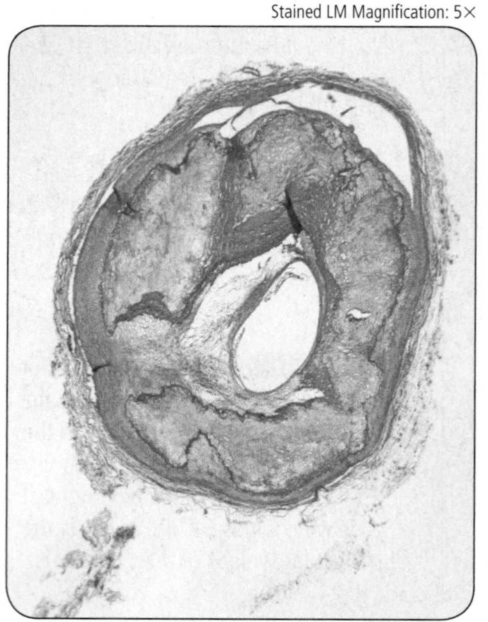

**Reading Check Summarize** the factors that cause coronary artery disease.

## Degenerative Diseases

Some diseases called **degenerative diseases** (dih JEH nuh ruh tihv • dih ZEEZS) are the result of a part of the body wearing out. This can be due to the natural aging process. However, in many cases, degenerative conditions occur sooner than would be expected in a person's lifetime. Degenerative arthritis and arteriosclerosis (ar tir ee oh skluh ROH sus), which is also referred to as hardening of the arteries, are examples of degenerative diseases. Degenerative arthritis is common. Most people have the disease by the age of 70 years, and the disease is found in almost all vertebrate animals. Because many degenerative diseases also have a genetic component, some individuals might be more likely to develop a disease because of their genetic makeup.

## Metabolic Diseases

**Metabolic disease** results from an error in a biochemical pathway. Some metabolic diseases result in the inability to digest specific amino acids or to regulate body processes. When the pancreas does not make the proper amount of insulin and glucose does not enter body cells normally, the condition known as Type 1 diabetes results. This results in high glucose levels in the bloodstream, which causes damage to many organs including the kidneys and the retinas of the eyes. Metabolic diseases can have a genetic component but also can involve environmental factors such as diet.

## Cancer

In Chapter 9, you learned about cancer. Cancer is characterized by abnormal cell growth. Normally, certain regulatory molecules in the body control the beginning and end of the cell cycle. If this control is lost, abnormal cell growth results that could lead to various types of tumors, as shown in **Figure 37.16.** The abnormal cells can interfere with normal body functions and can travel throughout the body. Cancer can develop in any body tissue or organ, including the blood cells. Cancer in the blood cells is called leukemia. Both genetic and environmental factors have been shown to cause cancer.

**Connection to History** Cancer has been a disease that affects humans since ancient times. Egyptian mummies show evidence of bone cancer, and ancient Greek scientists described different kinds of cancer. Medieval manuscripts have reported details about cancer.

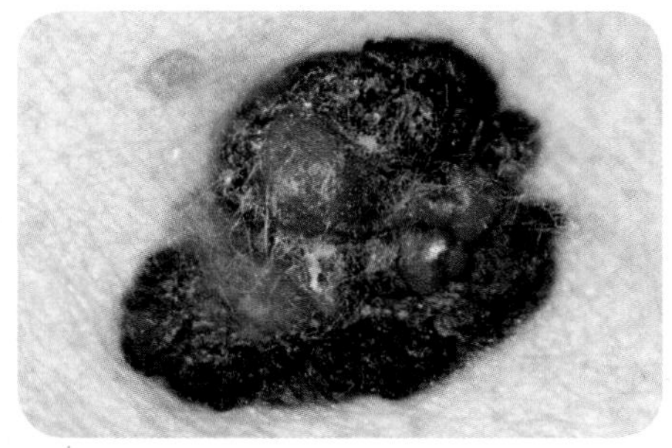

**Figure 37.16** Cancer is due to an abnormal increase in cell division in the body, which results in a tumor such as this skin tumor. **Infer** ***Why is this large growth so life-threatening?***

## MiniLab 37.2

### Compare Cancerous and Healthy Cells

**How do cancerous cells and healthy cells differ in appearance?** Observe and compare liver cells afflicted with this common noninfectious disease to healthy liver cells.

**Procedure**

1. Read and complete the lab safety form.
2. Place a prepared **slide of healthy human liver cells** on a **microscope.** **WARNING:** ***Never touch broken microscope slides or other broken glass materials.***
3. Observe the healthy liver cells under several different magnifications.
4. Sketch a diagram of several healthy liver cells.
5. Repeat steps 2–4 with a prepared **slide of cancerous human liver cells.**

**Analysis**

1. **Compare and contrast** the features of healthy liver cells with those of cancerous liver cells.
2. **Infer** why it would not be dangerous to handle an object that was handled by a patient with liver cancer.
3. **Describe** how cancer disrupts the body's homeostasis.

LM Magnification: 50×

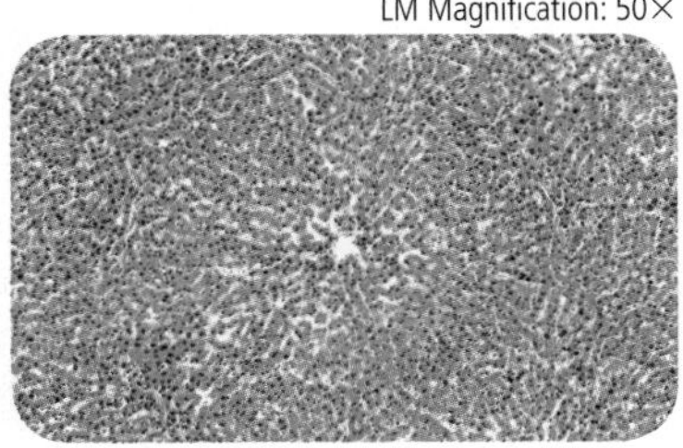

**Healthy cells**

LM Magnification: 50×

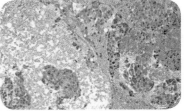

**Cancerous cells**

## Inflammatory Diseases

Inflammatory diseases, such as allergies and autoimmunity, are diseases in which the body produces an inflammatory response to a common substance. Recall from Section 2 that infectious diseases also result in an inflammatory response. However, the inflammatory response in an infectious disease enhances the overall immune response. This inflammatory response is a result of the immune system removing bacteria or other microorganisms from the body. In inflammatory disease, the inflammatory response is not helpful to the body.

**Allergies** Certain individuals might have an abnormal reaction to environmental antigens. A response to environmental antigens is called an **allergy.** These antigens are called allergens and include things such as plant pollens, dust, dust mites, and various foods, as illustrated in **Table 37.4.** An individual becomes sensitized to the allergen and has localized inflammatory response with swollen itchy eyes, stuffy nose, sneezing, and sometimes a skin rash. These symptoms are the result of a chemical called histamine that is released by certain white blood cells. Antihistamine medications can help alleviate some of these symptoms.

**Reading Check** **Explain** how allergies are related to the immune system.

**Table 37.4 Common Allergens**

Concepts In Motion
**Interactive Table** To explore more about common allergens, visit biologygmh.com.

| Allergen | Example | Description |
|---|---|---|
| **Dust mite** | Color-Enhanced SEM Magnification: 170× | Dust mites are found in mattresses, pillows, and carpets. Mites and mite feces are allergens. |
| **Plant pollen** | Color-Enhanced SEM Magnification: 2300× | Different parts of the country have very different pollen seasons; people can react to one or more pollens, and a person's pollen allergy season might be from early spring to late fall. |
| **Animal dander** | Color-Enhanced SEM Magnification: 80× | Dander is skin flakes; cat and dog allergies are the most common, but people also are allergic to pets such as birds, hamsters, rabbits, mice, and gerbils. |
| **Peanut** | | Allergic reaction to peanuts can result in anaphylaxis. Peanut allergy is responsible for more fatalities than any other type of allergy. |
| **Latex** | | Latex comes from the milky sap of the rubber tree, found in Africa and Southeast Asia; the exact cause of latex allergy is unknown. |

Severe allergic reactions to particular allergens can result in **anaphylactic** (an uh fuh LAK tik) **shock,** which causes a massive release of histamine. In anaphylactic shock, the smooth muscles in the bronchioles contract, which restricts air flow into and out of the lungs.

Common allergens that cause severe allergic reactions are bee stings, penicillin, peanuts, and latex, which is used to make balloons and surgical gloves. People who are extremely sensitive to these allergens require prompt medical treatment if exposed to these agents because anaphylactic reactions are life-threatening. Allergies and anaphylactic reactions are known to have an inherited component.

**Autoimmunity** During the development of the immune system, the immune system learns not to attack proteins produced by the body. However, some people develop autoimmunity (aw toh ih MYOON ih tee) and do form antibodies to their own proteins, which injures their cells.

**Figure 37.17** shows the hands of a person with rheumatoid arthritis—a form of arthritis in which antibodies attack the joints. Degenerative arthritis, the form of arthritis that you read about earlier in the section on degenerative diseases, is not caused by autoimmunity.

Rheumatic fever and lupus (LEW pus) are other examples of autoimmune disorders. Rheumatic fever is an inflammation in which antibodies attack the valves of the heart. This can lead to damage to the heart valves and cause the valves to leak or not close properly as blood moves through the heart. Lupus is a disorder in which antibodies against cell nuclei, called antinuclear antibodies, are formed. As a result, many organs are vulnerable to attack by the body's own immune system.

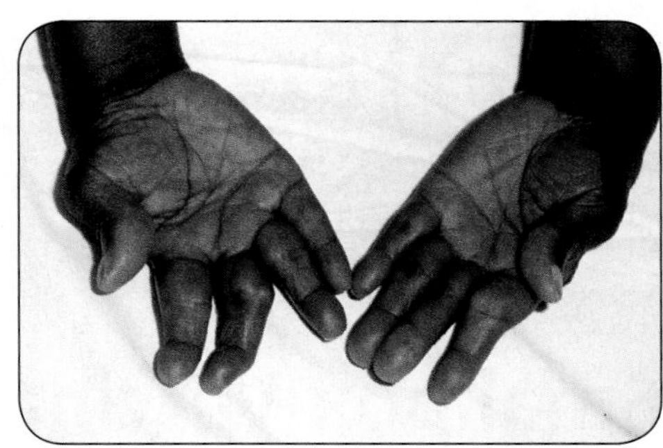

■ **Figure 37.17** The large knobs on these fingers are due to rheumatoid arthritis—an autoimmune disease.

**CAREERS IN BIOLOGY**

**Rheumatologist** A rheumatologist is a doctor who specializes in the diagnosis and treatment of diseases of the muscles and joints. For more information on biology careers, visit biologygmh.com.

# Section 37.3 Assessment

## Section Summary

- Noninfectious disorders often have both a genetic and an environmental component.
- The inflammatory response to an infectious disease enhances the immune response, but the inflammatory response to an inflammatory disease is not helpful to the body.
- Allergies are due to an overactive immune response to allergens found in the environment.
- Anaphylactic shock is a severe hypersensitivity to particular allergens.
- Autoimmunity results in an immune attack on body cells.

## Understand Main Ideas

1. MAIN Idea **Identify** the type of noninfectious disease shown in **Figure 37.15.**
2. **Explain** the role of allergens in allergies.
3. **Sketch** a diagram demonstrating the process of anaphylactic shock.
4. **Categorize** the following diseases into the categories used in this section: sickle cell disease, diabetes, vertebral degeneration, autoimmunity, and leukemia.

## Think Scientifically

5. *Hypothesize* several causes of chronic bronchitis (inflammation of the bronchioles) found in coal miners.
6. *Create a plan* A child is found to be allergic to cat dander. Create a plan that limits the child's exposure to the allergen.
7. WRITING in Biology Create a pamphlet explaining the symptoms of allergies and listing common allergens.

# Biology & Society

## Smallpox Vaccination and Bioterrorism

The smallpox virus spreads quickly among people and can kill up to 30% of those infected. Because smallpox is so lethal, the government has debated for years whether there should be mandatory vaccination of the American public. The debate still goes on today.

**Smallpox as a Disease** Smallpox is caused by a virus for which there is no cure; however, in 1796, Edward Jenner developed the smallpox vaccine, which helped save an enormous number of lives by preventing the disease. It is widely believed that the virus currently exists only in laboratories in the United States and Russia. However, there are concerns that terrorists might obtain the virus and release it.

**Bioterrorism and Smallpox** The last case of smallpox in the U.S. occurred in 1949, and routine vaccination in the U.S. ended in 1972. Smallpox persisted in other countries well into the 1970s until vaccination programs were able to completely eliminate the disease. It was declared to be wiped out in 1980.

Immunity developed from vaccination lasts for about three to five years. Vaccination also prevents infection or lessens the effects of infection if given within a few days after exposure. If bioterrorists were to obtain smallpox and spread it into the U.S. population, the Centers for Disease Control and Prevention (CDC) has a plan to provide vaccines to people exposed to the virus within three days to lessen the effect of the disease or to prevent the disease altogether. The U.S. supply of vaccine is securely stored in the event of an outbreak so that there is enough vaccine for everyone. However, even with all the precautions the U.S. government has in place there is no guarantee that an outbreak could be prevented.

If smallpox is so lethal, why not just vaccinate everyone in the U.S. on a regular basis? Mandatory vaccination is not necessarily an option because many people would suffer consequences from the vaccine. For example, at least 25 percent of our population has suppression of the immune system due to drugs or illness. Receiving the smallpox vaccine could result in serious complications for these individuals because their immune systems are in a weakened state.

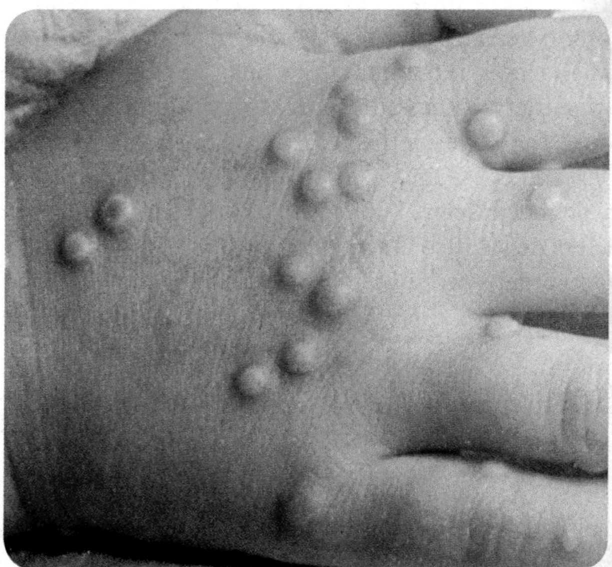

The term *smallpox* refers to the bumps that appear on the face and body as a result of infection with the smallpox virus.

The U.S. government and the CDC take the possibility of smallpox outbreaks very seriously, and the debate over mandatory vaccination will likely continue as long as bioterrorism is a threat.

**DEBATE in Biology**

Should the entire population be vaccinated on a regular basis against smallpox? Conduct additional research about smallpox and bioterrorism at biologygmh.com and then split up into teams to debate the issue.

# BIOLAB

## FORENSICS: HOW DO YOU FIND PATIENT ZERO?

**Background: Imagine that a new disease—"Cellphonitis"—has invaded your school. One of the symptoms of this disease is the urge to use a cell phone during class. Cellphonitis is easily transferred from person to person by direct contact and there is no natural immunity to the disease. A student in your class has the disease, and is Patient Zero. The disease is spreading in your class and you need to track the disease to prevent the spread of an epidemic.**

**Question:** *Is it possible to track a disease and determine the identity of Patient Zero?*

### Materials

Pasteur pipets (1 per group)
numbered test tubes of water, one infected with simulated "cellphonitis" (1 per group)
test tube racks (1 per group)
small paper cups (1 per group)
pencil and paper
testing indicator

### Safety Precautions

### Procedure

1. Read and complete the lab safety form.
2. Prepare a table to keep track of the contacts you make. Select a test tube and record the number of the test tube.
3. Use a Pasteur pipet and move a small amount of the fluid from the test tube to a paper cup.
4. Your teacher will divide your class into groups. When your group is called, you will simulate the sharing of saliva during drinking water by using your pipets to exchange the fluid in your test tubes with another member of your group.
5. Record who you exchanged with in your tables.
6. Roll the test tube gently between your hands to mix and repeat Step 4 every time your group is told to exchange. Be sure to pick someone different to exchange with each time.
7. When the exchanges are complete, your teacher will act as the epidemiologist and use the testing indicator to see who has the disease.
8. Share the information and work together as groups to see if you can determine the identity of Patient Zero.
9. Once each group has made their hypothesis, test the original fluid in each cup to see who really was Patient Zero.
10. Return the test tubes. Dispose of the other materials you used as instructed by your teacher.

### Analyze and Conclude

1. **Analyze** Use your data and draw a diagram for each possible Patient Zero. Use arrows to show who should be infected with each possible Patient Zero.
2. **Compare and Contrast** How was the spread of "cellphonitis" in this simulation similar to the spread of disease in real life? How was it different?
3. **Think Critically** If this simulation were run in a large class, why might the disease not be passed in later exchanges?
4. **Error Analysis** What problems did you run into as you tried to determine the identity of Patient Zero?

### COMMUNICATE

**Newscast** Use newspapers and other sources to learn about a current disease epidemic. Prepare a newscast of how epidemiologists are searching for the source of disease and present it to your class. To find out more about tracking disease, visit BioLabs at biologygmh.com.

# Chapter 37 Study Guide

FOLDABLES **Infer** the conditions under which each type of immunity would be used to deter pathogens.

| Vocabulary | Key Concepts |
|---|---|
| **Section 37.1 Infectious Diseases** | |
| • antibiotic (p. 1082)<br>• endemic disease (p. 1081)<br>• epidemic (p. 1081)<br>• infectious disease (p. 1076)<br>• Koch's postulates (p. 1077)<br>• pandemic (p. 1081)<br>• pathogen (p. 1076)<br>• reservoir (p. 1078) | MAIN Idea Pathogens are dispersed by people, other animals, and objects.<br>• Pathogens, such as bacteria, viruses, protozoans, and fungi, cause infectious diseases.<br>• Koch's postulates demonstrate how to show that a particular pathogen causes a certain disease.<br>• Pathogens are found in disease reservoirs and are transmitted to humans by direct and indirect methods.<br>• The symptoms of disease are caused by invasion of the pathogen and the response of the host immune system.<br>• Treatment of infectious disease includes the use of antibiotics and antiviral drugs. |
| **Section 37.2 The Immune System** | |
| • antibody (p. 1086)<br>• B cell (p. 1086)<br>• complement protein (p. 1085)<br>• cytotoxic T cell (p. 1088)<br>• helper T cell (p. 1088)<br>• immunization (p. 1089)<br>• interferon (p. 1085)<br>• lymphocyte (p. 1086)<br>• memory cell (p. 1089) | MAIN Idea The immune system has two main components: nonspecific immunity and specific immunity.<br>• The nonspecific immune response includes the skin barrier, secreted chemicals, and cellular pathways that activate phagocytosis.<br>• The specific immune response involves the activation of B cells, which produce antibodies, and T cells, which include helper T cells and cytotoxic T cells.<br>• Passive immunity involves receiving antibodies against a disease.<br>• Active immunity results in immune memory against a disease.<br>• HIV attacks helper T cells, causing an immune system failure. |
| **Section 37.3 Noninfectious Disorders** | |
| • allergy (p. 1094)<br>• anaphylactic shock (p. 1095)<br>• degenerative disease (p. 1092)<br>• metabolic disease (p. 1093) | MAIN Idea Noninfectious disorders include genetic disorders, degenerative diseases, metabolic diseases, cancer, and inflammatory diseases.<br>• Noninfectious disorders often have both a genetic and an environmental component.<br>• The inflammatory response to an infectious disease enhances the immune response, but the inflammatory response to an inflammatory disease is not helpful to the body.<br>• Allergies are due to an overactive immune response to allergens found in the environment.<br>• Anaphylactic shock is a severe hypersensitivity to particular allergens.<br>• Autoimmunity results in an immune attack on body cells. |

# CHAPTER 37 Assessment

## Section 37.1

### Vocabulary Review

*Match the definitions below with a vocabulary term from the Study Guide page.*

**1.** A(n) __________ is an agent that causes an infectious disease.

**2.** When a disease becomes widespread in a particular area, it is called a/an __________.

**3.** A source of disease organisms is called a __________.

### Understand Key Concepts

**4.** Which national organization tracks disease patterns in the United States?
**A.** The Centers for Disease Control and Prevention
**B.** National Disease Center
**C.** World Health Organization
**D.** United Nations

**5.** Which scientist established a method for determining whether a microorganism caused a specific disease?
**A.** Koch **C.** Sagan
**B.** Hooke **D.** Mendel

**6.** Which is the most common way that humans acquire an infectious disease?
**A.** contaminated water
**B.** mosquito bites
**C.** sick animals
**D.** infected humans

*Use the photo below to answer question 7.*

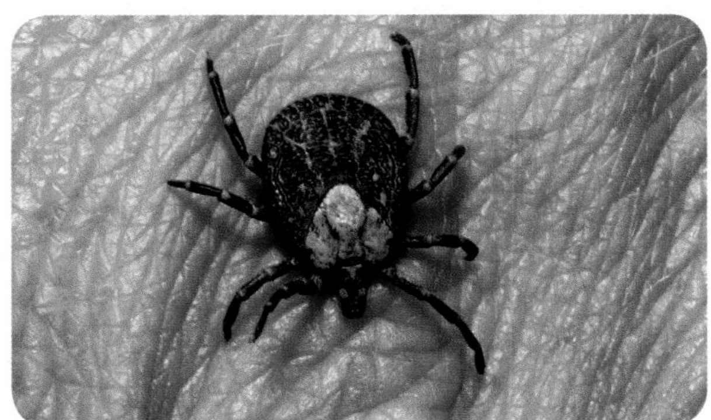

**7.** Which type of disease transmission is shown above?
**A.** direct contact **C.** object transmission
**B.** air transmission **D.** vector transmission

*Use the photo below to answer question 8.*

**8.** Which substance is secreted by the organism shown above?
**A.** anthrax **C.** gentamicin
**B.** influenza **D.** penicillin

### Constructed Response

**9. Open Ended** Explain how you could prove that a particular bacteria was causing an infectious disease in a mouse population.

**10. Open Ended** Explain how the Centers for Disease Control and Prevention would be able to determine if an epidemic was occurring in your city.

**11.** CAREERS IN BIOLOGY Imagine you are the school nurse. Describe to students more than one way the cold virus could be transmitted from one person to another.

### Think Critically

**12. Design** a feasible plan that could decrease the spread of infectious disease within your school.

**13. Evaluate** why growing viruses in cell cultures would be an exception to Koch's postulates.

## Section 37.2

### Vocabulary Review

*For questions 14–16, match each definition with a vocabulary term from the Study Guide page.*

**14.** a chemical produced by B cells in response to antigen stimulation

**15.** a cell that activates B cells and cytotoxic T cells

**16.** a type of white blood cell produced in the bone marrow that includes B and T cells

## Understand Key Concepts

*Use the diagram below to answer questions 17 and 18.*

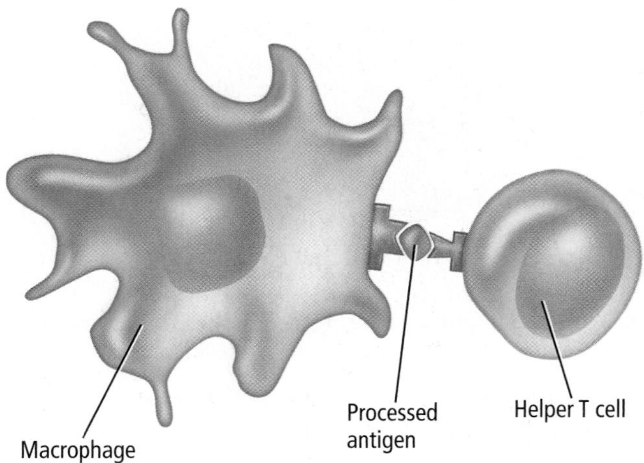


17. What kind of immune response is demonstrated in the diagram above?
    **A.** genetic
    **B.** nonspecific
    **C.** specific
    **D.** hormonal

18. To which does the activated helper T cell present its antigen?
    **A.** a pathogen
    **B.** bone marrow
    **C.** a B cell
    **D.** the thymus gland

19. Which is the first defense your body has against infectious disease?
    **A.** the helper T cell
    **B.** an antibody
    **C.** your skin
    **D.** phagocytosis

20. What is the role of complement proteins, found in the plasma, in the immune response?
    **A.** enhance phagocytosis
    **B.** activate phagocytes
    **C.** enhance destruction of a pathogen
    **D.** all of the above

21. Where are lymphocytes produced?
    **A.** bone marrow
    **B.** thymus gland
    **C.** spleen
    **D.** lymph nodes

## Constructed Response

22. **Short Answer** Describe how the thymus is involved in the development of immunity.

23. **Open Ended** Evaluate why the body needs both a nonspecific and a specific immune response.

24. **Open Ended** Form a hypothesis as to why the proportion of unvaccinated Americans is increasing.

## Think Critically

25. **Organize** the sequence of events that occur to activate an antibody response to tetanus bacteria.

26. **Compare** the role of helper T cells and cytotoxic T cells in the specific immune response.

# Section 37.3

## Vocabulary Review

*Use a vocabulary term from the Study Guide page to answer questions 27–29.*

27. What type of reaction is a hypersensitivity to an allergen such as a bee sting?

28. Which type of disease happens when people abnormally respond to environmental antigens?

29. Which type of disease is caused by a body part wearing out?

## Understand Key Concepts

*Use the photo below to answer question 30.*

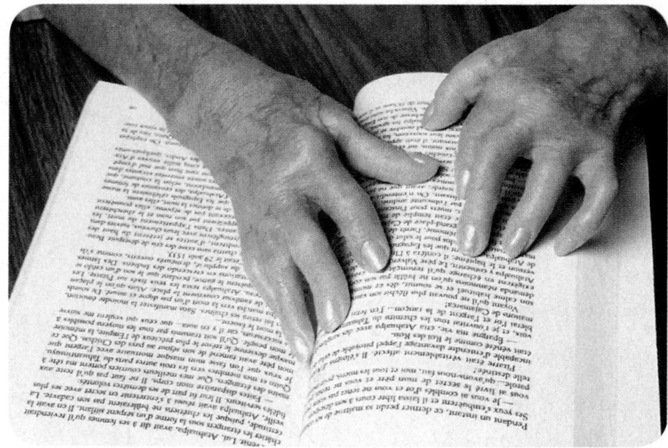

30. The above photo demonstrates which disease?
    **A.** tetanus
    **B.** sickle-cell disease
    **C.** rheumatoid arthritis
    **D.** allergy

31. Which type of noninfectious disease is defined as a problem in a biochemical pathway in the body?
    **A.** inflammatory disease
    **B.** metabolic disease
    **C.** degenerative disease
    **D.** cancer

32. Which of the following substances is released in the body to cause most of the symptoms of allergies?
  - **A.** insulin
  - **B.** allergens
  - **C.** histamine
  - **D.** acetylcholine

33. Individuals can have a dangerous response to particular allergens, such as latex, and go into anaphylactic shock. What will be the result?
  - **A.** breathing problems
  - **B.** epileptic seizures
  - **C.** atherosclerosis
  - **D.** arthritis

34. In autoimmunity, which attacks the body's own proteins?
  - **A.** antigens
  - **B.** allergens
  - **C.** antibodies
  - **D.** antihistamines

## Constructed Response

35. **Short Answer** Describe how an allergy differs from a common cold, considering that the symptoms are similar.

36. **Short Answer** Discuss the effects on the organs of the body when the smooth muscles in the bronchioles constrict, causing breathing to be difficult.

37. **Short Answer** Evaluate why lupus causes systemic problems in the body.

## Think Critically

38. **Construct** a table listing each of the types of noninfectious disease and give an example of each type.

*Use the graph below to answer question 39.*

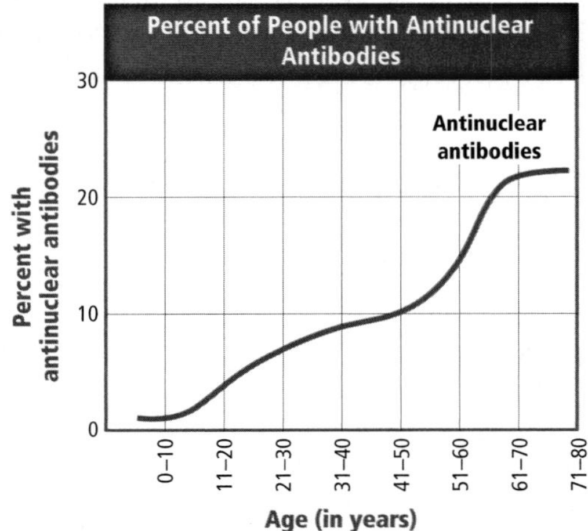


39. **Summarize** the relationship between antinuclear antibodies and age.

## Additional Assessment

40.   **Biology** Construct an analogy comparing the immune system to a castle being attacked by invaders from a neighboring territory.

### Document-Based Questions

*The table below illustrates the effectiveness of using vaccinations to prevent the contraction of disease. There was a large decrease in cases of the diseases listed after the use of vaccinations.*

Data obtained from: Mandell, G. L., et al. 1995. *Principles and Practice of Infectious Diseases*, 4th ed. Churchill Livingstone, and Centers for Disease Control and Prevention. 2000. *Morbidity and Mortality Weekly Report* 48: 1162-1192.

| Disease | Maximum Number of Cases in a Year | Number of Cases in 1999 in U.S. | Percent Change |
|---|---|---|---|
| **Measles** | 894,134 | 60 | –99.99 |
| **Mumps** | 152,209 | 352 | –99.77 |
| **Polio (paralytic)** | 21,269 | 0 | –100.0 |
| **Tetanus** | 1560 | 33 | –97.88 |
| **Hepatitis B** | 26,611 | 6495 | –75.59 |

41. Which disease has shown the greatest change in occurrence since the year of its maximum number of cases?

42. Tetanus has shown a large decline since the United States started vaccinating. Explain why this disease will not be completely eradicated.

43. Create a bar graph showing the percent change in number of cases as a result of vaccination for each disease.

## Cumulative Review

44. Describe the biome in your area, including the abiotic factors that help define the biome and at least five species that are prevalent. **(Chapter 3)**

45. Based on your knowledge of bird adaptations, design the perfect bird for a cold, marshy area inhabited by fish and other invertebrates. **(Chapter 29)**

# Standardized Test Practice

**Cumulative**

## Multiple Choice

1. In the digestive system, complex carbohydrates are broken down into which substance?
   A. amino acids
   B. fatty acids
   C. simple sugars
   D. starches

*Use the diagram below to answer questions 2 and 3.*

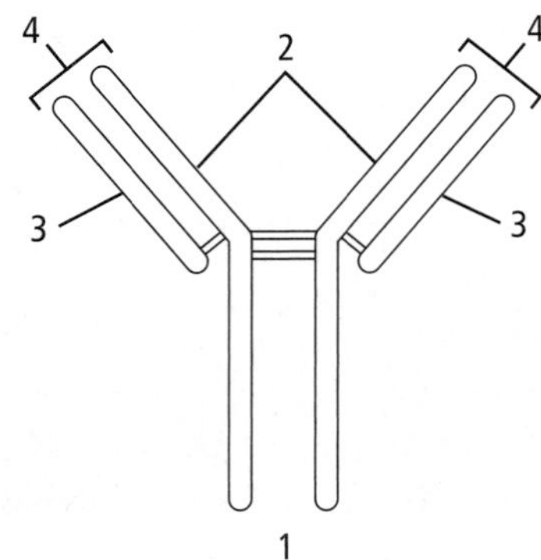


2. The diagram above shows the basic structure of an antibody. Which part of the diagram corresponds to the antigen binding site?
   A. 1
   B. 2
   C. 3
   D. 4

3. Why are parts 2 and 3 of the diagram above important for the formation of antibodies?
   A. They allow for an enormous number of possible antibodies to form.
   B. They are created by the T cells in the immune system.
   C. They help reduce the number of antibodies that form.
   D. They help stimulate the inflammatory response.

4. Which is the role of estrogen during puberty in females?
   A. It causes development of the female body.
   B. It causes eggs to begin to mature in the ovaries.
   C. It causes meiosis to start to produce an egg.
   D. It causes ovaries to release mature eggs.

5. Which is true of the appendix?
   A. It absorbs sodium hydrogen carbonate to neutralize acid.
   B. It has no known function in the digestive system.
   C. It helps break down fats.
   D. It secretes acids to help break down foods.

*Use the diagram below to answer question 6.*

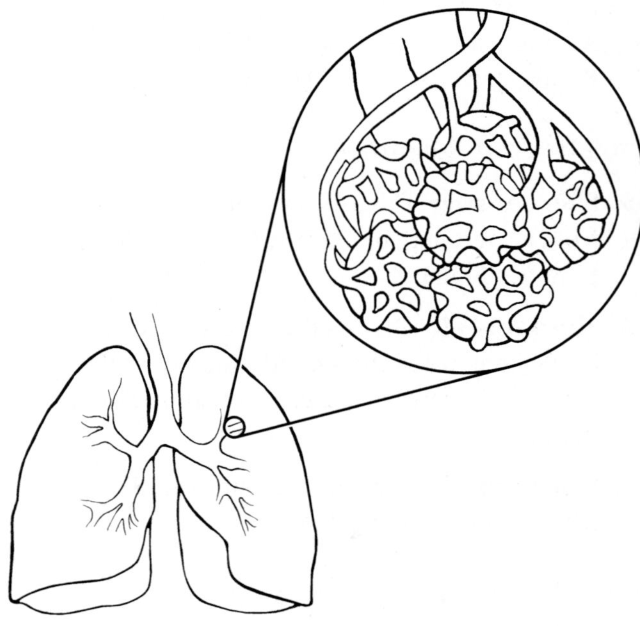

6. Which happens in the blood in these structures?
   A. Carbon dioxide and oxygen are exchanged.
   B. Carbon dioxide and oxygen remain constant.
   C. Nitrogen and carbon dioxide are exchanged.
   D. Nitrogen and carbon dioxide remain constant.

7. Puberty takes place during which transition in life?
   A. adolescence to adulthood
   B. childhood to adolescence
   C. fetus to infant
   D. zygote to fetus

8. What is the role of hormones in the body?
   A. to act as reaction catalysts
   B. to control breathing process
   C. to help synthesize proteins
   D. to regulate many body functions

## Short Answer

*Use the graph below to answer questions 9 and 10.*

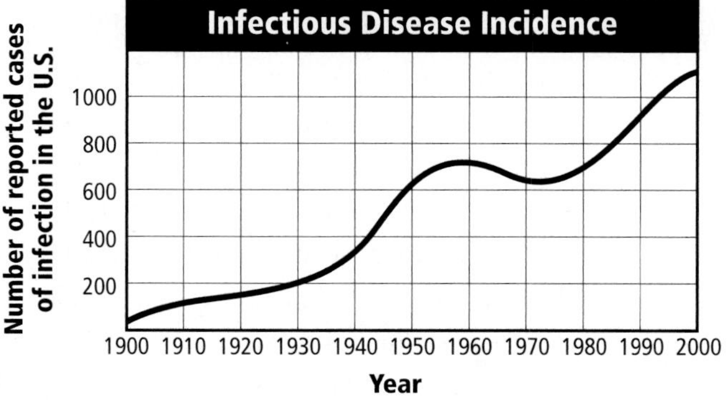


**9.** What is the overall trend shown in the above graph?

**10.** What are two possible explanations for the pattern in the above graph?

**11.** What characteristics are used to classify protists into three groups?

**12.** Describe the process of dilation during birthing. Assess why it is important.

**13.** Identify the function of the large intestine.

**14.** Assess how the respiratory system of most reptiles is adapted for life on land.

**15.** Free-living flatworms have some unique body structures: eyespots, a ganglion, and auricles that detect chemical stimuli. How are these body structures related to each other?

## Extended Response

**16.** Arthropods first moved onto land about 400 million years ago and have survived several mass extinctions. Propose a hypothesis about why arthropods have been so successful.

**17.** Compare the production of sperm cells and egg cells during meiosis.

## Essay Question

Scientist Mark Lappé wrote the following in 1981, in a book called *Germs That Won't Die:*

"Unfortunately, we played a trick on the natural world by seizing control of these [natural] chemicals, making them more perfect in a way that has changed the whole microbial constitution of the developing countries. We have organisms now proliferating that never existed before in nature. We have selected them. We have organisms that probably caused a tenth of a percent of human disease in the past that now cause twenty, thirty percent of the diseases that we're seeing. We have changed the whole face of the earth by the use of antibiotics."

*Using the information in the paragraph above, answer the following question in essay format.*

**18.** As Lappé predicted in 1981, many diseases have emerged in forms that are resistant to treatment by antibiotics and other powerful drugs. Have antibiotics "changed the whole face of the earth" for the better or for the worse? In an organized essay, discuss the pros and cons of antibiotics as they are used today.

**NEED EXTRA HELP?**

| If You Missed Question . . . | 1 | 2 | 3 | 4 | 5 | 6 | 7 | 8 | 9 | 10 | 11 | 12 | 13 | 14 | 15 | 16 | 17 | 18 |
|---|---|---|---|---|---|---|---|---|---|---|---|---|---|---|---|---|---|---|
| Review Section . . . | 35.2 | 37.2 | 37.2 | 36.2 | 35.1 | 34.2 | 36.2 | 35.2 | 37.1 | 37.1 | 19.1 | 36.2 | 35.1 | 29.1 | 25.1 | 26.1 | 36.1 | 37.1 |

## For students and parents/guardians

This skillbuilder handbook helps you sharpen your problem-solving skills so you can get the most out of reading and understanding scientific writing and data. Improving skills such as making comparisons, analyzing information, reading time lines, and using graphic organizers also can help you boost your test scores. In addition, you'll find useful instructions on how to hold a debate and a review of math skills.

The reference handbook is another tool that will assist you. The classification tables, word origins, and the periodic table of the elements are resources that will help increase your comprehension.

# Table of Contents

# Make Comparisons

## Why learn this skill?

Suppose you want to buy portable MP3 music player, and you must choose between three models. You would probably compare the characteristics of the three models, such as price, amount of memory, sound quality, and size to determine which model is best for you. In the study of biology, you often make comparisons between the structures and functions of organisms. You will also compare scientific discoveries or events from one time period with those from another period.

## Learn the Skill

When making comparisons, you examine two or more items, groups, situations, events, or theories. You must first decide what will be compared and which characteristics you will use to compare them. Then identify any similarities and differences.

For example, comparisons can be made between the two illustrations on this page. The different structures of the animal cell can be compared to the different structures of the plant cell. By reading the labels, you can see that both types of cells have a nucleus.

## Practice the Skill

Create a table with the heading *Animal and Plant Cells.* Make three columns. Label the first column *Cell Structures.* Label the second column *Animal Cells.* Label the third column *Plant Cells.* List all the cell structures in the first column. Place a check mark under either *Animal Cell* or *Plant Cell* or both if that structure is shown in the illustration. When you have finished the table, answer these questions.

1. What items are being compared? How are they being compared?
2. What structures do animal and plant cells have in common?
3. What structures are unique to animal cells? What structures are unique to plant cells?

## Apply the Skill

**Make Comparisons** On pages 708 and 712 respectively, you will find illustrations for a sponge's life cycle and a jellyfish's life cycle. Compare the two illustrations carefully. Then, identify the similarities and the differences between the two cycles.

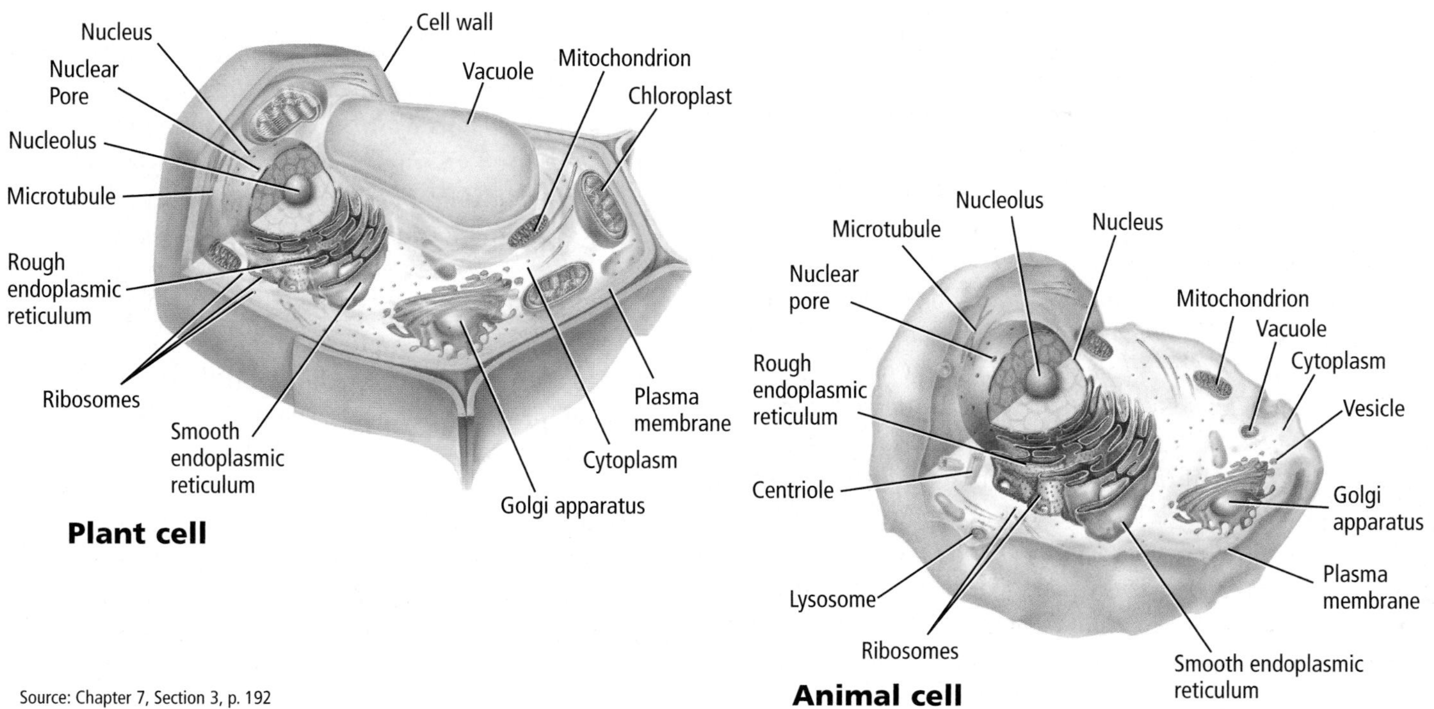


Source: Chapter 7, Section 3, p. 192

# Analyze Information

## Why learn this skill?

Analyzing, or looking at separate parts of something to understand the entire piece, is a way to think critically about written work. The ability to analyze information is important when determining which ideas are the most important.

## Learn the Skill

To analyze information, use the following steps:

- identify the topic being discussed
- examine how the information is organized—identify the main points
- summarize the information in your own words, and then make a statement based on your understanding of the topic and what you already know

## Practice the Skill

Read the following excerpt from *National Geographic*. Use the steps listed above to analyze the information and answer the questions that follow.

*Like something straight out of a Jules Verne novel, an enormous tentacled creature looms out of the inky blackness of the deep Pacific waters. But this isn't science fiction. A set of extraordinary images captured by Japanese scientists marks the first-ever record of a live giant squid* (Architeuthis) *in the wild.*

*The animal—which measures roughly 8 meters long—was photographed 900 meters beneath the North Pacific Ocean. Japanese scientists attracted the squid toward cameras attached to a baited fishing line. The scientists say they snapped more than 500 images of the massive cephalopod before it broke free after snagging itself on a hook. They also recovered one of the giant squid's two longest tentacles, which severed during its struggle.*

*The photo sequence, taken off Japan's Ogasawara Islands in September 2004, shows the squid homing in on the baited line and enveloping it in "a ball of tentacles." Tsunemi Kubodera of the National Science Museum in Tokyo and Kyoichi Mori of the Ogasawara Whale Watching Association report their observations in the journal* Proceedings of the Royal Society B.

"Architeuthis *appears to be a much more active predator than previously suspected, using its elongated feeding tentacles to strike and tangle prey," the researchers write. They add that the squid was found feeding at depths where no light penetrates even during the day.*

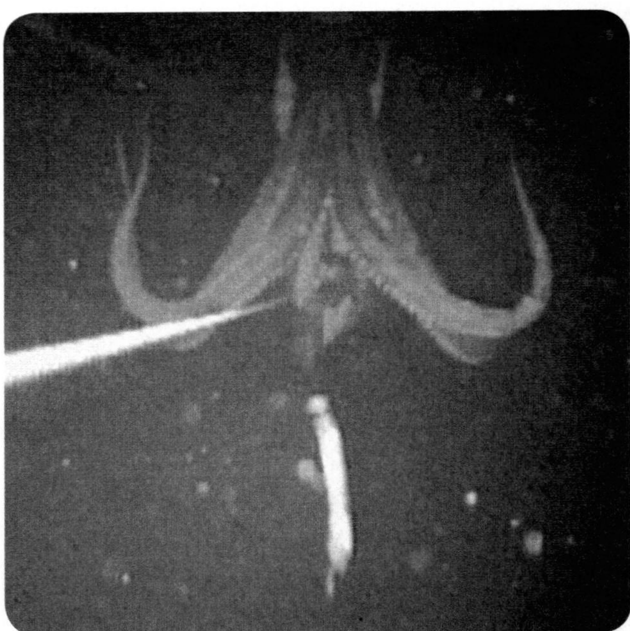

**Giant squid on a fishing line**

*Squid expert Martin Collins of the British Antarctic Survey based in Cambridge, England is especially interested in clues the images might provide to the way giant squid swim and hunt in the deep ocean.*

*Collins says there were two competing schools of thought among giant squid experts. "One was the idea that [giant squid] were fairly inactive and just drifted around, dangling their tentacles below them like fishing lures to catch what came by," he said.*

*"The other theory was that they were actually quite active. This new evidence supports this, suggesting they are active predators which can move reasonably quickly. The efforts the squid went to untangle itself [from the baited fishing line] also shows they are capable of quite strong and rapid movement," he added.*

1. What topic is being discussed?
2. What are the main points of the article?
3. Summarize the information in this article, and then provide your analysis based on this information and your own knowledge.

## Apply the Skill

**Analyze Information** Analyze a short, informative article on a new scientific discovery or new science technology, such as the hybrid car. Summarize the information and make a statement of your own.

# Synthesize Information

## Why learn this skill?

The skill of synthesizing involves combining and analyzing information gathered from separate sources or at different times to make logical connections. Being able to synthesize information can be a useful skill for you as a student when you need to gather data from several sources for a report or a presentation.

## Learn the Skill

Follow these steps to synthesize information:

- select important and relevant information
- analyze the information and build connections
- reinforce or modify the connections as you acquire new information

Suppose you need to write a research paper on endangered species. You would need to synthesize what you learn to inform others. You could begin by detailing the ideas and information you already have about endangered species. A table such as the one below could help you categorize the facts.

**Table SH.1 Endangered Species Statistics**

| Group | October 2000 | | October 2005 | |
|---|---|---|---|---|
| | U.S. | Foreign | U.S. | Foreign |
| Mammals | 63 | 251 | 68 | 251 |
| Birds | 78 | 175 | 77 | 175 |
| Reptiles | 14 | 64 | 14 | 64 |
| Amphibians | 10 | 8 | 12 | 8 |
| Fishes | 69 | 11 | 71 | 11 |
| Clams | 61 | 2 | 62 | 2 |
| Snails | 20 | 1 | 24 | 1 |
| Insects | 30 | 4 | 35 | 4 |
| Arachnids | 6 | 0 | 12 | 0 |
| Crustaceans | 18 | 0 | 19 | 0 |

Source: U.S. Fish and Wildlife Service

Then you could select a passage about endangered species like the sample below, which is adapted from Chapter 5.

*Stable ecosystems can be changed by the activity of other organisms, climate, or natural disasters. This natural process of extinctions is not what scientists are worried about. Many worry about a recent increase in the rate of extinction.*

*One of the factors that is increasing the current rate of extinction is the overexploitation, or excessive use, of species that have economic values. Historically, overexploitation was the primary cause of species extinction. However, the number one cause of species extinction today is the loss or destruction of habitat.*

*There are several ways that species can lose their habitats. If a habitat is destroyed or disrupted, the native species might have to relocate or die. For example, humans are clearing areas of tropical rain forests and are replacing the native plants with agricultural crops or grazing lands.*

## Practice the Skill

Use the table and the passage on this page to answer these questions.

1. What information is presented in the table?
2. What is the main idea of the passage? What information does the passage add to your knowledge about the topic?
3. By synthesizing the two sources and using your own knowledge, what conclusions can you draw about habitat conservation practices for endangered species?
4. Using what you learned in your studies and from this activity, contrast two types of habitat changes and their effects on the ecosystem.

## Apply the Skill

**Synthesize Information** Find two sources of information on the same topic and write a short report. In your report, answer the following questions: What are the main ideas of each source? How does each source add to your understanding of the topic? Do the sources support or contradict each other? What conclusions can you draw from the sources?

# Take Notes and Outline

## Why learn this skill?

One of the best ways to remember something is to write it down. Taking notes—writing down information in a brief and orderly format—not only helps you remember, but also makes studying easier.

## Learn the Skill

There are several styles of note taking, but all explain and put information in a logical order. As you read, identify and summarize the main ideas and details that support them and write them in your notes. Paraphrase, that is, state in your own words, the information rather then copying it directly from the text. Using note cards or developing a personal "shorthand"—using symbols to represent words—can help.

You might also find it helpful to create an outline when taking notes. When outlining material, first read the material to identify the main ideas. In textbooks, section headings provide clues to main topics. Identify the subheadings. Place supporting details under the appropriate heading. The basic pattern for outlines is as follows:

MAIN TOPIC
- I. FIRST IDEA OR ITEM
  - A. FIRST DETAIL
    - 1. SUBDETAIL
    - 2. SUBDETAIL
  - B. SECOND DETAIL
- II. SECOND IDEA OR ITEM
  - A. FIRST DETAIL
  - B. SECOND DETAIL
    - 1. SUBDETAIL
    - 2. SUBDETAIL
- III. THIRD IDEA OR ITEM

## Practice the Skill

Read the following excerpt from *National Geographic*. Use the steps you just read about to take notes or create an outline. Then answer the questions that follow.

*Mapping the three billion letters of the human genome has helped researchers better understand the 99.9 percent of DNA that is identical in all humans. Now a new project aims to map the 0.1 percent of DNA where differences occur. The International HapMap Project will look at variations that dictate susceptibility to genetic influences, such as environmental toxins and inherited diseases.*

*Researchers "read" DNA code by its structural units called nucleotides. These chemical building blocks are designated by the letters A (adenine), C (cytosine), G (guanine), and T (thymine). Single-letter variations in genes—called single nucleotide polymorphisms, or SNPs (pronounced "snips")—are often the culprits behind a wide range of genetic diseases. For example, changing an A to a T in the gene for the blood molecule hemoglobin causes sickle cell anemia.*

*But most diseases and disorders are not caused by a single gene. Instead they are caused by a complex combination of linked genetic variations at multiple sites on different chromosomes.*

*Haplotypes are sets of adjacent SNPs that are closely associated and are inherited as a group. Certain haplotypes are known to have a role in diseases, including Alzheimer's, deep vein thrombosis, type 2 diabetes, and age-related macular degeneration, a leading cause of blindness.*

1. What is the main topic of the article?
2. What are the first, second, and third ideas?
3. Name one detail for each of the ideas.
4. Name one subdetail for each of the details.

## Apply the Skill

**Take Notes and Outline** Go to Section 2.1 and take notes by paraphrasing and using shorthand or by creating an outline. Use the section title and headings to help you create your outline. Summarize the section using only your notes.

# Understand Cause and Effect

## Why learn this skill?

In order to understand an event, you should look for how that event or chain of events came about. When scientists are unsure of the cause for an event, they often design experiments. Although there might be an explanation, an experiment should be performed to be certain the cause created the event you observed. This process examines the causes and effects of events.

## Learn the Skill

Every human body regulates its own temperature to maintain conditions suitable for survival. Exercise *causes* a body to heat up. The stimulated nerves in the skin are the *effect,* or result, of exercise. The figure below shows how one event—the **cause**—led to another—the **effect.**

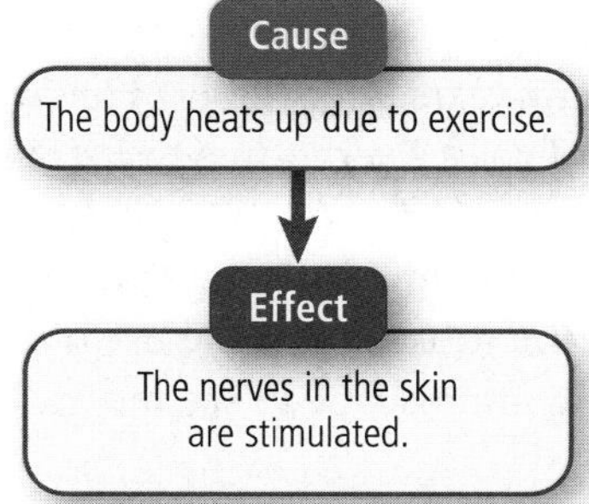


You can also identify cause-and-effect relationships in sentences from clue words such as:

| | |
|---|---|
| **because** | **thus** |
| **that is why** | **due to** |
| **led to** | **for this reason** |
| **so that** | **produced** |
| **consequently** | **therefore** |
| **as a result** | **in order to** |

Read the sample sentences below.

**"A message is sent to sweat glands. As a result, perspiration occurs."**

In the example above, the cause is a message being sent. The cause-and-effect clue words "as a result" tell you that the perspiration is the effect of the message.

In a chain of events, an effect often becomes the cause of other events. The next chart shows the complete chain of events that occur when exercise raises body temperature and the body returns to homeostasis.

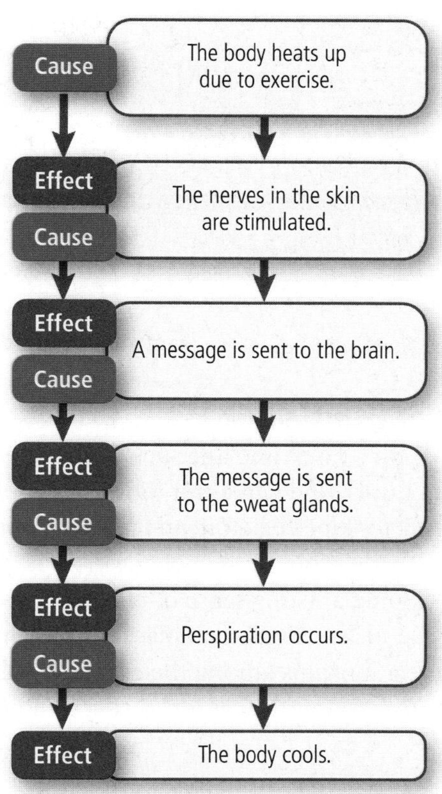


## Practice the Skill

Make a chart, like the one above, showing which events are causes and which are effects using these sentences. Use Chapter 33 to help you.

1. The hair cells respond by generating nerve impulses in the auditory nerve and transmitting them to the brain.
2. As the stapes vibrates, it causes the oval window to move back and forth.
3. Sound waves enter the auditory canal and cause the eardrum to vibrate.
4. Vibrations cause the fluid inside the cochlea to move like a wave against the hair cells.
5. Vibrations travel through the malleus, the incus, and the stapes.

## Apply the Skill

**Understand Cause and Effect** Read an account of a recent scientific event or discovery in a science article. Determine the causes and effects that lead to the event or discovery. Show the chain of events in a chart.

Skillbuilder Handbook

# Read a Time Line

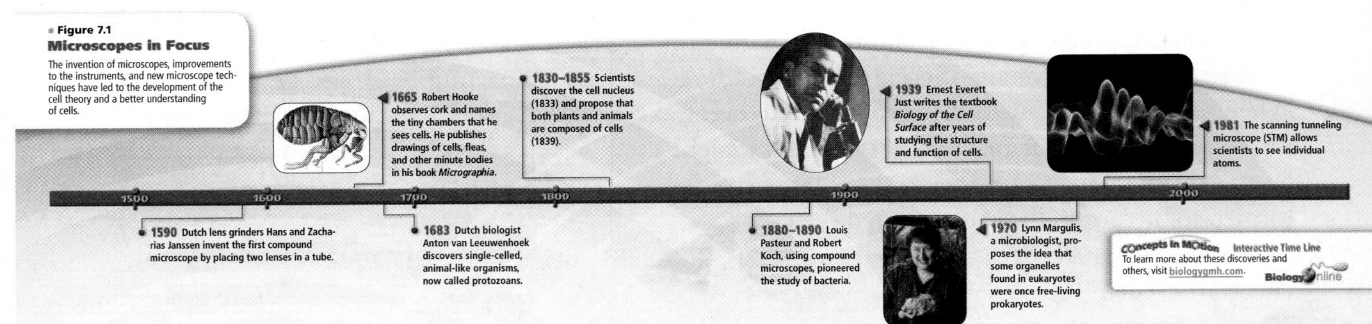

Figure 7.1
Microscopes in Focus
The invention of microscopes, improvements to the instruments, and new microscope techniques have led to the development of the cell theory and a better understanding of cells.
1500
1600
1700
1800
1900
2000
1590 Dutch lens grinders Hans and Zacharias Janssen invent the first compound microscope by placing two lenses in a tube.
1665 Robert Hooke observes cork and names the tiny chambers that he sees cells. He publishes drawings of cells, fleas, and other minute bodies in his book Micrographia.
1683 Dutch biologist Anton van Leeuwenhoek discovers single-celled, animal-like organisms, now called protozoans.
1830–1855 Scientists discover the cell nucleus (1833) and propose that both plants and animals are composed of cells (1839).
1880–1890 Louis Pasteur and Robert Koch, using compound microscopes, pioneered the study of bacteria.
1939 Ernest Everett Just writes the textbook Biology of the Cell Surface after years of studying the structure and function of cells.
1970 Lynn Margulis, a microbiologist, proposes the idea that some organelles found in eukaryotes were once free-living prokaryotes.
1981 The scanning tunneling microscope (STM) allows scientists to see individual atoms.
Concepts in Motion Interactive Time Line
To learn more about these discoveries and others, visit biologygmh.com.
Biology Online


Source: Chapter 7, Section 1 pp. 182–183

## Why learn this skill?

When you read a time line such as the one above, you see not only when an event took place, but also what events took place before and after it. A time line can help you develop the skill of chronological thinking. Developing a strong sense of chronology—when and in what order events took place—will help you examine relationships among the events. It will also help you understand the causes or effects of events.

## Learn the Skill

A time line is a linear chart that list events that occurred on specific dates. The number of years between dates at the begining and end of the time line is the time span. A time line that begins in 1910 and ends in 1920 has a ten-year time span. Some time lines span centuries. Examine the time lines below. What time spans do they cover?

Time lines are usually divided into smaller parts called time intervals. On the two time lines below, the first time line has a 300-year time span divided into 100-year time intervals. The second time line has a six-year time span divided into two-year time intervals.

## Practice the Skill

Study the time line above and then answer these questions.

1. What time span and intervals appear on this time line?
2. Which scientist was the first to observe cells with a microscope?
3. How many years after Robert Hooke observed cork did Ernest Everett Just write *Biology of the Cell Surface?*
4. What was the time span between the creation of the first microscope and the use of the scanning tunneling microscope to see individual atoms.

## Apply the Skill

**Read a Time Line** Sometimes a time line shows events that occurred during the same period, but related to two different subjects. The time line above shows events related to cells between 1500 and 2000. Copy the time line and events onto a piece of paper. Then use a different color to add events related to genetics during this same time span. Use the chapters in Unit 3 to help you.

# Analyze Media Sources

## Why learn this skill?

To stay informed, people use a variety of media sources, including print media, broadcast media, and electronic media. The Internet has become an especially valuable research tool. It is convenient to use, and the information contained on the Internet is plentiful. Whichever media source you use to gather information, it is important to analyze the source to determine its accuracy and reliability.

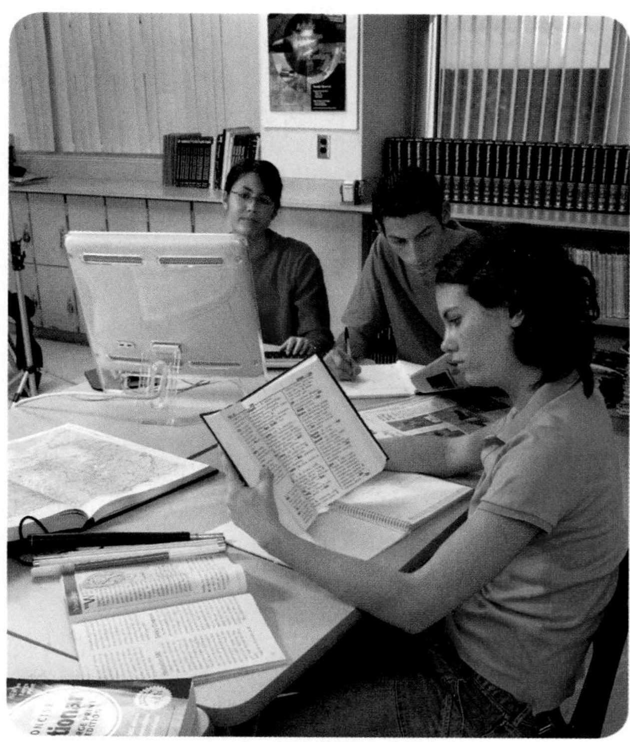

## Learn the Skill

There are a number of issues to consider when analyzing a media source. Most important is to check the accuracy of the source and content. The author and publisher or sponsors should be credible and clearly indicated. To analyze print media or broadcast media, ask yourself the following questions:

- Is the information current?
- Are the resources revealed?
- Is more than one resource used?
- Is the information biased?
- Does the information represent both sides of an issue?
- Is the information reported firsthand or secondhand?

For electronic media, ask yourself these questions in addition to the ones above.

- Is the author credible and clearly identified? Web site addresses that end in .edu, .gov, and .org tend to be credible and contain reliable information.
- Are the facts on the Web site documented?
- Are the links within the Web site appropriate and current?
- Does the Web site contain links to other useful resources?

## Practice the Skill

To analyze print media, choose two articles, one from a newspaper and the other from a newsmagazine, on an issue on which public opinion is divided. Then, answer these questions.

1. What points are the articles trying to make? Were the articles successful? Can the facts be verified?
2. Did either article reflect a bias toward one viewpoint or another? List any unsupported statements.
3. Was the information reported firsthand or secondhand? Do the articles seem to represent both sides fairly?
4. How many resources can you identify in the articles? List them.

To analyze electronic media, visit biologygmh.com and select Web Links. Choose one link from the list, read the information on that Web site, and then answer these questions.

1. Who is the author or sponsor of the Web site?
2. What links does the Web site contain? How are they appropriate to the topic?
3. What resources were used for the information on the Web site?

## Apply the Skill

**Analyze Sources of Information** Think of an issue in the nation on which public opinion is divided. Use a variety of media resources to read about this issue. Which news source more fairly represents the issue? Which news source has the most reliable information? Can you identify any biases? Can you verify the credibility of the news source?

# Use Graphic Organizers

## Why learn this skill?

While you read this textbook, you will be looking for important ideas or concepts. One way to arrange these ideas is to create a graphic organizer. In addition to Foldables™, you will find various other graphic organizers throughout your book. Some organizers show a sequence, or flow, of events. Other organizers emphasize the relationship between concepts. Develop your own organizers to help you better understand and remember what you read.

## Learn the Skill

An **events chain concept map** describes a sequence of events, such as stages of a process or procedure. When making an events-chain map, first identify the event that starts the sequence and add events in chronological order until you reach an outcome.

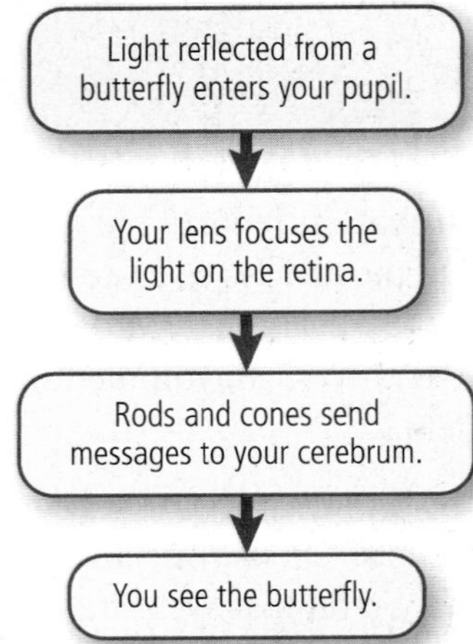


In a **cycle concept map,** the series of events do not produce a final outcome. The event that appears to be the final event relates back to the event that appears to be the initiating event. Therefore, the cycle repeats itself.

**Blood Flow in the Body**

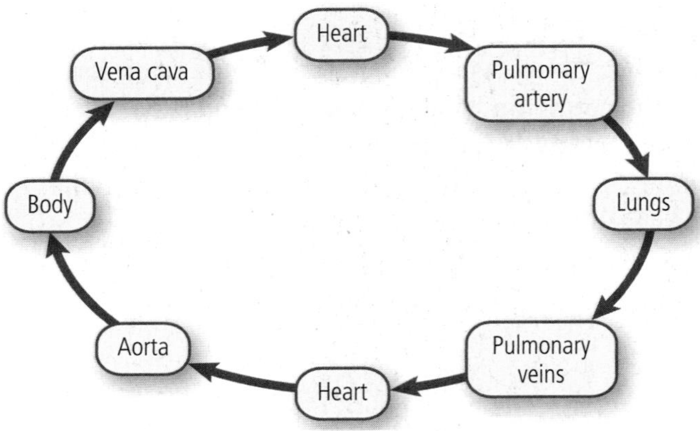


A **network tree concept map** shows the relationship among concepts, which are written in order from general to specific. The words written on the lines between the circles, called linking words, describe the relationships among the concepts; the concepts and the linking words can form a sentence.

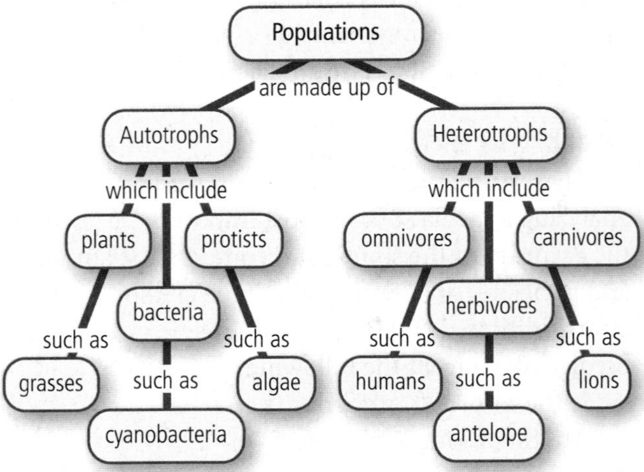


## Practice the Skill

1. Create an events chain concept map that describes the process of hearing the ring of a bell. Begin with sound waves entering the outer ear. End with hearing the bell ring. Use Chapter 33 to help you.
2. Create a cycle concept map of human respiration. Make sure that the cycle is complete with the event that appears to be the final event relating back to the event that appears to be the starting event. Go to Chapter 34 for help.
3. Create a network tree concept map with these words: *Biomes, aquatic biomes, terrestrial biomes, marine biomes, estuary biomes, freshwater biomes, desert, grasslands, temperate forest, salt water, mixed waters, freshwater, sparse plant life, grasses,* and *broad-leaved trees.* Add linking words to describe the relationships between concepts. Refer to Chapter 3 for help.

## Apply the Skill

**Use Graphic Organizers** Create an events chain concept map of succession using information from Chapter 3. Create a cycle concept map of the water cycle using information from Chapter 2. Create a network tree concept map of animals that includes invertebrates and vertebrates, characteristics of each type, and examples. Use Chapters 24–30 to help you.

# Debate Skills

New research leads to new scientific information. There are often opposing points of view on how this research is conducted, how it is interpreted, and how it is communicated. The *Biology and Society* features in your book offer a chance to debate a current controversial topic. Here is an overview on how to conduct a debate.

## Choose a Position and Research

First, choose a scientific issue that has at least two opposing viewpoints. The issue can come from current events, your textbook, or your teacher. These topics could include human cloning or environmental issues. Topics are stated as affirmative declarations, such as "Cloning human beings is beneficial to society."

One speaker will argue the viewpoint that agrees with the statement, called the positive position, and another speaker will argue the viewpoint that disagrees with the statement, called the negative position. Either individually or with a group, choose the position for which you will argue. The viewpoint that you choose does not have to reflect your personal belief. The purpose of debate is to create a strong argument supported by scientific evidence.

After choosing your position, conduct research to support your viewpoint. Use resources in your media center or library to find articles, or use your textbook to gather evidence to support your argument. A strong argument is supported by scientific evidence, expert opinions, and your own analysis of the issue. Research the opposing position also. Becoming aware of what points the other side might argue will help you to strengthen the evidence for your position.

## Hold the Debate

You will have a specific amount of time, determined by your teacher, in which to present your argument. Organize your speech to fit within the time limit: explain the viewpoint that you will be arguing, present an analysis of your evidence, and conclude by summing up your most important points. Try to vary the elements of your argument. Your speech should not be a list of facts, a reading of a newspaper article, or a statement of your personal opinion, but an analysis of your evidence in an organized manner. It is also important to remember that you must never make personal attacks against your opponent. Argue the issue. You will be evaluated on your overall presentation, organization and development of ideas, and strength of support for your argument.

**Additional Roles** There are other roles that you or your classmates can play in a debate. You can act as the timekeeper. The timekeeper times the length of the debaters' speeches and gives quiet signals to the speaker when time is almost up (usually a hand signal).

You can also act as a judge. There are important elements to look for when judging a speech: an introduction that tells the audience what position the speaker will be arguing, strong evidence that supports the speaker's position, and organization. The speaker also must speak clearly and loudly enough for everyone to hear. It is helpful to take notes during the debate to summarize the main points of each side's argument. Then, decide which debater presented the strongest argument for his or her position. You can have a class discussion about the strengths and weaknesses of the debate and other viewpoints on this issue that could be argued.

Skillbuilder Handbook

# Math Skills

Experimental data is often quantitative and is expressed using numbers and units. The following sections provide an overview of the common system of units and some calculations involving units.

## Measure in SI

The International System of Measurement, abbreviated SI, is accepted as the standard for measurement throughout most of the world. The SI system contains seven base units. All other units of measurement can be derived from these base units.

**Table SH.2 SI Base Units**

| Measurement | Unit | Symbol |
|---|---|---|
| Length | Meter | m |
| Mass | Kilogram | kg |
| Time | Second | s |
| Electric current | Ampere | A |
| Temperature | Kelvin | K |
| Amount of substance | Mole | mol |
| Intensity of light | Candela | cd |

Some units are derived by combining base units. For example, units for volume are derived from units of length. A liter (L) is a cubic decimeter ($dm^3 = dm \times dm \times dm$). Units of density (g/L) are derived from units of mass (g) and units of volume (L).

When units are multiplied by factors of ten, new units are created. For example, if a base unit is multiplied by 1000, the new unit has the prefix *kilo-*. Prefixes for some units are shown in **Table SH.3.**

To convert a given unit to a unit with a different factor of ten, multiply the unit by a conversion factor. A conversion factor is a ratio equal to one. The equivalents in **Table SH.3** can be used to make such a ratio. For example, 1 km = 1000 m. Two conversion factors can be made from this equivalent.

$$\frac{1000 \text{ m}}{1 \text{ km}} = 1 \quad \text{and} \quad \frac{1 \text{ km}}{1000 \text{ m}} = 1$$

To convert one unit to another factor of ten, choose the conversion factor that has the unit you are converting from in the denominator. For example, to convert one kilometer to meters, use the following equation.

$$1 \cancel{\text{km}} \times \frac{1000 \text{ m}}{1 \cancel{\text{km}}} = 1000 \text{ m}$$

A unit can be multiplied by several conversion factors to obtain the desired unit.

**Table SH.3 Common SI Prefixes**

| Prefix | Symbol | Equivalents |
|---|---|---|
| mega | m | $1 \times 10^6$ base units |
| kilo | k | $1 \times 10^3$ base units |
| hecto | h | $1 \times 10^2$ base units |
| deka | da | $1 \times 10^1$ base units |
| deci | d | $1 \times 10^{-1}$ base units |
| centi | c | $1 \times 10^{-2}$ base units |
| milli | m | $1 \times 10^{-3}$ base units |
| micro | $\mu$ | $1 \times 10^{-6}$ base units |
| nano | n | $1 \times 10^{-9}$ base units |
| pico | p | $1 \times 10^{-12}$ base units |

**Practice Problem 1** How would you change 1000 micrometers to kilometers?

## Convert Temperature

The following formulas can be used to convert between Fahrenheit and Celsius temperatures. Notice that each equation can be obtained by algebraically rearranging the other. Therefore, you only need to remember one of the equations.

**Conversion of Fahrenheit to Celsius**

$$°C = \frac{(°F) - 32}{1.8}$$

**Conversion of Celsius to Fahrenheit**

$$°F = 1.8(°C) + 32$$

## Make and Use Tables

Tables help organize data so that it can be interpreted more easily. Tables are composed of several components—a title describing the contents of the table, columns and rows that separate and organize information, and headings that describe the information in each column or row.

| Table SH.4 | Effects of Exercise on Heart Rate | |
|---|---|---|
| Pulse taken | Individual heart rate (Beats per min) | Class average (Beats per min) |
| At rest | 73 | 72 |
| After exercise | 110 | 112 |
| 1 minute after exercise | 94 | 90 |
| 5 minutes after exercise | 76 | 75 |

Looking at this table, you should not only be able to pick out specific information, such as the class average heart rate after five minutes of exercise, but you should also notice trends.

**Practice Problem 2** Did the exercise have an effect on the heart rate one minute after exercise? How can you tell? What can you conclude about the effects of exercise on heart rate during and after exercise?

## Make and Use Graphs

After scientists organize data in tables, they often display the data in graphs. A graph is a diagram that shows relationships among variables. Graphs make interpretation and analysis of data easier. The three basic types of graphs used in science are the line graph, the bar graph, and the circle graph.

**Line Graphs** A line graph is used to show the relationship between two variables. The independent variable is plotted on the horizontal axis, called the *x*-axis. The dependent variable is plotted on the vertical axis, called the *y*-axis. The dependent variable *(y)* changes as a result of a change in the independent variable *(x)*.

Suppose a school started a bird-watching group to observe the number of birds in the school courtyard. The number of birds in the courtyard was recorded each day for four months. The average number of birds per month was calculated. A table of the birds' visitations is shown below.

| Table SH.5 | Average Number of Birds Viewed |
|---|---|
| Time (days) | Average Number of Birds per Day |
| 30 | 24 |
| 60 | 27 |
| 90 | 30 |
| 120 | 32 |

To make a graph of the average number of birds over a period of time, start by determining the dependent and independent variables. The average number of birds after each period of time is the dependent variable and is plotted on the *y*-axis. The independent variable, or the number of days, is plotted on the *x*-axis.

Plain or graph paper can be used to construct graphs. Draw a grid on your paper or a box around the squares that you intend to use on your graph paper. Give your graph a title and label each axis with a title and units. In this example, label the number of days on the *x*-axis. Because the lowest average of birds viewed was 24 and the highest was 32, you know that you will have to start numbers on the *y*-axis at least 24 and number to at least 32. You could decide to number 20–40 by intervals of two spaced at equal distances.

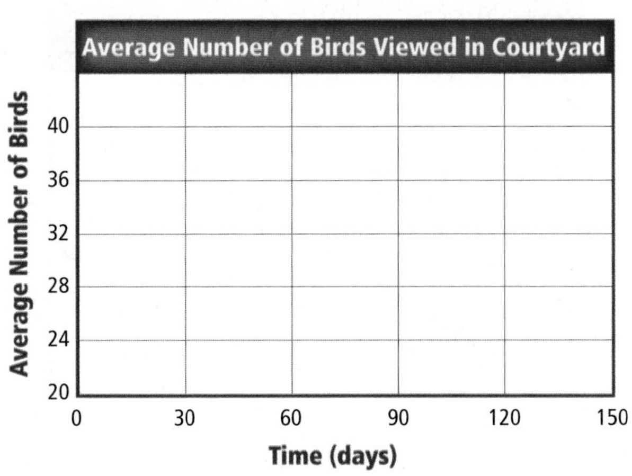

Begin plotting points by locating 30 days on the $x$-axis and 24 on the $y$-axis. Where an imaginary vertical line from the $x$-axis and an imaginary horizontal line from the $y$-axis meet, place the first data point. Place other data points using the same process. After all the points are plotted, draw a "best fit" straight line through all the points.

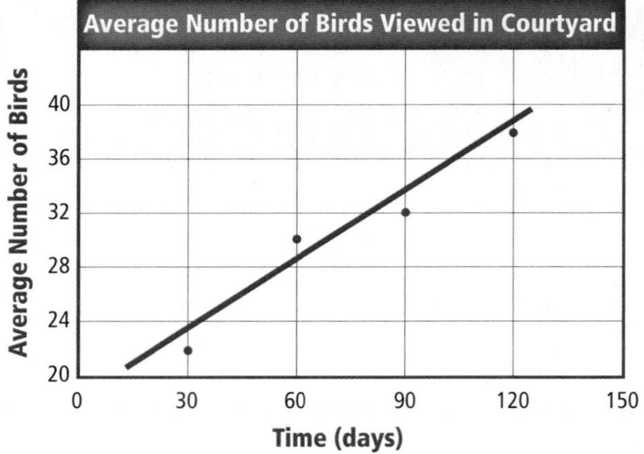


The bird-watching group also recorded the average number of brown-feathered birds they observed in the school courtyard. In the first month they averaged 21 brown-feathered birds per day. In the second month they averaged 24 brown-feathered birds. An average of 28 brown-feathered birds per day was observed in the third month. In the final month an average of 30 brown-feathered birds was observed.

What if you want to compare the average number of birds viewed with the average number of brown-feathered birds? The average brown-feathered bird data can be plotted on the same graph. Include a key with different lines indicating different sets of data.

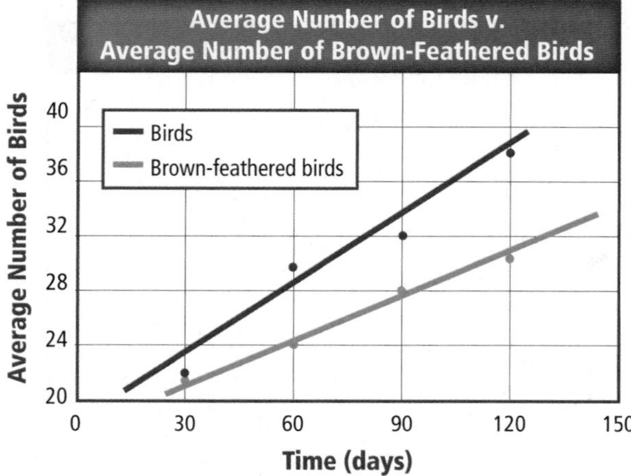


**Practice Problem 3** Between 30 days and 120 days, what is the change in the average number of birds viewed?

**Practice Problem 4** For the 120 days how did the average number of brown-feathered birds change as the average number of birds changed?

**Slope of a Linear Graph** The slope of a line is a number determined by any two points on the line. This number describes how steep the line is. The greater the absolute value of the slope, the steeper the line. Slope is the ratio of the change in the $y$-coordinates (rise) to the change in the $x$-coordinates (run) as you move from one point to the other.

The graph below shows a line that passes through (5, 4) and (9, 6).

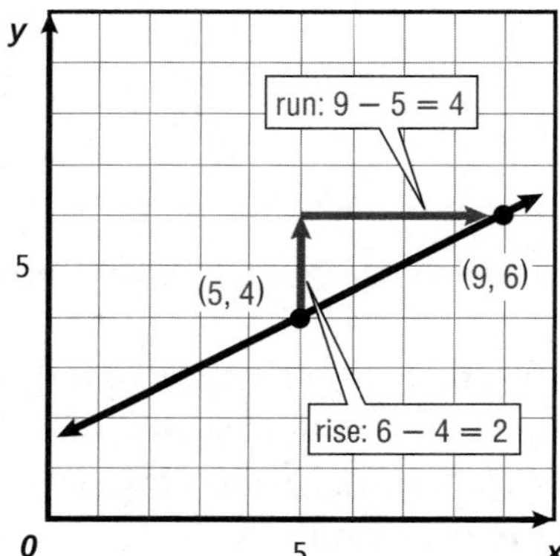


$$\text{Slope} = \frac{\text{rise}}{\text{run}}$$

$$= \frac{\text{change in } y\text{-coordinates}}{\text{change in } x\text{-coordinates}}$$

$$= \frac{6-4}{9-5}$$

$$= \frac{2}{4} \text{ or } \frac{1}{2}$$

So, the slope of the line is $\frac{1}{2}$.

A linear relationship can be translated into equation form. The equation for a straight line is

$$y = mx + b$$

where $y$ represents the dependent variable, $m$ is the slope of the line, $x$ represents the independent variable, and $b$ is the y-intercept, which is the point where the line crosses the $y$-axis.

**Linear and Exponential Trends** Two types of trends you are likely to see when you graph data in biology are linear trends and exponential trends. A linear trend has a constant increase or decrease in data values. In an exponential trend the values are increasing or decreasing more and more rapidly. The graphs below are examples of these two common trends.

In the graph below, there are two lines describing two frog species. Both lines show an increasing linear trend. As the temperature increases, so does the call pulse rates of the frogs. The rate of increase is constant.

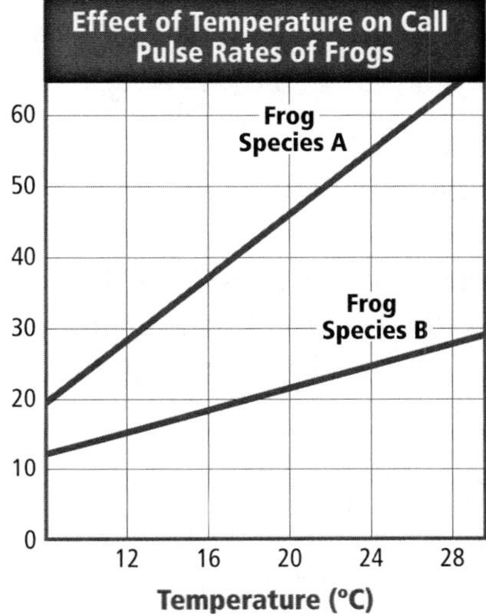


Source: Chapter 28, Section 3, p. 837

The example below shows how a mouse population would grow if the mice were allowed to reproduce unhindered. At first the population would grow slowly. The population growth rate soon accelerates because the total number of mice that are able to reproduce has increased. Notice that the portion of the graph where the population is increasing more and more rapidly is J-shaped. A J-shaped curve generally indicates exponential growth.

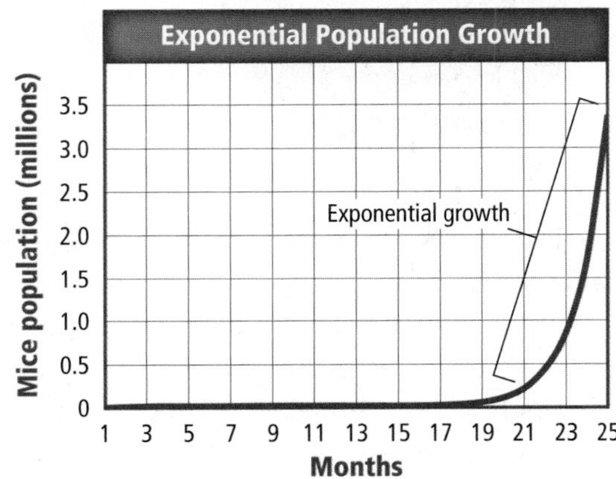


Source: Chapter 4, Section 1, p. 97

**Bar Graphs** A bar graph displays a comparison of different categories of data by representing each category with a bar. The length of the bar is related to the category's frequency. To make a bar graph, set up the x-axis and y-axis as you did for the line graph. Plot the data by drawing thick bars from the x-axis up to the y-axis point.

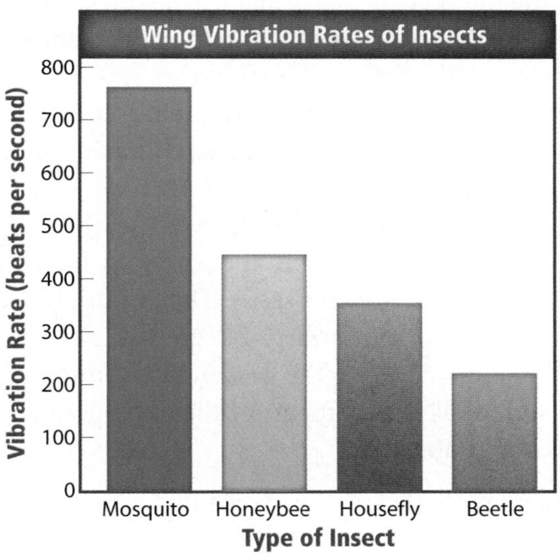


Look at the graph above. The independent variable is the type of insect. The dependent variable is the number of wing vibrations per second.

Bar graphs can also be used to display multiple sets of data in different categories at the same time. A bar graph that displays two sets of data is a called double bar graph. Double bar graphs have a legend to denote which bars represent each set of data. The graph below is an example of a double bar graph.

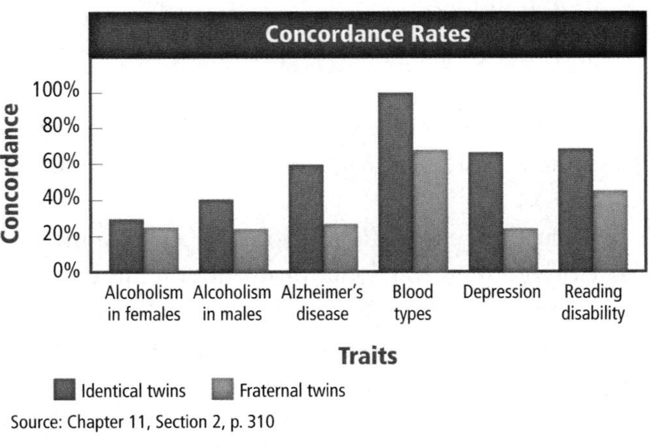


Source: Chapter 11, Section 2, p. 310

**Practice Problem 5** Which type of insect has the highest number of wing vibrations per second? Is this more than twice as fast as the housefly? Explain.

**Circle Graphs** A circle graph consists of a circle divided into sections that represent parts of a whole. When all the sections are placed together, they equal 100 percent of the whole.

Suppose you want to make a circle graph to show the number of seeds that germinate in a package. You would first determine the total number of seeds and the numbers of seeds that germinate out of the total. You plant 143 seeds. Therefore, the whole circle represents this amount. You find that 129 seeds germinate. The seeds that germinate make up one section of the circle graph and the seeds that do not germinate make up another section.

To find out how much of the circle each section should cover, divide the number of seeds that germinate by the total number seeds. Then multiply the answer by 360, the number of degrees in a circle. Round your answer to the nearest whole number. The sum of all the segments of the circle graph should add up to 360°.

$$\text{Segment of circle for seeds that germinated} = \frac{\text{Seeds that germinated}}{\text{Total number of seeds}}$$

Divide $= \frac{129}{143}$

Multiply by number of degrees in a circle $= 0.902 \times 360°$

$= 324.72°$

Round to nearest whole number $= 325°$

Segment of circle for seeds that did not germinate $= 360° - 325°$

$= 35°$

To draw your circle graph, you will need a compass and a protractor. First, use the compass to draw a circle.

Then, draw a straight line from the center to the edge of the circle. Place your protractor on this line, and mark the point on the circle where 35° angle will intersect the circle. Draw a straight line from the center of the circle to the intersection point. This is the section for the seeds that did not germinate. The other section represents the group of seeds that did germinate.

Next, determine the percentages for each part of the whole. Calculate percentages by dividing the part by the total and multiplying by 100. Repeat this calculation for each part.

$$\text{Percent of seeds that germinate} = \frac{\text{Seeds that germinated}}{\text{Total number of seeds}}$$

$= \frac{129}{143}$

Multiply by 100 and add the % $= 0.902 \times 100$

$= 0.902$

$= 90.2\%$

Percent of seeds that do not germinate $= 100\% - 90.2\%$
$= 9.8\%$

Complete the graph by labeling the sections of the graph with percentages and giving the graph a title. Your completed graph should look similar to the one below.

If your circle graph has more than two sections, you will need to construct a segment for each entry. Place your protractor on the last line segment that you have drawn and mark off the appropriate angle. Draw a line segment from the center of the circle to the new mark on the circle. Continue this process until all of the segments have been drawn.

**Percentage of Germinating and Non-Germinating Seeds**

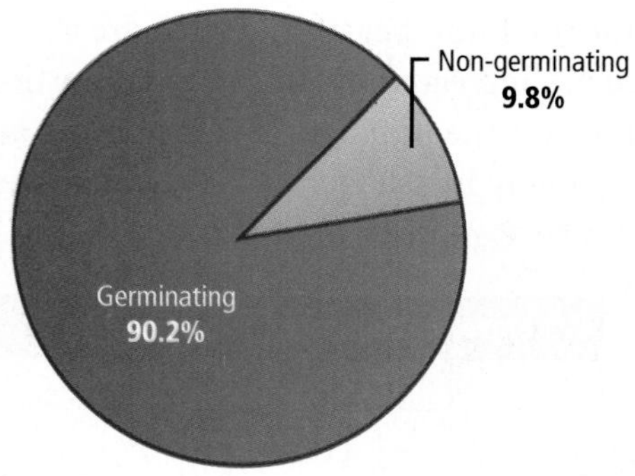


**Practice Problem 6** There are 25 varieties of flowering plants growing around the high school. Construct a circle graph showing the percentage of each flowers' color. Two varieties have yellow blooms, five varieties have blue-purple blooms, eight varieties have white blooms, and ten varieties have red blooms.

## Six-Kingdom Classification

The classification used in this text combines information gathered from the systems of many different fields of biology. For example, phycologists—biologists who study algae—have developed their own system of classification, as have mycologists—biologists who study fungi. The naming of animals and plants is controlled by two completely different sets of rules. The six-kingdom system, although not ideal for reflecting the phylogeny of all life, is useful for showing relationships. Taxonomy is an area of biology that evolves just the like species it studies. In **Table RH.1,** only the major phyla are listed, and one genus is named as an example. For more information about each taxon, refer to the chapter in the text in which the group is described.

**Table RH.1** **Six-Kingdom Classification**

Concepts In Motion
**Interactive Table** To explore more about classification, visit biologygmh.com.

| Kingdom | Phylum/Division* (Common Name) | Typical Example (Common Name) | Characteristics |
|---|---|---|---|
| **Eubacteria** | Actinobacteria | *Mycobacterium* | • unicellular<br>• most absorb food from surroundings<br>• some are photosynthetic<br>• some are chemosynthetic<br>• many are parasites<br>• many are round, spiral, or rod-shaped<br>• some form colonies |
| | Omnibaceria | *Salmonella* (salmonella) | |
| | Spirochaetae (spirochetes) | *Treponema* | |
| | Chloroxybacteria | *Prochloron* | |
| Salmonella<br>Source: Chapter 18, Section 1, p. 519 | Cyanobacteria (blue green algae) | *Nostoc* (nostoc) | |
| **Archaebacteria** | Aphragmabacteria | *Mycoplasma* | • unicellular<br>• some absorb food from surroundings<br>• some are photosynthetic<br>• some are chemosynthetic<br>• many are found in extremely harsh environments including salt ponds, hot springs, swamps, and deep-sea hydrothermal vents |
| | Halobacteria | *Halobacerium* | |
| Methanococcus jannaschii<br>Source: Chapter 18, Section 1, p. 516 | Methanocreatrices | *Methanobacillus* | |
| **Protista** | Sarcodina (amoeba) | *Amoeba* (amoeba) | • unicellular<br>• take in food<br>• free-living or parasitic<br>• move by means of pseudopods |
| | Ciliophora (ciliates) | *Paramecium* (paramecium) | • unicellular<br>• take in food<br>• have large numbers of cilia |
| Amoeba<br>Source: Chapter 19, Section 1, p. 543 | Apicomplexa (apicomplexan) | *Plasmodium* (plasmodium) | • unicellular<br>• take in food<br>• no means of movement<br>• are parasites in animals |

*In the Kingdom Plantae the major phyla are referred to as "divisions."

| Kingdom | Phylum/Division* (Common Name) | Typical Example (Common Name) | Characteristics |
|---|---|---|---|
| **Protista** *(continued)* | Zoomastigina (zooflagellates) | *Trypanosoma* | • unicellular<br>• take in food<br>• free-living or parasitic<br>• have one or more flagella |
| | Euglenophyta (euglenoids) | *Euglena* (euglena) | • unicellular<br>• photosynthetic or take in food<br>• most have one flagellum |
| Diatom<br>Source: Chapter 19, Section 3, p. 554 | Bacillariophyta (diatoms) | *Navicula* | • unicellular<br>• photosynthetic<br>• have unique double shells made of silica |
| | Pyrrophyta (dinoflagellates) | *Gonyaulax* | • unicellular<br>• photosynthetic<br>• contain red pigments<br>• have two flagella |
| | Rhodophyta (red algae) | *Chondrus* | • most are multicellular<br>• photosynthetic<br>• contain red pigments<br>• most live in deep, salt water |
| | Phaeophyta (brown algae) | *Laminaria* | • most are multicellular<br>• photosynthetic<br>• contain brown pigments<br>• most live in salt water |
| Red algae<br>Source: Chapter 19, Section 3, p. 559 | Chlorophyta (green algae) | *Ulva* | • unicellular, multicellular, or colonies<br>• photosynthetic<br>• contain chlorophyll<br>• live on land, in freshwater, or salt water |
| | Acrasiomycota (cellular slime mold) | *Dictyostelium* | • unicellular or multicellular<br>• absorb food<br>• change form during life cycle<br>• cellular and plasmodial slime molds |
| | Myxomycota (acellular slime mold) | *Physarum* | |
| Slime mold<br>Source: Chapter 19, Section 4, p. 561 | Oomycota (water mold/ downy mildew | *Phytophthora* | • multicellular<br>• are either parasites or decomposers<br>• live in freshwater or salt water |

*In the Kingdom Plantae the major phyla are referred to as "divisions."

| Kingdom | Phylum/Division* (Common Name) | Typical Example (Common Name) | Characteristics |
|---|---|---|---|
| **Fungi** | Zygomycota (common mold) | *Rhizopus* (bread mold) | • multicellular<br>• absorb food<br>• spores are produced in sporangia |
| | Ascomycota (sac fungi) | *Saccharomyces* (yeast) | •unicellular and multicellular<br>• absorb food<br>• spores produced in asci |
| | Basidiomycota (club fungi) | *Crucibulum* (bird's nest fungus) | • multicellular<br>• absorb food<br>• spores produced in basidia |
| Bread mold<br>Source: Chapter 20, Section 2, p. 583 | Deuteromycota (imperfect fungi) | *Penicillium* (penicillum) | • members with unknown reproductive structures<br>• imperfect fungi |
| | Chytridiomycota | *Chytrids* | • some are saprobes<br>• some parasitize protists, plants, and animals |
| **Plantae** | Hepaticophyta (liverworts) | *Pellia* | • multicellular nonvascular plants<br>• reproduce by spores produced in capsules<br>• green<br>• grow in moist, land environments |
| | Anthocerophyta (hornworts) | *Anthoceros* | |
| | Bryophyta (moss) | *Polytrichum* (haircap moss) | |
| Liverwort<br>Source: Chapter 21, Section 2, p. 612 | Lycophyta (club moss) | *Lycopodium* (wolf's claw) | • multicellular vascular plants<br>• spores are produced in cone-like structures<br>• live on land<br>• photosynthetic |
| | Arthrophyta | *Equisetum* (horsetails) | • vascular plants<br>• ribbed and jointed stems<br>• scale-like leaves<br>• spores produced in cone-like structures |
| | Pterophyta (ferns) | *Polypodium* (ferns) | • vascular plants<br>• leaves called fronds<br>• spores produce in clusters or sporangia called sori<br>• live on land or in water |
| Wood fern<br>Source: Chapter 21, Section 3, p. 614 | Ginkgophyta (ginko) | *Ginkgo* (ginko) | • deciduous trees<br>• only one living species<br>• have fan-shaped leaves with branching veins and fleshy cones with seeds |

*In the Kingdom Plantae the major phyla are referred to as "divisions."

Reference Handbook

| Kingdom | Phylum/Division* (Common Name) | Typical Example (Common Name) | Characteristics |
|---|---|---|---|
| **Plantae** *(continued)*<br>Welwitschia<br>Source: Chapter 21, Section 4, p. 618 | Cycadophyta (cycad) | *Cyas* (palm tree) | • palm-like plants<br>• have large, feather-like leaves<br>• produce seeds in cones |
| | Coniferophyta (conifer) | *Pinus* (pine tree) | • deciduous or evergreen<br>• trees or shrubs<br>• needle-like or scale-like leaves<br>• seeds produced in cones |
| | Gnetophyta (gnetophyte) | *Welwitschia* (welwitschia) | • shrubs or woody vines<br>• seeds produced in cones<br>• division contains only three genera |
| | Anthophyta (flowering plant) | *Rhododendron* (rhododendron) | • dominant group of plants<br>• flowering plants<br>• have fruit with seeds |
| **Animalia**<br>Sponge<br>Source: Chapter 24, Section 3, p. 707 | Porifera (sponges) | *Spongilla* (sponge) | • aquatic organisms that lack true tissues and organs<br>• asymmetrical and sessile |
| | Cnidaria (cnidarians) | *Hydra* (hydra) | • radially symmetrical<br>• digestive cavity with one opening<br>• most have tentacles armed with stinging cells<br>• live in aquatic environments singly or in colonies |
| | Platyhelminthes (flatworms) | *Dugesia* (planaria) | • unsegmented, bilaterally symmetrical<br>• no body cavity<br>• digestive cavity, if present, has only one opening<br>• parasitic and free-living species |
| | Nematoda (roundworms) | *Trichinella* (trichinella) | • pseudocoelomate, unsegmented, bilaterally symmetrical<br>• tubular digestive tract<br>• without cilia<br>• live in great numbers in soil and aquatic sediments |
| Abalone<br>Source: Chapter 25, Section 3, p. 742 | Mollusca (mollusks) | *Nautilus* (nautilus) | • soft-bodied coelomates<br>• bodies are divided into three parts: head-foot, visceral mass, and mantle<br>• many have shells<br>• almost all have a radula<br>• aquatic and terrestrial species |

*In the Kingdom Plantae the major phyla are referred to as "divisions."

| Kingdom | Phylum/Division* (Common Name) | Typical Example (Common Name) | Characteristics |
|---|---|---|---|
| **Animalia** *(continued)* | Annelida (segmented worms) | *Hirudo* (leech) | • coelomate, serially segmented, bilaterally symmetrical<br>• complete digestive tract<br>• most have setae on each segment that anchor them during crawling<br>• terrestrial and aquatic species |
| | Arthropoda (arthopods) | *Colias* (butterflies) | • chitinous exoskeleton covering segmented bodies<br>• paired, jointed appendages<br>• many have wings<br>• land and aquatic species |
| Sand dollar<br>Source: Chapter 27, Section 1, p. 798 | Echinodermata (echinoderm) | *Cucumaria* (sea cucumber) | • marine organisms<br>• have spiny or leathery skin and a water-vascular system with tube feet<br>• radially symmetrical |
| | Chordata (chordates) | | • segmented coelomates with a notochord<br>• possess a dorsal nerve cord, pharyngeal slits, and a tail at some stage of life<br>• most have paired appendages |
| | **Chordata Subphylum:** Urochordata | *Polycarpa* (sea squirt) | • young have all of the main chordate features; adults have only pharyngeal gill slits |
| | **Chordata Subphylum:** Cephalochordata | *Branchiostoma* (amphioxus) | • adults have all of the main features of chordates |
| Sea otter<br>Source: Chapter 30, Section 1, p. 880 | **Chordata Subphylum:** Vertebrata | *Panthera* (panther) | • the hallmark feature of all vertebrates is a spinal column |

*In the Kingdom Plantae the major phyla are referred to as "divisions."

# Three-Domain Classification

Increasingly, biologists are classifying organisms into categories larger than kingdoms called domains. The three domains are: Domain Bacteria, which includes the Kingdom Eubacteria; Domain Archaea, which includes the Kingdom Archaebacteria; and the Domain Eukarya, which includes protists, fungi, plants, and animals. With discoveries, this classification system may change.

| DOMAIN | Bacteria | Archaea | Eukarya | | | |
|---|---|---|---|---|---|---|
| KINGDOM | Eubacteria | Archaebacteria | Protista | Fungi | Plantae | Animalia |

# Scientific Word Origins

This list of prefixes, suffixes, and roots is provided to help you understand science terms used throughout this biology textbook. The list identifies whether the prefix, suffix, or root is of Greek *(G)* or Latin *(L)* origin. Also listed is the meaning of the prefix, suffix, or root and a science word in which it is used.

| Origin | Meaning | Example |
|---|---|---|
| **A** | | |
| ad *(L)* | to, toward | adaxial |
| aero *(G)* | air | aerobic |
| an *(G)* | without | anerobic |
| ana *(G)* | up | anaphase |
| andro *(G)* | male | androceium |
| angio *(G)* | of seed | angiosperm |
| anth/o *(G)* | flower | anthophyte |
| anti *(G)* | against | antibody |
| aqu/a *(L)* | of water | aquatic |
| archae *(G)* | ancient | achaebacteria |
| arthro, artio *(G)* | jointed | arthropod |
| askos *(G)* | bag | ascospore |
| aster *(G)* | star | Asteroidea |
| autos *(G)* | self | autoimmune |
| **B** | | |
| bi *(L)* | two | bipedal |
| bio *(G)* | life | biosphere |
| **C** | | |
| carn *(L)* | flesh | carnivore |
| ceph *(G)* | head | cephalopod |
| chloros *(G)* | light green | chlorophyll |
| chroma *(G)* | pigmented | chromosome |
| cide *(L)* | to kill | insecticide |
| circ *(L)* | circular | circadian |
| cocc/coccus *(G)* | small and round | streptococcus |
| con *(L)* | together | convergent |
| cyte *(G)* | cell | cytoplasm |
| **D** | | |
| de *(L)* | remove | decompose |
| dendron *(G)* | tree | dendrite |
| dent *(L)* | tooth | edentate |
| derm *(G)* | skin | epidermis |
| di *(G)* | two | disaccharide |
| dia *(G)* | apart | diaphragm |
| dorm *(L)* | sleep | dormancy |

| Origin | Meaning | Example |
|---|---|---|
| **E** | | |
| echino *(G)* | spiny | echinoderm |
| ec *(G)* | outer | ecosystem |
| ella(e) *(L)* | small | organelle |
| endo *(G)* | within | endosperm |
| epi *(G)* | upon | epidermis |
| eu *(G)* | true | eukaryote |
| exo *(G)* | outside | exoskeleton |
| **F** | | |
| fer *(L)* | to carry | conifer |
| **G** | | |
| gastro *(G)* | stomach | gastropod |
| genesis *(G)* | to originate | oogenesis |
| gen/(e)(o) *(G)* | kind | genotype |
| gon *(G)* | reproductive | archegonium |
| gravi *(L)* | heavy | gravitropism |
| gymn/o *(G)* | naked | gymnosperm |
| gyn/e *(G)* | female | gynecium |
| **H** | | |
| hal(o) *(G)* | salt | halophyte |
| hapl(o) *(G)* | single | haploid |
| hemi *(G)* | half | hemisphere |
| hem(o) *(G)* | blood | hemoglobin |
| herb/a(i) *(L)* | vegetation | herbivore |
| heter/o *(G)* | different | heterotrophic |
| hom(e)/o *(G)* | same | homeostasis |
| hom *(L)* | human | hominid |
| hydr/o *(G)* | water | hydrolysis |
| **I** | | |
| inter *(L)* | between | internode |
| intra *(L)* | within | intracellular |
| is/o *(G)* | equal | isotonic |
| **J** | | |
| jug *(L)* | to join | jugular |

| Origin | Meaning | Example |
|---|---|---|
| **K** | | |
| kary *(G)* | nucleus | ekaryote |
| kera *(G)* | hornlike | keratin |
| **L** | | |
| leuc/o *(G)* | white | leukocyte |
| logy *(G)* | study of | biology |
| lymph/o *(L)* | water | lymphocyte |
| lysis *(G)* | break up | dialysis |
| **M** | | |
| macr/o *(G)* | large | macromolecule |
| meg/a *(G)* | great | megaspore |
| meso *(L)* | in the middle | mesophyll |
| meta *(G)* | after | metaphase |
| micr/o *(G)* | small | microscope |
| mon/o *(G)* | only one | monocotyledon |
| morph/o *(G)* | form | morphology |
| **N** | | |
| nema *(G)* | a thread | nematode |
| neuro *(G)* | nerve | neuron |
| nod *(L)* | knot | nodule |
| nomy(e) *(G)* | system of laws | taxonomy |
| **O** | | |
| olig/o *(G)* | small, few | oligochaete |
| omn *(L)* | all | omnivore |
| orni(s) *(G)* | bird | ornithology |
| oste/o *(G)* | bone formation | osteocyte |
| ov *(L)* | an egg | oviduct |
| **P** | | |
| pal(a)e/o *(G)* | ancient | paleontology |
| para *(G)* | beside | parathyroid |
| path/o *(G)* | suffering | pathogen |
| ped *(L)* | foot | centipede |
| per *(L)* | through | permeable |
| peri *(G)* | around, about | peristalsis |
| phag/o *(G)* | eating | phagocyte |
| phot/o *(G)* | light | photosynthesis |
| phyl *(G)* | race, class | phylogeny |
| phyll *(G)* | leaf | chlorophyll |
| phyte *(G)* | plant | epiphyte |
| pinna *(L)* | feather | pinnate |

| Origin | Meaning | Example |
|---|---|---|
| **P continued** | | |
| plasm/o *(G)* | to form | plasmodium |
| pod *(G)* | foot | gastropod |
| poly *(G)* | many | polymer |
| post *(L)* | after | posterior |
| pro *(G) (L)* | before | prokaryote |
| prot/o *(G)* | first | protocells |
| pseud/o *(G)* | false | pseudopodium |
| **R** | | |
| re *(L)* | back to original | reproduce |
| rhiz/o *(L)* | root | rhizoid |
| **S** | | |
| scope *(G)* | to look | microscope |
| some *(G)* | body | lysome |
| sperm *(G)* | seed | gymnosperm |
| stasis *(G)* | remain constant | homeostasis |
| stom *(G)* | mouthlike opening | stomata |
| syn *(G)* | together | synapse |
| **T** | | |
| tel/o *(G)* | end | telophase |
| terr *(L)* | of Earth | terrestrial |
| therm *(G)* | heat | endotherm |
| thylak *(G)* | sack | thylakoid |
| trans *(L)* | across | transpiration |
| trich *(G)* | hair | trichome |
| trop/o *(G)* | a change | gravitropism |
| trophic *(G)* | nourishment | heterotrophic |
| **U** | | |
| uni *(L)* | one | unicellular |
| **V** | | |
| vacc/a *(L)* | cow | vaccine |
| vore *(L)* | eat greedily | omnivore |
| **X** | | |
| xer/o *(G)* | dry | xerophye |
| **Z** | | |
| zo/o *(G)* | living being | zoology |
| zygous *(G)* | two joined | homozygous |

Reference Handbook

## PERIODIC TABLE OF THE ELEMENTS

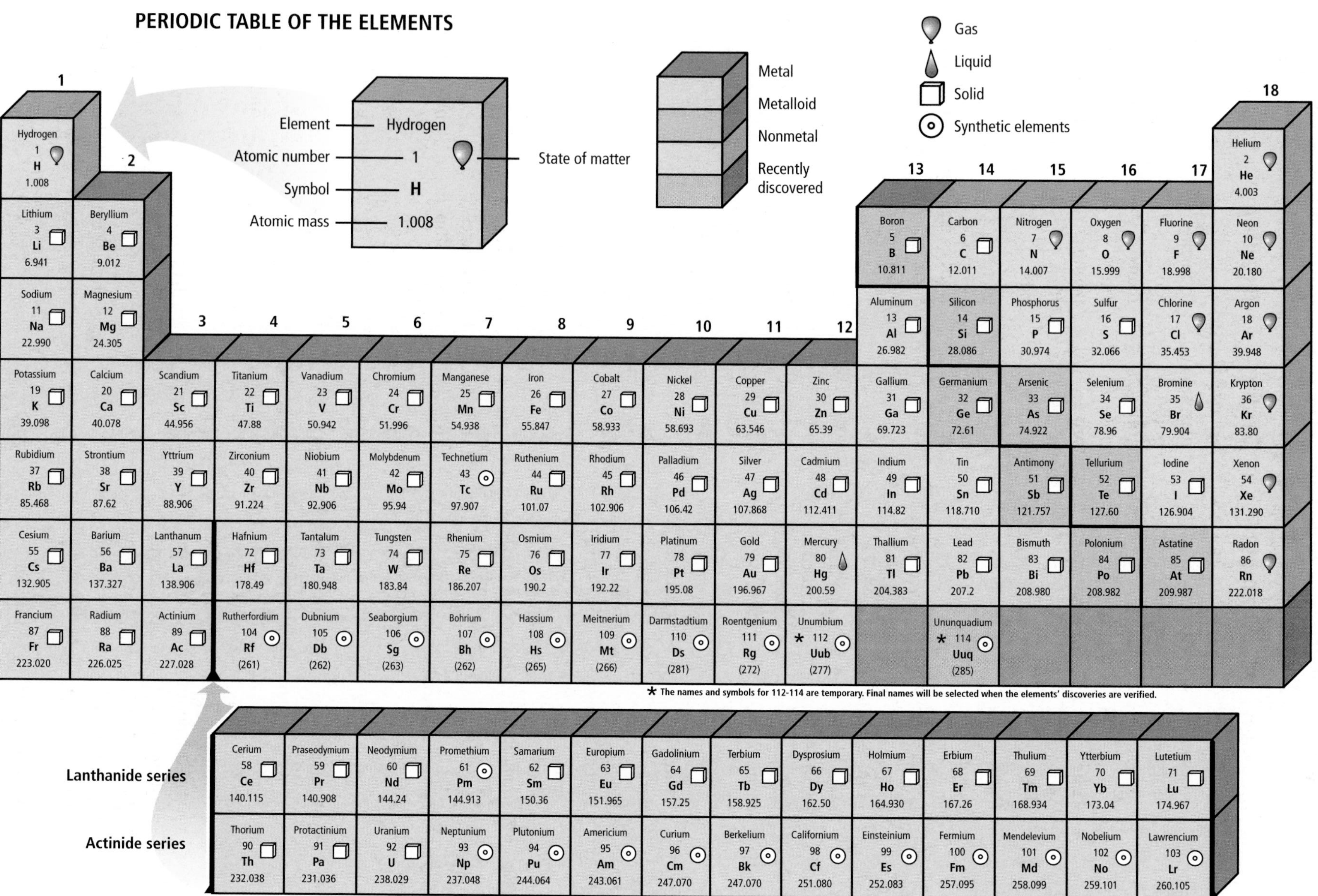


| | 1 | 2 | 3 | 4 | 5 | 6 | 7 | 8 | 9 | 10 | 11 | 12 | 13 | 14 | 15 | 16 | 17 | 18 |
|---|---|---|---|---|---|---|---|---|---|---|---|---|---|---|---|---|---|---|
| 1 | Hydrogen 1 H 1.008 | | | | | | | | | | | | | | | | | Helium 2 He 4.003 |
| 2 | Lithium 3 Li 6.941 | Beryllium 4 Be 9.012 | | | | | | | | | | | Boron 5 B 10.811 | Carbon 6 C 12.011 | Nitrogen 7 N 14.007 | Oxygen 8 O 15.999 | Fluorine 9 F 18.998 | Neon 10 Ne 20.180 |
| 3 | Sodium 11 Na 22.990 | Magnesium 12 Mg 24.305 | | | | | | | | | | | Aluminum 13 Al 26.982 | Silicon 14 Si 28.086 | Phosphorus 15 P 30.974 | Sulfur 16 S 32.066 | Chlorine 17 Cl 35.453 | Argon 18 Ar 39.948 |
| 4 | Potassium 19 K 39.098 | Calcium 20 Ca 40.078 | Scandium 21 Sc 44.956 | Titanium 22 Ti 47.88 | Vanadium 23 V 50.942 | Chromium 24 Cr 51.996 | Manganese 25 Mn 54.938 | Iron 26 Fe 55.847 | Cobalt 27 Co 58.933 | Nickel 28 Ni 58.693 | Copper 29 Cu 63.546 | Zinc 30 Zn 65.39 | Gallium 31 Ga 69.723 | Germanium 32 Ge 72.61 | Arsenic 33 As 74.922 | Selenium 34 Se 78.96 | Bromine 35 Br 79.904 | Krypton 36 Kr 83.80 |
| 5 | Rubidium 37 Rb 85.468 | Strontium 38 Sr 87.62 | Yttrium 39 Y 88.906 | Zirconium 40 Zr 91.224 | Niobium 41 Nb 92.906 | Molybdenum 42 Mo 95.94 | Technetium 43 Tc 97.907 | Ruthenium 44 Ru 101.07 | Rhodium 45 Rh 102.906 | Palladium 46 Pd 106.42 | Silver 47 Ag 107.868 | Cadmium 48 Cd 112.411 | Indium 49 In 114.82 | Tin 50 Sn 118.710 | Antimony 51 Sb 121.757 | Tellurium 52 Te 127.60 | Iodine 53 I 126.904 | Xenon 54 Xe 131.290 |
| 6 | Cesium 55 Cs 132.905 | Barium 56 Ba 137.327 | Lanthanum 57 La 138.906 | Hafnium 72 Hf 178.49 | Tantalum 73 Ta 180.948 | Tungsten 74 W 183.84 | Rhenium 75 Re 186.207 | Osmium 76 Os 190.2 | Iridium 77 Ir 192.22 | Platinum 78 Pt 195.08 | Gold 79 Au 196.967 | Mercury 80 Hg 200.59 | Thallium 81 Tl 204.383 | Lead 82 Pb 207.2 | Bismuth 83 Bi 208.980 | Polonium 84 Po 208.982 | Astatine 85 At 209.987 | Radon 86 Rn 222.018 |
| 7 | Francium 87 Fr 223.020 | Radium 88 Ra 226.025 | Actinium 89 Ac 227.028 | Rutherfordium 104 Rf (261) | Dubnium 105 Db (262) | Seaborgium 106 Sg (263) | Bohrium 107 Bh (262) | Hassium 108 Hs (265) | Meitnerium 109 Mt (266) | Darmstadtium 110 Ds (281) | Roentgenium 111 Rg (272) | Ununbium * 112 Uub (277) | | Ununquadium * 114 Uuq (285) | | | | |

* The names and symbols for 112-114 are temporary. Final names will be selected when the elements' discoveries are verified.

| | | | | | | | | | | | | | | |
|---|---|---|---|---|---|---|---|---|---|---|---|---|---|---|
| Lanthanide series | Cerium 58 Ce 140.115 | Praseodymium 59 Pr 140.908 | Neodymium 60 Nd 144.24 | Promethium 61 Pm 144.913 | Samarium 62 Sm 150.36 | Europium 63 Eu 151.965 | Gadolinium 64 Gd 157.25 | Terbium 65 Tb 158.925 | Dysprosium 66 Dy 162.50 | Holmium 67 Ho 164.930 | Erbium 68 Er 167.26 | Thulium 69 Tm 168.934 | Ytterbium 70 Yb 173.04 | Lutetium 71 Lu 174.967 |
| Actinide series | Thorium 90 Th 232.038 | Protactinium 91 Pa 231.036 | Uranium 92 U 238.029 | Neptunium 93 Np 237.048 | Plutonium 94 Pu 244.064 | Americium 95 Am 243.061 | Curium 96 Cm 247.070 | Berkelium 97 Bk 247.070 | Californium 98 Cf 251.080 | Einsteinium 99 Es 252.083 | Fermium 100 Fm 257.095 | Mendelevium 101 Md 258.099 | Nobelium 102 No 259.101 | Lawrencium 103 Lr 260.105 |

# Glossary/Glosario

A multilingual science glossary at biologygmh.com includes Arabic, Bengali, Chinese, English, Haitian Creole, Hmong, Korean, Portuguese, Russian, Tagalog, Urdu, and Vietnamese.

## Pronunciation Key

Use the following key to help you sound out words in the glossary.

| | | | |
|---|---|---|---|
| **a** | back (BAK) | **ew** | food (FEWD) |
| **ay** | day (DAY) | **yoo** | pure (PYOOR) |
| **ah** | father (FAH thur) | **yew** | few (FYEW) |
| **ow** | flower (FLOW ur) | **uh** | comma (CAHM uh) |
| **ar** | car (CAR) | **u** (+ con) | rub (RUB) |
| **e** | less (LES) | **sh** | shelf (SHELF) |
| **ee** | leaf (LEEF) | **ch** | nature (NAY chur) |
| **ih** | trip (TRIHP) | **g** | gift (GIHFT) |
| **i** (i + con + e) | idea, life (i DEE uh, life) | **j** | gem (JEM) |
| **oh** | go (GOH) | **ing** | sing (SING) |
| **aw** | soft (SAWFT) | **zh** | vision (VIHZH un) |
| **or** | orbit (OR but) | **k** | cake (KAYK) |
| **oy** | coin (COYN) | **s** | seed, cent (SEED, SENT) |
| **oo** | foot (FOOT) | **z** | zone, raise (ZOHN, RAYZ) |

**Cómo usar el glosario en español:**
1. Busca el término en inglés que desees encontrar.
2. El término en español, junto con la definición, se encuentran en la columna de la derecha.

Glossary/ Glosario

## A

### English

**abdomen: (p. 763)** in arthropods, posterior body region of an arthropod that contains fused segments, digestive structures, reproductive organs, and bears additional legs; in humans, part of body that is between the diaphragm and pelvis.

**abiotic (ay bi AH tihk) factor: (p. 35)** any nonliving factor in an organism's environment, such as soil, water temperature, and light availability.

**abyssal zone: (p. 81)** deepest, very cold region of the open ocean.

**acid: (p. 164)** substance that releases hydrogen ions ($H^+$) when dissolved in water; an acidic solution has a pH less than 7.

**acoelomate (ay SEE lum ayt): (p. 701)** animal with a solid body that lacks a fluid-filled body cavity between the gut and the body wall.

**acrasin (uh KRA sun): (p. 563)** chemical given off by starving amoeba-like cells that serves as a signal to the cells to form a sluglike colony.

**actin: (p. 948)** protein filament in muscle cells that functions with myosin in contraction.

**action potential: (p. 964)** nerve impulse.

### Español

**abdomen: (pág. 763)** región posterior del cuerpo de un artrópodo, la que contiene segmentos fusionados, estructuras digestivas, los órganos reproductores y que sostiene patas adicionales.

**factor abiótico: (pág. 35)** todo factor inanimado en el ambiente de un organismo, como el suelo, el agua, la temperatura del agua y la disponibilidad de luz.

**zona abisal: (pág. 81)** la zona más profunda y más fría del océano.

**ácido: (pág. 164)** sustancia que libera iones hidrógeno (H+) cuando se halla disuelta en agua; una solución ácida contiene un pH menor que 7.

**acelomado: (pág. 701)** animal de cuerpo sólido que carece de una cavidad corporal llena de fluido entre las órganos internos y las paredes del cuerpo.

**acrasina: (pág. 563)** sustancia química que liberan ciertas células ameboides, cuando tienen hambre, y que sirve de señal para que estas células formen una colonia viscosa.

**actina: (pág. 948)** filamento proteico de las células musculares que, junto con la miosina, participan en la contracción muscular.

**potencial de acción: (pág. 964)** un impulso nervioso.

**activation energy: (p. 158)** minimum amount of energy needed for reactants to form products in a chemical reaction.

**active site: (p. 160)** specific place where a substrate binds on an enzyme.

**active transport: (p. 205)** energy-requiring process by which substances move across the plasma membrane against a concentration gradient.

**adaptation (a dap TAY shun): (p. 10)** inherited characteristic of a species that develops over time in response to an environmental factor, enabling the species to survive.

**adaptive radiation: (p. 439)** diversification of a species into a number of different species, often over a relatively short time span.

**addiction: (p. 981)** psychological and/or physiological dependence on a drug.

**adenosine triphosphate (uh DEN uh seen • tri FAHS fayt) (ATP): (p. 221)** energy-carrying biological molecule, which, when broken down, drives cellular activities.

**adolescence (a dul ES unts): (p. 1063)** developmental phase that begins with puberty and ends at adulthood.

**adulthood: (p. 1064)** developmental phase that occurs at the end of adolescence, when physical growth is complete.

**aerobic process: (p. 228)** a metabolic process that requires oxygen.

**aerobic respiration: (p. 228)** metabolic process in which pyruvate is broken down and electron-carrier molecules are used to produce ATP through electron transport.

**age structure: (p. 104)** in any population, the number of individuals in their pre-reproductive, reproductive, and post-reproductive years.

**agonistic (ag oh NIHS tihk) behavior: (p. 917)** threatening or combative behavior between two members of the same species that usually does not result in injury or death.

**air sac: (p. 863)** in birds, the posterior and anterior structure used in respiration, resulting in only oxygenated air moving through the lungs.

**aldosterone (al DAWS tuh rohn): (p. 1035)** steroid hormone produced by the adrenal cortex that acts on the kidneys and is important for sodium reabsorption.

**allele: (p. 278)** alternative form that a single gene may have for a particular trait.

**allergy: (p. 1094)** overactive immune response to environmental antigens.

**allopatric speciation: (p. 437)** occurs when a population divided by a geographic barrier evolves into two or more populations unable to interbreed.

**energía de activación: (pág. 158)** cantidad mínima de energía que requieren los reactivos para formar productos durante una reacción química.

**sitio activo: (pág. 160)** lugar específico donde un sustrato se une a una enzima.

**transporte activo: (pág. 205)** proceso que requiere energía y que le permite a una sustancia atravesar la membrana plasmática contra un gradiente de concentración.

**adaptación: (pág. 10)** característica heredada de una especie; esta característica evoluciona a lo largo del tiempo en respuesta a un factor ambiental y le ayuda a la especie a sobrevivir.

**radiación adaptativa: (pág. 439)** diversificación de una especie en diferentes especies, a menudo en un período relativamente corto.

**adicción: (pág. 981)** dependencia psicológica o fisiológica a una droga.

**trifosfato de adenosina (ATP): (pág. 221)** molécula biológica que transporta energía, y que al desdoblarse, hace funcionar las actividades celulares.

**adolescencia: (pág. 1063)** fase del desarrollo que se inicia en la pubertad y termina al comenzar la edad adulta.

**edad adulta: (pág. 1064)** fase del desarrollo que empieza al terminar la adolescencia, cuando se completa el crecimiento físico.

**proceso aeróbico: (pág. 228)** proceso metabólico que requiere oxígeno.

**respiración aeróbica: (pág. 228)** proceso metabólico en que se desdobla el piruvato y las moléculas transportadoras de electrones ayudan a producir ATP mediante el transporte de electrones.

**estructura etaria: (pág. 104)** el número de individuos en edad prereproductora, reproductora y postreproductora en una población.

**comportamiento agonístico: (pág. 917)** comportamiento amenazador o combativo entre dos miembros de la misma especie y que normalmente no produce heridas o muerte.

**sacos aéreos: (pág. 863)** estructuras anteriores y posteriores de las aves que participan en la respiración celular y permiten sólo el paso de sangre oxigenada por los pulmones.

**aldosterona: (pág. 1035)** hormona esteroide producida por la corteza adrenal, la cual actúa sobre los riñones y es importante para la reabsorción de sodio.

**alelo: (pág. 278)** forma alternativa de un gene determinado para un rasgo dado.

**alergia: (pág. 1094)** acentuada respuesta inmune a un antígeno del ambiente.

**especiación alopátrica: (pág. 437)** sucede cuando una población separada en dos por una barrera geográfica, evoluciona y se convierte en dos poblaciones incapaces de entrecruzarse.

# G

**gametangium (ga muh TAN jee um): (p. 583)** reproductive hyphal structure of zygomycetes that contains a haploid nucleus.

**gametangio: (pág. 583)** estructura reproductora de las hifas de los cigomicetos: contiene un núcleo haploide.

**gamete: (p. 271)** a haploid sex cell, formed during meiosis, that can combine with another haploid sex cell and produce a diploid fertilized egg.

**gameto: (pág. 271)** célula sexual haploide, formada durante la meiosis, que se puede combinar con otra célula sexual haploide y producir un huevo diploide fecundado.

**ganglion: (p. 728)** group of nerve-cell bodies that coordinates incoming and outgoing nerve impulses.

**ganglio: (pág. 728)** conjunto de cuerpos celulares de neuronas que se encargan de coordinar la entrada y salida de impulsos nerviosos.

**gastrovascular (gas troh VAS kyuh lur) cavity: (p. 711)** in cnidarians, the space surrounded by an inner cell layer, where digestion take place.

**cavidad gastrovascular: (pág. 711)** en los cnidarios, espacio rodeado por una capa interna de células y en que ocurre la digestión.

**gastrula (GAS truh luh): (p. 696)** two-cell-layer sac with an opening at one end that forms from the blastula during embryonic development.

**gástrula: (pág. 696)** saco de dos células de espesor, con una apertura en uno de sus extremos, que se forma a partir de la blástula durante el desarrollo embrionario.

**gel electrophoresis: (p. 365)** process that involves using electric current to separate certain biological molecules by size.

**electroforesis en gel: (pág. 365)** proceso en que se usa corriente eléctrica para separar ciertas moléculas biológicas, según su tamaño.

**gene: (p. 270)** functional unit that controls inherited trait expression that is passed on from one generation to another generation.

**gene: (pág. 270)** unidad funcional que controla la expresión de un rasgo heredado y que se transmite de una generación a otra.

**gene regulation: (p. 342)** ability of an organism to control which genes are transcribed in response to the environment.

**regulación génica: (pág. 342)** capacidad de un organismo para controlar los genes que se transcriben en respuesta a un ambiente.

**gene therapy: (p. 378)** technique to correct mutated disease-causing genes.

**terapia génica: (pág. 378)** técnica para corregir genes con mutaciones que causan enfermedades.

**genetic diversity: (p. 116)** variety of inheritable characteristics or genes in an interbreeding population.

**diversidad genética: (pág. 116)** variedad de características o genes heredables en una población que se entrecruza.

**genetic drift: (p. 433)** random change in allelic frequencies in a population.

**deriva genética: (pág. 433)** cambio aleatorio de frecuencias alélicas en una población.

**genetic engineering: (p. 363)** technology used to manipulate an organism's DNA by inserting the DNA of another organism.

**ingeniería genética: (pág. 363)** tecnología que se aplica para manipular el DNA de un organismo, mediante la inserción del DNA de otro organismo.

**genetic recombination: (p. 283)** new combination of genes produced by crossing over and independent assortment.

**recombinación genética: (pág. 283)** nueva combinación de genes producida por el entrecruzamiento y la distribución independiente de genes.

**genetics: (p. 277)** science of heredity.

**genética: (pág. 277)** ciencia que estudia la herencia.

**genome: (p. 364)** total DNA in each cell nucleus of an organism.

**genoma: (pág. 364)** todo el DNA en el núcleo de cada célula de un organismo.

**genomics: (p. 378)** study of an organism's genome.

**genómica: (pág. 378)** estudio del genoma de un organismo.

**genotype: (p. 279)** an organism's allele pairs.

**genotipo: (pág. 279)** pares de alelos de un organismo.

**genus: (p. 487)** taxonomic group of closely related species with a common ancester.

**género: (pág. 487)** grupo taxonómico de especies estrechamente emparentadas que comparten un antepasado común.

**geologic time scale: (p. 396)** model showing major geological and biological events in Earth's history.

**escala del tiempo geológico: (pág. 396)** modelo que muestra los principales eventos geológicos y biológicos de la historia de la Tierra.

**germination: (p. 678)** process in which a seed's embryo begins to grow.

**gestation: (p. 887)** species-specific amount of time during which the young develop in the uterus before they are born.

**gibberellins: (p. 649)** group of plant hormones that are transported in vascular tissue and that can affect seed growth, stimulate cell division, and cause cell elongation.

**gill (p. 738)** respiratory structure of most mollusks and aquatic arthropods.

**gizzard: (p. 746)** muscular sac in birds that contains hard particles that help grind soil and food before they pass into the intestine.

**gland: (p. 887)** an organ or group of cells that secretes a substance for use elsewhere in the body.

**glucagon (GLEW kuh gahn): (p. 1034)** hormone produced by the pancreas that signals liver cells to convert glycogen to glucose and release glucose into the blood.

**glycolysis: (p. 229)** anaerobic process; first stage of cellular respiration in which glucose is broken down into two molecules of pyruvate.

**Golgi apparatus: (p. 195)** flattened stack of tubular membranes that modifies, sorts, and packages proteins into vesicles and transports them to other organelles or out of the cell.

**gradualism: (p. 440)** theory that evolution occurs in small, gradual steps over time.

**granum: (p. 223)** one of the stacks of pigment-containing thylakoids in a plant's chloroplasts.

**grassland: (p. 70)** biome characterized by fertile soils with a thick cover of grasses.

**ground tissue: (p. 638)** plant tissue consisting of parenchyma, collenchyma, and sclerenchyma.

**growth: (p. 9)** process that results in mass being added to an organism; may include formation of new cells and new structures.

**guard cell: (p. 636)** one of a pair of cells that function in the opening and closing of a plant's stomata by changes in their shape.

**germinación: (pág. 678)** proceso que inicia el crecimiento del embrión de una semilla.

**gestación: (pág. 887)** período específico para cada especie, durante el cual las crías se desarrollan en el útero, antes de nacer.

**giberelinas: (pág. 649)** grupo de hormonas vegetales que son transportadas por el tejido vascular y que pueden afectar el crecimiento de las semillas, y estimular la división y la elongacion celular.

**branquia: (pág. 738)** estructura respiratoria de la mayoría de los moluscos.

**molleja: (pág. 746)** saco muscular que contiene partículas duras que ayudan a moler el suelo y los alimentos, antes de que pasen al intestino.

**glándula: (pág. 887)** grupo de células que secretan una sustancia a usarse en alguna otra parte del cuerpo.

**glucagón: (pág. 1034)** hormona producida por el páncreas; les indica a las células del hígado que conviertan glucógeno en glucosa y que liberen la glucosa hacia el torrente sanguíneo.

**glucólisis: (pág. 229)** proceso anaeróbico; primera etapa de la respiración celular, en la cual la glucosa se transforma en dos moléculas de piruvato.

**aparato de Golgi: (pág. 195)** conjunto de membranas tubulares aplanadas que modifica, acomoda y empaca proteínas en vesículas y luego las transporta hacia otros organelos o hacia afuera de la célula.

**gradualismo: (pág. 440)** teoría que señala que la evolución sucede gradualmente, en pasos pequeños, a lo largo del tiempo.

**grana: (pág. 223)** conjunto de tilacoides con pigmentos de los cloroplastos de una planta.

**pradera: (pág. 70)** bioma caracterizado por suelos fértiles con una espesa cubierta de pastos.

**tejido fundamental: (pág. 638)** tejido vegetal que consiste en parénquima, colénquima y esclerénquima.

**crecimiento: (pág. 9)** proceso que provoca el aumento de masa en un organismo; puede incluir la formación de células y estructuras nuevas.

**célula guardiana: (pág. 636)** una de las células del par de células cuya función es abrir y cerrar, mediante cambios en su forma, los estomas de la planta.

## H

**habitat: (p. 38)** physical area in which an organism lives.

**habitat fragmentation: (p. 127)** habitat loss from separation of an ecosystem into small pieces of land.

**hábitat: (pág. 38)** área física en que vive un organismo.

**fragmentación del hábitat: (pág. 127)** pérdida de hábitat como resultado de la partición de un ecosistema en terrenos pequeños.

**Okazaki fragment:** **(p. 334)** short segment of DNA synthesized discontinuously in small segments in the 3' to 5' direction by DNA polymerase.

**omnivore** **(AHM nih vor):** **(p. 42)** heterotroph that consumes both plants and animals.

**oocyte** **(OH uh site):** **(p. 1050)** immature egg inside an ovary.

**open circulatory system:** **(p. 739)** blood is pumped out of vessels into open spaces surrounding body organs.

**operant conditioning:** **(p. 913)** learned behavior that occurs when an association is made between a response to a stimulus and a punishment or a reward.

**operculum** **(oh PUR kyuh lum):** **(p. 824)** movable, protective flap that covers a fish's gills and helps to pump water that enters the mouth and moves over the gills.

**operon:** **(p. 342)** section of DNA containing genes for proteins required for a specific metabolic pathway—consists of an operator, promoter, regulatory gene, and genes coding for proteins.

**opposable first digit:** **(p. 452)** a digit, either a thumb or a toe, that is set apart from the other digits and can be brought across the palm or foot so that it touches or nearly touches the other digits; this allows animals to grasp an object in a powerful grip.

**order:** **(p. 488)** taxonomic group that contains related families.

**organelle:** **(p. 186)** specialized internal cell structure that carries out specific cell functions such as protein synthesis and energy transformation.

**organism:** **(p. 6)** anything that has or once had all the characteristics of life.

**organization:** **(p. 8)** orderly structure shown by living things.

**osmosis** **(ahs MOH sus):** **(p. 203)** diffusion of water across a selectively permeable membrane.

**ossification:** **(p. 942)** formation of bone from osteoblasts.

**osteoblast:** **(p. 942)** bone-forming cell.

**osteoclast:** **(p. 943)** cell that breaks down bone cells.

**osteocyte:** **(p. 942)** living bone cell.

**overexploitation:** **(p. 124)** overuse of species with economic value—a factor in species extinction.

**oviduct** **(OH vuh duct):** **(p. 1050)** tube that transports an egg released from an ovary to the uterus.

**fragmento Okazaki:** **(pág. 334)** segmento corto de DNA que la enzima polimerasa de DNA sintetiza discontinuamente en segmentos pequeños en la dirección de 3' a 5'.

**omnívoro:** **(pág. 42)** heterótrofo que consume tanto plantas como animales.

**oocito:** **(pág. 1050)** óvulo inmaduro dentro de un ovario.

**sistema circulatorio abierto:** **(pág. 739)** la sangre se bombea fuera de los vasos hacia los espacios abiertos que rodean los órganos corporales.

**condicionamiento operante:** **(pág. 913)** comportamiento adquirido que ocurre al asociar una respuesta con un estímulo y un castigo o una recompensa.

**opérculo:** **(pág. 824)** protector móvil que cubre las agallas de los peces y ayuda a bombear el agua que entra a la boca y se desplaza sobre las agallas.

**operón:** **(pág. 342)** sección de DNA que contiene los genes para las proteínas requeridas para un trayecto metabólico específico; consiste en un operador, un promotor, un gene regulador y un código de genes para las proteínas.

**primer dígito oponible:** **(pág. 452)** dígito, ya sea un pulgar o un dígito del pie, que se diferencia del resto de los dígitos y el cual se puede cruzar a través de la palma de la mano o del pie y puede tocar o casi tocar los otros dígitos; esto les permite a los animales asir objetos fuertemente.

**orden:** **(pág. 488)** agrupación taxonómica de familias relacionadas.

**organelo:** **(pág. 186)** estructura celular especializada interna con funciones celulares específicas como la síntesis y la transformación de energía.

**organismo:** **(pág. 6)** cualquier cosa que tuvo o tiene todas las características de la vida.

**organización:** **(pág. 8)** estructura ordenada de todos los seres vivos.

**osmosis:** **(pág. 203)** difusión del agua a través de una membrana de permeabilidad selectiva.

**osificación:** **(pág. 942)** formación ósea a partir de los osteoblastos.

**osteoblasto:** **(pág. 942)** célula formadora de hueso.

**osteoclasto:** **(pág. 943)** célula que destruye las células óseas.

**osteocito:** **(pág. 942)** célula ósea viva.

**sobre-explotación:** **(pág. 124)** uso excesivo de las especies con un valor económico; es un factor en la extinción de especies.

**oviducto:** **(pág. 1050)** conducto que transporta un óvulo desde el ovario hasta el útero.

# P

**pacemaker:** **(p. 995)** heart's sinoatrial node, which initiates contraction of the heart.

**marcapaso:** **(pág. 995)** nódulo atrioventricular del corazón que inicia la contracción cardíaca.

**paleontologist** **(pay lee ahn TAH luh just):** **(p. 394)** scientist who studies fossils.

**paleontólogo:** **(pág. 394)** científico que estudia los fósiles.

**palisade mesophyll** **(mehz uh fihl):** **(p. 644)** leaf-tissue layer that contains many chloroplasts and is the site where most photosynthesis takes place.

**mesófilo en empalizada:** **(pág. 644)** capa de tejido de la hoja que contiene muchos cloroplastos y donde se ubica la mayor parte de la fotosíntesis.

**pandemic:** **(p. 1081)** widespread epidemic.

**pandemia:** **(pág. 1081)** epidemia que se extiende a muchos países.

**parasitism** **(PER uh suh tih zum):** **(p. 40)** symbiotic relationship in which one organism benefits at the expense of another organism.

**parasitismo:** **(pág. 40)** relación simbiótica en la cual un organismo se beneficia a expensas de otro.

**parasympathetic nervous system:** **(p. 972)** branch of the autonomic nervous system that controls organs and is most active when the body is at rest.

**sistema nervioso parasimpático (SNP):** **(pág. 972)** división del sistema nervioso autónomo que controla los órganos y es más activo cuando el cuerpo está en reposo.

**parathyroid hormone:** **(p. 1034)** substance produced by the parathyroid gland that increases blood calcium levels by stimulating bones to release calcium.

**hormona paratiroides:** **(pág. 1034)** sustancia producida por la glándula tiroides que aumenta los niveles de calcio en la sangre al estimular la liberación de calcio en los huesos.

**parenchyma** **(puh RENG kuh muh)** **cell:** **(p. 632)** spherical, thin-walled cell found throughout most plants that can function in photosynthesis, gas exchange, protection, storage, and tissue repair and replacement.

**célula de parénquima:** **(pág. 632)** célula esférica con paredes delgadas que se encuentra en la mayoría de las plantas y que funciona en la fotosíntesis, el intercambio de gases, la protección, el almacenamiento y reparación o reemplazo de tejidos.

**pathogen:** **(p. 1076)** agent, such as a bacterium, virus, protozoan, or fungus, that causes infectious disease.

**patógeno:** **(pág. 1076)** agente, como las bacterias, los virus, los protozoarios o los hongos, causante de enfermedades infecciosas.

**pedicellaria** **(peh dih sih LAHR ee uh):** **(p. 793)** small pincher that helps echinoderms catch food and remove foreign materials from the skin.

**pedicelarios:** **(pág. 793)** pinza minúscula de los equinodermos que los ayuda a obtener alimento y eliminar objetos extraños de la piel.

**pedigree:** **(p. 299)** diagrammed family history that is used to study inheritance patterns of a trait through several generations and that can be used to predict disorders in future offspring.

**pedigrí:** **(pág. 299)** historia familiar diagramada que se emplea para el estudio de los patrones hereditarios de un rasgo a través de varias generaciones, capaz de predecir trastornos en la progenie futura.

**pedipalp:** **(p. 772)** one of a pair of arachnid appendages used for sensing and holding prey and in male spiders used for reproduction.

**pedipalpo:** **(pág. 772)** uno de un par de apéndices de los arácnidos utilizado para manipular la presa y, en las arañas macho, para la reproducción.

**peer review:** **(p. 14)** a process in which the procedures used during an experiment may be repeated and the results are evaluated by scientists who are in the same field or are conducting similar research.

**evaluación de compañeros:** **(pág. 14)** proceso en que los procedimientos que se usan durante un experimento pueden repetirse y otros científicos en el mismo campo de estudio o que realizan investigaciones similares pueden evaluar los resultados.

**pellicle:** **(p. 547)** membrane layer that encloses a paramecium and some other protists.

**película:** **(pág. 547)** capa membranosa que encierra un paramecio.

**pepsin:** **(p. 1021)** digestive enzyme involved in the stomach's chemical digestion of proteins.

**pepsina:** **(pág. 1021)** enzima digestiva presente en la digestión química de las proteínas.

**perennial:** **(p. 621)** plant that can live for several years.

**perenne:** **(pág. 621)** planta que vive por varios años.

**pericycle:** **(p. 640)** plant tissue that produces lateral roots.

**periciclo:** **(pág. 640)** tejido vegetal que produce raíces laterales.

**period: (p. 396)** subdivision of an era on the geologic time scale.

**período: (pág. 396)** subdivisión de una era en la escala geológica.

**peripheral nervous system: (p. 968)** consists of sensory and motor neurons that transmit information to and from the central nervous system.

**sistema nervioso periférico (SNP): (pág. 968)** compuesto por neuronas sensoriales y motoras que transportan información desde y hacia el sistema nervioso central.

**peristalsis (per uh STAHL sus): (p. 1021)** rhythmic, wavelike muscular contractions that move food throughout the digestive tract.

**peristaltismo: (pág. 1021)** serie de contracciones musculares rítmicas ondulantes que mueven el alimento por el esófago.

**petal: (p. 668)** colorful flower structure that attracts pollinators and provides them a landing place.

**pétalo: (pág. 668)** estructura floral colorida que atrae a los agentes polinizadores y les provee un lugar de aterrizaje.

**petiole (PET ee ohl): (p. 644)** stalk that connects a plant's blade to the stem.

**pecíolo: (pág. 644)** tallito de la hoja que une la lámina foliar con el tallo.

**pH: (p. 165)** measure of the concentration of hydrogen ions ($H^+$) in a solution.

**pH: (pág. 165)** medida de la concentración de iones de hidrógeno ($H^+$) en una solución.

**pharmacogenomics (far muh koh jeh NAH mihks): (p. 378)** study of how genetic inheritance affects the body's response to drugs in order to produce safer and more specific drug dosing.

**farmacogenética: (pág. 378)** estudio de la influencia de la herencia genética en la respuesta corporal a los medicamentos a fin de producir posologías más seguras y específicas.

**pharyngeal pouch: (p. 804)** in chordate embryos, one of the paired structures connecting the muscular tube lining the mouth cavity and the esophagus.

**bolsa faríngea: (pág. 804)** en los embriones de los cordados, una de las estructuras pareadas que conectan el conducto muscular que cubre la cavidad bucal con el esófago.

**pharynx (FER ingks): (p. 727)** in free-living flatworms, the tubelike muscular organ that can extend out of the mouth and suck food particles into the digestive tract.

**faringe: (pág. 727)** en las planarias, el órgano muscular tubular que se extiende desde la boca y chupa las partículas de alimento hacia el tubo digestivo.

**phenotype: (p. 279)** observable characteristic that is expressed as a result of an allele pair.

**fenotipo: (pág. 279)** apariencia externa que se expresa como resultado de un par de alelos.

**pheromone (FER uh mohn): (p. 768)** chemical secreted by an animal species to influence the behavior of other members of the same species.

**feromona: (pág. 768)** señal química que secreta una especie animal para influir en el comportamiento de otros miembros de la misma especie.

**phloem (FLOH em): (p. 638)** vascular plant tissue composed of sieve tube members and companion cells that conducts dissolved sugars and other organic compounds from the leaves and stems to the roots and from the roots to the leaves and stems.

**floema: (pág. 638)** tejido vascular vegetal formado por los miembros del tubo criboso y células acompañantes que transporta azúcares disueltos y otros compuestos orgánicos de las hojas y tallos hacia las raíces; y de allí a las hojas y tallos.

**phospholipid bilayer: (p. 188)** plasma membrane layers composed of phospholipid molecules arranged with polar heads facing the outside and nonpolar tails facing the inside.

**bicapa fosfolípida: (pág. 188)** capas membranosas del plasma compuestas por moléculas fosfolípidas cuyas cabezas polares miran hacia fuera y cuyas colas no polares miran hacia adentro.

**photic zone: (p. 80)** open-ocean zone shallow enough for sunlight to penetrate.

**zona fótica: (pág. 80)** zona a mar abierto lo suficientemente baja para que penetre la luz solar.

**photoperiodism (foh toh PIHR ee uh dih zum): (p. 672)** flowering response of a plant based on the number of hours of darkness it is exposed to.

**fotoperiodicidad: (pág. 672)** respuesta de floración de una planta al número de horas de oscuridad a la cual se expone.

**photosynthesis: (p. 220)** two-phase anabolic pathway in which the Sun's light energy is converted to chemical energy for use by the cell.

**fotosíntesis: (pág. 220)** sendero anabólico bifásico por medio del cual la energía luminosa solar se transforma en energía química para uso de la célula.

**phylogeny (fy LAH juh nee): (p. 491)** evolutionary history of a species.

**filogenia: (pág. 491)** historia evolutiva de una especie.

**phylum (FI lum): (p. 488)** taxonomic group of related classes.

**pigment: (p. 223)** light-absorbing colored molecule, such as chlorophyll and carotenoid, in the thylakoid membranes of chloroplasts.

**pilus: (p. 518)** hairlike, submicroscopic structure made of protein that can help a bacterial cell attach to environmental surfaces and act as a bridge between cells.

**pistil: (p. 669)** flower's female reproductive structure; it is usually composed of a stigma, a style, and an ovary.

**pituitary gland: (p. 1033)** endocrine gland located at the base of the brain; called the "master gland" because it regulates many body functions.

**placenta: (p. 887)** in most mammals, the specialized organ that provides food and oxygen to the developing young and removes their wastes.

**placental mammal: (p. 891)** mammal that has a placenta and gives birth to young that need no further development within a pouch.

**placental stage: (p. 1063)** birthing stage in which the placenta and umbilical cord are expelled from the mother's body.

**plankton: (p. 77)** tiny marine or freshwater photosynthetic, free-floating autotrophs that serve as a food source for many fish species.

**plasma: (p. 997)** clear, yellowish fluid portion of the blood.

**plasma membrane: (p. 185)** flexible, selectively permeable boundary that helps control what enters and leaves the cell.

**plasmid: (p. 366)** any of the small, circular, double-stranded DNA molecules that can be used as a vector.

**plasmodium (plaz MOH dee um): (p. 562)** feeding stage of a slime mold in which it is a mobile cytoplasmic mass with many diploid nuclei but no separate cells.

**plastron (PLAS trahn): (p. 857)** ventral part of a turtle's shell.

**platelet: (p. 997)** flat cell fragment that functions in blood clotting.

**plate tectonics: (p. 400)** geologic theory that Earth's surface is broken into several huge plates that move slowly on a partially molten rock layer.

**polar body: (p. 1051)** tiny cell that is produced and eventually disintegrates in the development of an oocyte.

**polar molecule: (p. 161)** molecule with oppositely charged regions.

**filo: (pág. 488)** agrupación taxonómica de clases que se relacionan.

**pigmento: (pág. 223)** molécula de color que absorbe la luz, como la clorofila y la carotenoide, en la membranas tilacoides de los cloroplastos.

**pilus: (pág. 518)** estructura submicroscópica filiforme compuesta por proteína que ayuda a una célula bacteriana a adherirse a las superficies ambientales y actuar como puente entre las células.

**pistilo: (pág. 669)** estructura reproductora femenina de la flor, compuesta generalmente por un estigma, un estilo y un ovario.

**glándula pituitaria: (pág. 1033)** glándula endocrina localizada en la base del cerebro, conocida como la "glándula maestra" puesto que regula muchas funciones corporales.

**placenta: (pág. 887)** en la mayoría de los mamíferos, el órgano especializado que provee alimento y oxígeno a la cría en desarrollo y elimina sus desechos.

**mamífero placentario: (pág. 891)** mamífero con placenta que pare a las crías que no requieren desarrollarse adicionalmente en una bolsa.

**etapa placentaria: (pág. 1063)** etapa de alumbramiento en la cual la placenta y el cordón umbilical se expulsan del cuerpo de la madre.

**plancton: (pág. 77)** diminutos autótrofos fotosintéticos marinos o de agua dulce, que flotan libremente y constituyen la fuente alimenticia de muchas especies de peces.

**plasma: (pág. 997)** porción fluida clara y amarillenta de la sangre.

**membrana plasmática: (pág. 185)** frontera flexible, selectivamente permeable, que ayuda a controlar lo que entra y sale de la célula.

**plásmido: (pág. 366)** cualquiera de las pequeñas moléculas de DNA circulares de filamento doble que pueden usarse como vector.

**plasmodio: (pág. 562)** etapa alimenticia de un hongo plasmódico en la cual es una masa de citoplasma móvil con muchos núcleos diploides pero sin membranas separadas.

**plastrón: (pág. 857)** parte ventral del caparazón de una tortuga.

**plaqueta: (pág. 997)** fragmentos celulares planos que funcionan en la coagulación de la sangre.

**tectónica de placas: (pág. 400)** teoría geológica que afirma que la corteza terrestre se divide en varias placas enormes que se mueven lentamente sobre una capa rocosa parcialmente fundida.

**cuerpo polar: (pág. 1051)** célula diminuta que se produce y posteriormente se desintegra en el desarrollo de un oocito.

**molécula polar: (pág. 161)** molécula con regiones cargadas opuestamente.

**polar nuclei:** **(p. 674)** in anthophytes, the two nuclei in the center of a megaspore.

**polygenic trait:** **(p. 309)** characteristic, such as eye color or skin color, that results from the interaction of multiple gene pairs.

**polymer:** **(p. 167)** large molecule formed from smaller repeating units of identical, or nearly identical, compounds linked by covalent bonds.

**polymerase chain reaction (PCR):** **(p. 368)** genetic engineering technique that can make copies of specific regions of a DNA fragment.

**polyp** **(PAH lup):** **(p. 712)** tube-shaped, sessile body form of cnidarians.

**polyploidy:** **(p. 285)** having one or more extra sets of all chromosomes, which, in polyploid plants, can often result in greater size and better growth and survival.

**pons:** **(p. 970)** part of the brain stem that helps control breathing rate.

**population:** **(p. 36)** group of organisms of the same species that occupy the same geographic place at the same time.

**population density:** **(p. 92)** number of organisms per unit of living area.

**population growth rate:** **(p. 97)** how fast a specific population grows.

**postanal tail:** **(p. 803)** chordate structure used primarily for locomotion.

**posterior:** **(p. 700)** tail end of an animal with bilateral symmetry.

**postzygotic isolating mechanism:** **(p. 437)** occurring after formation of a zygote.

**predation** **(prih DAY shun):** **(p. 38)** act of one organism feeding on another organism.

**preen gland:** **(p. 862)** oil-secreting gland located near the base of a bird's tail.

**prehensile tail:** **(p. 456)** functions like a fifth limb, provides the ability to grasp tree limbs or other objects and can support the body weight of some animals.

**prezygotic isolating mechanism:** **(p. 437)** occurring before breeding; produces a fertilized egg, or zygote.

**primary succession:** **(p. 62)** establishment of a community in an area of bare rock or bare sand, where no topsoil is present.

**prion** **(PREE ahn):** **(p. 531)** protein that can cause infection or disease.

**product:** **(p. 157)** substance formed by a chemical reaction; located on the right side of the arrow in a chemical equation.

**profundal zone:** **(p. 77)** deepest, coldest area of a large lake with little light and limited biodiversity.

**núcleos polares:** **(pág. 674)** en las antofitas, los dos núcleos en el centro de una megáspora.

**rasgo poligénico:** **(pág. 309)** característica, como el color de los ojos o de la piel, que resulta de la interacción de múltiples pares de genes.

**polímero:** **(pág. 167)** molécula gigante formada por unidades pequeñas, repetitivas, idénticas, o casi idénticas, de compuestos unidos por enlaces covalentes.

**reacción en cadena de polimerasa (RCP):** **(pág. 368)** técnica de ingeniería genética capaz de hacer copias de regiones específicas de un fragmento de DNA.

**pólipo:** **(pág. 712)** cuerpo sésil cilíndrico de los cnidarios.

**poliploide:** **(pág. 285)** que tiene uno o más grupos de todos los cromosomas que, en plantas poliploides, puede resultar en un mayor tamaño y mejor crecimiento y supervivencia.

**pons:** **(pág. 970)** parte del bulbo raquídeo que ayuda a controlar el ritmo de la respiración.

**población:** **(pág. 36)** grupo de organismos de la misma especie que viven en la misma localidad geográfica al mismo tiempo

**densidad demográfica:** **(pág. 92)** número de organismos por unidad de área o superficie habitable.

**tasa de crecimiento demográfico:** **(pág. 97)** el grado de rapidez con que crece una población específica.

**cola postnatal:** **(pág. 803)** estructura de los cordados que se usa principalmente para la locomoción.

**posterior:** **(pág. 700)** extremo de la cola de un animal con simetría bilateral.

**mecanismo aislado postcigótico:** **(pág. 437)** que ocurre después de la formación de un cigoto.

**depredación:** **(pág. 38)** modo de nutrición de un organismo al alimentarse de otro.

**uropigio:** **(pág. 862)** glándula secretora de aceite localizada cerca de la base de la cola de un ave.

**cola prensil:** **(pág. 456)** funciona como una quinta extremidad y permite que algunos animales se agarren de las ramas de los árboles u otros objetos y la cual puede sostener el peso de algunos animales.

**mecanismo aislado precigótico:** **(pág. 437)** que ocurre antes de la procreación; produce un óvulo fecundado o cigoto.

**sucesión primaria:** **(pág. 62)** colonización en un área de roca o arena desnudas, sin mantillo (capa vegetal superior).

**prión:** **(pág. 531)** proteína que puede causar infecciones o enfermedades.

**producto:** **(pág. 157)** sustancia formada por una reacción química; localizada en el lado derecho de la flecha en una ecuación química.

**zona profunda:** **(pág. 77)** el área más fría y profunda de un lago grande, con poca luz y una biodiversidad limitada.

**proglottid (proh GLAH tihd): (p. 730)** continuously formed, detachable section of a tapeworm that contains male and female reproductive organs, flame cells, muscles, and nerves; breaks off when its eggs are fertilized and passes out of the host's intestine.

**proglótido: (pág. 730)** sección de una tenia que contiene músculos, nervios, bulbos ciliados y órganos reproductores; desprende cuando sus huevos son fecundados y sale por el intestino del huésped.

**prokaryotic cell: (p. 186)** microscopic, unicellular organism without a nucleus or other membrane-bound organelles.

**célula procariótica: (pág. 186)** organismo unicelular, microscópico, sin núcleo u otros organelos limitados por membranas.

**prophase: (p. 248)** first stage of mitosis, during which the cell's chromatin condenses into chromosomes.

**profase: (pág. 248)** primera etapa de la mitosis, durante la cual la cromatina celular se condensa para formar cromosomas.

**protein: (p. 170)** organic compound made of amino acids joined by peptide bonds; primary building block of organisms.

**proteína: (pág. 170)** compuesto orgánico formado por aminoácidos unidos por enlaces pépticos; piedra angular de los organismos.

**proteomics: (p. 379)** study of the structure and function of proteins in the human body.

**proteómica: (pág. 379)** estudio de la estructura y función de proteínas en el cuerpo humano.

**prothallus (pro THA lus): (p. 665)** heart-shaped, tiny fern gametophyte.

**prótalo: (pág. 665)** gametofito diminuto de helecho, en forma de corazón.

**protist: (p. 501)** unicellular, multicellular, or colonial eukaryote whose cell walls may contain cellulose; can be plantlike, animal-like, or funguslike.

**protista: (pág. 501)** eucariota unicelular, multicelular o colonial cuyas paredes celulares pueden contener celulosa; pueden tener forma vegetal, animal o fungosa.

**proton: (p. 148)** positively charged particle in an atom's nucleus.

**protón: (pág. 148)** particular cargada positivamente en el núcleo de un átomo.

**protonema: (p. 664)** small, threadlike structure produced by mosses that can develop into the gametophyte plant.

**protonema: (pág. 664)** estructura filamentosa pequeña producida por musgos, capaz de desarrollarse en la planta gametofita.

**protostome (PROH tuh stohm): (p. 702)** coelomate animal whose mouth develops from the opening in the gastrula.

**protostomado: (pág. 702)** animal celomado cuya boca se desarrolla de la abertura de la gástrula.

**protozoan (proh tuh ZOH un): (p. 542)** heterotrophic, unicellular, animal-like protist.

**protozoario: (pág. 542)** protista unicelular heterótrofo parecido a un animal.

**pseudocoelom (soo duh SEE lum): (p. 701)** fluid-filled body cavity between the mesoderm and the endoderm.

**seudoceloma: (pág. 701)** cavidad corporal llena de fluido entre el mesodermo y el endodermo.

**pseudopod (SEW duh pahd): (p. 550)** temporary cytoplasmic extension that sarcodines use for feeding and movement.

**seudópodos: (pág. 550)** extensión citoplásmica temporal que emplean los sarcodinos en la alimentación y locomoción.

**puberty: (p. 1049)** growth period during which sexual maturity is reached.

**pubertad: (pág. 1049)** período durante el cual se llega a la madurez sexual.

**punctuated equilibrium: (p. 440)** theory that evolution occurs with relatively sudden periods of speciation followed by long periods of stability.

**equilibrio puntuado: (pág. 440)** teoría que sostiene que la evolución ocurre con períodos relativamente súbitos de especiación, seguido de largos períodos de estabilidad.

**pupa (PYEW puh): (p. 778)** nonfeeding stage of complete metamorphosis in which the insect changes from the larval form to the adult form.

**pupa: (pág. 778)** etapa no alimenticia de la metamorfosis completa de un insecto en la cual el insecto cambia de la forma larval a la adulta.

## R

**radial (RAY dee uhl) symmetry: (p. 700)** body plan that can be divided along any plane, through a central axis, into roughly equal halves.

**simetría radial: (pág. 700)** plano corporal que, a través de un eje central a lo largo de cualquier plano, puede dividirse en casi dos partes iguales.

**radicle:** **(p. 679)** first part of the embryo to emerge from the seed and begin to absorb water and nutrients from the environment.

**radiometric dating:** **(p. 395)** method used to determine the age of rocks using the rate of decay of radioactive isotopes.

**radula (RA juh luh):** **(p. 738)** rasping tonguelike organ with rows of teeth that many mollusks use in feeding.

**reactant:** **(p. 157)** substance that exists before a chemical reaction starts; located on the left side of the arrow in a chemical equation.

**recessive:** **(p. 278)** Mendel's name for a specific trait hidden or masked in the $F_1$ generation.

**recombinant DNA:** **(p. 366)** newly generated DNA fragment containing exogenous DNA.

**red blood cell:** **(p. 997)** hemoglobin-containing, disc-shaped, short-lived blood cell that lacks a nucleus and that transports oxygen to all the body's cells.

**red bone marrow:** **(p. 942)** type of marrow that produces red and white blood cells and platelets.

**reflex arc:** **(p. 963)** nerve pathway consisting of a sensory neuron, an interneuron, and a motor neuron.

**regeneration:** **(p. 728)** ability to replace or regrow body parts missing due to predation or damage.

**relative dating:** **(p. 394)** method used to determine the age of rocks by comparing the rocks with younger and older rock layers.

**renewable resource:** **(p. 130)** any resource replaced by natural processes more quickly than it is consumed.

**reproduction:** **(p. 9)** production of offspring.

**reservoir:** **(p. 1078)** source of a pathogen in the environment.

**response:** **(p. 9)** organism's reaction to a stimulus.

**restriction enzyme:** **(p. 364)** bacterial protein that cuts DNA into fragments.

**retina:** **(p. 974)** innermost layer of the eye that contains rods and cones.

**retrovirus:** **(p. 530)** RNA virus, such as HIV, with reverse transcriptase in its core.

**rhizoid (RIH zoyd):** **(p. 583)** type of hypha formed by a mold that penetrates a food's surface.

**rhizome:** **(p. 615)** fern's thick underground stem that functions as a food-storage organ.

**ribosomal RNA (rRNA):** **(p. 336)** type of RNA that associates with proteins to form ribosomes.

**radícula:** **(pág. 679)** primera parte del embrión que emerge de la semilla y comienza a absorber agua y nutrientes del medio ambiente.

**datación radiométrica:** **(pág. 395)** método utilizado para determinar la edad de las rocas mediante la tasa de desintegración de los isótopos radioactivos.

**rádula:** **(pág. 738)** órgano raspador parecido a una lengua con hileras de dientes que emplean muchos moluscos para alimentarse.

**reactivo:** **(pág. 157)** sustancia que existe antes de empezar una reacción química; localizada al lado izquierdo de la flecha en una ecuación química.

**recesivo:** **(pág. 256)** nombre de Mendel para una rasgo específico oculto o encubierto en la generación $F_1$.

**DNA recombinante:** **(pág. 366)** fragmento de DNA recién generado que contiene DNA exógeno.

**glóbulo rojo:** **(pág. 997)** célula sanguínea de corta vida, esférica, anucleada, que contiene hemoglobina y que transporta oxígeno a todas las células del cuerpo.

**médula roja:** **(pág. 942)** tipo de médula que produce glóbulos rojos, glóbulos blancos y plaquetas.

**arco reflejo:** **(pág. 963)** trayecto nervioso que consiste en una neurona sensorial, una interneurona y una neurona motora.

**regeneración:** **(pág. 728)** capacidad de reemplazar o regenerar partes corporales perdidas debido a la depredación o daños.

**datación relativa:** **(pág. 394)** método empleado para determinar la edad de las rocas al compararlas con capas rocosas más recientes y más antiguas.

**recurso renovable:** **(pág. 130)** cualquier recurso reemplazable por procesos naturales de manera más rápida de lo que se consume.

**reproducción:** **(pág. 9)** producción de la progenie.

**reservorio:** **(pág. 1078)** fuente de un patógeno en el medio ambiente.

**respuesta:** **(pág. 9)** la reacción de un organismo a un estímulo.

**enzima restrictiva:** **(pág. 364)** proteína bacterial que corta el DNA en fragmentos.

**retina:** **(pág. 974)** capa más interna del ojo que contiene bastoncillos y conos.

**retrovirus:** **(pág. 530)** virus RNA, como el HIV, con transcriptasa inversa en su núcleo.

**rizoide:** **(pág. 583)** tipo de hifa formada por un musgo que penetra la superficie del alimento.

**rizoma:** **(pág. 615)** el tallo grueso subterráneo de un helecho que funciona como órgano de almacenamiento de alimento.

**RNA ribosomal (rRNA):** **(pág. 336)** tipo de RNA que se asocia con las proteínas para formar ribosomas.

**ribosome: (p. 193)** simple cell organelle that helps manufacture proteins.

**ribosoma: (pág. 193)** organelo celular simple que ayuda a elaborar proteínas.

**RNA: (p. 336)** ribonucleic acid; guides protein synthesis.

**RNA: (pág. 336)** ácido ribonucleico; guía la síntesis de proteínas.

**RNA polymerase: (p. 337)** enzyme that regulates RNA synthesis.

**RNA polimerasa: (pág. 337)** enzima que regula la síntesis de RNA.

**rod: (p. 974)** one of the light-sensitive cells in the retina that sends action potentials to the brain via neurons in the optic nerve.

**bastoncillo: (pág. 974)** una de las células de la retina que es sensible a la luz y que envía potenciales de acción al cerebro mediante las neuronas del nervio óptico.

**root cap: (p. 639)** layer of parenchyma cells that covers the root tip and helps protect root tissues during growth.

**piloriza: (pág. 639)** capa de células del parénquima que cubre la punta de las raíces y ayuda a proteger su tejido durante el crecimiento.

**rubisco: (p. 226)** enzyme that converts inorganic carbon dioxide molecules into organic molecules during the final step of the Calvin cycle.

**rubisco: (pág. 226)** enzima que convierte las moléculas inorgánicas de dióxido de carbono en moléculas orgánicas durante la etapa final del ciclo de Calvin.

## S

**safety symbol: (p. 21)** logo representing a specific danger such as radioactivity, electrical or biological hazard, or irritants that may be present in a lab activity or field investigation.

**símbolo de seguridad: (pág. 21)** logotipo que advierte acerca de algún peligro, como radioactividad, agentes irritantes, riesgos eléctricos o biológicos, que pudieran presentarse en una actividad de laboratorio o investigación de campo.

**sarcomere: (p. 948)** in skeletal muscle, the functional unit that contracts and is composed of myofibrils.

**sarcómero: (pág. 948)** en el músculo esquelético, la unidad funcional que se contrae y se compone de miofibrilla muscular.

**scale: (p. 823)** small, flat, platelike structure near the surface of the skin of most fishes; can be ctenoid, cycloid, placoid, or ganoid.

**escama: (pág. 823)** estructura pequeña, plana y lameliforme, cerca de la superficie de la piel de la mayoría de los peces; puede ser serrada, cicloide, placoidea o ganoidea.

**science: (p. 11)** a body of knowledge based on the study of nature.

**ciencia: (pág. 11)** conjunto de conocimiento basado en el estudio de la naturaleza y su entorno físico.

**scientific methods: (p. 16)** a series of problem-solving procedures that might include observations, forming a hypothesis, experimenting, gathering and analyzing data, and drawing conclusions.

**método científico: (pág. 16)** una serie de procedimientos de solución de problemas que pueden incluir observaciones, formulación de una hipótesis, experimentación, recopilación y análisis de datos y sacar conclusiones.

**sclerenchyma (skle RENG kuh muh) cell: (p. 633)** plant cell that lacks cytoplasm and other living components when mature, leaving thick, rigid cell walls that provide support and function in transport of materials.

**célula esclerénquima: (pág. 633)** célula vegetal carente de citoplasma y de otros componentes vitales en su etapa madura, caracterizada por paredes celulares gruesas y rígidas que proveen soporte y funcionan en el transporte de materiales.

**scolex (SKOH leks): (p. 730)** parasitically adapted, knob-like anterior end of a tapeworm, having hooks and suckers that attach to the host's intestinal lining.

**escólex: (pág. 730)** extremidad adaptada parasitariamente con forma de perilla que poseen las tenias; posee ganchos y chupones que se adhieren a la cubierta intestinal del huésped.

**sebaceous gland: (p. 937)** oil-producing gland in the dermis that lubricates skin and hair.

**glándula sebácea: (pág. 937)** glándula productora de aceite en la dermis que lubrica la piel y el cabello.

**secondary succession: (p. 63)** orderly change that occurs in a place where soil remains after a community of organisms has been removed.

**sucesión secundaria: (pág. 63)** cambio ordenado que ocurre en el suelo de los lugares que experimentaron la expulsión de una comunidad de organismos.

**sediment: (p. 75)** material deposited by water, wind, or glaciers.

**sedimento: (pág. 75)** material depositado por el agua, el viento o los glaciares.

**seed: (p. 607)** adaptive reproductive structure of some vascular plants that contains an embryo, nutrients for the embryo, and is covered by a protective coat.

**seed coat: (p. 677)** protective tissue that forms from the hardening of the outside layers of the ovule.

**selective breeding: (p. 360)** directed breeding to produce plants and animals with desired traits.

**selective permeability (pur mee uh BIH luh tee): (p. 187)** property of the plasma membrane that allows it to control movement of substances into or out of the cell.

**semen (SEE mun): (p. 1049)** fluid that contains sperm, nourishment, and other fluids of the male reproductive system.

**semicircular canal: (p. 975)** inner-ear structure that transmits information about body position and balance to the brain.

**semiconservative replication: (p. 333)** method of DNA replication in which parental strands separate, act as templates, and produce molecules of DNA with one parental DNA strand and one new DNA strand.

**seminiferous tubule (se muh NIHF rus • TEW byul): (p. 1049)** tubule of the testis in which sperm develop.

**sepal: (p. 668)** flower organ that protects the bud.

**septum: (p. 578)** cross-wall that divides a hypha into cells.

**serendipity: (p. 18)** occurrence of accidental or unexpected but fortunate outcomes.

**sessile (SEH sul): (p. 706)** organism permanently attached to one place.

**seta (SEE tuh): (p. 747)** tiny bristle that digs into soil and anchors an earthworm as it moves forward.

**sex chromosome: (p. 305)** X or Y chromosome; paired sex chromosomes determine an individual's gender—XX individuals are female and XY individuals are male.

**sex-linked trait: (p. 307)** characteristic, such as red-green color blindness, controlled by genes on the X chromosome; also called an X-linked trait.

**sexual selection: (p. 436)** change in the frequency of a trait based on competition for a mate.

**short-day plant: (p. 672)** plant that flowers in the winter, spring, or fall, when the number of hours of darkness is greater than the number of hours of light.

**SI: (p. 14)** system of measurements used by scientists, abbreviation of the International System of Units.

**sieve tube member: (p. 638)** nonnucleated, cytoplasmic cell of the phloem.

**single nucleotide polymorphism: (p. 376)** variation in a DNA sequence occurring when a single nucleotide in a genome is altered.

**semilla: (pág. 607)** estructura reproductora y adaptable de algunas plantas vasculares que contiene un embrión con su fuente de nutrientes y una capa protectora.

**tegumento: (pág. 677)** tejido protector formado del endurecimiento de las capas externas del óvulo.

**criaza selectiva: (pág. 360)** crianza dirigida hacia la producción de plantas y animales con rasgos deseados.

**permeabilidad selectiva: (pág. 187)** propiedad de la membrana plasmática que le permite controlar el movimiento de las sustancias dentro o fuera de la célula.

**semen: (pág. 1049)** fluido que contiene espermatozoides, nutrientes y otros fluidos del sistema reproductor masculino.

**canal semicircular: (pág. 975)** estructura interna del oído que transmite al cerebro información relativa a la posición y equilibrio corporales.

**replicación semiconservadora: (pág. 333)** método de replicación del DNA mediante el cual los filamentos paternos se separan, actúan como plantillas y producen moléculas de DNA con un filamento paterno de DNA y otro nuevo de DNA.

**túbulo seminífero: (pág. 1049)** túbulo del teste donde se desarrollan los espermatozoides.

**sépalo: (pág. 668)** órgano de la flor que protege el botón.

**septo: (pág. 578)** tabique que divide una hifa en células.

**serendipia: (pág. 18)** hecho accidental o inesperado con resultados favorables.

**sésil: (pág. 706)** organismo que permanece adherido a una superficie.

**seta: (pág. 747)** pequeña cerda que penetra en el suelo y provee el soporte que requiere una lombriz al avanzar.

**cromosoma sexual: (pág. 305)** cromosoma X o Z; los cromosomas sexuales pareados determinan el sexo del individuo: los individuos XX son femeninos y los XY, masculinos.

**rasgo ligado al sexo: (pág. 307)** característica, como el daltonismo, controlada por los genes en el cromosoma X; también denominado rasgo ligado a la X.

**selección sexual: (pág. 436)** cambio de la frecuencia de un rasgo basado en la rivalidad por una pareja.

**planta de días cortos: (pág. 672)** planta que florece en el invierno, primavera u otoño cuando el número de horas de oscuridad es mayor que el número de horas diurnas.

**SI: (pág. 14)** sistema de medición que usan los científicos, abreviatura del Sistema Internacional de Unidades.

**miembro de los tubos cribosos: (pág. 638)** célula citoplasmática del floema que carece de núcleo.

**polimorfismo de un nucleótido simple: (pág. 376)** variación en una secuencia de DNA que ocurre al alterarse un solo nucleótido en un genoma.

**siphon (p. 741)** tubular organ through which octopuses and squids eject water, at times so rapidly that their movement appears jet-propelled.

**sister chromatid: (p. 248)** structure that contains identical DNA copies and is formed during DNA replication.

**skeletal muscle: (p. 948)** striated muscle that causes movement when contracted and is attached to bones by tendons.

**small intestine: (p. 1022)** longest part of the digestive tract; involved in mechanical and chemical digeston.

**smooth muscle: (p. 947)** muscle that lines many hollow internal organs, such as the stomach and uterus.

**solute: (p. 163)** substance dissolved in a solvent.

**solution: (p. 163)** homogeneous mixture formed when a substance (the solute) is dissolved in another substance (the solvent).

**solvent: (p. 163)** substance in which another substance is dissolved.

**somatic nervous system: (p. 971)** part of the peripheral nervous system that transmits impulses to and from skin and skeletal muscles.

**sorus: (p. 616)** fern structure formed by clusters of sporangia, usually on the undersides of a frond.

**spawning: (p. 826)** process by which male and female fishes release their gametes near each other in the water.

**species: (p. 9)** group of organisms that can interbreed and produce fertile offspring.

**species diversity: (p. 117)** in a biological community, the number and abundance of different species.

**spindle apparatus: (p. 250)** structure made of spindle fibers, centrioles, and aster fibers that is involved in moving and organizing chromosomes before the cell divides.

**spinneret: (p. 772)** in spiders, the structure that spins silk from a fluid protein secreted by their glands.

**spiracle (SPIHR ih kul): (p. 767)** opening in the arthropod body through which air enters and waste gases leave.

**spongy bone: (p. 942)** less dense inner-bone layer with many cavities that contain bone marrow.

**spongy mesophyll: (p. 644)** loosely packed, irregularly shaped cells with spaces around them located below the palisade mesophyll.

**spontaneous generation: (p. 401)** idea that life arises from nonliving things.

**sporangium: (p. 581)** sac or case in which fungal spores are produced.

**sifón: (pág. 741)** órgano tubular por el cual los pulpos y los calamares expulsan agua, a veces tan rápido, que asemeja una propulsión a chorro.

**cromátides hermanas: (pág. 248)** estructura formada durante la replicación del DNA, que contiene copias idénticas de DNA.

**músculo óseo: (pág. 948)** músculo estriado que causa movimiento al contraerse, adherido a los huesos por los tendones.

**intestino delgado: (pág. 1022)** parte más larga del tracto digestivo; presente en la digestión mecánica y química.

**músculo liso: (pág. 947)** músculo que recubre las paredes de muchos órganos internos, como el estómago y el útero.

**soluto: (pág. 163)** sustancia disuelta en un disolvente.

**solución: (pág. 163)** mezcla homogénea formada al disolverse una sustancia (el soluto) en otra sustancia (el disolvente).

**disolvente: (pág. 163)** sustancia en la cual se disuelve otra sustancia.

**sistema nervioso somático: (pág. 971)** porción del sistema nervioso periférico que transmite impulsos hacia y desde la piel a los músculos esqueléticos.

**soro: (pág. 616)** estructura de helecho formada por grupos de esporangios, ubicada generalmente en la super ficie inferior de una fronda.

**desove: (pág. 826)** proceso mediante el cual tanto los peces macho como las hembras liberan sus gametos cerca uno del otro en el agua.

**especie: (pág. 9)** grupo de organismos que pueden cruzarse y producir progenies fértiles.

**diversidad de especies: (pág. 117)** en una comunidad biológica, el número y la abundancia de diferentes especies.

**huso: (pág. 250)** estructura compuesta por fibras de microtúbulos, centriolos y áster encargada de movilizar y organizar los cromosomas antes de la división celular.

**hileras: (pág. 772)** en las arañas, la estructura productora de seda a partir del fluido proteico que segregan sus glándulas.

**espiráculo: (pág. 767)** abertura en el cuerpo de los artrópodos a través de la cual entra el aire y salen los gases de desecho.

**hueso esponjoso: (pág. 942)** capa de hueso interno menos densa con muchos orificios que contienen médula.

**mesófilo esponjoso: (pág. 644)** células irregulares, ligeramente empacadas, con espacios circundantes localizados bajo el mesófilo en empalizada.

**generación espontánea: (pág. 401)** idea de que la vida surge de la materia no viva.

**esporangio: (pág. 581)** en los hongos, un saco o envoltura donde se producen las esporas.

**spore:** **(p. 580)** reproductive haploid (*n*) cell with a hard outer shell that forms a new organism without the fusion of gametes and is produced in the asexual and sexual life cycles of most fungi and some other organisms.

**stabilizing selection:** **(p. 434)** most common form of natural selection in which organisms with extreme expressions of a trait are removed.

**stamen:** **(p. 669)** male reproductive organ of most flowers composed of a filament and an anther.

**stem cell:** **(p. 256)** unspecialized cell that can develop into a specialized cell under the right conditions.

**sternum** **(STUR num):** **(p. 862)** in birds, the large breastbone to which flight muscles are attached.

**stimulant:** **(p. 978)** substance/drug that increases alertness and physical activity.

**stimulus:** **(p. 9)** any change in an organism's internal or external environment that causes the organism to react.

**stolon** **(STOH lun):** **(p. 583)** type of hypha formed by a mold that spreads over a food's surface.

**stomata:** **(p. 606)** openings in the outer cell layer of leaf surfaces and some stems that allow the exchange of water, carbon dioxide, oxygen, and other gases between a plant and its environment.

**strobilus** **(STROH bih lus):** **(p. 613)** compact cluster of spore-bearing structures in some seedless vascular plant sporophytes.

**stroma:** **(p. 223)** fluid-filled space outside the grana in which light-dependent reactions take place.

**substrate:** **(p. 160)** reactant to which an enzyme binds.

**sustainable use:** **(p. 130)** use of resources at a rate that they can be replaced or recycled.

**swim bladder:** **(p. 827)** gas-filled internal space in bony fishes that allows them to regulate their buoyancy.

**swimmeret:** **(p. 771)** crustacean appendage used as a flipper during swimming.

**symbiosis** **(sihm bee OH sus):** **(p. 39)** close mutualistic, parasitic, or commensal association between two or more species that live together.

**symmetry** **(SIH muh tree):** **(p. 700)** balance or similarity in body structures of organisms.

**sympathetic nervous system:** **(p. 972)** branch of the autonomic nervous system that controls organs and is most active during emergencies or stress.

**sympatric speciation:** **(p. 437)** occurs when a species evolves into a new species in an area without a geographic barrier.

**espora:** **(pág. 580)** célula reproductora haploide (n) con una cubierta protectora dura capaz de formar un nuevo organismo sin la fusión de gametos; y se produce en los ciclos vitales sexuales y asexuales de la mayoría de los hongos.

**selección estabilizadora:** **(pág. 434)** la selección natural más común, mediante la cual se eliminan los organismos con expresiones extremas de un rasgo.

**estambre:** **(pág. 669)** órgano reproductor masculino de la mayoría de las flores, compuesto por un filamento y una antera.

**célula madre:** **(pág. 256)** célula no especializada capaz de desarrollarse en una célula especializada bajo las condiciones adecuadas.

**esternón:** **(pág. 862)** en las aves, hueso pectoral grande al cual se adhieren los músculos de vuelo.

**estimulante:** **(pág. 978)** sustancia / droga que aumenta la agudeza y actividad física.

**estímulo:** **(pág. 9)** cualquier cambio en el ambiente interno o externo de un organismo que ocasiona una reacción en el organismo.

**estolón:** **(pág. 583)** tipo de hifa formada por un hongo que se extiende sobre la superficie de los alimentos.

**estomas:** **(pág. 606)** aberturas en la capa celular externa superficial de las hojas y de algunos tallos que permiten el intercambio de agua, dióxido de carbono y otros gases entre una planta y su medioambiente.

**estróbilo:** **(pág. 613)** racimo compacto de estructuras que contienen esporas en algunos esporófitos de plantas vasculares sin semilla.

**estroma:** **(pág. 223)** espacio relleno de fluido fuera de las granas donde suceden reacciones lumino-dependientes.

**sustrato:** **(pág. 160)** reactivo al cual se adhiere una enzima.

**uso sostenible:** **(pág. 130)** uso de los recursos a una tasa tal que puedan reemplazarse o reciclarse.

**vejiga natatoria:** **(pág. 827)** espacio interno relleno de gas en los peces óseos que les ayuda a controlar su flotabilidad.

**pleópodo:** **(pág. 771)** apéndice crustáceo empleado como aleta durante la natación.

**simbiosis:** **(pág. 39)** asociación estrecha mutualista, parasítica o comensal entre dos o más especies que viven juntas.

**simetría:** **(pág. 700)** equilibrio o similitud en las estructuras corporales de los organismos.

**sistema nervioso simpático:** **(pág. 972)** rama del sistema nervioso autónomo que controla los órganos y es muy activo durante las emergencias o el estrés.

**especiación simpátrica:** **(pág. 437)** ocurre cuando una especie evoluciona en una especie nueva dentro de un área sin frontera geográfica.

**synapse (SIH naps): (p. 967)** gap between one neuron's axon and another nueron's dendrite.

**sinapsis: (pág. 967)** brecha entre el axón de una neurona y las dendritas de otra.

# T

**taste bud: (p. 973)** one of a number of specialized chemical receptors on the tongue that can detect sweet, sour, salty, and bitter tastes.

**papila gustativa: (pág. 973)** una de un número de receptores químicos especializados de la lengua que detectan los sabores dulces, agrios, salados y amargos.

**taxon: (p. 487)** named group of organisms, such as a phylum, genus, or species.

**taxón: (pág. 487)** grupo nombrado de organismos, como un filo, un género o una especie.

**taxonomy (tak SAH nuh mee): (p. 485)** branch of biology that identifies, names, and classifies species based on their natural relationships.

**taxonomía: (pág. 485)** rama de la biología que identifica, nombra y clasifica las especies en base a su morfología y comportamiento.

**technology (tek NAH luh jee): (p. 15)** application of knowledge gained from scientific reasearch to solve society's needs and problems and improve the quality of life.

**tecnología: (pág. 15)** aplicación del conocimiento derivado de la investigación científica a fin de resolver los problemas y necesidades de la sociedad y mejorar la calidad de vida.

**telomere: (p. 311)** protective cap made of DNA that is found on the ends of a chromosome.

**telómero: (pág. 311)** capa protectora de DNA que se encuentra en los extremos de un cromosoma.

**telophase: (p. 251)** last stage of mitosis in which nucleoli reappear. Two new nuclear membranes begin to form, but the cell has not yet completely divided.

**telofase: (pág. 251)** fase final de la mitosis en que reaparecen los nucléolos. Comienzan a formarse dos nuevas membranas nucleares sin que la célula haya terminado de dividirse.

**temperate forest: (p. 69)** biome south of the boreal forest characterized by broad-leaved, deciduous trees, well-defined seasons, and average yearly precipitation of 75–150 cm.

**bosque templado: (pág. 69)** bioma al sur del bosque boreal compuesto por árboles caducifolios de hojas anchas, estaciones bien definidas y entre 70 y 150 cm de precipitación promedio anual.

**tendon: (p. 948)** tough connective-tissue band that connects muscle to bone.

**tendón: (pág. 948)** banda dura de tejido conectivo que adhieren los músculos a los huesos.

**territorial behavior: (p. 918)** competitive behavior in which an animal tries to adopt and defend a physical area against others of the same species.

**comportamiento territorial: (pág. 918)** comportamiento competitivo mediante el cual un animal trata de adoptar y defender un área física de otros animales de la misma especie.

**test: (p. 550)** hard, porous, shell-like covering of an amoeba.

**testa: (pág. 550)** cubierta dura, porosa, con forma de cáscara, de una ameba.

**test cross: (p. 362)** breeding that can be used to determine an organism's genotype.

**cruzamiento de prueba: (pág. 362)** cruce que puede ayudar a determinar el genotipo de un organismo.

**tetrapod: (p. 830)** four-footed animal with legs that have feet and toes with joints.

**tetrápodo: (pág. 830)** animal cuadrúpedo cuyas patas tienen pies y dedos con articulaciones.

**thallose (THAL lohs): (p. 612)** liverwort with a fleshy, lobed body shape.

**talosa: (pág. 612)** hepática con forma corporal carnosa lobulada.

**theory: (p. 14)** explanation of a natural phenomenon based on many observations and investigations over time.

**teoría: (pág. 14)** explicación de un fenómeno natural basado en muchas observaciones y experimentos con el correr del tiempo.

**theory of biogenesis (bi oh JEN uh sus): (p. 402)** states that only living organisms can produce other living organisms.

**teoría de la biogénesis: (pág. 402)** plantea que sólo los organismos vivos pueden producir otros organismos vivos.

**therapsid: (p. 896)** extinct mammal-like reptile from which the first mammals probably arose.

**terápsido: (pág. 896)** reptil extinto parecido a un mamífero del cual probablemente surgieron los primeros mamíferos.

**thermodynamics: (p. 218)** study of the flow and transformation of energy in the universe.

**termodinámica: (pág. 218)** estudio del flujo y transformación de la energía del universo.

**thorax:** **(p. 763)** middle body region of an arthropod consisting of three fused main segments that may bear legs and wings.

**threshold:** **(p. 964)** minimum stimulus needed to produce a nerve impulse.

**thylakoid:** **(p. 223)** in choroplasts, one of the stacked, flattened, pigment-containing membranes in which light-dependent reactions occur.

**thyroxine:** **(p. 1034)** thyroid hormone that increases the metabolic rate of cells.

**tolerance:** **(p. 61)** organism's ability to survive biotic and abiotic factors. **(p. 981)** as the body becomes less responsive to a drug, an individual needs larger and more frequent doses to achieve the same effect.

**trachea:** **(p. 1001)** tube that carries air from the larynx to the bronchi.

**tracheal (TRAY kee ul) tube:** **(p. 767)** in most terrestrial arthropods, one of a system of tubes that branch into smaller tubules and carry oxygen throughout the body.

**tracheid (TRAY key ihd):** **(p. 637)** long, cylindrical plant cell in which water passes from cell to cell through pitted ends.

**transcription (trans KRIHP shun):** **(p. 337)** process in which mRNA is synthesized from the template DNA.

**transfer RNA:** **(p. 336)** type of RNA that transports amino acids to the ribosome.

**transformation:** **(p. 367)** process in which bacterial cells take up recombinant plasmid DNA.

**transgenic organism:** **(p. 370)** organism that is genetically engineered by inserting a gene from another organism.

**translation:** **(p. 338)** process in which mRNA attaches to the ribosome and a protein is assembled.

**transpiration:** **(p. 645)** process in which water evaporates from the inside of leaves to the outside through stomata.

**transport protein:** **(p. 189)** protein that moves substances or wastes through the plasma membrane.

**trichinosis (trih kuh NOH sus):** **(p. 733)** disease caused by eating raw or undercooked meat, usually pork, infected with *Trichinella* larvae.

**trichocyst (TRIH kuh sihst):** **(p. 547)** elongated, cylindrical structure that can discharge a spinelike structure that may function in defense, as an anchoring device, or to capture prey.

**trophic (TROH fihk) level:** **(p. 42)** each step in a food chain or food web.

**tropical rain forest:** **(p. 72)** hot, wet biome with year-round humidity; contains Earth's most diverse species of plants and animals.

**tórax:** **(pág. 763)** región del cuerpo medio de un artrópodo compuesta por tres segmentos principales fusionados capaz de soportar patas y alas.

**umbral:** **(pág. 964)** estímulo mínimo requerido para producir un impulso nervioso.

**tilacoide:** **(pág. 223)** en los cloroplastos, una de las membranas apiladas y aplanadas que contienen pigmento donde ocurren las reacciones lumino-dependientes.

**tiroxina:** **(pág. 1034)** hormona tiroidea que aumenta la tasa metabólica de las células.

**tolerancia:** **(pág. 61)** capacidad de un organismo de sobrevivir factores bióticos y abióticos. **(pág. 981)** a medida que el cuerpo se vuelve menos sensible a una droga, un individuo necesita dosis más frecuentes y mayores para obtener el mismo efecto.

**tráquea:** **(pág. 1001)** conducto que lleva el aire desde la laringe hasta los bronquios.

**tubo traqueal:** **(pág. 767)** en la mayoría de los artrópodos terrestres, uno entre un sistema de conductos que se ramifican en otros más pequeños y transportan el oxígeno por todo el cuerpo.

**traqueida:** **(pág. 637)** célula vegetal alargada y cilíndrica en la cual pasa el agua de célula a célula a través de extremos picados.

**transcripción:** **(pág. 337)** proceso en que el mRNA se sintetiza del patrón de DNA.

**RNA de transferencia:** **(pág. 336)** tipo de RNA que transporta los aminoácidos a los ribosomas.

**transformación:** **(pág. 367)** proceso en el cual las células bacterianas recogen el DNA plásmido recombinante.

**organismo transgénico:** **(pág. 370)** organismo generado genéticamente al insertar el gene de un organismo distinto.

**traducción:** **(pág. 338)** proceso mediante el cual el mRNA se adhiere al ribosoma y se sintetiza una proteína.

**transpiración:** **(pág. 645)** proceso en el cual el agua se evapora de adentro hacia fuera de las hojas a través de los estomas.

**proteína de transporte:** **(pág. 189)** proteína que mueve sustancias o desechos a través de la membrana plasmática.

**triquinosis:** **(pág. 733)** enfermedad causada por la carne cruda o poco cocinada, generalmente de cerdo, infectada con larvas de la *Trichinella.*

**tricocisto:** **(pág. 547)** estructura alargada y cilíndrica que puede descargar una estructura husiforme capaz de reaccionar como defensa, como sistema de anclaje o captura de presa.

**nivel trófico:** **(pág. 42)** cada paso de una cadena o red alimenticia.

**pluviselva tropical:** **(pág. 72)** bioma caliente, lluvioso, con una humedad anual continua; contiene las especies más diversas de plantas y animales terrestres.

**tropical savanna: (p. 71)** biome characterized by grasses and scattered trees, and herd animals such as zebras and antelopes.

**tropical seasonal forest: (p. 71)** biome characterized by deciduous and evergreen trees, a dry season, and animal species that include monkeys, elephants, and Bengal tigers.

**tropism (TROH pih zum): (p. 651)** response to an external stimulus in a specific direction.

**tube foot: (p. 795)** one of the muscular, small, fluid-filled tubes with suction-cuplike ends that enable echinoderms to move and collect food.

**tundra: (p. 68)** treeless biome with permanently frozen soil under the surface and average yearly precipitation of 15–25 cm.

**tympanic (tihm PA nihk) membrane: (p. 837)** eardrum.

**sabana tropical: (pág. 71)** bioma caracterizado por hierbas, árboles dispersos y animales que se agrupan en manadas, como cebras y antílopes.

**bosque estacional tropical: (pág. 71)** bioma caracterizado por árboles caducifolios y siempreverdes, una estación seca y especies de animales que incluyen a los monos, los elefantes y los tigres de Bengala.

**tropismo: (pág. 651)** crecimiento de una planta en respuesta a estímulos externos proveniente de una dirección específica.

**pie ambulacral: (pág. 795)** uno de los conductos musculares pequeños rellenos de fluido y con ventosas de los equinodermos que posibilita el movimiento y la recolección de alimento.

**tundra: (pág. 68)** bioma carente de árboles, con suelo permanentemente congelado bajo la superficie; y una precipitación promedio anual de 15-25 cm.

**membrana timpánica: (pág. 837)** tímpano.

## U



**urea: (p. 1006)** nitrogenous waste product of the excretory system.

**urethra (yoo REE thruh): (p. 1049)** tube that conducts semen and urine out of the body through the penis in males and transports urine out of the body in females.

**uterus: (p. 887)** saclike muscular female organ in which embryos develop.

**urea: (pág. 1006)** producto de desecho nitrogenado del sistema excretorio.

**uretra: (pág. 1049)** conducto que conduce el semen y la orina fuera del cuerpo a través del pene en los machos y transporta la orina fuera del cuerpo de las hembras.

**útero: (pág. 887)** órgano femenino muscular con forma de saco hueco donde se desarrollan los embriones.

## V

**vacuole: (p. 195)** membrane-bound vesicle for temporary storage of materials such as food, enzymes, and wastes.

**valve: (p. 994)** one of the tissue flaps in veins that prevents backflow of blood.

**van der Waals forces: (p. 155)** attractive forces between molecules.

**vascular cambium: (p. 634)** thin cylinder of meristematic tissue that produces new transport cells.

**vascular plant: (p. 606)** type of plant with vascular tissues adapted to land environments; most widely distributed type of plant on Earth.

**vascular tissue: (p. 606)** specialized tissue that transports water, food, and other substances in vascular plants and can also provide structure and support.

**vacuola: (pág. 195)** espacio encerrado por una membrana para el almacenamiento temporal de materiales como alimento, enzimas y desechos.

**válvula: (pág. 994)** uno de los opérculos de los tejidos en las venas que evita que la sangre fluya hacia atrás.

**fuerzas de van der Waals: (pág. 155)** fuerzas de atracción entre las moléculas.

**cámbium vascular: (pág. 634)** cilindro delgado de tejido meristémico que produce células de transporte nuevas.

**planta vascular: (pág. 606)** tipo de planta con tejido vascular adaptada a ambientes terrestres; tipo de planta ampliamente distribuida en la Tierra.

**tejido vascular: (pág. 606)** tejido especializado que transporta agua, alimento y otras sustancias en las plantas vasculares y también proveen estructura y soporte.

**vas deferens (VAS • DEF uh runz): (p. 1049)** duct through which sperm move away from the testis and toward the urethra.

**conducto deferente: (pág. 1049)** ducto por el cual los espermatozoides se alejan de los testículos hacia la uretra.

**vegetative reproduction: (p. 662)** asexual reproduction in which new plants grow from parts of an existing plant.

**reproducción vegetativa: (pág. 662)** reproducción asexual en la cual crecen plantas nuevas de las partes de una planta existente.

**vein: (p. 994)** blood vessel that carries deoxygenated blood back to the heart.

**vena: (pág. 994)** vaso sanguíneo que devuelve la sangre desoxigenada al corazón.

**ventral (VEN trul): (p. 700)** underside or belly of an animal with bilateral symmetry.

**ventral: (pág. 700)** la superficie inferior o barriga de un animal con simetría bilateral.

**ventricle: (p. 824)** the heart chamber that pumps blood from the heart to the gills.

**ventrículo: (pág. 894)** la cavidad cardíaca que bombea la sangre del corazón a las agallas.

**vertebrate: (p. 693)** animal with an endoskeleton and a backbone.

**vertebrado: (pág. 693)** animal que posee endoesqueleto y columna vertebral.

**vessel element: (p. 637)** elongated, tubular plant cell that forms xylem strands (vessels) and conducts water and dissolved substances.

**elemento vascular: (pág. 637)** células vegetales alargadas, tubulares, que forman filamentos de xilema (vasos) y conducen agua y sustancias disueltas.

**vestigial structure: (p. 425)** reduced form of a functional structure that indicates shared ancestry.

**estructura vestigial: (pág. 425)** forma reducida de una estructura funcional que indica ascendencia compartida.

**villus (VIH luhs): (p. 1023)** fingerlike structure through which most nutrients are absorbed from the small intestine.

**vellosidad: (pág. 1023)** estructura en forma de dedos por la cual el intestino delgado absorbe la mayor parte de los nutrientes.

**virus: (p. 525)** nonliving strand of genetic material that cannot replicate on its own, has a nucleic acid core, a protein coat, and can invade cells and alter cellular function.

**virus: (pág. 525)** hebra sin vida, de material genético, incapaz de duplicarse por sí misma; tiene un núcleo de ácido nucleico, un revestimiento de proteína y puede invadir las células y alterar sus funciones.

**vitamin: (p. 1028)** fat-soluble or water-soluble organic compound needed in very small amounts for the body's metabolic activities.

**vitamina: (pág. 1028)** compuesto orgánico liposoluble o hidrosoluble, que se necesita en porciones muy pequeñas para las actividades metabólicas del cuerpo.

**voluntary muscle: (p. 948)** consciously controlled skeletal muscle.

**músculo voluntario: (pág. 948)** músculo esquelético controlado en forma consciente.

## W

**water-vascular system: (p. 795)** system of fluid-filled, closed tubes that allow echinoderms to control movement and get food.

**sistema vascular acuático: (pág. 795)** sistema de conductos cerrados, rellenos de fluido, que permite a los equinodermos controlar el movimiento y obtener alimento.

**weather: (p. 65)** atmospheric conditions such as temperature and precipitation at a specific place and time.

**tiempo: (pág. 65)** condiciones atmosféricas, como la temperatura y la precipitación, en un lugar y tiempo específico.

**wetland: (p. 78)** water-saturated land area that supports aquatic plants.

**humedal: (pág. 78)** terreno saturado de agua que mantiene a las plantas acuáticas.

**white blood cell: (p. 998)** large, nucleated, disease-fighting blood cell produced in the bone marrow.

**glóbulo blanco: (pág. 998)** célula sanguínea gigante y nucleada que combate las enfermedades y se produce en la médula ósea.

**woodland: (p. 69)** biome characterized by small trees and mixed shrub communities.

**zona boscosa: (pág. 69)** bioma caracterizado por árboles pequeños y comunidades de arbustos mixtas.

**xylem** **(ZI lum): (p. 637)** vascular plant tissue that transports water and dissolved minerals away from the roots throughout the plant and is composed of vessel elements and tracheids.

**xilema: (pág. 637)** tejido vegetal vascular que transporta el agua y los minerales disueltos desde las raíces hacia el resto de la planta, compuesto por elementos de los vasos y traqueidas.

**yellow bone marrow: (p. 942)** type of marrow that consists of stored fat.

**médula ósea amarilla: (pág. 942)** tipo de médula que consiste en grasas almacenadas.

## Z

**zero population growth (ZPG): (p. 104)** occurs when the birthrate equals the death rate.

**zygote** **(ZI goht): (p. 695)** fertilized egg formed when a sperm cell penetrates an egg.

**crecimiento demográfico nulo (CDN): (pág. 104)** sucede cuando la tasa de natalidad es igual a la tasa de mortalidad.

**cigoto: (pág. 695)** óvulo fecundado que se forma cuando un espermatozoide fecunda un óvulo.

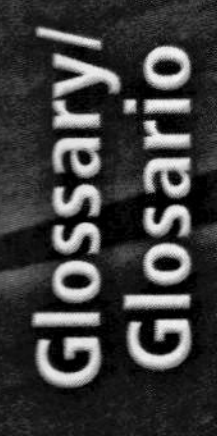